THE LAWS
OF SCOTLAND

———•———

STAIR MEMORIAL
ENCYCLOPAEDIA

Volume 12

THE LAWS OF SCOTLAND

STAIR MEMORIAL ENCYCLOPAEDIA

Volume 12

The Law Society of Scotland
Butterworths

Edinburgh   1992

The Law Society of Scotland
The Law Society's Hall, 26 Drumsheugh Gardens, EDINBURGH EH3 7YR

Butterworths

United Kingdom	Butterworth & Co (Publishers) Ltd, 4 Hill Street, EDINBURGH EH2 3JZ and 88 Kingsway, LONDON WC2B 6AB
Australia	Butterworths Pty Ltd, SYDNEY, MELBOURNE, BRISBANE, ADELAIDE, PERTH, CANBERRA and HOBART
Canada	Butterworth & Co (Canada) Ltd, TORONTO and VANCOUVER
Ireland	Butterworth (Ireland) Ltd, DUBLIN
Malaysia	Malayan Law Journal Sdn Bhd, KUALA LUMPUR
New Zealand	Butterworths of New Zealand Ltd, WELLINGTON and AUCKLAND
Singapore	Butterworth & Co (Asia) Pte Ltd, SINGAPORE
USA	Butterworth Legal Publishers, ST PAUL, Minnesota, SEATTLE, Washington, BOSTON, Massachusetts, AUSTIN, Texas and D & S Publishers, CLEARWATER, Florida

First published 1992

© The Law Society of Scotland 1992

British Library Cataloguing in Publication Data

The Laws of Scotland: Stair memorial encyclopaedia.
  Vol 12
  1. Law — Scotland — Dictionaries
  I. Law Society of Scotland
  344.1108′6   KDC150

ISBN (complete set) 0 406 237 00 X
        (this volume) 0 406 237 12 3

Typeset and printed in Scotland by Thomson Litho Ltd, East Kilbride,
on Bannockburn Fine Wove made by Guardbridge Papers Co Ltd of
Fife and supplied by James McNaughton Paper Group. Bound by Bath
Press using cloth supplied by Watson Grange of Linwood, Paisley.

GENERAL EDITORS

1981–88

THE LATE SIR THOMAS SMITH QC, DCL, LLD, FRSE, FBA
Honorary Bencher of Gray's Inn
Professor Emeritus of Scots Law in the University of Edinburgh

1988–

ROBERT BLACK QC, LLB, LLM, FRSA
Professor of Scots Law in the University of Edinburgh
Formerly Deputy and Joint General Editor

DEPUTY GENERAL EDITORS

HAMISH McN HENDERSON MA, LLB
Advocate in Aberdeen
Formerly University Fellow and Senior Lecturer in
Scots Law in the University of Edinburgh

JOSEPH M THOMSON LLB
Regius Professor of Law in the University of Glasgow

KENNETH MILLER LLB, LLM, PHD
Professor of Law in the University of Strathclyde

CO-ORDINATOR TO THE GENERAL EDITORS

JOAN ROSE BA

OFFICE BEARERS OF THE LAW SOCIETY OF SCOTLAND

President 1991–92
James H Campbell BL

Vice-President 1991–92
Brian C Adair TD, LLB

Secretary
Kenneth W Pritchard BL, WS

Convener, Encyclopaedia Committee
Professor J Ross Harper CBE, MA, LLB

Member of the Encyclopaedia Committee
C W R Gemmill BA, LLB

BUTTERWORTHS' EDITORIAL STAFF

Text Editor
R Peter Moore, LLB
of Lincoln's Inn, Barrister

Editorial Manager
Margaret Cherry LLB

Sub-editor
Joan Lyle LLB

Sub-editor
Margaret Hannan

INDEXER
Ann Barrett
Member, the Society of Indexers

Contributors to this volume

HUMAN RIGHTS IN EUROPE

Rebecca M M Wallace MA, LLB, PHD
Reader in Law in the University of Strathclyde

IMMIGRATION AND EXTRADITION

Robin M White LLB, LLM, CERT SOC ANTH, AIL, JP
Senior Lecturer in Law in the University of Dundee

INDUSTRIAL AND PROVIDENT SOCIETIES, CREDIT UNIONS AND FRIENDLY SOCIETIES

Ian Swinney LLB, Solicitor
Lecturer in Private Law in the University of Glasgow

INSURANCE

A D M Forte MA, LLB
Senior Lecturer in Law in the University of Edinburgh

INTEREST

Paragraphs 1001–1031
Nicolas J S Lockhart LLB(Hons)

Paragraphs 1032–1038
Hamish McN Henderson MA, LLB, Advocate in Aberdeen
Formerly University Fellow and Senior Lecturer in Scots Law in the University of Edinburgh

INTERPRETATION OF STATUTES, DEEDS AND OTHER DOCUMENTS

INTERPRETATION OF STATUTES

J Fleming Wallace QC

INTERPRETATION OF DEEDS AND OTHER DOCUMENTS

Professor J A M Inglis CBE, MA, LLB, Solicitor
Professor of Conveyancing in the University of Glasgow

INVESTOR PROTECTION

THE FINANCIAL SERVICES ACT 1986

Deborah C Adams LLB
Company Secretary, Ivory & Sime PLC

Alastair J Gordon MA, LLB, WS, NP

INSIDER DEALING

Alistair M Clark LLB, PHD
Senior Lecturer in Law in the University of Strathclyde

The law stated in this volume is in general that in force on 30 April 1991 but later developments have been noted wherever possible.

Contributors to this volume

HUMAN RIGHTS IN EUROPE

Rebecca M M Wallace, MA, LLB, PhD
Reader in Law in the University of Strathclyde

IMMIGRATION AND EXTRADITION

Robin M White, BA, LLB, Dip Soc Anthropology
Senior Lecturer in Law in the University of Dundee

INDUSTRIAL AND PROVIDENT SOCIETIES, CREDIT UNIONS AND FRIENDLY SOCIETIES

Ian Snaith, LLM, Solicitor
Lecturer in Law in the University of Leicester

INSURANCE

A D M Forte, LLB
Senior Lecturer in Law in the University of Aberdeen

INTEREST

[illegible]

[illegible]
William J L Henderson, MA, LLB, Advocate in Aberdeen
Formerly University Fellow, and Senior Lecturer in Scots Law in the University of Edinburgh

INTERPRETATION OF STATUTES, DEEDS AND OTHER DOCUMENTS

Francis J Wallace QC

INTERPRETATION OF DEEDS AND OTHER DOCUMENTS

E [illegible], MA, LLB, CA, CA, Solicitor
Professor, Clinical Studies in the University of Glasgow

INVESTOR PROTECTION

[illegible]

Deborah A Sabalot
Company Secretary, [illegible] Ltd

Alistair [illegible], BA, LLB, [illegible]

PUBLIC DEALING

Alan E M Clark, LLB, [illegible]
Senior Lecturer in Law in the University of Strathclyde

The law stated in this volume is in general that in force on 30 April 1991 but later developments have been noted wherever possible.

Contents

List of Abbreviations xi
Table of Statutes 1
Table of Orders, Rules and Regulations 25
Table of Other Enactments 33
Table of Cases 41

HUMAN RIGHTS IN EUROPE

Table of Contents I
1. The European Convention for the Protection of Human Rights and
   Fundamental Freedoms (paras 1–23) I
2. The Rights as Developed Through the Jurisprudence of the European
   Court of Human Rights (paras 24–100) 25

IMMIGRATION AND EXTRADITION

Table of Contents 99
1. Immigration (paras 101–500) 101
2. Extradition (paras 501–600) 254

INDUSTRIAL AND PROVIDENT SOCIETIES, CREDIT UNIONS AND FRIENDLY SOCIETIES

Table of Contents 303
1. Introduction (paras 601–605) 304
2. Industrial and Provident Societies (paras 606–655) 306
3. Credit Unions (paras 656–678) 338
4. Friendly Societies (paras 679–800) 349

INSURANCE

Table of Contents 397
1. Introduction (paras 801–802) 398
2. Classification of Insurance (paras 803–805) 400
3. The Provision of Insurance and Insurance Services (paras 806–817) 401
4. Formation of Insurance Contracts (paras 818–825) 409
5. The Insurance Policy (paras 826–844) 415
6. Assignation (paras 845–847) 425
7. Insurable Interest (paras 848–857) 426
8. Misrepresentation and Non-Disclosure (paras 858–872) . . . 431
9. Warranties (paras 873–878) 441
10. Causation (paras 879–1000) 445

INTEREST

Table of Contents 465
1. Introduction (para 1001) 465
2. Interest Due by Contractual Stipulation (paras 1002–1011) . . 467
3. Wrongful Withholding of Sums Due (paras 1012–1021) . . 474
4. Interest on Trust and Executry Funds (paras 1022–1031). . . 485
5. Interest on Damages and Decrees (paras 1032–1034) . . 491
6. Interest on Arbitration Awards (para 1035) 494
7. Interest on Tribunal Awards (para 1036) . . . 495
8. Rate of Interest (para 1037) 496
9. Compound Interest (paras 1038–1100) 497

INTERPRETATION OF STATUTES, DEEDS AND OTHER DOCUMENTS

Table of Contents 501
1. Interpretation of Statutes (paras 1101–1212) . . . 502
2. Interpretation of Deeds and Other Documents (paras 1213–1300) . 565

INVESTOR PROTECTION

Table of Contents 603
1. The Financial Services Act 1986 (paras 1301–1500) . . 604
2. Insider Dealing (paras 1501–1536) 680

INDEXES

INDEXES. 703

Abbreviations

AC	Law Reports, Appeal Cases (House of Lords and Privy Council) 1890–
AD	Appellate Division (S Africa) 1910–46
AD	Annual Digest and Reports of Public International Law Cases 1919–1949
AFDI	*Annuaires français de droit international* (1955–)
A-G	Attorney-General
AJCL	American Journal of Comparative Law
AJIL	American Journal of International Law (1907–)
ALR	Argus Law Reports (Australia) 1895–1973, and Australian Law Reports 1973–
AMS	Ancient Manuscripts of Scotland
APS	Acts of the Parliament of Scotland
AS	Act of Sederunt
AYIL	Australian Yearbook of International Law
Act of Adj	Act of Adjournal
Ad & El	Adolphus and Ellis's Reports (King's Bench and Queen's Bench) (England) 1834–42
Adam	Adam's Justiciary Reports 1894–1919
All ER	All England Law Reports 1936–
All ER Rev	All England Law Reports Annual Review 1982–
App Cas	Law Reports, Appeal Cases (House of Lords) 1875–90
App D	Appellate Division (S Africa) 1910–46
App Div	Appellate Division (New York Supreme Court) 1896–1955; 2d, 1955–
Arkley	Arkley's Justiciary Reports 1846–48
Arnot	Arnot's Criminal Trials 1536–1784
Asp MLC	Aspinall's Maritime Law Cases 1870–1943
ATC	Annotated Tax Cases 1922–
Aust	Australia
B & Ad	Barnewall and Adolphus's Reports (King's Bench) (England) 1830–34
B & Ald	Barnewall and Alderson's Reports (King's Bench) (England) 1817–22
B & C	Barnewall and Cresswell's Reports (King's Bench) (England) 1822–30
B & CR	Bankruptcy and Companies Winding up Reports 1918–41
B & S	Best and Smith's Reports (Queen's Bench) (England) 1861–70
BCC	British Company Cases (1983–)
BCLC	Butterworths Company Law Cases 1983–
BCR	British Columbia Reports 1867–1947
BILC	British International Law Cases
BTLC	Butterworths Trading Law Cases 1986–
BTR	British Tax Review 1956–
BYIL	British Yearbook of International Law 1920–
Beav	Beavan's Reports (Rolls Court) (England) 1838–66
Bell App	S S Bell's Scotch Appeals (House of Lords) 1842–50
Bell Fol Cas	P Bell's Folio Cases (Court of Session) 1794–95
Bell Oct Cas	P Bell's Octavo Cases (Court of Session) 1790–92
Bing	Bingham's Reports (Common Pleas) (England) 1822–34
Bing NC	Bingham's New Cases (Common Pleas) (England) 1834–40
Biss & Sm	Bisset and Smith's Digest (S Africa)

Bligh	Bligh's Reports (House of Lords) 1819–21
Bligh NS	Bligh's Reports, New Series (House of Lords) 1827–37
Bos & P	Bosanquet and Puller (England) 1796–1804
Broun	Broun's Justiciary Reports 1842–45
Brown's Supp	Brown's Supplement to Morison's Dictionary of Decisions (Court of Session) 1622–1794
Brown's Syn	Brown's Synopsis of Decisions (Court of Session) 1532–1827
Bruce	Bruce's Decisions (Court of Session) 1714–15
Buchan	Buchanan's Reports (Court of Session) 1800–13
C	Command Papers 1833–99
CA	Court of Appeal
CAR	Commonwealth Arbitration Reports 1905–65
C & P	Carrington and Payne's Reports (Nisi Prius) (England) 1823–41
CB	Common Bench (England) 1845–56
CBNS	Common Bench, New Series (England) 1856–65
CCR	County Court Rules (England)
CDE	*Cahiers de Droit Européen* (1965–)
CFI	Court of First Instance
CL	Current Law 1947–
CLJ	Cambridge Law Journal
CLR	Commonwealth Law Reports (Australia) 1903–
CLY	Current Law Year Book 1947–
CMLR	Common Market Law Reports 1962–
CML Rev	Common Market Law Review (1963–)
CPD	Law Reports, Common Pleas Division (England) 1875–80
CYIL	Canadian Yearbook of International Law
Camb LJ	Cambridge Law Journal 1921–
Camp	Campbell's Reports (Nisi Prius) (England) 1807–16
Cas tep Talb	Cases in Equity temp Talbot
Cd	Command Papers 1900–18
Ch	Law Reports, Chancery Division (England) 1890–
Ch App	Law Reports, Chancery Appeals (England) 1865–75
Ch D	Law Reports, Chancery Division (England) 1875–90
Ch Rob	Christopher Robinson's Reports (Admiralty) (England) 1798–1808
Cl & Fin	Clark and Finnelly's Reports (House of Lords) 1831–46
Cm	Command Papers 1986–
C-MAC	Courts-Martial Appeal Court
Cmd	Command Papers 1919–56
Cmnd	Command Papers 1956–86
Com Cas	Commercial Cases 1895–1941
Com Dig	Comyn's Digest 1792 (England)
Com LR	Commercial Law Reports 1981–
Cornell ILJ	Cornell International Law Journal
Coup	Couper's Justiciary Reports 1868–85
Cox CC	Cox's Criminal Cases (England) 1843–1941
Cr App Rep	Criminal Appeal Reports (England) 1908–
Crim LR	Criminal Law Review (England) 1954–
D	Dunlop's Session Cases 1838–62
DC	Divisional Court
D (HL)	House of Lords cases in Dunlop's Session Cases 1838–62
DLR	Dominion Law Reports (Canada) 1912–55; 2d, 1956–67; 3d, 1968–83; 4th 1984–
DNB	Dictionary of National Biography
Dalr	Dalrymple's Decisions (Court of Session) 1698–1718

Deas & And	Deas and Anderson's Decisions (Court of Session) 1829–32
De G & J	De Gex and Jones's Reports (Chancery) (England) 1857–59
De G & Sm	De Gex and Smale's Reports (Chancery) (England) 1846–52
De G F & J	De Gex, Fisher and Jones's Reports (Chancery) (England) 1859–62
De G J & Sm	De Gex, Jones and Smith's Reports (Chancery) (England) 1862–65
De G M & G	De Gex, Macnaghten and Gordon's Reports (Chancery) (England) 1851–57
Dirl	Dirleton's Decisions (Court of Session) 1665–77
Dods	Dodson's Reports (Admiralty) (England) 1811–22
Dow	Dow's Reports (House of Lords) 1812–18
Dow & Cl	Dow and Clark's Reports (House of Lords) 1827–32
Durie	Durie's Decisions (Court of Session) 1621–42
EAT	Employment Appeal Tribunal
E & B	Ellis and Blackburn's Reports (Queen's Bench) (England) 1852–58
E & E	Ellis and Ellis's Reports (Queen's Bench) (England) 1858–61
E B & E	Ellis, Blackburn and Ellis's Reports (Queen's Bench) (England) 1858–60
EC	European Communities
ECHR	European Court of Human Rights
ECJ	European Court of Justice (Court of Justice of the European Communities)
ECR	European Court of Justice Reports 1954–
ECSC	European Coal and Steel Community
EEC	European Economic Community
EG	Estates Gazette 1858–
EGD	Estates Gazette Digest 1902–
EHD	English Historical Documents
EHR	Economic History Review
EHRR	European Human Rights Reports 1979–
ER	English Reports 1220–1865
Edgar	Edgar's Decisions (Court of Session) 1724–26
Elchies	Elchies' Decisions (Court of Session) 1733–54
Eng Judg	Decisions of English Judges during the Usurpation 1655–61
Eq Rep	Equity Reports (England) 1853–55
Euratom	European Atomic Energy Community
EuR	*Europarecht* (1966–)
Eur LR	European Law Review (1955–)
Eur YB	European Yearbook (1962–)
Ex D	Law Reports, Exchequer Division (England) 1875–80
Exch	Exchequer Reports (England) 1847–56
F	Fraser's Session Cases 1898–1906 (preceded by year and volume number); Federal Reporter (USA) 1880–1924; 2d, 1924– (preceded by volume number and followed by year)
FC	Faculty Collection (Court of Session) 1752–1825
F (HL)	House of Lords cases in Fraser's Session Cases 1898–1906
F (J)	Justiciary cases in Fraser's Session Cases 1898–1906
FLR	Family Law Reports (1980–)
FSR	Fleet Street Reports 1963–
F Supp	Federal Supplement (USA) 1932–
Falc	Falconer's Decisions (Court of Session) 1744–51
Fam	Law Reports, Family Division (England) 1972–
Ferg	Ferguson's Consistorial Decisions 1811–17

Forbes	Forbes' Journal of the Sessions 1705–13
Fount	Fountainhall's Decisions (Court of Session) 1678–1712
GA Resoln	General Assembly Resolution
GWD	Green's Weekly Digest 1986–
GYIL	German Yearbook of International Law
Gaz LR	Gazette Law Reports (New Zealand) 1898–1953
Gil & Fal	Gilmour's and Falconer's Decisions (Court of Session) 1661–66, 1681–86
H & C	Hurlstone and Coltman's Reports (Exchequer) (England) 1862–66
H & N	Hurlstone and Norman's Reports (Exchequer) (England) 1856–62
HC	High Court
HL	House of Lords
HL Cas	House of Lords Cases 1847–66
HLR	Housing Law Reports 1981–
Hague Recueil	Hague Academy of International Law Recueil de Cours
Hailes	Hailes' Decisions (Court of Session) 1766–91
Hale PC	Hale's Pleas of the Crown 1678
Harc	Harcarse's Decisions (Court of Session) 1681–91
Hawk PC	Hawkin's Pleas of the Crown
Home	Clerk Home's Decisions (Court of Session) 1735–44
Hume	Hume's Decisions (Court of Session) 1781–1822
ICJ	International Court of Justice
ICJR	International Court of Justice Reports
ICLQ	International and Comparative Law Quarterly (1952–)
ICLQR	International and Comparative Law Quarterly Review 1952–
ICR	Industrial Cases Reports (England) 1972–
IH	Inner House
IL	The International Lawyer
ILJ	Industrial Law Journal
ILM	International Legal Materials
ILR	Irish Law Reports 1838–50
ILT	Irish Law Times 1867–
ILT Jo	Irish Law Times Journal 1867–
IR	Irish Reports 1893–
IRLR	Industrial Relations Law Reports 1972–
ITR	Industrial Tribunal Reports 1966–78
Imm AR	Immigration Appeal Reports 1972–
Ind JIL	Indian Journal of International Law (1960–)
Int Aff	International Affairs (1922–)
Int LR	International Law Reports
Irv	Irvine's Justiciary Reports 1851–68
J	Justice
JC	Justiciary Cases 1917–
JCMS	Journal of Common Market Studies (1962–)
JDI	_Journal de Droit International_ (1915–)
J Juris	Journal of Jurisprudence 1857–91
JLSS	Journal of the Law Society of Scotland 1956–
JO CECA	_Journal Officiel de la Communauté Européen du Charbon et de l'Acier_ (1952–58)
JP	Justice of the Peace Reports (England) 1837–
JP Jo	Justice of the Peace and Local Government Review (England) 1837–

JPL	Journal of Planning Law 1948–53; Journal of Planning and Property Law 1954–72; and Journal of Planning and Environment Law 1973–
J Shaw	J Shaw's Justiciary Reports 1848–51
JR	Juridical Review 1889–
JSPTL	Journal of the Society of Public Teachers of Law
Jur Soc P	Juridical Society Papers 1858–74
JWTL	Journal of World Trade Law (1967–)
KB	Law Reports, King's Bench Division (England) 1900–52
KIR	Knight's Industrial Reports (England) 1966–75
K & W Dic	Kames' and Woodhouselee's Dictionary of Decisions (Court of Session) 1540–1796
Kames Rem Dec	Kames' Remarkable Decisions (Court of Session) 1716–28
Kames Sel Dec	Kames' Select Decisions (Court of Session) 1752–68
Kilk	Kilkerran's Decisions (Court of Session) 1738–52
LA	Lord Advocate
LC	Lord Chancellor
LCJ	Lord Chief Justice
LGR	Knight's Local Government Reports 1902–
LIEI	Legal Issues of European Integration (1974–)
LJ	Law Journal newspaper (England) 1866–1965; Lord Justice
L J-C	Lord Justice-Clerk
LJ Ch	Law Journal, Chancery (England) 1831–1946
LJ Ex	Law Journal, Exchequer (England) 1831–75
L J-G	Lord Justice-General
LJKB	Law Journal, King's Bench (England) 1900–52
LJP	Law Journal, Probate, Divorce and Admiralty (England) 1875–1946
LJPC	Law Journal, Privy Council 1865–1946
LJQB	Law Journal, Queen's Bench Division (England) 1831–1900
LJR	Law Journal Reports (England) 1947–49
LQR	Law Quarterly Review 1885–
LR A & E	Law Reports, Admiralty and Ecclesiastical (England) 1865–75
LRCCR	Law Reports, Crown Cases Reserved (England) 1865–75
LRCP	Law Reports, Common Pleas (England) 1865–75
LR Eq	Law Reports, Equity (England) 1865–75
LR Exch	Law Reports, Exchequer (England) 1865–75
LRHL	Law Reports, House of Lords (England and Ireland) 1866–75
LR Ir	Law Reports, Ireland 1877–93
LR P & D	Law Reports, Probate and Divorce (England) 1865–75
LRPC	Law Reports, Privy Council 1865–75
LRQB	Law Reports, Queen's Bench (England) 1865–75
LRRP	Law Reports, Restrictive Practices 1957–
LR Sc & Div	Law Reports, House of Lords (Scotch and Divorce) 1866–75
LS Gaz	Law Society's Gazette (England) 1903–
LT	Law Times Reports (England) 1859–1947
LT Jo	Law Times newspaper (England) 1843–1947
LTOS	Law Times Reports, Old Series (England) 1843–59
LVAC	Lands Valuation Appeal Court
Land Ct	Scottish Land Court
Law Com	Law Commission (England)
Ll L Rep	Lloyd's List Law Reports 1919–50
Lloyd's Rep	Lloyd's List Law Reports 1951–67; Lloyd's Law Reports 1968–
LoNJ	League of Nations Journal
LoNTS	League of Nations Treaty Series
Lyon Ct	Court of the Lord Lyon

M	Macpherson's Session Cases 1862–73
M (HL)	House of Lords cases in Macpherson's Session Cases 1862–73
M & S	Maule and Selwyn (England) 1813–17
M & W	Meeson and Welsby (England) 1836–47
MLR	Modern Law Review 1937–
MR	Master of the Rolls
Mac & G	Macnaghten and Gordon's Reports (Chancery) (England) 1849–52
MacF	MacFarlane's Jury Trials (Court of Session) 1838–39
Macl & R	Maclean and Robinson's Scotch Appeals (House of Lords) 1839
Maclaurin	Maclaurin's Arguments and Decisions 1670–1770
Macq	Macqueen's House of Lords Reports 1851–65
Misc	New York Miscellaneous Reports 1892–1955; 2d, 1955–
Moore Int Arb	Moore's History and Digest of International Arbitrations
Mor	Morison's Dictionary of Decisions (Court of Session) 1540–1808
Mun LR	Municipal Law Reports 1903–13
Murr	Murray's Jury Court Cases 1815–30
NI	Northern Ireland Law Reports 1925–
NJW	*Niue Juristische Wochenschrift* (1947–)
NLJ	New Law Journal (England) 1965–
NMS	National Manuscripts of Scotland
NY	New York Court of Appeals Reports 1847–1955; 2d, 1956–
NYS	New York Supplement 1888–1937; 2d, 1938–
NZ	New Zealand
NZLR	New Zealand Law Reports 1883–
NZULR	New Zealand University Law Review 1963–
OCR	Ordinary Cause Rules
OH	Outer House
OJ	Official Journal of the European Communities; C, Information; L, Legislation
OJLS	Oxford Journal of Legal Studies (1981–)
OLR	Ontario Law Reports 1901–30
OR	Ontario Reports 1931–73; 2d, 1974–
P	Law Reports, Probate, Divorce and Admiralty Division (England) 1890–1971
P & CR	Planning and Compensation Reports 1949–67; Property and Compensation Reports 1968– (England)
PC	Judicial Committee of the Privy Council
PCIJ	Permanent Court of International Justice Reports
PD	Law Reports, Probate, Divorce and Admiralty Division (England) 1875–90
PE Debs	European Parliament Debates
PL	Public Law
Pat	Paton's House of Lords Appeal Cases 1726–1821
Paters	Paterson's House of Lords Appeals 1851–73
Pitc	Pitcairn's Criminal Trials 1488–1624
Pol Q	Political Quarterly
QB	Queen's Bench Reports (England) 1841–52 (volume number precedes)
QB	Law Reports, Queen's Bench Division (England) 1891–1901, 1952– (year precedes)
QBD	Law Reports, Queen's Bench Division (England) 1875–90
QC	Queen's Counsel

R	Rettie's Session Cases 1873–98
RA	Rating Appeals 1965–
RBDI	*Revue belge de droit international* (1965–)
RC	Rules of the Court of Session
RdC	*Recueil des Cours* (Hague Recueil) (1923–)
RDE	*Revista di diritto europeo* (1961–)
RDI	*Revista di diritto internazionale* (1896–)
RFSP	*Revue française des sciences politiques*
RGDIP	*Revue général de droit international public* (1896–)
RGS	Register of the Great Seal of Scotland
RHDI	*Revue hellenique de droit international* (1948–)
R (HL)	House of Lords cases in Rettie's Session Cases 1873–98
RICS	Royal Institution of Chartered Surveyors, Scottish Lands Valuation Appeal Reports
R (J)	Justiciary cases in Rettie's Session Cases 1873–98
RMC	*Revue du Marché Commun* (1958–)
RPC	Reports of Patents, Designs and Trade Marks Cases 1884–; Restrictive Practices Court
RRC	Ryde's Rating Cases (England) 1956–
RSC	Rules of the Supreme Court (England)
RTDE	*Revue trimestrielle de droit européen* (1965–)
RTR	Road Traffic Reports 1970–
RVR	Rating and Valuation Reports (England) 1960–
Robert	Robertson's Scotch Appeals (House of Lords) 1707–27
Robin	Robinson's Scotch Appeals (House of Lords) 1840–41
Ross LC	G Ross's Leading Cases in the Law of Scotland (Land Rights) 1638–1849
S	P Shaw's Session Cases 1821–38 (NE indicates New Edition)
SA	South African Law Reports 1947–
SALJ	South African Law Journal
SAL Rev	South African Law Review
SAR	South African Supreme Court Reports 1881–92
S & D Just	Shaw and Dunlop's Justiciary Cases 1819–31
SC	Session Cases 1907–; Supreme Court
SCCR	Scottish Criminal Case Reports 1981–
SCCR Supp	Scottish Criminal Case Reports Supplement 1950–80
SC (HL)	House of Lords cases in Session Cases 1907–
SC (J)	Justiciary Cases in Session Cases 1907–16
SCLR	Scottish Civil Law Reports 1987–
SCOLAG	The journal of the Scottish Legal Action Group
SCR	Summary Cause Rules
SC Resoln	Security Council Resolution
Sel Cas Ch	Select Cases in Chancery (England) 1724–33
SI	Statutory Instruments
SJ	Scottish Jurist 1829–73
SLCR	Scottish Land Court Reports in Scottish Law Review (1913–63) (preceded by year and volume number), and Scottish Land Court Reports 1982– (preceded by year)
SLCR App	Appendix to the annual reports of the Scottish Land Court 1963–
SLG	Scottish Law Gazette 1933–
SLJ	Scottish Law Journal and Sheriff Court Record 1858–61
SLM	Scottish Law Magazine and Sheriff Court Reporter 1862–67
SLR	Scottish Law Reporter 1865–1925
SL Rev	Scottish Law Review and Sheriff Court Reporter 1885–1963
SLT	Scots Law Times 1893–1908 (preceded by year and volume number), and 1909– (preceded by year)

SLT (ECCN)	Scots Law Times European Court Case Notes (1984–)
SLT (Land Ct)	Scottish Land Court Reports in Scots Law Times 1964–
SLT (Lands Trib)	Lands Tribunal for Scotland Reports in Scots Law Times 1971–
SLT (Lyon Ct)	Lyon Court Reports in Scots Law Times 1950–
SLT (Notes)	Notes of Recent Decisions in Scots Law Times 1946–1981
SLT (Sh Ct)	Sheriff Court Reports in Scots Law Times 1893–
SN	Session Notes 1925–48
SO	Standing Orders
SPD	State Papers Domestic
SPLP	Scottish Planning Law and Practice 1980–
SR & O	Statutory Rules and Orders
SRR	Scots Revised Reports 1707–1873, 1898–1908
STC	Simon's Tax Cases 1973–
Scot Law Com	Scottish Law Commission
Scot Hist Rev	Scottish Historical Review
Sh & Macl	P Shaw and Maclean's House of Lords Appeal Cases 1835–38
Sh App	P Shaw's Scotch Appeals (House of Lords) 1821–26
Sh Ct Rep	Sheriff Court Reports in Scottish Law Review 1885–1963
Shaw Just	P Shaw's Justiciary Reports 1819–31
Shaw Teind	P Shaw's Teind Court Decisions 1821–31
Sim	Simon's Reports (Chancery) (England) 1826–52
Sim & St	Simon & Stuart's Reports (Chancery) (England) 1822–26
Sim NS	Simon's Reports, New Series (Chancery) (England) 1850–52
Smith LC	Smith's Leading Cases (England)
Sol Jo	Solicitors' Journal (England) 1856–
Stair Rep	Stair's Reports (Court of Session) 1661–81
Stair Soc	Stair Society
State Tr	State Trials 1163–1820
State Tr NS	State Trials, New Series 1820–58
Stuart	Stuart, Milne and Peddie's Reports (Court of Session) 1851–53
Swin	Swinton's Justiciary Reports 1835–41
Syme	Syme's Justiciary Reports 1826–29
TC	Tax Cases 1875–
TLR	Times Law Reports (England) 1884–1952
TR	Taxation Reports 1939–
TS	United Kingdom Treaty Series
Taunt	Taunton's Reports (Common Pleas) (England) 1807–19
Term Rep	Term Reports (England) 1785–1800
Tul LR	Tulane Law Review (1929–)
UNRIAA	United Nations Reports of International Arbitral Awards
UNTS	United Nations Treaty Series
US	United States Supreme Court Reports 1754–
VATTR	Value Added Tax Tribunal Reports 1973–
V-C	Vice-Chancellor
VLR	Victorian Law Reports 1875–1956
VR	Victorian Reports 1870–72, and 1957–
Ves	Vesey Junior's Reports (Chancery) (England) 1789–1817
Ves Sen	Vesey Senior's Reports (Chancery) (England) 1747–56
WALR	West Australian Law Reports 1898–1959
WAR	Western Australian Reports 1960–
W & S	Wilson and Shaw's House of Lords Cases 1825–34
WLR	Weekly Law Reports (England) 1953–
WN	Law Reports, Weekly Notes (England) 1866–1952
WR	Weekly Reporter (England) 1852–1906

WS	Writer to the Signet
WWR	Western Weekly Reports (Canada) 1911–1950, and 1955–
West	West's House of Lords Reports 1839–41
White	White's Justiciary Reports 1885–93
WuW	*Wirtschaft und Wettbewerb* (1951–)
YB	Year Books
YBILC	Yearbook of the International Law Commission
YBWA	Yearbook of World Affairs
YEL	Yearbook of European Law (1981–)
ZaöRV	*Zeitschrift für ausländisches öffentliches Recht und Völkerrecht* (1929–)

Table of Statutes

	PARA
Accumulations Act 1800 (c 98)	1264
Administration of Estates (Small Payments) Act 1965 (c 32)	
s 1(1)	628
2	626
3	628
7(5)	628
Sch 1—	
Pt I	628
Sch 2	626
Sch 3, 4	628
Administration of Justice Act 1956 (c 46)	
s 47	1154
Administration of Justice Act 1970 (c 31)	
s 31	63
Administration of Justice (Scotland) Act 1933 (c 41)	
s 16	1037
Administration of Justice (Scotland) Act 1972 (c 59)	
s 1	63
3	725
4	1037
Age of Majority (Scotland) Act 1969 (c 39)	
s 1	1268
(2)	1218, 1231
(3)	613, 615, 618
Sch 1—	
Pt I	613, 615, 618
Agricultural Credits (Scotland) Act 1929 (c 13)	
s 5	641
(1)	641
6	641
(1)–(4)	641
7	641
(1)	641
8	641
(1)	641
9	641
Agricultural Holdings (Scotland) Act 1908 (c 64)	
s 18	1166
Agricultural Holdings (Scotland) Act 1949 (c 75)	
s 1	1235
Agriculture Act 1967 (c 22)	617
Aliens Act 1793 (c 4)	104
Aliens Act 1798 (c 50)	104
Aliens Act 1798 (c 77)	104
Aliens Act 1802 (c 92)	104
Aliens Act 1803 (c 155)	104
Aliens Act 1814 (c 155)	104
Aliens Act 1815 (c 54)	104
Aliens Act 1816 (c 86)	104

	PARA
Aliens Act 1818 (c 96)	104
Aliens Act 1818 (c 97)	104
Aliens Act 1820 (c 105)	104
Aliens Act 1826 (c 54)	104
Aliens Act 1905 (c 13)	106
Aliens Restriction Act 1914 (4 & 5 Geo 5 c 12)	106
Aliens Restriction (Amendment) Act 1919 (c 92)	106
s 1	106
Arbitration Act 1950 (c 27)	
s 21	725
Armed Forces Act 1976 (c 52)	
s 22(5)	865
Sch 9—	
para 20(4), (5)	865
Armed Forces Act 1981 (c 55)	
s 28(1)	865
Sch 4—	
para 2(2)	865
Aviation Security Act 1982 (c 36)	
Pt I (s 1–9)	532
s 4, 7, 40	532
Sch 2—	
para 7	532
Backing of Warrants (Republic of Ireland) Act 1965 (c 45)	501, 510, 512, 526, 532, 533, 581, 582
s 1	527
(1)(a)	528, 555
(b)	555, 561
(2)	528, 555
(a)–(c)	528
(3)	543, 555
(b)	528
(4)	561
2(1)	543, 555, 561, 564
(2)	316, 529, 543, 548, 555, 564
(a)	532, 535, 564
(b)	540, 543
(c), (d)	539
(e)	535
(4)	564
2A(1)–(5), (7), (10)–(12)	573
3(1)	564
(2)	572
4(1)	558
(2)	558, 561
(3)	561, 564
(4), (6)	564
5(5)	564
6(1), (2)	572
7(a)	555, 567
(b), (c)	567
8(1)	555
10(1)	555
(3)	528, 555, 558, 561, 564

PARA

Backing of Warrants (Republic of ireland) Act 1965—*contd*
Schedule—
para 5, 6 564
Ballot Act 1872 (c 33)
s 2, 28 1177
Sch 1 1177
Banking Act 1979 (c 37) 656
s 2(1) 656
Sch 1—
para 11 656
Banking Act 1987 (c 22) 666, 1325, 1391
s 2 .... 1325, 1520
5(1)–(5) 666
108 666
(1) 666, 1325
Sch 6—
para 7(1), (2) 666
27(1) 1325
Sch 7—
Pt I 666
Bankruptcy (Scotland) Act 1985 (c 66)
s 75(1) 911
Sch 7—
para 4 911
Benefit Building Societies Act 1836
(c 32) 602
Bills of Exchange Act 1882 (c 61)
s 100 1126
Bills of Sale Act (1878) Amendment
Act 1882 (c 43) 1178
Blank Bonds and Trusts Act 1696
(c 25) 1228
Bretton Woods Agreements Act 1945
(c 19)
s 3(1) 130
British Nationality Act 1948 (c 56) 107,
118, 153, 549
s 1(2) 107
2(1) 120
6(2) 118
34(3) 106
Sch 4—
Pt II 106
British Nationality Act 1965 (s 34)
s 1 120
British Nationality Act 1981 (c 61) 107,
109, 118, 127, 220, 324, 549
s 1 127
(3) 121
(5) 279
4 121
(5), (6) 107
5 220
6 121
11 107
18 121
23, 26 107
Pt IV (s 30–35) 120, 220
s 30 .... 107, 549
(a) 120
31 .... 107, 549
33 120

PARA

British Nationality Act 1981—*contd*
s 37 .... 107, 512, 549
39 339
(2) 118, 153
(4) 128
(6) 118, 120, 122–124, 128,
130, 131, 135, 136, 138,
150, 153, 161, 162, 166,
170, 184–187, 193, 196,
200, 205, 206, 208, 214,
215, 329, 336, 342, 352,
358
51(3) 132
52(8) 122
Sch 1—
para 1–4 121
Sch 3 .... 512, 520
Sch 4—
para 2 .... 118, 120, 122–124, 128,
130, 131, 135, 136, 138,
150, 153, 161, 162, 170,
184–187, 193, 196, 200,
205, 206, 208, 214, 215,
329, 336
3(1) 166, 336, 352, 358
5 128
7 .... 120, 342
Sch 6 520
Sch 9 122
British Nationality and Status of
Aliens Act 1914 (c 17)
See Status of Aliens Act 1914 (c 17)
British Nationality (Falkland Islands)
Act 1983 (c 6) 324
s 4(3) 132
British Nationality (Hong Kong) Act
1990 (c 34) 107, 220
Building Societies Act 1874 (c 42) 602
Building Societies Act 1986 (c 53)
s 119 1308
120(1) 624
Sch 18—
Pt I—
para 6 624
Burgh Police (Scotland) Act 1892
(c 55) 1129, 1142
s 4(2) 1168
11, 21, 22 1165
38 1119
233 1142
430 1120
Capital Transfer Tax Act 1984 (c 51)
See Inheritance Tax Act 1984 (c 51)
Carriage by Air Act 1932 (c 36)
Sch 1—
art 8 1178
Carriage by Air Act 1961 (c 27)
s 1(1) 1154
Channel Tunnel Act 1987 (c 53)
s 1(7) 162
Child Abduction Act 1984 (c 37)
s 2 532
11(4) 532

PARA

Children and Young Persons Act 1969
(c 54)
s 7 63
Civil Aviation Act 1982 (c 16)
s 93 514
Coal Nationalisation Act 1946 (c 59) 1243
s 5 1243
Sch 1 1243
Commonwealth Immigrants Act 1962
(c 21) 107, 153, 158, 198, 324
s 2(2) 125
Commonwealth Immigrants Act 1968
(c 9) 107, 158, 198, 324
s 2 125
Commonwealth Secretariat Act 1966
(c 10) 130
s 1(2) 130
Schedule—
para 6 130
Companies Act 1967 (c 81)
s 130(4) 705
Sch 8—
Pt V 705
Companies Act 1980 (c 22) 1501
Pt IV (s 68–73) 1501
Companies Act 1985 (c 6) 650, 680, 731,
906, 1325, 1330, 1405,
1506, 1510, 1535
Pt I, Ch I (s 1–24) 731
s 4–6, 8 731
35 613
Pt V, Ch VII (s 159–181) 1325
Pt VI (s 198–220) 1501
s 317(8) 1506
318(6) 1506
319(7) 1506
320(3) 1506
323–330 1501
378 651
Pt XI, Ch V (s 384–394A) 637, 715
s 389(1) 637, 715
434–436 1330
459–461 1535
Pt XVIII, Ch I (s 462–466) 641
s 517(2) 641
617(3) 641
651 906
Pt XXII, Ch II (s 680–690) 1510
s 716 680
735(1) 1506
736 1506
741(1), (2) 1506
744 1507
Companies Act 1989 (c 40) 1341, 1362
s 25, 50 .... 637, 715
72 1341
(2), (3) 1330
73 1341
(5) 1415
74 1341
(2)–(4), (6) 1533
75, 76 1341
108 613

PARA

Companies Act 1989—*contd*
s 141(2), (3) 906
144(1) 1506
153 1309
Pt VIII (s 192–206) 1341
s 192 .... 1341, 1342
193 1362
(1) 1341, 1376, 1412
(2) 1310
194 .... 1335, 1341, 1356
200(1) 1305
203(2) 1312, 1313
204(1) 1312
205(1) 1322
206(1) 812, 1305, 1312, 1313,
1318, 1333, 1340, 1356,
1402, 1409
212 .... 1330, 1340, 1356, 1409
Sch 20—
para 26 1312
Sch 23 1341
para 2 .... 1340, 1356
3 1340
(2) 1402
4, 5 1340
6 .... 1340, 1409
7 .... 812, 1333
8 1318
13(2), (3) 1305
14(2) 1312
15(3) 1305
16 1312
21 .... 1312, 1313
Sch 24 .... 906, 1330, 1340, 1341,
1356, 1409
Companies Consolidation (Consequential Provisions) Act 1985
(c 9)
s 26(2)–(4) 641
30 .... 609, 614, 617, 637, 638,
650, 651, 715, 733, 808,
814
Sch 2 .... 609, 614, 617, 637, 638,
650, 651, 715, 733, 808,
814
Companies (Floating Charges and
Receivers) (Scotland) Act 1972
(c 67)
s 10 641
Company Securities (Insider Dealing)
Act 1985 (c 8) 1387, 1393,
1501–1506, 1511, 1512,
1514, 1516–1519, 1523,
1525, 1527, 1531, 1534,
1535
s 1 .... 1502, 1517, 1518, 1523,
1525, 1526, 1531–1535
(1) 1502, 1503, 1505, 1506,
1508–1511, 1520, 1536
(2) 1502, 1511, 1514, 1515,
1520, 1526, 1536
(3), (4) 1502, 1506, 1512, 1513,
1536

PARA

Company Securities (Insider Dealing)
  Act 1985—*contd*
  s 1(5) 1502, 1514–1516, 1526,
                               1530
    (6) 1502, 1516, 1526
    (7) 1502, 1503, 1517, 1526
    (8) 1502, 1503, 1517, 1518,
                               1526
  2 .... 1502, 1519, 1520, 1523,
                1525, 1526, 1531–1535
    (1) 1519, 1522, 1536
    (2) 1520
    (3) 1502, 1521, 1522
    (4)–(6) 1520
  3 .... 1502, 1503, 1511, 1512,
         1514, 1517, 1518, 1521–
            1523, 1526, 1532
    (1) 1526
      (a) 1526, 1527
      (b) 1526, 1528
      (c), (d) 1526, 1529
    (2) 1526, 1530
  4 .... 1502, 1525, 1526,
                    1531–1535
    (1) 1523, 1524, 1526
    (2) 1526
  5 .... 1502, 1526, 1531–1535
    (1) 1525
    (2), (3) 1525, 1526
  6 .... 1523, 1526
    (1), (2) 1531
  7 1526
    (1), (2) 1532
  8(1) 1534
    (3) 1535
  9(a) 1505
    (b) 1505, 1507
  10 1536
    (a) 1504
    (b) 1504, 1509
  11(a), (b) 1506
  12(a), (b) 1510
    (c) 1523
  13(1), (1A), (2) 1510
    (3)–(5) 1524
  14 1514
  16(1) 1503, 1520, 1534
    (1A) 1503
    (2) 1506, 1507
Conjugal Rights (Scotland) Act 1861
  (c 86)
  s 16 1191
Consolidation of Enactments (Procedure) Act 1949 (c 33) 1158
Consular Relations Act 1968 (c 18) 130
  s 12(1) 130
  Sch 1 130
Consumer Credit Act 1974 (c 39) 656,
                669, 833, 1037
  s 10 656
  11(1) 833
  12(a) 833
  16(5) 669, 833
  137–140 1037

PARA

Contempt of Court Act 1981 (c 49) 95
Convention Penalties Act 1962 (South
  Africa)
  s 1, 4 835
Conveyancing Amendment (Scot-
  land) Act 1938 (c 24)
  s 9(1), (3) 1244
Conveyancing and Feudal Reform
  (Scotland) Act 1970 (c 35) 623,
              1247, 1248, 1258
  s 1 .... 1149, 1247
    (2), (3) 1248
    2 1247
    3 1249
    (5) 1249
    4, 6 1249
  Pt II (s 9–32) 1254, 1258
  s 9(2) 1255
    (3) 1254
    10 .... 1235, 1255
    (2) 1255
    11 1255
    (2) 1235
    13 1255
    31, 32 1258
    40 1257
    45 1234
    54(2) 1254
  Sch 2—
    Form A 1235
  Sch 3 .... 1235, 1255
  Sch 9 1257
Conveyancing (Scotland) Act 1874
  (c 94)
  s 4(2) 1249
    27 1237
    28 .... 1218, 1228
    32 .... 1235, 1260
    38 1228
    39 .... 1218, 1227
    40 1218
    54 1227
    61 1241
  Sch A 1249
Conveyancing (Scotland) Act 1924
  (c 27)
  s 8 1241
    (1) 1241
    14(1) 1235
    18(1) 1126
    48 1240
  Sch D 1241
Co-operative Development Agency
  Act 1978 (c 21) 607
Co-operative Development Agency
  and Industrial Development Act
  1984 (c 57)
  s 6 607
  Sch 2, Pt II 607
Counterfeit Currency (Convention)
  Act 1935 (c 25) 510
Court of Session Act 1808 (c 151)
  s 19 1032

PARA

Court of Session Act 1988 (c 36)
s 5 1037
42 1032
Credit Unions Act 1979 (c 34) 603,
656–658, 662, 663, 672,
677, 678
s 1 658
(1) 662
(2), (3) 661, 662
(4) 661, 662, 664
(5) 661
(6) 661, 664
2 .... 657, 658
(1) 657
(4) 658
(5), (6) 657, 658
3 .... 656, 663
(1)–(3) 658
(4) 657, 658
4 658
(1) 662, 663
(2) 663
(3), (5) 657
5 .... 658, 663
(1) 664
(2) 664, 665
(3) 665, 673
(5), (6) 664
6 .... 657, 658, 663
(1) 657, 664
(2), (5) 664, 673
(6) 664
7 658
(1)–(5) 665
8 658
(2), (5) 666
9 658
(1) 657, 666
(2) 666, 670
(3)–(5) 666
10 658
(1)–(6) 666
11 .... 656, 658, 663
(1)–(7) 669
12 658
(1)–(4) 667
(5) 667, 678
(6) 667
13 .... 658, 666
(1)–(6) 666
14 .... 658, 670
(1)–(7) 670
15 .... 658, 662, 663
(1)–(4) 668
16 658
(1)–(3) 668
17 658
(1) 657, 674
(2), (3) 674
18 658
(1)–(3) 675
19 658
(1)–(6) 676

PARA

Credit Unions Act 1979—*contd*
s 20 .... 657, 658
(1) 657, 677
(2) 677
21 .... 657, 658, 672
(1)–(4) 672
22 .... 657, 658, 672, 673
23 .... 657, 658
(1)–(3) 673
24 658
(1) 671
(2) 657, 671
25 .... 658, 659
26 658
27 .... 658, 662
(b)–(d) 668
28 .... 657, 658
(1), (3)–(6) 678
29, 30 658
31 .... 657, 658
(1) 666
(2) 663
(3) 657
32, 33 658
Sch 1 .... 657, 658, 663
para 4, 8, 9, 12–24 663
Sch 2 .... 658, 676
para 6 676
Sch 3 658
Criminal Appeal Act 1968 (c 19) 34
s 29(1) 34
56 34
Criminal Damage Act 1971 (c 48)
s 1(2) 532
Criminal Jurisdiction Act 1975 (c 59)
s 1 539
3 539
4(4) 539
Sch 3—
para 1 539
Criminal Justice Act 1967 (c 80)
s 92 655
106(2) 655
Sch 3—
Pt I 655
Criminal Justice Act 1982 (c 48)
s 44(2) 1301
54 .... 161, 622, 630, 645, 655,
744
55(2) 666, 735, 1534
(3) 655
56 .... 655, 666
64 213
77 .... 206, 865
Sch 6—
para 20 655
Sch 10—
para 1, 2 213
Sch 14—
para 36, 37 865
Sch 15—
para 15 206

PARA

Criminal Justice Act 1988 (c 33)
Pt I (s 1–22) 510
s 1 568
22(2)–(5) 532
123(6) 865
134 .... 508, 532
170(1) 666, 1301
Sch 1—
para 2 568
5 573
Sch 8—
para 9 865
Sch 15—
para 58(b) 666, 1301
Criminal Justice (International Co-
operation) Act 1990 (c 5) 501
s 6(1), (6) 119
Criminal Justice (Scotland) Act 1980
(c 62)
s 34 .... 619, 707
83(2) 865
Sch 3—
para 1 .... 619, 707
Sch 7—
para 24 865
Criminal Law Act 1609 (c 1) 504
Criminal Law Act 1773 (c 31) 504
Criminal Law Act 1967 (c 58)
s 10(2) 515
Sch 3—
Pt III 515
Criminal Law Act 1977 (c 45)
s 63(1) 655, 666, 735, 1301,
1534
Sch 11—
para 5 .... 655, 666, 735, 1301,
1534
Criminal Procedure Act 1701 (c 6) 504
Criminal Procedure (Scotland) Act
1975 (c 21) 555, 745
s 289B 735
(6) 666, 1301, 1534
289C 655
289F 161, 622, 630, 645, 744
289G 161, 622, 630, 645, 655,
744
289H 655
442 .... 619, 707
461(1) 206
Sch 7D 655
Sch 9—
para 47 206
Crofters (Scotland) Act 1955 (c 21)
s 16(9) 1168
16A(2) 1168
Crofting Reform (Scotland) Act 1976
(c 21)
s 13(3) 1168
Damages (Scotland) Act 1976 (c 13)
s 1 1191
Decimal Currency Act 1969 (c 19) 686
s 3 1231
6 690

PARA

Decimal Currency Act 1969—*contd*
s 9 1231
Sch 1 1231
Deeds Act 1696 (c 15) 1190
Diplomatic Immunities (Conferences
with Commonwealth Countries
and Republic of Ireland) Act 1961
(c 11) 130
s 1 130
Diplomatic Privileges Act 1964 (c 81) 130
District Courts (Scotland) Act 1975
(c 20)
s 5(7) 528
Divorce Jurisdiction, Court Fees and
Legal Aid (Scotland) Act 1983
(c 12)
s 6(1) 269
Sch 1—
para 13 269
Divorce (Scotland) Act 1938 (c 50) 1191
Drugs (Prevention of Misuse) Act
1964 (c 64)
s 1(1) 1147
Education (Scotland) Act 1946 (c 72) 90
s 29(1) 90
Education (Scotland) Act 1962 (c 47) 90
s 29(1) 90
Education (Scotland) Act 1980 (c 44) 95
s 28(1) 90
31 26
135(1) 1220
Employers' Liability (Compulsory
Insurance) Act 1969 (c 57) 805, 910
s 1(3) 910
Employment Act 1980 (c 42) 95
Employment Act 1982 (c 46)
s 21(2) 1036
Sch 3—
para 7 1036
Employment Protection (Consolidation) Act 1978 (c 44) 1036
s 128(3) 1036
Sch 9—
para 6A 1036
Enterprise and New Towns (Scotland) Act 1990 (c 35)
s 4(3) 617
Equal Pay Act 1970 (c 4) 1147
European Communities Act 1972
(c 68) 114, 219, 235, 1205
s 2 219
(2) 114, 137, 235
3 219
(2) 235
9 613
European Communities (Amendment) Act 1986 (c 58)
s 2 219
(b) 235
Explosive Substances Act 1883 (c 3)
s 2, 3 532
Extradition Act 1843 (cc 75, 76) 519

PARA

Extradition Act 1870 (c 52) 510, 533, 536,
538, 544, 566, 1146

s 2 .... 508, 514
  3(1) 316, 532, 1146
  (2) 540, 541
  (3), (4) 562
  4 508
  7 .... 550, 553
  8 .... 556, 562
  (1) 553
  9 .... 544–546, 562
  10 .... 544–546, 562, 568
  11 .... 562, 568, 574
  11A, 12 568
  13 559
  14, 15 565
  16 .... 514, 568
  (1) 553, 562
  17 508
  19 577
  21 508
  22 559
  26 .... 514, 536, 548, 556
Sch 1 .... 171, 514
Extradition Act 1873 (c 60) 510
Extradition Act 1895 (c 33) 510
Extradition Act 1906 (c 15) 510
Extradition Act 1932 (c 39) 510
Extradition Act 1989 (c 33) 501, 507,
510–512, 514, 519, 520,
522, 523, 530, 533, 534,
544, 554, 563, 575, 577

Pt I (s 1–5) 516
s 1 .... 508, 510
  (1) 513, 516
  (2) 519, 520
  (3) 508, 510–514, 532, 536,
541, 545, 550, 553, 556,
559, 562, 565, 568, 574,
577
2 .... 522, 548
  (1)–(3) 515, 548
  (4) 515
3 580
  (1) 511, 542
  (2) 512
  (3) 511
4 513
  (1) 511, 517
  (2) 511, 516
  (3)–(5) 511
  5(1), (2), (6) 520
Pt II (s 6) 516
s 6 .... 511, 523
  (1) 523
    (a) 516, 533
    (b)–(d) 516, 534
  (2) 516, 536
  (3) 516, 523, 538
  (4)–(6) 516, 540, 542
  (7) 523, 542
  (8) 523, 533
  (9) 532–534

PARA

Extradition Act 1989—*contd*

s 6(10) 534
Pt III (s 7–17) 511, 513, 516, 533, 534
s 7(1) 551, 554
  (2) 551, 563
  (3) 514
  (4), (5) 554
8 563
  (1)(a) 554
    (b) 557
  (2) 554, 557, 563
  (3) 554, 557
  (4) 557
  (5) 554, 560
  (6) 554
9 571
  (1) 557, 560, 563
  (2), (3) 563
  (4) 546, 563, 578, 580
  (5)–(7) 557
  (8) 546, 563
    (a) 546, 563, 578, 580
    (b) 563
  (9)–(11) 563
10(1), (2) 571
  (3) 514, 571
  (4)–(13) 571
11(1) 570
  (2) 570, 575
  (3), (4) 570
  (5) 570, 575
  (6) 570
12 570
  (1)–(6) 575
13(1)–(4) 575
14(1) 570
  (2) 514
  (3) 514, 570
  (4) 570
15(1)–(3) 511
16(1)–(5) 570
18 577
19 579
20 .... 511, 577, 579
21 501
22 508
  (1), (3)–(5) 546
  (6) 515
23(1), (2) 532
24(1)–(4) 532
25(1), (2) 532
26 565
  (1), (2) 566
27(1)–(4) 566
28(1) 553
37 510
  (3) 514, 545
  (5) 573
38(2), (3) 514
Sch 1 .... 508, 510, 511, 533, 538
  para 1(2) 532
    (3) 540, 541
    (4), (5) 562

PARA

Extradition Act 1989—*contd*
Sch 1—*contd*
para 4(1) 550
(2), (3) 553
5(1)(a) 553
(b) 556
(2) 556
(3) 556, 562
(4) 556
6 545
(1), (2) 562
7 545
(1)–(3) 562
8(1) 562, 568
(2), (3) 574
9(1) 568
(2) 514
(3), (4) 568
10 .... 568, 574
11 559
12 565
13 .... 514, 568
(1) 553, 559, 562
(2) 562
14 .... 508, 514
15 .... 512, 514
17 577
18 559
19 514
20 .... 513, 514, 536, 548, 556,
559
Sch 2 510
Extradition Acts 1870–1935 .... 510, 512
Extradition with England Act 1612
(c 2) 504
Factories Act 1937 (c 67) 1121
Pt II (s 12–40) 1121
s 22(1) 1182
24(1) 1156
26(1) 1121
Factories Act 1961 (c 34)
s 29(1) 1118, 1121
Family Law Act 1986 (c 55)
s 46 269
Family Law Reform Act 1969 (c 46)
s 19(2) 628
28(4) 628
Family Law (Scotland) Act 1985 (c 37)
s 1(1) 853
Finance Act 1933 (c 19)
s 31 1117
(1) 1117
Sch D—
Case I 1117
Finance Act 1960 (c 44)
s 47, 48 1105
Finance Act 1965 (c 25)
Sch 7—
para 15(2) 1207
Sch 18—
para 3 1207
Finance Act 1971 (c 68)
s 69(7) 623

PARA

Finance Act 1971—*contd*
Sch 14—
Pt VI 623
Finance Act 1975 (c 7) 1231
s 19(1) 1231
22 1231
49(5) 1231
Finance (No 2) Act 1975 (c 45)
s 46(1) 1037
52(4) 687
Sch 9—
para 1–3 687
Finance Act 1980 (c 48)
s 57(2) 688
61(3) 1037
62(2) 1037
Finance Act 1985 (c 54)
s 41(4) 687
98(6) 687
Sch 27—
Pt V—
Note 5 687
Finance Act 1986 (c 41)
s 100(1) 1231
Finance Act 1987 (c 16)
s 30(4) 690
Finance Act 1989 (c 26)
s 156, 158, 178, 179 1037
Finance Act 1990 (c 29)
s 48 689
49 .... 689, 690
(3), (4) 688
(5) 689
Sch 9—
para 6, 7 689
Finance Act 1991 (c 31) 689, 690
s 50 .... 689, 690
Sch 9—
para 1 689
3 690
4 689
Financial Services Act 1986 (c 60) ... 656, 691,
802, 804, 806, 807, 811,
1301–1303, 1305, 1307–
1309, 1311, 1312, 1314–
1360, 1320–1322, 1325,
1329, 1333, 1341, 1342,
1348, 1353, 1354, 1356,
1362, 1368, 1377, 1386,
1387, 1400, 1412, 1423,
1429, 1520, 1524, 1531
Pt I (s 1–128) 1313
s 1(1) 807, 812, 1308
(2) 812, 1307
2 1307
Pt I, Ch II–XII (s 3–113) 1310
s 3 .... 1301, 1306, 1321, 1324,
1325
4(1), (2) 1301
5 1412
(1)–(3) 1412
6 1412
(1), (2) 1324

PARA

Financial Services Act 1986—*contd*

s 6(3) 1324, 1332
  (5)–(9) 1324
Pt I, Ch III (s 7–34) 1301, 1306
s 7(1), (2) 1312
  8(1), (2) 1312
  9(1) 1312
  (2)–(5) 1312, 1322
  (6) 1312
  10(1), (2), (4) 1312
  (5) 1314
  11(1)–(6) 1314
  12(1)–(3) 1314
  15(1), (2) 1313
  16(1), (2) 1313
  17(1) 1313
  18(1)–(3) 1313
  (4) 1314
  19(1), (2) 1314
  20(1)–(3) 1314
  22 .... 807, 1312, 1339
  (a), (b) 1316
  23 1312
  (1) 691, 1317
  24 .... 1318, 1328, 1339
  (a), (b) 1318
  25 .... 1310, 1339
  26 1417
  (1), (2) 1310
  27 1319
  (1), (2) 1310, 1319
  (3)–(5) 1310
  28 .... 1342, 1413
  (1) 691, 1311
  (2) 691
  (3)–(5) 1311
  29(1) 1311, 1417
  (4) 1311
  30(1)–(4) 1310
  31 .... 1312, 1339
  (1)–(3) 1320
  32(1) 1320, 1342, 1417
  33 1320
  (3) 1417
  34(1) 1320, 1417
  (4) 1320
Pt I, Ch IV (s 35–46) 1301, 1306
s 35 1321
  36(1) 1322
  37(1), (2), (4) 1322
  38(1) 1322
  39(1), (2), (4) 1322
  40(1), (2) 1322
  42, 43 .... 1307, 1321
  44 .... 812, 1307, 1378
  (1) 1323, 1361
  (2)–(6) 1361
  (9) 1332
  45 1307
  (1)–(3) 1323
  46 1307
  (1) 1323

PARA

Financial Services Act 1986—*contd*

Pt I, Ch V (s 47–63C) 1339, 1410,
                                  1412, 1417
s 47 .... 810, 1324, 1395, 1410
  (1), (2) 810, 1332
  (3)–(6) 1332
  47A 1341
  (1)–(4) 1342
  47B(1), (2), (4) 1342
  48 .... 691, 1331, 1340
  (1) 1356
  (2) 1356, 1395
  (3)–(5) 1356
  (6) 1395
  (7) 1332
  (8) 1332, 1531
  49 .... 1340, 1402
  50 .... 1339, 1340, 1410, 1412,
                                  1417
  51 .... 819, 1340
  (1), (2) 1336
  52 1340
  53 .... 1340, 1429
  (1) 1429
  54 1340
  (1), (2) 1429
  (3) 1421
  55 .... 1340, 1409
  56 .... 1324, 1339, 1410, 1417
  (1) 812, 1340, 1333
  (2)–(5) 1334
  (7) 812, 1334
  (7A), (8) 1334
  57 .... 1366, 1410
  (1) 1335, 1337
  (2) 1337, 1423
  (3)–(8) 1337
  58 1337
  (3) 1337, 1410, 1412
  59 .... 1339, 1342, 1410, 1415,
                                  1417
  (1)–(3) 1338
  (4) 1338, 1417
  (5) 1338
  (6) 1338, 1412
  (8) 1338
  60 1342
  (1) 1339
  (2) 1339, 1417
  (3)–(5) 1339
  61 .... 1410–1412, 1535
  (1) 1342, 1410, 1411
  (2) 1410
  (3) 1411, 1535
  (4) 1411
  (5) 1411, 1535
  (6), (7) 1411
  (8), (9) 1410, 1411
  62 .... 1341, 1362, 1376, 1387,
                1397, 1398, 1412, 1535
  (1) 821, 1412, 1535
  (2), (3) 1412

PARA

Financial Services Act 1986—*contd*

s 62A 1341, 1362, 1376, 1387
　(1), (2) 1412
63A 1335, 1341
　(1) 1356
Pt I, Ch VI (s 64–71) 1417
s 64(1), (3), (4) 1413
65 1413
66 1413
67(1), (3) 1413
68, 69 1413
70 1417
　(1), (3), (5) 1413
72(1)–(3), (5) 1412
75(1) 1307, 1308, 1325
　(2)–(7) 1325
　(8) 1307, 1308, 1325
　(9) 1307, 1325
76 1367
　(1) 1326
　(2) 1326, 1367
　(3)–(7) 1326
77 1327
　(2)–(5) 1328
78 1325
　(1)–(8) 1327
79(1), (4) 1327
80 1327
81 . . . . 1327, 1328
82(1)–(3) 1327
83 1327
85 . . . . 1327, 1328, 1363
86 . . . . 1318, 1326, 1400
　(1)–(5) 1328
　(7) 1399
　(8) 1318, 1328
87 1329
　(1)–(3), (5) 1328
88 1329
　(1)–(8) 1328
89 1328
90(1), (2) 1328
91(1), (2), (5) 1329
92(1), (3), (4) 1329
93(1) 1329
　(4) 1329
94(1)–(5), (7), (7A) 1330
　(8), (8A), (8B), (9) 1330
Pt I, Ch IX (s 96–101) 1305
s 96(1)–(4) 1416
　(6) 1416, 1418
97(1)–(5) 1417
98(1) 1418, 1419
　(2)–(5) 1419
99 1419
100 1417
　(1)–(5) 1419
102–104 1415
105 1415
　(1), (3), (4), (6), (9), (10) 1415
106 1415
114 . . . . 1319, 1331, 1429, 1520
　(1) 1305, 1310

PARA

Financial Services Act 1986—*contd*

s 114(3) 1520
　(4), (5) 1310
　(6) 1310, 1322
115 1305
117(1), (2) 1305
119 1322
　(1) 1312
120 1322
　(1), (2) 1312
121(2), (3) 1305
122, 123 1312
129 . . . . 807, 820, 1316
130(2) 810
132(1), (3), (6) 807, 835
133 . . . . 808, 859
137 820
140 . . . . 691, 1317, 1356
Pt IV (s 142–157) 1301, 1520
Pt V (s 158–171) 1301
Pt VI (s 172) 1301
Pt VII (s 173–178) 1301
s 173(1) 1502, 1519, 1520, 1522
　(2) 1520
174(1) 1526, 1529
　(2) 1526
　(3) 1523, 1524, 1526
　(4) 1510, 1524
175 . . . . 1523, 1531
176 1510
177(1), (2), (2A), (3)–(5) 1533
　(5A), (7), (8), (10) 1533
178 1533
188(1) 1305
207(1) 1306, 1312, 1325, 1386,
　　　　　　　　　　　　　　　　　　　1520
　(2), (3) 1337
211(1) 1340, 1429, 1510
212(2) 1503
　(3) 1510
Sch 1 1360
　Pt I (para 1–11) 1308
　　para 1 . . . . 1325, 1332
　　　note 1308
　　2 . . . . 1325, 1332
　　3 . . . . 1308, 1325, 1332
　　4, 5 . . . . 1325, 1332
　　6 1325
　　7 1308
　　9 . . . . 1308, 1510
　　10 . . . . 807, 812, 1325
　Pt II (para 12–16) 1307, 1332, 1412
　　para 12, 13 1307
　　15 812
　Pt III (para 17–25B) 1332, 1412
　　para 17–19 1307
　　20 1307
　　　(4) 1325
　　21–25, 25A, 25B 1307
　Pt IV (para 26, 27) 1307, 1332, 1412
Sch 3 1313
Sch 4 1322
　para 5 1322

PARA

Financial Services Act 1986—*contd*
Sch 5 1321
Sch 6—
   para 1–3 1416
     4(1), (2) 1416
     5 1418
Sch 7—
   para 1 1305
Sch 10 812
   para 2(1), (2) 1316
     3(1) 1316
     4 1399
     5 820
     7(2) 1316
Sch 11 691
   Pt II (para 2–12) 691, 1317
     para 4(2) 691
       10 691
   Pt III (para 13–27) 1317
     para 14 .... 691, 1399
       17 691
       22B 1341
       23(1) 691
   Pt IV (para 28–37) 691
     para 28(1), (4) 1520
Sch 16—
   para 28(a), (b) 1503
Sch 17 1510
Firearms Act 1968 (c 27)
  s 16 532
   17(1) 532
Fishings Act 1661 (c 279) 103
Food and Drugs Act 1938 (c 56)
  s 3(1) 1151
Foreign Judgments (Reciprocal Enforcement) Act 1933 (c 13)
  s 8(1) 1149
Foreign Marriage Act 1892 (c 23)
  s 1(2) 220
Foreign Marriage (Amendment) Act 1988 (c 44)
  s 1(2) 220
France Act 1491 (Apr 28 c 2) 103
French Subject Act 1558 (c 6) 103
Friendly and Industrial and Provident Societies Act 1968 (c 55) ... 603, 630, 680
  s 1 640
   (1), (2) 630
   2 640
   (1), (2) 630
   3 .... 631, 640
   (1)–(3) 631
   (4) 632
   (5) 635, 671
   (7) 630, 631
   4 .... 613, 636
   (1) 639
   (2) 636
   (5) 639
   (6), (7) 636
   5 613
   (1) 639
     proviso 639

Friendly and Industrial and Provident Societies Act 1968—*contd*
  s 5(2) 639
   6 613
   (1)–(9) 639
   7 613
   (1)–(3) 637
   8 .... 613, 639
   (1)–(3) 638
   (4) 639
   (5) 638
   9 613
   (1)–(7) 640
   10 .... 613, 640
   11(1) 634
   (2) 632
   (5) 635
   13(1)–(5) 633
   14(1), (2), (4) 633
   15 .... 633, 638
   (1)–(4), (6)–(9) 633
   17(5) 699, 713
   20(1)(a) 634, 654
   (b) 630
  Sch 1—
   para 10 634
     11 654
Friendly Societies Act 1793 (c 54) 602
Friendly Societies Act 1834 (c 40) 602
  s 4 602
Friendly Societies Act 1846 (c 27) 602
  s 10 602
Friendly Societies Act 1875 (c 60) 602, 683, 697, 703
Friendly Societies Act 1896 (c 25) 683, 717, 725
  s 2, 8, 22 683
   36 704
   56, 62, 64–67 683
   78 704
   101, 103, 104 683
  Sch 2—
   Pt I, II 683
Friendly Societies Act 1908 (c 32)
  s 9 745
Friendly Societies Act 1955 (4 Eliz 2 c 19)
  s 3(3) 705
Friendly Societies Act 1971 (c 66)
  s 11(5) 630
   14 639
  Sch 2—
   para 49 639
Friendly Societies Act 1974 (c 46) 603, 604, 630, 679, 683–687, 690, 691, 694, 695, 697, 699, 700, 703–705, 707, 708, 710, 711, 717, 719, 724–726, 736–738, 741, 743–745, 1317
  s 1(2), (3) 604
   2(3) 604
   4(1), (3) 604

Friendly Societies Act 1974—*contd*

PARA

s 5(1), (2) 604
7 687
  (1) 684, 699, 700, 704, 720,
                     1317
    (a) 684, 686
    (b) 685, 693
    (c), (d) 685, 694
    (e) 685, 694, 699
    (f) 685, 694
  (2) 697, 699–701, 703–708,
          713, 715, 719, 725, 737
    (a) 698
    (b) 699
  (3), (3A) 687, 688
  (5) 687
8 611
  (1) 695, 704
  (2) 695, 707
  (3) 699
9(2) 695
  (3) 695, 717
10 .... 605, 696, 697, 703
11(1) 697, 707
  (2) 697
12 697
  (1) 707
13 697
14 .... 697, 699
15 695
16(1), (2) 695
17 698
18 .... 699, 703, 711
  (1) 703
  (2) 699
19 703
20 703
  (1) 703
22(2) 706
23 .... 702, 721
  (1) 702, 721
  (2), (3) 721
24 708
  (1)–(4) 708
  (5) 708, 710
25 .... 707, 710, 712
26 .... 707, 708
27 .... 702, 707
  (2) 707
28 .... 707, 708
  (1)–(3) 707
29 .... 700, 710
  (1) 714, 716
  (2)–(4) 714
30 710
  (1)–(7) 714
  (8) 710, 714, 744
31 710
  (1)–(5) 715
32 710
  (1)–(3) 715
  (4) 744
33 .... 710, 715

Friendly Societies Act 1974—*contd*

PARA

s 33(1)–(3) 715
34 710
  (1)–(5) 715
35 710
  (1)–(6) 715
36 .... 710, 715
  (1) 715
37 .... 710, 715
  (1), (2) 715
38 710
  (1)–(5) 716
39 710
  (1), (2) 716
40 .... 710, 716
41 .... 700, 714, 717, 718
  (1)–(6) 717
42 .... 700, 717
  (4), (5) 717
43(1)–(3), (5), (6) 718
44 714
  (1) 714
45 714
  (b) 717
46 .... 708, 715
  (1) 709, 719
  (2) 719
47 .... 701, 719
48 720
  (2) 720
49 .... 702, 720
  (a) 720
  (b)–(d) 702, 720
50 .... 702, 719–721
  (1)–(3), (5) 720
51 .... 702, 719
  (1)–(4) 719
52 .... 702, 719
  (1) 719
53 .... 702, 719, 721
  (1) 702
54 719
  (1), (3) 708
58 708
59 708
  (1), (2) 707
60(1) 699, 704
  (2) 704, 738
61 699
63 702
64 .... 688, 690
  (1B) 690
  (2) 722
65(2) 699, 701
66 711
  (1)–(8) 722
67(1)–(3) 723
68(1) 709, 723
  (2), (3) 723
69(1) 723
  (2) 722
70(1), (2) 724
71 724

PARA

Friendly Societies Act 1974—*contd*

s 71(1), (2)	692
(3)	680
(4)	692
(5)	744
72	686
(1)	724
73	724
(2)	686
(5)	744
74	686, 724
75	701
76	725
(1)	725
(2)	725, 739
(3)–(5)	725
77	708, 725
(1)	725
(2)	725, 727
(3)	725, 727, 739
(4)	725
78(1)	725
(3)	725, 739
79	725
(1)	725, 727
(2)–(4)	725
80(1), (2)	725
81(1), (2)	699
82	728
(1)	727
(2), (3)	728
(4)	727
(5)	728, 736
(6)	729
(7)	727
83	727
(1)–(8)	727
84(1), (2)	731
(3)	731, 736
(4)	731
85(1)–(3)	730
(4)	730, 736
(5), (6)	730
86(1)	699, 713, 727
(2)	713, 727
(3), (4)	727
87	733
(1)–(4)	733
88	735
(1), (2)	735
(3)	727, 735
(4)–(9)	735
89	734
(1)–(3)	734
(4)	734, 744
(5)–(7)	734
90	700, 739
(1)–(4)	713, 732
(5), (6)	732
(7)	713
91	711
(1)/(7)	736
92	736

PARA

Friendly Societies Act 1974—*contd*

s 92(2)	736
93(1), (2)	737, 738
(3)	738, 739
(4)	738
94	708
(2)–(7)	738
95(1)–(7)	739
96	739
97	738, 739
98(1)–(4)	744
(5)–(8)	743
99	745
(1)	744
(2)	708, 709, 745
(3)–(5)	745
(6)	708, 709, 745
(7)	744, 745
100	744
101(1)	743
(2), (3)	742
103(1)	708, 741
(2)–(7)	741
106	724
111(1)	697, 699, 707, 719
(3)	604, 605
(4)	714
116(2)	683, 704
(4)	632, 635–637, 683
Sch 1	684, 691, 699, 1317
para (1)	686, 688
(2)	688
(a)–(c)	686
(d)	686, 724
(e)	686
(3)	686, 704
(4), (5)	686, 688
(6), (7)	686
Sch 2	701
Pt I (para 1–11)	698
para 2	699
3(1)	699, 704–706
(2)	699, 701
4	699, 703, 713
5	697, 699, 701, 707, 708
6	699, 700, 715, 719
7, 8	699
9	699, 725
10	700
11(1), (2)	699
Pt II (para 12–15)	698
para 12, 13	700
14	700, 737
15	700
Sch 3	707
Sch 5	724
para 2	724
Sch 6	686
para 3	686, 692, 724
5	686, 704, 724
6, 7	686
8	724

PARA

Friendly Societies Act 1974—*contd*
Sch 10—
    para 7–13 683
Sch 11 .... 632, 635–637, 683
Friendly Societies Act 1981 (c 50) 603,
    683
Friendly Societies Act 1984 (c 62) 603,
    683
Fugitive Offenders Act 1881 (c 69) 519
Fugitive Offenders Act 1967 (c 68) 171,
    501, 510, 519, 522, 538,
    544, 577
  s 3(1) 548
    4(1) 316
      (a) 532
      (b), (c) 534
     (2) 538
     (3) 540
    5(3) 554
    6(1) 563
     (4), (5) 554
    7 .... 544, 546
     (1), (2) 544, 563
     (3) 563
     (4) 544, 563
    8(2) 575
     (3) 570
    9(1)–(6) 575
    11 566
Game Act 1670 (c 25) 1107
  s 3 1107
Genocide Act 1969 (c 12)
  s 2(1) 532
Gipsies Act 1609 (c 20) 103
Greenock Corporation Act 1909
  (c cxxix)
  s 251 1113
Guardianship of Infants Act 1925
  (c 45)
  s 10 1229
Habeas Corpus Act 1679 (c 2) 504
Highways (Scotland) Act 1771 (c 53)
  s 1 1179
House of Commons Disqualification
  Act 1975 (c 24)
  s 1 331
    10(2) 139
  Sch 1, Pt II 331
  Sch 3 139
Housing Act 1985 (c 68)
  Pt III (s 58–78) 160
Housing Act 1988 (c 50)
  s 59 .... 648, 649
  Sch 6—
    para 2 .... 648, 649
Housing Associations Act 1985 (c 69) 617
  s 1 719
    5(3) 610
    16, 17 619
    19 616
    21(1), (2) 648, 649
     (3) 650
     (4) 653

PARA

Housing Associations Act 1985—*contd*
  s 21(5) 652
    22(1) 653
    23 .... 652, 653
    25 .... 636, 637, 639
Housing (Consequential Provisions)
  Act 1985 (c 71)
  s 4 .... 621, 719
  Sch 2—
    para 8 621
    26 719
Housing (Scotland) Act 1930 (c 40)
  s 16 1174
Housing (Scotland) Act 1987 (c 26)
  Pt II (s 24–43) 160
Immigration Act 1971 (c 77) 8, 105–107,
    109, 110, 117–119, 123,
    125, 128, 130, 131, 133,
    134, 137, 138, 141, 143,
    150, 153, 155, 160, 162,
    166, 167, 190, 198, 235,
    269, 316, 331, 350, 354
  s 1 .... 133, 134
    (1) 117, 123
    (2) 119
    (3) 122
    (4) 110, 141, 170
    (5) 110, 125, 208
    2 .... 118, 153
    (1), (2) 118, 153
    3 .... 119, 147, 354
    (1) 119, 123
     (a) 198
     (b) 119, 120
     (c) 119, 170, 177
    (2) 110, 138, 141
    (3) 119, 244
     (a) 119, 177, 253
     (b) 119, 176, 177, 253, 342
    (4) 119, 120, 176, 177
    (5) 119, 120, 138, 203
     (a) 126, 186, 204, 205
     (b) 126, 204, 207
     (c) 126, 204, 208
    (6) 119, 120, 126, 203, 204,
     206
    (7) 135, 136, 203
    (8) 118, 126, 153
    (9) 118, 151, 339
    4 193
    (1) 112, 131, 138, 141, 142,
     146, 170, 178, 180
    (2) 111, 138, 140, 142, 143,
     147, 161–163, 165, 167,
     169, 170, 173, 185, 196–
     201, 213, 345
    (3) 119, 138, 175, 190
    (4) 138, 184
    5 .... 138, 147
    (1) 120, 202, 212, 342
    (2) 214, 342
    (3) 208, 342
    (4) 120, 208, 269, 342

PARA

Immigration Act 1971—*contd*

s 5(4)(a), (b) 208
  (5) 211, 212, 213
  (6) 215
6 .... 119, 138
  (1)–(3) 206
  (6) 211
  (7) 206
7 .... 119, 206
  (1)–(5) 126
8 .... 119, 128, 146, 148
  (1) 119, 129, 161, 196
    (a)–(c) 129
  (2) 128, 151
  (3) 128, 130
  (3A) 130
  (4) 128, 131
  (5), (5A) 128
  (6) 131
9 119
  (1) 123
  (2) 122–124, 175
  (3) 124
  (4) 122–124
  (5)–(7) 122
10 119
11(1) 146
  (1A) 146
  (2) 146, 147
  (3) 146
  (4) 122
12 139
  (b) 330, 331
13 330
  (1), (2) 336
  (3) 150, 339
  (4) 333, 339
  (5) 338, 339
14 .... 329, 330
  (1) 178, 336
  (2) 336
  (3), (4) 340
  (5) 212, 340
15 330
  (1) 205, 214, 336
  (2) 208, 211
  (3) 207, 342
  (4) 177, 214, 342
  (5), (6) 342
  (7) 330
16 .... 201, 330
  (1) 336, 341
  (2), (3) 341
  (4) 333, 341
  (4A) 199
17 .... 201, 330
  (1) 336, 341, 343
  (2), (3) 336
  (4), (5) 343
18 330
  (1) 211, 345
  (2) 345
19 330

PARA

Immigration Act 1971—*contd*

s 19(1) 110, 333
  (2) 112, 333
  (3), (4) 333
20 .... 330, 348, 350, 357, 366
  (1) 334
  (2) 334, 366
  (3) 334
21 .... 330, 367
  (1) 330
22 169
  (4) 352
  (5) 358
24(1) 185–187
  (a) 170, 185, 195
  (b) 178, 186, 205
  (c) 186, 195
  (d) 165, 187
  (e) 169, 187
  (f) 187
  (g) 135, 136, 187
  (1A) 186
  (2) 185–187
  (3) 185, 186
26(1) 166, 175
  (a), (b) 166
  (c) 166, 175
  (d), (e) 166
  (f) 175
  (g) 166, 190
27 200
  (a)–(d) 161
28 .... 185, 186
29 215
33(1) 110, 123, 129, 147, 150,
                    198, 342
  (2) 120, 342
  (2A) 120, 342
  (5) 105, 106, 108
35(1) 125
36 123
Sch 2 .... 142, 146
para 1(1) 138, 140, 142
  (2) 138, 140, 143
  (3) 111
  2 .... 129, 162
  (1) 146
  (2) 143, 165
  (3) 162, 165
  3 .... 141, 147
  (1) 193
  4(1), (2), (2A), (3), (4) 162
  5 163
  6 173
  (1) 120, 170, 345
  (2) 170
  (3), (4) 162, 170
  8 .... 145, 185, 197
  (1), (2) 200
  9 .... 147, 185, 198, 200
  10 .... 147, 185
  (1)–(3) 200
  11 .... 167, 200

PARA

Immigration Act 1971—*contd*
  Sch 2—*contd*
    para 12 129
      (1) 196
      (2) 196, 200
     13 .... 129, 201
      (1) 196
      (2) 196, 200
     14 .... 129, 200
     15 200
     16 146
      (1) 167, 199
      (2) 199
      (3) 167, 199
      (4A) 167
     17 .... 146, 169
      (1) 168, 199
      (2) 168
     18 146
      (1)–(4) 167
     19, 20 146
     21 .... 146, 169, 199
     22 .... 146, 167, 199
      (1)–(3) 169
     23 .... 146, 199
      (2) 169
     24 .... 146, 199
      (1)–(3) 169
     25 .... 146, 169, 199
     26 133
      (1), (2) 161
     27(1), (2) 161
     27A 161
     28(1) 200, 201
      (2) 212
      (3) 199, 200
      (4) 200
      (5), (6) 200, 201
     29 .... 199, 213
      (1)–(6) 199
     30 .... 199, 213
      (2) 199
     31, 32 .... 199, 213
     33 199
  Sch 3 .... 119, 147, 202
    para 1 212
      (4) 212
     2 211
      (1), (1A), (2)–(6) 213
     3 .... 212, 213
     4–6 213
  Sch 4 .... 199, 122, 123
    para 1(1)–(5) 123
     2 123
     3(1), (2) 123
     4 123
  Sch 5 139
    para 1 331
     2(1), (2) 331
     3 331
     5 .... 330, 331
     6–9 331
     11 330

PARA

Immigration Act 1971—*contd*
  Sch 5—*contd*
    para 12 .... 330, 331
     14 331
Immigration Act 1988 (c 14) ... 109, 114, 118,
             137, 146, 235, 316, 322
  s 1 .... 110, 125
   2 118
    (1)–(4) 118
   3 339
    (1) 118
   4 130
   5 322
   6(1) 186
   7(1), (2) 114, 137, 235
   8 .... 150, 152, 162, 165, 170,
                    172
    (1)–(3) 162
    (4) 129, 162
    (5), (6) 162
    (7) 146, 150, 162
    (8) 162
   10 .... 119, 120, 150, 162, 169,
        170, 176, 177, 187, 197,
        200, 212, 213, 215, 329,
              340, 342
  Schedule—
    para 1 .... 119, 176, 177, 342
     2 215
     3 .... 212, 329, 340
     5 150
     6 162
     7 170
     8 170
      (1) 120
      (2) 162
      (3) 120
     9 200
      (1), (4) 197
     10(1) 169
      (2) 213
      (3) 187
      (4) 169, 187, 213
Immigration Appeals Act 1969 (c 21) 106
Immigration (Carriers' Liability) Act
  1987 (c 24) 109, 316, 317
  s 1(1), (2), (4) 161, 317
Income and Corporation Taxes Act
  1970 (c 10)
  s 340A 659
   540(3) 1212
Income and Corporation Taxes Act
  1988 (c 1) 679, 683, 687, 690
  s 154 1120
   267 689
   329 1034
    (2), (4) 1034
   360–633 617
  Pt XII, Ch II (s 459–467) 687
  s 459 680
   460(1)–(3) 689
    (4A), (4B) 689
    (5)–(12) 689

PARA

Income and Corporation Taxes Act
  1988—*contd*
  s 464 .... 688, 690
    (1)–(3) 690
    (4A), (4B) 690
    (5)–(7) 690
  465 689
  466(1) 688
    (2) 689
  487 659
  620(9) 690, 738
  844 .... 688, 1105
    (1) 687
    (4) 687, 722
  Sch 15—
    para 3 689
      (1), (2), (5)–(11) 689
  Sch 29—
    para 13 .... 687, 688
      32 .... 687, 1105
  Sch 31 722
Income Tax Act 1952 (c 10)
  s 25(3) 1105
  161(1), (3) 1120
**Increase of Rent and Mortgage
  Interest (Restrictions) Act 1920
  (c 17)**
  s 7 1117
**Industrial and Provident Societies Act
  1852 (c 31)** 602
**Industrial and Provident Societies Act
  1876 (c 45)** 602
**Industrial and Provident Societies Act
  1893 (c 39)** 607, 626, 653
**Industrial and Provident Societies Act
  1952 (c 17)** 621
**Industrial and Provident Societies Act
  1961 (c 28)** 621
**Industrial and Provident Societies Act
  1965 (c 12)** 603, 607–613, 615,
                      619, 637, 647, 654, 656,
                      657, 670, 677, 678
  s 1 .... 612, 657
    (1) 607, 615, 616, 619, 621,
                  622, 624, 626, 636
      (b) 607, 613
    (2) 607, 610
      (a) 608, 611
      (b) 609, 611
    (3) 607, 608
  2(1), (2) 610, 657
    (3) 610, 662
  3 .... 610, 657
  4 .... 607, 613, 653
  5 .... 613, 616, 657
    (1)–(5) 613
    (6) 613, 655
    (7) 655
  6 .... 613, 618, 657
    (1)–(4) 621
  7 .... 613, 657
    (1)–(3), (6) 622
  8 .... 605, 610, 616

PARA

Industrial and Provident Societies Act
  1965—*contd*
  s 10 .... 613, 616
    (1) 616
    (2) 613
    (3) 616, 657
  11 657
  12 .... 611, 615, 623, 657
  13(1), (2) 615
    (3) 654
    (4) 615
  14(1) 614, 616
    (2) 616
    (3) 607
  15 618
    (2) 655
  16 .... 608, 609, 611, 658
    (1) 677
      (a) 611, 657
      (b) 611
      (c) 611, 645, 677
    (2) 611
    (4) 645
    (5) 655
  17 .... 657, 658
    (1) 611, 677
    (2)–(6) 611
  18 .... 610, 611, 616, 677
    (1) 610
  19 657
    (1), (2) 618
  20 .... 613, 615, 618, 619, 666
  21 .... 615, 623, 657
  22(1), (2) 625
  23 .... 613, 618, 620
    (1)–(6) 626
  24 .... 613, 620, 629
    (1)–(3) 627
  25 .... 613, 620, 628, 629
    (1), (2) 628
  26 .... 618, 620
    (1), (2) 629
  27 .... 628, 629
  30 .... 615, 657
  31 .... 613, 624, 657
  32 624
  34(1)–(5) 623
  36 613
  37, 38 630
  39 .... 618, 630
    (1) 632, 634, 657, 671
    (2), (2A), (3) 634
    (4) 634, 652
    (5) 635
  40 .... 635, 671
  41 .... 615, 620
    (1)–(3) 619
  42 620
    (1)–(4) 619
  44(1) 618, 643
    (5) 618
  45(1), (2) 642
  46 .... 615, 618

PARA

Industrial and Provident Societies Act
  1965—*contd*
s 46(1), (2) 643
  47 618
    (1)–(4) 644
  48 .... 611, 674
    (1) 645, 657
    (2) 645, 655
    (3) 645
  49 675
    (1)–(4) 646
    (5), (6) 646, 675
    (7) 646
  50 .... 657, 672
    (1) 648
    (2)–(5) 648–650
  51 .... 657, 672
    (1)–(3) 649
  52 .... 657, 673
    (1)–(3), (5) 650
  53 673
    (1), (2) 651, 657
    (3)–(7) 651
  54 648–650
    (4) 650
  55 .... 618, 653
    (a) 653
    (b) 634, 652
  56 .... 645, 653
  57 621
    (a)–(e) 653
  58 .... 618, 652
    (2), (3) 652
    (4) 652, 655
    (5)–(9) 652
  59 .... 649, 650, 652, 653
  60 .... 615, 647
    (1)–(3), (7)–(9) 647
  61 .... 655, 657, 678
  62 .... 620, 654, 657, 678
  63 .... 654, 657, 678
  64 .... 657, 678
    (1) 654, 655
    (2) 655
  65 .... 655, 657, 678
  66 .... 620, 657, 678
    (1) 654
    (2) 654, 678
  67 654
  68 .... 654, 657, 678
  71(2) 654
  73 604
    (1) 605, 610, 613
  74 .... 619, 647, 654
  78 604
Sch 1 .... 607, 610, 612, 615, 657
  para 1–4 613
       5 .... 613, 616
       6 .... 613, 619
       7 .... 613, 621
       8 .... 613, 622
       9 .... 613, 621
      10 .... 613, 636

PARA

Industrial and Provident Societies Act
  1965——*contd*
Sch 1—*contd*
  para 11 .... 613, 618, 626
       12, 13 613
       14 .... 613, 624
  Sch 2 622
  Sch 3—
    Pt II—
      Forms C–E 623
  Sch 4—
    Pt II 615, 619
Industrial and Provident Societies Act
  1967 (c 48) 603, 641
s 3 641
    (3) 641
  4(1)–(4) 641
Industrial and Provident Societies Act
  1975 (c 41) 603, 621
s 3(3) 651
Industrial and Provident Societies Act
  1978 (c 34) 603
Industrial and Provident Societies
  Acts 1965–1978 .... 672, 677
Industrial Assurance Act 1923 (c 8) .. 680, 701
s 1(2) 680, 682
  6 699
  8 701
  19 713
    (1)–(3) 699
  23 705
  39(5) 743
  Sch 1 701
  Sch 4 701
Industrial Assurance Acts 1923–1968: 680, 682
Industrial Assurance and Friendly
  Societies Act 1929 (c 28) 680
  Schedule 701
Industrial Assurance and Friendly
  Societies Act 1948 (c 39) 680
Industrial Assurance and Friendly
  Societies Act 1948 (Amendment)
  Act 1958 (c 27) 680
Industrial Assurance (Juvenile Socie-
  ties) Act 1926 (c 35) 680
Industrial Common Ownership Act
  1976 (c 78) 617
Inheritance Tax Act 1984 (c 51)
s 4, 273 1231
  Sch 6—
    para 1 1231
Inner Urban Areas 1978 (c 50) 617
Insolvency Act 1985 (c 65)
s 109(1) 906
  235(1) 904, 905, 907, 908
  Sch 6—
    para 45 906
  Sch 8—
    para 7(2) 904, 905, 907
         (4) 908
  Sch 9—
    para 9 906

PARA

Insolvency Act 1986 (c 45) 620, 653,
　　　　　　　　　　　　　680, 733
　Pt I (s 1–7) 904
　Pt II (s 8–27) 653
　Pt IV (s 73–219) 653, 740
　　Ch VI–X (s 117–219) 740
　　Ch VI (s 117–162) 733, 740
　　Ch VII–IX (s 163–205) 740
　　Ch X (s 206–219) 653, 740
　Pt V (s 220–229) 740
　s 220 740
　　(1) 680
　Pt VI (s 230–246) 653
　s 439(2) 653, 733, 904, 905, 907
　　440 733
　Sch 14 .... 653, 733, 904, 905, 907
Insurance Brokers (Registration) Act
　　1977 (c 46) 806, 811, 813
　s 1(1) 813
　　2–4, 6, 7 813
　　9(1) 813
　　10(1) 813
　　11 813
　　12(2) 813
　　13, 15, 22 813
Insurance Companies Act 1982 (c 50) 668,
　　　　　　802, 806, 807, 810, 811,
　　　　　　　　　　　　　1316
　s 1 .... 699, 717
　　(1) 1308
　　2 .... 807, 835
　　(1) 807
　　(2) 680, 807
　　(5) 807
　　3 .... 807, 1316
　　(1), (3) 807
　　4 .... 807, 1316
　　6, 7 807
　　9(2) 807
　　11(2) 807
　　13(2A) 1316
　　14(1) 807
　Pt II (s 15–71) 1316
　s 16 .... 807, 1316
　　28 807
　　29(7) 807
　　32 807
　　(3) 807
　　37 .... 808, 1316
　　38–44 1316
　　45 1316
　　(1) 808
　　46 .... 808, 1316
　　47–53 1316
　　54 .... 808, 1316
　　55 1316
　　(3) 807
　　56–71 1316
　　75–78 820
　　95(a) 802
　　99(2) 668
　Sch 1 .... 699, 717, 807, 820, 1308

PARA

Insurance Companies Act 1982—*contd*
　Sch 2 807
　　Pt I 844
　Sch 5—
　　para 20 668
Insurance Contracts Act 1984 (Aus-
　　tralia)
　s 17 850
Interception of Communications Act
　　1985 (c 56) 95
Interest on Damages (Scotland) Act
　　1958 (c 61) 1001, 1032
　s 1(1), (1A), (2) 1032
Interest on Damages (Scotland) Act
　　1971 (c 31) 1001, 1032
　s 1(1) 1032
International Development Associ-
　　ation Act 1960 (c 35)
　s 3(1) 130
International Finance Corporation Act
　　1955 (c 5)
　s 3(1) 130
International　Headquarters　and
　　Defence Organisation Act 1964
　　(c 5) 131
　s 1 131
International Organisations Act 1968
　　(c 48) 130
　s 1 130
　　(2) 130
　　5(1), (2) 130
　　6(2) 130
　　12(5) 130
　Sch 1 130
Interpretation Act 1889 (c 63) 1206, 1231
　s 1(1) 1207
　　9 1202
　　11(1) 1197
　　(2) 1195
　　31 1164
　　38(1) 1196
　　(2) 1194, 1197
Interpretation Act 1978 (c 30) 1195,
　　　　　1197, 1206, 1212, 1231
　s 3 1202
　　4 1231
　　5 .... 220, 666, 1171, 1211,
　　　　　　　　　　　　　1301
　　6 .... 1207, 1231
　　7 1208
　　8 1209
　　11 1164
　　12(1) 1210
　　15 1197
　　16(1) 1194, 1197
　　17(1) 1195
　　(2) 1196
　　20(2) 1212
　Sch 1 .... 220, 666, 1171, 1211,
　　　　　　　　　　　　　1301
　Sch 2—
　　para 4, 5 1211

PARA

Interpretation of Acts Act 1850 (c 21) ... 1206, 1207
s 4 1137
Judicial Factors (Scotland) Act 1889 (c 39)
s 11A 911
Juries Act 1825 (c 50) 104
Land Compensation (Scotland) Act 1963 (c 51)
s 40 .... 1036, 1037
Land Compensation (Scotland) Act 1973 (c 56) 1150
Land Registration (Scotland) Act 1979 (c 33) 1256, 1259
s 1 1235
 3(1) 1244
 4(2) 1238, 1259
 5(2), (4) 1246
 6 1246
 (4) 1218
 9 .... 1227, 1234
 (3), (4) 1218
 16 .... 1235, 1250
 17 .... 1235, 1251
 (1) 1260
 18 .... 1235, 1260
 19–23 1235
 28 1259
 (1) 1218, 1259
 30 1235
 (2) 1260
Land Tenure Reform (Scotland) Act 1974 (c 38) 1251
s 1(1), (2) 1249
 2(1), (2) 1249
 4 1249
 (7) 1249
 5 1249
 (1), (7), (12) 1249
 6 1249
 8(1) 1251
 9(1), (4) 1251
 12 1244
 16, 17 1251
 24(2) 1249
Law Reform (Husband and Wife) (Scotland) Act 1985 (c 37)
s 28(1) 269
Sch 1—
 para 8 269
Law Reform (Miscellaneous Provisions) Act 1934 (c 41)
s 3 1036
Law Reform (Miscellaneous Provisions) (Scotland) Act 1966 (c 19)
s 6 1264
Law Reform (Miscellaneous Provisions) (Scotland) Act 1968 (c 70)
s 6(2), (3) 1265
 18 1264
 22(5) 1265
Law Reform (Miscellaneous Provisions) (Scotland) Act 1980 (c 55)
s 18 .... 1036, 1037

PARA

Law Reform (Miscellaneous Provisions) (Scotland) Act 1985 (c 73) 1234
s 4–7 1251
 8 1234
 (1), (2), (4)–(6), (9) 1234
 9 1234
 (2), (4), (7), (8) 1234
 13(6) 1231
Law Reform (Parent and Child) (Scotland) Act 1986 (c 9)
s 1(4) 628, 723
 10(1) 1229
 Sch 1 .... 628, 723
 para 4 1229
Legal Aid (Scotland) Act 1967 (c 43)
s 1(7) 52
Legal Aid (Scotland) Act 1986 (c 47)
s 22 52
Licensing (Scotland) Act 1903 (c 25) 1158
Life Assurance Act 1774 (c 48) .. 835, 848, 856
s 1 .... 835, 848
 4 848
Limitation Act 1939 (c 21) 1105
Limitation Act 1963 (c 47) 1105
 Pt I (s 1–7) 1105
 Pt II (s 8–13) 1105
Lloyd's Act 1982 (c xiv) 1303
Loan Societies Act 1840 (c 110) 656
Local Government (Financial Provisions) (Scotland) Act 1963 (c 12)
s 14(1) 1170
Local Government (Scotland) Act 1973 (c 65)
s 96(5) 1171
Local Government (Scotland) Act 1975 (c 30)
s 18 1171
Magistrates' Courts Act 1980 (c 43)
s 154 206
Sch 7—
 para 104 206
Manufactures Act 1661 (c 280) 103
March Dykes Act 1661 (c 284) 1112
Marine and Aviation Insurance (War Risks) Act 1952 (c 57)
s 7(1) 828
Marine Insurance Act 1906 (c 41) 830, 848, 860, 864
s 4(1), (2) 835, 848
 5(2) 850
 6(1) 855, 857
 17 858
 18 860
 (1) 859, 860, 864
 (2) 869
 (4) 864
 22 828
 23 para (1) 828
 24(1) 828
 26(1) 828
 27(2) 830, 888
 (3) 830

PARA

Marine Insurance Act 1906—*contd*

s 28 831
  32(1), (2) 913
  33(1) 876
    (3) 875
  35(2), (3) 874
  50(1) 845
    (2) 846
    (3) 847
  51 845
  55(1) 879
  69 para (1) 886
  79 896
    (1) 894
  81 893
  84(2) 835
    (3) 857
  Sch 1—
    r 1 857
Married Women's Policies of Assurance (Scotland) Act 1880 (c 26) 853
Married Women's Policies of Assurance (Scotland) (Amendment) Act 1980 (c 56)
  s 1 853
Matrimonial Causes Act 1950 (c 25)
  s 16 1125
    (2) 1125
Matrimonial Homes (Family Protection) (Scotland) Act 1981 (c 59)
  s 1 1231
  6(3) 1231
    (4) 1259
  8(2) 1231
Matrimonial Proceedings (Polygamous Marriages) Act 1972 (c 38)
  s 2 269
Medical Act 1956 (c 76)
  s 28(1) 680
  52(2) 680
  54(1) 680
Medical Act 1983 (c 54)
  s 47 680
  56(1) 680
  Sch 6—
    para 11, 20 680
Mental Health Act 1959 (c 72) 41
  Pt VIII (s 100–121) 629
  s 104 629
Mental Health Act 1983 (c 20)
  Pt VII (s 93–113) 629
  s 98 629
Mental Health (Scotland) Act 1984 (c 36) 629
  s 83 .... 147, 216
Merchant Shipping Act 1894 (c 60)
  s 2 1156
    (1), (2) 1156
  158 1159
  373 1156
  503 1156
Merchant Shipping Act 1970 (c 36) 129
  s 70 129

PARA

Merchant Shipping (International Labour Conventions) Act 1925 (c 42)
  s 1(1) 1159
Mines and Quarries Act 1954 (c 70)
  s 48(1) 1183
  81(1) 1156
  108, 157 1183
National Health Service (Scotland) Act 1972 (c 58)
  s 64(1) 187
  Sch 6—
    para 155 187
National Health Service (Scotland) Act 1978 (c 29)
  s 109 187
  Sch 15—
    para 10 187
Naturalisation Act 1669 (c 12) 103
Nautical Assessors (Scotland) Act 1894 (c 40)
  s 2 1166
Northern Ireland Assembly Disqualification Act 1975 (c 25)
  s 5(2) 139
  Sch 3—
    Pt I 139
Northern Ireland Constitution Act 1973 (c 36)
  s 41(1) 219
  Sch 6—
    Pt I 219
Nuclear Materials (Offences) Act 1983 (c 18) 508, 532
Obscene Publications Act 1959 (c 66) 81
Obscene Publications Act 1964 (c 74) 81
Offences against the Person Act 1861 (c 100)
  s 4 532
  9 515
  18, 20–24, 28–30, 48, 55, 56 532
Official Secrets Act 1911 (c 28) 1146
  s 1 1146
Official Secrets Act 1920 (c 75) 1108
  s 3 1125
  7 1108
Overseas Development and Co-operation Act 1980 (c 63)
  s 9 130
Partnership Act 1890 (c 39) 1037, 1261
  s 18 1261
  24(3) 1037
  25 1261
  33(1) 1261
Petroleum (Production) Act 1934 (c 36) 1243
  s 1 1243
Pneumoconiosis etc (Workers' Compensation) Act 1979 (c 41) 906
Policies of Assurance Act 1867 (c 144) 845
  s 2 846
  5 847
  Schedule 847

PARA

Policyholders Protection Act 1975
  (c 75) 806, 814
  s 6, 7, 11, 16, 17 814
Prescription and Limitation (Scotland)
  Act 1973 (c 52)
  s 3 1259
  Pt II (s 17–23) 1105
Prevention of Crime Act 1871 (c 112)
  s 7, 20 1140
Prevention of Fraud (Investments) Act
  1939 (c 16) 1302
  s 10 609
Prevention of Fraud (Investments) Act
  1958 (c 45) 1302–1304
  s 17 1302
  Sch 1 1302
Prevention of Terrorism (Temporary
  Provisions) Act 1989 (c 4) 117, 119,
                         122, 138, 142, 145, 163
  s 4 .... 134, 147
  (4) 134
  5 134
  (4) 117
  6 134
  (4) 117
  7 134
  (4) 117
  8(1) 134
  16 .... 133, 138, 142, 145
  20(1) 134
  (3) 133, 134
  Sch 2 .... 134, 147
  para 1 134
       2 134
       (3) 134
       3 134
       (1)–(10) 134
       4 134
       5 134
       (3), (4) 134
       6 134
       (3), (4) 134
       7 134
       (3), (4) 134
       9(2)–(5) 134
  Sch 3 133
  Sch 5 .... 138, 142
  para 1 .... 133, 145
       2–10 133
  Sch 6 .... 133, 142
Princess Sophia Naturalisation Act
  1705 (c 16) 1125
Protection from Eviction Act 1964
  (c 97) 1253
Public Expenditure and Receipts Act
  1968 (c 14)
  s 5 724
  Sch 3 724
Public Houses Acts Amendment
  (Scotland) Act 1862 (c 35) 1111
  s 2 1111
Race Relations Act 1976 .... 190, 865
  s 20(1), (2) 865

PARA

Registration of Aliens Act 1836 (c 11) 104
Registration of Leases (Scotland) Act
  1857 (c 26)
  s 1 1251
  3(2) 1251
Rehabilitation of Offenders Act 1974
  (c 53) 807, 865
  s 1(1) 865
  4(3) 865
  5(1) 865
  (2) 865
     Table A, B 865
Removings Act 1555 (c 12) 1253
Rent (Scotland) Act 1984 (c 58) 1253
  Pt I (s 1–10) 1253
  Pt II (s 11–21) 1253
  s 23 1253
  Sch 2 1253
Representation of the People Act 1983
  (c 2)
  s 1(1) 121
Representation of the People (Scotland) Act 1832 (c 65)
  s 11 1166
Representation of the People (Scotland) Act 1868 (c 48) 1145
  s 20 1207
  27 1145
  28(2) 1145
Reserve and Auxiliary Forces (Protection of Civil Interests) Act 1951
  (c 65) 705
  Pt VI (s 54–59) 705
  s 54 705
  55–57 .... 680, 705
  58 705
Restriction of Offensive Weapons Act
  1959 (c 37) 1107
  s 1(1) 1107
Restriction of Offensive Weapons Act
  1961 (c 22)
  s 1 1107
Restrictive Trade Practices Act 1956
  (c 68)
  s 20 1122
Restrictive Trade Practices Act 1976
  (c 34) 614, 617
  s 32 614
  33 .... 614, 617
Rivers Pollution Prevention Act 1876
  (c 75) 1127
Road Traffic Act 1988 (c 52) 911
  s 3 1104
  Pt VI (s 143–162) 805, 825
  s 148(1), (2), (5) 911
  151(9) 864, 869
  152(1) 911
  (2) 859, 911
  (3) 911
  153(1), (2) 911
  170(2) 1109

PARA

Road Traffic (Consequential Provisions) Act 1988 (c 54)
s 4 814
Sch 3—
para 14 814
Road Traffic Offenders Act 1988 (c 53)
s 1(1) 1173
Royal and Parliamentary Titles Act
1927 (c 4)
s 2(2) 220
Sale of Goods Act 1979 (c 54) 1009
s 20 850
49(3) 1009
Sex Discrimination Act 1975 (c 65)
s 29(1), (2) 865
45 865
Sex Disqualification (Removal) Act
1919 (c 71)
s 1 1145
Sexual Offences Act 1956 (c 69)
s 1, 20 532
Sheriff Courts (Scotland) Act 1907
(c 51)
s 5 1128
Sheriff Courts (Scotland) Extracts Act
1892 (c 17)
s 9 1037
Slave Trade Act 1873 (c 88) 510
Social Security Act 1973 (c 38)
s 51(3)(a) 690
Social Security Act 1986 (c 50) 160
Pt II (s 20–31) 160
Social Work (Scotland) Act 1968 (c 49)
s 49(1) 1173
Societies Borrowing Powers Act 1898
(c 15) 721
Status of Aliens Act 1914 (c 17) 106
Statute Law (Repeals) Act 1986 (c 12)
s 1(1) 269
Sch 1—
Pt I 269
Statute Law Revision Act 1867 (c 59) 1244
Statutory Declaration Act 1835 (c 62) 1262
Street Offences Act 1959 (c 57)
s 1(1) 1115
Succession (Scotland) Act 1964 (c 41) ... 1264,
1268
s 23 1218
(2) 1268
28 1229
30 1271
31 1266
Summary Jurisdiction (Scotland) Act
1954 (c 48)
s 62 619
Summary Procedure (Scotland) Act
1864 (c 53)
s 18(2) 1178
Sch K 1178
Suppression of Terrorism Act 1978
(c 26) 532
s 1 532
2(1) 532

PARA

Suppression of Terrorism Act 1978—
contd
s 2(2) 535
5 532
Supreme Court Act 1981 (c 54)
s 33 63
Taking of Hostages Act 1982 (c 28) . 508, 532
s 1 532
3(2) 532
Taxes Management Act 1970 (c 9)
s 86 1037
95(1), (2) 1105
Telecommunications Act 1984 (c 12)
s 109(1) 1259
Sch 4—
para 71 1259
Tenures Abolition Act 1746 (c 50)
s 10 1244
Term and Quarter Days (Scotland)
Act 1990 (c 22)
s 1(1), (2) 1218
3(2) 1218
Third Parties (Rights against Insurers)
Act 1930 .... 904, 905, 907, 908, 910,
911
s 1(1) 904, 905, 907
(3) 907
3 908
Titles to Land Consolidation (Scotland) Act 1868 (c 101)
s 8 .... 1235, 1250
20 1161
139 1229
144 1227
149 1228
Sch (B) 1235
Town and Country Planning (Scotland) Act 1947 (c 53)
Sch 11 1036
Town and Country Planning (Scot-
land) Act 1972 (c 52)
Sch 24 1036
Trade Act 1681 (c 78) 103
Trade Union and Labour Relations
Act 1974 (c 52) 77, 95
s 1(2) 77
Sch 1—
para 6(5) 77
Trade Union and Labour Relations
(Amendment) Act 1976 (c 7)
s 1(e) 77
Transmission of Moveable Property
(Scotland) Act 1862 (c 85)
Sch A–C 847
Tribunals and Inquiries Act 1971 (c 62)
s 14 725
(2) 1130
Trustee Investments Act 1961 (c 62) 624,
666, 719, 1272
Sch 1—
Pt I, II 666
Trustee Savings Banks Act 1969 (c 50)
s 14(1) 624

PARA

Trustee Savings Banks Act 1985 (c 58)
  s 4(3) 666, 719
  7(3) 666, 719
  Sch 4 ....666, 719
Trusts (Scotland) Act 1921 (c 58) .. 1229, 1272
  s 2 1229
  3, 4 1272
Trusts (Scotland) Act 1961 (c 57) 1264
  s 5 1264
Unfair Contract Terms Act 1977
  (c 50) 802, 837
  s 15(3) 802, 837
Union with England Act 1707 (c 7)
  art 20 1112
Union with Ireland Act 1800 (c 67) 101
Universities (Scotland) Act 1889
  (c 55) 45
  s 14 1145

PARA

Usury Act 1713 (c 15) 1037
Usury Laws Repeal Act 1854 (c 90) 1037
Valuation and Rating (Scotland) Act
  1956 (c 60)
  s 7(2), (3) 1170
Valuation of Lands (Scotland) Act
  1854 (c 91)
  s 5 1122
  9 1172
  30 1122
Vehicles (Excise) Act 1971 (c 10) 911
Visiting Forces Act 1952 (c 67) 131
  s 1 ....131, 501
  13 501
Waterworks Clauses Act 1847 (c 17)
  s 28 1166
Winter Herding Act 1686 (c 11) 1182

Table of Orders, Rules and Regulations

PARA

Act of Adjournal (Consolidation) 1988, SI 1988/110
r 149(2) 558
150, 151 564
152 555
(1)–(3) 567
Sch 1—
Form 82 558
83 564
Act of Sederunt (Interest in Sheriff Court Decrees or Extracts) 1975, SI 1975/948 1037
Act of Sederunt (Rules of Court, consolidation and amendment) 1965, SI 1965/321
RC 66 .... 1036, 1037
Administration of Estates (Small Payments) (Increase of Limit) Order 1975, SI 1975/1137 628
art 3(a) 626
Administration of Estates (Small Payments) (Increase of Limit) Order 1984, SI 1984/539 628
art 2 .... 722, 723
(a) 626
Agricultural and Horticultural Co-operation Scheme 1971, SI 1971/415 617
Agricultural Credits (Scotland) Regulations 1929, SR & O 1929/495 641
Albania (Extradition) Order in Council 1927, SR & O 1927/605 507
Aliens Order 1920, SR & O 1920/448 106
Aliens Order 1953, SI 1953/1671 207
Austria (Extradition) (Extension) Order 1972, SI 1972/1581 507
Austria (Extradition) Order 1970, SI 1970/1111 507
Sch 1—
art 4 549
Belgium (Extradition) (Amendment) Order 1975, SI 1975/1034 507
Belgium (Extradition) (Amendment) Order 1985, SI 1985/1634 507
Boarding-out of Children (Foster Placement) Regulations 1988, SI 1988/2184 63
Boarding-Out of Children Regulations 1955, SI 1955/1377 63
reg 10 63
British Nationality (Hong Kong) (Selection Scheme) Order 1990, SI 1990/2292 .... 107, 220
Building Societies (Deferred Shares) Order 1991, SI 1991/701 1308

PARA

Channel Tunnel (Fire Services, Immigration and Prevention of Terrorism) Order 1990, SI 1990/2227
art 3 .... 138, 146, 147, 161, 162, 165, 167, 193, 199, 200
4 133
Sch 1 .... 138, 146, 147, 161, 162, 165, 167, 193, 199, 200
Sch 2 133
Child Benefit (General) Regulations 1976, SI 1976/965
reg 12 269
Chocolate, Sugar Confectionery and Cocoa Products Order 1949, SI 1949/781 1131
Church of Scotland Trust Orders 1932 to 1985 1321
Companies Act 1989 (Commencement No 3, Transitional Provisions and Transfer of Functions under the Financial Services Act 1986) Order 1990, SI 1990/354 1342
Companies Act 1989 (Eligibility for Appointment as Company Auditor) (Consequential Amendments) Regulations 1991, SI 1991/1997
reg 2, 4 .... 637, 638, 715
Schedule—
para 20(2) 637
(3) 638
24(2), (3) 715
Companies Consolidation (Consequential Provisions) (Northern Ireland) Order 1986, SI 1986/1035
art 23 .... 808, 814
Sch 1—
Pt II 808, 814
Companies (Tables A to F) Regulations 1985, SI 1985/805 612
Conduct of Employment Agencies and Employment Business Regulations 1976, SI 1976/715 311
Consumer Credit (Exempt Agreements) Order 1980, SI 1980/52 833
Co-operative Development Agency (Winding Up and Dissolution) Order 1990, SI 1990/279 607
art 4 607
Credit Unions Act 1979 (Commencement No 1) Order 1979, SI 1979/936 658
Credit Unions Act 1979 (Commencement No 2) Order 1980, SI 1980/481 658

PARA

Credit Unions (Authorised Banks) (Termination of Powers of Chief Registrar) Order 1980, SI 1980/736 656

Credit Unions (Authorised Investments) Order 1979, SI 1979/866 .... 606, 656, 666

Credit Unions (Increase of Limits of Shareholding of Deposits by persons too young to be members and of Loans) Order 1989, SI 1989/2423

art 3 665

4 666

5 669

Criminal Damage (Northern Ireland) Order 1977, SI 1977/426

art 3(2) 532

Czechoslovakia Extradition Order in Council 1926, SR & O 1926/1466 507

Decimal Currency (End of Transitional Period) Order 1971, SI 1971/1123 1231

Denmark (Extradition) (Amendment) Order 1979, SI 1979/1311 507

Denmark (Extradition) Order in Council 1936, SR & O 1936/405 507

Employers' Liability (Compulsory Insurance) General Regulations 1971, SI 1971/1117 910

reg 2(1) 910

Employment Agencies Act 1973 (Charging Fees to Au Pairs) Regulations 1981, SI 1981/1481 311

Estonia (Extradition) Order in Council 1926, SR & O 1926/840 507

European Communities (Immunities and Privileges of the North Atlantic Salmon Conservation Organisation) Order 1985, SI 1985/1773 130

European Convention on Extradition Order 1990, SI 1990/1507 ...... 507, 508

art 5 507

Sch 5 507

Extradition, Argentine Republic Order in Council 1894, SR & O 1894/76 507

Extradition (Aviation Security) Order 1991, SI 1991/1699 508

Extradition, Belgium Order in Council 1902, SR & O 1902/208 507

Extradition, Belgium Order in Council 1907, SR & O 1907/544 507

Extradition, Belgium Order in Council 1911, SR & O 1911/793 507

Extradition, Bolivia Order in Council 1898, SR & O 1898/597 507

Extradition, certain foreign states (white slave traffic) Order in Council 1923, SR & O 1923/971 .... 507, 508

PARA

Extradition, Chile Order in Council 1898, SR & O 1898/597 507

Extradition, Columbia Order in Council dated 28 November 1889 507

Extradition (Cuba, Italy, Luxemburg, Switzerland and Yugo-Slavia) (White Slave Traffic) Order in Council 1934, SI 1934/500 508

Extradition, Cuba Order in Council 1905, SR & O 1905/558 507

Extradition, Denmark Order in Council dated 26 June 1873 507

Extradition (Designated Commonwealth Countries) Order 1991, SI 1991/1700 520

Extradition (Drug Trafficking) Order 1991, SI 1991/1701 508

Extradition, Ecuador Order in Council dated 26 June 1886 507

Extradition, France and Tunis Order in Council 1909, SR & O 1909/1458 507

Extradition, France Order in Council dated 16 May 1878 507

Extradition, France Order in Council 1896, SR & O 1896/54 507

Extradition (Genocide) Order 1970, SI 1970/147 508

Extradition, Greece Order in Council 1912, SR & O 1912/193 507

Extradition, Guatemala Order in Council dated 26 November 1886 507

Extradition, Guatemala Order in Council 1914, SR & O 1914/1323 507

Extradition, Hayti Order in Council dated 5 February 1876 507

Extradition (Hijacking) Order 1971, SI 1971/2102 508

Extradition, Hungary Order in Council dated 17 March 1874 507

Extradition (Internationally Protected Persons) Order 1979, SI 1979/453 508

Extradition, Italy Order in Council dated 24 March 1873 507

Extradition, Liberia Order in Council 1894, SR & O 1894/114 507

Extradition, Luxembourg Order in Council dated 2 March 1881 507

Extradition, Mexico Order in Council dated 6 April 1889 507

Extradition, Monaco Order in Council dated 9 May 1892 507

Extradition, Netherlands Order in Council 1899, SR & O 1899/83 507

Extradition, Nicaragua Order in Council 1906, SR & O 1906/382 507

Extradition, Norway and Sweden Order in Council dated 30 November 1873 507

PARA

Extradition, Norway Order in Council 1907, SR & O 1907/545 507

Extradition Order in Council (Russia) dated 7 March 1887 507

Extradition, Panama Order in Council 1907, SR & O 1907/648 507

Extradition, Paraguay Order in Council 1911, SR & O 1911/662 507

Extradition, Peru Order in Council 1907, SR & O 1907/383 507

Extradition, Portugal Order in Council 1894, SR & O 1894/102 507

Extradition (Protection of Nuclear Material) Order 1971, SI 1971/1720 508

Extradition, Roumania Order in Council 1894, SR & O 1894/119 507

Extradition, Salvador Order in Council dated 16 December 1882 507

Extradition, San Marino Order in Council 1900, SR & O 1900/168 507

Extradition, Servia Order in Council 1901, SR & O 1901/586 507

Extradition, Siam Order in Council 1911, SR & O 1911/1151 507

Extradition (Suppression of Terrorism) Order 1978, SI 1978/1106 508

Extradition, Switzerland Order in Council dated 18 May 1881 507

Extradition, Switzerland Order in Council 1905, SR & O 1905/616 507

Extradition (Taking of Hostages) Order 1985, SI 1985/751 508

Sch 4 508

Extradition (Tokyo Convention) Order 1971, SI 1971/2103 508

Extradition (Torture) Order 1991, SI 1991/1702 508

Extradition, Uruguay Order in Council dated 5 March 1885 507

Extradition, Uruguay Order in Council dated 24 November 1891 507

Federal Republic of Germany (Extradition) (Amendment) Order 1978, SI 1978/1403 507

Federal Republic of Germany (Extradition) Order 1960, SI 1960/1375 507

Sch 1—
art iv 549

Financial Services Act 1986 (Delegation) (No 2) Order 1988, SI 1988/738 1326

Financial Services Act 1986 (Delegation) Order 1987, SI 1987/942 .... 819, 1324, 1329–1331, 1335, 1336, 1338, 1339, 1410–1415, 1417, 1429

art 3 1310

Sch 1, 2 1310

Financial Services Act 1986 (Delegation) Order 1991, SI 1991/200 1411

PARA

Financial Services Act 1986 (Extension of Scope of Act) Order 1991, SI 1991/1104 1308

Financial Services Act 1986 (Extension of Scope of Act and Meaning of Collective Investment Scheme) Order 1988, SI 1988/496 ..... 1307, 1308

Financial Services Act 1986 (Investment Advertisements) (Exemptions) (No 2) Order 1988, SI 1988/716 1337

Financial Services Act 1986 (Investment Advertisements) (Exemptions) Order 1988, SI 1988/316 1337

Financial Services Act 1986 (Investment Advertisements) (Exemptions) Order 1990, SI 1990/27 1337

Financial Services Act 1986 (Miscellaneous Exemptions) (No 2) Order 1988, SI 1988/723 1323

Financial Services Act 1986 (Miscellaneous Exemptions) Order 1988, SI 1988/350 1323

Financial Services Act 1986 (Miscellaneous Exemptions) Order 1991, SI 1991/493 1323

Financial Services Act 1986 (Restriction of Right of Action) Regulations 1991, SI 1991/489 .... 1362, 1376, 1387

reg 2, 3 1412

Financial Services Act 1986 (Restriction of Scope of Act and Meaning of Collective Investment Scheme) (No 2) Order 1990, SI 1990/1493 1307

Financial Services Act 1986 (Restriction of Scope of Act and Meaning of Collective Investment Scheme) Order 1988, SI 1988/803 1307

Financial Services Act 1986 (Restriction of Scope of Act and Meaning of Collective Investment Scheme) Order 1990, SI 1990/349 .... 1307, 1308

Financial Services Act 1986 (Restriction of Scope of Act) Order 1988, SI 1988/318 1307

Financial Services Act 1986 (Single Property Schemes) (Exemption) Regulations 1989, SI 1989/28 1326

Financial Services Act 1986 (Transfer of Functions Relating to Friendly Societies) (Transitional Provisions) Order 1987, SI 1987/2069 .... 683, 691

Financial Services (Designated Countries and Territories) (Overseas Collective Investment Schemes) (Bermuda) Order 1988, SI 1988/2284 1328

PARA

Financial Services (Designated Countries and Territories) (Overseas Collective Investment Schemes) (Guernsey) Order 1988, SI 1988/2148 1328

Financial Services (Designated Countries and Territories) (Overseas Collective Investment Schemes) (Jersey) Order 1988, SI 1988/2149 1328

Financial Services (Designated Countries and Territories) (Overseas Collective Investment Schemes) Order 1988, SI 1988/2015 1328

Financial Services (Transfer of Functions Relating to Friendly Societies) Order 1987, SI 1987/925 .. 683, 691

Financial Services Tribunal (Conduct of Investigations) Rules 1988, SI 1988/351 1416
    r 3 1417
    4(1), (2) 1417
    5 1417
    6–12 1418
    16, 17 1419
    18 1418

Finland (Extradition) Order 1976, SI 1976/1037 507

Firearms (Northern Ireland) Order 1981, SI 1981/155
    art 6(1) 532
    17 532
    18(1) 532
    Sch 4—
    para 5 532

France (Extradition) (Amendment) Order 1978, SI 1978/455 507

France (Extradition) Order in Council 1928, SR & O 1928/575 507

Friendly Societies (Limits of Benefits) Order 1982, SI 1982/1353 683

Friendly Societies (Limits of Benefits) Order 1984, SI 1984/513 683

Friendly Societies (Long Term Insurance Business) Regulations 1987, SI 1987/2132 .... 683, 717
    reg 3–6 717
    11 717

Friendly Societies (Proxy Voting) Regulations 1971, SI 1971/1946 . 683, 713

Friendly Societies (Qualifications of Actuaries) Regulations 1968, SI 1968/1481 .... 683, 695
    reg 2 695

Friendly Societies Regulations 1975, SI 1975/205 .... 683, 703
    reg 2 .... 695–697, 699, 703, 708,
                   713, 717, 725, 727, 728,
                   731, 732, 736, 738, 739
    4 696
    5–7 703
    8 727
    9, 10 728

PARA

Friendly Societies Regulations 1975—
    contd
    reg 11 731
    12 728
    13 736
    14 738
    16 695
    Sch 1—
    Form A 695, 717
        B, C 695
        D 696
        E 697, 717
        F, G 697
        H–N 703
        P–R 699
        S 708
        T 725
        U 727
        V 727, 728, 731
        W–Y 728
        Z 731
        AA 728
        AC 713, 732
        AD, AH 736
        AI, AIb, AJ–AL 738
        AM–AO 739
    Sch 2 695

Friendly Societies (Valuation) Regulations 1969, SI 1969/201 683
    reg 2, 3 717
    4 717
    (6) 717

Friendly Societies (Valuation) Regulations 1985, SI 1985/1919 ..... 683, 717
    reg 4A 717

Hong Kong (British Nationality) Order 1986, SI 1986/948 .... 120, 220
    art 7(9) 132

Housing (Northern Ireland) Order 1988, SI 1988/1990
    Pt II 160

Hungary (Extraction) Order in Council 1937, SR & O 1937/719 507

Iceland (Extradition) Order in Council 1939, SR & O 1939/825 507

Immigration Act 1971 (Commencement) Order 1972, SI 1972/1514 125

Immigration Act 1988 (Commencement No 1) Order 1988, SI 1988/1133
    art 2 322
    3 110
    (1) 125
    (2) 118
    Schedule 322

Immigration Act 1988 (Commencement No 2) Order 1991, SI 1991/1001 .... 119, 176, 342

Immigration Appeals (Notices) Regulations 1984, SI 1984/2040 109
    reg 3 170
    (1) 211, 345
    (2) 345

PARA

Immigration Appeals (Notices) Regu-
　lations 1984—*contd*
　reg 3(4) 211, 345, 348
　　4(1) 345, 349
　　　(2) 345
　　6 .... 211, 345
Immigration Appeals (Procedure)
　(Amendment) Rules 1991, SI
　1991/1543 352
Immigration Appeals (Procedure)
　Rules 1984, SI 1984/2041 ...... 109, 169
　r 2(1) 141
　　4(1)–(6) 348
　　(7) 211, 348
　　(8)–(11) 348
　　5(1) 211, 348
　　(2) 348
　　6(1)–(8) 346
　　7(1)–(3) 347
　　8(1), (2) 349
　　(3) 337, 348–350
　　(4) 349
　　11 350
　　　(1) 348
　　　(2) 349
　　12(1) 346, 351
　　14(1) 357, 358
　　(2) 358
　　15(1)–(4) 359
　　16(2)–(4) 361
　　(5) 360, 361
　　(7), (8) 361
　　17(1)–(4) 362
　　18(1)–(3) 365
　　20(a)–(c) 363
　　21 366
　　23 .... 199, 213
　　24–27 352
　　28 352
　　(a), (b) 352
　　29(1) 353
　　(2), (3) 352
　　31 333
　　(1), (2) 354
　　32(1)–(4) 352
　　33 352
　　34(1)–(5) 355
　　35 .... 351, 363
　　36, 37 352
　　39(1)–(3) 356
　　40 356
　　41 367
　　42 330
　　(c) 350
　　43(1) 348
　　44 .... 346, 359
　　(1) 355
Immigration (Carriers' Liability Pre-
　scribed Sum) Order 1991, SI
　1991/1497 .... 161, 317
Immigration (Control of Entry
　through Republic of Ireland)
　Order 1972, SI 1972/1610 ...... 122, 124

PARA

Immigration (Control of Entry
　through Republic of Ireland)
　Order 1972—*contd*
　art 3 124
　　(1), (2) 124
　　4(1), (2), (4)–(7) 124
Immigration (Exemption from Con-
　trol) Order 1972, SI 1972/1613
　art 2(1) 130
　　3 130
　　4(a)–(l) 130
　　5(1) 132
　　(a)–(c) 132
　　(d), (e) 129
　　(2), (3) 129, 132
　Schedule 130
Immigration (Guernsey) Order 1972,
　SI 1972/1719 123
Immigration (Hotel Records) Order
　1972, SI 1972/1689
　art 3–5 184
Immigration (Isle of Man) Order
　1991, SI 1991/2630 123
Immigration (Jersey) Order 1972, SI
　1972/1813 123
Immigration (Landing and Embar-
　kation Cards) 1975, SI 1975/65 146
　art 4, 5 163
Immigration (Particulars of Passen-
　gers and Crew) Order 1972, SI
　1972/1667 161
Immigration (Ports of Entry) Order
　1987, SI 1987/177
　art 2 161
　Schedule 161
Immigration (Registration with Pol-
　ice) Regulations 1972, SI 1972/
　1758 119
　reg 3 175
　　4(1) 175
　　5 175
　　(1) 175
　　7 175
　　(3) 175
　　8 175
　　(a) 243
　　9 175
　　(2), (3) 175
　　10(1)–(3) 175
　　11(1) 175
　　(2) 175, 190
　Schedule 175
Immigration (Restricted Right of
　Appeal against Deportation)
　(Exemption) (No 2) Order 1988,
　SI 1988/1203
　art 1 322
　　2(a) 316, 322, 342
　　(b) 342
　　3 342
　　(a) 322
　　(b) 316, 322

PARA

Immigration (Variation of Leave)
Order 1976, SI 1976/1572 ...... 109, 211
  reg 3 179
    (1)–(3) 178
Increase of Criminal Penalties etc
  (Scotland) Order 1984, SI 1984/
  526
  art 3 .... 666, 735, 1301, 1534
    4 .... 161, 622, 630, 645, 655,
                                        744
Industrial and Provident Societies
  (Credit Unions) Regulations
  1979, SI 1979/937 .... 606, 656
  reg 4 662
    6 663
    17 662
  Sch 1—
    Form CU1 662
      CU5–CU7 663
  Sch 2 662
Industrial and Provident Societies
  (Group Accounts) Rules 1969, SI
  1969/1037 .... 606, 633
Industrial and Provident Societies
  (Increase in Deposit-taking Li-
  mits) Order 1981, SI 1981/394 606
  art 3 622
Industrial and Provident Societies
  (Increase in Shareholding Limit)
  Order 1981, SI 1981/395 606
  art 3 621
Industrial and Provident Societies
  Regulations 1965, SI 1965/1995 606
  reg 2 .... 614, 647–650, 652, 653
    4 616
    6 .... 648, 649
    8, 9 650
    10 652
    13 .... 610, 612
  Sch 1—
    Form D–G 616
      T 648, 650
      U 649, 650
      V 648–650
      W 649
      X, Y 650
      AA, AB, AE, AF 652
      AG 649, 650, 652, 653
      AH 647
  Sch 2 .... 610, 612, 616
Industrial and Provident Societies
  Regulations 1967, SI 1967/1310 . 606, 641
  reg 4–6, 8, 9 641
  Schedule—
    Form AK, AN–AP 641
Industrial Assurance and Friendly So-
  cieties (Death Certificates) (Scot-
  land) Regulations 1949, SI
  1949/1066 724
Industrial Tribunals (Interest) Order
  1990, SI 1990/479 1036
Insider Dealing (Public Servants)
  Order 1989, SI 1989/2164 1520

PARA

Insider Dealing (Recognised Stock
  Exchange) (No 2) Order 1990, SI
  1990/47 1503
Insider Dealing (Recognised Stock
  Exchange) Order 1989, SI 1989/
  2165 1503
Insurance Brokers Registration Coun-
  cil (Accounts and Business
  Requirements) Rules Approval
  Order 1979, SI 1979/489 813
Insurance Brokers Registration Coun-
  cil (Code of Conduct) Approval
  Order 1978, SI 1978/1394 813
Insurance Brokers Registration Coun-
  cil (Constitution of the Disciplin-
  ary Committee) Rules Approval
  Order 1978, SI 1978/1457 813
Insurance Brokers Registration Coun-
  cil (Constitution of the Investi-
  gating Committee) Rules
  Approval Order 1978, SI 1978/
  1456 813
Insurance Brokers Registration Coun-
  cil (Indemnity Insurance and
  Grants Scheme) Rules Approval
  Order 1987, SI 1987/1496 813
Insurance Companies (Assistance)
  Regulations 1987, SI 1987/2130
  reg 2(a) 835
    (b) 844
  Schedule 844
Insurance Companies Regulations
  1981, SI 1981/1654 .... 807, 818, 819,
                                       821
  reg 3–21 807
    23 807
    67–69 811
    70(1) 820
  Sch 10, 11 820
Iraq (Extradition) Order in Council
  1933, SR & O 1933/357 507
Israel (Extradition) (Amendment)
  Order 1978, SI 1978/1623 507
Israel (Extradition) Order 1960, SI
  1960/1660 507
Land Registration (Scotland) Rules
  1980, SI 1980/1413
  r 3, 7 1246
    14 1259
  Sch A—
    Form 6 1259
Latvia (Extradition) Order in Council
  1925, SR & O 1925/1029 507
Licensed Dealers (Conduct of Busi-
  ness) Rules 1960, SI 1960/1216 1303
Licensed Dealers (Conduct of Busi-
  ness) Rules 1983, SI 1983/585 1303
Lithuania (Extradition) Order in
  Council 1927, SR & O 1927/504 507
Luxembourg (Extradition) Order in
  Council 1951, SI 1951/1170 507

PARA

Magistrates' Courts (Backing of Warrants) Rules 1965, SI 1965/1906 . 555, 558

Merchant Shipping (Seamen's Documents) Regulations 1987, SI 1987/408 129

National Health Service (Charges to Overseas Visitors) (Scotland) Regulations 1989, SI 1989/364 160

National Savings Bank Regulations 1972, SI 1972/764
reg 10 719

Norway (Extradition) (Amendment) Order 1985, SI 1985/1637 507

Occupational Pension Schemes (Friendly Society) Regulations 1976, SI 1976/598
reg 6 .... 701, 703

Poland Extradition Order in Council 1934, SR & O 1934/209 507

Portugal (Extradition) Order in Council 1933, SR & O 1933/678 507

Prevention of Terrorism (Temporary Provisions) (Designated Ports) Order 1991, SI 1991/2649 133

Prison (Amendment) Rules 1976, SI 1976/503 95

Prison Rules 1964, SI 1964/388 44
r 37A 95

Registration of Births, Deaths and Marriages (Fees) (Scotland) Order 1989, SI 1989/2370
reg 2 724
Sch 1 724

Rehabilitation of Offenders Act 1974 (Exceptions) Order 1975, SI 1975/1023 807

Road Traffic (Northern Ireland Consequential Amendments) Order 1981, SI 1981/160 814

Savings Banks (Ordinary Deposits) (Limits) Order 1969, SI 1969/939 624

Social Security and Family Allowances (Polygamous Marriages) Regulations 1975, SI 1975/561 269

Social Security (Northern Ireland) Order 1986 160
Pt III 160

Spain (Extradition) Order 1986, SI 1986/766 507

PARA

Suppression of Terrorism Act 1978 (Application of Provisions) (United States of America) Order 1986, SI 1986/2146 532

Suppression of Terrorism Act 1978 (Designation of Countries) Orders—
1978, SI 1978/1245 .... 508, 532
1979, SI 1979/497 .... 508, 532
1980, SI 1980/357, 1392 .... 508, 532
1981, SI 1981/1389, 1507 .... 508, 532
1986, SI 1986/271, 1137 .... 508, 532
1987, SI 1987/2137 .... 508, 532
1989, SI 1989/2210 508
1990, SI 1990/1272 508

Suppression of Terrorism Act 1978 (Hong Kong) Order 1987, SI 1987/2045 508

Suppression of Terrorism Act 1978 (Overseas Territories) Order 1986, SI 1986/2019 508

Sweden (Extradition) Order 1966, SI 1966/226 507

Switzerland (Extradition) Order in Council 1935, SR & O 1935/676 507

Taking of Hostages Act 1982 (Overseas Territories) Order 1982, SI 1982/1540 508

Taking of Hostages (Guernsey) Order 1982, SI 1982/1539 508

Taking of Hostages (Isle of Man) (No 2) Order 1982, SI 1982/1839 508

Taking of Hostages (Jersey) Order 1982, SI 1982/1533 508

Town and Country Planning (General Development) (Scotland) Order 1959, SI 1959/1361
art 3(3) 1177

Transfer of Functions (Immigration Appeals) Order 1987, SI 1987/465 .... 139, 169, 329, 331
art 2(c) 330, 331
3(2), (3) 330, 331

Transfer of Functions (Minister for the Civil Service and Treasury) Order 1981, SI 1981/1670 ...... 139, 331

United States of America (Extradition) (Amendment) Order 1986, SI 1986/2020 507

United States of America (Extradition) Order 1976, SI 1976/2144 507

Table of Other Enactments

PARA

Act of Accession (1972)
Protocol 3—
art 6 220
African Charter on Human and
Peoples' Rights (1981) 6
Agreement with Israel (1960) 507
Exchange of Notes (1978) 507
American Convention on Human
Rights (1969) 6
Charter of the United Nations (1945) 3
preamble 3
art 1, para 3 3
55(c) 3
56, 73 3
76(c) 3
Convention against Discrimination in
Education (1960) 5
Convention against Illicit Traffic in
Narcotic Drugs and Psychotropic
Substances (1989) 508
Convention against Torture and other
Cruel, Inhuman or Degrading
Treatment or Punishment
(1985) 5, 508
art 3(1) 26
Convention for the Protection of
Human Rights and Fundamental
Freedoms (1950) 4, 6, 8, 9, 11–15,
17, 22, 24, 38, 41, 42, 52,
53, 57, 69, 80, 81, 94, 95,
109, 115, 233, 575, 1153
preamble 6, 79
art 1 6
Sect I (art 2–18) 6
art 2 ....6, 24–26, 31
para 1 25
2(a)–(c) 25
3 ....6, 26, 27, 31, 115, 575
4 ....6, 28, 31
para 1, 2 28
3(a)–(d) 28
5 ....6, 24, 26, 28, 29, 33, 39,
42, 52, 115
para 1 ....34, 35, 38–41
(a) 29, 34, 35
(b) 29
(c) 29, 30, 35, 40
(d) 29, 39
(e) 29, 41
(f) 29, 38
2 29
3 29–31
4 ....29, 33, 35–39, 41
5 29
6 ....6, 8, 24, 26, 43–45, 50, 51,
54, 57–60, 64, 69
para 1 ...32, 43–46, 49–51, 54, 56, 84
2 ....43, 53

PARA

Convention for the Protection of
Human Rights and Fundamental
Freedoms (1950)—contd
art 6 para 3 52
(a) 43, 51
(b) 43
(c) 43, 52
(d) 43, 55, 56
(e) 43, 51
7 ....6, 31, 61
para 1, 2 61
8 ....6, 8, 15, 39, 44, 52, 62–70,
73, 78, 79, 84, 115
para 1 ....62, 66, 68, 78
2 .....24, 62, 63, 65, 66, 68, 69,
78, 79, 81
9 ....6, 72, 73, 77–79
para 1 ....72, 78
2 ....24, 72, 78, 79, 81
10 ....6, 73, 74, 77–79, 81, 82
para 1 ....73, 78
2 ....24, 73, 78, 79, 81, 82
11 ....6, 73, 75–79, 83
para 1 ....24, 75, 76, 78
2 ....24, 75, 78, 79, 81, 83
12 ....6, 15, 71, 115
13 ....6, 52, 69, 77, 84
14 ....6, 8, 26, 65, 72, 76, 85, 115
15 ....25, 26, 30, 31
para 1 31
2 ....25, 26, 31
3 ....31, 32
16 6
17 ....6, 90
18 6
19 10
(1), (2) 10
20, para 1 11
2, 3 14
21, para 1, 3 11
22, para 1 11
23 11
24 ....14, 15
25 ....14–16, 19, 20
para 1–5 14
26 14
27 15
para 1, 2 15
28, para 1, 2 15
29 15
30 16
para 1 15
proviso 15
2, 3 15
31 16
para 1–3 15
32, para 1 15
33, 34 15

PARA

Convention for the Protection of
Human Rights and Fundamental
Freedoms (1950)—*contd*
art 36 11
38 12
39, para 1, 3 12
40, para 1, 3, 7 12
43–45 17
46 .... 12, 15, 17
47 17
48 .... 15, 17
(a) 14, 17
(b)–(d) 17
49 20
50 .... 20, 21, 94
51, para 1, 2 20
52 20
53 .... 20, 94
54 20
55 12
56, para 1, 2 12
63, para 1, 2 26
64, para 1 90
Protocol 1 .... 6, 87, 90
art 1 .... 87, 88
2 .... 26, 87, 89–92
3 .... 87, 93
Protocol 2 .... 6, 23, 87
art 1, para 1, 2 23
3, para 1, 2 23
Protocol 3 .... 6, 87
Protocol 4 .... 6, 87, 115
Protocol 5 .... 6, 12, 87
Protocol 6 .... 6, 26, 87
Protocol 7 .... 6, 87
Protocol 8 .... 6, 11, 12, 14, 15, 17, 87
Protocol 9 .... 6, 87
Convention for the Suppression of
Unlawful Acts against the Safety
of Civil Aviation (1971) 508, 518
Protocol (1988) 508
Convention for the Suppression of
Unlawful Seizure of Aircraft
(1970) 508, 518, 525
Convention for the Unification of
Certain Rules relating to Inter-
national Carriage by Air (1933) 1154
Convention on Offences and certain
other Acts committed on Board
Aircraft (1963) 508, 518, 525
Convention on the Abolition of Slav-
ery, the Slave Trade and Insti-
tutions and Practices similar to
Slavery (1956) 2
Convention on the Elimination of All
Forms of Discrimination against
Women (1979) 5
Convention on the Physical Protec-
tion of Nuclear Material (1980) 508
Convention on the Prevention and
Punishment of Crimes against
Internationally Protected Per-
sons, including Diplomatic
Agents (1973–1974) 508

PARA

Convention on the Prevention and
Punishment of the Crime of
Genocide (1948) 5, 508, 518, 525
Convention on the Rights of the Child
1989 5
Convention relating to the Status of
Refugees (1951) 116, 151, 203,
314–318, 320–323,
342, 509
art 1 314
(c) 314
26, 28, 31–33 314
Protocol 116, 203, 314–317, 320,
509
Convention relating to the Status of
Stateless Persons (1954) 151
Covenant of the League of Nations
(1919) 2
art 22 2
Core Conduct of Business Rules 1340,
1356, 1362, 1368, 1386,
1397, 1399–1401
r 1 .... 1357, 1359, 1362
2 .... 1348, 1358, 1359, 1362
3 .... 1359, 1362
4 .... 1360, 1373
(1)–(4) 1360
5 .... 1366, 1367, 1398, 1400,
1423
(1) 1363, 1367
(2), (3) 1367
(4) 1367, 1373
6 .... 1366–1368, 1400
7 .... 1366, 1368, 1369
(1), (2) 1369
8 .... 1366, 1368, 1370
9 .... 1347, 1366, 1367, 1371
(1), (2) 1371
10 .... 1347, 1366, 1372, 1398
11 .... 1364, 1366
(1), (2) 1364
12 .... 1363, 1366
(1), (2) 1363
13 .... 1361, 1366, 1378
(1)–(4) 1378
14 1375
(1), (2) 1375
15 1376
(1)–(3) 1376
16 .... 1346, 1373
(1), (2) 1373
17 .... 1360, 1365
(1)–(6) 1365
18 1374
(1), (2) 1374
19 1377
(1), (2) 1377
20 1379
21 1380
(1), (2) 1380
22 .... 1359, 1381
(1)–(5) 1381
23 1382

PARA

Core Conduct of Business Rules—
  contd
  r 24 .... 1379, 1383
    25 1384
    26 1385
    (1), (2) 1385
    27 .... 1386, 1398
    28 1387
    (1)–(3) 1387
    29 1388
    30 1389
    31 .... 1352, 1390
    32 1391
    33 1392
    34 .... 1351, 1352, 1393
    (1)–(3) 1393
    35 1394
    (1), (2) 1394
    36 .... 1384, 1395
    (1)–(4) 1395
    37 1396
    (1), (2) 1396
    38 1397
    (1)–(3) 1397
    39 1398
    (1), (2) 1398
    40 .... 1367, 1368, 1399
    (1) 1399
    (2) 1367, 1368, 1400
    (3) 1401
Declaration by the United Kingdom
  replacing the Declaration on the
  Definition of the Term 'Nation-
  als' (1982) 220
Declaration of Representatives of
  Governments of Member States
  meeting in Council (1964) 222
EC Council Directive—
  68/366 .... 221, 225, 236
    art 1 223
    2(1)–(3) 224
    3(1) 233
    (2) 223, 225
    4(1) 226, 227
    (2)–(4) 230
    6(1) 226, 230
    (2) 227
    (3) 226, 230
    7(1) 227, 237
    (2) 227
    8(1) 222, 226, 230
    Annex 230
  72/194 .... 221, 232
  73/148 221
    art 1 225
    (1) 222, 223
    (2) 223
    2(1)–(3) 224
    3(1) 225
    (2) 223, 225
    4(1) 226, 227, 230, 237
    (2) 117, 226, 230
    (3) 230
    5 226

PARA

EC Council Directive—*contd*
  73/148—*contd*
    art 6(1), (2) 230
    8 232
  75/34 .... 221, 228
    art 2(1), (2) 228
    3(1) 223
    (2) 223, 228
    4(2) 228
    5(1), (2) 228
    6 230
    (2) 229
    8(2) 228
    9 232
  75/35 221
  77/486
    art 2, 3 231
  85/384 221
  85/611 1328
  89/592 1536
    art 1(1) 1536
  90/364–366 .... 221, 222, 226
EC Council Regulation—
  1612/68 .... 221, 223, 232
    preamble—
    6th recital 222
    art 1(1) 222
    7, 8 231
    10 231
    (1), (2) 223
    11, 12 231
    47 222
  1251/70 .... 221, 228, 232
    art 2(1), (2) 228
    3(1) 223
    (2) 223, 228
    4(2) 228
    5(1), (2) 228
    6 230
    (2) 229
    8(2) 228
  1408/71 .... 221, 222
  574/72 221
  311/76 221
  312/76 221
EEC Council Directive—
  64/221 .... 221, 234
    art 1 232
    2(1) 232
    (2) 233
    3(1), (3) 233
    (4) 224, 233
    4 233
    6–8 234
    9(1), (2) 234
    10 232
    Annex 233
EEC Treaty 219–223, 1320
  art 7 221
    48 .... 114, 221, 232
    (2) 221
    (3) 221, 232
    (b) 224–226

PARA

EEC Treaty—*contd*
art 48(2)(c) 228
  49–51 114
  52 .... 114, 221, 222, 232
  53–55 114
  56 114
  57 .... 114, 221
  58 114
  59 .... 114, 222
  60 .... 114, 221
  61–65 114
  66 .... 114, 232
  189 235
    2nd, 3rd para 219
  227(5) 220
  235 228
European Agreement on Transfer of
  Responsibility for Refugees
  (1980) 314
European Convention for the Prevention of Torture and Inhuman or
  Degrading Treatment or Punishment (1987) 5, 27
  art 1 27
European Convention on Extradition
  (1957) 503, 507, 508, 511,
                  512, 515, 517, 544
  Additional Protocol 503, 508
  Second Protocol 503, 508
European Convention on the Sup-
  pression of Terrorism (1977) ... 508, 532
European Social Charter (1961) 7, 76
  Pt I 7
  art 20, para 1(a) 7
Exchange of Notes with Austria con-
  cerning the Abolition of Visas
  (1971) 162
Exchange of Notes with Monaco con-
  cerning Arrangements to Facili-
  tate Travel (1961) 162
Exchange of Notes with Switzerland
  concerning Arrangements to
  Facilitate Travel (1961) 162
Final Act of the Conference on Security and Co-operation in Europe
  (1975) 4
Financial Services (Cancellation)
  Rules 1989 1340
  r 2.01 1336
  2.02(1)–(3), (6) 1336
  2.03–2.05 1336
  Schedule—
    Form 1A, 1B 1336
Financial Services (Clients' Money)
  Regulations 1987 .... 1340, 1409
  reg 1.3(1) 1409
  1.4(1)–(5) 1409
  2.1(1)–(3) 1409
  2.2 1409
  2.3 1409
  (6), (7) 1409
  3.1 1409

PARA

Financial Services (Common Unsolicited Calls) Regulations 1991 1333,
                      1335, 1340
Financial Services (Compensation of
  Investors) Rules 1988 1421
Financial Services (Compensation of
  Investors) Rules 1990 .... 1340, 1421,
                      1422, 1429
  r 1.03(2) 1421
  2.01 1422
  2.02(2), (3), (5) 1422
  2.06 1422
  2.07(1), (2) 1422
  2.08, 2.09 1422
  Annex 1—
    para 2 1421
  Annex 2 1421
Financial Services (Conduct of Business) Rules 1990 ...... 1340, 1386, 1531
  Pt 10 (r 10.01–10.07) 1388
Financial Services (Financial Supervision) Rules 1990 .... 1340, 1402
  r 1.04(1), (2) 1402
  (3) 1402
    Core Rule A 1403
             B 1404–1406
             C 1407
             D 1406
             E 1405
  2.01–2.04 1403
  3.01 1403
  4.02, 4.03 1403
  5.02, 5.08–5.11 1403
  6.02 1403
  7.01–7.05 1404
  8.01–8.03 1406
  9.01(2) 1408
  10.02 1405
Financial Services (Investment Business Clients' Money) (Chartered
  Accountants) Regulations 1988 1340
Financial Services (Notification)
  Regulations 1988 1340
Financial Services (Promotion of Un-
  regulated Collective Investment
  Schemes) Regulations 1991 1326
Financial Services (Regulated
  Schemes) Regulations 1991 .. 1327, 1328
Financial Services (Single Property
  Schemes) (Supplementary)
  Regulations 1989 1326
General Programme for the abolition
  of restrictions on freedom of
  establishment (1962) 221
General Programme for the abolition
  of restrictions on freedom to pro-
  vide services (1961) 221
Immigration Rules 109–112, 114–116,
                  119, 120, 125, 127, 128,
                  137, 138, 141, 146, 148–
                  153, 155, 158–160, 162,
                  170–175, 177, 181, 182,
                  198, 207, 209, 214, 215,

PARA

Immigration Rules—*contd*

          221, 235, 236, 240, 242,
          266, 267, 269, 279, 281,
          297, 305, 309, 310, 316–
          318, 320, 321, 325, 326,
          333, 343, 354, 375, 376

para 1 . . . . 120, 153, 191, 326
    2 . . . . 171, 269
    3 . . . . 208, 269
    4, 5 269
Sect 1 (para 6–93) 236
Pt I (para 6–21) 110
para 6 . . . . 164, 170
    7 . . . . 162, 171
    8 . . . . 151, 153, 171
    9 . . . . 120, 171
    10 . . . . 162, 170, 171
    11 . . . . 119, 173
    12 122
    13 151
    14 . . . . 119, 150, 151, 292
    15 . . . . 119, 151, 152
    16 . . . . 119, 141, 150–152, 244
    17 . . . . 119, 150, 292
     (a)–(c) 172
    19 . . . . 170, 171, 173, 305
    20 160
    21 . . . . 116, 171, 316–318
Pt II (para 22–33) 149, 292
para 22 . . . . 151, 160, 174, 305, 306
    23 . . . . 143, 151, 305, 306
    24 . . . . 151, 154, 174, 242, 246,
                   250
    25 . . . . 151, 173, 305, 309
    26 . . . . 151, 160, 266, 292, 293
    27, 28 293
    29 . . . . 154, 173, 241, 292, 293
    30 . . . . 154, 173, 174, 292, 294,
                   296
    31 . . . . 173, 174, 293, 301–303
    32 . . . . 151, 154, 173, 292, 295
    33 . . . . 151, 154, 173, 174,
                   310–312
Pt III (para 34–48) 110, 149
para 34 . . . . 112, 119, 140, 151, 154,
                   240
    35 . . . . 110, 119, 151, 155, 173,
                   242, 243
    36 . . . . 151, 154, 174, 261
    37 . . . . 151, 154, 160, 173, 174,
                   263, 266
    38 . . . . 151, 154, 173, 246,
                   249
     (a) 160, 247
     (b) 247
    39 . . . . 151, 154, 246, 247,
                   249
    40 . . . . 151, 154, 246, 249
     (a)–(f) 247
    41 . . . . 151, 154, 173, 246,
                   250–252
    42, 43 . . . . 151, 154, 251, 252

PARA

Immigration Rules—*contd*

para 44 . . . . 151, 154, 160, 173, 258,
                   259
    45 . . . . 151, 154, 160, 173, 254,
                   255
    46 . . . . 174, 264, 265
    47 . . . . 115, 151, 160, 268, 274
     (a)–(c) 274, 275
     (d), (e) 274, 276
    48 . . . . 115, 151, 173, 174, 268,
                   274
Pt IV (para 49–60) 149, 154
para 49 . . . . 112, 119, 151, 158–160,
                   173, 325, 326
    50 . . . . 115, 151, 160, 173, 268
     (a)–(c) 270, 271
     (d), (e) 270, 272
     note 120, 270
    51 . . . . 115, 151, 173, 268, 270
    52 . . . . 151, 159, 160, 173, 264,
                266, 268, 280, 282, 283,
                285, 287, 289, 326
    53 . . . . 151, 172, 173, 266, 268,
                279, 280, 285
     (a)–(f) 281
    54 . . . . 151, 173, 266, 268, 280,
                   285
     (a), (b) 281
    55 . . . . 151, 173, 266, 268, 280,
                282, 285
    56 . . . . 151, 173, 264, 266, 268,
                285, 287, 288
    57 . . . . 151, 173, 264, 266, 268,
                285, 286
    58 . . . . 120, 125, 150, 151, 173,
                176, 177
    59 . . . . 120, 125, 151, 173, 176,
                177
    60 . . . . 119, 120, 151, 173, 176,
                342
Pt V (para 61–67) 149
para 61 127
    64 . . . . 127, 151
    65 . . . . 127, 286
    67 127
Pt VI (para 68–74) 149, 151, 174
para 68 . . . . 137, 236, 268
    69 . . . . 137, 236
    70 . . . . 137, 236, 237
    71, 72 . . . . 137, 236
    73, 74 . . . . 137, 175, 236
Pt VII (para 75) 149
para 75 . . . . 116, 316–319, 322
Pt VIII (para 76, 77) 149
para 76 175
     (a)–(c) 175
    77 175
Pt IX (para 78–89) 149
para 78 . . . . 110, 119, 120, 149, 152,
                170–172, 177, 181
    79 170
    80 . . . . 165, 170, 171
    81 . . . . 143, 170, 171

PARA

Immigration Rules—*contd*

para 82	170, 171
83	152, 170
84, 85	170, 171
86	170, 171
(a), (b)	171
87, 88	170
89	167
Pt X (para 90–93)	149
Sect 2 (para 94–180)	127
Pt XI (para 94–154)	119, 149, 292
para 94	177
95	177, 181
96	177
98	316
99	181
100	180, 181
101	181
102	154, 157, 181, 241
103	249
105	307, 309
106	307
107	241, 263, 266, 297, 308
109	299, 308, 313
110	299
111	292
112	299
113	241, 293, 296, 299, 300, 303
114	154, 241, 300
115	154, 241, 299, 300, 308
116	293, 304
117	154, 244, 245
118	245
119	240, 241, 243, 245
120	157, 181, 240, 241, 297, 308
121	297, 308, 312
122	140, 154, 243, 244, 266
123	240, 248, 249, 266
124	248, 249
125	240
126	252, 257
127	253, 266
128	240, 256, 257, 266
129	260, 266
130	277
131	277, 278, 297, 308, 313
(a)–(h)	277, 278
132	270, 277
133–137	127
139	149, 154, 182, 241, 244, 249, 253, 257, 260, 262, 266, 268, 285, 291
140	116, 316, 320
142, 143	175, 183
144	178
146	235
147	235, 237
(a)–(c)	237, 238
148, 149	235, 237
150	235, 237, 238
151	235, 237, 239

PARA

Immigration Rules—*contd*

para 152	235, 238
153	235, 237
154	235
(a)–(e)	239
Pt XII (para 155–180)	149
para 155	126
(a)–(d)	204
156	203
157	335, 368
158	205
161	116, 316, 321
162	210
164	180, 208–210, 215, 342
165	181, 206, 207, 215
166	178, 205, 210, 329, 342
167	207
168	208, 215
169	208, 342
170–172	208
173	116, 203, 316, 321
174	211
175	212
176	198
177	200, 212, 343
178	206, 215
179, 180	214
Appendix	119, 150, 151
International Agreement for the Suppression of the White Slave Traffic (1904)	508
Protocol (1949)	508
International Convention against the Taking of Hostages (1979)	508, 532
International Convention for the Suppression of the Traffic in Women and Children (1921)	2
International Convention for the Suppression of the White Slave Traffic (1910)	508
Protocol (1949)	508
International Convention on Certain Questions relating to the Conflict of Nationality Laws (1930)	222
International Convention on the Elimination of All Forms of Racial Discrimination (1966)	5, 116
International Convention on the Suppression and Punishment of the Crime of Apartheid (1973)	5
International Convention relating to the Arrest of Sea-going Ships 1960	1154
International Convention with the object of securing the Abolition of Slavery and the Slave Trade (1926)	2
International Covenant on Civil and Political Rights (1966)	4, 116
International Covenant on Economic, Social and Cultural Rights (1966)	4

PARA

International Labour Organisation
Convention No 29 on Forced
Labour (1930) 28
  art 2, para 2 28
International Labour Organisation
Convention No 105 on the Abol-
ition of Forced Labour (1957) 5, 28
International Labour Organisation
Convention No 122 on Employ-
ment Policy (1964) 5
Proclamation of Tehran 1968 4
Protocol of Conference Relative to the
Abolition of the Slave Trade by
France (1815) 2
Rules of Procedure of the European
Commission of Human Rights
  1990 11
  r 3, 4 19
    32 15
    36 17
    43, para 1–3 15
    44, para 1(a)–(f) 15
        2(a)–(e) 15
        4, 5 15
    45–47 15
    48 15
      para 2(b) 19
    49–52 15
    54 16
  Ch V 15
  r 57, para 1, 3 15
    60 15
  Addendum—
    r 1(a), (b) 19
      2 19
      (a), (b) 19
      3, para 1, 2 19
      4, para 1, 2 19
      5, para 1, 2 19
      6, 7 19
Rules of Procedure of the European
Court of Human Rights 1959 12
Rules of Procedure of the European
Court of Human Rights 1982 12
  r 30 18
    31, para 2 18
    36 17
    51, para 2 17
    57 20
      para 1 20
    58 20
      para 1 20
    59–67 23
Rules regarding International Claims
1971
  r VII, VIII 14
Single European Act
  preamble 9
    3rd, 5th para 9
  art 16(3) 222
Statements of Principle (1990) 1342,
              1353–1356, 1369

PARA

Statements of Principle (1990)—*contd*
  Introduction—
    para (1), (2), (5) 1342
    principle 1 .... 1343, 1353
          2 1344
          3 .... 1345, 1353, 1354
          4 1346
          5 .... 1347, 1363, 1364, 1371,
                      1372
          6 .... 1348, 1353, 1355, 1358,
                  1383, 1395
          7 .... 1349, 1391
          8 .... 1350, 1402
          9 .... 1351, 1402
          10 ...... 1352, 1390, 1393, 1402
Statute of the Council of Europe
(1949)
  art 3 6
Treaty of Accession (1972) 220
  Protocol 3—
    art 2, 4, 6 220
  Final Act 220
  UK Declaration on 'Nationals' 220
Treaty of Accession (1985) 124
Treaty with Albania (1926) 507
Treaty with the Argentine Republic
(1889) 507
  Exchange of Notes (1979) 507
Treaty with Austria (1963) 507
  Exchange of Notes (1971) 507
Treaty with Belgium (1901)
  Exchange of Notes (1928, 1975 and
    1985) 507
  Supplementary Conventions (1907,
    1911 and 1923) 507
Treaty with Bolivia (1892) 507
Treaty with Chile (1897) 507
Treaty with Colombia (1888) 507
Treaty with Cuba (1904) 507
Treaty with Czechoslovakia (1924) 507
Treaty with Denmark (1873) 507
  Supplementary Convention (1938) 507
  Exchange of Notes (1979) 507
Treaty with Ecuador (1880) 507
Treaty with El Salvador (1881) 507
Treaty with Estonia (1925) 507
Treaty with Finland (1975) 507
  Exchange of Notes (1975 and
    1976) 507
Treaty with France (1876) 507
  Agreements (1899 and 1909) 507
  Conventions (1896 and 1908) 507
  Exchange of Notes (1923 and
    1978) 507
Treaty with Germany (1872) 507
  Agreement (1960) 507
  Exchange of Notes (1978) 507
Treaty with Greece (1910) 507
Treaty with Guatemala (1885) 507
  Protocol (1914) 507
Treaty with Haiti (1874) 507
Treaty with Hungary (1873) 507
  Declaration (1901) 507
  Supplementary Treaty (1936) 507

PARA

Treaty with Iceland (1938) 507
Treaty with Iraq (1932) 507
Treaty with Italy (1873) 507
Treaty with Latvia (1924) 507
Treaty with Liberia (1892) 507
Treaty with Lithuania (1926) 507
Treaty with Luxembourg (1880) 507
  Supplementary Convention (1939) 507
Treaty with Mexico (1886) 507
Treaty with Monaco (1891) 507
Treaty with the Netherlands (1898) 507
Treaty with Nicaragua (1905) 507
Treaty with Norway (1873) 507
  Agreement (1907) 507
  Exchange of Notes (1985) 507
Treaty with Panama (1906) 507
Treaty with Paraguay (1908) 507
Treaty with Peru (1904) 507
Treaty with Poland (1932) 507
Treaty with Portugal (1892) 507
  Protocol (1892) 507
  Supplementary Convention (1932) 507
Treaty with Roumania (1893) 507
  Protocol (1893) 507

PARA

Treaty with Russia (1886) 507
Treaty with San Marino (1899) 507
Treaty with Servia (1900) 507
Treaty with Sweden (1963) 507
  Exchange of Notes (1980) 507
Treaty with Switzerland (1880) 507
  Supplementary Conventions (1904
   and 1934) 507
Treaty with Siam (1911) 507
Treaties with the United States of
  America (1931) (1972) 507
  Supplementary Treaty (1985) 507
  Exchange of Notes (1986) 507, 545
Treaty with Uruguay (1884) 507
  Protocol (1891) 507
Universal Declaration of Human
  Rights (1948) 4, 116
  art 1–21 4
   29(2) 4
Vienna Convention on Consular
  Relations (1963) 130
Vienna Convention on the Law of
  Treaties (1969)
  art 30, 60 26

Table of Cases

A

A B v Northern Accident Insurance Co Ltd (1896) 24 R 258, 4 SLT 213 884
A G Securities v Vaughan, Antoniades v Villiers [1990] AC 417, [1988] 3 All ER 1058,
   HL 1252
Abbott v Minister for Lands [1895] AC 425, PC 1194
Abchurch SS Co Ltd v Stinnes 1911 SC 1010, 1911 2 SLT 72 1224
Abdulaziz, Cabales and Balkandali v United Kingdom (Ser A No 94, Judgment 28 May 1985) 7
   EHRR 471, E Ct HR 8, 17, 26, 65, 86, 115, 271
Abel v Lee (1871) LR 6 CP 365 1116
Aberdeen Harbour Board v Heating Enterprises (Aberdeen) Ltd 1989 SCLR 716, 1990 SLT
   416 852
Aberdeen Magistrates v Watt (1901) 3 F 787, 9 SLT 36 1171
Aberdeen Rly Co v Blaikie Bros (1854) 1 Macq 461, HL 1355
Aberdeen Suburban Tramways Co v Aberdeen Magistrates 1927 SC 683, 1927 SLT 468 ... 1198
Aberdeen, Corpn of Tailors of, v Coutts (1834) 2 Sh & Macl 609, HL (further proceedings
   (1840) 1 Robin 296, HL) 1232, 1246
Aberdein, Re [1896] WN 154 707
Abernethy v Forbes (1835) 13 S 263 1228
Abid Hussain v Entry Clearance Officer, Islamabad [1989] Imm AR 46, IAT 240, 271
Adam's Executrix v Maxwell 1921 SC 418, 1921 1 SLT 221 1268
Adamson v Melbourne and Metropolitan Board of Works [1929] AC 142, PC 1132
Adamson (T H) & Sons v Liverpool and London and Globe Insurance Co Ltd [1953] 2 Lloyd's
   Rep 355 881
Addison v Duguid (1793) Mor 7077 801
Adler v George [1964] 2 QB 7, [1964] 1 All ER 628, DC 1125
Admiralty v Burns 1910 SC 531, 1910 1 SLT 277 .... 1166, 1167, 1224, 1251
Adoui and Cornuaille v Belgium (Case 115, 116/81) [1982] ECR 1665, [1982] 3 CMLR 631,
   ECJ 233
Advocate (HM) v Bryce (unreported; noted in (1981) 2 Co Law 178) 1502
Advocate (HM) v Graham 1985 SLT 498 1178
Advocate (HM) v M'Donald 1984 JC 94, 1984 SLT 426 1178
Advocate (Lord) v M'Culloch (1874) 2 R 27 1237
Advocate (Lord) v Robertson (1897) 24 R (HL) 42 1185
Advocate (Lord) v Scotsman Publishers Ltd 1989 SLT 705, HL 8
Advocate (Lord) v Sprot's Trustees (1901) 3 F 440, 8 SLT 403 1157
Advocate (Lord) v Wemyss (1899) 2 F (HL) 1, 7 SLT 172 1238
Afza Mussarat v Secretary of State for the Home Department [1972] Imm AR 45 269
Agee v Lord Advocate 1977 SLT (Notes) 54 .... 115, 207
Agyen-Frempong v Immigration Appeal Tribunal [1988] Imm AR 262, CA 120, 125
Aiken's Executors v Aiken 1937 SC 678, 1937 SLT 414 847
Ailsa Craig Fishing Co Ltd v Malvern Fishing Co Ltd 1982 SC (HL) 14, 1982 SLT 377 843
Airedale Co-operative Worsted Manufacturing Society Ltd, Re [1933] Ch 639 .... 613, 622
Airey v Ireland (Ser A No 32, Judgment 9 October 1979) 2 EHRR 305, E Ct HR . 44, 62, 63, 77
Aitken v Finlayson, Bousfield & Co Ltd 1914 SC 770, 1914 2 SLT 27 844
Aitken's Trustees v Aitken 1927 SC 374, 1927 SLT 308 1270
Alam Bi v Immigration Appeal Tribunal [1979–80] Imm AR 146, CA 333, 357
Albert and Le Compte v Belgium (Ser A No 58, Judgment 10 February 1983) 5 EHRR 533, E Ct
   HR 26, 45, 75
Alexander v Immigration Appeal Tribunal [1982] 2 All ER 766, [1982] 1 WLR 1076, [1982]
   Imm AR 50, HL 110
Alexander v Mackenzie 1947 JC 155, 1948 SLT 68 1142
Algemeene Bankvereeniging v Langton (1935) 40 Com Cas 247, CA 839
Ali v Immigration Appeal Tribunal [1973] Imm AR 33, CA 343
Ali (M M H) v Secretary of State for the Home Department [1978] Imm AR 126, IAT 210
Allan v Stark (1901) 8 SLT 468, OH 1264

References are to paragraphs

Allgemeine Gold- und Silberscheideanstalt v Customs and Excise Comrs [1980] QB 390, [1980] 2 All ER 137, CA 8

Allgemeine Gold- und Silberscsheideanstalt v United Kingdom (Ser A No 108, Judgment 24 October 1986) 9 EHRR 1, E Ct HR 88

Allied Investors Trust Ltd v Board of Trade [1956] Ch 232, [1956] 1 All ER 162 1327

Allis-Chalmers Co v Maryland Fidelity and Deposit Co (1916) 114 LT 433, HL 818, 863

Altrincham Union Assessment Committee v Cheshire Lines Committee (1885) 15 QBD 597, CA 1203

Al-Tuwaidji v Chief Immigration Officer, London (Heathrow) Airport [1974] Imm AR 34, IAT 165, 171

Amarjit Singh Grewal v Secretary of State for the Home Department [1979–80] Imm AR 119, IAT 180

Ambatielos v Anton Jurgens Margarine Works [1923] AC 175, HL 1168

Ambatielos Arbitration (1956) 12 UNRIAA 83 14

Amer v Secretary of State for the Home Department [1979–80] Imm AR 87, IAT 299

Amicable Society of Lancaster, Ex parte (1801) 6 Ves 98 707

Amin, Re [1983] 2 AC 818, [1983] 2 All ER 864, HL 325, 326

Amministrazione delle Finanze dello Stato v Simmenthal SpA (Case 106/77) [1978] ECR 629, [1978] 3 CMLR 263, ECJ 219

Anand v Secretary of State for the Home Department [1978] Imm AR 36, IAT 208

Ancaster (Earl of) v Doig 1960 SC 203, 1960 SLT 257 .... 1225, 1251

Anderson v Commercial Union Assurance Co (1885) 55 LJQB 146, CA 890

Anderson v Dickie 1915 SC (HL) 79, 1915 1 SLT 393 1223

Anderson v Fitzgerald (1853) 4 HL Cas 484 .... 835, 858

Anderson v Jenkins Express Removals Ltd 1944 1136

Anderson v Lambie 1954 SC (HL) 43, 1954 SLT 73 1234

Anderson v Morice (1875) LR 10 CP 609, Ex Ch; (1876) 1 App Cas 713, HL 856

Anderson v Smoke (1898) 25 R 493, 5 SLT 309 1271

Anderson v Valentine 1957 SLT 57, OH 1232, 1247

Andronicou v Chief Immigration Officer, London (Heathrow) Airport [1974] Imm AR 87 150

Anglo-African Merchants Ltd v Bayley [1970] 1 QB 311, [1969] 2 All ER 421 839

Angur Begum v Secretary of State for the Home Department, Rutshanda Begum v Secretary of State for the Home Department [1990] Imm AR 1, CA 268

Angus Assessor v George Ogilvie (Montrose) Ltd 1968 SLT 348 1170

Angus Group Ltd v Lincoln Industries Ltd [1990] 3 NZLR 82 1035

Aradi v Immigration Officer, Heathrow [1985] AR 184, IAT 222, 223

Argy Trading Development Co Ltd v Lapid Developments Ltd [1977] 1 Lloyd's Rep 67, [1977] 1 WLR 444 890

Argyll (Duke of) v Campbell 1912 SC 458, 1912 1 SLT 316 1242

Argyllshire Commissioners of Supply v Campbell (1885) 12 R 1255 1239

Arif v Excess Insurance Group Ltd 1982 SLT 183, OH 865

Arif v Excess Insurance Group Ltd 1987 SLT 473, OH 851

Arkins, Re [1966] 3 All ER 651, [1966] 1 WLR 1593, DC 555, 564

Arshad v Immigration Officer, London (Heathrow) Airport [1977] Imm AR 19, IAT 172

Artico v Italy (Ser A No 37, Judgment 13 May 1980) 3 EHRR 1, E Ct HR 52

Arton, Re (No 1) [1896] 1 QB 108 .... 532, 534

Ashbury Railway Carriage and Iron Co v Riche (1875) LR 7 HL 653 613

Ashingdane v United Kingdom (Ser A No 93, Judgment 28 May 1985) 7 EHRR 528, E Ct HR 41

Ashley, Re, ex parte Corser (1801) 6 Ves 441 707

Ashraf v Immigration Appeal Tribunal [1989] Imm AR 234, CA 150, 172, 337

Aslan v Murphy (No 1) and (No 2), Wynne v Duke [1989] 3 All ER 130, CA 1252

Assheton Smith v Owen [1906] 1 Ch 179 1113

Associated Newspapers Ltd v Registrar of Restrictive Trading Agreements [1964] 1 All ER 55, [1964] 1 WLR 31, HL 1122

Associated Provincial Picture Houses Ltd v Wednesbury Corpn [1948] 1 KB 223, [1947] 2 All ER 680 316

Athanassiadis v Government of Greece [1971] AC 282, [1969] 3 All ER 293, HL 536, 550

Atkinson v United States of America Government [1971] AC 197, [1969] 3 All ER 1317, HL 536, 568

Attorney General v Guardian Newspapers Ltd (No 2) [1990] 1 AC 109, [1983] 3 All ER 546, HL 1153

References are to paragraphs

Attorney General v Prince Ernest Augustus of Hanover [1957] AC 436, [1957] 1 All ER 49,
  HL 103, 1125, 1136
Attorney-General v Theobald (1890) 24 QBD 557 1193
Attorney-General v Times Newspapers Ltd [1973] QB 710, [1972] 3 All ER 1136, DC 74
Attorney-General v Times Newspapers Ltd [1973] QB 710, [1973] 1 All ER 815, CA 74
Attorney-General v Times Newspapers Ltd [1974] AC 273, [1973] 3 All ER 54, HL 74
Attorney-General v Vernazza [1960] AC 965, [1960] 3 All ER 97, HL 1192
Attorney-General's Reference (No 1 of 1988) [1989] AC 971, [1989] 3 All ER 571, HL 1502,
                                                                                     1513
Attorney-General for Canada v Hallet and Carey Ltd [1952] AC 427, PC 1102
Attorney General for Colony of Hong Kong v Kwok-a-Sing (1873) LR 5 PC 179 514
Auchterarder Presbytery v Earl of Kinnoull (1839) Macl & R 220, HL 1123
Auer v Ministère Public (Case 271/82) [1983] ECR 2727, [1985] 1 CMLR 123, ECJ 221
Australia and New Zealand Bank Ltd v Colonial and Eagle Wharves Ltd [1960] 2 Lloyd's Rep
  241 860
Australian Agricultural Co v Saunders (1875) LR 10 CP 668, Ex Ch 915
Austria v Italy (Application 788/60) 4 YBHR 116, 6 YBHR 796 14
Avco Financial Services Ltd v McQuire 1976 SLT (Sh Ct) 33 1003
Axen v Germany (Ser A No 72, Judgment 8 December 1983) 6 EHRR 195, E Ct HR 49
Ayettey v Secretary of State for the Home Department [1972] Imm AR 261, IAT 293
Ayr Magistrates v Dobbie (1898) 25 R 1184, 6 SLT 110 1239
Ayrshire Employers Mutual Insurance Association Ltd v Inland Revenue Comrs 1946 SC (HL)
  1, 1946 SLT 235 1117

B

B v Austria (Ser A No 175, Judgment 28 March 1990) 13 EHRR 20, E Ct HR 32, 47
B v United Kingdom (Ser A No 121, Judgment 8 July 1987) 10 EHRR 87, E Ct HR 64
Babatunde Michael Olaleye v Secretary of State for the Home Department [1987] Imm AR 51,
  IAT 130
Badrul Bari v Immigration Appeal Tribunal [1987] Imm AR 13, CA 263
Bahadur Singh v Immigration Appeal Tribunal [1988] Imm AR 582, CA 125
Baijal v Secretary of State for the Home Department [1976] Imm AR 34, IAT 263
Bain v Duke of Hamilton (1865) 3 M 821 1221
Bain v Mackay (1875) 2 R (J) 32 1198
Bainbridge v Campbell 1912 SC 92, 1911 2 SLT 373 1232
Baird's Trustees v Duncanson (1892) 19 R 1045 1030
Balfour v Beaumont [1984] 1 Lloyd's Rep 272, CA 841
Baljinder Singh v Hammond [1987] 1 All ER 829, [1987] 1 WLR 283, DC 164
Ballantine v Employers' Insurance Co of Great Britain Ltd (1893) 21 R 305 884
Ballingall's Judicial Factor v Hamilton 1973 SLT 236 1271
Balogun v Secretary of State for the Home Department [1989] Imm AR 603, CA 150, 176
Bamgbose, Re [1990] Imm AR 135, CA 118, 190
Bank of Scotland v Bruce 1968 SLT (Sh Ct) 58 1003
Bank of Scotland v Davis 1982 SLT 20 .... 1001, 1002, 1003, 1037
Bank of Scotland v Logie 1986 SLT (Sh Ct) 47 1004
Banque Financière de la Cité SA v Westgate Insurance Co Ltd [1990] 2 All ER 947, HL (affg
  [1989] 2 All ER 952, CA) 858, 863
Barber v Guardian Royal Exchange Assurance Group (Case 262/88) [1990] 2 CMLR 513, ECJ ... 9
Barberà, Messegué and Jabardo v Spain (Ser A No 146, Judgment 6 December 1988) 11 EHRR
  360, E Ct HR 53, 59
Barclay v Barclay (1850) 22 SJ 354 1008
Barfod v Denmark (Ser A No 149, Judgment 22 February 1989) 13 EHRR 493, E Ct HR 74
Barnes v Jarvis [1953] 1 All ER 1061, [1953] 1 WLR 649, DC 1116
Barnett (Arthur) Ltd v National Insurance Co of New Zealand Ltd [1965] NZLR 874 (NZ SC) . 899
Barras v Aberdeen Steam Trawling and Fishing Co 1933 SC (HL) 21, 1933 SLT 338 1159
Barrett v Markham (1872) LR 7 CP 405 745
Barrett Bros (Taxis) Ltd v Davies [1966] 2 All ER 972, [1966] 1 WLR 1334, CA 883
Barthold v Germany (Ser A No 90, Judgment 25 March 1985) 7 EHRR 383, E Ct HR 81

References are to paragraphs

Barty v Hill 1907 SC (J) 36, 14 SLT 616 1120
Bashir (alias Ayoub) v Secretary of State for the Home Department [1978] Imm AR 150,
    IAT 207, 209
Basset v Basset (1744) 3 Atk 203 1161
Bastin v Davies [1950] 2 KB 579, [1950] 1 All ER 1095, DC 1151
Beach v Pearl Assurance Co Ltd [1938] IAC Rep 3 818
Bedford Insurance Co Ltd v Instituto de Resseguros do Brasil [1985] QB 966, [1984] 3 All ER
    766 807
Belgian Linguistic Case (No 2) (Ser A No 6, Judgment 23 July 1968) 1 EHRR 252,
    E Ct HR 17, 62, 85, 86, 89
Belgium (Government of) v Postlethwaite [1988] AC 924, [1987] 2 All ER 985, HL 511
Bell v Hay 1979 SC 237, 1980 SLT 110 1191
Bell Bros v Hudson Bay Insurance Co (1911) 44 SCR 419 (Can SC) 833
Bellencontre, Re [1891] 2 QB 122, DC 553
Ben Challum Ltd v Buchanan 1955 SC 348, 1955 SLT 294 1248
Benthem v Netherlands (Ser A No 97, Judgment 23 October 1985) 8 EHRR 1, E Ct HR 45
Benzie v Mickel 1945 JC 47, 1945 SLT 166 1166
Bernard v Entry Clearance Officer, Kingston, Jamaica [1976] Imm AR 7, IAT 282
Berrehab v Netherlands (Ser A No 138, Judgment 21 June 1988) 11 EHRR 322, E Ct HR ... 65
Beswick v Beswick [1968] AC 58, [1967] 2 All ER 1197, HL 1147, 1148, 1158
Bethlem Hospital, Re (1875) LR 19 Eq 457 1116
Bezicheri v Italy (Ser A No 164, Judgment 25 October 1989) 12 EHRR 210, E Ct HR 33
Bhagat Singh v Entry Clearance Officer, New Delhi [1978] Imm AR 134, IAT 306
Bhagat v Secretary of State for the Home Department [1972] Imm AR 189, IAT 293, 349
Bibi and Purvez v Immigration Appeal Tribunal [1988] Imm AR 298, CA 120
Bibi Bagas v Entry Clearance Officer, Bombay [1978] Imm AR 85, IAT 286
Birdi v Secretary of State for Home Affairs 11 February 1975 8
Birmingham Corpn v Minister of Housing and Local Government and Habib Ullah [1964] 1
    QB 178, [1963] 3 All ER 668, DC 1156
Birrell Ltd v City of Edinburgh District Council 1982 SLT 111, affd 1983 SC (HL) 75, 1982 SLT
    363, HL 1036
Bishop v Hooper [1905] VLR 220 1171
Bisset v Royal Exchange Assurance Co (1822) 1 S 174 (NE 165) 890
Black v Glasgow Corpn 1958 SC 260, 1959 SLT 219 1179
Blackburn Philanthropic Assurance Co Ltd, Re [1914] 2 Ch 430 731
Black-Clawson International Ltd v Papierwerke Waldhof-Aschaffenburg AG [1975] AC 591,
    [1975] 1 All ER 810, HL 1149, 1150
Blair v Assets Co (1896) 25 R (HL) 36, 4 SLT 13 1226
Blair v Duncan (1901) 4 F (HL) 1, 9 SLT 390 1271
Blair v Murray (1843) 5 D 1315 1038
Blair's Trustees v Payne (1884) 12 R 104 .. 1001, 1007, 1008, 1011, 1012, 1014, 1016, 1018, 1020
Bliersbach v MacEwen 1959 SC 43, 1959 SLT 81 269
Blythe v Birtley [1910] 1 Ch 228, CA 731
Boag v Standard Marine Insurance Co Ltd [1937] 2 KB 113, [1937] 1 All ER 714, CA 898
Boardman v Phipps [1967] 2 AC 46, [1966] 3 All ER 721, HL 1535
Bodén v Sweden (Ser A No 125B, Judgment 27 October 1987) 10 EHRR 367, E Ct HR .. 44, 96
Bogie's Trustees v Christie (1882) 9 R 453 1268
Bolton District National Independent Order of Oddfellows v National Independent Order of
    Oddfellows (1895) FS Cases 55 697
Bönisch v Austria (Ser A No 92, Judgment 6 May 1985) 9 EHRR 191, E Ct HR 56
Bonsignore v Stadt Köln (Case 67/74) [1975] ECR 297, [1975] 1 CMLR 472, ECJ 233
Booth (Vic) (Joiners) Ltd, 14 January 1986 (unreported), Lands Trib 1247
Boots the Chemist Ltd v GA Estates Ltd (1991) Scotsman, 4 July, OH 1032
Borthwick-Norton v Gavin Paul & Sons 1947 SC 659, 1948 SLT 89 1242
Borthwick's Trustees v Borthwick 1955 SC 227 1268
Bouamar v Belgium (Ser A No 129, Judgment 29 February 1988) 11 EHRR 1, E Ct HR 39
Bourne v Keane [1919] AC 815, HL 1163
Bovell v Entry Clearance Officer, Georgetown, Guyana [1973] Imm AR 37, IAT 281
Bowers v Gloucester Corpn [1963] 1 QB 881, [1963] 1 All ER 437, DC 1184
Bowie v Semple's Executors 1978 SLT (Sh Ct) 9 .... 1010, 1013
Boyd v Greig 1913 1 SLT 398, OH 1001, 1026
Boyd v Hamilton 1907 SC 912, 15 SLT 57 1239

References are to paragraphs

Boyle v Wilson [1907] AC 45, HL 1158
Boyle and Rice v United Kingdom (Ser A No 131, Judgment 27 April 1988) 10 EHRR 425, E Ct
   HR 21, 69, 84
Bozano v France (Ser A No 111, Judgment 18 December 1986) 9 EHRR 297, E Ct HR 38
Bradley v Eagle Star Insurance Co Ltd [1989] AC 957, [1989] 1 All ER 961, HL 905, 906
Braid Hills Hotel Co Ltd v Manuels 1909 SC 120, 16 SLT 523 1245
Brazier v Skipton Rock Co Ltd [1962] 1 All ER 955, [1962] 1 WLR 471 1183
Bricmont v Belgium (Ser A No 158, Judgment 7 July 1989) 12 EHRR 217, E Ct HR 58
British Linen Bank v Gammie (1948) 64 Sh Ct Rep 23 847
Britt v Buckinghamshire County Council [1964] 1 QB 77, [1963] 2 All ER 175, CA 1164
Broatch v Jenkins (1866) 4 M 1030 858
Broekmeulen v Huisarts Registratie Commissie (Case 246/80) [1981] ECR 2311, [1982] 1
   CMLR 91, ECJ 221
Brogan v United Kingdom (Ser A No 125B, Judgment 30 May 1989) 13 EHRR 439, E Ct HR .. 21
Brogan v United Kingdom (Ser A No 145B, Judgment 29 November 1988) 11 EHRR 117, E Ct
   HR 30
Brook v Trafalgar Insurance Co Ltd (1947) 79 Ll L Rep 365, CA 882
Brown v Bonnyrigg and Lasswade Magistrates 1936 SC 258, 1936 SLT 304 1174
Brown v Edinburgh Magistrates 1931 SLT 456 1201
Brown v Entry Clearance Officer, Kingston, Jamaica [1976] Imm AR 119, IAT 152, 282
Brown v Lord Advocate 1973 SLT 205 1182
Brown v National Coal Board [1962] AC 574, [1962] 1 All ER 81, HL 1183
Brown v North British Rly Co (1906) 8 F 534, 13 SLT 797 1240
Brown v Royal Insurance Co (1859) 1 E & E 853 890
Brownlee v Robb 1907 SC 1302, 15 SLT 261 847
Brownlie v Campbell (1880) 5 App Cas 925, HL 864
Brozicek v Italy (Ser A No 167, Judgment 19 December 1989) 12 EHRR 371, E Ct HR 51
Bruce v Whyte (1900) 2 F 823, 7 SLT 436 1203
Brydekirk (Minister) v Minister of Heritors of Hoddam (1877) 4 R 798 1136
Buchan v J Marr (Aberdeen) Ltd 1987 SCLR 96, 1987 SLT (Notes) 521, OH 1032
Buchan (Earl of) v Scottish Widows Fund Society (1857) 19 D 551 1228
Buchanan v Andrew (1873) 11 M (HL) 13 1216
Buchanan v Buchanan (1876) 3 R 556 1264
Buckie Magistrates v Dowager Countess of Seafield's Trustees 1928 SC 525, 1928 SLT 362: 1138
Budh Singh, Re, 13 July 1988 (unreported) 8
Bugdaycay v Secretary of State for the Home Department, Nelidow Santis v Secretary of State
   for the Home Department, Norman v Secretary of State for the Home Department, Re
   Musisi [1987] AC 514, [1987] 1 All ER 940, [1987] Imm AR 250, HL 198, 316, 317,
                                                  318, 319, 320, 321, 322, 344
Buist v Scottish Equitable Life Assurance Society (1878) 5 R (HL) 64 846
Bulmer (H P) Ltd v J Bollinger SA [1974] Ch 401, [1974] 2 All ER 1226, CA 1205
Bunten v Hart (1902) 9 SLT 476, OH 1014, 1038
Burke v Amalgamated Society of Dyers [1906] 2 KB 583 703
Burnand v Rodocanachi Sons & Co (1882) 7 App Cas 333, HL 830, 886, 895, 899, 900, 902
Burnley Equitable Co-operative and Industrial Society Ltd [1891] 1 QB 75 613
Bute v More (1870) 9 M 180 1201
Butler v Springmount Dairy Society [1906] 2 IR 193 616
Butter v Bennett [1963] Ch 185, [1962] 3 All ER 204, CA 1120

C

C (an infant) v Entry Clearance Officer, Hong Kong [1976] Imm AR 165, IAT 261
Cadell v Allan (1905) 7 F 606, 13 SLT 10 1239
Cairns v MacDiarmid (Inspector of Taxes) (1982) 56 TC 556, [1983] STC 178, CA 1034
Calder v Stevens (1871) 9 M 1074 1187
Caldwell (1871) 10 M 99 .... 1226, 1233
Caledonian Insurance Co v Gilmour (1892) 20 R (HL) 13, [1983] AC 85 827
Caledonian Rly Co v Glasgow Corpn (1901) 3 F 526, 8 SLT 457 1166
Caledonian Rly Co v Glenboig Union Fireclay Co Ltd 1911 SC (HL) 72, 1911 1 SLT 416 .. 1242
Caledonian Rly Co v North British Rly (1881) 8 R (HL) 23 .... 1106, 1110
Caledonian Rly Co v Symington 1912 SC (HL) 9, 1911 2 SLT 411 1242

References are to paragraphs

Callander v Smith (1900) 2 F 11408 SLT 132 1189
Calvin's Case (1608) 7 Co Rep 1a 104
Camden (Marquis) v Inland Revenue Comrs [1914] 1 KB 641, CA 1152
Came v City of Glasgow Friendly Society 1933 SC 69, 1933 SLT 90 823
Cameron v Macniven (1894) 21 R (J) 31, 1 SLT 467 1129
Campbell v Clydesdale Banking Co (1868) 6 M 943 1248
Campbell v Duke of Atholl (1869) 8 M 308 1178
Campbell v McCutcheon 1963 SC 505, 1963 SLT 290 1243
Campbell v Paterson (1896) 4 SLT 79 1239
Campbell v Western Isles Islands Council 1989 SLT 602 (affg 1988 SLT (Lands Trib) 4) ...1251
Campbell and Cosans v United Kingdom (Ser A No 48, Judgment 25 February 1982) 4 EHRR
   293, E Ct HR 26, 89, 90, 91, 95
Campbell and Fell v United Kingdom (Ser A No 80, Judgment 28 June 1984) 7 EHRR 165, E Ct
   HR 48, 52, 84
Campbell's Trustee v Welsh 1952 SC 343, 1952 SLT 352 1268
Campbell's Trustees v Campbell 1920 SC 297, 1920 1 SLT 188 1271
Campbell's Trustees v Campbell 1921 SC (HL) 12, 1921 1 SLT 50 1271
Campbell's Trustees v O'Neill 1911 SC 188, 1910 2 SLT 392 1116
Canada (Government of) v Aronson [1990] 1 AC 579, [1989] 2 All ER 1025, HL .522, 548, 563
Canada Southern Rly Co v International Bridge Co (1883) 8 App Cas 723, PC 1157
Canada Sugar Refining Co Ltd v R [1898] AC 735, PC 1119
Canadian National Railways v Canada SS Lines Ltd [1945] AC 204, PC 1168
Canavan 1929 SLT 636, OH 740
Canning v Farquhar (1886) 16 QBD 727, CA 818
Cantiere Meccanico Brindisino v Janson [1912] 3 KB 452, CA 860
Capper v Baldwin [1965] 2 QB 53, [1965] 1 All ER 787, DC 1102
Caprino v United Kingdom No 6871/75 (1980) 4 EHRR 97 ....207, 396
Caravans and Automobiles v Southall Borough Council [1963] 2 All ER 533, [1963] 1 WLR
   690, DC 1156
Carmichael v Caledonian Rly Co (1870) 8 M (HL) 119 ....1001, 1009, 1011, 1012, 1016,
                                    1017, 1021, 1029, 1031, 1037
Carmichael v Carmichael's Executrix 1919 SC 636, 1919 2 SLT 89 ....692, 724, 848, 853
Carmichael v Carmichael's Executrix 1920 SC (HL) 195, 1920 2 SLT 285 ...692, 848, 853, 1248
Carr and Sun Fire Insurance Co, Re (1897) 13 TLR 186, CA 846
Carreras v Cunard Steamship Co [1918] 1 KB 118 893
Carrick Furniture House Ltd v General Accident, Fire and Life Assurance Corpn Ltd 1977 SC
   308, 1978 SLT 65 886
Carroll v Piling [1939] LJNCCR 148 725
Carswell v Goldie 1967 SLT 339 1247
Carter v Boehm (1766) 3 Burr 1905 858
Cartledge v E Jopling & Sons Ltd [1963] AC 758, [1963] 1 All ER 341, HL 1105
Casher v Holmes (1831) 2 B & Ad 592 1169
Cassel v Lancashire and Yorkshire Accident Insurance Co Ltd (1885) 1 TLR 495 881
Castellain v Preston (1883) 11 QBD 380, CA 886, 894, 895, 900
Castioni, Re [1891] 1 QB 149, DC 532
Champion v Duncan (1867) 6 M 17 853
Champion v Gwent Chief Constable [1990] 1 All ER 116, [1990] 1 WLR 1, HL 8
Chancellor v Mosman (1872) 10 M 995 1237
Chanda v Immigration Officer, London (Heathrow) Airport [1981] Imm AR 88, IAT 172
Chandler v Director of Public Prosecutions [1964] AC 763, [1962] 3 All ER 142, HL: 1137, 1146
Chapman v Pole, PO (1870) 22 LT 306 ....830, 831
Chappell v United Kingdom (Ser A No 152, Judgment 30 March 1989) 12 EHRR 1, E Ct HR ..70
Chase Manhattan Equities Ltd v Goodman The Times 23 May 1991 1535
Chavda v Entry Clearance Officer, Bombay [1978] AR 40, IAT 287
Cheng v Governor of Pentonville Prison [1973] AC 931, [1973] 2 All ER 204, HL 532
Chernack v Mill 1938 JC 39, 1938 SLT 10 1168
Chinwo v Secretary of State for the Home Department [1985] Imm AR 74, IAT 299
Choudhry v Immigration Appeal Tribunal [1990] Imm AR 211, CA 271
Christie v Jackson (1898) 6 SLT 245, OH 1244
Christie v Matheson (1871) 10 M 9 1008
Christie v North British Insurance Co (1825) 3 S 519 (NE 360) 818, 828
Christodoulidou v Secretary of State for the Home Department [1985] Imm AR 179, IAT ..118

References are to paragraphs

Chrystal's Trustees v Haldane 1960 SC 127, 1961 SLT 25 1264
City Tailors Ltd v Evans (1921) 126 LT 439, CA 830, 880
Ciulla v Italy (Ser A No 148, Judgment 22 February 1989) 13 EHRR 346, E Ct HR 17, 40
Claddagh SS Co Ltd v Steven & Co 1919 SC 184, 1918 2 SLT 89, OH (approved 1919 SC (HL)
    132, 1919 2 SLT 170) 1225
Clancy v Dixon's Ironworks Ltd 1955 SC 17, 1955 SLT 36 1032
Clark v City of Glasgow Life Assurance Co (1854) 17 D (HL) 27 1246
Claveria v Immigration Officer, London (Heathrow) Airport [1978] Imm AR 176, IAT: 172, 198
Clerc v France (Ser A No 176, Judgment 26 April 1990), E Ct HR 22
Clidero v Scottish Accident Insurance Co (1892) 19 R 355 .... 841, 844
Clyde Navigation Trustees v Kelvin Shipping Co Ltd 1927 SC 622, 1927 SLT 436 1038
Clyde Navigation Trustees v Laird & Son (1883) 10 R (HL) 77 1113
Clydesdale Bank (Moore Place) Nominees Ltd v Snodgrass 1939 SC 805, 1940 SLT 46 1345
Coates v Diment [1951] 1 All ER 890 1197
Cochrane v Black (1855) 17 D 321 1027
Cochrane v Graham and Sibbald 1987 SLT 622 1019
Colak v Germany (Ser A No 147, Judgment 6 December 1988) 11 EHRR 513, E Ct HR 60
Coleman v Myers [1977] 2 NZLR 225, N.Z. CA 1535
Coleman's Depositories Ltd and Life and Health Assurance Association, Re [1907] 2 KB 798,
    CA 825
Collingridge v Royal Exchange Assurance Corpn (1877) 3 QBD 173 894
Collins v Barrowfield United Oddfellows 1915 SC 190, 1914 2 SLT 401 725
Colonial Sugar Refining Co Ltd v Irving [1905] AC 369, PC 1192
Colozza v Italy (Ser A No 89, Judgment 12 February 1985) 7 EHRR 516, E Ct HR 50, 96
Colquhoun v Brooks (1888) 21 QBD 52, CA 1165
Colquhoun v Brooks (1889) 14 App Cas 493, HL 1119
Colquhoun v Dumbarton Magistrates 1907 SC (J) 57, 14 SLT 847 1211
Colquhoun v Society of Contributors to the Widows' Fund of the Faculty of Procurators in
    Glasgow 1908 SC (HL) 10, 15 SLT 1049 705
Coltman, Re, Coltman v Coltman (1881) 19 Ch D 64, CA 719, 720
Commercial Bank of Scotland v Rhind (1860) 3 Macq 643, HL 1016
Commercial Union Assurance Co v Lister (1874) 9 Ch App 483 .... 896, 899
Commercial Union Assurance Co v Temple (1898) 29 SCR 206 (Can SC) 915
Commonwealth, The [1907] P 216, CA 903
Condogianis v Guardian Assurance Co Ltd [1921] 2 AC 125, PC 842
Confédération Française Démocratique du Travail v European Communities [1979] 2 CMLR
    229, Eur Com HR 9
Congested Districts (Ireland) Board (1895) RCR 3 721
Connelly v Simpson 1991 SCLR 295, OH 1012
Constitution Insurance Co of Canada v Kosmopoulos (1987) 34 DLR (4th) 208 (Can SC) ... 850
Container Transport International Inc and Reliance Group Inc v Oceanus Mutual Underwrit-
    ing Association (Bermuda) Ltd [1984] 1 Lloyd's Rep 476, CA 859, 869, 870
Cook v Deeks [1916] 1 AC 554, PC 1535
Coomber v Ross 1987 SLT 266, OH 1216
Cooper, Re [1911] 2 KB 550, CA 1034
Cooper's Trustees v Stark's Trustees (1898) 25 R 1160 1242
Cooper Scott v Gill Scott 1924 SC 309, 1924 SLT 204 .... 1221, 1237
Coppin, Re (1866) 2 Ch App 47 536
Cording v Halse [1955] 1 QB 63, [1954] 3 All ER 287, DC 1188
Corinthian Securities v Cato [1970] 1 QB 377, [1969] 3 All ER 1168, CA 1034
Cornish v Accident Insurance Co (1889) 23 QBD 453, CA 842
Cossey v United Kingdom (Ser A No 184, Judgment 27 September 1990) 13 EHRR 622, E Ct
    HR 67, 71
Costa v ENEL (Case 6/64) [1964] ECR 585, [1964] CMLR 425, ECJ 219
Council of Civil Service Unions v Minister for the Civil Service [1985] AC 374, [1984] 3 All ER
    935, HL 35
Council of Civil Service Unions v United Kingdom (Application 11603/85) (1987) 10 EHRR
    269, E Com HR 24
Couper v Mackenzie (1906) 8 F 1202, 13 SLT 870 1156
Coutts & Co v Allan & Co (1758) Mor 11549 1216
Coventry v Coventry (1834) 12 S 895 .... 1235, 1236
Cowper v Callender (1872) 10 M 353 1177

References are to paragraphs

Craig v Imperial Union Accident Assurance Co (1894) 1 SLT 646, OH 858, 865, 867
Cramas Properties Ltd v Connaught Fur Trimmings Ltd [1965] 2 All ER 382, [1965] 1 WLR
    892, HL 1121
Crawford (Earl of) v Duke of Montrose (1853) 1 Macq 401, HL 1112
Crawford and Stark v Bertram 15 May 1812, FC 1011
Crichton Stuart v Ogilvie 1914 SC 888, 1914 2 SLT 116 1166
Cromertie (Countess of) v Lord Advocate (1871) 9 M 988 1012
Cruikshank v Northern Accident Insurance Co Ltd (1895) 23 R 147, 3 SLT 167 .... 862, 875
Cuffy v Entry Clearance Officer, Georgetown, Guyana [1976] Imm AR 66, IAT 282
Cumming's Executors v Cumming 1967 SLT 68, OH 1271
Cunningham v Anglian Insurance Co Ltd 1934 SLT 273, OH 909
Cunninghame v Cunninghame's Trustees 1961 SC 32, 1961 SLT 194 1268
Currie v Campbell's Trustees (1888) 16 R 237 .... 1225, 1240
Currie's Trustees v Currie (1904) 7 F 364, 12 SLT 613 1230
Curtis v Stovin (1889) 22 QBD 513, CA 1123
Customs and Excise Officers' Mutual Guarantee Fund, Robson, Re v Attorney-General [1917]
    2 Ch 18 737
Cyprus v Turkey (Applications 6780/74, 6950/75) 2 Decisions and Reports 125 14

D

D (K) (a minor), Re [1988] AC 806, [1988] 1 All ER 577, HL 8
Dagdalen v Secretary of State for the Home Department [1988] Imm AR 425, CA 170
Dalby v India and London Life Assurance Co (1854) 15 CB 365, Ex Ch 854
Dalgleish v John Buchanan & Co (1854) 16 D 332 852
Dalhousie's (Earl of) Tutors v Lochlee Minister (1890) 17 R 1060 1239
Darby v Sweden (Ser A No 187, Judgment 23 October 1990), E Ct HR 62
Darrell v Tibbits (1880) 5 QBD 560, CA 900
Davendranath Doorga v Secretary of State for the Home Department [1990] Imm AR 98, CA . 292
David v S P A De Silva [1934] AC 106, PC 1131
Davidson v Guardian Royal Exchange Assurance 1979 SC 192, 1981 SLT 81 . 837, 842, 843, 890
Davidson v Johnston (1903) 6 F 239, 11 SLT 503 1139
Davie v Colinton Friendly Society (1870) 9 M 96 .... 695, 703
Dawsons Ltd v Bonnin 1922 SC (HL) 156, 1922 SLT 444 .... 823, 874, 875
De Becker v Belgium (Ser A No 4, Judgment 27 March 1962) 1 EHRR 43, E Ct HR 22
De Becker v Belgium Application 214/56 2 YBHR 214 14
De Cubber v Belgium (Ser A No 86, Judgment 26 October 1984) 7 EHRR 236, E Ct HR ... 48
De Geer v Stone (1882) 22 Ch D 243 104
De Jong, Baljet and Van den Brink v Netherlands (Ser A No 77, Judgment 22 May 1984) 8
    EHRR 20, E Ct HR 30, 31
De Maurier (Jewels) Ltd v Bastion Insurance Co Ltd [1967] 2 Lloyd's Rep 550 ... 874, 875, 878
De Wilde, Ooms and Versyp v Belgium (No 1) (Ser A No 12, Judgment 18 June 1971) 1 EHRR
    373, E Ct HR 18, 28, 42, 69
Dean Warwick Ltd v Borthwick 1983 SLT 533 .... 1012, 1013, 1014, 1015
Degan v Dundee Corpn 1940 SC 457, 1940 SLT 375 1180
Delcourt v Belgium (Ser A No 11, Judgment 17 January 1970) 1 EHRR 355, E Ct HR 60
Dempster (R and J) Ltd v Motherwell Bridge and Engineering Co Ltd 1964 SC 308, 1964 SLT
    353 .... 1012, 1032
Denmark, Norway, Sweden and the Netherlands v Greece (Applications 3321–3323, 3344/67)
    11 YBHR 690, 12 YBHR 1 14
Dennison v Jeffs [1896] 1 Ch 611 738
Department of Trade and Industry v St Christopher Motorists Association Ltd [1974] 1 All ER
    395, [1974] 1 WLR 99 802
Derrick v Secretary of State for the Home Department [1972] Imm AR 109, IAT 209
Dervish v Secretary of State for the Home Department [1972] Imm AR 48, IAT 214
Dewar v Inland Revenue Comrs [1935] 2 KB 351, (1935) 19 TC 561, CA 1034
Deweer v Belgium (Ser A No 35, Judgment 27 February 1980) 2 EHRR 439, E Ct HR 60
Diamond v Minter [1941] 1 KB 656, [1941] 1 All ER 390 .... 504, 511
Diatta v Land Berlin (Case 267/83) [1985] ECR 567, [1986] 2 CMLR 164, ECJ 223
Dick-Lauder v Leather-Cully 1920 SC 48, 1919 2 SLT 241 1237
Dilworth v Stamps Comrs [1899] AC 99, PC 1140

References are to paragraphs

Director of Public Prosecutions v Bhagwan [1972] AC 60, [1970] 3 All ER 97, HL 105
Director of Public Works v Ho Po Sang [1961] AC 901, [1961] 2 All ER 721, PC 1194
Dixon v Thompson (1891) FS Cases 46 701
Dobinson v Hawks (1848) 10 Sim 407 704
Donnison v Employers' Accident and Live Stock Insurance Co (1897) 24 R 681 875
Dora, The [1989] 1 Lloyd's Rep 69 .... 858, 862, 865
Dorchester Studios (Glasgow) Ltd v Stone 1975 SC (HL) 56, 1975 SLT 153 1251
Douglas v Douglas's Trustees (1867) 5 M 827 1038
Dow v Kilgour's Trustees (1877) 4 R 403 1269
Driscoll, Re Driscoll v Driscoll (1918) 1 IR 152 903
Drummond v Law Society of Scotland 1980 SC 175, OH 1012
Drylie v Alloa Coal Co Ltd 1913 SC 549, 1913 1 SLT 167 844
Duckett v Williams (1834) 2 Cr & M 348 835
Dudgeon v United Kingdom (Ser A No 45, Judgment 23 September 1981) 4 EHRR 149, E Ct
    HR 66, 78, 81, 95
Dumfries and Galloway Regional Council v M 1990 SLT 272 1178
Dunbar v A and B Painters Ltd [1986] 2 Lloyd's Rep 38, CA 862, 909
Dunbar v Scott's Trustees (1872) 10 M 982 1270
Dunbar & Co v Scottish County Investment Co Ltd 1920 SC 210, 1920 1 SLT 136 1128
Dunbar Magistrates v Duchess of Roxburghe (1835) 3 Cl & Fin 335, HL 1163
Duncan v Jackson (1905) 8 F 323, 13 SLT 932 1166
Duncan, Galloway & Co Ltd v Duncan, Falconer & Co 1913 SC 265, 1912 2 SLT 420 1012
Dunlop Pneumatic Tyre Co Ltd v New Garage and Motor Co Ltd [1915] AC 79, HL 1002
Dunlop v Goudie (1895) 22 R (J) 34 1187
Dunlop v Mundell 1943 SLT 286, OH 1129, 1180
Dunn (James) & Co v Anderston Foundry Co Ltd (1894) 21 R 880 1019

E

Eagle Star Insurance Co v Renton & Son 1941 SLT 61, OH 875
East African Asians v United Kingdom (1981) 3 EHRR 76, E Ct HR 115
East Coast Amusement Co Ltd v British Transport Board [1965] AC 58, [1963] 2 All ER 775,
    HL 1131
East India Co v Campbell (1749) 1 Ves Sen 246 504
Eclipse Mutual Benefit Association, Re (1854) Kay App 30 738
Edinburgh Life Assurance Co v Inland Revenue, Scottish Widows' Fund v Inland Revenue
    (1875) 2 R 394 1185
Edinburgh Magistrates v Begg (1883) 11 R 352 1246
Edinburgh Welfare Housing Trust v Edinburgh Assessor 1939 SC 279, 1939 SLT 184 1191
Ekbatani v Sweden (Ser A No 134, Judgment 26 May 1988) 13 EHRR 504, E Ct HR 50
Elcock v Thomson [1949] 2 KB 755, [1949] 2 All ER 381 .... 830, 888
Electricity Co of Sofia and Bulgaria Case (1939) PCIJ Ser A/B No 77 14
Ellen Street Estates Ltd v Minister of Health [1934] 1 KB 590, CA 1198
Emanuel (Lewis) & Son Ltd v Hepburn [1960] 1 Lloyd's Rep 304 841
Emmanuel v Secretary of State for the Home Department [1972] Imm AR 69, IAT 281
Engel v Netherlands (No 1) (Ser A No 22, Judgment 8 June 1976) 1 EHRR 647, E Ct
    HR 30, 40
Entry Certificate Officer, Bombay v Sacha [1973] Imm AR 5, IAT 171, 287
Entry Certificate Officer, Hong Kong v Lai [1974] Imm AR 98, IAT 306
Entry Certificate Officer, Lagos v Amusu [1974] Imm AR 16, IAT 293
Entry Clearance Officer v Sobanjo [1978] Imm AR 22, IAT 293
Entry Clearance Officer, Colombo v Hanks [1976] Imm AR 74, IAT 306
Entry Clearance Officer, Kingston, Jamaica v Holmes [1975] Imm AR 20, IAT 281
Entry Clearance Officer, Kingston, Jamaica v SS Martin [1978] Imm AR 100, IAT 281
Entry Clearance Officer, Kingston, Jamaica v Thompson [1981] Imm AR 148, IAT 281
Entry Clearance Officer, New Delhi v Bhambra [1973] Imm AR 14, IAT 333
Entry Clearance Officer, New Delhi v Kumar [1978] Imm AR 185, IAT 306
Equitable Fire and Accident Office Ltd v Ching Wo Hong [1907] AC 96, PC 915
Eriksson v Sweden (Ser A No 156, Judgment 22 June 1989) 12 EHRR 183, E Ct HR 64
Erkner and Hofauer v Austria (Ser A No 117, Judgment 23 April 1987) 9 EHRR 464, E Ct HR .. 88
Errington v Errington and Woods [1952] 1 KB 290, [1952] 1 All ER 149, CA 1252

References are to paragraphs

Escoigne Properties Ltd v Inland Revenue Comrs [1958] AC 549, [1958] 1 All ER 406, HL: 1147
Escritt v Todmorden Co-operative Society [1896] 1 QB 461, DC 628
Esso Petroleum Co Ltd v Hall Russell & Co Ltd [1989] AC 643, 1988 SLT 874, HL ... 894, 900
Eugene v Entry Clearance Officer, Bridgetown [1975] Imm AR 111, IAT 281
Ewing v Mathieson (1904) 41 SLR 594, OH 1029
Exchange Theatre Ltd v Iron Trades Mutual Insurance Co Ltd [1984] 1 Lloyd's Rep 149, CA: 863

F

F v Switzerland (Ser A No 128, Judgment 18 December 1987) 10 EHRR 411, E Ct HR 71
F (T) v Ravenscraig Hospital Management Committee and Managers 1988 SCLR 327, 1987
    SLT (Sh Ct) 76 8
Factortame Ltd v Secretary of State for Transport [1990] 2 AC 85, [1989] 2 All ER 692,
    HL 219
Fanti, The, The Padre Island [1990] 2 All ER 705, HL 907
Fanti, The, The Padre Island (No 2) [1989] 1 Lloyd's Rep 239, CA 907
Farida Begum v Immigration Officer, London (Heathrow) Airport [1978] Imm AR 107,
    IAT 172
Farquharson v Whyte (1886) 13 R (J) 29 1137
Farrans (Construction) Ltd v Dunfermline District Council 1988 SCLR 272, 1988 SLT
    466 .... 1010, 1013, 1021, 1035
Farrell v Federated Employers' Insurance Association Ltd [1970] 3 All ER 632, [1970] 1 WLR
    1400, CA 910
Faulds v British Steel Corpn 1977 SLT (Notes) 18 1229
Fehilly v General Accident Fire and Life Assurance Corpn 1982 SC 163, 1983 SLT 141 852
Feldbrugge v Netherlands (Ser A No 99, Judgment 29 May 1986) 8 EHRR 425, E Ct HR 45, 60
Ferguson v Aberdeen Parish Council 1916 SC 715, 1916 1 SLT 393 .... 848, 852
Fergusson v Skirving (1852) 1 Macq 232, HL 1200
Fergusson's Trustees v Buchanan 1973 SLT 41 1271
Fernandez v Government of Singapore [1971] 2 All ER 691, [1971] 1 WLR 989, HL 534
Fernandez v Secretary of State for the Home Department [1981] Imm AR 1, CA 115
Finch v Oake (1896) 1 Ch 409, CA 705
Findlater v Maan 1990 SLT 465 890
Finnish Shipowners Arbitration (1934) 3 UNRIAA 1479 14
Fisher v Bell [1961] 1 QB 394, [1960] 3 All ER 731, DC 1107
Fisherrow Harbour Comrs v Musselburgh Real Estate Co Ltd (1903) 5 F 367, 10 SLT 512 . 1239
Fleming v Baird (1841) 3 D 1015 1239
Fleming v Ure (1896) 4 SLT 26 1247
Fleming and Ferguson Ltd v Paisley Magistrates 1948 SC 547, 1948 SLT 457 1179
Flensburg Steam Shipping Co v Seligmann (1871) 9 M 1011 1032
Floor v Davis [1980] AC 695, [1979] 2 All ER 677, HL 1207
Foon v Secretary of State for the Home Department [1983] Imm AR 29, IAT 307
Forbes v Forbes (1869) 8 M 85 1008
Forbes (Sir William) & Co v Edinburgh Life Assurance Co (1832) 10 S 451 866
Forbes's Trustees v Tennant 1926 SC 294, 1926 SLT 135 1264
Ford v Ford's Trustees 1961 SC 122, 1961 SLT 128, OH 1264
Forrest and Barr v Henderson (1869) 8 M 187 1009
Forster v Forster (1871) 9 M 397 1139
Fortune v Orr [1894] FS Cases 539 738
Foss v Harbottle (1843) 2 Hare 461 1535
Fothringham v Passmore 1984 SC (HL) 96, 1984 SLT 401 1239
Fox, Campbell and Hartley v United Kingdom (Ser A No 182, Judgment 30 August 1990) 13
    EHRR 157, E Ct HR 30
France, Norway, Denmark, Sweden and the Netherlands v Turkey (Applications 9940–9944/
    82) 6 EHRR 241 14
Francis v Secretary of State for the Home Department [1972] Imm AR 162, IAT 346
Fraser v B N Furman (Productions) Ltd, Miller Smith & Partners Third Parties [1967] 3 All ER
    57, [1967] 1 WLR 898, CA 841
Fraser v J Morton Wilson Ltd (No 2) 1966 SLT 22, OH 1032
Freshwater v Western Australian Assurance Co Ltd [1933] 1 KB 515, CA 909
Fuji v State of California 28 Cal 2d, 242 P 2d 617 (1952), ILR 19 (1952) 3

References are to paragraphs

G

Gaima v Secretary of State for the Home Department [1989] Imm AR 205, CA 320
Gall v Loyal Glenbogie Lodge of the Oddfellows Friendly Society (1900) 2 F 1187, 8 SLT 140: 725
Galwey, Re [1896] 1 QB 230, DC 549
Gardiner v Admiralty Comrs 1964 SC (HL) 85, 1964 SLT 194 1121
Gardner v Beresford's Trustees (1878) 5 R (HL) 105 .... 1189, 1190, 1192
Garland v British Rail Engineering Ltd [1983] 2 AC 751, [1982] 2 All ER 402, HL 1153
Garland and Flexman v Wisbech Corpn [1962] 1 QB 151, [1961] 3 All ER 342 1204
Garthland's Trustees v M'Dowall, 26 May 1820 FC 1001, 1008
Gartside v Inland Revenue Comrs [1968] AC 553, [1968] 1 All ER 121, HL 1115
Gaskin v Liverpool City Council [1980] 1 WLR 1549, CA 63
Gaskin v United Kingdom (Application No 10454/83) (1989) 11 EHRR 402, E Com HR 63
Gaskin v United Kingdom (Ser A No 160, Judgment 7 July 1989) 12 EHRR 36, E Ct HR   21, 63
Gatehouse v Shaw (1919) CR Rep, Part A, 58 (Parliamentary Papers for 1920, vol 37) 741
Gedge v Royal Exchange Assurance Corpn [1900] 2 QB 214 848
Genc v Secretary of State for the Home Department [1984] Imm AR 180, IAT 202, 207
General Accident Insurance Corpn v Cronk (1901) 17 TLR 233 .... 818, 822
General Railway Workers Union v Macdonald (1900) 37 SLR 721 741
George and Goldsmiths and General Burglary Insurance Association Ltd, Re [1899] QB 595,
    CA 839
Germany (Government of the Federal Republic of) v Sotiriadis [1975] AC 1, [1974] 1 All ER
    692, HL 550, 556, 562, 568, 570
Ghassemian and Mirza v The Home Office [1989] Imm AR 42, CA 119, 176
Ghosh v Entry Clearance Officer, Calcutta [1976] Imm AR 60, IAT 293
Giangregorio v Secretary of State for the Home Department [1985] Imm AR 104, [1983] 3
    CMLR 472, IAT 222, 238
Gibson v Bonnington Sugar Refining Co Ltd (1869) 7 M 394 1239
Giffard v Queens Insurance Co (1869) 12 NBR 432 857
Gifto Fancy Goods Ltd v Ecclesiastical Insurance Office plc 1991 GWD 2-117, OH 870
Gilchrist v Gilchrist's Trustees (1889) 16 R 1118 1031
Gillegao v Secretary of State for the Home Department [1989] Imm AR 174, IAT 333
Gillies v Glasgow Royal Infirmary 1960 SC 438, 1961 SLT 93 1263
Gillow v United Kingdom (Ser A No 109, Judgment 24 November 1986) 11 EHRR 335, E Ct
    HR 62, 70, 79, 81
Gilmour's Trustees v Gilmour 1922 SC 753, 1922 SLT 596 1031
Glasgow Corpn v Glasgow Tramway and Omnibus Co Ltd (1898) 25 R (HL) 77, 6 SLT 129: 1224
Glasgow District of Ancient Order of Foresters v Stevenson (1899) 2 F 14, 7 SLT 163 .. 707, 725
Glasgow Feuing and Building Co v Watson's Trustees (1887) 14 R 610 1234
Glasgow Gas-Light Co v Barony Parochial Board of Glasgow (1868) 6 M 406 ...... 1006, 1013
Glasgow Provident Investment Society v Westminster Fire Office (1887) 14 R 947: 831, 886, 914
Glasgow Provident Investment Society v Westminster Fire Office (1888) 15 R (HL) 89 831,
                                                                        886, 890, 914
Glasgow Training Group (Motor Trade) Ltd v Lombard Continental plc 1989 SLT 375,
    OH 838, 839, 840
Glenlight Shipping Ltd v Excess Insurance Co Ltd 1983 SLT 241 .... 843, 844
Glen's Trustees v Lancashire and Yorkshire Accident Insurance Co Ltd (1906) 8 F 915, 14 SLT
    168 .... 841, 1233
Glicksman v Lancashire and General Assurance Co Ltd [1927] AC 139, HL 858
Goffar v Entry Clearance Officer, Dacca [1975] Imm AR 142, IAT 293
Golder v United Kingdom (Ser A No 18, Judgment 21 February 1975) 1 EHRR 524, E Ct
    HR 4, 17, 21, 44, 46, 62, 69, 79, 95
Good Luck, The [1990] 1 QB 818, [1989] 3 All ER 628, CA 858, 875
Gordon v Grant (1850) 13 D 1 1242
Gordon (William S) & Co Ltd v Thomson Partnership 1985 SLT 122 1261
Gore-Browne-Henderson's Trustees v Grenfell 1968 SC 73, 1968 SLT 237 1269
Gorham v Bishop of Exeter (1850) 5 Exch 630 1144
Grabemann v Germany (Application 12748/87), E Com MR 15
Graham v Graham (1816) 1 Ross LC 46 1237
Graham v Graham's Trustees 1927 SC 388, 1927 SLT 237 1269
Graham v Irving (1899) 2 F 29 1112
Grandison's Trustees v Jardine (1895) 22 R 925, 3 SLT 54 1010

References are to paragraphs

Granger v United Kingdom (Ser A No 174, Judgment 28 March 1990) 12 EHRR 469, E Ct
    HR 21, 52
Grant v Borg [1982] 2 All ER 257, [1982] 1 WLR 638, HL 186
Grant v Grant's Trustees (1898) 25 R 948 sub nom Armstrong v Grant 6 SLT 38 1037
Grant v Ullah 1987 SLT 639, OH 1019
Grant's Trustees v Grant (1898) 25 R 929 1270
Grant's Trustees v Morison (1875) 2 R 377 1222
Gray v Crofters Commission 1980 SLT (Land Ct) 2 1168
Gray v MacLeod 1979 SLT (Sh Ct) 17 1239
Gray v St Andrews and Cupar District Committees of Fife County Council 1911 SC 266, 1910
    2 SLT 354 1179
Greece (Royal Government of) v Governor of Brixton Prison [1971] AC 250, [1969] 3 All ER
    1337, HL 532, 550
Greece v United Kingdom (Applications 175/56, 299/57) 2 YBHR 182, 186 14
Green v Hendry (1890) Times, 19 May, CA (affg (1890) 25 L Jo 93) 697
Green (F W) & Co Ltd v Brown and Gracie Ltd 1960 SLT (Notes) 43, HL 1012, 1020,
                                                                                                1021, 1032
Greenlees v Port of Manchester Insurance Co 1933 SC 383, 1933 SLT 319 909
Greenock Harbour Trustees v Glasgow and South-Western Rly Co 1909 SC (HL) 49, 1909 2
    SLT 53 .... 1007, 1010
Grey v Pearson (1857) 6 HL Cas 61 1109
Griffiths v J P Harrison (Watford) Ltd [1963] AC 1, [1962] 1 All ER 909, HL 1132
Groppera Radio AG v Switzerland (Ser A No 173, Judgment 28 March 1990) 12 EHRR 321,
    E Ct HR 17, 73
Gross, Re, ex parte Treasury Solicitor [1968] 3 All ER 804, [1969] 1 WLR 12, DC 532
Groves v Cardiff Coal Trimmers Superannuation Society (1922) RCR 12 705
Guerin, Re (1888) 60 LT 538, DC 549
Guinness plc v Saunders [1990] 2 AC 663, [1990] 1 All ER 652, HL 1535
Gulten Ibrahim v Immigration Appeal Tribunal [1989] Imm AR 111, CA 208
Gunatilake v Entry Clearance Officer, Colombo [1975] Imm AR 23, IAT 263
Gunford Ship Co Ltd (in Liquidation) v Thames and Mersey Marine Insurance Co Ltd 1910 SC
    1072, 1910 2 SLT 154 (revsd in part 1911 SC (HL) 84, 1911 SLT 185) 848
Guzzardi v Italy (Ser A No 39, Judgment 6 November 1980) 3 EHRR 333, E Ct HR 26, 40
Gwawr-y-Gweithyr Industrial and Provident Society Ltd, Re, Dovey v Morgan [1901] 2 KB
    477, DC 625
Gwydyr v Lord Advocate (1894) 2 SLT 280, OH 1012

H

H v Belgium (Ser A No 127B, Judgment 30 November 1987) 10 EHRR 399, E Ct HR 60
H v United Kingdom (Ser A No 120, Judgment 8 July 1987) 10 EHRR 95, E Ct HR 64
H (a minor), Re [1982] Fam 121 [1982] 3 All ER 84 279
H K (an infant), Re [1967] 2 QB 617, [1967] 1 All ER 226, DC 164, 170
H M V Fields Properties Ltd v Skirt 'n' Slack Centre of London Ltd 1982 SLT 477 1251
H M V Fields Properties Ltd v Skirt 'n' Slack Centre of London Ltd 1987 SLT 2, OH 1012,
                                                                                                1015
Hadden v Bryden (1899) 1 F 710 6 SLT 362 848
Hadley v Baxendale (1854) 9 Exch 341 .... 1018, 1019, 1020
Hair v Prudential Assurance Co Ltd [1983] 2 Lloyd's Rep 667 .... 866, 867
Haji v Secretary of State for the Home Department [1978] Imm AR 26, IAT 251
Hak Rok Djang (or Chang) v Secretary of State for the Home Department [1985] Imm AR 125,
    IAT 162
Håkansson and Sturesson v Sweden (Ser A No 171, Judgment 21 February 1990) 13 EHRR 1,
    E Ct HR 54
Haldane v Ogilvy (1871) 10 M 62 1012
Haldane v Speirs (1872) 10 M 537 1008
Hall and Tawse Construction Ltd v Strathclyde Regional Council 1990 SLT 774 1019
Hamilton v National Coal Board 1960 SC (HL) 1, 1960 SLT 24 .... 1156, 1182
Hamilton v Secretary of State for Scotland 1991 GWD 10-624, OH 1153
Hamilton Gell v White [1922] 2 KB 422, CA 1194
Hamilton Magistrates v Bent Colliery Co 1929 SC 686, 1929 SLT 569 1239

References are to paragraphs

Hamlyn v Crown Accidental Insurance Co Ltd [1893] 1 QB 750, CA 844
Hampton v Toxteth Co-operative Provident Society Ltd [1915] 1 Ch 721 613
Handyside v United Kingdom (Ser A No 24, Judgment 7 December 1976) 1 EHRR 737, E Ct
   HR 73, 74, 81, 88
Hanover (Prince Ernest Augustus of) v Attorney-General [1956] Ch 188, [1955] 3 All ER 647,
   CA 1125
Harbant Kaur v Secretary of State for the Home Department [1982] Imm AR 84, IAT 287
Hardev Kaur v Entry Clearance Officer, New Delhi [1979–80] Imm AR 76, IAT 289
Hare v Gocher [1962] 2 QB 641, [1962] 2 All ER 763, DC 1173
Hargreaves v Alderson [1964] 2 QB 159, [1962] 3 All ER 1019, DC 1164
Harmail Singh v Immigration Appeal Tribunal [1978] Imm AR 140, CA 282
Harrington v Pearl Life Assurance Co Ltd (1913) 30 TLR 24 863
Harrington v Pearl Life Assurance Co Ltd (1914) 30 TLR 613, CA 818, 863
Harse v Pearl Life Assurance Co [1904] 1 KB 558 835
Hartdegen v Fanner 1980 SLT (Notes) 23, OH 858
Hashim v Secretary of State for the Home Department [1982] Imm AR 113, IAT 307
Hassan Temel v An Immigration Appeal Adjudicator [1988] Imm AR 496, CA 355
Hauer v Land Rheinland-Pfalz (Case 44/79) [1979] ECR 3727, [1980] 3 CMLR 42, ECJ 9
Hauschildt v Denmark (Ser A No 154, Judgment 24 May 1989) 12 EHRR 266, E Ct HR 48
Hawke v Niagara District Mutual Fire Insurance Co (1876) 23 Grant 139 825
Hearts of Oak Assurance Co Ltd v Attorney-General [1932] AC 392, HL 732
Henry v Sutherland (1801) Mor 'Annual-Rent' App p 1 1011
Hercules Insurance Co v Hunter (1836) 14 S 1137 886
Heriot's (George) Trust Governors v Paton's Trustees 1912 SC 1123, 1912 2 SLT 116 1200
Heriot's Hospital Governors v Ferguson (1774) 3 Pat 674, HL 1232
Heriot's Trust v Caledonian Rly Co 1915 SC (HL) 52, 1915 1 SLT 347 1116
Heritable Reversionary Co v Millar (1892) 19 R (HL) 43 1114
Heston and Isleworth Urban District Council v Grout [1897] 2 Ch 306, CA 1194
Heydon's Case (1584) 2 Co Rep 7a 1115
Highlands Insurance Co v Continental Insurance Co [1987] 1 Lloyd's Rep 109n 858, 859,
   860, 870
Hill v East and West India Dock Co (1884) 9 App Cas 448, HL 1114
Hill v Orkney Islands Council 1983 SLT (Lands Tr) 2 1138
Hills v Burns (1826) 2 W & S 80, HL 1271
Hislop v MacRitchie's Trustees (1881) 8 R (HL) 95 1248
Hobbs v Marlowe [1978] AC 16, [1977] 2 All ER 241, HL 897, 899
Hoekstra (née Unger) v Bestuur der Bedrijfsvereniging voor Detailhandel en Ambachten
   (Case 75/63) [1964] ECR 177, [1964] CMLR 319, ECJ 222
Hogg v Auchtermuchty Parochial Board (1880) 7 R 986 1185
Holburnhead Salmon Fishing Co v Scrabster Harbour Trustees 1982 SC 65 1203
Holdsworth v Gordon Cumming 1910 SC (HL) 49, 1910 2 SLT 136 .... 1223, 1225
Holmes Oil Co Ltd v Pumpherston Oil Co Ltd (1891) 18 R (HL) 52 1035
Hoosha Kumari Hanif v Secretary of State for the Home Department [1985] Imm AR 57,
   IAT 205, 209
Hope v Bennewith (1904) 6 F 1004, 12 SLT 243 1239
Horse, Carriage and General Insurance Co Ltd v Petch (1916) 33 TLR 131 898
Hoth v Secretary of State for the Home Department [1985] Imm AR 20, IAT 222, 226,
   235, 236, 237
Houldsworth v Gordon Cumming 1910 SC (HL) 49, 1910 2 SLT 136 1238
Houstoun v Barr 1911 SC 134, 1910 2 SLT 286 1239
How Group Northern v Sun Ventilating Co 1979 SLT 277 1222
Howard v Bodington (1877) 2 PD 203 1176
Howard v Lancashire Insurance Co (1885) 11 SCR 92 (Can SC) 857
Howard v Secretary of State for the Home Department [1972] Imm AR 93, IAT 281
Howard de Walden Estates Ltd v Bowmaker Ltd 1965 SC 163, 1965 SLT 254 1248
Howden v Rocheid (1869) 7 M (HL) 110 1156
Huda v Entry Clearance Officer, Dacca, New Delhi [1976] Imm AR 109, IAT 306
Hughes v Hardy [1885] FS Cases 402 .... 626, 722
Hughes v Liverpool Victoria Legal Friendly Society [1916] 2 KB 482, CA 835
Hunter v Fox 1964 SC (HL) 95, 1964 SLT 201 .... 1216, 1219, 1223, 1233
Hunter v General Accident Fire and Life Assurance Corpn 1909 SC (HL) 30, 1909 2 SLT
   99 .... 1223, 1232

References are to paragraphs

Hunter v Livingston Development Corpn 1984 SLT 10, OH 1002, 1012, 1014, 1019, 1037
Hunter v Lord Advocate (1869) 7 M 899 1239
Hutchison v National Loan Fund Life Assurance Society (1845) 7 D 467 861
Hutchison's Trustees v Downie's Trustees 1923 SLT 49, OH 1117
Huvig v France (Ser A No 176B, JUDGMENT 24 APRIL 1990) 12 EHRR 528, E Ct HR 68
Hynd's Trustee v Hynd's Trustees 1955 SC (HL) 1, 1955 SLT 105 1126

I

Ibrahim v Visa Officer, Islamabad [1978] Imm AR 18, IAT 281
Immigration Officer, London (Gatwick) Airport v Darboe [1981] Imm AR 210, IAT 306
Immigration Officer, London (Heathrow) Airport v Bhatti TH/57482/80 (1719), IAT 171
Income Tax General Purposes Comrs for City of London v Gibbs [1942] AC 402, [1942] 1 All
    ER 415, HL 1188
Income Tax Special Purposes Comrs v Pemsel [1891] AC 531, HL 1162, 1187, 1188
Incorporated General Insurances Ltd v Shooter t/a Shooter's Fisheries 1987 (1) SA 842 879
Industrial Development Consultants Ltd v Cooley [1972] 2 All ER 162, [1972] 1 WLR 443 . 1535
Inglis v British Airports Authority 1978 SLT (Lands Tr) 30 1150
Inglis v Buttery & Co (1878) 5 R (HL) 87 .... 1215, 1222
Inglis v Robertson and Baxter (1898) 25 R (HL) 70 M'Ewan v Perth Magistrates (1905) 7 F 714,
    12 SLT 846 1138
Inland Revenue Comrs v Bates [1965] 3 All ER 64, [1965] 1 WLR 1133, CA (affd in part [1968]
    AC 483, [1967] 1 All ER 84, HL) 1117
Inland Revenue Comrs v City of Glasgow Police Athletic Association 1952 SC 102, 1952 SLT
    136 1188
Inland Revenue Comrs v Hinchy [1960] AC 748, [1960] 1 All ER 505, HL 1105, 1142, 1158
Inland Revenue Comrs v Littlewoods Mail Order Stores Ltd [1963] AC 135, [1962] 2 All ER
    279, HL 1141
Inland Revenue Comrs v Saunders [1958] AC 285, [1957] 3 All ER 43, HL 1185
Inland Revenue v Luke 1963 SC (HL) 65, 1963 SLT 129 1106
Interhandel Case (Preliminary Objections) 1959 ICJR 6 14
Internationale Handelsgesellschaft mbH v Einfuhr- und Vorratsstelle für Getreide und Futter-
    mittel (Case 11/70) [1970] ECR 1125, [1972] CMLR 255, ECJ 9
Inverness County Council v Inverness Magistrates 1909 SC 386, 15 SLT 966, OH 1165
Inverness County Council v Inverness Magistrates 1909 SC 386, 1909 1 SLT 59 1165
Inverness Golf Club v James Parr & Associates 12 Jan 1987 (unreported) 1019
Inze v Austria (Ser A No 126, Judgment 28 October 1987) 10 EHRR 394, E Ct HR 86
Ionides v Pender (1874) LR 9 QB 531 880
Ireland v United Kingdom (Applications 5310/71, 5451/72) 41 Coll HR 1 14
Ireland v United Kingdom (Ser A No 25, Judgment 18 January 1978) 2 EHRR 25, E Ct
    HR 6, 14, 17, 22, 26, 30, 31
Isaacs v Royal Insurance Co (1870) LR 5 Exch 296 836
Islam v Secretary of State for the Home Department [1975] Imm AR 106, IAT 333

J

Jacobs v Hart (1900) 2 F (J) 33 7 SLT 425 1141
Jacobsson (Allan) v Sweden (Ser A No 163, Judgment 25 October 1989) 12 EHRR 56, E Ct
    HR 54, 88
Jahangard v Entry Clearance Officer, Vienna [1985] Imm AR 69, IAT 149, 259
James v Insurance Brokers Registration Council (1984) The Times, 16 February 813
James v United Kingdom (Ser A No 98, Judgment 21 February 1986) 8 EHRR 123, E Ct HR .. 88
Jamieson's Executors 1982 SC 1, 1982 SLT 198 1263
Jason v British Traders' Insurance Co Ltd [1969] 1 Lloyd's Rep 281 .... 842, 879
Jefford v Gee [1970] 2 QB 130, [1970] 1 All ER 1202, CA 1034
Jenkins v Deane (1933) 47 Ll L R 342 915
Joel v Law Union and Crown Insurance Co [1908] 2 KB 863, CA 860, 871
John O'Gaunt Lodge of Oddfellows v Bell (1883) FS Cases 67 707
Johnston v Gordon (1805) Hume 822 1251
Johnston v Ireland (Ser A No 112, Judgment 18 December 1986) 9 EHRR 203, E Ct
    HR 71, 86, 96

References are to paragraphs

Johnston v Robson (1868) 6 M 800 1184
Johnston v Royal Ulster Constabulary Chief Constable (Case 22/84) [1986] ECR 1651, [1986] 3
    CMLR 240, ECJ 9
Johnstone v Stott (1802) 4 Pat App 274, HL ....:....1200
Johnstone v The Walker Trustees (1897) 24 R 1061, 5 SLT 86 1248
Jones v Smart (1875) 1 Term Rep 44 1107
Jordan v Secretary of State for the Home Department [1972] Imm AR 201, IAT 209, 210
Judson v Ellesmere Port Ex-Servicemen's Club Ltd [1948] 2 KB 52, [1948] 1 All ER 844, CA .647
Juiakumaran, Ex parte (unreported) 318
Julita Esterm Florentine v Secretary of State for the Home Department [1987] Imm AR 1, IAT .130
Julius v Lord Bishop of Oxford (1880) 5 App Cas 214, HL 1179
Juma v Secretary of State for the Home Department [1974] Imm AR 96, IAT 299, 353

                                    K

Kamal v United Kingdom No 8378/78 (1980) 2 EHRR 244 115
Kamasinski v Austria (Ser A No 168, Judgment 19 December 1989) 13 EHRR 36, E Ct
    HR 21, 51
Karantoni v Secretary of State for the Home Department [1987] Imm AR 518, CA 208
Kaur v Lord Advocate 1980 SC 319, 1981 SLT 322, OH 8, 115, 1153
Kaur v Secretary of State for the Home Department 1987 SCLR 550, OH 112, 200, 201
Kearney v General Accident Fire and Life Assurance Corpn Ltd [1968] 2 Lloyd's Rep 240 ...909
Kearon v Thomson's Trustees 1949 SC 287, 1949 SLT 286 1037
Kedder v Reid (1840) 1 Robin, HL 1227
Keiller v Dundee Magistrates, Scott v Dundee Magistrates 1239
Keir Ltd v East of Scotland Water Board 1976 SLT (Notes) 72, OH 1001, 1012
Keith v Smyth (1884) 12 R 66 1239
Keith v Texaco Ltd 1977 SLT (Lands Tr) 16 1149
Kelly v Kelly 1986 SLT 101, OH 1535
Kemp v Largs Magistrates 1939 SC (HL) 6, 1939 SLT 228 1247
Kemp (James) (Leslie) Ltd v Robertson 1967 SC 229, 1967 SLT 213, OH 1136
Kennedy v Smith 1975 SC 266, 1976 SLT 110 ....841, 842, 876, 1232
Kerr 1968 SLT (Sh Ct) 61 1264
Khahiq v Secretary of State for the Home Department TH/5037/75 (459) (unreported) 171
Khan v Secretary of State for the Home Department [1977] 3 All ER 538, [1977] 1 WLR 1466,
    CA 198
Khawaja v Secretary of State for the Home Department [1984] AC 74, [1983] 1 All ER 765,
    [1982] Imm AR 139, HL 110, 119, 166, 171, 172, 177, 181, 198, 201, 207, 339, 341
Kidd v Kidd (1863) 2 M 227 1270
Kinnear and Brymer v Whyte (1868) 6 M 804 ....1127, 1178
Kirkness v John Hudson & Co Ltd [1955] AC 696, [1955] 2 All ER 345, HL 1160
Kirkpatrick's Trustee v Kirkpatrick (1874) 1 R (HL) 37 1161
Kjeldsen, Busk Madsen and Pederson v Denmark (Ser A No 23, Judgment 7 December 1976) 1
    EHRR 711, E Ct HR 86, 90, 91, 92
Klass v Germany (Ser A No 28, Judgment 6 September 1978) 2 EHRR 214, E Ct HR ...30, 68,
                                                                           79, 81, 84
Knoors v Secretary of State for Economic Affairs (Case 115/78) [1979] ECR 399, [1979] 2
    CMLR 357, ECJ 221
Kolbin & Sons v Kinnear & Co 1931 SC (HL) 128, 1931 SLT 464 1021
Kostovski v Netherlands (Ser A No 166, Judgment 20 November 1989) 12 EHRR 434, E Ct
    HR 17, 59
Kostovski v Netherlands (Ser A No 170, Judgment 29 March 1990), E Ct HR 21
Kpoma v Secretary of State for the Home Department [1973] Imm AR 25, IAT 293, 299
Kristinsson (Jón) v Iceland (Ser A No 171, Judgment 1 March 1990) 13 EHRR 238, E Ct HR ..22
Krupp v John Menzies Ltd 1907 SC 903, 15 SLT 36 1233
Kruslin v France (Ser A No 176A, JUDGEMENT 24 APRIL 1990) 12 EHRR 547, E Ct HR 68
Kuku v Secretary of State for the Home Department [1990] Imm AR 27, CA 176, 292
Kumar v Life Insurance Corpn of India [1974] 1 Lloyd's Rep 147 ....835, 858, 859
Kutner v Phillps [1891] 1 QB 267 1198

References are to paragraphs

König v Germany (Ser A No 27, Judgment 28 June 1978) 2 EHRR 170, E Ct HR 45, 46, 47

L

Lafferty v Barrhead Co-operative Society Ltd 1919 1 SLT 257, OH 613
Laidlaw v John M Monteath & Co 1979 SLT 78, OH 838, 842
Laing v Reed (1869) 5 Ch App 4 703
Laing's Trustees v Horsburgh 1965 SC 339, 1965 SLT 215 1221
Laird & Sons v Clyde Navigation Trustees (1879) 6 R 756 (affd (1883) 10 R (HL) 77) 1141
Lakhani v Immigration Appeal Tribunal [1988] Imm AR 474, CA 170
Lamb v Lord Advocate 1976 SC 110, 1976 SLT 151 1266
Lambert v Co-operative Insurance Society Ltd [1975] 2 Lloyd's Rep 485, CA 858, 863,
  864, 865, 870
Lamont v Glasgow Magistrates (1887) 14 R 603 1230
Lamy v Belgium (Ser A No 151, Judgment 30 March 1989) 11 EHRR 529, E Ct HR 36
Langborger v Sweden (Ser A No 155, Judgment 22 June 1989) 12 EHRR 416, E Ct HR .. 48, 60
Langridge v Secretary of State for the Home Department [1972] Imm AR 38, IAT 171
Largs Hydropathic Ltd v Largs Town Council 1966 SLT 117, OH 1237
Largs Hydropathic Ltd v Largs Town Council 1967 SC 1, 1967 SLT 23 .... 1221, 1237
Laurence v Davies [1972] 2 Lloyd's Rep 231 839
Law Accident Insurance Society v Boyd 1942 SC 384, 1942 SLT 207 863
Lawless v Ireland (No 1) (Ser A No 1, Judgment 14 November 1960) 1 EHRR 1, E Ct
  HR 12, 24, 30
Lawless v Ireland (No 2) (Ser A No 2, Judgment 7 April 1961) 1 EHRR 13, E Ct HR 12
Lawless v Ireland (No 3) (Ser A No 3, Judgment 1 July 1961) 1 EHRR 15, E Ct HR .. 12, 30, 31
Lawrence v Scott 1965 SC 403, 1965 SLT 390 1248
Le Compte, Van Leuven and De Meyere v Belgium (Ser A No 43, Judgment 23 June 1981) 4
  EHRR 1, E Ct HR 45, 75, 96
Leach v R [1912] AC 305, HL 1126
Lead Co's Workmen's Fund Society, Re, Lowes v Governor & Co for Smelting Down Lead
  with Pit and Sea Coal [1904] 2 Ch 196 680
Leander v Sweden (Ser A No 116, Judgment 26 March 1987) 9 EHRR 433, E Ct HR 63
Ledingham v Ontario Hospital Services Commission (1974) 46 DLR (3d) 699 (Can SC) 903
Lee v Alexander (1883) 10 R (HL) 91 1215
Lee v Knapp [1967] 2 QB 442, [1966] 3 All ER 961, DC 1109
Lee (David) & Co (Lincoln Ltd) v Coward Chance [1991] Ch 259, [1991] 1 All ER 668 1395
Lee's Trustee v Bensted 1916 SC 188, 1915 2 SLT 382 1034
Legal Consequences for States of the Continued Presence of South Africa in Namibia (South
  West Africa) notwithstanding Security Council Resolution 276 (Advisory Opinion) (1971)
  ICJR 16 at 56, 57, ICJ 3
Lendrum v Chakravarti 1929 SLT 96, OH 269
Leney v Craig 1982 SLT (Lands Trib) 9 1247
Leroy Rennie v Entry Clearance Officer, Kingston, Jamaica [1979–80] Imm AR 117, IAT .. 281
Leslie v Forbes (1749) Mor 4636 104
Levin v Staatssecretaris van Justitie (Case 53/81) [1982] ECR 1035, [1982] 2 CMLR 454,
  ECJ 221, 222
Lewis v Paulton (1907) 14 SLT 818, OH 725
Leyland Shipping Co Ltd v Norwich Union Fire Insurance Society Ltd [1918] AC 350, HL . 879
Liberto v Immigration Officer, London (Heathrow) Airport [1975] Imm AR 61, IAT 171
Lickiss v Milestone Motor Policies at Lloyds [1966] 2 All ER 972, [1966] 1 WLR 1334, CA . 883
Liddall v Duncan (1898) 25 R 1119, 6 SLT 77 1247
Life and Health Assurance Association Ltd v Yule (1904) 6 F 437, 11 SLT 690 862
Life Association of Scotland v Foster (1873) 11 M 351 ... 858, 860, 861, 864, 869, 871, 876, 1232
Lindsay v Barmcotte (1851) 13 D 718 853
Lingens v Austria (Ser A No 103, Judgment 8 July 1986) 8 EHRR 407, E Ct HR 73, 74, 81
Linlithgow Oil Co Liquidators v North British Rly Co (1904) 12 SLT 421, OH 1016, 1017
Lister v Romford Ice and Cold Storage Co Ltd [1957] AC 555, [1957] 1 All ER 125, HL 894, 897
Lithgow v United Kingdom (Ser A No 102, Judgment 8 July 1986) 8 EHRR 329, E Ct
  HR 84, 86, 88
Litster v Forth Dry Dock and Engineering Co Ltd (In Receivership) [1990] 1 AC 546, 1989 SLT
  540, HL 219, 1172

References are to paragraphs

Liverpool Borough Bank v Turner (1860) 30 LJ Ch 379 1176
Liverpool Victoria Legal Friendly Society v Head (1915) 50 LJCC 75 724
Liversidge v Anderson [1942] AC 206, [1941] 3 All ER 338, HL 369
Lloyd v Brassey [1969] 2 QB 98, [1969] 1 All ER 382, CA 1141
Locker and Woolf Ltd v Western Australian Insurance Co Ltd [1936] 1 KB 408, CA 860
London and Clydesdale Estates Ltd v Aberdeen District Council 1980 SC (HL) 1, 1980 SLT
    81 1177
London and Lancashire Fire Insurance Co Ltd v Bolands Ltd [1924] AC 836, HL 839
London and North Eastern Rly Co v Glasgow Assessor 1937 SC 309, 1937 SLT 167 1187
London County Commercial Reinsurance Office Ltd, Re [1922] 2 Ch 67 835
London General Insurance Co v General Marine Underwriters' Association [1921] 1 KB 104 . 860
Lonrho plc, Re [1990] 2 AC 154, [1989] 2 All ER 1100, HL 8
Looker v Law Union and Rock Insurance Co Ltd [1928] 1 KB 554 .... 818, 863
Lorimer's Executors v Hird 1959 SLT (Notes) 8, OH 1263
Lovejoy v Mulkern (1877) 46 LJ Ch 630, CA 699, 706
Lubbersen v Secretary of State for the Home Department [1984] Imm AR 56, [1984] 3 CMLR
    77, IAT 225, 226, 227, 230, 236, 237, 238
Lubetkin v Secretary of State for the Home Department [1979–80] Imm AR 162, IAT 178
Lucas (L) Ltd v Export Credits Guarantee Department [1973] 2 All ER 984, [1973] 1 WLR 914,
    CA 894, 901
Lucas (L) Ltd v Export Credits Guarantee Department [1974] 2 All ER 889, [1974] 1 WLR 909,
    HL 894
Lucena v Craufurd (1806) 2 B & PNR 269, HL 850
Lundie v Falkirk Magistrates (1890) 18 R 60 1158
Lutz v Germany (Ser A No 123, Judgment 25 August 1987) 10 EHRR 182, E Ct HR 53
Lynedoch (Lord) v Ouchterlony (1832) 11 S 60 .... 1024, 1026

M

M'Ara v Edinburgh Magistrates 1913 SC 1059, 1913 2 SLT 110 1201
Macarthys v Smith [1979] 3 All ER 325, [1979] 1 WLR 1189, [1979] 3 CMLR 44, 381, CA .. 219
Macaura v Northern Assurance Co Ltd [1925] AC 619, HL 851, 852
Macbeth v Ashley (1874) 1 R (HL) 14, 2 LR Sc & Div 352 1111
M'Caig v Glasgow University 1907 SC 231, 14 SLT 600 1270
McCallum v United Kingdom (Ser A No 183, Judgment 30 August 1990) 13 EHRR 597, E Ct
    HR 69
M'Cartney v Laverty 1968 SC 207, 1968 SLT (Notes) 50, OH 818, 823, 874
MacCormick v Lord Advocate 1953 SC 396, 1953 SLT 255 1201
M'Cowan v Stewart 1936 JC 36, 1936 SLT 370 1188
Macdonald v Douglas 1963 SC 374, 1963 SLT 191 1248
Macdonald v Glasgow Corpn 1973 SC 53, 1973 SLT 107 1033
Macdonald v Keeper of the General Register of Sasines 1914 SC 854, 1914 2 SLT 90 1238
MacDonald v National Mutual Life Assurance of Australasia Ltd (1906) 14 SLT 173, OH; 249,
    OH 854
Macdonald v Refuge Assurance Co Ltd (1890) 17 R 955 884
Macdonald (Lord) v Finlayson (1884) 12 R 228 1190
MacDougall v Chitnavis 1937 SC 390, 1937 SLT 421 269
McEllistrim v Ballymacelliogott Co-operative Agricultural and Dairy Sociey [1919] AC 548,
    HL 725
M'Elroy v Duke of Argyll (1902) 4 F 885, 10 SLT 156 1244
M'Elroy v London Assurance Corpn (1897) 24 R 287, 4 SLT 241 .... 828, 834
Macfarlane's Trustees v Henderson (1878) R 288 1271
McGillivary v Secretary of State for the Home Department [1972] Imm AR 63, IAT 281
McGlade v Royal London Mutual Insurance Society Ltd [1910] 2 Ch 169, CA 731
M'Govern v James Nimmo & Co Ltd 1938 SC (HL) 18, 1938 SLT 403 1032
M'Gowan v Glasgow Friendly Society 1913 SC 991, 1913 2 SLT 40 725
McGregor (John G) (Contractors) Ltd v Grampian Regional Council 1991 SLT 136 1035
M'Innes v Dunsmuir and Jackson 1908 SC 1021, 16 SLT 214 844
Macintyre v Grimond's Trustees (1905) 7 F (HL) 90, 12 SLT 760 1271
Mackay v London General Insurance Co (1935) 51 Ll L Rep 201 858
Mackie v European Assurance Society (1869) 21 LT 102 825
Mackintosh v May (1895) 22 R 345, 2 SLT 471 1251
Maclean v Campbell (1856) 18 D 609 1038

References are to paragraphs

M'Lean's Trustees v M'Lean (1891) 18 R 892 1023
MacLellan (P and W) v Peattie's Trustees (1903) 5 F 1031, 11 SLT 245 1217
McLennan (A & C) (Blairgowrie) Ltd v MacMillan 1964 JC 1, 1964 SLT 2 1174
M'Millan v Accident Insurance Co Ltd 1907 SC 484, 14 SLT 710 862
McMillan v HM Advocate 1982 SCCR 309, 1983 SLT 24 1172
Macmillan & Co v Dent [1907] 1 Ch 107, CA 1115
M'Mullan v Lochgelly Iron and Coal Co 1933 SC (HL) 64, 1934 SLT 114 1181
M'Murray v M'Murray's Trustees (1852) 14 D 1048 1031
McNealy v Pennine Insurance Co Ltd [1978] 2 Lloyd's Rep 18, CA 862
M'Phail v Lothian Regional Council 1981 SC 119, 1981 SLT 173, OH 1014, 1018
M'Phee v Royal Insurance Co Ltd 1979 SC 304, 1979 SLT (Notes) 54 .... 824, 859, 861, 876
Macpherson v Tytler (1853) 15 D 706 1008
M'Phersons v Haggarts (1881) 9 R 306 1225
Macrorie's Executors v McLaren 1984 SLT 271 1263
M'Taggart v M'Douall (1867) 5 M 534 1239
McVey v Glasgow Corpn 1973 SLT (Lands Trib) 15 1247
Macao v Officers of State 14 November 1820 FC; 1 Sh App 138, HL 103
Madden v Rhodes [1906] 1 KB 534, DC 745
Magor and St Mellons Rural District Council v Newport Corpn [1952] AC 189, [1951] 2 All ER
    839, HL 1107, 1116
Mahboub Iqbal Ahmed Malik, Re [1985] Imm AR 96, CA 333
Malcolm's Executors v Malcolm (1869) 8 M 272 1027
Malhi v Secretary of State for Home Affairs 1989 SLT 43, OH 112, 198
Malik v Secretary of State for the Home Department [1972] Imm AR 37 279
Malik v Secretary of State for the Home Department [1982] Imm AR 183, IAT 152
Malone v Metropolitan Police Comr (No 2) [1979] Ch 344, [1979] 2 All ER 620 68
Malone v United Kingdom (Ser A No 82, Judgment 2 August 1984) 7 EHRR 14, E Ct HR . 17,
                                                                        68, 79, 95
Mamon v Immigration Appeal Tribunal [1988] Imm AR 364, CA 112, 247, 248, 249
Manickavasagar v Metropolitan Police Comr [1987] Crim LR 50, DC 186
Manmohan Singh v Entry Clearance Officer, New Delhi [1975] Imm AR 118, IAT 306
Mann v Houston 1957 SLT 89 1252
Manz v Butler's Trustees 1973 SLT (Lands Trib) 2 1247
Mar (Earl of) v Ramsay (1838) 1 D 116 1244
March Cabaret Club and Casino Ltd v London Assurance [1975] 1 Lloyd's Rep 169 858
Marckx v Belgium (Ser A No 31, Judgment 13 June 1979) 2 EHRR 330, E Ct HR 26, 62,
                                                                        71, 86, 88, 96
Markt Intern and Beermann v Germany (Ser A No 165, Judgment 20 November 1989) 12
    EHRR 161, E Ct HR 17, 73
Marshall v Southampton and South-West Hampshire Area Health Authority (Teaching) (Case
    152/84) [1986] ECR 723, [1986] 1 CMLR 688, ECJ 9
Marshall and Scottish Employers' Liability and General Insurance Co Ltd, Re (1901) 85 LT
    757 915
Martin v City of Edinburgh District Council 1988 SCLR 90, 1988 SLT 329, OH 8
Martin v Secretary of State for the Home Department [1972] Imm AR 71, IAT 281
Mason v Harvey (1853) 8 Exch 819 884
Masson (William) Ltd v Scottish Brewers Ltd 1966 SC 9 1225
Matheson v Gemmell (1903) 5 F 448, 10 SLT 625 1238
Mathieson Gee (Ayrshire) Ltd v Quigley 1952 SC (HL) 38, 1952 SLT 239 822
Mathieu v Entry Clearance Officer, Bridgetown [1979–80] Imm AR 157, IAT 279
Matthew's Trustees v Matthew (1905) 13 SLT 470, OH 1030
Matthieu-Mohin and Clerfayt v Belgium (Ser A No 113, Judgment 2 March 1987) 10 EHRR 1,
    E Ct HR 93
Mattison v Hart (1854) 14 CB 357 1109
Mavrommatis Palestine Concessions Case (Jurisdiction) (1924) PCIJ Ser A No 2 14
May's Trustees v Paul (1900) 2 F 657, 7 SLT 402 1029
Mayfair Property Co, Re, Bartlett v Mayfair Property Co [1898] 2 Ch 28, CA 1115
Mayne Nickless v Pegler (1974) 1 NSWLR 228 822
Meacher v Blair-Oliphant 1913 SC 417, 1913 1 SLT 131 1242
Mecca Bookmakers (Scotland) Ltd v East Lothian District Licensing Board 1988 SLT 520,
    OH 1180
Medical Defence Union Ltd v Department of Trade [1980] Ch 82, [1979] 2 All ER 421 802

References are to paragraphs

Mehmet v Secretary of State for the Home Department [1977] Imm AR 68, CA 126
Mellacher v Austria (Ser A No 169, Judgment 19 December 1989) 12 EHRR 391, E Ct HR .. 88
Melrose v Adams (Edinburgh Savings Bank) (1897) 24 R 483, 34 SLR 346 .... 647, 725
Melville v Noble's Trustees (1896) 24 R 243, 4 SLT 198 .... 1025, 1037
Memi v Secretary of State for the Home Department [1976] Imm AR 129, IAT 247
Mendis v Immigration Appeal Tribunal and Secretary of State for the Home Department
    [1989] Imm AR 6, CA 320
Mensah v Secretary of State for the Home Department 1991 GWD 4-218, OH ... 110, 112, 333
Menzies v Caledonian Canal Comrs (1900) 2 F 953, 8 SLT 87 1248
Menzies v Marquess of Breadalbane (1901) 4 F 55 1239
Menzies v North British Insurance Co (1847) 9 D 694 840
Merchant v Entry Clearance Officer, Bombay [1975] Imm AR 49, IAT 279
Meunier, Re [1894] 2 QB 415, DC 532
Middleton v Tough 1908 SC (J) 32, 15 SLT 991 .... 1112, 1200
Mikeover Ltd v Brady [1989] 3 All ER 618, CA 1252
Millar v Galashiels Gas Co Ltd 1949 SC (HL) 31, 1949 SLT 223 1182
Millar's Trustees v Polson (1897) 24 R 1038, 5 SLT 94 1028
Miller's Cash Stores Ltd v West Ham Corpn [1955] 3 All ER 282, [1955] 1 WLR 1121, DC: 1196
Milner v Bradford Warehousemans Society (1909) RCR 12 705
Minister of Pensions v Ballantyne 1948 SC 176, 1948 SLT 242 .... 1166, 1167
Minter (F G) Ltd v Welsh Health Technical Services Organisation (1980) 13 Build LR 1,
    CA 1018, 1019
Minton v Secretary of State for the Home Department [1990] Imm AR 199, CA 170
Miss Jay Jay, The [1987] 1 Lloyd's Rep 32, CA 879
Mitchell v Secretary of State for the Home Department [1981] Imm AR 140, IAT 207
Mohamed Din v Entry Clearance Officer, Karachi [1978] Imm AR 56, IAT 306
Mohammad Zaman v Entry Certificate Officer, Lahore [1973] Imm AR 71, IAT 287
Mohan Singh v Entry Certificate Officer, New Delhi [1973] Imm AR 9, IAT 306
Mohd Meharban v Entry Clearance Officer, Islamabad [1989] Imm AR 57, IAT 271
Mokuola and Ogunbiyi v Secretary of State for the Home Department [1989] Imm AR 51,
    CA 118, 119, 198
Monaghan v Glasgow Corpn 1955 SC 80, 1955 SLT 89 1179
Monnell and Morris v United Kingdom (Ser A No 115, Judgment 2 March 1987) 10 EHRR
    205, E Ct HR 34, 50, 86
Montagu (Samuel) & Co Ltd v Swiss Air Transport Co Ltd [1966] 2 QB 306, [1966] 1 All ER
    814, CA 1178
Moorcock, The (1889) 14 PD 64, CA 1006
Moore v Secretary of State for Scotland 1985 SLT 38 .... 8, 1153
Moray and Nairn Assessor v Charles Meldrum & Sons 1968 SLT 366 1170
Moray County Council v Maclean 1962 SC 601, 1962 SLT 236, OH 1194
Morris v Ford Motor Co Ltd [1973] QB 792, [1973] 2 All ER 1084, CA 894, 897
Morson and Jhanjan v Netherlands (Joined Cases 35, 36/82) [1982] ECR 3723, [1983] 2 CMLR
    221, ECJ 222, 223
Morton v Cameron & Co 1987 SLT (Sh Ct) 44 1009
Morton v French 1908 SC 171, 15 SLT 517 .... 626, 722
Morton's Executor 1985 SLT 14 1263
Moss' Empires Ltd v Glasgow Assessor 1917 SC (HL) 1, 1916 2 SLT 215 .... 1122, 1166
Muhammad Idrish v Secretary of State for the Home Department [1985] Imm AR 155,
    IAT 119, 146, 205, 210, 211, 329
Muhammad v Suna 1956 SC 366, 1956 SLT 175, OH 269
Muir's Trustees (1869) 8 M 53 1230
Muirden v Garden's Executors 1981 SLT (Notes) 9 1229
Muirhead v Forth and North Sea Steamboat Mutual Insurance Association (1893) 21 R (HL) 1,
    1 SLT 325 891
Mukhopadyay v Entry Clearance Officer, Calcutta [1975] Imm AR 42, IAT 287
Müller v Switzerland (Ser A No 133, Judgment 24 May 1988) 13 EHRR 212, E Ct HR .. 73, 81
Müller & Co v Weber and Schaer (1901) 3 F 401, 8 SLT 401 1222
Munro v Butler Johnstone (Corehead) (1868) 7 M 250 1227
Munro v Dunbartonshire County Council 1954 SC 126, 1954 SLT 186 1207
Munro's Executors v Munro (1890) 18 R 122 1230
Mure v Kaye (1811) 4 Taunt 34 504
Murfitt v Royal Insurance Co Ltd (1922) 38 TLR 334 .... 818, 828

References are to paragraphs

Murgai v Entry Clearance Officer, New Delhi [1975] Imm AR 86, IAT 293, 333
Murray v Inland Revenue 1918 SC (HL) 111 1917 2 SLT 115 1193
Murray v Legal and General Assurance Society Ltd [1970] 2 QB 495, [1969] 3 All ER 794 .. 910
Murray's Trustee v Wood (1887) 14 R 856 1238
Murrayfield Ice Rink Ltd v Scottish Rugby Union 1972 SLT (Lands Trib) 20 (on appeal 1973
    SC 21, 1973 SLT 99) 1247
Musgrove v Chun Teeong Toy [1891] AC 272, PC 105
Musselburgh Magistrates v Musselburgh Real Estate Co Ltd (1904) 7 F 308, 12 SLT 636 .. 1239
Mustafa v Secretary of State for the Home Department [1979–80] Imm AR 32, IAT 343
Muthulakshmi v Secretary of State for the Home Department [1972] Imm AR 231, IAT ... 346
Mutual and Federal Insurance Co Ltd v Oudtshoorn Municipality 1985 (1) SA 419 858
Mutual Life Insurance Co of New York v Ontario Metal Products Co Ltd [1925] AC 344, PC . 871
Myeen-Ur-Rashid v Entry Clearance Officer, Dacca [1976] Imm AR 12, IAT 293

N

N S H v Secretary of State for the Home Department [1988] Imm AR 389, CA 318
N V Algemene Transport-en Expeditie Onderneming van Gend en Loos v Nederlandse Tarief
    Commissie (Case 26/62) [1963] ECR 1, [1963] CMLR 105, ECJ 219
Nairn v St Andrews and Edinburgh University Courts 1908 SC 113, 15 SLT 471 1145
Nairn v St Andrews and Edinburgh University Courts 1909 SC (HL) 10, 16 SLT 619: 1145, 1207
Nairobi v Kivan Seth, Entry Clearance Officer, [1979–80] Imm AR 63, IAT 290
Napier v Gordon (1831) 5 W & S 745, HL 1015, 1017, 1038
Napier v Spiers' Trustees (1831) 9 S 655 1018
Nash Dredging (UK) Ltd v Kestrel Marine Ltd 1986 SLT 67, OH 1038
National Association of Local Government Officers v Bolton Corpn [1943] AC 166, [1942] 2
    All ER 425, HL 1167
National Benefit Assurance Co Ltd, Re [1931] 1 Ch 46 835
National Benefit Trust Ltd v Coulter 1911 SC 544, 1911 1 SLT 190 818
National Employers Mutual General Insurance Association Ltd v Haydon [1980] 2 Lloyd's Rep
    149, CA 914, 916
National Farmers Union Mutual Insurance Society Ltd v Dawson [1941] 2 KB 424 911
National Farmers' Union Mutual Insurance Society Ltd v Tully 1935 SLT 574, OH 862
National Smokeless Fuels Ltd v Inland Revenue Comrs [1986] STC 300 8
National Union of Belgian Police v Belgium (Ser A No 19, Judgment 27 October 1975) 1
    EHRR 578, E Ct HR 76, 77, 85
Neil v South East Lancashire Insurance Co 1932 SC 35, 1932 SLT 29 .... 825, 875
Neilson v Stewart 1990 SLT 346 1008
Neilson v Stewart 1991 SLT 523, HL 1007, 1008
Nelson v British Broadcasting Corpn (No 2) [1980] ICR 110, [1979] IRLR 346, CA 1036
Netherlands Insurance Co Est 1845 Ltd v Karl Ljungberg & Co AB [1986] 3 All ER 767, [1986]
    2 Lloyd's Rep 19, PC 899
Neumeister v Austria (No 1) (Ser A No 8, Judgment 27 June 1968) 1 EHRR 91, E Ct
    HR 32, 47
New Plymouth Corpn v Taranaki Electric-Power Board [1933] AC 680, PC 1133
Nichols & Co v Scottish Union and National Insurance Co (1885) 14 R 1094 914
Nicholson v Glasgow Asylum for the Blind 1911 SC 391, 1911 1 SLT 37 1245
Nicol's Trustees v Sutherland 1951 SC (HL) 21, 1951 SLT 201 1126
Nielsen v Denmark (Ser A No 144, Judgment 28 November 1988) 11 EHRR 175, E Ct HR .. 39
Nielsen, Re [1984] AC 606, [1984] 2 All ER 81, HL 515, 548, 553, 562, 569, 573
Nijssen v Immigration Officer, London (Heathrow) Airport and Immigration Officer, Sheer-
    ness [1978] Imm AR 226, IAT 222, 233
Nimmo v Alexander Cowan & Sons Ltd 1967 SC (HL) 79, 1967 SLT 277 1118
Nisa v Secretary of State for the Home Department [1979–80] Imm AR 20, IAT 287
Nisbet's Trustees v Nisbet (1871) 9 M 937 1229
Noblet v Condon [1935] SASR 329 1109
Nokes v Doncaster Amalgamated Collieries Ltd [1940] AC 1014, [1940] 3 All ER 549,
    HL 1123
Nold (J), Kohlen- und Baustoffgroßhandlung v EC Commission (Case 4/73) [1974] ECR 491,
    [1974] 2 CMLR 338, ECH 9
Normid Housing Association Ltd v Ralphs [1989] 1 Lloyd's Rep 265, CA 908

References are to paragraphs

Norris v Ireland (Ser A No 142, Judgment 26 October 1988) 13 EHRR 186, E Ct HR ...17, 66
North British and Mercantile Insurance Co v London, Liverpool and Globe Insurance Co
   (1877) 5 Ch D 569, CA 914
North British and Mercantile Insurance Co v Stewart (1871) 9 M 534 836
North British Rly Co v Hawick Magistrates (1862) 1 M 200 1240
North British Rly Co v Moon's Trustee (1879) 6 R 640 1240
North of England Pure Oil-Cake Co v Archangel Maritime Insurance Co (1875) LR 10 QB
   249, DC 845
Northern Rock Building Society v Davies [1969] 3 All ER 1310, [1969] 1 WLR 1742 727
Notman v Anchor Assurance Co (1858) 4 CBNS 476 827
Nuland [1988] Crim LR 690, DC 515
Nuland, Re [1988] Crim LR 690, DC 515, 568

O

O v United Kingdom (Ser A No 120, Judgment 8 July 1987) 10 EHRR 82, E Ct HR 64
Obermeier v Austria (Ser A No 179, Judgment 28 June 1990), 13 EHRR 290, E Ct HR 21
Observer and Guardian v United Kingdom, Times 27 November 1991, E Ct HR 74
O'Connor v BHD Kirby & Co [1972] 1 QB 90, [1971] 2 All ER 1415, CA 862
Oddy v Phoenix Assurance Co Ltd [1966] 1 Lloyd's Rep 134 840
O'Donnell v Brownieside Coal Co Ltd 1934 SC 534, 1934 SLT 493 1229
O'Flynn v Equitable Fire Insurance and Trust Co and Commercial Assurance Co (1866) 1
   Roscoe's Rep 372 (Cape SC) 915
Ogilvie's Legatees v Hamilton (1833) 12 S 189 1029
Oldham Our Ladies Sick and Burial Society v Taylor (1887) 3 TLR 472, CA 680
Oloniluyi v Secretary of State for the Home Department [1989] Imm AR 135, CA 176
Olsson v Sweden (Ser A No 130, Judgment 24 March 1988) 11 EHRR 259, E Ct HR 64, 79
Olympic, The [1913] P 92 1159
Oram v Hutt [1914] 1 Ch 98, CA 699
Ormond Investment Co Ltd v Betts [1928] AC 143, HL 1160
Orr v Mitchell (1893) 20 R (HL) 27 .... 1221, 1237
Orton v Bristow (1916) 32 TLR 352, CA (affg (1915) 32 TLR 129) 703
Osama v Immigration Officer, London (Gatwick) Airport [1978] Imm AR 8, IAT 171
Oskar v Government of Australia [1988] AC 366, [1988] 1 All ER 183, HL 566, 570, 575

P

Padmore v Secretary of State for the Home Department [1972] Imm AR 1, IAT 349
Page v Scottish Insurance Corpn Ltd (1929) 98 LJKB 308, CA 894, 896
Pakelli v Germany (Ser A No 64, Judgment 25 April 1983) 6 EHRR 1, E Ct HR 52
Papayianni v United Kingdom [1974] Imm AR 7 115
Parekh, Re [1988] Crim LR 832, DC 568
Parker & Co (Sandbank) Ltd v Western Assurance Co 1925 SLT 131, OH 825, 828
Parlement Belge, The (1879) 4 PD 129 8
Parvez v Immigration Officer, London (Heathrow) Airport [1979–80] Imm AR 84 171
Patel v Entry Clearance Officer, Bombay [1978] Imm AR 154, IAT 306
Patel v Immigration Appeal Tribunal [1983] Imm AR 76, CA 293
Patel (Girishkumar Samabhai) v Secretary of State for the Home Department [1989] Imm AR
   246 8
Patmor Ltd v City of Edinburgh District Licensing Board 1988 SLT 850 1180
Pattison's Trustees v University of Edinburgh (1888) 16 R 73, OH 1227, 1263
Pauwels v Belgium (Ser A No 135, Judgment 26 May 1988) 11 EHRR 238, E Ct HR 31
Pawley v Wharldall [1966] 1 QB 373, [1965] 2 All ER 757, DC 1104
Pearson v Commercial Union Assurance Co (1876) 1 App Cas 498, HL 841
Pearson v Immigration Appeal Tribunal [1978] Imm AR 212, CA 112, 154, 344
Peat v Fowler (1886) 55 LJQB 271, DC 694
Pecastaing v Belgium (Case 98/79) [1980] ECR 691, [1980] 3 CMLR 685, ECJ 9
Percival v Wright [1902] 2 Ch 421 1535
Pereira v Entry Clearance Officer, Bridgetown [1979–80] Imm AR 79, IAT 279
Perera v Immigration Officer, London (Heathrow) Airport [1979–80] Imm AR 58, IAT 162

References are to paragraphs

Perth Local Board of Health v Maley (1904) 1 CLR 702 1156
Perth Water Comrs v M'Donald (1879) 6 R 1050 1187
Peters v General Accident Fire and Life Assurance Corpn Ltd [1938] 2 All ER 267, CA 845
Phillips v Entry Certificate Officer, Kingston, Jamaica [1973] Imm AR 47, IAT 286, 287
Phillips v Parnaby [1934] 2 KB 299 1157
Phillips v Phillips (1866) LR 1 P & D 169 1114
Phoenix Assurance Co v Spooner [1905] 2 KB 753 898
Phoenix General Insurance Co of Greece SA v Halvanon Insurance Co Ltd [1988] QB 216,
   [1987] 2 All ER 152, CA 807
Piara Singh v Entry Clearance Officer, Kingston, Jamaica [1977] Imm AR 1, IAT 247
Pickards v Pickard 1963 SC 604, 1963 SLT 56 1222
Pickles v Insurance Brokers Registration Council [1984] 1 All ER 1073, [1984] 1 WLR 748, DC: 813
Piersack v Belgium (Ser A No 53, Judgment 1 October 1982) 5 EHRR 169, E Ct HR 48
Pilkington Bros Ltd Workmen's Pension Fund, Re [1953] 2 All ER 816, [1953] 1 WLR 1084: 708
Pioneer Concrete (UK) Ltd v National Employers Mutual General Insurance Association Ltd
   [1985] 1 Lloyd's Rep 274 909
Plaine v Thomson (1836) 15 S 194 1030
Plattform 'Ärzte für das Leben' v Austria (Ser A No 139, Judgment 21 June 1988) 13 EHRR 204,
   E Ct HR 72
Poiss v Austria (Ser A No 117, Judgment 23 April 1987) 10 EHRR 231, E Ct HR 88
Poll v Lord Advocate (1899) 1 F 823, 5 SLT 167 105
Pollexfen v Stewart (1841) 3 D 1215 1026
Pomphrey's Trustees v Royal Naval Benevolent Trust 1967 SLT 61, OH 1271
Porter v Campbell's Trustees 1923 SC (HL) 94, 1923 SLT 619 1247
Port-Glasgow and Newark Sailcloth Co v Caledonian Rly Co (1892) 19 R 608 894
Portobello Magistrates v Edinburgh Magistrates (1882) 10 R 130 1127
Post Office v Estuary Radio Ltd [1967] 3 All ER 663, [1967] 1 WLR 847 1152
Post Office v Estuary Radio Ltd [1968] 2 QB 740, [1967] 3 All ER 679, CA 8
Post Office v Norwich Union Fire Insurance Society Ltd [1967] 2 QB 363, [1967] 1 All ER 577,
   CA 905
Powell v Cleland [1948] 1 KB 262, [1947] 2 All ER 672, CA 1156
Powell v Tokeley (1906) CR Rep, Part A, 134 (Parliamentary Papers for 1907, vol 78), DC . 703
Powell and Rayner v United Kindgom (Ser A No 172, Judgment 21 February 1990) 12 EHRR
   355, E Ct HR 84
Practice Note [1970] 1 All ER 1119, [1970] 1 WLR 663, CA 34
Practice Note [1980] 1 All ER 555, [1980] 1 WLR 270, CA 34
Practice Statement (Judicial Precedent) [1966] 3 All ER 77, [1966] 1 WLR 1234, HL 198
Praet (Julien) & Cie SA v H G Poland Ltd [1960] 1 Lloyd's Rep 416, CA 825
Prajapati, Ex parte [1981] Imm AR 199, DC 152
Prawdzic-Lazarska v Prawdzic-Lazarski 1954 SC 98, 1954 SLT 41, OH 269
Prentice v Chalmers 1985 SLT 168 1032
Prestwick Cinema Co Ltd v Gardiner 1951 SC 98, 1951 SLT 69 . . . . 1010, 1013
Pretto v Italy (Ser A No 71, Judgment 8 December 1983) 6 EHRR 182, E Ct HR 49
Price & Co v A1 Ships' Small Damage Insurance Association (1889) 22 QBD 580, CA 841
Printers and Transferrers Amalgamated Trades Protection Society, Re [1899] 2 Ch 184 737
Prior v Kelvin Shipping Co Ltd 1954 SLT (Notes) 12, OH 1166
Pritpal Singh v Secretary of State for the Home Department [1972] Imm AR 154, IAT 251
Provincial Insurance Co Ltd v Morgan [1933] AC 240, HL 878
Prudential Insurance Co v Inland Revenue Comrs [1904] 2 KB 658 802
Public Prosecutor v Oie Hee Koi [1968] AC 829, [1968] 1 All ER 419, PC 1177
Pudas v Sweden (Ser A No 125A, Judgment 27 October 1987) 10 EHRR 380, E Ct HR . 44, 45
Purcell Meats (Scotland) Ltd v McLeod 1986 SCCR 672, 1987 SLT 528 1511
Puttick v Secretary of State for the Home Department [1984] Imm AR 118, IAT 233
Pyx Granite Co Ltd v Ministry of Housing and Local Government [1960] AC 260, [1959] 3 All
   ER 1, HL 1204

Q

Queen Insurance Co v Parsons (1881) 7 App Cas 96, PC 825
Qurasha Begum v Immigration Officer, London (Heathrow) Airport [1978] Imm AR 158,
   IAT 172

References are to paragraphs

Qureshi v Immigration Officer, London (Heathrow) Airport [1977] Imm AR 113, IAT: 172, 292

R

R v Ayu [1958] 3 All ER 636, [1958] 1 WLR 1264, CCA 215
R v Bangoo [1976] Crim LR 746, CA 198
R v Bates [1952] 2 All ER 842 1135
R v Bennett [1978] Crim LR 44 (NZ CA) 577
R v Bouchereau (Case 30/77) [1977] ECR 1999, [1977] 2 CMLR 800, [1978] QB 732, [1981] 2
    All ER 924, ECJ 233
R v Bow Street Magistrates' Court, ex parte Choudbury 1990 Times, 9 April 8
R v Bow Street Magistrates Court, ex parte Van der Holst (1986) 83 Cr App Rep 114,
    DC 556, 559, 560, 562, 566
R v Bow Street Magistrates, ex parte Mackeson (1982) 75 Cr App Rep 24, DC 553, 577
R v Brabrook (1893) 69 LT 718, DC 703
R v Britton [1967] 2 QB 51, [1967] 1 All ER 486, CA 1140
R v Chief Immigration Officer, Bradford Airport, ex parte Ashiq Hussain [1969] 3 All ER
    1601, [1970] 1 WLR 9, DC 293
R v Chief Immigration Officer, Gatwick Airport, ex parte Kharrazi [1980] 3 All ER 373, [1980]
    1 WLR 1396, CA 110, 293, 299
R v Chief Immigration Officer, Heathrow Airport, ex parte Salamat Bibi [1976] 3 All ER 843,
    [1976] 1 WLR 979, CA 8, 115, 164, 268
R v Chief Immigration Officer, Manchester Airport, ex parte Insah Begum [1973] 1 All ER
    594, [1973] 1 WLR 141, CA 170
R v Chief Metropolitan Stipendiary Magistrate, ex parte Secretary of State for the Home
    Department [1989] 1 All ER 151, [1988] 1 WLR 1204, DC 515
R v Chief Registrar of Friendly Societies, ex parte Evans (1900) CR Rep, Part A, 89 (Parliamen-
    tary Papers for 1901, vol 72), 16 TLR 346, CA 739
R v Chiswick Police Station Superintendent, ex parte Sacksteder [1918] 1 KB 578, CA 501
R v Clarke [1985] AC 1037, [1985] 2 All ER 777, HL 190
R v Collier (unreported; see Financial Times 2 July 1987) 1502
R v Cross [1990] BCC 239, CA 1502
R v Davies (1983) 76 Cr App Rep 120, CA 577
R v Davis (1866) WN 24 695
R v Dickensen (unreported; noted in (1982) 3 Co Law 185) 1502, 1506
R v East Grinstead Justices, ex parte Doeve [1969] 1 QB 136, [1968] 3 All ER 666, DC 215
R v Edgehill [1963] 1 QB 593, [1963] 1 All ER 181, CCA 206
R v Entry Clearance Officer, Bombay, ex parte Amin [1980] 2 All ER 837, [1970] 1 WLR 1530,
    DC 159, 344
R v Gill [1976] 2 All ER 893, [1977] 1 WLR 78, CA 190
R v Governor of Ashford Remand Centre, ex parte Bouzagou [1985] Imm AR 69, CA 146,
                                                             166, 198
R v Governor of Brixton Prison, ex parte Armah [1968] AC 192, [1966] 3 All ER 177, HL . 544
R v Governor of Brixton Prison, ex parte Caborn-Waterfield [1960] 2 QB 498, [1960] 2 All ER
    178, DC 536
R v Governor of Brixton Prison, ex parte Guerin (1907) 51 Sol Jo 571, DC 549
R v Governor of Brixton Prison, ex parte Kahan [1989] QB 716, [1989] 2 All ER 368, DC .. 520
R v Governor of Brixton Prison, ex parte Kolczynski [1955] 1 QB 540, [1955] 1 All ER 31,
    DC 532, 562
R v Governor of Brixton Prison, ex parte Minervini [1959] 1 QB 155, [1958] 3 All ER 318, DC: 515
R v Governor of Brixton Prison, ex parte Rush [1969] 1 All ER 316, [1969] 1 WLR 165,
    DC 514, 515
R v Governor of Brixton Prison, ex parte Soblen [1963] 2 QB 243, [1962] 3 All ER 641,
    CA 207, 501, 553
R v Governor of Brixton Prison, ex parte Thompson [1911] 2 KB 82, DC 553
R v Governor of Pentonville Prison, ex parte Budlong, R v Governor of Pentonville Prison, ex
    parte Kember [1980] 1 All ER 701, [1980] 1 WLR 1110, DC 532
R v Governor of Pentonville Prison, ex parte Naghdi [1990] 1 All ER 257, [1990] 1 WLR 317,
    DC 515, 553
R v Governor of Pentonville Prison, ex parte Passingham [1983] 2 AC 464, [1983] 2 All ER 123,
    HL 562

References are to paragraphs

R v Governor of Pentonville Prison, ex parte Sinclair [1990] 2 QB 112, [1990] 2 All ER 789,
DC 568, 570
R v Governor of Pentonville Prison, ex parte Singh [1981] 3 All ER 23, [1981] 1 WLR 1031,
DC 562
R v Governor of Pentonville Prison, ex parte Teja [1971] 2 QB 274, [1971] 2 All ER 11, DC . 563
R v Governor of Pentonville Prison, ex parte Voets [1986] 2 All ER 630, [1986] 1 WLR 470,
DC 565
R v Governor of Winson Green Prison, Birmingham, ex parte Littlejohn [1975] 3 All ER 208,
[1975] 1 WLR 893, DC 532, 534
R v Hancock and Brooks (unreported; see Financial Times 9 November 1984 and 7 March
1985) 1502
R v Hodges (1967) 51 Cr App Rep 361, CA 215
R v Immigration Appeal Tribunal, ex parte Acqvah, Rahman, Gonzales-Rojas [1988] Imm AR
78 170
R v Immigration Appeal Tribunal, ex parte Ahluwalia [1979–80] Imm AR 1, DC 119, 333
R v Immigration Appeal Tribunal, ex parte Aisha Khatoon Ali [1979–80] Imm AR 195, CA . 333
R v Immigration Appeal Tribunal, ex parte Ajaib Singh [1978] Imm AR 59, DC 171
R v Immigration Appeal Tribunal, ex parte Ali Ajmal [1982] Imm AR 102, CA 8, 115
R v Immigration Appeal Tribunal, ex parte Amirbeaggi (1982) Times, 25 May, DC 353
R v Immigration Appeal Tribunal, ex parte Anilkumar Rabindrabhai Patel [1988] AC 910,
[1988] 2 All ER 378, [1988] Imm AR 434, HL 194, 198, 202, 207
R v Immigration Appeal Tribunal, ex parte Armstrong [1977] Imm AR 80, DC 359
R v Immigration Appeal Tribunal, ex parte Aurangzeb Khan [1989] Imm AR 524 271
R v Immigration Appeal Tribunal, ex parte Bashir [1985] Imm AR 231, CA 110
R v Immigration Appeal Tribunal, ex parte Bastiampillai [1983] 2 All ER 844, [1983] Imm AR
1, DC 287
R v Immigration Appeal Tribunal, ex parte Cheema [1982] Imm AR 124, CA 207
R v Immigration Appeal Tribunal, ex parte Chhinderpal Singh and Gurdip Singh [1989] Imm
AR 69 160
R v Immigration Appeal Tribunal, ex parte Chumun and Bano-Ovais [1987] Imm AR 92, DC . 348
R v Immigration Appeal Tribunal, ex parte Chundawadra [1988] Imm AR 161, CA 115
R v Immigration Appeal Tribunal, ex parte Coomasaru [1983] 1 All ER 208, [1983] 1 WLR 14,
[1982] Imm AR 77, CA 333
R v Immigration Appeal Tribunal, ex parte Florent [1985] Imm AR 141, CA 207
R v Immigration Appeal Tribunal, ex parte Hassanin [1987] 1 All ER 74, [1986] 1 WLR 1448,
[1986] Imm AR 502, CA 333
R v Immigration Appeal Tribunal, ex parte Hazrabibi Ibrahim Mohamed Kara [1989] Imm AR
120 282
R v Immigration Appeal Tribunal, ex parte Hoque and Singh [1988] Imm AR 216, CA 271
R v Immigration Appeal Tribunal, ex parte Hubbard [1985] Imm AR 110, DC 333, 345
R v Immigration Appeal Tribunal, ex parte Hussanin [1987] 1 All ER 74, [1986] 1 WLR 1448,
CA 353
R v Immigration Appeal Tribunal, ex parte Jaspal Singh [1977] Imm AR 105n, DC 345
R v Immigration Appeal Tribunal, ex parte Jonah [1985] Imm AR 7, IAT 318
R v Immigration Appeal Tribunal, ex parte Joseph [1977] Imm AR 70, DC 251
R v Immigration Appeal Tribunal, ex parte Khan [1975] Imm AR 26, IAT 293, 333
R v Immigration Appeal Tribunal, ex parte Khan [1983] Imm AR 32 207
R v Immigration Appeal Tribunal, ex parte Khan [1983] QB 790, [1983] 2 All ER 420, [1982]
Imm AR 134, CA 207
R v Immigration Appeal Tribunal, ex parte Kotecha [1983] 2 All ER 289, [1983] 1 WLR 487,
[1982] Imm AR 88, CA 353
R v Immigration Appeal Tribunal, ex parte Kumar [1986] Imm AR 446, CA 271
R v Immigration Appeal Tribunal, ex parte Kwok On Tong [1981] Imm AR 214, DC 333
R v Immigration Appeal Tribunal, ex parte Lila [1978] Imm AR 50, DC 357
R v Immigration Appeal Tribunal, ex parte Mahendra Singh [1984] Imm AR 1, DC ... 365, 366
R v Immigration Appeal Tribunal, ex parte Martin [1972] Imm AR 275, DC 333
R v Immigration Appeal Tribunal, ex parte Mehmet [1977] 2 All ER 602, [1977] 1 WLR 795,
[1977] Imm AR 56, DC 208, 345
R v Immigration Appeal Tribunal, ex parte Mehra [1983] Imm AR 156, DC 345
R v Immigration Appeal Tribunal, ex parte Miller [1988] Imm AR 1, DC 318, 320
R v Immigration Appeal Tribunal, ex parte Mohammed Khatab [1989] Imm AR 313, DC .. 271
R v Immigration Appeal Tribunal, ex parte Muruganandarajah [1986] Imm AR 382, CA ... 322

References are to paragraphs

R v Immigration Appeal Tribunal, ex parte Owusu-Sekyere [1987] Imm AR 425, CA 207
R v Immigration Appeal Tribunal, ex parte Palacio [1979–80] Imm AR 178, DC 171
R v Immigration Appeal Tribunal, ex parte Peikazadi [1979–80] Imm AR 191, IAT 251
R v Immigration Appeal Tribunal, ex parte Perween Khan [1972] 3 All ER 297, [1972] 1 WLR
    1058, [1972] Imm AR 268, DC 293
R v Immigration Appeal Tribunal, ex parte R P Mehta [1976] Imm AR 38, CA 348
R v Immigration Appeal Tribunal, ex parte Rafique [1990] Imm AR 235 275
R v Immigration Appeal Tribunal, ex parte Rahman [1987] Imm AR 313, CA 251
R v Immigration Appeal Tribunal, ex parte Rashid [1978] Imm AR 71, DC 333, 353
R v Immigration Appeal Tribunal, ex parte Ruhul Amin, R v Immigration Appeal Tribunal, ex
    parte Rahman, R v Immigration Appeal Tribunal, ex parte Haque [1987] 3 All ER 705,
    [1987] 1 WLR 1538, [1987] Imm AR 587, CA 125
R v Immigration Appeal Tribunal, ex parte Sajid Mahmood [1988] Imm AR 121 281
R v Immigration Appeal Tribunal, ex parte Secretary of State for the Home Department [1990]
    3 All ER 652, [1990] 1 WLR 1126, CA 149, 318, 319, 339
R v Immigration Appeal Tribunal, ex parte Shaikh [1981] 3 All ER 29, [1981] 1 WLR 1107,
    DC 293
R v Immigration Appeal Tribunal, ex parte Suleman [1976] Imm AR 147, DC 359
R v Immigration Appeal Tribunal, ex parte Surinder Mohan [1985] Imm AR 84, CA .. 277, 333
R v Immigration Appeal Tribunal, ex parte Swaran Singh [1987] 3 All ER 690, [1987] Imm AR
    563, CA 287
R v Immigration Appeal Tribunal, ex parte Tohur Ali [1988] Imm AR 237, CA 279
R v Immigration Appeal Tribunal, ex parte V M Mehta [1976] Imm AR 174, CA 348
R v Immigration Appeal Tribunal, ex parte Vinod Bhatia [1985] Imm AR 59, CA 271
R v Immigration Appeal Tribunal, ex parte Weerasuriya [1983] 1 All ER 195, [1982] Imm AR
    23, DC 333, 349, 353
R v Immigration Appeal Tribunal, ex parte Wirdestedt [1982] Imm AR 186, IAT 268, 269
R v Immigration Appeal Tribunal, ex parte Wirdestedt [1990] Imm AR 20, CA 268, 269
R v Immigration Appeal Tribunal, ex parte Zandfani [1984] Imm AR 213, DC 259
R v Inland Revenue Comrs, ex parte Rossminster [1980] AC 952, [1980] 1 All ER 80, HL .. 168
R v Jenkins (unreported; see Financial Times 18 July 1987) 1502
R v Kettle and Thorneywork (unreported; see Financial Times 18, 20 September 1984) 1502
R v Kirk (Case 63/83) [1984] ECR 2689, [1984] 3 CMLR 522, ECJ 9
R v London County Quarter Sessions Appeals Committee, ex parte Rossi [1956] QB 682,
    [1956] 1 All ER 670, CA 348
R v Long [1960] 1 QB 681, [1959] 3 All ER 559, CCA 1172
R v Loxdale (1758) 1 Burr 445 1156
R v McCartan [1958] 3 All ER 140, [1958] 1 WLR 933, CCA 215
R v Morris [1972] 1 All ER 384, [1972] 1 WLR 228, CA 1132
R v Naerger (unreported; see The Guardian 30 April 1986) 1502
R v Nazari [1980] 3 All ER 880, [1980] 1 WLR 1366, CA 205, 206
R v Oakes [1959] 2 QB 350, [1959] 2 All ER 92, CCA 1108
R v Officer Commanding Depot Battalion RASC Colchester, ex parte Elliott [1949] 1 All ER
    373, DC 577
R v Panel on Take-overs and Mergers, ex parte Datafin plc [1987] QB 815, [1987] 1 All ER 564,
    CA 1520
R v Peters (1886) 16 QBD 636 1152
R v Pieck (Case 157/79) [1980] ECR 2171, [1981] QB 571, [1981] 3 All ER 46, ECJ ... 114, 175,
                        221, 226, 230, 233, 235, 236, 238
R v Plymouth Justices, ex parte Driver [1986] QB 95, [1985] 2 All ER 681, DC 577
R v Saunders (Case 175/78) [1979] ECR 1129, [1979] 2 CMLR 216, [1980] QB 72, [1979] 2 All
    ER 267, ECJ 221, 226, 230
R v Secchi [1975] 1 CMLR 383, CA 222, 233
R v Secretary of State for Home Affairs, ex parte Duke of Chateau Thierry [1917] 1 KB 552,
    DC 501
R v Secretary of State for Home Affairs, ex parte Harniak Singh [1969] 2 All ER 867, [1969] 1
    WLR 835, DC 306
R v Secretary of State for the Home Department, ex parte Adesina [1988] Imm AR 442, CA . 190
R v Secretary of State for the Home Department, ex parte Alaa Mohamed el Sayed Hasem
    [1987] Imm AR 577 .... 316, 319, 320

References are to paragraphs

R v Secretary of State for the Home Department, ex parte Anosike [1971] 2 All ER 1405, [1971] 1 WLR 1136, DC 138, 167

R v Secretary of State for the Home Department, ex parte Arjumand [1983] Imm AR 123, DC . 306

R v Secretary of State for the Home Department, ex parte Ayub [1983] Imm AR 20, [1983] 3 CMLR 140, DC 223, 236

R v Secretary of State for the Home Department, ex parte Badaike (1977) Times, 4 May ... 170

R v Secretary of State for the Home Department, ex parte Bagga [1991] 1 QB 485, [1991] 1 All ER 777, CA 130

R v Secretary of State for the Home Department, ex parte Bhajan Singh [1976] QB 198, [1975] 2 All ER 1081, CA 8, 1153

R v Secretary of State for the Home Department, ex parte Bhatti (1982) 132 NLJ 743, CA 112, 325

R v Secretary of State for the Home Department, ex parte Brind [1991] 1 AC 696, [1991] 1 All ER 720, HL 8

R v Secretary of State for the Home Department, ex parte Choudhary [1978] 3 All ER 790, [1978] 1 WLR 1177, CA 198

R v Secretary of State for the Home Department, ex parte Dannenberg [1984] QB 766, [1984] 2 All ER 481, CA 234

R v Secretary of State for the Home Department, ex parte Dhirubhai Gordhanbhai Patel [1986] Imm AR 515, CA 198

R v Secretary of State for the Home Department, ex parte Draz [1985] Imm AR 215, DC .. 348

R v Secretary of State for the Home Department, ex parte Fauzia Wamar Din Bagga Khan [1987] Imm AR 543, CA 211

R v Secretary of State for the Home Department, ex parte Fazor Ali [1988] Imm AR 274, CA . 198

R v Secretary of State for the Home Department, ex parte Gurmeet Singh [1987] Imm AR 489, DC 200, 316, 317, 318, 319, 320, 321

R v Secretary of State for the Home Department, ex parte Hindjou [1989] Imm AR 24 .... 112, 201, 293, 294, 333

R v Secretary of State for the Home Department, ex parte Hosenball [1977] 3 All ER 452, [1977] 1 WLR 776, CA 110, 115, 207, 369

R v Secretary of State for the Home Department, ex parte Ibrahim (1980) Times, 29 March: 198

R v Secretary of State for the Home Department, ex parte Jayakody [1982] 1 All ER 461, [1982] 1 WLR 405, CA 172

R v Secretary of State for the Home Department, ex parte Khan [1985] 1 All ER 40, [1984] 1 WLR 1337, [1984] Imm AR 68, CA 112, 279

R v Secretary of State for the Home Department, ex parte Khera, R v Secretary of State for the Home Department, ex parte Khaweja [1984] AC 74, [1983] 1 All ER 765, [1982] Imm AR 139, HL 316

R v Secretary of State for the Home Department, ex parte Kirkwood [1984] 2 All ER 390, [1984] 1 WLR 913 .... 8, 553, 575

R v Secretary of State for the Home Department, ex parte Kuku [1989] Imm AR 38 329

R v Secretary of State for the Home Department, ex parte Lapinid [1984] 3 All ER 257, [1984] 1 WLR 1269, CA 198

R v Secretary of State for the Home Department, ex parte McAvoy [1984] 3 All ER 417, [1984] 1 WLR 1408 8

R v Secretary of State for the Home Department, ex parte Maqbool Hussain [1976] 1 WLR 97, DC 198

R v Secretary of State for the Home Department, ex parte Mehmet [1977] 2 All ER 602, [1977] 1 WLR 795, [1977] Imm AR 56, DC 211, 348

R v Secretary of State for the Home Department, ex parte Mughal [1974] QB 313, [1973] 3 All ER 796, CA 164, 170

R v Secretary of State for the Home Department, ex parte Nkiti [1989] Imm AR 182, CA .. 171

R v Secretary of State for the Home Department, ex parte Oladehinde [1991] 1 AC 254, [1990] 2 All ER 367, CA (affd [1991] 1 AC 254, [1990] 3 All ER 393, HL) 138, 142, 202

R v Secretary of State for the Home Department, ex parte Parshottam Singh [1989] Imm AR 469, CA 200

R v Secretary of State for the Home Department, ex parte Parvaz Akhtar [1981] 1 QB 46, [1980] 2 All ER 735, CA 118

R v Secretary of State for the Home Department, ex parte Phansopkar [1976] QB 606, [1975] 3 All ER 497, CA 118, 268

R v Secretary of State for the Home Department, ex parte Rajinder Kaur [1987] Imm AR 278, DC 112

References are to paragraphs

R v Secretary of State for the Home Department, ex parte Ram [1979] 1 All ER 687, [1979] 1
    WLR 148, DC 118, 198
R v Secretary of State for the Home Department, ex parte Samya and Younes Ounejma, R v
    Secretary of State for the Home Department, ex parte Hassan [1989] Imm AR 75, DC . 141
R v Secretary of State for the Home Department, ex parte Sandhu [1982] 2 CMLR 553 180
R v Secretary of State for the Home Department, ex parte Sandhu (1985) Times, 10 May,
    HL 223, 238
R v Secretary of State for the Home Department, ex parte Santillo (Case 131/79) [1980] ECR
    1585, [1980] 2 CMLR 308, [1981] QB 778, [1981] 2 All ER 897, ECJ 234
R v Secretary of State for the Home Department, ex parte Subramaniam [1977] QB 190, [1976]
    1 All ER 915, [1976] Imm AR 155, CA 119, 146, 205, 211
R v Secretary of State for the Home Department, ex parte Swati [1986] 1 All ER 717, [1986] 1
    WLR 477, [1986] Imm AR 88, CA 110, 112, 201, 333, 345
R v Secretary of State for the Home Department, ex parte Taj Mohammed Khan [1985] Imm
    AR 104, CA 146, 169
R v Secretary of State for the Home Department, ex parte Tolba, Bettancourt, Akinsanmi .. 170
R v Secretary of State for the Home Department, ex parte Vashist (1983) Times, 18 January,
    CA 205
R v Secretary of State for the Home Department, ex parte Yassin Talmasani [1987] Imm AR 32,
    CA 216
R v Secretary of State for the Home Department, ex parte Yeboah, R v Secretary of State for the
    Home Department, ex parte Draz [1987] 3 All ER 999, [1987] 1 WLR 1586, [1987] Imm
    AR 414, CA 211, 345
R v Secretary of State for the Home Department, ex parte Zamir [1980] AC 930, [1980] 2 All ER
    768, HL 166, 198
R v Secretary of State for Trade and Industry, ex parte R [1989] 1 All ER 647, [1989] 1 WLR 372,
    DC 1415
R v Serry (1980) Times, 31 October, CA 206
R v Tidd Pratt (1865) 6 B & S 672 ....699, 703
R v Titheridge and Titheridge (unreported; noted in (1983) 4 Co Law 117) 1502
R v Titterton [1895] 2 QB 61, DC 1156
R v United Kingdom (Ser A No 121, Judgment 8 July 1987) 10 EHRR 74, E Ct HR 64
R v Weil (1882) 9 QBD 701, CA 553
R v West Riding of Yorkshire County Council [1906] 2 KB 676, CA 1144
R v Williams [1982] 3 All ER 1092, [1982] 1 WLR 1398, CA 215
Rabin v Gerson Berger Association Ltd [1985] 1 All ER 1041, [1985] 1 WLR 595 1271
Rahim Miah v Secretary of State for the Home Department [1989] Imm AR 559, CA .. 119, 198
Rahman v Secretary of State for the Home Department [1989] Imm AR 325, IAT 314, 317
Rahmani v Diggines [1986] AC 475, [1986] 1 All ER 921, [1986] Imm AR 195, HL 351, 355
Raj v Entry Clearance Officer, New Delhi [1985] Imm AR 151, IAT 271
Rajput v Immigration Appeal Tribunal [1989] Imm AR 350, CA 110
Ralston v HM Advocate 1988 SCCR 590, 1989 SLT 474 8
Ramesh Kumar v Entry Clearance Officer, New Delhi [1985] Imm AR 242, IAT 152, 164
Ramjane v Chief Immigration Officer, Gatwick Airport [1973] Imm AR 84, IAT 172
Ramos v Immigration Appeal Tribunal [1989] Imm AR 148, CA 281
Rapp (Leo) Ltd v McClure [1955] 1 Lloyd's Rep 292 838
Rasmussen v Denmark (Ser A No 87, Judgment 28 November 1984) 7 EHRR 371, E Ct
    HR 85, 86
Ravat v Entry Clearance Officer, Bombay [1974] Imm AR 79, IAT 281
Rayner v Preston (1881) 18 Ch D 1, CA 890
Rees v United Kingdom (Ser A No 106, Judgment 17 October 1986) 9 EHRR 56, E Ct
    HR 67, 71
Rees, Re [1986] AC 937, [1986] 2 All ER 321, HL 553, 554, 556, 565
Rees and Kirby Ltd v Swansea City Council (1985) 30 Build LR 1, CA 1018
Regal (Hastings) Ltd v Gulliver [1942] 1 All ER 378, HL 1535
Regina Fur Co Ltd v Bossom [1957] 2 Lloyd's Rep 466, affd [1958] 2 Lloyd's Rep 425, CA . 860
Rehman v Secretary of State for the Home Department [1978] Imm AR 80, IAT 126
Renfrewshire County Council v Trustees of Orphan Homes of Scotland (1898) 1 F 186, 6 SLT
    229 1136
Reyners v Belgian State (Case 2/74) [1974] ECR 631, [1974] 2 CMLR 305, ECJ 221
Reynolds v Phoenix Assurance Co Ltd [1978] 2 Lloyd's Rep 440 ....865, 886
Rhemtulla v Immigration Appeal Tribunal [1979–80] Imm AR 168, CA 345

References are to paragraphs

Rhondda's (Viscountess) Claim [1922] 2 AC 339, HL 1145
Rice v Connolly [1966] 1 QB 414, [1966] 2 All ER 649, DC 190
Rice v Sioux City Memorial Park Cemetery Inc 245 Iowa 147, 60 NW 2d 110 (1953), ILR 20
 (1953) 3
Riches v Westminster Bank Ltd 1947 AC 390, [1947] 1 All ER 469, HL 1034
Rimmer (W T) & Co v Perth and Kinross Assessor 1965 SLT 406 1170
Ringeisen v Austria (No 1) (Ser A No 13, Judgment 16 July 1971) 1 EHRR 455, E Ct HR .. 32,
 45, 47
Ringeisen v Austria (No 2) (Ser A No 15, Judgment 22 June 1972) 1 EHRR 504, E Ct HR ... 20
Ringeisen v Austria (No 3) (Ser A No 16, Judgment 23 June 1973), 1 EHRR 513, E Ct HR .. 20
Rivière's Trade Mark, Re (1884) 26 Ch D 48 743
Robb v Logiealmond School Board (1875) 2 R 417 1186
Roberts v Avon Insurance Co [1956] 2 Lloyd's Rep 240 866
Roberts v Plaisted [1989] 2 Lloyd's Rep 341, CA 862, 866
Robertson v Adamson (1876) 3 R 978 1177
Robertson v Day (1879) 5 App Cas 63, PC 1132
Robertson v Thomson (1900) 3 F 5, 8 SLT 202 1126
Robertson Construction Co (Denny) Ltd v Taylor 1990 SCLR 304, 1990 SLT 698, OH ... 1001
Robertson's Judicial Factor v Robertson 1968 SLT 32, OH 1268
Robinson v Barton-Eccles Local Board (1883) 8 App Cas 798, HL 1140
Robinson v Currey (1881) 7 QBD 465, CA 743
Roger v J and P Cochrane & Co 1910 SC 1, 1909 2 SLT 277 1032
Roissard v Scott's Trustees (1897) 24 R 861, 4 SLT 322, OH 1018, 1019
Rojas 1967 SLT (Sh Ct) 24 269
Rose v Medical Invalid Life Assurance Co (1848) 11 D 151 818
Ross v British Railways Board 1972 SC 154, 1972 SLT 174 1033
Ross v Ross (1896) 23 R 802 .... 1031, 1037
Ross, Ex parte (1802) 6 Ves 802 707
Ross (James) & Son v Lord Advocate 1952 SLT (Notes) 77, OH 1131
Ross and Coulter v Inland Revenue 1948 SC (HL) 1, 1948 SLT 303 1185
Ross's Judicial Factor v Martin 1954 SC 18, 1954 SLT 49 1266
Rothes (Countess of) v Kirkcaldy Waterworks Comrs (1882) 9 R (HL) 108 1203
Rowlands (Mark) Ltd v Berni Inns Ltd [1986] QB 211, [1985] 3 All ER 473, CA 848, 850
Royal Bank of Scotland plc v Geddes 1983 SLT (Sh Ct) 32 .... 1002, 1004
Royal Bank of Scotland v Briggs 1982 SLT (Sh Ct) 46 1037
Royal Crown Derby Porcelain Co v Russell [1949] 2 KB 417, [1949] 1 All ER 749, CA ... 1159
Royal Liver Friendly Society, Re (1887) 35 Ch D 332 707
Royer (Case 48/75) [1976] ECR 497, [1976] 2 CMLR 619, ECJ 225, 226, 230, 232, 233, 234
Rubinat v Italy (Ser A No 89, Judgment 12 February 1985) 7 EHRR 512, E Ct HR 22, 96
Russell v Hereford Friendly Society (1899) CR Rep, Part A, 21 (Parliamentary Papers for 1900,
 vol 91) 738
Rust v Abbey Life Insurance Co Ltd [1979] 2 Lloyd's Rep 334, CA 818, 822
Rutili v Minister for the Interior (Case 36/75) [1975] ECR 1219, [1976] 1 CMLR 140,
 ECJ 9, 114, 115, 219, 232, 233, 234
Rutterford Ltd v Allied Breweries Ltd 1990 SCLR 186, 1990 SLT 249, OH 890

S

S 1979 SLT (Sh Ct) 37 1173
St Monance Magistrates v Mackie (1845) 7 D 582 1238
Sadlers' Co v Badcock (1743) 2 Atk 554 856
Saftar 1991 GWD 15-940, OH 110, 112, 271
Salabiaku v France (Ser A No 141A, Judgment 7 October 1988) 13 EHRR 379, E Ct HR 53
Salmon v Customs and Excise Comrs [1967] 2 QB 116, [1966] 3 All ER 971, CA 8
Salomon v A Salomon & Co Ltd [1897] AC 22, HL 1102
Salomon v Customs and Excise Comrs [1967] 2 QB 116, [1966] 3 All ER 871, CA 1152
Saltoun (Lord) v HM Advocate-General for Scotland (1860) 3 Macq 659, HL 1188
Salvin v James (1805) 6 East 571 834
Sanchez-Reisse v Switzerland (Ser A No 107, Judgment 21 October 1986) 9 EHRR 71, E Ct
 HR 37
Sangster's Trustees v General Accident Assurance Corpn Ltd (1896) 24 R 56, 4 SLT 163: 840, 841

References are to paragraphs

Sargeant v Butterworth (1907) 51 Sol Jo 429 705
Sattar v Secretary of State for the Home Department [1988] Imm AR 190, CA 198
Scheele v Immigration Officer, Harwich [1976] Imm AR 1, IAT 171
Schenk v Switzerland (Ser A No 140, Judgment 12 July 1988) 13 EHRR 242, E Ct HR 60
Schiesser v Switzerland (Ser A No 34, Judgment 4 December 1979) 2 EHRR 417, E Ct HR ..31
Schmidt v Secretary of State for Home Affairs [1969] 2 Ch 149, [1969] 1 All ER 904, CA ...105
Schmidt and Dalström v Sweden (Ser A No 21, Judgment 6 February 1976) 1 EHRR 637, E Ct
    HR 15, 76, 86
Scholfield v Vause (1886) 36 WR 170n, CA 697
Schtraks v Government of Israel [1964] AC 556, [1962] 3 All ER 529, HL 532, 1146
Schönenberger and Durmaz v Switzerland (Ser A No 137, Judgment 20 June 1988) 11 EHRR
    202, E Ct HR 69
Scott v Craig's Representative (1897) 24 R 462, OH, 4 SLT 173 1193
Scott v Handyside's Trustees (1868) 6 M 753 1038
Scott v McIntosh 1876 Guthries Sh Ct Cases (1st series) 211 743
Scott v Scottish Accident Insurance Co (1889) 16 R 630 827
Scott v Wilson (1893) 9 TLR 492 745
Scottish Amicable Heritable Securities Association Ltd v Northern Assurance Co (1883) 11 R
    287 ....802, 890, 912, 914
Scottish Cinema and Variety Theatres Ltd v Ritchie 1929 SC 350, 1929 SLT 323 1113
Scottish Co-operative Wholesale Society Ltd v Finnie 1937 SC 835, 1938 SLT 78 ....1245, 1248
Scottish Drainage and Improvement Co v Campbell (1889) 16 R (HL) 16 1203
Scottish Equitable Life Assurance Society v Buist (1877) 4 R 1076 ....846, 859
Scottish Marine Insurance Co v Turner (1853) 1 Macq 334, HL 879
Scottish Provident Institution v Cohen & Co (1886) 16 R 112 847
Scottish Residential Estates Development Co Ltd v Henderson 1989 GWD 22–932 (Sh Ct) . 1252
Scottish Union and National Insurance Co v Davis [1970] 1 Lloyd's Rep 1, CA 903
Scottish Widow's Fund and Life Assurance Society v Buist (1876) 3 R 1078 ....846, 859
Second Edinburgh and Leith Building Society v Aitken (1892) 19 R 603 738
Secretary of State for the Home Department v Campbell [1972] Imm AR 115, IAT 281
Secretary of State for the Home Department v Enorzah [1975] Imm AR 7, IAT 333
Secretary of State for the Home Department v Fardy [1972] Imm AR 192, IAT 333
Secretary of State for the Home Department v Gold and Gold [1985] Imm AR 66, IAT: 153, 336
Secretary of State for the Home Department v Grant [1974] Imm AR 64, IAT 263
Secretary of State for the Home Department v Jones [1978] Imm AR 161, IAT 255
Secretary of State for the Home Department v L G Patel [1972] Imm AR 227, IAT 287
Secretary of State for the Home Department v Mahli [1990] Imm AR 275, CA 342
Secretary of State for the Home Department v Mansour and Mansour [1985] Imm AR 1,
    IAT 120, 170, 198
Secretary of State for the Home Department v Oh [1972] Imm AR 236, IAT 293
Secretary of State for the Home Department v Otchere [1988] Imm AR 21, IAT 318
Secretary of State for the Home Department v Purushothaman [1972] Imm AR 176, IAT ...333
Secretary of State for the Home Department v Pusey [1972] Imm AR 240, IAT 281
Secretary of State for the Home Department v Rohr [1983] Imm AR 95, IAT 259
Secretary of State for the Home Department v Sanusi [1975] Imm AR 114, IAT 214
Secretary of State for the Home Department v Sarwar [1978] Imm AR 190, IAT 247
Secretary of State for the Home Department v Stillwaggon [1975] Imm AR 132, IAT ..155, 254
Secretary of State for the Home Department v Thaker [1976] Imm AR 114, IAT 181, 353
Secretary of State for the Home Department v Thirukumar [1989] Imm AR 402, CA 162,
                                                                              170, 318
Secretary of State for the Home Department v Two Citizens of Chile [1977] Imm AR 36, IAT . 318
Secretary of State for the Home Department v Udoh [1972] Imm AR 89, IAT 214
Secretary of State for the Home Department v Vethamony [1981] Imm AR 144, IAT 244
Secretary of State for the Home Department v 'X' (a Chilean citizen) [1978] Imm AR 73, IAT . 317
Secretary of State for the Home Department v Zalihe Huseyin [1988] Imm AR 129, CA 125
Secretary of State for Trade v Markus [1976] AC 35, [1975] 1 All ER 958, HL 1332
Securities and Investments Board v Financial Intermediaries Managers and Brokers Regulatory
    Association Ltd [1991] 4 All ER 398, [1991] 3 WLR 889 1422
Securities and Investments Board v Pantell SA [1990] Ch 426, [1989] 2 All ER 673 1324
Selkrig v Pitcairn and Scott (1808) Mor 'Insurance' Appendix no. 10 801
Seward v The 'Vera Cruz' (1884) 10 App Cas 59, HL 1198
Shah v Barnet London Borough Council [1983] 2 AC 309, [1983] 1 All ER 226, HL ...120, 342

References are to paragraphs

Shah v Secretary of State for the Home Department [1972] Imm AR 56, IAT 159
Shahib Al-Mehdawi v Secretary of State for the Home Department [1990] Imm AR 140,
    HL 351, 355
Shannon Realties Ltd v Ville de St Michel [1924] AC 185, PC 1123
Shaw v William Grant (Minerals) Ltd 1989 SLT 121, OH 1234
Sheffield Order of Druids Society, Re (1892) 8 TLR 389 697
Shetland Islands Council v BP Petroleum Development Ltd 1989 SCLR 48, 1990 SLT 82, OH: 1001
Shiells v Scottish Assurance Corpn Ltd (1889) 16 R 1014 ....875, 882, 883
Shop and Store Developments v Inland Revenue Comrs [1967] 1 AC 472, [1967] 1 All ER 42,
    HL 1103
Sickness and Accident Assurance Association Ltd v General Accident Assurance Corpn Ltd
    (1892) 19 R 977 ....818, 834, 836, 913, 914
Silver v United Kingdom (Ser A No 61, Judgment 25 March 1983) 5 EHRR 347, E Ct
    HR 44, 69, 78, 79, 81, 84
Simcock v Scottish Imperial Insurance Co Ltd (1902) 10 SLT 286, OH 853
Simpkin Marshall Ltd, Re [1959] Ch 229, [1958] 3 All ER 611 1196
Simpson v Selkirkshire Assessor 1948 SC 270, 1948, SLT 221, LVAC 1178
Simpson & Co v Thomson (1877) 5 R (HL) 40 ....894, 895, 901
Simson v Simson (1883) 10 R 1247 1263
Sinclair v HM Advocate (1890) 17 R (J) 38 577
Sinclair v National Coal Board 1963 SC 586, 1963 SLT 296 1183
Singh v Immigration Appeal Tribunal [1986] 2 All ER 721, [1986] 1 WLR 910, [1986] Imm AR
    352, HL 110, 205, 209, 210
Singh v Secretary of State for the Home Department 1990 SLT 300, OH 211, 345
Singh v Secretary of State for the Home Department 1991 GWD 9-547 ....112, 345
Skärby v Sweden (Ser A No 180B, Judgment 28 June 1990) 13 EHRR 90, E Ct HR 21, 44
Skoogström v Sweden (Ser A No 83, Judgment 2 October 1984) 7 EHRR 263, E Ct HR 96
Sloans Dairies v Glasgow Corpn 1977 SC 223, 1979 SLT 17 850
Sloley v Entry Clearance Officer, Kingston, Jamaica [1973] Imm AR 54, IAT 281
Smellie's Executrix v Smellie 1933 SC 725 , 1933 SLT 623 1008
Smith v Callander (1901) 3 F (HL) 28, 9 SLT 39 1189
Smith v Cammell Laird & Co Ltd [1940] AC 242, [1939] 4 All ER 381, HL 1182
Smith v Chambers' Trustees (1878) 5 R 97 (affd (1878) 5 R (HL) 151 1226
Smith v Galloway [1898] 1 QB 71, DC 703
Smith v Hughes [1960] 2 All ER 859, [1960] 1 WLR 830, DC 1115
Smith v Lerwick Harbour Trustees (1903) 5 F 680, 10 SLT 742 1239
Smith v Middleton 1972 SC 30, 1972 SLT (Notes) 3, OH 1032
Smith v Pearl Assurance Co [1939] 1 All ER 95, CA 909
Smyth v Allan (1813) 4 Pat 699, HL 1239
Soering v United Kingdom (Ser A No 161, Judgment 7 July 1989) 11 EHRR 439, E Ct
    HR 17, 21, 26, 575
Soering, Re [1988] Crim LR 307, DC 575
Soering, Re, Guardian, 22 November 1989, DC, [1989] CLY 1719 570
Sofi v Prudential Insurance Co Ltd (1990), CA (unreported) 876
Solicitors, Re a Firm of, The Times, 20 June 1991, CA 1395
Somchai Liangsiriprasert v United v United States Government [1991] 1 AC 225, [1990] 2 All
    ER 866, PC 577
Somervell's Trustee v Edinburgh Life Assurance Co 1911 SC 1069, 1911 2 SLT 87 1001,
                                                                        1012, 1014, 1016
Sons of Temperance Friendly Society 1926 SC 418, 1926 SLT 273 697
Southern Cross Assurance Co Ltd v Australian Provincial Assurance Co (1939) 39 SR (NSW)
    174 818
Spathari, The 1924 SC 182, 1924 SLT 126 ....858, 859, 860, 865
Spathari, The 1925 SC (HL) 6, 1925 SLT 322 ....858, 859, 860, 865
Spencer's Trustees v Ruggles 1981 SC 289, 1982 SLT 165 1268
Spiers v Ardrossan Canal Co (1827) 5 S 764 (NE 714) 1010
Spook Erection (Northern) Ltd v Kaye 1990 SLT 676, OH 1535
Sporrong and Lönnroth v Sweden (Ser A No 52, Judgment 23 September 1982) 5 EHRR 35,
    E Ct HR 88, 96
Standard Life Assurance Co v Weems (1884) 11 R (HL) 48 ....823, 835, 874, 875
Star Fire and Burglary Insurance Co Ltd v Davidson & Sons Ltd (1902) 5 F 83, 10 SLT
    282 ....818, 822, 823

References are to paragraphs

Stauder v City of Ulm (Case 26/69) [1969] ECR 419, [1970] CMLR 112, ECJ 9
Steadfast Insurance Co Ltd v F and B Trading Co Pty Ltd (1972) 46 ALJR 10 (Aust HC) ... 915
Stearns v Village Main Reef Gold Mining Co Ltd (1905) 21 TLR 236, CA 902
Steelclad Ltd v Iron Trades Mutual Insurance Co Ltd 1984 SC 71, 1984 SLT 304 916
Stephen v Scottish Boatowners Mutual Insurance Association 1986 SLT 234 OH (revsd 1989
    SLT 52, 2nd Div; 2nd Div upheld 1989 SLT 283, HL) 876, 878
Stephens v Cuckfield Rural District Council [1960] 2 QB 373, [1960] 2 All ER 716, CA ... 1164
Stepney Election Petition, Re, Isaacson v Durant (1886) 17 QBD 54 104
Stevenson v Hunter (1903) 5 F 761, 10 SLT 360, OH 1165
Stewart v Chapman [1951] 2 KB 792, [1951] 2 All ER 613, DC 1173
Stewart v Morison (1779) Mor 7080 858
Stewart v Oriental Fire and Marine Insurance Co Ltd [1985] QB 988, [1984] 3 All ER 777 .. 807
Stewart v Wilsons and Clyde Coal Co (1902) 5 F 120, 10 SLT 366 844
Stewart's Trustees v Whitelaw 1926 SC 701, 1926 SLT 400 1268
Stirling's Trustees 1977 SC 139, 1977 SLT 229 1271
Stirling's Trustees v Legal and General Assurance Society Ltd 1957 SLT 73, OH 1268
Stockton v Mason [1978] 2 Lloyd's Rep 430, CA 825, 828, 862
Stögmüller v Austria (Ser A No 9, Judgment 10 November 1969) 1 EHRR 155, E Ct HR ... 32
Stooke v Mutual Provident Alliance (1891) FS Cases 195, DC 703
Strachan v M'Dougle (1835) 13 S 954 847
Strasburger v Secretary of State for the Home Department [1978] Imm AR 165, IAT 296
Strathern v Padden 1926 JC 9, 1925 SLT 650 .... 1120, 1140
Stuart v Freeman [1903] 1 KB 47, CA 834
Sturrock v Rankin's Trustees (1875) 2 R 850 1270
Sudhakaran v Entry Clearance Officer, Madras [1976] Imm AR 3, IAT 152, 171
Sunday Times v United Kingdom (Ser A No 30, Judgment 26 April 1979) 2 EHRR 245, E Ct
    HR 17, 73, 74, 79, 81, 95
Sunday Times v United Kingdom, Times 27 November 1991, E Ct HR 74
Sunday Times v United Kingdom (No 2) (Ser A No 38, Judgment 6 November 1980) 3 EHRR
    317, E Ct HR 21
Sunshine Porcelain Potteries Pty Ltd v Nash [1961] AC 927, [1961] 3 All ER 203, PC 1191
Suruk Miah, Re (1976) Times, 4 February, CA 155
Suthendran v Immigration Appeal Tribunal [1977] AC 359, [1976] 3 All ER 611, [1977] Imm
    AR 44, HL 119, 146, 178, 205, 211, 340
Sutherland v Society of the Sun Fire Office (1852) 14 D 775 890
Sutherland's Trustee v Verschoyle 1968 SLT 43 1270
Sutter v Switzerland (Ser A No 74, Judgment 22 February 1984) 6 EHRR 272, E Ct HR . 49, 50
Sutton & Co v Ciceri & Co (1890) 17 R (HL) 40 1215
Swedish Engine Drivers' Union v Sweden (Ser A No 20, Judgment 6 February 1976) 1 EHRR
    617, E Ct HR 76, 84
Sweet (Inspector of Taxes) v Henderson 1921 SC 92, 1920 2 SLT 411 1034
Symington & Co v Union Insurance Society of Canton Ltd (1928) 45 TLR 181, CA 825
Symington's Executor v Galashiels Co-operative Store Co (1894) 21 R 371, 1 SLT 400 . 647, 725

T

Tahir v Immigration Appeal Tribunal [1989] Imm AR 98, CA 333, 345, 354
Tancred, Arrol & Co v Steel Co of Scotland Ltd (1890) 17 R (HL) 31 1215
Taylor v Allon [1966] 1 QB 304, [1965] 1 All ER 557, DC 818, 825
Taylor v John Lewis Ltd 1927 SC 891, 1927 SLT 625 1221
Taylor v Taylor (1871) 9 M 893 1191
Taylor's Executrices v Thom 1914 SC 79, 1913 2 SLT 337 1263
Tejpartap Singh Rehal v Secretary of State for the Home Department [1989] Imm AR 576,
    CA 119, 162, 170, 198
Tekle v Visa Officer, Prague [1986] Imm AR 71, IAT 316, 317
Templeton v Burgh of Ayr 1912 1 SLT 421, OH 1027
Tennant v Smith (1892) 19 R (HL) 1 1185
Tennent v Partick Magistrates (1894) 21 R 735, 1 SLT 594 .... 1119, 1129, 1136
Tesco Supermarkets Ltd v Nattrass [1972] AC 152, [1971] 2 All ER 127, HL 1511
Thameside Estates Ltd v Greater London Council (1979) 249 EG 347, 448, Lands Trib 1036
Theobald v Railway Passengers Assurance Co (1854) 10 Exch 45 830

References are to paragraphs

Thiem's Trustees v Collie (1899) 1 F 764, 7 SLT 4 1008
Thomas v Kelly (1888) 13 App Cas 506, HL 1178
Thompson v Thompson [1956] P 414, [1956] 1 All ER 603 1125
Thomson v Bent Colliery Co Ltd 1912 SC 242, 1912 1 SLT 53 1199
Thomson v Geekie (1861) 23 D 693 1007
Thomson v Mutter, Howey & Co 1913 SC 619, 1913 1 SLT 213 844
Thomson v Vernon 1983 SLT (Sh Ct) 17 1010
Thorogate and Royal Co-operative Collecting Society (1947) Reports of Selected Disputes
    referred to the Industrial Assurance Commissioner 1938–1949, 67 722
Thynne, Wilson and Gunnell v United Kingdom (Ser A No 190, Judgment 25 October 1990) 13
    EHRR 309, E Ct HR 35
Thynne, Wilson and Gunnell v United Kingdom (Applications 1178/85, 11978/86, 12009/86)
    13 EHRR 135, E Com HR 35
Tiffney v Bachurzewski 1983 SLT (Sh Ct) 45 1021
Tiffney v Bachurzewski 1984 SC 108, 1985 SLT 165 1019
Tombofa v Secretary of State for the Home Department [1988] Imm AR 400, CA 223, 232
Tough v Provincial Insurance Co of Canada (1875) 20 LCJ 168 825
Trans Barwil Agencies (UK) Ltd v John S Braid & Co Ltd 1989 SCLR 647, 1990 SLT 182,
    OH 1013, 1017, 1020, 1037
Travis v Nederland Life Insurance Co 104 Fed Rep 486 (1900) 818
Tre Traktörer Ab v Sweden (Ser A No 159, Judgment 7 July 1989) 13 EHRR 309, E Ct
    HR 54, 88
Turnbull & Co v Scottish Provident Institution (1896) 34 SLR 146, OH 853, 854
Turnbull's Trustees v Lord Advocate 1918 SC (HL) 88, 1918 1 SLT 112 1271
Turner (1869) 8 M 222 1186
Tweeddale (Marquis of) v Aytoun (1842) 4 D 862 1018
Tweeddale (Marquis of) Case (1793) 1 Anst 143 1163
Twentieth Century Equitable Friendly Society, Re [1910] WN 236 740
Tyrer v United Kingdom (Ser A No 26, Judgment 25 April 1978) 2 EHRR 1, E Ct HR .. 15, 26

U

Union Nationale des Entraîneurs et Cadres techniques Professionnels du Football v Heylens
    (Case 222/86) [1987] ECR 4097, [1989] 1 CMLR 901, ECJ 9
United Kingdom Life Assurance Co v Dixon (1838) 16 S 1277 847
United Law Clerks Society, Re [1947] Ch 150, [1946] 2 All ER 674 719
United States Diplomatic and Consular Staff in Tehran Case 1980 ICJR 3 4
United States Government v Bowe [1990] 1 AC 500, [1989] 3 All ER 315, PC 553, 562, 568
United States of America (Government of) v Jennings [1983] AC 624, [1982] 3 All ER 104, HL . 515
Unterpertinger v Austria (Ser A No 110, Judgment 24 November 1986) 13 EHRR 175, E Ct
    HR 57
Unwin v Hanson [1891] 2 QB 115, CA 1132
Uppal v United Kingdom (1981) 3 EHRR 391 115
Ure v Anderson (1834) 12 S 494 1240
Urquhart v Urquhart (1853) 1 Macq 658, HL 1190

V

Vacher & Sons Ltd v London Society of Compositors [1913] AC 107, HL 1135
Vainqueur José, The [1979] 1 Lloyd's Rep 557 883
Van der Leer v Netherlands (Ser A No 170, Judgment 21 February 1990) 12 EHRR 567, E Ct
    HR 21, 41
Van der Mussele v Belgium (Ser A No 70, Judgment 23 November 1983) 6 EHRR 163, E Ct
    HR 28, 86
Van der Sluijs, Zuiderveld and Klappe v Netherlands (Ser A No 78, Judgment 22 May 1984), E
    Ct HR 31
Van Droogenbroeck v Belgium (Ser A No 50, Judgment 24 June 1982) 4 EHRR 443, E Ct
    HR 28, 35
Van Duyn v Home Office (Case 41/74) [1974] ECR 1337, [1975] 1 CMLR 1, [1975] Ch 358,
    [1975] 3 All ER 190, ECJ 219, 232, 233, 235

References are to paragraphs

Van Marle v Netherlands (Ser A No 101, Judgment 26 June 1986) 8 EHRR 483, E Ct HR ... 88
Van Oosterwijk v Belgium (Ser A No 40, Judgment 6 November 1980) 3 EHRR 557, E Ct
    HR 15, 67
Vauxhall Estates Ltd v Liverpool Corpn [1932] 1 KB 733 1198
Veerabhadra v Secretary of State for the Home Department TH/1198/71/36 (unreported) ... 171
Verelst's Administratrix v Motor Union Insurance Co Ltd [1925] 2 KB 137 881
Visa Officer, Aden v Thabet [1977] Imm AR 75, IAT 333
Visa Officer, Islamabad v Mohd Altar [1979–80] Imm AR 141, IAT 353
Visa Officer, Islamabad v Shukar [1981] Imm AR 58, IAT 287
Visa Officer, Islamabad v Waheed Akhtar [1981] Imm AR 109, IAT 281
Visa Officer, Jerusalem v Awadallah [1978] Imm AR 5, IAT 171
Visa Officer, Karachi v Hussan Mohammad [1978] Imm AR 168, IAT 333, 353
Von Mehren & Co v Edinburgh Roperie and Sailcloth Co (1901) 4 F 232, 9 SLT 335 1217

                                              W

W v United Kingdom (Ser A No 121, Judgment 8 July 1987) 10 EHRR 29, E Ct HR 64
Waddell's Trustees v Crawford 1926 SC 654, 1926 SLT 457 .... 1023, 1025, 1029, 1031
Waddington v Miah [1974] 2 All ER 377, [1974] 1 WLR 683, HL 115
Wadia v Secretary of State for the Home Department [1977] Imm AR 92, IAT 333, 352
Walker v Lamb 1892 19 R (J) 50 1166
Walker (Peter) & Son (Edinburgh) Ltd v Church of Scotland General Trustees 1967 SLT 297: 1247
Walker Trustees v Lord Advocate 1912 SC (HL) 12, 1911 2 SLT 455 1112
Wallace v Earl of Eglinton (1835) 13 S 564 1018
Walsh v Griffiths-Jones [1978] 2 All ER 1002 1252
Wan Ping Nam v Federal German Republic Minister of Justice 1972 JC 43, 1972 SLT
    220 .... 549, 556, 562, 568
Warburton v Huddersfield Industrial Society [1892] 1 QB 817 613
Warburton v Loveland (1831) 2 Dow & Cl 480, HL 1121
Warburton v Loveland d Ivie (1828) 1 Hud & B 623, Ex Ch 1106
Warner v Metropolitan Police Comr [1969] 2 AC 256, [1968] 2 All ER 356, HL 1147
Warren v Henry Sutton & Co [1976] 2 Lloyd's Rep 276, CA 862
Watson and Belmann (Case 118/75) [1976] ECR 1185, [1976] 2 CMLR 552, ECJ 114, 219,
                                                                              222, 225, 230
Watson v Neuffert (1863) 1 M 1110 1215
Watson v Winch [1916] 1 KB 688 1196
Watson, Gow & Co Ltd v Glasgow Assessor 1910 SC 807, 1910 1 SLT 189 1172
Watson's Trustees v Watson 1913 SC 1133, 1913 2 SLT 172 1269
Watters v Hunter 1927 SC 310, 1927 SLT 232 1251
Wayne Tank and Pump Co Ltd v Employers' Liability Assurance Corpn Ltd [1974] QB 57,
    [1973] 3 All ER 825, CA 879
Weddell v Road Transport and General Insurance Co Ltd [1932] 2 KB 563 916
Weeks v Thames Water Authority (1980) 39 P & CR 208, [1979] JPL 774, Lands Trib 1036
Weeks v United Kingdom (Ser A No 114, Judgment 2 March 1987) 10 EHRR 293, E Ct
    HR 34, 35
Welch, Re, ex parte Trustees of Oddfellows Society (1894) 63 LJQB 524 707
Wemhoff v Germany (Ser A No 7, Judgment 27 June 1968) 1 EHRR 55, E Ct HR ... 30, 32, 46
West v National Motor and Accident Insurance Union Ltd [1955] 1 All ER 800, [1955] 1 WLR
    343, CA 875
West Derby Union v Metropolitan Life Assurance Society [1897] AC 647, HL 1165
West Midlands Police Chief Constable v Billingham [1972] 2 All ER 182, [1979] 1 WLR 747,
    DC 1132
West of England and South Wales District Bank, Re, ex parte Swansea Friendly Society (1879)
    11 Ch D 768 707
West of England Fire Insurance Co v Isaacs [1897] 1 QB 226, CA 898
Westminster Bank Ltd v Zang [1966] AC 182, [1966] 1 All ER 114, HL 1102
Westminster Fire Office v Glasgow Provident Investment Society (1888) 15 R (HL) 89 1187
What Every Woman Wants (1971) Ltd v Wholesale Paint and Wallpaper Co Ltd 1984 SLT 133: 1251
White v Cotton (1846) 8 D 872 853
White's Trustees v Whyte (1877) 4 R 786 1264
Whiteman v Sadler [1910] AC 514, HL 1165

References are to paragraphs

Whitwell v Autocar Fire and Accident Insurance Co (1927) 27 Ll L Rep 418 863
Wick Harbour Trustees v The Admiralty 1921 2 SLT 109, OH 1229
Wier, Re, ex parte Wier (1871) 6 Ch App 875 1164
Wight v Brown (1845) 11 D 459 853
Wilkie v Dunlop & Co (1834) 12 S 506 1229
Wilkinson v Wilkinson (1871) LR 12 Eq 604 1270
Will v Charles Will Ltd 1980 SLT (Notes) 37, OH 1032
Williams v Baltic Insurance Association of London Ltd [1924] 2 KB 282 857
Williams v Secretary of State for the Home Department [1972] Imm AR 207, IAT 281
Williams, Re, Wiles v Madgin [1985] 1 All ER 964, [1985] 1 WLR 905 1271
Williamson v Williamson's Trustee 1948 SLT (Notes) 72, OH 1008
Willows v Lewis [1981] TR 437, 125 Sol Jo 792 1212
Wilmot v Grace [1892] 1 QB 812 739
Wilson v Wilson 1939 SC 102, 1939 SLT 97 1191
Wimpey (George) & Co Ltd v British Overseas Airways Corpn [1955] AC 169, [1954] 3 All ER
   661, HL 1126
Windsor, Re (1865) 6 B & S 522 514
Winestone v Wolifson 1954 SC 77, 1954 SLT 153 1008
Winter v Inland Revenue Comrs [1963] AC 235, [1961] 3 All ER 855, HL 1188
Winterwerp v Netherlands (Ser A No 33, Judgment 24 October 1979) 2 EHRR 387, E Ct HR .. 41
Wishart v Wyllie (1853) 1 Macq 389, HL 1239
Wolf and Wolf v Forfar Potato Co 1984 SLT 100 890
Woodifield v Bond [1922] 2 Ch 40 1117
Woods v Co-operative Insurance Society 1924 SC 692, 1924 SLT 529 914
Woodward v Sarsons (1875) LR 10 CP 733 1175
Woolcott v Excess Insurance Co Ltd [1979] 1 Lloyd's Rep 231, CA 863, 870
Woolcott v Excess Insurance Co Ltd (No 2) [1979] 2 Lloyd's Rep 210 .... 862, 863
Woolcott v Sun Alliance and London Insurance Ltd [1978] 1 All ER 1253, [1978] 1 WLR
   493 ....822, 865
Wylie's Executrix v M'Jannet (1901) 4 F 195, 9 SLT 326 847
Wyndham Rather Ltd v Eagle, Star and British Dominions Insurance Co (1925) 21 Ll L Rep
   214, CA 825

X

X v United Kingdom (Ser A No 55, Judgment 18 October 1982) 5 EHRR 192, E Ct HR 41
X and Y v Netherlands (Ser A No 91, Judgment 26 March 1985) 8 EHRR 235, E Ct HR 62

Y

Yager and Guardian Assurance Co, Re (1912) 108 LT 38, DC 818, 863
Yanus Suleman Patel v Immigration Appeal Tribunal [1989] Imm AR 416, CA 207
Yau Yak Wah v The Home Office [1982] Imm AR 16, CA 333
Yeats v Yeats' Trustees (1833) 11 S 915 1229
Yeong Hoi Yuen v Secretary of State for the Home Department [1977] Imm AR 34, IAT ..241
Yew Bon Tew v Kenderaan Bas Mara [1983] 1 AC 553, [1982] 3 All ER 833, PC ...1190, 1192
Yorke v Yorkshire Insurance Co Ltd [1918] 1 KB 662 860
Yorkshire Dale Steamship Co Ltd v Minister of War Transport [1942] AC 691, [1942] 2 All ER
   6, HL 879
Yorkshire Insurance Co Ltd v Campbell [1917] AC 218, PC 875
Yorkshire Insurance Co Ltd v Nisbet Shipping Co Ltd [1962] 2 QB 330, [1961] 2 All ER
   487 ....894, 895, 900
Young v Baillie (1830) 8 S 624 1011
Young v Carmichael (1671) Mor 9636 1238
Young v Sun Alliance and London Insurance Ltd [1976] 3 All ER 561, [1977] 1 WLR 104,
   CA 838, 840

References are to paragraphs

Young, James and Webster v United Kingdom (Ser A No 44, Judgment 26 June 1981) 4 EHRR
    38, E Ct HR 73, 77, 78, 81, 84, 95

                                              Z

Zafar Igbal and Aris Sussain, Re [1982] NLJ 297, CA 172
Zamir v Secretary of State for the Home Department [1980] AC 930, [1980] 2 All ER 768, HL . 110
Zessa, Re [1983] AC 46, [1982] 2 All ER 513, HL 536
Zetland (Earl of) v Hislop (1882) 9 R (HL) 40 .... 1247, 1248
Zimmermann and Steiner v Switzerland (Ser A No 66, Judgment 13 July 1983) 6 EHRR 17, E
    Ct HR 47
Zurich General Accident and Liability Insurance Co Ltd v Leven 1940 SC 406, 1940 SLT
    350 .... 823, 858, 864, 865, 859, 860, 869, 875, 876
Zurich General Accident and Liability Insurance Co Ltd v Morrison [1942] 2 KB 53, [1942] 1
    All ER 529, CA 858, 859, 869

HUMAN RIGHTS IN EUROPE

PARA

1. **THE EUROPEAN CONVENTION FOR THE PROTECTION OF HUMAN RIGHTS AND FUNDAMENTAL FREEDOMS** 1

2. **THE RIGHTS AS DEVELOPED THROUGH THE JURISPRUDENCE OF THE EUROPEAN COURT OF HUMAN RIGHTS** 24
   (1) General 24
   (2) Life, Torture, Slavery etc 25
   (3) Liberty and Security of Person 29
   (4) Fair and Public Hearing 43
   (5) Retrospective Criminality 61
   (6) Family Life 62
       (a) The Right to Respect for Private and Family Life . . . 62
       (b) The Right to marry 71
   (7) Freedom of Thought, Conscience and Religion . . . 72
   (8) Freedom of Expression 73
   (9) Peaceful Assembly 75
   (10) Restrictions on Rights relating to Family, Thought, Conscience, Religion, Expression and Assembly 78
   (11) Availability of Effective Remedy 84
   (12) Discrimination 85
   (13) Rights to Property, Education and Free Elections . . . 87
   (14) The Impact of the Convention 94
   Appendix: Bibliography 97

The Author acknowledges with gratitude the research assistance given by Rhona Smith in the preparation of this title.

1. THE EUROPEAN CONVENTION FOR THE PROTECTION OF HUMAN RIGHTS AND FUNDAMENTAL FREEDOMS

1. Introduction. The term 'human rights' suggests certain rights which individuals, by virtue of their being human beings, are entitled to expect to be guaranteed to them. What these rights are or may be gives rise to constant jurisprudential debate[1]. A comprehensive and exhaustive universally applicable list of human rights is impossible to achieve. The content and expression of human rights will differ from state to state. Moreover, these will be determined by the political thinking prevalent in a state at a particular time, as well as by its social and economic development and the underlying culture of its society.

1 See eg J J Shestack 'The Jurisprudence of Human Rights' in *Human Rights in International Law: Legal and Policy Issues* (1984, ed T Meron) I, p 69; and M Cranston 'What are Human Rights' in *Human Rights Reader* (ed W Z Laqueur and B Rubin, 1980).

2. Historical overview before 1945. Until the twentieth century, a state's treatment of its own nationals was regarded as being its exclusive preserve and not susceptible to external review. Such treatment was not the domain of international law but of domestic law. One notable exception was slavery, which since 1815 was recognised by customary international law as an affront to humanity[1]. Minority groups — that is, persons of different religion, language or race from the majority group of the state in which they lived — were afforded certain rights by way of minority treaties.

At the conclusion of the 1914–18 war the opportunity was taken to establish a network of obligations *vis-à-vis* such minority groups[2]. These provided for the protection of life and liberty and religious freedom without discrimination on grounds of language, race or religion. Minority group nationals of the treaty parties enjoyed equality before the law with respect to civil and political rights and freedom of organisation for religious and educational purposes as well as provision by the state for the elementary instruction of their children in their own language in districts where a minority formed a considerable proportion of the population. The Council of the League of Nations was responsible for guaranteeing the 'rights'. The various provisions could not be modified without the assent of a majority of council members[3].

In addition to such minority rights, the Covenant of the League of Nations introduced the mandate system for those persons in ex-enemy colonies 'not yet able to stand by themselves in the strenuous conditions of the modern world'[4]. Under the mandate system, the power responsible for administering the mandate was obliged to guarantee freedom of conscience and religion.

Save for these instances, and the duty incumbent upon a state under international law to afford a certain minimum standard to foreigners in their territory[5] and certain regulations relating to the treatment of individuals in time of war[6], international regulation on the treatment of individuals was minimal prior to the 1939–45 war.

1 See eg the Protocol of the Conference Relative to the Abolition of the Slave Trade by France (Paris, 26 July 1815; 3 BFSP 195), reaffirmed in the International Convention with the object of securing the Abolition of Slavery and the Slave Trade (Geneva, 25 September 1926; 60 LNTS; TS 16 (1927); Cmd 2910). See also the International Convention for the Suppression of the Traffic in Women and Children (Geneva, 30 September 1921; 60 UNTS 416; TS 26 (1923); Cmd 1986); and the Convention on the Abolition of Slavery, the Slave Trade and Institutions and Practices similar to Slavery (Geneva, 7 September 1956; 266 UNTS 3; TS 59 (1957); Cmnd 257).
2 Minority treaties were established between the principal allies and associated powers and Poland, the Serbo-Croat-Slovene state, Romania, Greece and Czechoslovakia. Special minority clauses were to be found in the peace treaties concluded with Austria, Bulgaria, Hungary and Turkey, and also in the special conventions relating to Danzig, Upper Silesia and Memel Territory.
3 C A Macartney *National States and National Minorities* (1934); H L Jones 'National Minorities: A Case Study in International Protection' (1949) 14 LCP 559, 610–624; I L Claude *National Minorities: An International Problem* (1955); C H R Thornberry 'Is There a Phoenix in the Ashes — International Law and Minority Rights' (1980) 15 Texas ILJ 421.
4 Covenant of the League of Nations (Versailles, 28 June 1919; TS 4 (1919); Cmd 153), art 22.
5 See PUBLIC INTERNATIONAL LAW, vol 19, para 686.
6 See vol 19, paras 706–710.

3. Historical overview after the 1939–45 war. In the aftermath of the 1939–45 war, the treatment of individuals ceased to be regarded as exclusively a domestic issue and became a focus for international regulation. Since then there has been a plethora of international and regional organisations which give cognisance to human rights. The United Nations Charter expresses the determination of the member states to reaffirm faith 'in fundamental human rights, in the dignity and worth of the human person, in the equal rights of men and women . . .'[1]. Moreover, one of the purposes of the organisation is 'promoting and encouraging respect for human rights and for fundamental freedom for all without distinction as to race, sex, language or religion'[2]. The charter goes on to endorse these principles and pledge the United Nations as an organisation to promote universal respect for, and observance of, human rights and fundamental freedoms for all, regardless of race, sex, language or religion[3]; and pledges member states to take joint and separate action in co-operation with the organisation for the achievement of these purposes[4].

In addition, the trusteeship system[5], which replaces the mandate system of the League of Nations, had as one of its basic objectives the encouragement of respect for human rights and for the fundamental freedoms. The charter recognised the interests of the inhabitants of non-self-governing territories as paramount, the obligation to promote to the utmost the well-being of these territories being described as a 'sacred trust'[6]. However, the deficiency of the charter is that the language employed is vague and the commitment of member states is general and does not require to be fulfilled within a prescribed period of time[7].

1 Charter of the United Nations (San Francisco, 26 June 1946; TS 67 (1946); Cmd 7015), preamble.
2 Ibid, art 1, para 3.
3 Ibid, art 55(c).
4 Ibid, art 56.
5 The trusteeship system applied to eleven territories: ten former mandated territories and Somalia taken from Italy. Other than the Pacific islands, north of the equator, all are now independent states or have been incorporated into independent states.
6 Charter of the United Nations, art 73. The charter is addressed to member states and does not confer rights on individuals: see eg *Fuji v State of California* 28 Cal 2d, 242 P 2d 617 (1952), ILR 19 (1952) at 312; *Rice v Sioux City Memorial Park Cemetery Inc* 245 Iowa 147, 60 NW 2d 110 (1953), ILR 20 (1953) at 244; *Legal Consequences for States of the Continued Presence of South Africa in Namibia (South West Africa) notwithstanding Security Council Resolution 276* (Advisory Opinion) (1971) ICJR 16 at 56, 57, ICJ.
7 Charter of the United Nations, art 76(c).

4. The Universal Declaration of Human Rights.

The Universal Declaration of Human Rights[1] was one of the first instruments of the United Nations in the field of human rights. It was adopted on 10 December 1948 without a dissenting vote[2]. In the words of Mrs Eleanor Roosevelt[3] it is intended as 'a common standard of achievement for all peoples of all nations'. The declaration articulates in thirty articles wide-ranging rights of a political, civil, economic, social and cultural nature[4]. These rights are to be enjoyed by all persons without distinction of any kind, such as race, colour, sex, language, religion, political or other opinion, national or social origin, property, birth or other status[5]. It provides that the exercise of the rights should be subject only to lawful restrictions designed to secure 'due recognition and respect for the rights and freedoms of others and of meeting the just requirements of morality, public order and the general welfare in a democratic society'[6]. Although not legally binding[7], the declaration has served as a blueprint for constitutions adopted by newly independent states, and at least many of the rights, if not all, have crystallised into customary international law[8].

In August 1975, the Final Act of the Conference on Security and Co-operation in Europe in Helsinki was signed by representatives of thirty-five states including the United States and the USSR[9]. Section VII relates to respect for human rights and fundamental freedoms including the freedom of thought, conscience, religion or belief. The text of this Section is primarily a commitment to act in conformity with existing obligations in the field of human rights and it should not be over-exaggerated as innovative in respect of human rights, being as much related to security and disarmament as to human rights[10].

The rights and freedoms identified in the Universal Declaration of Human Rights have subsequently been more precisely defined in two separate covenants, both of which entered into force in 1976, the International Covenant on Civil and Political Rights[11], and the International Covenant on Economic,

Social and Cultural Rights[12]. The Covenant on Civil and Political Rights is concerned with those rights to be found in articles 1 to 21 of the declaration, whereas the Covenant on Economic, Social and Cultural Rights is concerned with the rights in articles 22 to 27 of the declaration. The former covenant requires contracting parties to fulfil their obligations immediately upon ratification, while the latter provides for the progressive achievement of the rights it seeks to guarantee.

1 Universal Declaration of Human Rights (Paris, 10 December 1948; UN 2 (1949); Cmd 7622); GA Resolution 217 A III, GAOR 3rd session, Pt I, Resolutions p 71.

2 Byleorussian SSR, Czechoslovakia, Poland, Ukranian SSR, USSR, Yugoslavia and Saudi Arabia abstained.

3 Mrs Roosevelt was the United States representative to the General Assembly and chairman of the United Nations Committee on Human Rights at the time the declaration was being drafted.

4 The rights include inter alia the right to life, liberty and security of person; freedom from slavery or servitude; the right to recognition as a person before the court; equality before the law; the right to an effective remedy by the competent national tribunal for acts violating the fundamental rights granted to a person by the constitution or by law; freedom from arbitrary arrest, detention or exile; the right to a fair and public hearing by an independent and impartial tribunal; the right to be presumed innocent until found guilty; the right to freedom of movement and residence; the right to nationality; the right to marry and found a family; the right to own property; the right to freedom of thought, conscience and religion; the right to freedom of opinion and expression; the right to social security; the right to work; the right to rest and leisure; the right to education; and the right to participate in the cultural life of the country.

5 Universal Declaration of Human Rights, art 2, which continues, 'Furthermore, no distinction shall be made on the basis of the political, jurisdictional or international status of the country or territory to which a person belongs, whether it be independent, trust, non self-governing or under any other limitation of sovereignty'.

6 Ibid, art 29(2).

7 Only General Assembly resolutions pertaining to procedural and budgetary matters are of a binding character.

8 See E Schwelb 'The Influence of the Universal Declaration of Human Rights on International and National Law' 1959 PASIL 217; J P Humphrey 'The United Nations Charter and the Universal Declaration of Human Rights' in *The International Protection of Human Rights* (1967, ed E Luard) ch 3; J P Humphrey 'The Universal Declaration of Human Rights' in *Human Rights: Thirty Years after the Universal Declaration* (1979, ed B G Ramcharan). See also the Proclamation of Tehran 1968 (UN sponsored International Conference on Human Rights), endorsing the declaration as 'an obligation for members of the international community' (23 GAOR A/CONF 32/41). See *Golder v United Kingdom* (Ser A No 18, Judgment 21 February 1975) 1 EHRR 524, E Ct HR, where the court invoked the declaration to assist in the interpretation of the Convention for the Protection of Human Rights and Fundamental Freedoms (Rome, 4 November 1950; TS 71 (1953); Cmd 8969); and *United States Diplomatic and Consular Staff in Tehran Case* 1980 ICJR 3 at 42 (para 91).

9 Final Act of the Conference on Security and Co-operation in Europe (Helsinki, 1 August 1975; 14 ILM (1975) 1292; Cmnd 6198). The Final Act is not legally binding but is rather a statement of intent: see eg H S Russell 'The Helsinki Declaration: Brobdingnag or Lilliput?' (1976) 70 AJIL 242, and O Schachter 'The Twilight Existence of Non-Binding International Agreements' (1977) 71 AJIL 296.

10 I Brownlie *Basic Documents on Human Rights* (2nd edn, 1981) p 320.

11 International Covenant on Civil and Political Rights (New York, 19 December 1966; TS 6 (1977); 6 ILM 368; Cmnd 6702).

12 International Covenant on Economic, Social and Cultural Rights (New York, 19 December 1966; TS 6 (1977); 6 ILM 360; Cmnd 6702).

5. International activity in the field of human rights. The list of international efforts to guarantee rights and freedoms is extensive. It includes inter alia conventions on genocide[1], on the abolition of forced labour[2], on discrimination in education[3], on employment policy[4], on racial discrimination[5], on apartheid[6], on discrimination against women[7], on torture and other cruel, inhuman or degrading treatment or punishment[8], and on the rights of the child[9].

1 Convention on the Prevention and Punishment of the Crime of Genocide (Paris, 9 December 1948; TS 58 (1970); Cmnd 4421). See R Lenkin *Axis Rule in Occupied Europe* (1944); N Robinson *The Genocide Convention* (1960); and *Genocide and Human Rights* (1982, ed J N Porter).
2 International Labour Organisation Convention No 105 on the Abolition of Forced Labour (Geneva, 25 June 1957; 320 UNTS 291; Cmnd 328). The International Labour Organisation was initially established in 1919 and was expanded in 1949.
3 Convention against Discrimination in Education (Paris, 15 December 1960; TS 44 (1962); 429 UNTS 93; Cmnd 1760). The convention emanated from the United Nations Educational, Scientific and Cultural Organisation, which was established in 1945.
4 International Labour Organisation Convention No 122 on Employment Policy (Geneva, 9 July 1964; TS 65 (1967); 569 UNTS 65; Cmnd 3360).
5 International Convention on the Elimination of All Forms of Racial Discrimination (New York, 7 March 1966; TS 77 (1969); Cmnd 4108). See N Lerner *The UN Convention on the Elimination of All Forms of Racial Discrimination: A Commentary* (1970).
6 International Convention on the Suppression and Punishment of the Crime of Apartheid (New York, 30 November 1973; 13 ILM 50).
7 Convention on the Elimination of All Forms of Discrimination against Women (New York, 18 December 1979; 19 ILM 33; TS 2 (1989); Cm 643).
8 Convention against Torture and other Cruel, Inhuman or Degrading Treatment or Punishment (New York, 4 February 1985; TS 107 (1991); Cm 1775; 23 ILM (1984) 1027, 24 ILM (1985) 535); European Convention for the Prevention of Torture and Inhuman or Degrading Treatment or Punishment (Strasbourg, 26 November 1987; Misc 5 (1988); ETS 126; Cm 339): see para 27 below.
9 Convention on the Rights of the Child 1989 (New York, 20 November 1989; Misc 17 (1991); Cm 1668; 28 ILM (1989) 1448) (not yet in force).

6. The European Convention on Human Rights. Simultaneous with the efforts at international regulation of human rights and freedoms, steps were taken to guarantee such rights and freedoms at a regional level. The most notable regional convention is the European Convention for the Protection of Human Rights and Fundamental Freedoms[1] drawn up by the ten original member states of the Council of Europe[2]. It was signed on 4 November 1950 and entered into force in September 1953[3].

Section I of the convention seeks to guarantee what may be characterised as civil and political rights, namely the right to life[4]; freedom from torture, inhuman or degrading treatment or punishment[5]; freedom from slavery or servitude or forced or compulsory labour[6]; the right to liberty and security of person and freedom from detention except by procedures prescribed and administered by law[7]; a right to the fair administration of justice[8] and protection against the retroactivity of the criminal law[9]; the right to respect for private and family life, home and correspondence[10]; the right to marry and to found a family[11]; the right to freedom of thought, conscience and religion[12]; the right to freedom of expression[13]; the right to freedom of peaceful assembly and to freedom of association with others[14]; the right to an effective remedy in the event of any right or freedom set forth in the convention being violated[15]; and the right to enjoy all such rights and freedoms contained in the convention 'without discrimination on any ground such as sex, race, colour, language, religion, political or other opinion, national or social origin, association with a national minority, property, birth or other status'[16].

Rights and freedoms additional to those in the convention are guaranteed by subsequent Protocols. The rights of property, education and free elections conducted by secret ballot are the subject of Protocol 1[17]. The Fourth Protocol provides that no one should be deprived of liberty solely on an inability to fulfil a contractual obligation and protects the right of free movement, the right of a person to choose his or her residence and the right to enter his or her national state[18]. The Sixth Protocol calls for the abolition of the death penalty in peace time[19], and the Seventh Protocol seeks to protect certain rights of aliens lawfully resident in the territory of a state and those convicted of a criminal offence[20].

Article 1 of the convention places an obligation on the contracting parties to the convention to secure to everyone within their jurisdiction the rights and freedoms defined in Section I of the convention[21]. Article 1 only comes into operation when taken in conjunction with the provisions contained in Section I. A violation of article 1 follows automatically from, but adds nothing to, a breach of those provisions: 'when the court has found such a breach, it has never held that article 1 has been violated'[22].

In the case of *Ireland v United Kingdom*, the European Court of Human Rights took the opportunity 'to clarify the nature of the engagements placed under [the court's] supervision'[23]. The court stated that:

> 'unlike international treaties of the classic kind, the Convention comprises more than reciprocal engagements between Contracting States. It creates, over and above a network of mutual, bilateral undertakings, objective obligations which, in the words of the Preamble, benefit from a "collective enforcement" . . . By substituting the words "shall secure" for the words "undertake to secure" in the text of Article 1, the drafters of the Convention also intended to make it clear that the rights and freedoms set forth in Section I would be directly secured to anyone within the jurisdiction of the Contracting States. That intention finds a particular faithful reflection in those instances where the Convention has been incorporated into domestic law'[24].

The protection afforded by the convention is not absolute. The rights and freedoms are restricted by limitations which may be justifiably invoked to serve the needs of public order, public security and the rights and freedoms of others[25]. Such limitations are legitimate if prescribed by law and necessary in a democratic society. The right to freedom of expression, the right to freedom of peaceful assembly and association and the right to the enjoyment of all rights and freedoms guaranteed in the convention without discrimination are not designed to prevent the contracting parties from imposing restrictions on the political activity of aliens[26]. Nor is anything in the convention to be 'interpreted as implying for any State, group or person any right to engage in any activity or perform any act aimed at the destruction of any of the rights and freedoms set forth herein or at their limitation to a greater extent than is provided for in the Convention'[27]. However, the restrictions permitted by the convention are not to be applied for any purpose other than those for which they have been prescribed[28].

The impact of the convention as will be illustrated below[29] has been to identify specific deficiences in the domestic legal systems of Contracting States, that is, systems which generally conform to the standards enunciated in the convention and which are representative of the 'common heritage of political traditions, ideals, freedom and the rule of law'[30].

---

1 Convention for the Protection of Human Rights and Fundamental Freedoms (Rome, 4 November 1950; 213 UNTS 221; TS 71 (1953); Cmd 8969).

2 There are now twenty-five members of the Council of Europe: Austria, Belgium, Cyprus, Czechoslovakia, Denmark, Finland, France, Germany, Greece, Hungary, Iceland, Ireland, Italy, Liechtenstein, Luxembourg, Malta, the Netherlands, Norway, Portugal, San Marino, Slovak Federal Republic, Spain, Sweden, Switzerland, Turkey and the United Kingdom. All except Czechoslovakia, Hungary and Slovak Federal Republic have ratified the convention. On admission to the Council of Europe (independent of the convention), every member of the council must accept the principles of the rule of law and of the enjoyment by all persons within its jurisdiction of human rights and fundamental freedoms: Statute of the Council of Europe (London, 5 May 1949; TS 51 (1949); Cmd 7778), art 3.

3 The Council of Europe was established in 1949 with a view to being the vehicle on which to promote European political integration. However, the organisation has achieved most fame for the production and supervision of the convention. It was the first organisation which attempted to regulate human rights at a regional level. Since then other regional organisations have also

turned to the protection of human rights and freedoms and have promulgated conventions in furtherance of this. These include inter alia the American Convention on Human Rights (San José, Costa Rica, 22 November 1969; (1970) 9 ILM 673; YBHR 390), which addresses the protection of civil and political rights but seeks also to promote the progressive realisation of economic, social, scientific and cultural rights; and the African Charter on Human and Peoples' Rights (Banjul, June 1981; 21 ILM (1982) 59).

4 See the Convention for the Protection of Human Rights and Fundamental Freedoms, art 2, and para 25 below. Section I comprises arts 2–18.

5 See ibid, art 3, and para 26 below.

6 See ibid, art 4, and para 28 below.

7 See ibid, art 5, and paras 29 ff below.

8 See ibid, art 6, and paras 43 ff below.

9 See ibid, art 7, and para 61 below.

10 See ibid, art 8, and paras 62 ff below.

11 See ibid, art 12, and para 71 below.

12 See ibid, art 9, and para 72 below.

13 See ibid, art 10, and paras 73, 74, below.

14 See ibid, art 11, and paras 75/77 below.

15 See ibid, art 13, and para 84 below.

16 See ibid, art 14, and para 85 below.

17 Convention for the Protection of Human Rights and Fundamental Freedoms, Protocol 1 (Paris, 20 March 1952; ETS 9; TS 46 (1954); Cmd 9221): see paras 87 ff below. The protocol entered into force on 18 May 1954.

18 Convention for the Protection of Human Rights and Fundamental Freedoms, Protocol 4 (Strasbourg, 16 September 1963; ETS 46; Misc 6 (1964); Cmnd 2309). The protocol entered into force on 2 May 1968.

19 Convention for the Protection of Human Rights and Fundamental Freedoms, Protocol 6 (Strasbourg, 28 April 1983; ETS 114; 22 ILM 538; 5 EHRR 167). The protocol entered into force on 1 March 1985.

20 Convention for the Protection of Human Rights and Fundamental Freedoms, Protocol 7 (Strasbourg, 22 November 1984; 7 EHRR 1), which entered into force on 1 November 1988, but the United Kingdom is not a signatory. The other protocols relate to procedural matters pertaining to the Council of Europe institutions charged with supervision of the application of the convention. Protocol 2 (Strasbourg, 6 May 1963; TS 104 (1970); Cmnd 4551), which entered into force on 21 September 1970, confers upon the European Court of Human Rights the competence to give advisory opinions: see para 23 below. Protocol 3 (Strasbourg, 6 May 1963; TS 106 (1970); Cmnd 4552), Protocol 5 (Strasbourg, 20 January 1966; TS 48 (1972); Cmnd 4963) and Protocol 8 (Vienna, 19 March 1985; Misc 9 (1985); Cmnd 9556), modify the text of the convention itself and are now incorporated into the text, the latest text being that issued in May 1990 (H (90) Strasbourg). Protocol 9 on the individual's right to bring a case before the court (ETS 140) was open for signature on 6 November 1990. The United Kingdom is a party to Protocol 1 with reservation, has signed but not ratified Protocol 4 and is not a signatory to either Protocol 6 or Protocol 9.

21 Convention for the Protection of Human Rights and Fundamental Freedoms, art 1. Section I comprises arts 2–18, which specify the rights provided by the convention.

22 *Ireland v United Kingdom* (Ser A No 25, Judgment 18 January 1978) 2 EHRR 25 at 103, E Ct HR, at para 238.

23 *Ireland v United Kingdom*, at para 239.

24 *Ireland v United Kingdom*, at para 239. For the relationship of the convention to domestic law, see para 8 below.

25 See paras 78 ff below.

26 Convention for the Protection of Human Rights and Fundamental Freedoms, art 16.

27 Ibid, art 17.

28 Ibid, art 18.

29 See paras 24 ff below. See also paras 94–96 below.

30 Convention for the Protection of Human Rights and Fundamental Freedoms, preamble.

7. Social and economic rights. Social and economic rights come within the ambit of the European Social Charter[1], which entered into force on 26 February 1965.

The European Social Charter does not place an obligation on contracting states to guarantee the rights and principles which it articulates. Part I lists nineteen rights and principles which are to be regarded as 'a declaration of the aims which each Contracting Party will pursue by all appropriate means'[2]:

(1) everyone shall have the opportunity to earn his living in an occupation freely entered upon;

(2) all workers have the right to just conditions of work;

(3) all workers have the right to safe and healthy working conditions;

(4) all workers have the right to fair remuneration sufficient for a decent standard of living for themselves and their families;

(5) all workers and employers have the right to freedom of association in national or international organisations for the protection of their economic and social interests;

(6) all workers and employers have the right to bargain collectively;

(7) children and young persons have the right to a special protection against the physical and moral hazards to which they are exposed;

(8) employed women, in case of maternity, and other employed women as appropriate, have the right to special protection of their work;

(9) everyone has the right to appropriate facilities for vocational guidance with a view to helping him choose an occupation suited to his personal aptitude and interests;

(10) everyone has the right to appropriate facilities for vocational training;

(11) everyone has the right to benefit from any measures enabling him to enjoy the highest possible standard of health attainable;

(12) all workers and their dependents have the right to social security;

(13) anyone without adequate resources has the right to social and medical assistance;

(14) everyone has the right to benefit from social welfare services;

(15) disabled persons have the right to vocational training, rehabilitation and resettlement, whatever the origin and nature of their disability;

(16) the family as a fundamental unit of society has the right to appropriate social, legal and economic protection to ensure its full development;

(17) mothers and children, irrespective of marital status and family relations, have the right to appropriate social and economic protection;

(18) the nationals of any one of the contracting parties have the right to engage in any gainful occupation in the territory of any one of the others on a footing of equality with the nationals of the latter, subject to restrictions based on cogent economic or social reasons;

(19) migrant workers who are nationals of a contracting party and their families have the right to protection and assistance in the territory of any other contracting party[3].

1 European Social Charter (Turin, 18 October 1961; TS 38 (1965); 529 UNTS 89; Cmnd 2643). The United Kingdom signed and ratified the charter on 11 July 1962. This charter is, of course, a different document from the EC Social Charter, currently the subject of much debate within the European Communities.

2 European Social Charter, art 20, para 1(a).

3 For the procedural provisions of the charter and the supervision machinery, which is flexible and leaves much discretion to contracting parties, see M Evans in *The European Social Charter, Fundamental Rights* (ed J W Bridge, D Lasok, R O Plender and D L Perrott); D Harris 'The European Social Charter' (essay, 1973).

8. Relation of the convention to United Kingdom domestic law. The Convention for the Protection of Human Rights and Fundamental Freedoms is not part of United Kingdom domestic law[1]. The convention is no different from any other international treaty to which the United Kingdom is a party, and international treaty law becomes incorporated into domestic law only by a deliberate act of the domestic legislature[2]. The United Kingdom adopts a dualistic approach to international treaty law[3]. Accordingly, an obligation to incorporate into domestic law can itself be an obligation only at the international law level[4]. Although the United Kingdom courts will endeavour to construe domestic law so as to conform to the convention[5], if a rule of domestic law should be contrary to the convention then the domestic law will prevail so far as the domestic court is concerned. In these circumstances, liability would be incurred at the domestic level. Notwithstanding comments by Lord Denning[6], the Scottish courts have expressed a more rigid dualistic approach[7]. In *Kaur v Lord Advocate*, Lord Ross stated:

> 'In my opinion the Convention cannot be regarded in any way as part of the municipal law of Scotland. I accept that the Convention sets forth a number of very important principles relating to human rights, but the provisions of the Convention have never entered into the law of Scotland. As I understand it, the law of Scotland is to be found partly in enactments by a body with legislative power and partly in the common law. A Treaty or a Convention is not part of the law of Scotland unless and until Parliament has passed legislation giving effect to the treaty provisions'[8].

Lord Ross was even unable to identify with the position adopted by English judges that the convention was relevant when construing a statute. He found the position 'extremely difficult to comprehend'[9]. Accordingly, Lord Ross held:

> 'If the Convention does not form part of the municipal law, I do not see why the Court should have regard to it at all. It was His Majesty's Government in 1950 which was a High Contracting Party to the Convention. The Convention has been ratified by the United Kingdom.... Under our constitution, it is the Queen in Parliament who legislates and not Her Majesty's Government, and the Court does not require to have regard to acts of Her Majesty's Government when interpreting the law.... The government may be ... bound, but I do not see how or why the Courts should be bound by the Convention'[9].

Lord Ross's assertion was endorsed in 1985 by the Inner House of the Court of Session in *Moore v Secretary of State for Scotland*, where it was stated:

> 'In our view Lord Ross was perfectly correct in holding that the Convention plays no part in our municipal law so long as it has not been introduced into it by legislation'[10].

However, in *Re Budh Singh*[11], Lord Morrison made the following statement:

> 'The second ground upon which it was maintained that the decision was unreasonable was that it proceeded upon the basis of a standard generally adopted by the Home Office which involved no proper respect for family life. Article 8 of the European Convention of Human Rights was referred to as laying down the principle involved but I regard it as unnecessary for me to determine whether the Court is bound by the provisions of this Article: if the policy of the Home Office is one which ignores the obvious humanitarian principle of respect for family life, it would in my view be unreasonable and subject to the Court's review. But the fact that, as indicated in the Minister's letter, there must be something out of the ordinary in regard to family circumstances to justify departure from the general practice of removing illegal entrants does not in my opinion involve any contravention of the humanitarian principle founded on. In this connection I agree with observations made with regard to Article 8 of the Convention in the context of illegal entry, by the European Court of Human Rights in the case of *Abdulaziz, Cabales and Balkandali*[12] ... dealing with an issue similar to that raised in the present case'.

Here there is at least a recognition that a principle enshrined in an article of the convention is one which should be reflected in Home Office policy, admittedly not because it is contained in the convention but rather because of its obvious humanitarian basis. Nevertheless Lord Morrison not only made reference to a judgment of the European Court of Human Rights but utilised the judgment handed down in that case to assist him in the case before him[13]. However, in *Lord Advocate v Scotsman Publishers Ltd* Lord Templeman observed:

'In my opinion, it is for Parliament to determine the restraints on freedom of expression which are necessary in a democratic society. The courts of this country should follow any guidance contained in a statute. If that guidance is inconsistent with the requirements of the Convention then that will be a matter for the Convention authorities and for the United Kingdom government. It will not be a matter for the courts'[14].

Lord Templeman placed the responsibility for legislation conforming with the convention exclusively on Parliament: no mention is made of the courts construing legislation so as to conform with the convention. In *T F v Ravenscraig Hospital Management Committee and Managers*, on a patient's right of appeal from a sheriff in mental health matters, the sheriff principal, who was upheld by the Inner House, observed that the appeal rights:

'may well have been introduced as a result of certain pressures created when the European Court of Human Rights decided that under its fundamental convention those detained in hospital should have [a] right of recourse to judicial review. However, . . . there was nothing in the material presented to me to suggest what degree of judicial review would have been required to comply with the said convention. . . . I find in effect that I cannot get much assistance from the judgments of the European Courts of Human Rights which I was asked to consider, for the effect of the new appeal procedures must be extracted from the actual terms of the legislation'[15].

Acknowledgment of the convention was noted by Lord Murray in *Martin v City of Edinburgh District Council*, when he identified that the case was:

'not about the legality or morality of apartheid. Prima facie South African apartheid would not be legally enforceable in Scotland, if only because of its apparent incompatibility with the [race relations legislation] and with article 14 of the European Convention on Human Rights'[16].

In *Ralston v HM advocate*, where the fair hearing guarantee contained in article 6 of the convention was raised, the High Court of Justiciary, while acknowledging that the convention was not part of Scottish municipal law, stated that:

'even if article 6 of the European Convention on Human Rights is regarded as showing the sort of rights which every citizen enjoys, there was no question in the present case of the appellant being denied a fair and public hearing by the court'[17].

The Scottish decisions thus reflect a difference in approach to the convention from that taken in the English courts, but the trend would appear to suggest a slight softening in attitude from the rigid dualistic approach of Lord Ross in *Kaur v Lord Advocate*. The English courts have consistently been more sympathetic in the cognisance they are prepared to give to the convention whilst still maintaining an essentially dualistic approach[18]. Accordingly, the English judicial approach can be summarised as being that legislation should be construed as far as possible to be in conformity with the convention unless to do so would clearly be contrary to the intention of Parliament, with the convention being employed as guidance[19].

1 The position is stated by J E S Fawcett *The Application of the European Convention on Human Rights* (1969) at p 17: '. . . the Convention has not been given statutory form, either directly or by reference, in the United Kingdom. Since the ratification of the Convention is plainly not an exercise by the Crown of its prerogative rights to conduct war and make peace, and since its provisions have not been incorporated into a United Kingdom statute, they are not justiciable in any Court in the United Kingdom'.

2 To allow otherwise would enable the Crown to legislate without consulting Parliament. The authoritative case is *The Parlement Belge* (1879) 4 PD 129. See Sir R Philimore at 154.

3 The two schools of thought which have predominated on the relationship of international law to domestic law are the monistic and the dualistic. Monists essentially maintain that there is one legal order of which municipal law and international law are part. In contrast, dualists regard international law and domestic law as being separate and unrelated to each other both actually and potentially. See PRIVATE INTERNATIONAL LAW, vol 19, para 652.

4 Ibid. See also W Finnie 'The European Convention on Human Rights, Domestic Status' (1980) 25 JLSS 434.

5 It is a presumption of statutory interpretation that Parliament does not intend to infringe international law: see inter alia *Salmon v Customs and Excise Comrs* [1967] 2 QB 116, [1966] 3 All ER 971, CA; *Post Office v Estuary Radio Ltd* [1968] 2 QB 740, [1967] 3 All ER 679, CA; *National Smokeless Fuels Ltd v Inland Revenue Comrs* [1986] STC 300. As to the convention, 'The court can and should take the Convention into account. They should take it into account whenever interpreting a statute which affects the rights and liberties of the individual. It is to be assumed that the Crown, in taking its part in legislation, would do nothing which was in conflict with treaties. So the court should now construe the Immigration Act 1971 [c 77] so as to be inconformity with a Convention and not against it': *R v Secretary of State for the Home Department, ex parte Bhajan Singh* [1976] QB 198 at 207, [1975] 2 All ER 1081 at 1083, CA, per Lord Denning MR. See also Lord Denning MR in *R v Chief Immigration Officer, Heathrow Airport, ex parte Salamat Bibi* [1976] 3 All ER 843 at 847, [1976] 1 WLR 979 at 984, CA: '. . . if there is any ambiguity in our statutes or uncertainty in our law, then these courts can look at the convention as an aid to clear up the ambiguity and uncertainty, seeking always to bring them into harmony with it. Furthermore, when Parliament is enacting a statute or the Secretary of State is framing rules, the court will assume that they had regard to the provisions of the convention and intended to make the enactment accord with the convention, and will interpret them accordingly. But I would dispute altogether that the convention is part of our law. Treaties and conventions do not become part of our law until they are made law by Parliament'. In this case Lord Denning made it clear what the position should be between the convention and a domestic legislative measure, and showed that the weight of the convention should be moral force only. In an earlier unreported case, *Birdi v Secretary of State for Home Affairs* 11 February 1975 (cited in *R v Secretary of State for the Home Department, ex parte Bhajan Singh* [1976] QB 198, [1975] 2 All ER 1081, CA), Lord Denning had stated that if an Act of Parliament did not conform to the convention he might be inclined to hold it invalid. However, in the *Bhajan Singh* case at 207 and at 1083 Lord Denning characterised the foregoing remark as 'a very tentative statement' and one which 'went too far'. See also *R v Secretary of State for the Home Department, ex parte Brind* [1991] 1 AC 696, [1991] 1 All ER 720, HL.

As to the status of the convention in other member states of the Council of Europe, see A Z Drzemczewski *European Human Rights Convention in Domestic Law: A Comparative Study* (1983), and A Z Drzemczewski 'The Authority of the Findings of the Organs of the European Human Rights Convention in Domestic Courts' in *Legal Issues of European Integration* 1979/1, p 1.

6 See note 5 above.

7 This may indeed be the one area of international law where Scotland and England have adopted a different stance.

8 *Kaur v Lord Advocate* 1980 SC 319 at 324, 1981 SLT 322 at 327, OH.

9 1980 SC 319 at 328, 1981 SLT 322 at 329, OH.

10 *Moore v Secretary of State for Scotland* 1985 SLT 38 at 41.

11 *Re Budh Singh* 13 July 1988 (Lexis transcript).

12 *Abdulaziz, Cabales and Balkandali v United Kingdom* (Ser A No 94, Judgment 28 May 1985) 7 EHRR 471, E Ct HR.

13 Lord Morrison said: 'In para 68 of the judgment [in the *Abdulaziz* case 7 EHRR 471 at 498] the European Court [of Human Rights] observed that "The duty imposed by Article 8 [of the convention] cannot be considered as extending to a general obligation . . . to respect the choice by married couples of the country of their matrimonial residence and to accept the non-national spouses for settlement in that country". The policy applied by the Home Office whereby only exceptional circumstances are held to justify departure from the practice of removing illegal entrants whether or not they are married could not be described as one which involves a lack of respect for family life, unless there existed a general obligation such as the European Court rejected. There is nothing in the petitioner's family circumstances which is not of the ordinary, and the immigration officer was therefore entitled to apply the general policy of removal to this case'.

14 *Lord Advocate v Scotsman Publications Ltd* 1989 SLT 705 at 710, HL.

15 *T F v Ravenscraig Hospital Management Committee and Managers* 1988 SCLR 327 at 331, 1987 SLT (Sh Ct) 76 at 78.

16 *Martin v City of Edinburgh District Council* 1988 SCLR 90 at 91, 1988 SLT 329 at 330, OH.

17   *Ralston v HM Advocate* 1988 SCCR 590 at 608, 1989 SLT 474 at 478.

18   Recent judicial pronouncements on the relation of the convention with English law include *Allgemeine Gold- und Silberscheideanstalt v Customs and Excise Comrs* [1980] QB 390 at 403, [1980] 2 All ER 137 at 141, 142, CA, per Lord Denning MR; *R v Immigration Appeal Tribunal, ex parte Ali Ajmal* [1982] Imm AR 102 at 107, CA; *R v Secretary of State for the Home Department, ex parte Kirkwood* [1984] 2 All ER 390 at 394, 395, [1984] 1 WLR 913 at 918, 919; *R v Secretary of State for the Home Department, ex parte McAvoy* [1984] 3 All ER 417 at 421, [1984] 1 WLR 1408 at 1414; *Re K D (a minor)* [1988] AC 806 at 823, [1988] 1 All ER 577 at 587, HL, per Lord Oliver of Aylmerton; *Girishkumar Samabhai Patel v Secretary of State for the Home Department* [1989] Imm AR 246 at 252; *Re Lonrho plc* [1990] 2 AC 154 at 208, [1989] 2 All ER 1100 at 1116, HL; *R v Bow Street Magistrates' Court, ex parte Choudbury* 1990 Times, 9 April; *Champion v Gwent Chief Constable* [1990] 1 All ER 116 at 125, [1990] 1 WLR 1 at 14, HL, per Lord Ackner.

19   Note must now be taken of the statement of Lord Bridge of Harwich in *R v Secretary of State for the Home Department, ex parte Brind* [1991] 1 AC 696 at 748, [1991] 1 All ER 720 at 723, HL, where he refuted the contention that when a statute confers upon an administrative authority a discretion capable of being exercised in a way which infringes any basic human right protected by the convention, it may similarly be presumed that the legislative intention was that the discretion should be exercised within the limits which the convention imposes. Although recognising the 'considerable persuasive force' of the submission, he nevertheless maintained that 'where Parliament has conferred on the executive an administrative discretion without indicating the precise limits within which it must be exercised, to presume that it must be exercised within Convention limits would be to go far beyond the resolution of an ambiguity'.

9. Human rights and European Community law.

On a number of occasions the European Court of Justice has stated that the principles enshrined in the Convention for the Protection of Human Rights and Fundamental Freedoms constitute the human rights of all citizens of the member states of the European Community:

> '... respect for fundamental rights forms an integral part of the general principles of law protected by the Court of Justice. The protection of such rights, whilst inspired by the constitutional traditions common to the Member States, must be ensured within the framework of the structure and objectives of the Community'[1].

There now exists a fairly extensive jurisprudence in which the European Court of Justice has made reference to human rights[2]. While that court has recognised that the principles enshrined in the convention are reflected in Community law, it has not found the convention *per se* to be part of Community law. It is not competent for the European Court of Justice to consider the compatibility of domestic legislation with the convention; nor is the institutional machinery of the convention applicable to Community law[3]. However, the court's cognisance has been complemented and supplemented by the other Community institutions. In 1976 the EC Commission submitted a report to the European Parliament[4], and the following year a joint declaration was issued by the Parliament, the EC Council and the EC Commission, stressing:

> 'the prime importance they attach to the protection of human rights, as derived in particular from the constitutions of the Member States and the European Convention for the Protection of Human Rights and Fundamental Freedoms'[5].

The preamble of the Single European Act speaks of:

> 'the fundamental rights recognised in the constitutions and laws of the Member States, in the Convention for the Protection of Human Rights and Fundamental Freedoms and the European Social Charter ...'[6],

and of a:

> 'responsibility incumbent upon Europe to aim at speaking ever increasingly with one voice and to act with consistency and solidarity in order more effectively to protect its common interests and independence, in particular to display the principles of democracy and compliance with the law and with human rights to which they are attached ...'[7].

The EC Commission is currently seeking to secure the Community's accession to the convention[8].

1 Case 11/70 *Internationale Handelsgesellschaft mbH v Einfuhr- und Vorratsstelle für Getreide und Futtermittel* [1970] ECR 1125 at 1134, [1972] CMLR 255 at 283, ECJ, where the court endorsed its recognition in Case 26/69 *Stauder v City of Ulm* [1969] ECR 419 at 425, [1970] CMLR 112 at 119, ECJ, that 'the fundamental rights enshrined in the general principles of Community law and protected by the Court' was a general principle of Community law.

2 Case 4/73 *J Nold, Kohlen- und Baustoffgroßhandlung v EC Commission* [1974] ECR 491 at 505, [1974] 2 CMLR 338 at 352, 353, ECJ; Case 36/75 *Rutili v Minister for the Interior* [1975] ECR 1219 at 1232, [1976] 1 CMLR 140 at 155, ECJ; Case 44/79 *Hauer v Land Rheinland-Pfalz* [1979] ECR 3727 at 3745, [1980] 3 CMLR 42 at 64, ECJ; Case 98/79 *Pecastaing v Belgium* [1980] ECR 691 at 716, [1980] 3 CMLR 685 at 708, ECJ; Case 63/83 *R v Kirk* [1984] ECR 2689, [1984] 3 CMLR 522, ECJ; Case 22/84 *Johnston v Royal Ulster Constabulary Chief Constable* [1986] ECR 1651, [1986] 3 CMLR 240, ECJ; Case 152/84 *Marshall v Southampton and South-West Hampshire Area Health Authority (Teaching)* [1986] ECR 723, [1986] 1 CMLR 688, ECJ; Case 222/86 *Union Nationale des Entraîneurs et Cadres techniques Professionnels du Football v Heylens* [1987] ECR 4097, [1989] 1 CMLR 901, ECJ; Case 262/88 *Barber v Guardian Royal Exchange Assurance Group* [1990] 2 CMLR 513, ECJ.

3 See *Confédération Française Démocratique du Travail v European Communities* [1979] 2 CMLR 229, Eur Com HR, where an allegation submitted by a French trade union to the commission was declared inadmissible as the European Community was not a party to the convention.

4 *The Protection of Fundamental Rights in the European Community* Bull EC Supp 5/76.

5 OJ C103, 5.4.77, p 1.

6 Single European Act, preamble, 3rd para.

7 Ibid, preamble, 5th para.

8 EC Commission's programme for 1990, Bull EC Supp 1.90 at p 12. See also the Commission's report *Accession of the Communities to the European Convention on Human Rights* Bull EC Supp 2/79, and the favourable response of the European Parliament to accession in OJ C127, 21.5.79, p 69. For further literature on the relationship of Community law and the convention, see inter alia M Zulug 'Fundamental Rights and the Law of the European Communities' (1971) 8 CML Rev 446; U Scheuner 'Fundamental Rights in European Community Law and in National Constitutional Law' (1975) 12 CML Rev 171; A G Toth *The Individual and Community Law, Legal Protection of Individuals in the European Communities* (1978), ch 3; A Z Drzemczewski 'The Authority of the Findings of the Organs of the European Human Rights Convention in Domestic Courts' *Legal Issues of European Integration* 1979/1, p 1; M Mendelson 'The European Court of Justice and Human Rights' (1981) YBEL 1; J McBride and L N Brown 'The United Kingdom, the European Community and the European Convention on Human Rights' (1981) YBEL 167; S Ghandi 'Interaction between the Protection of Fundamental Rights in the European Economic Community and under the European Convention on Human Rights' *Legal Issues of European Integration* 1981/2, p 1; P Pescatore 'The Context and Significance of Fundamental Rights in the Law of the European Communities' (1981) 2 Human Rights LJ 295; P D Degtaglou 'Human Rights and European Community Law' (1981) Tul LR 295; A Z Drzemczewski 'The Domestic Application of the European Human Rights Convention as European Community Law' (1981) 30 ICLQ 118; M A Davies 'The Protection of Fundamental Rights in the Community Legal Order' (1985) 10 EL Rev 398; J Schwarze 'The Administrative Law of the Community and the Protection of Human Rights' (1986) CML Rev 401; R R Churchill and N G Foster 'Double Standards in Human Rights? The Treatment of Spanish Fishermen by the European Community' (1987) 12 EL Rev 430; N G Foster 'The European Court of Justice and the European Convention for the Protection of Human Rights' (1987) 8 Human Rights LJ 245; L Collins *European Community Law in the United Kingdom* (4th edn, 1990), pp 8–13; and H G Schermers 'The European Communities bound by Fundamental Human Rights' (1990) 27 CML Rev 249.

10. Enforcement of the convention. It is the supervisory mechanism responsible for overseeing the application of the Convention for the Protection of Human Rights and Fundamental Freedoms which has given credence to the effectiveness of the convention as an instrument furthering the protection of human rights.

Three organs participate in the application of the convention: the European Commission of Human Rights[1], the European Court of Human Rights[2] (both organs having been established for the purpose of ensuring 'the observance of the engagements undertaken by the High Contracting Parties'[3]), and the Committee of Ministers[4].

1 For the composition of the Commission, see para 11 below, and for its powers and functions, see para 14 below. The Commission is established under the Convention for the Protection of Human Rights and Fundamental Freedoms (Rome, 4 November 1950; 213 UNTS 221; TS 71 (1953); Cmd 8969), art 19(1).

2 For the composition of the court, see para 12 below, and for its jurisdiction, see para 17 below. The court is established under ibid, art 19(2).

3 Ibid, art 19.

4 The Committee of Ministers is the executive organ of the Council of Europe, and consists of a representative (normally a member of the government) from each member state of the Council. Within the institutional framework of the Council of Europe there is a Consultative Assembly, but this is primarily a deliberative organ and as such does not participate in the overseeing of the convention.

11. Composition of the European Commission of Human Rights.

The European Commission of Human Rights is made up of commissioners, the number being equal to the number of High Contracting Parties to the Convention for the Protection of Human Rights and Fundamental Freedoms[1]. No two members of the Commission may be nationals of the same state[1].

Commissioners are elected by the Committee of Ministers by an absolute majority of votes[2] for a term of six years, and are eligible for re-election[3]. The office is a part-time office, and the majority of Commissioners hold other appointments, such as that of university professor and legal adviser[4]. Commissioners, who sit in their individual capacity[5], must be of high moral character and must either possess the qualifications required for appointment to high judicial office or be persons of recognised competence in national or international law[6].

The seat of the Commission is in Strasbourg, and its official languages are English and French. The Commission has drawn up its own rules of procedure in accordance with the convention[7].

1 Convention for the Protection of Human Rights and Fundamental Freedoms (Rome, 4 November 1950; 213 UNTS 221; TS 71 (1953); Cmd 8969), art 20, para 1 (renumbered by Protocol 8). As to the protocols, see para 6 above.

2 Ibid, art 21, para 1, under which a list of candidates is drawn up by the Bureau of the Consultative Assembly, each group of the Representatives of the High Contracting Parties submitting three candidates of whom two at least are its nationals.

3 Ibid, art 22, para 1. Elections are staggered, and are held every three years.

4 Commissioners may not hold any position which is incompatible with their independence and impartiality as members of the Commission or the demands of the office: ibid, art 23 (amended by Protocol 8).

5 Ibid, art 23.

6 Ibid, art 21, para 3 (added by Protocol 8).

7 Ibid, art 36. The current Revised Rules of Procedure (which take account of the entry into force of Protocol 8) were adopted by the Commission on 4 September 1990 and entered into force on 1 October 1990.

12. Composition of the European Court of Human Rights.

The European Court of Human Rights[1] consists of a number of judges equal to the members of the Council of Europe[2]. No two judges may be nationals of the same state[3]. Judges are elected by the Consultative Assembly from a list of persons nominated by member states of the Council of Europe[4]. They are elected for nine-year terms, and may be re-elected[5]. Candidates must be of high moral character and must either possess the qualifications required for appointment to high judicial office or be jurisconsults of recognised competence[6]. The appointment to the office of judge is a part-time one[7], but the judges, who sit in their individual capacities, are prohibited from holding any position which is incompatible with their independence and impartiality as members of the court or the demands of the office of judge[8].

In accordance with the Convention for the Protection of Human Rights and Fundamental Freedoms[9], the court has drawn up its own rules and determined its own procedure. The initials Rules of the Court, which were adopted in 1959, were the subject of various amendments and were completely revised on 24 November 1982. The new text came into force on 1 January 1983. Amendments to the rules were adopted on 26 January 1989 and 23 May 1991.

The seat of the court is in Strasbourg, and its official languages are English and French.

1 The court became operational in 1955 after the necessary eight declarations recognising the compulsory jurisdiction of the court (see the Convention for the Protection of Human Rights and Fundamental Freedoms (Rome, 4 November 1950; 213 UNTS 221; TS 71 (1953); Cmd 8969), art 46, and art 56, para 1) had been lodged. No case could be brought before the court before the first election of its members (art 56, para 2), which took place on 21 January 1959. The first cases brought before the court were *Lawless v Ireland (No 1)* (Ser A No 1, Judgment 14 November 1960) 1 EHRR 1, E Ct HR; *Lawless v Ireland (No 2)* (Ser A No 2, Judgment 7 April 1961) 1 EHRR 13, E Ct HR; *Lawless v Ireland (No 3)* (Ser A No 3, Judgment 1 July 1961) 1 EHRR 15, E Ct HR. The United Kingdom did not make a declaration recognising the court until 14 January 1966. All members of the Council of Europe have now made such declarations.
2 Convention for the Protection of Human Rights and Fundamental Freedoms, art 38.
3 Ibid, art 38. As a rule each member of the Council of Europe has had a national as a judge, but a Canadian national, Mr Ronald Macdonald, is the judge in respect of Liechtenstein.
4 Ibid, art 39, para 1, under which each member state nominates three candidates, of whom two at least must be its nationals.
5 Ibid, art 40, para 1. Provision for staggered elections is made in art 40, para 3 (added by Protocol 5). As to the protocols, see para 6 above.
6 Ibid, art 39, para 3.
7 The court is not in permanent session.
8 Convention for the Protection of Human Rights and Fundamental Freedoms, art 40, para 7 (added by Protocol 8).
9 Ibid, art 55.

13. Supervision of application of the convention. The supervisory machinery of the Convention for the Protection of Human Rights and Fundamental Freedoms is tripartite in structure, involving the participation of the three organs identified above:

(1) the European Commission of Human Rights considers the admissibility of petitions; promotes friendly settlements; and, if necessary, gives opinions on whether petitions identify convention violations;

(2) the European Court of Human Rights gives final and binding judgments on cases referred to it by the Commission or by a Contracting Party concerned; and

(3) the Committee of Ministers gives final and binding decisions on cases which cannot be referred to the court (namely those cases arising before the establishment of the court or subsequently involving a contracting party which has not recognised the court's jurisdiction) or on cases which for one reason or another are not referred to the court[1].

One possible measure identified for improving and accelerating the procedure under the convention has been the idea of merging the Commission and the court into a single full-time body. This was the subject of a report by the Committee of Experts for the Improvement of Procedures for the Protection of Human Rights (DH-PR) to the Steering Committee for Human Rights (CDDH)[2]. Such a radical far-reaching reform proposal has proved controversial. The existing supervisory machinery is overburdened and a merger might provide a remedy to the problems which currently beset the system — not least that ensuing from the prominence which would be given to judicial means for the enforcement of human rights at international level[3].

1 See the Convention for the Protection of Human Rights and Fundamental Freedoms (Rome, 4 November 1950; 213 UNTS 221; TS 71 (1953); Cmd 8969), art 32.
2 H (89) 2 Strasbourg, 2 May 1989, set out in 11 EHRR 412.
3 The DH-PR considered the arguments for and against merger as well as the principal features of the system which could result therefrom. No single and decisive argument for or against a merger emerged, and the report concluded with the DH-PR requesting the CDDH '(a) to decide whether or not it is desirable, at the present time, to pursue consideration of the possibility of merging the Commission and Court; (b) if appropriate, to provide the DH-PR with specific guidelines for such further consideration (eg that the DH-PR should set out the skeleton of a single Court system, examine methods of implementation, and at a suitable moment seek information on the budgetary implications of the matters under discussion)'. In October 1988 the CDDH instructed the DH-PR to draw up the detailed structure of such a system.

14. The European Commission of Human Rights. All petitions alleging a violation of the Convention for the Protection of Human Rights and Fundamental Freedoms are considered by the European Commission of Human Rights as to their admissibility. A petition may be either an inter-state complaint as provided for in article 24 of the convention[1] or an individual petition as provided for in article 25[2].

The right of individual petition is dependent upon the state against which the alleged violation is being lodged having made a declaration under article 25 recognising the Commission's competence to receive such a petition[3]. A declaration under article 25 is optional[4], and may be made for a specific period[5].

The Commission sits in plenary session, in Chambers and in committees[6]. Chambers of at least seven members may be established to deal with petitions submitted under article 25 if such petitions can be dealt with on the basis of established case law or raise no serious question affecting either the interpretation or application of the convention[7]. The Commission may set up committees, each composed of at least three members, with the power, exercisable by a unanimous vote, to declare inadmissible or strike from its list of cases a petition submitted under article 25, when such a decision can be taken without further examination[8]. A Chamber or a committee may at any time relinquish jurisdiction in favour of the plenary Commission, which may also order the transfer to it of any petition referred to a Chamber or committee[9]. However, only the plenary Commission has the competence to examine applications made under article 24 (inter-state petitions) or to bring a case before the European Court of Human Rights as provided by article 48(a)[10].

The Commission is competent to entertain a petition only after all domestic remedies have been exhausted, according to the generally recognised rules of international law, and within a period of six months from the date on which the final decision was taken[11].

1 Any High Contracting Party may refer to the Commission, through the Secretary General of the Council of Europe, any alleged breach of the provisions of the convention by another Contracting Party: Convention for the Protection of Human Rights and Fundamental Freedoms (Rome, 4 November 1950; 213 UNTS 221; TS 71 (1953); Cmd 8969), art 24. To date eighteen such applications have been lodged with the Commission involving six situations: (1) Applications 175/56, 299/57 *Greece v United Kingdom* 2 YBHR 182, 186 (concerning Cyprus); (2) Application 788/60 *Austria v Italy* 4 YBHR 116, 6 YBHR 796; (3) Applications 3321–3323, 3344/67 *Denmark, Norway, Sweden and the Netherlands v Greece* 11 YBHR 690, 12 YBHR 1; (4) Applications 5310/71, 5451/72 *Ireland v United Kingdom* 41 Coll HR 1; (5) Applications 6780/74, 6950/75 *Cyprus v Turkey* 2 Decisions and Reports 125; and (6) Applications 9940–9944/82 *France, Norway, Denmark, Sweden and the Netherlands v Turkey* 6 EHRR 241. Only one came before the court: *Ireland v United Kingdom* (Ser A No 25, Judgment 18 January 1978) 2 EHRR 25, E Ct HR.

2 The Commission may receive petitions addressed to the Secretary General of the Council of Europe from any person, non governmental organisation or group of individuals claiming to be the victim of a violation by one of the High Contracting Parties of the rights under the convention, providing the High Contracting Party against which the complaint is lodged has declared that it recognises the competence of the Commission to receive such petitions, and a High Contracting Party which make such a declaration undertakes not to hinder in any way the effective exercise of this right: Convention for the Protection of Human Rights and Fundamental Freedoms, art 25, para 1.

3 Ibid, art 25, para 1.

4 All Contracting Parties have made declarations under ibid, art 25.

5 Ibid, art 25, para 2. The United Kingdom made its initial declaration under art 25 on 14 January 1966. Its current declaration, which commenced on 14 January 1991, is for five years. It excludes issues arising in respect of the Isle of Man and the British Virgin Islands.

6 Ibid, art 20, paras 2, 3 (added by Protocol 8). As to the protocols, see para 6 above.

7 Ibid, art 20, para 2 (as so added).

8 Ibid, art 25, para 3 (as so added).

9 Ibid, art 25, para 4 (as so added).

10 Ibid, art 25, para 5 (as so added). For art 48(a), see para 17 below.

11 Ibid, art 26. For the relevant international law, see *Ambatielos Arbitration* (1956) 12 UNRIAA 83: 'Local remedies embrace not only judicial courts and tribunals but also the use of the procedural facilities which municipal law makes available to litigants before such courts and tribunals. It is the whole system of legal protection, as provided by municipal law'. See also *Finnish Shipowners Arbitration* (1934) 3 UNRIAA 1479; *Interhandel Case* (Preliminary Objections) 1959 ICJR 6 at 26–29; 1961 Harvard Draft Convention on the International Responsibility of States for Injuries to Aliens, art 19; International Law Commission Draft Articles on State Responsibility (1978) 2 YBILC (Pt II) 78; Rules regarding International Claims (Foreign and Commonwealth Office) 1971, r VII. There is no obligation to exhaust 'ineffective' remedies: r VIII. See also *Mavrommatis Palestine Concessions Case* (Jurisdiction) (1924) PCIJ Ser A No 2 at p 12; *Finnish Shipowners Arbitration* (1934) 3 UNRIAA 1479; *Electricity Co of Sofia and Bulgaria Case* (1939) PCIJ Ser A/B No 77 at 79. See generally PUBLIC INTERNATIONAL LAW, vol 19, para 744; and Application 214/56 *De Becker v Belgium* 2 YBHR 214 at 233, 234, where the Commission recognised the concept of a continuing violation and so circumvented the six-months rule.

15. Lodging a petition. The European Commission of Human Rights will not consider any petition submitted under article 25 of the Convention for the Protection of Human Rights and Fundamental Freedoms which is anonymous[1], or is substantially the same as an issue which has already been examined by the Commission, or which has been submitted to another procedure of international investigation or settlement and if it contains no relevant new information[2]. Also inadmissible will be any petition submitted under article 25 which the Commission considers to be incompatible with the provisions of the convention, manifestly ill-founded, or an abuse of the right of petition[3].

The Commission can deal only with complaints pertaining to the rights and freedoms guaranteed by the convention and protocols. Complaints to the Commission can relate only to matters which are the responsibility of a public authority of the state concerned. The Commission is not a court of appeal from national courts, and it cannot annul or change their decisions. Nor can the Commission intervene directly on behalf of the complainant with the national authority concerned. All petitions must be intimated in writing to the Commission's Secretary. The petition must identify the state against which the complaint is being made, give a brief outline of the complaint or complaints, an indication of the right or rights and/or freedom or freedoms allegedly violated, a list of the remedies which have been attempted in the state concerned, and a list of the official decisions concerning the case, including the date of each decision, the court or authority which took it and brief details of the decision itself. The Secretary in his response may indicate how the Commission has interpreted the convention in previous cases of a similar nature. In the event of the Secretary perceiving an obvious obstacle to the admission of the complaint, the complainant will be advised of this. However, the Secretary is precluded from giving advice about the law and practices of the state against which the complaint is made. If it appears from the necessary correspondence with the Secretary that the complaint is one which may constitute a formal application or petition to the Commission, then the complainant if wishing to proceed will be provided with the necessary form on which to submit the application[4]. At this stage complainants are advised, if possible, to instruct a lawyer to represent their case[5]. Legal aid, although it may be available at a later stage in the proceedings[6], cannot be granted at the time of lodging the application.

The Commission deals with the admissibility of petitions in accordance with its own Rules of Procedure[7]. The Commission meets in camera[8], and its decision is final. Decisions of the Commission are taken by a majority of the members present and voting[9]. If an application is rejected, there is no appeal against that decision[10].

In the event of the Commission accepting a petition, its function then is to examine the facts of the case and the arguments of the parties and to place itself at the disposal of the parties with a view to attaining a friendly settlement[11]. The emphasis is on obtaining a friendly settlement[12]. A friendly settlement is to have regard to the general interest as well as to the interests of the parties to the dispute[13]. In the event of a friendly settlement being achieved the Commission must issue a brief report containing a description of the parties, their representatives and advisers; a statement of the facts; and the terms of the settlement reached[14]. This report is then transmitted to the states concerned, to the Committee of Ministers and to the Secretary General of the Council of Europe for publication[15].

In the event of the Commission failing to reach a friendly settlement, it draws up a report of the case and gives its opinion as to whether the facts reveal a violation of one or more rights and freedoms by the state concerned[16]. The report, which may contain the individual opinions of members of the Commission[16], is transmitted to the Committee of Ministers and to the states concerned, who are not at liberty to publish the report or disclose its contents even to the applicant[17]. In transmitting the report to the Committee of Ministers the Commission may make such proposals as it thinks fit[18]. At this stage, two possibilities arise: the case may be sent within three months to the European Court of Human Rights in accordance with article 48[19], or the Committee of Ministers will decide by a two-thirds majority on whether there has been a violation of the convention[20].

There are no rules in either the convention or the Rules of Procedure as to which organ, the court or the Committee of Ministers, should have the task of determining the final decision[21]. Contracting Parties possibly favour the forum of the Committee of Ministers because of the confidentiality and flexibility of the proceedings. Practice leads to the conclusion that if the Commission is either unanimous or feels by a large majority that the convention has not yet been violated, the case will be referred to the Committee of Ministers. However, the complexity or the importance of the issues may be such as to favour a referral to the court in cases where there is no strong conviction that the convention has been violated[22]. A close decision of the Commission finding for a violation of the convention is likely to lead to a referral to the court.

---

1 Convention for the Protection of Human Rights and Fundamental Freedoms (Rome, 4 November 1950; 213 UNTS 221; TS 71 (1953); Cmd 8969), art 27, para 1(a).
2 Ibid, art 27, para 1(b).
3 Ibid, art 27, para 2. Also inadmissible, of course, will be any petition submitted before local remedies have been exhausted: art 26. After it has accepted a petition submitted under art 25, the Commission may decide by a two-thirds majority to reject the petition if, in the course of its examination, it finds that the existence of one of the grounds for non-acceptance provided for in art 27 has been established, and in such a case the decision must be communicated to the parties:

art 29 (amended by Protocol 8). As to the protocols, see para 6 above. The Commission may at any stage of the proceedings decide to strike a petition out of its list where the circumstances lead to the conclusion that (1) the applicant does not intend to pursue his petition, or (2) the matter has been resolved, or (3) for any other reason established by the Commission, it is no longer justified to continue the examination of the petition: art 30, para 1 (substituted by Protocol 8). However, the Commission must continue the examination if respect for human rights as defined in the convention so requires: art 30, para 1 proviso (as so substituted). If the Commission decides to strike out the petition after having accepted it, it must draw up a report containing a statement of the facts and the decision to strike out, with reasons, and must transmit the report to the parties, as well as to the Committee of Ministers for information; and the Commission may publish it: art 30, para 2 (as so substituted). The Commission may decide to restore a petition to its list if it considers that the circumstances justify such a course: art 30, para 3 (as so substituted).

4   The Rules of Procedure of the European Commission of Human Rights 1990 provide that any application under art 24 or art 25 of the convention must be submitted in writing, signed by the applicant or the applicant's representative: r 43, para 1. Where an application is submitted by a non-governmental organisation or a group of individuals, it must be signed by the persons competent to represent it, and the Commission must determine any question as to whether the signatories are so competent: r 43, para 2. Where applicants are represented in accordance with r 32, a power of attorney or written authorisation must be supplied by their representative or representatives: r 43, para 3.

The application form must set out (1) the applicant's name, age, occupation and address; (2) the name, occupation and address of any representative; (3) the name of the High Contracting Party against which the complaint is made; (4) the object of the application and the provision of the convention alleged to have been violated; (5) a statement of the facts and arguments; (6) any relevant documents and, in particular, the decisions, whether judicial or not, relating to the object of the application: r 44, para 1(a)–(f).

Applicants must furthermore (a) provide information enabling it to be shown that the conditions laid down in art 26 of the convention have been satisfied; (b) indicate whether they have submitted their complaints to any other procedure of international investigation or settlement; (c) indicate in which of the official languages (English or French) they wish to receive the Commission's decisions; (d) indicate whether they do or do not object to their identity being disclosed to the public; and (e) declare that they will respect the confidentiality of the proceedings before the Commission: r 44, para 2(a)–(e).

Failure to comply with these requirements may result in the application not being registered by the Commission. The date of introduction of the application will in general be considered to be the date of the first communication from the applicant setting out, even summarily, the object of the application, but the Commission may for good cause decide that a different date be considered. Applicants must keep the Commission informed of any change of their address and of all circumstances relevant to the application: see r 44, paras 4, 5.

5   This is not, however, a prerequisite for lodging an application.

6   See para 19 below.

7   See the Rules of Procedure of the European Commission of Human Rights 1990, rr 45–52.

8   Convention for the Protection of Human Rights and Fundamental Freedoms, art 33.

9   Ibid, art 34 (substituted by Protocol 8), which applies save where in accordance with art 20, 3rd para, unanimity is required and art 29 where a two-thirds majority is required.

10   See *Van Oosterwijk v Belgium* (Ser A No 40, Judgment 6 November 1980) 3 EHRR 557, E Ct HR, where the court refused to consider the merits of the case on the ground that domestic remedies had not been fully exhausted. This was in spite of the Commission declaring the petition admissible and identifying unanimously a violation of art 8 of the convention and a violation of art 12 by seven votes to three.

11   Ibid, art 28, para 1 (substituted by Protocol 8), provides that on accepting a petition the Commission must (1) with a view to ascertaining the facts, undertake together with the parties' representatives an examination of the petition and, if need be, an investigation, for the effective conduct of which the states concerned must furnish all necessary facilities, after an exchange of views with the Commission; (2) at the same time place itself at the disposal of the parties concerned with a view to securing a friendly settlement on the basis of respect for human rights as defined in the convention. For the procedure to be employed after admission of the application, see the Rules of Procedure of the European Commission of Human Rights 1990, ch V.

12   On statistical data available for 1989, the Commission adopted seven reports in respect of a friendly settlement: Application 12748/87 *Grabemann v Germany*, E Com MR.

13   See eg *Tyrer v United Kingdom* (Ser A No 26, Judgment 25 April 1978) 2 EHRR 1 at 7, 8, E Ct HR, at paras 24–27.

14   Rules of Procedure of the European Commission of Human Rights 1990, r 57, para 1.

15 Convention for the Protection of Human Rights and Fundamental Freedoms, art 28, para 2 (substituted by Protocol 8). The report must also be sent to the applicant: Rules of Procedure of the European Commission of Human Rights 1990, r 57, para 3.
16 Convention for the Protection of Human Rights and Fundamental Freedoms, art 31, para 1 (as so substituted). See also Rules of Procedure of the European Commission of Human Rights 1990, r 60.
17 Convention for the Protection of Human Rights and Fundamental Freedoms, art 31, para 2.
18 Ibid, art 31, para 3.
19 For ibid, art 48, see para 17 below.
20 Ibid, art 32, para 1.
21 An exception is ibid, art 46: thus reference may be made to the court only if the state concerned has accepted the court's jurisdiction.
22 See eg *Schmidt and Dalström v Sweden* (Ser A No 21, Judgment 6 February 1976) 1 EHRR 637, E Ct HR.

16. The workload of the Commission. In the last full year for which statistics are available, 1990, the Commission's Secretariat opened 4942 provisional files and registered 1657 individual petitions as applications within the meaning of article 25 of the Convention for the Protection of Human Rights and Fundamental Freedoms[1].

Among the 1216 applications decided upon in 1990, 1056 were declared inadmissible or struck off the list, either *de plano* or after communication to the respondent government[2], and 151[3] were declared admissible. During the same period, the Commission gave notice of 355 individual applications to the respondent government, adopted 77 reports on the merits[4], 12 reports on friendly settlements[5] and one report after having struck the case off its list[6].

On 31 December 1990, the total number of applications pending before the Commission was 2298[7]. Of that number 1509 were still awaiting the first examination by the Commission[8]. The Commission's workload is such that the time lapse between lodgment of a petition and a first consideration by the Commission is, on average, eighteen months. The increase in the number of applications is compounded by the fact that Commission members work only on a part-time basis.

1 The total number of applications received by the Commission in the first year of its operation was 138. For the Convention for the Protection of Human Rights and Fundamental Freedoms (Rome, 4 November 1950; 213 UNTS 221; TS 71 (1953); Cmd 8969), art 25, see para 15 above.
2 Ie approximately 88 per cent.
3 Ie approximately 12.5 per cent.
4 Ie under the Convention for the Protection of Human Rights and Fundamental Freedoms, art 31: see para 15 above.
5 Ie under ibid, art 30: see para 15 above.
6 Ie under the Rules of Procedure of the European Commission of Human Rights 1990, r 54.
7 On 31 December 1987 that figure was 1029; on 31 December 1989 it was 1788.
8 Ie 66 per cent.

17. The European Court of Human Rights. The jurisdiction of the European Court of Human Rights extends to all cases concerning the interpretation and application of the Convention for the Protection of Human Rights and Fundamental Freedoms which the High Contracting Parties or the European Commission of Human Rights refer to the court in accordance with article 48 of the convention[1]. Only the High Contracting Parties and the Commission have the right to bring a case before the court[2]. The court's jurisdiction may be exercised only in relation to states which have either deposited with the Secretary General of the Council of Europe a declaration that they recognise as compulsory *ipso facto* that jurisdiction or consented to the case being referred to the court[3]. Under article 48 a case may be brought before the court by:
(1) the Commission, or

(2) a High Contracting Party whose national is alleged to be a victim, or
(3) a High Contracting Party which referred the case to the Commission, or
(4) a High Contracting Party against which the complaint has been lodged[4].
A case m ay be referred to the court only after the Commission has acknowledged the failure of efforts for a friendly settlement and within a period of three months from the transmission of the Commission's report[5] to the Committee of Ministers[6].

For the consideration of each case brought before it the court forms a Chamber of nine judges including, as *ex officio* members, the President or Vice-President and the judge who is a national of any state party concerned[7]. If the 'national' judge is unable to sit or withdraws, or if there is none, the state in question is entitled to appoint a member of the court (an elected judge of a different nationality) or a person from outside the court (an *ad hoc* judge). The names of the other judges are drawn by lot by the President before the opening of the case[8].

The Chamber thus constituted may, or must under certain circumstances, relinquish jurisdiction in favour of the plenary court. Plenary jurisdiction is optional at any stage in the proceedings where a case pending before a Chamber raises one or more serious questions affecting the interpretation of the convention. Relinquishment is obligatory where the resolution of such question or questions might have a result inconsistent with a judgment previously delivered by a Chamber or the plenary court. Reasons need not be given for the decision to relinquish jurisdiction[9]. To date a Chamber has relinquished jurisdiction in favour of the plenary court in some seventy-one cases[10].

The first stage of the judicial procedure is generally written; memorials and other documents are lodged with the court's Registry in accordance with conditions and time limits prescribed by the President of the Court. Once the case is ready for hearing a date for oral proceedings is determined by the President. The oral proceedings are in principle in public.

1 Convention for the Protection of Human Rights and Fundamental Freedoms (Rome, 4 November 1950; 213 UNTS 221; TS 71 (1953); Cmd 8969), art 45.
2 Ibid, art 44.
3 Ibid, art 48. As to the declaration, see art 46.
4 Ibid, art 48(a)–(d).
5 Ie under ibid, art 32: see para 15 above.
6 Ibid, art 47.
7 Ibid, art 43 (amended by Protocol 8). As to the protocols, see para 6 above. To date the nomination of an *ad hoc* judge has occurred in fourteen cases.
8 Before a Chamber is constituted, interim measures may be granted by the court at the court's initiative, or at the request of the Commission, the applicant or any other person, or *proprio motu*: Rules of Procedure of the European Court of Human Rights 1982 (amended 26 January 1989), r 36. The rules as amended came into force on 1 April 1989. The granting of interim measures is of considerable practical importance. The power to indicate interim measures is also enjoyed by the Commission under the Rules of Procedure of the European Commission of Human Rights 1990, r 36, if this seems desirable in the interests of the parties or the proper conduct of proceedings before it.
9 Rules of Procedure of the European Court of Human Rights 1982, r 51, para 1. The convention does not provide for plenary jurisdiction.
10 See eg *Belgian Linguistic Case (No 2)* (Merits) (Ser A No 6, Judgment 23 July 1968) 1 EHRR 252, E Ct HR; *Golder v United Kingdom* (Ser A No 18, Judgment 21 February 1975) 1 EHRR 524, E Ct HR; *Ireland v United Kingdom* (Ser A No 25, Judgment 18 January 1978) 2 EHRR 25, E Ct HR; *Sunday Times v United Kingdom* (Ser A No 30, Judgment 26 April 1979) 2 EHRR 245, E Ct HR; *Malone v United Kingdom* (Ser A No 82, Judgment 2 August 1984) 7 EHRR 14, E Ct HR; *Abdulaziz, Cabales and Balkandali v United Kingdom* (Ser A No 94, Judgment 28 May 1985) 7 EHRR 471, E Ct HR; *Norris v Ireland* (Ser A No 142, Judgment 26 October 1988) 13 EHRR 186, E Ct HR; *Ciulla v Italy* (Ser A No 148, Judgment 22 February 1989) 13 EHRR 346, E Ct HR; *Soering v United Kingdom* (Ser A No 161, Judgment 7 July 1989) 11 EHRR 439, E Ct HR; *Markt Intern and Beermann v Germany* (Ser A No 165, Judgment 20 November 1989) 12 EHRR 161, E Ct

HR;*Kostovski v Netherlands* (Ser A No 166, Judgment 20 November 1989) 12 EHRR 434, E Ct HR; *Groppera Radio AG v Switzerland* (Ser A No 173, Judgment 28 March 1990) 12 EHRR 321, E Ct HR. The plenary court, when the case has been referred to it, may either retain jurisdiction over the whole case or may, after deciding the interpretation question or questions, order that the case be referred back to the Chamber, which then, in regard to the remaining part of the case, recovers its original jurisdiction: Rules of Procedure of the European Court of Human Rights 1982, r 51, para 2.

18. Parties to proceedings before the court. The state or states concerned are parties to the case. The Commission participates[1], but it does not assume the role of a party. The primary function of the Commission is to assist the court and to enlighten the court through fulfilling its task as 'defender of the public interest'. Under the convention, individual applicants do not enjoy *locus standi* as parties before the court. Notwithstanding this, the court's Rules of Procedure provide that although the applicant may be represented by an advocate authorised to practise in any one of the contracting states and resident in the territory of one of them, or by any person approved by the President, an applicant may be given leave by the President to present his own case, subject, if need be, to his being assisted by an advocate or other person so approved[2]. Unless decided otherwise by the President, the advocate or other person representing or assisting the applicant, or the applicant himself if he seeks leave to present his own case, must have an adequate knowledge of one of the court's official languages[3].

1 Ie by way of one or more of its members appointed as delegate or delegates for this purpose.
2 Rules of Procedure of the European Commission of Human Rights 1982, r 30. In the so-called 'Vagrancy' cases, *De Wilde, Ooms and Versyp v Belgium (No 1)* (Ser A No 12, Judgment 18 June 1971) 1 EHRR 373, E Ct HR (question of procedure), the court held that under the Rules of Procedure, r 29, para 1, whereby Commission delegates 'may be assisted by other persons', assistance could be rendered by any person of their choice.
3 Ibid, r 31, para 2.

19. Legal aid. An applicant may be granted legal aid to present his case before the European Commission of Human Rights. The Commission, either at the request of an applicant lodging an application under article 25 of the Convention for the Protection of Human Rights and Fundamental Freedoms or *proprio motu*, may grant free legal aid to the applicant in connection with the representation of the case:

(1) where observations in writing on the admissibility of the application have been received from the High Contracting Party concerned in pursuance of rule 48, paragraph 2(b), of the Rules of Procedure of the European Commission of Human Rights[1], or where the time limit for their submission has expired; or
(2) where the application has been declared admissible[2].

Free legal aid may be granted only where the Commission is satisfied:

(a) that it is essential for the proper discharge of the Commission's duties;
(b) that the applicant has not sufficient means to meet all or part of the costs involved[3].

If the applicant has been granted legal aid, such aid is continued before the European Court of Human Rights[4]. If legal aid has not been granted for the presentation of a case before the Commission, the President of the Court may at any time grant legal aid at the applicant's request[5].

1 Under the Rules of Procedure of the European Commission of Human Rights 1990, r 48, para 2(b), the Commission may invite the High Contracting Party against which a complaint has been made to make written representations on the admissibility of the application.
2 Ibid, Addendum, r 1(a), (b).
3 Ibid, Addendum, r 2(a), (b). In order to determine whether an applicant has sufficient means, the Commission must require him to complete a declaration stating his income, capital assets and

financial commitments to dependants or other financial obligations, and have the declaration certified by the appropriate domestic authorities: r 3, para 1. Before granting free legal aid the Commission must request the High Contracting Party concerned to submit written comments: r 3, para 2. Fees are payable only to a barrister, solicitor, professor of law or professionally qualified person of similar status, but may be paid to more than one such lawyer: r 4, para 1. Legal aid may be granted to cover not only lawyers' fees but also travelling and subsistence expenses and other necessary out-of-pocket expenses incurred by the applicant or lawyer: r 4, para 2. The rate of fees to be paid is fixed by the Commission Secretary by agreement with the appointed lawyer: r 5, para 1. The rate agreed is notified to the Secretary General of the Council of Europe: r 5, para 2. If the Commission finds that the conditions of r 2 are no longer satisfied, it may revoke its grant in whole or in part: r 6. In case of urgency when the Commission is not in session the President or a Vice-President may exercise the Commission's legal aid powers: r 7.

4 Rules of Procedure of the European Commission of Human Rights 1990, r 3.
5 Ibid, r 4. However, he must be satisfied (1) that the applicant lacks sufficient means to meet all or part of the costs involved, and (2) that such a course is necessary for the proper conduct of the case before the court: r 4.

20. The judgment of the court. The court reaches its judgment by a majority vote[1]. Reasons must be given by the court for its judgment[2]. Any judge who has taken part in the consideration of the case is entitled to annex to the judgment a separate opinion, concurring with or dissenting from the whole or a part of the judgment[3]. The court's judgment is final[4] and is binding upon the parties to the case[5].

In certain circumstances, the court may entertain requests for the interpretation or review of its judgments as provided for in the Rules of Court[6]. A request for an interpretation of a judgment must be made within a period of three years following the delivery of that judgment[7]. To date there has been only one such request[8]. In its interpretation judgment[9] the court denied that a request for an interpretation being addressed to the court itself constituted 'an appeal' undermining the 'sole object' of article 52 of the Convention[10]. In considering the request the court held that it was exercising inherent jurisdiction and that an interpretation went 'no further than to clarify the meaning and scope which it intended to give to a previous decision which issued from its own deliberations, specifying if need be what it thereby decided with binding force'.

A revision of judgment may be sought in the event of the discovery of a fact which might, by its nature, have a decisive influence and which was unknown at the time judgment was delivered. A request for revision must be made within six months of the fact coming to light[11].

Execution of the court's judgment is supervised by the Committee of Ministers[12]. In certain circumstances the court may afford 'just satisfaction' to the victim of a violation of the convention[13].

1 In common with other such bodies, the court decides all disputes regarding its jurisdiction: see the Convention for the Protection of Human Rights and Fundamental Freedoms (Rome, 4 November 1950; 213 UNTS 221; TS 71 (1953); Cmd 8969), art 49.
2 Ibid, art 51, para 1.
3 Ibid, art 51, para 2.
4 Ibid, art 52.
5 The High Contracting Parties undertake to abide by the court's decision in any case to which they are parties: ibid, art 53.
6 Rules of Procedure of the European Court of Human Rights 1982, rr 57, 58, respectively.
7 Ibid, r 57, para 1.
8 The Commission requested an interpretation of the court's judgment in *Ringeisen v Austria (No 2)* (Ser A No 15, Judgment 22 June 1972) 1 EHRR 504, E Ct HR.
9 *Ringeisen v Austria (No 3)* (Interpretation of Judgment of 22 June 1972) (Ser A No 16, Judgment 23 June 1973), 1 EHRR 513, E Ct HR.
10 Ie 'to make the Court's judgment not subject to any appeal to another authority': *Ringeisen v Austria (No 2)*, at para 17 (1 EHRR 508), cited in *Ringeisen v Austria (No 3)*, at para 13 (1 EHRR at 518). For the Convention for the Protection of Human Rights and Fundamental Freedoms, art 25, see para 15 above.

11 Rules of Procedure of the European Court of Human Rights 1982, r 58, para 1. No such request has so far been made to the court.
12 Convention for the Protection of Human Rights and Fundamental Freedoms, art 54. The Committee of Ministers has adopted rules with respect to arts 32, 54.
13 See ibid, art 50, and para 21 below.

21. 'Just satisfaction'. Article 50 of the Convention for the Protection of Human Rights and Fundamental Freedoms enables the European Court of Human Rights to afford 'just satisfaction' to an injured party. Article 50 provides as follows:

> 'If the Court finds that a decision or a measure taken by a legal authority or any other authority of a High Contracting Party is completely or partially in conflict with the obligations arising from the present Convention, and if the internal law of the said Party allows only partial reparation to be made for the consequences of this decision or measure, the decision of the Court shall, if necessary, afford just satisfaction to the injured party'[1].

The court is not competent to strike down the domestic legislation of Contracting Parties to the convention, nor to order that specific measures be taken. However, states do take 'general measures' to comply with judgments, and the court does possess the authority to accord such 'just satisfaction' as it deems appropriate in the circumstances. 'Just satisfaction', if accorded, may be granted at the time of the judgment[2] or subsequently[3].

There have been occasions when a friendly settlement has been reached[4]. 'Just satisfaction' may take the form of a finding for the applicant[5], or an award of costs and expenses[6] and/or compensation for pecuniary or non-pecuniary damage[7]. The amount awarded in any given case is dependent on the circumstances of that case and is peculiar to that case. The award is made in the currency deemed most appropriate and relevant[8]. Where appropriate, the applicable rate of exchange is as at the date of judgment[9]. Examples may be cited[10].

1 Convention for the Protection of Human Rights and Fundamental Freedoms (Rome, 4 November 1950; 213 UNTS 221; TS 71 (1953); Cmd 8969), art 50.
2 Eg *Boyle and Rice v United Kingdom* (Ser A No 131, Judgment 27 April 1988) 10 EHRR 425, E Ct HR.
3 Eg *Sunday Times v United Kingdom (No 2)* (Ser A No 38, Judgment 6 November 1980) 3 EHRR 317, E Ct HR.
4 Eg *Kostovski v Netherlands* (Ser A No 170, Judgment 29 March 1990), E Ct HR. Such friendly settlement must be approved by the court before it will deem it appropriate to strike the case out of its list: see *Kostovski* at para 7.
5 Eg *Golder v United Kingdom* (Ser A No 18, Judgment 21 February 1975) 1 EHRR 524 at 541, E Ct HR, where the court stated at para 46 that it was 'not necessary to afford to the applicant any just satisfaction other than resulting from the finding of a violation of his rights'. See also *Brogan v United Kingdom* (Ser A No 152B, Judgment 30 May 1989) 13 EHRR 439, E Ct HR.
6 *Soering v United Kingdom* (Ser A No 161, Judgment 7 July 1989) 11 EHRR 439, E Ct HR.
7 *Obermeier v Austria* (Ser A No 179, Judgment 28 June 1990), 13 EHRR 290, E Ct HR.
8 Eg *Kamasinski v Austria* (Ser A No 168, Judgment 19 December 1989)13 EHRR 36, E Ct HR, where the award of costs payable by Austria took the form of US $5,000.
9 *Gaskin v United Kingdom* (Ser A No 160, Judgment 7 July 1989) 12 EHRR 36, E Ct HR.
10 Eg £26,752.80 and 5,030.60 French francs (*Soering v United Kingdom* (Ser A No 161, Judgment 7 July 1989) 11 EHRR 439, E Ct HR); 15,000 Dutch guilders costs and expenses (*Van der Leer v Netherlands* (Ser A No 170, Judgment 21 February 1990) 12 EHRR 567, E Ct HR); £1,000 damages plus £7,000 costs and expenses (*Granger v United Kingdom* (Ser A No 174, Judgment 28 March 1990) 12 EHRR 469, E Ct HR); 77,408 Swedish crowns costs and expenses (*Skärby v Sweden* (Ser A No 180B, Judgment 28 June 1990) 13 EHRR 90, E Ct HR).

22. Statistics of the court. Since its creation, the European Court of Human Rights has had 203 cases referred to it[1]. In forty-five cases the court held that there had been no violation of the Convention for the Protection of Human

Rights and Fundamental Freedoms, whereas it found for one or more breaches in 118 cases. Eleven cases have been struck out of the court's list, one with the applicant's agreement following the amendment of the legislation complained of[2], one because the applicant's release from prison following a pardon and the lasting silence which he observed thereafter[3], and the remaining nine following the conclusion of a friendly settlement between the applicant and the respondent government[4].

1 The figures given here relate to statistics available in September 1990. Of these only one has been an inter-state case: *Ireland v United Kingdom* (Ser A No 25, Judgment 18 January 1978) 2 EHRR 25, E Ct HR.
2 *De Becker v Belgium* (Ser A No 4, Judgment 27 March 1962) 1 EHRR 43, E Ct HR.
3 *Rubinat v Italy* (Ser A No 89, Judgment 12 February 1985) 7 EHRR 512, E Ct HR.
4 The most recent instances are *Jón Kristinsson v Iceland* (Ser A No 171, Judgment 1 March 1990) 13 EHRR 238, E Ct HR, and *Clerc v France* (Ser A No 176, Judgment 26 April 1990), E Ct HR.

23. Advisory opinions. Under Protocol 2 to the Convention for the Protection of Human Rights and Fundamental Freedoms the European Court of Human Rights is competent to give advisory opinions, at the request of the Committee of Ministers, on legal questions concerning the interpretation of the convention[1], but not on questions relating to the content or scope of the rights and freedoms defined in the convention, or on any other question which the Commission, the court or the Committee of Ministers might have to consider in consequence of any proceedings which could be instituted in accordance with the convention[2]. For the consideration of a request for an advisory opinion the court sits in plenary session[3], and reasons must be given for any advisory opinion[4]. To date such a request has never been made to the court.

1 Convention for the Protection of Human Rights and Fundamental Freedoms, Protocol 2 (Strasbourg, 6 May 1963; TS 104 (1970); Cmnd 4551), art 1, para 1.
2 Ibid, art 1, para 2.
3 Ibid, art 3, para 1.
4 Ibid, art 3, para 2. See also the Rules of Procedure of the European Court of Human Rights 1982, rr 59–67.

2. THE RIGHTS AS DEVELOPED THROUGH THE JURISPRUDENCE OF THE EUROPEAN COURT OF HUMAN RIGHTS

(1) GENERAL

24. Introduction. Since its inception in 1959 the European Court of Human Rights has had more than two hundred cases referred to it. It is the law emanating from these decisions which is articulated below. The court's activity has been increasing steadily, and currently it is considering on average about twenty cases each year[1]. In the light of this, the court's jurisprudence on many of the articles of the Convention for the Protection of Human Rights and Fundamental Freedoms is now quite substantial. Consequently, in the treatment in this part of the title, where the court has handed down many decisions on particular articles[2], only the leading cases are expounded[3], whereas with regard to other articles all the case law has been considered. In the treatment of the case law particular prominence has been given to cases of United Kingdom, and notably Scottish, origin.

The general treatment below is schematic in character; however, the articles are not all treated in the same manner[4], and the reader will find that chronological consistency has not been maintained[5]. Where there is no case law[6] the effect of the article is set out for reference purposes.

The volume of judicial decisions has rendered consideration of the opinions of the European Commission of Human Rights impractical, other than in passing. This is not to deny the importance of the Commission's contribution to the development of the substantive law. This is particularly the case where the court has not had the opportunity to interpret a provision of the convention[7].

Citation of cases is by what may be termed the primary source, that is, Series A of the publications of the court, although references to the European Human Rights Reports have been added where appropriate. The law is that stated by the court as of 30 June 1990, although in some instances judgments delivered since that date have been noted, particularly if the case is of United Kingdom origin.

1 In 1960 the court heard one case: *Lawless v Ireland (No 1)* (Preliminary objections and questions of procedure) (Ser A No 1, Judgment 14 November 1960) 1 EHRR 1, E Ct HR. In 1989 twenty-one cases came before the court.
2 Eg the Convention for the Protection of Human Rights and Fundamental Freedoms (Rome, 4 November 1950, 213 UNTS 221; TS 71 (1953); Cmd 8969), arts 5, 6.
3 The court has displayed admirable judicial consistency.
4 Eg like and related subject matter have been treated together.
5 Eg the permitted derogations contained in the paragraph 2 of each of arts 8–11 of the convention are dealt with together.
6 Eg ibid, art 2.
7 Eg the Convention for the Protection of Human Rights and Fundamental Freedoms, art 11(1), in *Council of Civil Service Unions v United Kingdom* (Application 11603/85) (1987) 10 EHRR 269, E Com HR.

25. The right to life: article 2. Article 2 of the Convention for the Protection of Human Rights and Fundamental Freedoms provides:

'1. Everyone's right to life shall be protected by law. No one shall be deprived of his life intentionally save in the execution of a sentence of a court following his conviction of a crime for which this penalty is provided by law[1].

2. Deprivation of life shall not be regarded as inflicted in contravention of this Article when it results from the use of force which is no more than absolutely necessary:

  (a) in defence of any person from unlawful violence;
  (b) in order to effect a lawful arrest or to prevent the escape of a person lawfully detained;
  (c) in action lawfully taken for the purpose of quelling a riot or insurrection'[2].

The European Court of Human Rights has never been given an opportunity of interpreting or applying this article. As may be anticipated, it could give rise to questions relating to issues such as abortion and euthanasia. However, such philosophical discussion is outwith the scope of this study. Article 15 does not permit derogation from article 2 except in respect of deaths resulting from lawful acts of war[3].

1 Convention for the Protection of Human Rights and Fundamental Freedoms (Rome, 4 November 1950; 213 UNTS 221; TS 71 (1953); Cmd 8969), art 2, para 1.
2 Ibid, art 2, para 2(a)–(c).
3 Ibid, art 15, para 2: see para 31 below.

26. Torture and inhuman or degrading treatment or punishment: article 3. Article 3 of the Convention for the Protection of Human Rights and Fundamental Freedoms provides that 'No one shall be subjected to torture or to inhuman or degrading treatment or punishment'.

The right guaranteed in article 3 is an absolute right from which no derogation is allowed in any circumstances. Article 15, which allows derogation in 'time of war or other public emergency threatening the life of the nation', expressly prohibits derogation from article 3[1].

Article 3 was discussed in the Scottish case of *Campbell and Cosans*[2], concerning corporal punishment in state schools in Scotland. The central issue in the case was the use of the 'tawse' in Scottish schools. Application was made by two mothers, Mrs Grace Campbell and Mrs Jane Cosans, with respect to the possibility of their sons being subject to corporal punishment as a disciplinary measure in school. At the time, such punishment could be administered in Scottish state schools for misconduct by pupils. Neither families in the application before the European Commission of Human Rights could afford the alternative of private education. Strathclyde Regional Council refused to guarantee to Mrs Campbell that her son would not receive corporal punishment during his school career[3], whereas in respect of Jeffrey Cosans his refusal to accept corporal punishment led to his suspension from school. The failure to obtain an assurance that he would not be disciplined in such a manner resulted in his not returning to school and on obtaining his sixteenth birthday[4], eight months later, he was not required to do so. The application was accepted by the Commission. The Commission and the court shared the view that the boys concerned were not victims of 'torture' or 'inhuman treatment'. Although the threat of conduct prohibited by article 3 could be sufficient to violate that article, because of the 'circumstances obtaining in Scotland', it was not established that pupils at schools using such punishment were 'solely by reason of the risk of being subjected thereto, humiliated or debased in the eyes of others to the requisite degree or at all'[5]. As to whether the applicants' sons were humiliated or debased in their own eyes, the court acknowledged that a threat directed to an exceptionally insensitive person may have no significant effect on him, but, nevertheless, could be incontrovertibly degrading; and conversely, an exceptionally sensitive person might be deeply affected by a threat that could be described as degrading only by a distortion of the ordinary and usual meaning of the word. However, in the case before it, the court endorsed the Commission's opinion that insufficient medical evidence had been produced to establish that the two children had suffered any adverse psychological or other effects[6]. Whilst it was conceded that Jeffrey Cosans might have experienced apprehension or disquiet, these were not deemed to be sufficient to amount to degrading treatment within the meaning of article 3 and any feelings that Gordon Campbell might have experienced certainly did not constitute either humiliation or debasement. Accordingly, with respect to the alleged violation of article 3 the court held that no such contravention had been established[7].

Campbell and Cosans can be compared with the earlier case of *Tyrer*[8], concerning judicial corporal punishment in the Isle of Man[9]. Anthony Tyrer was sentenced to three strokes of the birch following his conviction of assault occasioning bodily harm. His appeal to the Staff of Government Division of the High Court of Justice of the Isle of Man was dismissed and on that day (28 April 1972) the sentence was carried out at a police station in the presence of Tyrer's father and a doctor. Later that year Tyrer lodged an application with the Commission alleging that the sentence of judicial corporal punishment was contrary to article 3 of the convention. The Commission endorsed[10] Tyrer's allegation in its report of 14 December 1976, when it characterised the punishment he had received as degrading. Similarly, the European Court of Human Rights was of the view that Tyrer's punishment constituted neither 'torture'[11] nor 'inhuman treatment' and assessed whether the punishment inflicted on Tyrer fell within the ambit of its understanding of degrading punishment. The court did note that an individual could be humiliated by mere criminal conviction, but that that was *per se* insufficient to constitute a breach of article 3. For article 3 to be violated the humiliation must arise from the punishment as a consequence of the conviction. The punishment is what must be assessed in the context of the circumstances peculiar to the case.

The court considered the deterrent argument advanced in favour of birching[12] but was unsympathetic, maintaining that 'a punishment does not lose its degrading character just because it is believed to be or actually is an effective deterrent or aid to crime control'[13]. The court was at pains to emphasise that 'it is never permissible to have recourse to punishments which are contrary to Article 3, whatever their deterrent effect may be'[13]. The court then addressed itself to the issue of no publicity — the punishment was administered in private and the name of the offender was not published. The court refuted the contention that the absence of publicity could serve to prevent a particular type of punishment being characterised as degrading; it may well suffice that the victim is humiliated in his own eyes, even if not in the eyes of others'[14]. The court decided in the affirmative that the punishment to which Tyrer had been subjected was degrading for the following reasons:

● it was institutionalised violence carried out by strangers;
● it was an assault on his dignity and integrity; and
● it gave rise to mental anguish[15].

Accordingly the court concluded[16] that the applicant had been subjected to punishment in which the elements of humiliation attained the level inherent in the notion of degrading punishment[17].

The only inter-state case to have come before the court is *Ireland v United Kingdom*[18], and because of the subject matter it is one of the best known of the court's judgments. Among the issues discussed by the court was the scope and application of article 3. Initially, the court was asked to consider the alleged violation of article 3 with respect to the forms of interrogation employed against detainees in Northern Ireland[19]. The court[20] was also of the view[21] that the practices employed were inhuman and degrading but that they fell short of torture[22]. The treatment was characterised 'inhuman' because, although the techniques did not give rise to actual bodily injury, the detainees experienced severe and intense mental and physical suffering which led to acute psychiatric disturbances during interrogation. The practices employed were 'degrading' because 'they were such as to arouse in their victims feelings of fear, anguish and inferiority capable of humiliating and debasing them and possibly breaking their physical or moral resistance'[22]. The practices, however, did not amount to torture[23] as they had not produced 'suffering of the particular intensity and cruelty implied by the word torture'[24]. The court distinguished between torture and inhuman and degrading treatment. Torture is 'deliberate inhuman treatment causing serious and cruel suffering'. The court's interpretation reflected article 1 of Resolution 3452 (XXX) adopted by the United Nations General Assembly on 9 December 1975[25]. Article 3 of the convention was also raised in the context of ill treatment at certain specified locations. The court held unanimously that a practice constituting inhuman treatment had been in operation at Palace Barracks and had been used by members of the Royal Ulster Constabulary against persons being held in custody there. However, again the court refuted[26] that the practice was one of torture[27].

Finally, the court unanimously rejected that the Irish government's request that the United Kingdom be ordered to institute criminal or disciplinary proceedings in accordance with its domestic law against those members of the security forces who had committed the breaches.

A recent judgment of the court on article 3 is worthy of mention. In the *Soering* case[28] the court unanimously decided that *in the event* (emphasis added) of the implementation of the decision of the United Kingdom Secretary of State to extradite the applicant to the United States, when he might be sentenced to capital punishment, there *would be* (emphasis added) a violation of article 3[29]. It was not the death penalty *per se* which the applicant and the court maintained was contrary to article 3[30], but rather the time the applicant could spend on death row. The court also acknowledged that present day attitudes in the Contracting States to capital punishment were relevant for an assessment as to whether the acceptable threshold of suffering or degradation had been exceeded. In the case before it, however, what the court took account of was the circumstances prevailing in death row and in particular the time span from trial to execution if the available appeal procedure was fully exhausted[31]. The court concluded that with regard 'to the very long period of time spent on death row in such extreme conditions, with the ever present and mounting anguish of awaiting execution of the death penalty, and to the personal circumstances of the applicant, especially his age and mental state at the time of the offence[32], the applicant's extradition to the United States would expose him to real risk of treatment going beyond the threshold set by Article 3'[33]. The court was not purporting to subject the Virginian legal system to external judicial review[34].

The *Soering* case crystallises what has evolved from the court's jurisprudence as the established scope of article 3 and also suggests an extension of article 3 to cover situations in which that article would not have previously been invoked. The court in *Soering* reiterated its earlier judgments in *Ireland v United Kingdom* and *Tyrer* that treatment is 'inhuman because it was premeditated, and was applied for hours at a stretch and caused, if not actual bodily injury, at least intense physical and mental suffering and is degrading because it arouses in its victims feelings of fear, anguish and inferiority capable of humiliating and debasing them and possibly breaking their physical or moral resistance'. In order for a punishment or treatment associated with it to be 'inhuman' or 'degrading', the suffering or humiliation involved must in any event go beyond that inevitable element of suffering or humiliation connected with a given form of legitimate treatment.

Treatment, certain aspects of which the applicants may feel to be humiliating[35], unpleasant or even irksome[36] or where there is no aim of debasement or affecting personality[37], will not be deemed contrary to article 3. In holding in *Soering* a potential action as being in violation of article 3, the court has only endorsed what it said in the *Campbell and Cosans* case that a mere threat of conduct provided it is sufficiently real and immediate may be prohibited by article 3. However, the violation in question in this instance would occur outside the territory of any of the Contracting States to the convention: the *Soering* judgment is therefore an instance of the extra-territorial application of the effects principle.

The judgment places the United Kingdom in an anomalous position under international law. The United Kingdom, by adhering to the court's judgment, is unable to fulfil its obligations to the United States as imposed by the extradition treaty existing between the two states. Alternatively, if the United Kingdom were to honour these obligations it would be violating the text of the convention and the court's interpretation thereof. It is an invidious situation to which international law does not provide the answer[38]. The court's judgment on the fate of Mr Soering can be contrasted with the fate of Mohamed Amekrane in 1972[39]. On an international level the current position is that:

'No state shall expel or return or extradite a person to another state where there are substantial grounds for believing that he would be in danger of being subjected to torture'[40].

The European Court of Human Rights has gone one step further in that the *Soering* judgment suggests that extradition should be denied where an individual is going to be subject to 'inhuman or degrading treatment'.

1 Convention for the Protection of Human Rights and Fundamental Freedoms (Rome, 4 November 1950; 213 UNTS 221; TS 71 (1953); Cmd 8969), art 15, para 2.
2 *Campbell and Cosans v United Kingdom* (Ser A No 48, Judgment 25 February 1982) 4 EHRR 293, E Ct HR. See further paras 90, 91, below.
3 In fact he never did.
4 Sixteen is the upper age limit for compulsory education in Scotland: Education (Scotland) Act 1980 (c 44), s 31.
5 *Campbell and Cosans,* at para 29 (4 EHRR 301).
6 *Campbell and Cosans,* at para 30 (4 EHRR 302).
7 The court then focused its attention on the alleged violation of the Convention for the Protection of Human Rights and Fundamental Freedoms, Protocol 1, art 2 (the right to education): see para 89 below.
8 *Tyrer v United Kingdom* (Ser A No 26, Judgment 25 April 1978) 2 EHRR 1, E Ct HR.
9 The current United Kingdom declaration under art 63, paras 1, 4, of the convention of 14 January 1966 excludes matters pertaining to the Isle of Man.
10 The voting was fourteen to one.
11 *Tyrer,* at para 29 (2 EHRR 9). For what constitutes 'torture' in the court's interpretation, see *Ireland v United Kingdom* (Ser A No 25, Judgment 18 January 1978) 2 EHRR 25 at 80, E Ct HR, at paras 167, 174, discussed below.
12 It was alleged that the majority of islanders favoured retaining the birch.
13 *Tyrer,* at para 31 (2 EHRR 10).
14 *Tyrer,* at para 32 (2 EHRR 10).
15 The anguish was produced by anticipating the punishment and the delay in the police station.
16 The voting was six to one.
17 This case also raised the question of the position of an applicant who seeks to withdraw a petition made to the Commission, discussed above.
18 *Ireland v United Kingdom* (Ser A No 25, Judgment 18 January 1978) 2 EHRR 25, E Ct HR. As to *locus standi,* see para 18 above.
19 The Commission in 1976 was of the view that the methods employed (sleep deprivation, hooding, subjection to noise, wall standing and deprivation of food and drink) constituted a practice of inhuman treatment and torture.
20 The court gave judgment although the United Kingdom government had accepted the Commission's findings and had given an unqualified undertaking that the practices would not in 'any circumstances be reintroduced as an aid to interrogation'. In addition to considering the scope and application of article 3 of the convention, the court also considered arts 5, 6, 14 and 15: see paras 29 ff, 43 ff, 85, 31, below, respectively.
21 The voting was sixteen to one.
22 *Ireland v United Kingdom,* at para 167 (2 EHRR 80).
23 The voting was thirteen to four.
24 *Ireland v United Kingdom,* at para 167 (2 EHRR 80).
25 'Torture constitutes an aggravated and deliberate form of cruel, inhuman or degrading treatment or punishment'.
26 The voting was fourteen to three.
27 The court held that it was not established that the practice continued beyond the autumn of 1971. The court decided by fifteen votes to two that violations had been been established as regards the other places named in the application.
28 *Soering v United Kingdom* (Ser A No 161, Judgment 7 July 1989) 11 EHRR 439, E Ct HR.
29 The case centred on the application of Jens Soering, a German national, being held in prison in England pending extradition to the United States to face charges in the State of Virginia of the murder of his girlfriend's parents. His girlfriend had already been convicted and sentenced for her part in the murders (forty-five years imprisonment on each count). However, Virginia maintains the death penalty and although the United Kingdom sought an assurance that the death penalty would not be imposed on the applicant (see *Soering,* at para 20; 11 EHRR 445), no further guarantee could be given.
30 The Convention for the Protection of Human Rights and Fundamental Freedoms, art 2 (see para 25 above), recognises capital punishment as a qualification to the right to life guaranteed by that

article. However, as noted by the court (*Soering*, at para 102; 11 EHRR 473), the death penalty is not in normal usage in the territories of any of the Contracting Parties to the convention, and thirteen members of the Council of Europe have become Contracting Parties to Protocol 6 (Strasbourg, 28 April 1983; ETS 114; 22 ILM 538; 5 EHRR 167), which calls for the abolition of the death penalty. The United Kingdom is not a signatory.
31 The average period between trial and execution in Virginia (on the basis of seven executions since 1977) is six to eight years.
32 His age was eighteen years.
33 *Soering*, at para 111 (11 EHRR 478).
34 The democratic character of the Virginian legal system in general and the positive features of Virginian trial, sentencing and appeal procedures in particular are beyond doubt: *Soering*, at para 111 (11 EHRR 478).
35 *Marckx v Belgium* (Ser A No 31, Judgment 13 June 1979) 2 EHRR 330, E Ct HR.
36 *Guzzardi v Italy* (Ser A No 39, Judgment 6 November 1980) 3 EHRR 333, E Ct HR.
37 *Albert and Le Compte v Belgium* (Ser A No 58, Judgment 10 February 1983) 5 EHRR 533, E Ct HR; *Abdulaziz, Cabales and Balkandali v United Kingdom* (Ser A No 94, Judgment 28 May 1985) 7 EHRR 471, E Ct HR.
38 The Vienna Convention on the Law of Treaties (Vienna, 23 May 1969; TS 58 (1980); Cmnd 7964), art 30, deals only with inconsistent treaties pertaining to the same subject matter, and art 60 on material breach (see PUBLIC INTERNATIONAL LAW, vol 19 para 631) is inapplicable in this case.
39 Mohamed Amekrane was a Moroccan national and a lieutenant-colonel in the Moroccan Air Force who participated in an abortive assassination attempt on King Hassan of Morocco. Amekrane sought political asylum in Gibraltar. This was refused, and within twenty-four hours he was handed over to representatives of the Moroccan government, who returned him to Morocco. On his return he was tried, convicted and sentenced to death by a military tribunal, and was executed on 15 January 1973. Prior to his execution an application was made in his name by his wife and children alleging a violation of article 3 of the Convention for the Protection of Human Rights and Fundamental Freedoms on the grounds that it was known that he would be prosecuted if returned to Morocco for a political offence and, if convicted, that the punishment was the death penalty. There was then no extradition treaty between the United Kingdom and Morocco. The question whether Mr Amekrane had suffered a violation of art 3 was not addressed as the United Kingdom made an *ex gratia* payment (£37,500 in full and final settlement) without any implication of guilt being acknowledged on the part of the United Kingdom.
40 Convention against Torture and other Cruel, Inhuman or Degrading Treatment or Punishment (New York, 4 February 1985; TS 107 (1991); Cm 1775; 23 ILM (1984) 1027; 24 ILM (1985) 535), art 3(1).

27. The European Convention for the Prevention of Torture and Inhuman or Degrading Treatment or Punishment.

The European Convention for the Prevention of Torture and Inhuman or Degrading Treatment or Punishment, signed in 1987, establishes a European Committee to examine, by visits at short notice to prisons in Contracting States, the treatment of persons deprived of liberty with a view to strengthening, if necessary, the protection of such persons from torture and from inhuman or degrading treatment or punishment[1]. The convention is designed to supplement and reinforce the position which the Council of Europe has adopted through the European Commission and Court of Human Rights on article 3 of the Convention for the Protection of Human Rights and Fundamental Freedoms.

1 European Convention for the Prevention of Torture and Inhuman or Degrading Treatment or Punishment (Strasbourg, 26 November 1987; Misc 5 (1988); ETS 126; Cm 339), art 1.

28. Slavery and compulsory labour: article 4.

Article 4 of the Convention for the Protection of Human Rights and Fundamental Freedoms provides that:

'1. No one shall be held in slavery or servitude[1].
2. No one shall be required to perform forced or compulsory labour[2].
3. For the purpose of this Article the term "forced or compulsory labour" shall not include:
   (a) any work required to be done in the ordinary course of detention imposed

according to the provisions of Article 5 of this Convention[3] or during conditional release from such detention;

    (*b*) any service of a military character or, in case of conscientious objectors in countries where they are recognised, service exacted instead of compulsory military service;

    (*c*) any service exacted in case of an emergency or calamity threatening the life or well-being of the community;

    (*d*) any work or service which forms part of normal civic obligations'[4].

There have been no United Kingdom cases in the European Court of Human Rights pertaining to this article. The European Court of Human Rights was confronted with providing an interpretation of paragraphs 2 and 3(d) of article 4 in the *Van der Mussele* case[5], which involved a Belgium pupil avocat, Eric Van der Mussele, who had been officially appointed by the Legal Advice and Defence Office of the Antwerp Bar to defend Mr Ebrine, a Gambian national. As a consequence of Mr Ebrine's lack of financial resources, Mr Van der Mussele received no remuneration for his services, but had he refused to provide such services he would have 'run the risk of having the Council of the Ordre strike his name off the roll of pupils or reject his application for entry on the register of avocats'. The court examined article 4 in the light of International Labour Organisation Conventions 29 and 105[6]. Read against the definition of 'forced or compulsory' contained in Convention 29[7], the court held that the services rendered by Mr Van der Mussele were neither 'forced' nor 'compulsory'. 'Forced' in the court's view denoted the 'idea of physical or mental constraint', a factor which was absent in the case before it, whereas 'compulsory' could not refer to just any form[8] of legal compulsion or obligation[9].

Existence of 'menace of penalty' was prima facie evidence of 'compulsory' labour in the instant case. This was refuted in part by the consensual nature of the provision of free services. Services of the type complained of were known and accepted to be an inevitable characteristic of pupillage, although the court conceded that 'a considerable and unreasonable imbalance between the aim pursued — to qualify as an *avocat* — and the obligations undertaken in order to achieve that aim would alone be capable of warranting the conclusion that the services exacted of Mr Van der Mussele in relation to legal aid were compulsory despite his consent'[10]. The court noted 'that the respective laws of numerous Contracting States have evolved or are evolving, albeit in varying degrees, towards the assumption by the public purse of the cost of paying lawyers or trainee lawyers appointed to act for indigent litigants'[10]. Accordingly paragraph 2 of article 4 had not been violated and the court was not required to determine possible justification under or in terms of paragraph 3(d).

In the *Van Droogenbroeck* case[11] the court upheld the application of paragraph 3(a) of article 4 with respect to work performed in prison by inmates. Work required of vagrants as part of a rehabilitation programme does not exceed the 'ordinary' limits within the meaning of paragraph 3(a)[12]. The court was of this view because the work had as its *raison d'être* rehabilitation and had equivalents in several Contracting States.

1 Convention for the Protection of Human Rights and Fundamental Freedoms (Rome, 4 November 1950; 213 UNTS 221; TS 71 (1953); Cmd 8969), art 4, para 1.
2 Ibid, art 4, para 2.
3 As to ibid, art 5, see paras 29 ff below.
4 Ibid, art 4, para 3(a)–(d).
5 *Van der Mussele v Belgium* (Ser A No 70, Judgment 23 November 1983) 6 EHRR 163, E Ct HR.
6 International Labour Organisation Convention No 29 on Forced Labour (Geneva, 28 June 1930; Cmd 3693); International Labour Organisation No 105 on the Abolition of Forced Labour (Geneva, 25 June 1957; 320 UNTS 291; Cmnd 328). These conventions are binding on Belgium and nearly all other member states of the Council of Europe. The court highlighted the deliberate

'striking similarity' between Convention 29, art 2, para 2, and the Convention for the Protection of Human Rights and Fundamental Freedoms, art 4, para 3.

7 Ie 'all work or service exacted from any person under the menace of any penalty and for which the said person has not offered himself voluntarily'.

8 Eg work to be performed pursuant to a freely negotiated labour services contract would not be an example of compulsory labour.

9 *Van der Mussele*, at para 34 (6 EHRR 173).

10 *Van der Mussele*, at para 40 (6 EHRR 178).

11 *Van Droogenbroeck v Belgium* (Ser A No 50, Judgment 24 June 1982) 4 EHRR 443, E Ct HR.

12 *De Wilde, Ooms and Versyp v Belgium (No 1)* (Ser A No 12, Judgment 18 June 1971) 1 EHRR 373 at 411, E Ct HR, at para 90.

(3) LIBERTY AND SECURITY OF PERSON

29. Introduction: article 5. Article 5 of the Convention for the Protection of Human Rights and Fundamental Freedoms provides as follows:

'1. Everyone has the right to liberty and security of person. No one shall be deprived of his liberty save in the following cases and in accordance with a procedure prescribed by law:

   (a) the lawful detention of a person after conviction by a competent court;

   (b) the lawful arrest or detention of a person for non-compliance with the lawful order of a court in order to secure the fulfilment of any obligation prescribed by law;

   (c) the lawful arrest or detention of a person effected for the purpose of bringing him before the competent legal authority on reasonable suspicion of having committed an offence or when it is reasonably considered necessary to prevent his committing an offence or fleeing after having done so[1];

   (d) the detention of a minor by lawful order for the purpose of educational supervision or his lawful detention for the purpose of bringing him before the competent legal authority[2];

   (e) the lawful detention of persons for the prevention of the spreading of infectious diseases, of persons of unsound mind[3], alcoholics or drug addicts or vagrants[4];

   (f) the lawful arrest or detention of a person to prevent his effecting an unauthorised entry into the country or of a person against whom action is being taken with a view to deportation or extradition[5].

2. Everyone who is arrested shall be informed promptly, in any language which he understands, of the reasons for his arrest and of any charge against him[6].

3. Everyone arrested or detained in accordance with the provisions of paragraph 1(c) of this Article shall be brought promptly before a judge or other officer authorised by law to exercise judicial power and shall be entitled to trial within a reasonable time or to release pending trial. Release may be conditioned by guarantees to appear for trial[7].

4. Everyone who is deprived of his liberty by arrest or detention shall be entitled to take proceedings by which the lawfulness of his detention shall be decided speedily by a court and his release ordered if the detention is not lawful[8].

5. Everyone who has been the victim of arrest or detention in contravention of the provisions of this Article shall have an enforceable right to compensation'[8].

1 See para 30 below.

2 See para 39 below.

3 See para 41 below.

4 See para 42 below.

5 Convention for the Protection of Human Rights and Fundamental Freedoms (Rome, 4 November 1950; 213 UNTS 221; TS 71 (1953); Cmd 8969), art 5 para 1(a)–(f). As to extradition and deportation, see paras 37, 38, below.

6 Ibid, art 5, para 2.

7 Ibid, art 5, para 3: see paras 30, 32, below.
8 Ibid, art 5, para 4: see paras 33, 35, below.
9 Ibid, art 5, para 5.

30. Right to be brought before a judicial person or body. Under paragraph 3 of article 5 of the Convention for the Protection of Human Rights and Fundamental Freedoms, everyone lawfully arrested or detained must be brought promptly before a judge or other officer authorised by law to exercise judicial power[1]. A leading case in this category is a United Kingdom case[2]. The four applicants had been arrested and detained under statutory power[3] on suspicion of involvement in acts of terrorism in Northern Ireland. The applicants were released after four to seven days[4] without being charged or appearing before a court. The applicants alleged that they had been victims of a breach of article 5.

Initially the European Court of Human Rights considered paragraph 1(c) of article 5[5], and stipulated that the absence of charges or failure to bring before a court did not necessarily mean that the purpose of detention was not in accordance with paragraph 1(c). The court maintained that the existence of such a purpose had to be considered independently of its achievement, and paragraph 1(c) did not 'presuppose that the police should have obtained sufficient evidence to bring charges, either at the point of arrest or while the applicants were in custody'[6].

Similarly a violation of paragraph 3 of article 5 is not precipitated simply on the ground that a person is neither charged nor brought before a court[7]. However, any delay in releasing the individual concerned may give rise to a breach of paragraph 3. If not released, the arrested person is entitled to a prompt appearance before a judge or judicial officer[7]. The assessment of 'promptness' has to be made in the light of the object and purpose of article 5, namely the protection of the individual against arbitrary interferences by the state with his right to liberty. An essential feature of the guarantee embodied in paragraph 3 is judicial control of interferences with an individual's liberty by the executive[8]. 'Promptness', the court has acknowledged, is to be assessed according to the circumstances of each case[9]. These circumstances, however, must never attain such importance that they impair the very essence of the right generated by paragraph 3 and so negate the state's obligation to ensure a prompt release or a prompt appearance before a judicial authority[10].

In an earlier case[11] the court acknowledged the diversity of the circumstances to be taken into account and the consequent variation of what may constitute legitimate detention[12]. Accordingly, the concern of the court in *Brogan* was to determine whether in light of the special circumstances advanced by the United Kingdom government such release could be considered as 'prompt'. In short, the court concluded that the special features of the case did not warrant the circumstances of the applicants' detention. To hold otherwise would be 'an unacceptably wide interpretation of the plain meaning of the word "promptly" and would entail a "serious weakening of a procedural guarantee to the detriment of the individual" '[13]. The court found that paragraph 3 of article 5 had been breached in respect of the four applicants notwithstanding the fact that their arrest and detention were inspired by the legitimate aim of protecting the community as a whole from terrorism. Such an aim *per se* is not sufficient to ensure compliance with the specific requirements of paragraph 3[13].

In the *Lawless* case[14] the court held that in the circumstances there had been a breach of article 5. However, the court was required to consider possible justification for the breach in terms of article 15[15]. Similarly, in *Ireland v United Kingdom*[16] the court held that prima facie there had been a breach of article 5, but the special circumstances prevailing demanded that the court consider article 5 in conjunction with article 15, which is considered in the paragraph which follows.

1 Convention for the Protection of Human Rights and Fundamental Freedoms (Rome, 4 November 1950; 213 UNTS 221; TS 71 (1953); Cmd 8969), art 5, para 3.
2 *Brogan v United Kingdom* (Ser A No 145B, Judgment 29 November 1988) 11 EHRR 117, E Ct HR.
3 Prevention of Terrorism (Temporary Provisions) Act 1984 (c 8), s 12.
4 The individuals were detained for different lengths of time.
5 In *Lawless v Ireland (No 3)* (Ser A No 3, Judgment 1 July 1961) 1 EHRR 15 at 27, E Ct HR, at para 14, the court stated that 'paragraph 1(c) of Article 5 can be construed only if read in conjunction with paragraph 3 of the same Article'. For para 1(c), see para 29 above.
6 *Brogan*, at para 53 (11 EHRR 131).
7 *Brogan*, at para 58 (11 EHRR 133).
8 *Brogan*, at para 58 (11 EHRR 134): judicial control is implied by the rule of law, 'one of the fundamental principles of a democratic society' (see eg *Engel v Netherlands (No 1)* (Ser A No 22, Judgment 8 June 1976) 1 EHRR 647 at 672, E Ct HR, at para 69, and *Klass v Germany* (Ser A No 28, Judgment 6 September 1978) 2 EHRR 214 at 234, E Ct HR, at para 55).
9 *Brogan*, at para 59 (11 EHRR 134). See also *Wemhoff v Germany* (Ser A No 7, Judgment 27 June 1968) 1 EHRR 55 at 76, E Ct HR, at para 10, and *De Jong, Baljet and Van den Brink v Netherlands* (Ser A No 77, Judgment 22 May 1984) 8 EHRR 20 at 39, E Ct HR, at para 52.
10 *Brogan*, at para 59. See also *Fox, Campbell and Hartley v United Kingdom* (Ser A No 182, Judgment 30 August 1990) 13 EHRR 157, E Ct HR, where the court held that although the arrest and detention of each of the applicants had been based on a bona fide suspicion that he or she was a terrorist, the court did not accept that the elements relied on by the United Kingdom government could, on their own, support the conclusion that there had been reasonable suspicion. In the court's opinion neither the previous convictions of Mr Cox and Ms Campbell some seven years earlier for acts of terrorism, nor the fact that all three applicants were questioned about specific terrorist acts during their detention, could, without further material, have satisfied an objective observer that the suspicion had been reasonable. In 1986 the applicants had been detained and asked about their suspected membership of the Provisional IRA, but were subsequently released without charge.
11 *Wemhoff v Germany* (Ser A No 7, Judgment 27 June 1968) 1 EHRR 55, E Ct HR.
12 *Wemhoff*, at para 10 (1 EHRR 76).
13 *Brogan*, at para 62 (11 EHRR 135, 136).
14 *Lawless v Ireland (No 1)* (Ser A No 1, Judgment 14 November 1960) 1 EHRR 1, E Ct HR. In 1957 Mr Lawless, an Irish national, was arrested and detained for five months without trial in the Republic of Ireland pursuant to the Offences Against the State Act 1939 (amended by the Offences Against the State (Amendment) Act 1940 (No 2 of 1940)), which was promulgated in order to meet the situation created by the activities of the IRA. Mr Lawless, who had been the subject of court proceedings under the 1939 Act, was rearrested in July 1957. He was interned, and in December 1957 appeared before the Detention Commission and gave a verbal undertaking that he would not participate in any of the activities prohibited by the 1939 Act.
15 For the Convention for the Protection of Human Rights and Fundamental Freedoms, art 15, see para 31 below.
16 *Ireland v United Kingdom* (Ser A No 25, Judgment 18 January 1978) 2 EHRR 25, E Ct HR. For the facts, see para 26 above.

31. Derogation in time of war etc: article 15. Article 15 of the Convention for the Protection of Human Rights and Fundamental Freedoms provides as follows:

'1. In time of war or other public emergency threatening the life of the nation any High Contracting Party may take measures derogating from its obligations under this Convention to the extent strictly required by the exigencies of the situation, provided that such measures are not inconsistent with its other obligations under international law[1].
2. No derogation from Article 2, except in respect of deaths resulting from lawful acts of war, or from Articles 3, 4 (paragraph 1) and 7 shall be made under this provision[2].
3. Any High Contracting Party availing itself of this right of derogation shall keep the Secretary-General of the Council of Europe fully informed of the measures which it has taken and the reasons therefor. It shall also inform the Secretary-General

of the Council of Europe when such measures have ceased to operate and the provisions of the Convention are again being fully executed'[3].

Article 15 does not release governments from their undertakings assumed in the convention, but it does give them the right 'in case of war or other public emergency threatening the life of the nation, to take measures derogating from its obligations under the Convention other than those named in Article 15(2), provided that such measures are strictly limited to what is required by the exigencies of the situation and also that they do not conflict with other obligations under international law'[4].

If article 15 is invoked, it is the European Court of Human Rights in Strasbourg which is responsible for determining whether the conditions laid down in the article have been fulfilled to the extent necessary to justify the permitted derogation[4]. The court further elaborated on this point in the case of *Ireland v United Kingdom*. After it acknowledged that the 'limits on the Court's powers of review ... are particularly apparent where Article 15 is concerned', the court stated that it was for 'each Contracting State with its responsibility for the life of [its] nation', to determine whether that life is threatened by a 'public emergency' and, if so, how far it is necessary to go in attempting to overcome the emergency. By reason of their direct and continuous contact with the pressing needs of the moment, the national authorities are, in principle, in a better position than an international judge to decide both on the nature and scope of derogations necessary to avert it. In this matter article 15, para 1, leaves the state authorities a wide discretion.

Nevertheless, states do not enjoy an unlimited power in this respect. The court, which, with the Commission, is responsible for ensuring the observance of the states' 'engagements ... is empowered to rule on whether the States have gone beyond the "extent strictly required by the exigencies" of the crisis. The domestic margin of appreciation is thus accompanied by a European supervision'[5]. The court's role is that of reviewing the lawfulness under the convention of the measures adopted. It is not the court's function to substitute any other assessment of what might have been the most prudent or most expedient policy for the member state concerned to have adopted. To fulfil its task, the court is required to 'reach its decision in the light, not of a purely retrospective examination of the efficiency of those measures, but of the conditions and circumstances reigning when they were originally taken and subsequently applied'[6].

As to the meaning to be ascribed to the words 'other public emergency threatening the life of the nation', the court has stated this 'is sufficiently clear; they refer to an exceptional situation of crisis or emergency which affects the whole population and constitutes a threat to the organised life of the community of which the State is composed'[7]. In *Ireland v United Kingdom* the court further provided that in the event of a state 'struggling against a public emergency threatening the life of the nation, it would be rendered defenceless if it were required to accomplish everything at once, to furnish from the outset each of its chosen means of action with each of the safeguards reconcilable with the priority requirements for the proper functioning of the authorities and for restoring peace within the Community', and thus the 'interpretation of Article 15 must leave a place for progressive adaptations'[8].

Returning to paragraph 3 of article 5, the court in *Schiesser* stated that 'officer' within the context of that provision is not identical with 'judge', although nevertheless having some of the latter's attributes, 'that is to say he must satisfy certain conditions each of which constitutes a guarantee for the person arrested'[9]. The court identified these conditions as follows:

(1) independence of the executive and of the parties — the officer may be to some extent subordinate to other judges or officers, provided that the latter enjoy similar independence;

(2) a procedural requirement whereby the officer is obliged to hear for himself the individual brought before him; and

(3) a substantive requirement whereby the officer is obliged to review the circumstances mitigating for or against detention, and by reference to legal criteria to decide whether there are reasons justifying detention and in the absence of such reasons order the release of the person concerned.

In both the foregoing cases the court held unanimously that the requirements of article 15 had been met and that the derogations from article 5 were not, in the respective circumstances of the cases, in breach of the convention.

In a more recent case, *Pauwels*[10], the issue was whether an individual in his capacity as chairman of a military Board of Inquiry afforded the guarantees of impartiality inherent in the concept of 'officer authorised by law to exercise judicial power'[11] when he could be, and in fact was, called upon to act in the same case, in respect of the same defendant, as prosecuting authority and thus as a party. The applicant's submission was that such an individual could not afford the required independence of either the parties or the executive. The court endorsed the submission on the grounds that the individual concerned combined these functions of investigation and prosecution. Accordingly, his impartiality did not have the appearance of being beyond doubt[12].

1 Convention for the Protection of Human Rights and Fundamental Freedoms (Rome, 4 November 1950; 213 UNTS 221; TS 71 (1953); Cmd 8969), art 15, para 1.

2 Ibid, art 15, para 2. For arts 2–4, see paras 25, 26, 28, above; and for art 7, see para 61 below.

3 Ibid, art 15, para 3.

4 *Lawless v Ireland (No 3)* (Ser A No 3, Judgment 1 July 1961) 1 EHRR 15 at 30, E Ct HR, at para 22.

5 *Ireland v United Kingdom* (Ser A No 25, Judgment 18 January 1978) 2 EHRR 25 at 92, E Ct HR, at para 207.

6 *Ireland v United Kingdom*, at para 214 (2 EHRR 95).

7 *Lawless v Ireland (No 3)*, at para 28 (1 EHRR 31).

8 *Ireland v United Kingdom*, at para 220 (2 EHRR 96).

9 *Schiesser v Switzerland* (Ser A No 34, Judgment 4 December 1979) 2 EHRR 417 at 426, E Ct HR, at para 31. Mr Schiesser had been brought before the Winterthur District Attorney, who ordered him to be placed in detention on remand. Mr Schiesser submitted that the district attorney was not an 'officer authorised by law to exercise judicial power'. In the instant case the court held that there had been no breach of the Convention for the Protection of Human Rights and Fundamental Freedoms, art 5, para 3.

10 *Pauwels v Belgium* (Ser A No 135, Judgment 26 May 1988) 11 EHRR 238, E Ct HR.

11 See the Convention for the Protection of Human Rights and Fundamental Freedoms, art 5, para 3.

12 The court thus endorsed its ruling in an earlier case that where an *auditeur militair* was liable to have to act in one and the same case as prosecuting authority after the case had been sent for trial by a court martial, he could not be independent of the parties at that preliminary stage precisely because he was liable to become one of the parties at the next stage of the procedure: see *De Jong, Baljet and Van den Brink v Netherlands* (Ser A No 77, Judgment 22 May 1984) 8 EHRR 20 at 38, E Ct HR, at para 49; and *Van der Sluijs, Zuiderveld and Klappe v Netherlands* (Ser A No 78, Judgment 22 May 1984), E Ct HR, at para 44.

32. Prolonged detention on remand. Every person is entitled to trial within a reasonable time[1]. What is a reasonable length of time was considered by the European Court of Human Rights in its early case law. The scope of the provision was established in the *Wemhoff* case[2], which concerned a West German national, Mr Wemhoff, who was arrested in November 1961 on suspicion of complicity in offences involving a breach of trust[3]. Following the completion of the official investigation by the West Berlin Prosecutor's office in 1964, a prosecution was initiated against Mr Wemhoff, who submitted that three years was an unreasonable period of detention and maintained that paragraph 3 of article 5 of the Convention for the Protection of Human Rights and Fundamental Freedoms had been breached[4]. The European Court of Human Rights stressed the importance of determining the scope of the provision, and denied that 'a purely grammatical interpretation' would suffice[5]. Such an interpretation would leave the judicial authorities with a choice between that of bringing the accused to trial within a reasonable time or releasing him, subject to guarantees, if need be, pending trial[6]. The court refuted such an interpretation on the ground that in the court's opinion it did not reflect the intention of the High Contracting Parties: in other words, that it was inconceivable that the High Contracting Parties should have intended to permit their judicial authorities, at the price of release of the accused, to protract proceedings beyond a reasonable time[7]. The court looked at paragraph 3 of article 5 in context and concluded that it was for the national authorities to determine whether the time which elapsed before judgment was passed on the accused exceeded at some stage a reasonable limit: in the words of the court, whether such time 'imposed a greater sacrifice than could, in the circumstances of the case, reasonably be expected of a person presumed to be innocent'[8]. What is of relevance is the provisional detention of accused persons and what is important is that such detention should not be prolonged beyond a reasonable time[9]. The question which still remained to be answered was what constituted the end of the detention period in terms of the article. Was it on the day on which a conviction became final or the one on which the charged was determined, even if only by a court of first instance? The court favoured the latter interpretation. The intention of the article is not to preclude taking into custody a person convicted at first instance who hitherto has been at liberty[10]. The court also maintained that reasonableness has to be assessed in each case according to its special features. The features warranting consideration can be extremely diverse, but the court did conclude that it is for national judicial authorities:

> 'to mention the circumstances which led them, in the general interest, to consider it necessary to detain a person suspected of an offence but not convicted. Likewise, such a person must, when exercising his remedies, have invoked reasons which tend to refute the conclusions drawn by the authorities from the facts established by them, as well as other circumstances which told in favour of his release', and that it is with reference to the foregoing that the European Court of Human Rights must determine 'whether the reasons given by the national authorities to justify continued detention are relevant and sufficient to show that detention was not unreasonably prolonged and contrary to article 5(3) of the Convention'[11].

Another case in point was that of *Ringeisen*[12], in which the court took cognisance of the principles which had evolved from the earlier cases. Most recently, in the case of *B v Austria*, the court maintained that 'persistence of reasonable suspicion that the person arrested has committed an offence is a condition *sine qua non* for the validity of the continued detention of the person concerned'[13]. Nevertheless, as the court noted in the *Stögmüller* case, paragraph 3 of article 5 'clearly implies, however, that the persistence of suspicion does not suffice to justify, after a certain lapse of time, the prolongation of the detention'[14], and the court must examine the reasons on which the domestic authorities based their decision[15]. The reasons given by the Austrian courts in the instant case were not only the gravity of the offences but the risk of the arrested person absconding, the possibility of collusion and the danger that he might commit other offences[16]. Regarding absconding, the court upheld what it had said in the *Wemhoff* judgment: '. . . while the severity of the sentence which the court may expect in the event of conviction may be legitimately regarded as a factor encouraging him to abscond — though the effect of such fear diminishes as detention continues and, consequently, the balance of the sentence which the accused may expect to have to serve is reduced, nevertheless the possibility of a severe sentence is not sufficient in this respect'[17]. The possibility of flight cannot therefore be assessed exclusively by reference to the severity of the penalties which may be involved. Other factors have to be taken into account, especially those relating to the character of the person involved, his morals, his home, his occupation, his assets, his family ties and all kinds of links with the country in which he is being prosecuted[18]. Nor does a danger of flight result from the possibility or ease with which the accused may cross a frontier[19]. In the case of *B v Austria* the court held that there had been no violation of paragraph 3 of article 5.

1 Convention for the Protection of Human Rights and Fundamental Freedoms (Rome, 4 November 1950; 213 UNTS 221; TS 71 (1953); Cmd 8969), art 5, para 3.
2 *Wemhoff v Germany* (Ser A No 7, Judgment 27 June 1968) 1 EHRR 55, E Ct HR.
3 The case before the domestic court was extremely complicated, not least because of the involvement of twelve co-accused.
4 Mr Wemhoff was convicted in 1965 and sentenced to six and a half years' penal service. There then followed a number of appeals in the domestic courts and eventually, after serving two-thirds of his sentence (the period of detention prior to his arrest being counted as part of the sentence), he was conditionally released in November 1966.
5 *Wemhoff*, at para 4 (1 EHRR 73).
6 See also *Neumeister v Austria (No 1)* (Ser A No 8, Judgment 27 June 1968) 1 EHRR 91, E Ct HR.
7 *Wemhoff*. Such an intention 'would, moreover, be flatly contrary to the provision in article 6(1)'. For the Convention for the Protection of Human Rights and Fundamental Freedoms, art 6, para 1, see para 43 below.
8 *Wemhoff*, at para 5 (1 EHRR 74).
9 *Wemhoff*. See also *Neumeister v Austria (No 1)* (Ser A No 8, Judgment 27 June 1968) 1 EHRR 91 at 125, E Ct HR, at para 4.
10 At this point the court noted the inter-relationship between the Convention for the Protection of Human Rights and Fundamental Freedoms, art 5, para 3, and art 6, para 1 (the latter article applying with regard to the trial and appeal procedure).
11 *Wemhoff*, at para 12 (1 EHRR 76).
12 *Ringeisen v Austria (No 1)* (Ser A No 13, Judgment 16 July 1971) 1 EHRR 455, E Ct HR.
13 *B v Austria* (Ser A No 175, Judgment 28 March 1990) 13 EHRR 20 at 30, E Ct HR, at para 42. See also *Stögmüller v Austria* (Ser A No 9, Judgment 10 November 1969) 1 EHRR 155, E Ct HR.
14 *Stögmüller v Austria; B v Austria*, at para 42.
15 *B v Austria*.
16 *B v Austria*, at para 43.
17 *Wemhoff*, at para 14. See also *B v Austria*, at para 44.
18 *Neumeister v Austria (No 1)*, at para 10 (1 EHRR 128).
19 *Stögmüller v Austria*, at para 15 (1 EHRR 194, 195). In this case the court observed that domestic courts have the competence to order the surrender of a passport.

33. Lawfulness of detention to be decided speedily. Everyone deprived of liberty by arrest or detention is entitled to take proceedings by which the lawfulness of his detention is decided speedily[1]. A major case involving this provision is that of *Bezicheri*[2]. Mr Bezicheri, a lawyer practising in Bologna, was arrested on suspicion inter alia of having been accessory to an aggravated murder. It was alleged that in the course of his professional activities he had acted as an intermediary between the murderers and the instigator of the crime, who was in prison. The applicant's submission was that the length of proceedings for the examination of his second application for release from detention amounted to a violation of this provision. The European Court of Human Rights held that the nature of detention on remand denotes short intervals between proceedings. This can be deduced from the assumption enshrined in article 5 of the Convention for the Protection of Human Rights and Fundamental Freedoms that detention on remand is of strictly limited duration 'because its *raison d'être* is essentially related to the requirements of an investigation which is to be conducted with expedition'[3]. The court conceded that the judge responsible for carrying out investigations must be given a certain amount of time in which to make the necessary inquiries, and concluded by noting that Contracting States are required under the convention to organise their legal systems so as to enable the courts to comply with its various requirements[4]. In the instant case, the investigations, which were of approximately five and a half months' duration, were held not to have been effected 'speedily' as required under paragraph 4 of article 5[5].

1 Convention for the Protection of Human Rights and Fundamental Freedoms (Rome, 4 November 1950; 213 UNTS 221; TS 71 (1953); Cmd 8969), art 5, para 4.
2 *Bezicheri v Italy* (Ser A No 164, Judgment 25 October 1989) 12 EHRR 210, E Ct HR.
3 *Bezicheri*, at para 21 (12 EHRR 214).
4 *Bezicheri*, at para 25 (12 EHRR 215).
5 *Bezicheri*, at para 26 (12 EHRR 215).

34. Setting off time in custody against custodial sentence. The case of *Monnell and Morris*[1] raised the question of setting off time in custody against a custodial sentence with respect to two British citizens, Mr Monnell and Mr Morris. Mr Monnell was convicted and sentenced to three years' imprisonment for burglary. Contrary to legal advice, Mr Monnell lodged various applications of appeal, all of which were unsuccessful. Consequently, pursuant to the Criminal Appeal Act 1968, the Court of Appeal ordered[2] that the fifty-six days spent by him in custody pending appeal should not count towards service of his sentence. Similarly Mr Morris acted contrary to legal advice in appealing against his conviction and sentence of three and a half years' imprisonment for conspiracy to supply heroin. In Mr Morris' case the fifty-six days which he spent in custody pending appeal did not count towards service of his sentence. The applicants contended that these periods of detention (which the Court of Appeal had ordered should not count towards the service of the sentences of imprisonment imposed on them at first instance) were not covered by any of the categories of permitted detention set out in paragraph 1 of article 5 of the Convention for the Protection of Human Rights and Fundamental Freedoms[3]. At the outset the European Court of Human Rights took the opportunity to restate that 'the word "after" in sub-paragraph (a) does not simply mean that the detention must follow the "conviction" in point of time: in addition, the detention must result from, follow and depend upon or occur by virtue of the "conviction" ... there must be a sufficient causal connection between the conviction and the deprivation of liberty at issue'[4]. The court drew attention to the fact that a direction that a period of detention should not count towards service of the sentence could not be regarded simply as a decision on the execution of the original sentence, since its effect was to extend the period of imprisonment[5]. The applicants' additional detention was imposed by the Court of Appeal for reasons independent of either the facts of the offence or the character and criminal record of the individuals concerned. In other words, it was unrelated to the circumstances which had led to the conviction and sentence at first instance and had been ordered in line with a clearly defined deterrent policy[6], namely to minimise unmeritorious applications for leave to appeal. The European Court of Human Rights also recognised that the loss of time ordered under such a direction may not be considered as part of any sentence of imprisonment being served[7]. In spite of these arguments, it nevertheless held that such periods of detention remained within the ambit of paragraph 1(a) of article 5 of the convention[8]. The court maintained that although the periods of detention pending appeal were not treated under English law as part of the applicants' sentences as such, they did constitute a consequential part of the period of detention hich results from the overall sentencing procedure following conviction. The court's attention was drawn to the fact that in many convention countries detention pending a criminal appeal was treated as detention on remand and that a convicted person does not commence serving his sentence until the conviction is finally pronounced. The appellate court in such systems has a sentencing competency and may also possess discretion in deciding whether, and if so to what extent, detention pending appeal may be deducted from the sentence[9]. The court maintained that the differences between the approaches of English law and continental systems in sentencing procedures was 'one of form and not of substance as far as effect on the convicted person'[10].

The permissible forms of legal machinery whereby a person may lawfully be the subject of a detention order 'after conviction' are not identified in paragraph 1 of article 5. Contracting Parties accordingly enjoy discretion, and may legitimately operate different sentencing procedures yet still comply with the requirements of paragraph 1(a). The court was of the view that the technical and formal differences of the United Kingdon's sentencing procedures *vis-à-vis* those of other convention countries was not 'such as to exclude the applicability of sub-paragraph (a) of Article 5(1)...'[10]. The court held that there was a sufficient and legitimate connection between the conviction of each applicant and the additional period of imprisonment following the loss-of-time order for the purposes of the deprivation of liberty permitted under paragraph 1(a) of article 5. The court concluded that the orders depriving Mr Monnell and Mr Morris of their liberty 'issued from and were executed by an appropriate authority and were not arbitrary', and that no breach of paragraph 1 of article 5 had occurred[11].

1 *Monnell and Morris v United Kingdom* (Ser A No 115, Judgment 2 March 1987) 10 EHRR 205, E Ct HR.
2 Ie pursuant to the Criminal Appeal Act 1968 (c 19), s 56.
3 For the Convention for the Protection of Human Rights and Fundamental Freedoms (Rome, 4 November 1950; 213 UNTS 221; TS 71 (1953); Cmd 8969), art 5, para 1, see para 29 above.
4 *Monnell and Morris*, at para 40 (10 EHRR 217). See also *Weeks v United Kingdom* (Ser A No 114, Judgment 2 March 1987) 10 EHRR 293, E Ct HR, considered in para 35 below.
5 *Monnell and Morris*, at para 43 (10 EHRR 218).
6 *Practice Note* [1970] 1 All ER 1119, [1970] 1 WLR 663, CA; *Practice Note* [1980] 1 All ER 555, [1980] 1 WLR 270, CA.
7 Criminal Appeal Act 1968, s 29(1). The European Court of Human Rights recognised that the power of the Court of Appeal was one exercised to discourage abuse of the court's own procedures and as such it was an inherent part of the criminal appeal following the conviction of an offender, and that it was in furtherance of a legitimate aim under the Convention for the Protection of Human Rights and Fundamental Freedoms, art 5, para 1.
8 *Monnell and Morris*, at para 45 (10 EHRR 219).
9 The example of the Federal Republic of Germany was cited.
10 *Monnell and Morris*, at para 47 (10 EHRR 219).
11 *Monnell and Morris*, at paras 50, 51 (10 EHRR 220). The applicants' argument that their applications for leave to appeal were neither hopeless nor frivolous were not entertained by the European Court of Human Rights, being a matter to be decided by the domestic court, and, except in so far as it was necessary to review the contested measure of deprivation of liberty for compatibility with the convention, the European Court of Human Rights was not competent to substitute its own assessment of the facts for that of the domestic court: *Monnell and Morris*, at para 49.

35. Detention of indeterminate length. An alleged violation of inter alia paragraph 4 of article 5 of the Convention for the Protection of Human Rights and Fundamental Freedoms[1] was raised in the United Kingdom case of *Weeks*[2]. Mr Weeks, a United Kingdom citizen, was sentenced to life imprisonment in December 1966[3]. He was released on licence in March 1976 but recalled to prison by a decision of the Home Secretary in June 1977. In October 1982 he was again released on licence but was re-detained in April 1985, his licence having been revoked by the Home Secretary in November 1984. In September 1985 he was released on licence for a third time. This was revoked in March 1986 but by this time Mr Weeks had fled to France.

The European Court of Human Rights was concerned with Mr Weeks' allegations regarding his first recall to prison in 1977 and the period of his imprisonment following his conviction in 1966[4]. The applicant's complaint in respect of paragraph 4 of article 5 was that he had been unable either on his recall to prison in 1977 or at reasonable intervals throughout his detention to take proceedings satisfying the requirements of that provision. The initial consideration which the court addressed was whether the requisite judicial control was incorporated in the original conviction. The court's task was to determine what new issues of lawfulness, if any, were capable of arising in relation to Mr Weeks' recall to prison and continued detention subsequent to sentence and whether the proceedings available complied with that paragraph 4 of article 5. The court maintained that for the purposes of that provision the lawfulness of arrest or detention was to be determined in the light 'not only of domestic law but also of the text of the Convention, the general principles embodied therein and the aim of the restrictions permitted by Article 5(1)'[5]. The court reiterated[6] what it had held in the context of its consideration of paragraph 1(c) of article 5, namely that the stated purpose of social protection and rehabilitation for which the 'indeterminate' sentence of life imprisonment was passed and the particular circumstances of the offences for which he was convicted put Mr Weeks' sentence in a 'special' category: unlike the case of a person sentenced to life imprisonment because of the gravity of the offence committed, the grounds upon which the judges had decided that Mr Weeks' detention and, therefore, liberty should be subject to the discretion of the executive for the rest of his life were by their nature susceptible of change with the passage of time[7].

Paragraph 4 of article 5 of the convention does not guarantee a right to judicial control of such scope as to empower the 'court' to consider all aspects of the case, such as questions of expediency, and substitute its own discretion for that of the original decision-making authority; however, the European Court of Human Rights did stipulate that review 'should be wide enough to bear on those conditions which, according to the Convention, are essential for the lawful detention of a person subject to the special kind of deprivation of liberty ordered against Mr Weeks'[8].

The court then turned to consider whether the proceedings available subsequent to conviction satisfied the requirements of paragraph 4 of article 5. That paragraph speaks of the detained individual being entitled to initiate proceedings, and the court made reference in this context to the United Kingdom system of parole for life prisoners, and concluded that in spite of certain, not negligible, safeguards there existed a certain procedural weakness in the case of a recalled prisoner. A prisoner is entitled to make representations with respect to his recall, not only in writing to the Parole Board but also orally to a member of the Local Review Committee. For the purpose of making such representations, he is also entitled to take legal advice. In addition, the prisoner concerned must, for the purpose of making representations, be sufficiently informed of the reasons for his recall. Notwithstanding these safeguards, the court was of the view that an absence of entitlement to full disclosure of any adverse material in the board's possession precluded proper participation of the individual adversely affected by the contested decision. Such participation, the court maintained, was one of the principal guarantees of a judicial procedure for the purposes of the convention and consequently the procedure followed in the instant case could not be regarded as 'judicial in character'[9]. The court concluded that neither in relation to consideration of Mr Weeks' recall to prison in 1977 nor in relation to periodic examination of his detention with a view to release on licence, could the Parole Board procedure be regarded as satisfying the requirements of paragraph 4 of article 5. Before concluding its considerations on the complaint *vis-à-vis* that provision, the court looked at the possibility of the decision of the Parole Board being subject to judicial review, recognising that prima facie shortcomings in one procedure may be made good by safeguards available in other procedures. The court acknowledged that an application for judicial review represented a useful supplement to the procedure before the Parole Board, by enabling the individual concerned to obtain review by the ordinary courts of the decisions of both the Parole Board and the Home Secretary. However, it was the court's opinion that the scope of the control afforded by judicial review was not sufficiently wide to bear on the conditions essential for the 'lawfulness' of Mr Weeks' detention; that is, whether it was consistent with and therefore justified by the objectives of the indeterminate sentence imposed on him[10]. Accordingly, the court held[11] that the judicial review procedure failed to provide by itself the proceedings required by paragraph 4 of article 5, nor did it serve to remedy the inadequacy of the procedure before the Parole Board. Thus that provision had been violated[12]. In the *Weeks* case the court consistently endorsed the principles enunciated in the earlier *Van Droogenbroeck* case[13], which concerned the detention of a recidivist in Belgium and his allegations that he had been denied the opportunity of having the lawfulness of his detention judicially reviewed[14].

1 For the Convention for the Protection of Human Rights and Fundamental Freedoms (Rome, 4 November 1950; 213 UNTS 221; TS 17 (1953); Cmd 8969), art 5, para 4, see para 29 above.

2 *Weeks v United Kingdom* (Ser A No 114, Judgment 2 March 1987) 10 EHRR 293, E Ct HR. A violation of the Convention for the Protection of Human Rights and Fundamental Freedoms, art 5, para 1 (see para 29 above), was also alleged, but the court concluded otherwise.

3 He was convicted of armed robbery, assaulting a police officer and being in unlawful possession of a firearm. At the time of his conviction he was aged seventeen.

4 Allegations regarding his re-detention from April 1985 were the subject of separate proceedings.

5 *Weeks*, at para 57 (10 EHRR 314). Mr Weeks did not dispute that at all times he could apply to the ordinary courts for judicial review.

6 *Weeks*, at para 49 (10 EHRR 312).

7 The sentencing judges had recognised that although Mr Weeks had been characterised as a 'dangerous young man', it was impossible for them to forecast how long his instability and personality disorders would endure. The European Court of Human Rights deduced from this that if the decision not to release him or the decision to re-detain him were based on grounds inconsistent with the objectives of the sentencing court, Mr Weeks' detention could not be regarded as being 'lawful' within paragraph 1(c) of article 5 of the convention, and from this argued that art 5, para 4, entitled Mr Weeks to apply to a 'court' having jurisdiction to decide 'speedily' whether his deprivation of liberty had become 'unlawful' in this sense. In other words, had the deprivation of liberty been transformed from one initially lawful to one which was arbitrary? Such entitlement, the court concluded, should have been available to Mr Weeks at the moment of any return to custody after being at liberty, and also at reasonable intervals during the course of his imprisonment: *Weeks*, at para 58 (10 EHRR 315).

8 *Weeks*, at para 59 (10 EHRR 315).

9 *Weeks*, at para 66 (10 EHRR 318).

10 *Weeks*, at para 69 (10 EHRR 319). Before reaching its conclusion the court made reference to the grounds of judicial review summarised by Lord Diplock in *Council of Civil Service Unions v Minister for the Civil Service* [1985] AC 374 at 410, 411, [1984] 3 All ER 935 at 950, 951, HL, namely 'illegality', 'irrationality' and 'procedural impropriety'.

11 Ie by thirteen votes to four.

12 *Weeks*, at para 60 (10 EHRR 315).

13 *Van Droogenbroeck v Belgium* (Ser A No 50, Judgment 24 June 1982) 4 EHRR 443, E Ct HR.

14 See also *Thynne, Wilson and Gunnell v United Kingdom* (Ser A No 190, Judgment 25 October 1990) 13 EHRR 666, E Ct HR. For the Commission proceedings, see *Thynne, Wilson and Gunnell v United Kingdom* (Applications 1178/85, 11978/86, 12009/86) 13 EHRR 135, E Com HR.

36. Access to files. In the *Lamy* case[1] it was alleged successfully that, notwithstanding Belgian domestic law, preventing the applicant's counsel from inspecting documents in his file throughout the applicant's first thirty days of custody was contrary to paragraph 4 of article 5 of the Convention for the Protection of Human Rights and Fundamental Freedoms[2]. The applicant argued that a review of the lawfulness of his detention should have been the occasion for objective, adversarial proceedings, and these could not be deemed to have taken place where the investigating judge and Crown counsel had had the opportunity to make their submissions in the full knowledge of a substantial file of documents whereas the applicant's defence lawyer could only present a case on the vague charges made in the arrest warrant. The European Court of Human Rights noted that during the first thirty days of custody, the applicant's counsel was, in accordance with the law as judicially interpreted, unable to inspect anything in the file, and in particular the reports made by the investigating judge and the Verviers police. This applied especially on the occasion of the applicant's first appearance before the *chambre du conseil*, which had to rule on the confirmation of the arrest warrant. The effect was that the applicant's counsel was denied the opportunity of effectively challenging the statements or views which the prosecution had based on these documents. The court maintained that access to these documents was essential for the applicant at what was a crucial stage in the proceedings, namely when the domestic court had to decide whether to remand him in custody or to release him. In particular, such access would have enabled Mr Lamy's counsel to address the court on the matter of the co-defendant's statements and attitudes[3]. In the view of the European Court of Human Rights inspection of the documents was a prerequisite to any effective challenge of the lawfulness of the arrest warrant[4]. The appraisal of the need to remand in custody and the subsequent assessment of guilt were too closely linked for access to documents to be refused in the former case when the law required it in the latter[4]. Accordingly, the court held unanimously that paragraph 4 of article 5 had been breached.

1 *Lamy v Belgium* (Ser A No 151, Judgment 30 March 1989) 11 EHRR 529, E Ct HR. Mr Lamy, a Belgian citizen, was the manager of a private limited company which filed a declaration of insolvency with the registry of the Verviers Commercial Court on 29 November 1982, and the court adjudged the company bankrupt the same day. In February 1983 Mr Lamy was brought before an investigating judge of the Verviers *tribunal de première instance* (regional court of first instance) and questioned, and subsequently, pursuant to a warrant for his arrest, he was taken into custody at the remand prison at Verviers.

2 For the Convention for the Protection of Human Rights and Fundamental Freedoms (Rome, 4 November 1950; 213 UNTS 221; TS 71 (1953); Cmd 8969), art 5, para 4, see para 29 above.

3 In March 1986 five co-defendants were committed for trial with Mr Lamy at the criminal court by the *chambre du conseil* of the Verviers *tribunal de première instance*.

4 *Lamy*, at para 29 (11 EHRR 538).

37. Detention prior to extradition. The *Sanchez-Reisse* case[1] concerned an Argentinian national, Leandres Sanchez-Reisse[2], who was arrested in Switzerland with a view to being extradited to Argentina, where he was wanted on charges of kidnapping a banker and holding him to ransom. Mr Sanchez-Reisse objected to his extradition and applied to the Federal Police Office for provisional release from detention. When this was refused he made three applications to the Federal Court, all of which were rejected[3]. It was the procedure adopted by the Federal Court which the applicant alleged violated paragraph 4 of article 5 of the Convention for the Protection of Human Rights and Fundamental Freedoms[4].

The first contention advanced by the applicant was that the Swiss system for appealing against detention prior to extradition did not afford adequate safeguards. The European Court of Human Rights refuted the argument that he had been denied access to a court, and held that the intervention of the Federal Police Office neither impeded the applicant's access to the Federal Court nor limited that court's power of review. Given the very nature of extradition and its effects on a state's international relations, the European Court of Human Rights considered that the participation of the executive could be regarded as expedient[5].

Secondly, Mr Sanchez-Reisse maintained that he had been denied the possibility of conducting his own defence because the exclusively written nature of the procedure in the Federal Court necessitated the assistance of a lawyer. He alleged that it was imperative that a detainee should be able to monitor the action taken by the lawyer, in particular by attending the oral proceedings, especially if the lawyer has been appointed by the Federal Police Office. This contention was likewise refuted by the European Court of Human Rights as having no basis in the text of paragraph 4 of article 5[6]. Such an allegation, the court continued, overlooked the fact that the requirement of a lawyer's assistance under Swiss law was intended to afford an important guarantee to the detainee who, by definition, is a foreigner, and therefore will often be unfamiliar with the Swiss legal system. Moreover, there was no evidence that the applicant's legal knowledge was sufficient to allow him to conduct matters himself.

Finally, the applicant alleged that he should have been given the opportunity (1) of replying to the opinion of the Federal Police Office, and (2) of appearing either as of right or on his application before a court to argue the case for his release[7]. It was contended that the lack of any contact with a court was incompatible with the very nature of *habeas corpus* and that it was particularly harsh in this case as detention prior to extradition afforded the detainee fewer points of reference than ordinary pre-trial detention[8]. The European Court of Human Rights expressed the view that paragraph 4 of article 5 required that Mr Sanchez-Reisse should have been provided in some way or another with the benefit of an adversarial procedure[9]. Affording him the possibility of submitting written comments on the opinion of the Federal Police Office would have been an appropriate means, but there was no evidence to suggest that this had been offered to him. The court acknowledged that while Mr Sanchez-Reisse had been allowed to indicate in his request the circumstances which he felt justified his release, this did not *per se* provide the indispensable 'equality of arms'[9]. The purpose of the provision would, the court continued, have been attained if the possibility of appearing in person before the Federal Court had been afforded to the applicant. The absence of this possibility led the court to conclude that the applicant had not received the benefit of a true adversarial procedure[9] and that the procedures employed did not, when viewed as a whole, comply with the guarantees afforded by the provision[10].

The court then turned its attention to the length of proceedings and whether the relevant decisions affecting Mr Sanchez-Reisse had been taken 'speedily'[11]. Such a term, the court argued, must be determined in the light of the circumstances of each case: it could not be defined in the abstract[12]. The court held that notwithstanding the relevance of the extradition issue, the applicant was entitled to a speedy decision — whether affirmative or negative — on the lawfulness of his custody[13]. The court concluded that there was no obvious reason[14] for depriving Mr Sanchez-Reisse of the guarantee of rapidity prescribed in paragraph 4 of article 5[15].

1 *Sanchez-Reisse v Switzerland* (Ser A No 107, Judgment 21 October 1986) 9 EHRR 71, E Ct HR.
2 He had for a number of years been resident with his wife and two children in Florida in the United States.
3 His first request was withdrawn and his second and third applications were rejected by the Federal Court in accordance with an opinion delivered by the Federal Police Office.

4 For the Convention for the Protection of Human Rights and Fundamental Freedoms (Rome, 4 November 1950; 213 UNTS 221; TS 71 (1953); Cmd 8969), art 5, para 4, see para 29 above.

5 *Sanchez-Reisse*, at para 45 (9 EHRR 81).

6 *Sanchez-Reisse*, at para 47 (9 EHRR 82).

7 This in the applicant's opinion contributed to the worsening of his state of health, the main ground on which his request for release was based.

8 Swiss courts hearing extradition cases review only compliance with the conditions of the relevant extradition treaty and not the merits of the charge.

9 *Sanchez-Reisse*, at para 51 (9 EHRR 83).

10 *Sanchez-Reisse*, at para 52 (9 EHRR 84).

11 The periods to be considered were thirty-one days and forty-six days.

12 *Sanchez-Reisse*, at para 56 (9 EHRR 85).

13 *Sanchez-Reisse*, at para 57 (9 EHRR 85).

14 Eg there was nothing to suggest that Mr Sanchez-Reisse's case raised complex issues necessitating detailed investigation and warranting lengthy consideration.

15 *Sanchez-Reisse*, at para 60 (9 EHRR 86).

38. Detention prior to deportation. In the case of *Bozano*[1] the issue before the European Court of Human Rights was detention with a view to deportation after the rejection of a request for extradition. The case concerned Mr Bozano, an Italian national who was convicted in Italy of various offences including murder. Prior to the final appeal hearing, Mr Bozano took refuge in France. Italy's request for his extradition was refused. Mr Bozano was subsequently charged in France[2] and committed for trial but released. During his release he was taken into custody and 'deported' to Switzerland without the opportunity to obtain legal advice[3]. Mr Bozano was finally extradited to Italy where, at the time of the Strasbourg proceedings, he was duly serving his life sentence. His application regarding violation of the Convention for the Protection of Human Rights and Fundamental Freedoms related to his 'abduction' and 'forcible removal' from France and the lack of remedies as guaranteed by paragraph 4 of article 5 of the convention. The court held that the main issue was to determine the 'lawfulness of the disputed detention and the protection of the individual from arbitrariness'. In the court's words 'not only was the individual's right to liberty at stake but also the individual's right to security of person'[4]. On the basis of the facts presented, the court had 'gravest doubts' as to whether the contested deprivation of liberty satisfied the legal requirements in the respondent state[5]. In particular, the court focused on the circumstances surrounding the applicant's removal to Switzerland[6]. In view of all the facts peculiar to the case, the court concluded that the applicant's deprivation of liberty with a view to his 'deportation' was neither 'lawful' within the meaning of paragraph 1(b) of article 5 nor compatible with the 'right to security of person'. The manner by which Mr Bozano was deprived of his liberty was characterised by the court as 'a disguised form of extradition' and not 'detention' as generally accepted as necessary prior to deportation[7]. In the light of the foregoing the court ruled unanimously that paragraph 1 of article 5 had been violated[8].

1 *Bozano v France* (Ser A No 111, Judgment 18 December 1986) 9 EHRR 297, E Ct HR.

2 The charges were fraud, forgery and falsification of administrative documents.

3 His 'deportation' was carried out in a somewhat irregular manner under duress by plain clothed policemen in an unmarked car.

4 *Bozano*, at para 54 (9 EHRR 313).

5 *Bozano*, at para 58 (9 EHRR 316).

6 *Bozano*, at para 59 (9 EHRR 316, 317). The court commented on the delay of more than a month between the issue and service of the deportation order, and on the manner in which he was apprehended.

7 *Bozano*, at para 60 (9 EHRR 317).

8 The court held that it had no jurisdiction to entertain the applicant's complaint in respect of the Convention for the Protection of Human Rights and Fundamental Freedoms, art 5, para 4. For art 5, para 1(f), see para 29 above.

39. Detention of minors. The *Nielsen* case[1] was concerned exclusively with article 5 of the Convention for the Protection of Human Rights and Fundamental Freedoms and its applicability to minors[2]. The issue before the European Court of Human Rights was the applicant's committal to the Child Psychiatric Ward at the State Hospital in Denmark on the authority of his mother, who was the sole holder of parental rights[3]. The court began its consideration by a general exposition of the scope and nature of parental rights:

> '... family life in the Contracting States encompasses a broad range of parental rights and responsibilities in regard to care and custody of minor children. The care and upbringing of children normally and necessarily require that the parents or an only parent decide where the child must reside and also impose, or authorise others to impose, various restrictions on the child's liberty. Thus the children in a school or other educational or recreational institution must abide by certain rules which limit their freedom of movement and their liberty in other respects. Likewise a child may have to be hospitalised for medical treatment. Family life in this sense, and especially the rights of parents to exercise parental authority over their children, having due regard to their corresponding parental responsibilities, is recognised and protected by the Convention, in particular by Article 8. Indeed the exercise of parental rights constitutes a fundamental element of family life'[4].

In the instant case, the court was of the view that the decision on the hospitalisation of the applicant was taken by the mother in her capacity as holder of parental rights and that the assistance rendered by the authorities was of a limited and subsidiary nature. The respective roles of the mother and the authorities was the salient factor in the court's determination that article 5 was not applicable. Hospitalisation of the applicant did not therefore amount to a deprivation of liberty by the state within the meaning of article 5, but was instead a responsible exercise by his mother of her custodial rights in the interests of the child[6].

Article 5 applies to everyone: the protection afforded therein therefore extends to minors provided the deprivation of liberty is occasioned by the state. This is illustrated in the case of *Bouamar*[7] where the applicant underwent successive placements in a remand prison as interim custody in accordance with domestic Belgian law. Criminal proceedings were never initiated against the applicant. Mr Bouamar complained that his detention in the remand prison on nine separate occasions throughout 1980 was contrary to paragraph 1 of article 5 of the convention and that the 'informal judicial set-up' of the juvenile court constituted a violation of paragraph 4 of article 5. Regarding paragraph 1, the main issue confronting the court was the assessment of the lawfulness of the detention periods. Not for the first time, the court stated that the interpretation and application of domestic law is the task of the national authorities, notably the courts. Nevertheless, the court concluded that the fruitless repetition of the nine placement orders had the effect of making them 'less and less "lawful"' under paragraph 1(d) of article 5, particularly in the absence of criminal proceedings[8]. The court held that the domestic appeal procedure 'had no practical effect'[9] because each of the applicant's appeals was declared inadmissible on the grounds that Mr Bouamar had been released from the disputed detention. The application was thus successful on both grounds[10].

1 *Nielsen v Denmark* (Ser A No 144, Judgment 28 November 1988) 11 EHRR 175, E Ct HR.
2 While the court held that in the circumstances of the case article 5 of the Convention for the Protection of Human Rights and Fundamental Freedoms (Rome, 4 November 1950; 213 UNTS 221; TS 71 (1953); Cmd 8969) was not applicable, it nevertheless made a number of pronouncements regarding the scope of article 5 in the context of the detention of minors. See especially art 5, para 1(d), and para 29 above.
3 The applicant was the subject of a custody dispute between his parents, who were unmarried. Under Danish law the mother prima facie held the full complement of parental rights. However,

the child had a better relationship with his father, and in spite of his mother's efforts this was ultimately recognised and the child was allowed to live permanently with his father, who was awarded custody.

4 *Nielsen*, at para 61 (11 EHRR 191, 192). For the Convention for the Protection of Human Rights and Fundamental Freedoms, art 8, see para 62 below.

5 *Nielsen*, at para 63 (11 EHRR 192, 193). The state assistance was that of the chief physician at the hospital and the social authorities which acquiesced in the mother's authorisation.

6 *Nielsen*, at para 73 (11 EHRR 196). The hospitalisation of the applicant followed his having lived 'underground' for more than three years and his running back to his father after his being returned to the lawful custody of his mother.

7 *Bouamar v Belgium* (Ser A No 129, Judgment 29 February 1988) 11 EHRR 1, E Ct HR.

8 *Bouamar*, at para 53 (11 EHRR 17).

9 *Bouamar*, at para 63 (11 EHRR 20).

10 The court was unanimous in its finding that there was a breach of the Convention for the Protection of Human Rights and Fundamental Freedoms, art 5, para 1, while the breach of art 5, para 4, was decided by six votes to one.

40. Compulsory residence. There are two cases concerning applicants who were the subjects of compulsory residence orders in Italy: *Guzzardi*[1] and *Ciulla*[2]. In each case the applicant was suspected of being involved in mafia-type organised crime, and compulsory residence was a preventive measure in terms of Italian Law no. 1423 of 1956 and Law no. 575 of 1965[3].

In the *Ciulla* case the European Court of Human Rights emphasised that under paragraph 1(c) of article 5 of the Convention for the Protection of Human Rights and Fundamental Freedoms deprivation of liberty is allowed only in connection with criminal proceedings[4]. However, the preventive procedure provided for under the 1956 Law had been designed for purposes other than criminal proceedings. The compulsory residence order could be based on suspicion rather than proof. The deprivation of liberty which in the present case had preceded that proof could not therefore be equated with pre-trial detention as governed by paragraph 1(c) of article 5[5].

Similarly, in the *Guzzardi* case the court stated that to use the term 'conviction' for a preventive or security measure would be cognisant neither with the principle of narrow interpretation to be observed in this area, nor with the fact that that word implies a finding of guilt[6]. In sum, the order in question was made outwith the context of criminal proceedings. The general background of the disputed detention and the importance of Italy's struggle against organised crime did not warrant an exception to paragraph 1 of article 5[7].

In its judgment in the *Guzzardi* case, the court reaffirmed that the starting point in any alleged deprivation of liberty within article 5 is the individual's particular situation, and criteria such as the type, duration, effects and manner of implementation of the measure in question must be taken into account[8].

1 *Guzzardi v Italy* (Ser A No 39, Judgment 6 November 1980) 3 EHRR 333, E Ct HR.

2 *Ciulla v Italy* (Ser A No 148, Judgment 22 February 1989) 13 EHRR 346, E Ct HR.

3 The latter was specifically directed against the Mafia.

4 *Ciulla*, at para 38 (13 EHRR 354). For the Convention for the Protection of Human Rights and Fundamental Freedoms (Rome, 4 November 1950; 213 UNTS 221; TS 71 (1953); Cmd 8969), art 5, para 1(c), see para 29 above.

5 *Ciulla*, at para 39 (13 EHRR 355).

6 *Guzzardi*, at para 100 (3 EHRR 366, 367).

7 *Ciulla*, at para 41 (13 EHRR 356): '. . . the exhaustive list of permissible exceptions in paragraph 1 of Article 5 . . . must be interpreted strictly'.

8 *Guzzardi*, at para 92 (3 EHRR 362, 363). The court had stated this earlier in *Engel v Netherlands (No 1)* (Ser A No 22, Judgment 8 June 1976) 1 EHRR 647 at 669, E Ct HR, at paras 58, 59.

41. Persons of unsound mind. The Convention for the Protection of Human Rights and Fundamental Freedoms does not state what is to be understood by the words 'persons of unsound mind' in paragraph 1(e) of article 5; nor is the term one which can be given a 'definitive interpretation'[1]. The European Court of Human Rights has acknowledged that it is a term whose meaning is 'continually evolving as research in psychiatry progresses, an increasing flexibility in treatment is developing and society's attitudes to mental illness change, in particular so that a greater understanding of the problems of mental patients is becoming more widespread'[2]: in deciding whether an individual 'should be detained as a "person of unsound mind", the national authorities are to be recognised as having a certain discretion since it is in the first place for the national authorities to evaluate the evidence adduced before them in a particular case'[3].

The task of the court is confined to applying the convention to the decisions adopted by the national authorities, with regard to the detention of a person deemed to be of unsound mind. In the *Winterwerp* case the court expressed the view that:

> 'except in emergency cases, the individual concerned should not be deprived of his liberty unless he has been reliably shown to be of "unsound mind". The very nature of what has to be established before the competent national authority — that is, a true mental disorder — calls for objective medical expertise. Further, the mental disorder must be of a kind or degree warranting compulsory confinement. What is more, the validity of continued confinement depends upon the persistence of such a disorder'[4].

The court's dicta in the *Winterwerp* judgment has been followed most notably from a United Kingdom standpoint in the case of *X v United Kingdom*[5].

1 *Winterwerp v Netherlands* (Ser A No 33, Judgment 24 October 1979) 2 EHRR 387, E Ct HR. For the Convention for the Protection of Human Rights and Fundamental Freedoms (Rome, 4 November 1950; 213 UNTS 221; TS 71 (1953); Cmd 8969), art 5, para 1(e), see para 29 above.
2 *Winterwerp*, at para 37 (2 EHRR 401).
3 *Winterwerp*, at para 40 (2 EHRR 403).
4 *Winterwerp*, at para 39 (2 EHRR 403).
5 *X v United Kingdom* (Ser A No 55, Judgment 18 October 1982) 5 EHRR 192, E Ct HR. The applicant, a United Kingdom citizen born in 1934, died in 1979. At the time of lodging his application with the European Court of Human Rights he was detained in Broadmoor Hospital, a special secure mental hospital for the criminally insane. His complaints were directed against his recall to Broadmoor in April 1974 following a three-year period of conditional discharge. He claimed that his recall was unjustified, that he was not promptly given sufficient reasons for his re-detention, and that he had no effective way of challenging the authorities' action. The relevant domestic legislation at that time was the Mental Health Act 1959 (c 72), which applied to England and Wales. The European Court of Human Rights concluded unanimously that there had been no breach of the Convention for the Protection of Human Rights and Fundamental Freedoms, art 5, para 1, although it found that there had been a breach of art 5, para 4. Both these decisions were followed in *Ashingdane v United Kingdom* (Ser A No 93, Judgment 28 May 1985) 7 EHRR 528, E Ct HR, and in *Van der Leer v Netherlands* (Ser A No 170, Judgment 21 February 1990) 12 EHRR 567, E Ct HR.

42. Vagrancy. In the 'Vagrancy' cases[1] the European Court of Human Rights unequivocally stated that although an individual may voluntarily surrender to detention, that does not remove him from the protective ambit of the Convention for the Protection of Human Rights and Fundamental Freedoms:

> 'the right to liberty is too important in a "democratic society" within the meaning of the Convention for a person to lose the benefit of the protection of the Convention for the single reason that he gives himself up to be taken into detention. Detention might violate Article 5 even although the person concerned might have agreed to it. When the matter is one which concerns *ordre public* within the Council of Europe, a scrupulous supervision by the organs of the Convention of all measures capable of violating the rights and freedoms which it guarantees is necessary in every case'[2].

As in other areas of activity, Contracting Parties retain discretion: but this discretion is not unfettered; it is subject to European supervision. Specifically with regard to vagrants and in particular with regard to the case before it, the court expressed the view that temporary distress or misery could drive a person to give himself up to the police to be detained, but this would not necessarily mean that the person so asking was in a state of vagrancy and even less that he was a professional beggar or that his state of vagrancy resulted from one of the circumstances — idleness, drunkenness or immorality — which, under Section 13 of the Belgian Act of 1891, could entail a more severe measure of detention[2].

1 *De Wilde, Ooms and Versyp v Belgium (No 1)* (Ser A No 12, Judgment 18 June 1971) 1 EHRR 373, E Ct HR.
2 *De Wilde, Ooms and Versyp v Belgium (No 1)*, at para 65 (1 EHRR 403).

(4) FAIR AND PUBLIC HEARING

43. Introduction: article 6. Article 6 of the Convention for the Protection of Human Rights and Fundamental Freedoms provides as follows:

'1. In the determination of his civil rights and obligations or of any criminal charge against him, everyone is entitled to a fair and public hearing within a reasonable time by an independent and impartial tribunal established by law. Judgment shall be pronounced publicly but the press and public may be excluded from all or part of the trial in the interest of morals, public order or national security in a democratic society, where the interests of juveniles or the protection of the private life of the parties so require, or to the extent strictly necessary in the opinion of the court in special circumstances where publicity would prejudice the interests of justice.
2. Everyone charged with a criminal offence shall be presumed innocent until proved guilty according to law.
3. Everyone charged with a criminal offence has the following minimum rights:
(*a*) to be informed promptly, in a language which he understands and in detail, of the nature and cause of the accusation against him;
(*b*) to have adequate time and facilities for the preparation of his defence;
(*c*) to defend himself in person or through legal assistance of his own choosing or, if he has not sufficient means to pay for legal assistance, to be given it free when the interests of justice so require;
(*d*) to examine or have examined witnesses against him and to obtain the attendance and examination of witnesses on his behalf under the same conditions as witnesses against him;
(*e*) to have the free assistance of an interpreter if he cannot understand or speak the language used in court'[1].

Article 6 is the article which has given rise to the highest number of cases before the European Court of Human Rights[2].

1 Convention for the Protection of Human Rights and Fundamental Freedoms (Rome, 4 November 1950; 213 UNTS 221; TS 71 (1953); Cmd 8969), art 6, paras 1–3.
2 Accordingly, only the leading and most recent cases will be dealt with in any great detail in the paragraphs which follow.

44. Right of access to court. The first United Kingdom case, *Golder*[1], concerned the applicant's allegation that paragraph 1 of article 6 of the Convention for the Protection of Human Rights and Fundamental Freedoms had been violated when he had been refused a consultation with a solicitor. He submitted that such refusal constituted a denial of access to a court. In its general observations, the European Court of Human Rights stated that a right of access exists to such an extent that 'in civil matters one can scarcely conceive of the rule of law without there being a possibility of having access to the courts'[2]. Furthermore,

> 'The principle whereby a civil claim must be capable of being submitted to a judge ranks as one of the universally "recognised" fundamental principles of law; the same is true of the principle of international law which forbids the denial of justice. Article 6(1) must be read in the light of these principles'[3].

The court continued:

> 'Were Article 6(1) to be understood as concerning exclusively the conduct of an action which had already been initiated before a court, a Contracting State could, without acting in breach of that text, do away with its courts, or take away their jurisdiction to determine certain classes of civil actions and entrust it to organs dependent on the Government. Such assumptions, indissociable from a danger of arbitrary power, would have serious consequences which are repugnant to the aforementioned principles and which the Court cannot overlook. It would be inconceivable . . . that Article 6(1) should describe in detail the procedural guarantees afforded to parties in a pending lawsuit and should not first protect that which alone makes it in fact possible to benefit from such guarantees, that is, access to a court. The fair, public and expeditious characteristics of judicial proceedings are of no value at all if there are not judicial proceedings. Taking all the preceding considerations together, it follows that the right of access constitutes an element which is inherent in the right stated by Article 6(1). This is not an extensive interpretation forcing new obligations on the Contracting States: it is based on the very terms of the first sentence of Article 6(1) read in its context and having regard to the object and purpose of the Convention, a lawmaking treaty, and to general principles of law'[4].

In sum the court emphasised:

> '. . . that Article 6(1) secures to everyone the right to have any claim relating to his civil rights and obligations brought before a court or tribunal. In this way the Article embodies the "right to a court", of which the right of access, that is the right to institute proceedings before courts in civil matters, constitutes one aspect only'[5].

The court nevertheless acknowledged that the right of access to the courts is not an absolute right[6], but confined itself to the issue before it, namely whether or not the application of the Prison Rules had violated the convention to the prejudice of Mr Golder. In other words, the court did not regard as its function an elaboration of a general theory of the limitations admissible in the case of convicted prisoners, nor even to rule *in abstracto* on the compatibility of the Prison Rules with the convention[7]. With respect to Mr Golder, the court held that his wish to consult a solicitor with a view to raising a legal action was justified, and that it was not the Home Secretary who should appraise the prospects of the action contemplated, but that that was the function of an independent and impartial court[8].

In respect of paragraph 1 of article 6, *Golder* was followed in *Silver*[9], *Pudas*[10], *Bodén*[1], and most recently in *Skarby*[12]. Another case which follows *Golder* is *Airey*[13], which, due to its facts, merits further consideration.

Mrs Airey, an Irish national, sought to obtain a decree of judicial separation on the grounds of her husband's alleged physical and mental cruelty to their children and herself[14]. Such a decree could be granted only by the Irish High Court, and legal aid was not available for that purpose. Consequently, due to lack of financial means, Mrs Airey was unable to instruct a lawyer. She contended that this led to a violation of paragraph 1 of article 6, her access to court being denied by the prohibitive cost involved. The Irish government argued that Mrs Airey had the right to appear on her own behalf before the High Court. The European Court of Human Rights was not receptive to this argument, as the right alleged by the Irish government was theoretical rather than practical or effective and it is the latter which the convention is designed to guarantee[15]. The court also rejected the attempt of the Irish government to distinguish the instant case from *Golder* on the ground that Mrs Airey had not encountered either a positive obstacle emanating from the state or a deliberate attempt by the state to impede access to the domestic court. The essence of the argument of the Irish government was that Ireland could not be held responsible for something which was directly attributable to Mrs Airey's personal financial circumstances[16]. The European Court of Human Rights acknowledged the difference in facts between the two cases, but did not support the conclusion drawn therefrom. To be hindered from pursuing an action could contravene the convention as much as a legal impediment: states may therefore be required to take positive measures to implement the convention as is the case with securing an effective right of access to the courts. Regarding Mrs Airey, the court held that with regard to all the circumstances of the case she did not enjoy an effective right of access to the High Court for the purpose of petitioning for a decree of judicial separation and accordingly paragraph 1 of article 6 had been breached[17].

1 *Golder v United Kingdom* (Ser A No 18, Judgment 21 February 1975) 1 EHRR 524, E Ct HR. Mr Golder, a prisoner at Parkhurst Prison, had petitioned the Home Secretary pursuant to the Prison Rules 1964, SI 1964/388, for permission to consult a solicitor as a preliminary to bringing civil proceedings for libel against a prison officer. The prison officer, following a disturbance at the prison, had made a statement implicating Mr Golder which was subsequently refuted to some extent by the officer himself and by others with the result that Mr Golder was cleared.
2 *Golder*, at para 34 (1 EHRR 535).
3 *Golder*, at para 35 (1 EHRR 535, 536).
4 *Golder*, at paras 35, 36 (1 EHRR 536).
5 *Golder*, at para 36 (1 EHRR 536).
6 *Golder*, at para 38 (1 EHRR 537).
7 *Golder*, at para 39 (1 EHRR 537).
8 *Golder*, at para 40 (1 EHRR 537). The court held by nine votes to three that the Convention for the Protection of Human Rights and Fundamental Freedoms (Rome, 4 November 1950; 213 UNTS 221; TS 71 (1953); Cmd 8969), art 6, para 1, had been violated. For art 6, see para 43 above. The applicant further contended that art 8, for which see para 62 below, had been violated.
9 *Silver v United Kingdom* (Ser A No 61, Judgment 25 March 1983) 5 EHRR 347, E Ct HR, where the facts were similar to those in *Golder*.
10 *Pudas v Sweden* (Ser A No 125A, Judgment 27 October 1987) 10 EHRR 380, E Ct HR, concerning procedures for challenging the revocation of a public transport licence.
11 *Bodén v Sweden* (Ser A No 125B, Judgment 27 October 1987) 10 EHRR 367, E Ct HR, concerning the challenge of an expropriation permit.
12 *Skärby v Sweden* (Ser A No 180B, Judgment 28 June 1990) 13 EHRR 90, E Ct HR, concerning the inability to challenge an exemption from a building plan.
13 *Airey v Ireland* (Ser A No 32, Judgment 9 October 1979) 2 EHRR 305, E Ct HR.
14 Divorce is not available in Ireland.
15 *Airey*, at para 24 (2 EHRR 314, 315).
16 *Airey*, at para 25 (2 EHRR 315, 316).
17 *Airey*, at para 28 (2 EHRR 318). The decision was by five votes to two.

45. Existence of dispute concerning a right. Before paragraph 1 of article 6 of the Convention for the Protection of Human Rights and Fundamental Freedoms[1] may be invoked, it is prerequisite that there exists a dispute concerning a right. The character of the 'dispute' as developed through the case law was succinctly summarised in the *Benthem* case[2] as follows:
(1) the word 'dispute' should be 'given a substantive rather than a formal meaning'[3].
(2) The dispute may relate not only to 'the actual existence of a right'[4] but also to its scope or the manner in which it may be exercised, and it may concern both 'questions of fact' and 'questions of law';
(3) the dispute must be genuine and of a serious nature[5]; and

(4) the result of the proceedings must be directly decisive for such a right[6].

The concept 'civil rights and obligations' is not interpreted solely by reference to the domestic law of the respondent state[7], nor does article 6 cover only 'private law disputes in the traditional sense, that is disputes between individuals or between an individual and the State to the extent that the latter had been acting as a private person, subject to private law' and not 'in its sovereign capacity'[8]. What is important in respect of the right is the 'character of the right at issue'[8] rather than the character of either the legislation which governs how the matter is to be determined or the authority which is invested with the jurisdiction in the matter[9]. The court is of the view that it is not required to provide an abstract definition of the concept of 'civil rights and obligations', but rather will consider the concept in the context of the relevant legislation at issue[10].

1 For the Convention for the Protection of Human Rights and Fundamental Freedoms (Rome, 4 November 1950; 213 UNTS 221; TS 71 (1953); Cmd 8969), art 6, para 1, see para 43 above.
2 See *Benthem v Netherlands* (Ser A No 97, Judgment 23 October 1985) 8 EHRR 1 at 8, E Ct HR, at para 32. This summary was approved in *Pudas v Sweden* (Ser A No 125A, Judgment 27 October 1987) 10 EHRR 380 at 387, E Ct HR, at para 31.
3 See *Le Compte, Van Leuven and De Meyere v Belgium* (Ser A No 43, Judgment 23 June 1981) 4 EHRR 1 at 16, E Ct HR, at para 45.
4 See *Le Compte, Van Leuven and De Meyere v Belgium*, at para 49 (4 EHRR 18).
5 See *Le Compte, Van Leuven and De Meyere v Belgium*, at para 51 (4 EHRR 19), and *Albert and Le Compte v Belgium* (Ser A No 58, Judgment 10 February 1983) 5 EHRR 533 at 541, 545, E Ct HR, at paras 29, 36.
6 See *Ringeisen v Austria (No 1)* (Ser A No 13, Judgment 16 July 1971) 1 EHRR 455, E Ct HR.
7 *König v Germany* (Ser A No 27, Judgment 28 June 1978) 2 EHRR 170, E Ct HR, at paras 88, 89.
8 *König v Germany* at para 90.
9 *Ringeisen v Austria (No 1)* at para 90.
10 This it did in *Feldbrugge v Netherlands* (Ser A No 99, Judgment 29 May 1986) 8 EHRR 425, E Ct HR, where it was called upon to examine the Dutch sickness insurance scheme and to determine whether the dispute in question fell within the sphere of public or private law. The court considered the scheme under a number of what it believed to be determining factors, namely (for public law) the character of the legislation, the compulsory nature of the legislation and the assumption by the state of responsibility for social protection; and (for private law) the personal and economic nature of the asserted right, the connection with the contract of employment, and affinities with insurance under the ordinary right: see paras 31–40 (8 EHRR 432–435).

46. Right to have case heard within a reasonable time. In the *Wemhoff* case[1] the European Court of Human Rights identified the precise aim of paragraph 1 of article 6 of the Convention for the Protection of Human Rights and Fundamental Freedoms[2] in criminal matters as being that of ensuring that accused persons do not have to lie under a charge for too long and that the charge is determined. As to the period to be taken into consideration for the purposes of applying this provision, the court stated conclusively that it should last as least until acquittal or conviction, even if this decision were to be reached on appeal. There was no reason why the protection against delay given to the persons concerned should end at the first hearing in a trial: unwarranted adjournments or excessive delays on the part of trial courts are as much to be avoided and if they occur may fall within paragraph 1 of article 6[3]. As to the commencement of the period to be taken into consideration, it is initiated from the date on which the person is charged[4]. It should be noted that the court has said that in civil matters it is conceivable that the reasonable time may in certain circumstances begin to run even before the issue of the writ commencing proceedings before the court[5].

1 *Wemhoff v Germany* (Ser A No 7, Judgment 27 June 1968) 1 EHRR 55, E Ct HR, discussed in para 32 above.

2 For the Convention for the Protection of Human Rights and Fundamental Freedoms (Rome, 4 November 1950; 213 UNTS 221; TS 71 (1953); Cmd 8969), art 6, para 1, see para 43 above.

3 *Wemhoff*, at para 18 (1 EHRR 78).

4 *Wemhoff*, at para 19 (1 EHRR 78).

5 *Golder v United Kingdom* (Ser A No 18, Judgment 21 February 1975) 1 EHRR 524 at 533, E Ct HR, at para 32; *König v Germany* (Ser A No 27, Judgment 28 June 1978) 2 EHRR 170 at 196, E Ct HR, at para 98.

47. What constitutes reasonableness? The European Court of Human Rights has articulated the factors which must be taken into account when an assessment is being made of the reasonableness of the duration of proceedings. These factors apply irrespective of whether the case is civil or criminal. Each case turns on its own facts, but regard will be given inter alia to the complexity of the case, the applicant's conduct and the manner in which the matter was dealt with by the administrative and judicial authorities[1].

1 *König v Germany* (Ser A No 27, Judgment 28 June 1978) 2 EHRR 170 at 197, E Ct HR, at para 99. See also *Neumeister v Austria (No 1)* (Ser A No 8, Judgment 27 June 1968) 1 EHRR 91 at 130, 131, E Ct HR, at paras 20, 21; *Ringeisen v Austria (No 1)* (Ser A No 13, Judgment 16 July 1971) 1 EHRR 455 at 495, 496, E Ct HR, at para 110; *Zimmermann and Steiner v Switzerland* (Ser A No 66, Judgment 13 July 1983) 6 EHRR 17 at 23, E Ct HR, at para 24; *B v Austria* (Ser A No 175, Judgment 28 March 1990) 13 EHRR 20 at 32 ff, E Ct HR, at paras 49 ff.

48. Independence and impartiality. In order to establish whether a body is independent both of the executive and of the parties to the case, regard will be given to the manner of appointment of its members and the duration of their term of office, the existence of guarantees against outside pressures and the question of whether the body presents an appearance of independence[1].

As the European Court of Human Rights has recognised, impartiality 'normally denotes absence of prejudice or bias', and its existence or otherwise can be tested in various ways[2]. Impartiality is established by the application of a subjective test 'that is on the basis of the personal conviction of a particular judge in a given case', and an objective test ascertaining whether the judge concerned 'offered guarantees sufficient to exclude any legitimate doubt in this respect'[3]. The personal impartiality of a judge is to be presumed unless there is proof to the contrary[4]. The objective test concerns ascertaining the existence of facts independent of the judge's personal conduct which call his impartiality into doubt. In this context, the court has held that even appearances may have a certain importance, as it is paramount, especially with regard to criminal proceedings, that the public in a democratic society has confidence in the court system[5]. Consequently, a judge in respect of whom there would be a legitimate reason to fear a lack of impartiality would be required to withdraw from a case[6]. The determination of such a fact is whether it 'can be held objectively justified'. Such a fear entertained by the accused would be recognised as being important but not decisive[7].

1 *Campbell and Fell v United Kingdom* (Ser A No 80, Judgment 28 June 1984) 7 EHRR 165 at 198, 199, E Ct HR, at para 78, endorsed in *Langborger v Sweden* (Ser A No 155, Judgment 22 June 1989) 12 EHRR 416 at 425, E Ct HR, at para 32.

2 *Piersack v Belgium* (Ser A No 53, Judgment 1 October 1982) 5 EHRR 169 at 179, 180, E Ct HR, at para 30.

3 See eg *Hauschildt v Denmark* (Ser A No 154, Judgment 24 May 1989) 12 EHRR 266 at 279, E Ct HR, at para 46.

4 *Hauschildt*, at para 47.

5 *Hauschildt*, at para 48.

6 *Hauschildt*, at para 48. See also *De Cubber v Belgium* (Ser A No 86, Judgment 26 October 1984) 7 EHRR 236 at 244, E Ct HR, at para 26.

7 *Hauschildt*, at para 48.

49. Public trial. In the context of public trial[1], the objective pursued by paragraph 1 of article 6 of the Convention for the Protection of Human Rights and Fundamental Freedoms[2] is to ensure scrutiny of the judiciary by the public with a view to safeguarding the right to a fair trial[3]. The public character of proceedings before judicial bodies is designed to protect litigants against the administration of 'justice' in secret with no public scrutiny. Publicity is thus seen by the European Court of Human Rights as a means of guaranteeing confidence in the court system at every level[4]. The court has recognised that the form of publicity given to a 'judgment' may not be uniform within Contracting States and that the form of publicity under the domestic law of the respondent state must be assessed in the light of the proceedings in question and by reference to the object and purpose of paragraph 1 of article 6[5].

1 This embraces both the right to a public hearing and the requirement that judgment should be pronounced publicly.
2 For the Convention for the Protection of Human Rights and Fundamental Freedoms (Rome, 4 November 1950; 213 UNTS 221; TS 71 (1953); Cmd 8969), art 6, para 1, see para 43 above.
3 See eg *Pretto v Italy* (Ser A No 71, Judgment 8 December 1983) 6 EHRR 182 at 189, E Ct HR, at para 27.
4 *Pretto*, at para 21 (6 EHRR 187). See also eg *Axen v Germany* (Ser A No 72, Judgment 8 December 1983) 6 EHRR 195 at 200, E Ct HR, at para 25; and *Sutter v Switzerland* (Ser A No 74, Judgment 22 February 1984) 6 EHRR 272 at 277, E Ct HR, at para 26.
5 *Axen*, at para 31 (6 EHRR 202, 203).

50. Trial *in absentia*. Although not expressly mentioned in paragraph 1 of article 6 of the Convention for the Protection of Human Rights and Fundamental Freedoms, the European Court of Human Rights has stated unequivocally that the object and purpose of that article taken as a whole is 'that a person "charged with a criminal offence" is entitled to take part in the hearing'[1]. Contracting States do, however, retain considerable discretion as regards the choice of means calculated to ensure that their legal systems are in compliance with the requirements of paragraph 1 of article 6 in respect of attendance. The court's task is not to indicate those means to the states, but to determine whether the result called for by the convention has been achieved[2]. Provided there has been a public hearing at first instance, the absence of 'public hearings' before a second or third instance may be justified by the special proceedings at issue. Leave-to-appeal proceedings involving only questions of law, and not questions of fact, may meet the requirements of article 6, even though the appellant was not given an opportunity of being heard in person by the appeal or cassation court[3].

1 *Colozza v Italy* (Ser A No 89, Judgment 12 February 1985) 7 EHRR 516 at 523, E Ct HR, at para 27. For the Convention for the Protection of Human Rights and Fundamental Freedoms (Rome, 4 November 1950; 213 UNTS 221; TS 71 (1953); Cmd 8969), art 6, para 1, see para 43 above.
2 *Colozza*, at para 30 (7 EHRR 525).
3 *Ekbatani v Sweden* (Ser A No 134, Judgment 26 May 1988) 13 EHRR 504 at 511, E Ct HR, at para 31, where the court noted the judgment in *Monnell and Morris v United Kingdom* (Ser A No 115, Judgment 2 March 1987) 10 EHRR 205, E Ct HR, and that in *Sutter v Switzerland* (Ser A No 74, Judgment 22 February 1984) 6 EHRR 272, E Ct HR, but highlighted that the underlying reason in the *Sutter* case was that the courts concerned did not have the task of establishing the facts of the case, but only that of interpreting the legal rules involved.

51. Right to the services of an interpreter. The right under article 6 of the Convention for the Protection of Human Rights and Fundamental Freedoms to the free assistance of an interpreter[1] applies not only to oral statements made at the trial hearing but also to documentary material and the pre-trial proceedings[2]. The convention does not demand a full written translation of written evidence or official documents. What is required is interpretation assistance which provides the defendant with knowledge of the case against him and enables him to defend himself, notably by submitting to the court his version of the facts in question[2]. To give practical and full effect to the right, the relevant authorities may not only be responsible for appointing an interpreter, but if they are alerted as to the particular circumstances may be responsible for ensuring that the interpretation provided is adequate[2].

Responsibility for not providing an interpreter will not be incurred if the state in question can establish that the applicant possesses sufficient command of its language to understand the nature of the charges against him[3].

1 See the Convention for the Protection of Human Rights and Fundamental Freedoms (Rome, 4 November 1950; 213 UNTS 221; TS 71 (1953); Cmd 8969), art 6, para 3(e), and para 43 above.
2 *Kamasinski v Austria* (Ser A No 168, Judgment 19 December 1989) 13 EHRR 36 at 65, E Ct HR, at para 74.
3 *Brozicek v Italy* (Ser A No 167, Judgment 19 December 1989) 12 EHRR 371, E Ct HR, where the applicant, a German national accused of offences committed in Italy, requested all correspondence to be in his mother tongue or in one of the official languages of the United Nations (ie English or French). The Italian authorities continued to serve all documents in Italian, a language with which the applicant was not sufficiently familiar. The court held by fifteen votes to five that there had been a violation of the Convention for the Protection of Human Rights and Fundamental Freedoms, art 6, paras 1, 3(a).

52. Legal assistance. The most recent case on legal assistance happens to be a Scottish case — the *Granger* case[1]. The trial of Thomas Lafferty and six others on charges relating, inter alia, to fire-raising and murder took place before the High Court of Justiciary in Glasgow in September 1984. Mr Granger appeared as a principal witness for the Crown. However, once in the witness box he denied all knowledge of any matters relevant to the crimes. He also denied that he had given statements, claiming instead that they had been made up by the police, who had pressurised him into signing them. Shortly afterwards, the applicant was arrested and prosecuted on indictment in the High Court of Justiciary for perjury. He was held in custody pending and during his trial. He was convicted after a month-long trial but appealed to the Court of Criminal Appeal, claiming a 'miscarriage of justice'. He was denied legal aid as his claim was deemed unsubstantiated in terms of the relevant legislation[2]. Consequently, he elected to represent himself and lost the appeal. His claim regarding the Convention for the Protection of Human Rights and Fundamental Freedoms was that the denial of free legal aid constituted a violation of paragraph 3(c) of article 6. Because of the complexity and importance of one of the issues raised in the appeal, the European Court of Human Rights considered that there should have been some means available to the competent authorities, including the High Court of Justiciary, which was responsible for ensuring the fair conduct of the appeal proceedings, to have the refusal of legal aid reconsidered. The European Court of Human Rights concluded that in all the circumstances of the case it would have been in the interests of justice for free legal assistance to have been given to the applicant, at least at the stage when the appeal was adjourned for evidence[4]. Such a course would have served the interests of justice and fairness by enabling the applicant to make an effective contribution to the proceedings[5]. The court concluded unanimously that there had been a violation of article 6.

The court has also stated that under the convention 'a person charged with a criminal offence who does not wish to defend himself in person must be able to have recourse to legal assistance of his own choosing'[6]. In conclusion, whenever compliance with paragraph 3 of article 6 is being reviewed, 'its basic purpose must not be forgotten, nor must it be severed from its roots'[7].

1 *Granger v United Kingdom* (Ser A No 174, Judgment 28 March 1990) 12 EHRR 469, E Ct HR.

2 Ie the Legal Aid (Scotland) Act 1967 (c 43), s 1(7) (repealed). See now the different provisions of the Legal Aid (Scotland) Act 1986 (c 47), s 22.
3 For the Convention for the Protection of Human Rights and Fundamental Freedoms (Rome, 4 November 1950; 213 UNTS 221; TS 71 (1953); Cmd 8969), art 6, para 3, see para 43 above. The applicant also claimed violations of arts 5, 8 and 13, but these allegations were not pursued before the court.
4 No review in fact took place.
5 *Granger*, at para 47 (12 EHRR 481).
6 *Pakelli v Germany* (Ser A No 64, Judgment 25 April 1983) 6 EHRR 1 at 10, E Ct HR, at para 31, approved in *Campbell and Fell v United Kingdom* (Ser A No 80, E Ct HR 28 June 1984) 7 EHRR 165 at 204, E Ct HR, at para 99.
7 *Artico v Italy* (Ser A No 37, Judgment 13 May 1980) 3 EHRR 1 at 12, E Ct HR, at para 32.

53. Presumption of innocence. Presumptions of fact or of law operate in every legal system, and although the Convention for the Protection of Human Rights and Fundamental Freedoms does not prohibit this, in principle it does require Contracting States to remain within certain limits in this respect as regards criminal law[1]. Thus paragraph 2 of article 6 provides that a person charged with a criminal offence is to be presumed innocent until proved guilty according to law. In the *Salabiaku* case the European Court of Human Rights stated that if the words 'according to law' in this provision could be defined by the national legislature, then a possible consequence would be 'to strip the trial court of any genuine power of assessment and deprive the presumption of innocence of its substance'[2]. Such a situation obviously could not be reconciled with the object and purpose of article 6. Paragraph 2 of this article does not regard presumptions of fact or of law with indifference: it requires states to confine such presumptions within reasonable limits which take into account the importance of what is at stake and maintain the rights of the defence[2]. Nor is the application of this paragraph limited to procedures where a prosecution ends in the conviction or acquittal of the accused: it will also be violated if, without the accused having previously been found guilty according to law, a judicial decision is reached which suggests that he is guilty of an offence[3].

1 *Salabiaku v France* (Ser A No 141A, Judgment 7 October 1988) 13 EHRR 379 at 387, E Ct HR, at para 26.
2 *Salabiaku*, at para 28 (13 EHRR 388).
3 *Lutz v Germany* (Ser A No 123, Judgment 25 August 1987) 10 EHRR 182 at 193, 194, E Ct HR, at para 44. See also *Barberà, Messegué and Jabardo v Spain* (Ser A No 146, Judgment 6 December 1988) 11 EHRR 360 at 392, E Ct HR, at para 91.

54. Judicial remedies against decision of administrative body. As previously stated, article 6 of the Convention for the Protection of Human Rights and Fundamental Freedoms secures to everyone the right to have any claim relating to civil rights and obligations brought before a court or tribunal[1]. In a number of primarily Swedish cases, the European Court of Human Rights has been called upon to consider proceedings for judicial review following a decision by an administrative body[2]. The common denominator in the cases was lack of provision in domestic law for any form of appeal or judicial review from the administrative decision in question. Taking the *Tre Traktörer* case as an example, the applicant, a Swedish limited company with a sole shareholder, took over a restaurant and obtained a licence to serve alcohol therein. This licence was subsequently revoked, and the complaint alleging violation of the convention related to the procedures for challenging that revocation[3].

1 See the Convention for the Protection of Human Rights and Fundamental Freedoms (Rome, 4 November 1950; 213 UNTS 221; TS 71 (1953); Cmd 8969), art 6, para 1, and paras 43, 44, above.

2 See eg *Tre Traktörer Ab v Sweden* (Ser A No 159, Judgment 7 July 1989) 13 EHRR 309, E Ct HR; *Allan Jacobsson v Sweden* (Ser A No 163, Judgment 25 October 1989) 12 EHRR 56, E Ct HR; *Håkansson and Sturesson v Sweden* (Ser A No 171, Judgment 21 February 1990) 13 EHRR 1, E Ct HR.

3 The court held by six votes to one that art 6, para 1, of the convention had been violated. The *Jacobsson* case concerned building prohibitions, whereas the *Håkansson and Sturesson* case concerned the grant of a requisite permit for holding agricultural estate. In both cases a violation of art 6, para 1, was held unanimously to have occurred.

55. Fairness to the accused. A person charged with a criminal offence is entitled to examine or have examined witnesses against him and to obtain the attendance and examination of witnesses on his behalf under the same conditions as witnesses against him[1]. The cases in this area relate to certain categories of witnesses: experts; biased witnesses (ex-spouse and stepdaughter); non compellable witnesses; and anonymous witnesses[2].

1 Convention for the Protection of Human Rights and Fundamental Freedoms (Rome, 4 November 1950; 213 UNTS 221; TS 71 (1953); Cmd 8969), art 6, para 3(d).
2 See paras 56–59 below.

56. Expert: the *Bönisch* case. Read literally, paragraph 3(d) of article 6 of the Convention for the Protection of Human Rights and Fundamental Freedoms relates to witnesses and not to experts[1]. Although the European Court of Human Rights will not depart from the definition employed in the relevant domestic legislation, the court cannot rely exclusively on that definition 'but must have regard to the procedural position and to the manner in which [the expert] performed his function'[2].

In the *Bönisch* case, the Austrian government maintained that under Austrian law an 'expert' was a neutral and impartial auxiliary of the domestic court appointed by the court itself, whereas the applicant was of the view that the individual in question could not be regarded as an 'expert' in the classic sense of the term but was rather a 'witness against the accused'[3]. The European Court of Human Rights was sympathetic to the applicant's contention, particularly when it came to light that it was the expert's report which led to the initiation of proceedings against the applicant. Thus the court concluded that the neutrality of the expert was open to doubt and that, relative to defence witnesses, he enjoyed a privileged position[4]. Consequently, the court concluded unanimously that there had been a breach of paragraph 1 of article 6.

1 *Bönisch v Austria* (Ser A No 92, Judgment 6 May 1985) 9 EHRR 191 at 199, E Ct HR, at para 29. For the Convention for the Protection of Human Rights and Fundamental Freedoms (Rome, 4 November 1950; 213 UNTS 221; TS 71 (1953); Cmd 8969), art 6, para 3(d), see para 55 above.
2 *Bönisch*, at para 31 (9 EHRR 200).
3 *Bönisch*, at para 30 (9 EHRR 199).
4 In his capacity of 'expert' he could attend throughout the hearings, put questions to the accused and to witnesses with the leave of the court and comment on their evidence at the appropriate moment: *Bönisch*, at para 33 (9 EHRR 200, 201).

57. Alleged bias: the *Unterpertinger* case. The witnesses in the *Unterpertinger* case[1] were the former spouse and stepdaughter of the applicant. He had been convicted in the national court of causing acute bodily harm to both women. Mr Unterpertinger alleged that he had been convicted exclusively on the basis of statements made to the police by the two women, which were subsequently read out at the trial. Both women declined to give evidence[2], and thus the applicant had no opportunity to question their statements. Furthermore, he was not permitted to call witnesses in support of his contention that the credibility of the two women was open to doubt. The European Court of Human Rights did not dispute the validity of the domestic legislation which allowed the women concerned to decline to give evidence. Such a provision is compatible with the Convention for the Protection of Human Rights and Fundamental Freedoms[3].

Although it did not hold that the women's statements should not have been read out when requested by the prosecution, the court stipulated that the use made of them as evidence had to comply with article 6, namely the protection of the right of the defence[4]. This is particularly the case when a person 'charged with a criminal offence' has a right 'to examine or have examined' witnesses against him and has not been given the opportunity at any stage in the earlier proceedings to question persons whose statements are read out at the earlier hearing[4]. The court held that by treating as conclusive the women's statements to the police, the national court had convicted Mr Unterpertinger 'on the basis of "testimony" in respect of which his defence rights were appreciably restricted'[5], and accordingly the court held unanimously that article 6 had been violated.

1 *Unterpertinger v Austria* (Ser A No 110, Judgment 24 November 1986) 13 EHRR 175, E Ct HR.
2 They were entitled to decline because of their relationship to the accused.
3 *Unterpertinger*, at para 30 (13 EHRR 183).
4 *Unterpertinger*, at para 31 (13 EHRR 183, 184).
5 *Unterpertinger*, at para 33 (13 EHRR 184).

58. 'Non-compellable' witnesses: the *Bricmont* case. The applicant in the *Bricmont* case[1] was the subject of criminal proceedings concerning forgery, uttering, breach of confidence and misappropriation of assets. A Belgian Prince joined the proceedings as a civil party seeking damages[2]. Under Belgian law, royal princes cannot be compelled to be witnesses, and this is permissible *vis-à-vis* conviction[3]. Most of the argument of the case before the European Court of Human Rights focused on the failure to make provision for a 'confrontation' between the royal family and the applicant. The court held that the circumstances of the case demanded that opportunity should have been given for any aspect of the complainant's account to be challenged either by way of a confrontation or an examination, either in public or, if necessary, at his home. That, the court held, would have made it possible for certain facts to have been clarified and provided the Prince with the opportunity of furnishing further details of — or even withdrawing — one or more of his charges[4]. In the light of the facts, the court concluded that Mr Bricmont's conviction in respect of three charges was based solely on the Prince's statements without affording Mr Bricmont the opportunity of elucidating evidence through an examination of or a confrontation with the Prince. Mr Bricmont had been convicted following proceedings which had infringed his defence rights[5].

1 *Bricmont v Belgium* (Ser A No 158, Judgment 7 July 1989) 12 EHRR 217, E Ct HR.
2 The applicant had been adviser and agent of the Prince, and the trial related to conduct during his employment.
3 'Special regulations governing the taking of evidence from, and the questioning of, high-ranking persons of State are to be found in the domestic legal systems of several Council of Europe member states. There are objective reasons for having them and they do not as such conflict with Article 6 of the Convention [for the Protection of Human Rights and Fundamental Freedoms]': *Bricmont*, at para 77 (12 EHRR 239, 240).
4 *Bricmont*, at para 81 (12 EHRR 240, 241).
5 The court held by five votes to two that article 6 of the convention had been violated.

59. Anonymous witness: the *Kostovski* case. In the *Kostovski* case[1] the applicant and others were convicted of armed robbery primarily on the basis of records of statements of two anonymous witnesses who were heard in the absence of counsel and the applicant by the police and subsequently a magistrate. The essence of Mr Kostovski's claim was that he had been denied a fair trial in that he had not been given the opportunity to have questions put to the anonymous witnesses and so had been unable to challenge their statements. The European Court of Human Rights, in accordance with its established case law, stated that its task was not to express a view as to whether the statements in question had been correctly admitted and assessed but rather to ascertain whether the proceedings considered as a whole, including the manner in which the evidence had been taken, were fair[2]. In relation to the case before it the court asserted that:

> 'If the defence is unaware of the identity of the person it seeks to question, it may be deprived of the very particulars enabling it to demonstrate that he or she is prejudiced, hostile or unreliable. Testimony or other declarations inculpating an accused may well be designedly untruthful or simply erroneous and the defence will scarcely be able to bring this to light if it lacks the information permitting it to test the author's reliability or cast doubt on his credibility. The dangers inherent in such a situation are obvious'[3].

The court responded to the Dutch government's submission that use of anonymous evidence stemmed from an increase in the intimidation of witnesses[4] by saying that:

> 'Although the growth in organised crime doubtless demands the introduction of appropriate measures, the Government's submissions appear to the Court to lay insufficient weight on what the applicant's counsel described as "the interest of everybody in a civilised society in a controllable and fair judicial procedure". The right to a fair administration of justice holds so prominent a place in a democratic society that it cannot be sacrificed to expediency. The Convention does not preclude reliance, at the investigation stage of criminal proceedings, on sources such as anonymous informants. However, the subsequent use of anonymous statements as sufficient evidence to found a conviction, as in the present case, is a different matter. It involved limitations on the rights of the defence which were irreconcilable with the guarantees contained in Article 6. In fact, the Government accepted that the applicant's conviction was based "to a decisive extent" on the anonymous statements'[5].

The court concluded unanimously with respect to Mr Kostovski that his rights of defence had been so constrained that he could not have been said to have received a fair trial and that Article 6 of the Convention for the Protection of Human Rights and Fundamental Freedoms had accordingly been breached.

1　*Kostovski v Netherlands* (Ser A No 166, Judgment 20 November 1989) 12 EHRR 434, E Ct HR.
2　*Kostovski*, at para 39 (12 EHRR 447), where the court referred back to its judgment in *Barberà, Messegué and Jabardo v Spain* (Ser A No 146, Judgment 6 December 1988) 11 EHRR 360 at 384, 385, E Ct HR, at para 68.
3　*Kostovski*, at para 42 (12 EHRR 448).
4　Their use therefore was based on a balancing of the interests of society, the accused and the witnesses.
5　*Kostovski*, at para 44 (12 EHRR 449).

60. Other examples of fairness to the individual.　The breadth of what may fall within the ambit of article 6 of the Convention for the Protection of Human Rights and Fundamental Freedoms may be illustrated by a reference to the following non-exhaustive list of instances[1]:

- the admission as evidence in a domestic court of an unlawfully obtained telephone conversation[2];
- extra-judicial assurances allegedly given to counsel in connection with the mitigation of his client's murder charge[3];
- the methods employed by a professional body[4] in connection with an application for reinstatement on the professional roll[5];
- the methods employed by an appeals board on an application for continuation of health insurance allowance[6];
- the methods employed by a rent review board and housing and tenancy court[7];

- the procedures utilised for the provisional closure of a business[8];
- the contested presence of a member of the Procureur General's department at the deliberations of the Belgian Court of Cassation[9].

1 A detailed analysis would serve no useful purpose as the cases turned primarily on the facts and circumstances peculiar to them.
2 *Schenk v Switzerland* (Ser A No 140, Judgment 12 July 1988) 13 EHRR 242, E Ct HR.
3 *Colak v Germany* (Ser A No 147, Judgment 6 December 1988) 11 EHRR 513, E Ct HR.
4 Ie in this instance the Council of the *Ordre des avocats* of Antwerp.
5 *H v Belgium* (Ser A No 127B, Judgment 30 November 1987) 10 EHRR 399, E Ct HR.
6 *Feldbrugge v Netherlands* (Ser A No 99, Judgment 29 May 1986) 8 EHRR 425, E Ct HR.
7 *Langborger v Sweden* (Ser A No 155, Judgment 22 June 1989) 12 EHRR 416, E Ct HR.
8 *Deweer v Belgium* (Ser A No 35, Judgment 27 February 1980) 2 EHRR 439, E Ct HR.
9 *Delcourt v Belgium* (Ser A No 11, Judgment 17 January 1970) 1 EHRR 355, E Ct HR.

(5) RETROSPECTIVE CRIMINALITY

61. Generally: article 7. Article 7 of the Convention for the Protection of Human Rights and Fundamental Freedoms provides that:

'1. No one shall be held guilty of any criminal offence on account of any act or omission which did not constitute a criminal offence under national or international law at the time when it was committed. Nor shall a heavier penalty be imposed than the one that was applicable at the time the criminal offence was committed.
2. This Article shall not prejudice the trial and punishment of any person for any act or omission which, at the time when it was committed, was criminal according to the general principles of law recognised by civilised nations'[1].

No cases have been referred to the European Court of Human Rights on article 7. The principles which the article seeks to guarantee are enshrined for the most part in the legal systems of the Contracting Parties.

1 Convention for the Protection of Human Rights and Fundamental Freedoms (Rome, 4 November 1950; 213 UNTS 221; TS 71 (1953); Cmd 8969), art 7, paras 1, 2.

(6) FAMILY LIFE

(a) The Right to Respect for Private and Family Life

62. Introduction: article 8. Article 8 of the Convention for the Protection of Human Rights and Fundamental Freedoms provides as follows:

'1. Everyone has the right to respect for his private and family life, his home and his correspondence.
2. There shall be no interference by a public authority with the exercise of this right except such as is in accordance with the law and is necessary in a democratic society in the interests of national security, public safety or the economic well-being of the country, for the prevention of disorder or crime, for the protection of health or morals, or for the protection of the rights and freedoms of others'[1].

The object of article 8 was said in the *Belgian Linguistic Case* to be 'essentially that of protecting the individual against arbitrary interference by the public authorities in his private family life'[2]. This has since been elaborated on by the European Court of Human Rights as not only requiring the state to abstain from such interference but to undertake positive obligations inherent in effective respect for private or family life[3]. These obligations may involve the adoption of measures designed to secure respect for private life even in the sphere of the relations of individuals between themselves[4]. The court has further held that article 8 applies to 'the "family life" of the "illegitimate" family as equally as it does to that of the "legitimate" family'[5]. 'Home' includes property from which there has been a prolonged absence but where the circumstances demonstrate a sufficient continuing link between the owners and the property concerned[6]. With respect to correspondence, article 8 embraces the right to initiate correspondence and not merely the supervision thereof[7].

1　Convention for the Protection of Human Rights and Fundamental Freedoms (Rome, 4 November 1950; 213 UNTS 221; TS 71 (1953); Cmd 8969), art 8, paras 1, 2.
2　*Belgian Linguistic Case (No 2)* (Merits) (Ser A No 6, Judgment 23 July 1968) 1 EHRR 252 at 282, E Ct HR, at para 7.
3　*Airey v Ireland* (Ser A No 32, Judgment 9 October 1979) 2 EHRR 305 at 319, E Ct HR, at para 32.
4　*X and Y v Netherlands* (Ser A No 91, Judgment 26 March 1985) 8 EHRR 235 at 239, 240, E Ct HR, at para 23. In this case the court considered the incompetence under Dutch law of a complaint by a father alleging a sexual assault on his daughter, aged sixteen, who by reason of mental handicap was unable to make the complaint herself, and held that there had been a violation of art 8.
5　*Marckx v Belgium* (Ser A No 31, Judgment 13 June 1979) 2 EHRR 330 at 341, 342, E Ct HR, at para 31.
6　*Gillow v United Kingdom* (Ser A No 109, Judgment 24 November 1986) 11 EHRR 335 at 349, E Ct HR, at para 46.
7　*Golder v United Kingdom* (Ser A No 18, Judgment 21 February 1975) 1 EHRR 524, E Ct HR.

63. Access to confidential personal records. The *Gaskin* case[1] brought before the European Court of Human Rights the issue of an individual's right of access to confidential records maintained by the relevant authorities during the time when he was in the care of the authorities. Mr Gaskin contended that he was ill-treated in care and when he attained majority he sought to obtain details of where he had been kept and with whom. He wanted this information not only to learn about his past but to assist him overcome problems he was experiencing[2]. On 9 October 1978 the applicant had been permitted by a social worker employed by Liverpool City Council to see the case records relating to him as kept by the council's Social Services Department. Mr Gaskin had removed these records without the council's consent and had retained them in his possession for three days. The following year, intent upon taking proceedings against the local authority for damages for negligence, Mr Gaskin made an application[3] for discovery of the local authority's case records made during his period in care. The application was heard by the High Court on 22 February 1980. The local authority objected to the grant of discovery of the records on the ground that disclosure and production would be contrary to the public interest. The applicant maintained that the case records held by the local authority should be made available to him, on the general principles of discovery, for the purpose of his proposed proceedings for personal injuries against the local authority. He also maintained that it was in the public interest that the standard of care provided by a local authority to a child in care be subject to at least one review. The judge in the proceedings maintained that the records in question should be regarded as private and confidential[4]. The Court of Appeal affirmed that decision and refused Mr Gaskin leave to appeal to the House of Lords. Subsequently, Mr Gaskin applied to the European Commission of Human Rights claiming that the council's refusal of access to the case records in question constituted a breach of his right to respect for his private and family life as guaranteed by article 8 of the Convention for the Protection of Human Rights and Fundamental Freedoms[5].

The European Court of Human Rights defined the issue before it as that of whether the United Kingdom, in handling Mr Gaskin's requests for access to his case records, was in breach of a positive obligation flowing from article 8 of the convention[6]. The court concluded that persons in the situation of Mr Gaskin do have:

> 'a vital interest, protected by the Convention, in receiving the information necessary to know and to understand their childhood and early development. On the other hand, it must be borne in mind that confidentiality of public records is of importance for receiving objective and reliable information, and that such confidentiality can also be necessary for the protection of third persons. Under the latter aspect, a system like the British one, which makes access to records dependent on the consent of the contributor, can in principle be considered to be compatible with the obligations under Article 8, taking into account the State's margin of appreciation. The Court considers, however, that under such a system the interests of the individual seeking access to records relating to his private and family life must be secured when a contributor to the records either is not available or improperly refuses consent. Such a system is only in conformity with the principle of proportionality if it provides that an independent authority finally decides whether access has to be granted in cases where a contributor fails to answer or withholds consent. No such procedure was available to the applicant in the present case'[7].

Thus the court concluded[8] that the procedures followed were deficient in that they failed to secure respect for Mr Gaskin's private and family life in the way required by article 8 of the convention[9].

1   *Gaskin v United Kingdom* (Ser A No 160, Judgment 7 July 1989) 12 EHRR 36, E Ct HR. The applicant, a United Kingdom citizen, spent most of his minority in the care of Liverpool City Council. During this time he was boarded out with various foster parents subject to the provisions of the Boarding-Out of Children Regulations 1955, SI 1955/1377 (revoked: see now the Boarding-out of Children (Foster Placement) Regulations 1988, SI 1988/2184). Under regulation 10 of the 1955 regulations the local authority was under a duty to maintain certain confidential records pertaining to children in care. The applicant ceased to be in the care of the council on attaining the age of majority in December 1977.

2   He had in 1974 appeared before Liverpool Juvenile Court and had pleaded guilty to a number of offences, including burglary and theft. The court had made a care order in respect of him under the Children and Young Persons Act 1969 (c 54), s 7.

3   Ie under the Administration of Justice Act 1970 (c 31), s 31 (repealed), which gave the High Court power to order such disclosure to a person who was likely to be a party to legal proceedings for personal injuries. See now the Supreme Court Act 1981 (c 54), s 33. The corresponding provision in Scotland is the Administration of Justice (Scotland) Act 1972 (c 59), s 1.

4   Boreham J said 'I am left in no doubt that it is necessary for the proper functioning of the child care service that the confidentiality of the relevant documents should be preserved. This is a very important service to which the interests — also very important — of the individual must, in my judgment, bow. I have no doubt that the public interest will be better served by refusing discovery and this I do' (quoted by Lord Denning MR in *Gaskin v Liverpool City Council* [1980] 1 WLR 1549 at 1552, CA).

5   Application No 10454/83 *Gaskin v United Kingdom* (1989) 11 EHRR 402, E Com HR. For the Convention for the Protection of Human Rights and Fundamental Freedoms (Rome, 4 November 1950; 213 UNTS 221; TS 71 (1953); Cmd 8969), art 8, see para 62 above.

6   Note the court's statement in *Airey v Ireland* (Ser A No 32, Judgment 9 October 1979) 2 EHRR 305 at 319, E Ct HR, at para 32: '... although the object of Article 8 is essentially that of protecting the individual against arbitrary interference by the public authorities, it does not merely compel the State to abstain from such interference: in addition to this primary negative undertaking, there may be positive obligations inherent in an effective respect for private or family life'.

7   *Gaskin v United Kingdom* (Ser A No 160, Judgment 7 July 1989) 12 EHRR 36 at 50, E Ct HR, at para 49.

8   Ie by eleven votes to six.

9   Another case concerning access to personal information is *Leander v Sweden* (Ser A No 116, Judgment 26 March 1987) 9 EHRR 433, E Ct HR. Mr Leander, a Swedish citizen, was required to leave his temporary employment as a museum technician at the Naval Museum at Karlskrona, following the unfavourable outcome of a personnel control. The museum is adjacent to a naval base which is a restricted military security zone. Mr Leander contended that the personnel

control as applied to his case gave rise to a breach of article 8 of the convention. The European Court of Human Rights accepted that by compiling, using and disclosing private information Sweden had interfered with rights under article 8. However, such interference was held to be justified in terms of the exceptions provided for in paragraph 2 of article 8, discussed in paras 78 ff below.

64. Child care. In the field of child care there are seven cases of importance before the European Court of Human Rights: five United Kingdom cases[1], which raise essentially the same issue, and two Swedish cases[2]. In the United Kingdom cases the issue before the court was the procedures followed and the remedies available for the committal of children into care. The Swedish cases were concerned primarily with the conditions of access and visitation rights by parents to their children in care. In all the cases it was not the merits of the decisions taken by the domestic judicial and local authorities but rather the procedures followed in reaching these decisions which were of concern to the European Court of Human Rights[3].

Looking initially at the United Kingdom cases, these were all concerned with the committal of juveniles to care and the terms of access allowed to their natural parents. For instance, in the case of *W v United Kingdom*, the alleged violation of article 8 of the Convention for the Protection of Human Rights and Fundamental Freedoms[4] was said to have arisen by reason of the procedures followed by the authority concerned in reaching its decisions to restrict and terminate the applicant's access to his child, the absence of remedies against those decisions and the length of certain related judicial proceedings. The European Court of Human Rights stressed the basic principle that 'the mutual enjoyment by parent and child of each other's company constitutes a fundamental element of family life' and, furthermore, that the natural family relationship is not terminated by reason of the fact that a child is taken into public care[5]. The court recognised that the decisions in question were of a sensitive nature and as a consequence the local authorities should be afforded a measure of discretion rather than be restricted to an inflexible procedure. Notwithstanding this, however, the court stated that it had to be remembered that such decisions might well prove to be irreversible. The court also recognised that where a child had been taken away from his parents and placed with alternative carers, he may in the course of time establish new bonds with them which it might not be in the child's intersts to disturb or interrupt by reversing a previous decision to restrict or terminate parental access. This, in the court's view, emphasised the need for there to be even greater than usual protection against arbitrary interferences with parent–child access. The court acknowledged that article 8 contained no explicit procedural requirements, but this was held 'not conclusive of the matter'. Although not looking to the merits of the decision made by the local authority, the court maintained that the local authority's decision-making process could not be entirely divorced from the substance of the decision. The decision-making process must have some influence on the decision, notably by ensuring that it is based on the relevant considerations, is not one-sided and thus neither is, nor appears to be, arbitrary. The relevant considerations were identified by the court as follows:

'The relevant considerations to be weighed by a local authority in reaching decisions on children in its care must perforce include the views and interests of the natural parents. The decision-making process must therefore, in the Court's view, be such as to secure that their views and interests are made known to and duly taken into account by the local authority and that they are able to exercise in due time any remedies available to them. In fact, the 1983 Code of Practice[6] stresses the importance of involving parents in access decisions.

There are three factors which have a bearing on the practicalities of the matter. Firstly, as the Commission pointed out, there will clearly be instances where the participation of the natural parents in the decision-making process either will not be possible or will not be meaningful — as, for example, where they cannot be traced or are under a physical or mental disability or where an emergency arises. Secondly, decisions in this area, whilst frequently taken in the light of case reviews or case conferences, may equally well evolve from a continuous process of monitoring on the part of the local authority's officials. Thirdly, regular contacts between the social workers responsible and the parents often provide an appropriate channel for the communication of the latter's views to the authority'[7].

In the light of these considerations, together with the serious nature of the decisions to be taken, the court stated that it had to be determined that the parents had been 'involved in the decision-making process, seen as a whole, to a degree sufficient to provide them with the requisite protection of their interests'. An absence of such involvement would, the court concluded, constitute a failure to respect their family life as guaranteed by article 8.

In the instant case, the court unanimously held that, in the circumstances of the case as before the court and notwithstanding the United Kingdom's margin of appreciation, there had been a violation of article 8 of the convention[9].

The *Olsson* case[10] raised not only the question of children in care but also the separation of the siblings. The court characterised such separation as an interference 'of a very serious order', and held that 'sufficiently sound and weighty considerations in the interests of the child' must be advanced before such a decision was taken. It is not enough that the child would be better off if placed in care[11]. In order to determine whether the required degree of sufficiency had been satisfied for the purposes of article 8, the court stated that it had to have regard to the case as a whole and in particular to the circumstances in which the decision was taken[11]. In *Olsson* the court concluded that the decision to take and to maintain in care was not in breach of article 8 but the manner in which the care decision was implemented (including the separation of siblings) was contrary to article 8. In the *Eriksson* case[12] the court held that there had been a violation of article 8 in respect of the applicant and her daughter in that subsequent to the termination of a care order there was insufficient mechanism within which to promote the relationship between mother and child with a view to reuniting them.

1 *O v United Kingdom* (Ser A No 120, Judgment 8 July 1987) 10 EHRR 82, E Ct HR; *H v United Kingdom* (Ser A No 120, Judgment 8 July 1987) 10 EHRR 95, E Ct HR; *W v United Kingdom* (Ser A No 121, Judgment 8 July 1987) 10 EHRR 29, E Ct HR, *B v United Kingdom* (Ser A No 121, Judgment 8 July 1987) 10 EHRR 87, E Ct HR; *R v United Kingdom* (Ser A No 121, Judgment 8 July 1987) 10 EHRR 74, E Ct HR.

2 *Olsson v Sweden* (Ser A No 130, Judgment 24 March 1988) 11 EHRR 259, E Ct HR; *Eriksson v Sweden* (Ser A No 156, Judgment 22 June 1989) 12 EHRR 183, E Ct HR.

3 See also the discussion of alleged violations of the Convention for the Protection of Human Rights and Fundamental Freedoms (Rome, 4 November 1950; 213 UNTS 221; TS 71 (1953); Cmd 8969), art 6, in paras 43 ff above.

4 For ibid, art 8, see para 62 above.

5 *W v United Kingdom*, at para 59 (10 EHRR 49) (*B v United Kingdom*, at para 60, and *R v United Kingdom*, at para 64, are identical); *Olsson*, at para 59 (11 EHRR 283) (also identical); *Eriksson*, at para 58 (12 EHRR 200).

6 Ie *Code of Practice on Access to Children in Care* (Department of Health and Social Security and Welsh Office, 1983).

7 *W v United Kingdom*, at paras 63, 64 (10 EHRR 49, 50).

8 *W v United Kingdom*, at para 64. The interference resulting from the decision would not be capable of being regarded as 'necessary' within the meaning of article 8.

9 *W v United Kingdom*, at para 70 (10 EHRR 53). Insufficient parental involvement with the decision-making process regarding care orders gave rise to a finding in *B v United Kingdom* and *R v United Kingdom* that article 8 had been breached. In *O v United Kingdom* the court refuted the

claim that the alleged lack of a right to a hearing before a court and of an effective legal remedy in respect of a claim for access to children was contrary to article 8.

10 *Olsson*, at para 72 (11 EHRR 287).

11 *Eriksson*, at paras 71, 72 (12 EHRR 203, 204).

65. Immigration. An alleged violation of article 8 of the Convention for the Protection of Human Rights and Fundamental Freedoms[1] was pleaded before the European Court of Human Rights in the case of *Abdulaziz, Cabales and Balkandali*[2]. The content of the applications was:

(1) that respect for family life encompassed the right of a person to establish his home in the state of his nationality or lawful residence, and subject only to the provisions of paragraph 2 of article 8[3], the dilemma either of having to move abroad or being separated from his spouse was inconsistent with this principle; and

(2) hindrance in fact was just as relevant as hindrance in law.

The court highlighted the fact that the three applicants had come to the United Kingdom as single persons and that they all subsequently married individuals who were known not to possess a right of permanent settlement in the United Kingdom[4]. The court held that article 8 could not be extended so as to place a general obligation on the Contracting Parties to respect the matrimonial residence of the married couples and thereby to have to accept the non-national spouses for settlement in that country. The applicants were deemed not to have produced any evidence of obstacles to establishing family life in their own or their husbands' home countries or to have shown that any special reasons existed why that could not be expected of them. Accordingly, there had been no 'lack of respect' for family life and no breach of article 8 had occurred[5].

In the *Berrehab* case[6] the court stated that it did not see *de facto* cohabitation as a *sine qua non* of family life parents and minor children. It was held that the relationship created between spouses by a lawful and genuine marriage — such as that contracted by Mr and Mrs Berrehab — had to be regarded as 'family life' and fall within the concept of family for the purposes of article 8; that a child born of such a union is *ipso jure* part of that relationship; and that from the moment of the child's birth and by the very fact of it, there exists between him and his parents a bond amounting to 'family life', even if the parents are not then living together[7].

Family life may be broken by subsequent events, but in the view of the European Court of Human Rights the frequency and regularity of Mr Berrehab's meetings with his daughter demonstrated that he 'very greatly valued' such meetings and the contention that the ties of family life had been broken could not be sustained. The court held by six votes to one that article 8 had been violated[8].

1 For the Convention for the Protection of Human Rights and Fundamental Freedoms (Rome, 4 November 1950; 213 UNTS 221; TS 71 (1953); Cmd 8969), art 8, see para 62 above.

2 *Abdulaziz, Cabales and Balkandali v United Kingdom* (Ser A No 94, Judgment 28 May 1985) 7 EHRR 471, E Ct HR. The case concerned three women lawfully and permanently settled in the United Kingdom whose respective husbands were not permitted to join them there and settle permanently with them. In the case of each woman the right to live in the United Kingdom existed before her marriage.

3 As to the Convention for the Protection of Human Rights and Fundamental Freedoms, art 8, para 2, see paras 78 ff below.

4 One was a visitor, one was a student, and, in the case of the Cabales, the marriage had taken place in the Philippines and the couple had never cohabited in the United Kingdom.

5 *Abdulaziz, Cabales and Balkandali*, at para 69 (7 EHRR 498). However, the court determined that there had been a breach of article 8 taken in conjunction with article 14 (for which see para 85 below): *Abdulaziz, Cabales and Balkandali*, at para 83 (7 EHRR 503).

6 *Berrehab v Netherlands* (Ser A No 138, Judgment 21 June 1988) 11 EHRR 322, E Ct HR.
7 The couple divorced before the birth of the child, but regular and frequent contact was maintained between father and daughter with the full co-operation of the mother. The applicant's request for a renewal of his residence permit was refused, and Mr Berrehab, a Moroccan national, became the subject of an exclusion order. This, he argued, was in violation of article 8 in that it meant that he could no longer have contact with his daughter.
8 Postscript: the couple remarried in August 1985.

66. Homosexuality. In the *Dudgeon* case[1] it was contended by the applicant that the criminal law of Northern Ireland, which prohibited certain homosexual acts between consenting adults even in private, amounted to a breach of article 8 of the Convention for the Protection of Human Rights and Fundamental Freedoms[2]. The essence of the applicant's contention was that although he had not been prosecuted he had 'experienced fear, suffering and psychological distress directly caused by the very existence of the laws in question'[3]. This fear which Mr Dudgeon had suffered and continued to suffer was in the view of the European Court of Human Rights an unjustified interference with his right to respect for his private life. Accordingly, a breach of article 8 had occurred[4]. Another case in point is the *Norris*[5] judgment, in which the court reaffirmed the position it adopted in the *Dudgeon* case[6].

1 *Dudgeon v United Kingdom* (Ser A No 45, Judgment 23 September 1981) 4 EHRR 149, E Ct HR.
2 For the Convention for the Protection of Human Rights and Fundamental Freedoms (Rome, 4 November 1950; 213 UNTS 221; TS 71 (1953); Cmd 8969), art 8, see para 62 above.
3 *Dudgeon*, at para 37 (4 EHRR 160).
4 It was held by fifteen votes to four. Much of the argument in this case centred on the recognised exceptions to paragraph 1 of article 8, contained in paragraph 2, which is discussed in paras 78 ff below.
5 *Norris v Ireland* (Ser A No 142, Judgment 26 October 1988) 13 EHRR 186, E Ct HR.
6 The only possible distinguishing factor suggested was that Mr Norris, unlike Mr Dudgeon, had not been the subject of any police investigation. However, the court held that its findings in the *Dudgeon* case had not been dependent upon this additional factor.

67. Transsexuality. The first case to come before the European Court of Human Rights concerning transsexuality was *Van Oosterwijk*[1]. In spite of the European Commission of Human Rights finding that the application was admissible[2], the court for the first and only time to date refuted this finding of admissibility and did not address the merits of the case[3]. More recently, the issue of transsexuality has been the subject of judicial consideration in the *Rees* case[4]. The applicant was a post-operative female to male transsexual who sought to have 'his' entry on the register of births altered to reflect 'his' changed status. This application had been refused by the Registrar General in 1980[5]. The alleged violation of article 8 of the Convention for the Protection of Human Rights and Fundamental Freedoms arose, the applicant maintained, from the constraints placed upon 'his' full integration into social life, and this was as a direct consequence of the failure of the United Kingdom government to provide measures that would legally constitute 'him' as a male for the purposes of the exhaustive classification of all citizens into male or female[6]. The European Court of Human Rights concluded that the United Kingdom had done all that it was required to do, by amending all other official documents, and the fact that 'he' was a female at birth was indisputable and unalterable. The entry in the register of births was and remains a true statement of the applicant's sex at birth. Accordingly in the light of the circumstances presented to it the court held that in the instant case article 8 had not been breached[7].

1 *Van Oosterwijk v Belgium* (Ser A No 40, Judgment 6 November 1980) 3 EHRR 557, E Ct HR.
2 The Commission also concluded unanimously that there had been a breach of the Convention for the Protection of Human Rights and Fundamental Freedoms (Rome, 4 November 1950; 213 UNTS 221; TS 71 (1953); Cmd 8969), art 8, for which see para 62 above.

3 The court held that there had been a failure to exhaust local remedies, as to which see para 14 above.

4 *Rees v United Kingdom* (Ser A No 106, Judgment 17 October 1986) 9 EHRR 56, E Ct HR.

5 All relevant personal documentation was in 'his' male name, but the register of births still showed 'his' sex as 'female'.

6 In particular the applicant claimed humiliation and embarrassment when required to produce a birth certificate, as the difference between 'his' apparent and legal sex was revealed.

7 The decision was by twelve votes to three. In *Cossey v United Kingdom* (Ser A No 184, Judgment 27 September 1990) 13 EHRR 622, E Ct HR, the court followed its ruling in the *Rees* case and held by ten votes to eight that the refusal of the United Kingdom government to issue the applicant (a post-operative male-to-female transsexual) with a birth certificate showing 'her' sex as 'female' did not constitute a violation of article 8 of the convention. However, the court did endorse what it had said in the *Rees* case, namely that it was 'conscious of the seriousness of the problems facing transsexuals and the distress they suffer', and that 'Since the Convention always has to be interpreted and applied in the light of present circumstances, it is important that the need for appropriate legal measures in this area should be kept under review': *Cossey*, at para 42.

68. Home and correspondence. Paragraph 1 of article 8 of the Convention for the Protection of Human Rights and Fundamental Freedoms has been interpreted so as to include telephone conversations within the ambit of 'private life' and 'correspondence'[1]. Possibly one of the best known cases to have come before the European Court of Human Rights and which concerns interference with correspondence has been that of *Malone*[2]. The applicant alleged a violation of article 8 under two heads:

(1) the interception of his postal and telephone communications by or on behalf of the police, or from the law and practice in England and Wales relevant thereto; and

(2) the 'metering' of his telephone by or on behalf of the police, or from the law and practice in England and Wales relevant thereto.

In 1977 Mr Malone, a United Kingdom citizen in business as an antique dealer, was charged with a number of offences relating to the dishonest handling of stolen goods. His trial in 1978 culminated in his being acquitted on certain counts whilst the jury disagreed on the rest. A retrial on the remaining charges took place in the spring of 1979, but again the jury failed to agree so Mr Malone was once more formally arraigned; the prosecution offered no evidence and he was acquitted.

At the trial in 1977 it emerged that details of a telephone conversation to which Mr Malone had been a party prior to his being charged were contained in the notebook of the police officer in charge of the investigations. Counsel for the prosecution accepted that this conversation had been intercepted on the authority of a warrant issued by the Secretary of State for the Home Department[3]. In addition to the instance revealed at the trial, Mr Malone contended that he believed that both his correspondence and telephone calls had been intercepted for a number of years and that he thought that such measures had continued since his acquittal on the charges against him[4]. Mr Malone further contended that his telephone had been 'metered' on behalf of the police by a device which automatically records all numbers dialled. As evidence for this belief, he asserted that when he was charged in March 1977 the premises of about twenty people whom he had recently telephoned were searched by the police. The government affirmed that the police had neither caused the applicant's telephone calls to be metred nor undertaken the alleged — or any — search operations on the basis of any list of numbers obtained from metering[5].

The court in *Malone* clearly stated that the issue of interception of communications in general was not one to which the court would address itself. The case before the court was 'directly concerned only with the question of interceptions effected by or on behalf of the police' — and not other government services such as HM Customs and Excise and the security services — 'within the general context of a criminal investigation, together with the legal and administrative framework relevant to such interceptions'[6]. The court unanimously concluded that there had been a breach of article 8 as regards both interception of communications and release of records of metering to the police. Much of the reasoning advanced by the court in reaching its conclusion turned on the legitimate exceptions permitted by paragraph 2 of article 8[7].

1   *Klass v Germany* (Ser A No 28, Judgment 6 September 1978) 2 EHRR 214, E Ct HR. For the Convention for the Protection of Human Rights and Fundamental Freedoms (Rome, 4 November 1950; 213 UNTS 221; TS 71 (1953); Cmd 8969), art 8, see para 62 above.
2   *Malone v United Kingdom* (Ser A No 82, Judgment 2 August 1984) 7 EHRR 14, E Ct HR.
3   In October 1978 Mr Malone instituted civil proceedings in the Chancery Division of the High Court against the Metropolitan Police Commissioner seeking inter alia a declaration that the interception, monitoring and recording of conversations on his telephone lines without his consent was unlawful, even if done pursuant to a warrant of the Secretary of State. The Solicitor General intervened on behalf of the Secretary of State, but without being made a party. The Vice-Chancellor dismissed Mr Malone's claim: see *Malone v Metropolitan Police Comr (No 2)* [1979] Ch 344, [1979] 2 All ER 620.
4   He based his belief on delay to and signs of interference with his correspondence. In particular, he produced to the European Commission of Human Rights bundles of envelopes which had been delivered to him either unsealed or sealed with adhesive tape of an identical kind. As to his telephone communications, he stated that he had heard unusual noises on his telephone and alleged that the police had possessed information which they could have obtained only by telephone tapping. No disclosure was made in any of the proceedings as to whether the applicant's own telephone had been tapped or whether other, and if so what other, telephone conversations to which the applicant was a party had been intercepted. The primary reason for withholding this information was that disclosure would or might frustrate the purpose of telephone interception, and might serve to identify and thus jeopardise other sources of police information, particularly informants. For similar reasons the government declined to disclose before the Commission or the court to what extent, if at all, the applicant's telephone calls and correspondence had been intercepted on behalf of the police. However, it was denied that the resealing or delivery unsealed of envelopes was attributable directly or indirectly to any interception. The government conceded that, as the applicant had been suspected of being concerned in receiving stolen property, he was one of a class of persons against whom measures of interception were liable to be employed.
5   The applicant's request to the Post Office and the police complaints department to remove suspected listening devices from his telephone met with the response that neither the Post Office nor the police had authority in the matter.
6   *Malone v United Kingdom*, at para 63 (7 EHRR 38).
7   See para 81 below. *Malone* was followed in *Kruslin v France* (Ser A No 176A, Judgement 24 April 1990) 12 EHRR 547, E Ct HR, and *Huvig v France* (Ser A No 176B, Judgment 24 April 1990) 12 EHRR 528, E Ct HR.

69. Prisoners' correspondence. The cases demanding consideration on the subject of prisoners' correspondence have, for the most part, been of United Kingdom origin[1].

The earliest case concerning the correspondence of convicted prisoners — and indeed the first case to come before the European Court of Human Rights alleging violation of the Convention for the Protection of Human Rights and Fundamental Freedoms by the United Kingdom — was that of *Golder*[2]. The applicant submitted that article 8 had been violated[3] when he had been denied contact with a solicitor under the Prison Rules 1964, SI 1964/388. The court unanimously held that there had been a violation of article 8 of the convention, although there had been no actual physical interference, such as prevention or censorship, with any communication between Golder and his solicitor or vice-versa. The violation had been incurred by the refusal of the Home Secretary of Mr Golder's petition, which had 'the direct and immediate effect of preventing Golder from contacting a solicitor by any means whatever, including that which in the ordinary way he would have used to begin with, correspondence'[4]. Impeding the initiation of correspondence constituted, in the court's view, the most far-reaching form of 'interference' with the exercise of the 'right to respect for correspondence'[4]. The court considered possible justifications for the interference[5] before reaching its affirmative conclusion[6].

Two cases before the European Court of Human Rights alleging a violation of article 8 have been of Scottish origin[7]. The court's decision in one of them, *Boyle and Rice*, did not contribute substantially to the law in this area but is of relevance with respect to article 13[8].

1 The two exceptions are *De Wilde, Ooms and Versyp v Belgium (No 1)* (Ser A No 12, Judgment 18 June 1971) 1 EHRR 373, E Ct HR, where the court acknowledged that the Convention for the Protection of Human Rights and Fundamental Freedoms (Rome, 4 November 1950; 213 UNTS 221; TS 71 (1953); Cmd 8969), art 8, protected the correspondence of detained vagrants in Belgium, and *Schönenberger and Durmaz v Switzerland* (Ser A No 137, Judgment 20 June 1988) 11 EHRR 202, E Ct HR, a case which concerns not a convicted prisoner but a suspect and his correspondence with a lawyer appointed by the suspect's wife.

2 *Golder v United Kingdom* (Ser A No 18, Judgment 21 February 1975) 1 EHRR 524, E Ct HR.

3 A violation of the Convention for the Protection of Human Rights and Fundamental Freedoms, art 6, was also maintained. For arts 6, 8, see paras 43, 62, above.

4 *Golder*, at para 43 (1 EHRR 538).

5 Ie those contained in the Convention for the Protection of Human Rights and Fundamental Freedoms, art 8, para 2: see para 78 below.

6 Similarly, in *Silver v United Kingdom* (Ser A No 61, Judgment 25 March 1983) 5 EHRR 347, E Ct HR, relating to the interception of prisoners' correspondence, the scope of the justification argument was the central issue.

7 *Boyle and Rice v United Kingdom* (Ser A No 131, Judgment 27 April 1988) 10 EHRR 425, E Ct HR; *McCallum v United Kingdom* (Ser A No 183, Judgment 30 August 1990) 13 EHRR 597, E Ct HR.

8 For the Convention for the Protection of Human Rights and Fundamental Freedoms, art 13, see para 84 below. Article 8 was violated when a letter written by Mr Boyle to a playwright friend was stopped by the prison governor in the mistaken belief that the contents were intended for publication. The United Kingdom government acknowledged that the rules had been wrongly applied owing to the fact that the letter was purely personal and in its final submissions to the court accepted that this constituted a breach of article 8: *Boyle and Rice*, at para 50 (10 EHRR 442). There was a similar finding with regard to article 8 in *McCallum*. Like *Boyle and Rice*, that case related to restrictions imposed on the correspondence of a convicted prisoner. Again the United Kingdom government did not contest the allegation in respect of article 8.

70. Violation of the home. Violation of a person's home has come before the European Court of Human Rights in two cases[1].

1 See *Gillow v United Kingdom* (Ser A No 109, Judgment 24 November 1986) 11 EHRR 335, E Ct HR, (where the refusal of a licence to occupy a house belonging to the applicants was held to be in breach of the Convention for the Protection of Human Rights and Fundamental Freedoms (Rome, 4 November 1950; 213 UNTS 221; TS 71 (1953); Cmd 8969), art 8, as being an interference with the exercise of their right to respect for their home which was disproportionate to the legitimate aim pursued by the relevant legislation); and *Chappell v United Kingdom* (Ser A No 152, Judgment 30 March 1989) 12 EHRR 1, E Ct HR, (where events during the simultaneous execution of an Anton Piller order and a search warrant at a home where video tapes, some alleged to be in breach of copyright and some to be obscene, were processed and stored and from which they were sold were held not to violate art 8).

(b) The Right to marry

71. Generally: article 12. Article 12 of the Convention for the Protection of Human Rights and Fundamental Freedoms provides that:

> 'Men and women of marriageable age have the right to marry and to found a family, according to the national laws governing the exercise of this right'.

The case of *F v Switzerland*[1] centred exclusively on article 12 and was concerned with the alleged violation of the article by the Swiss Civil Code's three-year prohibition on remarriage by the spouse deemed to be 'at fault' after divorce on the grounds of adultery[2]. The European Court of Human Rights noted that the Swiss domestic legislation was now unique in that no other Contracting State imposed a waiting period. The court also recognised 'that the stability of marriage is a legitimate aim which is in the public interest', although it expressed doubt as to whether the particular means used by Switzerland were appropriate for the achievement of that aim[3]. The court rejected unreservedly the argument that a temporary prohibition of remarriage could preserve the rights of others and in particular those of the future spouse of the divorced person. Article 12 is concerned only with the right to marry *per se* and therefore it extends an equal right of marriage to all persons, regardless of whether one is marrying for the first time or subsequent to divorce. In short, if domestic divorce legislation renders a person free to marry then that right must be upheld without reservation[4]. However, the convention does not demand that divorce be available in Contracting States and, if it is not available, the convention may not be invoked to provide a right of remarriage. This is illustrated by the case of *Johnston*[5], and was distinguished from the situation pertaining in the Swiss case[6]. Mr Johnston invoked article 12 in an unsuccessful attempt to secure a right to divorce in Ireland, where divorce is prohibited, although judicial separation is available. The European Court of Human Rights concluded 'that the ordinary meaning of the words "right to marry" is clear, in the sense that they cover the formation of marital relationship but not their dissolution'[7]. Even if, as was being suggested, 'the prohibition on divorce is to be seen as a restriction on capacity to marry', the court did not consider that, in a society adhering to the principle of monogamy, such a restriction could be regarded as undermining the substance of the right guaranteed by article 12[8]. Thus the court decided by sixteen votes to one that there was no violation of article 12. As stated, article 12 is concerned specifically with the right and the protection thereof to marry: the court has resisted the argument that article 12 embraces a right not to marry[9].

1 *F v Switzerland* (Ser A No 128, Judgment 18 December 1987) 10 EHRR 411, E Ct HR.
2 Swiss Civil Code, art 150. Following divorce on other grounds, the prohibition is a period fixed by the court 'of not less than one and not more than two years'.
3 *F v Switzerland*, at para 36 (10 EHRR 420).
4 The court decided in the affirmative, albeit narrowly (by nine votes to eight), that the Swiss Civil Code, art 150, violated the Convention for the Protection of Human Rights and Fundamental Freedoms (Rome, 4 November 1950; 213 UNTS 221; TS 71 (1953); Cmd 8969), art 12.
5 *Johnston v Ireland* (Ser A No 112, Judgment 18 December 1986) 9 EHRR 203, E Ct HR.
6 *F v Switzerland*, at para 38 (10 EHRR 421, 422).
7 *Johnston*, at para 52 (9 EHRR 218). See also *Rees v United Kingdom* (Ser A No 106, Judgment 17 October 1986) 9 EHRR 56 at 68, E Ct HR, at para 49, where the court said 'the right to marry guaranteed by Article 12 refers to the traditional marriage between persons of opposite biological sex'. A violation of art 12 was alleged in *Cossey v United Kingdom* (Ser A No 184, Judgment 27 September 1990) 13 EHRR 622, E Ct HR, but the court refuted it by fourteen votes to four and held that the applicant's inability to marry a woman did not stem from any legal impediment, and it could not be said that the right to marry had been impaired as a consequence of the provisions of domestic law: *Cossey*, at para 45 (13 EHRR 642). As to the applicant's inability to marry a man, the court held that the criteria adopted by English law reflected the concept of marriage to which the right guaranteed by article 12 refers, namely the traditional marriage between persons of opposite biological sex. The court observed that although some Contracting States would now regard as valid a marriage between a person in the applicant's situation and a man, the developments which had occurred to date could not be said to evidence any general abandonment of the traditional concept. In these circumstances the court maintained that it was not open to it to take a new approach to the interpretation of article 12 on this point and that the attachment to the traditional concept of marriage was sufficient reason for continuing to adopt biological criteria for determining sex for the purposes of marriage, and this was a matter encompassed within the power of the Contracting States to regulate by national law the exercise of the right to marry: *Cossey*, at para 46.
8 *Johnston*, at para 52 (9 EHRR 218, 219).
9 *Marckx v Belgium* (Ser A No 31, Judgment 13 June 1979) 2 EHRR 330 at 356, E Ct HR, at para 67.

(7) FREEDOM OF THOUGHT, CONSCIENCE AND RELIGION

72. Generally: article 9. Article 9 of the Convention for the Protection of Human Rights and Fundamental Freedoms provides as follows:

'1. Everyone has the right to freedom of thought, conscience and religion; this right includes freedom to change his religion or belief and freedom, either alone or in community with others and in public or private, to manifest his religion or belief, in worship, teaching, practice and observance.

2. Freedom to manifest one's religion or beliefs shall be subject only to such limitations as are prescribed by law and are necessary in a democratic society in the interests of public safety, for the protection of public order, health or morals, or for the protection of the rights and freedoms of others'[1].

A violation of article 9 was alleged in the case of *Darby*[2], but the European Court of Human Rights concluded unanimously that it was not necessary to examine the case under article 9 either alone or together with article 14.

1 Convention for the Protection of Human Rights and Fundamental Freedoms (Rome, 4 November 1950; 213 UNTS 221; TS (1953); Cmd 8969), art 9, paras 1, 2.
2 *Darby v Sweden* (Ser A No 187, Judgment 23 October 1990), E Ct HR. The case concerns the obligation to pay a church tax in Sweden.
3 For the Convention for the Protection of Human Rights and Fundamental Freedoms, art 14, see para 85 below.

(8) FREEDOM OF EXPRESSION

73. Introduction: article 10. Article 10 of the Convention for the Protection of Human Rights and Fundamental Freedoms provides as follows:

'1. Everyone has the right to freedom of expression. This right shall include freedom to hold opinions and to receive and impart information and ideas without interference by public authority and regardless of frontiers. This Article shall not prevent States from requiring the licensing of broadcasting, television or cinema enterprises.

2. The exercise of these freedoms, since it carries with it duties and responsibilities, may be subject to such formalities, conditions, restrictions or penalties as are prescribed by law and are necessary in a democratic society, in the interests of national security, territorial integrity or public safety, for the prevention of disorder or crime, for the protection of health or morals, for the protection of the reputation or rights of others, for preventing the disclosure of information received in confidence, or for maintaining the authority and impartiality of the judiciary'[1].

The freedom which article 10 is designed to guarantee has been characterised by the European Court of Human Rights as being one of the essential foundations of a democratic society, being one of the basic conditions for its progress and for the development of everyone[2]. Article 10 seeks to protect not only 'information' or 'ideas that are favourably received or regarded as inoffensive or as a matter of indifference', but also those that 'offend, shock or disturb the State or any sector of the population. Such are the demands of that pluralism, tolerance and broadmindedness without which there is no "democratic society"'[3].

Article 10 has been given a broad interpretation. As noted by the court in the *Müller* case, article 10 does not distinguish between the various forms of expression[4]; nor does it apply solely to certain types of information or ideas or forms of expression[5]. Article 10 embraces the freedom of artistic expression[6], the freedom of the press[7] and the medium of broadcasting[8].

States are permitted under paragraph 1 of article 10 to control by a licensing system the way in which broadcasting is organised in their territories, particularly in its technical aspects, but this does not remove licensing measures themselves from the application of paragraph 2 of the article. If this were the case, it would lead to a result 'contrary to the object and purpose of Article 10 taken as a whole'[9].

The right of expression includes the right to impart information and the right to receive information. The right to receive information as guaranteed by article 10 exists independently of the right to impart information[10]. The right contained in article 10 cannot be definitively distinguished from the right of correspondence guaranteed by article 8[11], the right to freedom of thought, conscience and religion guaranteed by article 9[12] and, arguably, the right of peaceful assembly and association guaranteed by article 11[13]. An overlap will become apparent when the legitimate exceptions to the rights guaranteed by the foregoing articles are discussed below[14].

1   Convention for the Protection of Human Rights and Fundamental Freedoms (Rome, 4 November 1950; 213 UNTS 221; TS 71 (1953); Cmd 8969), art 10, paras 1, 2.
2   *Handyside v United Kingdom* (Ser A No 24, Judgment 7 December 1976) 1 EHRR 737 at 754, E Ct HR, at para 49.
3   *Handyside*, at para 49. See also *Sunday Times v United Kingdom* (Ser A No 30, Judgment 26 April 1979) 2 EHRR 245 at 280, E Ct HR, at para 65, and *Lingens v Austria* (Ser A No 103, Judgment 8 July 1986) 8 EHRR 407 at 418, E Ct HR, at para 41.
4   *Müller v Switzerland* (Ser A No 133, Judgment 24 May 1988) 13 EHRR 212 at 225, E Ct HR, at para 27.
5   *Markt Intern and Beermann v Germany* (Ser A No 165, Judgment 20 November 1989) 12 EHRR 161 at 171, E Ct HR, at para 26.
6   *Müller*, at para 27.
7   *Sunday Times*.
8   *Groppera Radio AG v Switzerland* (Ser A No 173, Judgment 28 March 1990) 12 EHRR 321 at 337, E Ct HR, at para 55, where the court held that both broadcasting of programmes over the air and cable retransmissions of such programmes are covered by the right enshrined in article 10.
9   *Groppera Radio AG*, at para 61 (12 EHRR 338, 339).
10   See *Sunday Times*, at para 65 (2 EHRR at 280), where the court said that not only did the media have the task of imparting information and ideas but that the public had the right to receive them.
11   For the Convention for the Protection of Human Rights and Fundamental Freedoms, art 8, see para 62 above.
12   For ibid, art 9, see para 72 above.
13   See P Van Kyk and G J H Van Hoof *Theory and Practice of the European Convention on Human Rights* (1984) at pp 309, 210. For article 11 of the convention, see para 75 below.
14   See also the court's statement in *Young, James and Webster v United Kingdom* (Ser A No 44, Judgment 26 June 1981) 4 EHRR 38, E Ct HR, at para 66.

74. The freedom of the press. The *Sunday Times* case remains the leading statement by the European Court of Human Rights on the freedom of the press[1]. A domestic action was raised against the Sunday Times seeking an injunction to prevent the publication of articles by that newspaper on the development and manufacture of thalidomide in the United Kingdom[2]. The Sunday Times had earlier published an article entitled 'Our Thalidomide Children: A Case for National Shame'[3]. Civil proceedings were pending against the United Kingdom manufacturers of the drug, Distillers Co (Biochemicals) Ltd, and the injunction was sought on the grounds that the articles amounted to or would be a contempt of court. The injunction was granted by the Queen's Bench Division in November 1972. The newspaper proprietors appealed the decision, and the Court of Appeal ordered the discharge of the injunction[4]. On an appeal by the Attorney-General the House of Lords restored the injunction order on 18 July 1973[5]. The injunction was finally discharged on 23 June 1976, and the contentious article was published, albeit in a modified form, four days later on. The claim of the applicants[6] in the case before the European Court of Human Rights was that they had been the victims of a violation of article 10 of the Convention for the Protection of Human Rights and Fundamental Freedoms[7]. The violation, it was claimed, arose (1) by reason of the injunction granted by the English courts; and (2) by the continuing restraints to which the applicants were still subject arising from the width and lack of precision of the English law on contempt of court[8].

The court endorsed what it had said in the *Handyside* case, namely that freedom of expression is an essential foundation of a democratic society and highlighted the particular relevance of this freedom for the press[9]. The principles underlying freedom of expression were, the court maintained, 'equally applicable to the field of the administration of justice', as the latter 'serves the interests of the Community at large and requires the co-operation of an enlightened public'. Accordingly, the court concluded that although courts may be the *fora* for the settlement of disputes, this should not preclude prior discussion of disputes, in specialised journals, in the general press or among the public at large. In its observations, the court recognised the need for an equilibrium to be established between the mass media discharging its obligations to disseminate information whilst not interfering with the proper administration of justice[10]. However, in the instant case there had been a breach of article 10.

The next case concerning the issue of freedom of the press was that of *Lingens*[11]. The applicant, a journalist and magazine editor, had been convicted under the Austrian Criminal Code of publishing two defamatory articles which contained criticism of a leading political figure[12]. The applicant alleged that his conviction for defamation constituted an unjustified interference with his freedom of expression and was in breach of article 10. In its judgment, while the European Court of Human Rights acknowledged that the press 'may not overstep the bounds set, inter alia for the "protection of the reputation of others"', it also recognised the obligation incumbent on the press to 'impart information and ideas on political issues just as on those in other areas of public interest'[13]. The court maintained that freedom of the press afforded the public one of the best means of discovering and forming an opinion on the ideas and attitudes of political leaders. The court went so far as to say that freedom of political debate lies 'at the very core of the concept of a democratic society which prevails throughout the Convention'[14]. The court looked at the effect of the sanction imposed on Mr Lingens. Although the threat of criminal proceedings could not prevent the publication of the articles, it 'nonetheless amounted to a kind of censure, which would be likely to discourage him from making criticisms of that kind in the future'; it would be likely to deter journalists 'from contributing to public discussion of issues affecting the life of the Community' and would be 'liable to hamper the press in performing its task as purveyor of information and public watchdog'[15].

1 *Sunday Times v United Kingdom* (Ser A No 30, Judgment 26 April 1979) 2 EHRR 245, E Ct HR. For a case concerning publication of excerpts from a security agent's memoirs, see *Observer and Guardian v United Kingdom, Sunday Times v United Kingdom* Times, 27 November 1991, E Ct HR.
2 *Attorney-General v Times Newspapers Ltd* [1973] QB 710, [1972] 3 All ER 1136, DC.
3 The article was published in the Sunday Times on 24 September 1972.
4 *Attorney-General v Times Newspapers Ltd* [1973] QB 710, [1973] 1 All ER 815, CA.
5 *Attorney-General v Times Newspapers Ltd* [1974] AC 273, [1973] 3 All ER 54, HL.
6 Ie Times Newspapers Ltd (publishers), Mr Harold Evans (editor), and a group of journalists working on the Sunday Times.
7 For the Convention for the Protection of Human Rights and Fundamental Freedoms (Rome, 4 November 1950; 213 UNTS 221; TS 71 (1953); Cmd 8969), art 10, see para 73 above.
8 At the outset of the case, the European Court of Human Rights stated that it was concerned only with whether the decision of the House of Lords constituted a violation of the convention. That decision widened considerably the scope of the initial injunction, as it required the Divisional Court to order that 'Times Newspapers Ltd, by themselves, their servants, agents or otherwise, be restrained from publishing, or causing or authorising or procuring to be published or printed, any article or matter which prejudges the issues of negligence, breach of contract or breach of

duty, or deals with the evidence relating to any of the said issues arising in any actions pending or imminent against Distillers Co (Biochemicals) Ltd in respect of the development, distribution or use of the drug "thalidomide"': *Attorney-General v Times Newspapers Ltd* [1974] AC 273 at 327, [1973] 3 All ER 54 at 87, HL. The original order merely restrained Times Newspapers Ltd 'by themselves, their servants or agents or otherwise, from publishing or causing or authorising to be published an article in draft dealing, inter alia, with the development, distribution and use of the drug thalidomide' *Attorney-General v Times Newspapers Ltd* [1973] QB 710 at 713, [1972] 3 All ER 1136 at 1138, DC.

9 *Handyside v United Kingdom* (Ser A No 24, Judgment 7 December 1976) 1 EHRR 737 at 754, E Ct HR, at para 49.
10 Furthermore, whilst the mass media must not overstep the bounds imposed in the interests of the proper administration of justice, it is incumbent on them to impart information and ideas concerning matters that come before the courts just as in other areas of public interest. Not only do the media have the task of imparting such information and ideas: the public also has a right to receive them: *Sunday Times* at para 65 (2 EHRR 280).
11 *Lingens v Austria* (Ser A No 103, Judgment 8 July 1986) 8 EHRR 407, E Ct HR.
12 Ie Bruno Kreisky who was Federal Chancellor at the time the articles were published. The articles made reference to his alleged Nazi affiliation.
13 *Lingens*, at para 41 (8 EHRR 418).
14 *Lingens*, at para 42 (8 EHRR 418, 419).
15 *Lingens*, at para 44 (8 EHRR 420). In *Barfod v Denmark* (Ser A No 149, Judgment 22 February 1989) 13 EHRR 493 at 499, E Ct HR, at para 29, the court emphasised the great importance of ensuring that members of the public were not discouraged, through fear of criminal or other sanctions, from voicing their opinions on issues of public concern.

(9) PEACEFUL ASSEMBLY

75. Introduction: article 11. Article 11 of the Convention for the Protection of Human Rights and Fundamental Freedoms provides as follows:

'1. Everyone has the right to freedom of peaceful assembly and to freedom of association with others, including the right to form and to join trade unions for the protection of his interests.
2. No restrictions shall be placed on the exercise of these rights other than such as are prescribed by law and are necessary in a democratic society in the interests of national security or public safety, for the prevention of disorder or crime, for the protection of health or morals or for the protection of the rights and freedoms of others. This Article shall not prevent the imposition of lawful restrictions on the exercise of these rights by members of the armed forces, of the police or of the administration of the State'[1].

A professional organisation founded by the legislature and pursuing an aim which is in the general interest is not an 'association' within the meaning of article 11[2].

1 Convention for the Protection of Human Rights and Fundamental Freedoms (Rome, 4 November 1950; 213 UNTS 221; TS 71 (1953); Cmd 8969), art 11, paras 1, 2.
2 *Le Compte, Van Leuven and De Meyere v Belgium* (Ser A No 43, Judgment 23 June 1981) 4 EHRR 1 at 23, E Ct HR, at paras 64, 65; *Albert and Le Compte v Belgium* (Ser A No 58, Judgment 10 February 1983) 5 EHRR 533 at 547, E Ct HR, at para 44. The organisation in question in each case was the Belgian *Ordre des médecins*.

76. Scope of trade union freedom. Trade union freedom is one form, or a special aspect, of freedom of association. But article 11 of the Convention for the Protection of Human Rights and Fundamental Freedoms[1] does not guarantee any particular treatment of trade unions or their members by the state, such as the right to be consulted by the state. This was the conclusion of the European Court of Human Rights in the *National Union of Belgian Police* case[2], where the court held that a right to be consulted was not only excluded from paragraph 1 of article 11 but was not one recognised by Contracting States either in their national law or practice. Nor could it be argued that it was a right 'indispensable for the effective enjoyment of trade union freedom' and thus it was not 'an element necessarily inherent in a right guaranteed by the Convention'[3]. The court maintained that the purpose of the phrase 'the protection of his interests' is to protect the occupational interests of trade union members by trade union action, the conduct and development of which Contracting States are required both to permit and make possible. The court expressed the view that trade union members have, for the purpose of protecting their interests, a right that the trade union be heard. The mechanics of this are a matter of domestic discretion. Consultation is only one of the means available and is not required by the convention. What the convention does require 'is that under national law trade unions should be enabled in conditions not at variance with Article 11, to strive for the protection of their members' interests'[4]. The court in the instant case held that there had been no violation of paragraph 1 of article 11[5].

These principles were endorsed in the *Swedish Engine Drivers' Union* case[6] and the *Schmidt and Dalström* case[7], when the court noted that paragraph 1 of article 11 does not secure any particular treatment of trade unions or their members by the state, such as the conclusion of any collective agreement[8] or the right to benefits, such as salary increases, resulting from a new collective agreement[9]. In both these cases the court held article 11 as binding upon the 'State as employer' whether the latter's relations with its employees were governed by public or private law[10]. In *Schmidt and Dalström*, where the applicants averred that a right to strike was an 'organic right' included in article 11, the court responded by recognising the right to strike as only one of the means available for the protection of the occupational interests of trade union members[11]. In both cases, the court concluded unanimously that there had been no breach of article 11[12].

1 For the Convention for the Protection of Human Rights and Fundamental Freedoms (Rome, 4 November 1950; 213 UNTS 221; TS 71 (1953); Cmd 8969), art 11, see para 75 above.
2 *National Union of Belgian Police v Belgium* (Ser A No 19, Judgment 27 October 1975) 1 EHRR 578 at 590, 591, E Ct HR, at para 38.
3 *National Union of Belgian Police*, at para 38. The court also noted the existence within the Council of Europe framework of the European Social Charter (Turin, 18 October 1961; TS 38 (1965); 529 UNTS 89; Cmnd 2643) and its obligations on Contracting States 'to promote joint consultation between workers and employers'. As to the charter, see para 7 above.
4 *National Union of Belgian Police*, at para 38.
5 The applicant's complaint was founded on the failure of the Belgian government to recognise the National Union of Belgian Police as one of the most representative organisations of the police force. Membership of the union was open to all members of the municipal police force, and in 1974 its membership was about 50 per cent of the force. The municipal police force constituted less than 10 per cent of all municipal and provincial staff. The government's non-recognition meant that the union was excluded from consultation with the Ministry of the Interior on such matters as staff structures, conditions of recruitment and promotion, pecuniary status and salary scales of municipal and provincial staff. The applicants alleged that this exclusion, as regards both questions of interest to all such staff and questions peculiar to the municipal police, placed it at a disadvantage compared with the three trade unions open to that staff as a whole. Under a royal decree of 2 August 1966 (as amended in 1969) the only organisations regarded as the most representative of all municipal and provincial staff were to be those which were open to all staff and protected their occupational interests. The National Union of Belgian Police claimed that this greatly restricted its field of action and that as a consequence members of the municipal police were inclined to join those organisations which were considered to be 'representative' but which possessed a 'political' character incompatible with the 'special vocation' of the police. The union had sought an annulment of the royal decree by the *Conseil d'Etat*, but its application was dismissed in November 1969. The applicants claimed that the government's non-recognition of the union as one of the most representative organisation constituted a breach of the Convention for the Protection of Human Rights and Fundamental Freedoms.
6 *Swedish Engine Drivers' Union v Sweden* (Ser A No 20, Judgment 6 February 1976) 1 EHRR 617, E Ct HR.
7 *Schmidt and Dalström v Sweden* (Ser A No 21, Judgment 6 February 1976) 1 EHRR 637, E Ct HR.

8 *Swedish Engine Drivers' Union*, at para 39 (1 EHRR 627).
9 *Schmidt and Dalström*, at para 34 (1 EHRR 644).
10 *Swedish Engine Drivers' Union*, at para 37 (1 EHRR 627); *Schmidt and Dalström v Sweden*, para 34 (1 EHRR 644).
11 *Schmidt and Dalström v Sweden*, para 36 (1 EHRR 644). Again, reference was made to the European Social Charter.
12 In both cases a breach of the Convention for the Protection of Human Rights and Fundamental Freedoms, art 14 (see para 85 below), was alleged as well as a breach of art 11.

77. Closed shop agreements. In the case of *Young, James and Webster*[1] the applicants were former employees of British Rail who had been dismissed following their failure to join any one of the three trade unions[2] which were the subject of a 'closed shop' agreement concluded between British Rail and the trade unions concerned. Under the terms of the agreement, membership of one of the three unions was a condition of employment. The Trade Union and Labour Relations Act 1974 recognised refusal to join a trade union pursuant to a 'closed shop' agreement as a fair ground for dismissal except where the individual genuinely objected on grounds of religious belief[3]. All of the applicants believed that trade union membership should be a matter of individual choice, whilst Young and Webster took exception to trade union policies and activities and Young to the political affiliations of the particular trade unions concerned.

The applicants maintained that their dismissal was contrary inter alia to article 11 of the Convention for the Protection of Human Rights and Fundamental Freedoms[4], and the European Court of Human Rights acknowledged that the main issues of the case were concerned with that article[5]. The court further emphasised that its task was not to review the closed shop system as such in relation to the convention or to express an opinion on every consequence or form of compulsion which it may engender, but rather to examine the effects of the system on the applicants[6].

A substantial part of the pleadings presented to the court focused on whether article 11 guaranteed not only a freedom of association, including the right to form and to join a trade union, in the positive sense, but also, by implication, a 'negative right' not to be compelled to join either an association or union. The court for its part did not deem it necessary to become involved in the argument advanced by the United Kingdom government that such a right had been deliberately omitted from the convention[7]. Notwithstanding, the court did reiterate what it had said in the *National Union of Belgian Police* case[8]: that the right to form and to join trade unions is a special aspect of freedom of association[9]. However, such a notion of freedom implied 'some measure of freedom of choice as to its exercise'[9].

Even if the argument could be sustained that a negative right had been deliberately omitted from the convention, the court concluded, it did not follow that the negative aspect of a person's freedom of association fell outside the ambit of article 11 and that each and every compulsion to join a particular trade union was compatible with the intention of that provision. To construe article 11 as one sanctioning every kind of compulsion in the field of trade union membership 'would strike at the very substance of the freedom it is designed to guarantee'[10].

Turning to the facts of the case before it, the court found that the situation which had confronted the applicants was one clearly running 'counter to the concept of freedom of association in its negative sense'[11]. The court conceded, however, that if article 11 did not guarantee the negative aspect of that freedom to the same extent as the positive aspect, compulsion to join a particular trade union might not on every occasion be contrary to the convention[11]. In the instant case, the court characterised a threat of dismissal and a consequent loss of livelihood as 'a most serious form of compulsion'[12] and stated that such compulsion within the context of the particular circumstances was one which struck 'at the very substance of the freedom guaranteed by Article 11'[13]. On that basis the court concluded[14] that there had been an interference with that freedom as regards each of the three applicants.

The court also considered the restriction imposed on the applicants' right of choice regarding which trade unions they could join voluntarily. An individual could not be said to enjoy the right to freedom of association if in reality the freedom of action or choice which is available to him is either non-existent or so reduced as to be of no practical value[15]. The court held that this was the situation with respect to the three applicants. The court highlighted the complementary nature and consequential interaction of the convention's articles in the following way:

> 'The protection of personal opinion afforded by Articles 9 and 10 in the shape of freedom of thought, conscience and religion and of freedom of expression is also one of the purposes of freedom of association as guaranteed by Article 11. Accordingly, it strikes at the very substance of this Article to exert pressure, of the kind applied to the applicants, in order to compel someone to join an association contrary to his convictions'[16].

1 *Young, James and Webster v United Kingdom* (Ser A No 44, Judgment 26 June 1981) 4 EHRR 38, E Ct HR.

2 Ie the National Union of Railwaymen, the Transport Salaried Staff's Association and the Associated Society of Locomotive Engineers and Firemen.

3 Trade Union and Labour Relations Act 1974 (c 52), s 1(2), Sch 1, para 6(5) (amended by the Trade Union and Labour Relations (Amendment) Act 1976 (c 7), s 1(e)).

4 For the Convention for the Protection of Human Rights and Fundamental Freedoms (Rome, 4 November 1950; 213 UNTS 221; TS 71 (1953); Cmd 8969), art 11, see para 75 above. Breaches were also alleged of art 9 (see para 72 above), art 10 (see para 73 above) and art 13 (see para 84 below).

5 *Young, James and Webster*, at para 50 (4 EHRR 52).

6 *Young, James and Webster*, at para 53 (4 EHRR 54).

7 The United Kingdom had elucidated this argument from the text of the *Travaux préparatoires* for the convention.

8 *National Union of Belgian Police v Belgium* (Ser A No 19, Judgment 27 October 1975) 1 EHRR 578, E Ct HR.

9 *National Union of Belgian Police*, at para 38 (1 EHRR 590).

10 *Young, James and Webster*, at para 52 (4 EHRR 53).

11 *Young, James and Webster*, at para 55 (4 EHRR 54).

12 The court also noted that the compulsion was directed against any person who was engaged by British Rail before the introduction of the obligation to join a particular trade union.

13 *Young, James and Webster*, at para 55 (4 EHRR 54).

14 Ie by eighteen votes to three.

15 *Young, James and Webster*, at para 56 (4 EHRR 54, 55). The court here was again endorsing what it has said on a number of earlier occasions, that 'the Convention is intended to guarantee not rights that are theoretical or illusory but rights that are practical and effective': *Airey v Ireland* (Ser A No 32, Judgment 9 October 1979) 2 EHRR 305 at 314, E Ct HR, at para 24.

16 *Young, James and Webster*, at para 57 (4 EHRR 55).

(10) RESTRICTIONS ON RIGHTS RELATING TO FAMILY, THOUGHT, CONSCIENCE, RELIGION, EXPRESSION AND ASSEMBLY

78. Introduction. Restrictions on the exercise of the rights contained in articles 8 to 11 of the Convention for the Protection of Human Rights and Fundamental Freedoms[1], and which have received judicial congnisance by the European Court of Human Rights, are here dealt with together. The reason for this is that similar wording is used in the four articles concerned and consequently the court has adopted a common approach in interpretation. This is illustrated by the court's frequent cross-reference to the established case law on any of the four articles[2]. Paragraph 1 of each of articles 8, 9, 10 and 11 guarantee certain rights, but the guarantee is not unqualified. Under paragraph 2 of each of those articles there are three principal criteria justifying interference with the exercise of the right protected — the interference must be:

(1) in accordance with or prescribed by law;
(2) in pursuance of a legitimate aim;
(3) necessary in a democratic society.

These criteria are discussed in the paragraphs which follow.

1 For the text of the Convention for the Protection of Human Rights and Fundamental Freedoms (Rome, 4 November 1950; 213 UNTS 221; TS 71 (1953); Cmd 8969), arts 8–11, see paras 62, 72, 73, 75, above.
2 See eg *Dudgeon v United Kingdom* (Ser A No 45, Judgment 23 September 1981) 4 EHRR 149, E Ct HR, which refers to *Young, James and Webster v United Kingdom* (Ser A No 44, Judgment 26 June 1981) 4 EHRR 38 at 49, 50, E Ct HR, at para 43. See also *Silver v United Kingdom* (Ser A No 61, Judgment 25 March 1983) 5 EHRR 347 at 371, E Ct HR, at para 85, where the court stated that articles 8 and 10 'overlap as regards freedom of expression through correspondence and not to give them an identical interpretation could lead to different conclusions in respect of the same interference'.

79. 'In accordance with' or 'as prescribed by' law. Under the Convention for the Protection of Human Rights and Fundamental Freedoms, interference with the rights guaranteed by article 8 may be justified if it is inter alia 'such as is in accordance with the law'[1], and those guaranteed by articles 9 to 11 are subject only to such limitations, formalities, conditions, restrictions etc 'as are [inter alia] prescribed by law'[2].

The term 'prescribed by law' was considered in the *Sunday Times* case[3]. The European Court of Human Rights readily concluded that there had been an interference by a public authority with respect to the applicants' freedom of expression[4]. But as to whether that interference was legitimate, the court initially had to consider whether the interference was one 'prescribed by law'. The court identified the two requirements which in its view must flow from the expression 'prescribed by law'.

First, the law must be adequately accessible. By this the court meant that citizens should be provided with an indication as to what is adequate in the circumstances of the legal rules applicable to a given case[5]. Secondly, to be law, a norm must be formulated with sufficient precision so as to enable the citizen to regulate his conduct: thus he must be able, if need be with appropriate advice, to foresee to a degree that is reasonable in the circumstances the consequences which a given action might entail. However, it is not necessary for such consequences to be seen with absolute certainty; the court recognises that an equilibrium must be achieved between consistency and the flexibility necessary if the law is to develop and meet the contemporary needs of society[5].

The 'law', which may be statute or common law[6], must therefore be accessible and foreseeable. The law concerned must also be compatible with the 'rule of law'[7].

'The rule of law implies, *inter alia*, that an interference by the executive authorities with an individual's rights should be subject to an effective control which should normally be assured by the judiciary, at least in the last resort, judicial control offering the best guarantees of independence, impartiality and a proper procedure'[8].

The foregoing does not mean that the safeguards against arbitrary interference 'must be enshrined in the very text which authorises the imposition of restrictions'⁹. Notwithstanding the requirement that a norm manifests precision, '. . . law which confers a discretion must indicate the scope of that discretion'¹⁰.

1 Convention for the Protection of Human Rights and Fundamental Freedoms (Rome, 4 November 1950; 213 UNTS 221; TS 71 (1953); Cmd 8969), art 8, para 2.

2 Ibid, art 9, para 2; art 10, para 2; art 11, para 2. Although different terminology is employed in the English text of art 8 and of arts 9–11, in the French text *'prévue[s] par la loi'* is used in all four articles. This further explains why the court adopts a similar approach when required to decide whether the restriction complained of is actually justified.

3 *Sunday Times v United Kingdom* (Ser A No 30, Judgment 26 April 1979) 2 EHRR 245, E Ct HR.

4 *Sunday Times*, at para 45 (2 EHRR 269).

5 *Sunday Times*, at para 49 (2 EHRR 271).

6 *Sunday Times*, at para 47 (2 EHRR 270).

7 See the references in *Golder v United Kingdom* (Ser A No 18, Judgment 21 February 1975) 1 EHRR 524 at 534, 535, E Ct HR, at para 34, to the Convention for the Protection of Human Rights and Fundamental Freedoms, Preamble.

8 *Klass v Germany* (Ser A No 28, Judgment 6 September 1978) 2 EHRR 214 at 235, E Ct HR, at para 55. See also *Silver v United Kingdom* (Ser A No 61, Judgment 25 March 1983) 5 EHRR 347 at 373, E Ct HR, at para 90, and *Malone v United Kingdom* (Ser A No 82, Judgment 2 August 1984) 7 EHRR 14 at 40, E Ct HR, at para 67. In *Olsson v Sweden* (Ser A No 130, Judgment 24 March 1988) 11 EHRR 259 at 283, E Ct HR, at para 61(b), the court said 'The phrase "in accordance with the law" does not merely refer back to domestic law but also relates to the quality of the law, requiring it to be compatible with the rule of law; it thus implies that there must be a measure of protection in domestic law against arbitrary interferences by public authorities with the rights safeguarded' by the convention.

9 *Silver*, at para 90 (5 EHRR 373).

10 *Silver*, at para 88 (5 EHRR 372); *Malone*, at para 68 (7 EHRR 41); *Gillow v United Kingdom* (Ser A No 109, Judgment 24 November 1986) 11 EHRR 335 at 350, 351, E Ct HR, at para 51; *Olsson v Sweden* (Ser A No 130, Judgment 24 March 1988) 11 EHRR 259 at 283, E Ct HR, at para 61(a).

80. 'Legitimate aim'. The establishment of a legitimate aim under the Convention for the Protection of Human Rights and Fundamental Freedoms¹ has not proved contentious and does not merit in–depth discussion. The European Court of Human Rights seeks to establish whether the aim of the law is legitimate under the article in point.

1 See para 81, text and note 10 below.

81. 'Necessary is a democratic society'. Under the Convention for the Protection of Human Rights and Fundamental Freedoms, interferences with guaranteed rights and limitations, formalities, conditions, restrictions etc to which those rights are subject must be, inter alia, such 'as are necessary in a democratic society'¹.

The European Court of Human Rights has interpreted 'necessary' as not being synonymous with 'indispensable', but neither does it possess the flexibility of words such as 'admissible', 'ordinary', 'useful', 'reasonable' or 'desirable'². Furthermore, the court will not hold that a given action 'was not "necessary" simply because it could or would not have been granted under a different legal system'³. Contracting States enjoy a margin of discretion, but that discretion is not unfettered, being as it is subject to supervision by the court: it is for the court to give the final ruling on whether the interferences are compatible with the convention⁴.

To be justified through 'necessity', the interference complained of must be in response to a 'pressing social need'⁵. It is not sufficient that a state exercised its discretion reasonably, carefully and in good faith: a Contracting State which acts in such a way 'remains subject to the court's control as regards the compatibility of its conduct with the engagements it has undertaken under the Convention'⁶. The court has recognised that the scope of the discretion left to a state may depend on the aim being pursued. In the *Handyside* case, concerning the 'protection of morals'[7], the court acknowledged that it was:

> 'not possible to find in the domestic law of the various Contracting States a uniform European conception of morals. The view taken by their respective laws of the requirements of morals varies from time to time and from place to place, especially in an era which is characterised by a rapid and far-reaching evolution of opinions on the subject'[8].

Because of this and 'because of their direct and continuous contact with the vital focus of their countries', the court held that state authorities were as a rule better placed 'than the international judge to give an opinion on the exact content of these requirements as well as on the "necessity" of a "restriction" or "penalty" intended to meet them'[8]. This can be contrasted with what the court said in the *Sunday Times* case:

> 'the scope of the domestic power is not identical as regards each of the aims listed in Article 10, paragraph 2 . . . a more extensive European supervision corresponds to a less discretionary power of appreciation'[9].

Even if a restriction is seen to correspond to a 'pressing social need', the restriction itself has got to fulfil certain conditions. It has to be seen to be 'proportionate to the legitimate aim pursued'[10]. Accordingly a restriction may prima facie have the appearance of being legitimate but it will only be held to be compatible with the convention if it is proportionate to the aim being pursued and is the least onerous means of attaining that stated aim.

To be a justifiable restriction under the convention the curtailment of the right must according to the court's jurisprudence be 'necessary in a *democratic society*' (emphasis added). Expounding on this phrase, the court has identified the particular characteristics which it sees as being the hallmarks of a democratic society and which the convention must protect. Such characteristics are 'pluralism, tolerance and broadmindedness without which there is no "democratic society"'[11].

Finally, any exceptions to the exercise of a right guaranteed by the convention must be narrowly interpreted[12].

1 Convention for the Protection of Human Rights and Fundamental Freedoms (Rome, 4 November 1950; 213 UNTS 221; TS 71 (1953); Cmd 8969), art 8, para 2; art 9, para 2; art 10, para 2; art 11, para 2.
2 *Handyside v United Kingdom* (Ser A No 24, Judgment 7 December 1976) 1 EHRR 737 at 754, E Ct HR at para 48. See also eg *Sunday Times v United Kingdom* (Ser A No 30, Judgment 26 April 1979) 2 EHRR 245 at 275, 276, E Ct HR, at para 59.
3 *Sunday Times*, at para 61 (2 EHRR 277).
4 See *Handyside*, at para 49 (1 EHRR 754); *Sunday Times*, at para 59 (2 EHRR 276); *Silver v United Kingdom* (Ser A No 61, Judgment 25 March 1983) 5 EHRR 347 at 376, E Ct HR, at para 97; *Barthold v Germany* (Ser A No 90, Judgment 25 March 1985) 7 EHRR 383 at 402, E Ct HR, at para 55.
5 See eg *Handyside*, at para 48 (1 EHRR 754); *Sunday Times*, at para 59 (2 EHRR 275); *Dudgeon v United Kingdom* (Ser A No 45, Judgment 23 September 1981) 4 EHRR 149 at 164, 165, E Ct HR, at para 52; *Lingens v Austria* (Ser A No 103, Judgment 8 July 1986) 8 EHRR 407 at 418, E Ct HR, at para 39; *Gillow v United Kingdom* (Ser A No 109, Judgment 24 November 1986) 11 EHRR 335 at 352, 353, E Ct HR, at para 57.
6 *Sunday Times*, at para 59 (2 EHRR 276).
7 The *Handyside* case concerned the publication and distribution of *The Little Red Schoolbook* to minors which the United Kingdom government sought to restrain under the Obscene Publications Acts 1959 (c 66) and 1964 (c 74). The European Court of Human Rights held that the conviction of the applicant was justified under paragraph 2 of article 10 of the convention. The facts of the subsequent case of *Müller v Switzerland* (Ser A No 133, Judgment 24 May 1988), E Ct HR, should also be mentioned here as it, too, raised issues of morality. This case arose following an art exhibition open to the general public free of charge. Some of the paintings exhibited were deemed to be obscene. The artist and the exhibition organisers were convicted and fined and the

paintings were confiscated under Swiss law. It was alleged by the applicants that this was contrary to article 10 of the convention. The European Court of Human Rights endorsed the already established case law, notably that set out in the *Handyside* case.

8 *Handyside*, at para 48 (1 EHRR 753).

9 *Sunday Times*, at para 61 (2 EHRR 277). See also *Dudgeon v United Kingdom* (Ser A No 45, Judgment 23 September 1981) 4 EHRR 149, E Ct HR, where the court stated that not only the nature of the aim of the restriction but also the nature of the activities involved would affect the scope of the margin of appreciation.

10 *Handyside*, at para 49 (1 EHRR 754); *Sunday Times*, at para 62 (2 EHRR 277, 278); *Dudgeon*, at para 53 (4 EHRR 165); *Gillow v United Kindgom* (Ser A No 109, Judgment 24 November 1986) 11 EHRR 335 at 352, 353, E Ct HR, at para 57; *Müller v Switzerland* (Ser A No 133, Judgment 24 May 1988) 13 EHRR 212 at 228, E Ct HR, at para 32.

11 *Handyside*, at para 49 (1 EHRR 754); *Lingens v Austria* (Ser A No 103, Judgment 8 July 1986) 8 EHRR 407 at 418, E Ct HR, at para 41. This was extended in *Young, James and Webster v United Kingdom* (Ser A No 44, Judgment 26 June 1981) 4 EHRR 38 at 57, E Ct HR, at para 63, to include the attainment of a balance 'which ensures the fair and proper treatment of minorities and avoids any abuse of a dominant position'. In the *Müller* case, at para 33, the court acknowledged 'the exchange of ideas and opinions' as being essential for a democratic society.

12 See eg *Klass v Germany* (Ser A No 28, Judgment 6 September 1978) 2 EHRR 214 at 231, E Ct HR, at para 42.

82. Additional restriction.
Paragraph 2 of article 10 of the Convention for the Protection of Human Rights and Fundamental Freedoms[1] imposes a further restriction peculiar to the exercise of the right contained in article 10, namely a prohibition on 'the disclosure of information received in confidence, or for maintaining the authority and impartiality of the judiciary'.

1 For the Convention for the Protection of Human Rights and Fundamental Freedoms (Rome, 4 November 1950; 213 UNTS 221; TS 71 (1953); Cmd 8969), art 10, which relates to freedom of expression, see para 73 above.

83. Armed forces, police etc.
The last sentence of paragraph 2 of article 11 of the Convention for the Protection of Human Rights and Fundamental Freedoms[1] provides:

'This Article shall not prevent the imposition of lawful restrictions on the exercise of these rights by members of the armed forces, of the police or of the administration of the State'.

1 For the Convention for the Protection of Human Rights and Fundamental Freedoms (Rome, 4 November 1950; 213 UNTS 221; TS 71 (1953); Cmd 8969), art 11, which relates to peaceful assembly etc, see para 75 above.

(11) AVAILABILITY OF EFFECTIVE REMEDY

84. Generally: article 13.
Article 13 of the Convention for the Protection of Human Rights and Fundamental Freedoms provides as follows:

'Everyone whose rights and freedoms as set forth in this Convention are violated shall have an effective remedy before a national authority notwithstanding that the violation has been committed by persons acting in an official capacity'.

Article 13 is applicable only when a right guaranteed by another article of the convention has been violated[1]. Thus article 13 cannot be the sole basis of a complaint. However, article 13 does not mean that a person is entitled to a national remedy only if a 'violation' has occurred. It is not:

'a prerequisite for the application of Article 13 that the convention be in fact violated.
... Article 13 requires that where an individual considers himself to have been

prejudiced by a measure allegedly in breach of the Convention, he should have a remedy before a national authority in order both to have his claim decided and, if appropriate, to obtain redress. . . . Article 13 must be interpreted as guaranteeing an "effective remedy before a national authority" to everyone who *claims* that his rights and freedoms under the Convention have been violated'[2].

Article 13 does not prescribe a given manner for ensuring within the internal law of Contracting States the effective implementation of any of the provisions of the convention[3]. But it does guarantee the availability of a remedy at a national level to enforce — and hence to allege non-compliance with — the substance of the convention's rights and freedoms in whatever form they may happen to be secured in the domestic legal order[4]. Article 13 does not demand that there exists under domestic law a remedy in respect of any supposed grievance under the convention that an individual may have, however unmeritorious his complaint may be; the grievance must at least be arguable in terms of the convention[5]. As for the nature of the authority, it is not necessary that it be judicial but, if it is not, its powers and the guarantees which it affords are relevant in determining whether the remedy before it is effective[6]. Whereas a particular remedy may of itself not entirely satisfy the requirements of article 13, the aggregate of remedies provided under domestic law may do so[7].

The leading Scottish case alleging a violation of article 13 is that of *Boyle and Rice*[8]. The applicants claimed that no effective remedy had been available to them under Scots law in relation to their various complaints under the convention. The remedies available to the applicants were complaints to the prison governor, the relevant visiting committee, Parliament or the Secretary of State and judicial review by the courts. The applicants pursued the foregoing appeal procedures but were ultimately unsuccessful. This fact, the European Court of Human Rights maintained, did not in itself demonstrate that petition to the Secretary of State was an ineffective remedy for airing such complaints[9]. Accordingly the court held unanimously that however the applicants' grievance was construed there had been no violation of article 13[10].

The most recent case is *Powell and Rayner*[11], where the applicants contended that there existed no domestic remedy as required by article 13 with respect to their claims under paragraph 1 of article 6 and article 8 of the convention[12]. The court was unsympathetic to the applicants' submission due to the possibility available to any person under English law to raise an action in nuisance[13].

One of the four cases in which a violation of article 13 has been upheld is that of *Campbell and Fell*[14], where the court concluded unanimously that the refusal to allow confidential consultation with a lawyer and restrictions on personal correspondence amounted to violation of article 13.

1 *Swedish Engine Drivers' Union v Sweden* (Ser A No 20, Judgment 6 February 1976) 1 EHRR 617 at 631, E Ct HR, at para 50.
2 *Klass v Germany* (Ser A No 28, Judgment 6 September 1978) 2 EHRR 214 at 238, E Ct HR, at para 64, where the court refuted a literal reading of the Convention for the Protection of Human Rights and Fundamental Freedoms (Rome, 4 November 1950; 213 UNTS 221; TS 71 (1953); Cmd 8969), art 13, on the ground that to say that a person's entitlement to a national remedy was dependent on a violation having occurred was untenable.
3 *Swedish Engine Drivers' Union v Sweden*, at para 50.
4 *Young, James and Webster v United Kingdom* (Ser A No 44, Judgment 26 June 1981) 4 EHRR 38, E Ct HR, at para 57; *Silver v United Kingdom* (Ser A No 61, Judgment 25 March 1983) 5 EHRR 347 at 381, E Ct HR, at para 113; *Lithgow v United Kingdom* (Ser A No 102, Judgment 8 July 1986) 8 EHRR 329 at 397, E Ct HR, at para 205.
5 *Boyle and Rice v United Kingdom* (Ser A No 131, Judgment 27 April 1988) 10 EHRR 425 at 442, 443, E Ct HR, at para 52.
6 See eg *Klass*, at para 67 (2 EHRR at 239).
7 *Silver*, at para 113(c) (5 EHRR 381).

8 *Boyle and Rice v United Kingdom* (Ser A No 131, Judgment 27 April 1988) 10 EHRR 425, E Ct HR, discussed in para 69 above.
9 *Boyle and Rice v United Kingdom*, at para 75 (10 EHRR 449).
10 The court rejected the contention that that once a claim of an alleged violation of one of the substantive articles of the Convention for the Protection of Human Rights and Fundamental Freedoms has been declared 'manifestly ill-founded' it can no longer be regarded as 'arguable' for the purposes of art 13: *Boyle and Rice v United Kingdom*, at paras 54, 55 (10 EHRR 443, 444), endorsed in *Plattform 'Ärzte für das Leben' v Austria* (Ser A No 139, Judgment 21 June 1988) 13 EHRR 204 at 209, E Ct HR, at para 27.
11 *Powell and Rayner v United Kindgom* (Ser A No 172, Judgment 21 February 1990) 12 EHRR 355, E Ct HR.
12 The complaints related to noise level and disturbances attributable to air traffic using Heathrow Airport. Both the applicants' houses were in the flight path utilised by aircraft frequenting the airport. For the Convention for the Protection of Human Rights and Fundamental Freedoms, art 6, para 1, and art 8, see paras 43, 62, above.
13 The European Court of Human Rights held unanimously that there had been no violation of ibid, art 13, in respect of either applicant.
14 *Campbell and Fell v United Kingdom* (Ser A No 80, Judgment 28 June 1984) 7 EHRR 165, E Ct HR: see para 48 above.

(12) DISCRIMINATION

85. Generally: article 14. Article 14 of the Convention for the Protection of Human Rights and Fundamental Freedoms provides as follows:

'The enjoyment of the rights and freedoms set forth in this Convention shall be secured without discrimination on any ground such as sex, race, colour, language, religion, political or other opinion, national or social origin, association with a national minority, property, birth or other status'.

Article 14 does not form a right *per se*. It can only be invoked in conjunction with another article. In the words of the European Court of Human Rights, 'Although Article 14 has no independent existence, it is complementary to the other normative provisions of the Convention and Protocols'[1]. It thus follows that 'a measure which in itself is in conformity with the requirements of the Article enshrining the right or freedom in question may however infringe this Article when read in conjunction with Article 14 for the reason that it is of a discriminatory nature'[2]. Nevertheless, the application of article 14 does not necessarily presuppose a breach of the provisions of the convention — and to this extent it enjoys an autonomous meaning. However, there can be no room for its application unless the facts at issue fall within the ambit of one or more of the articles of the convention[3].

Article 14 should be viewed as forming an integral part of each of the articles of the convention which stipulate rights and freedoms:

'No distinctions should be made in this respect according to the nature of these rights and freedoms and of their correlative obligations, and for instance as to whether the respect due to the right concerned implies positive action or mere abstention. This is, moreover, clearly shown by the very general nature of the terms employed in Article 14: "the enjoyment of the rights and freedoms set forth in this Convention shall be secured"'[4].

However, article 14 does not forbid every difference in treatment in the exercise of the rights and freedoms recognised[5]. As the court stated, 'it is important to determine the criteria which may be utilised so as to determine whether or not a given difference in treatment, concerning ... the exercise of one of the rights and freedoms set forth, contravenes Article 14'[5]. In the court's view, based on the legal practice of a large number of democratic states, the principle of equality of treatment is violated if the distinction has no objective and reasonable justification. Justification is to be assessed in the light of the purpose and consequences of the measure being considered, regard being had to the principles which normally prevail in democratic societies. In addition, a difference in treatment must not only be in pursuance of a legitimate aim; there must exist a reasonable relationship of proportionality between the means employed and the aim sought to be realised[5]. The court, when confronted with having to determine whether or not there has been an arbitrary distinction, must give congnisance to the those legal and factual features which characterise the life of the state concerned as well as the particular circumstances pertinent to the case. Regarding article 14, the court has with other provisions recognised that Contracting States possess an inherent margin of appreciation and the court's review is concerned only with the conformity of these measures with the requirements of the convention[5].

1 *National Union of Belgian Police v Belgium* (Ser A No 19, Judgment 27 October 1975) 1 EHRR 578 at 592, E Ct HR at para 44.
2 *Belgian Linguistic Case (No 2)* (Merits) (Ser A No 6, Judgment 23 July 1968) 1 EHRR 252 at 283, E Ct HR, at para 9.
3 See eg *Rasmussen v Denmark* (Ser A No 87, Judgment 28 November 1984) 7 EHRR 371 at 377, E Ct HR, at para 29.
4 *Belgian Linguistic Case*, at para 9 (1 EHRR 283, 284).
5 *Belgian Linguistic Case*, at para 10 (1 EHRR 284).

86. Examples of alleged discrimination pleaded before the court. Discrimination has been alleged before the European Court of Human Rights on a wide variety of grounds, including sex[1], illegitimacy[2], religion[3], profession[4], trade union membership[5], freedom of person[6], financial means[7], liability for capital gains tax[8], and language[9].

1 *Rasmussen v Denmark* (Ser A No 87, Judgment 28 November 1984) 7 EHRR 371, E Ct HR; *Abdulaziz, Cabales and Balkandali v United Kingdom* (Ser A No 94, Judgment 28 May 1985) 7 EHRR 471, E Ct HR (see para 65 above).
2 *Marckx v Belgium* (Ser A No 31, Judgment 13 June 1979) 2 EHRR 330, E Ct HR; *Inze v Austria* (Ser A No 126, Judgment 28 October 1987) 10 EHRR 394, E Ct HR.
3 *Kjeldsen, Busk Madsen and Pederson v Denmark* (Ser A No 23, Judgment 7 December 1976) 1 EHRR 711, E Ct HR (see para 92 below).
4 *Van der Mussele v Belgium* (Ser A No 70, Judgment 23 November 1983) 6 EHRR 163, E Ct HR ('forced labour' of pupil advocate) (see para 28 above).
5 *Schmidt and Dalström v Sweden* (Ser A No 21, Judgment 6 February 1976) 1 EHRR 637, E Ct HR.
6 *Monnell and Morris v United Kingdom* (Ser A No 115, Judgment 2 March 1987) 10 EHRR 205, E Ct HR (loss of liberty of convicted persons held in custody pending appeal) (see para 34 above).
7 *Johnston v Ireland* (Ser A No 112, Judgment 18 December 1986) 9 EHRR 203, E Ct HR (lack of means to obtain divorce abroad which would be recognised by Irish law) (see para 71 above).
8 *Lithgow v United Kingdom* (Ser A No 102, Judgment 8 July 1986) 8 EHRR 329, E Ct HR.
9 *Belgian Linguistic Case (No 2)* (Merits) (Ser A No 6, Judgment 23 July 1968) 1 EHRR 252, E Ct HR (see para 62 above).

(13) RIGHTS UNDER PROTOCOL NO 1

87. Introduction. Protocol No 1 to the Convention for the Protection of Human Rights and Fundamental Freedoms enshrines three further rights. Article 1 of the Protocol is concerned with the so-called right to property[1], article 2 pertains to education[2], and article 3 enshrines the principle of free elections[3]. This is the only Protocol which has given rise to any case law[4].

1 For the Convention for the Protection of Human Rights and Fundamental Freedoms (Rome, 4 November 1950; 213 UNTS 221; TS 71 (1953); Cmd 8969), Protocol No 1, art 1, see para 88 below.

2 For ibid, Protocol No 1, art 2, see para 89 below.
3 For ibid, Protocol No 1, art 3, see para 93 below.
4 As to the subject matter of ibid, Protocols 2–9, see para 6 above.

88. The right to property. Article 1 of Protocol No 1 to the Convention for the Protection of Human Rights and Fundamental Freedoms provides as follows:

'Every natural or legal person is entitled to the peaceful enjoyment of his possessions. No one shall be deprived of his possessions except in the public interest and subject to the conditions provided for by law and by the general principles of international law.

The preceding provisions shall not, however, in any way impair the right of a State to enforce such laws as it deems necessary to control the use of property in accordance with the general interest or to secure the payment of taxes or other contributions or penalties'.

By recognising that everyone has the right to the peaceful enjoyment of his possessions, article 1 in substance guarantees the right of property[1]. The right of property includes the right of a person to dispose of his property, and this has been characterised by the European Court of Human Rights as being a traditional and fundamental aspect of that right[1]. This article does no more than enshrine the right of everyone to the peaceful enjoyment of 'his' possessions, and applies only to existing possessions. It does not guarantee the right to acquire possessions either on intestacy or through voluntary dispositions[2]. Under the second paragraph of article 1, a Contracting State remains competent to 'enforce such laws as it deems necessary to control the use of property in accordance with the general interest'. Contracting States are the sole judges of the 'necessity' for such a law[3]. As to what is 'in the public interest', the court will respect the judgment of the legislature unless that judgment is found to be 'manifestly without reasonable foundation'[4]. The reason for this is the court's recognition that it is natural that national legislatures should be allowed a wide margin of appreciation when implementing social and economic policies[5]. The role of the European Court of Human Rights is to review any contested measures under article 1 of Protocol No 1 and in fulfilment of this task to inquire into the facts with reference to which the national authorities acted[5]. In considering the article, the court has stipulated that the article is comprised of three distinct rules:

'The first rule, which is of a general nature, enounces the principle of peaceful enjoyment of property; it is set out in the first sentence of the first paragraph. The second rule covers deprivation of possessions and subjects it to certain conditions; it appears in the second sentence of the same paragraph. The third rule recognises that the States are entitled, amongst other things, to control the use of property in accordance with the general interest, by enforcing such laws as they deem necessary for the purpose; it is contained in the second paragraph'[6].

The three rules are not 'distinct' in the sense of being unconnected: the second and third rules are concerned with particular instances of interference with the right to peaceful enjoyment of property and should therefore be construed in the light of the general principle enunciated in the first rule[7]. As with other articles in the convention, the court has stated that it is necessary to determine whether a fair balance has been struck between the demands of the general interest of the community and the requirement that the individual's fundamental rights are protected[8]. More succinctly, there must be a fair balance between the means used and the intended aim[9].

1 *Marckx v Belgium* (Ser A No 31, Judgment 13 June 1979) 2 EHRR 330 at 354, E Ct HR, at para 61.
2 *Marckx*, at para 50 (2 EHRR 350).

3 *Handyside v United Kingdom* (Ser A No 24, Judgment 7 December 1976) 1 EHRR 737 at 760, E Ct HR, at para 62; *Marckx*, at para 64 (2 EHRR 355).

4 *James v United Kingdom* (Ser A No 98, Judgment 21 February 1986) 8 EHRR 123 at 142, E Ct HR, at para 46; *Mellacher v Austria* (Ser A No 169, Judgment 19 December 1989) 12 EHRR 391 at 409, E Ct HR, at para 45.

5 *James*, at para 46.

6 *Sporrong and Lönnroth v Sweden* (Ser A No 52, Judgment 23 September 1982) 5 EHRR 35 at 50, E Ct HR, at para 61, endorsed in subsequent cases, eg inter alia *Allgemeine Gold- und Silberscsheideanstalt v United Kingdom* (Ser A No 108, Judgment 24 October 1986) 9 EHRR 1 at 12, E Ct HR, at para 48; *Erkner and Hofauer v Austria* (Ser A No 117, Judgment 23 April 1987) 9 EHRR 464 at 487, E Ct HR, at para 73; *Poiss v Austria* (Ser A No 117, Judgment 23 April 1987) 10 EHRR 231 at 252, E Ct HR, at para 63; *Tre Traktörer Ab v Sweden* (Ser A No 159, Judgment 7 July 1989) 13 EHRR 309 at 323, E Ct HR, at para 54; *Allan Jacobsson v Sweden* (Ser A No 163, Judgment 25 October 1989) 12 EHRR 56 at 66, E Ct HR, at para 53; *Mellacher v Austria* (Ser A No 169, Judgment 19 December 1989) 12 EHRR 391 at 408, E Ct HR, at para 42.

7 *James*, at para 37 (8 EHRR at 139, 140); *Lithgow v United Kingdom* (Ser A No 102, Judgment 8 July 1986) 8 EHRR 329 at 367, E Ct HR, at para 106; *Tre Traktörer Ab v Sweden* (Ser A No 159, Judgment 7 July 1989) 13 EHRR 309 at 323, E Ct HR, at para 54.

8 *Sporrong and Lönnroth*, at para 69 (5 EHRR 52).

9 *Van Marle v Netherlands* (Ser A No 101, Judgment 26 June 1986) 8 EHRR 483 at 491, E Ct HR, at para 43.

89. The right to education: introduction. Article 2 of Protocol No 1 of the Convention for the Protection of Human Rights and Fundamental Freedoms provides as follows:

'No person shall be denied the right to education. In the exercise of any functions which it assumes in relation to education and to teaching, the State shall respect the right of parents to ensure such education and teaching in conformity with their own religious and philosophical convictions'.

The scope of this article was articulated by the European Court of Human Rights in the *Belgian Linguistics Case*[1]. Initially, the court considered the language employed by the article and concluded that in spite of the negative formulation[2] the article undoubtedly enshrined a right[3]. The court then proceeded to determine the content of this right and the consequential scope of the obligation placed upon Contracting Parties to the Protocol. The existence of the right did not require Contracting Parties to establish educational facilities at their own expense, or to subsidise education of any particular type or at any particular level.

However, it did not follow that Contracting States had no positive obligation in ensuring respect for the right guaranteed by article 2 of Protocol No 1. To determine scope, the court stated that it was important to look at the aim of the article. The court noted in this context that all member states of the Council of Europe possessed a general and official education system and therefore the question of requiring each state to establish such a system did not arise. All that was required was that persons subject to the jurisdiction of Contracting Parties be guaranteed 'the right in principle, to avail themselves of the means of instruction existing at a given time'[3].

The convention, however, does not set down specific obligations concerning the extent of these means and the manner of their organisation or subsidisation. In respect of the case before it, the court found that the article does not specify the language in which education must be conducted. Nevertheless, 'the right to education would be meaningless if it did not imply in favour of its beneficiaries, the right to be educated in the national language or in one of the national languages as the case may be'[3]. In its first sentence, the article guarantees:

'a right of access to educational institutions existing at a given time, but such access constitutes only a part of the right to education . . . the "right to education" to be effective' demands inter alia that:

> 'the individual who is the beneficiary should have the possibility of drawing profit from the education received, that is to say, the right to obtain, in conformity with the rules in force in each State, and in one form or another, official recognition of the studies which he has completed'[4].

The very nature of the right guaranteed by the first sentence of the article called for:

> 'regulation by State, regulation which may vary in time and place according to the needs and resources of the community and of individuals. It goes without saying that such regulation must never injure the substance of the right to education nor conflict with other rights enshrined in the Convention'[5].

Unlike the first sentence of the article, the second sentence does not guarantee a right to education. It only requires that states respect parents' religious and philosophical convictions, not their linguistic preferences[6]. To interpret the former as embracing the latter would amount to a distortion of the ordinary and usual meaning of the language and to read something into the convention which did not exist[6]. From the *travaux préparatoires*, it was evident that the object of the second sentence of the article was not to secure respect by the state of a right for parents to have education conducted in a language other than that of the country in question; indeed in June 1951 the Committee of Experts which had the task of drafting the Protocol set aside such a proposal. Several members of the committee believed that it was concerned with the general problem of ethnic minorities and that it consequently fell outside the scope of the convention[6].

The main case to be considered is that of *Campbell and Cosans*[7]. The court split the claim under this article into two: the general right to education[8] and the respect to be accorded to parental convictions[9]. The court opted to consider parental convictions first.

1 *Belgian Linguistic Case (No 2)* (Merits) (Ser A No 6, Judgment 23 July 1968) 1 EHRR 252, E Ct HR.
2 Ie 'No person shall be denied the right to education'.
3 *Belgian Linguistic Case*, at para 3 (1 EHRR 280, 281).
4 *Belgian Linguistic Case*, at para 4 (1 EHRR 281).
5 *Belgian Linguistic Case*, at para 5 (1 EHRR 281, 282).
6 *Belgian Linguistic Case*, at para 6 (1 EHRR 282).
7 *Campbell and Cosans v United Kingdom* (Ser A No 48, Judgment 25 February 1982) 4 EHRR 293, E Ct HR. For the facts, see para 26 above.
8 See para 91 below.
9 See para 90 below.

90. Parental convictions and education: the *Campbell and Cosans* case.

In the *Campbell and Cosans* case[1] the European Court of Human Rights first pointed out that 'the education of children is the whole process whereby, in any society, adults endeavour to transmit their beliefs, culture and other values to the young, whereas teaching or instruction refers in particular to the transmission of knowledge and to intellectual development'[2]. The court then proceeded to state that it considered it 'somewhat artificial to attempt to separate off matters relating to internal administration as if all such matters fell outside the scope of Article 2' of Protocol No 1 to the Convention for the Protection of Human Rights and Fundamental Freedoms[2]. 'The use of corporal punishment', the court continued, could 'be said to belong to the internal administration of a school, but at the same time it is, when used, an integral part of the process whereby a school seeks to achieve the object for which it was established, including the development and moulding of the character and mental powers of its pupils'[2].

The court then reiterated its earlier pronouncement in the Danish case of *Kjeldsen, Busk Madsen and Pederson*[3] that 'the second sentence of article 2 is binding upon the Contracting States in the exercise of "each and every" function that they undertake in the sphere of education and teaching, so that the fact that a given function may be considered to be ancillary is of no moment in this context'[4].

In response to arguments submitted by the government to the effect that the Scottish central or local government functions in the educational field did not extend to disciplinary matters, the court said:

'It may be true that the day-to-day maintenance of discipline in the schools in question is left to the individual teacher; when he administers corporal punishment he is exercising not a power delegated to him by the State but a power vested in him by the Common Law by virtue of his status as a teacher, and the law in this respect can be changed only by Act of Parliament. Nevertheless, in regard to education in Scotland, the State has assumed responsibility for formulating general policy and the schools attended by the applicants' children were State schools. Discipline is an integral, even indispensable, part of any educational system, with the result that the functions assumed by the State in Scotland must be taken to extend to questions of discipline in general, even if not to its everyday maintenance. Indeed, this is confirmed by the fact that central and local authorities participated in the preparation of the Code of Practice and that the Government themselves are committed to a policy aimed at abolishing corporal punishment'[5].

With respect to a further submission of the government, namely that the obligation to respect philosophical convictions arises only in relation to information and knowledge as opposed to all aspects of school administration, the government relied on a passage in the court's judgment in *Kjeldsen, Busk Madsen and Pederson*:

'The second sentence of Article 2 implies . . . that the State, in fulfilling the functions assumed by it in regard to education and teaching, must take care that information or knowledge included in the curriculum is conveyed in an objective, critical and pluralistic manner. The State is forbidden to pursue an aim of indoctrination that might be considered as not respecting parents' religious and philosophical convictions. That is the limit that must not be exceeded'[6].

The court responded by stating that the Danish case concerned the actual content of the instruction whereas 'the second sentence of Article 2 has a broader scope'[7]. This, the court continued, was confirmed in that same judgment when the court held 'that the said sentence is binding upon the Contracting States in the exercise, inter alia, of the function "consisting of the organisation and financing of public education"'[8].

When considering the government's argument that philosophical convictions could not be interpreted as encompassing opinions on internal school administration such as discipline, the court addressed itself to the interpretation of the word 'convictions' and concluded as follows:

'In its ordinary meaning the word "convictions", taken on its own, is not synonymous with the words "opinions" and "ideas", such as are utilised in Article 10 of the Convention, which guarantees freedoms of expression; it is more akin to the term "beliefs" (in the French text: "*convictions*") appearing in Article 9 — which guarantees freedom of thought, conscience and religion — and denotes views that attain a certain level of cogency, seriousness, cohesion and importance'[9].

The court then directed its attention to the adjective 'philosophical', and acknowledged that it is not capable of being afforded an exhaustive definition. Neither of the extreme interpretations (namely, a fully fledged system of thought and views on more or less trivial matters) was considered appropriate in the context of article 2 as the former would too narrowly restrict the scope of a right that is guaranteed to all parents and the latter might result in the inclusion of matters of insufficient weight or substance[10]. In conclusion, the court stated:

> 'Having regard to the Convention as a whole, including Article 17[11], the expression "philosophical convictions" in the present context denotes, in the Court's opinion, such convictions as are worthy of respect in a "democratic society" and are not incompatible with human dignity; in addition, they must not conflict with the fundamental right of the child to education, the whole of Article 2 being dominated by its first sentence'[12].

The court then turned to consider the complaint before it. Firstly, the applicants' views were stated as relating to 'the integrity of the person, the propriety of the infliction of corporal punishment and the exclusion of the distress pursuant to the risk of such punishment'. Such views were deemed to relate 'to a weighty and substantial aspect of human life and behaviour'[12]. Such characteristics distinguished the applicants' views from other opinions that might be held on other methods of discipline or on discipline in general[12].

In the alternative, the United Kingdom government maintained that the obligation to respect the applicants' convictions had been satisfied by the adoption of a policy of gradually eliminating corporal chastisement. Any other solution, the government contended, would be incompatible with the necessity of striking a balance between the opinions of supporters and opponents of this method of discipline and with the terms of the reservation to article 2 made by the United Kingdom at the time of signing Protocol No 1, which reads:

> '. . . in view of certain provisions of the Education Acts in force in the United Kingdom, the principle affirmed in the second sentence of Article 2 is accepted by the United Kingdom only so far as it is compatible with the provision of efficient instruction and training, and the avoidance of unreasonable public expenditure'[13].

The court in response to these arguments stated that:

> 'the duty to respect parental convictions in this sphere cannot be overridden by the alleged necessity of striking a balance between the conflicting views involved, nor is the Government's policy to move gradually towards the abolition of corporal punishment in itself sufficient to comply with this duty'[14].

As regards the United Kingdom's reservation, the court cited the relevant domestic law and concluded that the relevant section of the Education (Scotland) Act 1962[15] was no more than a re-enactment of an identical provision in the Education (Scotland) Act 1946 and therefore went no further than a law in force at the time when the reservation was made[16].

The court accepted that certain solutions canvassed — such as the establishment of a dual system whereby in each sector there would be separate schools for children of parents objecting to corporal punishment — would be incompatible, especially in the present economic situation, with the avoidance of unreasonable public expenditure. However, the court did not regard it as established that other means of respecting the applicants' convictions, such as a system of exemption for individual pupils in a particular school, would necessarily be incompatible with 'the provision of efficient instruction and training, and the avoidance of unreasonable public expenditure'[17].

The court concluded[18] in the light of its observation that with respect to Mrs Campbell and Mrs Cosans there had been a breach of the second sentence of article 2 of Protocol No 1.

---

1 *Campbell and Cosans v United Kingdom* (Ser A No 48, Judgment 25 February 1982) 4 EHRR 293, E Ct HR. See also para 26 above.
2 *Campbell and Cosans*, at para 33 (4 EHRR 303).
3 *Kjeldsen, Busk Madsen and Pederson v Denmark* (Ser A No 23, Judgment 7 December 1976) 1 EHRR 711, E Ct HR: see para 92 below.

4 *Campbell and Cosans*, at para 33 (4 EHRR 303).
5 *Campbell and Cosans*, at para 34 (4 EHRR 303).
6 *Campbell and Cosans*, at para 35 (4 EHRR 304), quoting from *Kjeldsen, Busk Madsen and Pederson v Denmark*, at para 53 (1 EHRR 730, 731).
7 *Campbell and Cosans*, at para 35.
8 *Campbell and Cosans*, at para 35, quoting from *Kjeldsen, Busk Madsen and Pederson v Denmark*, at para 50 (1 EHRR 728).
9 *Campbell and Cosans*, at para 36 (4 EHRR 304). For the Convention for the Protection of Human Rights and Fundamental Freedoms (Rome, 4 November 1950; 213 UNTS 221; TS 71 (1953); Cmd 8969), arts 9, 10, see paras 72, 73, above.
10 *Campbell and Cosans*, at para 36 (4 EHRR 304, 305).
11 The Convention for the Protection of Human Rights and Fundamental Freedoms, art 17, provides that nothing in the convention is to be interpreted as implying for any state, group or person any right to engage in any activity or perform any act aimed at the destruction of any of the rights and freedoms set forth therein or at their limitation to a greater extent than is provided for therein.
12 *Campbell and Cosans*, at para 36 (4 EHRR 305).
13 Reservation to Protocol No 1 signed by the United Kingdom government on 20 March 1952, the ratification being deposited on 3 November 1952.
14 *Campbell and Cosans*, at para 37 (4 EHRR 305, 306).
15 Ie the Education (Scotland) Act 1962 (c 47), s 29(1) (repealed), replacing the Education (Scotland) Act 1946 (c 72), s 29(1). See now the Education (Scotland) Act 1980 (c 44), s 28(1), which similarly provides that so far as is compatible with the provision of suitable instruction and training and the avoidance of unreasonable public expenditure, pupils are to be educated in accordance with the wishes of their parents.
16 A reservation in respect of any provision of the Convention for the Protection of Human Rights and Fundamental Freedoms is permitted only to the extent that any law in force in the territory of a state at the time the reservation is made is not in conformity with the provision: art 64, para 1.
17 *Campbell and Cosans*, at para 37 (4 EHRR 306).
18 Ie by six votes to one.

91. The general right to education: the *Campbell and Cosans* case. Having considered the parents' right to have their convictions respected under the second sentence of article 2 of Protocol No 1 to the Convention for the Protection of Human Rights and Fundamental Freedoms, the European Court of Human Rights in the *Campbell and Cosans* case[1] turned next to Mrs Cosans' allegation that her son Jeffrey had been denied the right to education which was guaranteed by the first sentence of article 2. The court adopted a different stance from that of the European Commission of Human Rights or the United Kingdom government. The court argued, contrary to the Commission, that the alleged violation of the first sentence of article 2 was not absorbed by the finding of a violation of the second. In other words, Mrs Cosans' allegation of a breach of the first sentence of article 2 constituted a separate complaint, and not merely a further legal submission or argument. The court affirmed[2] that the article must be viewed as a whole, the right set out in the second sentence being an adjunct of the fundamental right to education set out in the first sentence. Moreover, whereas the second sentence was concerned with the right of a parent, the first concerned the right of the child[3]. The right of education guaranteed by the first sentence by its very nature demands regulation by the state, but such regulation must never injure the substance of the right or conflict with other rights enshrined in the convention or its protocols[4]. Because the suspension of Jeffrey Cosans, being based on his refusal to be subject to corporal punishment, conflicted with his parent's right enshrined in the second sentence, it could not be described as reasonable, and, in any event, fell outside the state's power of regulation under the article[4].

1 *Campbell and Cosans v United Kingdom* (Ser A No 48, Judgment 25 February 1982) 4 EHRR 293, E Ct HR.
2 Ie affirmed what it had said in *Kjeldsen, Busk Madsen and Pederson v Denmark* (Ser A No 23, Judgment 7 December 1976) 1 EHRR 711 at 729, E Ct HR, at para 52.

3 *Campbell and Cosans*, at para 40 (4 EHRR 307).
4 *Campbell and Cosans*, at para 41 (4 EHRR 307).

92. Education: the *Kjeldsen, Busk Madsen and Pederson* case. In the earlier case of *Kjeldsen, Busk Madsen and Pederson*[1], a number of issues were discussed before the European Court of Human Rights that were not in point in the *Campbell and Cosans* case. The applicants, three Danish couples with children of school age, objected to integrated and hence compulsory, sex education as introduced into state-run primary schools by the domestic legislative measure, Act No 235 of 27 May 1970. The parents' requests that their children be exempted from sex education had been rejected by the competent authorities. The only alternatives available to persons holding such views were either to educate the children at home or to send them to private schools, which in Denmark receive very substantial subsidies from the state. First, the court acknowledged that the right to education extended to both private and public schools[2]. The *raison d'être* of the second sentence of article 2 of Protocol No 1 to the Convention for the Protection of Human Rights and Fundamental Freedoms emerged as being, in the court's view, that of safeguarding the possibility of pluralism in education, 'which possibly is essential for the preservation of the "democratic society" as conceived by the Convention'. This, in the light of the power of the modern state, will best be realised, the court concluded, through state teaching[2]. The court denied that article 2 permitted a distinction to be drawn between religious instruction and other subjects. Article 2 requires the state to respect parents' convictions, be they religious or philosophical, throughout the entire state education programme[3]. The court conceded that abuses could occur as to the manner in which legislative provisions were applied by a given school or teacher and that the competent authorities are under a duty to ensure that parents' religious and philosophical convictions are not disregarded at this level by 'carelessness, lack of judgment or misplaced proselytism'; however, the legislation in question did not amount to an attempt at indoctrination aimed at advocating a specific kind of sexual behaviour, nor did it make a point of 'exalting sex or inciting pupils to indulge precociously in practices that are dangerous for their stability, health or future or that many parents may consider reprehensible'. Further, it did not affect the right of parents to enlighten and advise their children, to exercise with regard to their children natural parental functions as educators, or to guide their children on a path in line with the parents' own religious or philosophical convictions[4].

In the case before it the court concluded[5] that the disputed legislation did not give rise to a breach of article 2 of Protocol No 1.

1 *Kjeldsen, Busk Madsen and Pederson v Denmark* (Ser A No 23, Judgment 7 December 1976) 1 EHRR 711, E Ct HR.
2 *Kjeldsen, Busk Madsen and Pederson v Denmark*, at para 50 (1 EHRR 728, 729).
3 *Kjeldsen, Busk Madsen and Pederson v Denmark*, at para 51 (1 EHRR 729, 730).
4 *Kjeldsen, Busk Madsen and Pederson v Denmark*, at para 54 (1 EHRR 731, 732).
5 Ie by six votes to one.

93. The right to free elections. Article 3 of Protocol No 1 to the Convention for the Protection of Human Rights and Fundamental Freedoms provides as follows:

> 'The High Contracting Parties undertake to hold free elections at reasonable intervals by secret ballot, under conditions which will ensure the free expression of the opinion of the people in the choice of the legislature'.

On the first occasion when the European Court of Human Rights was asked to consider an alleged violation of this article[1], the court deemed it necessary to give a detailed interpretation of the article. The applicants, both in their capacity as voters and elected representatives, complained of the method used for appointing the representatives of the administrative district of Halle-Vilvoorde on the Flemish Council[2].

Essentially the applicants' complaint was two-fold with regard to section 29(1) of the 1980 Special Act which determined the membership of the Flemish Council. Firstly, the applicants complained that it did not in practice enable French-speaking electors in the administrative district of Halle-Vilvoorde to appoint French-speaking representatives to the Flemish Council, while Dutch-speaking electors can appoint Dutch-speaking representatives. Secondly, they claimed that it prevented any parliamentarian elected in that electoral district and resident in one of the municipalities of the administrative district of Halle-Vilvoorde from sitting on the Flemish Council if he belonged to the French-language group in the House of Representatives or the Senate, and this obstacle was not encountered by the elected representatives belonging to a Dutch-language group and residing in one of the same municipalities.

The court heralded article 3 of Protocol No 1 as being of prime importance in the convention because it enshrined 'a characteristic principle of democracy'[3]. The court refuted a restrictive interpretation of article 3 in respect of the phrase 'The High Contracting Parties undertake'[4]. The court submitted that the reason for the use of 'the inter-state colouring of the wording of Article 3' lay apparently in a desire 'to give greater solemnity to the commitment undertaken and the fact that the primary obligation in the field concerned . . . is one of adoption by the State of positive measures to "hold" democratic elections'[5]. The court recognised that the rights enshrined in the article are not absolute[6]. This is because article 3 neither sets these out in express terms nor defines them. Accordingly, there is room for implied limitations to be imposed by states. Notwithstanding this wide margin of appreciation, it is for the court to determine in the last resort whether the requirements of Protocol No 1 have been complied with; it has to satisfy itself that the conditions do not curtail the rights in question to such an extent as to impair their very essence and deprive them of their effectiveness; that they are imposed in pursuit of a legitimate aim; and that the means employed are not disproportionate. In particular, such conditions must not thwart 'the free expression of the opinion of the people in the choice of the legislature'[6].

Article 3 applies only to the election of the 'legislature', or at least of one of its chambers if it has two or more. The word 'legislature' does not necessarily mean only the national parliament; it has to be interpreted in the light of the constitutional structure of the state in question[7].

The obligations arising from the article are confined to the provision of 'free' elections at 'reasonable intervals', 'by secret ballot' and 'under conditions which will ensure the free expression of the opinion of the people'. It does not require the introduction of any specific system such as proportional representation or majority voting with one or two ballots[8]. The court acknowledged here the wide margin of appreciation which Contracting States enjoy *vis-à-vis* the electoral system they operate and concluded that, for the purposes of article 3 of Protocol No 1, any electoral system must be assessed in the light of the political evolution of the country concerned; features that would be unacceptable in the context of one system could be jusitified in the context of another, provided that it guaranteed the chosen system the 'free expression of the opinion of the people in the choice of the legislature'[8].

Turning to the specific case before it, the court concluded that the requirements placed on the French-speaking electors in the district of Halle-Vilvoorde did not infringe these rights by the mere fact that they must vote either for candidates who would take the parliamentary oath in French and would accordingly join the French-language group in the House of Representatives or the Senate and sit on the French Community Council, or alternatively for candidates who would take the oath in Dutch and belong to the Dutch-language group in the House of Representatives or the Senate and sit on the Flemish Council. This did not constitute a disproportionate limitation such as would thwart 'the free expression of the opinion of the people in the choice of the legislature'[9]. Consequently, the court ruled[10] that there had been no breach of article 3 Protocol No 1.

1 *Matthieu-Mohin and Clerfayt v Belgium* (Ser A No 113, Judgment 2 March 1987) 10 EHRR 1, E Ct HR.
2 The following facts are spelt out in full because the circumstances surrounding the applicants' allegations are uniquely peculiar to Belgium. The administrative district of Halle-Vilvoorde was created in 1983, and comprises the municipalities of the former administrative district of Brussels, excluding those in the bilingual district of Brussels, but including the six 'peripheral municipalities with special status'. Halle-Vilvoorde comes within the Dutch-language region of the Flemish Region and thus under the authority of the Flemish Council and Executive, and is accordingly not subject to the authority of the French Community institutions or those of the Walloon Region. It nevertheless contains a sizable French-speaking minority: according to the applicants (whose figures were not disputed by the government) at least 100,000 people out of a total population of 518,962 at 1 January 1982. The French-speakers also claimed to be in the majority in the six 'peripheral municipalities', and the Belgian State is alleged to have acted against their wishes in hitherto refusing to incorporate these municipalities into the Brussels Region. Ordinarily, electoral districts in Belgium correspond to administrative ones. There is one exception, however. The administrative districts of Brussels-Capital and Halle-Vilvoorde together form a single electoral district for parliamentary and provincial elections, with Brussels as the principal town. The votes cast in the two administrative districts are consequently counted together, and it is impossible to distinguish between candidates elected by the one district and those elected by the other. The applicants claimed that the French-speaking voters in the Halle-Vilvoorde district can expect — given their numbers and the statutory quota — to return three or four members to the House of Representatives by their own votes alone. In the general election of 8 November 1981 there were 999,601 registered voters in the Brussels electoral district, who had to elect thirty-four Representatives and seventeen Senators. Nothing prevents French-speaking candidates — whether resident in Halle-Vilvoorde or not — from standing for election in that district, or the voters — whether French-speaking or not — from voting for them. If they are elected, they may take the parliamentary oath in French or Dutch as they wish, irrespective of the language they personally speak. If they take the oath in French (as the applicants did), their membership of the French-language group in the House of Representatives or the Senate entitles them to sit on the French Community Council (which has no responsibility for the district of Halle-Vilvoorde) but not on the Flemish Council — whether exercising its Community or its regional functions — nor on the Walloon Regional Council. Conversely, if they take the oath in Dutch, they will be members of a Dutch-language group and will accordingly sit on the Flemish Council but not on the French Community Council nor on the Walloon Regional Council; and they will lose the right to vote in a French-language group on those matters in respect of which the constitution requires special majorities. Correspondingly, the French-speaking voters in Halle-Vilvoorde cannot be represented on the Flemish Council other than by parliamentarians who have taken the oath in Dutch. Candidates are not under any obligation to state in advance which language group they will join, and they do not usually do so.
3 *Matthieu-Mohin and Clerfayt*, at para 47 (10 EHRR 15).
4 Ie as opposed to the more usual terminology, 'Everyone has the right', or 'no one shall'.
5 *Matthieu-Mohin and Clerfayt*, at para 50 (10 EHRR 15, 16).
6 *Matthieu-Mohin and Clerfayt*, at para 52 (10 EHRR 16).
7 *Matthieu-Mohin and Clerfayt*, at para 53 (10 EHRR 16).
8 *Matthieu-Mohin and Clerfayt*, at para 54 (10 EHRR 17).
9 *Matthieu-Mohin and Clerfayt*, at para 57 (10 EHRR 18).
10 Ie by thirteen votes to five.

(14) THE IMPACT OF THE CONVENTION

94. Introduction. The Convention for the Protection of Human Rights and Fundamental Freedoms is regarded as enshrining those rights and freedoms which should be enjoyed by all persons living in a democratic society. One of the most notable features of the convention when compared to other guarantees of human rights is the sophisticated supervisory machinery employed for (1) examining complaints of alleged violations of the convention, and (2) ensuring compliance with the convention. The European Court of Human Rights is not competent to strike down offending national laws, nor can the court sanction 'offenders' other than by way of article 50[1]. Nevertheless, Contracting Parties do like to be seen to be acting in conformity with the convention as interpreted by the court. Consequently, Contracting Parties do as a norm respond affirmatively and remove the offending deficiency so as to comply with the court's decision in respect of the case to which they are a party, as the instances cited in the following paragraphs illustrate[2].

  1   For the Convention for the Protection of Human Rights and Fundamental Freedoms (Rome, 4 November 1950; 213 UNTS 221; TS 71 (1953); Cmd 8969), art 50, see para 21 above.
  2   See also ibid, art 53, whereby the High Contracting Parties undertake to abide by the decision of the court in any case to which they are parties.

95. United Kingdom examples. Among the instances in which the United Kingdom government has responded to decisions of the European Court of Human Rights are the *Sunday Times* case[1], which prompted the Contempt of Court Act 1981 (c 49)[2]; the *Young, James and Webster* case[3], which led to the amendment of the Trade Union and Labour Relations Act 1974 (c 52) by the Employment Act 1980 (c 42); the *Dudgeon* case[4], which resulted in the Homosexual Offences (Northern Ireland) Order 1982; the *Campbell and Cosans* case[5], following which the Education (Scotland) Act 1980 (c 44) was passed; the *Golder* case[6], leading to an amendment to the Prison Rules 1964[7]; and the *Malone* case[8], in response to which the Interception of Communications Act 1985 (c 56) was enacted.

This list, and that in the following paragraph, are not intended to be exhaustive, but rather to illustrate that a judgment of the European Court of Human Rights may have consequences of a general scope in that law reform may be either initiated or accelerated by it.

  1   *Sunday Times v United Kingdom* (Ser A No 30, Judgment 26 April 1979) 2 EHRR 245, E Ct HR (see para 74 above).
  2   For a discussion as to whether the Contempt of Court Act 1981 (c 49) brought United Kingdom law into line with the Convention for the Protection of Human Rights and Fundamental Freedoms, see S H Bailey 'The Contempt of Court Act 1981' (1982) 45 MLR 301 at 306.
  3   *Young, James and Webster v United Kingdom* (Ser A No 44, Judgment 26 June 1981) 4 EHRR 38, E Ct HR (see para 77 above).
  4   *Dudgeon v United Kingdom* (Ser A No 45, Judgment 23 September 1981) 4 EHRR 149, E Ct HR (see para 66 above).
  5   *Campbell and Cosans v United Kingdom* (Ser A No 48, Judgment 25 February 1982) 4 EHRR 293, E Ct HR (see paras 26, 90, 91, above).
  6   *Golder v United Kingdom* (Ser A No 18, Judgment 21 February 1975) 1 EHRR 524, E Ct HR (see paras 44, 69, above).
  7   The Prison Rules 1964, SI 1964/388, r 37A, was added by the Prison (Amendment) Rules 1976, SI 1976/503.
  8   *Malone v United Kingdom* (Ser A No 82, Judgment 2 August 1984) 7 EHRR 14, E Ct HR (see para 68 above).

96. Non-United Kingdom examples. Among the instances in which governments other than that of the United Kingdom have responded to decisions of the European Court of Human Rights are the *Marckx* case[1], which led to the amendment of various Belgian legal provisions relating to affiliation, the *Le Compte, Van Leuven and De Meyere* case[2], as a result of which disciplinary proceedings before the Belgian Appeals Councils of the *Ordre des médecins* and the *Ordre des pharmaciens* are now, subject to certain conditions, to be held in public; the *Sporrong and Lönnroth* case[3], which prompted new Swedish legislation on town planning and construction; the *Skoogström* case[4], after which the Swedish Code of Judicial Practice was amended; the *Colozza* and *Rubinat* cases[5], which led to a new Italian Code of Criminal Procedure 1988; the *Johnston* case[6], resulting in the Irish Status of Children Act 1987; and the *Bodén* case[7], after which legislation was passed in Sweden extending the review competence of the Supreme Administrative Court.

1 *Marckx v Belgium* (Ser A No 31, Judgment 13 June 1979) 2 EHRR 330, E Ct HR.
2 *Le Compte, Van Leuven and De Meyere v Belgium* (Ser A No 43, Judgment 23 June 1981) 4 EHRR 1, E Ct HR.
3 *Sporrong and Lönnroth v Sweden* (Ser A No 52, Judgment 23 September 1982) 5 EHRR 35, E Ct HR.
4 *Skoogström v Sweden* (Ser A No 83, Judgment 2 October 1984) 7 EHRR 263, E Ct HR.
5 *Colozza v Italy* (Ser A No 89, Judgment 12 February 1985) 7 EHRR 516, E Ct HR; *Rubinat v Italy* (Ser A No 89, Judgment 12 February 1985) 7 EHRR 512, E Ct HR.
6 *Johnston v Ireland* (Ser A No 112, Judgment 18 December 1986) 9 EHRR 203, E Ct HR (see para 71 above).
7 *Bodén v Sweden* (Ser A No 125B, Judgment 27 October 1987) 10 EHRR 367, E Ct HR.

APPENDIX

97–100. Bibliography. The following texts on international law contain chapters on human rights:

I Brownlie *Principles of Public International Law* (Oxford, 4th edn 1990)
M Dixon *Textbook on International Law* (Blackstone Press, 1990)
N A M Green *International Law* (Pitman, 3rd edn 1987)
D W Greig *International Law* (Butterworths, 2nd edn 1976)
D J Harris *Cases and Materials on International Law* (Sweet & Maxwell, 3rd edn 1983)
M Shaw *International Law* (Grotius, 2nd edn 1986)
J C Starke *Introduction to International Law* (Butterworths, 10th edn 1989)
R M M Wallace *International Law* (Sweet & Maxwell, 1986).

The following are general texts on human rights:

I Brownlie (ed) *Basic Documents on Human Rights* (Clarendon, Oxford, 3rd edn 1983)
M Cranston *What are Human Rights?* (Taplinger, New York, 1973)
J Donnelly *The Concept of Human Rights* (Croom Helm 1985)
H Lauterpacht *International Law and Human Rights* (Stevens, 1950)
E Luard (ed) *The International Protection of Human Rights* (Thames & Hudson, 1967)
M S McDougal *Human Rights and World Public Order: The Basic Policies of an International Law of Human Dignity* (Yale, 1950)
B O'Connor (ed) *International Human Rights: A Bibliography 1970–1975* (University of Notre Dame Law School, 1980)
E F Paul, J Paul and F D Miller (eds) *Human Rights* (Oxford, 1984)
A H Robertson *Human Rights in the World* (Manchester University Press, 2nd edn 1972)

P Sieghart *The International Law of Human Rights* (Clarendon, Oxford, 1983)
P Sieghart *The Lawful Rights of Mankind* (Oxford, 1985)
Writers and Scholars Educational Trust *The Human Rights Handbook* Part I (Macmillan, 1979).

Texts on human rights within Europe include:

R Beddard *Human Rights and Europe* (Sweet & Maxwell, 2nd edn 1980)
V Berger *Case Law of the European Court of Human Rights*, vol 1 1960–1987 (Round Hall Press, 1989)
A Z Drzemczewski *European Human Rights Convention in Domestic Law: A Comparative Study* (Clarendon, Oxford, 1983)
S Ercmen *Guide to Case Law, European Convention on Human Rights* (Wein Braumuller, 1981)
M P Furmston *The Effect on English Domestic Law of Membership and of Ratification of the European Convention on Human Rights* (Nijhoff, 1983)
F G Jacobs *The European Convention on Human Rights* (Clarendon, Oxford, 1975)
L Mikaelsen *European Protection of Human Rights: The Practice and Procedure of the European Commission on the Admissibility of Applications from Individuals and States* (Sijthoff & Noordhoff, 1980)
C C Morrison Jnr *The Dynamics of Development in the European Human Rights Convention System* (Nijhoff, 1981)
Z M Nedjati *Human Rights under the European Convention* (North Holland, 1978)
T Opsahl and T Ouchterlary *The European Convention on Human Rights* (Leiden Sitjoff, 1974)
H Petzold *The European Convention on Human Rights: Cases and Materials* (Koln, 4th edn, 1981)
A H Robertson *The Council of Europe* (Stevens, 1961)
A H Robertson *Human Rights in Europe* (Manchester University Press, 2nd edn, 1987)
W Ullah *European Community Law and Human Rights: Casebook* (London HLT, 1989)
P Van Dyk and G J M Van Hoof *Theory and Practice of the European Convention on Human Rights* (Nijhoff, 1983).

The following are publications of the Council of Europe:

Yearbook of the European Convention on Human Rights K Academic Publishers (Nijhoff: published annually since 1959 (except 1961))
Digest of Strasbourg Case Law relating to the European Convention on Human Rights (6 vols, C Heymanns Verlag, 1984)
Human Rights of Aliens in Europe K Academic Publishers (Nijhoff, 1985)
Collected Texts of the European Convention on Human Rights K Academic Publishers (Nijhoff, 1986)
European Court of Human Rights, Series A: Decisions of the European Court of Human Rights
European Court of Human Rights, Series B: Pleadings, Oral Arguments, Documents of the European Court of Human Rights
Human Rights Terminology in International Law: A Thesaurus Council of Europe Publications Catalogue (1990).

There are two human rights journals:

Human Rights Law Journal (HRLJ), N P Engel (monthly from January 1991)
Human Rights Quarterly: A Comparative and International Journal of the Social Services, Humanities and Law (John Hopkins University Press).

Cases before the European Court of Human Rights are reported in the European Human Rights Reports (EHRR).

The British Yearbook of International Law (BYIL) and the *Yearbook of European Law* feature articles on the Convention for the Protection of Human Rights and Fundamental Freedoms as well as an annual summary of the activities of the Council of Europe. The European Law Review (ELR) publishes a regular current summary of those activities, while other legal periodicals which feature articles on human rights generally and the convention in particular include inter alia the American Journal of Comparative Law (AJCJ), the American Journal of International Law (AJIL), the International and Comparative Law Quarterly (ICLQ), the Law Quarterly Review (LQR), the Modern Law Review (MLR), the Journal of the Law Society of Scotland (JLSS), the Scots Law Times (SLT) and the Juridical Review (JR).

IMMIGRATION AND EXTRADITION

	PARA
1. IMMIGRATION .	101
(1) History and Purposes of Immigration Law .	101
(2) Sources and Status of Rules on Control .	108
(a) Municipal Law and Practice .	108
(b) Community Law .	114
(c) International Law .	115
(3) Right of Abode .	117
(4) Leave to Enter or Remain .	119
(a) Introduction .	119
(b) Common Travel Area .	122
(c) Groups Subject to Immigration Control but with Protected Status .	125
(d) Groups Exempted from Immigration Control .	128
(e) Special Limitations on Movement .	133
(f) Community Law .	137
(5) Institutions of Control .	138
(a) Central Control .	138
(b) Local Control .	141
(6) Processes of Control .	146
(a) Introduction .	146
(b) Control before Entry .	150
(A) Entry Clearance .	150
(B) Work Permits .	154
(C) Special Vouchers .	158
(D) Sponsorship and Public Funds .	160
(c) Control on Entry .	161
(d) Control after Entry .	177
(A) Remaining in the United Kingdom .	177
(B) Offences and Removal .	185
(C) Other Post-Entry Controls and Checks .	189
(e) Control of Departure .	192
(A) Introduction .	192
(B) Administrative Removal .	194
(C) Deportation .	202
(D) Other Forms of Control .	215
(7) Categories of Entrant under Community Law without the Right of Abode .	219
(a) Community Law .	219
(b) Community Law as Mediated by the Immigration Rules .	235
(8) Categories of Entrant not under Community Law without a Right of Abode .	240
(a) Introduction .	240
(b) Persons in Employment, Business and Related Categories .	241
(A) Introduction .	241
(B) Work-Permit Holders .	242
(C) Permit-Free Employment .	246
(D) Businessmen and the Self-Employed .	250
(E) Writers and Artists .	254

(F) Persons of Independent Means 258
(G) Commonwealth Citizens with United Kingdom
       Ancestry 261
(H) Commonwealth Citizen Working Holidaymakers . . 263
(I) Dependants 264
(c) Family Reunion and Creation by Settlement . . . 267
(A) Introduction 267
(B) Admission of Spouse 269
(C) Admission of Fiances and Fiancees 274
(D) Settlement by virtue of Marriage of those Admitted other
       than as Spouse, Fiancée or Fiancé 278
(E) Admission of Children 279
(F) Admission of Parents, Grandparents and other Relatives 285
(d) Students, Visitors and Au Pairs 291
(A) Introduction 291
(B) Students 292
(C) Dependants of Students 301
(D) Visitors 305
(E) Au Pairs 310
(e) Refugees and Political Asylees 314
(A) International Law 314
(B) United Kingdom Law 316
(f) United Kingdom Passport Holders 324
(9) Appeals and Related Processes 329
(a) Introduction 329
(b) System of Appeal 330
(c) Appealable and Non-Appealable Decisions . . . 336
(d) Procedure 345
(A) Procedure on First Stage Appeal (other than 'Security'
       Cases) 345
(B) Procedure on Further Appeal (other than 'Security' Cases) 357
(C) Procedure on Reference from the Secretary of State . 367
(D) Procedure in 'Security' Deportation Cases . . . 368
(e) Representations by Members of Parliament 370

2. **EXTRADITION** 501
(1) Introduction 501
(2) Historical Background 502
(3) Purposes 505
(4) Sources and Authority 506
(a) Extradition to Foreign States 506
(b) Extradition to Commonwealth Countries . . . 518
(c) Extradition to the Republic of Ireland 525
(d) Extradition to the United Kingdom 530
(5) General Restrictions on Return 531
(a) Political Offences 531
(b) Rule on Contumacy 536
(c) Previous Acquittal or Conviction 538
(d) Speciality 540
(e) The Prima Facie Rule 544
(f) Other Restrictions 548
(6) Extradition from the United Kingdom 550
(a) Requisition and the Order of the Secretary of State . . 550
(b) Authority to proceed 553
(c) Informal Requisition or Request and Provisional Warrants . 556

(d) Executing the Warrant 559
(e) Hearing and Committal 562
(f) Authentication of Documents 565
(g) Review 568
(h) Secretary of State's Order to surrender or return . . . 574
(7) Extradition to the United Kingdom 577
(a) Foreign States. 577
(b) Commonwealth Countries 579
(c) Republic of Ireland 581

The General Editors and the author express warm appreciation to Professor Paul O'Higgins, who, at an early stage in the preparation of the title, kindly lent a copy of his PhD thesis 'The Law of Extradition, with particular reference to British practice'. Thanks are also due to Ian Dickinson and Judge David Edward for comments and advice received on the first draft of the title.

1. IMMIGRATION

(1) HISTORY AND PURPOSES OF IMMIGRATION LAW

101. Immigration to the United Kingdom. There is a long history of immigration[1]. Since the inception of the United Kingdom in 1801[2], emigration from it has exceeded immigration in almost every year[3]. Apart from this considerable emigration (chiefly to the settler colonies and their successor states) and the secular drift of population from periphery to centre, three major migratory flows, internal or external, have affected the United Kingdom.

After 1845 large numbers of Irish people entered Great Britain because of the Potato Famine[4]. Many moved on to the United States of America but many remained in Scotland[5]. Also until the mid-1960s, considerable seasonal and permanent migration from Ireland continued[6].

Between 1871 and 1905 a considerable number of Jews fleeing anti-Semitic policies in Eastern Europe entered the United Kingdom, although again many moved on[7].

Chiefly from the late 1950s until 1962, a significant number of people from the parts of the 'black Commonwealth' and Hong Kong entered to take employment, and their dependants are in some cases still seeking entry[8]. Originally this was frequently immigration to work and return, but later favoured settlement[9]. However, many of those immigrants have now returned to their country of origin[10].

In addition there has been a continuous but variable flow of immigrants, chiefly to work, from foreign countries[11], but including return migration from the Dominions in the 1930s[12]; recruitment of continental European workers in the late 1940s[13], and occasional groups of refugees or near refugees such as those from Hungary in 1956, Czechoslovakia in 1968, Kenya in 1968, Uganda in 1972, Cyprus in 1974 and Vietnam around 1980[14]. Emigration from Hong Kong may be anticipated in the light of the change of regime in 1997[15].

Since 1973 workers and businessmen from member states of the European Community have had almost unrestricted entry, but few have settled[16]. In addition, an enormous number of tourists and other visitors enter annually. They are not immigrants but are controlled by what is termed immigration law.

1 A number of books on immigration history and law have been written: see eg those cited in J M Evans *Immigration Law* (2nd edn, 1983) p 40, notes 11, 13. See also S Abbott *The Prevention of*

Racial Discrimination in Britain (1971) chs 2, 3; V Bevan *Development of British Immigration Law* (1986); D A Coleman *Demography of Immigrants and Minority Groups in the United Kingdom* (1982) (especially the essays by W Brass, C Holmes, P R Jones, C Peach and V Robinson); *Colour and Citizenship* (1969, Institute of Race Relations) chs 5–16, 26, 27, 29, 30; *Britain's Black Population* (1980, Runnymede Trust and Radical Statistics Race Group) chs 1, 2, 7; *Role of Immigrants in the Labour Market* (1975, Unit for Manpower Studies (Department of Employment and Productivity)); and J Walvin *Passage to Britain* (1984).

2 Ie under the Union with Ireland Act 1800 (c 67).

3 *Role of Immigrants in the Labour Market* para B2. As to recent years, see Office for Population Censuses and Surveys 'International Migration' (Series MN) (annual since 1974); T Devis 'International Migration: return migrant and remigrant flows' (1985) 41 Population Trends 13; L Bulusu 'Recent Patterns of Migration from and to the United Kingdom' (1986) 46 Population Trends 35. Approximately one-third of migrants entering the United Kingdom each year were born in it, ie they are *return* migrants.

4 *Role of Immigrants in the Labour Market* para B3.

5 Ibid, para B3 and Table B1.

6 Ibid, Tables B2, B8, B9, B12.

7 See ibid, para B4, and note 5 above.

8 See ibid, para B13 and Tables B10–B16, B24, D8, and the annual Control of Immigration Statistics 1976 to date. See also Fifth Report from the Home Affairs Committee (HC Paper (1981–82) no. 90) (Immigration from the Indian Sub-Continent) and the government's reply (Cmnd 8725) (1982); the Second Report from the Home Affairs Committee (HC Papers (1984–85) no. 102) (Chinese community in Britain) and the government's reply (Cmnd 9586) (1985); the Second Report from the Home Affairs Committee (HC Papers (1985–86) no. 67) (Immigration from the Indian Sub-continent) and the government's reply (Cm 199) (1987); and the First Report from the Home Affairs Committee (HC Papers (1986–87) no. 96) (Bangladeshis in Britain) and the government's reply (Cm 193) (1987).

9 *Role of Immigrants in the Labour Market* paras C2–C7.

10 T Devis (1985) 41 Population Trends 13, and the sources quoted therein.

11 *Role of Immigrants in the Labour Market* para B24, Tables B3–B7, D1, and the annual Control of Immigration Statistics 1976 to date.

12 *Role of Immigrants in the Labour Market* para B6.

13 Ibid, paras B5–B11.

14 See, in relation to the Vietnamese, the Third Report from the Home Affairs Committee (HC Paper (1984–85) no. 72) (refugees and asylum, with special reference to the Vietnamese) and the government's reply (Cmnd 9626) (1985).

15 See para 107 below.

16 *Role of Immigrants in the Labour Market* paras D10–D22 and Tables D2, D3, and the annual Control of Immigration Statistics 1976 to date.

102. Reasons for migration to the United Kingdom in the twentieth century.

People wish to migrate for various reasons and for various lengths of time. Generally speaking they may do so to improve their economic prospects, or to avoid political pressure, or (to extend the meaning of 'migrate') for tourism[1]. However, migration is possible only if a host country will accept the migrant. The relative 'market power' of migrant and host will vary.

The United Kingdom has pursued a generally restrictive posture in the twentieth century[2]. Nevertheless, as an economically developed country, it has required labour and has both actively and passively recruited people from elsewhere[3]. Generally these people have come from economically less developed countries and been willing to take less attractive jobs, although many do not[4]. This is true of North-West Europe generally[5]. These immigrants have been termed 'replacement labour'. Latterly, generally, only highly-skilled people have been accepted.

Since immigration control was first applied, its chief instrument has been the work permit[6]. Thus the number of permits, and the jobs for which they are issued, largely reflect government economic policy. Further, the number of immigrants, their length of stay, and their countries of origin also largely reflect this. In order to increase the net benefit of the system, access to social benefits is limited to some extent[7].

Businessmen and people of independent means, and some specific sorts of employees, are admitted on broadly similar principles[8]. The whole is modified by Community law. Essentially, this does not remove the boundaries of the system, but expands them to those of the European Community[9].

The economic bases are modified by other principles. Immediate dependants of those admitted are also admitted, and all may qualify for permanent settlement after some years[10]. There is also a desire to facilitate entry of descendants of those born in the United Kingdom[11], to abide by international and Commonwealth obligations[12], to admit some refugees[13] and, to a limited extent, to allow unification of families[14]. Immigration control has been seen as a method of reducing racial tension, but this is a highly controversial point[15].

Large numbers of short-term migrants enter as students and tourists who, with few exceptions, cannot thereby qualify for permanent settlement[16].

Immigration law has developed mainly as a series of responses to, and attempts to regulate, particular pressures rather than as a positive means of achieving preconceived social or economic aims[17].

1 *Role of Immigrants in the Labour Market* (1975, Unit for Manpower Studies (Department of Employment and Productivity)) Part I, Section C.
2 See eg J M Evans *Immigration Law* (2nd edn, 1983) ch 1 *passim*.
3 *Role of Immigrants in the Labour Market* Part I, Section C, Part II, Section E.
4 Ibid, Part II, relevant Tables and Annexes 2–4, and the annual Control of Immigration Statistics 1976 to date.
5 *Role of Immigrants in the Labour Market* Part I, Section C, Part II, Section E and Annex 3. See also J Salt and H D Clout *Migration in Post-war Europe: Geographical Essays* (1976).
6 *Role of Immigrants in the Labour Market* paras B5, B11, and related Tables, and *Evans* ch 1, especially pp 23–26.
7 Ie chiefly by the requirement not to resort to 'public funds': see the Statement of Changes in Immigration Rules (HC Paper (1989–90) no. 251) (the Immigration Rules), paras 22, 26, 42, 47, and paras 240 ff below. As to the Immigration Rules, see para 110 below.
8 See paras 240, 241, 250–253, below.
9 See paras 114, 221 ff below.
10 See paras 264–266 below.
11 See paras 261, 263, below.
12 See paras 115, 116, 235, 316, below.
13 See paras 316–321 below.
14 See paras 267 ff below.
15 *Evans* pp 28–32; *Macdonald's Immigration Law and Practice* (3rd edn, 1991, eds I A Macdonald and N J Blake) pp 16, 17.
16 See paras 291 ff, 305–309 below. See also the annual Control of Immigration Statistics 1976 to date.
17 See eg *Evans* ch 1, and the First Report from the Select Committee on Race Relations and Immigration (HC Paper (1977–78) (no. 303-II) (Immigration vol 2) p 1. See also the sources cited in para 101, note 1, above.

103. Immigration law until the Union. Little reference to freedom of entry or control of it appears in the cases or among the institutional writers. The latter distinguish subjects and aliens but generally question if an alien might hold heritable property[1].

The 'auld alliance' statute of 1491[2] asserted reciprocity of freedoms and privileges for the Scots in France and the French in Scotland and intended the advancement of the good of merchants. Reciprocal '*naturalité*' for Scots and French within each other's countries, and specified advantages relating to lands, heritage, office, dignities and benefices were granted by statute in 1558[3]. Craig refers to both, but only in the context of heritable property[4]. Buchanan, though concerned (unlike the institutional writers) with public law subjects, does not address the subject[5].

A number of seventeenth-century statutes provided for naturalisation of 'foreigners' setting up home or business in Scotland[6]. The Act setting up the Bank of Scotland naturalised any 'foreigner' becoming a partner and described resulting advantages without mention of rights of entry[7].

Banishment existed as a common law and statutory punishment[8]. A Privy Council proclamation of 1603 and the Gipsies Act 1609 also banished all 'Egyptians'[9]. In trials of gipsies under this provision the defence was raised, unsuccessfully, that it applied only to those in the realm at the time, but not, apparently, the defence that it should not apply because they were subjects[10].

Thus no clear assertion exists that certain people, subjects or aliens, could be refused entry, save those banished. The advantages of naturalisation were seen chiefly in terms of land and office holding and trade, but these advantages are worthless without free entry. Therefore, it may tentatively be argued that subjects had a right of entry and others did not, subject to banishment. No system of control existed.

1 Craig *Jus Feudale* l,2,64; Erskine *Institute* III,10,10; Stair *Institutions* (5th edn, 1832) vol 1, More's Notes, Note A,x.
2 Ie the France Act 1491 (Apr 28 c 2) (repealed).
3 Ie under the French Subjects Act 1558 (c 6) (repealed).
4 *Craig* l,14,7. A list of these and other related resources is recorded in Mackenzie *Observations* (1687) pp 159 ff.
5 See eg G Buchanan *De Jure Regni Apud Scotos* (translated by D N MacNeil, as *The Art and Science of Government Among the Scots* (1964)) which is silent on the issue.
6 See eg the Fishings Act 1661 (c 279); the Manufactures Act 1661 (c 280); the Naturalization Act 1669 (c 12); and the Trade Act 1681 (c 78) (all repealed).
7 Ie APS ix, 494, c 88 (see generally BANKING AND FINANCIAL INSTITUTIONS, vol 2, para 1115). The provision was considered repealed as contrary to the Act of Union in *Macao v Officers of State* 14 Nov 1820 FC; (1822) 1 Sh App 138, HL. *Attorney General v Prince Ernest Augustus of Hanover* [1957] AC 436, [1957] 1 All ER 49, HL, is inconsistent, as noted by T B Smith in 'British Nationality and the Union of 1707' 1956 SLT (News) 89; T B Smith *Studies Critical and Comparative* (1962) pp 20–27, 32; T B Smith *British Justice: The Scottish Contribution* (1961) pp 24–27; and CONSTITUTIONAL LAW, vol 5, para 716. Neither forensic view assists on the question of entry.
8 Hume *Commentaries* I,528.
9 *Hume* I,468. The Gipsies Act 1609 (c 20) is repealed.
10 *Hume* I,468 ff.

104. Immigration law in Great Britain and the United Kingdom to the end of the nineteenth century.

The Revolutionary and Napoleonic Wars produced several statutes[1] controlling entry of aliens, discussed by Bell[2]. For instance, one required registration of aliens entering[3]. A common law prohibition on aliens cannot be inferred from this[4].

Other public general statutes permitting naturalisation as a reward or otherwise were passed, as well as private Acts[5], but contained no reference to rights of entry.

The occasional case referring to subjects did so in relation to heritable property[6]. English cases parallel this[7].

1 See eg the Aliens Acts 1793 (c 4), 1798 (cc 50, 77), 1802 (c 92), 1803 (c 155), 1814 (c 155), 1815 (c 54), 1816 (c 86), 1818 (cc 96, 97), 1820 (c 105) (all repealed); the Juries Act 1825 (c 50); and the Aliens Act 1826 (c 54) (the Peace Alien Act) (repealed).
2 Bell *Principles* s 2134.
3 See the Registration of Aliens Act 1836 (c 11) (repealed).
4 The First Report from the Select Committee on Race Relations and Immigration (HC Paper (1977–78) (no. 303-I) (Immigration vol 1) para 20 asserts 'The settlement of aliens in the United Kingdom has always been controlled. There never has been any right of settlement . . . [for aliens]'. No authority for this is offered. It continues '[I]n earlier centuries aliens who did settle were under severe disabilities'. The only example offered is land holding, on the authority of

5 Coke Rep 502 (an erroneous citation for an unknown case, but in any event before the Acts of Union), and it is further asserted that all rights were enjoyed 'by favour of the Royal Prerogative'.

5 C Parry *Nationality and Citizenship Laws of the Commonwealth and of the Republic of Ireland* (1957) pp 5, 6, 34–40 (relating to pre-Union England only), pp 47–77 (spanning the seventeenth to the nineteenth centuries). Parry, like most other writers on nationality until the 1960s, referred to immigration barely, if at all.

6 See eg *Leslie v Forbes* (1749) Mor 4636.

7 See eg *De Geer v Stone* (1882) 22 Ch D 243; *Calvin's Case* (1608) 7 Co Rep 1a (concerning the union of the crowns). *Re Stepney Election Petition, Isaacson v Durant* (1886) 17 QBD 54, is unusual in relating to Parliamentary elections.

105. Common law on immigration from the late nineteenth century. Whether an alien had a right of entry is usually considered to have first been considered in *Musgrove v Chun Teeong Toy*[1]. A statute of Victoria (Australia) taxed Chinese immigrants on entry. It was argued that the royal prerogative did not extend to excluding aliens. There was also dispute as to whether proper procedures had been followed and whether the statute was *intra vires*. The Privy Council, however, avoided the fundamental issue, deciding only that an alien could not bring an action in the circumstances. In *Poll v Lord Advocate*[2] an alien fishing boat was prevented from landing its catch. On the assertion of the Lord Advocate, the Lord Ordinary held the action an act of state, so not capable of question in court by an alien.

In *Schmidt v Secretary of State for Home Affairs*[3] the English Court of Appeal declared by a majority that on the basis of the current statutory regime an alien could be refused entry without reason given. Lord Denning MR and Widgery LJ considered obiter that aliens had no right of entry at common law and might be deported although there might be a duty to act fairly in deportations[4].

A decade after it ceased to exist, a common law right of subjects to enter was unequivocally declared by the House of Lords in *Director of Public Prosecutions v Bhagwan*[5]. It follows that there is no right to deport them (banishment not then being used[6]).

The prerogative rights of the Crown in respect of aliens are expressly preserved by the Immigration Act 1971[7]. This might indicate a lack of such powers in relation to subjects.

1 *Musgrove v Chun Teeong Toy* [1891] AC 272, PC.

2 *Poll v Lord Advocate* (1899) 1 F 823, 5 SLT 167.

3 *Schmidt v Secretary of State for Home Affairs* [1969] 2 Ch 149, [1969] 1 All ER 904, CA.

4 [1969] 2 Ch 149 at 168, 169, 171, [1969] 1 All ER 904 at 907, 908, 909, per Lord Denning MR, and at 172–174, and at 910–912, per Widgery LJ, CA.

5 *Director of Public Prosecutions v Bhagwan* [1972] AC 60, [1970] 3 All ER 97, HL.

6 However, as to the powers in respect of the prevention of terrorism, see paras 133, 134, below.

7 Immigration Act 1971 (c 77), s 33(5).

106. Statute law concerning entry of aliens in the twentieth century. Immigration law effectively commenced with the Aliens Act 1905[1], which arose out of a royal commission[2] on the immigration of Eastern European Jews, and laid the foundations of the current scheme[3]. It required aliens in immigrant ships over a certain size to land only at designated ports and gave immigration officers the right to refuse entry to those appearing undesirable on health, economic or criminal grounds. They could be deported on similar grounds. There was a right of appeal.

The Aliens Restriction Act 1914[4], an emergency measure on the outbreak of the 1914–18 war, replaced the 1905 Act and, with amendments, was made permanent by way of the Aliens Restriction (Amendment) Act 1919[5]. These Acts (and delegated legislation under them[6]) built what remains essentially the current system by creating the work permit scheme[7], and remained in force until replaced by the Immigration Act 1971. That Act came into force on 1 January 1973, on the same date as the major exception in favour of European Community nationals in pursuance of the principles of free movement of workers and establishment[8]. Appeals, abolished in 1914, were reintroduced by the Immigration Appeals Act 1969[9]. The Immigration Act 1971 expressly preserved prerogative powers in relation to aliens[10].

1 The Aliens Act 1905 (c 13) is repealed.
2 *Report of the Commission on Alien Immigration* (Cd 1741) (1903).
3 Ie the British Nationality and Status of Aliens Act 1914 (c 17), which is now known as the Status of Aliens Act 1914 (c 17): see the British Nationality Act 1948 (c 56), s 34(3), Sch 4, Pt II. The 1914 Act altered the methods of acquisition of the status of British subject as did later British nationality legislation, but none referred to rights of entry until that of 1981.
4 The Aliens Restriction Act 1914 (c 12) is repealed.
5 Ie renewed annually by the Expiring Laws Continuance Acts: see the Aliens Restriction (Amendment) Act 1919 (c 92), s 1 (repealed).
6 Ie the Aliens Order 1920, SR & O 1920/488 (revoked).
7 See para 102, note 6, above, and paras 154–157 below.
8 See paras 114, 219 ff below.
9 The Immigration Appeals Act 1969 (c 21) is repealed.
10 Immigration Act 1971 (c 77), s 33(5).

107. Statute law concerning entry of British subjects/Commonwealth citizens in the twentieth century. British subjects (also known as Commonwealth citizens since the British Nationality Act 1948[1]) were free of any statutory control until the Commonwealth Immigrants Act 1962 (c 21), passed as a reaction to immigration from the 'black Commonwealth'. It restricted the right of entry to those born in the United Kingdom; or who were citizens of the United Kingdom and Colonies holding a passport issued by the United Kingdom government (as opposed to the government of a colony); or who were included on the passport of a person with the right. This excluded the vast majority of British subjects including a significant proportion of citizens of the United Kingdom and Colonies, chiefly those born in colonies. All others, including British subjects from the Indian sub-continent and West Indies required leave to enter, and two categories of citizens of the United Kingdom and Colonies resulted: those with a right of entry to the United Kingdom and those without (who would, however, have a right of entry to a colony). The chief category of leave to enter was that of holders of employment vouchers (essentially work permits)[2]. Once entered, such a person and his dependants had a right to remain permanently.

On the independence of the East African dependencies, people of Indian sub-continent origin were in general not allowed the new local citizenship as of right but required to register. Those not so doing remained citizens of the United Kingdom and Colonies, and held passports from the United Kingdom government, there being no longer any relevant colonial government to issue them. Thus they had the right of entry. In 1968 many of these people were in effect expelled from Uganda but on attempting to enter the United Kingdom had their right of entry removed by the Commonwealth Immigrants Act 1968[3], which introduced the requirement of an ancestral connection with the United Kingdom. Many were therefore 'shuttlecocked' between airports until admitted by other countries as an act of mercy[4]. The Act produced three classes of citizens of the United Kingdom and Colonies: those with a right of entry to the United Kingdom, those without but with a right of entry to a colony, and those with no right of entry anywhere despite a United Kingdom passport (unless by virtue of dual nationality or rights of entry to a third country).

The United Kingdom was subject to considerable moral, legal and political pressure on this issue through the European Commission of Human Rights and otherwise. 'Special vouchers' were issued administratively for the gradual admission of East African Asians[5]. This system is still in operation[6].

The Immigration Act 1971 (c 77), broadly speaking, put British subjects without a right of entry in the same position as aliens. For example, entry on a work permit no longer gave the right to remain permanently. Those with a right of entry (now termed 'right of abode') were termed 'patrials', and the category was expanded to include most British subjects who were first or second generation descendants of people born in the United Kingdom, and wives of 'patrials'. The chief beneficiaries were citizens of Australia, Canada and New Zealand.

The British Nationality Act 1981, amending the Immigration Act 1971, formalised the entry categories. Broadly, citizens of the United Kingdom and Colonies:

(1) who were patrials became British citizens[7];
(2) with a right of entry to a colony became British Dependent Territories citizens[8]; and
(3) with no right of entry became British Overseas citizens[9].

Changes in the methods of acquisition also occurred, and the term 'British subject' was applied in a fundamentally different way[10]. The overall category, hitherto called 'British subject' or 'Commonwealth citizen' is now only to be called 'Commonwealth citizen'.

Because of fears for the future after the resumption of power by China in 1997, the British Nationality Act 1981 included a section permitting certain British Dependent Territories citizen colonial civil servants and the like to be registered as British citizens[11]. Few have been so registered[12]. The British Nationality (Hong Kong) Act 1990 (c 34) sets up schemes whereby those holding another form of British nationality who are considered essential to the running of the territory, and their spouses and minor children, may be registered as British citizens, and thereby obtain a right of abode in the United Kingdom. The government considered that a total of 225,000 might finally be registered, but that few would in fact enter the United Kingdom[13].

The right of abode is now subject to 'exclusion orders', a form of internal banishment, under the prevention of terrorism powers[14].

1 See the British Nationality Act 1948 (c 56), s 1(2) (repealed). 'British subject', since 1 January 1983, describes only that small group hitherto known as British subjects without citizenship, and 'Commonwealth citizen' is the only proper term for the general category: see the British Nationality Act 1981 (c 61), ss 30, 31, 37, and NATIONALITY AND CITIZENSHIP, vol 14, paras 1903, 1906 ff.

2 Originally employment vouchers were seen as a method of rationing entry as such, but the division into types of voucher related to job prospects, and the rapid deletion of category C vouchers (for those with no specific job, nor a highly desired skill) shows the economic influence: see J M Evans *Immigration Law* (2nd edn, 1983) p 152, note 63.

3 The Commonwealth Immigrants Act 1968 (c 9) is repealed.

4 See eg D Steel *No Entry* (1969); D Humphrey and M Ward *Passports and Politics* (1974). Official publications are more mealy-mouthed: see eg the First Report from the Select Committee on Race Relations and Immigration (HC Paper (1977–78) no. 303-I) (Immigration vol 1) paras 113, 114; the Fifth Report from the Home Affairs Committee (HC Paper (1981–82) no. 90-I) (Immigration from the Indian Sub-Continent vol 1) paras 68, 69; and the Second Report from the Home Affairs Committee (HC Paper (1980–81) no. 158) (Numbers and Legal Status of Future British Overseas Citizens without other Citizenship) which, while substantially concerning such East African Asians, omitted to discuss how they acquired their unenviable position.

5 As to special vouchers, see para 158 below.

6 See paras 115, 324, below.

7 See the British Nationality Act 1981, s 11, and vol 14, para 1906.

8 See ibid, s 23, and vol 14, para 1933.

9 See ibid, s 26, and vol 14, para 1942.
10 See ibid, ss 30, 31, 37, and vol 14, paras 1950, 1953, 1954. See also the British Nationality (Hong Kong) (Selection Scheme) Order 1990, SI 1990/2292.
11 See the British Nationality Act 1981, s 4(5), (6), and vol 14, para 1914.
12 See eg 170 HC Official Report (5th series) col 1597.
13 See 170 HC Official Report (5th series) col 1566.
14 See para 134 below.

(2) SOURCES AND STATUS OF RULES ON CONTROL

(a) Municipal Law and Practice

108. Common law. Common law powers are dealt with above[1]. They are largely of historical interest only, since the statutory regime is a comprehensive code. Prerogative powers in relation to aliens are nevertheless preserved[2].

1 See paras 103–105 above.
2 Immigration Act 1971 (c 77), s 33(5).

109. Legislation. The Immigration Act 1971 as amended[1] is the principal and, read with the Immigration Act 1988, the sole Act of substance. It is significantly affected by European Community law[2] and most detail is delegated to statutory instruments and the Immigration Rules[3]. There is also considerable administrative discretion[4]. The European Convention on Human Rights is not used as an interpretive device[5].

Some statutory instruments are made under the 1971 Act, in particular concerning appeals procedure[6].

1 Ie chiefly by the British Nationality Act 1981 (c 61) and the Immigration Act 1988 (c 14). See also the Immigration (Carriers' Liability) Act 1987 (c 24).
2 See paras 114, 221 ff below.
3 See para 110 below.
4 See paras 111, 112, below.
5 See para 115 below.
6 The principal statutory instruments are the Immigration (Variation of Leave) Order 1976, SI 1976/1572 (amended by SI 1989/1005); the Immigration Appeals (Notices) Regulations 1984, SI 1984/2040; and the Immigration Appeals (Procedure) Rules 1984, SI 1984/2041. The other statutory instruments are mentioned in the relevant paragraphs below.

110. The Immigration Rules. The Secretary of State is required to lay before Parliament rules laid down by him as to the practice to be followed in the administration of the Immigration Act 1971 for regulating entry into and stay in the United Kingdom of persons required by that Act to have leave to enter[1]. They are published as House of Commons Papers and Command Papers[2], under the title 'Statement of Changes in Immigration Rules' but are referred to as the 'Immigration Rules'[3]. Conditions are imposed on their content[4] and they are subject to negative resolution procedure[5].

Their status is unclear. They are drafted in large measure as glosses on the legislation and description of practice[6]. They are frequently modified by terms such as 'normally' or 'usually'[7] and satisfaction of their formal requirements may not be conclusive[8], and they are rarely specific enough to grant an indefeasible entitlement or bind an official. Nor do they cover all foreseeable situations[9]. In English cases it has been decided that they are not delegated legislation[10], and indeed not rules of law[11] nor of legislative or statutory force[12]. Rather they are guidelines[13] and can at least on occasion be ignored by courts[14] and normal rules of statutory interpretation are inappropriate[15]. Nevertheless, a ground of appeal against an immigration officer's decision is that it was not in accordance with an immigration rule applying to the case[16]. Also such failure, and improper exercise of discretion granted in a rule, has been held ground for judicial review in England[17].

Where the Immigration Rules are unclear or do not cover a situation (and indeed in any case), the Secretary of State may exercise his power to decide 'outside the Rules'[18].

Immigration Rules have been re-issued, usually only with minor changes, very many times, so transitional provisions are very important[19].

1 Immigration Act 1971 (c 77), s 3(2).
2 The current rules are the Statement of Changes in Immigration Rules (HC Paper (1989–90) no. 251) (the Immigration Rules) (amended by HC Paper (1989–90) no. 454; HC Paper (1990–91) nos. 160, 320, 356; Cm 1219 (1990); Cm 1220 (1990); Cm 1491 and 1672 (1991)).
3 See the Immigration Act 1971, ss 3(2), 33(1).
4 See ibid, ss 1(4), (5), 3(2) (s 1(5) is repealed subject to exceptions: see the Immigration Act 1988 (c 14), s 1, and the Immigration Act 1988 (Commencement No 1) Order 1988, SI 1988/1133, art 3).
5 Immigration Act 1971, s 3(2).
6 See eg the Immigration Rules, Part I (paras 6–21) and Part III (paras 34–48). Cumming Bruce LJ described an earlier, essentially similar, version as a 'curious amalgam of information and description of executive procedures': *R v Secretary of State for the Home Department, ex parte Hosenball* [1977] 3 All ER 452 at 466, [1977] 1 WLR 766 at 788, CA. Lord Bridges observed that they 'do not purport to enact a precise code having statutory force, and on their face, frequently offer no more than broad guidelines as to how discretion is to be exercised in different typical situations. Insofar as they lay down principles to be applied they generally do so in loose and imprecise terms . . .': *Singh v Immigration Appeal Tribunal* [1986] 2 All ER 721, [1986] 1 WLR 910, [1986] Imm AR 352, HL.
    They are not rules of law. They are rules of practice laid down for the guidance of immigration officers and tribunals who are entrusted with the administration of the Act: *R v Secretary of State for the Home Department, ex parte Hosenball* [1977] 3 All ER 452 at 459, [1977] 1 WLR 766 at 780, CA, per Lord Denning. '[If] Parliament disapproves of the rules they are not thereby abrogated': at 463, and at 785, per Geoffrey Lane LJ.
7 See eg the Immigration Rules, para 35. As to the meaning of 'not normally', see *R v Immigration Appeal Tribunal, ex parte Bashir* [1985] Imm AR 231, CA.
8 See eg the Immigration Rules, para 78.
9 Eg that of a person applying for a work permit from within the United Kingdom.
10 *R v Secretary of State for the Home Department, ex parte Hosenball* [1977] 3 All ER 452, [1977] 1 WLR 766, CA. See especially at 459, and at 780, per Lord Denning. They are 'quite unlike ordinary delegated legislation': *Singh v Immigration Appeal Tribunal* [1986] 2 All ER 721, [1986] 1 WLR 910, [1986] Imm AR 352, HL, per Lord Bridge.
11 *R v Secretary of State for the Home Department, ex parte Hosenball* [1977] 3 All ER 452, [1977] 1 WLR 776, CA.
12 [1977] 3 All ER 452 at 466, [1977] 1 WLR 766 at 788, per Cumming Bruce LJ, CA; *Zamir v Secretary of State for the Home Department* [1980] AC 930, [1980] 2 All ER 768, HL (not followed on another point in *Khawaja v Secretary of State for the Home Department* [1984] AC 74, [1983] 1 All ER 765, [1982] Imm AR 139, HL). See also J M Evans *Immigration Law* (2nd edn, 1983) pp 400–407.
13 *Alexander v Immigration Appeal Tribunal* [1982] 2 All ER 766 at 770, [1982] 1 WLR 1076 at 1080, [1982] Imm AR 50 at 54, HL, per Lord Roskill.
14 *R v Secretary of State for the Home Department, ex parte Hosenball* [1977] 3 All ER 452, [1977] 1 WLR 766, CA. Indeed, they are subject to the *ultra vires* principle: eg *Rajput v Immigration Appeal Tribunal* [1989] Imm AR 350, CA.
15 *Alexander v Immigration Appeal Tribunal* [1982] 2 All ER 766 at 770, [1982] 1 WLR 1076 at 1080, [1982] Imm AR 50 at 54, HL, per Lord Roskill.
16 Immigration Act 1971, s 19(1)(a)(i).
17 *R v Chief Immigration Officer, Gatwick Airport, ex parte Kharrazi* [1980] 3 All ER 373, [1980] 1 WLR 1396, CA. However, see now *R v Secretary of State for the Home Department, ex parte Swati* [1986] 1 All ER 717, [1986] 1 WLR 477, [1986] Imm AR 88, CA. As to judicial review in Scotland, see *Mensah v Secretary of State for the Home Department* 1991 GWD 4-218, OH, and *Saftar* 1991 GWD 15-940, OH.

18 See para 112 below.
19 The previous Immigration Rules were Statement of Changes in Immigration Rules (HC Papers (1988–89) no. 388), itself preceded by HC Paper (1982–83) no. 169 (the Former Immigration Rules) (as amended by HC Paper (1984–85) nos 293, 503; HC Paper (1985–86) nos 306, 584; HC Paper (1986–87) no. 154; HC Paper (1987–88) no. 208; Cmnd 9539 (1985); and Cmnd 9914 (1986)). Changes are usually discussed in the periodical 'Immigration and Nationality Law and Practice'.

111. Instructions to immigration officers and medical inspectors. The Secretary of State may give instructions consistent with the Immigration Rules to immigration officers and medical inspectors[1]. These are unpublished, but are assumed to give guidance on the exercise of discretion, and their contents can occasionally be inferred[2].

1 Immigration Act 1971 (c 77), s 4(2), Sch 2, para 1(3).
2 Thus, eg, changes in the treatment of returning residents were inferred in 1979: see L Grant and I Martin *Immigration Law and Practice* (1982) p 163, note 7. Extracts appear in *Immigration Control Procedures: Report of a Formal Investigation* (1985, Commission for Racial Equality) paras 3.1.2, 3.19.1. The periodical 'Immigration and Nationality Law and Practice' carries articles discussing the application of the law and the discretion under it. The instructions current in 1979 can be viewed at the office of the Joint Council for the Welfare of Immigrants.

112. Ministerial discretion. The Secretary of State has the power to decide cases 'outside the Rules'[1], and whether the Immigration Rules are clear or not[2].

The number and distribution of work permits is within the discretion of the Department of Employment, the criteria being published through leaflets, press releases, Written Answers to either House of Parliament etc[3]. The number and distribution of 'special vouchers' may be an exercise of the prerogative[4] and in any case proceeds according to largely unpublished rules[5]. Guidelines are occasionally issued as to how discretion will be exercised in other areas[6]. Amnesties for illegal entrants have been made twice.

Exercises of ministerial discretion are subject to judicial review, but few Scottish cases are reported[7].

1 See the Immigration Act 1971 (c 77), s 19(2). The power may be inferred from s 4(1), and may be inherent as an exercise of the prerogative. An example is 'authorisation' by the Secretary of State to remain after limited leave has expired, but which is not leave to remain as such: see para 146, note 8, below. For ad hoc examples, see eg *R v Secretary of State for the Home Department, ex parte Rajinder Kaur* [1987] Imm AR 278, DC, and *Mamon v Immigration Appeal Tribunal* [1988] Imm AR 364, CA.
2 *Pearson v Immigration Appeal Tribunal* [1978] Imm AR 212, CA.
3 See the Statement of Changes in Immigration Rules (HC Paper (1989–90) no. 251) (the Immigration Rules), para 34. Numbers to be issued are announced in Parliament.
4 *R v Secretary of State for the Home Department, ex parte Bhatti* (1982) 132 NLJ 743, CA.
5 See the Immigration Rules, para 49. Principles for distribution have been inferred: see L Grant and I Martin *Immigration Law and Practice* (1982) pp 44–47, and 'First Supplement' (1984) pp 29, 30. See also the Fifth Report from the Home Affairs Committee (HC Paper (1981–82) no. 90) (Immigration from the Indian Sub-Continent) and the government's reply (Cmnd 8725) (1982). As to refugees, see para 323 below.
6 Eg in relation to bringing a child to the United Kingdom for adoption (currently Circular RON 117 (D)): L Grant and I Martin *Immigration Law and Practice* (1982) p 163, note 7. These guidelines raised a legitimate expectation which could not be removed without an opportunity to make representations and after full and serious considerations as to whether there was an over-riding public interest in doing so: *R v Secretary of State for the Home Department, ex parte Khan* [1985] 1 All ER 40, [1984] 1 WLR 1337, [1984] Imm AR 68, CA.
7 Principles for judicial review in England were laid down in *R v Secretary of State for the Home Department, ex parte Swati* [1986] 1 All ER 717, [1986] 1 WLR 477, [1986] Imm AR 88, CA. The court declared that purely factual challenges should go through the normal appeal machinery,

and the judicial review was only available on 'Wednesbury principles'. See also *R v Secretary of State for the Home Department, ex parte Hindjou* [1989] Imm AR 24. Scottish judicial review cases includes *Kaur v Secretary of State for the Home Department* 1987 SCLR 550, OH; *Malhi v Secretary of State for Home Affairs* 1989 SLT 43, OH; *Mensah v Secretary of State for the Home Department* 1991 GWD 4-218, OH; *Singh v Secretary of State for the Home Department* 1991 GWD 9-547; *Saftar* 1991 GWD 15-940, OH.

113. Decisions of courts and tribunals. There is a specialised series of Immigration Appeal Reports published by Her Majesty's Stationery Office[1]. The great majority of cases have been decided in England.

1 Until 1986 very few immigration cases were reported, and there was heavy reliance upon unreported cases. Since then the Immigration Appeal Reports ('Imm AR') have been reasonably extensive and regular. Reference to unreported cases is eschewed here. The periodical 'Immigration and Nationality Law and Practice' carries brief notes on unreported cases.

(b) Community Law

114. Direct effect of Community law. Community law concerns immigration in so far as it enshrines the principles of free movement of persons and services[1]. The Immigration Act 1988 declares that leave to enter or remain is not required of any person exercising a relevant Community right or a right under any provision made by virtue of the European Communities Act 1972[2], and empowers the Secretary of State, by order, to give leave to enter for a limited period to any class of Community nationals with such a right[3].

The Immigration Rules provide a specific regime for Community nationals and their families. However, much of the relevant Community law has direct effect and must be applied by national courts in preference to inconsistent national law[4]. Inconsistent Immigration Rules and associated legislation have been held to contravene Community law and to that extent are inapplicable to Community nationals[5].

1 See the EEC Treaty, arts 48–66, the associated secondary legislation, and paras 221 ff below.
2 Ie under the European Communities Act 1972 (c 68), s 2(2): Immigration Act 1988 (c 14), s 7(1).
3 Immigration Act 1988, s 7(1), (2). No such order has yet been made.
4 Case 36/75 *Rutili v Minister for the Interior* [1975] ECR 1219, [1976] 1 CMLR 140, ECJ; Case 118/75 *Watson and Belmann* [1976] ECR 1185, [1976] 2 CMLR 552, ECJ; Case 157/79 *R v Pieck* [1980] ECR 2171, [1981] QB 571, [1981] 3 All ER 46, ECJ.
5 Case 157/79 *R v Pieck* [1980] ECR 2171, [1981] QB 571, [1981] 3 All ER 46, ECJ. The relevant Immigration Rules were changed as a result.

(c) International Law

115. The European Convention on Human Rights. The United Kingdom is a party to the European Convention on Human Rights[1], which requires parties to make their law conform to the principles of the Convention. Several of the rights and freedoms guaranteed by the Convention have had application in immigration cases, including article 3 (freedom from torture and inhuman and degrading treatment or punishment), article 5 (right to liberty and security of person), article 8 (right to respect for privacy and family life), article 12 (right of men and women of marriageable age to marry and found a family) and article 14 (freedom from discrimination in the enjoyment of rights and freedoms guaranteed by the Convention)[2]. A Protocol dealing with citizenship and guaranteeing a right to enter one's country of nationality has not been ratified by the United Kingdom[3]. The Convention is not mentioned in the legislation or the Immigration Rules.

The United Kingdom recognises the right of individual petition to the European Commission on Human Rights, and this has been used several times, notably in the *East African Asians* case[4] and the *Abdulaziz* case[5]. The last mentioned reached the European Court of Human Rights, and settlements have been achieved in several[6]. None directly affects United Kingdom law, but the *East African Asians* case was influential in the operation of the 'special voucher' scheme, and the *Abdulaziz* case also caused changes in the Immigration Rules[7]. Also the Secretary of State and immigration officers may take the Convention into account although they are not obliged to[8].

The European Court of Justice has held that the Convention applies to acts taken in derogation of the principle of free movement[9]. Thus it may be partly incorporated via Community law.

The House of Lords suggested that the Convention can be used as an aid in interpreting statute[10]. This view was unequivocally rejected in a deportation case before the Outer House[11]. It was held that the Convention is not part of Scots law, and further that a court was therefore not entitled to use it as an aid to construction or otherwise. It was also held that the principle *quod fieri debet infectum valet* (the government having failed to pass legislation required by the Convention) did not apply to give a remedy. That the Convention might be incorporated via Community law was not accepted on the facts, as there was no Community element in the case.

In England the courts have been more equivocal, but the Court of Appeal has generally set its face against any form of adoption[12].

1 Convention for the Protection of Human Rights and Fundamental Freedoms (Rome, 4 November 1950; TS 71 (1953); Cmd 8969).
2 For ibid, art 3, see HUMAN RIGHTS IN EUROPE, para 26 above; for art 5, see paras 29 ff above; for art 8, see paras 62 ff above; for art 12, see para 71 above, and for art 14, see paras 85, 86, above.
3 Protocol No 4 (Strasbourg, 16 September 1963; Misc 6 (1964); Cmnd 2309).
4 *East African Asians v United Kingdom* (1981) 3 EHRR 76, E Ct HR.
5 *Abdulaziz, Cabales and Balkandali v United Kingdom* (1985) 7 EHRR 471, E Ct HR. Other cases have included *Papayianni v United Kingdom* [1974] Imm AR 7; *Agee v Lord Advocate* 1977 SLT (Notes) 54; and *Kamal v United Kingdom* No 8378/78 (1980) 2 EHRR 244.
6 See eg *Uppal v United Kingdom* (1981) 3 EHRR 391.
7 See the Statement of Changes in Immigration Rules (HC Paper (1982–83) no. 169) (the Former Immigration Rules), paras 41–44, 46–49 (amended by HC Paper (1984–85) no. 503, paras 8–10, subject to savings in paras 27, 28, 30 (all revoked). See now the Statement of Changes in Immigration Rules (HC Paper (1989–90) no. 251) (the Immigration Rules), paras 47, 48, 50, 51.
8 See in respect of the Secretary of State *Fernandez v Secretary of State for the Home Department* [1981] Imm AR 1, CA (reaffirmed in *R v Immigration Appeal Tribunal, ex parte Chundawadra* [1988] Imm AR 161, CA), and in respect of immigration officers *R v Chief Immigration Officer, Heathrow Airport, ex parte Salamat Bibi* [1976] 3 All ER 843, [1976] 1 WLR 979, CA (doubted in a related issue in *R v Secretary of State for the Home Department, ex parte Hosenball* [1977] 3 All ER 452, [1977] 1 WLR 776, CA).
9 Case 36/75 *Rutili v Minister for the Interior* [1975] ECR 1219, [1976] 1 CMLR 140, ECJ. See also HUMAN RIGHTS IN EUROPE, para 9 above.
10 *Waddington v Miah* [1974] 2 All ER 377, [1974] 1 WLR 683, HL.
11 *Kaur v Lord Advocate* 1980 SC 319, 1981 SLT 322, OH. See also HUMAN RIGHTS IN EUROPE, para 8 above.
12 *R v Chief Immigration Officer, Heathrow Airport, ex parte Salamat Bibi* [1976] 3 All ER 843, [1976] 1 WLR 979, CA; *R v Immigration Appeal Tribunal, ex parte Ali Ajmal* [1982] Imm AR 102, CA.

116. Other international law obligations. Various international conventions have a bearing on immigration including the Universal Declaration of

Human Rights[1], the International Convention on the Elimination of all Forms of Discrimination[2], the International Covenant on Civil and Political Rights[3], and the Convention on the Status of Refugees[4]. International Labour Organisation Resolutions may also apply, and international customary law may create obligations[5]. None of these obligations has direct effect, but the Immigration Rules require full account to be taken of the Convention on the Status of Refugees[6].

1 Universal Declaration of Human Rights (Paris, 10 December 1948; UN 2 (1949); Cmd 7662): see HUMAN RIGHTS IN EUROPE, para 4 above. For the text see *Basic Documents on Human Rights* (3rd edn, 1983, ed I Brownlie) p 250.
2 International Convention on the Elimination of All Forms of Racial Discrimination (New York, 7 March 1966; TS 77 (1969); Cmnd 4108). For the text see *Brownlie* p 302.
3 International Covenant on Civil and Political Rights with Optional Protocol (New York, 19 December 1966; TS 6 (1977); Cmnd 6702). For the text see *Brownlie* p 270.
4 Convention relating to the Status of Refugees (Geneva, 28 July 1951; TS 39 (1954); Cmd 9171) and Protocol relating to the Status of Refugees (New York, 31 January 1967; TS 15 (1969); Cmnd 3906).
5 See eg L Oppenheim *International Law* (8th edn, 1955) vol 1, pp 645, 646; R Plender *International Migration Law* (2nd rev edn, 1988); G S Goodwin-Gill *International Law and the Movement of Persons Between States* (1978). See also *R v Secretary of State for the Home Department, ex parte Thakrar* [1974] QB 684, [1974] 2 All ER 261.
6 Statement of Changes in Immigration Rules (HC Paper (1989–90) no. 251) (the Immigration Rules), paras 21, 75, 140, 161, 173.

(3) RIGHT OF ABODE

117. Meaning of 'right of abode'. The right of abode denotes the freedom to come and go into, and from, the United Kingdom without let or hindrance except such as may be required under and in accordance with the Immigration Act 1971 to enable the right to be established or as may be otherwise lawfully imposed[1]. (This last includes exclusion orders under the Prevention of Terrorism (Temporary Provisions) Act 1989[2] and, in the case of those not British citizens, 'hostage' orders and 'safety' orders[3].) One form of temporary residence permit for Community nationals is also, confusingly, referred to as a 'right of abode'[4].

The right of abode is to be distinguished from indefinite leave to enter or remain, and 'settlement'[5].

1 Immigration Act 1971 (c 77), s 1(1).
2 See the Prevention of Terrorism (Temporary Provisions) Act 1989 (c 4), ss 5(4), 6(4), 7(4), and para 117 below.
3 As to 'hostage' and 'safety' orders, see para 217 below.
4 See EC Council Directive 73/148 (OJ L172, 28.6.73, p 14), art 4(2), and para 230 below.
5 See para 120 below.

118. Who has the right of abode. All British citizens, and those Commonwealth citizens who are not British citizens but who immediately before the commencement of the British Nationality Act 1981 had a right of abode under the appropriate provisions of the Immigration Act 1971[1] have the right of abode[2]. The former category of 'patrials' no longer exists[3]. A person asserting British citizenship bears the burden of proof[4], and a person claiming the right of abode must prove his right of entry by either producing a United Kingdom passport describing him as a British citizen or citizen of the United Kingdom and Colonies with the right of abode, or by producing a certificate of settlement[5].

Special provisions apply in respect of persons exercising Community rights and nationals of member states[6].

1 Ie under the Immigration Act 1971 (c 77), s 2(1)(d) or s 2(2), as then in force: see note 2 below.

2 Ibid, s 2(1) (substituted by the British Nationality Act 1981 (c 61), s 39(2)). Commonwealth citizens who had the right of abode under the Immigration Act 1971, s 2(1)(d) (as originally enacted), before the commencement of the 1981 Act were those born to or legally adopted by a parent who at the time was a citizen of the United Kingdom and Colonies by birth in the United Kingdom or Islands.

    Commonwealth citizens who had the right of abode under the Immigration Act 1971, s 2(2) (as originally enacted), before the commencement of the 1981 Act were those married to a man who had a right of abode himself, or who had been married to such a man, or who had been married to a man who was a British subject and would, but for his death, have been on the commencement of the British Nationality Act 1948 (c 56) a citizen of the United Kingdom and Colonies by his birth, adoption, naturalisation or registration in the United Kingdom or Islands or by his birth to or legal adoption by a parent who held that citizenship by one of those means (except for a woman registered as a citizen by virtue of s 6(2) of the 1948 Act unless registered by virtue of marriage to a citizen before the passing of the 1971 Act) or that parent's birth to or adoption by a parent who at that time had that citizenship.

    The Immigration Act 1988 (c 14) prevents certain polygamous wives and widows from exercising their right of abode in order to enter the United Kingdom (see s 2), or from obtaining a certificate of entitlement under the Immigration Act 1971 (see s 3(9) (substituted by the Immigration Act 1988, s 3(1))). Those affected are defined with some complexity. Essentially, they are those who:

(1) have the right of abode because they are Commonwealth citizens who are or were married to a man with a right of abode; and

(2) are polygamously or potentially polygamously married to that man; and

(3) have not been in the United Kingdom between the marriage and 1 August 1988; and

(4) have a co-wife or co-widow who has entered the United Kingdom (other than as a visitor or as an illegal entrant) or has been granted a certificate of entitlement:

see the Immigration Act 1988, s 2(1)–(3), and the Immigration Act 1988 (Commencement No 1) Order 1988, SI 1988/1133, art 3(2).

    A wife or widow who had already entered the United Kingdom since the marriage, but at a time when there was no co-wife, is unaffected: Immigration Act 1988, s 2(4). The provision does not affect those who are British citizens (so have the right of abode in their own right), nor the children of polygamous marriages, except in so far as they enter as dependants. Nor does it actually remove the right of abode of those it does affect, but merely declares that the Immigration Act 1971 applies to them as it applies to a person not having a right of abode: Immigration Act 1988, s 2(3). It is thought that very few women are covered by the provision.

    The right of abode is statutory and cannot be acquired by exercise of discretion, and nor can estoppel, or in Scotland, personal bar apply: *Christodoulidou v Secretary of State for the Home Department* [1985] Imm AR 179, IAT (distinguishing *R v Secretary of State for the Home Department, ex parte Ram* [1979] 1 All ER 687, [1979] 1 WLR 148, DC).

    As to British subjects, Commonwealth citizens and citizenship of the United Kingdom and Colonies, see NATIONALITY AND CITIZENSHIP, vol 14, paras 1906 ff.

3 'Patrial' was a term first used in 1629 (according to the Shorter Oxford English Dictionary) and revived by the Immigration Act 1971, s 2 (as originally enacted), and described those with the right of abode, a term invented by that Act: see para 117 above. Those who were patrial retain the right of abode.

4 Immigration Act 1971, s 3(8) (amended by the British Nationality Act 1981, s 39(6), Sch 4, para 2). See also *R v Secretary of State for the Home Department, ex parte Phansopkar* [1976] QB 606, [1975] 3 All ER 497, CA; *R v Secretary of State for the Home Department, ex parte Parvaz Akhtar* [1981] 1 QB 46, [1980] 2 All ER 735, CA. A person erroneously assumed to be a British citizen requires leave to enter, so if admitted, is an illegal entrant: *Mokuola and Ogunbiyi v Secretary of State for the Home Department* [1989] Imm AR 51, CA; *Re Bamgbose* [1990] Imm AR 135, CA. As to British citizenship, see vol 14, paras 1906 ff.

5 Immigration Act 1971, s 3(9) (substituted by the Immigration Act 1988, s 3(1)). As to certificates of entitlement and proof of right of abode, see para 153 below.

6 See para 114 above, and para 137 below.

(4) LEAVE TO ENTER OR REMAIN

(a) Introduction

119. Leave to enter and leave to remain. All those without a right of abode (unless exempted[1]) require permission to live, work or settle, and are subject to regulation and control of entry, stay and departure imposed by the Immigration Act 1971[2] (subject always to Community law[3]). Such a person may require entry clearance or other permission before entry[4], and specifically requires leave to enter[5] unless exempted[6]. Leave to enter may be given for an indefinite or limited period[7] and, if limited, may be subject to conditions restricting employment and requiring registration with the police[8]. It is normally given for a limited period[9]. Also the Secretary of State is accepted as able to give 'authorisation' (which is not leave to remain) outside the Immigration Rules to a person in the United Kingdom whose limited leave has expired. This renders his presence lawful (but does not preclude a decision to make a deportation order)[10]. A person requiring leave may be deported on specified grounds[11].

Leave to enter may be varied by extending[12] or restricting its duration, by adding, varying or revoking conditions, or by removing the time limit (which thereby cancels any other conditions)[13], and in the case of a person who has already entered, is referred to as 'leave to remain'[14].

In the case of limited leave, the limitation and any conditions may be imposed so that they will apply to any subsequent leave obtained after a temporary absence within the duration of that leave[15].

This creates no entitlement to re-entry, since leave lapses by departure outwith the common travel area (with one exception)[16]. A person requiring leave to enter is thus subject to control upon return after any departure (other than in the exceptional case)[17]. Those whose previous leave was limited who do seek re-entry, should be dealt with in the light of all relevant circumstances. The same time limits and conditions will continue unless it is decided to supersede them and deal with the person as a new arrival[18]. Those whose previous leave was indefinite are dealt with below[19].

Leave to enter or remain will not normally be given to a person who does not satisfy the conditions for one of the categories of the Immigration Rules[20]. It is also subject to the Prevention of Terrorism Act 1989[21].

Leave obtained by deception may be invalid[22].

Leave to enter is to be distinguished from 'temporary admission'[23].

---

1 See generally para 117 above. Exemption is possible under the Immigration Act 1971 (c 77), ss 8, 9: see paras 128–132 below. A prisoner in the United Kingdom under a warrant to give evidence or be identified or otherwise assist in an investigation in the United Kingdom of an offence, is not subject to the Immigration Act 1971 while the warrant subsists: see the Criminal Justice (International Co-operation) Act 1990 (c 5), s 6(1), (6). As to Community nationals, see paras 221 ff below.

2 Immigration Act 1971, s 1(2).

3 See ibid, s 7, and para 114 above, and paras 221 ff below.

4 See the Statement of Changes in Immigration Rules (HC Paper (1989–90) no. 251) (the Immigration Rules), paras 14–17, 34, 35, 49, and paras 150 ff below.

5 See the Immigration Act 1971, s 3(1), and paras 119 ff below.

6 See ibid, ss 8–10, Sch 4, and para 128 below.

7 Ibid, s 3(1)(b).

8 See the Immigration Act 1971, ss 3(1)(c), 4(3) and the Immigration (Registration with Police) Regulations 1972, SI 1972/1758 (amended by SI 1976/2018, SI 1981/534, SI 1982/502, SI 1982/1024, SI 1983/442, and SI 1990/400). Currently the power is exercised only in relation to aliens.

9 Immigration Rules, para 11. As to 'codes' used on passport stamps, see para 170, notes 2, 13, above.

10 *R v Secretary of State for the Home Department, ex parte Subramaniam* [1977] QB 190, [1976] 1 All ER 915, [1976] Imm AR 155, CA; *Suthendran v Immigration Appeal Tribunal* [1977] AC 359, [1976] 3 All ER 611, [1977] Imm AR 44, HL; *Muhammad Idrish v Secretary of State for the Home Department* [1985] Imm AR 155, IAT.

11 See the Immigration Act 1971, ss 3(5), (6), 6, Sch 3, and paras 202 ff below.

12 Extension of leave does not have to be mentioned explicitly: *R v Immigration Appeal Tribunal, ex parte Ahluwalia* [1979–80] Imm AR 1, DC.

13 See the Immigration Act 1971, s 3(3)(a), and the Immigration Rules, para 11, and Pt XI (paras 94–154).

14 Immigration Act 1971, s 3(1)(b).

15 Ibid, s 3(3)(b) (amended by the Immigration Act 1988 (c 14), s 10, Schedule, para 1, as from 16 May 1991: see the Immigration Act 1988 (Commencement No 2) Order 1991, SI 1991/1001). See also the Immigration Rules, para 60. 'Re-entry visas' are no longer required of visa nationals returning to the United Kingdom during periods granted on an earlier occasion, provided that leave was for more than six months: see para 14, Appendix (amended and substituted by the Statement of Changes in Immigration Rules (HC Paper 1990–91), no. 356).

16 Immigration Act 1971, s 3(4). This provision commonly creates difficulties for the unwary: see para 176, notes 2, 3, below. See also *Ghassemian and Mirza v The Home Office* [1989] Imm AR 42, CA. The exception is in the case of certain seamen and aircrew: Immigration Act 1971, s 8(1), and para 129 below. As to common travel areas, see para 122 below.

17 See the Immigration Rules, para 60. However, see also the Immigration Act 1971, s 3(3)(b) (as amended: see note 15 above), and para 176, notes 2, 3, below.

18 Immigration Rules, para 60. However, see the Immigration Act 1971, s 3 (as so amended), and para 176, notes 2, 3, below.

19 See paras 120, 176, below.

20 See the Immigration Rules, para 78, and paras 171, 172, below.

21 See paras 133, 134, below.

22 *Khawaja v Secretary of State for the Home Department* [1984] AC 74, [1983] 1 All ER 765, [1982] Imm AR 139, HL. It may be that deception not known of by the person does not invalidate leave: *Rahim Miah v Secretary of State for the Home Department* [1989] Imm AR 559, CA. However, see *Mokuola and Ogunbiyi v Secretary of State for the Home Department* [1989] Imm AR 51, CA. As to leave given by mistake, see *Tejpartap Singh Rehal v Secretary of State for the Home Department* [1989] Imm AR 576, CA.

23 See paras 146, 169, below.

120. Indefinite leave to enter or to remain and 'settlement'. Indefinite leave to enter or remain, that is leave without restriction on the period for which the person may remain, may be given[1]. In such cases, no other conditions may be imposed. The person, though without a right of abode, and still subject to immigration control, is free to stay, work, leave and re-enter (unless absent for over two years, or assisted to leave with public funds)[2]. He is not, however, exempt from deportation[3].

A person with indefinite leave who is ordinarily resident is said to be 'settled' if he did not enter or remain in breach of the immigration laws, or, if he did, subsequently entered lawfully or has been lawfully granted leave to remain[4].

Departure outwith the common travel area nullifies indefinite leave[5]. However, a person who received indefinite leave, returning within two years, will normally be admitted as a 'returning resident'[6]. A longer period may possibly be accepted considering all the relevant circumstances, including having spent most of his life in the United Kingdom. A British Overseas citizen holding a United Kingdom passport will normally be admitted as a 'returning resident'[7].

In any case a British Dependent Territories citizen, British National (Overseas), British Overseas citizen, British protected person or in some cases a British subject[8] holding a United Kingdom passport issued in the United Kingdom or the Republic of Ireland, before 1 April 1973, should be freely admitted unless his passport is endorsed to show he is subject to immigration control[9].

1 Immigration Act 1971 (c 77), s 3(1)(b) (amended by the British Nationality Act 1981 (c 61), s 39(6), Sch 4, para 2). Where the date stamp on a passport was illegible, it was conceded that

since it was not possible to determine the period of leave, indefinite leave has been granted in accordance with the 1971 Act, Sch 2, para 6(1) (as amended), despite evidence that limited leave was intended: *Secretary of State for the Home Department v Mansour and Mansour* [1985] Imm AR 1, IAT. However, see now the effect of the Immigration Act 1971, Sch 2, para 6(1) (as further amended by the Immigration Act 1988 (c 14), s 10, Schedule, para 8(1), (3)). As to deception, see the cases cited in para 119, note 22, above.

2 As to returning residents, see the Statement of Changes in Immigration Rules (HC Paper (1989–90) no. 251) (the Immigration Rules), paras 58, 59, and para 176 below.

3 See the Immigration Act 1971, ss 3(5), (6), 5(1), (4), and paras 126, 202 ff below.

4 See the Immigration Act 1971, s 33(2A) (added by the British Nationality Act 1981, Sch 4, para 7), and the Immigration Rules, para 1. See also *Agyen-Frempong v Immigration Appeal Tribunal* [1988] Imm AR 262, CA. The somewhat different meanings attached to the word 'settlement' by different parts of the Immigration Rules were discussed by the Court of Appeal in *Bibi and Purvez v Immigration Appeal Tribunal* [1988] Imm AR 298, CA. For the purposes of settlement of a spouse, a person in HM Forces stationed in the United Kingdom, but serving abroad, is regarded as present and settled in the United Kingdom: Immigration Rules, para 50, note.

   'Ordinarily resident', the meaning of which is modified by the Immigration Act 1971, s 33(2), was discussed and effectively defined by the House of Lords in *Shah v Barnet London Borough Council* [1983] 2 AC 309, [1983] 1 All ER 226, HL.

5 Immigration Act 1971, s 3(4).

6 See the Immigration Rules, paras 58–60. Those who received public funds to leave are ineligible: para 58. Where a person has been treated as settled only by virtue of an earlier deception of which he was ignorant, it appears that para 78 is sufficient to permit the immigration officer to refuse entry.

7 Ibid, para 9.

8 The meaning of 'British subject' is restricted by the British Nationality Act 1981, Pt IV (ss 30–35), to the category previously known as 'British subjects without citizenship' (including those claiming such status under the British Nationality Act 1948 (c 56), s 2(1) (repealed)). The case in which such a person is enabled to take advantage of the rule is that of those referred to in the British Nationality Act 1981, s 30(a), ie those who were aliens and registered as British subjects without citizenship (or cognate category) under the British Nationality Act 1965 (c 34), s 1, on marriage to a man who has such status. The power to register still exists under the British Nationality Act 1981, s 33, but those registering after its commencement cannot, *semble*, take advantage of the rule. For more detail, see NATIONALITY AND CITIZENSHIP, vol 14, para 1950.

   The category of British Nationals (Overseas) was created by the Hong Kong (British Nationality) Order 1986, SI 1986/948: see vol 14, paras 1946–1949. As to the meaning of 'British Dependent Territories citizen', 'British Overseas citizen' and 'British protected person', see vol 14, paras 1932 ff.

9 Immigration Rules, para 9.

121. 'Settlement', naturalisation and registration as a citizen. 'Settlement'[1] as such does not affect nationality. For many immigrants 'settlement' is a satisfactory status for long-term or permanent residence. The possibility of deportation remains[2] but is, under current legislation, a remote one for most of those 'settled'. Rights attaching to citizenship, such as the franchise[3], and entitlement to a passport are not acquired by 'settlement'. However, the relevant citizenship for such purposes is normally Commonwealth citizenship[3], which is held by British Dependent Territories citizens, British Overseas citizens, British Nationals (Overseas), British subjects (without citizenship) and citizens of all independent Commonwealth countries as well as British citizens[4]. Thus such rights are held by those citizens present in the country irrespective of their immigration status.

The position in relation to passports is more complicated since passports for British citizens, British Dependent Territories citizens, British Overseas citizens, British Nationals (Overseas) and British subjects (without citizenship) are all in some sense 'British' passports, while those of other independent Commonwealth countries are not[5]. Certainly, however, a person becoming 'settled' acquires no rights to a passport from the United Kingdom government thereby.

Also an advantage of 'settlement' over naturalisation as a citizen is that the country of nationality or origin may require relinquishment of its nationality upon acquisition of another (as the United Kingdom does not). 'Settlement' is a precondition for naturalisation in the case of the United Kingdom (together with requirements of recent actual residence, good character, relevant language and lack of breach of immigration laws)[6]. Naturalisation is, however, at the discretion of the Secretary of State[7].

Apart from acquisition by naturalisation, citizenship can be acquired by registration in certain cases. 'Settlement' is a precondition of some of these forms[8], but not all[9].

1 As to the meaning of 'settlement', see para 120, note 4, above.
2 See para 120, note 3, above.
3 See eg the Representation of the People Act 1983 (c2), s 1(1), and ELECTIONS.
4 As to these forms of citizenship, see generally NATIONALITY AND CITIZENSHIP, vol 14, paras 1906 ff.
5 See PASSPORTS.
6 As to naturalisation, see the British Nationality Act 1981 (c61), ss 6, 18, Sch 1, especially paras 1–4, and vol 14, paras 1920, 1921, 1937. Requirements vary somewhat depending upon whether the applicant is married to a citizen, and whether British citizenship or British Dependent Territories citizenship is sought.
7 See ibid, s 6, and vol 14, paras 1922, 1923.
8 See ibid, s 4 (see vol 14, para 1914) and vicariously s 1(3)(a) (second limb).
9 As to citizenship by registration, see vol 14, paras 1912 ff.

(b) Common Travel Area

122. 'Local journeys' exempted from immigration control. The United Kingdom, the Channel Islands, the Isle of Man, and the Republic of Ireland are collectively referred to as 'the common travel area'[1]. The Secretary of State, by statutory instrument, may exclude the Republic of Ireland from the area for any reason specified in the instrument, and any of the Islands if it appears to him necessary by reason of differences of immigration laws[2]. Travel within the area on a 'local journey' is not subject to control, so leave is not normally required, except in relation to any place excluded[3]. 'Local journey' is defined as one beginning and ending within the area, on a ship or aircraft beginning and ending its voyage within the area, having called at no place outside it[4].

There are exceptional cases. A person may be subject to an exclusion order under the Prevention of Terrorism (Temporary Provisions) Act 1989 (c4)[5]. A person seeking entry on a local journey who is not a British citizen may, subject to Schedule 4 of the Immigration Act 1971, be refused, if refused entry in the past, and not subsequently given leave to enter or remain, or if given on arrival written notice that the Secretary of State has issued directions that his exclusion is conducive to the public good in the interests of national security[6]. A person arriving in the United Kingdom will be refused entry if there is reason to believe he intends to enter another part of the area and is not acceptable to the immigration authorities there[7].

In the case of those entering the United Kingdom on local journeys, having entered the common travel area from outside it, special rules of considerable complexity apply[8]. They also apply to those who received leave to enter the United Kingdom, but whose leave expired while elsewhere in the common travel area[8].

The position of the Channel Islands in relation to the European Community raises further questions[9].

1 See the Statement of Changes in Immigration Rules (HC Paper (1989–90) no. 251) (the Immigration Rules), para 12; and the Immigration Act 1971 (c 77), ss 1(3), 11(4).
2 See the Immigration Act 1971, s 9(5)–(7) (amended by the British Nationality Act 1981 (c 61), s 52(8), Sch 9).
3 Immigration Rules, para 12.
4 Immigration Act 1971, s 11(4).
5 See para 134 below.
6 Immigration Act 1971, s 9(4) (amended by the British Nationality Act 1981, s 39(6), Sch 4, para 2).
7 Immigration Rules, para 12.
8 See the Immigration Act 1971, s 9(2) (as amended: see note 6 above), and the Immigration (Control of Entry through Republic of Ireland) Order 1972, SI 1972/1610 (amended by SI 1979/730, SI 1980/1859, 1982/1028, SI 1985/1854, and SI 1987/2092), and para 124 below.
9 See para 220 below.

123. Entry to the United Kingdom via the Channel Islands or the Isle of Man. The Immigration Act 1971 is extended, with exceptions, adaptations and modifications, to the Islands[1], and control is thereby in part delegated[2]. Some independent local legislation exists[3]. This involves control over those with a right of abode, and is not affected by section 1(1) of the Immigration Act 1971 since that applies only to the United Kingdom.

If a person's presence in any of the Islands is unlawful, he requires leave to enter the United Kingdom[4]. In other cases, where a person has been given leave to enter or remain in any of the Islands, or has been refused leave, then if he is not a British citizen, the leave or refusal has effect as if given or made in the United Kingdom[5]. Limited leave given in any of the Islands subject to conditions which could be imposed in the United Kingdom[6] is treated as if given by notice on arrival in the United Kingdom[7]. Any such leave may be varied or revoked in relation to the United Kingdom as if given under the Act (and takes effect as if so given *ab initio*) and is similarly subject to appeal[8]. No right of appeal is thereby given in the United Kingdom against a decision taken in any of the Islands[9]. If during an absence from the United Kingdom the person has required leave to enter the Islands, his leave to enter the United Kingdom lapses[10].

The power exists to impose restrictions and conditions upon those entering the United Kingdom from the Islands on a local journey having come from outside the common travel area, or whose limited leave to remain in the United Kingdom expires while in any of the Islands, if such person is neither a British citizen nor covered by Schedule 4 of the Act[11].

A deportation order under the immigration laws of any of the Islands has effect as if made under the Act if the person is not a British citizen[12]. However, the Secretary of State may direct that such an order does not apply, and in any case such an order will not prevent entry to the United Kingdom from that island[13].

Subject to the general requirements of Schedule 4 of the Act, a person refused leave to enter or remain in the United Kingdom (and not subsequently granted leave), or who is given on arrival written notice of the directions of the Secretary of State that his exclusion is conducive to the public good in the interests of national security, requires leave to enter the United Kingdom[14].

1 'The Islands' means the Channel Islands and the Isle of Man: Immigration Act 1971 (c 77), s 33(1).
2 Ibid, s 36. See also the Immigration (Guernsey) Order 1972, SI 1972/1719 (amended by SI 1982/1834 and SI 1983/1897); the Immigration (Jersey) Order 1972, SI 1972/1813 (amended by SI 1982/1836, SI 1984/1690 and SI 1989/488); and the Immigration (Isle of Man) Order 1991, SI 1991/2630.
3 See the Loi sur les Etrangers 1973 (Jersey); the Housing (Jersey) Law 1949; the Housing (General Provisions) (Jersey) Regulations 1970; and the Control of Employment Act 1975 (Isle of Man).

4 Immigration Act 1971, s 9(1), Sch 4, para 4 (amended by the British Nationality Act 1981 (c 61), s 39(6), Sch 4, para 2).

5 Immigration Act 1971, Sch 4, para 1(1) (as so amended).

6 Ie under ibid, s 3(1): see para 119 above.

7 Ibid, Sch 4, para 1(2) (as amended: see note 4 above).

8 Ibid, Sch 4, para 1(3), (4).

9 Ibid, Sch 4, para 1(5).

10 Ibid, Sch 4, para 2.

11 Ibid, s 9(2) (as amended: see note 4 above). At the date at which this volume states the law, no order has been made.

12 Ibid, Sch 4, para 3(1) (as so amended).

13 Ibid, Sch 4, para 3(2).

14 Ibid, s 9(4)(a).

124. Entry to the United Kingdom via the Republic of Ireland. A person other than a British citizen, entering the United Kingdom on a local journey, having entered the Republic of Ireland from outside the common travel area, or whose limited leave to enter or remain in the United Kingdom has lapsed while in another part of the area, is subject to such restrictions on time and conditions on employment and registration with the police as are imposed by statutory instrument[1]. The instrument imposes a particular regime upon certain people who might broadly be termed 'doubtful cases'. They are:

(1) those (not being citizens of the Republic) arriving by aircraft from the Republic, but who started the journey outside the area and received no leave to land in the Republic[2]; and

(2) those on a local journey from the Republic, satisfying any of four conditions:

    (a) being a visa national with no valid United Kingdom visa;

    (b) having entered the Republic unlawfully from outside the area;

    (c) having entered the Republic after having unlawfully entered the United Kingdom and Islands, or having overstayed limited leave to enter or remain there, but in neither case having subsequently received leave; and

    (d) being a person in respect of whom the Secretary of State has given directions that exclusion is conducive to the public good[3].

Such people require leave to enter as they are treated as if not arriving in the United Kingdom on a local journey within the common travel area[4].

Subject to exceptions, certain other people not 'doubtful cases' are admitted for specified periods, but without permission to engage in any occupation for reward or employment. These are those who (having no right of abode, nor being citizens of the Republic, and not already covered by the Order or the Immigration Act 1971[5]) enter the United Kingdom on a local journey having either entered the Republic from outside the common travel area (in which case the period is three months), or whose limited leave to enter or remain in the United Kingdom expired while outside the United Kingdom (in which case the period is seven days)[6]. The exceptions are that those who are Community nationals may engage in an occupation for reward or employment (subject to transitional arrangements still in effect for the nationals of Spain and Portugal)[7], and those who are visa nationals whose visa contains the words 'short visit' are admitted for one month of entering from outside the area instead of three months (the seven-day period remaining unchanged)[8].

These restrictions and conditions are automatic and no application for leave to enter is required, but appeal is available[9]. They may be varied and appeal against refusal is possible[10].

In the case of Community nationals, the limitation of time to three months is not of itself in contravention of Community law, since it applies to all such nationals, not just those coming to pursue economic activities. In the case of Community nationals coming for such purposes they fall under the general regulation in respect of that category rather than that of the common travel area[11]. Indeed the municipal law is presumably to that extent repealed by Community law[11].

1 See the Immigration Act 1971 (c 77), s 9(2) (amended by the British Nationality Act 1981 (c 61), s 39(6), Sch 4, para 2), and the Immigration (Control of Entry through Republic of Ireland) Order 1972, SI 1972/1610 (amended by SI 1979/730, SI 1980/1859, 1982/1028, SI 1985/1854 and SI 1987/2092).
2 Ibid, art 3(1)(a).
3 Ibid, art 3(1)(b)(i)–(iv) (amended by SI 1970/730). For the meaning of 'visa national', see para 151 below.
4 Ibid, art 3(2).
5 Ie the Immigration (Control of Entry through Republic of Ireland) Order 1972, art 3, and the Immigration Act 1971, s 9(4) (see para 122 above): Immigration (Control of Entry through Republic of Ireland) Order 1972, art 4(2).
6 Ibid, art 4(1), (3), (4), (7) (amended by SI 1980/1859, SI 1982/1028, SI 1985/1854 and SI 1987/2092).
7 Ibid, art 4(4)(b), (c) (amended by SI 1980/1859, SI 1985/1854 and SI 1987/2092). The transitional arrangements end on 1 January 1993: Treaty of Accession (1985) (Cmnd 9634).
8 Ibid, art 4(5)–(7). See also the Immigration Act 1971, s 9(4), and para 122 above. For the meaning of 'visa national', see para 151 below.
9 Ibid, s 9(2), (3) (as amended: see note 1 above).
10 Ibid, s 9(3).
11 See para 114 above, and paras 137, 221 ff below.

(c) Groups Subject to Immigration Control but with Protected Status

125. Commonwealth citizens with protected rights of entry. Commonwealth citizens settled on 1 January 1973 and their wives and dependent children are not exempted from control, but the Immigration Rules were until 1988 required to be so drafted that the freedom of such persons to enter and leave the United Kingdom was not less than it was under the previous law[1]. This preserved the right of a settled Commonwealth citizen man to bring in, without submitting to the test of proving adequate maintenance and accommodation, his wife and his children under sixteen years of age who might remain indefinitely and work[2]. This right has now been removed, except in respect of wives and children whose entry clearance was applied for before 1 August 1988[3]. The right, in so far as it remains, can be lost by being away from the United Kingdom for more than two years although a person who has lived in the United Kingdom for most of his life, and others, may be admitted thereafter[4].

1 Immigration Act 1971 (c 77), s 1(5) (repealed with savings: see note 3 below). This provision was brought into force on 1 January 1973: see s 35(1), and the Immigration Act 1971 (Commencement) Order 1972, SI 1972/1514. See also *R v Immigration Appeal Tribunal, ex parte Ruhul Amin, R v Immigration Appeal Tribunal, ex parte Rahman, R v Immigration Appeal Tribunal, ex parte Haque* [1987] 3 All ER 705, [1987] 1 WLR 1538, [1987] Imm AR 587, CA; *Secretary of State for the Home Department v Zalihe Huseyin* [1988] Imm AR 129, CA; and *Agyen-Frempong v Immigration Appeal Tribunal* [1988] Imm AR 262, CA. 'Wives' does not include husbands: *Bahadur Singh v Immigration Appeal Tribunal* [1988] Imm AR 582, CA.
2 Commonwealth Immigrants Act 1962 (c 21), s 2(2) (amended by the Commonwealth Immigrants Act 1968 (c 9), s 2) (both repealed). Cf the Statement of Changes in Immigration Rules (HC Paper (1982–83) no. 169) (the Former Immigration Rules) para 48 (saved by the Statement of Changes in Immigration Rules (HC Paper (1984–85) no. 503) paras 10, 26) (both revoked).
3 See the Immigration Act 1971, s 1(5) (repealed with savings: see the Immigration Act 1988 (c 14), s 1, and the Immigration Act 1988 (Commencement No 1) Order 1988, SI 1988/1133, art 3(1)).

4 Statement of Changes in Immigration Rules (HC Paper (1989–90) no. 251) (the Immigration Rules), paras 58, 59.

126. Commonwealth citizens and citizens of the Republic of Ireland protected against deportation. Commonwealth citizens and citizens of the Republic of Ireland having such status and being ordinarily resident on 1 January 1973 cannot be deported if ordinarily resident for the last five years:

(1) preceding a decision to deport[1] (which is a question of fact and may differ from the date of notice[2]) in the cases of deportation[3] for the following:

    (a) breach of conditions of limited leave to enter or remain;

    (b) where the Secretary of State deems it conducive to the public good; and

    (c) where the person is a member of the family of a person ordered to be deported[4]; or

(2) preceding a recommendation for deportation by a court[5].

Time spent in breach of immigration laws does not count as ordinary residence, and periods of imprisonment or detention imposed on conviction for six months or more do not count towards the last five years[6]. It is for the person concerned to prove exemption[7].

While exempt from deportation, such a person is not exempt from the requirement of leave to enter, should he leave voluntarily and wish to return.

1 *Mehmet v Secretary of State for the Home Department* [1977] Imm AR 68, CA.
2 *Rehman v Secretary of State for the Home Department* [1978] Imm AR 80, IAT.
3 Immigration Act 1971 (c 77), s 7(1)(b). As more than five years have elapsed since 1 January 1973, s 7(1)(b) now incorporates s 7(1)(a).
4 See ibid, s 3(5)(a)–(c), and the Statement of Changes in Immigration Rules (HC Paper (1989–90) no. 251) (the Immigration Rules), para 155.
5 See the Immigration Act 1971, s 7(1)(c), applying s 3(6), and the Immigration Rules, para 155.
6 Immigration Act 1971, s 7(2)–(4).
7 Ibid, s 7(5), applying s 3(8).

127. Children born in the United Kingdom who are not British citizens. It is possible since the British Nationality Act 1981 for children, although born in the United Kingdom, not thereby to acquire a British nationality, and therefore to require leave to enter if they have left[1].

Before embarking, such a child under eighteen years of age and unmarried should[2], on application, be given (irrespective of the normal rules on maintenance and accommodation[3]) leave to remain for the same period as his parents, except in certain cases[4]. These are that if the parents have different periods, the child should receive the longer (unless the parents are separated, in which case he should receive the same as the parent with day-to-day responsibility), and that, if the child is to remain with a parent with a right of abode, or if he is in the care of a local authority, he should be given indefinite leave[5]. He may also be given leave under other provisions[6] of the Immigration Rules[7].

Such a child who wishes to re-enter and does not already have leave should be given (irrespective of the normal rules on maintenance and accommodation) leave for the same period as his parents if the immigration officer is satisfied that he was born in the United Kingdom and has not been away for more than two years and is coming with, or to join, parents, with the same exceptional cases[8]. Also, the child need have no entry clearance if travelling alone or with parents who need none, except in the case of a visa national[9]. If neither parent has current leave (nor right of abode) the child will be refused entry (except that if both parents are in fact in the United Kingdom and unlikely to be removed in the immediate future, and there is no person outside the United Kingdom who could reasonably be expected to look after him, he may be granted leave for a limited period)[10].

In all cases, 'parent' includes a step-parent where the natural parent is dead, and the father and mother of an illegitimate child, or, where there has been a genuine transfer of parental responsibility on the ground of the parents' inability to care for the child, another person[11].

1 See the British Nationality Act 1981 (c61), s1, and NATIONALITY AND CITIZENSHIP, vol14, para 1908.
2 Ie under the Statement of Changes in Immigration Rules (HC Paper (1989–90) no. 251) (the Immigration Rules), paras 61, 62, 133.
3 Ibid, para 135.
4 Ibid, para 134.
5 Ibid, paras 134, 136.
6 Ie under any paragraph of ibid, Section 2 (paras 94–180).
7 Ibid, para 137.
8 Ibid, paras 64, 65.
9 Ibid, para 64.
10 Ibid, para 67.
11 Ibid, paras 65, 134.

(d) Groups Exempted from Immigration Control

128. Introduction. Certain groups are specifically exempted from control by the Immigration Act 1971[1], and the Secretary of State has power to exempt, by order, any persons or classes of person, conditionally or otherwise, from all or any of the provisions of the Act which relate to those not British citizens[2]. Such persons, while having no leave to enter, appear to be 'authorised' in terms of the Immigration Rules[3]. If the order relates to a class, it is to be made by statutory instrument[4]. A person already holding limited leave to enter the United Kingdom who becomes entitled to an exemption continues to hold it if he later loses the exemption, unless it has expired meantime[5]. Presumably indefinite leave is, *a fortiori*, unaffected, and time spent in the United Kingdom exempted under an order may be regarded as spent settled if the order so provides[6]. However, time spent in the United Kingdom by virtue of an exemption under the former immigration laws corresponding to the current exemptions for certain diplomats[7], or as a member of a Commonwealth or other visiting force[8], is not to be regarded as time spent settled in the United Kingdom[9].

1 Ie under the Immigration Act 1971 (c77), s8: see paras 129ff below.
2 Ibid, s8(2) (amended by the British Nationality Act 1981 (c61), s39(6), Sch4, para2).
3 See para 112, note 1, para 119, note 10, above, and para 146, note 8, para 178, note 5, para 205, note 3, and para 211, note 4, below.
4 Immigration Act 1971, s8(2).
5 Ibid, s8(5).
6 Ibid, s8(5A) (added by the British Nationality Act 1981, s39(4)).
7 Ie under Immigration Act 1971, s8(3): see para 130 below.
8 Ie under ibid, s8(4)(b), (c): see para 131 below.
9 Ibid, s8(5) (amended by the British Nationality Act 1981, Sch4, para5).

129. Seamen and aircrew. A member of the crew of a ship or aircraft arriving in the United Kingdom but required, under engagement, to leave on that ship or within seven days on that or another aircraft, as a member of its crew, does not require leave to enter, and may enter until the ship or aircraft departs, except in three cases[1]. These are:
(1) where a deportation order is in force against him;
(2) where he has been refused leave to enter in the past (and not subsequently granted it); and

(3) where he is required to submit to examination[2] by an immigration officer[3]. Also, a member of the crew of an aircraft (but not a ship) already given leave to enter, and returning within the period for which he had leave as a crew member required under an engagement requiring him to leave within seven days, requires no leave unless falling within the same three exceptional cases (save that the second is expressed as excluding a person who has entered unlawfully and not subsequently been granted leave to enter or remain)[4].

Any Commonwealth citizen or British protected person holding a British seaman's card, or any citizen of the Republic of Ireland, who in either case was engaged as a member of the crew of a ship (but not an aircraft) within the common travel area, and is discharged from that engagement on arrival in the United Kingdom, requires no leave, except in the same three cases (save with the same modification as for returning aircraft crew with leave)[5].

'Crew' means all persons actually employed in the working or service of a ship or aircraft, including the captain[6]. 'Captain' means the master of a ship or commander of an aircraft[6]. 'Aircraft' includes hovercraft[6]. 'British seaman's card' means a valid card issued under regulations made under the Merchant Shipping Act 1970[7] or card having the same effect[8].

1 Immigration Act 1971 (c 77), s 8(1). Crew with leave are normally in 'permit free employment': see para 247 below.
2 Ie in accordance with ibid, Sch 2, para 2 (which must now be read with the Immigration Act 1988 (c 14), s 8(4)), which empowers immigration officers to examine crews to the same extent as others, not the Immigration Act 1971, Sch 2, paras 12–14, which concern crews entering the United Kingdom to join ships and aircraft: see para 162, below.
3 Ibid, s 8(1)(a)–(c).
4 Immigration (Exemption from Control) Order 1972, SI 1972/1613, art 5(1)(e), (2).
5 Ibid, art 5(1)(d), (2), (3).
6 Immigration Act 1971, s 33(1).
7 Ie under the Merchant Shipping Act 1970 (c 36), s 70: Immigration (Exemption from Control) Order 1972, art 5(3). For the current regulations, see the Merchant Shipping (Seamen's Documents) Regulations 1987, SI 1987/408, and SHIPPING.
8 Immigration (Exemption from Control) Order 1972, art 5(3).

130. Diplomats, consuls and related groups. Members of missions within the meaning of the Diplomatic Privileges Act 1964 (c 81), members of their families who form part of their households, and those entitled to the immunity from jurisdiction conferred upon diplomatic agents, are exempted from the provisions of the Immigration Act 1971 which relate to those who are not British citizens[1].

In addition, certain groups are exempted from all provisions of that Act relating to those who are not British citizens, and certain others from all such provisions save those in relation to deportation. The first type of group comprises any consular officer or consular employee (other than one who is part-time or who is engaged in the United Kingdom in any private occupation for gain), in the service of a specified state and a member of such a person's family who forms part of his household[2].

The second type of group comprises some three classes, in each case including members of the family forming part of the household[3]. The three classes are:
(1) any person upon whom immunity from jurisdiction is conferred by Order in Council[4] under the Consular Relations Act 1968, and any consular officer (other than an honorary one) or consular employee not already covered by section 8(3) of the Immigration Act 1971[5];
(2) any member of the government of another territory visiting the United Kingdom on the business of that government (unless the Secretary of State otherwise directs); any person (not already exempted by section 8(3) of the Immigration Act 1971) visiting as the representative, or member of the

official staff of the representative, of the government of a country to which
the Diplomatic Immunities (Conferences with Commonwealth Countries
and Republic of Ireland) Act 1961[6] applies provided his name appears in a list
published under the 1961 Act; and any officer or servant of the Commonwealth Secretariat who falls within the Schedule[7] of the Commonwealth
Secretariat Act 1966[8];

(3) any person immune from legal process in respect of official acts[9]; any person
(not already exempted by section 8(3) of the Immigration Act 1971)
immune from suit and legal process by virtue of an Order in Council[10]
under the International Organisations Act 1968; any representative and
officer[11] of the North Atlantic Salmon Conservation Organisation[12].

1 Immigration Act 1971 (c 77), s 8(3) (amended by the British Nationality Act 1981 (c 61), s 36(6),
Sch 4, para 2, and the Immigration Act 1988 (c 14), s 4). In the case of a member of a mission other
than a diplomatic agent, the Immigration Act 1971, s 8(3), applies only if he enters or has entered
the United Kingdom as a member of that mission, or in order to take up a post as such a member
which was offered to him before his arrival: s 8(3A) (added by the Immigration Act 1988, s 4). See
also *Julita Esterm Florentine v Secretary of State for the Home Department* [1987] Imm AR 1, IAT;
Babatunde Michael Olaleye v Secretary of State for the Home Department [1987] Imm AR 51, IAT.
Exemption lasts only as long as the diplomatic appointment: *R v Secretary of State for the Home
Department, ex parte Bagga* [1991] 1 QB 485, [1991] 1 All ER 777, CA.
2 Immigration (Exemption from Control) Order 1972, SI 1972/1613, art 3 (amended by SI
1982/1649). The specified states are Austria, Belgium, Bulgaria, Czechoslovakia, Denmark,
France, German Democratic Republic, Greece, Federal Republic of Germany, Hungary, Italy,
Japan, Mexico, Mongolia, Norway, Poland, Roumania, Sweden, Spain, Union of Soviet
Socialist Republics, United States of America, and Yugoslavia: Schedule (amended by SI
1977/693). 'Consular employee' and 'consular officer' have the meanings respectively assigned
to them by the Vienna Convention on Consular Relations (Vienna, 24 April 1963; TS 14 (1973);
Cmnd 5219), art 1, as set out in the Consular Relations Act 1968 (c 18), Sch 1: Immigration
(Exemption from Control) Order 1972, art 2(1).
3 Ibid, art 4(l) (added by SI 1985/1809).
4 Ie an Order in Council made under the Consular Relations Act 1968, s 12(1): Immigration
(Exemption from Control) Order 1972, art 4(f).
5 Immigration (Exemption from Control) Order 1972, art 4(f), (h), (i).
6 Ie the Diplomatic Immunities (Conferences with Commonwealth Countries and Republic of
Ireland) Act 1961 (c 11), s 1 (repealed): Immigration (Exemption from Control) Order 1972,
art 4(e). See now the International Organisations Act 1968 (c 48), s 1, Sch 1.
7 Ie the Commonwealth Secretariat Act 1966 (c 10), s 1(2), Schedule, para 6.
8 Immigration (Exemption from Control) Order 1972, art 4(a), (e), and art 4(j) (added by SI
1977/693).
9 Ie any act performed by him in his official capacity under any Order in Council made under the
Bretton Woods Agreements Act 1945 (c 19), s 3(1) (the International Monetary Fund and the
International Bank); the International Finance Corporation Act 1955 (c 5), s 3(1) (International
Finance Corporation); and the International Development Association Act 1960 (c 35), s 3(1)
(International Development Association) (all repealed): Immigration (Exemption from Control)
Order 1972, art 4(b)–(d). See now the International Organisations Act 1968, Sch 1, and the
Overseas Development and Co-operation Act 1980 (c 63), s 9.
10 Ie under the International Organisations Act 1968, ss 1(2), 5(1), 6(2), except such person
mentioned in s 5(2)(c)–(e), or by Order in Council continuing to have effect by virtue of s 12(5):
Immigration (Exemption from Control) Order 1972, art 4(g) (amended by SI 1977/693).
11 Ie under the European Communities (Immunities and Privileges of the North Atlantic Salmon
Conservation Organisation) Order 1985, SI 1985/1773.
12 Immigration (Exemption from Control) Order 1972, art 4(b)–(d), (g), and art 4(k) (added by SI
1985/1809).

131. Members of certain armed forces. Certain members of certain armed
forces are exempted from the provisions of the Immigration Act 1971, other
than those relating to British citizens, except in relation to deportation[1]. They
comprise:
(1) any person subject to service law as a member of the home forces (that is any
of Her Majesty's forces other than a Commonwealth force or force raised

under the law of an associated state, colony, protectorate or protected state)[2];

(2) any person undergoing training in the United Kingdom with any unit of the home forces, who is a member of a Commonwealth force (that is a force to which the provisions of the Visiting Forces Act 1952 (c 67) apply without an Order in Council under section 1 of that Act[3]) or a force raised under the law of an associated state, colony, protectorate or protected state[4]; or

(3) any person posted for service in the United Kingdom as a member of a visiting force or any other of Her Majesty's forces, or as a member of an international headquarters or defence organisation designated[5] under the International Headquarters and Defence Organisations Act 1964[6].

1 Immigration Act 1971 (c 77), s 8(4) (amended by the British Nationality Act 1981 (c 61), s 39(6), Sch 4, para 2).
2 Immigration Act 1971, s 8(4)(a), (6).
3 See ARMED FORCES, vol 2, para 786.
4 Immigration Act 1971, s 8(4)(b), (6).
5 Ie designated under the International Headquarters and Defence Organisations Act 1964 (c 5), s 1: see ARMED FORCES, vol 2, para 787.
6 Immigration Act 1971, s 8(4)(c). 'Visiting force' means a body, contingent or detachment of the forces of a country to which the provisions of the International Headquarters and Defence Organisation Act 1964, s 1, apply, being a body, contingent or detachment for the time being present in the United Kingdom on the invitation of Her Majesty's government in the United Kingdom: Immigration Act 1971, s 8(6).

132. Persons exempted by reason of holding a relevant passport. Members of several classes, not being British citizens, are exempted from immigration control by reason of holding a relevant passport[1]. They are:

(1) any British Dependent Territories citizen, British Overseas citizen or British National (Overseas) holding British visitors passports issued in the United Kingdom and Islands[2];

(2) any Commonwealth citizen or British protected person included in a collective passport issued in the United Kingdom or one of the Islands[3]; and

(3) any Commonwealth citizen, British protected person, or citizen of the Republic of Ireland returning from a no-passport excursion to France, Belgium or the Netherlands holding an identity document, issued under approved arrangements, in the authorised form[4].

The exemption does not, however, apply in the case of anyone subject to a deportation order, or who has entered unlawfully and not subsequently received leave to enter or remain[5].

1 Immigration (Exemption from Control) Order 1972, SI 1972/1613, art 5(1) (amended by SI 1982/1649).
2 See ibid, art 5(1)(a), and the British Nationality Act 1981 (c 61), s 51(3)(a) (amended by the British Nationality (Falkland Islands) Act 1983 (c 6), s 4(3), and the Hong Kong (British Nationality) Order 1986, SI 1986/948, art 7(9)).
3 Immigration (Exemption from Control) Order 1972, art 5(1)(b), (3).
4 Ibid, art 5(1)(c), (3) (amended by SI 1975/617).
5 Ibid, art 5(2).

(e) Special Limitations on Movement

133. Port and border controls under the prevention of terrorism powers. Any person (including, therefore, any British citizen or other person with a right of abode) who has arrived in or seeks leave to enter Great Britain or Northern Ireland may be examined by an examining officer[1] for the purpose of determining if he is involved in terrorism, is subject to an exclusion order or has committed certain related offences, and may be detained for that purpose[2]. Such a person must produce certain documents if requested, and may be searched[3].

Ships and aircraft making certain journeys for reward within the common travel area may do so using only designated ports, unless authorised by an examining officer[4], and the Secretary of State may designate control areas for embarkation and disembarkation of passengers, and captains of ships and aircraft are obliged to take all reasonable steps to secure that their passengers can be examined by examining officers, and must supply various details of such passengers[5]. These powers should not be confused with the similar power under the Immigration Act 1971[6].

1 Ie constables, immigration officers and customs and excise officers: see the Prevention of Terrorism (Temporary Provisions) Act 1989 (c 4), s 16, Sch 5, para 1.
2 See ibid, Sch 5, paras 2, 6, 7 (amended by the Channel Tunnel (Fire Services, Immigration and Prevention of Terrorism) Order 1990, SI 1990/2227, art 4, Sch 2). As to exclusion orders, see para 134 below. The exercise of the examination and detention powers conferred by the Prevention of Terrorism (Temporary Provisions) Act 1989, Sch 5, paras 2–6, are subject to supervision in accordance with Sch 3. These powers may be exercised notwithstanding the rights conferred by the Immigration Act 1971 (c 77), s 1: Prevention of Terrorism (Temporary Provision) Act 1989, s 20(3).
3 See ibid, Sch 5, paras 3–5 (as so amended). See also note 2 above.
4 See ibid, Sch 5, para 8 and Sch 6 (amended by the Prevention of Terrorism (Temporary Provisions) (Designated Ports) Order 1991, SI 1991/2649).
5 See the Prevention of Terrorism (Temporary Provision) Act 1989, Sch 5, paras 9, 10 (as amended: see note 2 above).
6 See the Immigration Act 1971, Sch 2, para 26, and para 161 below.

134. Exclusion orders under the prevention of terrorism powers. The Secretary of State may make an exclusion order, where it appears expedient to him to prevent acts of terrorism designed to influence public opinion or government policy with respect to Northern Ireland, against a person who he is satisfied is, or has been concerned in, or is seeking entry with a view to being concerned in, the commission, preparation or instigation of acts of terrorism[1]. Notice of the making of the order must be served on the person concerned, provided that the person is in the United Kingdom, including details of the right to make representations[2]. Otherwise it may be served on the person by posting it to him at his last known address[3].

Such an order may exclude the person from the entire United Kingdom, or from Great Britain, or from Northern Ireland, except in certain cases relating to British citizens as follows[4]. If a British citizen is ordinarily resident in Great Britain and has been for the last three years, or is subject to an exclusion order in relation to Northern Ireland, he cannot be excluded from Great Britain[5]. If a British citizen is ordinarily resident in Northern Ireland and has been for the last three years or is subject to an exclusion order in relation to Great Britain, he cannot be excluded from Northern Ireland[6]. A British citizen cannot be excluded from the United Kingdom[7].

In addition, in the case of a person ordinarily resident in the United Kingdom, Great Britain or Northern Ireland against whom an exclusion order can be made, the Secretary of State must have regard to whether his connection with another country or territory is such as to make it appropriate to make an order[8].

Time spent in breach of an exclusion order, the Immigration Act 1971 (c 77) or similar law passed subsequently, or in imprisonment or detention for six months or more following conviction, does not count as ordinary residence[9] for the purpose of calculating the three years[10].

Failure to comply with an exclusion order is an offence[11], and a person may be removed after notice has been given if he consents, or if seven days have elapsed and he has made no representations, or if he has made representations but the Secretary of State has notified him that he will not revoke the order[12].

There is no appeal, but representations may be made in writing to the Secretary of State with a request for a personal interview with a person appointed by the Secretary of State to advise him[13]. Such representations must be made within seven days of the notice being served, but if the person concerned consents to removal the Secretary of State may make them within fourteen days, although the personal interview need not be granted unless the Secretary of State considers it reasonably practicable to do so within a reasonable time in Northern Ireland, Great Britain or the Republic of Ireland as appropriate[14]. The Secretary of State must consider the representations and advice and give notice of his decision in writing[15].

The Secretary of State may revoke an exclusion order at any time, and all exclusion orders expire after three years (without prejudice to a further order)[16].

1　See the Prevention of Terrorism (Temporary Provisions) Act 1989 (c 4), ss 4–7, Sch 2. 'Terrorism' means the use of violence for political ends and includes any use of violence for the purpose of putting the public or any section of the public in fear: s 20(1). This power may be exercised notwithstanding the rights conferred by the Immigration Act 1971 (c 77), s 1: Prevention of Terrorism (Temporary Provision) Act 1989, s 29(3).
2　See ibid, s 4(4), Sch 2, paras 2, 3.
3　Ibid, Sch 2, para 2(3).
4　See ibid, Sch 2, paras 5–7.
5　Ibid, s 5(4).
6　Ibid, s 6(4).
7　Ibid, s 7(4).
8　Ibid, ss 5(3), 6(3), 7(3).
9　Ie in Great Britain for the purposes of ibid, s 5(4)(a), or in Northern Ireland for the purposes of s 6(4)(a): Sch 2, para 9(2).
10　Ibid, Sch 2, para 9(2)–(5).
11　Ibid, s 8(1).
12　Ibid, Sch 2, para 5. As to removal directions, see Sch 2, para 6.
13　Ibid, Sch 2, para 3(1).
14　See ibid, Sch 2, para 3(2)–(10).
15　See ibid, Sch 2, para 4.
16　Ibid, Sch 2, para 1.

135. 'Hostage' orders. An Order in Council may be made prohibiting nationals or citizens of a country (who are not British citizens) from embarking in the United Kingdom or from doing so elsewhere than at a port of exit, or imposing restrictions or conditions upon embarkation, where it appears proper to do so by reason of restrictions or conditions imposed on British citizens, British Dependent Territories citizens or British Overseas citizens leaving or seeking to leave any country or the territory subject to the government of any country of such nationals or citizens[1]. No appeal exists and contravention is an offence[2].

1　Immigration Act 1971 (c 77), s 3(7) (amended by the British Nationality Act 1981 (c 61), s 39(6), Sch 4, para 2).
2　Immigration Act 1971, s 24(1)(g).

136. 'Safety' orders. An Order in Council may be made to prohibit, in the interests of safety, those who are not British citizens from embarking upon a specified or indicated ship or aircraft[1]. No appeal exists and contravention is an offence[2].

1　Immigration Act 1971 (c 77), s 3(7) (amended by the British Nationality Act 1981 (c 61), s 39(6), Sch 4, para 2). The drafting is ambiguous but it appears that such orders, separate from 'hostage'

orders, are possible. However, this view is unorthodox: see eg *Macdonald's Immigration Law and Practice* (3rd edn, 1991, eds I A Macdonald and N J Blake) p 75.
2 Immigration Act 1971, s 24(1)(g).

(f) Community Law

137. Community nationals and their families. Nationals of member states of the European Community were not mentioned in the Immigration Act 1971 (c 77). The Immigration Act 1988, however, declares that Community nationals exercising 'an enforceable Community right' or one in 'a provision made under section 2(2) of the European Communities Act 1972' do not require leave to enter or remain[1]. The Secretary of State may also, by order, give leave to enter for a limited period to any class of Community national, without such entitlement[2].

The Immigration Rules (broadly reflecting Community law) create a specific regime for Community nationals if coming to pursue economic activities, which is markedly less rigorous for them (and their families) than for others, and exempts them from the normal requirements for a work permit or the like, and from specifically limited leave to enter[3]. The definition of 'family' used is also broader[4].

The Treaty rules applying the principles of freedom of movement for persons and services mean that such persons have Community law rights, proof against contrary national legislation (except to a limited degree in relation to documentation and the public policy proviso) and have thereby a general right to enter the United Kingdom without permission[5]. Moreover, their rights can be altered only by Community legislation.

1 Immigration Act 1988 (c 14), s 7(1). The European Communities Act 1972 (c 68), s 2(2), enables Orders in Council or regulations to be made to implement Community obligations.
2 Immigration Act 1988, s 7(2). The right does not extend to family members who are not Community nationals. At the date at which this volume states the law, no order under s 7(2) had been made.
3 Statement of Changes in Immigration Rules (HC Paper (1989–90) no. 251) (the Immigration Rules), Pt VI (paras 68–74).
4 Ibid, para 70.
5 See paras 221 ff below.

(5) INSTITUTIONS OF CONTROL

(a) Central Control

138. The Secretary of State and the Home Office. Responsibility for the system of immigration control[1] rests with primarily the Secretary of State, in particular for issuing Immigration Rules[2], giving or varying leave to remain[3], appointing immigration officers and medical inspectors[4], making regulations under the Immigration Act 1971[5], and in relation to deportation[6]. He is also responsible for the operation of the Prevention of Terrorism (Temporary Provisions) Act 1989 which includes controls on entry provisions[7].

In practice the Secretary of State is chiefly the Home Secretary (although actual administration is in the hands of a minister of state), and the Home Office contains the Immigration and Nationality Department[8]. Home Office staff (along with some Foreign and Commonwealth Office staff) also man British missions abroad issuing entry clearances. The police are involved in immigration control and the Home Office thus is involved in so far as it bears responsibility for the police[9].

The Home Office contracts with Property Guards Ltd, Security Express Ltd, Securicor Ltd and Group 4 Total Security Ltd to guard those wishing to enter the United Kingdom who are detained at Heathrow, Gatwick, Birmingham and Manchester Airports and to provide escorts between immigration offices[10].

1 Invaluable guides to the general operation of the immigration control are provided by the relevant reports of the Home Affairs Committee, and the annual reports of the Immigration and Nationality Department.

2 See the Immigration Act 1971 (c 77), s 3(2), and para 110 above.

3 Ibid, s 4(1).

4 See ibid, s 4(2), Sch 2, para 1(1), (2) (s 4(2)(b) being amended by the Channel Tunnel (Fire Services, Immigration and Prevention of Terrorism) Order 1990, SI 1990/2227, art 3, Sch 1). With the consent of the Commissioners for Customs and Excise, customs and excise officers may be appointed immigration officers: see para 142 below.

5 Immigration Act 1971, s 4(3), (4) (amended by the British Nationality Act 1981 (c 61), s 39(6), Sch 4, para 2).

6 See the Immigration Act 1971, ss 3(5), 5, 6, and paras 202 ff below. As to the power of the Secretary of State to devolve deportation decisions to immigration inspectors, see *R v Secretary of State for the Home Department, ex parte Oladehinde* [1991] 1 AC 254, [1990] 2 All ER 367, CA (affd [1991] 1 AC 254, [1990] 3 All ER 393, HL).

7 See the Prevention of Terrorism (Temporary Provisions) Act 1989 (c 4), s 16, Sch 5, and para 133 above.

8 See eg the Home Office annual *Report on the Work of the Immigration and Nationality Department* (1984 to date); Sixth Report from the Home Affairs Committee (HC Paper (1984–85) no. 277) (Immigration and Nationality Department of the Home Office); First Report from the Select Committee on Race Relations and Immigration (HC Paper (1977–78 no. 303) (Immigration); Fifth Report from the Home Affairs Committee (HC Paper (1986–87) no. 247) (Passport Control) and the government's reply (Cm 313); Fifth Report from the Home Affairs Committee (HC Paper (1989–90) no. 319) (Administrative Delays in the Immigration and Nationality Department).

9 See para 144 below.

10 See P Green *Private Sector Involvement in the Immigration Detention Centres* (1989) and the sources cited therein. See also *R v Secretary of State for the Home Department, ex parte Anosike* [1971] 2 All ER 1405, [1971] 1 WLR 1136, DC.

139. The Lord Chancellor. The Lord Chancellor appoints adjudicators and the Immigration Appeal Tribunal[1].

1 See the Immigration Act 1971 (c 77), s 12, Sch 5 (amended by the House of Commons Disqualification Act 1975 (c 24), s 10(2), Sch 3; the Northern Ireland Assembly Disqualification Act 1975 (c 25), s 5(2), Sch 3, Pt I; the Transfer of Functions (Minister for the Civil Service and Treasury) Order 1981, SI 1981/1670; and the Transfer of Functions (Immigration Appeals) Order 1987, SI 1987/465).

140. Other government departments. The Department of Employment issues work permits and must approve leave to remain in the case of some work-permit holders[1]. The Foreign and Commonwealth Office provides some staff for British missions abroad issuing entry clearances[2]. The Commissioners of Customs and Excise may consent to the employment of customs and excise officers as immigration officers[3] and the Minister of Health and Social Security or other appropriate minister of the Government of Northern Ireland may, in Northern Ireland, appoint medical inspectors in pursuance of arrangements made between him and the Secretary of State[4]. The Secretary of State for Health appoints medical inspectors in Great Britain[5].

The Secretary of State for Scotland has no responsibility for immigration control save in so far as he has responsibility for Scottish police forces and may authorise removal of a mental patient from the United Kingdom[6].

1 See the Statement of Changes in Immigration Rules (HC Paper (1989–90) no. 251) (the Immigration Rules), paras 34, 122. Work permits are dealt with by the Overseas Labour Section of the Department of Employment: Communication from Overseas Labour Section. As to work permits, see para 154 below.
2 See First Report from the Select Committee on Race Relations and Immigration (HC Paper (1977–78) no. 303) (Immigration), para 35.
3 Immigration Act 1971 (c 77), s 4(2), Sch 2, para 1(1).
4 Ibid, Sch 2, para 1(2).
5 HC Paper no. 303, para 36.
6 See paras 144, 216, below.

(b) Local Control

141. Entry clearance officers. Entry clearance officers grant or refuse entry clearance at British missions abroad[1]. They are not mentioned in the Immigration Act 1971 but only in the Immigration Rules, where they are subsumed for that purpose to immigration officers[2].

1 See eg First Report from the Select Committee on Race Relations and Immigration (HC Paper (1977–78) no. 303) (Immigration) para 35, and Home Office annual *Report on the Work of the Immigration and Nationality Department* (1984 to date). See also paras 150–153, 158, below. Their function is to determine whether certain facts required by the Statement of Changes in Immigration Rules (HC Paper (1989–90) no. 251) (the Immigration Rules) are fulfilled, rather than to exercise discretion (*R v Secretary of State for the Home Department, ex parte Samya and Younes Ounejma, R v Secretary of State for the Home Department, ex parte Hassan* [1989] Imm AR 75, DC), because the Immigration Act 1971 (c 77), s 3(2) read with s 1(4) (see para 110 above), and Sch 2, para 3, require the Secretary of State to make Immigration Rules defining the discretion of immigration officers, and no discretion is thereby given to entry clearance officers.
2 Immigration Rules, para 16. See also the Immigration Appeals (Procedure) Rules 1984, SI 1984/2041, r 2(1) (entry clearance officer). The fact that the rules bind immigration officers (who are by the Immigration Act 1971, s 4(1), expressed to exercise certain discretion) to refuse entry to those refused entry clearance by an entry clearance officer, does not mean that the Immigration Rules are *ultra vires*: *R v Secretary of State for the Home Department, ex parte Samya and Younes Ounejma, R v Secretary of State for the Home Department, ex parte Hassan* [1989] Imm AR 75, DC.

142. Immigration officers. Immigration officers operate control on entry and have the power to grant or to refuse entry to the United Kingdom to those subject to immigration control and some other powers devolved upon them by the Secretary of State. They also have other related powers of examination, detention etc, and powers under the Prevention of Terrorism (Temporary Provisions) Act 1989[1]. They are appointed by the Secretary of State, and may, with the consent of the Commissioners of Customs and Excise, be customs and excise officers[2].

1 See the Immigration Act 1971 (c 77), s 4(1), (2), Sch 2 (see paras 161, 162, 165–170, below), and the Prevention of Terrorism (Temporary Provisions) Act 1989 (c 4), s 16, Schs 5, 6 (see para 133 above). See also *R v Secretary of State for the Home Department, ex parte Oladehinde* [1991] 1 AC 254, [1990] 2 All ER 367, CA (affd [1991] 1 AC 254, [1990] 3 All ER 393, HL).
2 See the Immigration Act 1971, s 4(1), (2), Sch 2, para 1(1).

143. Medical inspectors. Medical inspectors, who must be fully qualified medical practitioners, may be appointed for the purposes of the Immigration Act 1971[1]. They have power to require a person seeking entry to submit to a test or examination[2]. With certain exceptions, a person subject to immigration control may be refused entry where a medical inspector advises it is undesirable on medical grounds[3].

1 Immigration Act 1971 (c 77), s 4(2), Sch 2, para 1(2).
2 See ibid, Sch 2, para 2(2), the Statement of Changes in Immigration Rules (HC Paper (1989–90) no. 251) (the Immigration Rules), paras 23, 81, and para 165, below.
3 See the Immigration Rules, para 81, and paras 171, 172, below.

144. Police. The police have certain functions, principally in relation to the registration of aliens[1].

1 See para 183 below. See also the Scottish Home and Health Department Circulars to Chief Constables No 6/1972 (Immigration Act 1971), para 10, and No 10/1973 (Immigration Act 1971: Police Registration and Hotel Records).

145. Examining officers. All constables, immigration officers, customs and excise officers employed as immigration officers, and, in Northern Ireland, members of Her Majesty's forces specified by the Secretary of State, are examining officers for the purposes of the Prevention of Terrorism (Temporary Provisions) Act 1989[1].

1 See the Prevention of Terrorism (Temporary Provisions) Act 1989 (c 4), s 16, Sch 5, para 1, and para 133 above.

(6) PROCESSES OF CONTROL

(a) Introduction

146. Definition of terms in respect of entry. The definition of 'arrival', 'disembarkation', 'landing', 'admission', 'admission in a temporary capacity', 'temporary admission', 'temporary release', 'entry' and 'authorisation' are distinct from each other and are in part defined in the legislation.

'Arrival' is used to denote mere physical arrival in the United Kingdom including especially the position of a person who has not disembarked from a ship or aircraft or left the Channel Tunnel system, but also including that of a person in a control area in an approved port, or detained for inquiries, or given temporary admission or bail under Schedule 2[1] of the Immigration Act 1971[2], and is given an ad hoc meaning by the Immigration Act 1988[3].

'Disembarkation' is used to denote actual exit from a ship or aircraft on arrival (except from a local journey within the common travel area), and 'landing' is used similarly[4].

'Admission' is used in relation to temporary admission, a process whereby those actually arrived and disembarked are allowed into the country without leave to enter, pending inquiries, and 'temporary release' refers to release without bail after detention; bail may also be granted to such a person who has been detained instead of being given temporary admission[5]. Such temporary admission is to be distinguished from 'admission in a temporary capacity', that is being given leave to enter for a limited period[6]. 'Admission' as such is used in its obvious meaning.

'Entry' is not defined in the legislation, but excludes presence in a control area in an approved port, being detained, being temporarily admitted, or being temporarily released. It may be inferred to apply to the process of becoming at large within the United Kingdom, not subject to restraint de facto and presumptively lawfully[7].

'Authorisation' is used in the Immigration Rules and appears to refer to those who need no leave to enter[8] and those whose limited leave has expired but who, without further leave being given, are permitted by the Secretary of State, as an indulgence, to remain temporarily[9].

1 Ie under the Immigration Act 1971 (c 77), Sch 2, paras 16–25: see paras 167, 169, below.
2 Ibid, s 11(1), (1A), (3) (s 11(1A) added by the Channel Tunnel (Fire Services, Immigration and Prevention of Terrorism) Order 1990, SI 1990/2227, art 3, Sch 1).
3 See the Immigration Act 1988 (c 14), s 8(7).
4 See the Immigration Act 1971, s 11(2)(a), (3), and the Immigration (Landing and Embarkation Cards) Order 1975, SI 1975/65. As to the common travel area, see paras 122–124 above.
5 See the Immigration Act 1971, Sch 2, paras 21–25, and para 169 below.
6 *R v Secretary of State for the Home Department, ex parte Taj Mohammed Khan* [1985] Imm AR 104, CA. As to leave to enter for a limited period, see para 119 above, and para 173 below.
7 See the Immigration Act 1971, ss 4(2), 11(1), (1A) (as added: see note 2 above), and Sch 2, para 2(1) (amended by the Channel Tunnel (Fire Services, Immigration and Prevention of Terrorism) Order 1990, Sch 1). See also *R v Governor of Ashford Remand Centre, ex parte Bouzagou* [1985] Imm AR 69, CA.
8 Ie under the Immigration Act 1971, s 8: see paras 128 ff above.
9 *R v Secretary of State for the Home Department, ex parte Subramaniam* [1977] QB 190, [1976] 1 All ER 915, [1976] Imm AR 155, CA; *Suthendran v Immigration Appeal Tribunal* [1977] AC 359, [1976] 3 All ER 611, [1977] Imm AR 44, HL; *Muhammad Idrish v Secretary of State for the Home Department* [1985] Imm AR 155, IAT.

147. Definition of terms in respect of departure. 'Embarkation' means entering a ship or aircraft, except for the purpose of a local journey within the common travel area[1]. 'Removal' is not defined, but in immigration law bears its obvious meaning, except that it is restricted to the expulsion of those refused leave to enter or who have entered as illegal entrants, or against whom a deportation order is in force[2]. 'Deportation' is thus removal under a deportation order[3]. Removal is also possible under the mental health legislation[4]. 'Exclusion' applies to exclusion under an exclusion order under the prevention of terrorism legislation[5], or simple refusal of entry[6].

1 Immigration Act 1971 (c 77), s 11(2). Leaving the United Kingdom by way of the Channel Tunnel is not 'embarkation': see s 4(2), Sch 2, para 3 (amended by the Channel Tunnel (Fire Services, Immigration and Prevention of Terrorism) Order 1990, SI 1990/2227, art 3, Sch 1).
2 See the Immigration Act 1971, ss 4(2), 33(1) ('illegal entrant'), Sch 2, paras 8–10 (as so amended), and paras 202 ff below.
3 See ibid, s 5, Sch 3, and paras 202 ff below.
4 See the Mental Health (Scotland) Act 1984 (c 36), s 83, which applies to all those with no right of abode, and para 216 below.
5 See the Prevention of Terrorism (Temporary Provisions) Act 1989 (c 4), s 4, Sch 2, and para 134 above.
6 See the Immigration Act 1971, s 3, and para 170 below.

148. The four phases of control. Immigration control can be divided into four phases: (1) control before entry; (2) control on entry; (3) control after entry; and (4) control of departure.

Control before entry is heavily stressed, and is a filter[1]. The decision upon grant or refusal of leave to enter is in part decided before (or indeed instead of) seeking leave to enter, and by entry clearance officers, rather than immigration officers. Those wishing to enter may, and in some cases must, obtain an entry clearance, 'special voucher' or work permit before departure[2]. Nevertheless it is not referred to at length in the legislation or the Immigration Rules[3].

Control on entry[4] is reduced in importance in that a person with entry clearance, 'special voucher', or work permit will normally be admitted. Leave to enter is nevertheless required and to a large extent the Immigration Rules are concerned with this. There are circumstances in which entry will be refused to those with entry clearance, 'special voucher' or work permit, as it can be refused to those without, including general grounds applicable to all, and specific grounds applicable to different categories. The Immigration Rules are largely drafted in terms of control on entry.

Control after entry[5] has traditionally not been regarded as extensive. Leave to enter may be limited in duration and conditions relating to employment and to registration with the police may be imposed. Such limits and conditions can be varied or removed. No general requirement to produce a passport exists although it is sometimes the practice of various authorities to request or require it. This form of control has been alleged to have increased informally but substantially[6].

Control of departure exists in that certain people may be removed administratively and others deported or subjected to related processes[7].

1 See eg the Immigration Act 1988 (c 14), s 8, and para 150, text to note 6, para 152, text to note 9, para 162, text to note 1, and para 170, text to note 9, below.
2 See paras 150 ff below.
3 Ie the Statement of Changes in Immigration Rules (HC Paper (1989–90) no. 251) (the Immigration Rules).
4 See paras 161 ff below.
5 See paras 177 ff below.
6 See paras 189–191 below.
7 See paras 192 ff below.

149. Categories under the immigration rules. A person requiring leave to enter must normally apply for leave relating to one of the categories laid down in the Immigration Rules[1] (and consequently must consider any relevant control before entry)[2]. A person may fall into more than one category, in which case his situation is to be considered 'in the round'[3]. The Secretary of State may give leave 'outside the rules', but this is rare[4]. The Immigration Rules define the conditions for each category, although fulfilment of them creates no entitlement to leave to enter[5].

The categories are drafted in three broad groups:
(1) 'Passengers coming for temporary purposes', which includes visitors, students and au pairs[6]. This group is assumed to be ineligible for settlement[7].
(2) 'Passengers coming for employment or business, as persons of independent means, or for marriage', which includes those on work permits, Commonwealth citizens coming to work who have a grandparent born in the United Kingdom, young Commonwealth citizens on working holidays, those in permit-free employment, businessmen and self-employed persons, persons of independent means, writers and artists, dependants of any of the preceding, and fiancés and fiancées[8]. This group is generally eligible for eventual settlement although the Immigration Rules are on occasion ambiguous[9].
(3) 'Passengers coming for settlement', which includes United Kingdom passport holders, spouses, other relatives, parents, grandparents and other relatives, and returning residents[10]. This group seeks indefinite leave to enter or remain, that is permanent settlement, as such.
Three other groups are referred to:
(a) 'Children born in the United Kingdom who are not British citizens'[11].
(b) 'Nationals of European Community countries and their families'[12].
(c) 'Asylum'[13].

The Immigration Rules equally lay down conditions for variation of leave, including removal of conditions[14], and for deportation[15] as well as for registration with the police[16], general grounds of refusal of leave to enter[17], and rights of appeal[18].

1 Ie the Statement of Changes in Immigration Rules (HC Paper (1989–90) no. 251) (the Immigration Rules): see generally para 110 above.

2 Ibid, para 78. As to control before entry, see paras 150 ff below.
3 *Jahangard v Entry Clearance Officer, Vienna* [1985] Imm AR 69, IAT. See also *R v Immigration Appeal Tribunal, ex parte Secretary of State for the Home Department* [1990] 3 All ER 652, [1990] 1 WLR 1126, CA.
4 See para 112 above. The constitutional basis of this power is unclear.
5 Immigration Rules, para 78.
6 See ibid, Pt II (paras 22–33) and Pt IX (paras 78–89), and paras 291 ff below.
7 See ibid, para 139. As to settlement, see paras 120, 121, above.
8 See ibid, Pt III (paras 34–48), Pt IX, and paras 241 ff below.
9 Ibid, para 139.
10 See ibid, Pt IV (paras 49–60), and paras 267 ff, 324 ff, below.
11 See ibid, Pt V (paras 61–67), and para 284 below.
12 See ibid, Pt VI (paras 68–74), and paras 219 ff below.
13 See ibid, Pt VII (para 75), and paras 316 ff below.
14 See ibid, Pt XI (paras 94–154), and paras 177 ff below.
15 See ibid, Pt XII (paras 155–180), and paras 202 ff below.
16 See ibid, Pt VIII (paras 76, 77), and para 175 below.
17 See ibid, Pt IX (paras 78–89), and para 170 below.
18 See ibid, Pt X (paras 90–93). As to appeals, see paras 329 ff below.

(b) Control before Entry

(A) ENTRY CLEARANCE

150. Introduction. 'Entry clearance' means a visa, letter of consent or entry certificate, and these are taken, in accordance with the Immigration Rules, as evidence of the eligibility of a person (other than a British citizen) to enter[1]. It does not include a work permit[2]. All entry clearances take the form of a stamp in the passport, except a Home Office letter of consent, which is a separate document. An entry clearance is dated and specifies a period within which it must be used (which is usually six months). It is valid for use only once, except in the case of a visa stipulating that it may be used more than once[3].

Possession of entry clearance does not ensure entry, but the possessor of a current entry clearance may be refused entry only on certain grounds[4]. It also permits appeal from within the United Kingdom against refusal of entry at a port of entry[5]. Immigration procedures appropriate for control on entry may be undergone before entry, and a passport stamp given which states that leave to enter has been given, in which case the person is deemed to have been given such leave on arrival[6].

1 See the Immigration Act 1971 (c 77), s 33(1) (amended by the British Nationality Act 1981 (c 61), s 39(6), Sch 4, para 2, and the Immigration Act 1988 (c 14), s 10, Schedule, para 5), and the Statement of Changes in Immigration Rules (HC Paper (1989–90) no. 251) (the Immigration Rules), para 14 (amended by HC Paper (1990–91) no. 356), para 16. The Appendix (substituted by HC Paper (1990–91) no. 356), lists visa countries as follows:

Countries or Territorial Entities whose Nationals or Citizens need Visas for the United Kingdom

Afghanistan	Burundi	Cuba
Albania	Cambodia	Djibouti
Algeria	Cameroon	Egypt
Angola	Cape Verde	Equatorial Guinea
Bangladesh	Central Africa	Ethiopia
Benin	Republic	Gabon
Bhutan	Chad	Ghana
Bulgaria	China	Guinea
Burkina	Comoros	Guinea-Bissau
Burma	Congo	Haiti

India	Mozambique	Sri Lanka
Indonesia	Nepal	Sudan
Iran	Nigeria	Syria
Iraq	Oman	Taiwan
Jordan	Pakistan	Thailand
Korea (North)	Philippines	Togo
Laos	Poland	Tunisia
Lebanon	Romania	Turkey
Liberia	Rwanda	Uganda
Libya	Sao Tome e	US Pacific
Madagascar	Principe	Territories
Mali	Saudi Arabia	Vietnam
Mauritania	Senegal	Yemen
Mongolia	Somalia	Zaïre
Morocco	Soviet Union	

Except (a) those who qualify for admission to the United Kingdom as returning residents in accordance with para 58; and

(b) those who seek leave to enter the United Kingdom within the period of their earlier leave unless that leave:

(i) was for a period of six months or less; or

(ii) was extended by statutory instrument.

2 Nor does it include a 'visa exempt' stamp: *Balogun v Secretary of State for the Home Department* [1989] Imm AR 603, CA.

3 *Andronicou v Chief Immigration Officer, London (Heathrow) Airport* [1974] Imm AR 87. Copies of entry clearance documents are reproduced in L Grant and I Martin *Immigration Law and Practice* (1982) Appendix 2.

4 See the Immigration Rules, para 17 (as originally enacted). Any entry clearance obtained by false representations is ineffective for entry so cannot be 'current', except for the purpose of appeal against the decision rendering it invalid: *Ashraf v Immigration Appeal Tribunal* [1989] Imm AR 234, CA. See also para 172 below.

5 See the Immigration Act 1971, s 13(3), and paras 336, 339, below.

6 See the Immigration Act 1988 (c 14), s 8, and para 152, text to note 9, para 162, text to notes 1, 2, and para 170, text to note 9, below. The stamp is valid for seven days: see s 8(7). At the date at which this volume states the law, the system was not in use.

151. Who needs entry clearance. Visas have been required of nationals of certain foreign countries for some time, but the regime has now extended to Commonwealth countries[1]. Entry certificates were introduced as a form of visa within the Commonwealth in 1969, ostensibly to enable Commonwealth citizens to ascertain their eligibility before departure and thus to minimise the possibility of refusal at the port of entry[2]. However, in relation to dependants from the Indian sub-continent, it appears that the system may be being used as a means of rationing entry and delaying or denying exercise of a presumptive entitlement from the Indian sub-continent, although the Home Office does not accept this[3].

A 'visa national' wishing to enter requires a visa issued for the purpose for which entry is sought, except that visa nationals who are 'returning residents' or are returning within the period of leave greater than six months already granted do not need one[4]. A 'visa national' is a national of any state specified in the Appendix to the Immigration Rules, a stateless person, or the holder of a 'non-national document'[5]. 'Non-national document' is not defined, but presumably includes travel documents other than those issued by a state[6].

Foreign nationals who are not 'visa nationals' (nor are nationals of European Community countries seeking entry to pursue economic activities, or their families[7]) may seek entry clearance to determine eligibility to enter but only from outwith the common travel area[8].

In any case, entry clearance is required of all those wishing to enter for:

(1) 'permit-free employment'[9];

(2) as businessmen or self-employed persons[10];

(3) as a person of independent means[11];

(4) as a writer or artist[12];

(5) as a fiancé or fiancée[13]; and

(6) for settlement whether as a spouse[14], child[15], or parent, grandparent or other relative[16].

Special voucher holders as such do not require entry clearance, but their dependants do[17].

Visitors[18], au pairs[19], work permit holders[20], doctors and dentists seeking post-graduate training[21], young Commonwealth citizens on working holidays[22], and United Kingdom-born children who are not British citizens (provided they are not entering with parents requiring entry clearance) do not require entry clearance unless visa nationals[23]. Nor do settled 'returning residents' not absent for over two years[24]. In the case of Commonwealth citizens with a United Kingdom-born grandparent[25] and of students[26] the Immigration Rules are ambiguous. In practice the former are not usually required to produce entry clearance. In the case of the latter, and of work-permit holders and even visitors, it may be advisable to obtain entry clearance, at least in the case of those from countries where it is presumed there is 'pressure to emigrate'[27].

Although they do not require entry clearance, certain people with the right of abode require certificates of entitlement[28].

1 See the Statement of Changes in Immigration Rules (HC Paper 1989–90) no. 251) (the Immigration Rules), para 14, Appendix, and para 150, note 1, above.

2 *Report of the Committee on Immigration Appeals* (the Wilson Report) (Cmnd 3387) (1967).

3 The chief criticism is found in *Immigration Control Procedures: Report of a Formal Investigation* (1985, Commission for Racial Equality) especially ch 4, and the Annual Reports of the Joint Council for the Welfare of Immigrants. Several of the Commission's conclusions were anticipated in M Akram and S Leigh *Where Do You Keep Your String Beds?* (1984); M Akram and J Elliot *Appeal Dismissed* (1977); Z Chowdhury *Split Families: an Examination of the Immigration Control System Relating to Dependants in Bangladesh* (1982). For Home Office rejoinders, see the Home Office annual *Report on the Work of the Immigration and Nationality Department* (1984 to date). See also First Report from the Select Committee on Race Relations and Immigration (HC Paper (1977–78) no. 303) (Immigration); Fifth Report from the Home Affairs Committee (HC Paper (1981–82) no. 90) (Immigration from the Indian Sub-continent); Sixth Report from the Home Affairs Committee (HC Paper (1984–85) no. 277) (Immigration and Nationality Department of the Home Office).

4 See the Immigration Rules, paras 14–16 (amended by HC Paper (1990–91) no. 356). The requirements may, it seems, be waived for air passengers in transit provided they have entry facilities for their country of destination and transit visas for any other country en route, even if they must change between the various London airports: see L Grant and I Martin *Immigration Law and Practice* (1982) pp 60, 61. See also the Immigration Rules, para 13. As to returning residents, see para 120, text and note 6, above.

5 Ibid, para 14.

6 The documents accepted are a refugee travel document (issued under the Convention relating to the Status of Refugees (Geneva, 28 July 1951; TS 39 (1954); Cmd 9171)), a stateless person's travel document (issued under the Convention relating to the Status of Stateless Persons (New York, 28 September 1954; TS 41 (1960); Cmnd 1098)), and any *laissez-passer* (issued by an international organisation whose officials are exempted by statutory instrument under the Immigration Act 1971 (c 77), s 8(2): see para 128 above).

7 See the Immigration Rules, Pt VI (paras 68–74): see para 137 above, and paras 221 ff below.

8 See ibid, para 15.

9 See ibid, paras 38–40, and paras 246 ff below.

10 See ibid, paras 41–43, and paras 250–253 below.

11 See ibid, para 44, and paras 258–260 below.

12 See ibid, para 45, and paras 254–257 below.

13 See ibid, paras 47, 48, and paras 274 ff below.

14 See ibid, paras 50, 51, and paras 269–273 below.

15 See ibid, paras 53–55, and paras 279–284 below.

16 See ibid, para 52, 56, 57, and paras 285–290 below.

17 See ibid, para 49, and para 326 below.

18 See ibid, paras 22–25, and paras 305–309 below.
19 See ibid, para 33, and paras 310–313 below.
20 See ibid, paras 34, 35, and paras 154–157, 242–245 below.
21 See ibid, para 32, and para 292 below.
22 See ibid, para 37, and para 263 below.
23 See ibid, para 64, and para 290 below.
24 See ibid, paras 58–60, and para 119 above.
25 See ibid, para 36, and para 261 below.
26 See ibid, para 26, and paras 292 ff below.
27 The phrase, of obvious import, was popularised and criticised in *Immigration Control Procedures: Report of a Formal Investigation* (1985, Commission for Racial Equality).
28 See the Immigration Act 1971, s 3(9), the Immigration Rules, paras 8, 16, and para 153 below.

152. Application for grant of entry clearance and refusal. Entry clearance should be applied for from the nearest High Commission, Embassy or Consulate in the country in which the applicant is living, outside the common travel area[1]. It is not clear if the requirement is mandatory or directory. A form is available, but is not mandatory provided the application is quite unambiguous[2]. An interview may be required of the applicant, and possibly also of the sponsor[3]. Entry clearance is granted or refused in accordance with the provisions of the Immigration Rules, but applications are decided in the light of the circumstances existing at the time of the decision (except that a child will not be refused clearance for settlement solely because he becomes over age between receipt of the application and the date of the decision on it)[4]. Thus, broadly, the same evidence is required as would be to show eligibility under the relevant Immigration Rules for leave to enter, for example family relationship to and dependency upon a person already settled, and an applicant can also be referred for a medical examination[5]. Thus, broadly also, the grounds for refusal of entry clearance are presumed to be the same as for refusal of entry although the Immigration Rules do not refer to the issue except in passing[6].

It has been argued that the burden of proof has been raised or reversed in practice in applications relating to the Indian sub-continent[7]. Delays in obtaining an interview, and thereafter a decision, are usually considerable in the case of such applications[8]. A procedure whereby actual leave to enter may be granted before entry exists[9].

1 Statement of Changes in Immigration Rules (HC Paper (1989–90) no. 251) (the Immigration Rules), para 15.
2 Form IM2. See also *Ex parte Prajapati* [1981] Imm AR 199, DC; *Brown v Entry Clearance Officer, Kingston, Jamaica* [1976] Imm AR 119, IAT; *Malik v Secretary of State for the Home Department* [1982] Imm AR 183, IAT.
3 An entry clearance officer is not acting judicially when interviewing, but administratively: *Ramesh Kumar v Entry Clearance Officer, New Delhi* [1985] Imm AR 242, IAT. Cf para 164, text to and note 2, below.
4 Immigration Rules, para 16.
5 Ibid, para 83. See also *Sudhakaran v Entry Clearance Officer, Madras* [1976] Imm AR 3, IAT.
6 See the Immigration Rules, para 78.
7 *Immigration Control Procedures: Report of a Formal Investigation* (1985, Commission for Racial Equality) para 11.6.5 ff. It has been suggested that this is the result of discrimination, and some evidence was produced: see eg Annex B, paras 11, 40.
8 Ibid, Table 4.2. See also the annual 'Control of Immigration into the United Kingdom Statistics'. There are not only lengthy waits for interviews, but more than one interview may be required and the decision can then take a further lengthy period.
9 See the Immigration Act 1988 (c 14), s 8, and para 150, text to note 6, above, para 162, text to notes 1, 2, and para 170, text to note 9, below.

153. Certificates of entitlement and proof of right of abode. Those with a right of abode[1] do not require entry clearance. However, a person asserting British citizenship bears the burden of proof[2], which requires to be discharged by production of a United Kingdom passport describing him as a British citizen, or as a citizen of the United Kingdom and Colonies with the right of abode[3], or a certificate of entitlement (previously known as a certificate of patriality[4]) issued by or on behalf of the United Kingdom government. In other words the certificate of entitlement performs the same function as an entry certificate. Those already in the United Kingdom will normally have their passports stamped to show the right of abode, or will be British citizens and entitled to a passport which exempts them from any need for a certificate of entitlement, and in any case will be settled[5], having indefinite leave to remain.

Also requiring a certificate of entitlement are those who are Commonwealth citizens, but not British citizens, who nevertheless have a right of abode because of descent from a United Kingdom-born parent, or because of marriage to a man with a right of abode[6]. Such people were given the right of abode by the Immigration Act 1971 as originally enacted (having lost it under the Commonwealth Immigrants Act 1962)[7]. The right is continued (but not further transmissible) under the Immigration Act 1971[8].

A certificate of patriality issued in error to an unentitled person is accepted as capable of 'cancellation' even in the absence of fraud, misrepresentation or concealment of material facts[9].

There is no requirement to acquire a certificate of entitlement in order to enter, only if a right of abode is asserted. Thus, visitors do not need them, nor any person who can successfully obtain leave to enter under another category of the Immigration Rules. It is also likely that a large number of those with the right of abode who are not British citizens do not know that they have it.

1 See paras 117, 118, above.
2 Immigration Act 1971 (c 77), s 3(8) (amended by the British Nationality Act 1981 (c 61), s 39(6), Sch 4, para 2).
3 A person who has not renewed his passport since 1 January 1983 might bear one describing him as a citizen of the United Kingdom and Colonies.
4 See para 118 above.
5 Statement of Changes in Immigration Rules (HC Paper (1989–90) no. 251) (the Immigration Rules), para 1. See also para 120 above.
6 Ibid, para 8.
7 They acquired it by virtue of the Immigration Act 1971, s 2(1)(d), (2) (as originally enacted). All Commonwealth citizens born to, or adopted by a parent (of either sex) who had citizenship of the United Kingdom and Colonies by birth in the United Kingdom or Islands were included: s 2(1)(d) (as originally enacted). This provision introduced a measure of sexual equality, as citizenship descended only in the male line, but increasingly the right of entry was seen as the primary dependent right. On the other hand, it was noted that nearly all those benefiting (and benefiting from other parts of s 2) were in the 'white' Commonwealth and hardly any in the 'non-white' Commonwealth. This apparent anomaly was exacerbated by the fact that the right was being restored to people who had lost it a decade earlier under the Commonwealth Immigrants Act 1962 (c 21) (repealed).

    Also included were all Commonwealth citizens married to men who were citizens of the United Kingdom and Colonies by any means whatsoever and had a right of entry: Immigration Act 1971, s 2(2) (as originally enacted). Widows and the divorced wives of such men and those of men who would have been such citizens with a right of entry had they not died before the new dispensation of the British Nationality Act 1948 (c 56) (which invented the citizenship of the United Kingdom and Colonies) and the Immigration Act 1971 itself, were also included.
8 See the Immigration Act 1971, s 2 (substituted by the British Nationality Act 1981, s 39(2)).
9 *Secretary of State for the Home Department v Gold and Gold* [1985] Imm AR 66, IAT. Such cancellation is not a 'refusal' so no appeal lies: see para 336 below.

(B) WORK PERMITS

154. Introduction. Work permits are the major form of control over entry for economic activity (except in the case of Community nationals). They are not required for entry by those who:

(1) require leave to enter and who seek indefinite leave[1];

(2) seek entry for 'permit-free employment'[2];

(3) are Commonwealth citizens seeking entry for employment and can prove a United Kingdom-born grandparent[3];

(4) are young Commonwealth citizens on a working holiday[4];

(5) are au pairs[5];

(6) are writers and artists[6];

(7) are businessmen or self-employed persons[7]; or

(8) are persons of independent means[8].

Visitors are also free to transact business[9]. Students may have a condition prohibiting employment, or merely restricting it, that is, requiring Home Office consent[10], except that student nurses, midwives, doctors or dentists are subject to special rules[11]. Otherwise a person seeking employment, including 'on the job' training[12], in the United Kingdom requires a work permit[13].

A work permit is granted only for a specific job to be performed by a specific person for a specific period, and may be applied for only by an employer[14]. Limited possibilities of change of employment exist. However, the leave to enter is capable of renewal for up to four years, and indefinite leave may be granted thereafter[15]. Thus the system may be distinguished from the '*gastarbeiter*' system imposed elsewhere, under which work and entitlement to entry last for the duration of a fixed-term contract, which may be renewed, but cannot result in permanent settlement[16].

The numbers, types and distribution of work permits are, as noted, entirely a matter for the government of the day, not requiring parliamentary approval, and largely reflect economic policies in relation to employment as a whole and to specific industries with labour shortages[17]. Thus specific allotments to particular industries or particular territories have been made[18]. However, the overall number of work permits issued has declined and for a number of years they have in general been allotted only in respect of highly-skilled workers and trainees[19]. There is no appeal against refusal to grant a work permit[20].

At the date at which this volume states the law, a new system of distribution of work permits was under discussion.

1 See the Statement of Changes in Immigration Rules (HC Paper (1989–90) no. 251) (the Immigration Rules), Pt IV (paras 49–60), and paras 267 ff below.

2 See ibid, paras 38–40, and paras 246–249 below.

3 See ibid, para 36, and para 261 below.

4 See ibid, para 37, and para 263 below.

5 See ibid, para 33, and paras 310–313 below.

6 See ibid, para 45, and paras 254–257 below.

7 See ibid, paras 41–43, and paras 250–253 below.

8 See ibid, para 44, and paras 258–260 below.

9 See ibid, para 24, and paras 305–309 below.

10 See ibid, para 30, and paras 292 ff below.

11 See ibid, paras 29, 32, 102, 114, 115, and para 295 below.

12 See ibid, para 117, and paras 244, 245, below.

13 See ibid, para 34, and paras 242–245 below.

14 See Department of Employment leaflets OW5 'Employment of Overseas Workers in the United Kingdom'; OW17 'Employment in the United Kingdom: a guide for workers from non-EC countries'; OW21 'Employment of Overseas Workers in the United Kingdom: Training and work experience'; and OW1 'Application to Employ an Overseas Worker'. These and other related pamphlets should be available from the Professional and Executive Register of local job centres. In addition, changes in practice may be intimated by a mere 'Press Notice', eg that of the Department of Employment dated 31 December 1979 phasing out certain types of work permit: see I A Macdonald *Immigration Law and Practice* (2nd edn, 1987) p 194, note 7. They do not require renewal as such, but may specify a period of employment which will indicate the length of leave to enter which will be given: see para 244, text to note 1, para 245, text to note 1, below.

15 Immigration Rules, paras 122, 139. As already noted the work permit as such is not renewable. Renewal of leave to enter or remain is dependent upon the Department of Employment approving the continued employment, unless the permit is issued for four years: see paras 242, 243, 245, below.

 After four years in 'work-permit employment', settlement is normally granted: see para 244 below.

16 See eg E H Hönekopp and H Ullman 'Status of Immigrant Workers in the Federal Republic of Germany' in E J Thomas *Immigrant Workers in Europe: their legal status: a comparative study* (1982).

17 See para 112 above.

18 Eg to the textile and clothing industry in the early 1970s, and to the hotel and catering trade more recently; there have also been allotments to specific dependencies: see J M Evans *Immigration Law* (2nd edn, 1983) p 155; I A Macdonald *Immigration Law and Practice* (2nd edn, 1987) p 194; *Role of Immigrants in the Labour Market* (1975, Unit for Manpower Studies (Department of Employment and Productivity)) Part II, especially paras F21–F39, F64–F92.

19 The two principal recipient states in recent years have been Japan and the United States: see the annual 'Control of Immigration into the United Kingdom Statistics'.

20 *Pearson v Immigration Appeal Tribunal* [1978] Imm AR 212, CA: see para 344 below.

155. Allotment of work permits for skilled work and for trainees. No indication is given in the Immigration Act 1971, the statutory instruments thereunder, nor the Immigration Rules as to the criteria for allotment of work permits or the method of application, save that they are issued by the Department of Employment in respect of a specific post and that in general a work permit should be obtained before the person sets out for the United Kingdom[1]. Criteria and method are ascertained from Department of Employment leaflets, and press releases, and ministerial statements and Written Answers in Parliament[2].

For a post to be considered for a work permit, a genuine vacancy must exist[3] for a worker in one of the following categories:

(1) those with recognised professional qualifications;

(2) administrative and executive staff;

(3) highly qualified technicians with specialised experience;

(4) other key workers with a high or scarce qualification in an industry or occupation requiring specific expert knowledge or skills;

(5) highly skilled or experienced workers for senior posts in hotel and catering work who have successfully completed appropriate full-time training courses of at least two years' duration at approved schools abroad or, exceptionally, have acquired other specialised or uncommon skills and experience;

(6) established entertainers, including self-employed entertainers coming to fulfil engagements;

(7) sportsmen and sportswomen who meet the appropriate skills criteria (professional sportsmen and sportswomen taking part in competitions of international standing do not normally require permits);

(8) other persons only if, in the opinion of the Secretary of State for Employment, their employment is in the national interest; and

(9) those coming for a limited period of training on the job or work experience[4].

The post must have been advertised locally, nationally and in the trade press, and must not be capable of being filled by a candidate possessing equal skills or qualifications, by promotion, transfer or training or from elsewhere within the European Community. The employer must be prepared to pay for an applicant resident in the United Kingdom but at a distance to come to interviews or to take up employment. Wages and conditions of employment must be no worse than those locally available for similar work[5].

For a person to be considered for a work permit for such a post, he must be between twenty-three and fifty-three years of age except in the case of trainees (where the minimum age is eighteen) or sportsmen and women (where there is no lower age limit) and must have a good command of English, and fulfil the criteria for the post[6].

The employer applies (preferably at least eight weeks in advance) to the local Department of Employment office (except in the case of sportsmen and women, who are dealt with centrally), enclosing documentary evidence that he has advertised as required, and the results of such advertising, and references and other evidence relating to the proposed worker[7].

The Department of Employment then decides whether or not to issue a work permit. It will not do so if it considers that suitable labour is available resident in the United Kingdom, that inadequate advertising has occurred within the European Community, or that the person specified does not have the necessary qualifications, skills or experience. Fulfilment of all criteria does not entitle the applicant to have a work permit issued[8].

If issued, the work permit is, in the case of aliens (except Pakistanis), sent to the employer to forward, and in the case of Commonwealth citizens (and Pakistanis) to the relevant High Commission (or embassy) in order that further checks, including medical examination, can be made before forwarding[9].

1 Statement of Changes in Immigration Rules (HC Paper (1989–90) no. 251) (the Immigration Rules), para 35.
2 See the examples set out in para 154, note 14, above.
3 See the Department of Employment leaflet ow5 'Employment of Overseas Workers in the United Kingdom', para 9.
4 Ibid, para 8. See also *Secretary of State for the Home Department v Stillwaggon* [1975] Imm AR 132, IAT.
5 Leaflet ow5, paras 9, 10.
6 Ibid, paras 7–9.
7 See ibid, paras 12–16, and the Department of Employment leaflet ow1 'Application to Employ an Overseas Worker'.
8 *Re Suruk Miah* (1976) Times, 4 February, CA.
9 Leaflet ow5, para 18.

156. Allotment of work permits in other cases.
In cases where a quota of work permits is granted to a particular type of employment, or in favour of a particular territory, similar arrangements apply as for work permits allotted in respect of skilled work except for the criteria of skill[1].

1 Communication from the Overseas Labour Division of Department of Employment. As to the arrangements in respect of skilled work, see para 155 above.

157. Application for a work permit in the case of a person resident in the United Kingdom.
In general a work permit will not be issued in respect of a person present in the United Kingdom, but may be in the cases of nurses or midwives trained in the United Kingdom[1]. Visitors or students may be granted extensions of stay as trainees if the Department of Employment considers the offer satisfactory and if there is no reason to believe that the person does not intend to leave on completion of the training[2].

1 Statement of Changes in Immigration Rules (HC Paper (1989–90) no. 251) (the Immigration Rules), para 102.
2 Ibid, para 120.

(C) SPECIAL VOUCHERS

158. Introduction.
The position of the 'East African Asians' has been noted above, that is, in brief, that they retained the right of entry under the Common-

wealth Immigrants Act 1962 (c 21), that the Commonwealth Immigrants Act 1968 (c 9) removed it when they attempted to exercise it, but that there was much political moral pressure applied to the United Kingdom[1]. The 'special voucher' scheme was introduced: this was expressed to be for the purpose of allowing orderly entry for settlement, so that a claim was acknowledged[2]. The Immigration Rules envisage that such a person may receive entry clearance in lieu of a special voucher[3].

1 See para 107, above.
2 759 HC Official Report (5th series) col 1256.
3 Statement of Changes in Immigration Rules (HC Paper (1989–90) no. 251) (the Immigration Rules), para 49.

159. Allocation of special vouchers. Although the Immigration Rules do refer briefly to 'United Kingdom passport holders', the rules say nothing about the allocation of vouchers[1]. Nor does any other official published source lay down authoritative guidelines, and details are therefore to be gleaned from parliamentary statements and the like[2]. It appears that special vouchers may be granted to a British Overseas citizen or British subject (without citizenship) or British protected person, provided he is not a dual national, who is a head of household and who is in Kenya or Uganda and regarded as being under pressure to leave, or who has left and is resident in India, or in the case of British Overseas citizens only, in other countries.

A woman is regarded as a head of household only if she is single, widowed or divorced, or if her husband has such a disability as to prevent him from being regarded as head of household. In all cases she must be over eighteen years of age.

The voucher covers dependent children under eighteen years of age and may cover those up to twenty-five years of age even if they could qualify separately.

Thus, a family, the male head of which adopted local citizenship, is wholly ineligible even if all other members of the family are British Overseas citizens, and his wife and children cannot benefit (except in the case of any independent children over twenty-five years of age). Equally a daughter otherwise eligible, marrying a man who cannot be eligible, loses all eligibility.

The annual allocation of special vouchers is determined by the Secretary of State. Those wishing to apply do so at a United Kingdom High Commission office. Priorities are operated in allocation in favour of certain groups.

Entry clearance also has to be obtained for dependants of the special voucher holder, and the entry clearance officer must be satisfied that there will be adequate accommodation which is owned or occupied by the special voucher holder and that they can be maintained adequately without, in either case, resort to public funds[3].

There is no appeal against refusal of a special voucher as they are not entry clearances[4], but United Kingdom passport holders who have entry clearance, which the Immigration Rules envisage, would[5].

1 See the Statement of Changes in Immigration Rules (HC Paper (1989–90) no. 251) (the Immigration Rules), para 49.
2 See eg 759 HC Official Report (5th series) col 1256; 818 HC Official Report (5th series) col 380; 849 HC Official Report (5th series) col 656; 890 HC Official Report (5th series) written answers col 23; 10 HC Official Report (6th series) written answers cols 439–444. Some details are given in the Fifth Report from the Home Affairs Committee (HC Paper (1981–82) no. 90) (Immigration from the Indian Sub-Continent) paras 68–132, and the government's reply (Cmnd 8725) (1982) paras 14, 15, and the First Report from the Select Committee on Race Relations and Immigration (HC Paper (1977–78) no. 303) (Immigration) paras 113–123. More recently, a leaked letter from the Department of Education and Science to the Home Office shows an apparent attempt to arrange exceptional measures to speed the entry of teachers to fill London vacancies: The

Independent, 3 August 1990. Most information on the subject has been gleaned by the Joint Council for the Welfare of Immigrants and appears in L Grant and I Martin *Immigration Law and Practice* (1982), First Supplement (1985) paras 3.8–3.13, and more recently in the periodical 'Immigration and Nationality Law and Practice'.
3 Immigration Rules, paras 49, 52.
4 *Shah v Secretary of State for the Home Department* [1972] Imm AR 56, IAT; *R v Entry Clearance Officer, Bombay, ex parte Amin* [1980] 2 All ER 837, [1970] 1 WLR 1530, DC.
5 Immigration Rules, para 49. As to appeals, see para 336, below.

(D) SPONSORSHIP AND PUBLIC FUNDS

160. Sponsorship and public funds generally. Nothing is said in the Immigration Act 1971 or statutory instruments thereunder concerning sponsorship. However, in the case of most categories under the Immigration Rules, it is a requirement that there be adequate maintenance and accommodation available for the person seeking entry, without recourse to public funds[1]. This requirement has been translated into a requirement, under the rubric 'public funds', for a sponsor who may be asked to give an undertaking in writing to be responsible for such maintenance and accommodation and who is warned that any income support in fact paid may be recovered from the sponsor[2]. Consequently entry clearance officers may require a notarised 'sponsorship declaration', particularly in settlement or Indian sub-continent cases. No official form for this exists, but the declaration must clearly identify the sponsor and his immigration status, employment, income etc and details of the accommodation[3]. Sponsors may be asked to provide authority for the Inland Revenue to release tax information to the entry clearance officer[4].

The sponsorship undertaking is also to include any variation of leave[5]. Thus agreement to be responsible for a particular period is likely to have effects upon applications to extend leave to a longer period.

1 See the Statement of Changes in Immigration Rules (HC Paper (1989–90) no. 251) (the Immigration Rules), paras 22, 26, 37, 38(a), 44, 45, 47, 49, 50, 52. 'Public funds' means housing under the Housing Act 1985 (c 68), Pt III (ss 58–78), the Housing (Scotland) Act 1987 (c 26), Pt II (ss 24–43) (see HOUSING, vol 11, paras 2037 ff) and the Housing (Northern Ireland) Order 1988, SI 1988/1990, Pt II; and income support, family credit and housing benefit under the Social Security Act 1986 (c 50), Pt II (ss 20–31), and the Social Security (Northern Ireland) Order 1986, Pt III. Savings from supplementary benefit are 'public funds': *R v Immigration Appeal Tribunal, ex parte Chhinderpal Singh and Gurdip Singh* [1989] Imm AR 69. There may also be police inquiries: see the Scottish Home and Health Department Police (Chief Constable) Circular No 6/1972 (Immigration Act 1971 (c 77)) para 34. It does not refer to the position under the national health service: cf the National Health Service (Charges to Overseas Visitors) (Scotland) Regulations 1989, SI 1989/364, and the Scottish Home and Health Department Circular 1982 (Gen) 29 (Treatment of Overseas Visitors).
2 Immigration Rules, para 20. The power to recover is under the Social Security Act 1986, and the Social Security (Northern Ireland) Order 1986.
3 L Grant and I Martin *Immigration Law and Practice* (1982) pp 171, 172, and First Supplement (1985) p 89, gives a useful description and advice and points out that a local authority may attest the suitability of accommodation.
4 *Immigration Control Procedures: Report of a Formal Investigation* (1985, Commission for Racial Equality) para 4.6.5.
5 Immigration Rules, para 20.

(c) Control on Entry

161. Requirements as to place and manner of entry. The Secretary of State may from time to time, by written notice to the owners or agents of ships and aircraft or the Concessionaires of the Channel Tunnel and those concerned in the management of ports, designate control areas in ports for the purpose of the embarkation and disembarkation of passengers, and specify conditions and restrictions to be observed there[1]. Those given notice are to take all reasonable steps to secure that passengers embark or disembark only in such control areas, and subject to such conditions and restrictions[1]. This power should not be confused with that under the prevention of terrorism powers[2].

Except with the approval of the Secretary of State, owners and agents of ships or aircraft carrying passengers for reward may not arrange for the ship or aircraft to call at any port in order to disembark passengers except a designated port of entry, if any passenger requires leave to enter[3]. Nor in such circumstances may they embark passengers unless they have reasonable cause to believe them all to be British citizens[4].

Breach of these requirements is an offence punishable on summary conviction with a fine of not more than level 4 on the standard scale or imprisonment not exceeding six months, or both, but no passenger can commit the offence[5].

The captain of a ship or aircraft must take the necessary steps to ensure that passengers and crew do not disembark unless examined by an immigration officer (in which case he must take steps to secure that the examination is orderly); or in accordance with arrangements approved by an immigration officer; or, in the case of crew members, unless they are entitled to enter without leave[6] the United Kingdom[7].

The Secretary of State may, by statutory instrument, require captains of all ships and aircraft, or such as arrive from certain places only, to provide immigration officers with a passenger list showing names and nationalities of passengers, and particulars of crew members, and to allow immigration officers to dispense with such requirements[8].

Breach of these requirements is an offence punishable on summary conviction by a fine not exceeding level 4 on the standard scale or imprisonment or both[9].

Owners or agents of a ship or aircraft are liable to a fine where a person arriving by such ship or aircraft requires leave to enter and fails to produce a valid passport with photograph or other document satisfactorily establishing identity and nationality, or, in the case of a visa national, to produce a visa[10]. Proof that such document was produced before embarkation, or that its falsity was not reasonably apparent, is a defence[11].

1 Immigration Act 1971 (c 77), s 4(2), Sch 2, paras 26(1), (2), 27A (amended and substituted by the Channel Tunnel (Fire Services, Immigration and Prevention of Terrorism) Order 1990, SI 1990/2227, art 3, Sch 1).

2 See para 133 above.

3 Immigration Act 1971, Sch 2, para 26(1). The designated seaports and hoverports are Dover, Felixstowe, Folkestone, Harwich, Hull, London, Newhaven, Plymouth, Portsmouth, Ramsgate, Sheerness, Southampton and Tyne; and the designated airports are Aberdeen, Belfast, Birmingham, Bournemouth (Hurn), Bristol, Cardiff (Wales), East Midlands, Edinburgh, Gatwick-London, Glasgow, Heathrow-London, Leeds/Bradford, Liverpool, Luton, Manchester, Newcastle, Norwich, Prestwick, Southampton, Southend, Stansted-London and Teesside: Immigration (Ports of Entry) Order 1987, SI 1987/177, art 2, Schedule.

4 Immigration Act 1971, Sch 2, para 26(1) (amended by the British Nationality Act 1981 (c 61), s 39(6), Sch 4, para 2).

5 See the Immigration Act 1971, s 27(b)(i), (ii), (c). As to level 4 of the standard scale, see the Criminal Procedure (Scotland) Act 1975 (c 21), ss 289F, 289G (added by the Criminal Justice Act 1982 (c 48), s 54). At the date at which this volume states the law, level 4 is £1,000: see the Increase of Criminal Penalties etc (Scotland) Order 1984, SI 1984/526, art 4. See also PROCEDURE, vol 17, para 575, note 1.

6 Ie under the Immigration Act 1971, s 8(1): see para 129 above.

7 Ibid, Sch 2, para 27(1).

8 Ibid, Sch 2, para 27(2). See also the Immigration (Particulars of Passengers and Crew) Order 1972, SI 1972/1667 (amended by SI 1975/980).

9 Immigration Act 1971, s 27(a)(i) and s 27(d)(ii) (added by the Channel Tunnel (Fire Services, Immigration and Prevention of Terrorism) Order 1990, Sch 1).

10 Immigration (Carriers' Liability) Act 1987 (c 24), s 1(1). At the date at which this volume states the law, the fine is £2,000: s 1(1) (amended by the Immigration (Carriers' Liability Prescribed Sum) Order 1991, SI 1991/1497).

11 Ibid, s 1(2), (4).

162. Examination on arrival to establish identity, nationality etc. Unless he has undergone appropriate immigration procedure before arrival, a person arriving in the United Kingdom, whether or not seeking entry and whether or not requiring leave to enter, may be examined by an immigration officer to determine whether or not he is a British citizen; if not, whether he requires leave to enter; and if he does require leave, whether it should be given and on what conditions[1]. Appropriate immigration procedures before arrival require the person to have had a passport or other travel document, which bears a stamp placed on it by an immigration officer, which states that he may enter the United Kingdom either for an indefinite period or for a limited one, and in the latter case states the conditions imposed[2]. Such a person is deemed to have been given such leave timeously on arrival, and is not to be examined as if arriving without such leave, but only for the purpose of establishing that he is such a person[3]. Such leave may be cancelled, however, within twenty-four hours (subject to certain constraints)[4]. 'Arrival' is given a restricted meaning in this context[5].

'Examination' is not defined but can include acquiring information from other people as well as an interview[6]. A person arriving in the United Kingdom, unless he has undergone appropriate immigration procedure before arrival, may be required in writing to submit to further examination, provided that he is not prevented from leaving on his intended ship or aircraft if he is a transit passenger or a member of a crew arriving on, or for the purpose of joining, a ship or aircraft[7].

A person examined must produce all such information as is required for the purpose of examination, and in particular a valid passport with photograph or other document satisfactorily identifying him and his nationality[8]. Such document may be detained by an immigration officer until the person is given leave to enter or is about to be removed or deported[9]. National passports or travel documents issued by a territorial entity or authority not reecognised by Her Majesty's government as a state, or not dealt with as a government by it, or which does not accept valid United Kingdom passports, may not be acceptable, and neither may such documents failing to comply with international passport practice[10]. In the case of nationals of member states of the European Community (except Ireland, which, like the United Kingdom, does not have them), valid identity cards are acceptable[11]. In other cases, where an agreement to that effect has been concluded, national identity cards in conjunction with visitors' cards may be accepted for visits of less than six months and not for employment[12].

A person examined must declare whether he is carrying any documents of any description which an immigration officer considers relevant for the examination, and if so must produce it[13]. The person may be searched to discover if he is carrying such a document, but a girl or woman may be searched only by a woman[14]. Any document produced or discovered, other than a passport, may be detained for up to seven days, or, if the immigration officer is of the opinion that it will be needed for an appeal under the Immigration Act 1971, until he is satisfied it is not so needed[15].

1 See the Immigration Act 1971 (c 77), s 4(2), Sch 2, para 2 (amended by the British Nationality Act 1981 (c 61), s 39(6), Sch 4, para 2, and the Channel Tunnel (Fire Services, Immigration and Prevention of Terrorism) Order 1990, SI 1990/2227, art 3, Sch 1), the Immigration Act 1988

(c 14), s 8, and the Statement of Changes in Immigration Rules (HC Paper (1989–90) no. 251)
(the Immigration Rules), para 7.

2 See the Immigration Act 1988, s 8(1), and para 150, text to note 6, para 152, text to note 9, above,
and para 170, text to note 9, below.

3 Ibid, s 8(2)–(4). The provision also exempts medical examination: see para 165 below.

4 Ibid, s 8(5), (6) (applying the Immigration Act 1971, Sch 2, para 6(3), (4)) (amended by the
Immigration Act 1988, s 10, Schedule, para 8(2))). For the purposes of the Immigration Act
1988, s 8(6), a reference to a port at which a person seeks to enter the United Kingdom includes
the terminal area in the tunnel system at Cheriton, Folkestone, and the service and maintenance
area at the Old Dover Colliery site referred to in the Channel Tunnel Act 1987 (c 53), s 1(7)(b):
Immigration Act 1988, s 8(8) (added by the Channel Tunnel (Fire Services, Immigration and
Prevention of Terrorism) Order 1990, Sch 1).

5 For the purposes of the Immigration Act 1988, s 8, references to a person's arrival in the United
Kingdom are references to the first occasion on which he arrives after the time when the stamp in
question was placed in his passport or travel document, being an occasion not later than seven
days after that time: s 8(7).

6 *Perera v Immigration Officer, London (Heathrow) Airport* [1979–80] Imm AR 58, IAT. The 'interview' is not necessarily the whole of the 'examination': *Secretary of State for the Home Department v
Thirukumar* [1989] Imm AR 402, CA. An examination can be too perfunctory to be an examination for this purpose: *Tejpartap Singh Rehal v Secretary of State for the Home Department* [1989]
Imm AR 576, CA.

7 Immigration Act 1971, Sch 2, para 2(3).

8 See ibid, Sch 2, para 4(1), (2), and the Immigration Rules, para 7.

9 Immigration Act 1971, Sch 2, para 4(2A) (added by the Immigration Act 1988, Schedule, para 6).

10 Immigration Rules, r 10. Territorial entities or authorities not recognised for this purpose are
currently Bophuthatswana, Ciskei, Federation of Micronesia, Korean Democratic Republic,
Republic of the Marshall Islands, Taiwan, Transkei, Turkish Republic of North Cyprus and
Venda: Communication from the Immigration and Nationality Department. This list excludes
the Imamate of Oman States and Yemen (Royalist authorities) mentioned by L Grant and
I Martin *Immigration Law and Practice* (1982), First Supplement (1985) para 5.3. In the case of other
countries, an *ad hoc* decision to refuse to accept may be taken, and acceptability may depend upon
the category of the Immigration Rules under which entry is sought: *Hak Rok Djang (or Chang) v
Secretary of State for the Home Department* [1985] Imm AR 125, IAT.

11 Immigration Rules, para 7.

12 Ibid, para 7. The countries are: Austria (Exchange of Notes with Austria concerning the
Abolition of Visas (Vienna, 12 July 1971; TS 74 (1971); Cmnd 4785)); Monaco (Exchange of
Notes with Monaco concerning Arrangements to Facilitate Travel (London 29 March 1961 and
Monaco 11 April 1961; TS 62 (1961); Cmnd 1430)); and Switzerland and Liechtenstein (Ex-
change of Notes with Switzerland concerning Arrangements to Facilitate Travel (Berne, 27
February 1961; TS 33 (1961); Cmnd 1371)). The format of these British visitors' cards are found
in the appendices to the treaties, but are not reprinted in the United Kingdom Treaty Series.

13 Immigration Act 1971, Sch 2, para 4(2)(b).

14 Ibid, Sch 2, para 4(3).

15 Ibid, Sch 2, para 4(4).

163. Requirement to complete a landing card.
Any person without the
right of abode and aged sixteen years or more may be required to complete a
landing card supplied on the ship or aircraft (in a form directed by the Secretary
of State) and produce it to an immigration officer, unless on a local journey
within the common travel area (except for a person having entered the Republic
of Ireland and not obtained leave to enter there, intending to enter the United
Kingdom or one required to do so under the Prevention of Terrorism (Temporary Provisions) Act 1989 (c 4))[1]. The details required are name, place and date of
birth, nationality or citizenship, occupation, and the address at which the person
will be staying in the United Kingdom.

1 See the Immigration Act 1971 (c 77), s 4(2), Sch 2, para 5, and the Immigration (Landing and
Embarkation Cards) 1975, SI 1975/65, arts 4, 5. As to the exceptions, see paras 124, 133, 134,
above.

164. Conduct of examination.
Immigration officers are required to carry
out their duties without regard to the race, colour or religion of those seeking

entry[1] and must act honestly and fairly, although, as an administrative officer rather than a judicial one, he does not have to follow a set procedure so long as he gives the passenger a real opportunity to state his case and is satisfied before taking a particular decision[2].

It is for the passenger to show his entitlement, and there is no obligation upon immigration officers to suggest other grounds or further evidence[3].

1 Statement of Changes in Immigration Rules (HC Paper (1989–90) no. 251) (the Immigration Rules), para 6. However, see *Immigration Control Procedures: Report of a Formal Investigation* (1985, Commission for Racial Equality) paras 4.29.1–4.29.12, also ch 9. Examination need not take place at the time of entry or port of entry: *Baljinder Singh v Hammond* [1987] 1 All ER 829, [1987] 1 WLR 283, DC.

2 *Re HK (an infant)* [1967] 2 QB 617, [1967] 1 All ER 226, DC; *R v Secretary of State for the Home Department, ex parte Mughal* [1974] QB 313, [1973] 3 All ER 796, CA. See also *Ramesh Kumar v Entry Clearance Officer, New Delhi* [1985] Imm AR 242, IAT.

3 *R v Chief Immigration Officer, Heathrow Airport, ex parte Salamat Bibi* [1976] 3 All ER 843, [1976] 1 WLR 979, CA.

165. Medical examination of those seeking entry. A person seeking entry may be examined by a medical inspector or other qualified person carrying out a test or examination required by a medical inspector, and may be required in writing to submit for further examination, provided that he is not prevented from leaving on the intended ship or aircraft in the case of a transit passenger, or a member of a crew arriving on or for the purpose of joining, a ship or aircraft[1]. It appears that the requirement may be applied to those with a right of abode, since although they cannot be refused entry they are seeking entry, but it cannot be applied to those who have undergone appropriate immigration procedure before arrival as they are not subject to examination[2].

Immigration officers are normally to refer to a medical inspector any passengers intending to remain for more than six months, any who mention health or medical treatment as a reason for the visit, and any appearing not to be in good health, or to be mentally or physically abnormal[3]. Otherwise the power is to be used sparingly[3]. This is presumably intended to apply only in the case of those without a right of abode, since referral is with a view to possible refusal of entry. However, further examination may be required after entry on public health grounds[4]. There is no method of appeal against a medical inspector's conclusion or advice[5]. Vaginal examinations are now not to be made[6]. Breach of the requirement to submit to a medical examination is an offence[7].

1 Immigration Act 1971 (c 77), s 4(2), Sch 2, para 2(2), (3) (amended by the Channel Tunnel (Fire Services, Immigration and Prevention of Terrorism) Order 1990, SI 1990/2227, art 3, Sch 1).

2 See the Immigration Act 1988 (c 14), s 8, and para 162 above.

3 Statement of Changes in Immigration Rules (HC Paper (1989–90) no. 251) (the Immigration Rules) para 80.

4 Ie under the Immigration Act 1971, Sch 2, para 2(3): see para 171, text to note 13, and para 172, text to note 10, below.

5 *Al-Tuwaidji v Chief Immigration Officer, London (Heathrow) Airport* [1974] Imm AR 34, IAT. See also paras 171, 172, below.

6 L Grant and I Martin *Immigration Law and Practice* (1982) p 78, note 14. See also 'The Medical Examination of Immigrants: Report to the Home Secretary by the Chief Medical Officer' (1980).

7 See the Immigration Act 1971, s 24(1)(d), and para 187 below.

166. Failure to comply with examination requirements. Failure without reasonable excuse to submit to examination on entry, to produce information or documents (or a landing card) in the course of such examination, or to make a return, statement or representation in the course of such examination or otherwise which is known to be false or not believed to be true, are offences[1]. So is to alter without lawful entitlement any document issued, made under, or for the purposes of the Immigration Act 1971 or to have in possession such a document or a passport known, or for which there is reasonable cause to believe, to be false[2]. So, further, is it to obstruct an immigration officer or other person lawfully acting in execution of the Act[3]. All are punishable on summary conviction by a fine not exceeding level 4 on the standard scale, or with imprisonment for not more than six months, or both[4].

Thus no right of silence exists. However, mere non-disclosure of material facts is not of itself fraud or deception[5].

1 Immigration Act 1971 (c 77), s 26(1)(a)–(c), (e). See also *R v Governor of Ashford Remand Centre, ex parte Bouzagou* [1985] Imm AR 69, CA.
2 Immigration Act 1971, s 26(1)(d) (amended by the British Nationality Act 1981 (c 61), s 39(6), Sch 4, para 3(1)).
3 Immigration Act 1971, s 26(1)(g).
4 Ibid, s 26(1). As to level 4 on the standard scale, see para 161, note 5, above.
5 *Khawaja v Secretary of State for the Home Department* [1984] AC 74, [1983] 1 All ER 765, [1982] Imm AR 139, HL (not following *R v Secretary of State for the Home Department, ex parte Zamir* [1980] AC 930, [1980] 2 All ER 768, HL).

167. Detention for examination on arrival and identification. A person required to submit to examination on arrival may be detained by an immigration officer until examined and until a decision is reached[1]. Any person on a ship or aircraft, or in a vehicle after arrival through the tunnel system, may be removed from it by an immigration officer, or prevented from disembarking, if refused leave, in which case the captain may detain him[2]. In other cases, detention may be in any place that the Secretary of State has directed[3].

Any person detained may be taken into the custody of a constable, or of any person acting under the authority of an immigration officer, to and from any place where his attendance is required in order to ascertain his citizenship or nationality, or to make arrangements for admission to another country or territory, or to any other place where he is required to be for the purposes of the Immigration Act 1971[4]. Such custody is deemed lawful[5]. Also there is no time limit to detention, subject to the right to request bail[6].

Any person detained may be photographed, measured or subjected to any other reasonably necessary steps to identify him by an immigration officer, constable, police officer or any other person authorised by the Secretary of State[7].

If such a person is to be removed he may be placed, under the authority of an immigration officer, on board any ship or aircraft in which he is to be removed under directions[8].

1 Immigration Act 1971 (c 77), s 4(2), Sch 2, para 16(1). This power is distinct from that under the prevention of terrorism legislation: see paras 133, 134, above.
2 Ibid, Sch 2, para 16(3) and para 16(4A) (added by the Channel Tunnel (Fire Services, Immigration and Prevention of Terrorism) Order 1990, SI 1990/2227, art 3, Sch 1).
3 See the Immigration Act 1971, Sch 2, para 18(1), and the Immigration (Places of Detention) Direction 1972 (this is not a statutory instrument and is not published).
4 Immigration Act 1971, Sch 2, para 18(3).
5 Ibid, Sch 2, para 18(4).
6 See ibid, Sch 2, para 22, and the Statement of Changes in Immigration Rules (HC Paper (1989–90) no. 251) (the Immigration Rules), para 89. See also *R v Secretary of State for the Home Department, ex parte Anosike* [1971] 2 All ER 1405, [1971] 1 WLR 1136, DC.
7 Immigration Act 1971, Sch 2, para 18(2).
8 Ibid, Sch 2, para 11. As to removal, see paras 194 ff below.

168. Search warrant and arrest. A constable or immigration officer may arrest without warrant a person liable to be detained pending examination[1]. A sheriff, magistrate or justice of the peace may grant to a constable of the relevant police area a warrant, valid for a month, to search named premises for a person liable to such arrest, and to arrest him[2]. It is not clear that the person to be arrested need be named[3].

1 Immigration Act 1971 (c 77), s 4(2), Sch 2, para 17(1).
2 Ibid, Sch 2, para 17(2)(b).
3 Cf *R v Inland Revenue Comrs, ex parte Rossminster* [1980] AC 952, [1980] 1 All ER 80, HL, which related to the granting of warrants to search premises for unspecified documents in relation to unspecified alleged tax frauds.

169. Temporary admission and release and bail. Where a person is liable to detention on arrival, he may be temporarily admitted without leave to enter, by written authority of an immigration officer, though without prejudice to later detention, and subject to such restrictions as to residence, employment or occupation and reporting to the police as the immigration officer requires from time to time in writing[1]. A person actually detained on arrival may be temporarily released thereafter in similar fashion[2]. This power is in either case more likely to be exercised where there are compassionate circumstances, or close relations in the United Kingdom, and less likely in the case of men of working age, those whose refusal would be obligatory, and those believed to have practised deception[3]. It is commonly used where representations are made to the Secretary of State by a member of Parliament, and in asylum cases.

A person actually detained on arrival and not given temporary release may apply to an adjudicator for bail seven days after arrival[4]. The bail bond is conditional upon appearance before an immigration officer at a stated time and place or as notified by the immigration officer, and subject to any other conditions appearing to the adjudicator likely to result in appearance as ordered[5]. The bail bond may be taken by another person at the adjudicator's discretion[6]. Bail may be declared forfeit by the adjudicator if the terms of the bail bond are not complied with, and be transmitted to the sheriff court having jurisdiction, and is treated as having been forfeit there[7].

If he has reasonable grounds for believing that a person is likely to breach any condition of his bail bond or has breached one, an immigration officer or constable may arrest him without warrant, and the power to issue a search warrant for a detained person[8] applies equally here[9]. A person arrested must be brought before an immigration officer within twenty-four hours or, if that is not practicable, a sheriff[10]. The adjudicator or sheriff, if of the opinion that the condition of bail was, or is likely to be, breached, may direct the person's detention or liberation on the original or new bail, but must otherwise liberate him on the original bail[11].

The Lord Chancellor may make rules for applications to adjudicators and has done so[12].

Temporary admission, release and bail conditions in relation to detention pending an appeal against removal following refusal of leave to enter are as dealt with below, save that where no directions for removal are in force, the consent of the Secretary of State is not required[13].

1 Immigration Act 1971 (c 77), s 4(2), Sch 2, para 21 (amended by the Immigration Act 1988 (c 14), s 10, Schedule, para 10(1), (4)). 'Temporary admission' is to be distinguished from 'admission in a temporary capacity' (as to which see para 146 above): *R v Secretary of State for the Home Department, ex parte Taj Mohammed Khan* [1985] Imm AR 104, CA. Breach, without reasonable excuse, of such restrictions is an offence: see the Immigration Act 1971, s 24(1)(e), and para 187 below.

2 See ibid, Sch 2, para 21 (as amended).
3 L Grant and I Martin *Immigration Law and Practice* (1982) para 13.10.
4 Immigration Act 1971, Sch 2, para 22(1).
5 Ibid, Sch 2, para 22(1), (2).
6 Ibid, Sch 2, para 22(3).
7 Ibid, Sch 2, para 23(2).
8 Ie under ibid, Sch 2, para 17: see para 168 above.
9 Ibid, Sch 2, para 24(1)(a).
10 Ibid, Sch 2, para 24(2).
11 Ibid, Sch 2, para 24(3).
12 See ibid, s 22, and Sch 2, para 25 (s 22 being amended by the Transfer of Functions (Immigration Appeals) Order 1987, SI 1987/465); and the Immigration Appeals (Procedure) Rules 1984, SI 1984/2041.
13 See para 197 below.

170. Grant or refusal of leave to enter. Any person without a right of abode may require leave to enter, which is granted or refused by immigration officers[1]. This has been dealt with in general terms above, and lapse of leave and variation of leave (including extension and removal of time limits) are dealt with below[2] as are conditions imposed in respect of employment and registration with the police[3].

Immigration officers are required to carry out their duties without regard to the race, colour or religion of people seeking entry and should act honestly and fairly[4].

Grounds of refusal are set out in the Immigration Rules[5], but fulfilment of the conditions of entry for any particular category under the rules is no guarantee of entry[6]. In any case, the rules are frequently modified by terms such as 'usually' or 'normally'.

Broadly speaking two types of ground for refusal exist, that is the 'general grounds' applicable to most or all requiring leave to enter (except those exempted from their operation)[7], and specific grounds relating only to the particular category of the Immigration Rules under which entry is sought[8].

Refusal of leave may be given only by a chief immigration officer or immigration inspector[9]. Notice of grant or refusal is to be given in writing[10] except where the requirement is specifically waived, for example in the case of local journeys within the common travel area[11]. Where the person seeking entry appears to be in the charge of a responsible person, notice may be given to the latter[12].

In fact notice is normally given by way of a stamp in the person's passport. An entry stamp is rectangular and identifies the immigration officer, the date, and the port of entry. There may also be further stamps indicating length of entry permitted, that employment is prohibited or restricted (that is it may be taken only with the consent of the Department of Employment or the Home Office), that registration with the police is required, that re-admission will be permitted after an absence, or that indefinite leave is given[13]. Where only an entry stamp is given, the person is deemed to be given indefinite leave[14]. A refusal of entry stamp is the same as an entry stamp but bears a large overprinted cross. In all cases, other information may be recorded, for example that the person was referred for further examination[15].

The notice is to be given within twenty-four hours of the conclusion of examination[16]. However, this includes further examination and further medical examination, and since there is no formal limitation on how long this may continue (except in the cases of transit passengers and crew members), subject to a court order for liberation on bail[17], there is no necessity for the twenty-four hours even to commence. Indeed examination finishes only when all relevant information is obtained and the moment for decision arrived at[18]. If the twenty-four hour period does elapse without notice being given, limited leave of six months with a prohibition on employment is deemed to be given[19].

Any notice which is given may be cancelled by further notice in writing within twenty-four hours in any case[20]. Leave given can then be refused, and leave refused given[20]. In the latter case it is deemed to be leave limited to six months, subject to a condition prohibiting employment, unless the notice declares it to be indefinite[21].

A person refused entry may be removed, and entry is an offence[22]. Where refusal occurs it should normally be exercised to secure removal to the country in which he boarded the ship or aircraft that brought him to the United Kingdom, although circumstances may justify removal to an entirely different country[23]. 'Temporary admission' may be sought[24], and special arrangements apply to asylum seekers[25]. Before removal a person should be permitted to telephone friends, relations, his High Commission or consul[26].

1   Immigration Act 1971 (c 77), ss 1(4), 4(1).
2   See paras 176 ff below. As to visitors' 'checkout' coding, see note 13 below, and para 305, especially note 6, below.
3   See the Immigration Act 1971, s 3(1)(c), and paras 174, 175, below. These are the only conditions which may be imposed.
4   Statement of Changes in Immigration Rules (HC Paper (1989–90) no. 251) (the Immigration Rules), para 6. However, see eg *Immigration Control Procedures: Report of a Formal Investigation* (1985, Commission for Racial Equality) paras 4.19.1–4.19.12 and ch 9. See also *Re HK (an infant)* [1967] 2 QB 617, [1967] 1 All ER 226, DC; and *R v Secretary of State for the Home Department, ex parte Mughal* [1974] QB 313, [1973] 3 All ER 796, CA.
5   See below, and paras 171, 172, below.
6   Immigration Rules, para 78. However, a person able to take advantage of the appropriate procedure for obtaining before entry a passport stamp stating that the person may enter is deemed on entry to have been given leave to enter: see the Immigration Act 1988 (c 14), s 8, and para 150, text to note 6, para 152, text to note 9, and para 162, text to notes 1, 2, above.
7   See the Immigration Rules, paras 10, 19, 78–86.
8   See paras 235–239, 240 ff below.
9   Immigration Rules, para 79.
10 See the Immigration Act 1971, s 4(1), and the Immigration Appeals (Notices) Regulations 1984, SI 1984/2040, reg 3. For the effect of illegible stamps, which may constitute no notice at all, and thus give leave by default (as to which see text to note 19 above), see *Secretary of State for the Home Department v Mansour and Mansour* [1985] Imm AR 1, IAT; *R v Secretary of State for the Home Department, ex parte Tolba, Bettancourt, Akinsanmi; R v Immigration Appeal Tribunal, ex parte Acqvah, Rahman, Gonzales-Rojas* [1988] Imm AR 78; *Lakhani v Immigration Appeal Tribunal* [1988] Imm AR 474, CA (all majority decisions); and *Minton v Secretary of State for the Home Department* [1990] Imm AR 199, CA. However, where a person requiring leave to enter was 'waved through' by mistake, he was an illegal entrant: *Tejpartap Singh Rehal v Secretary of State for the Home Department* [1989] Imm AR 576, CA.
11 As to the common travel area, see paras 122–124 above.
12 Immigration Act 1971, s 4(2), Sch 2, para 6(4). Cf *R v Chief Immigration Officer, Manchester Airport, ex parte Insah Begum* [1973] 1 All ER 594, [1973] 1 WLR 141, CA.
13 L Grant and I Martin *Immigration Law and Practice* (1982) Appendix 2 gives illustrations, but does not refer to the distinction between 'Code 5N' (normal) admission stamp, and the 'Code 3' ('checkout') admission stamp: see para 305, note 6, below.
14 *R v Secretary of State for the Home Department, ex parte Badaike* (1977) Times, 4 May.
15 *Grant and Martin*, Appendix 2.
16 Immigration Act 1971, Sch 2, para 6(1) (amended by the Immigration Act 1988 (c 14), s 10, Schedule, para 7). As to examination, see paras 162, 164, 165, above. However, this did not operate where, by mistake, a person requiring leave was 'waved through' immigration control: *Tejpartap Singh Rehal v Secretary of State for the Home Department* [1989] Imm AR 576, CA.
17 As to bail, see para 169 above.
18 *Secretary of State for the Home Department v Thirukumar* [1989] Imm AR 402, CA.
19 Immigration Act 1971, Sch 2, para 6(1) (amended by the Immigration Act 1988, Schedule, para 8).

20 Immigration Act 1971, Sch 2, para 6(2), (3) (as amended: see notes 16, 19, above). As to illegible
   stamps, see note 10 above. The power to cancel a notice includes the power to vary reasons given
   within a notice: *Dagdalen v Secretary of State for the Home Department* [1988] Imm AR 425, CA.
21 Ibid, Sch 2, para 6(3) (as amended: see note 19 above).
22 Ibid, s 24(1)(a). The offence is punishable on summary conviction with a fine not exceeding level
   4 on the standard scale (as to which see para 161, note 5, above) or with imprisonment for not
   more than six months: s 24(1)(a) (amended by the British Nationality Act 1981 (c 61), s 39(6), Sch
   4, para 2). As to removal, see paras 194–201 below.
23 Immigration Rules, para 87.
24 See para 146 above.
25 See paras 314 ff below.
26 Immigration Rules, para 88.

**171. Refusal of leave to enter in the case of a person not holding entry
clearance.** Failure to fulfil the specific requirements of the particular category
of the Immigration Rules under which entry is sought is a ground for refusal[1].
These requirements are dealt with below in relation to each category[2]. In
particular, however, failure to obtain entry clearance, work permit or a special
voucher where required, justifies refusal[3]. In addition, any one of the following
seven 'general' grounds justifies refusal.

(1) Failure to hold an acceptable passport or other travel document[4].
(2) 'Restricted returnability', that is, where a person fails to satisfy the immi-
    gration officer that he will be admitted to another country after a stay in the
    United Kingdom[5]. In the case of those whose permission to enter another
    country must be exercised before a given date, leave may be given but will
    terminate at least two months before that date[5]. In the case of someone
    whose travel document restricts the period for which he may be abroad (that
    is, is subject to an exit visa) he may obtain leave, terminating before that
    period expires, but in any case leave will not be given to terminate after the
    expiry of a travel document[5]. None of these restrictions apply, however, to
    a person eligible for settlement or seeking entry with, or to join, a spouse
    already settled[5]. Nor, it appears, do they apply in the case of a person
    seeking entry as a refugee[6]. Also, of course, once entered, a person may
    apply for leave to be extended, or to change category by seeking asylum or
    otherwise.
(3) Previous immigration offences or deception, that is, for example, where a
    person has ignored a time limit or conditions on previous leave to enter or
    remain, or where deception has been employed to obtain entry clearance or
    leave to remain[7]. The deception need not have been practised by the person
    concerned[8].
(4) Medical reasons, that is, where a medical inspector advises that it is undesir-
    able to admit the person (unless there are strong compassionate grounds[9]) or
    where a person declines to submit to medical examination[10]. Also, where a
    medical inspector advises that a person suffers from a specified disease or
    condition which may interfere with his ability to support himself and any
    dependants, this is to be taken into account (and presumably 'strong com-
    passionate grounds' are not necessary)[11]. As described above, any person
    seeking entry may be referred for medical examination (excluding vaginal
    examination), and this will normally be done where entry is sought for a
    period exceeding six months; where the person mentions health or medical
    treatment as a reason for the visit; and where the person appears not to be in
    good health or appears to be mentally or physically abnormal[11].
    The medical inspector's conclusion and advice cannot be challenged as
such (except conceivably by judicial review of a decision taken upon it, if it
were wholly unreasonable). Although there may be an appeal against refusal
of leave, the immigration officer should follow the advice (unless there are

strong compassionate circumstances), at least if it is unequivocal[12].

Returning residents, and the spouses and children under eighteen years of age of people settled in the United Kingdom are exempt from refusal on this ground, but such a person who would otherwise be refused leave can be given notice requiring him to submit to further examination and treatment after entry[13]. So can a person admitted on the 'compassionate grounds' exemption, and, indeed, any other case if the medical inspector so recommends[13]. However, in the case of European Community nationals, the effective ambit of the power to refuse is presumably limited in freedom of movement cases by the 'public policy proviso'[14].

(5) Criminal record, that is conviction in any country of an offence included in the list of extradition crimes[15] or for which a person is returnable[16], and does not apply to the wife or a child under eighteen years of age of a person who is settled, nor where the immigration officer considers there are strong compassionate circumstances[17]. This phrase has been in general interpreted restrictively[18]. However, the Divisional Court of the Queen's Bench Division held that, although the words are hard to apply, the court would not lay down guidelines[19]. Nevertheless it rejected re-interpreting the phrase to mean 'reasons of a totally compelling or exceptional nature'[19].

(6) Being subject to a deportation order[20]. The person is to be advised that he may seek revocation of the order[21]. This ground does not cover exclusion orders under the prevention of terrorism legislation[22]. However, that of being 'conducive to the public good' undoubtedly does.

(7) Exclusion is conducive to the public good[23]. This may result from a personal direction from the Secretary of State, or by decision of the immigration officer on information available to him, for example as to the person's character, conduct, or associations[24]. Thus a marriage of convenience coupled with allegations of employment of overstayers was sufficient[25]. Personal attributes do not exhaust the category, since seeking entry to marry a girl of fourteen and a half years was sufficient, even though the person himself had not manipulated immigration procedures[26]. The power is not, however, to be used lightly or in trivial circumstances[27]. This ground cannot be used against a wife or a child under eighteen years of age of a person who is settled[28].

An exclusion order served against a national of the European Community must comply with the substantive and procedural requirements of Community law[29].

1 Statement of Changes in Immigration Rules (HC Paper (1989–90) no. 251) (the Immigration Rules), para 78.
2 Ie categories of entrant under Community law (see paras 219 ff below), and categories of entrant not under Community law (see paras 240 ff below).
3 See paras 150 ff above.
4 See the Immigration Rules, paras 7–10, and paras 153, 162, above.
5 Ibid, para 19.
6 See ibid, para 21, and paras 314 ff below.
7 Ibid, para 78.
8 *Khawaja v Secretary of State for the Home Department* [1984] AC 74, [1983] 1 All ER 765, [1982] Imm AR 139, HL.
9 *Visa Officer, Jerusalem v Awadallah* [1978] Imm AR 5, IAT (references to *Veerabhadra v Secretary of State for the Home Department* TH/1198/71/36 (unreported) and *Khahiq v Secretary of State for the Home Department* TH/5037/75 (459) (unreported)). See also *Entry Certificate Officer, Bombay v Sacha* [1973] Imm AR 5, IAT; *Parvez v Immigration Officer, London (Heathrow) Airport* [1979–80] Imm AR 84; *Immigration Officer, London (Heathrow) Airport v Bhatti* TH/57482/80 (1719), IAT (referred to in *Parvez v Immigration Officer, London (Heathrow) Airport* [1979–80] Imm AR 84 at 86 footnote); *R v Immigration Appeal Tribunal, ex parte Palacio* [1979–80] Imm AR 178, DC.
10 Immigration Rules, para 81.
11 See ibid, para 80, and para 165 above.

12 *Al-Tuwaidji v Chief Immigration Officer, London (Heathrow) Airport* [1974] Imm AR 34, IAT;
   Sudhakaran v Entry Clearance Officer, Madras [1976] Imm AR 3, IAT.
13 Immigration Rules, para 82.
14 See para 232 below.
15 Ie contained in the Extradition Act 1870 (c 52), Sch 1 (repealed) (see para 514 below): Immigration Rules, para 84.
16 Ie under the Fugitive Offenders Act 1967 (c 68) (repealed) (see para 522 below): Immigration
   Rules, para 84.
17 Ibid, para 84.
18 See *Langridge v Secretary of State for the Home Department* [1972] Imm AR 38, IAT; *Liberto v
   Immigration Officer, London (Heathrow) Airport* [1975] Imm AR 61, IAT; *Visa Officer, Jerusalem v
   Awadallah* [1978] Imm AR 5, IAT.
19 *R v Immigration Appeal Tribunal, ex parte Palacio* [1979–80] Imm AR 178, DC.
20 See the Immigration Rules, para 85, and paras 202 ff below.
21 Ibid, para 85.
22 See para 134 above.
23 Immigration Rules, para 86.
24 Ibid, para 86(a), (b). An immigration officer may refuse entry to a person acquitted of a serious
   offence if he thinks on the balance of probabilities that he did commit it: *R v Secretary of State for
   the Home Department, ex parte Nkiti* [1989] Imm AR 182, CA.
25 *Osama v Immigration Officer, London (Gatwick) Airport* [1978] Imm AR 8, IAT.
26 *R v Immigration Appeal Tribunal, ex parte Ajaib Singh* [1978] Imm AR 59, DC. However, there is
   now an age rule for spouses: see the Immigration Rules, para 2.
27 *Scheele v Immigration Officer, Harwich* [1976] Imm AR 1, IAT.
28 Immigration Rules, para 86.
29 See paras 232–234 below.

**172. Refusal of leave to enter in the case of a person holding an entry
clearance.** Possession of entry clearance[1] exempts the possessor from refusal
on grounds of failure to fulfil the specific requirements of the particular category
of the Immigration Rules under which entry is sought, since they will have been
applied by the entry clearance officer already[2]. However, the exemption is not
indefeasible since refusal is possible on two grounds. If false representations
were employed or material facts not disclosed, whether in writing or not, for the
purpose of obtaining entry clearance, refusal is justified even if the holder did
not know of the deception[3]. There is no requirement that the false representations be material, although no doubt they usually will be[4]. Facts not disclosed
include statements of intention, for example as to the purpose of the visit, but to
justify refusal these must be material[5]. A material fact has been defined as one
which, if disclosed, would have justified refusal, and the test is subjective[6].

Also, refusal is justified if there has been a change of circumstance since the
entry clearance was issued, which removes the basis of the holder's claim to
admission, unless the change is merely that the person is a child who has become
over age since application[7]. Thus, for example, since admission of children as
dependants of a settled person normally requires both parents to be settled in the
United Kingdom already, or to become so at the same time as the child, so that
where between receipt of entry clearance and arrival one settled parent leaves the
United Kingdom permanently, a relevant change has occurred[8]. The House of
Lords (retreating from an earlier view) held that mere non-disclosure of relevant
facts is not of itself deception[9].

Possession of an entry clearance does not exempt the holder from the 'general
grounds' of refusal[10].

Possession of entry clearance does permit appeal against refusal of leave to
enter to be heard before the person is removed[11].

1 For the originally expressed aim of entry certificates (the main form or entry clearance), see para
  151 above.
2 Statement of Changes in Immigration Rules (HC Paper (1989–90) no. 251) (the Immigration
  Rules), para 78. See also the Immigration Act 1988 (c 14), s 8, and para 162 above.

3 Immigration Rules, para 17(a). See also *Khawaja v Secretary of State for the Home Department* [1984] AC 74, [1983] 1 All ER 765, [1982] Imm AR 139, HL. As to the effects on applications for entry clearance obtained by deception, see *Chanda v Immigration Officer, London (Heathrow) Airport* [1981] Imm AR 88, IAT; *Ashraf v Immigration Appeal Tribunal* [1989] Imm AR 234, CA.

4 *Claveria v Immigration Officer, London (Heathrow) Airport* [1978] Imm AR 176, IAT.

5 See eg *Ramjane v Chief Immigration Officer, Gatwick Airport* [1973] Imm AR 84, IAT; *Qureshi v Immigration Officer, London (Heathrow) Airport* [1977] Imm AR 113, IAT; *Farida Begum v Immigration Officer, London (Heathrow) Airport* [1978] Imm AR 107, IAT; *Qurasha Begum v Immigration Officer, London (Heathrow) Airport* [1978] Imm AR 158, IAT.

6 *R v Secretary of State for the Home Department, ex parte Jayakody* [1982] 1 All ER 461, [1982] 1 WLR 405, CA; *Re Zafar Igbal and Aris Sussain* [1982] NLJ 297, CA.

7 Immigration Rules, para 17(b).

8 Ibid, para 53. Cf *Arshad v Immigration Officer, London (Heathrow) Airport* [1977] Imm AR 19, IAT, where the change occurred between interview and issue.

9 *Khawaja v Secretary of State for the Home Department* [1984] AC 74, [1983] 1 All ER 765, [1982] Imm AR 139, HL.

10 Ie because of (1) restricted returnability; (2) medical reasons; (3) criminal record; (4) deportation order; (5) conduciveness to the public good: see the Immigration Rules, para 17(c), and para 171 above.

11 See paras 336, 339, below.

173. Time limits on grant of leave to enter. Leave to enter may be given subject to time limits (and the phrase 'limited leave' denotes such a limit), and such a limit is normally imposed[1]. Its length will vary with the category of the Immigration Rules under which leave is being given, and with other circumstances of the case, but rarely exceeds twelve months[2] (although it is renewable). In the case of a passport shortly to expire, or subject to an exit visa, the time limit will not postdate the expiry date or a date two months before the lapse of the exit visa, respectively[3]. The time limit will be recorded in the person's passport by a stamp[4].

The alternative to a time limit is indefinite leave, granted normally only on settlement[5], that is where the person is permitted to remain permanently. This is also recorded by a stamp in the passport[6].

1 Statement of Changes in Immigration Rules (HC Paper (1989–90) no. 251) (the Immigration Rules), para 11. See also the Immigration Act 1971 (c 77), s 4(2), Sch 2, para 6, and para 170 above.

2 See the Immigration Rules, paras 25, 29, 30, 31 (visitors), para 32 (post-graduate doctors and dentists), para 33 (au pairs), paras 35, 37, 38, 41 (employment or business), para 44 (persons of independent means), para 45 (writers and artists), para 48 (fiancés and fiancées), and para 51 (spouses), and paras 236–239, 240 ff below.

3 See ibid, para 19, and para 171 above.

4 For illustration of the stamps used, see L Grant and I Martin *Immigration Law and Practice* (1982) Appendix 2.

5 See the Immigration Rules, paras 49–60, and paras 119–121 above.

6 See *Grant and Martin* Appendix 2.

174. Employment conditions imposed on grant of leave to enter. As a principal strand in immigration policy is the protection of the labour market[1], permission to take employment is given only in the case of those given leave to enter in specific categories of the Immigration Rules. However, this does not prevent transaction of business[2].

In the case of those given leave to pursue an economic activity, the permission will normally be a restricted one, that is for the economic activity specified in the entry clearance or work permit, unless the consent of the Secretary of State for Employment is obtained for a change of employment or that of the Secretary of State for the Home Department is obtained to engage in a business or profession[3] and this appears from the passport stamp[4]. Community nationals are subject to separate rules[5].

In the case of those given leave for other purposes, there will normally be a complete prohibition upon employment[6], but in some cases a restricted permission may be given (that is variation of leave is required)[7], or even unrestricted permission[8].

In the case of those given leave for settlement, no restriction or prohibition is possible[9]. In the cases of Commonwealth citizens with at least one United Kingdom born grandparent, leave is given for four years, at least if entry clearance has been obtained, and no restriction upon employment is imposed, even though (or indeed if) the stated purpose for seeking leave to enter is employment[10]. Also, anomalously, young Commonwealth citizens on a working holiday normally have no restriction or prohibition upon employment imposed[11].

1 See para 102 above.
2 Statement of Changes in Immigration Rules (HC Paper (1989–90) no. 251) (the Immigration Rules), para 24. 'Employment' and 'transaction of business' are not defined. The distinction is not parallel to that of 'contract of service' and 'contract of services' since independent contractors would normally require work permits or enter as 'businessmen'. However, the Community law category of 'provider of services' may bear comparison: see paras 221, 222, below. The essence appears to be the brevity of the visit, but no cases are reported.
3 Ie variation of leave is obtained: see para 177 below.
4 For illustrations of the stamps used, see L Grant and I Martin *Immigration Law and Practice* (1982) Appendix 2.
5 See the Immigration Rules, Pt VI (paras 68–74), and paras 221 ff below.
6 See ibid, para 22 (visitors), para 33 (au pair), and para 48 (fiancés and fiancées).
7 See ibid, para 30 (students) and para 46 (dependants of persons coming for employment or business or persons of independent means).
8 See ibid, paras 31, 46.
9 See para 120 above.
10 Immigration Rules, para 36.
11 See ibid, para 37, and para 263 below.

175. Police registration conditions on grant of leave to enter. Conditions requiring registration with the police may be imposed by statutory instrument[1]. The power is exercised only in relation to aliens (including Community nationals) and requires registration of all those given limited leave with a condition so stipulating (or treated as such)[2]. In other words, the requirement is in effect sub-delegated. The Immigration Rules exercise this apparent sub-delegation and assert that registration may exceptionally be required of any alien if the immigration officer thinks it necessary to ensure the alien complies with the terms of his leave, and may normally be required in certain other cases[3]. These other cases are:

(1) all work-permit holders and those in permit-free employment (save only ministers of religion and the like and private servants of diplomats) where the leave exceeds three months[4];

(2) students, doctors and dentists in postgraduate training, au pairs, businessmen, persons of independent means, writers and artists, and members of the family of a Community national entering for economic activities who are not themselves Community nationals, provided in all cases the leave exceeds six months[5]; and

(3) spouses and children of all those required to register (save of doctors, dentists and au pairs (who by definition may not be married))[6].

Also, where a person is not required to register but later granted variation of leave placing him in one of those categories, the requirement is to be imposed[7]. Community nationals as such are not normally required to register (regardless of their reason for entering)[8]. A fee is required[9].

The register is kept by the chief officer of police for a police area, and registration is effected at the chief police station for the area of the person's ordinary residence or (if he has no ordinary residence) for where he is[10]. Registration must occur within seven days of the requirement to register being applied[11]. The details registered are extensive, and a photograph is required[12]. The registered person must attend in person and produce all information necessary to complete registration[13].

The registered person receives a certificate of registration which must be a separate document, not a passport stamp, and is in booklet form[14]. Variation of details must be registered, and the person may be required to produce information in person[15]. Where a person has an ordinary residence in the United Kingdom, and is to be away from it for more than two continuous months, he must report both this and his return[16].

A registered person may be required to produce the registration certificate to a police officer or immigration officer on demand, or within forty-eight hours at a specified police station[17].

It is an offence to give false information or to fail to register or to register changes of details[18].

1 See the Immigration Act 1971 (c 77), s 4(3).
2 Immigration (Registration with Police) Regulations 1972, SI 1972/1758, reg 3. See also Scottish Home and Health Police (Chief Constables) Circular 10/1973 (Immigration Act 1971: Police Registration and Hotel Records). The effect of the Regulations in respect of Community nationals is limited by Community law: see Case 157/79 *R v Pieck* [1980] ECR 2171, [1981] QB 571, [1981] 3 All ER 46, ECJ, and paras 114, 137, above, and paras 219–239 below.
3 Statement of Changes in Immigration Rules (HC Paper (1989–90) no. 251) (the Immigration Rules), paras 76, 77. See also paras 142, 143, above and para 183 below. Those entering via the common travel area or whose leave expired while outside the United Kingdom are subject to the requirement: see the Immigration Act 1971, s 9(2), and paras 122–124 above.
4 Immigration Rules, para 76(a).
5 Ibid, para 76(b).
6 Ibid, para 76(c). As to what is an au pair, see para 311, below.
7 Ibid, para 142.
8 Ibid, paras 73, 74. See also Case 157/79 *R v Pieck* [1980] ECR 2171, [1981] QB 571, [1981] 3 All ER 46, ECJ.
9 Immigration (Registration with Police) Regulations 1972, reg 10(3) (substituted by SI 1990/400, and amended by SI 1991/965).
10 Ibid, reg 4(1).
11 Ibid, reg 5(1).
12 See ibid, regs 5, 9, Schedule.
13 See ibid, regs 5, 11(1).
14 Ibid, reg 10(1), (2) (substituted by SI 1990/400).
15 See ibid, regs 7, 8, 9(2), (3).
16 Ibid, reg 7(3).
17 Ibid, reg 11(2).
18 Immigration Act 1971, s 26(1)(c), (f). The penalty on summary conviction is a fine not exceeding level 4 on the standard scale or with imprisonment for not more than six months or both: s 26(1). As to level 4 on the standard scale, see para 161, note 5, above.

176. Lapse of leave to enter or remain and 'returning residents'. If a person leaves the common travel area, leave to enter or remain lapses[1]. However, a person with indefinite leave to remain will normally be re-admitted as a 'returning resident' if the absence has not been greater than two years and, exceptionally, even if it has[2]. Also, a person with limited leave to enter will normally be re-admitted on the same conditions if he returns within the time-limit originally imposed and his relevant circumstances have not changed[3].

1 Immigration Act 1971 (c 77), s 3(4). See also *Ghassemian and Mirza v The Home Office* [1989] Imm AR 42, CA. This provision commonly creates difficulties for the unwary who leave the country and find they cannot re-enter even though they are within the period for entry originally granted. It was described as a 'trap' by the Master of Rolls in *Oloniluyi v Secretary of State for the Home Department* [1989] Imm AR 135 at 136, CA. In that case (distinguished in *Kuku v Secretary of State*

for the Home Department [1990] Imm AR 27, CA), the Court of Appeal held that assurances given
by the Immigration and Nationality Department staff that re-entry would be permitted created
legitimate expectations sufficient to allow the court to question an immigration officer's decision
to refuse leave to re-enter. As to the common travel area, see paras 122–124 above.

2 See the Immigration Act 1971, s 3(4), and the Statement of Changes in Immigration Rules (HC
   Paper (1989–90) no. 251) (the Immigration Rules), paras 58, 59.

3 Ibid, para 60. Home Office practice where a person requiring leave to enter who cannot take
   advantage of the rule in favour of 'returning residents' wishes to leave the United Kingdom
   temporarily and seeks advice, is to stamp the passport with an Immigration Act 1971 's 3(3)(b)
   enabling stamp' and if necessary a 'visa exempt stamp': *Kuku v Secretary of State for the Home
   Department* [1990] Imm AR 27, CA. An Immigration Act 1971 's 3(3)(b) enabling stamp' has
   been required since 16 May 1991: see the Immigration Act 1971, s 3(3)(b) (amended by the
   Immigration Act 1988 (c 14), s 10, Schedule, para 1), and the Immigration Act 1988 (Commencement No 2) Order 1991, SI 1991/1001. The immigration officer at the port of entry still
   has discretion to alter the limitation and any conditions, or to refuse leave to enter. In *Oloniluyi v
   Secretary of State for the Home Department* [1989] Imm AR 135, CA (decided when the Immigration Act 1971 's 3(3)(b) enabling stamps' were discretionary), the Master of the Rolls
   observed that a re-entrant should be treated as an entrant *de novo* only if it benefited him. A 'visa
   exempt' stamp is not a visa: *Balogun v Secretary of State for the Home Department* [1989] Imm AR
   603, CA. See also para 342, text to notes 2–12, below.

(d) Control after Entry

(A) REMAINING IN THE UNITED KINGDOM

177. Variation of leave. A person given indefinite leave to enter cannot have
the leave varied except in the sense:
(1) that absence from the United Kingdom causes it to lapse and it will normally
     be regranted only if return occurs within two years[1]; and
(2) that indefinite leave does not exclude the possibility of deportation[2] (other
     than in relation to exempted categories[3]) or of an exclusion order under the
     prevention of terrorism legislation[4].
It is also always possible that leave granted may be later decided to have resulted
from material fraud or deception, and hence to be vitiated[5].

A person given limited leave to enter may have that leave varied by being
given leave to remain and, equally, leave to remain may be varied[6]. Such leave
lapses on leaving the common travel area, but will normally be renewed on the
same terms if the person returns within the period for which leave was originally
granted, if relevant circumstances have not changed[7]. The decision is normally
taken by Home Office staff in the name of the Home Secretary, rather than by
immigration officers, but in some cases it is taken by the Home Secretary
personally[8].

Variation means restriction, enlargement or removal of the time limit, and
addition, variation and revocation of employment and police registration conditions, and this is taken, in principle, to include change of category under the
Immigration Rules[9]. If the time limit is removed, any other condition must be
removed[10].

Specific considerations relating to different categories are set out in the
Immigration Rules and are dealt with below in relation to each category[11].
General considerations applying to some or all categories are also set out, and are
dealt with below[12]. In any case, meeting all formal requirements specified is not
conclusive[13].

It is possible for variation decisions to be taken 'outside the rules'[14]. Also
variation may be conditional upon a sponsor giving an undertaking in writing to

be responsible for the applicant's maintenance and accommodation for the duration of any extension[15]. The Department of Social Security is stated to be able to recover any income support payments made to such an applicant[16].

The position of European Community nationals is dealt with below[17].

1 See the Immigration Act 1971 (c 77), s 3(4), and the Statement of Changes in Immigration Rules (HC Paper (1989–90) no. 251) (the Immigration Rules), paras 58, 59. As to leave to enter or remain generally, see paras 119–120 above.
2 See paras 202 ff below.
3 See para 126 above.
4 See para 134 above.
5 *Khawaja v Secretary of State for the Home Department* [1984] AC 74, [1983] 1 All ER 765, [1982] Imm AR 139, HL. See also the Immigration Rules, para 78.
6 See the Immigration Act 1971, s 3(3)(a), and the Immigration Rules, paras 94, 95. See also para 120 above.
7 Immigration Act 1971, s 3(3)(b), (4) (amended by the Immigration Act 1988 (c 14), s 10, Schedule, para 1).
8 See eg the Immigration Act 1971, s 15(4). Entry clearance officers and immigration officers act administratively not judicially, when conducting interviews and otherwise: see para 152, note 3, and para 164, text to note 2, above. It is likely that a decision on variation of leave would be similarly classified.
9 See ibid, s 3(3)(a), and the Immigration Rules, para 95. To become settled (see para 120 above) involves a change of category under the Immigration Rules.
10 See the Immigration Act 1971, s 3(3)(a), and the Immigration Rules, para 95. Conditions may be as to employment, occupation and police registration only: Immigration Act 1971, s 3(1)(c).
11 See paras 235, 236, 240 ff below.
12 See para 181 below.
13 Immigration Rules, para 95.
14 See para 112 above.
15 Immigration Rules, para 96. This appears apt to include an undertaking in respect of a grant of indefinite leave to remain which would therefore be of indeterminate duration. Such an interpretation runs contrary to the purpose expressed in para 95 that all conditions are to be removed upon grant of indefinite leave.
16 Ibid, para 96.
17 See paras 225 ff below.

178. Application for variation of leave. Application for variation of leave is made to the Home Office. It may be made in person but is usually made by post[1]. No official form for application is provided. Information required includes name, date of birth, marital status, address in the United Kingdom, evidence of continued ability to fulfil the requirements of the category, and an explanation of the reason for seeking extension of stay. Passport and police registration certificate should be included[2], and Home Office reference number if possible[3]. An interview may be required, which may take place locally or in London.

Application should be made before leave expires, since otherwise the criminal offence of overstaying applies from the date of expiry[4], and there is a right of appeal against refusal[5]. Application dates from posting, not arrival[6], and, where made timeously, results in automatic extension of leave on the same employment and registration conditions until twenty-eight days after the decision is made (unless it is made more than twenty-eight days before expiry of the original leave or the automatic extension is already operating in favour of the applicant)[7]. The date of decision is deemed, if posted, to be the day of posting, and in any other case, to be the day the notice was served[8].

The decision on variation is (exceptional cases apart) to be given in writing[9]. This is done by a mitre shaped stamp in the passport giving the date, and a rectangular one stating the time limit and conditions (if any) or that indefinite leave has been given, where variation is granted[10]. Where it is refused, the date of expiry on the entry stamp or previous variation of leave stamp will be underlined[10].

1 Details are given in the 'Report on the Work of the Immigration and Nationality Department' (1984, Home Office) Ch 6, paras 3–11. See also the Home Office annual 'Report on the Work of the Immigration and Nationality Department' (1985 to date).
2 As to registration with the police, see para 183 below.
3 The reference number is found on all correspondence with the Home Office and may be indorsed on the back of the passport.
4 Ie under the Immigration Act 1971 (c 77), s 24(1)(b)(i): see para 186 below.
5 See ibid, s 14(1), and para 336 below. See also *Suthendran v Immigration Appeal Tribunal* [1977] AC 359, [1976] 3 All ER 611, [1977] Imm AR 44, HL.
6 *Lubetkin v Secretary of State for the Home Department* [1979–80] Imm AR 162, IAT.
7 Immigration (Variation of Leave) Order 1976, SI 1976/1572, reg 3(1), (2) (amended by SI 1989/1005). This does not constitute an 'authorisation': see the Statement of Changes in Immigration Rules (HC Paper (1989–90) no. 251) (the Immigration Rules), para 166, and para 211, text and note 4, and para 212, text to note 4, below.
8 Immigration (Variation of Leave) Order 1976, reg 3(3).
9 See the Immigration Act 1971, s 4(1), and the Immigration Rules, para 144.
10 L Grant and I Martin *Immigration Law and Practice* (1982) Appendix 2.

179. Lapse of application. Where a person has applied to vary leave and requests his passport back for the purpose of travel outside the common travel area (*sed quaere* for requests for other purposes), the application to vary leave is deemed to have been withdrawn, unless it has already been determined[1].

1 Ie under the Immigration (Variation of Leave) Order 1976, SI 1976/1572, reg 3 (amended by SI 1989/1005). As to the common travel area, see paras 122–124 above.

180. Variation of leave without application. Variation of leave may occur without application and thus contrary to the wishes of the person concerned[1]. It is not clear in what circumstances this can occur, but the 'general considerations' permit 'curtailment' as well as refusal and it is enjoined in certain cases where a court which might have recommended deportation did not do so[2]. It is thought to be rarely used.

1 See the Immigration Act 1971 (c 77), s 4(1), and the Statement of Changes in Immigration Rules (HC Paper (1989–90) no. 251) (the Immigration Rules), para 100. See also *Amarjit Singh Grewal v Secretary of State for the Home Department* [1979–80] Imm AR 119, IAT; *R v Secretary of State for the Home Department, ex parte Sandhu* [1982] 2 CMLR 553.
2 See the Immigration Rules, para 164, and para 181 below.

181. General considerations for curtailment or refusal of variation. General considerations for curtailment or refusal of an application for variation are set out in the Immigration Rules and apply in all cases (subject to Community law)[1]. They fall into five broad categories.

First, two considerations expressly concern change of category under the Immigration Rules[2]. Such application must be refused if it is to change to a category for which entry clearance is required and the applicant has no such clearance[3]. There are exemptions for any person seeking settlement, where clearly it is inappropriate, and for a spouse of a person settled in the United Kingdom[3]. Such application must also be refused if it is to change to employment for which a work permit is required, with an exception for visitors or students seeking variation to become trainees[4], and for nurses and midwives on completion of training in the United Kingdom, provided the training was not financed by an international scholarship agency or home government[5].

Secondly, five considerations apply to past or future ability to fulfil the formal requirements of the Immigration Rules. Leave may be curtailed or refused if the applicant ceases to meet the requirements of the rules under which entry was granted; if he has failed to comply with any conditions attached to leave or to maintain and accommodate himself and any dependants without recourse to public funds; or if he has made false representations or not disclosed material facts in order to obtain original leave to enter or previous variation of leave[6]. Misrepresentation without the knowledge of the applicant is not expressly included, as it is in relation to refusal of entry[7], but it is unclear what effect this difference has. However, the interpretation of the refusal of entry rule in relation to misrepresentations presumably applies[8]. Leave may also be refused (but not, it appears, curtailed) if the applicant has failed to honour any declaration or undertaking given orally or in writing as to intended duration and purpose of stay, or, in the case of a person sponsored by Her Majesty's government, an international scholarship agency, or by his home government, on the ground of failure to show that the sponsoring authority is content for further leave to be granted[9].

Thirdly, two considerations relate to the applicant's character. Leave may be refused or curtailed if his character, conduct or associations make it undesirable to permit him to remain, or if he represents a danger to national security[10].

Fourthly, leave may be refused (but not it appears, curtailed) if, were the applicant permitted to stay for the requested period, he might not be permitted to return to another country[11].

Finally, further leave may be refused (but not, it appears, curtailed) if an applicant takes an unreasonable time to produce documents or other evidence required to establish his claim under the rules[11].

This is not an exhaustive list, in that specific requirements apply in each category[12] and conviction by a court which might have recommended deportation but did not is mentioned elsewhere[13]. Previous Immigration Rules also referred to the need to take account of all relevant facts and (as in refusal of entry cases) emphasised that satisfaction of the formal requirements is not conclusive[14]. Deletion of such phrases may not reflect the deletion of such considerations, but this cannot be assumed.

1 See the Statement of Changes in Immigration Rules (HC Paper (1989–90) no. 251) (the Immigration Rules), paras 99–102, and references to 'principles' in para 95. The 'general considerations' have been considerably tightened over the years: *Secretary of State for the Home Department v Thaker* [1976] Imm AR 114, IAT.
2 For the categories, see paras 219 ff below (categories of entrant under Community law without the right of abode), and paras 240 ff below (categories of entrant not under Community law without the right of abode).
3 See the Immigration Rules, para 102.
4 Ie under ibid, para 120: see para 240 below.
5 Ibid, para 102.
6 Ibid, para 100.
7 See ibid, para 78, and paras 171, 172, above.
8 *Khawaja v Secretary of State for the Home Department* [1984] AC 74, [1983] 1 All ER 765, [1982] Imm AR 139, HL.
9 Immigration Rules, para 101.
10 Ibid, para 100.
11 Ibid, para 101.
12 See paras 235–239, 240 ff below.
13 See the Immigration Rules, para 165, and para 206 below.
14 Statement of Changes in Immigration Rules (HC Paper (1982–83) no. 169) (the Former Immigration Rules), para 97 (revoked).

182. Variation of leave for settlement. As noted, only certain categories of persons may seek settlement[1]. The Immigration Rules specifically limit the possibility to those given leave to enter:

(1) in approved employment (that is work-permit holders);

(2) in permit-free employment (except in the case of some doctors and dentists);
(3) to set up in business;
(4) for self-employment;
(5) as a writer or artist;
(6) as a person of independent means;
(7) as a worker or work-seeker with a grandparent born in the United Kingdom; or
(8) as close relatives of those already settled[2].

In all cases (except that of close relatives) the person must have been in that capacity for four years and all relevant circumstances including the general considerations, and, in the case of work-permit holders, the likelihood of continued employment, is to be considered[2]. 'Close relatives' presumably includes spouses.

1 Statement of Changes in Immigration Rules (HC Paper (1989–90) no. 251) (the Immigration Rules), para 139, and para 149 above.
2 Ibid, para 139.

183. Registration with the police.
The process is described above, including registration of changes of address and other particulars[1].

If registration with the police is required on entry, it can be expected to be continued on any variation of leave, save variation for settlement[2]. Although it is competent to apply to vary leave by removing the condition of registration this is unlikely to be successful[2]. Also if it is not imposed on entry, but the person, by subsequent variation of leave, falls into one of the categories requiring registration, the condition will be imposed[3].

The police registration certificate or satisfactory reason for non-production may be demanded of an alien at any time by an immigration officer or constable[4]. If not produced, production may be required within forty-eight hours at a nominated police station[4].

1 See para 175 above.
2 See the Statement of Changes in Immigration Rules (HC Paper (1989–90) no. 251) (the Immigration Rules), para 143.
3 See ibid, para 142.
4 See para 175 above.

184. Hotel records.
The Secretary of State is specifically empowered to make by statutory instrument provision appearing expedient to him requiring records of people staying in hotels and other lodging or sleeping accommodation, and for those staying there to provide the necessary information[1]. This applies to British citizens as well as others[1]. The power has been exercised and requires those keeping hotels and like premises to keep for twelve months records of the full name and nationality of all guests over sixteen years of age[2]. In addition, the number and places of issue of the passport (or other document establishing identity and nationality) and the address of the next destination of alien guests are to be recorded[3]. The record is open to any constable or person authorised by the Secretary of State[4]. Guests are required to supply the information and failure to do so is an offence, as is failure to maintain the register[5].

1 Immigration Act 1971 (c 77), s 4(4) (amended by the British Nationality Act 1981 (c 61), s 39(6), Sch 4, para 2).
2 See the Immigration (Hotel Records) Order 1972, SI 1972/1689, arts 3, 5, and HOTELS AND TOURISM, vol 11, para 1730.
3 See ibid, art 4, and vol 11, para 1730.
4 See ibid, art 5, and vol 11, para 1730.
5 See ibid, arts 4, 5, and vol 11, para 1730, note 1.

(B) OFFENCES AND REMOVAL

185. Illegal entry. Knowingly to enter in breach of a deportation order, or without leave, is an offence[1]. It is also ground for removal[2].

1　Immigration Act 1971 (c 77), s 24(1)(a). The offence is an arrestable one (s 24(2)), and is punishable on summary conviction with a fine not exceeding level 4 on the standard scale or with imprisonment for not more than six months or both (s 24(1) (amended by the British Nationality Act 1981 (c 61), s 39(6), Sch 4, para 2)). As to level 4, see para 161, note 5, above. As to the extended time limit for prosecution, see the Immigration Act 1971, ss 24(3), 28. As to deportation, see paras 202 ff below.

2　See ibid, s 4(2), Sch 2, paras 8–10, and paras 194 ff below.

186. Overstaying and breach of conditions. It is an offence to stay beyond the time limit imposed in the case of limited leave to enter or remain, subject to any automatic extension resulting from an application to vary leave or to appeal against a refusal to vary (or to vary leave in the way requested)[1]. Equally it is an offence to breach conditions imposed, for example requiring an individual to register with the police and either not to work at all, or to do so only with the consent of the Department of Employment or Home Office[2]. Such breaches are also grounds for deportation[3].

1　Immigration Act 1971 (c 77), s 24(1)(b)(i), (c). The offence under s 24(1)(b) is to overstay 'knowingly'. This was interpreted to mean that one knew one was overstaying, not that one knew it was an offence: *Grant v Borg* [1982] 2 All ER 257, [1982] 1 WLR 638, HL. This case concerned the Immigration Act 1971, s 24(1)(b)(i), before s 24(1A) was added by the Immigration Act 1988 (c 14), s 6(1), to which extent it is no longer authority in respect of expiration of leave after 10 July 1988. The offences under the Immigration Act 1971, s 24(1)(b), (c), are arrestable ones (s 24(2)) and are punishable on summary conviction with a fine not exceeding level 4 on the standard scale or with imprisonment for not more than six months or both (s 24(1) (amended by the British Nationality Act 1981 (c 61), s 39(6), Sch 4, para 2)). As to level 4, see para 161, note 5, above. As to application to vary leave, see paras 177, 178, above. As to the extended time limit for prosecution, see the Immigration Act 1971, ss 24(3), 28.

2　Ibid, s 24(1)(b)(ii). The offence is a continuing one: *Manickavasagar v Metropolitan Police Comr* [1987] Crim LR 50, DC. As to the penalty, see note 1 above.

3　Immigration Act 1971, s 3(5)(a) (as amended: see note 1 above). As to deportation, see paras 202 ff below.

187. Breach of other requirements. It is an offence:
(1) to fail, without reasonable excuse, to comply with a requirement to report to a chief administrative medical officer of a Health Board or to submit to a test or examination by him as required by a medical inspector upon entry[1];
(2) to fail, without reasonable excuse, to observe a requirement as to residence, as to his employment or occupation, or as to reporting to the police or to an immigration officer, imposed when given temporary admission, temporary release, or bail pending a decision on leave to enter or pending deportation[2];
(3) to disembark after being placed on board a ship or aircraft with a view to deportation or other removal[3]; or
(4) to embark in contravention of a restriction imposed under a 'hostage' or 'safety' order[4].

All, except the first of these, are arrestable offences, but none is, of itself, ground for deportation or other removal[5].

1　Immigration Act 1971 (c 77), s 24(1)(d) (amended by the National Health Service (Scotland) Act 1972 (c 58), s 64(1), Sch 6, para 155, and the National Health Service (Scotland) Act 1978 (c 29), s 109, Sch 15, para 10). As to medical examination, see paras 165, 166, above. The offence is punishable on summary conviction with a fine not exceeding level 4 on the standard scale or with imprisonment for not more than six months or both: Immigration Act 1971, s 24(1) (amended by the British Nationality Act 1981 (c 61), s 39(6), Sch 4, para 2). As to level 4, see para 161, note 5, above.

2 Immigration Act 1971, s 24(1)(e) (amended by the Immigration Act 1988 (c 14), s 10, Schedule, para 10(3), (4)). As to temporary admission and release, see para 169 above. For the penalty, see note 1 above.

3 Immigration Act 1971, s 24(1)(f). For the penalty, see note 1 above.

4 Ibid, s 24(1)(g). As to hostage and safety orders, see paras 135, 136, above. For the penalty, see note 1 above.

5 Ibid, s 24(2). As to the grounds for removal or deportation, see paras 196, 204, below.

188. Tracing overstayers and related processes. Landing cards can be matched by computer to embarkation cards to permit checking of overstaying[1]. Also the Immigration and Nationality Department maintains an 'intelligence unit' which has an index of persons known or suspected of immigration offences and related information[2]. There is also a police 'intelligence unit' on immigration matters and immigration is the concern of a police force's Special Branch[3]. Further there are certain routine exchanges of information between the Home Office and the Department of Health and Social Security and probably other organs of government, including registrars of births, marriages and deaths[4].

1 See para 163 above (landing cards), and para 193 below (embarkation cards). The computer system (INDECS) is described in the Sixth Report from the Home Affairs Committee (HC Paper (1984–85) no. 277) (Immigration and Nationality Department of the Home Office), paras 23–27, and *Immigration Control Procedures: Report of a Formal Investigation* (1985, Commission for Racial Equality) paras 8.5.1–8.5.3, 8.6.1–8.6.7. It does not appear to be very effective. In practice INDECS checks are usually made only on those regarded as worth checking by immigration officers, generally those admitted in 'Code 3': see para 305, note 6, below. An Overstayers Tracing and Intelligence Section of the Immigration and Nationality Department follows up 'no trace of embarkation' (NTE) cases. There are some tens of thousands annually, but very few are traced, and it appears that a significant proportion of NTE reports are due to inaccurate recording, ie 'fake alarms': see eg *Immigration Control Procedures: Report of a Formal Investigation* para 8.8.2.

2 Ie the Immigration Service Intelligence Unit (ISIU): *Immigration Control Procedures: Report of a Formal Investigation* paras 8.5.1–8.5.3. Concern has been expressed as to the accuracy of the information recorded: P Gordon *Policing Immigration: Britain's Internal Controls* (1985) pp 46–49, 95–99.

3 Ie the Central Illegal Immigration Intelligence Unit (CIIIU), with a 'steering committee' representing the Immigration and Nationality Department, the Association of Chief Police Officers, the Metropolitan Police and HM Customs and Excise: *Macdonald's Immigration Law and Practice* (3rd edn, 1991, eds I A Macdonald and N J Blake) pp 346, 347; *Immigration Control Procedures: Report of a Formal Investigation* paras 8.5.2, 8.7.1, 8.7.2. The Fourth Report from the Home Affairs Committee (HC Paper (1984–85) no. 71) (Special Branch), pp xi–xii (guidelines on the work of the Special Branch, para 11), describes the work of the Special Branch in England and Wales, but it appears that the same position holds in Scotland: *Gordon* pp 46–49, 96, 97.

4 *Immigration Control Procedures: Report of a Formal Investigation* paras 8.10.1–8.10.3, 8.16.1, 8.16.2; *Gordon* pp 62, 63, 97.

(C) OTHER POST-ENTRY CONTROLS AND CHECKS

189. Introduction. It has been orthodox to assume that post-entry controls are minimal, largely because controls before and on entry obviated the need (added to the lack of land boundaries of the state) and because there was a traditional dislike of internal controls of any kind on the United Kingdom. The position is contrasted with that pertaining in some continental European countries where identity cards for the population as a whole are normal, and in some cases required.

However, it is now asserted by many that in fact a considerable, if very variable, number of unofficial and other controls operate. Further, it is agreed, because most of the post-war immigrants have been from the 'black Commonwealth', these unofficial controls operate chiefly upon black or coloured people (even if British-born) rather than upon those with limited leave to enter[1].

Since these controls are not formally part of the immigration control system, and are in some cases unofficial, and possibly unlawful, it is difficult to know how they operate.

1 *Immigration Control Procedures: Report of a Formal Investigation* (1985, Commission for Racial Equality) ch 6; P Gordon *Policing Immigration: Britain's Internal Controls* (1985).

190. Police checks and 'passport raids'. Arrest for immigration offences is commonly effected by the police. It has been reported from time to time that people who are questioned by the police on matters unrelated to immigration have been asked or apparently required to produce a passport or give information on their immigration status and on occasion detained[1]. There is an obligation upon aliens registered with the police to produce their police registration card[2], but no obligation applies to them, or, *a fortiori* to Commonwealth citizens, to produce passports[3]. Whether refusal to produce a passport or answer inquiries could amount to obstruction of a constable in the execution of his duty under the Immigration Act 1971, in such circumstances, is a question of fact but must be doubted, as must whether there is reasonable cause for arrest or detention[4]. The Scottish Office has issued guidance to chief constables on inquiries concerning illegal immigrants[5]. Also guidance has been issued in relation to deportation which, inter alia, requests reports of serious offences committed by aliens, Commonwealth citizens and Irish citizens who entered after the Immigration Act 1971 came into force[6].

'Passport raids' refers to large scale operations in which the police have questioned and detained at one time substantial numbers of people gathered together in premises such as a place of work, shop or restaurant. This is done as a result of information suggesting that the group to be questioned includes illegal entrants or overstayers[7].

How far arrest and questioning by the police is lawful under these circumstances is a matter for discussion[8].

1 L Grant and I Martin *Immigration Law and Practice* (1982) pp 214, 215; *Macdonald's Immigration Law and Practice* (3rd edn, 1991, eds I A Macdonald and N J Blake) pp 346, 347; P Gordon *Policing Immigration: Britain's Internal Controls* (1985) pp 57–60 *et passim*; *Evidence of the Royal Commission on Criminal Procedure* (1979, Joint Council for the Welfare of Immigrants) paras 9–20, and the facts of cases such as *R v Clarke* [1985] AC 1037, [1985] 2 All ER 777, HL; *R v Secretary of State for the Home Department, ex parte Adesina* [1988] Imm AR 442, CA; and *Re Bamgbose* [1990] Imm AR 135, CA.
2 See the Immigration Act 1971 (c 77), s 4(3), the Immigration (Registration with Police) Regulations 1972, SI 1972/1758, art 11(2), and para 175 above.
3 This is reported to have been confirmed by the then Minister of State at the Home Office, Mr Raison: *The Guardian* 28 April 1980.
4 Ie under the Immigration Act 1971, s 26(1)(g): see para 166 above. See also *R v Clarke* [1985] AC 1037, [1985] 2 All ER 777, HL; *R v Gill* [1976] 2 All ER 893, [1977] 1 WLR 78, CA; and *Rice v Connolly* [1966] 1 QB 414, [1966] 2 All ER 649, DC.
5 Scottish Home and Health Police (Chief Constables) Circular 42/1973 (Immigration Act 1971: Illegal Entrants), which enjoins police on illegal entrant inquiries to 'avoid any action which might be construed as harassment of immigrants as such: for example, a request to inspect the passport of someone who comes to notice in connection with a minor offence but whom there is no reason to suspect of being in the country illegally': para 7. See also para 8.
6 Scottish Home and Health Police (Chief Constables) Circular 9/1973 (Immigration Act 1971: Deportation) para 7.
7 See eg the 'Report on the Work of the Immigration and Nationality Department' (1984, Home Office) ch 9, para 11; *Immigration Control Procedures: Report of a Formal Investigation* (1985,

Commission for Racial Equality) paras 8.9.1–8.9.6; *Evidence of the Royal Commission on Criminal Procedure* (1979, Joint Council for the Welfare of Immigrants) para 20; *Macdonald* pp 347–349; *Grant and Martin* para 10.10; *Gordon* pp 51–57. Some such acts are presumably unlawful by virtue of the Race Relations Act 1976 (c 74).

8 *Macdonald* pp 347–349; *Gordon, passim.*

191. Welfare state facilities and employment. It has been reported from time to time that people have been asked to produce passports or other evidence to obtain access to education, housing and social work facilities, in order to check their entitlement or to obtain employment[1]. In some cases entitlement may indeed depend upon immigration status, as for instance in the case of income support, in so far as a person is admitted, provided he has no recourse to public funds[2]. It may be doubted if all those controlling access to such facilities are sufficiently conversant with immigration law and practice to be able to determine entitlement from a passport[3]. Also it has been suggested that in fact it is only those who are black or coloured who are asked, and that they are asked even when British-born, and that, in any case, unjustified refusals of access result[4]. In the case of employment, the employer does nothing unlawful by employing a person with no right to work[5].

Because of difficulties in relation to access to health services, similar to those in relation to education etc, coupled with assertions as to the racially discriminating effect of inquiries made in practice, a new statutory regime has been applied, together with circular guidance from the Scottish Office on admission to hospitals[6]. The tenor of this guidance is to restrict requests as to immigration status severely, and in particular for passports.

1 See eg P Gordon *Policing Immigration: Britain's Internal Controls* (1985) ch 4.
2 Statement of Changes in Immigration Rules (HC Paper (1989–90) no. 251) (the Immigration Rules), para 1.
3 EC draft directive on the harmonisation of laws to combat illegal immigration and illegal employment (R/2655/76): see Report 20 from the Select Committee on the European Communities (HL Papers (1976–77) no. 91) (Illegal immigration).
4 *Gordon* ch 4.
5 However, he may be guilty, art and part, presumably.
6 Scottish Home and Health Department NHS circular 1982 (GEN) 29 (NHS treatment of Overseas Visitors). For the statutory regime, see HEALTH SERVICES, vol 11, para 1318. No equivalent regime covers general practitioner services.

(e) Control of Departure

(A) INTRODUCTION

192. Requirements as to place and manner of embarkation. The Secretary of State has equivalent powers to control the place and manner of embarkation as he has to control disembarkation[1].

1 See para 161 above.

193. Requirements to submit to examination, to complete an embarkation card, and other formalities. Those leaving the United Kingdom may be required to be examined to determine whether they are British citizens and, if not, their identity[1], to complete embarkation cards under the equivalent circumstances as for landing cards[2]. The person's passport may be indorsed with a triangular stamp indicating the date and port of exit[3]. Various other markings may be used[3].

1 Immigration Act 1971 (c 77), s 4, Sch 2, para 3(1) (amended by the British Nationality Act 1981 (c 61), s 39(6), Sch 4, para 2, and the Channel Tunnel (Fire Services, Immigration and Prevention of Terrorism) Order 1990, SI 1990/2227, art 3, Sch 1). Cf para 162 above.
2 See para 163 above.
3 See L Grant and I Martin *Immigration Law and Practice* (1982) Appendix 2.

(B) ADMINISTRATIVE REMOVAL

194. What constitutes administrative removal. Administrative removal is removal of those considered never to have entered (or in one limited case, remained) lawfully. Procedural safeguards are limited and, with one minor exception, there is no right of appeal. Judicial review may, however, be available. In England and Wales administrative removal has been a fecund source of *habeas corpus* applications, and the area is one of considerable civil liberties interest.

Administrative removal is to be distinguished from deportation[1].

1 See paras 202 ff below. However, removal and deportation are not mutually exclusive: *R v Immigration Appeal Tribunal, ex parte Anilkumar Rabindrabhai Patel* [1988] AC 910, [1988] 2 All ER 378, [1988] Imm AR 434, HL.

195. Who is liable to administrative removal. Two broad categories of people are liable to administrative removal, that is, those refused entry on arrival, and those considered illegal entrants. In addition crews of ships and aircraft may be removed administratively in certain circumstances for remaining (rather than entering) unlawfully[1]. Entry after refusal, illegal entry of any other type and overstaying by such crew members are also offences[2]. Prosecutions appear to be rare. The provisions apply to Community nationals subject to Community law[3].

1 See para 196 below.
2 See the Immigration Act 1971 (c 77), s 24(1)(a), (c), and paras 185, 186, above.
3 See paras 219 ff below.

196. Grounds for administrative removal of ship and aircraft crews. Ship and aircraft crew are allowed to enter, without leave, to join a ship or aircraft[1] or to receive hospital treatment[2], or, having arrived as crew on a ship or aircraft, because leaving shortly in the same capacity[3]. If overstaying or reasonably suspected of it, such a person may be removed administratively[4].

1 Immigration Act 1971 (c 77), s 4(2), Sch 2, para 12(1). As to seamen and aircrew generally, see para 129 above.
2 Ibid, Sch 2, para 13(1)(b).
3 See ibid, s 8(1), and para 129 above.
4 See ibid, Sch 2, paras 12(2), 13(2) (amended by the British Nationality Act 1981 (c 61), s 39(6), Sch 4, para 2). As to the procedure for administrative removal, see para 200 below.

197. Refusal of leave to enter as a ground for administrative removal. Who requires leave to enter and grounds for refusal of leave to enter is dealt with elsewhere in this title[1]. Such refusal is a ground for administrative removal[2]. Refusal of leave is not a ground for administrative removal, and removal after any subsequent overstaying must be dealt with as deportation (subject to the special provision in relation to ship and aircraft crew)[3].

1 See para 119 above. However, there are special cases in respect of the common travel area and the European Communities: see paras 122–124, 137, above.
2 See the Immigration Act 1971 (c 77), s 4(2), Sch 2, para 8 (amended by the Immigration Act 1988 (c 14), s 10, Schedule, para 9(1), (4)). Refugees may be exempted: see paras 314 ff below.

3 As to deportation, see paras 202 ff below.

198. Illegal entry as a ground for administrative removal. The definition of 'illegal entry' has caused much discussion. Its development before the current legislation is of interest but is not dealt with here[1]. As currently defined, it is a ground for removal[2].

Under the current legislation, 'illegal entrant' is defined as a person unlawfully entering or seeking to enter in breach of a deportation order or of the immigration laws and includes a person who has so entered[3]. Being 'in breach of a deportation order' is straightforward[4], and 'immigration laws' is defined as referring to the Immigration Act 1971 and any law for similar purposes in force in the United Kingdom or Islands (apparently excluding the Immigration Rules)[5].

There are two difficulties. First, the person must be entering not only in breach of a deportation order or of the immigration laws, but also, it seems, 'unlawfully' since that adverb modifies the whole phrase. Thus a specific requirement is apparently added. This could require that the act be intentional for example[6]. However, this line was rejected by the English Court of Appeal and the word appears to have no effect[7]. The second difficulty is in the phrase 'in breach ... of the immigration laws'. This clearly includes entering despite failure to obtain leave to enter where required contrary to the Immigration Act 1971[8] (for instance by entering at a non-designated port or at no port at all). This situation is sometimes referred to as 'clandestine entry'. It was not, however, originally thought (even, it seems, by the government of the day) to cover a situation where leave is in fact obtained, but by means of forged documents or untrue statements[9]. This situation is sometimes referred to as 'entry by deception'[10].

However, during the 1970s the Home Office brought a number of cases which enabled the courts to interpret illegal entry to include various forms of entry by deception, not least where the person concerned had no knowledge of the deceit[11]. At the high point of this process, the House of Lords held that there was a positive duty of candour upon those seeking entry to reveal all material facts they knew or ought to have known to an immigration officer[12].

The House of Lords retreated from this extreme position in the *Khawaja* case[13]. The position established was that a person is an illegal entrant 'by deception' if he uses deception or fraud, typically if he breaches specific provision of the law by making a statement knowing it to be false or not believing it true and thus causes the immigration officer to grant leave where he would not otherwise have done so[14]. There is no 'duty of candour', and in particular mere non-disclosure cannot constitute making a false statement. The burden of proof lies on the Secretary of State for the Home Department, and whether a person is an illegal entrant is to be decided on the balance of probabilities, the balance taking into account the nature and gravity of the issue. That the immigration officer considered he had reasonable grounds does not dispose of the issue. It would appear in the light of this decision that a number of earlier cases must be regarded as wrongly decided[15].

Leave given by mistake in the absence of deceit is valid[16]. Mere lapse of time, or subsequent leave (for example as a 'returning resident' or indefinite leave to remain after four years' approved employment), after original illegal entry do not mend the original deceit[17]. Also the duty to submit to examination is absolute where a person arrives but is not met by an immigration officer, so that it is difficult lawfully to disembark at all in such circumstances[18].

1 However, see eg L Grant and I Martin *Immigration Law and Practice* (1982), ch 12 (and Supplement (1985)); *Macdonald's Immigration Law and Practice* (3rd edn, 1991, eds I A Macdonald and N J

Blake) chs 15, 17. It is important to note that illegal entry had no meaning in respect of Commonwealth citizens before the Commonwealth Immigrants Act 1962 (c 21), and that until the Commonwealth Immigrants Act 1968 (c 9) (repealed) amended that Act, there was no obligation upon Commonwealth citizens to seek leave to enter, no offence was committed by failing to obtain leave, and removal on the grounds of failure to have obtained leave was impossible after twenty-four hours: see further para 107, above. The effect was that any such person remaining for more than a day was not an illegal entrant: see eg L Grant and I Martin *Immigration Law and Practice* (1982) para 12.11.

2 Immigration Act 1971 (c 77), s 4(2), Sch 2, para 9.

3 Ibid, s 33(1). A person erroneously assumed to be a British citizen and admitted without leave is an illegal entrant even where personally blameless: *Mokuola and Ogunbiyi v Secretary of State for the Home Department* [1989] Imm AR 51, CA; *Tejpartap Singh Rehal v Secretary of State for the Home Department* [1989] Imm AR 576, CA. However, a returning resident refused entry on the ground of deception practised on the original entry is not: *Sattar v Secretary of State for the Home Department* [1988] Imm AR 190, CA. See also the text to and note 6 below.

4 See paras 202 ff below, especially para 212 below. However, as to returned deportees, see the Statement of Changes in Immigration Rules (HC Paper (1989–90) no. 251) (the Immigration Rules), para 176.

5 Immigration Act 1971, s 33(1). The status of the Immigration Rules is ambiguous: see para 110 above.

6 *R v Governor of Ashford Remand Centre, ex parte Bouzagou* [1985] Imm AR 69, CA. See also *Khan v Secretary of State for the Home Department* [1977] 3 All ER 538, [1977] 1 WLR 1466, CA, where the person seeking entry was wholly innocent but presented a passport obtained on her behalf by a third party and which was a fake: this was no defence. In *Rahim Miah v Secretary of State for the Home Department* [1989] Imm AR 559, CA, the Court of Appeal considered it relevant whether the entrant knew of the deception but expressly declined to consider whether the decision in the *Khan* case was, in the light of *Khawaja v Secretary of State for the Home Department* [1984] AC 74, [1983] 1 All ER 765, [1982] Imm AR 139, HL, correctly decided. However, see note 3 above.

7 *R v Governor of Ashford Remand Centre, ex parte Bouzagou* [1985] Imm AR 69, CA.

8 Ie under the Immigration Act 1971, s 3(1)(a).

9 *Grant and Martin* paras 12.1 (especially note 3)–12.3, and Supplement, paras 12.1, 12.2; *Macdonald* pp 417 ff, 418 ff. Presumably because of surprise at the success of the new Home Office view, two amnesties were granted to certain of those who were retrospectively affected. For the principal reported cases showing the change of view, see note 11 below.

10 Several types of deception can be distinguished, eg deception as to identity (by using a false or forged passport); deception as to entitlement (by falsely claiming to be settled when a 'returning resident', or to be a dependent child); and deception as to intention (eg by falsely claiming an intention to leave when seeking entry as a visitor or student): see *Macdonald* pp 417, 418.

11 The principal reported cases were *R v Secretary of State for the Home Department, ex parte Maqbool Hussain* [1976] 1 WLR 97, DC; *R v Bangoo* [1976] Crim LR 746, CA; *Khan v Secretary of State for the Home Department* [1977] 3 All ER 538, [1977] 1 WLR 1466, CA; *R v Secretary of State for the Home Department, ex parte Choudhary* [1978] 3 All ER 790, [1978] 1 WLR 1177, CA; *R v Secretary of State for the Home Department, ex parte Ibrahim* (1980) Times, 29 March. However, see the text to and note 15 below.

12 *R v Secretary of State for the Home Department, ex parte Zamir* [1980] AC 930, [1980] 2 All ER 768, HL. The unreasonableness of this is clear. To know what facts are material requires a good working knowledge of the Immigration Act 1971, the statutory instruments thereunder, the Immigration Rules currently in force, and conceivably the unpublished instructions to immigration officers (see para 111 above).

13 *Khawaja v Secretary of State for the Home Department* [1984] AC 74, [1983] 1 All ER 765, [1982] Imm AR 139, HL.

14 Their Lordships' *ratio decidendi* on this part of the *Khawaja* case is closely tied to the facts, and has been explained further in subsequent cases, especially *Bugdaycay v Secretary of State for the Home Department, Nelidow Santis v Secretary of State for the Home Department, Norman v Secretary of State for the Home Department, Re Musisi* [1987] AC 514, [1987] 1 All ER 940, [1987] Imm AR 250, HL, and *R v Immigration Appeal Tribunal, ex parte Anilkumar Rabindrabhai Patel* [1988] AC 910, [1988] 2 All ER 378, [1988] Imm AR 434, HL. It is irrelevant whether the person is seeking settlement or entry in a temporary capacity, and whether, had he told the full facts, he would have been admitted in a different category. Lord Bridges in the *Patel* case also explained and retracted his remarks in the *Khawaja* case relating to deportation on the grounds of 'conduciveness to the public good' (involving use of the *Practice Statement (Judicial Precedent)* [1966] 3 All ER 77, [1966] 1 WLR 1234, HL). The principle in the *Khawaja* case, as explained, has been applied in Scotland in *Malhi v Secretary of State for Home Affairs* 1989 SLT 43, OH.

15 Eg most of those mentioned in note 11 above. See eg comments on *Khan v Secretary of State for the Home Department* [1977] 3 All ER 538, [1977] 1 WLR 1466, CA, in *R v Immigration Appeal Tribunal, ex parte Anilkumar Rabindrabhai Patel* [1988] AC 910, [1988] 2 All ER 378, [1988] Imm AR 434, HL. The Court of Appeal has also regarded a number of cases of purported returning residents whose previous leave depended upon deceit as simple 'port refusals' rather than as cases of illegal entry, as for example in *R v Secretary of State for the Home Department, ex parte Fazor Ali* [1988] Imm AR 274, CA, with effect that the principle in the *Khawaja* case does not fall to apply.

16 *R v Secretary of State for the Home Department, ex parte Ram* [1979] 1 All ER 687, [1979] 1 WLR 148, DC; *Secretary of State for the Home Department v Mansour and Mansour* [1985] Imm AR 1, IAT. However, a person 'waved through' immigration control was an illegal entrant (*Tejpartap Singh Rehal v Secretary of State for the Home Department* [1989] Imm AR 576, CA), and silent production of a passport known to be false is deception (*R v Secretary of State for the Home Department, ex parte Dhirubhai Gordhanbhai Patel* [1986] Imm AR 515, CA).

17 *R v Secretary of State for the Home Department, ex parte Lapinid* [1984] 3 All ER 257, [1984] 1 WLR 1269, CA. See also *Claveria v Immigration Officer, London (Heathrow) Airport* [1978] Imm AR 176, IAT, discussed in *Grant and Martin* Supplement para 12.4; *Macdonald* p 227.

18 *R v Governor of Ashford Remand Centre, ex parte Bouzagou* [1985] Imm AR 69, CA.

199. Detention for administrative removal. Those liable to removal may be detained pending removal, and pending appeal[1], and may be removed from a ship or aircraft or, if arriving by way of the Channel Tunnel, may be removed from a vehicle or prevented from disembarking on one, and may be arrested without warrant[2]. They may be given temporary admission or release on bail on the same conditions as those detained on arrival, except when appealing[3]. However, in such case a chief immigration officer or police inspector may, with the consent of the Home Secretary, liberate a person so detained conditional upon:

(1) a bail bond for appearance before an adjudicator or the Immigration Appeal Tribunal;

(2) sufficient bail; and

(3) other conditions necessary to ensure appearance[4].

An adjudicator or the tribunal may do likewise (and may allow another to take the bail), and is required to if giving leave to appeal to the tribunal or where no such leave is required for such an appeal, except in certain circumstances such as where the applicant is likely to commit an offence[5].

1 Immigration Act 1971 (c 77), s 4(2), Sch 2, paras 16(1), (2), 28(3). Those liable to removal must not be detained on board a ship or aircraft so as to compel him to leave whilst the appeal is pending: Sch 2, para 28(3).

2 Ibid, Sch 2, paras 16(3), (4A), 17(1) (s 16(4A) being added by the Channel Tunnel (Fire Services, Immigration and Prevention of Terrorism) Order 1990, SI 1990/2227, art 3, Sch 1). A bail application may be made: see the Immigration Appeals (Procedure) Rules 1984, SI 1984/2041, r 23.

3 See the Immigration Act 1971, Sch 2, paras 21–25 (temporary admission or release: see para 169 above), and Sch 2, paras 29–33 (bail).

4 See ibid, Sch 2, paras 29(1), (2), (5), 30.

5 See ibid, Sch 2, paras 29(3)–(6), 30. The exceptions are where the person (1) has broken bail; (2) is likely to commit offences; (3) is a danger to public health; (4) is mentally disordered and it is in his own interests or for the protection of any other person; and (5) is under seventeen years of age and arrangements for his care in case of release are necessary but have not been made: Sch 2, para 30(2)(a)–(e).

200. Procedure for administrative removal. In the case of a person who may be removed administratively, an immigration officer may give directions to the captain of the ship or aircraft on which the person arrived to remove him in that ship or aircraft, or to the owners or agents of that ship or aircraft to remove him on another ship or aircraft of which they are owners or agents or on another ship or aircraft specified (or, in the cse of a person who has arrived by way of the Channel Tunnel, the Concessionaires of the Channel Tunnel)[1]. If on another ship or aircraft, the directions will specify a destination which must be a country of which the person removed is a national or citizen, or from which he holds a passport or document of identity, or from which he embarked, or to which there is reason to believe he will be admitted[2]. The same powers apply in the case of overstaying ship or aircraft crew[3]. In the case of those refused entry such directions must be given within two months of the refusal or notice of intention to give directions[4].

Alternatively, where it appears to the Secretary of State that it is not practicable for such directions to be given, or that they would be ineffective, or that the two-month limit for such directions, or notice of intention, in respect of those refused leave has not been complied with, then he may give directions in accordance with such arrangements as he may make, or specifically to owners or agents of any ship, to remove such a person (in which case he may specify the ship or aircraft and the destination)[5]. The destination in any case must be one to which an immigration officer may direct removal[5].

A person in respect of whom directions for removal have been given may be placed, under the authority of an immigration officer, on board the ship or aircraft in which he is to be removed[6].

1 Immigration Act 1971 (c 77), s 4(2), Sch 2, para 8(1)(a)–(c) (amended by the Channel Tunnel (Fire Services, Immigration and Prevention of Terrorism) Order 1990, SI 1990/2227, art 3, Sch 1).

2 Immigration Act 1971, Sch 2, para 8(1)(c)(i)–(iv) (as so amended). It is an offence for the captain or agent, or the Concessionaires of the Channel Tunnel, to fail to make the necessary arrangements: see s 27 (as amended), and para 161 above.

3 See ibid, Sch 2, paras 12(2), 13(2) (amended by the British Nationality Act 1981 (c 61), s 39(6), Sch 4, para 2). For these purposes there is an extra power to remove to a country or territory where he was engaged as a member of the crew of the ship or aircraft which he came to the United Kingdom to join: Immigration Act 1971, Sch 2, paras 12(2)(c)(iv), 13(2)(c)(iv).

4 Ibid, Sch 2, paras 8(2), 9 (para 8(2) being amended by the Immigration Act 1988 (c 14), s 10, Schedule, para 9). In calculating the two-month period, any time while an appeal is pending is discounted (see the Immigration Act 1971, Sch 2, para 28(1), (4)–(6) (as so amended)). The Statement of Changes in Immigration Rules (HC Paper (1989–90) no. 251) (the Immigration Rules), para 177, repeats the requirement as to distinction but stipulates also that the public interest, and expense, are to be considered. The amendment of Sch 2, para 8(2), allows 'notice of intention to give directions' to be given within the two-month period instead of directions themselves. This effectively removes any time limit. See also *R v Secretary of State for the Home Department, ex parte Gurmeet Singh* [1987] Imm AR 489, DC, on the provision before amendment.

5 See the Immigration Act 1971, Sch 2, para 10(1), (2) (as so amended). The Secretary of State bears the cost: Sch 2, para 10(3). The Secretary of State has similar powers in respect of seamen and aircrews: see Sch 2, para 14. Where the Secretary of State issues such directions they must be issued *de novo* and may not be a variation of those spent directions originally issued by the immigration officer. The words 'might have been given' in Sch 2, para 10(1)(b), do not mean 'might have been but have not' but 'were competent': *Kaur v Secretary of State for the Home Department* 1987 SCLR 550, OH; *R v Secretary of State for the Home Department, ex parte Parshottam Singh* [1989] Imm AR 469, CA. See also the commentary at 558, 559, noting inter alia erroneous use of the term 'patrial' instead of 'British citizen'.

6 Immigration Act 1971, Sch 2, paras 11, 15. However, this does not apply if detained pending appeal: see Sch 2, para 28(3), (5), (6).

201. Challenging removal. There is a severely limited right of appeal against administrative removal which can in some cases be pursued only from abroad[1], although appeal against refusal of leave as such is possible in a relevant case and removal may not be effected while the appeal is pending[2].

Challenge is possible by way of judicial review. Few reported cases of this appear in Scotland, but it has been common in England, chiefly by way of *habeas corpus*[3]. A confusing series of decisions, viewed as a decline of the effectiveness of *habeas corpus*, has been overtaken by the decision of the House of Lords in the *Khawaja* case[4].

1 See the Immigration Act 1971 (c 77), ss 16, 17, and paras 336, 341, 343, 344, below.
2 Ie under ibid, s 4(2), Sch 2, para 28(1), (5), (6): see para 200 above. As to appeals, see s 13, and paras 336, 339, below.
3 *Kaur v Secretary of State for the Home Department* 1987 SCLR 550, OH. For discussion of English cases, see L Grant and I Martin *Immigration Law and Practice* (1982) paras 13.15–13.19; *Macdonald's Immigration Law and Practice* (3rd edn, 1991, eds I A Macdonald and N J Blake) pp 494–500; and more recently *R v Secretary of State for the Home Department, ex parte Swati* [1986] 1 All ER 717, [1986] 1 WLR 477, [1986] Imm AR 88, CA, and *R v Secretary of State for the Home Department, ex parte Hindjou* [1989] Imm AR 24.
4 *Khawaja v Secretary of State for the Home Department* [1984] AC 74, [1983] 1 All ER 765, [1982] Imm AR 139, HL. As to the burden of this decision, see para 198 above.

(C) DEPORTATION

202. What is deportation. Deportation is the process whereby, on certain grounds, the Secretary of State may, if he thinks fit, order certain people who have entered, whether lawfully or otherwise[1], to be removed[2]. Thus it is to be distinguished from administrative removal[3].

It is useful to distinguish the deportation decision (after which appeal against the decision is normally available[4]) and the deportation order requiring departure and which may effect removal. In the case of deportations following a court recommendation, appeal against conviction or sentence (including the recommendation itself) in the normal fashion is available, rather than through the immigration appeal system.

In deciding to make an order the Secretary of State must take certain general considerations into account[5] and balance the public interest against compassionate circumstances, and seek consistency[6].

1 See eg *Genc v Secretary of State for the Home Department* [1984] Imm AR 180, IAT. He may devolve part of the process to immigration inspectors, but not all: *R v Secretary of State for the Home Department, ex parte Oladehinde* [1991] 1 AC 254, [1990] 2 All ER 367, CA (affd [1991] 1 AC 254, [1990] 3 All ER 393, HL).
2 See the Immigration Act 1971 (c 77), s 5(1), Sch 3, and paras 212, 213, below.
3 See paras 194 ff above. However, deportation and removal are not mutually exclusive: *R v Immigration Appeal Tribunal, ex parte Anikumar Ravindrabhai Patel* [1988] AC 910, [1988] 2 All ER 378, [1988] Imm AR 434, HL.
4 In most cases, appeal is available through the immigration appeal system: see paras 329 ff, 336, 341, 344, below. In certain 'security' cases there is no appeal at all but possible recourse to the 'Three Wise Men' procedure: see paras 335, 368, 369, below.
5 See para 209 below.
6 See para 210 below.

203. Who is liable to deportation. Any person who is not a British citizen, (unless falling into one of the categories of those protected from deportation and certain diplomats, consuls and persons in related groups) may be deported if the relevant grounds are fulfilled[1]. In relation to European Community nationals, however, the legislation is subject to Community law[2]. Also, a deportation order will not be made against a Convention[3] refugee if the only country to which he can be deported is that from which he is a refugee[4].

1 See the Immigration Act 1971 (c 77), s 3(5)–(7), the Statement of Changes in Immigration Rules (HC Paper (1989–90) no. 251) (the Immigration Rules), para 156, and paras 126, 130, 135, 136, above. Thus British Dependent Territories citizens, British Overseas citizens and British Nationals (Overseas), British subjects and British protected persons may be deported, as may other

Commonwealth citizens (and of course aliens, but subject to Community law: see para 137 above, and paras 221 ff below) even if settled (see para 121 above). For the definition of these terms, see NATIONALITY AND CITIZENSHIP, vol 14, paras 1906 ff.

2 See para 137 above, and paras 221 ff below.

3 Convention relating to the Status of Refugees (Geneva, 28 July 1951; TS 39 (1954); Cmd 9171) and Protocol relating to the Status of Refugees (New York, 31 January 1967; TS 15 (1969); Cmnd 3906).

4 Immigration Rules, para 173. See further paras 314 ff below.

204. Grounds for a deportation decision. There are four grounds on which the Secretary of State may decide to deport. They are:

(1) remaining beyond the time permitted in a limited leave to enter (that is 'overstaying'), or failure to observe any condition attached to leave to enter (that is, working without permission or failing to register with the police)[1];

(2) in the case of a person over seventeen years of age, a recommendation from a court upon conviction in certain circumstances[2];

(3) where deportation is deemed by the Secretary of State conducive to the public good[3]; and

(4) membership of the family of a person deported[4].

1 See the Immigration Act 1971, s 3(5)(a); the Statement of Changes in Immigration Rules (HC Paper (1989–90) no. 251) (the Immigration Rules), para 155(a); and para 205 below.

2 See the Immigration Act 1971, s 3(6); the Immigration Rules, para 155(d); and para 206 below.

3 See the Immigration Act 1971, s 3(5)(b); the Immigration Rules, para 155(b); and para 207 below.

4 See the Immigration Act 1971, s 3(5)(c); the Immigration Rules, para 155(c); and para 208 below.

205. Overstaying or breach of conditions. Deportation is normally the proper course in the case of overstaying or breach of conditions[1], but certain general circumstances will be taken into account[2]. Ignorance of being an overstayer is no barrier[3]. Overstaying is also a criminal offence[4]. Thus, there is a choice between deportation, prosecution, or both. Also, since the offence is imprisonable, conviction could further lead to a court recommendation to deport, providing alternative grounds[5]. Acquittal of the offence does not preclude deportation on the ground of overstaying as such[6].

1 Immigration Act 1971 (c 77), s 3(5)(a) (amended by the British Nationality Act 1981 (c 61), s 39(6), Sch 4, para 2).

2 Statement of Changes in Immigration Rules (HC Paper (1989–90) no. 251) (the Immigration Rules), para 166. See also *R v Nazari* [1980] 3 All ER 880, [1980] 1 WLR 1366, CA. A person relying on the protection of the Immigration Act 1971, s 15(1), against deportation while his appeal is pending (see para 211, note 4, below) does not thereby have 'authorisation' for the purpose of the Immigration Rules, para 158. Thus a deportation order may be made against him. Nor, it appears, does the protection of the Immigration Act 1971, s 15(1), require that he be not removed until any application for judicial review of an appeal decision (as opposed to any appeal as such) is determined: *R v Secretary of State for the Home Department, ex parte Subramaniam* [1977] QB 190, [1976] 1 All ER 915, [1976] Imm AR 155, CA; *Suthendran v Immigration Appeal Tribunal* [1977] AC 359, [1976] 3 All ER 611, [1977] Imm AR 44, HL; *Muhammad Idrish v Secretary of State for the Home Department* [1985] Imm AR 155, IAT. One circumstance is the effect on third parties: *Singh v Immigration Appeal Tribunal* [1986] 2 All ER 721, [1986] 1 WLR 910, [1986] Imm AR 352, HL. See also para 209, text to note 1, below.

3 *Hoosha Kumari Hanif v Secretary of State for the Home Department* [1985] Imm AR 57, IAT. However, it may be a compassionate circumstance to be taken into account: see para 210 below.

4 See the Immigration Act 1971, s 24(1)(b), and para 186 above.

5 See para 186 above. Alternative means of appeal would also exist.

6 *R v Secretary of State for the Home Department, ex parte Vashist* (1983) Times, 18 January, CA. It has been suggested that prosecution is more likely where the person has few connections with the United Kingdom, and that students are particularly at risk. Deportation is the more useful alternative where a party has a strong case for extension, but has failed to apply for it or to appeal against refusal: L Grant and I Martin *Immigration Law and Practice* (1982) para 11.17.

206. Court recommendation. When a sheriff court or the High Court of Justiciary convicts a person of seventeen years or more of an offence punishable by imprisonment (including life imprisonment) it may recommend deportation in the case of a person liable to deportation except that the High Court of Justiciary may do so on appeal only if the appeal is against conviction or sentence on indictment[1]. Any enactment restricting young offenders or first offenders is to be ignored in determining whether an offence is imprisonable, and if a person is found to have committed an offence it is to be regarded as a conviction even if the court does not proceed to conviction[2].

The recommendation may not be made unless the person has had seven days' notice in writing that British citizens cannot be deported, and describing who are British citizens, and describing the groups exempted from deportation[3], and the court may adjourn for this purpose[4].

Certain principles have been laid down by the courts in England as to recommendations. In *R v Nazari*[5] the Court of Appeal in England enunciated some six principles as follows:

(1) whether the person's continued presence is detrimental, because of the seriousness of the crime or the length of criminal record (but excluding general deterrence)[6];

(2) that the harshness of the regime to which the person would return is irrelevant to the court (though the Home Secretary may take it into account);

(3) the effect on the family and other innocent persons must be considered;

(4) unilateral promises to leave at the end of any sentence should be given little weight;

(5) mental instability is a good reason for a recommendation;

(6) in the case of 'illegal immigrants'[7], a recommendation should normally be made.

In addition it was held under the earlier law that sentence should not be reduced because a recommendation is made[8].

It has been argued that it is unnecessary for a court recommendation to be a separate ground for deportation[9].

1 Immigration Act 1971 (c 77), ss 3(6), 6(1) (s 3(6) being amended by the British Nationality Act 1981 (c 61), s 39(6), Sch 4, para 2). The High Court is given power to make rules by Act of Adjournal: Immigration Act 1971, s 6(7). Potentially problems arise in so far as Scots and English criminal law are not coterminous: see para 207, note 4, below.

2 Ibid, s 6(3) (amended by the Criminal Justice Act 1982 (c 48), s 77, Sch 15, para 15). Under the earlier Immigration Rules, in such cases, 'supervised departure' with a prohibition on re-entry could be imposed. This is no longer specifically enjoined, but a supervised departure is referred to in the Statement of Changes in Immigration Rules (HC Paper (1989–90) no. 251) (the Immigration Rules), para 178, and as a possibility where a court has not recommended departure in para 165.

3 Ie under the Immigration Act 1971, s 7: see para 126 above.

4 See ibid, s 6(2) (amended by the Criminal Procedure (Scotland) Act 1975 (c 21), s 461(1), Sch 9, para 47; the Magistrates' Courts Act 1980 (c 43), s 154, Sch 7, para 104; and the British Nationality Act 1981, Sch 4, para 2).

5 *R v Nazari* [1980] 3 All ER 880, [1980] 1 WLR 1366, CA.

6 Receipt of supplementary benefit was held not to be a factor if the offence is minor: *R v Serry* (1980) Times, 31 October, CA.

7 'Illegal immigrant' is not a term of art. 'Illegal entrant' is defined (see para 198, text to note 3, above), and excludes those overstaying in breach of conditions.

8 *R v Edgehill* [1963] 1 QB 593, [1963] 1 All ER 181, CCA.

9 Eg see *Macdonald's Immigration Law and Practice* (3rd edn, 1991, eds I A Macdonald and N J Blake) pp 391, 392, and notes.

207. Conduciveness to the public good. The ground of conduciveness to the public good is wholly undefined. The House of Lords originally observed

that the ground was intended for cases where continued presence is objectionable on specific grounds, not to remove a respectable person for circumstances
concerned with his original entry; but the House later specifically retracted that
view[1]. The Immigration Rules assert that general rules on the use of the ground
cannot be laid down, but that all relevant circumstances known to the Secretary
of State, including the general considerations, will be taken into account[2]. These
include past conduct as well as future[3].

It appears that the power has been used in two principal types of case, that is
those where a 'marriage of convenience' (however defined) is alleged[4], and
political cases[5]. The distinction has considerable importance for the appeal
procedure[6]. In addition, the power has been used in a variety of miscellaneous
cases, including where there has been criminal activity but no court recommendation or even no conviction or no likelihood of further offence, and the
Immigration Rules specifically hold out this possibility[7].

1 *Khawaja v Secretary of State for the Home Department* [1984] AC 74, [1983] 1 All ER 765, [1982]
    Imm AR 139, HL, per Lord Bridge; *R v Immigration Appeal Tribunal, ex parte Anilkumar
    Rabindrabhai Patel* [1988] AC 910, [1988] 2 All ER 378, [1988] Imm AR 434, HL.
2 Statement of Changes in Immigration Rules (HC Paper (1989–90) no. 251) (the Immigration
    Rules), para 167. As to the general considerations, see para 209 below.
3 *Bashir (alias Ayoub) v Secretary of State for the Home Department* [1978] Imm AR 150, IAT.
4 What constitutes a 'marriage of convenience' is unclear. It covers 'bogus' marriages entered
    solely to achieve entry including where facts are suppressed (*Yanus Suleman Patel v Immigration
    Appeal Tribunal* [1989] Imm AR 416, CA (distinguishing *Khawaja v Secretary of State for the Home
    Department* [1984] AC 74, [1983] 1 All ER 765, [1982] Imm AR 139, HL)), but is complicated by
    the 'primary purpose' rules (see paras 270, 271, 274, 275, below). See also *R v Immigration Appeal
    Tribunal, ex parte Cheema* [1982] Imm AR 124, CA; *R v Immigration Appeal Tribunal, ex parte
    Khan* [1983] QB 790, [1983] 2 All ER 420, [1982] Imm AR 134, CA; *R v Immigration Appeal
    Tribunal, ex parte Owusu-Sekyere* [1987] Imm AR 425, CA. However, see *R v Immigration Appeal
    Tribunal, ex parte Khan* [1983] Imm AR 32, which was disapproved in *R v Immigration Appeal
    Tribunal, ex parte Anilkumar Rabindrabhai Patel* [1988] AC 910, [1988] 2 All ER 378, [1988] Imm
    AR 434, HL. Deportation must relate to continued presence, not solely fraud on original entry,
    but no restriction on time or place of relevant events exists and deceitful use of marriage is a
    ground under the Immigration Act 1971 (c 77), s 3(5)(b) (see para 204 above): *Genc v Secretary of
    State for the Home Department* [1984] Imm AR 180, IAT.
      Problems could arise in so far as Scots law and English law diverge on the constitution of
    marriage: see para 269, note 1, below. Sir Thomas Smith quotes the case of an American in
    Scotland expelled on a deportation order from London because he intended to marry in Scotland
    an 'infant' ward of an English court and observes that the illegality of the conduct and desirability
    of deportation should 'have been decided by the Scottish courts': T B Smith *British Justice: The
    Scottish Contribution* (1961) p 28, citing A E Anton and Ph Franceskakis 'Modern Scots "Runaway
    Marriages"' 1958 JR 253 at 270 note 71. It is not clear under what power the man was deported.
    The contemporary legislation was the Aliens Order 1953, SI 1953/1671 (spent). Currently,
    deportation is at the discretion of the Secretary of State (ie effectively the Home Secretary: see
    para 138 above) subject only to appeal to the ad hoc United Kingdom immigration appeals
    system (see paras 329 ff below). The courts are involved only in so far as they may recommend
    deportation upon conviction of an imprisonable offence (see para 206 above), or may review the
    judicial decision of the Secretary of State or the immigration appeal system. For a more recent
    case on somewhat similar facts, see R M White 'Foreign Marriages: Some Validity and Immi-
    gration Issues' 1986 SCOLAG 79 at 79, 80. See also para 329, note 3, below.
5 See eg *R v Governor of Brixton Prison, ex parte Soblen* [1963] 2 QB 243, [1962] 3 All ER 641, CA;
    Dutschke (unreported but see B A Hepple 'Aliens and Administrative Justice: The Dutschke
    Case' (1971) 34 MLR 501); *Caprino v United Kingdom* No 6871/75 (1980) 4 EHRR 97; *R v Secretary
    of State for the Home Department, ex parte Hosenball* [1977] 3 All ER 452, [1977] 1 WLR 776, CA;
    Agee v Lord Advocate 1977 SLT (Notes) 54.
6 Where the ground of deportation is conduciveness to the public good in the interests of national
    security or of the relations between the United Kingdom and any other country, or other reasons
    of a political nature, there is no appeal (Immigration Act 1971, s 15(3)), although there is the
    'Three Wise Men' procedure (see paras 368, 369, below).
7 Immigration Rules, para 165. See eg *Mitchell v Secretary of State for the Home Department* [1981]
    Imm AR 140, IAT; *R v Immigration Appeal Tribunal, ex parte Florent* [1985] Imm AR 141, CA.

208. Membership of the family of a deportee. Where a person is or has been ordered to be deported, her children under eighteen years of age (if a woman), or his wife and his or her children under eighteen years of age (if a man), may also be deported[1]. 'Wife' includes polygamous wives, and 'child' includes both legally adopted children and others treated as adopted, but illegitimate children (unless adopted or treated as such) are regarded only as children of their mother[2]. A deportation order cannot be made against a family member eight weeks or more after the principal deportee has left, disregarding time while an appeal is pending[3].

Where a wife is qualified for settlement other than as a dependant, an order will not normally be made[4]. Also a person ceases to be liable to family deportation if he ceases to belong to the family[5]. This normally includes a divorced wife, a woman and children living apart from the husband and father, children who have reached eighteen years of age, or are near that age and have spent some years in the United Kingdom, children who have left the family home on taking employment or if married, and children of school age if the effect on their education will be disruptive, and realistic plans for their care and maintenance exist if the parent or parents are deported[6]. Further, the eventual return of family members may be a relevant factor[7].

Yet further, an abbreviated list of general considerations explicitly applies in place of the usual list[8], including

(1) length of residence in the United Kingdom;
(2) ties with the United Kingdom other than as dependants of the principal deportee;
(3) ability to be maintained without recourse to public funds for the foreseeable future;
(4) any compassionate or other relevant circumstances; and
(5) any representations[9].

Immigration history is a relevant circumstance[10].

These considerations are drafted on the assumption that the prinicpal deportee is a husband or father, so it is unclear how far they apply if she is a wife or mother.

---

1 Immigration Act 1971 (c 77), ss 3(5)(c), 5(4)(a), (b) (s 3(5)(c) being amended by the British Nationality Act 1981 (c 61), s 39(6), Sch 4, para 2). The power exists where a notice of deportation is made against the principal deportee and does not require a deportation order to have been made: *Gulten Ibrahim v Immigration Appeal Tribunal* [1989] Imm AR 111, CA (overturning to that extent *R v Immigration Appeal Tribunal, ex parte Mehmet* [1977] 2 All ER 602, [1977] 1 WLR 795, [1977] Imm AR 56, DC).
2 Immigration Act 1971, s 5(4). Cf s 1(5) (see para 125 above), and the Statement of Changes in Immigration Rules (HC Paper (1989–90) no. 251) (the Immigration Rules), para 3.
3 See the Immigration Act 1971, ss 5(3), 15(2), and the Immigration Rules, para 168. A family deportation order falls if the principal order does: *R v Immigration Appeal Tribunal, ex parte Mehmet* [1977] 2 All ER 602, [1977] 1 WLR 795, [1977] Imm AR 56, DC.
4 See the Immigration Rules, para 170.
5 Immigration Act 1971, s 5(3).
6 Immigration Rules, paras 170, 171. The phrase 'near that age' means 'near but below that age': *Karantoni v Secretary of State for the Home Department* [1987] Imm AR 518, CA.
7 See the Immigration Rules, para 172.
8 See ibid, para 164, and para 209 below.
9 Ibid, para 169.
10 *Anand v Secretary of State for the Home Department* [1978] Imm AR 36, IAT.

---

209. General considerations in making a decision or giving effect to a court recommendation. The Immigration Rules require every relevant factor known to the Secretary of State to be taken into account by him, including

nine specified ones, in deciding whether to give effect to a court recommendation for deportation or making a decision on the grounds of overstaying, breach
of conditions or conduciveness to the public good[1]. These are:

(1) age;
(2) length of residence in the United Kingdom;
(3) strength of connections with the United Kingdom;
(4) personal history, including character, conduct and employment record;
(5) domestic circumstances;
(6) nature of the offence of which the person was convicted (in relevant cases);
(7) previous criminal record (where relevant);
(8) compassionate circumstances; and
(9) any representations made on the person's behalf[2] (such representations do
    not require the Secretary of State to make a new decision[3]).

It is not possible to make general statements as to how these factors operate in
actual cases[4], although where the Secretary of State decides to deport, his
decisions are not readily overturned in the immigration appeal process[5]. One
specific relevant circumstance is, for example, immigration history if revealing
deception[6].

It has been stressed that representations, particularly if revealing new factors,
and from members of Parliament, can be effective (although the power of
members of Parliament to make representations has been reduced)[7].

1 Statement of Changes in Immigration Rules (HC Paper (1989–90) no. 251) (the Immigration
  Rules), para 164. A more restricted list applies in the case of members of the deportee's family:
  see para 208 above.
2 Ibid, para 164. The list is not to be regarded as exhaustive and may include eg impact on a third
  party: *Singh v Immigration Appeal Tribunal* [1986] 2 All ER 721, [1986] 1 WLR 910, [1986] Imm
  AR 352, HL.
3 *Hoosha Kumari Hanif v Secretary of State for the Home Department* [1985] Imm AR 57, IAT.
4 L Grant and I Martin *Immigration Law and Practice* (1982) ch 11, refers to numerous unrepresent-
  ative cases. See also *Derrick v Secretary of State for the Home Department* [1972] Imm AR 109, IAT.
5 See eg *Jordan v Secretary of State for the Home Department* [1972] Imm AR 201, IAT.
6 *Bashir (alias Ayoub) v Secretary of State for the Home Department* [1978] Imm AR 150, IAT.
7 *Grant and Martin* para 11.39.

**210. Balance of public interest and compassionate circumstances and
consistency.** The public interest is to be balanced against compassionate circumstances[1]. This is logically difficult to reconcile with the requirements of the
general considerations. Consistency is also to be sought[2].

1 Statement of Changes in Immigration Rules (HC Paper (1989–90) no. 251) (the Immigration
  Rules), para 162. See eg *M M H Ali v Secretary of State for the Home Department* [1978] Imm AR
  126, IAT; *Jordan v Secretary of State for the Home Department* [1972] Imm AR 201, IAT; *Muhammad
  Idrish v Secretary of State for the Home Department* [1985] Imm AR 155, IAT. The Immigration
  Rules, para 162, is to be read in conjunction with what are now paras 164 and 166: *Singh v
  Immigration Appeal Tribunal* [1986] 2 All ER 721, [1986] 1 WLR 910, [1986] Imm AR 352, HL.
2 Immigration Rules, para 162.

211. Notice of decision to deport and appeals. When the Secretary of State
has decided to make a deportation order, the person must be notified in writing
of the decision and reasons and informed of the right to appeal as soon as
practicable at his last known or usual address, or address provided for receipt of
notice, unless there is no knowledge of his whereabouts, in which case service of
the notice is unnecessary[1]. Unsuccessful service does not preclude deportation[2].
This notice allows appeal which must be entered within fourteen days of the
decision (not, therefore, of the sending or receipt of the notice) except in special
circumstances[3] and there can be no deportation order while an appeal is pending[4]. Appeals are dealt with below[5].

Service of notice also permits detention[6].

1 See the Immigration Act 1971 (c 77), s 18(1); the Statement of Changes in Immigration Rules (HC Paper (1989–90) no. 251) (the Immigration Rules), para 174; and the Immigration Appeals (Notices) Regulations 1984, SI 1984/2040, regs 3(1), (4), 6. Delay in taking the decision cannot 'estop' the Secretary of State: *R v Secretary of State for the Home Department, ex parte Fauzia Wamar Din Bagga Khan* [1987] Imm AR 543, CA.
2 *R v Secretary of State for the Home Department, ex parte Mehmet* [1977] 2 All ER 602, [1977] 1 WLR 795, [1977] Imm AR 56, DC; *R v Secretary of State for the Home Department, ex parte Yeboah, R v Secretary of State for the Home Department, ex parte Draz* [1987] 3 All ER 999, [1987] 1 WLR 1586, [1987] Imm AR 414, CA (followed in *Singh v Secretary of State for the Home Department* 1990 SLT 300, OH, on appeal 1991 GWD 9–547).
3 Immigration Appeals (Procedure) Rules 1984, SI 1984/2041, rr 4(7), 5(1).
4 Immigration Act 1971, s 15(2). As to appeal against the recommendation of the court for deportation, see s 6(6). See also the Immigration (Variation of Leave) Order 1976, SI 1976/1572 (amended by SI 1989/1005), and *R v Secretary of State for the Home Department, ex parte Subramaniam* [1977] QB 190, [1976] 1 All ER 915, [1976] Imm AR 155, CA; *Suthendran v Immigration Appeal Tribunal* [1977] AC 359, [1976] 3 All ER 611, [1977] Imm AR 44, HL; *Muhammad Idrish v Secretary of State for the Home Department* [1985] Imm AR 155, IAT.
5 See paras 329 ff below.
6 See the Immigration Act 1971, s 5(5), Sch 3, para 2, and para 213 below.

212. Deportation orders. Where the Secretary of State decides to deport a person, and no appeal is made, or the appeal is rejected, the Secretary of State may sign a deportation order[1]. The effect of a deportation order is to require the deportee to leave and to prohibit him from re-entering[2].

The Secretary of State may also give directions to the captain of a ship or aircraft about to leave the United Kingdom, or to owners or agents of a ship or aircraft, requiring them to make arrangements (or he may make his own arrangements) for the removal of the deportee to a country of which he is a national or citizen, or to which there is reason to believe he will be admitted, taking into account the public interest and expense[3].

Such directions are of no effect while an appeal in respect of a deportation order is pending[4].

1 See the Immigration Act 1971 (c 77), s 5(1), and the Statement of Changes in Immigration Rules (HC Paper (1989–90) no. 251) (the Immigration Rules), para 175. The order must contain a summary of the facts and, where appropriate, confirmation that an appeal has been rejected: para 175, which makes reference to the 'Three Wise Men' procedure (see para 368 below). The Secretary of State may decide not to sign the order if a supervised or voluntary departure is arranged: see para 215 below.
2 Immigration Act 1971, s 5(1). The order also causes any appeal against variation of leave to lapse: s 14(5) (added by the Immigration Act 1988 (c 14), s 10, Schedule, para 3).
3 See the Immigration Act 1971, s 5(5), Sch 3, para 1, and the Immigration Rules, para 177. He may pay all or part of the consequential expenditure: see the Immigration Act 1971, Sch 3, para 1(4).
4 Ibid, Sch 2, para 28(2), applied by Sch 3, para 3.

213. Detention pending deportation order, appeal or removal. A person subject to a court recommendation for deportation, not otherwise detained or liberated on bail, may be detained by the court making the recommendation[1]. That court may liberate him, on account of an appeal or otherwise, as may the Secretary of State[2]. A court liberating such a person may make restrictions as to residence, employment or occupation and reporting to the police[3]. These restrictions may be added, varied or removed by the court directing liberation or (where liberation was directed on appeal) by either the High Court of Justiciary or the sheriff court from which the appeal came on application by the deportee, or constable or an immigration officer[4].

A person who has received notice of a decision to deport and who is not otherwise detained or liberated on bail, and a person subject to a deportation order, may be detained under the authority of the Secretary of State, or subject to such restrictions as to residence, employment or occupation and reporting to the police as the Secretary of State requires by written notice pending the order, removal or departure, as appropriate[5].

1 Immigration Act 1971 (c 77), s 5(5), Sch 3, para 2(1) (amended by the Criminal Justice Act 1982 (c 48), s 64, Sch 10, para 1).
2 Immigration Act 1971, Sch 3, para 2(1), (1A) (amended and added by the Criminal Justice Act 1982, Sch 10, para 1). As to the effect of appeals, see the Immigration Act 1971, Sch 3, para 3, and para 212, text and note 4, above. Applications for bail may be made: see the Immigration Appeals (Procedure) Rules 1984, SI 1984/2041, r 23.
3 Immigration Act 1971, Sch 3, para 4 (added by the Criminal Justice Act 1982, Sch 10, para 2, and amended by the Immigration Act 1988 (c 14), s 10, Schedule, para 10(2), (4)). Cf the Immigration Act 1971, s 4(2), Sch 2, paras 29–32, applied by Sch 3, para 3, and para 199 above.
4 See the Immigration Act 1971, Sch 3, paras 5, 6 (as so added).
5 See ibid, Sch 3, paras 2(2)–(6), 5, 6 (substituted and added by the Criminal Justice Act 1982, Sch 10, paras 1, 2, and amended by the Immigration Act 1988, Schedule, para 10(2), (4)).

214. Revocation of a deportation order. A deportation order lapses if the person becomes a British citizen and may be revoked by the Secretary of State[1]. The chief considerations for the Secretary of State are a material alteration in circumstances, or fresh information[2]. Passage of time is relevant but at least three years will normally be expected to have passed, and in a case of a serious criminal record a long period of years will apply[3]. The public interest (including maintenance of immigration control) is to be balanced against the individual's interests[4].

There is a right of appeal against refusal to revoke unless the Secretary of State has personally certified exclusion to be conducive to the public good[5].

Revocation does not entitle the person to enter again, so he must qualify under the Immigration Rules[6].

1 Immigration Act 1971 (c 77), s 5(2) (amended by the British Nationality Act 1981 (c 61), s 39(6), Sch 4, para 2).
2 Statement of Changes in Immigration Rules (HC Paper (1989–90) no. 251) (the Immigration Rules), para 180.
3 Ibid, para 180. See eg *Secretary of State for the Home Department v Udoh* [1972] Imm AR 89, IAT; *Dervish v Secretary of State for the Home Department* [1972] Imm AR 48, IAT; *Secretary of State for the Home Department v Sanusi* [1975] Imm AR 114, IAT.
4 Immigration Rules, para 180.
5 See the Immigration Act 1971, s 15(1)(a), (4), and the Immigration Rules, para 179. As to the public good, see para 207 above.
6 Ibid, para 179.

(D) OTHER FORMS OF CONTROL

215. Supervised and voluntary departure and curtailment of stay. The Immigration Rules provide that a supervised departure with a prohibition on re-entry may be arranged as an alternative to deportation[1], and point out that in the case of family members subject to deportation, it is possible to leave voluntarily[2]. The Secretary of State may provide travelling and other expenses of those liable to deportation, but not having a deportation order made against them, and intending to live permanently abroad[3].

In cases where a court recommendation to deport might have been made but was not, curtailment of stay with a prohibition on re-entry may be imposed instead of deportation[4].

Payments including travelling expenses are also available to others, other than British citizens, leaving with the intention of residing permanently abroad if they wish to and it is in their interests[5].

In a small number of cases English courts have declined to issue an injunction or have bound over a person on condition that he leave the United Kingdom[6]. The Court of Appeal has approved the practice subject to guidelines[7]. No Scottish cases appear to have been reported.

1 Statement of Changes in Immigration Rules (HC Paper (1989–90) no. 251) (the Immigration Rules), para 178. As to certain difficulties in the procedure, see L Grant and I Martin *Immigration Law and Practice* (1982) para 11.45. The current Immigration Rules no longer mention supervised departures in respect of young offenders: see the Immigration Rules, para 164 (formerly the Statement of Changes in Immigration Rules (HC Paper (1982–83) no. 169) (the Former Immigration Rules), para 156 (revoked)).
2 Immigration Rules, para 168.
3 Immigration Act 1971 (c 77), s 5(6) (amended by the Immigration Act 1988 (c 14), s 10, Schedule, para 2).
4 Immigration Rules, para 165. See also paras 177, 180, 181, above. There is no specific power to revoke prohibition on re-entry, nor any appeal, so that expulsion under this power may be more draconian than deportation.
5 Immigration Act 1971, s 29 (amended by the British Nationality Act 1981 (c 61), s 39(6), Sch 4, para 2).
6 *R v McCartan* [1958] 3 All ER 140, [1958] 1 WLR 933, CCA; *R v Ayu* [1958] 3 All ER 636, [1958] 1 WLR 1264, CCA; *R v Hodges* (1967) 51 Cr App Rep 361, CA; *R v East Grinstead Justices, ex parte Doeve* [1969] 1 QB 136, [1968] 3 All ER 666, DC. See also A J Chislett 'Recognisances and Conditions' [1958] Crim LR 734, and H A H Walter 'Recognisances' [1960] Crim LR 113.
7 *R v Williams* [1982] 3 All ER 1092, [1982] 1 WLR 1398, CA.

216. Removal of mental patients. The Secretary of State may authorise the removal of a mental patient if it is in the patient's interests and proper arrangements have been made for care and treatment[1]. No appeal is possible.

1 See the Mental Health (Scotland) Act 1984 (c 36), s 83, and MENTAL HEALTH, vol 14, para 1470. The power is rarely used: *Macdonald's Immigration Law and Practice* (3rd edn, 1991, eds I A Macdonald and N J Blake) p 400. It appears that the appropriate Secretary of State is the Secretary of State for Scotland, and that he, or the Home Secretary may, in the case of a person with mental illness, proceed instead under the power to deport, at least when there is no evidence that the illness is of such severity as to require such 'proper arrangements' at the destination: *R v Secretary of State for the Home Department, ex parte Yassin Talmasani* [1987] Imm AR 32, CA. As to deportation, see paras 202 ff above.

217. 'Hostage' and 'safety' orders. The Secretary of State has power to make provision to control the exit of persons of certain nationalities under certain circumstances[1].

1 See paras 135, 136, above.

218. Extradition and related processes. Extradition and related processes, including return of prisoners and deserters, is dealt with separately[1].

1 See paras 501 ff below.

(7) CATEGORIES OF ENTRANT UNDER COMMUNITY LAW WITHOUT THE RIGHT OF ABODE

(a) Community Law

219. United Kingdom law and Community law. Community law[1] is, in its own terms, independent of and superior to the national law of any member state[2], and if directly effective and directly applicable overrides incompatible national law, whether that national law precedes or succeeds the Community law[3]. Where there is incompatibility, national courts must, therefore, apply Community law in preference to national law (subject to the possibility of referral of the question of interpretation of Community law to the European Court of Justice)[4].

There are various forms of Community legislation. Provisions of the EEC Treaty and regulations are binding in their entirety and take direct effect in each member state[5]. Directives are, in principle, binding as to the result to be achieved, but form and method are left to national authorities[6]. However the European Court of Justice has held that, in certain circumstances, directives may be directly effective[7], and thus can be relied upon in litigation in national courts, without the necessity of intervening national legislation[8].

The United Kingdom having acceded to the Treaty concerning the accession of the United Kingdom to the European Economic Community, the Euratom and the European Coal and Steel Community, parliament enacted the European Communities Act 1972 to render municipal law conform to Community law[9]. A principal effect of this is to oblige United Kingdom courts to recognise the precedence of Community law. Broadly speaking, this precedence has been recognised in practice[10].

1 See CONSTITUTIONAL LAW, vol 5, paras 320–325, 329, 354, EUROPEAN COMMUNITY LAW AND INSTITUTIONS, vol 10, paras 1 ff, and SOURCES OF LAW (FORMAL), vol 22, paras 204–214.
2 Case 26/62 *NV Algemene Transport-en Expeditie Onderneming van Gend en Loos v Nederlandse Tarief Commissie* [1963] ECR 1, [1963] CMLR 105, ECJ; Case 106/77 *Amministrazione delle Finanze dello Stato v Simmenthal SpA* [1978] ECR 629, [1978] 3 CMLR 263, ECJ.
3 Case 6/64 *Costa v ENEL* [1964] ECR 585, [1964] CMLR 425, ECJ.
4 Case 6/64 *Costa v ENEL* [1964] ECR 585, [1964] CMLR 425, ECJ; Case 118/76 *Watson and Belmann* [1976] ECR 1185, [1976] 2 CMLR 552, ECJ.
5 EEC Treaty, art 189, 2nd para.
6 Ibid, art 189, 3rd para.
7 See vol 22, paras 206, 207; Case 6/64 *Costa v ENEL* [1964] ECR 585, [1964] CMLR 425, ECJ; Case 41/74 *Van Duyn v Home Office* [1974] ECR 1337, [1975] 1 CMLR 1, ECJ.
8 Case 41/74 *Van Duyn v Home Office* [1974] ECR 1337, [1975] 1 CMLR 1, ECJ; Case 36/75 *Rutili v Minister for the Interior* [1975] ECR 1219, [1976] 1 CMLR 140, ECJ.
9 See the European Communities Act 1972 (c 68), s 2 (amended by the Northern Ireland Constitution Act 1973 (c 36), s 41(1), Sch 6, Pt I) and the European Communities Act 1972, s 3 (amended by the European Communities (Amendment) Act 1986 (c 58), s 2).
10 See eg *Macarthys v Smith* [1979] 3 All ER 325, [1979] 1 WLR 1189, [1979] 3 CMLR 44, 381, CA. See now *Litster v Forth Dry Dock and Engineering Co Ltd* [1990] 1 AC 546, 1989 SLT 540, HL; *Factortame Ltd v Secretary of State for Transport* [1990] 2 AC 85, [1989] 2 All ER 692, HL.

220. Nationality, territorial extent and Community law rights. Rights under Community law relevant to immigration depend, in part, upon nationality[1]. On accession to the EEC Treaty, the United Kingdom made a declaration as to the meaning of 'United Kingdom national' for Community purposes[2]. Changes in United Kingdom nationality law[3] rendered that definition meaningless, and a further declaration was made[4]. This declares British citizens, British subjects (without citizenship), and British Dependent Territories citizens by virtue of a connection with Gibraltar[5] to be such 'United Kingdom nationals'. However, it has been doubted whether this declaration has any effect[6]. The definition is not likely to be further amended to take account of more recent legislation[7], but there are certain oddities in it[8].

In any case, special provisions relate to the inhabitants of the Isle of Man and the Channel Islands (which are not part of the United Kingdom)[9]. The EEC Treaty specifically limits its operation in respect of these Islands to the extent necessary to ensure the implementation of the arrangements for those Islands set out in the United Kingdom Accession Treaty[10]. The Accession Treaty[11] did not specifically apply the freedom of movement provisions to the Islands, so they are outside the territorial scope of those provisions. Also, the Accession Treaty defined 'Channel Islanders and Manxmen'[12], declares their rights in respect of the United Kingdom to be unaffected, but also declares that such persons do not benefit from the Community provisions relating to the freedom of movement of persons and services[13]. However, the Accession Treaty also requires the authorities of the Channel Islands and Isle of Man to apply the same treatment to all natural and legal persons of the Community[14].

This, it has been suggested, means that nationals of other member states are on a par with British citizens in that they can visit the Islands (within the ambit of the common travel area and subject to the prevention of terrorism provisions[15]), but are subject to local restrictions upon residence and employment[16].

1 See generally NATIONALITY AND CITIZENSHIP, vol 14, para 1903.
2 As to the United Kingdom the terms 'nationals', 'nationals of member states' or 'nationals of member states and overseas countries and territories' wherever used in the Treat[ies], establishing the European Community, the Euratom, and the European Coal and Steel Community or in any of the Community Acts deriving from those Treaties are to be understood to refer to (1) persons who are citizens of the United Kingdom and Colonies or British subjects not possessing that citizenship or the citizenship of another Commonwealth country or territory, who in either case, have the right of abode in the United Kingdom, and are therefore exempt from United Kingdom immigration control; (2) persons who are citizens of the United Kingdom and Colonies by birth or by registration or naturalisation in Gibraltar, or whose father was so born, registered or naturalised: Treaty of Accession (1972), Final Act, United Kingdom Declaration on the Definition of 'Nationals' (superseded). 'United Kingdom national' has been defined in other ways for other purposes: see eg the Foreign Marriage Act 1892 (c 23), s 1(2) (added by the Foreign Marriage (Amendment) Act 1988 (c 44), s 1(2)).
3 Ie under the British Nationality Act 1981 (c 61).
4 As to the United Kingdom the terms 'nationals', 'nationals of member states' or 'nationals of member states and overseas countries and territories' wherever used in the Treat[ies] establishing the European Community, the Euratom and the European Coal and Steel Community or in any of the Community Acts deriving from those Treaties are to be understood to refer to (1) British citizens; (2) persons who are British subjects by virtue of the British Nationality Act 1981, Pt IV (ss 30–35), and who have the right of abode in the United Kingdom and are therefore exempt from United Kingdom immigration control; (3) British Dependent Territories citizens who acquire their citizenship from a connection with Gibraltar: Declaration by the United Kingdom replacing the Declaration on the Definition of the term 'Nationals' (Rome, 31 December 1982; TS 67 (1983); Cmnd 9062; OJ C23, 28.1.83, p 1).
    The reference in respect of the Channel Islands and Isle of Man to 'any citizen of the United Kingdom and Colonies' is to be understood as referring to 'any British citizen': Act of Accession (1972), Protocol 3, art 6.
5 Those connected with Gibraltar are specifically mentioned because they have the right of free movement within the European Community, and thus a right to enter the United Kingdom for certain purposes, although they have no right of abode. This is reflected in the British Nationality Act 1981, s 5: see vol 14, para 1915.
6 Ie on the ground that it is a unilateral declaration, not a Treaty document, had no statutory or other parliamentary approval, nor was it the judgment of a competent court: *Macdonald's Immigration Law and Practice* (3rd edn, 1991, eds I A Macdonald and N J Blake) p 147, note 10.
7 The Hong Kong (British Nationality) Order 1986, SI 1986/948, creates the category of British Nationals (Overseas) (as to which see vol 14, paras 1946–1949), but this status is irrelevant for present purposes. The British Nationality (Hong Kong) Act 1990 (c 34), allows some inhabitants of Hong Kong to register as British citizens, in which case they will fall under the second declaration (as to which see note 4 above). See the British Nationality (Hong Kong) (Selection Scheme) Order 1990, SI 1990/2292.
8 Ie that those with a right of abode who are not British citizens are not included, but that British Dependent Territories citizens by virtue of a connection with Gibraltar, who have no right of abode in the United Kingdom (unless registered under the British Nationality Act 1981, s 5, as British citizens), are: *Macdonald* p 147.
9 Interpretation Act 1978 (c 30), s 5, Sch 1 ('British Islands'). Cf the Royal and Parliamentary Titles Act 1927 (c 4), s 2(2). Special rules apply to the Channel Islands as part of the common travel area and to preserve employment and residence for local inhabitants: see para 122 above.
10 EEC Treaty, art 227(5)(c).

11 Ie the Treaty of Accession (1972).

12 Ie any citizen of the United Kingdom and Colonies who holds that citizenship by virtue of the fact that he, a parent or grandparent was born, adopted, naturalised or registered in the island in question; but such a person is not for this purpose regarded as a Channel Islander or Manxman if he, a parent or grandparent was born, adopted, naturalised or registered in the United Kingdom: ibid, Protocol 3, art 6. Nor is he so regarded if he has at any time been ordinarily resident in the United Kingdom for five years: Protocol 3, art 6. The reference to citizen of the United Kingdom and Colonies must now be read with the Declaration of 1982: see note 4 above. However, the doubts referred to in text and note 6 above should be noted.

13 Ibid, Protocol 3, art 2.

14 Ibid, Protocol 3, art 4.

15 See paras 122–124 above.

16 *Macdonald* p 147.

221. Freedom of movement of persons and services. The EEC Treaty established the principles of free movement of workers, freedom of establishment and freedom to provide services within the Community, and also prohibits discrimination within the scope of the Treaty on the grounds of nationality.

Freedom of movement of persons involves the right to take up and to seek offers of employment; to travel within the Community for these purposes; and to stay in a member state, including sojourn, after employment ceases[1]. The freedom of establishment includes the right of the self-employed to carry on non-wage earning activities and to set up and manage companies[2]. The freedom to provide services includes the right to do so temporarily in another member state[3]. Regulations and directives further detail the rights, and expand them (for example in relation to recipients of services)[4].

The freedoms are, however, subject to the entitlement of the member states to limit the rights granted, on the grounds of public policy, public security or public health[5].

Discrimination on the ground of nationality within the scope of the EEC Treaty, and without prejudice to any special provisions in it, is prohibited[6]. Abolition of such discrimination between workers as regards terms and conditions of employment is specifically required[7].

The Immigration Rules provide a specific regime for Community nationals and their families. Inconsistent Immigration Rules and associated legislation have been held to contravene Community law and to that extent be inapplicable to Community nationals[8].

1 See the EEC Treaty, art 48. See also Case 53/81 *Levin v Staatssecretaris van Justitie* [1982] ECR 1035, [1982] 2 CMLR 454, ECJ.

2 EEC Treaty, art 52.

3 Ibid, art 60.

4 Ie principally EEC Council Directive 64/221 (OJ 1964, p 850 (S Edn 1963–64, p 117)); EC Council Directives 68/360 (OJ L257, 19.19.68, p 13 (S Edn 1968 (II), p 485)), 72/194 (OJ L121, 26.5.72, p 32 (S Edn 1972 (II), p 474)), 73/148 (OJ L172, 28.6.73, p 14)), 75/34 (OJ L14, 20.1.75, p 10), 75/35 (OJ L14, 20.1.75, p 14), 90/364 (OJ L180, 13.7.90, p 26), 90/365 (OJ L180, 13.7.90, p 28), 90/366 (OJ L180, 13.7.90, p 30); EC Council Regulations 1612/68 (OJ L257, 19.19.68, p 2 (S Edn 1968 (II), p 475)), 1251/70 (OJ L142, 30.6.70, p 24 (S Edn, 1970 (II), p 402)), 1408/71 (OJ L149, 5.7.71, p 2 (S Edn 1971 (II), p 416)), 574/72 (OJ L74, 16.3.72, p 1 (S Edn 1972 (I), p 122)), 311/76 (OJ L39, 14.2.76, p 1) and 312/76 (OJ L39, 14.2.76, p 2). Updated versions of the full text of all such instruments are found in the *Encyclopedia of European Community Law* vol c, binders I, VI. The relevant Treaty provisions also require General Programmes for the advancement of freedom of establishment and to provide services: see General Programme for the abolition of restrictions on freedom of establishment (JO 1962, p 36 (S Edn (2nd Series) IX, p 7)) and General Programme for the abolition of restrictions on freedom to provide services (Brussels, 18 December 1961: JO 1962, p 32 (S Edn (2nd Series) IX, p 3)). These were to be implemented by directive and many were issued. However, the European Court of Justice found the relevant provisions of the EEC Treaty to be directly effective and no more directives were issued: see eg Case 2/74 *Reyners v Belgian State* [1974] ECR 631, [1974] 2 CMLR 305, ECJ. Other EEC Treaty

provisions (eg art 57) require progress towards equivalence of diplomas etc: see eg EC Council Directive 85/384 (OJ L223, 21.8.85, p 15).
5 See the EEC Treaty, art 48(3), and paras 232–234 below.
6 Ibid, art 7.
7 See ibid, art 48(2), and EC Council Regulation 1612/68. The proscription prevents member states from discrimination against their own nationals as well as in favour of them: Case 175/78 *R v Saunders* [1979] ECR 1129, [1979] 2 CMLR 216, [1980] QB 72, ECJ; Case 115/78 *Knoors v Secretary of State for Economic Affairs* [1979] ECR 399, [1979] 2 CMLR 357, ECJ; Case 246/80 *Broekmeulen v Huisarts Registratie Commissie* [1981] ECR 2311, [1982] 1 CMLR 91, ECJ; Case 271/82 *Auer v Ministère Public* [1983] ECR 2727, [1985] 1 CMLR 123, ECJ.
8 Case 157/79 *R v Pieck* [1980] ECR 2171, [1981] QB 571, [1981] 3 All ER 46, ECJ.

222. 'Primary right' holders. Workers, the self-employed and providers and recipients of services, as such, are given rights[1]. 'Worker' is not defined in the EEC Treaty but has a Community law meaning, that is, a person in or in bona fide search of any form of employment available for further work regardless of motive for working[2]. For certain purposes, the legislation distinguishes 'temporary workers', 'frontier workers' and 'seasonal workers' from others. 'Frontier workers' are those who have residence in one member state to which they return as a rule each day or at least once a week, but are employed in the territory of another[3]. The rights normally depend upon a worker being a national of a member state (but irrespective of his place of residence), and upon the worker being a migrant[4].

The beneficiaries of the right of establishment are not defined, but they must be nationals of a member state, and (a few circumstances apart) need not be resident, nor actually employed or in business when seeking to enter[5]. Providers of services include those wishing to provide services, who must be nationals of a member state[6].

Recipients of services are not referred to in the EEC Treaty, but are specifically included in Community legislation. They must, presumably, include those wishing to receive services as well as those already in receipt, and be nationals of a member state[6]. The extent of the category is unclear[7].

Nationality remains a matter for national law. 'Community national' means a national of a member state in accordance with the laws of that state[8].

Stateless persons and refugees, even when resident within a member state, have no freedom of movement, of establishment, or to provide or to receive services. However, they do acquire benefits under the legislation on social security for migrant workers, and a declaration asserts that refugees resident in one member state wishing to work in another should be viewed with particular favour[9].

The EC Council may extend the provisions dealing with services to non-nationals established in a member state[10].

1 EC Council Directives 90/364 (OJ L180, 13.7.90, p 26), 90/365 (OJ L180, 13.7.90, p 28) and 90/366 (OJ L180, 13.7.90, p 30), require member states to extend certain Community rights of residence to other Community nationals and their immediate families by 30 June 1992.
2 Case 75/63 *Hoekstra (née Unger) v Bestuur der Bedrijfsvereniging voor Detailhandel en Ambachten* [1964] ECR 177, [1964] CMLR 319, ECJ; *R v Secchi* [1975] 1 CMLR 383, CA; *Nijssen v Immigration Officer, London (Heathrow) Airport and Immigration Officer, Sheerness* [1978] Imm AR 226, IAT; Case 53/81 *Levin v Staatssecretaris van Justitie* [1982] ECR 1035, [1982] 2 CMLR 454, ECJ; *Giangregorio v Secretary of State for the Home Department* [1985] Imm AR 104, [1983] 3 CMLR 472, IAT; *Hoth v Secretary of State for the Home Department* [1985] Imm AR 20, IAT. As to those seeking work, see para 236, text and note 1, below.
3 EC Council Directive 68/360 (OJ L257, 19.19.68, p 13 (S Edn 1968 (II), p 485)), art 8(1)(b).
4 EC Council Regulation 1612/68 (OJ L257, 19.19.68, p 2 (S Edn 1968 (II), p 475)), preamble, 6th recital, arts 1(1), 47. See also Joined Cases 35, 36/82 *Morson and Jhanjan v Netherlands* [1982] ECR 3723, [1983] 2 CMLR 221, ECJ; and *Aradi v Immigration Officer, Heathrow* [1985] AR 184, IAT.
5 See the EEC Treaty, art 52, and EC Council Directive 73/148 (OJ L172, 28.6.73, p 14), art 1(1)(a). However, see para 236, text and note 1, below.

6 See the EEC Treaty, art 59, and EC Council Directive 73/148, art 1(1)(a).

7 Case 118/75 *Watson and Belmann* [1976] ECR 1185, [1976] 2 CMLR 552, ECJ. Those receiving 'professional services' are no doubt included. Tourists, although receiving services, are no doubt not included.

8 See para 220 above. In *Aradi v Immigration Officer, Heathrow* [1985] AR 184, IAT, the tribunal observed that the relevant Community legislation does not refer to dual nationality and, without seeking a preliminary ruling from the European Court of Justice, concluded that in the case of dual nationals, a member state should apply the International Convention on Certain Questions relating to the Conflict of Nationality Laws (The Hague, 12 April 1930; TS 33 (1937); Cmd 5553).

9 EC Council Regulation 1408/71 (OJ L149, 5.7.71, p 2 (S Edn 1971 (II), p 416)); Declaration of Representatives of Governments of Member States meeting in Council (JO 22.5.64, p 1225).

10 EEC Treaty, art 59 (amended by the Single European Act, art 16(3)).

223. 'Secondary right' holders. Families are not mentioned in the EEC Treaty. Secondary legislation broadly gives to families the same rights as primary right holders, irrespective of nationality. Families of those providing or receiving services, and of temporary, frontier and seasonal workers are not mentioned and so are possibly excepted; those not nationals of member states may be required to obtain a visa (although they must be afforded every facility for obtaining one)[1]. In the case of workers family rights to instal themselves with the primary right holder depend upon the availability of housing[2].

'Family' includes spouses, descendants who are either under twenty-one years of age or who are dependent (or in the case of the self-employed and providers of services, are both), and dependent relatives in the ascending line[3]. Their rights are, however, only triggered by the exercise by the primary right holder of his right to free movement[4]. Other relatives have no entitlement, but, if dependent, must be favoured by the member state[5]. A person ceasing to be a member of a family terminates his rights. These rights may also depend upon residence with the primary right holder[6].

The death of the primary right holder does not necessarily terminate family rights[7].

1 EC Council Directive 68/360 (OJ L257, 19.19.68, p 13 (S Edn 1968 (II), p 485)), art 3(2); EC Council Directive 73/148 (OJ L172, 28.6.73, p 14), art 3(2). These apply only where the primary right holder is outside his own member state or receiving services outside it: *Tombofa v Secretary of State for the Home Department* [1988] Imm AR 400, CA.

2 EC Council Regulation 1612/68 (OJ L257, 19.19.68, p 2 (S Edn 1968 (II), p 475)). This is not to give rise to discrimination on the ground of nationality.

3 EC Council Directive 68/360, art 1; EC Council Regulation 1612/68, art 10(1); EC Council Directive 73/148, art 1(1). It is not clear if adopted children are included. Divorced or separated spouses may not have the right, but do not necessarily have to live with the primary right holder: Case 267/83 *Diatta v Land Berlin* [1985] ECR 567, [1986] 2 CMLR 164, ECJ; *R v Secretary of State for the Home Department, ex parte Sandhu* (1985) Times, 10 May, HL.

4 Joined Cases 35, 36/82 *Morson and Jhanjan v Netherlands* [1982] ECR 3723, [1983] 2 CMLR 221, ECJ; *R v Secretary of State for the Home Department, ex parte Ayub* [1983] Imm AR 20, [1983] 3 CMLR 140, DC (this may be *per incuriam*). In *Aradi v Immigration Officer, Heathrow* [1985] AR 184, IAT, the tribunal decided, without seeking a preliminary ruling from the European Court of Justice, that a British citizen/Irish citizen dual national should be treated as a British citizen and that it followed that she could not trigger such rights for a dependant: see para 222, text and notes 2, 8, above.

5 EC Council Regulation 1612/68, art 10(2); EC Council Directive 73/148, art 1(2).

6 Case 267/83 *Diatta v Land Berlin* [1984] ECR 567, [1986] 2 CMLR 164, ECJ; *R v Secretary of State for the Home Department, ex parte Sandhu* (1985) Times, 10 May, HL.

7 EC Council Regulation 1251/70 (OJ L142, 30.6.70, p 24 (S Edn 1970 (II), p 402)), art 3(1), (2); EC Council Directive 75/34 (OJ L14, 20.1.75, p 10), art 3(1), (2).

224. Right to depart and return. Member states must grant primary right holders who are Community nationals and secondary right holders, whether or not Community nationals, permission to leave their territory[1]. The holder is entitled by right to an identity card or passport issued by the competent national authority and valid for at least five years (unless another document allowing departure is available), without requirement of an exit visa, and for entry to all other member states and any intervening countries[2]. He is entitled to be re-admitted without formality even if the travel document has expired or his nationality is disputed[3].

1 EEC Treaty, art 48(3)(b); EC Council Directive 68/360 (OJ L257, 19.19.68, p 13 (S Edn 1968 (II), p 485)), art 2(1); EC Council Directive 73/148 (OJ L172, 28.6.73, p 14), art 2(1).
2 EEC Treaty, art 48(3)(b); EC Council Directive 68/360, art 2(2), (3); EC Council Directive 73/148, art 2(2), (3).
3 EEC Council Directive 64/221 (OJ 1964, p 850 (S Edn 1963–64, p 117)), art 3(4). Presumably they need only re-admit them if they are entitled under Community law or as nationals.

225. Right to enter. Member states must admit primary right holders to take up their economic activity, and accompanying secondary right holders, provided they hold a valid identity card or passport[1]. Visas may be required only of non-national secondary right holders[2]. In the case of workers, the right includes a right to enter for three months to seek work as well as indefinitely actually to take up work[3].

1 EEC Treaty, art 48(3)(b); EC Council Directive 68/360 (OJ L257, 19.19.68, p 13 (S Edn 1968 (II), p 485)), art 3(2); EC Council Directive 73/148 (OJ L172, 28.6.73, p 14), arts 1, 3(1).
2 EC Council Directive 68/360, art 3(2); EC Council Directive 73/148, art 3(2).
3 Case 48/75 *Royer* [1976] ECR 497, [1976] 2 CMLR 619, ECJ; Case 118/75 *Watson and Belmann* [1976] ECR 1185, [1976] 2 CMLR 552, ECJ, per Advocate General Trabucchi. See also T C Hartley *European Economic Community Immigration Law* (1978) p 105, quoting the Council Minutes in relation to EC Council Directive 68/360, and *Lubbersen v Secretary of State for the Home Department* [1984] Imm AR 56, [1984] 3 CMLR 77, IAT. See further para 236, text and note 1, below.

226. Right to reside for the purpose of employment etc. Member states must permit primary and secondary right holders (except in the cases of those seeking work, temporary workers, providers and recipients of services, and their families, and some other families) to reside indefinitely and to move freely within their territories[1]. The right is drafted in part in terms of the right to a residence permit. The former is, however, not dependent upon the grant of the latter of which it is merely proof[2].

Workers may be required to produce the travel document used to enter the country and specified evidence of employment: thus those seeking work acquire no right to reside and may be refused a residence permit[3]. Temporary workers receive a right to residence for the duration of employment, whether seasonal or not[4]. In the former case the evidence of employment must state the period of employment, and in the latter, that the expected duration of employment will be sufficient to cover his stay[5]. Frontier workers have a right to reside in the member state of employment[6].

Those exercising the right of establishment automatically acquire the right to reside[7].

Providers and recipients of services acquire a right to reside for as long as the services are provided[8].

Freedom to reside does not preclude restrictions upon entry to part of the territory in the application of normal criminal law[9].

1 EEC Treaty, art 48(3)(b); EC Council Directive 68/360 (OJ L257, 19.19.68, p 13 (S Edn 1968 (II), p 485)), art 6(1)(a); EC Council Directive 73/148 (OJ L172, 28.6.73, p 14), art 5. Member states are required to extend certain rights of residence to other Community nationals and their immediate families by 30 June 1992: see EC Council Directives 90/364 (OJ L180, 13.7.90, p 26); 90/365 (OJ L180, 13.7.90, p 28); and 90/366 (OJ L180, 13.7.90, p 30).

2　Case 48/75 *Royer* [1976] ECR 497, [1976] 2 CMLR 619, ECJ; Case 157/79 *R v Pieck* [1980] ECR 2171, [1981] QB 571, [1981] 3 All ER 46, ECJ.

3　EC Council Directive 68/360, art 4(1). See also *Lubbersen v Secretary of State for the Home Department* [1984] Imm AR 56, [1984] 3 CMLR 77, IAT; and *Hoth v Secretary of State for the Home Department* [1985] Imm AR 20, IAT.

4　EC Council Directive 68/360, arts 6(3), 8(1)(a), (c).

5　Ibid, art 8(1)(a).

6　Ibid, art 8(1)(b).

7　EC Council Directive 73/148, art 4(1). See also *Hoth v Secretary of State for the Home Department* [1985] Imm AR 20, IAT, and para 236, text and note 1, below.

8　EC Council Directive 73/148, art 4(2).

9　Case 175/78 *R v Saunders* [1979] ECR 1129, [1980] QB 72, [1979] 2 All ER 267, ECJ.

227. Termination of the rights to reside. Temporary rights to reside terminate automatically. It is not clear if they can be renewed. Otherwise the right to reside is unlimited unless terminated. How termination occurs is largely to be deduced from grounds for terminating or not renewing residence permits. Although the right to reside does not depend on grant of a residence permit, there is no point in withdrawing or refusing to renew one unless the right to reside is thereby terminated.

Withdrawal of a full residence permit is justified by absence of six consecutive months or more unless for military service[1]. No mention is made of its effect on temporary residence permits or the providers and recipients of services confusingly termed 'right of abode'[2].

In the case of workers, unemployment due to temporary incapacity resulting from illness or accident, or which is involuntary (if duly confirmed by the competent employment office), does not of itself justify withdrawal[3]. On first renewal of the residence permit, but not subsequently, restriction to a further twelve months is possible[4]. Workers with permanent incapacity may acquire the right to remain after the ending of their employment[5].

In the case of the self-employed, unemployment resulting from temporary incapacity due to illness or accident does not of itself justify withdrawal of a residence permit[6].

1　EC Council Directive 68/360 (OJ L257, 19.19.68, p 13 (S Edn 1968 (II), p 485)) art 6(2); EC Council Directive 73/148 (OJ L172, 28.6.73, p 14) art 4(1).

2　See para 230 below.

3　EC Council Directive 68/360, art 7(1). 'Involuntary' is not defined.

4　Ibid, art 7(2). Presumably continuous unemployment, voluntary or involuntary (except in cases of permanent or temporary incapacity) justifies withdrawal: see T C Hartley *European Economic Community Immigration Law* (1978) p 117, and *Lubbersen v Secretary of State for the Home Department* [1984] Imm AR 56, [1984] 3 CMLR 77, IAT.

5　See para 228 below.

6　EC Council Directive 73/148, art 4(1). Presumably unemployment for other causes does not.

228. Right to remain after employment. Member states must permit those who have been workers or self-employed (but not those who are providers or recipients of services) to remain after employment has ended, in three cases:

(1)　those wishing to retire;

(2)　those permanently incapacitated for work by reason of illness or injury; and

(3)　those frontier workers who wish to retain the right to reside by reason of employment[1].

A person wishing to retire acquires the right to remain if he has reached the age at which he is entitled to an old age pension in the member state in which he wishes to remain (or if not entitled because self-employed, the age of sixty-five years); has been a worker or self-employed there for at least twelve months preceding retirement; and has resided there for at least three consecutive years[2].

An employed or self-employed person who was not qualified by reason of having left the relevant member state but was resident in it for a long period, must have his re-admission for retirement facilitated[3].

A person permanently incapacitated acquires the right if he was a worker or self-employed in the member state in which he wishes to remain, or if he ceased work because of a permanent incapacitation, and either has resided continuously in that state for the preceding two years or has an incapacity resulting from an accident at work or an occupational disease which entitles him to a pension for which that state is wholly or partly responsible[4]. Those unqualified by reason of having left the relevant member state but who were resident for a long period, must have re-admission facilitated[5].

A frontier worker acquires a right to remain in the member state where he worked or was self-employed if he had the right to reside there and worked or was self-employed there for three continuous years, even if he commences employment in a third member state. Further, periods of such employment are to be considered to have been completed in the 'state of residence' for the purposes of acquiring the right to remain on retirement or permanent incapacitation[6].

In the cases of retirement and incapacity, the residence requirement does not apply if the spouse of the person seeking the right to remain is a national of the member state concerned (or was, but lost that nationality upon marriage)[7].

In all cases continuous residence is to be attested by any normal method used in the relevant country. It is not affected by absences of less than three months per year, or on military service. Continuous employment is not interrupted by periods of involuntary unemployment, provided it is duly recorded by the competent employment office, nor by absences due to illness or accident, in the case of workers, nor by periods of incapacity due to circumstances outside the control of the person concerned or of inactivity owing to illness or accident in the case of self-employment[8].

No formality may be required by a member state for the exercise of the right to remain and, in the case of retirement and incapacity, absences for two years after acquiring the right may not adversely affect it[9].

Families residing with a primary right holder who have acquired the right, also acquire the right, and continue to have it after his death. If the primary right holder dies during his working life and before acquiring the right to remain, the family acquires that right only if he had resided there continuously for the two years preceding his death; the death resulted from an accident at work or occupational disease; and the surviving spouse is a national of the state of residence (or was, but lost that nationality upon marriage)[10].

1 EEC Treaty, arts 48(3)(c), 235; EC Council Regulation 1251/70 (OJ L142, 30.6.70, p 24 (S Edn 1970 (II), p 402)); EC Council Directive 75/34 (OJ L14, 20.1.75, p 10).
2 EC Council Regulation 1251/70, art 2(1)(a); EC Council Directive 75/34, art 2(1)(a).
3 EC Council Regulation 1251/70, art 8(2); EC Council Directive 75/34. 'Long period' is not defined, and 'facilitate' appears to create no liability.
4 EC Council Regulation 1251/70, art 2(1)(b); EC Council Directive 75/34, art 2(1)(b).
5 EC Council Regulation 1251/70, art 8(2); EC Council Directive 75/34, art 8(2). As to the meaning of 'long period' and 'facilitate', see note 3 above.
6 EC Council Regulation 1251/70, art 2(1)(c); EC Council Directive 75/34, art 2(1)(c). The 'state of residence' is presumably the 'state of actual residence'.
7 EC Council Regulation 1251/70, art 2(2); EC Council Directive 75/34, art 2(2). Loss of nationality on marriage appears to cover voluntary as well as automatic loss.
8 EC Council Regulation 1251/70, art 4(2); EC Council Directive 75/34, art 4(2).
9 EC Council Regulation 1251/70, art 5(1), (2); EC Council Directive 75/34, art 5(1), (2).
10 EC Council Regulation 1251/70, art 3(2); EC Council Directive 75/34, art 3(2). As to loss of nationality on marriage, see note 7 above.

229. Termination of the right to remain after employment. No means of terminating the right to remain after employment is mentioned. However, since a residence permit can be withdrawn or not renewed by reason of absences greater than six consecutive months, unless for military service, such absence terminates the right to remain[1].

1 EC Council Regulation 1251/70 (OJ L142, 30.6.70, p 24 (S Edn 1970 (II), p 402)), art 6(2); 75/34 (OJ L14, 20.1.75, p 10), art 6(2).

230. Residence permits for those 'primary' right holders coming to work and their families. Member states are required to issue a residence permit free of charge (or at the normal cost of an identity card) to primary right holders with a right to reside (unless resident for less than three months or unless the primary right holder is a provider or recipient of services)[1]. Those claiming a residence permit must produce the document on which they entered and, in the case of workers, the specified evidence of employment. The self-employed must produce proof that they are self-employed 'primary' right holders[2]. Formalities must not hinder immediate commencement of employment[3]. Specific wording is required in the case of workers[4].

In the case of temporary workers (whether seasonal or not), those expected to be employed for less than three months are not entitled to a residence permit[5]. Temporary workers expected to be employed for more than three months, if seasonal workers, or between three months and one year if not, are entitled to a temporary residence permit which, in the latter case, may be limited to the expected period of employment[6]. No limit is specified in the former[6].

No reference is made to those without a temporary residence permit whose employment unexpectedly exceeds three months, or the stated amount. Presumably the former become entitled to a temporary residence permit and the latter to a renewal or to a full residence permit.

In the case of frontier workers, there is no right to a residence permit in the member state of employment, but it may issue them with a special residence permit valid for five years and automatically renewable[7].

Full residence permits must be valid for at least five years and renewable automatically (assuming the right to reside continues or is replaced by a right to remain), and throughout the territory of the member state (subject to any limitations imposed by the normal criminal law)[8]. It is not clear if the latter characteristics also apply to temporary residence permits.

Providers and recipients of services are not entitled to a residence permit, but to a confusingly entitled 'right of abode' if their right to reside exceeds three months. They do not require one for a lesser period but may be required to report their presence to the police[9].

Secondary right holders, that is, families of primary right holders, have the same entitlement to a residence permit in so far as they have the right to reside on production of the same documents as the worker, together with, in the case of a worker's family, a document from the state of origin, or whence they came, testifying that they are dependent, or do live under the same roof, but it is not clear if families of temporary or frontier workers, or of those providing or receiving services, have any right to reside[10].

While the right to reside does not depend upon grant of a residence permit, member states may require residence permits to be held on pain of a penalty[11].

Member states may refuse to issue a residence permit on one of the grounds of the public policy proviso, but must decide as soon as possible, and in any case within six months, and must allow the person concerned to enter pending a decision. It is not clear if failure to refuse within six months bars refusal completely.

1 EC Council Directive 68/360 (OJ L257, 19.19.68, p 13 (S Edn 1968 (II), p 485)), art 4(2); EC
    Council Directive 73/148 (OJ L172, 28.6.73, p 14), art 4(1); EC Council Regulation 1251/70 (OJ
    L142, 30.6.70, p 24 (S Edn 1970 (II), p 402)), art 6; EC Council Directive 75/34 (OJ L14, 20.1.75,
    p 10), art 6. See also *Lubbersen v Secretary of State for the Home Department* [1984] Imm AR 56,
    [1984] 3 CMLR 77, IAT.
2 EC Council Directive 73/148, art 6(2).
3 EC Council Directive 68/360, art 6(1).
4 Ibid, Annex.
5 Ibid, art 8(1)(a).
6 Ibid, arts 6(3), 8(1)(c).
7 Ibid, art 8(1)(b).
8 Ibid, art 6(1); EC Council Directive 73/148, art 6(1). See also Case 175/78 *R v Saunders* [1979]
    ECR 1129, [1980] QB 72, [1979] 2 All ER 267, ECJ.
9 EC Council Directive 73/148, art 4(2).
10 EC Council Directive 68/360, art 4(3), (4); EC Council Directive 73/148, art 4(3).
11 Case 48/75 *Royer* [1976] ECR 497, [1976] 2 CMLR 619, ECJ; Case 157/79 *R v Pieck* [1980] ECR
    2171, [1981] QB 571, [1981] 3 All ER 46, ECJ; Case 118/75 *Watson and Belmann* [1976] ECR 1185,
    [1976] 2 CMLR 552, ECJ.

231. Other rights. Workers have a right to equality of treatment with national
workers in employment, social and tax matters, including trade union membership and access to housing[1]. Workers' spouses and dependent children under
twenty-one years have the right to take employment, and workers' resident
dependent children have the right to general educational, apprenticeship and
vocational training courses as if nationals; and member states are to encourage
such participation[2]. In particular, member states are to give free tuition in their
own official languages to such children and promote mother tongue teaching
and the national culture[3].

1 EC Council Regulation 1612/68 (OJ L257, 19.19.68, p 2 (S Edn 1968 (II), p 475)), arts 7, 8, 10.
2 Ibid, arts 11, 12.
3 EC Council Directive 77/486 (OJ L199, 6.8.77, p 32), arts 2, 3.

232. Public policy proviso. There are permitted derogations from the rights
of free movement, freedom of establishment and provision and receipt of
services, even if they result in discrimination against foreign nationals (in so far
as a state may not exclude its own nationals)[1]. The European Court of Justice has
held that limitations on free movement within a member state are not justified
by the public policy proviso unless they are applied where national law permits
them to be applied to nationals. In particular, the proviso applies to all measures
concerning entry into a state, issue or renewal of residence permits, and expulsion, and may apply to persons with a primary or secondary right[2]. However,
application of the proviso is to be exceptional[3].
   The precise wording of the proviso applying to workers differs from that
applying to the right of establishment and to providers and recipients of services, but the principles are the same, and allow such derogation on the grounds
of public policy, public security or public health. These terms are undefined and
interpretation is left to national governments, subject to the limits imposed by
Community law[4].

1 Ie under the EEC Treaty, arts 48(3), 52, 66; EEC Council Directive 64/221 (OJ 1964, p 850
    (S Edn 1963–64, p 117)), art 10; EC Council Directive 72/194 (OJ L121, 26.5.72, p 32 (S Edn 1972
    (II), p 474)); EC Council Directive 73/148 (OJ L172, 28.6, 73, p 14), art 8; EC Council Directive
    75/34 (OJ L14, 20.1.75, p 10), art 9, but not under EC Council Regulation 1612/68 (OJ L257,
    19.19.68, p 2 (S Edn 1968 (II), p 475)) or EC Council Regulation 1251/70 (OJ L142, 30.6.70, p 24

(S Edn 1970 (II), p 402)), although this is not significant since both are subject to the EEC Treaty, art 48, by virtue of Case 41/74 *Van Duyn v Home Office* [1974] ECR 1337, [1975] 1 CMLR 1, [1975] Ch 358, [1975] 3 All ER 190, ECJ.

2 EEC Council Directive 64/221, arts 1, 2(1). Families are protected only if the 'primary right' holder is outside his member state or receiving services outside it: *Tombofa v Secretary of State for the Home Department* [1988] Imm AR 400, CA.

3 Case 41/74 *Van Duyn v Home Office* [1974] ECR 1337, [1975] 1 CMLR 1, [1975] Ch 358, [1975] 3 All ER 190, ECJ; Case 36/75 *Rutili v Minister for the Interior* [1975] ECR 1219, [1976] 1 CMLR 140, ECJ.

4 Case 41/74 *Van Duyn v Home Office* [1974] ECR 1337, [1975] 1 CMLR 1, [1975] Ch 358, [1975] 3 All ER 190, ECJ; *Rutili v Minister for the Interior* [1975] ECR 1219, [1976] 1 CMLR 140, ECJ; Case 48/75 *Royer* [1976] ECR 497, [1976] 2 CMLR 619, ECJ.

233. Substantive limits of the public policy proviso. The public policy proviso may not be invoked for economic ends, although they may be part of public policy[1]. Thus, for example, exclusion of the unemployed as such would not be permissible, but there are individual cases of persons being refused entry when purporting to be seeking work because they are not in fact believed to be doing so[2]. Only listed diseases or disabilities justify refusal of entry or of a first residence permit on that ground, and if occurring later do not justify refusal to renew or expulsion[3]. Measures taken on the ground of public policy or public security must be based exclusively on the personal conduct of the person[4]. This includes voluntary actions generally, including present involvement in an organisation against which actions are taken, but possibly excluding mere sympathy, and in general excluding past associations[5]. Previous criminal convictions as such do not justify measures, even as general deterrence, but measures based on individual deterrence and possibly even prevention or retaliation might[6].

The expiry of a travel document does not justify expulsion or refusal to re-admit (but may justify non-admission *ab initio*)[7]. Nor does failure to hold a travel document, even in contravention of national law, if the person is exercising a Community right[8]. Exercise of a Community law right as such (and possibly of a right under the European Convention on Human Rights[9]) cannot justify use of the proviso[10].

In all cases, there must be an actual policy to justify use of the proviso, it must safeguard a fundamental interest of society and the threat to it must be genuine and sufficiently serious[10]. Thus a principle of proportionality may be applied[11]. The activities against which measures are taken need not be made illegal provided at least the competent authority has defined its standpoint and has adopted with respect to its own nationals repressive or otherwise genuine and effective measures intended to combat the activities[12].

1 EEC Council Directive 64/221 (OJ 1964, p 850 (S Edn 1963–64, p 117)), art 2(2).
2 *R v Secchi* [1975] 1 CMLR 383, CA; *Nijssen v Immigration Officer, London (Heathrow) Airport and Immigration Officer, Sheerness* [1978] Imm AR 226, IAT.
3 EEC Council Directive 64/221, art 4 and Annex. The list in the Annex to the directive includes drug addiction.
4 Ibid, art 3(1).
5 Case 41/74 *Van Duyn v Home Office* [1974] ECR 1337, [1975] 1 CMLR 1, [1975] Ch 358, [1975] 3 All ER 190, ECJ; *Puttick v Secretary of State for the Home Department* [1984] Imm AR 118, IAT.
6 Case 67/74 *Bonsignore v Stadt Köln* [1975] ECR 297, [1975] 1 CMLR 472, ECJ; Case 30/77 *R v Bouchereau* [1977] ECR 1999, [1977] 2 CMLR 800, [1978] QB 732, [1981] 2 All ER 924, ECJ; Joined Cases 115, 116/81 *Adoui and Cornuaille v Belgium* [1982] ECR 1665, [1982] 3 CMLR 631, ECJ.
7 EEC Council Directive 64/221, art 3(3), (4).
8 EC Council Directive 68/360 (OJ L257, 19.19.68, p 13 (S Edn 1968 (II), p 485)), art 3(1). See also Case 48/75 *Royer* [1976] ECR 497, [1976] 2 CMLR 619, ECJ; Case 157/79 *R v Pieck* [1980] ECR 2171, [1981] QB 571, [1981] 3 All ER 46, ECJ.

9 Ie the Convention for the Protection of Human Rights and Fundamental Freedoms (Rome, 4 November 1950; TS 71 (1953); Cmd 8969).
10 Case 36/75 *Rutili v Minister for the Interior* [1975] ECR 1219, [1976] 1 CMLR 140, ECJ.
11 See T C Hartley *European Economic Community Immigration Law* (1978) pp 157, 158.
12 Case 41/74 *Van Duyn v Home Office* [1974] ECR 1337, [1975] 1 CMLR 1, [1975] Ch 358, [1975] 3 All ER 190, ECJ.

234. Procedural limits. When a decision is taken relying on the public policy proviso, the person concerned must be informed of the grounds on which it was taken, unless this would be contrary to the security interests of the relevant state[1]. The grounds must be precise and comprehensive[2]. In the case of refusal of a residence permit, or of expulsion, the person must also be officially notified and, save in cases of urgency, given at least one month to leave or, where a residence permit has not yet been granted, fifteen days[3]. The urgency would probably have to be justified under the proviso[4].

A person refused entry, issue or renewal of a residence permit, or expelled, must have the same legal remedies as nationals of the member state in respect of acts of administration[5]. In the cases of renewal of a residence permit or of expulsion of a person holding a residence permit:
(1) if there is no right of appeal to a court of law, or
(2) where there is one but only in respect of the legal validity of the decision, or
(3) where there is one but the appeal can have no suspensory effect,
no decision may be taken (except in cases of urgency) until opinion is obtained from a 'competent authority'[6]. This competent authority must be one before which the person enjoys the rights of defence and assistance or representation as domestic law provides and must be separate from the authority empowered to refuse renewal or to expel[6]. A person refused issue of a first residence permit or expulsion before issue of a residence permit must be referred to the same competent authority for consideration, and the person is entitled to defend himself in person unless this would be contrary to national security[7].

What is a 'competent authority' is largely at the discretion of member states, provided that it fulfils the criteria of EEC Council Directive 64/221, and in the United Kingdom recommendation by a criminal court may satisfy the requirements. However, lapse of time between the opinion and the decision purportedly based on it may deprive the opinion of its validity for the purpose since new factors may emerge[8].

1 EEC Council Directive 64/221 (OJ 1964, p 850 (S Edn 1963–64, p 117)), art 6.
2 Case 36/75 *Rutili v Minister for the Interior* [1975] ECR 1219, [1976] 1 CMLR 140, ECJ.
3 EEC Council Directive 64/221, art 7.
4 Case 48/75 *Royer* [1976] ECR 497, [1976] 2 CMLR 619, ECJ.
5 EEC Council Directive 64/221, art 8.
6 Ibid, art 9(1). See also *R v Secretary of State for the Home Department, ex parte Dannenberg* [1984] QB 766, [1984] 2 All ER 481, CA.
7 EEC Council Directive 64/221, art 9(2).
8 Case 131/79 *R v Secretary of State for the Home Department, ex parte Santillo* [1980] ECR 1585, [1980] 2 CMLR 308, [1981] QB 778, [1981] 2 All ER 897, ECJ.

(b) Community Law as Mediated by the Immigration Rules

235. Relationship of Community law and United Kingdom law. Most of the relevant Community law is directly effective[1]. The Immigration Act 1971 makes no reference to the European Community, but the Immigration Act 1988 and the Immigration Rules do[2]. The 1988 Act specifically asserts that a person entitled by virtue of an enforceable Community right or of any provision made under the European Communities Act 1972[3] does not require leave to enter or remain[4]. The 1988 Act also permits the Secretary of State to give leave for a limited period to any class of persons who are Community nationals but are not entitled to enter under the principal provision[5]. The Immigration Rules have not necessarily reflected Community law accurately in the past[6].

1 See the EEC Treaty, art 189, and the European Communities Act 1972 (c 68), s 3(2) (amended by the European Communities Act 1986 (c 58), s 2(b)). See also Case 41/74 *Van Duyn v Home Office* [1974] ECR 1337, [1975] 1 CMLR 1, [1975] Ch 358, [1975] 3 All ER 190, ECJ.
2 See the Statement of Changes in Immigration Rules (HC Paper (1989–90) no. 251) (the Immigration Rules), paras 146–154.
3 Ie under the European Communities Act 1972, s 2(2). At the date at which this volume states the law, no relevant provisions have been made.
4 Immigration Act 1988 (c 14), s 7(1).
5 Ibid, s 7(2). At the date at which this volume states the law, no order has been made under s 7(2).
6 Case 157/79 *R v Pieck* [1980] ECR 2171, [1981] QB 571, [1981] 3 All ER 46, ECJ. See also *Hoth v Secretary of State for the Home Department* [1985] Imm AR 20, IAT.

236. Entry. Under the Immigration Rules, a national of a member state, except, until 1993, a Portuguese or Spanish national, is entitled to be admitted to take or seek employment, to set up in business, to become self-employed or otherwise to exercise the right of establishment and of the provision or receipt of services[1].

Families of Community nationals entitled to be admitted are to be admitted on the same basis as the 'primary right' holder, whether or not themselves Community nationals, but require entry clearance if they are not[2]. 'Family' includes spouse, children under twenty-one years of age and, if dependent, other children and grandchildren, parents, grandparents and great-grandparents[3].

'Primary' and 'secondary right' holders may be refused admission only if exclusion is conducive to the public good on grounds of public policy, security or health[4].

Those admitted are free to remain for up to six months without further formality (provided they do not become a charge upon public funds), but must thereafter apply for a residence permit[5]. However, refusal to grant a permit does not of itself terminate the right of residence in Community law[6].

A national of a member state who would be entitled to enter to seek or take work will normally be admitted for six months without any restriction upon employment, even if not in fact seeking or taking work, provided that he satisfies the immigration officer that he is not likely to become a charge upon public funds or liable to refusal of leave under the general grounds[7]. This is not expressed to cover families[7].

Police registration is not normally required except in the case of family members who are not themselves Community nationals[8].

Other restrictions applied by Section One of the Immigration Rules[9] are stated to apply to the extent permitted by Community law[10].

1 Statement of Changes in Immigration Rules (HC Paper (1989–90) no. 251) (the Immigration Rules), para 69. In *Hoth v Secretary of State for the Home Department* [1985] Imm AR 20, IAT, the tribunal asserted that the right to enter to seek work is founded upon the Immigration Rules and the right of residence of a person in work upon EC Council Directive 68/360 (OJ L257, 19.19.68, p 13 (S Edn 1968 (II), p 485): see para 237, text and note 2, below).
2 See the Immigration Rules, para 70. However, see *R v Secretary of State for the Home Department, ex parte Ayub* [1983] Imm AR 20, [1983] 3 CMLR 140, DC (which may be *per incuriam*).
3 Immigration Rules, para 70. This is apparently narrower than the Community law definition for freedom of movement purposes: see para 223 above, and para 235, text and note 6 above.
4 Ibid, para 71. As to primary and secondary right holders, see paras 222, 223, above, and as to the public policy proviso, see paras 232–234 above.

5 Ibid, para 72. As to residence permits, see para 230 above.
6 Cf para 227 above. See also Case 157/79 *R v Pieck* [1980] ECR 2171, [1981] QB 571, [1981] 3 All ER 46, ECJ; *Lubbersen v Secretary of State for the Home Department* [1984] Imm AR 56, [1984] 3 CMLR 77, IAT.
7 Immigration Rules, para 73. See also *Hoth v Secretary of State for the Home Department* [1985] Imm AR 20, IAT.
8 Immigration Rules, para 74.
9 Ibid, Section One, comprises paras 6–93.
10 Ibid, para 68. This preserves to that extent a large number of provisions including those concerning subjection to immigration control and leave to enter, the common travel area, entry clearance, restricted returnability and particular requirements in relation to visitors, students, au pairs and those entering in various economic categories or of independent means, and their dependants, fiancés, fiancées and those seeking settlement.

237. Residence and residence permits. After six months a person applying for a residence permit for a national of a member state of the European Communities will receive one if fulfilling one of three conditions[1]. These are:
(1) that he has entered employment;
(2) that he has established himself in business, or in a self-employed capacity or otherwise, in accordance with Community law on the right of establishment and the rights relating to provision or receipt of services; or
(3) that he is a member of the family of such a person[2].
Such a person will not normally be required to register with the police[3]. A family member who is not a Community national will not receive a residence permit but an extension of leave and may be required to register with the police[4].

However, in the case of a person who has not entered employment or who has become a charge on public funds, a residence permit is to be refused, and in the case of a person who cannot produce evidence that he has established himself in business or become self-employed, it may be refused, or a short extension granted to complete arrangements for establishment[5].

A person who becomes a charge on public funds before the first issue of a residence permit, or who fails either to enter employment or to establish himself in business or to become self-employed, or otherwise be in accordance with Community law on the rights of establishment and the provision or receipt of services, may be required to leave the United Kingdom, subject to appeal[6].

In the case of a person expected to be employed for between three and twelve months, the permit is limited to the expected duration, but for others in employment, or established in business, self-employment or otherwise in accordance with Community law on the rights of establishment the provision or receipt of services, the permit is for five years[7]. A member of a family receives a residence permit if he is a Community national, or extension of stay if not, on the same terms as the 'primary right' holder.

A person issued with a residence permit for five years, resident in the United Kingdom for four of them and being in employment, self-employment, or the member of the family of such a person throughout that time, may have the residence permit indorsed to indicate permission to remain indefinitely, but in the case of a person involuntarily unemployed for twelve consecutive months, a renewal of twelve months only may be given[8]. Members of families who are not Community nationals are given extension of stay in the same terms[9].

1 Statement of Changes in Immigration Rules (HC Paper (1989–90) no. 251) (the Immigration Rules), para 147.
2 Ibid, para 147(a)–(c). For the meaning of 'family', see para 70, and para 236 above, and see further para 223 above. See also *Hoth v Secretary of State for the Home Department* [1985] Imm AR 20, IAT.
3 Immigration Rules, para 153.
4 Ibid, paras 147(c), 153.

5 Ibid, para 148, 149. See also *Lubbersen v Secretary of State for the Home Department* [1984] Imm AR 56, [1984] 3 CMLR 77, IAT; *Hoth v Secretary of State for the Home Department* [1985] Imm AR 20, IAT, and para 236, note 1, above. For the meaning of 'public funds', see para 160, note 1, above.

6 Immigration Rules, para 150. This is more restrictive than EC Council Directive 68/360 (OJ L257, 19.19.68, p 13 (S Edn 1968 (II), p 485)), art 7(1) and EC Council Directive 73/148 (OJ L172, 28.6.73, p 14), art 4(1). See also *Hoth v Secretary of State for the Home Department* [1985] Imm AR 20, IAT, and para 236, note 1, above.

7 Immigration Rules, paras 148, 149.

8 Ibid, 151. As to involuntary employment, see *Lubbersen v Secretary of State for the Home Department* [1984] Imm AR 56, [1984] 3 CMLR 77, IAT.

9 Immigration Rules, para 147(c).

238. Termination of the right to reside. A residence permit may be curtailed, after a written warning and subject to appeal, if the person no longer fulfils the requirements of employment, self-employment etc or membership of the family of such a person[1]. However, in the case of a worker, this will not be done where he is no longer employed on account of temporary incapacity for work as a result of illness or accident, or of involuntary unemployment[2].

A secondary right holder's entitlement to reside depends upon the primary right holder exercising his right[3]. Expiry of limited leave or the decision to curtail a permit do not of themselves terminate the right of residence. Where voluntary unemployment is the reason this must be established by the Home Office and on evidence other than receipt of supplementary benefit (or any successor benefit) alone, although the burden of proof is on the worker[4]. A person who has entered employment, is self-employed etc, or the member of the family of such a person[5], will not be deported on the ground that his presence is not conducive to the public good, unless this is justified on the grounds of public policy, security or health[6].

1 Ie under the Statement of Changes in Immigration Rules (HC Paper (1989–90) no. 251) (the Immigration Rules), para 147(a)–(c) (see para 237 above): para 150.

2 Ibid, para 150. However, see *Giangregorio v Secretary of State for the Home Department* [1985] Imm AR 104, [1983] 3 CMLR 472, IAT; and *Lubbersen v Secretary of State for the Home Department* [1984] Imm AR 56, [1984] 3 CMLR 77, IAT.

3 *R v Secretary of State for the Home Department, ex parte Sandhu* (1985) Times, 10 May, HL.

4 *Giangregorio v Secretary of State for the Home Department* [1985] Imm AR 104, [1983] 3 CMLR 472, IAT; *Lubbersen v Secretary of State for the Home Department* [1984] Imm AR 56, [1984] 3 CMLR 77, IAT.

5 Ie under the Immigration Rules, para 147(a)–(c) (see para 237 above): para 152.

6 Ibid, para 152. See also Case 157/79 *R v Pieck* [1980] ECR 2171, [1981] QB 571, [1981] 3 All ER 46, ECJ. For the public policy proviso, see para 232 above.

239. Right to remain after employment. A person who has had his residence permit renewed after five years (or in the case of a family member who is not a national of a member state, his leave to remain so extended) may expect to have it indorsed (or varied) for indefinite leave to remain[1].

In addition, the time limit should be removed in the case of a Community national

(1) who has reached the age of entitlement to a state retirement pension, was in employment for the twelve months preceding in any member state, and who has had three continuous years of residence in the United Kingdom;

(2) who has ceased employment on account of permanent incapacity for work arising out of an accident at work or occupational disease entitling him to a state disability pension (or, if continuously resident in the United Kingdom, any permanent incapacity for work);

(3) who is a member of the family of a person in either preceding group; or

(4) who is a member of the family of a person who dies during his working life,
     either having two years continuous residence in the United Kingdom or
     who dies as a result of an industrial accident or occupational disease[2].

1 Statement of Changes in Immigration Rules (HC Paper (1989–90) no. 251) (the Immigration
   Rules), para 151.
2 Ibid, para 154(a)–(e).

(8) CATEGORIES OF ENTRANT NOT UNDER COMMUNITY LAW WITHOUT A RIGHT OF ABODE

(a) Introduction

240. Role of the Immigration Rules categories and change of category. A person must in general fulfil the requirements of one of the categories of the Immigration Rules in order to obtain entry clearance, leave to enter or leave to remain[1]. Changes of category are in principle possible but (other than to settlement) rare[2].

1 This is a clear implication of the way the Immigration Rules are drafted: see eg Statement of
   Changes in Immigration Rules (HC Paper (1989–90) no. 251) (the Immigration Rules), paras 34,
   119, 123, 125, 128. A person who cannot make his intention clear cannot expect to be successful:
   Abid Hussain v Entry Clearance Officer, Islamabad [1989] Imm AR 46, IAT.
2 See the Immigration Rules, para 120.

(b) Persons in Employment, Business and Related Categories

(A) INTRODUCTION

241. Categories leading to settlement. Those who enter in any of the employment, business or related categories may seek settlement, generally after four years in the United Kingdom[1]. Thus entry clearance (or a work permit) is normally required. In two cases, however, settlement is not available, that is, those of work-permit holders who are trainees and young Commonwealth citizen working holidaymakers[2].

Change into one of the categories of employment etc from a 'non-settlement' category is in most cases explicitly prohibited[3]. Thus all applications to enter those categories must normally be applications for entry clearance, and from outwith the United Kingdom. In the following five cases such change is possible:

(1) visitors and students may be permitted to change category to trainee (that is
     to become a work-permit holder)[4];
(2) a person in any capacity who fulfils the requirements for young Common-
     wealth citizen working holidaymakers may change to that category (which
     does not require entry clearance or a work permit)[5];
(3) nurses and midwives who have trained in a United Kingdom hospital
     (provided they were not financed by an international scholarship agency or
     home government) may change to employment in that capacity (which
     requires a work permit)[6];
(4) graduates of United Kingdom medical schools may be given an extension
     for up to twelve months to undertake pre-registration house officer
     employment as required for full registration with the General Medical
     Council[7]; and

(5) doctors and dentists on post-graduate training may change category to employed doctor or dentist (that is to become a work-permit holder)[8].

In the two first-mentioned cases, the work cannot lead to settlement.

It may not always be clear which is the appropriate category for an intending entrant[9].

1 Statement of Changes in Immigration Rules (HC Paper (1989–90) no. 251) (the Immigration Rules), para 139.
2 See ibid, paras 107, 119. However, it is envisaged that settlement is possible for others: see the penultimate sentence of para 139.
3 See ibid, para 102. In practice exceptions are known.
4 See ibid, para 120, and paras 297, 308, below.
5 See ibid, para 107, and para 263 below.
6 See ibid, para 120, and paras 297, 308, below.
7 See ibid, paras 29, 113, and para 293 below.
8 See ibid, paras 114, 115, and para 300 below.
9 See eg *Yeong Hoi Yuen v Secretary of State for the Home Department* [1977] Imm AR 34, IAT. Nurses and midwives in training, and doctors and dentists in post-graduate training or working as house officers are regarded as students: see paras 292 ff below.

(B) WORK–PERMIT HOLDERS

242. Introduction. The requirement for a work permit and the method of distribution are dealt with above, as is the need or otherwise for entry clearance[1].

Similarly the general provisions relating to control before, on and after entry and on departure (where applicable) apply[2]. The Immigration Rules specifically enjoin an immigration officer to refuse leave on grounds of false representations or concealment of material facts (with or without the holder's knowledge), or because the holder's age excludes him, or he does not intend to take, or is incapable of taking, the employment[3]. That the validity of the permit has expired is not a reason, if circumstances beyond the holder's control delayed him and the job is still open[3].

Persons admitted as visitors are permitted to transact business without a work permit, but this does not permit work for which a permit is required[4].

1 See paras 150 ff above.
2 See paras 161 ff above.
3 Statement of Changes in Immigration Rules (HC Paper (1989–90) no. 251) (the Immigration Rules), para 35.
4 Ibid, para 24.

243. Change of employment. As the work permit is valid for employment in the job specified only, change of employment requires Department of Employment consent, and this is granted or withheld on the same grounds as for the original issue[1]. Trainees may not change to ordinary employment and only in very limited circumstances may anyone else[2].

Changes in employment are recorded in the police registration certificate of aliens and certificate of employment of Commonwealth citizens[3].

1 See the Statement of Changes in Immigration Rules (HC Paper (1989–90) no. 251) (the Immigration Rules), paras 35, 122. As to the issue of work permits, see para 154 above.
2 Ibid, para 119. See also para 241 above, and para 245 below.
3 Immigration (Registration with Police) Regulations 1972, SI 1972/1758, reg 8(a).

244. Extension of leave and settlement of work-permit holders, other than trainees. Work permits are not renewed, so operate essentially as a form of entry clearance, although strictly speaking they are not such clearance[1]. Leave to enter will normally have been given for the period specified therein and it will be for four years or less[2]. Leave to enter or remain of a work-permit holder may be extended as a normal example of variation of leave[3]. Where, as is usual, it is granted for less than four years, it will normally be extended for up to a maximum of four years by the Home Office if the extension is approved by the Department of Employment, but not otherwise[4].

After four years' approved employment, such a person may apply for indefinite leave, which is considered in the light of all relevant circumstances including the general grounds for refusal or curtailment of leave and whether the employer wishes to continue employing the applicant[5].

1 See the Statement of Changes in Immigration Rules (HC Paper (1989–90) no. 251) (the Immigration Rules), paras 16, 122. See also para 245, text and note 1, below.
2 See ibid, paras 117, 122.
3 See the Immigration Act 1971 (c 77), s 3(3), and the Immigration Rules, para 122, and paras 177 ff above.
4 Ibid, para 122. In *Secretary of State for the Home Department v Vethamony* [1981] Imm AR 144, IAT, an extension was given even though the person was not in approved employment, as he was in comparable employment.
5 Immigration Rules, para 139.

245. Extension of leave of trainees. Work-permit holders training 'on the job' may apply for extension to continue or complete training, which may be given if the Department of Employment confirms that the training is continuing and progress is satisfactory and there is no reason to believe that the holder does not intend to leave the United Kingdom on completion of his training[1].

Work-permit holders in short-term employment not leading to qualifications or skills but widening experience and knowledge of English may apply for extension, but the approval of the Department of Employment is a pre-requisite, and this will be given only in exceptional circumstances[2].

In neither case may the trainee transfer to an ordinary work permit, nor is the employment 'approved employment' for the purpose of seeking indefinite leave, so the permit cannot lead to settlement[3].

1 Statement of Changes in Immigration Rules (HC Paper (1989–90) no. 251) (the Immigration Rules), para 117.
2 Ibid, para 118. See also para 156 above, and the Department of Employment leaflet OW21 'Employment of Overseas Workers in the United Kingdom: Training and work experience'.
3 Immigration Rules, para 119.

(C) PERMIT-FREE EMPLOYMENT

246. Introduction. Those in permit-free employment require (with one minor exception) entry clearance, and are subject to the general grounds of refusal of leave to entry clearance holders[1]. They are normally admitted for twelve months, but in one case for an appropriate period not exceeding four years[2].

Persons admitted as visitors are permitted to transact business without fulfilling the requirements for this category but this does not permit work falling into the permit-free category[3].

1 As to entry clearance, see paras 150–152, 172, above. As to control of entry generally, see paras 148, 154 ff above, and as to control on entry, see paras 161 ff, 177 above.
2 See the Statement of Changes in Immigration Rules (HC Paper (1989–90) no. 251) (the Immigration Rules), paras 38–40, and para 247 below.
3 See ibid, paras 24, 34.

247. What is permit-free employment. Persons in certain forms of employment do not require a work permit to be issued[1]. They are:

(1) ministers of religion, missionaries and members of religious orders[2];

(2) representatives of overseas newspapers, news agencies and broadcasting organisations on long-term assignment to the United Kingdom[3];

(3) representatives of foreign firms which have no branch, subsidiary or other representative in the United Kingdom[4];

(4) private servants (aged sixteen years or more) of members of the staff of diplomatic or consular missions or of members of the family forming part of the household of such persons[5];

(5) persons coming for employment by an overseas government or in the employment of the United Nations Organisation or other international organisation of which the United Kingdom is a member[6];

(6) teachers and language assistants coming to schools under approved exchange schemes[7];

(7) seamen under contract to join a ship in British waters[8];

(8) operational ground staff (but not other staff) of overseas-owned airlines[9]; and

(9) seasonal workers at agricultural camps under approved schemes[10].

In the case of the category under head (1), the persons must be coming to work full-time in that capacity and be able to maintain and accommodate themselves and any dependants without recourse to public funds[11]. Difficulties of definition can arise[12].

1 Until 1985 doctors and dentists were in permit-free employment, but now require work permits or are self-employed. As to students, see paras 292 ff below.

2 Statement of Changes in Immigration Rules (HC Paper (1989–90) no. 251) (the Immigration Rules), para 38(a).

3 Ibid, para 38(b).

4 Ibid, para 39.

5 Ibid, para 40(a). There are ad hoc extensions to others, other than diplomats, apparently 'outside the rules': *Macdonald's Immigration Law and Practice* (3rd edn, 1991, eds I A Macdonald and N J Blake) pp 215, 216. This is exemplified in *Mamon v Immigration Appeal Tribunal* [1988] Imm AR 364, CA: see para 112 above.

6 Immigration Rules, para 40(b).

7 Ibid, para 40(c). They must be approved by 'the Education Departments' (sic) or administered by the Central Bureau for Educational Visits and Exchanges or the League for the Exchange of Commonwealth Teachers.

8 Ibid, para 40(d). These are to be distinguished from crews landing in the United Kingdom with a view to leaving, as crews, shortly thereafter, who do not need leave: see para 129 above.

9 Ibid, para 40(e).

10 Ibid, para 40(f). 'Approved schemes' is not defined.

11 Ibid, para 38(a). Members of religious orders engaged in teaching are allowed to teach at establishments maintained by their own order without a work permit: para 38(a). For the meaning of 'public funds', see para 160, note 1, above.

12 Some formal qualifications, experience and a formal invitation from an organisation are desirable. A 'panel of experts' exists to sift applications: L Grant and I Martin *Immigration Law and Practice* (1982) para 7.15. See also *Memi v Secretary of State for the Home Department* [1976] Imm AR 129, IAT; *Piara Singh v Entry Clearance Officer, Kingston, Jamaica* [1977] Imm AR 1, IAT; and *Secretary of State for the Home Department v Sarwar* [1978] Imm AR 190, IAT.

248. Change of employment. It appears that persons in permit-free employment may change employment within their category[1].

1 See the Statement of Changes in Immigration Rules (HC Paper (1989–90) no. 251) (the Immigration Rules), paras 123, 124. However, for an example of a servant admitted 'outside the rules', see *Mamon v Immigration Appeal Tribunal* [1988] Imm AR 364, CA.

249. Extension of leave. All those in permit-free employment may have leave extended if still in the same category of employment[1]. This will normally be for three years, given in three annual extensions[2]. In the case of crew members, extension will be given only as necessary to enable them to join their ship or aircraft[3]. In the case of a language teacher under an exchange scheme, the extension is two years, and in the case of a seasonal worker, until 30 November in any year[4].

After four years, such a person other than a private servant, language teacher, seaman or seasonal worker may apply for indefinite leave, which is considered in the light of all circumstances, including the general grounds for refusal or curtailment of leave, and whether the employer wishes to continue employ-ment[5].

1 See the Statement of Changes in Immigration Rules (HC Paper (1989–90) no. 251) (the Immi-gration Rules), paras 123, 124. However, as to a servant admitted 'outside the rules', see *Mamon v Immigration Appeal Tribunal* [1988] Imm AR 364, CA.

2 Immigration Rules, para 123. Representatives of overseas firms are admitted for an appropriate period not exceeding four years (para 39); others for an appropriate period not greater than twelve months (paras 38, 40). Where the representative of an overseas firm is granted extensions of stay, the aggregate of his periods of stay in such a capacity may not exceed the qualifying period for settlement: para 124.

3 See ibid, paras 103, 123.

4 Ibid, para 123.

5 Ibid, para 139. As to representatives of overseas firms, see note 2 above.

(D) BUSINESSMEN AND THE SELF-EMPLOYED

250. Introduction. Businessmen and the self-employed (whether intending to work on their own account or in partnership) require entry clearance and may be admitted for twelve months, subject to the general grounds of refusal of leave to entry clearance holders[1].

Persons admitted as visitors are permitted to transact business without fulfil-ling the requirements of this category, but demarcation disputes do occasionally occur[2].

1 Statement of Changes in Immigration Rules (HC Paper (1989–90) no. 251) (the Immigration Rules), para 41. As to refusal of leave to enter, see para 172 above. Similarly the general provisions relating to control on entry, after entry and on departure, where applicable, apply: see paras 161 ff above.

2 Ibid, para 24. As to the difficulties, see *Macdonald's Immigration Law and Practice* (3rd edn, 1991, eds I A Macdonald and N J Blake) pp 234, 235.

251. Conditions for entry clearance. A businessman or self-employed per-son must show (1) that he is putting his own money into the business; (2) that his investment is proportional to his interest; (3) that he can bear his share of the liabilities; (4) that he will be occupied full-time in the business; and (5) that there is a genuine need for his services and investment[1]. The investment must be at least £200,000 which is under his control and disposable in the United King-dom[2].

In the case of a person taking over a business or joining as partner, he must show that his share of profits is sufficient to maintain and accommodate him and his dependants[3]. Audited accounts and a written statement of the terms of take-over must be produced, and he must show evidence that new paid full-time employment in the business for persons settled in the United Kingdom will be created[3]. In particular, entry clearance is to be refused if the occupation amounts to disguised employment, or if income will have to be supplemented by recourse to employment or public funds[4].

In the case of a person establishing a new business, he must show that he is bringing in sufficient funds of his own to establish an enterprise that can realistically be expected to maintain him and any dependants without recourse to employment or public funds, and that new paid full-time employment in the business for persons settled in the United Kingdom will be provided[5].

1 Statement of Changes in Immigration Rules (HC Paper (1989–90) no. 251) (the Immigration Rules), para 41. Under the similar rules applying earlier (see Statement of Changes in Immigration Rules (HC Paper (1979–80) no. 394 (superseded)) it was decided that available assets and all circumstances should be looked at 'in the round', but it is not clear if 'family money' or loans may be counted: *R v Immigration Appeal Tribunal, ex parte Joseph* [1977] Imm AR 70, DC; *Haji v Secretary of State for the Home Department* [1978] Imm AR 26, IAT; *R v Immigration Appeal Tribunal, ex parte Peikazadi* [1979–80] Imm AR 191, IAT. Those rules do not permit a person to enter to inherit a family business: *R v Immigration Appeal Tribunal, ex parte Rahman* [1987] Imm AR 313, CA.
2 Immigration Rules, para 41. The capital limit is in fact waived in some cases: *Macdonald's Immigration Law and Practice* (3rd edn, 1991, eds I A Macdonald and N J Blake) pp 229, 230.
3 Immigration Rules, para 42.
4 Ibid, para 42. See also *Pritpal Singh v Secretary of State for the Home Department* [1972] Imm AR 154, IAT. For the meaning of 'public funds', see para 160, note 1, above.
5 Immigration Rules, para 43.

252. Change of employment.

252. Change of employment. Businessmen and the self-employed are specifically to be refused entry clearance or extension of leave if engaging in employment of any kind, and the conditions also clearly imply that they may not enter a new business without clearance or leave applied for *de novo*[1].

1 Statement of Changes in Immigration Rules (HC Paper (1989–90) no. 251) (the Immigration Rules), paras 41–43, 126.

253. Extension of leave.

253. Extension of leave. Those admitted as businessmen or self-employed may have leave extended if there is evidence that the conditions required for entry clearance continue to be fulfilled, in which case extensions, not exceeding in the aggregate the qualifying period for settlement with a restriction on employment may be given[1].

After four years such a person may apply for indefinite leave, which is considered in the light of all relevant circumstances, including the general grounds for refusal or curtailment of leave[2].

1 Statement of Changes in Immigration Rules (HC Paper (1989–90) no. 251) (the Immigration Rules), paras 126, 127. As to the general provisions in respect of variation, limitation and conditions attached to limited leave to enter or remain in the United Kingdom, see the Immigration Act 1971 (c 77), s 3(3)(a), (b), and paras 119, 177, above.
2 Immigration Rules, para 139.

(E) WRITERS AND ARTISTS

254. Introduction. A writer or artist requires entry clearance and may be admitted for an initial period of up to four years with a restriction upon employment[1].

'Artist' apparently relates only to the fine arts and not the performing arts, since 'entertainers' are excluded and must, therefore, apply for work permits[2].

1 Statement of Changes in Immigration Rules (HC Paper (1989–90) no. 251) (the Immigration Rules), para 45. However, they may engage in 'business which is part and parcel of an artist's and

writer's profession such as the holding of an exhibition': Home Secretary 979 HC Official Report (5th series) written answers col *189* (20 February 1980).

2 *Secretary of State for the Home Department v Stillwaggon* [1975] Imm AR 132, IAT.

255. Conditions for entry clearance.
A writer or artist must show that he does not intend to do work other than as writer or artist and can maintain and accommodate himself and any dependants from his own resources, without recourse to public funds[1].

1 Statement of Changes in Immigration Rules (HC Paper (1989–90) no. 251) (the Immigration Rules), para 45. This apparently excludes 'family funds' since the phrase 'own resources' was added after *Secretary of State for the Home Department v Jones* [1978] Imm AR 161, IAT, where the issue concerned a person supported entirely from external funds.

256. Change of employment.
It is implied that a writer or artist is not expected to take other employment, although no explicit bar to extension of leave is created by taking employment other than that for which a work permit is required[1].

1 Statement of Changes in Immigration Rules (HC Paper (1989–90) no. 251) (the Immigration Rules), para 128.

257. Extension of leave.
Those admitted as writers or artists may have leave extended if able to produce satisfactory evidence that they have maintained and accommodated themselves and any dependants without recourse to public funds or work for which a work permit is necessary, but not exceeding in the aggregate the qualifying period for settlement[1].

After four years such a person may apply for indefinite leave, which is considered in the light of all relevant circumstances including the general grounds for refusal or curtailment of leave[2].

1 Statement of Changes in Immigration Rules (HC Paper (1989–90) no. 251) (the Immigration Rules), para 128.
2 Ibid, para 139.

(F) PERSONS OF INDEPENDENT MEANS

258. Introduction.
A person of independent means requires entry clearance and may be admitted for an initial period of up to four years with a prohibition upon employment subject to the general grounds for refusal of leave to enter for entry-clearance holders[1].

1 Statement of Changes in Immigration Rules (HC Paper (1989–90) no. 251) (the Immigration Rules), para 44. As to refusal of leave to enter in the case of a person holding an entry clearance, see para 172 above. Similarly the general provisions relating to control on entry, after entry and on departure, where applicable, apply: see paras 161 ff above.

259. Conditions for entry clearance.
A person of independent means must show he has control of £200,000 or more, or an income of £20,000 or more, disposable in the United Kingdom[1]. He must also be able to maintain, support and accommodate himself and any dependants indefinitely without working, without assistance from others, and without recourse to public funds, and demonstrate either a close connection with the United Kingdom (such as close relatives or long residence) or that admission would be in the general interests of the United Kingdom[2].

1 Statement of Changes in Immigration Rules (HC Paper (1989–90) no. 251) (the Immigration Rules), para 44. However, an entry clearance is not to be granted solely because the financial conditions are met: para 44. Access to the resources must be legally enforceable: *Secretary of State for the Home Department v Rohr* [1983] Imm AR 95, IAT.

2 Immigration Rules, para 44. The older cases concerning 'frugal living' are now irrelevant. 'Without working' appears to mean 'without working anywhere in the world': *Jahangard v Entry Clearance Officer, Vienna* [1985] Imm AR 69, IAT, *obiter*, referring to two unreported cases of the Immigration Appeal Tribunal, one a majority decision. As to 'close connection with the United Kingdom', see *R v Immigration Appeal Tribunal, ex parte Zandfani* [1984] Imm AR 213, DC, and as to the 'general interests of the United Kingdom', see *Secretary of State for the Home Department v Rohr* [1983] Imm AR 95, IAT.

260. Extensions of leave. A person of independent means continuing to fulfil the requirements for entry clearance may be granted an extension not exceeding in the aggregate the qualifying period for settlement with a prohibition on employment[1].

After four years, such a person may apply for indefinite leave which is considered in the light of all relevant circumstances including the general grounds for refusal or curtailment of leave[2].

1 Statement of Changes in Immigration Rules (HC Paper (1989–90) no. 251) (the Immigration Rules), para 129.
2 Ibid, para 139.

(G) COMMONWEALTH CITIZENS WITH UNITED KINGDOM ANCESTRY

261. Introduction. A Commonwealth citizen who can prove that one of his grandparents was born in the United Kingdom and who wishes to take or seek employment will be granted entry clearance and will be admitted (subject to the general grounds for refusal) for a period of four years[1]. It is not clear that entry clearance is in fact required.

1 Statement of Changes in Immigration Rules (HC Paper (1989–90) no. 251) (the Immigration Rules), para 36. The paternal grandparent of an illegitimate child is insufficient: *C (an infant) v Entry Clearance Officer, Hong Kong* [1976] Imm AR 165, IAT. See also FAMILY LAW, vol 10, para 1186, and NATIONALITY AND CITIZENSHIP, vol 14, para 1908. As to the general grounds of refusal, see para 172 above. The general conditions on control on entry, after entry and on departure, where applicable, apply: see paras 161 ff above.

262. Extension of leave. After four years, Commonwealth citizens with United Kingdom ancestry may apply for indefinite leave to remain without fulfilling any particular further requirements[1]. Leave may be granted in the light of all relevant circumstances including the general grounds for refusal or curtailment of leave[1].

The provisions are in marked contrast to the provisions concerning employment and family reunion generally and effectively extend the 'right of abode', although deportation is still possible[2].

1 Statement of Changes in Immigration Rules (HC Paper (1989–90) no. 251) (the Immigration Rules), para 139.

2 See paras 244, 245, 249, 253, 257, 260, above (employment), and paras 267 ff below (family reunion). The contrast is less marked than under earlier Immigration Rules, when indefinite leave was given on arrival: see eg Statement of Changes in Immigration Rules (HC Paper (1982–83), no. 169) (the Former Immigration Rules), para 29 (superseded).

(H) COMMONWEALTH CITIZEN WORKING HOLIDAYMAKERS

263. Commonwealth citizen working holidaymakers generally. Commonwealth citizens aged between seventeen and twenty-seven years inclusive who wish to enter for an extended holiday before settling in their own country, and intend to take employment only incidental to such holiday and have the means to pay for a return journey, may be admitted for up to two years on the understanding that they will have no recourse to public funds[1]. No entry clearance is required.

This provision, allowing any work, and for up to two years provided it is incidental to a holiday, is in marked contrast to the provisions concerning employment and family reunion generally[2]. However, no extension beyond two years is normally possible[3] (although persons in other categories may be able to vary leave by entering this category)[4].

1 Statement of Changes in Immigration Rules (HC Paper (1989–90) no. 251) (the Immigration Rules), para 37. As to 'incidental', see *Baijal v Secretary of State for the Home Department* [1976] Imm AR 34, IAT; *Secretary of State for the Home Department v Grant* [1974] Imm AR 64, IAT; *Badrul Bari v Immigration Appeal Tribunal* [1987] Imm AR 13, CA, and as to eventual settlement, see *Gunatilake v Entry Clearance Officer, Colombo* [1975] Imm AR 23, IAT. The general conditions on control on entry, after entry and on departure, where applicable, including general grounds of refusal, apply: see paras 161 ff above.
2 See paras 242 ff above, and paras 269 ff below.
3 Immigration Rules, paras 37.
4 Ibid, para 107.

(I) DEPENDANTS

264. Who is eligible as a dependant. Only wives and unmarried children under eighteen years of age can be dependants[1]. They are defined (*mutatis mutandis*) in essentially the same way as dependants entering for settlement[2]. They require entry clearance[3].

1 Statement of Changes in Immigration Rules (HC Paper (1989–90) no. 251) (the Immigration Rules), para 46. However, if the breadwinner becomes settled, other relatives may be eligible: see paras 46, 52, 56, 57.
2 See paras 268, 269, 279, below. Thus husbands may only be admitted 'outside the rules': see para 112 above.
3 Immigration Rules, para 46.

265. Conditions for entry clearance. Dependants of those in employment, business or related categories must be able to be maintained and accommodated by the breadwinner without recourse to public funds in accommodation of his own or which he occupies, and he may be required to give a written undertaking to this effect[1]. They will be prohibited from employment if the breadwinner is prohibited and should be admitted for the same period as the breadwinner[2].

1 Statement of Changes in Immigration Rules (HC Paper (1989–90) no. 251) (the Immigration Rules), para 46.

2 Ibid, para 46. Thus wives and children of businessmen and the self-employed, writers and artists
and persons of independent means will not normally be able to seek work, but those of others in
employment, business and related categories will.

266. Extension of leave and settlement. In general any extension granted to
a breadwinner should also be granted to dependants provided the maintenance
and accommodation requirements are still met[1]. In other cases, the rules are
silent, but the practice appears to be the same. In the case of Commonwealth
citizens with United Kingdom ancestry, the question does not arise since they
are admitted for four years, together with any dependants, and can normally
obtain indefinite leave thereafter[2]. In the case of Commonwealth citizen working holidaymakers the question also does not arise since they are normally
admitted for up to two years without the possibility of extension which exceeds
in the aggregate more than this period[3].

In all cases where the breadwinner may apply for settlement, dependants may
also apply[4]. There is an apparent contradiction with the Immigration Rules as to
whether only spouses and children are eligible, or whether other relatives
(limited to older children, parents, grandparents, siblings, uncles and aunts
under strict limitations) are also eligible[5].

1 See the Statement of Changes in Immigration Rules (HC Paper (1989–90) no. 251) (the Immigration Rules), para 122 (work-permit holders), para 123 (permit-free categories), para 127
   (businessmen and the self-employed), para 128 (writers and artists), and para 129 (persons of
   independent means).
2 See ibid, paras 26, 139, and paras 261, 262, above.
3 See ibid, paras 37, 107, and para 263 above.
4 See ibid, para 139.
5 Ibid, para 139. The Statement of Changes in Immigration Rules (HC Paper (1982–83) no. 169)
   (the Former Immigration Rules), para 133, did not specify which relatives were eligible, but had
   to be read with Pt IV (passengers coming for settlement), which in para 48 (amended by HC
   Paper (1984–85) no. 503) declared that 'other relatives' might seek settlement, and cross-referred
   to para 52 (all superseded). This referred to parents and, on exiguous conditions, to grandparents, siblings, older children, uncles and aunts. The current provision stipulates who is
   entitled to settle, which refers specifically to spouses and children only: Immigration Rules,
   para 139. However, paras 52–57 still refer to the wider range of relatives.

(c) Family Reunion and Creation by Settlement

(A) INTRODUCTION

267. Family reunion and creation by settlement generally. One of the
most controversial aspects of immigration control is its attitude to family
reunion and creation by settlement[1]. This is regarded by many as presenting a
considerable contrast between the ease with which even those with a relatively
distant ancestral connection, and thus a possible but not inevitable family link
with the United Kingdom, may obtain entry, and the difficulty with which
those with no ancestral connection, but with strong family connection, such as a
United Kingdom settled breadwinner or fiancée, creating a presumptive entitlement, contend. The former may benefit from holding a right of abode, from the
specific Immigration Rule[2] permitting settlement of those with merely ancestral
connection, or from the sexually discriminatory rules on admission of spouses
once applying. The latter must surmount the entry clearance system, the
'primary purpose' rule for spouses, fiancés and fiancées, the 'sole responsibility'
rule for children, or the exiguous requirements in relation to dependants other
than spouses or children.

Such contrasts have provided evidence in the view of many critics of racial discrimination in the fundamental policies on immigration and the opportunity for it in day-to-day administration. The Home Office view is that in fact the difference is explained by the need to protect the employment market, resulting in the need for tight controls upon those entering from countries where there is pressure to emigrate (since they will wish to seek work and may be tempted to enter illegally or overstay) and the lack of need for tight controls upon those entering from elsewhere.

The great majority of people entering for settlement since the mid-1960s have been families, reunited with breadwinners (largely because of the severe restrictions upon entry of others, sometimes referred to as 'primary immigrants').

It is also worth noting that the inherently sexually discriminatory nature of the Immigration Rules and their operation is most evident here. It is assumed broadly that there will be a male breadwinner settled and a dependent wife and children seeking to join him.

1 For the position of dependants of those not settled, see paras 264–266 above (dependants of those in employment, business and related categories), paras 301–304 below (dependants of students), and para 309 above (visitors).
2 Ie the Statement of Changes in Immigration Rules (HC Paper (1989–90) no. 251) (the Immigration Rules).

268. Who may seek settlement on grounds of family relationship.
Spouses, children under eighteen and, under exiguous conditions, parents, grandparents, siblings, older children, and aunts and uncles may seek entry for settlement on grounds of relationship to a person settled and present in the United Kingdom (and the relationship need not have subsisted when the person settled became settled)[1]. So may fiancés and fiancées, *mutatis mutandis*[2].

Entry clearance is required in all cases[3] except:

(1) where European Community law applies[4];
(2) where the applicant is a wife who acquired the right of abode upon marriage[5]; or
(3) where the person has already entered under another category and seeks variation of leave on the basis of a family relationship[6].

Admission with entry clearance is subject to the general grounds of refusal in the case of those with entry clearance[7].

1 See generally the Statement of Changes in Immigration Rules (HC Paper (1989–90) no. 251) (the Immigration Rules), paras 50–57. A stable homosexual relationship does not count: *R v Immigration Appeal Tribunal, ex parte Wirdestedt* [1982] Imm AR 186, IAT (on appeal [1990] Imm AR 20, CA). The sponsor must be physically present in the United Kingdom: *Angur Begum v Secretary of State for the Home Department, Rutshanda Begum v Secretary of State for the Home Department* [1990] Imm AR 1, CA.
2 Immigration Rules, paras 47, 48.
3 See ibid, paras 48, 51, 52; *R v Chief Immigration Officer, Heathrow Airport, ex parte Salamat Bibi* [1976] 3 All ER 843, [1976] 1 WLR 979, CA.
4 See the Immigration Rules, para 68, and paras 114, 137, 219 ff, above.
5 *R v Secretary of State for the Home Department, ex parte Phansopkar* [1976] QB 606, [1975] 3 All ER 497, CA.
6 Immigration Rules, para 139.
7 See para 172 above.

(B) ADMISSION OF SPOUSE

269. What is a spouse? 'Spouse' is a term referred to in the Immigration Rules, but is not defined[1].

Questions arise concerning polygamous marriages, as to which the position is uncertain in Scots law. It appears that the number of actually polygamous marriages where a spouse is in the United Kingdom is infinitesimal, but a second wife of a polygamous marriage where the husband was domiciled in a country permitting polygamy (and therefore recognised by English law), was held under the law then in force to be entitled as a wife[2]. Potentially polygamous marriages are those entered validly and in fact monogamously (at least so far) under a law permitting polygamy, and are considerably more common.

Scots law is unclear in its attitude to potentially polygamous marriages[3]. Matrimonial relief may be granted in such cases[4] and social security legislation specifically deals with the issue[5], and it is possible that such marriages would be recognised generally if valid. However, the major difficulty is perhaps whether such a marriage is in fact valid. Scots law may (as broadly speaking English law does)[6] consider the formal nature to be governed by the law of the place of celebration, but the capacity to be governed by the law of the domicile[7]. However, there are no relevant cases and such policy could produce injustice, for example in the case of a person resident in Scotland who goes to, say Pakistan, to contract a marriage which is not intended to be polygamous[8].

In the past it appears that wives of potentially polygamous marriages have been freely admitted as wives[9].

However, a woman is not to be given entry clearance, leave to enter, or variation of leave, as a wife if the marriage is polygamous or potentially polygamous, and another living wife has been admitted to the United Kingdom since her marriage (other than as a visitor) or granted a certificate of entitlement or entry clearance[10]. This does not, however, apply if she had been in the United Kingdom since her marriage before such other wife entered (or if she applied before 1 August 1988), or if any of the relevant people were present illegally[11].

Nor may a person under sixteen years of age of either sex be granted entry clearance, leave to enter or remain, or variation of leave, as a spouse[12].

Problems may also arise concerning the validity of extra-judicial divorces[13].

1 In the Former Immigration Rules (ie Statement of Changes in Immigration Rules (HC Paper (1982–83) no. 169) (the Former Immigration Rules), para 49 (superseded)), a woman in permanent association with a man as his wife (due account being taken of local custom and tradition tending to establish the permanence of the association) might be admitted as a wife, provided any previous marriage had broken down, and no previous wife had been admitted. This provision is now omitted from the rules, presumably deliberately. However, the Immigration Act 1971 (c 77) does declare in relation to deportation that 'wife' includes each of two or more wives: see s 5(4), and para 208 above. In *R v Immigration Appeal Tribunal, ex parte Wirdestedt* [1982] Imm AR 186, IAT (on appeal [1990] Imm AR 20, CA), the court rejected the contention that a stable homosexual relationship creates a 'close relative'. No doubt this rejection includes the creation of 'spouses'.

In so far as Scots law has different rules as to the creation of marriage to English law, problems could arise: see the case noted in A E Anton and Ph Francescakis 'Modern Scots "Runaway Marriages"' 1958 JR 253 at 270, note 71, also quoted in T B Smith *British Justice: The Scottish Contribution* (1961) p 28. See also R M White 'Foreign Marriages: Some Validity and Immigration Issues' 1986 SCOLAG 79.

2 *Afza Mussarat v Secretary of State for the Home Department* [1972] Imm AR 45. This point is elided in *Polygamous Marriages* (Law Com Working Paper No 83, Scot Law Com Consultative Memorandum No 56) Section B, paras 4.18–4.24, which deals with the question in relation to immigration, at least according to the law of England.

3 Ibid, Section C, *passim*. See also E M Clive *The Law of Husband and Wife in Scotland* (2nd edn, 1982) pp 128–135, which, inter alia questions the need for a notion of potentially polygamous marriages. See further *Lendrum v Chakravarti* 1929 SLT 96, OH; *Muhammad v Suna* 1956 SC 366, 1956 SLT 175, OH; *Prawdzic-Lazarska v Prawdzic-Lazarski* 1954 SC 98, 1954 SLT 41, OH; and M MacEwan 'Potentially Polygamous Marriages of Immigrants' 1979 SCOLAG 169. J M Thomson *Family Law in Scotland* (2nd edn, 1991) is silent on the subject.

4 See the Matrimonial Proceedings (Polygamous Marriages) Act 1972 (c 38), s 2 (amended by the Divorce Jurisdiction, Court Fees and Legal Aid (Scotland) Act 1983 (c 12), s 6(1), Sch 1, para 13;

Law Reform (Husband and Wife) (Scotland) Act 1984 (c 15), s 9(1), Sch 1, para 6; Family Law (Scotland) Act 1985 (c 37), s 28(1), Sch 1, para 8; and the Statute Law (Repeals) Act 1986 (c 12), s 1(1), Sch 1, Pt I). This also applies to actual polygamous marriages.

5 See the Social Security and Family Allowances (Polygamous Marriages) Regulations 1975, SI 1975/561 (amended by SI 1989/1642), and the Child Benefit (General) Regulations 1976, SI 1976/965, reg 12.

6 A V Dicey and J H C Morris *The Conflict of Laws* (11th edn, 1987 ed L Collins) pp 648–677; G C Cheshire and P M North *Private International Law* (11th edn, 1987 ed P M North and J J Fawcett) pp 594–616.

7 A E Anton *Private International Law* (1967) pp 279–283. See also *Lendrum v Chakravarti* 1929 SLT 96, OH; *MacDougall v Chitnavis* 1937 SC 390, 1937 SLT 421; *Bliersbach v MacEwen* 1959 SC 43, 1959 SLT 81; *Rojas* 1967 SLT (Sh Ct) 24.

8 The Scottish Law Commission has recommended legislation expressing the general principles that it should be possible to enter a potentially polygamous marriage abroad and that a potentially polygamous marriage valid in Scotland should be treated for all purposes as valid unless and until it becomes polygamous, and has produced a draft Bill: *Polygamous Marriages*, Appendix.

9 L Grant and I Martin *Immigration Law and Practice* (1982) para 8.25.

10 Statement of Changes in Immigration Rules (HC Paper (1989–90) no. 251) (the Immigration Rules) paras 3, 5.

11 Ibid, paras 4, 5.

12 Ibid, para 2.

13 Especially *talaq* divorces: see the Family Law Act 1986 (c 55), s 46, and FAMILY LAW, vol 10, para 945. See also *Macdonald's Immigration Law and Practice* (3rd edn, 1991, eds I A Macdonald and N J Blake) pp 255, 256; *Clive* pp 650–660. As to the current law, see vol 10, para 940.

270. Entry clearance and leave to enter and remain. Entry clearance is necessary for a spouse and, if the conditions are fulfilled[1], leave may be given for up to twelve months[2] subject to the general grounds for refusal of leave for entry clearance holders[3]. This is varied to indefinite leave if the Secretary of State is satisfied at the end of that period that the marriage is not terminated and that the spouses intend to live permanently together as spouses[4].

No mention is made of a prohibition upon employment.

1 Ie under the Statement of Changes in Immigration Rules (HC Paper (1989–90) no. 251) (the Immigration Rules), para 50(a)–(e): see paras 271, 272, below. The definition of 'settled' is, for this purpose, extended to include a member of Her Majesty's forces based in the United Kingdom but serving overseas: para 50, note.

2 Ibid, para 51.

3 See para 172 above.

4 Immigration Rules, para 132. See also para 271, text and note 4, below.

271. Nature of the marriage and 'primary purpose' as conditions for entry clearance. The entry clearance officer must be satisfied that the parties to the marriage have met; that they intend to live together permanently as spouses; and that the marriage was not entered into primarily to obtain admission to the United Kingdom[1]. These requirements were originally inserted only in relation to husbands, in the belief that marriage was used in order to permit entry of men, particularly from the Indian sub-continent, primarily to work. The issue was confused because of the arranged nature of marriage among most people of Indian sub-continent origin. The requirement was extended to wives as a result of the decision of the European Court of Human Rights that the rule was sexually discriminatory[2].

The 'primary purpose' rule, with the burden of proof upon the applicant, is designed to be and is likely to be in practice, a considerable hurdle. The guidance to entry clearance officers apparently emphasises the burden of proof and lists subjects for questioning[3].

The English Court of Appeal has laid down a test for 'primary purpose' cases which can be expressed in eight propositions, as follows:

(1) the onus falls on the applicant to satisfy the entry clearance officer on the balance of probabilities that the primary purpose of the marriage was not to obtain settlement, and that the other requirements of the rule are satisfied;

(2) the entry clearance officer is entitled to make inquiries of his own and to test the evidence the applicant puts forward;

(3) the applicant's intention is the central concern, but the intentions of both parties are relevant and so also, in an arranged marriage, are the intentions of the parents;

(4) the mere fact that there is an intention on the part of the spouses to live permanently together does not of itself mean that the marriage was not entered into primarily to obtain settlement, although it is their intention at the time of marriage which counts;

(5) however, the fact that the parties intend to live together permanently and have met is relevant to, and assists in proving that, the primary purpose of the marriage was not to obtain settlement;

(6) where the applicant comes from a community in which arranged marriages are the norm, the entry clearance officer is entitled to take this into consideration, but that fact does not show that the primary purpose was to obtain settlement;

(7) the very fact that an applicant is applying usually presupposes an intention to settle in the United Kingdom, so is not evidence that settlement is the primary purpose of the marriage;

(8) the same considerations apply when variation of leave to settlement is sought by a spouse after the initial twelve month leave to enter[4].

Previous history of attempts at settlement, or admissions that the marriage would not take place if the couple would have to live in the applicant's country of origin are likely to be fatal to an application, but a history of intermarriage between the families or evidence that the *mores* of the ethnic group in question accentuate religious bonds rather than national might assist.

1 Statement of Changes in Immigration Rules (HC Paper (1989–90) no. 251) (the Immigration Rules), para 50(a)–(c). The requirement of having 'met' is one of having 'made one another's acquaintance' (*Raj v Entry Clearance Officer, New Delhi* [1985] Imm AR 151, IAT), and to have done so in the context of marriage (*Mohd Meharban v Entry Clearance Officer, Islamabad* [1989] Imm AR 57, IAT).

2 *Abdulaziz, Cabales and Balkandali v United Kingdom* (1985) 7 EHRR 471, E Ct HR.

3 L Grant and I Martin *Immigration Law and Practice* (1982), First Supplement (1985) para 8.57A. See also *Abid Hussain v Entry Clearance Officer, Islamabad* [1989] Imm AR 46, IAT.

4 *R v Immigration Appeal Tribunal, ex parte Hoque and Singh* [1988] Imm AR 216, CA, which drew upon the earlier decisions in *R v Immigration Appeal Tribunal, ex parte Vinod Bhatia* [1985] Imm AR 59, CA, and *R v Immigration Appeal Tribunal, ex parte Kumar* [1986] Imm AR 446, CA, and was applied in *Saftar* 1991 GWD 15-940, OH. The court set forth its propositions in the context of the previous rules, but the test is equally applicable under the current rules: see para 110 above. The court in fact expounded the test in ten propositions, but two relate (*mutatis mutandis*) to fiancés and fiancées: see para 275 below. In *Choudhry v Immigration Appeal Tribunal* [1990] Imm AR 211, CA, the court (affirming its decision in *R v Immigration Appeal Tribunal, ex parte Hoque and Singh* [1988] Imm AR 216, CA, disapproving *R v Immigration Appeal Tribunal, ex parte Mohammed Khatab* [1989] Imm AR 313, DC, but approving *R v Immigration Appeal Tribunal, ex parte Aurangzeb Khan* [1989] Imm AR 524) observed that it would be useful to have a specific finding on the intention to live permanently together.

272. Maintenance and accommodation as conditions for entry clearance. The entry clearance officer must be satisfied that there will be adequate accommodation for the parties without recourse to public funds in accommodation of their own or which they occupy themselves, and that they will be able to maintain themselves and their dependants adequately without recourse to public funds[1].

1 Statement of Changes in Immigration Rules (HC Paper (1989–90) no. 251) (the Immigration Rules), para 50(d), (e). For the meaning of 'public funds', see para 160, note 1, above.

273. Proof of marriage. In practice the major difficulty for most spouses, at least in the case of wives coming from the Indian sub-continent, has been proof of marriage[1]. The problem arises largely because of lack of reliable documentary proof aggravated by the need to travel considerable distances for interviews conducted through interpreters, to obtain entry clearance, in countries with poor communications[2]. There are also allegations that the interviews are not well conducted and that the entry clearance system is used to delay or prevent entry of those with a presumptive entitlement[3]. Considerable queues have existed for many years for entry of such wives[4]. The Home Office considers that the process is an unavoidable result of the pressure to emigrate, and a consequent likelihood of deception[5].

1 See para 267 above. See also *Immigration Control Procedures: Report of a Formal Investigation* (1985, Commission for Racial Equality) ch 4.
2 Ibid, paras 4.7.1–4.8.7.
3 Ibid, paras 4.3.3, 4.4.5, 4.4.7, 4.9.1–4.12.8, 4.29.1– 4.29.12, especially paras 4.29.7, 4.35.1– 4.35.2 and 4.36.1.
4 Ibid, para 4.3.4, Table 4.2.
5 Ibid, paras 2.4.1–2.4.14. See also the Home Office annual 'Report on the Work of the Immigration and Nationality Department' (1984 to date).

(C) ADMISSION OF FIANCES AND FIANCEES

274. Entry clearance and leave to enter. Entry clearance is necessary for fiancés and fiancées and, if the conditions are fulfilled[1], leave may be given for six months, subject to the general grounds for refusal of leave for entry clearance holders[2]. The person is advised to apply, once the marriage has taken place, for an extension[3]. A prohibition on employment is imposed[3].

1 Ie the Statement of Changes in Immigration Rules (HC Paper (1989–90) no. 251) (the Immigration Rules), para 47(a)–(e): see paras 275, 276, below.
2 Ibid, paras 47, 48.
3 Ibid, para 48.

275. Nature of the marriage and 'primary purpose' as conditions of entry. The entry clearance officer must be satisfied in respect of fiancés and fiancées that it is not the primary purpose of the intended marriage to obtain admission to the United Kingdom; that the parties intend to live together permanently; and that they have met[1].

1 See Statement of Changes in Immigration Rules (HC Paper (1989–90) no. 251) (the Immigration Rules), para 47(a)–(c). As to the test for the 'primary purposes' rule which apply mutatis mutandis to fiancés and fiancées, see para 271 above. See also *R v Immigration Appeal Tribunal, ex parte Rafique* [1990] Imm AR 235, where the test was not applied.

276. Maintenance and accommodation as conditions for entry. The entry clearance officer must be satisfied in respect of fiancés and fiancées that adequate maintenance and accommodation without recourse to public funds will be available for the applicant until the date of the marriage[1]. He must also be satisfied that after the marriage there will be adequate accommodation for the parties without recourse to public funds in accommodation of their own or which they occupy themselves, and that they will be able to maintain themselves and their dependants adequately without recourse to public funds[2].

1 Statement of Changes in Immigration Rules (HC Paper (1989–90) no. 251) (the Immigration Rules), para 47(d). For the meaning of 'public funds', see para 160, note 1, above.
2 Ibid, para 47(e)(i), (ii).

277. Variation of leave after marriage. Leave will be varied after the initial six months only if the marriage has taken place and certain conditions fulfilled (in which case a further twelve-months' leave is given)[1] or if good cause is shown and certain other conditions are fulfilled[2].

The conditions applying after marriage are that the conditions for entry clearance continue to be fulfilled and that the marriage did not take place after a decision to deport, or a court recommendation to deport, has been made, and that the marriage has not been terminated[3]. No prohibition upon taking work is mentioned, and it can be assumed that none will be imposed.

If the Secretary of State is satisfied after the further twelve months, indefinite leave may be granted if two conditions are fulfilled, that is, that the marriage has not been terminated, and that both parties intend to live together permanently as spouses[4]. This last requirement is separate from the requirement that the marriage be genuine, and the Secretary of State must exercise his discretion in respect of it[5].

The conditions, in addition to 'good cause', applying if the marriage has not taken place are that satisfactory evidence that the marriage will soon take place and that the maintenance and accommodation requirements are still met[6].

1 Statement of Changes in Immigration Rules (HC Paper (1989–90) no. 251) (the Immigration Rules), paras 130, 131.
2 Ibid, para 130.
3 Ibid, para 131(a)–(h).
4 Ibid, para 132.
5 *R v Immigration Appeal Tribunal, ex parte Surinder Mohan* [1985] Imm AR 84, CA.
6 Immigration Rules, para 130.

(D) SETTLEMENT BY VIRTUE OF MARRIAGE OF THOSE ADMITTED OTHER THAN AS SPOUSE, FIANCEE OR FIANCE

278. Variation of leave of those who marry having been admitted for other purposes. A person admitted in any capacity other than spouse, fiancée or fiancé can seek to extend leave and become settled by virtue of marriage to a person settled in the United Kingdom[1]. The conditions imposed are the same as for a person admitted as fiancée or fiancé[2].

Failure to fulfil them does not affect the validity of the marriage but compels the settled spouse to leave or the spouses to separate when the limited leave expires (unless it is extended on some other ground).

Where both parties have limited leave, the same presumably applies *a fortiori*.

1 Statement of Changes in Immigration Rules (HC Paper (1989–90) no. 251) (the Immigration Rules), para 131.
2 See ibid, para 131(a)–(h). As to fiancés and fiancées, see paras 274 ff above.

(E) ADMISSION OF CHILDREN

279. What are child and parent for the purposes of admission for settlement of children? 'Child' is defined by the definition of 'parent'. 'Parent' includes both parents of an illegitimate child, step-parents, provided the equivalent natural parent is dead, and adoptive parents, but only where there has been a genuine transfer of responsibility which was on the ground of the natural parents' inability to care for the child, and not arranged to facilitate admission[1]. The adoption does not have to be one recognised in the United Kingdom but must be valid where it occurred[2].

The Immigration Rules do not deal with the case of a child entering in order to be adopted, but unpublished guidelines exist, issued in letter form, to inquirers[3]. These require that it be ascertained:

(1) that the adoption be not a mere device to obtain entry;

(2) that the child's welfare is assured;

(3) what his or her feelings are;

(4) that the natural parents (or guardians) agree;

(5) that the relevant authorities in the country of residence agree;

(6) that a court is likely to grant an adoption order; and

(7) that one prospective adopting parent be domiciled in the United Kingdom.

Considerable documentation is required. The Home Office also requires undertakings from the prospective adopters as to intentions and financial abilities and inquiries are made via social work departments. Entry clearance for six months is normally given. If either adopting parent is a British citizen and the adoption order is made by a United Kingdom court the child becomes a British citizen on the date of adoption[4]. Otherwise indefinite leave is given[5].

Where a child obtained leave to enter with a citizen uncle and aunt, having been turned out of its parents' home, a court considering its adoption was not bound by a refusal to extend leave (prospective adoption not having been mentioned), since under the relevant statute the welfare of the child was the primary consideration[6].

1 Statement of Changes in Immigration Rules (HC Paper (1989–90) no. 251) (the Immigration Rules), para 53. See also *Pereira v Entry Clearance Officer, Bridgetown* [1979–80] Imm AR 79, IAT. The word 'adoptive' in the Immigration Rules, para 53, is not limited to a formal adoption and permanency is the primary concern: *R v Immigration Appeal Tribunal, ex parte Tohur Ali* [1988] Imm AR 237, CA.

2 *Malik v Secretary of State for the Home Department* [1972] Imm AR 37; *Merchant v Entry Clearance Officer, Bombay* [1975] Imm AR 49, IAT; *Mathieu v Entry Clearance Officer, Bridgetown* [1979–80] Imm AR 157, IAT.

3 For the current letter, see RON 117 (D). The guidelines are discussed in *R v Secretary of State for the Home Department, ex parte Khan* [1985] 1 All ER 40, [1984] 1 WLR 1337, [1984] Imm AR 68, CA, where the letter issued no longer reflected policy applied. The court held that the new procedure could be used only after the recipient of the letter had been told of it, and given a chance to make representations, and only after full and serious consideration as to any overriding public interest justifying departure from the procedure described in the letter. It is understood that the letter was changed after this case.

4 See the British Nationality Act 1981 (c 61), s 1(5), and NATIONALITY AND CITIZENSHIP, vol 14, para 1910.

5 See L Grant and I Martin *Immigration Law and Practice* (1982), First Supplement (1985) para 8.42, and *Macdonald's Immigration Law and Practice* (3rd edn, 1991, eds I A Macdonald and N J Blake) pp 279 ff.

6 *Re H (a minor)* [1982] Fam 121 [1982] 3 All ER 84.

280. Entry clearance and leave to enter or remain.

Entry clearance is necessary (unless the child is already present in another capacity) and if the conditions are fulfilled, indefinite leave may be given on entry[1]. The conditions vary depending upon whether the child is under eighteen years of age and unmarried or not[2].

1 See the Statement of Changes in Immigration Rules (HC Paper (1989–90) no. 251) (the Immigration Rules), para 52.

2 See ibid, paras 53–55, and paras 281–283 below. Those under eighteen and married are not referred to specifically and presumably fall to be considered as if eighteen or more.

281. Conditions of admission (other than maintenance and accommodation requirements) for settlement of children under eighteen. The Immigration Rules require that a child does not acquire indefinite leave on arrival in advance of both parents, other than in exceptional cases, as the aim is the reunification of families[1]. Thus normally both parents (or the one surviving parent) must be already settled, or accepted for settlement on the same occasion[2]. If one of the two parents is given limited leave with a view to settlement instead, the child is given twelve months' leave[3].

If both parents are living (whatever their marital status) a child is admitted to join, or accompany, one parent only if that parent has sole responsibility for the child's upbringing, or if there are serious or compelling family or other considerations making exclusion undesirable, and suitable arrangements for the child's care have been made[4]. In such cases another settled relative may act as sponsor[5]. If the child is joining or accompanying a parent with limited leave with a view to settlement, and that parent has sole responsibility and there are serious or compelling considerations, the child is to be given leave for twelve months[6].

'Sole responsibility' is not to be construed literally, and is a question of fact to be determined according to the degree of support, and genuine interest and affection. A degree of delegation to others is accepted[7]. Legal responsibility is not dispositive.

'Serious and compelling family or other considerations' has been interpreted strictly[8]. Comparison between living conditions being experienced and those which would be experienced if leave to enter were given is not accepted and poverty as such is insufficient[9]. However, poverty, overcrowding and near abandonment have been sufficient[10], and a child under twelve years of age is regarded as one whose exclusion is undesirable, provided maintenance and accommodation requirements (here including a resident female relative) are fulfilled[11].

1 *Ibrahim v Visa Officer, Islamabad* [1978] Imm AR 18, IAT; *Visa Officer, Islamabad v Waheed Akhtar* [1981] Imm AR 109, IAT. Thus 'courier wives' are frowned on: *Immigration Control Procedures: Report of a Formal Investigation* (1985, Commission for Racial Equality) paras 4.24.1–4.24.3.

2 Statement of Changes in Immigration Rules (HC Paper (1989–90) no. 251) (the Immigration Rules), para 53(a)–(d).

3 Ibid, para 54(a).

4 Ibid, para 53(e), (f). The approach in *R v Immigration Appeal Tribunal, ex parte Sajid Mahmood* [1988] Imm AR 121, was approved in *Ramos v Immigration Appeal Tribunal* [1989] Imm AR 148, CA.

5 *Ravat v Entry Clearance Officer, Bombay* [1974] Imm AR 79, IAT.

6 Immigration Rules, para 54(b).

7 *McGillivary v Secretary of State for the Home Department* [1972] Imm AR 63, IAT; *Emmanuel v Secretary of State for the Home Department* [1972] Imm AR 69, IAT; *Martin v Secretary of State for the Home Department* [1972] Imm AR 71, IAT; *Secretary of State for the Home Department v Pusey* [1972] Imm AR 240, IAT; *Bovell v Entry Clearance Officer, Georgetown, Guyana* [1973] Imm AR 37, IAT; *Sloley v Entry Clearance Officer, Kingston, Jamaica* [1973] Imm AR 54, IAT; *Eugene v Entry Clearance Officer, Bridgetown* [1975] Imm AR 111, IAT; *Entry Clearance Officer, Kingston, Jamaica v SS Martin* [1978] Imm AR 100, IAT.

8 *Howard v Secretary of State for the Home Department* [1972] Imm AR 93, IAT; *Leroy Rennie v Entry Clearance Officer, Kingston, Jamaica* [1979–80] Imm AR 117, IAT; *Entry Clearance Officer, Kingston, Jamaica v Thompson* [1981] Imm AR 148, IAT.

9 *Secretary of State for the Home Department v Campbell* [1972] Imm AR 115, IAT; *Williams v Secretary of State for the Home Department* [1972] Imm AR 207, IAT.

10 *Entry Clearance Officer, Kingston, Jamaica v Holmes* [1975] Imm AR 20, IAT.

11 See L Grant and I Martin *Immigration Law and Practice* (1982) para 8.39; *Macdonald's Immigration Law and Practice* (3rd edn, 1991, eds I A Macdonald and N J Blake) p 275. See also para 283 below.

282. Conditions of admission (other than maintenance and accommodation requirements) for settlement of children of eighteen or over. Admission of persons aged eighteen years or more as children is possible only in the most exceptional compassionate circumstances, in the same fashion as other relatives, but the rigour is to be modified in the case of fully dependent unmarried daughters under twenty-one years of age who form part of the family unit overseas and have no other close relatives to turn to[1]. The maintenance and accommodation requirements apply as with other children[2].

1 See the Statement of Changes in Immigration Rules (HC Paper (1989–90) no. 251) (the Immigration Rules), paras 52, 55. See also *Bernard v Entry Clearance Officer, Kingston, Jamaica* [1976] Imm AR 7, IAT; *Brown v Entry Clearance Officer, Kingston, Jamaica* [1976] Imm AR 119, IAT; *Cuffy v Entry Clearance Officer, Georgetown, Guyana* [1976] Imm AR 66, IAT; *Harmail Singh v Immigration Appeal Tribunal* [1978] Imm AR 140, CA; *R v Immigration Appeal Tribunal, ex parte Hazrabibi Ibrahim Mohamed Kara* [1989] Imm AR 120.
2 See para 283 below.

283. Maintenance and accommodation requirements. The entry clearance officer must be satisfied in respect of children under the age of eighteen and, in exceptional circumstances, children under the age of twenty-one, that there will be adequate accommodation and that they will be maintained adequately without recourse to public funds[1].

1 Statement of Changes in Immigration Rules (HC Paper (1989–90) no. 251) (the Immigration Rules), para 52. As to 'public funds', see para 160, note 1, above.

284. Children born in the United Kingdom who are not British citizens. The position of children born in the United Kingdom who are not British citizens is dealt with above[1].

1 See para 127 above.

(F) ADMISSION OF PARENTS, GRANDPARENTS AND OTHER RELATIVES

285. Introduction. Certain relatives, other than spouses and children, may be admitted under exiguous conditions and require entry clearance, unless already present in another capacity[1].

1 Statement of Changes in Immigration Rules (HC Paper (1989–90) no. 251) (the Immigration Rules), para 139, read with paras 52–57. However, there is a contradiction between these provisions as to what relatives are eligible: see para 266, note 5, above.

286. What are parents and grandparents for the purpose of admission. In defining 'parents' and 'grandparents' for the purposes of admission as such, no cross-reference is made to the definition of 'parents' for the purposes of admission of children[1], but remarried parents are excluded except on certain conditions[2].

Eligible are widowed mothers, widowed fathers over sixty-five years of age, or under that age in certain situations[3], provided in all cases that there is a son or daughter already present and settled, or who is admitted for settlement on the same occasion or given limited leave with a view to settlement[4]. The eligibility rules are applied strictly, for example to exclude unmarried parents.

1 See para 279 above.
2 Ie that he or she must be unable to look for support to the children of the second marriage and the United Kingdom settled children must have sufficient means and accommodation to maintain

parent and step-parent and any children of the second marriage who would be admissible as dependants: Statement of Changes in Immigration Rules (HC Paper (1989–90) no. 251) (the Immigration Rules), para 57. See also *Bibi Bagas v Entry Clearance Officer, Bombay* [1978] Imm AR 85, IAT.

3 See para 288 below.

4 Immigration Rules, para 65. The provision does not in fact refer to grandparents as such at all, but is headed 'Parents, grandparents and other relatives', so plainly covers them: *Phillips v Entry Certificate Officer, Kingston, Jamaica* [1973] Imm AR 47, IAT. See also para 288 below.

287. Maintenance, accommodation and dependency requirements for admission of parents and grandparents falling within the normal age requirements.

The maintenance and accommodation requirements for parents and grandparents are the same as for children[1]. In addition the parent or grandparent must show specifically that he or she is wholly or mainly dependent upon sons or daughters settled in the United Kingdom who have the means to maintain the parent or grandparent and any other relatives admissible as dependants of the parents and adequate accommodation[2]. Further, the parent or grandparent must be without close relatives in his or her own country to turn to[2].

The dependency required can include physical or emotional dependency, where it is greater than ordinary family affection and is continuing[3]. It is, however, necessarily financial in part, and this is interpreted strictly as 'necessary dependence', in particular where alternative sources exist[4].

The requirement of a lack of close relatives to turn to has not been interpreted strictly, and requires it to be reasonable that such relatives be turned to and that they be willing and able to assist[5].

The dependency can arise while the parent or grandparent is in the United Kingdom as a visitor[6].

1 See the Statement of Changes in Immigration Rules (HC Paper (1989–90) no. 251) (the Immigration Rules), paras 52, 56, and para 276 above. See also *Phillips v Entry Certificate Officer, Kingston, Jamaica* [1973] Imm AR 47, IAT; *Secretary of State for the Home Department v L G Patel* [1972] Imm AR 227, IAT; *Nisa v Secretary of State for the Home Department* [1979–80] Imm AR 20, IAT.

2 Immigration Rules, para 56.

3 *Chavda v Entry Clearance Officer, Bombay* [1978] AR 40, IAT; *R v Immigration Appeal Tribunal, ex parte Bastiampillai* [1983] 2 All ER 844, [1983] Imm AR 1, DC; *R v Immigration Appeal Tribunal, ex parte Swaran Singh* [1987] 3 All ER 690, [1987] Imm AR 563, CA.

4 *Mohammad Zaman v Entry Certificate Officer, Lahore* [1973] Imm AR 71, IAT; *Visa Officer, Islamabad v Shukar* [1981] Imm AR 58, IAT; *R v Immigration Appeal Tribunal, ex parte Bastiampillai* [1983] 2 All ER 844, [1983] Imm AR 1, DC.

5 *Chavda v Entry Clearance Officer, Bombay* [1978] AR 40, IAT; *R v Immigration Appeal Tribunal, ex parte Bastiampillai* [1983] 2 All ER 844, [1983] Imm AR 1, DC; *R v Immigration Appeal Tribunal, ex parte Swaran Singh* [1987] 3 All ER 690, [1987] Imm AR 563, CA.

6 *Harbant Kaur v Secretary of State for the Home Department* [1982] Imm AR 84, IAT.

288. Maintenance, accommodation and dependency requirements for admission of parents and grandparents not falling within the normal age requirements.

In addition to the usual maintenance, accommodation and dependency requirements, parents and grandparents not falling within the normal age requirements[1], other than widowed mothers, must show that they are living alone in the most exceptional compassionate circumstances[2]. Occasional cases do occur[3].

1 Ie sixty-five: see para 286 above.

2 Statement of Changes in Immigration Rules (HC Paper (1989–90) no. 251) (the Immigration Rules), para 56. The previous specific requirement of a standard of living substantially below that of their own country is no longer mentioned: see the Statement of Changes in Immigration Rules (HC Paper (1982–83) no. 169) (the Former Immigration Rules), para 52 (superseded).

3 *Mukhopadyay v Entry Clearance Officer, Calcutta* [1975] Imm AR 42, IAT; *Entry Certificate Officer, Bombay v Sacha* [1973] Imm AR 5, IAT.

289. What other relatives are eligible for the purposes of admission.
Only sons, daughters, sisters, brothers, uncles and aunts are referred to (though without age restriction)[1]. Presumably no others are eligible.

1 Statement of Changes in Immigration Rules (HC Paper (1989–90) no. 251) (the Immigration Rules), para 52. The earlier Immigration Rules included other relations: see eg Statements of Changes in Immigration Rules (HC Paper (1972–73) no. 79), para 46 and (HC Paper (1972–73) no. 81) para 41 (both superseded). See also *Hardev Kaur v Entry Clearance Officer, New Delhi* [1979–80] Imm AR 76, IAT, concerning a widowed sister-in-law.

290. Maintenance, accommodation and dependency requirements for admission of other relatives. The conditions for admission for settlement of other relatives are the same as for parents and grandparents who do not fulfil the normal age requirements[1].

1 See para 288 above. See also *Entry Clearance Officer, Nairobi v Kivan Seth* [1979–80] Imm AR 63, IAT.

(d) Students, Visitors and Au Pairs

(A) INTRODUCTION

291. Categories not normally leading to settlement. A person in one of the categories of student, visitor or au pair cannot normally expect to achieve settlement[1]. Entry clearance is not specifically required for such persons although it may be advisable in some cases, especially that of students.

1 As to whom may apply for settlement, see the Statement of Changes in Immigration Rules (HC Paper (1989–90) no. 251) (the Immigration Rules), para 139, and para 241 above.

(B) STUDENTS

292. Introduction. The term 'student' is used to include school pupils, nurses and midwives in training, hospital house officers in pre-registration training and doctors and dentists in postgraduate training[1]. The requirements of this category do not apply to those who enter as dependants of others and who are entitled to state education (subject to the rules on overseas students[2]). Those wishing to enter as students will not be admitted unless fees are being paid; thus in relation to primary or secondary education they would require to be entering a fee-paying school[3]. Entry clearance is not specifically required of students (unless visa nationals) but may be desirable[4].

A student with entry clearance fulfilling the general requirements for entry clearance for students is to be admitted for an appropriate period depending upon the course and his means (subject to the general grounds for refusal of entry clearance holders[5]), and in any case with a restriction on employment[6]. A student who neither has entry clearance nor fulfils the requirements for entry clearance may be admitted in limited circumstances[7].

1 Statement of Changes in Immigration Rules (HC Paper (1989–90) no. 251) (the Immigration Rules), paras 26, 29, 32. Doctors and dentists in postgraduate training are treated as a specific

category in Pt II (paras 22–33) (in relation to entry), but are included among all students in Pt XI (paras 94–154) (in relation to variation of leave). In earlier Immigration Rules they were treated as students throughout: see eg Statement of Changes in Immigration Rules (HC Paper (1982–83) no. 169) (the Former Immigration Rules), para 23, before its amendment by Statement of Changes in Immigration Rules (HC Paper (1984–85) no. 293), para 1 (both superseded).

2 Ie in relation to fees and grants: see EDUCATION.

3 Immigration Rules, para 26.

4 'Cf the opening words of ibid, para 26, with those of para 30. Visa nationals are explicitly required to have entry clearance (see para 14 and cf para 111), unless they wish to take up postgraduate medical or dental training. Students from poorer countries, especially if they have relatives in the United Kingdom, may be refused entry even with an entry clearance as it is suspected that they intend to settle: *Qureshi v Immigration Officer, London (Heathrow) Airport* [1977] Imm AR 113, IAT; *Davendranath Doorga v Secretary of State for the Home Department* [1990] Imm AR 98, CA. Because of the delays experienced in obtaining entry clearance in the Indian sub-continent, it may be difficult to do so before the course starts. Students wishing to leave the United Kingdom briefly in the course of their studies should before leaving (because all leave lapses on departure outwith the common travel area) take steps to ensure that they will be readmitted, by contacting the Immigration and Nationality Department: see *Kuku v Secretary of State for the Home Department* [1990] Imm AR 27, CA, and para 176 above.

5 See the Immigration Rules, para 17, and para 172 above. See also note 4 above.

6 Ibid, para 30. 'Restriction' means that the consent of the Department of Employment and the Home Office must be obtained for the employment: see para 296, note 1, below.

7 See ibid, para 30.

293. General requirements for entry clearance for students (other than doctors or dentists seeking postgraduate training).

Entry clearance for students (other than doctors or dentists seeking postgraduate training) may be granted if five requirements are fulfilled[1]. These are:

(1) that he satisfies the entry clearance officer or immigration officer that he has been accepted for a course of study at a university, polytechnic or further education establishment, independent school or any bona fide private education establishment[2];

(2) that the course will occupy the whole or a substantial part of his time, and that there will be in general at least fifteen hours per week in organised daytime study of a single or related subjects[3];

(3) that he is able, and realistically intends, to follow the course of study[4];

(4) that he can meet the cost of the course and maintenance and accommodation for himself and any dependants without working and without recourse to public funds (and evidence of sponsorship by his home government or other official body is important)[5];

(5) that he intends to leave the United Kingdom at the completion of his studies[6].

'Course of study' has been interpreted liberally to include, for instance, first degrees followed by higher degrees, secondary education followed by tertiary, or even primary followed by secondary and then tertiary, provided at least there is a coherent and definite plan capable of being carried out by the student, and the plan is not disguised settlement[7].

In relation to the requirements under heads (1), (2) and (3), the fifteen hours per week requirement is not absolute where accompanied by genuine keen interest, evidence of work required and qualifications or sponsorship, but must have a definite end in view and be more than coaching[8]. In any case entry clearance may be granted where these conditions are not fulfilled, provided the prospective student produces evidence which satisfies the entry clearance officer that he has genuine and realistic intentions of study instead[9].

In relation to the requirement under head (4), the source may be scholarship, savings or 'family funds', but good documentary evidence is necessary of resources available in the United Kingdom[10]. Employment of the student may be permitted by the Department of Employment, and no restriction is put upon wives' employment if the student is not prohibited from working[11]. Earnings so acquired may not be taken into account in relation to extension of leave, so their possibility cannot be taken into account in relation to entry clearance, although that of wives can[12]. Students are presumed never to have husbands.

In relation to the requirement under head (5), there is a complicated history and comparatively lengthy case law, and it has been suggested that the provision is otiose and effectively a mere trap for the naive[13]. Clearly an intention to leave is difficult to prove, and it is accepted that it is consistent with seeking several qualifications in consecutive courses of study, and with a wish or belief in the possibility of settlement. Essentially the test is a 'primary purpose' rule[14], and earlier applications of it as a 'realism' or 'value for money' test[15] are probably overturned.

Those seeking entry for training as nurses or midwives having been accepted at a hospital are specifically mentioned as to be admitted unless there is evidence that the acceptance resulted from misrepresentation, or that he or she does not intend to follow the course[16]. As the restriction on meeting costs without working cannot apply here, it is not clear how far if at all this is in addition to or substitution for the general requirements. Graduates of United Kingdom medical schools are also specifically mentioned as 'admissible' for up to twelve months as house officers seeking to achieve registration with the General Medical Council[17].

1 These requirements do not apply to training as a nurse or midwife at a hospital: see Statement of Changes in Immigration Rules (HC Paper (1989–90) no. 251) (the Immigration Rules), para 29, and the text and note 16 below.

2 Ibid, para 26.

3 Ibid, paras 26, 27.

4 Ibid, para 27. This does not allow the entry clearance officer or immigration officer to interpose his judgment on academic matters (*R v Secretary of State for the Home Department, ex parte Hindjou* [1989] Imm AR 24), but the position is more restricted than under earlier Immigration Rules (*R v Chief Immigration Officer, Bradford Airport, ex parte Ashiq Hussain* [1969] 3 All ER 1601, [1970] 1 WLR 9, DC).

5 Immigration Rules, paras 26–28.

6 Ibid, paras 27, 28.

7 *R v Chief Immigration Officer, Gatwick Airport, ex parte Kharrazi* [1980] 3 All ER 373, [1980] 1 WLR 1396, CA. However, see *Myeen-Ur-Rashid v Entry Clearance Officer, Dacca* [1976] Imm AR 12, IAT.

8 *Entry Certificate Officer, Lagos v Amusu* [1974] Imm AR 16, IAT; *Kpoma v Secretary of State for the Home Department* [1973] Imm AR 25, IAT.

9 Immigration Rules, para 28.

10 *Bhagat v Secretary of State for the Home Department* [1972] Imm AR 189, IAT; *Ayettey v Secretary of State for the Home Department* [1972] Imm AR 261, IAT; *Murgai v Entry Clearance Officer, New Delhi* [1975] Imm AR 86, IAT.

11 Immigration Rules, paras 31, 113, 116.

12 Ibid, para 113.

13 *Macdonald's Immigration Law and Practice* (3rd edn, 1991, eds I A Macdonald and N J Blake) pp 191 ff. The provision appears otiose in that a work permit cannot normally be obtained from within the United Kingdom (see para 157 above), nor settlement obtained by a student (see para 299 below), and a trap for the naive since one might, if asked, readily agree that it could be pleasant to settle in the United Kingdom, without thereby intending to express any intention: *Entry Clearance Officer v Sobanjo* [1978] Imm AR 22, IAT.

14 Cf the 'primary purpose' test in respect of marriages: see paras 271, 275, above. See also *R v Immigration Appeal Tribunal, ex parte Perween Khan* [1972] 3 All ER 297, [1972] 1 WLR 1058, [1972] Imm AR 268, DC; *Secretary of State for the Home Department v Oh* [1972] Imm AR 236, IAT; *R v Immigration Appeal Tribunal, ex parte Khan* [1975] Imm AR 26, IAT; *Myeen-Ur-Rashid v Entry Clearance Officer, Dacca* [1976] Imm AR 12, IAT; *R v Immigration Appeal Tribunal, ex parte Shaikh* [1981] 3 All ER 29, [1981] 1 WLR 1107, DC; *R v Chief Immigration Officer, Gatwick Airport, ex parte Kharrazi* [1980] 3 All ER 373, [1980] 1 WLR 1396, CA; *Patel v Immigration Appeal Tribunal* [1983] Imm AR 76, CA.

15 *R v Immigration Appeal Tribunal, ex parte Khan* [1975] Imm AR 26, IAT; *Goffar v Entry Clearance Officer, Dacca* [1975] Imm AR 142, IAT; *Ghosh v Entry Clearance Officer, Calcutta* [1976] Imm AR 60, IAT.
16 Immigration Rules, para 29. Cf para 295 below.
17 See ibid, paras 29, 113. Cf para 295 below.

294. Entry of students without entry clearance (other than doctors or dentists seeking postgraduate training).

A student (other than doctors or dentists seeking postgraduate training) without entry clearance who is not a visa national may be admitted if either he fulfils the entry clearance requirements or he has genuine and realistic intentions[1] of studying, intends to leave at the end of the course of study and can meet the cost of the course and maintenance and accommodation for himself and any dependant without working and without recourse to public funds, but cannot fulfil the general requirements[2]. In the latter case admission is for a limited period with a prohibition on employment with advice to apply for variation of leave[2].

1 Ie he has not been accepted for a relevant course: see eg *R v Secretary of State for the Home Department, ex parte Hindjou* [1989] Imm AR 24.
2 Statement of Changes in Immigration Rules (HC Paper (1989–90) no. 251) (the Immigration Rules), para 30.

295. Entry requirements for doctors and dentists seeking postgraduate training.

A doctor or dentist eligible for full or limited registration with the General Medical Council or the General Dental Council may be admitted for postgraduate training in hospital, provided that he intends to leave on completion of training and he has not already spent an aggregate of four years in the United Kingdom for this purpose already[1]. He will be admitted for an appropriate period not exceeding twelve months[2].

1 Statement of Changes in Immigration Rules (HC Paper (1989–90) no. 251) (the Immigration Rules), para 32. Cf para 293, text to note 17, above.
2 Ibid, para 32.

296. Employment of students (other than doctors and dentists).

Students (other than doctors and dentists) are normally admitted with a restriction upon employment, that is, they require Department of Employment consent to take work during free time or vacation[1]. Occasional sales of art work by an art student do not constitute employment[2].

Although a requirement of entry is adequate means, and work lawfully undertaken may not be taken into account in assessing means, at least on applications for extension of leave, those of wives can[3].

1 Statement of Changes in Immigration Rules (HC Paper (1989–90) no. 251) (the Immigration Rules), paras 30, 113. They are expected to obtain consent via the local professional and executive register office, Jobcentre or employment office, and must provide satisfactory evidence that the work will not interfere with the course of study. In any case permission is given only if no suitable resident labour is available, and wages and conditions are not less favourable than those for similar work in the area: Department of Employment leaflet OW5 'Employment of Overseas Workers in the United Kingdom', para 3. As to the status of this leaflet, see para 112 above.
2 *Strasburger v Secretary of State for the Home Department* [1978] Imm AR 165, IAT.
3 Immigration Rules, para 113.

297. Change of category for students (other than doctors and dentists on postgraduate training).

Students (other than doctors and dentists on postgraduate training) may change category to spouse[1], to young Commonwealth working holidaymaker[2], or to au pair[3], provided the relevant conditions are fulfilled. In limited circumstances they may change category to a work-permit holding trainee[4]. No other change is explicitly permitted by the Immigration Rules.

1 See the Statement of Changes in Immigration Rules (HC Paper (1989–90) no. 251) (the Immigration Rules), para 131, and para 278 above.
2 See ibid, para 107, and para 263 above.
3 See ibid, para 121, and paras 310–313 below.
4 See ibid, para 120, and paras 241, 245, above.

298. Change of category for doctors and dentists on postgraduate training.
Doctors and dentists on postgraduate training are now in the same position as other students[1].

1 See para 297 above.

299. Extension of leave for students.
A student admitted without entry clearance may be given an extension (and any prohibition on employment reduced to a restriction) on satisfactory evidence of fulfilment of the entry clearance conditions for students provided he is not a visa national[1]. A student showing evidence (which may be verified[2]) that he

(1) is enrolled[3] as a student in a course fulfilling the admission requirements[4],
(2) is in regular attendance[5],
(3) can maintain and accommodate himself without working or recourse to public funds and continues to intend to leave at the end of his studies[6],

may be granted an extension[7] provided he is not moving from one course to another to continue as a student indefinitely[8]. More than four years on short courses (that is of less than two years) is unacceptable[8]. In the case of those financed by Her Majesty's government, by an international scholarship agency or by their home government, extension should not be granted beyond the duration of the award[9].

The earnings of the student's wife may be taken into account in assessing the adequacy of maintenance, but not his own[10]. Husbands of students are not envisaged.

1 See the Statement of Changes in Immigration Rules (HC Paper (1989–90) no. 251) (the Immigration Rules), paras 109, 115. It seems that even a visa national without entry clearance may obtain an extension to pursue postgraduate medical or dental training.
2 See ibid, para 109, and *Kpoma v Secretary of State for the Home Department* [1973] Imm AR 25, IAT.
3 'Enrolled' means having an unconditional confirmed place on a course: *Chinwo v Secretary of State for the Home Department* [1985] Imm AR 74, IAT.
4 Ie the entry clearance requirements: see para 293 above.
5 Ie judged at the time of application (*Juma v Secretary of State for the Home Department* [1974] Imm AR 96, IAT), and examination success is relevant (*Amer v Secretary of State for the Home Department* [1979–80] Imm AR 87, IAT).
6 Immigration Rules, para 109. As to public funds, see para 160, note 1, above.
7 See ibid, para 109, and *R v Chief Immigration Officer, Gatwick Airport, ex parte Kharrazi* [1980] 3 All ER 373, [1980] 1 WLR 1396, CA.
8 Immigration Rules, para 110.
9 Ibid, para 112.
10 Ibid, para 113.

300. Specific provisions on extension of leave in the case of medical students and doctors and dentists in postgraduate training.
A graduate of a United Kingdom medical school may be given a twelve-month extension to undertake pre-registration house officer employment as required for full registration with the General Medical Council[1].

A doctor or dentist may have a twelve-month extension for postgraduate training if he is registered with the General Medical Council or the General Dental Council, and there is no reason to believe he does not intend to undergo such training and to leave the United Kingdom thereafter[2]. Extensions are not to exceed an aggregate of four years and such period does not count towards settlement[3]. Visitors and students may be granted an extension for postgraduate medical or dental training on the same conditions[4].

It is not clear if these are in addition to or in substitution for the general grounds for extension for students.

1 Statement of Changes in Immigration Rules (HC Paper (1989–90) no. 251) (the Immigration Rules), para 113.
2 Ibid, para 114.
3 Ibid, para 114. As to settlement, see para 120 above.
4 Ibid, para 115.

(C) DEPENDANTS OF STUDENTS

301. Who is a dependant. Only a wife and children under eighteen years of age may be dependants of a student[1].

1 Statement of Changes in Immigration Rules (HC Paper (1989–90) no. 251) (the Immigration Rules), para 31. It is not clear if the 'common law wife' provision applies: see para 269, note 1, above. Presumably the 'primary responsibility' requirements in practice apply: see para 281, notes 1–3, above.

302. Conditions for entry of dependants. Dependants of students must be able to be maintained and accommodated without recourse to public funds and should be admitted for the same period as the student[1].

1 Statement of Changes in Immigration Rules (HC Paper (1989–90) no. 251) (the Immigration Rules), para 31. As to public funds, see para 160, note 1 above.

303. Employment of dependants. Where the student is prohibited from employment, the dependants should be too[1]. Otherwise they should not be restricted or prohibited[1]. A wife's earnings may be taken into account in calculating the adequacy of maintenance[2].

1 Statement of Changes in Immigration Rules (HC Paper (1989–90) no. 251) (the Immigration Rules), para 31.
2 Ibid, para 113.

304. Extension of leave. A student's dependants will normally be given the same extension and employment conditions as the student[1].

1 Statement of Changes in Immigration Rules (HC Paper (1989–90) no. 251) (the Immigration Rules), para 116.

(D) VISITORS

305. Introduction. 'Visitor' is a miscellaneous category and most people entering do so within it, chiefly as tourists, businessmen or the like[1]. Visitors do not need entry clearance (unless visa nationals), but may be well-advised to obtain it, if of working age and from a poor country, since it may be assumed that they intend to work and settle illegally[2]. Particular attention is paid to those seeking medical treatment[3].

A visitor will be admitted for up to six months with a prohibition upon employment[4] (which does not prevent the transaction of business[5]), if fulfilling the requirements of the Immigration Rules. 'Restricted returnability' may indicate a shorter period[6].

1 Statement of Changes in Immigration Rules (HC Paper (1989–90) no. 251) (the Immigration Rules), para 22.
2 See *Immigration Control Procedures: Report of a Formal Investigation* (1985, Commission for Racial Equality) ch 6, especially pp 90–94, and the Immigration Rules, para 22.
3 See ibid, para 23, and para 306 below.
4 Ibid, para 25.
5 Ibid, para 25. How 'transaction of business' differs from 'employment' is not wholly clear: see para 174, note 2, above.
6 See ibid, para 19, and para 171 above. Earlier rules specifically referred to other factors which may still operate, eg charter flight date, being in transit, 'or if his case ought to be subject to early review by the Home Office'. This appears to refer to the use of the 'Code 3' stamp on the visitor's passport (as distinct from the usual 'Code 5N' stamp) whereby an immigration officer indicates that he is doubtful about the passenger's intentions but has insufficient evidence to justify refusal: *Immigration Control Procedures: Report of a Formal Investigation*, para 6.9.2.

306. Conditions for entry of visitors, including visitors seeking medical treatment.

A visitor must be able to maintain and accommodate himself and any dependants adequately (or be maintained and accommodated by relatives) and meet the cost of the return journey without working or recourse to public funds[1]. A visitor seeking private medical treatment may be admitted but must show adequate funds and that he is no threat to public health, and may be required to produce evidence of arrangements for consultation and treatment[2].

In the case of those who might be considered to intend to work or overstay, stress is laid upon the need for an incentive to return and lack of incentive to stay[3]. In general this affects those from poor countries and can lead to hardship[4]. However, some evidence is required, and of intention rather than of wish (though the attitudes of others may be relevant)[5]. Moreover, the likelihood of an application for extension is no ground for refusal[6], nor is holding a United Kingdom passport, though it may be taken into account[7].

1 Statement of Changes in Immigration Rules (HC Paper (1989–90) no. 251) (the Immigration Rules), para 22. It is for the visitor to say how long he thinks funds will last, not for the immigration officer to suggest it: *R v Secretary of State for Home Affairs, ex parte Harniak Singh* [1969] 2 All ER 867, [1969] 1 WLR 835, DC.
2 Immigration Rules, para 23. A medical inspector must be satisfied that there is no public health risk, and that the person's means are sufficient for the likely cost: para 23. It is irrelevant that the treatment sought is available in the person's own country: *Mohan Singh v Entry Certificate Officer, New Delhi* [1973] Imm AR 9, IAT.
3 See eg *Entry Clearance Officer, Colombo v Hanks* [1976] Imm AR 74, IAT; *Huda v Entry Clearance Officer, Dacca, New Delhi* [1976] Imm AR 109, IAT; *Bhagat Singh v Entry Clearance Officer, New Delhi* [1978] Imm AR 134, IAT; *Entry Clearance Officer, New Delhi v Kumar* [1978] Imm AR 185, IAT.
4 See eg *Manmohan Singh v Entry Clearance Officer, New Delhi* [1975] Imm AR 118, IAT.
5 *Entry Certificate Officer, Hong Kong v Lai* [1974] Imm AR 98, IAT; *Entry Clearance Officer, New Delhi v Kumar* [1978] Imm AR 185, IAT; *Immigration Officer, London (Gatwick) Airport v Darboe* [1981] Imm AR 210, IAT.
6 *R v Secretary of State for the Home Department, ex parte Arjumand* [1983] Imm AR 123, DC.
7 *Mohamed Din v Entry Clearance Officer, Karachi* [1978] Imm AR 56, IAT; *Patel v Entry Clearance Officer, Bombay* [1978] Imm AR 154, IAT.

307. Extension of leave. Leave of less than six months for a visitor may be extended, if admission conditions continue to be fulfilled, to allow a visit of up to six months[1]. A visitor undergoing or wishing to undergo medical treatment should produce evidence of arrangements made, of progress and likely duration of treatment, and of funds sufficient for the purpose[2]. The intention to return must continue[3].

1 See the Statement of Changes in Immigration Rules (HC Paper (1989–90) no. 251) (the Immigration Rules), para 105. An explicit possibility of extensions to one year appeared in earlier rules: see eg Statement of Changes in Immigration Rules (HC Paper (1982–83) no. 169) (the Former Immigration Rules), para 103 (superseded). As to earlier rules allowing visitors to stay for up to one year, see *Hashim v Secretary of State for the Home Department* [1982] Imm AR 113, IAT; and *Foon v Secretary of State for the Home Department* [1983] Imm AR 29, IAT.
2 See the Immigration Rules, para 106. It appears that such extension is not subject to the requirement that a visit should not exceed six months.
3 Ibid, para 106.

308. Change of category. Generally a visitor may not change category. It is possible to do so in order to become a young Commonwealth citizen working holidaymaker[1], a student (including a doctor or a dentist on post-graduate training)[2], a trainee work-permit holder[3], an au pair[4], or a spouse[5], provided that the relevant conditions are fulfilled.

1 See the Statement of Changes in Immigration Rules (HC Paper (1989–90) no. 251) (the Immigration Rules), para 107, and para 263 above.
2 See ibid, para 109, 115, and paras 299, 300, above.
3 See ibid, para 120, and para 241 above.
4 See ibid, para 121, and para 312 below.
5 See ibid, para 131, and para 278 above.

309. Dependants. The Immigration Rules refer to dependants of visitors but give no definition[1]. Such dependants are clearly to some extent visitors in any case. Family groups can normally be expected to be treated all in the same way, but, where an intention to overstay is presumed or medical treatment is sought by one member only, differential treatment can apply.

1 Statement of Changes in Immigration Rules (HC Paper (1989–90) no. 251) (the Immigration Rules), paras 25, 105.

(E) AU PAIRS

310. Introduction. Au pairs may be admitted for up to two years with a prohibition upon employment, if coming within the definition in the Immigration Rules[1].

1 Statement of Changes in Immigration Rules (HC Paper (1989–90) no. 251) (the Immigration Rules), para 33.

311. What is an au pair. An au pair is an unmarried girl between seventeen and twenty-seven years inclusive, without dependants, who is a national of a specified country[1] who has come under an arrangement to learn English and to live as a member of an English-speaking family[2]. Full-time domestic employment is excluded[3].

No definition of 'arrangement' is given, nor any required characteristics such as 'pocket-money'[4].

1 Ie who is a national of any member state of the European Community, Andorra, Austria, Cyprus, The Faeroes, Finland, Greenland, Iceland, Liechtenstein, Malta, Monaco, Norway, San Marino, Sweden, Switzerland, Turkey or Yugoslavia: Statement of Changes in Immigration Rules (HC Paper (1989–90) no. 251) (the Immigration Rules), para 33.

2 Ibid, para 33. The age and nationality conditions function to exclude Filipino maids and other covert domestic employment: *Macdonald's Immigration Law and Practice* (3rd edn, 1991, eds I A Macdonald and N J Blake) p 202.

3 Immigration Rules, para 33.

4 *Macdonald* pp 201, 211, especially notes 11–13, compares this silence with the reference made to such issues in 'Au Pair in Britain' (1973, Central Office of Information) (which inter alia declares the relationship to accept social equality and suggests a level of 'pocket money'), in the Conduct of Employment Agencies and Employment Business Regulations 1976, SI 1976/715, and in the Employment Agencies Act 1973 (Charging Fees to Au Pairs) Regulations 1981, SI 1981/1481.

312. Extension of leave. An au pair may have leave extended for an aggregate of two years if the au pair arrangement is satisfactory[1].

1 See the Statement of Changes in Immigration Rules (HC Paper (1989–90) no. 251) (the Immigration Rules), paras 33, 121.

313. Change of category. An au pair could seek to change category to student or, presumably, visitor, but not otherwise except by marriage[1].

1 See the Statement of Changes in Immigration Rules (HC Paper (1989–90) no. 251) (the Immigration Rules), paras 109, 131, and para 278 above.

(e) Refugees and Political Asylees

(A) INTERNATIONAL LAW

314. What is a refugee. 'Refugee' is defined by the Convention Relating to the Status of Refugees, as complemented by the Protocol on the Status of Refugees, as a person who, owing to a well-founded fear of persecution on the grounds of race, religion, nationality, membership of a social group, or political opinions, is outside his country and is unable or unwilling to take its protection or to return to it[1]. Under the Convention, signatories agree not to return refugees to their countries of nationality or to other countries where they might also be persecuted ('non-refoulement') and to facilitate their settlement, to provide a travel document and to give other rights[2]. A refugee is given no right, as such, to enter any country.

Determination of who is a refugee may not be straightforward, and a stateless person is not necessarily a refugee. Refugee status may be lost[3].

1 See the Convention relating to the Status of Refugees (Geneva, 28 July 1951; TS 39 (1954); Cmd 9171), art 1, and the Protocol relating to the Status of Refugees (New York, 31 January 1967; TS 15 (1969); Cmnd 3906). See also the European Agreement on Transfer of Responsibility for Refugees (Strasbourg, 16 October 1980; TS 50 (1987); Cm 222), which was discussed in *Rahman v Secretary of State for the Home Department* [1989] Imm AR 325, IAT. The term 'refugee' is also used in other international conventions. I am grateful to Mr A Fortin of the Office of the United Nations High Commissioner for Refugees for information and opinions on the law relating to refugees. However, he bears no responsibility for what is written in this part of the title.

2 Convention relating to the Status of Refugees, arts 26, 28, 31–33 *et passim*.

3 Ibid, art 1(c). See also L Grant and I Martin *Immigration Law and Practice* (1982) paras 15.5, 15.23, and *Macdonald's Immigration Law and Practice* (3rd edn, 1991, eds I A Macdonald and N J Blake) pp 287 ff.

315. What is an asylee. 'Asylee' (or 'political' or 'diplomatic asylee') has no general definition. States may always give asylum to those who are not refugees

within the Refugee Convention definition[1], and may in practice deny asylum to
those who are refugees. The categories 'asylee' and 'refugee' thus appear to be
overlapping but not coincident.

1 Ie under the Convention relating to the Status of Refugees (Geneva, 28 July 1951; TS 39 (1954);
   Cmd 9171) and Protocol relating to the Status of Refugees (New York, 31 January 1967; TS 15
   (1969); Cmnd 3906): see para 314 above.

(B) UNITED KINGDOM LAW

316. The immigration legislation. The Immigration Acts 1971 (c 77) and
1988 (c 14) make no reference to asylum or to refugees. Nor does the Immigration (Carriers' Liability) Act 1987 (c 24), although it has considerable effect
upon them.

Other related legislation does refer to them[1], as do the Immigration Rules,
which state more than once that full account is to be taken of the Convention and
Protocol relating to the Status of Refugees[2] and that nothing in the rules is to be
construed as requiring action contrary to it[3]. Also several paragraphs refer to
asylum and refugees, without defining either term, and indeed effectively
regarding them as referring to identical situations[4].

The Convention and Protocol are referred to in recent cases, and have been
used as an interpretive device[5]. How far United Kingdom legislation and
practice fulfil the requirements of them is a matter for discussion. A *Handbook on
Procedures and Criteria for Determining Refugee Status* produced by the United
Nations High Commissioner for Refugees is not referred to in the rules, but has
been referred to as an interpretive device by the Immigration Appeal Tribunal[6].

The United Kingdom has had a practice of treating all those granted asylum as
if refugees under the Convention, and they are all therefore referred to below as
refugees. However, the problem for the potential refugee lies in establishing
that he is one, and recent decisions have been robust. Moreover, the House of
Lords has held that, subject only to the principles in the *Wednesbury* case, it is for
the Home Secretary to decide who is a refugee, not the courts[7].

An Asylum Bill was introduced in the House of Commons in November
1991 to amend the law in relation to the seeking of asylum.

1 Cf the Extradition Act 1870 (c 52), s 3(1), the Fugitive Offenders Act 1967 (c 68), s 4(1), (both
   repealed) and the Backing of Warrants (Republic of Ireland) Act 1965 (c 45), s 2(2), and
   paras 506 ff below. See also the Immigration (Restricted Right of Appeal against Deportation)
   (Exemption) (No 2) Order 1988, SI 1988/1203, arts 2(a), 3(b), and para 322 below.
2 Ie the Convention relating to the Status of Refugees (Geneva, 28 July 1951; TS 39 (1954); Cmd
   9171) and Protocol relating to the Status of Refugees (New York, 31 January 1967; TS 15 (1969);
   Cmnd 3906).
3 See the Statement of Changes in Immigration Rules (HC Paper (1989–90) no. 251) (the Immigration Rules), paras 21, 98, 161 (refugees) and paras 75, 173 (asylum). However, the House of
   Lords held that the discretion of the Secretary of State is not thereby limited in the absence of
   evidence that he has ignored the terms of the Convention (see note 2 above) (*Bugdaycay v
   Secretary of State for the Home Department, Nelidow Santis v Secretary of State for the Home
   Department, Norman v Secretary of State for the Home Department, Re Musisi* [1987] AC 514, [1987] 1
   All ER 940, [1987] Imm AR 250, HL), and determination of refugee status by him is only
   challengeable on the principles enunciated in *Associated Provincial Picture Houses Ltd v Wednesbury
   Corpn* [1948] 1 KB 223, [1947] 2 All ER 680, CA.
4 See the Immigration Rules, paras 21, 98, 161 (refugees) and paras 75, 140, 173 (asylum).
5 See eg *Bugdaycay v Secretary of State for the Home Department, Nelidow Santis v Secretary of State for
   the Home Department, Norman v Secretary of State for the Home Department, Re Musisi* [1987] AC
   514, [1987] 1 All ER 940, [1987] Imm AR 250, HL; *R v Secretary of State for the Home Department,
   ex parte Sivakumaran, R v Secretary of State for the Home Department, ex parte Vaithialingam, R v
   Secretary of State for the Home Department, ex parte Vilvarajah, R v Secretary of State for the Home*

Department, ex parte Vathanan, R v Secretary of State for the Home Department, ex parte Navaratham [1988] AC 958, [1988] 1 All ER 193, [1988] Imm AR 147, HL.

6 *Tekle v Visa Officer, Prague* [1986] Imm AR 71, IAT; *R v Secretary of State for the Home Department, ex parte Gurmeet Singh* [1987] Imm AR 489, DC; *R v Secretary of State for the Home Department, ex parte Alaa Mohamed el Sayed Hasem* [1987] Imm AR 577.

7 *Bugdaycay v Secretary of State for the Home Department, Nelidow Santis v Secretary of State for the Home Department, Norman v Secretary of State for the Home Department, Re Musisi* [1987] AC 514, [1987] 1 All ER 940, [1987] Imm AR 250, HL (distinguishing *R v Secretary of State for the Home Department, ex parte Khera, R v Secretary of State for the Home Department, ex parte Khaweja* [1984] AC 74, [1983] 1 All ER 765, [1982] Imm AR 139, HL).

317. Application of control before entry. United Kingdom immigration law stresses control before entry. This poses particular problems for potential refugees. Thus for example, the fact that under the Refugee Convention[1], a person must be outside his country of nationality to be regarded as a refugee was held to justify refusal of a request for asylum made to a British Embassy by a person still in his country of nationality[2]. Indeed, since the Immigration Rules do not explicitly envisage refugees as a specific category of entrant, it has been held that entry clearance officers do not have the power to grant visas to refugees[3]. In other words, a potential refugee must arrive in the United Kingdom by some other means and seek refugee status on arrival.

This raises the question of how a visa national may ever seek asylum. The answer appears to be that the Immigration Rules require full account to be taken of the Refugee Convention, and they are not to be construed as requiring action contrary to it[4], and specifically require grounds for refusal to be set aside in a refugee case[5]. Potential refugees and other asylees are therefore in practice likely to arrive without entry clearance. There may be a related propensity for them to adopt various tactics, even if they are genuine potential refugees, such as seeking forged documents, seeking entry in a category such as visitor or student, or seeking entry to one country which is not a safe refuge but is easy to enter, with a view to entering another, safer, refuge thereafter.

In respect of the first of these tactics, the effect of the Immigration (Carriers' Liability) Act 1987 is important. This Act makes it an offence for the owners or agents of a ship or aircraft to permit a person requiring leave to enter to fail on arrival to produce to an immigration officer, on request, a valid passport with photograph or other document satisfactorily establishing identity, and, in the case of a visa national, a valid visa[6]. The result is that a potential refugee may never reach the United Kingdom, as he will not be permitted to board the ship or aircraft in the first place[7]. The Act therefore constitutes a form of control before entry. The other two tactics may raise problems of control on entry.

1 Ie the Convention relating to the Status of Refugees (Geneva, 28 July 1951; TS 39 (1954); Cmd 9171) and Protocol relating to the Status of Refugees (New York, 31 January 1967; TS 15 (1969); Cmnd 3906).

2 *Secretary of State for the Home Department v 'X' (a Chilean citizen)* [1978] Imm AR 73, IAT.

3 *Tekle v Visa Officer, Prague* [1986] Imm AR 71, IAT. See also *Bugdaycay v Secretary of State for the Home Department, Nelidow Santis v Secretary of State for the Home Department, Norman v Secretary of State for the Home Department, Re Musisi* [1987] AC 514, [1987] 1 All ER 940, [1987] Imm AR 250, HL; *Rahman v Secretary of State for the Home Department* [1989] Imm AR 325, IAT.

4 Statement of Changes in Immigration Rules (HC Paper (1989–90) no. 251) (the Immigration Rules), para 21. However, note the difficulties raised by *R v Secretary of State for the Home Department, ex parte Gurmeet Singh* [1987] Imm AR 489, DC.

5 Immigration Rules, para 75.

6 Immigration (Carriers' Liability) Act 1987 (c 24), s 1(1) (amended by the Immigration (Carriers' Liability Prescribed Sum) Order 1991, SI 1991/1497). There is a defence in respect of documents held on embarkation but destroyed en route: s 1(2). A document is to be regarded as being what it purports to be unless its falsity is reasonably apparent: s 1(4).

7 The only point at which the carrier is likely to have the opportunity to examine the documents is at check-in at the airport, or equivalent at a seaport. This gives untrained airline and shipping

employees the obligation of judging the adequacy of the documents produced, with the knowledge that a mistake could result in a fine.

318. Application of control on entry to refugees seeking entry in that capacity. Under the Immigration Rules, special considerations are said to arise where a person seeking entry 'claims asylum' or where it appears to an immigration officer that he might be 'eligible for asylum'[1]. 'Asylum' is not defined. Such a case is to be referred to the Home Office regardless of any grounds which might appear to justify refusal of leave to enter (such as lack of entry clearance or forged documents)[1]. This does not constitute temporary leave to enter, although temporary admission is possible[2]. Under the general provision in the rules leave is not to be refused if to do so would breach the provisions of the Refugee Convention[3]. In particular, using the words of the Refugee Convention on 'non-refoulement', the Immigration Rules stipulate that asylum is not to be refused if the only country to which the person could be removed is one to which he is unwilling to go owing to a well-founded fear of being persecuted for reasons of race, religion, nationality, membership of a particular social group or political opinion[4].

The words used have been interpreted by the courts. The House of Lords decided that to show a 'well-founded fear' a person had to show that there were objective grounds (whether or not actually known to the applicant) for saying that there was a reasonable likelihood that he would be persecuted on the grounds mentioned in the Refugee Convention if he returned[5]. The Divisional Court of the Queen's Bench Division considered 'persecution' to bear its ordinary meaning of 'subjection to injurious action and oppression'[6]. 'Particular social group' has been held broad enough to encompass the Ghanaian Military Intelligence[7].

The protection afforded by the 'non-refoulement' provision is in any case not as great as may appear, for a refugee can be removed to a non-persecuting country[8], even without reference to the Home Office[9]. Thus an actual refugee who has arrived by way of another country may be subject to removal to that country, and this would not necessarily constitute acting contrary to United Kingdom obligations under the Refugee Convention.

If the Home Office decides to 'grant asylum', the person will be given leave to enter[10]. Normally twelve months' leave to enter, with no restriction on employment, will be given, succeeded by an extension of three years, with the requirement to register with the police removed, succeeded in turn by indefinite leave, although no extension is automatic[11].

If the Home Office decides not to 'grant asylum', the person will be examined to discover if he may be granted leave to enter under another provision[12]. If refused, a person should be given reasons[13]. On occasion 'exceptional leave to remain' is granted. This is leave 'outside the Rules', and may be given for a twelve-month, renewable, period[14]. If the Home Office decides not to 'grant asylum', and does not grant leave in any other category, nor 'exceptional leave to remain', the person will be removed, normally to the country from which he has come[15].

It has been argued that, in recent years, the immigration authorities have decided to remove applicants for asylum with excessive haste. This appears to have occurred, for instance, in the 'Tamil refugees' case[16]. Asylum applications at the port of entry are normally referred to the United Kingdom Immigrants Advisory Service if the applicant is not otherwise represented, although the Home Office reserves the right not to refer them.

1 Statement of Changes in Immigration Rules (HC Paper (1989–90) no. 251) (the Immigration Rules), para 75.

2 *Bugdaycay v Secretary of State for the Home Department, Nelidow Santis v Secretary of State for the Home Department, Norman v Secretary of State for the Home Department, Re Musisi* [1987] AC 514, [1987] 1 All ER 940, [1987] Imm AR 250, [1987] Imm AR 250, HL; *R v Secretary of State for the Home Department, ex parte Gurmeet Singh* [1987] Imm AR 489, DC.

3 Immigration Rules, para 21. As to the Refugee Convention, see para 314, note 1, above. For an account of the procedure adopted, see *Secretary of State for the Home Department v Thirukumar* [1989] Imm AR 402, CA.

4 Immigration Rules, para 75.

5 *R v Secretary of State for the Home Department, ex parte Sivakumaran, R v Secretary of State for the Home Department, ex parte Vaithialingam, R v Secretary of State for the Home Department, ex parte Vilvarajah, R v Secretary of State for the Home Department, ex parte Vathanan, R v Secretary of State for the Home Department, ex parte Navaratham* [1988] AC 958, [1988] 1 All ER 193, [1988] Imm AR 147, HL (the 'Tamil refugees' case: see note 16 below, and *Secretary of State for the Home Department v Thirukumar* [1989] Imm AR 402, CA, which refers to a 'political asylum questionnaire'). See further references to the unreported Queen's Bench decision of *Ex parte Juiakumaran* (unreported) cited in *R v Secretary of State for the Home Department, ex parte Gurmeet Singh* [1987] Imm AR 489, DC.

6 *R v Immigration Appeal Tribunal, ex parte Jonah* [1985] Imm AR 7, IAT. See also references to the unreported Queen's Bench decision of *Ex parte Juiakumaran* cited in *R v Secretary of State for the Home Department, ex parte Gurmeet Singh* [1987] Imm AR 489, DC.

7 *Secretary of State for the Home Department v Otchere* [1988] Imm AR 21, IAT.

8 *Secretary of State for the Home Department v Two Citizens of Chile* [1977] Imm AR 36, IAT; *Bugdaycay v Secretary of State for the Home Department, Nelidow Santis v Secretary of State for the Home Department, Norman v Secretary of State for the Home Department, Re Musisi* [1987] AC 514, [1987] 1 All ER 940, [1987] Imm AR 250, HL; *R v Secretary of State for the Home Department, ex parte Gurmeet Singh* [1987] Imm AR 489, DC. See also *R v Immigration Appeal Tribunal, ex parte Miller* [1988] Imm AR 1, DC.

9 *R v Secretary of State for the Home Department, ex parte Gurmeet Singh* [1987] Imm AR 489, DC.

10 Immigration Rules, para 75.

11 L Grant and I Martin *Immigration Law and Practice* (1982) para 15.15; *Macdonald's Immigration Law and Practice* (3rd edn, 1991, eds I A Macdonald and N J Blake) p 312. The Immigration Rules are unspecific on this point.

12 Immigration Rules, para 75.

13 *R v Secretary of State for the Home Department, ex parte Gurmeet Singh* [1987] Imm AR 489, DC. An example is found in *NSH v Secretary of State for the Home Department* [1988] Imm AR 389, CA.

14 *Grant and Martin* paras 15.17, 15.18. This is apparently increasingly used.

15 Immigration Rules, para 75.

16 See note 5 above, and eg N Blake 'The Road to Sivakumaran' [1988] INLP 12, and 'Life after the Lords; developments in the case of Sivakumaran and others' [1990] INLP 7. The Tamils were vindicated. For other Tamil refugee cases, see *Secretary of State for the Home Department v Thirukumar* [1989] Imm AR 402, CA, and *R v Immigration Appeal Tribunal, ex parte Secretary of State for the Home Department* [1990] 3 All ER 652, [1990] 1 WLR 1126, CA.

319. Application of control on entry to refugees not seeking entry in that capacity.

A potential refugee may seek leave to enter in a different category, such as visitor or student (in which the usual requirements as to entry clearance apply)[1]. This may be either because he considers an attempt to seek leave to enter as an asylee too risky[2], or because, having been admitted in a different category, he later decides to seek asylum because of a change of circumstances in his country.

If leave to enter is refused for the category requested, and asylum then sought, essentially the same procedure is laid down as for persons seeking entry as refugees, and the person will not be removed while the Home Office considers the case[3].

If leave to enter is in fact granted for a category other than refugee, then the question of asylum may only arise when the limited leave granted expires, and leave to remain is sought. However, a person who obtained entry in one category, although in reality seeking refugee status, might risk refusal or removal later, for example when seeking variation of leave to remain, on the ground that he did not present himself to the authorities without delay requesting asylum[4] or that he obtained entry by deception[5], respectively.

1 *R v Secretary of State for the Home Department, ex parte Gurmeet Singh* [1987] Imm AR 489, DC. See also *R v Secretary of State for the Home Department, ex parte Alaa Mohamed el Sayed Hasem* [1987] Imm AR 577.

2 See eg *R v Secretary of State for the Home Department, ex parte Alaa Mohamed el Sayed Hasem* [1987] Imm AR 577.

3 See the Statement of Changes in Immigration Rules (HC Paper (1989–90) no. 251) (the Immigration Rules), para 75; *R v Immigration Appeal Tribunal, ex parte Secretary of State for the Home Department* [1990] 3 All ER 652, [1990] 1 WLR 1126, CA; and para 318 above. How far this is effective may be doubtful: see eg *Bugdaycay v Secretary of State for the Home Department, Nelidow Santis v Secretary of State for the Home Department, Norman v Secretary of State for the Home Department, Re Musisi* [1987] AC 514, [1987] 1 All ER 940, [1987] Imm AR 250, HL.

4 *R v Secretary of State for the Home Department, ex parte Alaa Mohamed el Sayed Hasem* [1987] Imm AR 577.

5 See paras 320, 321, below. See also *Bugdaycay v Secretary of State for the Home Department, Nelidow Santis v Secretary of State for the Home Department, Norman v Secretary of State for the Home Department, Re Musisi* [1987] AC 514, [1987] 1 All ER 940, [1987] Imm AR 250, HL.

320. Application of control after entry. For reasons already mentioned, commonly it is after entry, and possibly several years after entry, that a person admitted in another category seeks asylum[1]. It may clearly be difficult for a person who dislikes the regime in his own country to apply for asylum. Such an action may risk courting unpopularity at home for himself and any family, and might be regarded in the United Kingdom as seeking 'back-door' settlement, precipitating non-renewal of leave to remain in the category in which leave to enter was granted.

According to the Immigration Rules, a person may seek asylum in the United Kingdom on the ground of a well-founded fear of persecution, in other words, as a Convention refugee[2]. In such a case, the claim 'is to be carefully considered in the light of all relevant circumstances'[3]. However, a major problem is that, as already noted, a person who desired refugee status, but who obtained leave to enter in another category and who seeks asylum later, may be refused on the ground of failing to seek asylum timeously[4] or considered thereby to have obtained that leave by false representations, the concealment of material facts or other deception[5]. There is no explicit mention of an application on other grounds, that is as an asylee other than a Convention refugee.

In any case, such an applicant may be extremely nervous of revealing his identity, or that he is seeking asylum. It has been suggested that it is very important that the application be in writing, supported by documentary evidence (or the lack of it explained), and that assistance is sought from the British section of Amnesty International, the British Refugee Council, the Joint Council for the Welfare of Immigrants, the United Kingdom Immigrants Advisory Service (Refugee Unit), or the London office of the United Nations High Commissioner for Refugees[6].

An interview will normally be required by the Home Office, and it has been suggested that it is preferable that this be done at the Immigration and Nationality Department offices rather than locally, and that the applicant be accompanied[6]. While a claim is being dealt with, the applicant remains subject to his original leave, extended if necessary in the usual fashion for applicants for variation of leave[7].

If accepted as a refugee, the same leave will be given, *mutatis mutandis*, as to an applicant accepted on arrival. If not accepted as a refugee, a person may nevertheless be granted 'exceptional leave to remain'[8].

1 See para 319 above.

2 Ie under the Convention relating to the Status of Refugees (Geneva, 28 July 1951; TS 39 (1954); Cmd 9171) and Protocol relating to the Status of Refugees (New York, 31 January 1967; TS 15 (1969); Cmnd 3906).

3 Statement of Changes in Immigration Rules (HC Paper (1989–90) no. 251) (the Immigration Rules), para 140. It is for the immigration officer or Home Secretary to decide what is a refugee: *Bugdaycay v Secretary of State for the Home Department, Nelidow Santis v Secretary of State for the Home Department, Norman v Secretary of State for the Home Department, Re Musisi* [1987] AC 514, [1987] 1 All ER 940, [1987] Imm AR 250, HL. See also eg *R v Secretary of State for the Home Department, ex parte Alaa Mohamed el Sayed Hasem* [1987] Imm AR 577; *Mendis v Immigration Appeal Tribunal and Secretary of State for the Home Department* [1989] Imm AR 6, CA; and *Gaima v Secretary of State for the Home Department* [1989] Imm AR 205, CA. The 'relevant circumstances' need not all relate to refugee status: *R v Immigration Appeal Tribunal, ex parte Miller* [1988] Imm AR 1, DC.

4 See *R v Secretary of State for the Home Department, ex parte Alaa Mohamed el Sayed Hasem* [1987] Imm AR 577, and para 319 above.

5 See *Bugdaycay v Secretary of State for the Home Department, Nelidow Santis v Secretary of State for the Home Department, Norman v Secretary of State for the Home Department, Re Musisi* [1987] AC 514, [1987] 1 All ER 940, [1987] Imm AR 250, HL, and para 319 above. A further difficulty is shown by *R v Secretary of State for the Home Department, ex parte Gurmeet Singh* [1987] Imm AR 489, DC.

6 L Grant and I Martin *Immigration Law and Practice* (1982), and First Supplement (1985) paras 15.8–15.12. Specialist assistance is essential.

7 See para 178 above. See also *Bugdaycay v Secretary of State for the Home Department, Nelidow Santis v Secretary of State for the Home Department, Norman v Secretary of State for the Home Department, Re Musisi* [1987] AC 514, [1987] 1 All ER 940, [1987] Imm AR 250, HL.

8 L Grant and I Martin *Immigration Law and Practice* (1982) paras 15.17, 15.18. This is apparently increasingly used.

321. Application of control of departure. No specific mention is made in the Immigration Rules of the administrative removal of refugees. This issue is of some moment:

(1) because of the limited possibility of appeal against removal;

(2) because a person refused entry as a refugee will normally be removed to the country he claims to be fleeing;

(3) because of the likelihood of those seeking asylum doing so only after obtaining leave to enter in another category, with the risk of this being regarded as a false representation, the concealment of material facts or other deception[1]; and

(4) because the decision as to who is a refugee is for the immigration service on behalf of the Home Secretary[2].

In relation to deportation, it is reiterated in the Immigration Rules that full account is to be taken of the Refugee Convention and that nothing in the rules is to be construed as requiring action contrary to it[3]. It is also specifically provided that a refugee will not be deported if he can be deported only to the persecuting country[4].

1 *Bugdaycay v Secretary of State for the Home Department, Nelidow Santis v Secretary of State for the Home Department, Norman v Secretary of State for the Home Department, Re Musisi* [1987] AC 514, [1987] 1 All ER 940, [1987] Imm AR 250, HL; *R v Secretary of State for the Home Department, ex parte Gurmeet Singh* [1987] Imm AR 489, DC.

2 *Bugdaycay v Secretary of State for the Home Department, Nelidow Santis v Secretary of State for the Home Department, Norman v Secretary of State for the Home Department, Re Musisi* [1987] AC 514, [1987] 1 All ER 940, [1987] Imm AR 250, HL.

3 Statement of Changes in Immigration Rules (HC Paper (1989–90) no. 251) (the Immigration Rules), para 161. As to the Refugee Convention, see para 314, note 1, above.

4 Immigration Rules, para 173.

322. Application of appeal and related processes. There is no appeal against refusal of refugee status as such, only the usual power to appeal against refusal of leave to enter, against refusal to vary leave to enter or remain, or against deportation (subject to an exception), and the limited appeal against removal[1]. The restrictions upon the right of appeal against deportation contained in the Immigration Act 1988[2] are, however, partly mitigated in the case of refugees. They may appeal on the grounds either that, on the facts of the case, there is in law no power to make a deportation order on the ground stated in the notice of deportation, or that deportation would be contrary to United Kingdom obligations under the Refugee Convention[3].

Judicial review of the decision to remove or deport is available[4].

There is no mention of removal or deportation of those given 'exceptional leave to remain'.

1 See paras 333, 336, 344, below, and *Bugdaycay v Secretary of State for the Home Department, Nelidow Santis v Secretary of State for the Home Department, Norman v Secretary of State for the Home Department, Re Musisi* [1987] AC 514, [1987] 1 All ER 940, [1987] Imm AR 250, HL. See also *R v Immigration Appeal Tribunal, ex parte Muruganandarajah* [1986] Imm AR 382, CA. Reference to the Home Office in the Statement of Changes in Immigration Rules (HC Paper (1989–90) no. 251) (the Immigration Rules), para 75, is not temporary leave to enter, so refusal is not appealable.

2 Ie under the Immigration Act 1988 (c 14), s 5 (brought into force on 1 August 1988: see the Immigration Act 1988 (Commencement No 1) Order 1988, SI 1988/1133, art 2, Schedule).

3 See the Immigration (Restricted Right of Appeal against Deportation) (Exemption) (No 2) Order 1988, SI 1988/1203, arts 1, 2(a), 3(a), (b) (as from 1 August 1988). As to the Refugee Convention, see para 314, note 1, above.

4 *Bugdaycay v Secretary of State for the Home Department, Nelidow Santis v Secretary of State for the Home Department, Norman v Secretary of State for the Home Department, Re Musisi* [1987] AC 514, [1987] 1 All ER 940, [1987] Imm AR 250, HL; *R v Secretary of State for the Home Department, ex parte Sivakumaran, R v Secretary of State for the Home Department, ex parte Vaithialingam, R v Secretary of State for the Home Department, ex parte Vilvarajah, R v Secretary of State for the Home Department, ex parte Vathanan, R v Secretary of State for the Home Department, ex parte Navaratham* [1988] AC 958, [1988] 1 All ER 193, [1988] Imm AR 147, HL.

323. Travel documents. A person accepted as a refugee will be given, on application, a Convention[1] travel document valid for all countries except that of the refugee's origin, valid for the period of his leave to remain in the United Kingdom or, if he has indefinite leave, for up to five years. The refugee's national passport will not be stamped with the leave to remain (which is stamped upon the Home Office letter intimating acceptance as a refugee), and should not be used[2].

A person not accepted as a refugee but given 'exceptional leave to remain' may be given a certificate of identity stamped with the leave to remain if he is unable to renew his passport. He may otherwise continue to use his passport[3].

Because of the rule on 'restricted returnability' a stateless person will normally be given leave to enter only if accepted by another state as stateless and issued with a travel document by it. The Home Office does, on occasion, issue travel documents to stateless persons[4].

1 Ie the Convention relating to the Status of Refugees (Geneva, 28 July 1951; TS 39 (1954); Cmd 9171).

2 L Grant and I Martin *Immigration Law and Practice* (1982) para 15.20.

3 *Grant and Martin* para 15.21.

4 *Grant and Martin* para 15.24.

(f) United Kingdom Passport Holders

324. What is a United Kingdom passport holder. In so far as any British citizen may hold a United Kingdom passport, the title 'United Kingdom passport holder' is misleading. However, it was adopted to describe those citizens of the United Kingdom and Colonies[1] who held passports issued by the United Kingdom government (as opposed to those issued by colonial governments, or by British consulates abroad), but whose right of entry to the United Kingdom was removed by the Commonwealth Immigrants Act 1968[2]. In practice, the most important group of such people were the 'East African Asians', that is, those of Asian descent, expelled from, or pressed to leave, the East African countries after independence, and who in general held no other citizenship. They were thus deprived of any right of entry to any country in the world[3]. They are now British Overseas citizens (although some British subjects and British Protected persons may be treated for this purpose as if British Overseas citizens[4]). The 'special voucher' scheme was created as a limited alleviation of their condition[5]. Many are now in the Indian sub-continent, having been admitted on a temporary basis by the relevant governments on humanitarian grounds (there being no legal obligation), because of the length of wait to obtain a special voucher, or because of ineligibility for one[6].

1 Ie the then existing nationality category relating specifically to the United Kingdom, trifurcated by the British Nationality Act 1981 (c 61) (amended by the British Nationality (Falkland Islands) Act 1983 (c 6)) into British citizen, British Dependent Territories citizen and British Overseas citizen: see para 107 above, and NATIONALITY AND CITIZENSHIP, vol 14, paras 1906 ff.
2 Under the first measure of immigration control over British subjects/Commonwealth citizens (ie the Commonwealth Immigrants Act 1962 (c 21) (repealed)), United Kingdom passport holders were one of the classes remaining free from control: see para 107 above.
3 See paras 107, 112, 153, 159, above and the references cited therein.
4 L Grant and I Martin *Immigration Law and Practice* (1982) para 3.9. For the meaning of 'British Overseas citizen', British subject (ie 'without citizenship') and British Protected person, see para 107 above, and vol 14, paras 1942, 1950, 1954.
5 See paras 107, 112, 158, 159, above and the references cited therein.
6 See the First Report from the Select Committee on Race Relations and Immigration (HC Paper (1977–78) no. 303-I) (Immigration) paras 118–123; Second Report from the Home Affairs Committee (HC Paper (1980–81) no. 158) (Numbers and Legal Status of Future British Overseas Citizens without other Citizenship) paras 11, 13, and pp 6 *et passim*; Fifth Report from the Home Affairs Committee (HC Paper (1981–82) no. 90-I) (Immigration from the Indian Sub-Continent) paras 68–76, and the government's reply (Cmnd 8725) (1982) pp 12–17; and the Second Report from the Home Affairs Committee (HC Papers (1985–86) no. 67) (Immigration from the Indian Sub-Continent) paras 65–68. See also Home Office annual 'Report on the Work of the Immigration and Nationality Department' (1984 to date).

325. Eligibility for entry for settlement. The Immigration Rules stipulate that a British Overseas citizen is to be admitted for settlement if he presents a special voucher, or entry clearance, but not otherwise[1]. They do not describe the conditions of eligibility for a special voucher, nor the principles of distribution (except that they are to be sought from a British government representative overseas), and these conditions and principles are not, as such, published at all[2]. They have nevertheless been elicited or inferred and are described above[3]. There is no appeal against refusal of a special voucher[4].

1 Statement of Changes in Immigration Rules (HC Paper (1989–90) no. 251) (the Immigration Rules), para 49.
2 See para 112 above. A special voucher is not an entry clearance: *Re Amin* [1983] 2 AC 818, [1983] 2 All ER 864, HL.
3 See para 159 above and the references cited therein.
4 It is an exercise of the royal prerogative (*R v Secretary of State for the Home Department, ex parte Bhatti* (1982) 132 NLJ 743, CA), and it is not an entry clearance (*Re Amin* [1983] 2 AC 818, [1983] 2 All ER 864, HL). See also paras 158, 159, above, and para 344 below.

326. Eligibility for settlement of dependants. The Immigration Rules stipulate that the dependants (presumably irrespective of nationality) of special-voucher holders are to be admitted, provided they have entry clearance[1], adequate accommodation which the special-voucher holder owns or occupies without recourse to public funds, and that the special-voucher holder is able and willing to support them without recourse of public funds[2]. This excludes reliance, inter alia, upon housing as a homeless person, income support, family credit and housing benefit[3].

What constitutes a dependant is, from the context of the Immigration Rules, the same as for 'family reunion' cases[4]. However, unmarried, unemployed children up to twenty-five years of age have been admitted, and 'sympathetic consideration' is given in other cases[5].

1 See paras 150–152 above. A special voucher is not an entry clearance: see *Re Amin*[1983] 2 AC 818, [1983] 2 All ER 864, HL.
2 See the Statement of Changes in Immigration Rules (HC Paper (1989–90) no. 251) (the Immigration Rules), paras 49, 52.
3 See ibid, para 1, and para 160, note 1, above.
4 See paras 161 ff above.
5 L Grant and I Martin *Immigration Law and Practice* (1982), First Supplement (1985) para 3.12.

327. Entry for other purposes. Nothing prevents a United Kingdom passport holder, or the dependant of one, from entering for a purpose other than settlement, such as visitor, if the relevant conditions are fulfilled[1]. However, such a person is likely to be scrutinised thoroughly and might be refused entry on the ground that settlement was in fact intended.

1 L Grant and I Martin *Immigration Law and Practice* (1982) para 3.12.

328. Change of category and extensions for United Kingdom passport holders and their dependants who have entered for purposes other than settlement. Nothing prevents a United Kingdom passport holder or dependant, entering for purposes other than settlement, from changing categories or obtaining extensions under the same conditions as others, and these persons could be accepted for settlement after four years, although this is not automatic[1].

1 L Grant and I Martin *Immigration Law and Practice* (1982) para 3.12.

(9) APPEALS AND RELATED PROCESSES

(a) Introduction

329. Origin and criticisms. Appeal available under the early legislation was not continued[1]. The present system was introduced as a result of the statutory limitation upon the common law right of British subjects to enter (as opposed to the aliens' 'privilege')[2]. Nevertheless the system applies equally to Commonwealth citizens and aliens. It has been criticised on several grounds, including:
(1) its lack of structural independence from the Home Office[3];
(2) alleged frequent unacceptable features of Home Office presentation of its case;
(3) alleged high propensity of adjudicators to accept too readily Home Office assertions and to fail to correct abuses;
(4) the requirement in a high proportion of cases that they be pursued from abroad; and
(5) the narrowness of appeals against use of the 'conducive' ground for deportation[4].
The success rate of appeals by applicants is not high[5].

A variation of leave or a requirement to depart which is appealed takes no effect until the appeal is disposed of[6].

Apart from the appeal procedure, members of Parliament may be willing to make representations to the Home Secretary on individual cases[7].

1 See para 106 above. See also J M Evans *Immigration Law* (2nd edn, 1983) pp 327–329.
2 *Report of the Committee on Immigration Appeals* (the Wilson Report) (Cmnd 3387) (1967). As a result of discussion following the 'Review of Appeals under the Immigration Act 1971: A Discussion Document' (1981, Home Office), various changes were made in the system.
3 This has largely been rectified by the transfer of the power of appointment etc from the Secretary of State to the Lord Chancellor with effect from 1 April 1987: see the Transfer of Functions (Immigration Appeals) Order 1987, SI 1987/465. However, in *R v Secretary of State for the Home Department, ex parte Kuku* [1989] Imm AR 38 at 41, Macpherson J, felt able to say that where there was a conflict of evidence 'I am bound . . . to resolve that conflict in favour of the immigration authorities'.
4 See eg *Immigration Control Procedures: Report of a Formal Investigation* (1985, Commission for Racial Equality) ch 10 (which at para 10.21.3 asserts that 'the system gives every appearance of being biased against applicants'); *Evans* pp 326–374; *Macdonald's Immigration Law and Practice* (3rd edn, 1991, eds I A Macdonald and N J Blake) pp 431, 432; *Pivot of the System* (1981, Runnymede Trust).
5 *Immigration Control Procedures: Report of a Formal Investigation* (1985, Commission for Racial Equality) Tables 10.1–10.7, and paras 10.7.1–10.7.4; *Evans* pp 363–367.
6 See the Immigration Act 1971 (c 77), s 14 (amended by the British Nationality Act 1981 (c 61), s 39(6), Sch 4, para 2, and the Immigration Act 1988 (c 14), s 10, Schedule, para 3). However, the protection is not an 'authorisation' within the meaning of the Statement of Changes in Immigration Rules (HC Paper (1989–90) no. 251) (the Immigration Rules), para 166: *Muhammad Idrish v Secretary of State for the Home Department* [1985] Imm AR 155, IAT.
7 See para 370 below.

(b) System of Appeal

330. Appellate authorities. Where appeal exists it is normally to an adjudicator in the first instance[1] and, thereafter, to the Immigration Appeal Tribunal[2]. There is no further appeal. Judicial review is in principle available and has been widely used in England and Wales. Some appeals are direct to the tribunal[3] and some go to an extra-statutory panel of 'Three Wise Men'[4]. Where the adjudicator has dismissed an appeal and there has been no further appeal to the tribunal, or the tribunal has dismissed an appeal at first instance[5], confirmed an adjudication dismissing an appeal or reversed one allowing the appeal, the Secretary of State may refer matters not previously before the adjudicator or tribunal to them for consideration[6].

Adjudicators sit alone, in various locations (including Edinburgh and Glasgow normally) as directed by the Lord Chancellor[7], but the tribunal has invariably sat in London although it may sit where directed by the Lord Chancellor[8]. It may sit in divisions of three or greater uneven numbers[9], and certain functions may be carried out by the president or a chairman alone[10].

1 Ie under the Immigration Act 1971 (c 77), ss 13–19: see paras 333 ff below.
2 Ie under ibid, s 20; see para 334 below.
3 Ie an appeal (1) against deportation on the grounds of conduciveness to public good; (2) in respect of family relationship to a deportee, against refusal to revoke a family deportation order; or (3) where the appeal is related to such an appeal which is still pending: see ibid, s 15(7)(a)–(c), and paras 202–204, 207, 208, 214, above, and paras 336, 342, below.
4 See paras 368, 369, below.
5 Ie under the Immigration Act 1971, s 15 (see paras 336, 342, above): s 21(1)(a).
6 Ibid, s 21.
7 Ibid, s 12(b), Sch 5, para 5 (amended by the Transfer of Functions (Immigration Appeals) Order 1987, SI 1987/465, arts 2(c), 3(2), (3)).

8 Immigration Act 1971, Sch 5, para 11.
9 Ibid, Sch 5, para 12.
10 Immigration Appeals (Procedure) Rules 1984, SI 1984/2041, r 42.

331. Personnel of the appeal system. There are as many adjudicators as the Lord Chancellor, with the consent of the Treasury, determines[1]. One is Chief Adjudicator, who allocates duties[2]. Adjudicators need not be legally qualified[3]. There is no specific power in the Immigration Act 1971 to dismiss them, but the terms of appointment are in the hands of the Lord Chancellor[4]. Until 1987 these functions were carried out by the Secretary of State and the arrangements were criticised on the grounds of natural justice and otherwise[5].

There are as many members of the Immigration Appeal Tribunal as the Lord Chancellor appoints, one being president[6]. The president, and such number of the other members, must be an advocate, barrister or solicitor of at least seven years standing and every sitting must be presided over by a person so qualified[7]. Otherwise no member need be legally qualified. The terms of appointment are in the hands of the Lord Chancellor[8].

The 'Three Wise Men' for the non-statutory appeal may be anyone appointed by the Secretary of State[9].

1 Immigration Act 1971 (c 77), s 12(b), Sch 5, para 1 (amended by the Transfer of Functions (Minister for the Civil Service and Treasury) Order 1981, SI 1981/1670, and the Transfer of Functions (Immigration Appeals) Order 1987, SI 1987/465, arts 2(c), 3(2), (3)). The amendment by the Transfer of Functions (Immigration Appeals) Order 1987, which transferred the power of appointment from the Secretary of State to the Lord Chancellor, meets the criticism referred to in para 329, text and note 3, above. The adjudicators are remunerated (Immigration Act 1971, Sch 5, para 3 (amended by the Transfer of Functions (Immigration Appeals) Order 1987, arts 2(c), 3(2), (3)). There are approximately eighty, of whom ten are full-time, on a ten-year contract. It appears that as the full-time contracts fall in, they are replaced by part-time ones.
2 Immigration Act 1971, Sch 5, paras 1, 5 (amended by the Transfer of Functions (Immigration Appeals) Order 1987, arts 2(c), 3(2), (3)).
3 In practice they are almost all legally qualified.
4 Immigration Act 1971, Sch 5, paras 2(1), 3 (as amended: see note 2 above). They may resign: Sch 5, para 2(2) (as so amended).
5 See note 1 above. See also eg *Immigration Control Procedures: Report of a Formal Investigation* (1985, Commission for Racial Equality), paras 10.4, 10.14.1–10.14.4, 10.22.1–10.22.3, 10.23.1–10.23.3. Adjudicators were criticised individually and collectively: see eg para 10.23.3 (referring to 'colonial administrators'), and the *Pivot of the System* (1981, Runnymede Trust) p 26.
6 Immigration Act 1971, Sch 5, para 6. The Lord President apparently has no role. Members of the Immigration Appeal Tribunal are paid: Sch 5, para 9 (amended by the Transfer of Functions (Minister for the Civil Service and Treasury) Order 1981, and the Transfer of Functions (Immigration Appeals) Order 1987, arts 2(c), 3(2), (3)). They are disqualified from sitting in the House of Commons: House of Commons Disqualification Act 1975 (c 24), s 1, Sch 1, Pt II.
7 Immigration Act 1971, Sch 5, paras 7, 12, 14.
8 See ibid, Sch 5, paras 8, 9 (as amended: see note 6 above).
9 See paras 368, 369, below.

332. Effects of appeal upon leave to enter or remain. Application to appeal automatically extends leave to enter or remain upon the existing conditions as to employment and registration with the police until twenty-eight days after the decision is made[1].

1 See para 178, text and notes 7, 8, above.

333. Nature of first appeals subject to specified limits, other than in 'security' deportation cases. Appeal to an adjudicator (or to the Immigration Appeal Tribunal on first appeal) may be based on any of three grounds, that is that the decision complained of:
(1) was not in accordance with the law; or

(2) was not in accordance with the Immigration Rules, or

(3) involved an exercise of discretion by the Secretary of State or an officer which should have been exercised differently[1].

Head (1) is presumably not limited to immigration law, and includes failure to follow procedural requirements[2] or natural justice, or to take required reasons into account[3]. In the case of Community nationals, it must include Community law if free movement principles are involved[4]. Also, a question of fact on which the decision was taken (but not others) may be reviewed[5]. This includes examination of new evidence concerning facts in existence at the time of the decision, but there is an unwillingness to depart from a conclusion on credibility[6].

As to head (2), the status of the Immigration Rules, and their interpretation, is dealt with above[7]. Cases include those where irrelevant grounds are used or reliance on a mixture of Immigration Rule categories[8].

Under head (3), the power is not limited to whether exercise was reasonable, but whether it is right[9]. Failure of the Secretary of State to decide 'outside the Rules' is not, however, an exercise of discretion[10]. The burden of proof is normally upon the appellant[11].

Subject to certain limitations in regard to refusal of entry and removal[12], an appeal made out on one of these grounds is to be allowed[13], and the adjudicator or tribunal gives directions to effect the determination in principle (but not necessarily in detail[14]) which must be complied with, subject to further appeal, and may make recommendations[15].

At least in relation to decisions on control before entry or on entry[16], appeal rather than judicial review is the appropriate remedy in the absence of exceptional circumstances[17].

1 Immigration Act 1971 (c 77), s 19(1)(a)(i), (ii). The Court of Appeal has laid down principles for the application in England and Wales on judicial review in immigration cases, and tied them to 'Wednesbury principles': see *R v Secretary of State for the Home Department, ex parte Swati* [1986] 1 All ER 717, [1986] 1 WLR 477, [1986] Imm AR 88, CA. The appellant can adduce facts in existence at the relevant time but unknown to the Secretary of State: see *R v Immigration Appeal Tribunal, ex parte Hassanin* [1987] 1 All ER 74, [1986] 1 WLR 1448, [1986] Imm AR 502, CA. For the 'Wednesbury principles', see ADMINISTRATIVE LAW, vol 1, paras 236 ff.

2 *Secretary of State for the Home Department v Enorzah* [1975] Imm AR 7, IAT; *R v Immigration Appeal Tribunal, ex parte Ahluwalia* [1979–80] Imm AR 1, DC. However cf *Islam v Secretary of State for the Home Department* [1975] Imm AR 106, IAT.

3 *Entry Clearance Officer, New Delhi v Bhambra* [1973] Imm AR 14, IAT; *Murgai v Entry Clearance Officer, New Delhi* [1975] Imm AR 86, IAT; *Yau Yak Wah v The Home Office* [1982] Imm AR 16, CA; *R v Immigration Appeal Tribunal, ex parte Hubbard* [1985] Imm AR 110, DC; *Tahir v Immigration Appeal Tribunal* [1989] Imm AR 98, CA.

4 See paras 116, 137, 219 ff above.

5 Immigration Act 1971, s 19(2). See also *Wadia v Secretary of State for the Home Department* [1977] Imm AR 92, IAT. Adjudicators have been loth to overturn entry clearance officers' and immigration officers' views on credibility: *Alam Bi v Immigration Appeal Tribunal* [1979–80] Imm AR 146, CA.

6 *Secretary of State for the Home Department v Purushothaman* [1972] Imm AR 176, IAT; *R v Immigration Appeal Tribunal, ex parte Rashid* [1978] Imm AR 71, DC; *Visa Officer, Karachi v Hussan Mohammad* [1978] Imm AR 168, IAT; *Alam Bi v Immigration Appeal Tribunal* [1979–80] Imm AR 146, CA; *R v Immigration Appeal Tribunal, ex parte Weerasuriya* [1983] 1 All ER 195, [1982] Imm AR 23, DC.

7 See the Statement of Changes in Immigration Rules (HC Paper (1989–90) no. 251) (the Immigration Rules), and para 110 above.

8 *R v Immigration Appeal Tribunal, ex parte Martin* [1972] Imm AR 275, DC; *R v Immigration Appeal Tribunal, ex parte Khan* [1975] Imm AR 26, IAT; *R v Immigration Appeal Tribunal, ex parte Rashid* [1978] Imm AR 71, DC; *R v Immigration Appeal Tribunal, ex parte Aisha Khatoon Ali* [1979–80] Imm AR 195, CA. However, see now *R v Immigration Appeal Tribunal, ex parte Kwok On Tong* [1981] Imm AR 214, DC; and *R v Immigration Appeal Tribunal, ex parte Coomasaru* [1983] 1 All ER 208, [1983] 1 WLR 14, [1982] Imm AR 77, CA.

9 Where the Secretary of State refused an application inter alia upon a ground which is mandatory, it does not follow that he had not applied his mind to a discretion held under the same rule: *R v*

Immigration Appeal Tribunal, ex parte Surinder Mohan [1985] Imm AR 84, CA; *Re Mahboub Iqbal Ahmed Malik*[1985] Imm AR 96, CA. See also *R v Immigration Appeal Tribunal, ex parte Hubbard* [1985] Imm AR 110, DC; *Tahir v Immigration Appeal Tribunal* [1989] Imm AR 98, CA.

10 Immigration Act 1971, s 19(2).

11 See the Immigration Appeals (Procedure) Rules 1984, SI 1984/2041, r 31. See also *Tahir v Immigration Appeal Tribunal* [1989] Imm AR 98, CA.

12 Ie where an adjudicator is satisfied that the appellant is an illegal entrant: see the Immigration Act 1971, ss 13(4), 16(4), and paras 339, 341, below.

13 Ibid, s 19(1)(a).

14 *Secretary of State for the Home Department v Fardy* [1972] Imm AR 192, IAT; *Visa Officer, Aden v Thabet* [1977] Imm AR 75, IAT.

15 See the Immigration Act 1971, s 19(3), (4). Recommendations can only be made under the Act where the appeal is allowed and failure to make one is not a ground of appeal: *Gillegao v Secretary of State for the Home Department* [1989] Imm AR 174, IAT.

16 See para 336 below.

17 *R v Secretary of State for the Home Department, ex parte Swati* [1986] 1 All ER 717, [1986] 1 WLR 477, [1986] Imm AR 88, CA, explained in *R v Secretary of State for the Home Department, ex parte Hindjou* [1989] Imm AR 24. Lord Coulsfield held in a deportation case that while any statutory appeal ought to be pursued, the jurisdiction of the court was not excluded if the fundamental invalidity of the proceedings was in issue: *Mensah v Secretary of State for the Home Department* 1991 GWD 4-218, OH.

334. Nature of further appeal, other than in 'security deportation' cases.

Any party, if leave be given, may appeal, other than in 'security deportation' cases, to the Immigration Appeal Tribunal from the adjudicator if dissatisfied with his determination[1]. The tribunal may affirm the determination or make any other which the adjudicator could have made[2].

1 Immigration Act 1971 (c 77), s 20(1).
2 See ibid, s 20(2), (3).

335. Nature of appeals in 'security' deportation cases.

There is no right of appeal as such in 'security' cases except against destination when deported[1]. Where a person is to be deported under the 'conducive' ground, however, there is a non-statutory advisory procedure[2]. This does not amount to an appeal but to an opportunity for representations on a political or administrative decision.

1 See paras 342–344 below.
2 Ie under the Statement of Changes in Immigration Rules (HC Paper (1989–90) no. 251) (the Immigration Rules), para 157: see paras 339 ff below.

(c) Appealable and Non-Appealable Decisions

336. Decisions which may be appealed.

The following decisions may be appealed subject to certain limits[1]:

(1) control before entry decisions:
    (a) that entry clearance be refused[2];
    (b) that a certificate of entitlement be refused[3];
(2) control on entry decisions:
    (a) that leave to enter is required[4];
    (b) that leave to enter be refused[5];
(3) control after entry decisions:
    (a) that a variation of leave be made[6];
    (b) that a variation of leave be refused[6];
    (c) that particular limits or conditions be imposed after certain exemptions from control cease, or British citizenship is lost[7];

(4) control on departure decisions:
- (a) that a power exists to direct removal as an illegal entrant, as a person in breach of a deportation order, or as an overstaying crew member[8];
- (b) that a deportation order be made[9];
- (c) that a deportation order be not revoked[10];
- (d) that a particular destination be not chosen for removal after refusal of entry, after a deportation order, or after entry in breach of a deportation order[11].

1 See paras 337 ff below.
2 Immigration Act 1971 (c 77), s 13(2).
3 Ibid, s 13(2) (amended by the British Nationality Act 1981 (c 61), s 39(6), Sch 4, para 3(1)). A certificate issued in error to an unentitled person may be 'cancelled'. Such cancellation is not a 'refusal'. Therefore no appeal lies: see *Secretary of State for the Home Department v Gold and Gold* [1985] Imm AR 66, IAT.
4 Immigration Act 1971, s 13(1). There is no appeal against actual conditions imposed. Objection is made by an application for variation of leave: see paras 177 ff above. Refusal of such variation is appealable: see text to note 6 below.
5 Ibid, s 13(1).
6 Ibid, s 14(1).
7 Ibid, s 14(2) (amended by the British Nationality Act 1981, Sch 4, para 2).
8 Immigration Act 1971, s 16(1).
9 Ibid, s 15(1)(a).
10 Ibid, s 15(1)(b).
11 See ibid, s 17(1)–(3).

337. Forgery and wrong identity as a limit on appeals.

Forgery or issue to the wrong person of a document relating to entry may be raised as a preliminary issue objecting to the hearing of an appeal and, if successful, any right of appeal is effectively removed[1].

1 Immigration Appeals (Procedure) Rules 1984, SI 1984/2041, r 8(3)(a)(ii). As to the effect of entry clearance obtained by false representations, see para 150, note 4, above. Where a person arrives with an entry clearance obtained by false representations, it is ineffective, and is not 'current', but the subsequent refusal of entry founds the right of appeal, and the entry clearance is deemed 'current' for the purposes of appeal against the decision rendering it invalid: *Ashraf v Immigration Appeal Tribunal* [1989] Imm AR 234, CA.

338. Specific limits on control before entry decision appeals.

There is no appeal against refusal of entry clearance where the Secretary of State certifies that he personally directed the appellant not to be given leave to enter because his exclusion is conducive to the public good[1].

1 Immigration Act 1971 (c77), s 13(5).

339. Specific limits on control on entry decision appeals.

There is no appeal against the decision that leave to enter is required where the appellant claims the right of abode, unless he holds a relevant passport or certificate of entitlement[1], or if the 'conducive' ground applies[2].

Appeal against refusal of leave to enter is to be dismissed if the adjudicator is satisfied that at the time the appellant was an illegal entrant[3]. This does not appear to mean that an adjudicator can hold *ex proprio motu* that an appellant was an illegal entrant[4]. Refusal of leave to enter in one capacity does not prevent application for leave to enter in another, and appeal against refusal of that second application[5].

Such an appeal may not be pursued while the appellant is in the United Kingdom unless he was refused leave at a port of entry and held an entry clearance or a work permit[6].

1 See the Immigration Act 1971 (c 77), s 13(3) (amended by the British Nationality Act 1981 (c 61), s 39, and the Immigration Act 1988 (c 14), s 3), read with the Immigration Act 1971, s 3(9) (as so amended). A relevant passport is one describing him as a British citizen or as a citizen of the United Kingdom and Colonies having the right of abode in the United Kingdom: see paras 117, 118, 153, above.
2 Immigration Act 1971, s 13(5).
3 Ibid, s 13(4).
4 *Khawaja v Secretary of State for the Home Department* [1984] AC 74 at 119, [1983] 1 All ER 765 at 788, [1982] Imm AR 139 at 166, HL, per Lord Bridge.
5 *R v Immigration Appeal Tribunal, ex parte Secretary of State for the Home Department* [1990] 3 All ER 652, [1990] 1 WLR 1126, CA.
6 Immigration Act 1971, s 13(3).

340. Specific limits on control after entry appeals. There is no appeal at all against any variation made by statutory instrument (or by failure to make a statutory instrument)[1].

There is no appeal against variation of leave which reduces or does not increase or remove the limit on duration, if the decision is on the 'conducive' ground as personally taken, or certified, by the Secretary of State as being on security or other political grounds[2]. Nor may there be appeal against a refusal to vary leave if the application for variation was out of time[3]. Any appeal against variation of leave lapses when a deportation order is made[4].

1 Immigration Act 1971 (c 77), s 14(4).
2 Ibid, s 14(3). The 'Three Wise Men' procedure (see paras 368, 369, below) does not apply here.
3 *Suthendran v Immigration Appeal Tribunal* [1977] AC 359, [1976] 3 All ER 611, [1977] Imm AR 44, HL.
4 Immigration Act 1971, s 14(5) (amended by the Immigration Act 1988 (c 14), s 10, Schedule, para 3). As to deportation, see paras 202 ff above.

341. Specific limits on control of departure decision appeals relating to removal of illegal entrants etc. Appeal against directions for removal as an illegal entrant, as a person in breach of a deportation order, or as an overstaying crew member[1], may not be pursued from within the United Kingdom, unless the appeal is against directions effecting a deportation order and the appellant asserts he is not the person named[2], or possibly if he has entered in breach of a deportation order and seeks to be removed to a different country from that specified[3]. Nor, if the directions effect a deportation order, may the original validity of the order be disputed[4].

An appeal by a crew member is to be dismissed in any case if the adjudicator is satisfied that there was power to remove the appellant as an illegal entrant, but this does not appear to mean that he can decide this *ex proprio motu*[5].

1 Ie under the Immigration Act 1971 (c 77), s 16(1): see para 336 above.
2 Ibid, s 16(2).
3 Ibid, s 17(1)(c). This is not easy to reconcile with s 16(2).
4 Ibid, s 16(3).
5 See ibid, s 16(4), and *Khawaja v Secretary of State for the Home Department* [1984] AC 74 at 119, [1983] 1 All ER 765 at 788, [1982] Imm AR 139 at 166, HL.

342. Specific limits on control of departure decision appeals relating to deportation orders. There is no appeal against a deportation order made on the 'conducive' ground as being on security or other political grounds, whether or not the decision was made personally, or certified, by the Secretary of State[1]. Nor is there any appeal against a deportation order following a recommendation by a court, although appeal against that recommendation may be pursued within the criminal courts as an appeal against conviction.

In the case of a person given leave to enter (as opposed to leave to remain) less than seven years earlier (and a person is presumed to have been so given it unless he proves otherwise[2]), he may not appeal against a deportation order made by reason of overstaying, breach of conditions, or membership of a family of a person who is or had to be ordered to be deported for overstaying or breach of conditions, except on one ground[3]. That ground is that, on the facts, there is no power to make the deportation order for the reasons stated in the notice of the decision[4]. Thus, there is no appeal on the ground that the discretion to make the order should not have been exercised, given the relevant circumstances[5].

Indefinite leave will normally have been achieved by a person lawfully present in the United Kingdom who was last given leave to enter more than five years ago[6], and such a person will normally be ordinarily resident[7]. Thus a number of 'settled'[8] people are subject to the power in respect of family deportations.

The Secretary of State is empowered to exempt any persons to any extent by order, subject to parliamentary approval[9]. The power has been exercised in relation to two groups. The first is refugees, who may appeal against the deportation on the ground that deportation would be contrary to United Kingdom obligations under the Refugee Convention[10]. The second is certain persons who, having obtained entry more than seven years ago, travelled abroad but returned within the time limit originally imposed upon them[11]. Although normally in such cases, on return, the original conditions would re-apply, this is a new application for leave to enter[12]. Under this exemption, unless those terms are superseded, it is the earlier date of the original conditions which counts.

In family deportation cases generally, the appellant is not allowed to dispute any statement made to obtain entry clearance or leave to enter or remain, in order to show whether or not he belongs to a family, unless he shows that neither he, nor any person acting on his authority, made it, and that either he did not know it was being made, or was under eighteen years of age[13].

There is no appeal against a refusal to revoke a deportation order if refusal was made personally, or certified, by the Secretary of State (whether or not involving security or other political grounds)[14]. No appeal against revocation may be made from within the United Kingdom[15].

1 Immigration Act 1971 (c 77), s 15(3), (4). However, note the 'Three Wise Men' procedure: see paras 368, 369, below.
2 Immigration Act 1988 (c 14), s 5(4).
3 Ibid, s 5(1)(a), (b).
4 Ibid, s 5(1). The impact of this was diminished in *Secretary of State for the Home Department v Mahli* [1990] Imm AR 275, CA, where it was held that there can be no inquiry into the propriety of the proceedings leading up to the decision to deport.
5 Ie under the Statement of Changes in Immigration Rules (HC Paper (1989–90) no. 251) (the Immigration Rules), paras 164, 166, 169: see paras 205, 208, 209, above.
6 See paras 120, 121, above.
7 As to the meaning of 'ordinarily resident', see the Immigration Act 1971, s 33(2) and (2A) (added by the British Nationality Act 1981 (c 61), s 39(6), Sch 4, para 7), and *Shah v Barnet London Borough Council* [1983] 2 AC 309, [1983] 1 All ER 226, HL. See also para 120 above.
8 For the meaning of 'settled', see the Immigration Act 1971, s 33(1), (2A) (as so added).
9 Immigration Act 1988, s 5(2), (3).
10 Immigration (Restricted Right of Appeal against Deportation) (Exemption) (No 2) Order 1988, SI 1988/1203, arts 2(a), 3, and para 322 above. As to refugees, see paras 314, 316, 320, above. As to the Refugee Convention, see para 314, note 1, above.
11 Immigration (Restricted Right of Appeal against Deportation) (Exemption) (No 2) Order 1988, art 2(b).
12 Immigration Act 1971, s 3(3)(b) (amended by the Immigration Act 1988, s 10, Schedule, para 1, as from 16 May 1991: see the Immigration Act 1988 (Commencement No 2) Order 1991, SI 1991/1001). See also the Immigration Rules, para 60, and para 176, notes 1–3, above.
13 Immigration Act 1971, s 15(6).
14 Ibid, s 15(4).
15 Ibid, s 15(5).

343. Limits on control of departure decision appeals relating to removal destination. There is no appeal against removal to a particular destination after refusal of leave to enter, unless there is also appeal against the requirement of leave to enter, or the refusal was at a port of entry and entry clearance or a work permit were held[1]. Nor is such appeal available if there is also an appeal against refusal of entry or deportation as such, and it is not raised simultaneously[2].

In relation to deportation removals the Immigration Rules require that the country of nationality, or the country which most recently provided a travel document, should be the normal destination and that if the person seeks another destination, he must be able to show that that other country is willing to take him[3]. In such case the public interest and expense are to be considered[3].

1 Immigration Act 1971 (c 77), s 17(5). The words 'if at all' in s 17(1) are in effect ignored: *Mustafa v Secretary of State for the Home Department* [1979–80] Imm AR 32, IAT.
2 Immigration Act 1971, s 17(4).
3 Statement of Changes in Immigration Rules (HC Paper (1989–90) no. 251) (the Immigration Rules), para 177. See also *Ali v Immigration Appeal Tribunal* [1973] Imm AR 33, CA.

344. Decisions which are not appealable at all. No appeal is possible at all against refusal of a special voucher[1] or of a work permit[2] and refugee status as such[3].

1 *R v Entry Clearance Officer, Bombay, ex parte Amin* [1980] 2 All ER 837, [1970] 1 WLR 1530, DC.
2 *Pearson v Immigration Appeal Tribunal* [1978] Imm AR 212, CA.
3 *Bugdaycay v Secretary of State for the Home Department, Nelidow Santis v Secretary of State for the Home Department, Norman v Secretary of State for the Home Department, Re Musisi* [1987] AC 514, [1987] 1 All ER 940, [1987] Imm AR 250, HL.

(d) Procedure

(A) PROCEDURE ON FIRST STAGE APPEAL (OTHER THAN 'SECURITY' CASES)

345. Notice of appealable decision. Normally, written notice of any appealable decision is sent as soon as practicable to the relevant person or to another person who submitted the application on his behalf, but it may on occasion be dispensed with[1]. It must include statements:
(1) of reasons, which are conclusive[2],
(2) of intended destination on removal, where appropriate[3],
(3) of particulars of any right of appeal[4],
(4) of the manner of bringing an appeal[5],
(5) of time limits[6], and
(6) of facilities for advice or assistance[7],
unless it is a decision to vary leave and is not less favourable than that requested[8].

1 See the Immigration Act 1971 (c 77), s 18(1), and the Immigration Appeals (Notices) Regulations 1984, SI 1984/2040, reg 3(1), and para 211 above. As to the officers etc obliged to issue notices, see reg 3(2). There is no need for notice if the whereabouts or place of abode of the appellant is unknown (reg 3(4)), and the requirements are fulfilled by a registered letter or recorded delivery posted to the last known address (reg 6). See also *R v Immigration Appeal Tribunal, ex parte Mehmet* [1977] 2 All ER 602, [1977] 1 WLR 795, [1977] Imm AR 56, DC; *R v Immigration Appeal Tribunal, ex parte Jaspal Singh* [1977] Imm AR 105n, DC; *Rhemtulla v Immigration Appeal Tribunal* [1979–80] Imm AR 168, CA; *R v Secretary of State for the Home Department, ex parte Yeboah, R v Secretary of State for the Home Department, ex parte Draz* [1987] 3 All ER 999, [1987] 1 WLR 1586, [1987] Imm AR 414, CA (followed by the Inner House in *Singh v Secretary of State for the Home Department* 1991 GWD 9-547, upholding the decision of Lord Weir: see 1990 SLT 300, OH). There is no need to inform of an unappealable decision, eg grant of leave to enter, which is in any case given in writing: see the Immigration Act 1971, s 4(2), Sch 2, para 6(1), and para 170 above.

2 See the Immigration Appeals (Notices) Regulations 1984, reg 4(1)(a), and the Immigration Act 1971, s 18(2). This statement can be perfunctory: *R v Secretary of State for the Home Department, ex parte Swati* [1986] 1 All ER 717, [1986] 1 WLR 477, [1986] Imm AR 88, CA. However, a distinction was drawn between 'reasons' (which may not be added to) and 'grounds' (which may be) (*R v Immigration Appeal Tribunal, ex parte Mehra* [1983] Imm AR 156, DC), although this was doubted in *R v Immigration Appeal Tribunal, ex parte Hubbard* [1985] Imm AR 110, DC (where it was held that the appellate authorities were not confined to considering the matter in which the Secretary of State based his decision) and *Tahir v Immigration Appeal Tribunal* [1989] Imm AR 98, CA.
3 Immigration Appeals (Notices) Regulations 1984, reg 4(1)(b).
4 Ibid, reg 4(1)(c)(i).
5 Ibid, reg 4(1)(c)(ii).
6 Ibid, reg 4(1)(c)(iii).
7 Ibid, reg 4(1)(c)(iv). This is invariably the address of the United Kingdom Immigrants Advisory Service.
8 Ibid, reg 4(2).

346. Notice of first stage appeal. Notice of a first stage appeal is given by furnishing particulars, including grounds of appeal, in writing and signed[1], except in the case of a decision that leave is required, or that leave to enter be refused (provided such appeal may be pursued in the United Kingdom), when it may be given orally[2]. Variation or amplification of grounds of appeal is possible later[3]. An oral hearing should be requested if desired[4]. Notice is to be sent to any immigration officer where oral notice is permitted, but otherwise to a specified recipient[5].

The recipient refers the case to the appellate authorities with any other particulars given by the appellant either as soon as practicable or, in some cases, as soon as practicable after production of the explanatory statement[6]. This gives the respondent considerable control over the speed and order of appeals.

If the decision appealed against is altered, the appellant is given the opportunity to withdraw, amend or make a new appeal[7].

1 Ie signed by the appellant or either his authorised representative or by another on the appellant's behalf if he is incapable: Immigration Appeals (Procedure) Rules 1984, SI 1984/2041, r 6(5). Form 1 of the previous procedure rules is abandoned and the particulars required are name, date of birth, nationality, particulars of the decision and grounds of appeal: r 6(3)(a)–(c).
2 Ibid, r 6(1).
3 Ibid, r 6(4). Material changes may not be made, since they constitute a new ground of appeal: *Francis v Secretary of State for the Home Department* [1972] Imm AR 162, IAT; *Muthulakshmi v Secretary of State for the Home Department* [1972] Imm AR 231, IAT. The previous practice of giving notice of appeal with 'grounds to follow' appears no longer possible.
4 Immigration Appeals (Procedure) Rules 1984, r 12(1)(a).
5 Ie (1) the relevant entry clearance officer is specified in relation to appeals against refusal of entry clearance or certificate of entitlement; (2) the relevant immigration officer in an appeal against a decision that leave is required, that leave be refused, that the person be removed or removed to a particular destination; and (3) the Secretary of State in all other cases: ibid, r 6(2)(a)–(c). The Secretary of State may substitute another entry clearance officer or immigration officer or himself on certain grounds: see r 6(2), (8). Notice should be sent by registered letter or recorded delivery to the address indicated with the notice of an appealable decision already received (see para 345 above) or otherwise to the Immigration and Nationality Department (Appeals Section), Thanet House, 231 Strand, London WC2 1DA: r 44.
6 See ibid, rr 6(6)(a), (b), 8.
7 Ibid, r 6(7).

347. Parties to a first stage appeal. The respondent to a first stage appeal is the specified recipient, but the Secretary of State may substitute himself on certain grounds, or may be joined additionally[1]. Where the appellant is or claims to be a refugee, the United Kingdom representative of the United Nations High Commissioner for Refugees may be joined at his instance[2].

1 See the Immigration Appeals (Procedure) Rules 1984, SI 1984/2041, r 7(1), (2). As to the specified recipient, see para 346, note 5, above.
2 Ibid, r 7(3). As to who is a refugee, see para 314 above.

348. Time limits. Time limits for notice of appeal are in general brief. They are as follows:
(1) control before entry decisions:
    (a) on refusal of entry clearance, three months from refusal[1];
    (b) on refusal of certificate of entitlement, three months from refusal if application was to an entry clearance officer, or fourteen days if to the Secretary of State[2];
(2) control on entry decisions:
    (a) on requirement of leave to enter, twenty-eight days after departure (whether or not by removal)[3];
    (b) on refusal of leave to enter, twenty-eight days after departure (whether or not by removal)[4];
(3) control after entry decisions:
    (a) on variation of leave, fourteen days after decision[5];
    (b) on refusal to vary leave, fourteen days after decision[5];
    (c) on imposition of limited leave after exemption or loss of citizenship, fourteen days after the decision[6];
(4) control of departure decisions:
    (a) on power to remove as an illegal entrant etc, twenty-eight days after departure[7];
    (b) on making a deportation order, fourteen days after the decision[8];
    (c) on refusal to revoke a deportation order, twenty-eight days after the decision[9];
    (d) on destination on removal, until departure where refused leave to enter, and in other cases until departure but not later than fourteen days after the directions were given[10].

Where the time runs from a decision, the decision is deemed to have been taken on the day it would be delivered in the normal course of events (or, if proved, a later date on which it was in fact delivered) if posted, or otherwise, the day it was served[11]. This does not cover cases where notice is dispensed with[12].

The specified recipient may, if he thinks it just and right by reason of special circumstances, permit an appeal out of time, except in the case of an appellant subject to a deportation order[13]. In any case appeal out of time is possible by proceeding as if in time and having the matter dealt with as a preliminary issue if raised by the respondent within the same limits at the specified recipient's discretion[14]. This has been liberally interpreted to include, for example, error by the appellant's agents; it requires looking at all the materials, and may include consideration of the merits, but cannot include appeal against deportation after the deportation order has been signed[15]. Appeal to the Immigration Appeal Tribunal is possible[16].

1 Immigration Appeals (Procedure) Rules 1984, SI 1984/2041, r 4(4).
2 Ibid, r 4(2), (3).
3 Ibid, r 4(1). This operates whether the person can appeal from within the United Kingdom or not: see para 339 above.
4 Ibid, r 4(1).
5 Ibid, r 4(5).
6 Ibid, r 4(6).
7 Ibid, r 4(9).
8 Ibid, r 4(7).
9 Ibid, r 4(8).

10 Ibid, r 4(10).
11 See ibid, r 4(11), and *R v Immigration Appeal Tribunal, ex parte Chumun and Bano-Ovais* [1987] Imm AR 92, DC (disapproving as *per incuriam R v Secretary of State for the Home Department, ex parte Draz* [1985] Imm AR 215, DC, and following *R v London County Quarter Sessions Appeals Committee, ex parte Rossi* [1956] QB 682, [1956] 1 All ER 670, CA). It seems that if notice is undelivered then, following *R v Secretary of State for the Home Department, ex parte Mehmet* [1977] 2 All ER 602, [1977] 1 WLR 795, [1977] Imm AR 56, DC, the authorities could immediately rely upon the Immigration Appeals (Notices) Regulations 1984, SI 1984/2040, reg 3(4): see para 345, note 1, above. Where time expires on a Saturday or a Sunday or a public holiday, it is deemed to expire on the next working day: Immigration Appeals (Procedure) Rules 1984, r 43(1).
12 See para 345 above.
13 Immigration Appeals (Procedure) Rules 1984, r 5(1), (2). As to the specified recipient, see para 346, note 5, above.
14 Ibid, rr 8(3)(b), 11(1).
15 *R v Immigration Appeal Tribunal, ex parte R P Mehta* [1976] Imm AR 38, CA; *R v Immigration Appeal Tribunal, ex parte V M Mehta* [1976] Imm AR 174, CA; *R v Secretary of State for the Home Department, ex parte Draz* [1985] Imm AR 215, DC.
16 See the Immigration Act 1971 (c 77), s 20, and para 334 above.

349. Explanatory statement by the respondent. The respondent must, except in certain circumstances, produce as soon as practicable after notice of appeal is given a written statement of facts relating to the decision, and the reasons for it, and send copies to the appellate authorities and the appellant[1]. The exceptional circumstances are broadly two. First, where an immigration officer is respondent and he is of the opinion that it is not practicable to produce the statement in view of the time before the hearing, he must instead give written notice of this, and that an oral statement will be made[2]. Secondly, in the four circumstances where a preliminary issue can be raised a brief statement may be produced which includes the allegation and facts relevant to it only (although a full statement is required if proceedings continue)[3].

The respondent may amplify the written statement at the commencement of the hearing[4]. Nevertheless, the explanatory statement largely comprises the respondent's case (though other documents may be annexed), and so it is of fundamental importance.

The system has been heavily criticised[5]. It has been suggested that the procedure, in practice, allows the respondent to determine the speed and order of appeals by his rate of production of explanatory statements, since no time limit exists for their production. The statement is commonly prepared by one person from the notes of another, which themselves may rely on hearsay, and neither may be available for cross-examination, nor the other person's notes as evidence, and presenting officers are enjoined not to reveal notes. The appellant is perforce often not present and so not available as witness. Thus the assertions of the statement, it is argued, tend to be regarded as the facts of the case[6] and the burden of proof almost insurmountable (which is reflected in the appeal success rate[7]).

1 Immigration Appeals (Procedure) Rules 1984, SI 1984/2041, r 8(1). Cf the Immigration Appeals (Notices) Regulations 1984, SI 1984/2040, reg 4(1): see para 345 above. The explanatory statement is an explanation of the reasons given in the notice of an appealable decision, so may not be departed from: *Bhagat v Secretary of State for the Home Department* [1972] Imm AR 189, IAT.
2 Immigration Appeals (Procedure) Rules 1984, r 8(2), (4). This will usually only apply to refusals at the port of entry. In such cases the immigration officer ought usually to be available for cross-examination: *Padmore v Secretary of State for the Home Department* [1972] Imm AR 1, IAT.
3 See the Immigration Appeals (Procedure) Rules 1984, rr 8(3), 11(2), and para 350 below. However, since such matters will normally be dealt with at a preliminary hearing (see para 350 below) and at such hearing the appellate authority will probably want an indication as to the merits and strengths of the case, in practice full facts may be included.
4 Ibid, r 8(4). How far inadequate reasons are fatal to the respondent is unclear: *Padmore v Secretary of State for the Home Department* [1972] Imm AR 1, IAT.

5 See eg *Immigration Control Procedures: Report of a Formal Investigation* (1985, Commission for Racial Equality) especially paras 10.10.1–10.10.10, 10.11.1–10.11.6, 10.12.1–10.12.3, 10.24.1, 10.25.1; *Appeal Dismissed* (1977, Runnymede Trust); *Pivot of the System* (1981, Runnymede Trust).

6 In England the explanatory statement is evidence: *R v Immigration Appeal Tribunal, ex parte Weerasuriya* [1983] 1 All ER 195, [1982] Imm AR 23, DC.

7 See eg *Immigration Control Procedures: Report of a Formal Investigation* (1985, Commission for Racial Equality) Tables 10.1–10.7; J M Evans *Immigration Law* (2nd edn, 1983) pp 363–367, Tables I–III(c).

350. Preliminary issues. Four grounds of objection to a hearing may be raised by the respondent as preliminary issues. These are:

(1) that some specified provision of the Immigration Act 1971 prohibits the appeal;

(2) that the appellant's passport, entry clearance or like document was forged or related to another person;

(3) that the notice of appeal was not properly signed; or

(4) that the notice of appeal was out of time[1].

Appeal to the Immigration Appeal Tribunal from the determination on the preliminary issue is possible with leave[2].

1 See the Immigration Appeals (Procedure) Rules 1984, SI 1984/2041, r 11 as read with r 8(3). Where the Immigration Appeal Tribunal hears a case at first instance (see para 333 above) the President or a chairman acting alone may decide the matter: r 42(c)(i).

2 See the Immigration Act 1971 (c 77), s 20, and para 334 above.

351. Determination without a hearing and summary determination. An appeal may be determined without a hearing in seven circumstances, namely where:

(1) no party has requested a hearing[1];

(2) the appellate authority decides to allow the appeal having received representations from the appellant and having given the other parties an opportunity to reply[2];

(3) no person represents the appellant and the appellate authority is satisfied he is outside the United Kingdom or that it is impracticable to give him notice[3];

(4) the appellate authority is satisfied the appeal is only against removal to a particular destination and considers a hearing not warranted[4];

(5) a preliminary issue arises and the appellant has not used the opportunity to submit a statement rebutting the respondent's allegation, or the contents of such statement do not warrant a hearing[5];

(6) the decision is withdrawn or reversed and the appellate authority is satisfied written notice has been given to the appellant[6];

(7) it appears to the appellate authority that the issues have been determined already in previous proceedings to which the appellant was a party, and on essentially similar facts, provided that he gives the parties an opportunity to make representations that a hearing is required and notice of such determination must state the issues raised and specify the previous proceedings[7].

This case under head (7) is referred to as a 'summary determination'[7].

1 Immigration Appeals (Procedure) Rules 1984, SI 1984/2041, r 12(1)(a).

2 Ibid, r 12(1)(b).

3 Ibid, r 12(1)(c). See also *Rahmani v Diggines* [1986] AC 475, [1986] 1 All ER 921, [1986] Imm AR 195, HL, distinguished in *Shahib Al-Mehdawi v Secretary of State for the Home Department* [1990] Imm AR 140, HL.

4 Immigration Appeals (Procedure) Rules 1984, r 12(1)(d).

5 Ibid, r 12(1)(e). As to preliminary issues, see para 350 above.

6 Ibid, r 12(1)(f).

7 See ibid, r 35.

352. The hearing. The usual powers to fix time and place, give directions and transfer proceedings exist[1], and appeals may be combined with the assent of parties if there is a common question of law or fact, the appeals relate to members of the same family, or it is otherwise desirable[2].

The appellate authority may request particulars and may require attendance to produce documents or as a witness[3].

Parties may be represented but the leave of the appellate authority is required if the appellant's representative is not counsel, a solicitor, a consular officer or a person appointed by the United Kingdom Immigrants Advisory Service[4]. Hearings may be held in the absence of a party[5].

Hearings are in public[6], except in four cases. These are:

(1) where fraud in relation to an entry document is alleged and disclosure of the method of detection would be contrary to the public interest (in which case the appellant and his representatives can also be excluded)[7];

(2) where there is a request to that effect by a party (and the appellate authority accedes)[8];

(3) where a member of the public is behaving in a way likely to interfere with the proceedings[9]; or

(4) where the appellate authority considers that evidence relating to third parties is to be given, that such evidence should not be given in public, and no party requests that it should be given in public[10].

Parties are to be given an opportunity to address the appellate authority (including, in the respondent's case, to amplify the explanatory statement[11]), to give evidence, to call witnesses (who may be required to take the oath or affirm but cannot be compelled unless a court could compel them), to cross-examine and to make representations at the close of evidence[12]. Otherwise the appellate authority is master of its proceedings, which tend to formality[13].

It appears that the Home Office instructions to its presenting officers enjoin them to resist production of notes accompanying explanatory statements, which contain on occasion prejudicial statements, and, as noted, relevant officers are rarely available for cross-examination[14].

1 See the Immigration Appeals (Procedure) Rules 1984, SI 1984/2041, rr 24, 33 (which includes the power to transfer medical examination) and r 37.
2 Ibid, r 36.
3 See ibid, r 25 and r 27 (amended by the Immigration Appeals (Procedure) (Amendment) Rules 1991, SI 1991/1545). Witness expenses are payable, but it is thought that this power is rarely used.
4 See ibid, r 26.
5 See para 351 above.
6 Immigration Appeals (Procedure) Rules 1984, r 32(1).
7 See the Immigration Act 1971 (c 77), s 22(4) (amended by the British Nationality Act 1981 (c 61), s 39(6), Sch 4, para 3(1)), and the Immigration Appeals (Procedure) Rules 1984, r 32(2), (4).
8 Ibid, r 32(3)(a), (4).
9 Ibid, r 32(3)(b), (4).
10 Ibid, r 32(3)(c), (4).
11 See ibid, r 8(4), and para 349 above.
12 Ibid, rr 28(a), (b), 29(2), (3).
13 Ibid, r 28. Witnesses are commonly excluded until their evidence is given: *Wadia v Secretary of State for the Home Department* [1977] Imm AR 92, IAT; *Immigration Control Procedures: Report of a Formal Investigation* (1985, Commission for Racial Equality) para 10.15.1.
14 Ibid, paras 10.11.1–10.11.6, 10.24.1.

353. Evidence. The appellate authority may receive any evidence it considers relevant, irrespective of the normal rules of admissibility, provided the evidence relates to facts in existence at the time of the decision even if unknown to the decision-maker[1]. In relation to facts coming into existence after the decision, the general rule is that they are irrelevant, and a fresh application should be made[2]. Exceptions may be recognised[3].

1 Immigration Appeals (Procedure) Rules 1984, SI 1984/2041, r 29(1). See also *Visa Officer, Islamabad v Mohd Altar* [1979–80] Imm AR 141, IAT; *R v Immigration Appeal Tribunal, ex parte Rashid* [1978] Imm AR 71, DC; and *Visa Officer, Karachi v Hussan Mohammad* [1978] Imm AR 168, IAT. Self-serving evidence is unlikely to be admitted: *Juma v Secretary of State for the Home Department* [1974] Imm AR 96, IAT. See further *R v Immigration Appeal Tribunal, ex parte Hussanin* [1987] 1 All ER 74, [1986] 1 WLR 1448, CA (distinguishing *R v Immigration Appeal Tribunal, ex parte Weerasuriya* [1983] 1 All ER 195, [1982] Imm AR 23, DC, and *R v Immigration Appeal Tribunal, ex parte Kotecha* [1983] 2 All ER 289, [1983] 1 WLR 487, [1982] Imm AR 88, CA).

2 *R v Immigration Appeal Tribunal, ex parte Weerasuriya* [1983] 1 All ER 195, [1982] Imm AR 23, DC; *R v Immigration Appeal Tribunal, ex parte Kotecha* [1983] 2 All ER 289, [1983] 1 WLR 487, [1982] Imm AR 88, CA. Facts in evidence at the time of the decision, but unknown to the Secretary of State, may be admitted: *R v Immigration Appeal Tribunal, ex parte Hassanin* [1987] 1 All ER 74, [1986] 1 WLR 1448, [1986] Imm AR 502, CA.

3 *R v Immigration Appeal Tribunal, ex parte Amirbeaggi* (1982) Times, 25 May, DC. Earlier extensions of the principle as in *Secretary of State for the Home Department v Thaker* [1976] Imm AR 114, IAT, are now limited.

354. Burden of proof. The burden of proof is on the appellant. In particular it lies on him if he argues that he is not a person to whom the rule applied properly applies or relies on any fact which would have to be proved to the immigration authorities for the purposes of the Immigration Act 1971 or the Immigration Rules[1], or claims the right of abode[2].

1 Immigration Appeals (Procedure) Rules 1984, SI 1984/2041, r 31(1), (2). The standard of proof has been argued to be variable in practice: see the *Immigration Control Procedures: Report of a Formal Investigation* (1985, Commission for Racial Equality) para 10.17.1, quoting Home Office Guidance to Presenting Officers. See also *Tahir v Immigration Appeal Tribunal* [1989] Imm AR 98, CA. As to the Immigration Rules, see para 110 above.

2 See the Immigration Act 1971 (c 77), s 3, and paras 117, 118, above.

355. Hearing in the absence of a party. A hearing may take place in the absence of a party (or his representative) if, proper notice of time and place of hearing having been given, the party (or his representative) fails to appear without an explanation (although even with an explanation the appellate authorities may nevertheless consider it proper to continue)[1]. In particular, it may take place in the absence of the appellant if he is outwith the United Kingdom, or is suffering from a communicable disease, or by reason of illness or accident cannot attend, or it is impracticable to give him notice and no person is authorised to represent him[2]. In any such eventuality, the appellate authority may proceed on such evidence as is before it[3].

1 Immigration Appeals (Procedure) Rules 1984, SI 1984/2041, r 34(2), (3), (5)(b). Notice is presumed to have been received if sent by registered post or recorded delivery at least seven days before the hearing, unless the contrary is shown: rr 34(5)(a), 44(1). This is extremely short notice. An agent's negligence in informing an appellant of his appeal does not constitute procedural impropriety or denial of natural justice: *Shahib Al-Mehdawi v Secretary of State for the Home Department* [1990] Imm AR 140, HL, distinguishing *Rahmani v Diggines* [1986] AC 475, [1986] 1 All ER 921, [1986] Imm AR 195, HL. For a general discussion, see *Hassan Temel v An Immigration Appeal Adjudicator* [1988] Imm AR 496, CA.

2 Immigration Appeals (Procedure) Rules 1984, r 34(1)(a)–(d).

3 Ibid, r 34(4).

356. Determination and record of proceedings. The appellate authority may either give notice of the determination at the end of the proceedings, or reserve it[1]. In either case, reasons must be given and the whole written and sent to parties[2]. The authority is also required to keep a summary of the proceedings, unless there is a shorthand or mechanically made record[3].

1 Immigration Appeals (Procedure) Rules 1984, SI 1984/2041, r 39(1), (2).
2 Ibid, r 39(1)–(3).
3 Ibid, r 40.

(B) PROCEDURE ON FURTHER APPEAL (OTHER THAN 'SECURITY' CASES)

357. Appeal to the Immigration Appeal Tribunal. Any party dissatisfied with a determination of an adjudicator may, with leave, appeal to the Immigration Appeal Tribunal[1]. Appeal is therefore in law and fact[2].

1 Immigration Appeals (Procedure) Rules 1984, SI 1984/2041, r 14(1). See also the Immigration Act 1971 (c 77), s 20, and para 334 above. As the United Nations High Commissioner for Refugees can be a party where relevant (see para 347 above), he may appeal. No appeal is possible where the Immigration Appeal Tribunal hears the first stage appeal: see para 333 above. Interlocutory proceedings do not produce a 'determination' and therefore admit of no appeal: *R v Immigration Appeal Tribunal, ex parte Lila* [1978] Imm AR 50, DC.
2 However, overturning facts is unusual: *Alam Bi v Immigration Appeal Tribunal* [1979–80] Imm AR 146, CA.

358. Leave for further appeal. Leave is required in all cases, from either an adjudicator or the Immigration Appeal Tribunal itself[1]. However it must be granted where the appeal is against a decision:

(1) that leave to enter is required (provided that the applicant holds a certificate of entitlement)[2]; or

(2) that leave to enter be refused (provided that the applicant held an entry clearance and was not an illegal entrant)[3]; or

(3) that a person be removed to a country he is unwilling to enter for fear of persecution[4]; or

(4) that the appeal raises an arguable point of law (subject to an exception)[5].

1 Immigration Appeals (Procedure) Rules 1984, SI 1984/2041, r 14(1).
2 Immigration Act 1971 (c 77), s 22(5)(a) (amended by the British Nationality Act 1981 (c 61), s 39(6), Sch 4, para 3(1)).
3 Immigration Act 1971, s 22(5)(b).
4 Immigration Appeals (Procedure) Rules 1984, r 14(2)(b). Fear of such persecution renders a person a refugee: see para 314 above.
5 Ibid, r 14(2)(a). The exception is where the appeal is to the Immigration Appeal Tribunal on the ground of the adjudicator's misdirections on a point of law, in which case it may be refused if the adjudicator could have nevertheless made the same determination, even if the point of law might have been decided in favour of the appellant: r 14(2)(a).

359. Time limits. Application to an adjudicator for leave for further appeal must be made forthwith after the determination, if given *ex tempore*, and as soon as possible after presumed receipt if reserved[1].

Application to the Immigration Appeal Tribunal must be made within fourteen days (or forty-two days in the case of a person outwith the common travel area) of the determination if *ex tempore* or of presumed receipt if reserved[2].

1 Immigration Appeals (Procedure) Rules 1984, SI 1984/2041, r 15(1), (4). As to service of notice, see r 44, and para 346 above. 'Forthwith' has been used to mean within twenty-four hours of promulgation, even when not given *ex tempore*. Thus the date for leave to be requested can pass before notice of the determination has been received and the appellant must then seek leave to

appeal from the Immigration Appeal Tribunal which will not normally hear oral argument on the issue (see para 363 below): *Immigration Control Procedures: Report of a Formal Investigation* (1985, Commission for Racial Equality) para 10.18.1.

2 Immigration Appeals (Procedure) Rules 1984, r 15(2)–(4). See also *R v Immigration Appeal Tribunal, ex parte Suleman* [1976] Imm AR 147, DC; *R v Immigration Appeal Tribunal, ex parte Armstrong* [1977] Imm AR 80, DC.

360. Disposal of application. Applications for leave to appeal are to be disposed of without a hearing unless special circumstances render one desirable[1].

1 Immigration Appeals (Procedure) Rules 1984, SI 1984/2041, r 16(5). Where the matter is disposed of by the Immigration Appeal Tribunal, it may be determined by the President or other chairman.

361. Notice of application. Application for leave for further appeal may be made orally to an adjudicator[1]. If leave is granted, written application must thereafter be made within the usual time limit for application to the Immigration Appeal Tribunal but served on the adjudicator[2].

Such written application, and any application which is written *ab initio*, must contain specified particulars, including grounds of appeal[3]. Variation or amplification of the grounds is possible later[4].

Notice of application for leave for further appeal, where leave is granted, constitutes notice of appeal[5].

1 Immigration Appeals (Procedure) Rules 1984, SI 1984/2041, r 16(5).
2 Ibid, r 16(5). This appears possible whether the determination is *ex tempore* or not.
3 Details required are name, address, date of birth, nationality, particulars of determination appealed against and grounds of appeal: ibid, r 16(2)(a)–(c). The notice or application must be signed by the appellant or either by his authorised representative or by another on the appellant's behalf if he is incapable: r 16(3). Form 2 of the earlier procedure rules is abandoned.
4 Ibid, r 16(4).
5 Ibid, r 16(8). The adjudicator transmits it to the Immigration Appeal Tribunal: see r 16(7).

362. Parties. The parties to a further appeal are the same as before the adjudicator, but the Secretary of State may substitute himself or any entry clearance officer or immigration officer if the original officer is unable to take part[1]. The Secretary of State may also become a party at any time upon giving written notice[2], as may the United Kingdom Representative of the United Nations High Commissioner for Refugees, if a party is or claims to be a refugee[3].

1 Immigration Appeals (Procedure) Rules 1984, SI 1984/2041, r 17(1), (4). Cf parties to the first stage appeal: see para 347 above.
2 Ibid, r 17(2).
3 Ibid, r 17(3). As to who is a refugee, see para 314 above.

363. Determination without a hearing and summary determination. The Immigration Appeal Tribunal may determine a further appeal without a hearing in four circumstances:
(1) where no party has requested a hearing[1];
(2) where the appellant is the person against whom the decision was taken, he is not represented and the tribunal is satisfied he is outside the United Kingdom or that it is impracticable to give him notice[2];
(3) where leave has been granted automatically on certain grounds and after giving the appellant an opportunity to make representations, and the tribunal decides a hearing is not warranted[3];
(4) where the tribunal makes a summary determination[4].

1 Immigration Appeals (Procedure) Rules 1984, SI 1984/2041, r 20(a).
2 Ibid, r 20(b).
3 Ibid, r 20(c).
4 See ibid, r 35, and para 351 above.

364. The hearing. The powers and duties of the Immigration Appeal Tribunal are the same as for any appellate authority at first instance[1].

1 See para 352 above.

365. Evidence. The Immigration Appeal Tribunal receives the adjudicator's record of proceedings and may at its discretion receive fresh evidence adduced by a party (provided written notice is given) or which it has itself requested[1]. Where it does request further evidence, this evidence may, if written, be given in such manner as the tribunal directs and, if oral, be taken by the tribunal itself, or by an adjudicator to whom it is remitted[2].

1 See the Immigration Appeals (Procedure) Rules 1984, SI 1984/2041, r 18(1), (2), (3)(a), (b).
2 Ibid, r 18(3)(c). See also *R v Immigration Appeal Tribunal, ex parte Mahendra Singh* [1984] Imm AR 1, DC, and para 366, note 3, below.

366. Determination. The Immigration Appeal Tribunal on further appeal has the same powers as an appellate authority at first appeal[1]. Even if affirming, it may alter, add to or replace the adjudicator's direction or recommendations[2]. It may also remit to any adjudicator (who has the same powers to take fresh evidence) for determination in accordance with its directions where it thinks appropriate[3].

1 See the Immigration Act 1971 (c 77), s 20, and para 334 above.
2 Ibid, s 20(2). For a discussion of powers and duties where the Immigration Appeal Tribunal proposes to differ from the adjudicator, having heard oral evidence, see *R v Immigration Appeal Tribunal, ex parte Mahendra Singh* [1984] Imm AR 1, DC.
3 See the Immigration Appeals (Procedure) Rules 1984, SI 1984/2041, r 21.

(C) PROCEDURE ON REFERENCE FROM THE SECRETARY OF STATE

367. Powers. Where a matter is referred to an appellate authority by the Secretary of State, the authority may consider it in whatever manner it thinks appropriate[1].

1 Immigration Appeals (Procedure) Rules 1984, SI 1984/2041, r 41. As to such references, see the Immigration Act 1971 (c 77), s 21, and para 330 above.

(D) PROCEDURE IN 'SECURITY' DEPORTATION CASES

368. Representations to the 'Three Wise Men'. In the non-statutory 'security' deportation appeals, the person is informed, so far as possible, of the nature of the allegations against him and is given the opportunity to appear before three advisers appointed by the Secretary of State and make representations to them[1]. The advisers, who are known as the 'Three Wise Men', offer their advice to the Secretary of State[1].

1 See the Statement of Changes in Immigration Rules (HC Paper (1989–90) no. 251) (the Immigration Rules), para 157.

369. Criticisms of the procedure. In the few cases in which it has been employed, the procedure in respect of 'security' deportation cases has been criticised as being in breach of natural justice since the person concerned had little idea of the nature of the allegations (for no case was presented for the Home Office, and few or no documents revealed), and since there is no reason for a separate procedure at all[1].

In one case, the deportation order was revoked shortly before the procedure was to be invoked, possibly because the procedure was in breach of Community law[2]. The same case was also found admissible by the European Commission on Human Rights on the ground that no effective legal challenge to the person's detention existed[2] but the applicant lost on the merits.

1 For example *R v Secretary of State for the Home Department, ex parte Hosenball* [1977] 3 All ER 452, [1977] 1 WLR 776, CA. Cf *Liversidge v Anderson* [1942] AC 206, [1941] 3 All ER 338, HL, especially per Lord Atkin at 244, 245, and at 361. See also *Macdonald's Immigration Law and Practice* (3rd edn, 1991, eds I A Macdonald and N J Blake) pp 382–385.
2 *Caprino v United Kingdom* No 6871/75 (1980) 4 EHRR 97. See also *Macdonald* p 330.

(e) Representations by Members of Parliament

370. Introduction. Members of Parliament may be willing to make representations on a case to the Home Office in respect of their constituents, or friends or relations of their constituents. Members of the House of Lords may also be willing to make representations in some cases.

371. Home Office guidelines. The Home Office does not respond as readily to representations from members of Parliament as once it did[1], and issues to MPs a document called 'Guidelines on the Handling of Representations by Members of Parliament'. These guidelines list, non-exhaustively, the sort of inquiry an MP may wish to make, but admit that MPs may wish to raise other matters[2]. The list includes general inquiries about procedures; progress inquiries; supply on information; requests for return of documents; support for a case under appeal; representations about deportations; and support for citizenship applications. They also implicitly enjoin MPs to contact the Immigration and Nationality Department rather than the minister direct, and explicitly ask for sufficient information to identify the subject of the inquiry, including full name, and Home Office number, failing which, the subject's nationality, date of birth, and the date of any application.

The guidelines have no status other than as a published guide to the Home Office view of its role and practice in reacting to representations from MPs. The guidelines admit implicitly that it is not for the Home Office to limit the right of MPs to make representations[3].

1 See eg the account given in L Grant and I Martin *Immigration Law and Practice* (1982) pp 22, 87, 88, 201–204, 247, 248, 276, 341, of the procedure pertaining before the issue of the 'Guidelines on the Handling of Representations by Members of Parliament' (1988, Home Office).
2 Ibid, Annex, para 2.
3 Ibid, para 2.

372. General guidance. The Home Office guidelines outline the responses which will be made to representations. They declare that ministers expect members of Parliament to respect the convention that they do not take up cases involving other MPs' constituents, and that members of the House of Lords will first consult any relevant MP[1]. They record that the minister will review Home

Office decisions only where there is no right of appeal, or the appeal process has been exhausted and there is new and compelling evidence. Thus, the minister will not normally intervene to take an initial decision, to pre-empt an appellate decision, or to overturn a final appellate decision in the absence of new and compelling evidence. It also requests MPs to contact the Immigration and Nationality Department rather than the minister in any correspondence at this stage[2].

1 'Guidelines on the Handling of Representations by Members of Parliament' (1988, Home Office) para 4.
2 Ibid, paras 3, 5, Annex, paras 3, 4.

373. Representations in respect of refusal in entry clearance cases. In respect of entry clearance cases, the Home Office guidelines note that decisions overseas are the responsibility of the Foreign and Commonwealth Office. If a case is referred to the Home Office for decision it will take into account any representations, but the minister will not intervene[1].

Where there is appeal against the refusal, the general guidelines in respect of appeals apply[2].

1 'Guidelines on the Handling of Representations by Members of Parliament' (1988, Home Office) para 6.
2 Ibid, para 7. As to the general guidelines in respect of appeals, see para 372 above.

374. Representations in refusal of entry cases. In respect of refusal of entry cases, including those relating to illegal entrants detected on or shortly after arrival, the Home Office guidelines refer to the fact that in law a decision on refusal of entry is taken by the immigration officer, and that a right of appeal exists[1]. If the minister (or, out of working hours, the Home Office duty officer) receives representations, he may be willing to defer removal of a person for up to eight days, even in the case of an illegal entrant[2]. He will only do so, however, if there are demonstrated to exist exceptional and compelling reasons, such as a bereavement or sudden grave illness in the immediate family, which the immigration officer has had an opportunity to consider and has rejected[3]. The member of Parliament will be asked to provide written representations within the eight days. If he does not provide them, the minister will instruct removal arrangements, the MP will be informed, and removal will take place within four further days[4].

Where there is an application for political asylum and a safe third country to which the person can be removed, there will be no deferral, and all other cases will be dealt with on their merits, without any automatic deferral[5].

Where there is an appeal, the general guidelines in respect of appeals presumably apply[6].

1 'Guidelines on the Handling of Representations by Members of Parliament' (1988, Home Office) paras 8, 9, 11.
2 Ibid, paras 10, 11.
3 Ibid, paras 9, 10.
4 Ibid, para 10.
5 Ibid, para 12.
6 See para 372 above.

375. Representations in 'after entry' cases. In respect of 'after entry' cases, the Home Office guidelines state that representations will be taken into account in applications to extend or vary leave, but that the minister will not intervene[1].

Where there is an appeal pending, the person's leave is automatically extended[2], and (as the general guidelines in respect of appeals declare[3]) the minister will not normally intervene. The guidelines observe that unless there has been a significant change in circumstances there is no point in a member of Parliament making representations at this stage[4].

Representations after the appeal process is unsuccessfully concluded are stated to be unlikely to succeed unless, despite the dismissal of the appeal, the adjudicator has made a recommendation for exceptional treatment outside the Immigration Rules, or unless there is new and compelling evidence[5].

Where the right of appeal has not been exercised, or where no appeal is permitted, the minister is stated to be unlikely to reverse the decision in the absence of new and compelling evidence not known at the time of the decision[6].

1 'Guidelines on the Handling of Representations by Members of Parliament' (1988, Home Office) para 15.
2 See para 332 above.
3 See para 372 above.
4 'Guidelines on the Handling of Representations by Members of Parliament', para 17.
5 Ibid, para 18. As to the Statement of Changes in Immigration Rules (HC Paper (1989–90) no. 251) (the Immigration Rules), see para 110 above.
6 'Guidelines on the Handling of Representations by Members of Parliament', para 18.

376–500. Representations in respect of administrative removal and deportation decisions. In respect of deportation cases, including those of illegal entrants (other than cases dealt with as refusals of entry[1]) the Home Office guidelines declare that any representations will be taken into account before the deportation order is signed (as the Immigration Rules require[2]), but that requests for deferment of removal thereafter will be accepted only if there is new and compelling evidence which was not taken into account when the deportation order was signed[3]. Where such a request is accepted, the minister may defer removal for eight days. The member of Parliament will be asked to provide written representations within that period. If no such representations are received, the minister will give instructions for removal[3]. Where there is an appeal, the general guidelines on appeals presumably apply[4].

In respect of removal of an illegal entrant (other than one dealt with as a refusal of entry[5]), if there has been judicial review of the decision to remove, no request for deferment will be accepted without new and compelling evidence not previously taken into account[6]. The minister may be willing to defer removal for eight days in such cases, and the MP will be asked to provide written representations within the eight days. If he does not provide them, the minister will instruct removal arrangements, the MP will be informed, and removal will take place within four further days[7].

1 See para 374 above.
2 See para 209 above.
3 'Guidelines on the Handling of Representations by Members of Parliament' (1988, Home Office) para 20.
4 See para 372 above.
5 See para 374 above.
6 'Guidelines on the Handling of Representations by Members of Parliament', para 21.
7 Ibid, para 22.

2. EXTRADITION

(1) INTRODUCTION

501. What is extradition. There is no statutory or common law definition of 'extradition'. However, it may be defined as the process whereby a person is surrendered by the authorities of one state to the authorities of another, at the latter's request, because that person is accused of, or alleged to have been convicted of, a crime[1]. This distinguishes it from both refusal of entry and deportation (although on occasion these may constitute disguised extradition[2]). Also, does mere acquiescence by one state in the removal of a person from its territory by agents of another state constitute extradition?

Further, in the United Kingdom, traditionally, the term 'extradition' has been reserved for extradition to foreign states, permitted under the explicitly entitled extradition legislation. Extradition to Commonwealth territories was under separate legislation, the Fugitive Offenders Act 1967 (c 68), which referred to extradition as 'rendition' and employed somewhat different procedures. Extradition to the Republic of Ireland was and is under yet different legislation, the Backing of Warrants (Republic of Ireland) Act 1965 (c 45), employing procedures yet different again.

All these Acts have been amended, in some cases considerably, and the complexity has been modified and increased, at least in the short term, by the Extradition Act 1989 (c 33), which in part replaces the earlier legislation. Provision also exists in the legislation for repatriation of prisoners serving sentences abroad[3].

There is separate legislation governing the return of some other classes of person, for instance some military deserters[4], and in international co-operation in the suppression of crime by others' means[5].

1 For other definitions, see 18 *Halsbury's Laws of England* (4th edn) para 201; V E Hartley-Booth *British Extradition Law and Procedure* (1980) pp LI and 3, 4; I A Shearer *Extradition in International Law* (1971) pp 12, 21; I Stanbrook and C Stanbrook Extradition: The Law and Practice (1980) pp xxv–xxix.

2 See eg *R v Secretary of State for Home Affairs, ex parte Duke of Chateau Thierry* [1917] 1 KB 552, DC; *R v Superintendent of Chiswick Police Station, ex parte Sacksteder* [1918] 1 KB 578, CA; *R v Governor of Brixton Prison, ex parte Soblen* [1963] 2 QB 243, [1962] 3 All ER 641, CA. See also C H R Thornberry 'Dr Soblen and the Alien Law of the United Kingdom' (1963) 12 ICLQ 414; P O'Higgins 'Disguised Extradition: The Soblen Case' (1964) 27 MLR 521.

3 See the Extradition Act 1989 (c 33), s 21.

4 See the Visiting Forces Act 1952 (c 67), ss 1, 13, and ARMED FORCES, vol 2, para 786.

5 Ie under the Criminal Justice (International Co-operation) Act 1990 (c 5).

(2) HISTORICAL BACKGROUND

502. Ancient extradition. Some writers have traced extradition to ancient times, one as far as 1280 BC[1]. However, there is no evidence of theory and practice developing continuously to modern times.

The orthodox view has been that few treaties on the subject existed in Europe before the eighteenth century, but that extradition frequently occurred without benefit of treaty, and that most of those extradited were political opponents of the requesting regime[2]. More recent research strongly suggests the inaccuracy of each of these propositions[3].

It is not necessary to adjudicate between the views, for all the legislation is modern, and earlier periods are of antiquarian interest only. It is, however, worthy of note that one of the earliest medieval treaties was that of 1174 between Scotland and England[4].

1 I A Shearer *Extradition in International Law* (1971) p 5.

2 See eg Sir E Clarke *Extradition* (4th edn, 1903) pp 18–22.

3 P O'Higgins *The Law of Extradition, with particular reference to British practice* (unpublished, PhD thesis) ch 2 'The History of Extradition in British Practice'. I am grateful to Professor O'Higgins

for making this work available. See also (1965) 6 British Digest of International Law (ed C Parry, consulting ed Sir G Fitzmaurice) ch 17 'Extradition Rendition of Offenders' pp 444–449, '2 History of Extradition and Rendition of Offenders in the United Kingdom' especially pp 444, 445.
   4 *Sir E Clarke* p 18.

503. Modern extradition in international law. International customary law appears to have favoured some idea of extradition, although contrary opinions have been offered[1]. The first modern extradition treaties (in the sense that they express the major characteristics and principles which are still current) were concluded in the late eighteenth or early nineteenth centuries[2]. France was the chief innovator. Principles evolving in the common law world differed somewhat from those in the civil law world (for example, in relation to the requirement in common law countries of a prima facie case, and the exemption in the civil law countries of 'own nationals'), but through the influence of numerous multi-lateral treaties[3], the divergence is decreasing. Further, rendering of fugitives within the British Empire, not being between foreign countries, diverged fundamentally from extradition in other contexts. However, such divergences are now also much reduced.

Few entirely new bilateral extradition treaties have been concluded since 1914. So far as the United Kingdom is concerned, special arrangements within the Commonwealth have reduced the effect of the lack of new treaties. Also, since 1945 there has been a marked growth of an alternative to extradition, that is a deterritorialisation of criminal jurisdiction in relation to terrorist and like offences[4].

Most important of all, there has been the growth of a different framework for extradition. Bilateral treaties concerning all types of extradition are being replaced by multi-lateral ones concerning extradition for specific purposes[5].

   1 I A Shearer *Extradition in International Law* (1971) pp 22 ff, especially references to Grotius and Vattel and others (see p 24, notes 1–5).
   2 *Shearer* pp 7–19.
   3 See especially the European Convention on Extradition (1957), the Additional Protocol ETS 86 (1975), and the Second Protocol ETS 98 (1978) and paras 506–508 below.
   4 See para 508 below.
   5 See para 507 below.

504. Modern extradition in municipal law. At common law, there appears to be no power inhering in any authority in the United Kingdom to surrender a person to a foreign state[1], although no explicit statement to this effect appears. Barriers to the trial of those surrendered by foreign states to the United Kingdom, whether at common law or by statute, are more or less non-existent[2].

Hume, while discussing criminal jurisdiction over Scots abroad, skirts the subject but refers with approval to the Criminal Procedure Act 1701 (c 6) which he concluded to accord with precedent and sound principle[3]. This implicitly forbids extradition for trial abroad, and accepts a jurisdiction for the *forum delicti* without reference to the means of apprehension, if an accused be found within the jurisdiction[4]. However, arrangements for surrender between England and Scotland have existed for a long time[5].

Extradition from the United Kingdom is therefore entirely statutory, and extradition to it is almost entirely berefit of law.

   1 *Diamond v Minter* [1941] 1 KB 656, [1941] 1 All ER 390. For earlier English views, see Blackstone, *Commentaries on the Laws of England* (14th edn, 1803) vol 1, p 366; *East India Co v Campbell* (1749) 1 Ves Sen 246; *Mure v Kaye* (1811) 4 Taunt 34. See also *International Law Opinions* (1956, ed Lord McNair) II, 43.
   2 See paras 577 ff below.

3 Hume *Commentaries* II, 52. There is an English equivalent in the Habeas Corpus Act 1679 (c 2).
4 *Hume* p 57.
5 See eg the Extradition with England Act 1612 (c 2), the English statute the Criminal Law Act 1609 (c 1), and the Criminal Law Act 1773 (c 31) (all repealed).

(3) PURPOSES

505. Why extradite. Some features of law may be best explained as expressing a desire on the part of the state to get its fugitive criminals back, for which it is prepared to pay the price of reciprocity. Characteristics such as the exclusion of political offences, the speciality rule, the common law prima facie case requirement, and the civil law exemption for 'own nationals' are otherwise hard to explain.

Alternatives to extradition, such as trial *in absentia* by the *forum delicti*, or trial in the *forum deprehensionis* without prosecution witnesses, have obvious drawbacks. However, the growth of multi-lateral extradition agreements betokens a somewhat different policy, that is, a reciprocal interest in the suppression of crime.

(4) SOURCES AND AUTHORITY

(a) Extradition to Foreign States

506. International law generally. Customary international law on extradition is unclear. In practice, the subject is treated wholly as a matter of treaty[1].

1 See eg I A Shearer *Extradition in International Law* (1971) ch 2, especially pp 22–36; G Schwarzenberger *International Law* (3rd edn, 1957) vol 1, pp 256–260; L Oppenheim *International Law* (8th edn, 1983, ed Lauterpacht) vol 1, ss 327 ff.

507. Bilateral treaties. The United Kingdom currently has bilateral treaties with forty-four states, as follows: Albania[1], Argentine Republic[2], Austria[3], Belgium[4], Bolivia[5], Chile[6], Colombia[7], Cuba[8], Czechoslovakia[9], Denmark[10], Ecuador[11], Finland[12], France[13], Federal Republic of Germany[14], Greece[15], Guatemala[16], Haiti[17], Hungary[18], Iceland[19], Iraq[20], Israel[21], Italy[22], Liberia[23], Luxembourg[24], Mexico[25], Monaco[26], the Netherlands[27], Nicaragua[28], Norway[29], Panama[30], Paraguay[31], Peru[32], Poland[33], Portugal[34], Roumania[35], El Salvador[36], San Marino[37], Spain[38], Sweden[39], Switzerland[40], Thailand[41], United States of America[42], Uruguay[43], and Yugoslavia[44]. All such treaties are in broadly similar form, enjoining reciprocal extradition for certain acts, subject to certain limits, and following specified procedures, save that those in relation to Austria, Denmark, Finland, France, Federal Republic of Germany, Greece, Iceland, Israel, Italy, Luxembourg, the Netherlands, Norway, Portugal, Spain, Sweden and Switzerland continue only in relation to transitional cases and to dependencies of those countries to which the European Convention on Extradition does not apply[45]. Extradition to those countries now takes place under the aegis of that Convention[46].

A number of other treaties have been regarded as lapsed[47] (that is those with Estonia[48], Latvia[49], Lithuania[50] and Russia[51]), and other treaties appear to have expired (that is those with the Cameroons and Togo[52] and Tunisia)[53].

1 See the Treaty with Albania (Tirana, 22 July 1926; TS 20 (1927); Cmd 2920), and the Albania (Extradition) Order in Council 1927, SR & O 1927/605.

2 See the Treaty with the Argentine Republic (Buenos Ayres, 22 May 1889; TS 2 (1894); C 7260); the Exchange of Notes dated 19 November 1979; and the Extradition, Argentine Republic Order in Council 1894, SR & O 1894/76 (amended by SI 1980/185).

3 See the Treaty with Austria (Vienna, 9 January 1963; TS 68 (1970); Cmnd 4438); Exchange of Notes dated 25 August 1971. See also the Austria (Extradition) Order 1970, SI 1970/1111; and the Austria (Extradition) Order 1972, SI 1972/1581 (both revoked with savings by the European Convention on Extradition Order 1990, SI 1990/1507, art 5, Sch 5), and para 508, note 12, below.

4 See the Treaty with Belgium (Brussels, 29 October 1901; TS 7 (1902); Cd 1008); Supplementary Conventions (London 5 March 1907; TS 16 (1907); Cd 3580), (London, 3 March 1911; TS 21 (1911); Cd 5807), (London, 8 August 1923; TS 1 (1924); Cmd 2026); Exchanges of Notes (London, 28 June and 2 July 1928; TS 20 (1928); Cmd 3203), (Brussels, 15 May 1975; TS 107 (1975); Cmnd 6203), (London, 10 September 1985; TS 59 (1985); Cmnd 9659); the Extradition, Belgium Orders in Council 1902, SR & O 1902/208, 1907, SR & O 1907/544, 1911, SR & O 1911/793; the Extradition, certain foreign states (white slave traffic) Order in Council 1923, SR & O 1923/971; and the Belgium (Extradition) (Amendment) Orders 1975, SI 1975/1034, 1985, SI 1985/1634.

5 See the Treaty with Bolivia (Lima, 22 February 1892; TS 10 (1899); C 9239), and the Extradition, Bolivia Order in Council 1898, SR & O 1898/597.

6 See the Treaty with Chile (Santiago, 26 January 1897; TS 12 (1898); C 9051), and the Extradition, Chile Order in Council 1898, SR & O 1898/597.

7 See the Treaty with Colombia (Bogotá, 27 October 1888; 79 BFSP 12; C 5902), and the Extradition, Columbia Order in Council dated 28 November 1889.

8 See the Treaty with Cuba (Havana, 3 October 1904; TS 15 (1905); Cd 2530), and the Extradition, Cuba Order in Council 1905, SR & O 1905/558.

9 See the Treaty with Czechoslovakia (London, 11 November 1924; TS 31 (1926); Cmd 2779), and the Czechoslovakia Extradition Order in Council 1926, SR & O 1926/1466.

10 See the Treaty with Denmark (Copenhagen, 31 March 1873; 63 BFSP 5; C 779), Exchange of Notes dated 24 August 1979. See also Extradition, Denmark Order in Council dated 26 June 1873; the Denmark (Extradition) Order in Council 1936, SR & O 1936/405; and the Denmark (Extradition) (Amendment) Order 1979, SI 1979/1311 (all revoked with savings: see note 3 above), and para 508, note 12, below.

11 See the Treaty with Ecuador (Quito, 20 September 1880; 72 BFSP 137; C 4786), and the Extradition, Ecuador Order in Council dated 26 June 1886.

12 See the Treaty with Finland (London, 29 October 1975; TS 23 (1977); Cmnd 6741); Exchanges of Notes (Helsinki 12 May 1976; TS 23 (1977); Cmnd 6741), (London, 29 October 1975, TS 53 (1977); Cmnd 6843). See also the Finland (Extradition) Order 1976, SI 1976/1037 (revoked with savings: see note 3 above), and para 508, note 12, below.

13 See the Treaty with France (Paris, 14 August 1876; 67 BFSP 5; C 2008) (amended by Conventions (Paris, 13 February 1896; TS 4 (1896); C 7973), (Paris, 17 October 1908; TS 34 (1909); Cd 4965)); Exchange of Notes (Paris, 16 February 1978; TS 62 (1978); Cmd 7241). See also the Extradition, France Order in Council dated 16 May 1878; the Extradition, France Order in Council 1896, SR & O 1896/54; the Extradition, France and Tunis Order in Council 1909, SR & O 1909/1458; and the France (Extradition) (Amendment) Order 1978, SI 1978/455 (all revoked with savings: see note 3 above), and para 508, note 12, below.

14 See the Treaty with Germany (London, 14 May 1872; 62 BFSP 5; C 564); Agreement (Bonn, 23 February 1960; TS 70 (1960); Cmnd 1200); Exchange of Notes (London, 25–27 September 1978; TS 5 (1979); Cmnd 7421). See also the Federal Republic of Germany (Extradition) Order 1960, SI 1960/1375; and the Federal Republic of Germany (Extradition) (Amendment) Order 1978, SI 1978/1403 (both revoked with savings: see note 3 above), and para 508, note 12, below.

15 See the Treaty with Greece (Athens, 11 and 24 September 1910; TS 6 (1912); Cd 6074), and the Extradition, Greece Order in Council 1912, SR & O 1912/193 (revoked with savings: see note 3 above). See also para 508, note 12, below.

16 See the Treaty with Guatemala (Guatemala, 4 July 1885; 76 BFSP 72; C 4920); Protocol (Guatemala City, 30 May 1914; TS 12 (1914); Cd 7625); the Extradition, Guatemala Order in Council dated 26 November 1886; and the Extradition, Guatemala Order in Council 1914, SR & O 1914/1323.

17 See the Treaty with Haiti (Port au Prince, 7 December 1874; 65 BFSP 44; C 1385), and the Extradition, Hayti Order in Council dated 5 February 1876.

18 See the Treaty with Hungary (Vienna, 3 December 1873; 63 BFSP 213; C 916 (amended by Declaration (London, 26 June 1901; TS 13 (1902); C 1078))); Supplementary Treaty (Budapest, 18 September 1936; TS 32 (1937); Cmd 5550) (spent in relation to Austria); Extradition, Hungary Order in Council dated 17 March 1874; and the Hungary (Extradition) Order in Council 1937, SR & O 1937/719.

19 See the Treaty with Iceland (ie Supplementary Convention to Treaty with Denmark of 31 March 1873: see note 10 above) (London, 25 October 1938; TS 40 (1939); Cmd 6083), and the Iceland (Extradition) Order in Council 1939, SR & O 1939/825 (revoked with savings: see note 3 above). See also para 508, note 12, below.

20 See the Treaty with Iraq (Baghdad, 2 May 1932; TS 13 (1933); Cmd 4317), and the Iraq (Extradition) Order in Council 1933, SR & O 1933/357.

21 See the Agreement with Israel (London, 4 April 1960; TS 77 (1960); Cmnd 1223); Exchange of Notes (Tel Aviv/Jerusalem, 16 August 1978; TS 99 (1978); Cmnd 7375). See also the Israel (Extradition) Order 1960, SI 1960/1660; and the Israel (Extradition) (Amendment) Order 1978, SI 1978/1623 (both revoked with savings: see note 3 above), and para 508, note 12, below.

22 See the Treaty with Italy (Rome, 5 February 1873; 63 BFSP 19; C 708), and the Extradition, Italy Order in Council dated 24 March 1873 (revoked with savings: see note 3 above). See also para 508, note 12, below.

23 See the Treaty with Liberia (London, 16 December 1892; TS 6 (1894); C 7306), and the Extradition, Liberia Order in Council 1894, SR & O 1894/114.

24 See the Treaty with Luxembourg (Luxembourg, 24 November 1880; 71 BFSP 48; C 2803); Supplementary Convention (Luxembourg, 29 May 1939; TS 59 (1951); Cmd 8321). See also the Extradition, Luxembourg Order in Council dated 2 March 1881; and the Luxembourg (Extradition) Order in Council 1951, SI 1951/1170 (both revoked with savings: see note 3 above), and para 508, note 12, below.

25 See the Treaty with Mexico (Mexico City, 7 September 1886; 77 BFSP 1253; C 5670), and the Extradition, Mexico Order in Council dated 6 April 1889).

26 See the Treaty with Monaco (Paris, 17 December 1891; TS 10 (1892); C 6552), and the Extradition, Monaco Order in Council dated 9 May 1892.

27 See the Treaty with the Netherlands (London, 26 September 1898; TS 1 (1889); C 9089), and the Extradition, Netherlands Order in Council 1899, SR & O 1899/83 (revoked with savings: see note 3 above). See also para 508, note 12, below.

28 See the Treaty with Nicaragua (Managua, 19 April 1905; TS 7 (1906); Cd 3001), and the Extradition, Nicaragua Order in Council 1906, SR & O 1906/382.

29 See the Treaty with Norway (Stockholm, 26 June 1873; 63 BFSP 175; C 900); Agreement (Kristiania, 18 February 1907; TS 19 (1907); Cd 3606); Exchange of Notes (Oslo, 5 August 1985; TS 6 (1986); Cmnd 9707). See also the Extradition, Norway and Sweden Order in Council dated 30 September 1873; the Extradition, Norway Order in Council 1907, SR & O 1907/545; the Norway (Extradition) (Amendment) Order 1979, SI 1979/913; and the Norway (Extradition) (Amendment) Order 1985, SI 1985/1637 (all revoked with savings: see note 3 above), and para 508, note 12, below.

30 See the Treaty with Panama (Panama, 25 August 1906; TS 25 (1907); Cd 3648), and the Extradition, Panama Order in Council 1907, SR & O 1907/648.

31 See the Treaty with Paraguay (Asuncion, 12 September 1908; TS 19 (1911); Cd 5737), and the Extradition, Paraguay Order in Council 1911, SR & O 1911/662.

32 See the Treaty with Peru (Lima, 26 January 1904; TS 13 (1907); Cd 3498), and the Extradition, Peru Order in Council 1907, SR & O 1907/383.

33 See the Treaty with Poland (Warsaw, 11 January 1932; TS 10 (1934); Cmd 4552), and the Poland Extradition Order in Council 1934, SR & O 1934/209.

34 See the Treaty with Portugal (Lisbon, 17 October 1892; TS 7 (1894); C 7307); Protocol (Lisbon, 30 November 1892; TS 7 (1894); C 7307); Supplementary Convention (Lisbon, 20 January 1932; TS 28 (1933); Cmd 4401). See also the Extradition, Portugal Order in Council 1894, SR & O 1894/102; and the Portugal (Extradition) Order in Council 1933, SR & O 1933/678 (both revoked with savings: see note 3 above), and para 508, note 12, below.

35 See the Treaty with Roumania and Protocol (Bucharest, 21 March 1893; TS 14 (1894); C 7357), and the Extradition, Roumania Order in Council 1894, SR & O 1894/119.

36 See the Treaty with El Salvador (Paris, 23 June 1881; 72 BFSP 13; C 3445), and the Extradition, Salvador Order in Council dated 16 December 1882.

37 See the Treaty with San Marino (Florence, 16 October 1899; TS 9 (1900); Cd 40), and the Extradition, San Marino Order in Council 1900, SR & O 1900/168.

38 See the Treaty with Spain (London, 22 July 1985; TS 40 (1986); Cmnd 9615), and the Spain (Extradition) Order 1986, SI 1986/766 (revoked with savings: see note 3 above). See also para 508, note 12, below.

39 See the Treaty with Sweden (London, 26 April 1963; TS 62 (1966); Cmnd 3113); Exchange of Notes (Stockholm, 19 February 1980; TS 53 (1980); Cmnd 7946); and the Sweden (Extradition) Order 1966, SI 1966/226 (amended by SI 1980/566) (both revoked with savings: see note 3 above), and para 508, note 12, below.

40 See the Treaty with Switzerland (Berne, 26 November 1880; 71 BFSP 54; C 2885); Supplementary Conventions (London, 29 June 1904; TS 16 (1905); Cd 2532), (Berne, 19 December 1934; TS

29 (1935); Cmd 4975). See also the Extradition, Switzerland Order in Council dated 18 May 1881; the Extradition, Switzerland Order in Council 1905, SR & O 1905/616; and the Switzerland (Extradition) Order in Council 1935, SR & O 1935/676 (all revoked with savings: see note 3 above), and para 508, note 12, below.

41 See the Treaty with Siam (Bangkok, 4 March 1911; TS 23 (1911); Cd 5861), and the Extradition, Siam Order in Council 1911, SR & O 1911/1151.

42 See the Treaties with the United States of America (London, 22 December 1931; TS 18 (1935); Cmd 4928), (London, 8 June 1972; TS 16 (1977); Cmnd 6723); Supplementary Treaty (Washington, 25 June 1985; US 2 (1985); Cmnd 9565); Exchange of Notes (Washington, 19 and 20 August 1986; US 3 (1986); Cmnd 9915); the United States of America (Extradition) Order 1976, SI 1976/2144; and the United States of America (Extradition) (Amendment) Order 1986, SI 1986/2020 (amended by SI 1987/2046).

43 See the Treaty with Uruguay (Monte Video, 26 March 1884; 75 BFSP 18; C 4282); Protocol (Monte Video, 20 March 1891; TS 4 (1892); C 6593); and the Extradition, Uruguay Orders in Council dated 5 March 1885 and 24 November 1891.

44 See the Treaty with Servia (Belgrade, 6 December 1900; TS 8 (1901); Cd 797), and the Extradition, Servia Order in Council 1901, SR & O 1901/586.

45 Ie under the European Convention on Extradition Order 1990, which came into force on 14 May 1991 upon ratification of the Convention by the United Kingdom: see para 508, note 12, below.

46 See note 45 above. Also under the regime applied by the Extradition Act 1989 (c 33), these bilateral treaties will gradually decrease in importance, being replaced by multilateral agreements (see para 508 below), or 'ad hoc' extradition.

47 See 478 HC Official Report (5th Series) col 464.

48 See the Treaty with Estonia (London, 18 November 1925; TS 18 (1926); Cmd 2708), and the Estonia (Extradition) Order in Council 1926, SR & O 1926/840 (spent).

49 See the Treaty with Latvia (Riga, 16 July 1924; TS 44 (1924); Cmd 2519), and the Latvia (Extradition) Order in Council 1925, SR & O 1925/1029 (spent).

50 See the Treaty with Lithuania (Kaunas (Kovno), 18 May 1926; TS 15 (1927); Cmd 2897), and the Lithuania (Extradition) Order in Council 1927, SR & O 1927/504 (spent).

51 See the Treaty with Russia (London, 24 November 1886; 77 BFSP 107; C 4992), and the Extradition Order in Council (Russia) dated 7 March 1887 (spent).

52 See the Treaty with France (see note 13 above) applied by Exchange of Notes (London, 21 September and 13 November 1923; 117 BFSP 314), and the France (Extradition) Order in Council 1928, SR & O 1928/575.

53 See the Treaty with France (see note 13 above) applied by Agreements (Paris, 31 December 1889; 81 BFSP 55; C 5976), (Paris, 29 July 1909; TS 35 (1909); Cd 4966), and the France (Extradition) Order in Council 1928.

508. Multilateral agreements. In addition to bilateral treaties there are twelve multilateral agreements to which the United Kingdom is party, and which require parties variously to treat them as extradition arrangements, to extend their criminal jurisdiction, to extend the range of their extraditable offences, to narrow the political offence exemption to extradition, and to do other things[1]. They are:

(1) the International Convention for the Suppression of the White Slave Traffic[2];

(2) the Convention on the Prevention and Punishment of the Crime of Genocide[3];

(3) the Tokyo Convention on Offences Committed on Board Aircraft in Flight[4];

(4) the Hague Convention on Unlawful Seizure of Aircraft[5];

(5) the Montreal Convention for the Suppression of Unlawful Acts against the Safety of Civil Aviation and Protocol[6];

(6) the New York Convention on Crimes against Internationally Protected Persons[7];

(7) the European Convention on the Suppression of Terrorism[8];

(8) the International Convention against the Taking of Hostages[9];

(9) the Convention on the Physical Protection of Nuclear Material[10];

(10) the United Nations Convention against Torture and other Cruel, Inhuman or Degrading Treatment or Punishment[11];

(11) the European Convention on Extradition[12]; and
(12) the Vienna Convention against Illicit Narcotic Drugs and Psychotropic Substances[13].

1 Under the Extradition Act 1870 (c 52), ss 2, 4, 17 and 21 (as saved by the Extradition Act 1989 (c 33), s 1(3) and set out in Sch 1) the Extradition Acts are applied so as to render specified offences extraditable in respect of states signatory to the Conventions with which the United Kingdom has a bilateral extradition treaty (as to which see para 507 above).

2 Ie the International Agreement for the Suppression of the White Slave Traffic (Paris, 18 May 1904; TS 24 (1905); Cd 2689); the International Convention for the Suppression of the White Slave Traffic (Paris, 4 May 1910; TS 20 (1912); Cd 6326); and Protocol (Lake Success, 4 May 1949; TS 85 (1953); Cmd 9042). As to the application of the Convention, see note 1 above, the Extradition, certain foreign states (white slave traffic) Order in Council 1923, SR & O 1923/971 (as amended by SI 1951/1384; SI 1970/1111; SI 1978/1523; and SI 1986/766) (Belgium, France, Hungary, Monaco, Netherlands, Norway, Portugal, Thailand, Tunis (however, see para 507 text and note 52 above) and Uruguay); the Extradition (Cuba, Italy, Luxemburg, Switzerland and Yugoslavia) (White Slave Traffic) Order in Council 1931, SR & O 1931/718; and the Extradition (Denmark) (White Slave Traffic) Order in Council 1934, SR & O 1934/500.

3 Ie the Convention on the Prevention and Punishment of the Crime of Genocide (Paris, 9 December 1948; TS 58 (1970); Cmnd 4421). As to the application of the Convention in respect of the offence of genocide, see note 1 above, and the Extradition (Genocide) Order 1970, SI 1970/147 (amended by SI 1978/1886; SI 1981/209; SI 1982/145; SI 1986/2011; and SI 1987/453) (Albania, Argentina, Austria, Belgium, Chile, Columbia, Cuba, Czechoslovakia, Denmark, Ecuador, El Salvador, Finland, France, (Federal Republic of) Germany, Greece, Guatemala, Haiti, Hungary, Iceland, Iraq, Israel, Italy, Liberia, Luxembourg, Mexico, Monaco, Netherlands, Nicaragua, Norway, Panama, Peru, Poland, Romania, Spain, Sweden, Uruguay, Yugoslavia, and specified United Kingdom overseas territories).

4 Ie the Convention on Offences and certain other Acts committed on Board Aircraft ('the Tokyo Convention') (Tokyo, 14 September 1963; TS 126 (1969); Cmnd 4230). As to the application of the Convention in respect of offences on board aircraft in flight registered in states signatory to the Convention, see note 1 above, the Extradition Act 1989 (c 33), ss 1, 22, Sch 1, para 14, and the Extradition (Tokyo Convention) Order 1971, SI 1971/2103 (amended by SI 1982/149, SI 1985/1993, SI 1986/2016, and SI 1987/456) (Argentina, Austria, Belgium, Bolivia, Chile, Columbia, Czechoslovakia, Denmark, Ecuador, El Salvador, Finland, France, (Federal Republic of) Germany, Greece, Guatemala, Haiti, Hungary, Iceland, Iraq, Israel, Italy, Luxembourg, Mexico, Monaco, Netherlands, Nicaragua, Norway, Panama, Paraguay, Peru, Poland, Portugal, Romania, Spain, Sweden, Switzerland, Thailand, Uruguay, United States of America, Yugoslavia and specified United Kingdom overseas territories).

5 Ie the Convention for the Suppression of Unlawful Seizure of Aircraft ('the Hague Convention') (The Hague, 16 December 1970; TS 39 (1972); Cmnd 4956). As to the application of the Convention to render hijacking extraditable in respect of states signatory to the Convention, whether or not the United Kingdom has a bilateral extradition treaty with them, see note 1 above, the Extradition Act 1989, s 22, and the Extradition (Hijacking) Order 1971, SI 1971/2102 (amended by SI 1977/1237, SI 1978/1887, SI 1981/210, SI 1982/146, SI 1985/1989, SI 1986/2012, SI 1987/451, SI 1987/2041, and SI 1988/2243) ((1) Argentina, Austria, Belgium, Bolivia, Chile, Columbia, Czechoslovakia, Denmark, Ecuador, El Salvador, Finland, France, (Federal Republic of) Germany, Greece, Guatemala, Haiti, Hungary, Iceland, Iraq, Israel, Italy, Liberia, Luxembourg, Mexico, Monaco, Netherlands, Nicaragua, Norway, Panama, Paraguay, Peru, Poland, Portugal, Romania, Spain, Sweden, Switzerland, Thailand, United States of America, Uruguay and Yugoslavia (with which there are bilateral treaties); (2) Afghanistan, Bahrain, Benin, Brazil, Bulgaria, Byelorussia, Cape Verde, Chad, China, Congo, Costa Rica, Dominican Republic, Egypt, Ethiopia, Gabonese Republic, (Democratic Republic of) Germany, Guinea, Guinea-Bissau, Indonesia, Iran, Ivory Coast, Japan, Jordan, Korea, Kuwait, Lebanon, Libya, Mali, Mauritania, Mongolia, Morocco, Nepal, Niger, Oman, Pakistan, Philippines, Qatar, Saudi Arabia, Senegal, South Africa, Sudan, Surinam, Syria, Togo, Tunisia, Turkey, Ukraine, Union of Soviet Socialist Republics, United Arab Emirates, Venezuela, Vietnam, Yemen Arab Republic and Zaire (with which no bilateral extradition treaties exist); and (3) specified United Kingdom overseas territories).

6 Ie the Convention for the Suppression of Unlawful Acts against the Safety of Civil Aviation ('the Montreal Convention') (Montreal, 23 September 1971; TS 10 (1974); Cmnd 5524), and Protocol for the Suppression of Unlawful Acts of Violence at Airports serving International Civil Aviation (Montreal, 24 February 1988; TS 20 (1991); Cm 1470). As to the application of the Convention to render offences against the safety of aircraft extraditable in respect of states signatory to the Convention or Protocol, whether or not the United Kingdom has a bilateral

extradition treaty with them, see note 1 above, the Extradition Act 1989, s 22, and the Extradition (Aviation Security) Order 1991, SI 1991/1699 ((1) Argentina, Belgium, Bolivia, Chile, Colombia, Czech and Slovak Federal Republic, Ecuador, El Salvador, Guatemala, Haiti, Hungary, Iraq, Liberia, Mexico, Monaco, Nicaragua, Panama, Paraguay, Peru, Poland, Romania, Thailand, United States of America, Uruguay and Yugoslavia (parties to the Convention with which bilateral treaties exists); (2) Chile, Czech and Slovak Federal Republic, Hungary, Iran, Mexico, Peru, Yugoslavia (parties to the Protocol with which bilateral treaties exists); (3) Afghanistan, Bahrain, Bhutan, Brazil, Bulgaria, Burkina Faso, Cameroon, Cape Verde, Chad, China, Congo, Costa Rica, Dominican Republic, Egypt, Equatorial Guinea, Ethiopia, Gabon, Guinea, Guinea-Bissau, Honduras, Indonesia, Iran, Ivory Coast, Japan, Jordan, Republic of Korea, Kuwait, Laos, Lebanon, Libya, Madagascar, Mali, Mauritania, Mongolia, Morocco, Nepal, Niger, Oman, Philippines, Qatar, Rwanda, Saudi Arabia, Senegal, South Africa, Sudan, Suriname, Syria, Togo, Tunisia, Union of Soviet Socialist Republics, Byelorussian Soviet Socialist Republic, Ukrainian Soviet Socialist Republic, United Arab Emirates, Venezuela, Vietnam, Republic of Yemen, Zaire (parties to the Convention with which no bilateral treaties exist); and (4) Bulgaria, Republic of Korea, Kuwait, Mali, Saudi Arabia, Togo, Union of Soviet Socialist Republics, Byelorussian Soviet Socialist Republic and United Arab Emirates (parties to the Protocol with which no bilateral treaties exist)).

7 Ie the Convention on the Prevention and Punishment of Crimes against Internationally Protected Persons, including Diplomatic Agents (the Internationally Protected Persons Convention) (New York, 14 December 1973 – 31 December 1974; TS 3 (1980); Cmnd 7765. As to the application of the Convention to render offences against internationally protected persons extraditable in respect of states signatory to the Convention, whether or not the United Kingdom has a bilateral extradition treaty with them, see note 1 above, the Extradition Act 1989, s 22, and the Extradition (Internationally Protected Persons) Order 1979, SI 1979/453 (amended by SI 1982/147, SI 1985/1990, SI 1986/2013, SI 1987/454, SI 1987/2042 and SI 1988/2244 ((1) Argentina, Austria, Chile, Czechoslovakia, Denmark, Ecuador, El Salvador, Finland, (Federal Republic of) Germany, Greece, Guatemala, Haiti, Hungary, Iceland, Iraq, Israel, Italy, Liberia, Mexico, Nicaragua, Norway, Panama, Paraguay, Peru, Poland, Romania, Spain, Sweden, Switzerland, United States of America, Uruguay and Yugoslavia (with which there are bilateral treaties); (2) Bulgaria, Costa Rica, Gabon, (Democratic Republic of) Germany, Iran, Jordan, Korea, Mongolia, Niger, Oman, Pakistan, Philippines, Rwanda, Syria, Togo, Tunisia, Turkey, Union of Soviet Socialist Republics and Zaire (with which no bilateral extradition treaties exist); and (3) specified United Kingdom overseas territories).

8 Ie the European Convention on the Suppression of Terrorism (Strasbourg, 27 January 1977; TS 93 (1978); Cmnd 7390). As to the application of the Convention to prevent certain offences of violence, or in respect of aircraft, falling within the political offence exemption in respect of states signatory to the Convention or otherwise, and whether or not the United Kingdom has a bilateral treaty with them, as designated by the Secretary of State, see note 1 above, and the Extradition (Suppression of Terrorism) Order 1978, SI 1978/1106 (amended by SI 1980/398, SI 1980/1525, SI 1981/1544, SI 1986/220, SI 1986/1300, SI 1987/2206 and SI 1990/1306) (Austria, Belgium, Denmark, Finland, France, (Federal Republic of) Germany, Greece, Iceland, Italy, Luxembourg, the Netherlands, Norway, Portugal, Spain, Sweden and Switzerland).

As to the countries designated parties to the Convention, see the Suppression of Terrorism Act 1978 (Designation of Countries) Orders 1978, SI 1978/1245 (Austria, Denmark, (Federal Republic of) Germany (and West Berlin), Sweden); 1979, SI 1979/497 (Cyprus); 1980, SI 1980/357 (Norway); 1980, SI 1980/1392 (Iceland); 1981, SI 1981/1389 (Spain, Turkey); 1981, SI 1981/1507 (Luxembourg); 1986, SI 1986/271 (Belgium, Netherlands, Portugal, Switzerland); 1986, SI 1986/1137 (Italy, Liechtenstein); 1987, SI 1987/2137 (France); 1989, SI 1989/2210 (Republic of Ireland) and 1990, SI 1990/1272 (Finland, Greece).

The Convention is extended with exceptions, additions and modifications to Anguilla, Bermuda, British Indian Ocean Territory, British Virgin Islands, Cayman Islands, Falkland Islands, Falkland Islands Dependencies, Gibraltar, Montserrat, Pitcairn, Henderson, Ducie and Oeno Islands, St Helena, St Helena Dependencies, Sovereign Base Areas of Akrotiri and Dhekelia in the Island of Cyprus, and the Turks and Caicos Islands (see the Suppression of Terrorism Act 1978 (Overseas Territories) Order 1986, SI 1986/2019) and Hong Kong (see the Suppression of Terrorism Act 1978 (Hong Kong) Order 1987, SI 1987/2045).

9 Ie the International Convention against the Taking of Hostages (the Hostage Convention) (New York, 18–31 December 1979; TS 81 (1983); Cmnd 9100). As to the application of the Convention to render an offence under the Taking of Hostages Act 1982 (c 28) extraditable in respect of states signatory to the Convention, whether or not the United Kingdom has a bilateral extradition treaty with them, see note 1 above, the Extradition Act 1989, s 22, and the Extradition (Taking of Hostages) Order 1985, SI 1985/751 (amended by SI 1985/1992, SI 1986/2015, SI 1987/455, SI 1987/2044, and SI 1988/2246) (1) Austria, Chile, Czechoslovakia, Ecuador, El Salvador, Fin-

land, (Federal Republic of) Germany, Guatemala, Iceland, Italy, Norway, Panama, Portugal, Spain, Sweden, Switzerland, United States of America and Yugoslavia (with which there are bilateral treaties), and (2) Bhutan, Bulgaria, Cameroon, Egypt, (Democratic Republic of) Germany, Honduras, Japan, Jordan, Republic of Korea, Philippines, Senegal, Suriname and Togo (with which no bilateral treaty exists). The Taking of Hostages Act 1982 is (with additions, exemptions and modifications) extended to Jersey (Taking of Hostages (Jersey) Order 1982, SI 1982/1533), Guernsey (Taking of Hostages (Guernsey) Order 1982, SI 1982/1539), the Isle of Man (Taking of Hostages (Isle of Man) (No 2) Order 1982, SI 1982/1839), Anguilla, Bermuda, British Indian Ocean Territory, Cayman Islands, Falkland Islands, Falkland Islands and Dependencies, Gibraltar, Hong Kong, Montserrat, Pitcairn, Henderson, Ducie and Oeno Islands, St Helena and Dependencies, Sovereign Base Areas of Akrotiri and Dhekelia, Turks and Caicos Islands and the Virgin Islands (see the Taking of Hostages Act 1982 (Overseas Territories) Order 1982, SI 1982/1540 (amended by SI 1987/455)) and the Extradition (Taking of Hostages) Order 1985, Sch 4 (amended by SI 1987/455).

10 Ie the Convention on the Physical Protection of Nuclear Material (Misc 27 (1980); Cmnd 8112) (not yet issued in the United Kingdom Treaty Series). As to the application of the Convention to render offences under the Nuclear Materials (Offences) Act 1983 (c 18) extraditable in respect of states signatory to the Convention, whether or not the United Kingdom has a bilateral extradition treaty with them, see note 1 above, the Extradition Act 1989, s 22, and the Extradition (Protection of Nuclear Material) Order 1991, SI 1991/1720 ((1) Argentina, the Czech and Slovak Federal Republic, Guatemala, Hungary, Mexico, Paraguay, Poland, United States of America and Yugoslavia (with which bilateral treaties exist); and (2) Brazil, Bulgaria, China, Indonesia, Japan, Republic of Korea, Mongolia, Philippines and the Union of Soviet Socialist Republics (with which no bilateral treaties exist).

11 Ie the Convention against Torture and other Cruel, Inhuman or Degrading Treatment or Punishment (the Torture Convention) (New York, 4 February 1985; TS 107 (1991); Cm 1775). As to the application of the Convention to render torture, as defined by the Criminal Justice Act 1988 (c 33), s 134, extraditable in respect of the states signatory to the Convention whether or not the United Kingdom has a bilateral extradition treaty with them, see note 1 above, the Extradition Act 1989, s 22, and the Extradition (Torture) Order 1991, SI 1991/1702 ((1) Argentina, Chile, Colombia, Czech and Slovak Federal Republic, Ecuador, Guatemala, Hungary, Mexico, Panama, Paraguay, Peru, Poland, Romania, Uruguay (with which there are bilateral treaties); (2) Austria, Denmark, France, Germany, Greece, Italy, Luxembourg, Netherlands, Norway, Portugal, Spain, Sweden, Switzerland (with which bilateral treaties exist in respect of specified United Kingdom territories); (3) Afghanistan, Algeria, Brazil, Bulgaria, Cameroon, China, Egypt, Guinea, Libya, Philippines, Senegal, Somalia, Union of Soviet Socialist Republics (including the Byelorussian Soviet Socialist Republic and the Ukrainian Soviet Socialist Republic) Togo and Tunisia (with which no bilateral treaties exist); and (4) specified United Kingdom territories).

12 Ie the European Convention on Extradition (Paris, 13 December 1957; ETS 24 (1966); Cm 999); Additional Protocol (Strasbourg, 15 October 1975; ETS 86 (1975); Cm 999); and Second Protocol (Strasbourg, 17 March 1978; ETS 98 (1978); Cm 999). As to the application of the Convention as an arrangement under which extradition can occur as between signatories, see the European Convention on Extradition Order 1990, SI 1990/1507 (Austria, Cyprus, Denmark, Finland, France, (Federal Republic of) Germany, Greece, Iceland, Israel, Italy, Liechtenstein, Luxembourg, Netherlands, Norway, Portugal, Spain, Sweden, Switzerland and Turkey).

13 Ie the Convention against Illicit Traffic in Narcotic Drugs and Psychotropic Substances (Misc 14 (1989); Cm 804). As to the application of the Convention in respect of the states signatory to the Convention whether or not the United Kingdom has a bilateral extradition treaty with them: see note 1 above, the Extradition Act 1989, s 22, and the Extradition (Drug Trafficking) Order 1991, SI 1991/1701 ((1) Bolivia, Chile, Ecuador, Guatemala, Mexico, Nicaragua, Paraguay, United States of America and Yugoslavia (with which there are bilateral treaties); and (2) Bahrain, Bhutan, China, Costa Rica, Egypt, Guinea, Jordan, Madagascar, Oman, Qatar, Senegal, Togo, Tunisia, United Arab Emirates, Union of Soviet Socialist Republics and Byelorussian Soviet Socialist Republic (with which there are no bilateral treaties)).

509. Other agreements. The United Kingdom is a party to the Geneva Convention relating to the Status of Refugees and the Protocol to it[1], but has not altered municipal law as a result[2].

1 Ie the Convention relating to the Status of Refugees (Geneva, 28 July 1951; TS 39 (1954); Cmd 9171) and Protocol relating to the Status of Refugees (New York, 31 January 1967; TS 15 (1969); Cmnd 3906).

2 As to the position of refugees in immigration law, see paras 314 ff above.

510. Procedures under municipal law generally. The principal statute is
the Extradition Act 1989. This Act repeals and re-enacts, in consolidated form
with amendments, the Extradition Acts 1870 to 1935[1]. This regime, referred to
in this title as the '1870 procedure', applies to all extradition 'arrangements'[2]
already in force under the repealed Acts unless and until they are replaced by
'extradition arrangements'[3] under what is referred to in this title as the '1989
procedure' instituted by the substantive provisions of the Extradition Act 1989[4].

Under the 1870 procedure, where there is an 'arrangement' with a foreign
state, embodied in an Order in Council, then on receipt of a requisition from
that state, and after the requirements of sundry procedure are satisfied, and
provided certain restrictions upon return do not apply, the Secretary of State is
permitted to surrender a 'fugitive criminal' to that state[5].

Under the 1989 procedure[6], 'extradition arrangements', which may be 'general' or 'special', may be made with a foreign state. A 'general extradition
arrangement' must be embodied in an Order in Council. A 'special extradition
arrangement' need not. In either case, broadly as is the case under the older
regime, on receipt of a requisition from that state, after the requirements of
sundry procedure are satisfied, and provided certain restrictions upon return do
not apply, the Secretary of State is permitted to surrender to that state a person
liable to extradition.

The legislation for extradition to the Republic of Ireland is the Backing of
Warrants (Republic of Ireland) Act 1965 (c 45). This requires no 'arrangement',
and a warrant from the Republic, indorsed in the United Kingdom, permits
return of the named person[7].

The procedures are dealt with below[8].

1 Ie under the Extradition Act 1989 (c 33), ss 1, 37, Schs 1, 2. The Extradition Acts 1870 to 1935
   comprise the Extradition Acts 1870 (c 52) (repealed), 1873 (c 60), 1895 (c 33) (repealed), 1906
   (c 15) (repealed), 1932 (c 39) (repealed), the Slave Trade Act 1873 (c 88), and the Counterfeit
   Currency (Convention) Act 1935 (c 25).
2 See para 511 below.
3 See para 511 below.
4 See the Extradition Act 1989, s 1(3).
5 See paras 511–517, 550, 553, 556, 559, 562, 565, 568, 569, 574, below.
6 See paras 518–524, 551, 554, 557, 560, 563, 566, 570, 571, 575, below. The procedure was
   instituted by the Extradition Act 1989, and is intended progressively to replace the 1870
   procedure. In fact the process was that, following the Report of a Departmental Working Party,
   entitled 'A Review of the Law and Practice of Extradition in the United Kingdom' in 1982, and a
   Green Paper on *Extradition* (Cmnd 9421) (1985), and a short section in the White Paper on
   Criminal Justice (Cmnd 9658) (1986) (see paras 47–52), amendments to the Extradition Acts 1870
   to 1935 and the Fugitive Offenders Act 1967 (c 68) (repealed) were made in the Criminal Justice
   Bill 1987, which fell on the dissolution of Parliament. The Bill was re-introduced and became the
   Criminal Justice Act 1988 (c 33), Pt I (ss 1–22) (repealed) which amended the law of extradition.
   Part I of the 1988 Act never came into force, and its provisions were consolidated (with further
   amendments) into the Extradition Act 1989. The 1989 procedure is essentially the same as that
   under the Fugitive Offenders Act 1967, much of which it re-enacts with changes.
7 See paras 525–529, 552, 555, 558, 561, 564, 567, 572, 573, 576, below.
8 See paras 550 ff below.

511. Arrangements. Under the 1870 procedure (which continues to apply in
respect of any foreign state until replaced)[1], the requirement for an 'arrangement' was usually filled by a bilateral treaty, but could be filled by a multilateral
one[2]. Some multilateral treaties modify bilateral treaties. It is therefore important to consider, in any individual case, all multilateral treaties which might have

a bearing. All such arrangements were required to be embodied in Orders in Council, by which means they entered municipal law.

Under the 1989 procedure extradition arrangements (which will gradually replace the 1870 procedure) are defined as arrangements with a foreign state under which extradition procedures under Part III of the Extradition Act 1989 are available[3]. These may be general extradition arrangements or special extradition arrangements.

'General extradition arrangements' are arrangements of a general nature made with one or more states and relating to the operation of extradition procedures under Part III of the 1989 Act[4]. Thus both bilateral and multilateral treaties are included[5]. General extradition arrangements may be embodied in Orders in Council directing that the procedure in Part III of the 1989 Act, subject to any limitations, restrictions, exceptions and qualifications contained in the Order, applies in respect of the foreign state or states with which it has been made[6]. Such an Order in Council must in any case provide that it can be terminated, or unilaterally denounced, by notice of not more than one year[7]. It must also be in conformity with the provisions of the 1989 Act, and in particular with the restrictions on return[8]. However, the Order in Council is conclusive evidence that the arrangements contained in it comply with the Act, and that it applies Part III procedures to the foreign state or states mentioned[9]. Orders in Council must be laid before Parliament, and if they provide for return without the need for the requesting state to show a prima facie case against the person, then the Order is subject to the negative resolution procedure[10].

'Special extradition arrangements' are arrangements, relating to the operation of Part III of the 1989 Act procedures in particular cases, made with a state with which there are no general extradition arrangements[11]. Thus they are ad hoc extradition. They are available only when no general arrangements are in force in relation to that state[11] and may include limitations, restrictions, exceptions and qualifications[12]. The Secretary of State may issue a certificate specifying that special extradition arrangements exist with a state in respect of a certain person, and the certificate is conclusive evidence of all matters stated in it[13]. The same procedures apply to extradition under special extradition arrangements as under general extradition arrangements[14].

As observed, the law on extradition to the United Kingdom is such that there is no need for a treaty. However, surrenders to other states always require legislative authority[15].

1 See the Extradition Act 1989 (c 33), s 1(3), Sch 1, and para 510 above.
2 For the bilateral treaties and multilateral agreements, see paras 507, 508, above.
3 Extradition Act 1989, s 3(1). Part III comprises ss 7–17. See also s 20, and para 577 below.
4 Ibid, s 3(3)(a).
5 The United Kingdom has entered the European Convention on Extradition (see para 508 above), and it is contemplated that most extraditions will henceforth be under multilateral treaty. The word 'arrangement' does not specifically require a treaty, as the definition of 'special arrangements' demonstrates: see the text and note 11 below. However, since 'general arrangements' are to relate to the Extradition Act 1989, Pt III, procedures, it is difficult to see how they could fail to be treaties.
6 Ibid, s 4(1). Treaties do not of themselves alter municipal law, so some such power is necessary to incorporate the treaties into municipal law. The treaty may be an aid to interpretation on the Order in Council: *Government of Belgium v Postlethwaite* [1988] AC 924, [1987] 2 All ER 985, HL. The power is permissive, but there is no authority to surrender a person except under legislation: *Diamond v Minter* [1941] 1 KB 656, [1941] 1 All ER 390.
7 Extradition Act 1989, s 4(2)(a).
8 Ibid, s 4(2)(b). As to restrictions on return, see s 6 and paras 531 ff below.
9 Ibid, s 4(3). Challenge to such an Order is thus extremely limited.
10 Ibid, s 4(4), (5).
11 Ibid, s 3(3)(b).
12 Ibid, s 15(1).

13 ibid, s 15(2), (3). There is thus no parliamentary control over special extradition arrangements.
14 Ibid, s 3(1), (3)(b). Such extradition must also be in conformity with the provisions of the 1989 Act, and in particular with the restrictions on return under s 6: see paras 531 ff below.
15 *Diamond v Minter* [1941] 1 KB 656, [1941] 1 All ER 390.

512. Meaning of 'foreign state'. 'Foreign state' was not defined for the purposes of the 1870 procedure, but extradition was restricted to those states with which there was an arrangement embodied in an Order in Council[1]. However, the provision in the Extradition Act 1989, saving existing arrangements under the Extradition Acts 1870 to 1935 with foreign states, declares certain acts, wherever committed, to be within the jurisdiction of states to which that provision has effect, if they are offences against the law of such states, and constitute the United Kingdom offences described in the 1989 Act[2].

'Foreign state' is defined for the purposes of extradition under the 1989 procedure in the 1989 Act as, subject to an exception, any state other than:
(1) the United Kingdom[3];
(2) an independent Commonwealth country[4];
(3) a colony[5]; or
(4) the Republic of Ireland[6].
The exception is that any state which is a party to the European Convention on Extradition[7] may be (but is not required to be) treated as a foreign state[8].

1 As to arrangements, see para 511 above.
2 See the Extradition Act 1989 (c 33), s 1(3), Sch 1, para 15, and para 514 below. As to the Extradition Acts 1870 to 1935, see para 510, note 1, above.
3 Extradition Act 1989, s 3(2)(i).
4 Ie as mentioned in the British Nationality Act 1981 (c 61), s 37, Sch 3 (see para 520 below): Extradition Act 1989, s 3(2)(ii).
5 Ie a United Kingdom colony, which is not specifically defined in the 1989 Act: ibid, s 3(2)(iii).
6 Ibid, s 3(2)(iv). As to extradition arrangements with the Republic of Ireland, see paras 525 ff below.
7 See para 508 above.
8 Extradition Act 1989, s 3(2). Thus the Republic of Ireland could be so treated, and extraditions with it occur under the 1989 Act instead of the Backing of Warrants (Republic of Ireland) Act 1965 (c 45). Similarly extraditions with any Commonwealth country, such as Cyprus (which is a signatory) and Malta (which is not) could occur under this power instead of that relating to Commonwealth countries, although there is no reason why this should be done.

513. Who can be extradited to a foreign state. Under the 1870 procedure, fugitive criminals are liable to be extradited. 'Fugitive criminal' means any person accused or convicted of an extradition crime committed within the jurisdiction of any foreign state who is in or is suspected of being in some part of Her Majesty's dominions[1].

Under the 1989 procedure a person is liable to be extradited if he is accused in a foreign state of committing an extradition crime, or is alleged to be unlawfully at large after conviction of an extradition crime by a court in a foreign state, provided in either case that that foreign state has extradition arrangements with the United Kingdom permitting extradition under Part III of the Extradition Act 1989[2].

1 Extradition Act 1989 (c 33), s 1(3), Sch 1, para 20. The term is misleading since the person need be neither fugitive (in the sense of fleeing) nor a criminal (since he may be found not guilty).
2 Ibid, s 1(1). This requires, indirectly, an extradition arrangement embodied in an Order in Council: see s 4, and para 511 above. Part III comprises ss 7–17.

514. Extradition crime in relation to foreign states under the 1870 procedure. 'Extradition crime' under the Extradition Act 1870 procedure was defined by the list method. That is to say, it was defined as any crime which, if committed in England or within English (sic) jurisdiction would be a crime listed in the 1870 Act[1]. A person could be extradited, however, only if the relevant extraditable crime was also listed in the Order in Council embodying the arrangement under which his extradition was requested[2]. The alleged crime was required to have been in fact committed within the jurisdiction of the requesting state, which included every colony, dependency or constitutive part of it, including any area over which it exerted de facto control, and also including ships and aircraft[3]. Jurisdiction could extend to extra-territorial crimes and to those deemed to take place within a foreign state[4]. The offence was required to be one against the general law of the state[5].

This position is preserved in respect of extraditions under the 1870 procedure, as the saving provisions of the Extradition Act 1989 require the phrase 'extradition crime' to be construed by reference to the relevant Order in Council[6] as it had effect immediately before the coming into force of the Extradition Act 1989[7]. However, the Extradition Act 1989 anticipates that amendments made to that Order will have effect after the commencement of the 1989 Act, which was (for the most part) 27 September 1989[8].

1 See the Extradition Act 1870 (c 52), s 26, Sch 1 (repealed).
2 All such Orders in Council continue in force under the 1870 procedure until replaced, by virtue of the Extradition Act 1989 (c 33), s 1(3).
3 See the Extradition Act 1870, s 16, and the Civil Aviation Act 1982 (c 16), s 93 (both repealed). See now the Extradition Act 1989, s 1(3), Sch 1, paras 13, 14, and para 562 below.
4 *Attorney General for Colony of Hong Kong v Kwok-a-Sing* (1873) LR 5 PC 179. See now the Extradition Act 1989, Sch 1, paras 15, 19.
5 *Re Windsor* (1865) 6 B & S 522; *R v Governor of Brixton Prison, ex parte Rush* [1969] 1 All ER 316, [1969] 1 WLR 165, DC.
6 Ie the Order in Council made under the Extradition Act 1870, s 2 (repealed).
7 See the Extradition Act 1989, Sch 1, para 20. Thus the comprehensive list of extradition crimes in the Extradition Act 1870, Sch 1 (repealed), no longer has effect, and in respect of any extradition under the 1870 procedure, 'extradition crime' is defined by the Order in Council embodying the bilateral treaty, as amended. For the Orders in Council, see para 507 above.
8 Extradition Act 1989, ss 37(3), 38(2). The machinery provisions (ie ss 7(3), 10(3), 14(2), (3), 38(3), Sch 1, para 9(2)) came into force on the passing of the Act (ie 27 July 1989): s 38(3).

515. Extradition crime in relation to foreign states under the 1989 procedure. 'Extradition crime' under the 1989 procedure is defined not by the list method but by double-punishability. The definition includes conduct in the territory of a foreign state which, if it occurred in the United Kingdom[1], would constitute an offence punishable with imprisonment for a term of twelve months or any greater punishment, and which, however described in the law of the foreign state, is so punishable under that law[2]. The definition also extends to extra-territorial offences (rather than conduct) attracting the same level of punishment, provided one of two conditions is fulfilled[3]:

(1) that in corresponding circumstances equivalent conduct would constitute an extra-territorial offence against the law of the United Kingdom[4] punishable with imprisonment for a term of twelve months or any greater punishment[5].

(2) that the foreign state bases its jurisdiction on the nationality of the offender, that the conduct occurred outside the United Kingdom, and that if it occurred in the United Kingdom it would be an offence punishable with imprisonment for a term of twelve months or any greater punishment[6].

In any case, the law of a foreign state includes the law of any part of it, and similarly conduct in any colony or dependency, or in any vessel, aircraft or hovercraft of a foreign state is to be treated as conduct in that state[7]. The law of the United Kingdom includes the law of any part of it, and conduct in a vessel, aircraft or hovercraft of a colony of the United Kingdom is to be treated as conduct in that colony[8].

Certain offences arising out of international agreements are deemed to have taken place in the requesting foreign state irrespective of where they in fact took place[9].

1 If the conduct occurred in England, and was not an offence there, but was in Scotland, it is not clear what the position would be.

2 Extradition Act 1989 (c 33), s 2(1)(a). The phrase 'conduct . . . however described' follows the European Convention on Extradition (see para 508 above) and gets rid of the need to amend both the arrangements, and the Orders in Council embodying them, in order to include new offences, and of most of the difficulties of deciding whether the conduct was a particular offence or not under the foreign law, a drawback of the list method: see *Re Nielsen* [1984] AC 606, [1984] 2 All ER 81, HL. Though the foreign state will still have to indicate an offence alleged in order to show the severity of punishment. The double-punishability rule means that a slightly different range of offences is included, and in practice the range will be more extensive, including, for instance, revenue offences hitherto excluded: cf eg *Nuland* [1988] Crim LR 690, DC. However, see also *R v Chief Metropolitan Stipendiary Magistrate, ex parte Secretary of State for the Home Department* [1989] 1 All ER 151, [1988] 1 WLR 1204, DC.

3 Extradition Act 1989, s 2(1)(b).

4 Ie including the law of any part of the United Kingdom: ibid, s 2(4)(a).

5 Ibid, s 2(1)(b)(i), (2). 'Equivalent conduct' presumably means that the extra-territorial components of the offence would be outside the United Kingdom, and the intra-territorial within the United Kingdom (*R v Governor of Brixton Prison, ex parte Rush* [1969] 1 All ER 316, [1969] 1 WLR 165, DC; *R v Governor of Pentonville Prison, ex parte Naghdi* [1990] 1 All ER 257, [1990] 1 WLR 317, DC) although extra-territorial components may be admitted.

6 Extradition Act 1989, s 2(1)(b)(ii), (3). Few United Kingdom offences are extra-territorial or based on nationality (see eg the Offences against the Person Act 1861 (c 100), s 9 (amended by the Criminal Law Act 1967 (c 58), s 10(2), Sch 3, Pt III) (an English Act)); thus the United Kingdom might extradite to a destination in circumstances in which it could not request extradition because it had no jurisdiction, and even conceivably where the conduct was not criminal in the state in which it occurred, only in the state of the nationality of the person concerned, although the Secretary of State would presumably decline to extradite in such circumstances.

7 Extradition Act 1989, s 2(4)(a), (b). Thus offences in any part of a federation are included, whether state or federal: cf Government of the *United States of America v Jennings* [1983] AC 624, [1982] 3 All ER 104, HL. As to offences in respect of vessels, cf *R v Governor of Brixton Prison, ex parte Minervini* [1959] 1 QB 155, [1958] 3 All ER 318, DC. Offshore installations as such are not included.

8 Extradition Act 1989, s 2(4)(a), (c). Thus Scots law and Northern Irish law are accorded equal status with English law. Offshore installations as such are not included.

9 See ibid, s 22(6).

516. Restrictions on return to foreign states. Under the 1870 procedure there are certain restrictions upon return[1]. These include:

(1) an exemption for political offences;

(2) 'speciality', that is that the person may only be tried for the offence for which his extradition was ordered;

(3) a priority of unrelated criminal proceedings in the United Kingdom (or in England); and

(4) opportunities to challenge the surrender[2].

Under the 1989 procedure, the Extradition Act 1989 places restrictions upon return[3]. It does so indirectly. It delineates[4] who is liable to extradition where procedures under Part III of the 1989 Act are available[5], and places restrictions upon return of persons under Part III. These restrictions apply in the following situations:

(a) return is restricted in the case of:

(i) political offences;

(ii) offences under military law;

(iii) where the request is made for the purpose of persecution on account of race, religion, nationality or political opinions; and

(iv) where the trial might be prejudiced or the person punished, detained or restricted in his personal liberty by reason of his race, religion, nationality or political opinions[6];

(b) return is restricted where conviction was obtained in the person's absence, if it would not be in the interests of justice to return him[7];

(c) return is restricted where the person would, if charged in the United Kingdom, be entitled to be discharged on the ground of previous acquittal or conviction[8];

(d) return is restricted on grounds of 'speciality' on a narrower definition than under the 1870 procedure, that is that he will be tried only for the offence for which his return has been ordered, or an offence otherwise disclosed by the same facts (provided it is an offence for which extradition may be ordered), or for any other extradition crime to the trial of which the Secretary of State consents (provided again it is an offence for which extradition may be ordered)[9].

These restrictions[10] apply to all extradition arrangements, and in the case of general extradition arrangements the Order in Council must be in conformity with them, and must also provide that the arrangements terminate after one year, or may be denounced upon not more than one year's notice[11].

1 As to the '1870 procedure', see para 510 above.
2 See paras 531 ff below.
3 Ie under the Extradition Act 1989 (c 33), Pt II (s 6). As to the '1989 procedure', see para 510 above.
4 Ie under ibid, Pt I (ss 1–5).
5 See ibid, s 1(1), and para 513 above. Part III comprises ss 7–17.
6 Ibid, s 6(1)(a)–(d).
7 Ibid, s 6(2).
8 Ibid, s 6(3).
9 Ibid, s 6(4)–(6).
10 See paras 531 ff below.
11 Extradition Act 1989, s 4(2).

517. 'Ad hoc' extradition to foreign states. Under the 1870 procedure the requirement for an 'arrangement', as then defined, precluded extradition in the absence of a treaty[1].

The wider definition under the 1989 procedure, which includes 'special extradition arrangements' not requiring any treaty, permits ad hoc extradition to a foreign state providing there are no 'general extradition arrangements' in force in relation to it[1]. This power exists only in relation to foreign states[2]. However, 'foreign state' is defined to include any state party to the European Convention on Extradition[3].

1 See para 511 above.
2 See the Extradition Act 1989 (c 33), s 4(1), and para 511 above.
3 See paras 508, 512, above.

(b) Extradition to Commonwealth Countries

518. International law. No bilateral treaties exist on extradition between the United Kingdom and other Commonwealth countries, but some Commonwealth countries may be parties to some multilateral treaties[1].

An agreement in 1966[2] required parallel legislation between Commonwealth countries, to produce common principles to fulfil the role of bilateral treaties.

1 Australia, for example, is a party to the Genocide, Tokyo, Hague and Montreal Conventions, for which see para 508, notes 3–6, above.

2 Ie *Scheme relating to the Rendition of Fugitive Offenders within the Commonwealth* (Cmnd 3008) (1966).

519. Municipal law generally. Rendition of offenders (as it was originally called) was Empire-wide before the independence of most former dependencies. The statutory regime for extradition (as it is now called) within the Commonwealth is now found entirely within the Extradition Act 1989[1]. It operates upon broadly the same principles as does extradition to foreign states.

No arrangements are required, and on a requisition from a designated Commonwealth country or a colony, after the requirements of sundry procedure are satisfied, and provided that certain restrictions upon return do not apply, the Secretary of State is permitted to surrender to that country or colony a person liable to extradition[2]. Procedure is dealt with below[3].

1 Until the Extradition Act 1989 (c 33) the statutory regime for extradition was found in the Fugitive Offenders Act 1967 (c 68), and before that in the Fugitive Offenders Act 1881 (c 69) and yet earlier in the Extradition Act 1843 (cc 75, 76) (all repealed). For the history of the present provisions, see para 510, note 6, above. The 1989 procedure is essentially the same as that under the Fugitive Offenders Act 1967, which it re-enacts with changes.
2 Extradition Act 1989, s 1(2).
3 See paras 551, 554, 557, 560, 563, 566, 570, 575, below.

520. Designated Commonwealth countries and colonies. The Extradition Act 1989 provides a procedure for the designation of Commonwealth countries for the purposes of extradition[1]. Any Order in Council, which is subject to negative resolution procedure[2], may designate any country whose citizens are Commonwealth citizens listed in the British Nationality Act 1981[3], which in fact lists independent Commonwealth countries. Such countries are referred to as 'designated Commonwealth countries'[4].

'Colonies' is not defined, although the Act is stated to apply to all colonies[5].

1 Ie under the Extradition Act 1989 (c 33), s 5(1).
2 Ibid, s 5(6).
3 Ie under the British Nationality Act 1981 (c 61), Sch 3 (see NATIONALITY AND CITIZENSHIP, vol 14, para 1953): Extradition Act 1989, s 5(1).
4 Ibid, s 5(1). A country leaving the Commonwealth does not cease to be a designated Commonwealth country unless United Kingdom municipal law changes its status: *R v Governor of Brixton Prison, ex parte Kahan* [1989] QB 716, [1989] 2 All ER 368, DC. See also H McN Henderson 'South Africa Leaves the Commonwealth' 1961 SLT (News) 65, and the South Africa Act 1962 (c 23) (as amended). The Commonwealth countries designated are: Antigua and Barbuda, Australia, the Bahamas, Bangladesh, Barbados, Belize, Botswana, Brunei, Canada, Dominica, Fiji, the Gambia, Ghana, Grenada, Guyana, India, Jamaica, Kenya, Kiribati, Lesotho, Malawi, Malaysia, Maldives, Malta, Mauritius, Nauru, New Zealand, Nigeria, Papua New Guinea, Saint Christopher and Nevis, St Lucia, St Vincent and the Grenadines, Seychelles, Sierra Leone, Singapore, Solomon Islands, Sri Lanka, Swaziland, Tanzania, Tonga, Trinidad and Tobago, Tuvalu, Uganda, Vanuatu, Western Samoa, Zambia and Zimbabwe: Extradition (Designated Commonwealth Countries) Order 1991, SI 1991/1700.
5 Extradition Act 1989, s 5(2). The British Nationality Act 1981, Sch 6, lists British Dependent Territories (see vol 14, para 1932), but this includes eg the Sovereign Base Areas of Akrotiri and Dhekelia, and so is wider than 'colony'.

521. Who may be extradited to a designated Commonwealth country or colony. A person is liable to be extradited to a designated Commonwealth country or a colony if he is accused of an extradition crime or is alleged to be unlawfully at large after conviction of such an offence in any such country or colony[1].

1 Extradition Act 1989 (c 33), s 1(2). This closely, but not precisely, parallels the provision in relation to extradition to foreign states: see para 513 above. In respect of extradition to a

Commonwealth country or colony the words 'by a court' are omitted after 'conviction of such an [extradition] crime', but the difference is probably insignificant. For the designated Commonwealth countries, see para 520, note 4, above.

522. Extradition crime in respect of designated Commonwealth countries and colonies. 'Extradition crime' is defined in the Extradition Act 1989 for the purposes of extradition to designated Commonwealth countries and colonies *mutatis mutandis* identically as for the purposes of extradition to a foreign state[1].

1 See the Extradition Act 1989 (c 33), s 2, and para 515 above. Under the previous legislation in respect of Commonwealth countries and colonies (ie the Fugitive Offenders Act 1967 (c 68) (repealed)) the term 'relevant offence' was used. In *Government of Canada v Aronson* [1990] 1 AC 579, [1989] 2 All ER 1025, HL, a majority of the House of Lords held that an offence was only a 'relevant offence' if the ingredients of the offence in the other Commonwealth country, as disclosed in the charge, would constitute an offence in the United Kingdom had it been committed here. It was not enough that the evidence might allow the inference that there was such an offence. For the designated Commonwealth countries, see para 520, note 4, above.

523. Restrictions upon return to designated Commonwealth countries and colonies. The Extradition Act 1989 places restrictions upon return of persons whose extradition is sought[1]. These restrictions are the same as in respect of extradition to foreign states[2] with two exceptions.

In respect of arrangements made with a designated Commonwealth country or colony[3], such arrangements may be made for a particular case or may be of a more general nature[4]. In respect of an offence of a political character[5], this does not include an offence against the life or person of the Head of the Commonwealth or attempting or conspiring to commit, or assisting, counselling or procuring the commission of or being accessory before or after the fact to such an offence, or of impeding the apprehension or prosecution of persons guilty of such an offence[6].

1 Ie under the Extradition Act 1989 (c 33), s 6: see para 516 above.
2 See para 516 above.
3 Ie under the Extradition Act 1989, s 6(4): see para 516 above.
4 Ibid, s 6(7). For these purposes a certificate issued by or under the authority of the Secretary of State confirming the existence of an arrangement and stating its terms is conclusive evidence of the matters contained in the certificate: s 6(7). For the designated Commonwealth countries, see para 520, note 4, above.
5 Ie under ibid, s 6(1): see para 516 above.
6 Ibid, s 6(8).

524. 'Ad hoc' extradition to designated Commonwealth countries and colonies. No 'arrangements' are required for extradition to designated Commonwealth countries. In so far as the agreement of 1966[1] between Commonwealth countries constitutes a pan-Commonwealth arrangement in the non-technical sense, and involves common principles, no such extradition is ad hoc.

1 Ie *Scheme relating to the Rendition of Fugitive Offenders within the Commonwealth* (Cmnd 3008) (1966). For the designated Commonwealth countries, see para 520, note 4, above.

(c) Extradition to the Republic of Ireland

525. International law. No bilateral treaty exists with the Republic of Ireland, but the Republic is party to some relevant multilateral conventions[1].

There is broad agreement upon the principles of extradition law as between the Republic of Ireland and the United Kingdom.

1 Eg the Genocide, Tokyo and Hague Conventions: see para 508, notes 3–5, above.

526. Municipal law generally.
The procedure operating for extradition to the Republic of Ireland is essentially a survival of that in force when Ireland was part of the United Kingdom, and which still pertains as between Scotland and England. It is contained within the Backing of Warrants (Republic of Ireland) Act 1965 (c 45). On requisition from the authorities within the Republic of Ireland, after the requirements of sundry procedure are satisfied, the Secretary of State is permitted to surrender to that country a person liable to extradition. Procedure is dealt with below[1].

1 See paras 552, 555, 558, 561, 564, 567, 572, 573, 576, below.

527. Who may be extradited to the Republic of Ireland.
Any person is liable to extradition to the Republic of Ireland if a warrant in respect of him has been issued by a judicial authority in the Republic of Ireland in respect of certain types of crime[1].

1 Ie under the Backing of Warrants (Republic of Ireland) Act 1965 (c 45), s 1.

528. Extradition crime in relation to the Republic of Ireland.
There is no definition of 'extraditable crime' in relation to extradition to the Republic of Ireland. The types of offences for which a person may be extradited there are identified procedurally. They are, subject to certain limitations, either any indictable offence, or any offence punishable on summary conviction with imprisonment for six months, where, in either case, there is a warrant for arrest issued in the Republic which has been indorsed by a justice of the peace in the United Kingdom, or in Scotland by a sheriff[1].

The limitations are two. First, extradition is not available where it is sought for a summary offence, unless one of three conditions is fulfilled[2]. They are that:

(1) that person has failed to appear in court and he has been personally summonsed in either the Republic or the United Kingdom[3];

(2) having entered a recognisance for the trial in the Republic, he has failed to appear[4]; or

(3) having appeared before the court in the Republic, he has failed to appear at adjourned proceedings[5].

Secondly, extradition is not available where it is for imprisonment of a person alleged to be convicted of a summary offence, and the imprisonment would be for failure to pay a fine or other sum[6].

1 Backing of Warrants (Republic of Ireland) Act 1965 (c 45), s 1(1)(a). In Scotland, 'justice of peace' includes a sheriff and a magistrate: s 10(3). Stipendiary magistrates are *ex officio* justices of the peace: District Courts (Scotland) Act 1975 (c 20), s 5(7); see COURTS AND COMPETENCY, vol 6, para 1160. Except in this context, the term 'magistrate' in the 1965 Act, s 10(3), is probably now inappropriate. See also vol 6, para 1156.
2 Backing of Warrants (Republic of Ireland) Act 1965, s 1(2).
3 Ibid, s 1(2)(a).
4 Ibid, s 1(2)(b).
5 Ibid, s 1(2)(c).
6 Ibid, s 1(3)(b).

529. Restrictions on return to the Republic of Ireland.
Restrictions are imposed upon extradition to the Republic of Ireland on grounds of double criminality and the political offence exemption[1].

1 See the Backing of Warrants (Republic of Ireland) Act 1965 (c 45), s 2(2), and paras 531, 535, 548, below.

(d) Extradition to the United Kingdom

530. Extradition to the United Kingdom generally. The Extradition Act 1989 has few references to extradition to the United Kingdom. Questions of sources and authority in relation to such extradition are dealt with below[1].

1 See paras 577 ff below.

(5) GENERAL RESTRICTIONS ON RETURN

(a) Political Offences

531. Introduction. Political offences in general exempt the perpetrator from extradition. Provision for this is found in the legislation. In respect of foreign states, if they are still dealt with under the 1870 procedure, it reflects the bilateral treaty and, where relevant, the multilateral treaties[1]. In respect of foreign states, if they are dealt with under the 1989 procedure, and in respect of designated Commonwealth countries and colonies and the Republic of Ireland, it reflects presumed shared understandings, and the relevant multilateral treaties[2].

The tendency of most of the multilateral treaties is to restrict the ambit of the exemption. Where the exemption may be raised, it may be raised at several stages in the procedure, both executive (except in the case of extradition to the Republic of Ireland) and judicial.

1 See para 532 below.
2 See paras 533–535 below.

532. The political offence exemption under the 1870 procedure. Under the 1870 procedure[1], which, via the relevant Orders in Council, continues to operate in respect of countries with which the bilateral agreements still hold good, there is a twofold political offence exemption. First, certain offences may not be extraditable at all, because omitted from the list of extradition offences[2]. Secondly, a person committing an extradition offence which is either 'of a political character', or a person whose surrender has been sought 'with a view to try to punish him for an offence of a political character' is exempted[3]. This second, ill-drafted, form of exemption was interpreted in a number of cases, and some uncertain principles emerged. These are:
(1) the offence must have been committed by a person who was part of a group (albeit small);
(2) the group has to desire revolution, or to change a government or policies of a government;
(3) possibly, the group has to be in competition with other political bodies, although possibly it was enough for the offender to wish to escape from a government (at least a totalitarian one);
(4) the offence is required to be committed to further the group's aims; and
(5) probably, the offence has to be part of some civil disorder[4].
The exemption operates only if the requesting state was the target of the crime[5]. However, if that state is shown not to be intending to apply the normal criminal

law and procedure, but to punish the person from political motives, the offence is political irrespective, it seems, of the motives of the person committing the crime[6].

It is to be presumed that whether the person's cause was deemed good or bad is irrelevant, but it is easier to reconcile the cases if sympathy for the fugitive is taken into account. The exemption is not, however, disguised asylum (although it might be politically difficult to deport a person whose extradition had been refused).

The effect of the exemption has been limited by amending legislation, reflecting multilateral agreements. Genocide and attempts, conspiracy or incitement to commit genocide are not to be regarded as political, nor proceedings in respect of them as a criminal matter of a political character[7]. Also, the fact that the act of which a person is accused or convicted could not have been punished under the law in force at the time and place that they were committed cannot be raised as an objection to extradition proceedings[8].

Certain terrorist offences[9] are not to be regarded as political offences; nor are proceedings in respect of such an offence to be regarded as a criminal matter of a political character or as criminal proceedings of a political character, in relation to certain designated states or countries[10].

The designated countries are either those designated by order of the Secretary of State as parties to the European Convention on the Suppression of Terrorism[11] or those to which an order under the Suppression of Terrorism Act 1978[12] has been applied as foreign states, designated Commonwealth countries or United Kingdom dependencies which are not parties to the Convention[13].

A person who appears to the appropriate authorities[14] to be accused of, or has been convicted of, a crime elsewhere which is also an offence, or an attempt to commit an offence, under section 1 of the Taking of Hostages Act 1982 is not to be returned under certain circumstances[15]. Those circumstances are that a request has been received from a designated Commonwealth country which is a party to the Hostage Convention[16], and it appears to the appropriate authorities that he might, if returned, be prejudiced at his trial by reason of difficulties in his communication with the appropriate authorities[17] of the state representing him diplomatically or consularly[18].

A new, narrow, limb to the exemption is introduced, exempting from extradition a fugitive if the intention of the requesting state is to punish on the grounds of race, religion, nationality or political opinions[19].

1 As to the '1870 procedure', see para 510 above.
2 Eg treason. As to extraditable offences, see paras 514, 522, 528, above.
3 Extradition Act 1989 (c 33), s 1(3), Sch 1, para 1(2)(a), (b) (re-enacting the Extradition Act 1870 (c 52), s 3(1) (repealed)). The first limb also appeared in the Fugitive Offenders Act 1967 (c 68) (see s 4(1)(a) (repealed)) and still appears, with some variation, in the Backing of Warrants (Republic of Ireland) Act 1965 (c 45) (see s 2(2)(a)).
4 *Re Castioni* [1891] 1 QB 149, DC; *Re Meunier* [1894] 2 QB 415, DC; *Re Arton (No 1)* [1896] 1 QB 108; *R v Governor of Brixton Prison, ex parte Kolczynski* [1955] 1 QB 540, [1955] 1 All ER 31, DC; *Schtraks v Government of Israel* [1964] AC 556, [1962] 3 All ER 529, HL; *Re Gross, ex parte Treasury Solicitor* [1968] 3 All ER 804, [1969] 1 WLR 12, DC; *Royal Government of Greece v Governor of Brixton Prison* [1971] AC 250, [1969] 3 All ER 1337, HL; *Cheng v Governor of Pentonville Prison* [1973] AC 931, [1973] 2 All ER 204, HL; *R v Governor of Pentonville Prison, ex parte Budlong, R v Governor of Pentonville Prison, ex parte Kember* [1980] 1 All ER 701, [1980] 1 WLR 1110, DC. See also *R v Governor of Winson Green Prison, Birmingham, ex parte Littlejohn* [1975] 3 All ER 208, [1975] 1 WLR 893, DC (under the Backing of Warrants (Republic of Ireland) Act 1965).
5 *Cheng v Governor of Pentonville Prison* [1973] AC 931, [1973] 2 All ER 204, HL.
6 *R v Governor of Brixton Prison, ex parte Kolczynski* [1955] 1 QB 540, [1955] 1 All ER 31, DC.
7 Extradition Act 1989, s 23(1) (replacing the Genocide Act 1969 (c 12), s 2(1) (repealed)).
8 Extradition Act 1989, s 23(2).
9 Ie an offence to which the Suppression of Terrorism Act 1978 (c 26), s 1, applies, and which would be an offence if committed in the United Kingdom or its extraterritorial jurisdiction. The

offences are: (1) common law offences (ie murder; manslaughter or culpable homicide: rape; kidnapping, abduction or plagium; false imprisonment; assault occasioning actual physical harm or causing injury; wilful fireraising); (2) offences under the Offences against the Person Act 1861 (c 100), ss 4, 18, 20–24, 28–30, 48, 55, 56; (3) offences under the Explosive Substances Act 1883 (c 3), ss 2, 3; (4) offences under the Sexual Offences Act 1956 (c 69), ss 1, 20; (5) an offence under the Firearms Act 1968 (c 27), ss 16, 17(1); (6) an offence under the Criminal Damage Act 1971 (c 48), s 1(2); (7) an offence under the Criminal Damage (Northern Ireland) Order 1977, SI 1977/426, art 3(2); (8) an offence under the Firearms (Northern Ireland) Order 1981, SI 1981/155, arts 17, 18(1); (9) an offence under the Taking of Hostages Act 1982 (c 28); (10) an offence under the Aviation Security Act 1982 (c 36), Pt I (ss 1–9) (except ss 4, 7); (11) an offence under any provision of the Nuclear Material (Offences) Act 1983 (c 18); (12) an offence under the Child Abduction Act 1984 (c 37), s 2, or any corresponding provision in force in Northern Ireland; (13) the offence of torture under the Criminal Justice Act 1988 (c 33), s 134; (14) an offence of attempting to commit any of the above offences; and (15) an offence of conspiring to commit any of the above offences: Suppression of Terrorism Act 1978 (c 26), s 1, Sch 1 (amended by the Aviation Security Act 1982, s 40, Sch 2, para 7; the Taking of Hostages Act 1982, s 3(2); the Firearms (Northern Ireland) Order 1981, art 6(1), Sch 4, para 5; the Child Abduction Act 1984, s 11(4); and the Criminal Justice Act 1988, s 22(2)–(5)).

10 Extradition Act 1989, s 24(1), (2)(b).
11 Ibid, s 24(3)(a). The countries designated are Austria, Belgium, Cyprus, Denmark, France, (Federal Republic of) Germany, Iceland, Italy, Liechtenstein, Luxembourg, the Netherlands, Norway, Portugal, Spain, Sweden, Switzerland and Turkey: see the Suppression of Terrorism (Designation of Countries) Orders 1978, SI 1978/1245; 1979, SI 1979/497; 1980, SI 1980/357; 1980, SI 1980/1392; 1981, SI 1981/1389; 1981, SI 1981/1507; 1986, SI 1986/271; 1986, SI 1986/1137; and 1987, SI 1987/2137. As to the European Convention on the Suppression of Terrorism, see para 508 above.
12 Ie under the Suppression of Terrorism Act 1978, s 5.
13 Extradition Act 1989, s 24(3)(b). An order has been made in respect of the United States of America: see the Suppression of Terrorism Act 1978 (Application of Provisions) (United States of America) Order 1986, SI 1986/2146.
14 Ie the Secretary of State, the court of committal and the High Court or High Court of Justiciary on an application for *habeas corpus* or for review of the order of committal: Extradition Act 1989, s 6(9).
15 Ibid, s 25(1)(b).
16 Ie the International Convention against the Taking of Hostages (New York, 18–31 December 1979; TS 81 (1983); Cmnd 9100) (the Hostage Convention): Extradition Act 1989, s 25(3).
17 By what appears to be a drafting slip, these words, defined in ibid, s 6(9) (see note 14 above), are used in a sense inconsistent with this definition.
18 Ibid, s 25(1)(a), (3).
19 Ibid, Sch 1, para 1(2)(c) (added by s 24(4)), replacing the Suppression of Terrorism Act 1978, s 2(1) (repealed). Cf the Extradition Act 1870, s 3(1) (repealed).

533. The basic provision under the 1989 procedure and in relation to the Commonwealth.

No person may be returned under the 1989 procedure[1] or committed or kept in custody for the purposes of such return, if it appears to an appropriate authority that the alleged extradition offence is of a political character[2]. 'Appropriate authority' means the Secretary of State, the court of committal, or the High Court of Justiciary on an application for review of the order of committal[3]. The Extradition Act 1989 is a consolidating measure, therefore the interpretation of that phrase under the older law, discussed above, remains authoritative[4].

The basic provision applies to extradition to both foreign states and to Commonwealth countries and colonies. However, there is an exception in relation to Commonwealth countries and colonies. In relation to them, an offence against the life or person of the Head of the Commonwealth cannot be a political offence, and nor can attempting or conspiring to commit the offence[5].

1 Ie under any 'extradition arrangement' under the Extradition Act 1989 (c 33), Part III (ss 7–17), other than one of those remaining for the time being under the 1870 procedure or under the Backing of Warrants (Republic of Ireland) Act 1965 (c 45). As to the '1870 procedure' and the '1989 procedure', see para 510 above.

2 See the Extradition Act 1989, s 6(1)(a), and para 516 above.
3 Ibid, s 6(9). In England and Wales the High Court is substituted for the High Court of Justiciary. This provision reproduces the first and main limb of the political offence exemption under the Extradition Act 1870 (c 52) (repealed). See now the Extradition Act 1989, Sch 1, and para 532 above.
4 See para 532 above.
5 See the Extradition Act 1989, s 6(8), and para 523 above.

534. Variations upon the basic provision under the 1989 procedure and in relation to the Commonwealth. In addition to the basic provision on political offences[1], under the Extradition Act 1989 a person may not be returned under Part III of the Act[2], or committed or kept in custody for the purposes of return in two situations related to political offences. The first of these is that the offence for which extradition is sought is an offence under military law, but not under the general criminal law[3]. The second is where it appears to an appropriate authority that although the request purported to be made on account of an extradition crime, it was in fact made on account of certain other reasons[4]. Those other reasons are that the request was made for the purpose of prosecuting or punishing him on account of his race, religion, nationality or political opinions, or that he might, if returned, be prejudiced or restricted in his personal liberty on those grounds[5].

'Appropriate authority' has the same meaning as in the basic provision[6], and, for the purposes of its application to Commonwealth countries and colonies, 'race' includes tribe[7].

1 See para 533 above.
2 Ie under the Extradition Act 1989 (c 33), Pt III (ss 7–17).
3 See ibid, s 6(1)(b), and para 516 above. This achieves the effect previously achieved by the absence of such offences from the list of 'extradition crimes': see para 514 above.
4 Ibid, s 6(1)(c).
5 Ibid, s 6(1)(c), (d). This provision appeared in the Fugitive Offenders Act 1967 (c 68), s 4(1)(b), (c) (repealed). It has been suggested that a difference in drafting between the two is significant, ie that in the former case the appropriate authority must think that the request is 'in fact' made for the prohibited purpose, and that bad faith will not be assumed (*Re Arton (No 1)* [1896] 1 QB 108), while in the latter, it need only think that the prohibited consequence 'might' happen. Certainly, the former seems to require a particular intention on the part of the requesting state or country, while the latter does not: see *Fernandez v Government of Singapore* [1971] 2 All ER 691, [1971] 1 WLR 989, HL; *R v Governor of Winson Green Prison, Birmingham, ex parte Littlejohn* [1975] 3 All ER 208, [1975] 1 WLR 893, DC.
6 See the Extradition Act 1989, s 6(9), and para 533 above.
7 Ibid, s 6(10). Presumably this does not bar this usage in relation to foreign states, particularly given the vagueness of the word 'race'.

535. Political offence exemption and related restrictions on return in relation to the Republic of Ireland. In relation to the Republic of Ireland, the legislation forbids an order to deliver the person concerned to the Garda Síochána if it is shown to the satisfaction of the court of committal that one or more of three conditions is fulfilled.

The first condition is that the offence specified in the warrant under which the person was arrested is an offence of a political character, an offence under military law which is not an offence under the general criminal law, or an offence under an enactment relating to taxes, duties or exchange control[1].

The second condition is that there are substantial grounds for believing that the warrant was in fact issued in order to secure the return of the person for the purpose of prosecuting or punishing him on account of his race, religion, nationality or political opinions[2].

The third condition is that the person would, if returned, be prejudiced at his trial or punished, detained or restricted in his personal liberty by reason of his race, religion, nationality or political opinions[3].

1 Backing of Warrants (Republic of Ireland) Act 1965 (c 45), s 2(2)(a). As to the meaning of 'political offence', see para 532 above.
2 Ibid, s 2(2)(e)(i) (added by the Suppression of Terrorism Act 1978 (c 26), s 2(2)). For a discussion of the interpretation of a similar worded provision in respect of foreign states etc, see para 534, note 5, above.
3 Backing of Warrants (Republic of Ireland) Act 1965, s 2(2)(e)(ii) (as so added). As to interpretation, see para 534, note 5, above.

(b) Rule on Contumacy

536. 'Contumacy': conviction *in absentia* and injustice in conviction. The original rule on 'contumacy' exists largely because of the drafting of an earlier Act and the facts of a particular case[1]. The result was a rule in the Extradition Act 1870 treating a person convicted 'for contumacy' as one accused of a crime[2]. This is continued for extraditions under the 1870 procedure[3] and some bilateral treaties under the older regime follow this pattern in any case.

The meaning of the provision is, however, unclear. It has been taken to refer to conviction *in absentia*, where the matter may be re-opened if the accused later surrenders to the court, and possibly in other cases, the name of the process being irrelevant[4]. Clearly it was considered that substantial injustice may occur with convictions *in absentia*, and by no means all such convictions would be within the 'contumacy' rule.

Under the 1989 procedure, there is a simpler provision declaring that no person may be returned to a foreign state or committed or kept in custody for that purpose if it appears to the appropriate authority that the conviction was obtained in his absence and that it would not be in the interests of justice to return him on the ground of that conviction[5].

The House of Lords held in a case under the 1870 procedure that there is no judicial power to refuse to commit on grounds of injustice, as the discretion of the Secretary of State adequately covers the matter[6].

1 *Re Coppin* (1866) 2 Ch App 47.
2 See the Extradition Act 1870 (c 52), s 26 ('conviction') (repealed).
3 See the Extradition Act 1989 (c 33), s 1(3), Sch 1, para 20 ('conviction'). As to the '1870 procedure', see para 510 above.
4 See eg *R v Governor of Brixton Prison, ex parte Caborn-Waterfield* [1960] 2 QB 498, [1960] 2 All ER 178, DC (where a decision in France *par contumace* was distinguished from a *jugement-itératif défaut*); *Athanassiadis v Government of Greece* [1971] AC 282, [1969] 3 All ER 293, HL; *Re Zessa* [1983] AC 46, [1982] 2 All ER 513, HL. The version found in the renewed treaty with Spain refers specifically to convictions *in absentia* and enjoins a particular procedure.
5 Extradition Act 1989, s 6(2). For the meaning of 'appropriate authority', see para 533, text and note 3, above. As to the '1989 procedure', see para 510 above.
6 *Atkinson v United States of America Government* [1971] AC 197, [1969] 3 All ER 1317, HL.

537. 'Contumacy': conviction *in absentia* and injustice in conviction in relation to the Republic of Ireland. There is no provision in respect of contumacy or convictions *in absentia* in relation to extradition to the Republic of Ireland.

(c) Previous Acquittal or Conviction

538. Previous acquittal or conviction other than in the Republic of Ireland. The Extradition Act 1870 (c 52) did not contain any specific provision to prevent extradition of a person who claimed to have tholed his assize, having been tried for the offence already, save in the special case of 'contumacy'[1]. No such provision, therefore, is found in relation to the 1870 procedure[2].

The Fugitive Offenders Act 1967 did so provide[3], and this rule has been incorporated in the 1989 procedure[4]. No person may be returned, committed or kept in custody for the purposes of return if it appears to the appropriate authority that, if charged with the offence in the United Kingdom, he would be entitled to be discharged under any rule of law relating to previous acquittal or conviction[5].

1 As to 'contumacy', see para 536 above.
2 Ie under the Extradition Act 1989 (c 33), Sch 1: see para 510 above. As to arrangements, see para 511 above.
3 See the Fugitive Offenders Act 1967 (c 68), s 4(2) (repealed).
4 See para 510 above.
5 Extradition Act 1989, s 6(3). For the meaning of 'appropriate authority', see para 533, text and note 3, above.

539. Previous acquittal or conviction in relation to the Republic of Ireland. In relation to the Republic of Ireland, the legislation provides that the court of committal may not order delivery of a person to the Garda Síochána if he has been acquitted or convicted in a trial in Northern Ireland for an extra-territorial offence[1] in respect of the same act or omission as that in respect of which the arrest warrant is issued[2]. It also provides that the court of committal may not order such delivery where extradition is sought for an offence committed in Northern Ireland which is also an extra-territorial offence under the law[3] of the Republic of Ireland[4].

1 Ie as defined in the Criminal Jurisdiction Act 1975 (c 59), s 1: Backing of Warrants (Republic of Ireland) Act 1965 (c 45), s 2(2)(d) (added by the Criminal Jurisdiction Act 1975, s 4(4), Sch 3, para 1).
2 Backing of Warrants (Republic of Ireland) Act 1965, s 2(2)(d) (as so added).
3 Ie under the law of the Republic of Ireland as defined in the Criminal Jurisdiction Act 1975, s 3: Backing of Warrants (Republic of Ireland) Act 1965, s 2(2)(c) (as so added).
4 Ibid, s 2(2)(c) (as so added).

(d) Speciality

540. Introduction. Extradition legislation generally expresses the principle that a person extradited may be tried only for the offences specified in the request[1].

1 See the Extradition Act 1870 (c 52), s 3(2) (repealed) (re-enacted in the Extradition Act 1989 (c 33), Sch 1, para 1(3): see para 541 below); the Backing of Warrants (Republic of Ireland) Act 1965 (c 45), s 2(2)(b) (see para 543 below); the Fugitive Offenders Act 1967 (c 68), s 4(3) (repealed) (re-enacted in the Extradition Act 1989, s 6(4)–(6): see para 542, below).

541. Speciality under the 1870 procedure. Under the 1870 procedure[1] the speciality limitation is stringent, preventing return to the requesting state unless its law, or an 'arrangement' with it[2], prevents detention or trial for any offence other than the extradition crime for which the extradition was sought[3].

1 See para 510 above.
2 The drafting appears to envisage an ad hoc 'arrangement' requiring speciality, thus giving the word 'arrangement' a slightly different meaning from the general one (see para 511 above), although as an 'arrangement' is a precondition of extradition under the 1870 procedure, the distinction makes no difference. However, see para 542, note 7, below. As to the '1870 procedure', see para 510 above.

3 Extradition Act 1989 (c 33), s 1(3), Sch 1, para 1(3) (re-enacting the Extradition Act 1870 (c 52), s 3(2) (repealed)).

542. Speciality under the 1989 procedure. Under the 1989 procedure[1] the speciality limitation prevents a person from being returned to the requesting state unless provision is made by the relevant law or by an arrangement with the relevant foreign state, Commonwealth country or colony securing that he will not be dealt with for another offence[2], subject to two exceptions. First, it is permitted for other offences for which he could lawfully be returned[3] and which are disclosed by the facts in respect of which his return was ordered[4]. Secondly, it is permitted for any other extradition crime in respect of which the Secretary of State consents to his being dealt with, provided it does not appear to him that an order for return would not be lawful[5].

There are no 'extradition arrangements' as such with Commonwealth countries, except where that country may be party to a multilateral convention constituting an 'extradition arrangement'[6]. However, the Secretary of State is given power to enter an 'arrangement' with a designated Commonwealth country or colony for the purpose of introducing a speciality restriction, which may be for the particular case in question, or of a more general nature[7].

The word 'arrangement' in this context appears to bear a different meaning from that of 'extradition arrangement'[8].

1 See para 516 above.
2 Extradition Act 1989 (c 33), s 6(4)(a).
3 Ie which constitutes an extradition crime, and is subject to no other restriction upon return, such as the political offence exemption. Whether such a restriction operates may be decided by the court of committal (see para 563 below) or the Secretary of State (see para 575 below).
4 Extradition Act 1989, s 6(4)(b), (5).
5 Ibid, s 6(4)(c), (6). The provision enforces the other restrictions upon return, but leaves it to the Secretary of State alone to determine whether they apply, subject only to the possibility of judicial review.
6 See para 511 above.
7 See the Extradition Act 1989, s 6(7), and para 523 above. As to designated Commonwealth countries and colonies, see para 520 above.
8 See ibid s 3(1), and para 511 above. See also para 541, note 1, above.

543. Speciality in relation to the Republic of Ireland. In relation to the Republic of Ireland, there is no specific speciality provision as such. There is a limitation in respect of those whose extradition is sought in respect of a conviction. No warrant to arrest such a person may be indorsed (as the procedure requires[1]) except for the purpose of bringing him before a court in the Republic of Ireland for sentence in respect of the conviction or of taking him to serve imprisonment under such a sentence, provided it is not imprisonment in default of payment of a fine or other sum[2].

1 Ie under the Backing of Warrants (Republic of Ireland) Act 1965 (c 45), s 2(2)(b).
2 Ibid, s 1(3). See also s 2(1), (2), and paras 535, 539, above.

(e) The Prima Facie Rule

544. Introduction. Traditionally, the United Kingdom has imposed a requirement upon states requesting extradition that they provide a prima facie case against the person whose extradition is requested. The requirement under the Extradition Act 1870 took the form of requiring evidence which would, according to the law of England, justify magistrates in committing the person for trial[1], and a modified form appeared in the Fugitive Offenders Act 1967 designed to accommodate the fact that Scottish criminal procedure did not recognise such an institution[2]. The level of proof this implied was not clear. The House of Lords found by a bare majority that the version of the prima facie requirement found in the 1967 Act[3] meant that the court must consider there to be more than a mere possibility that the person did the act in question, but need not find near certainty[4].

The prima facie requirement is designed to ensure that a genuine case against the person existed, and so is related to the political offence[5], double criminality[6] and speciality[7] rules. However, civil law countries have no equivalent to the English committal procedure, and were said to find it onerous to fulfil the requirement[8]. Further, even within the United Kingdom, the committal procedure is not universally employed. It is, of course, unknown in Scotland (as noted), has never been required for extradition to the Republic of Ireland, and is in effect dispensed with in many English cases.

1 See the Extradition Act 1870 (c 52), ss 9, 10 (repealed).
2 See the Fugitive Offenders Act 1967 (c 68), s 7(1), (2), (5) (repealed).
3 Ie under ibid, s 7 (repealed).
4 *R v Governor of Brixton Prison, ex parte Armah* [1968] AC 192, [1966] 3 All ER 177, HL, especially at 229, 230, and at 184, per Lord Reid.
5 See paras 531–535 above.
6 See para 548 below.
7 See paras 540–543 above.
8 It was suggested (1) that up to one-third of all requests for extradition received by the United Kingdom in the years before the reforms contained in the Extradition Act 1989 (c 33), failed on this ground; (2) that Spain denounced its treaty for this reason and other states expressed concern; and (3) that it was seen as the principal reason why the United Kingdom could not sign the European Convention on Extradition: see *Extradition* (Cmnd 9421) (1985), the Green Paper on the subject, paras 2.5–2.10. It should be noted that Spain nevertheless entered a new treaty shortly thereafter. As to the European Convention on Extradition, see para 508 above.

545. The prima facie rule under the 1870 procedure. The prima facie rule continues to apply to extraditions under the 1870 procedure[1], unless the Orders in Council are amended[2].

1 See the Extradition Act 1989 (c 33), s 1(3), Sch 1, paras 6, 7 (re-enacting the Extradition Act 1870 (c 52), ss 9, 10 (repealed)). As to the '1870 procedure', see para 510 above.
2 Extradition Act 1989, s 37(3). See eg the amendment to the bilateral treaty with the United States: Exchange of Notes (Washington, 19 and 20 August 1986; US 3 (1986); Cmnd 9915).

546. The prima facie rule under the 1989 procedure. The earlier legislation required that the prima facie rule be applied in all cases (except for extradition to the Republic of Ireland)[1]. The 1989 procedure[2] allows the rule to be dispensed with. A prima facie case need not be shown if the request is from a foreign state and is made under a 'general arrangement' which, as embodied in an Order in Council, does not require it[3]. A prima facie case is required by the multilateral conventions in respect of relevant offences[4].

The prima facie rule does apply in respect of extradition under 'special extradition arrangements'[5].

1 Ie under the Extradition Act 1870 (c 52), ss 9, 10 (repealed) and the Fugitive Offenders Act 1967 (c 68), s 7: see para 544 above.
2 As to the '1989 procedure', see para 510 above.
3 See the Extradition Act 1989 (c 33), s 9(4), (8). As to 'general arrangements', and the requirement for them to be embodied in an Order in Council, see para 511 above.
4 See ibid, s 22(1), (3), (5). As to the multilateral conventions, see para 508 above. For the relevant offences, see s 22(4).

5 There is a general requirement that at the hearing before the court of committal there is required evidence sufficient to warrant the person's trial if the extradition crime had taken place within the jurisdiction of the court, unless the extradition is sought under an Order in Council giving effect to general extradition arrangements under which the extradition request was made otherwise provides: see ibid, s 9(8)(a), and para 563 below. As to 'general extradition arrangements' and 'special extradition arrangements', see para 511 above, and as to hearings before the court of committal, see paras 559–561 below.

547. The prima facie rule in relation to the Republic of Ireland. No requirement that a prima facie case be put to the court of committal before extradition to the Republic of Ireland exists.

(f) Other Restrictions

548. Double criminality. Extradition legislation requires double criminality in principle. That is, the conduct for which extradition is sought must be a crime in both countries[1].

Under the 1870 procedure, the 'list' method of defining extradition crimes is employed[2]. This requires the relevant offence to be identified as a specific crime in both jurisdictions[3].

Under the 1989 procedure, the 'double punishability' method is employed[4]. This clearly continues to involve double criminality[5]. However, certain extra-territorial offences raise difficulties[6].

In relation to the Republic of Ireland, the 'double punishability' method is also employed, but with a lower standard of punishability[7].

1 See (1) the Extradition Act 1870 (c 52), s 26 ('fugitive criminal') (repealed) (re-enacted in the Extradition Act 1989 (c 33), Sch 1, para 20), requiring the offence to be an extradition crime; (2) the Backing of Warrants (Republic of Ireland) Act 1965 (c 45), s 2(2), requiring the offence to also be an offence in the United Kingdom; and (3) the Fugitive Offenders Act 1967 (c 68), s 3(1)(c) (repealed) (re-enacted in the Extradition Act 1989, s 2), requiring the crime to be an extradition one.
2 See para 514 above. As to the '1870 procedure', see para 510 above.
3 Strictly speaking, under the 1870 procedure, the United Kingdom jurisdiction has to be English law: *Re Nielsen* [1984] AC 606, [1984] 2 All ER 81, HL.
4 See para 515 above. As to the '1989 procedure', see para 510 above.
5 In *Government of Canada v Aronson* [1990] 1 AC 579, [1989] 2 All ER 1025, HL, decided under the Fugitive Offenders Act 1967, s 3(1) (repealed), which employed the 'double punishability' method, the House of Lords held that the particulars on the charge must show the ingredients of the offence, not merely evidence from which guilt of United Kingdom offences could, *mutatis mutandis*, be inferred.
6 Ie principally those which are chiefly intra-territorial, but have an extra-territorial element: see the discussion in Colin J Warbrick 'The Criminal Justice Act 1988: The New Law on Extradition' [1989] Crim LR 4 at 8, 9, referring to what is now the Extradition Act 1989, s 2(1)(b)(i), (2), (3).
7 See the Backing of Warrants (Republic of Ireland) Act 1965, s 2(2).

549. 'Own nationals' exemption. It is common for states to exempt themselves from extraditing their own nationals either completely, or at the discretion of the government of the state[1]. The United Kingdom has acquired the right to refuse to extradite its nationals through the reciprocity of the bilateral agreements under the older regime[2]. However, it does not promote the practice, and does not take advantage of the possibility[3].

Where the question arises, the burden of proof in United Kingdom law lies on the person asserting his nationality[4]. Where there is a discretion, it is the executive's[5]. It may be unclear whether the treaty exempts completely, or at discretion[6].

Also, it is unclear who, in the United Kingdom case, the 'own nationals' would be. Most treaties refer to 'subjects'. This must have meant 'British subjects' at common law and under the relevant legislation before the British Nationality Act 1948 (c 56), since no other category existed. That category included, roughly, all those born within the Empire or Commonwealth, and their foreign-born descendants in the male line[7]. After the British Nationality Act 1948 (which added to the category the alternative title of 'Commonwealth citizen'[8]) the practice continued[9]. It does not seem that any attempt was made to limit the category to citizens of the United Kingdom and Colonies, a category created by the British Nationality Act 1948[10]. Thus the subsequent trifurcation of that citizenship by the British Nationality Act 1981 can in general be ignored.

However, the 1981 Act did transfer the title 'British subject' to a small group hitherto known as 'British subjects without citizenship'[11], while retaining the title 'Commonwealth citizen'[12], who would thus appear to be the 'own nationals' in question in the absence of any other relevant provision. The first treaty entered into after the British Nationality Act 1981 did nevertheless give a more restricted definition of 'nationals' for its own purposes, that is, the trifurcated successor statuses of citizenship of the United Kingdom and Colonies[13].

No 'own national' exemption operates between the United Kingdom and Commonwealth countries, nor between the United Kingdom and the Republic of Ireland.

1 All states with which the United Kingdom has bilateral agreements with under the 1870 procedure exempt their nationals, save for Ecuador, Israel and the United States of America. For the relevant treaties, see para 507 above.
2 See para 507 above.
3 Indeed it eschewed the possibility in the bilateral treaties with Spain and Sweden: see para 507 above.
4 *Re Guerin* (1888) 60 LT 538, DC; *R v Governor of Brixton Prison, ex parte Guerin* (1907) 51 Sol Jo 571, DC.
5 *Re Galwey* [1896] 1 QB 230, DC.
6 For a discussion, see V E Hartley-Booth *British Extradition Law and Procedure* (1980), vol 1, pp 70–72.
7 See NATIONALITY AND CITIZENSHIP, vol 14, paras 1902, 1904.
8 See vol 14, para 1902.
9 Eg in the new treaties with Austria (see the Austria (Extradition) Order 1970, SI 1970/1111, Sch 1, art 4), and the Federal Republic of Germany (see the Federal Republic of Germany (Extradition) Order 1960, SI 1960/1375, Sch 1, art iv). This extends the category of 'national' to British protected persons (see vol 14, paras 1914, 1954), and even, astonishingly, to citizens of the Republic of Ireland.
10 *Wan Ping Nam v Federal German Republic Minister of Justice* 1972 JC 43, 1972 SLT 220, proceeded on this basis.
11 British Nationality Act 1981 (c 61), ss 30, 31, and vol 14, para 1950.
12 See ibid, s 37, and vol 14, para 1953.
13 See the Treaty with Spain (London, 22 July 1985; TS 40 (1986); Cmnd 9615). The three statuses are British citizen, British Dependent Territories citizen, and British Overseas citizen.

(6) EXTRADITION FROM THE UNITED KINGDOM

(a) Requisition and the Order of the Secretary of State

550. Requisition under the 1870 procedure. The 1870 procedure commences (unless provisional warrant procedure is used[1]) with a requisition to the Secretary of State from a recognised diplomatic representative[2]. No formality is required unless imported by the relevant Order in Council[3].

1 See para 556 below.

2 Extradition Act 1989 (c 33), s 1(3), Sch 1, para 4(1) (re-enacting the Extradition Act 1870 (c 52), s 7). As to the '1870 procedure', see para 510 above.

3 See eg *Royal Government of Greece v Governor of Brixton Prison* [1971] AC 250, [1969] 3 All ER 1337, HL; *Athanassiadis v Government of Greece* [1971] AC 282, [1969] 3 All ER 293, HL; *Government of the Federal Republic of Germany v Sotiriadis* [1975] AC 1, [1974] 1 All ER 692, HL.

551. Request under the 1989 procedure. The 1989 procedure commences (unless provisional warrant procedure is used[1]) with a request to the Secretary of State from a recognised diplomatic or consular representative of a foreign state[2], or by or on behalf of the government of a designated Commonwealth state[3] or the governor of a colony[4].

The request must include the particulars of the person concerned, particulars of the relevant offence, and evidence sufficient to justify issue of a warrant under the 1989 procedure, and either a warrant issued in the requesting state, Commonwealth country or colony (in the case of an accused person), or a certificate of conviction and sentence (in the case of a convicted person)[5].

1 See para 557 below.
2 As to the meaning of 'foreign state', see para 512 above.
3 As to the meaning of designated 'Commonwealth country' and 'colony', see para 520 above.
4 Extradition Act 1989 (c 33), s 7(1). As to the '1989 procedure', see para 510 above.
5 Ibid, s 7(2)(a)–(d). Copies must be served on the person whose return is requested before he is brought before the court of committal: s 7(2).

552. Requests from the Republic of Ireland. No requisition or request is necessary or competent.

(b) Authority to proceed

553. Authority to proceed under the 1870 procedure. The Secretary of State may act on a requisition, but may decline if he thinks fit, if the offence is of a political character[1]. However, the 'arrangements' in the relevant Order in Council[2] permitting extradition may limit this discretion. It is unclear if a court would go behind this discretion[3]. If he acts, the Secretary of State may[4] signify to the metropolitan magistrate[5] that a requisition has been made and require him to issue a warrant to arrest the person[6].

Despite the requirement to issue, the metropolitan magistrate may, it appears, refuse to issue a warrant if there is insufficient evidence to justify it, had the offence occurred in England or Wales (sic)[7].

There is no limit to the number of orders the Secretary of State may make pursuant to a requisition, and a fresh order may be made even if the accused is in custody under an earlier order, without further requisition[8].

No power to seize goods is referred to, and the practice of searching the accused and his premises is of doubtful legality[9].

1 Extradition Act 1989 (c 33), s 1(3), Sch 1, para 4(3), (re-enacting the Extradition Act 1870 (c 52), s 7 (repealed) (as to which see *Re Rees* [1986] AC 937, [1986] 2 All ER 321, HL)). For a discussion of 'political character', see paras 531, 532, above. It appears that the Secretary of State is not obliged to refuse to act on a requisition concerning a political offence.
2 See para 511 above.
3 *R v Governor of Brixton Prison, ex parte Thompson* [1911] 2 KB 82, DC; *R v Governor of Brixton Prison, ex parte Soblen* [1963] 2 QB 243, [1962] 3 All ER 641, CA, especially at 300 and at 302, and at 659, 660, and at 661, per Lord Denning; *R v Bow Street Magistrates, ex parte Mackeson* (1982) 75 Cr App Rep 24, DC (concerning extradition to the United Kingdom); *R v Secretary of State for the Home Department, ex parte Kirkwood* [1984] 2 All ER 390, [1984] 1 WLR 913; *Re Rees* [1986] AC 937, [1986] 2 All ER 321, HL.

4 It appears that there is no obligation, and that therefore the reference to a political offence in the form, in which it appears, is otiose.

5 In the case of a crime committed on the high seas on a vessel or hovercraft which has put into any United Kingdom port, to any sheriff: Extradition Act 1989, Sch 1, para 13(1)(a) (re-enacting the Extradition Act 1870, s 16(1) (repealed)).

6 Extradition Act 1989, Sch 1, para 4(2), re-enacting the Extradition Act 1870, s 7 (repealed) with some changes. Thus the intimation does not now have to be 'under his hand and seal', although it still has to be 'under his hand': Extradition Act 1989, s 28(1). It does not appear that the Secretary of State need specify closely the details of the offence, since he is only issuing an instruction to a magistrate: *R v Governor of Pentonville Prison, ex parte Naghdi* [1990] 1 All ER 257, [1990] 1 WLR 317, DC.

7 Extradition Act 1989, Sch 1, para 5(1)(a) (re-enacting the Extradition Act 1870, s 8(1) (repealed) with the addition of 'Wales'). The level of evidence required is less than for a prima facie case to be made out: *R v Weil* (1882) 9 QBD 701, CA. Other grounds for refusal include that no extradition crime is disclosed (ie the double criminality rule: see para 548 above) as in *Re Bellencontre* [1891] 2 QB 122, DC; *Re Nielsen* [1984] AC 606, [1984] 2 All ER 81, HL. However, see *R v Governor of Pentonville Prison, ex parte Naghdi* [1990] 1 All ER 257, [1990] 1 WLR 317, DC.

8 *Re Rees* [1986] AC 937, [1986] 2 All ER 321, HL; *United States Government v Bowe* [1990] 1 AC 500, [1989] 3 All ER 315, PC.

9 See V E Hartley-Booth *British Extradition Law and Procedure* (1980), vol 1, p 39.

554. Authority to proceed under the 1989 procedure. The Secretary of State may act on an extradition request from a foreign state or designated Commonwealth country or colony unless[1] it appears to him that an order for the return of the person could not lawfully be made[2], or would not in fact be made[3], in accordance with the provisions of the Extradition Act 1989[4].

If he acts, the Secretary of State may[5] issue an authority to proceed[6] to the Sheriff of Lothian and Borders (or to the chief metropolitan stipendiary magistrate, or a designated metropolitan magistrate)[7], specifying the offence or offences under United Kingdom law which it appears to the Secretary of State would be constituted by equivalent conduct in the United Kingdom[8]. An authority to proceed may be withdrawn and a new one issued in the absence of a new request[9].

The authority to proceed entitles the sheriff or magistrate to issue a warrant for the arrest of the person, if he is supplied with such evidence as would justify the issue of the warrant for the arrest of a person accused (or convicted) within his jurisdiction[10], and if it appears to him that the conduct alleged would constitute an extradition crime[11]. The sheriff or magistrate thus appears to be able to decline to issue a warrant. Such a warrant may be executed in any part of the United Kingdom by any constable, without being backed[12].

Where a warrant is issued in respect of a crime of stealing or receiving stolen property (sic) or any other property offence in a designated Commonwealth country or a colony[13], any sheriff or justice of the peace (whether in Scotland or elsewhere in the United Kingdom) may issue a warrant to search for the property[14] as if the offence had been committed within his jurisdiction[15]. The powers do not exist in relation to property offences in foreign countries.

1 The following restrictions (where they apply) appear to bind the Secretary of State not to issue an authority to proceed.

2 Eg it would fall foul of one of the general restrictions on return: see paras 531 ff above.

3 This presumably refers to the Secretary of State's executive power, where there are no restrictions upon return, to decline to extradite a person.

4 Extradition Act 1989 (c 33), s 7(4) (re-enacting the Fugitive Offenders Act 1967 (c 68), s 5(3) (repealed)).

5 It appears that he is not obliged to issue an authority to proceed.

6 Extradition Act 1989, s 7(1).

7 Ibid, s 8(1)(a). 'Designated metropolitan magistrate' means a metropolitan stipendiary magistrate designated for the purpose by the Lord Chancellor: s 8(2).

8 Ibid, s 7(5).

9 *Re Rees* [1986] AC 937, [1986] 2 All ER 321, HL.

10 This is clearly less than is required to make out a prima facie case, since that requirement is no longer always necessary: see para 546 above. In any case this is clear from the case law on the equivalent provision under the 1870 procedure: see para 553, note 7, above.

11 Extradition Act 1989, s 8(1)(a), (3). The 'double criminality' rule is applied: see para 548 above. As to the meaning of 'extradition crime', see para 515 above.

12 Ibid, s 8(5) (re-enacting the Fugitive Offenders Act 1967, s 6(4) (repealed)).

13 See para 520 above.

14 Ie that involved in the offence only.

15 Extradition Act 1989, s 8(6) (re-enacting with changes the Fugitive Offenders Act 1967, s 6(5) (repealed)).

555. Authority to proceed in relation to the Republic of Ireland. A warrant issued in the Republic of Ireland for an indictable offence or (in certain circumstances) an offence punishable by six months' imprisonment on summary conviction, authorises a constable producing it, and stating on oath that he has reason to believe the named person is within the jurisdiction of the sheriff (or justice of the peace), to seek indorsement of that warrant from the sheriff (or justice)[1]. The Irish warrant must be issued by a court, judge or justice of the peace or peace commissioner[2]. The sheriff (or justice) may decline on the ground of speciality or, in the case of summary convictions, on procedural grounds[3].

1 See the Backing of Warrants (Republic of Ireland) Act 1965 (c 45), ss 1(1)(a), (b), (2), 2(2), 10(3), and paras 528, 535, 539, above.

2 Ibid, s 10(1). It is assumed valid if verified in the prescribed manner: s 7(a). The power of prescription is prescribed by rules made by Act of Adjournal under the standard legislation (ie now the Criminal Procedure (Scotland) Act 1975 (c 21): see the Backing of Warrants (Republic of Ireland) Act 1965, s 8(1)(b), and the Act of Adjournal (Consolidation) 1988, SI 1988/110, r 152. As to prescription in England, see the Magistrates' Courts (Backing of Warrants) Rules 1965, SI 1965/1906. See also *Re Arkins* [1966] 3 All ER 651, [1966] 1 WLR 1593, DC. The political offence exemption is relevant only at a later stage.

3 Backing of Warrants (Republic of Ireland) Act 1965, ss 1(2), (3), 2(1), (2), and paras 528, 535, 539, above.

(c) Informal Requisition or Request and Provisional Warrants

556. Provisional warrants under the 1870 procedure. Any justice of the peace in the United Kingdom (including in Scotland a sheriff), and in England the metropolitan magistrate, may issue a warrant on the strength of sufficient information or complaint, without an order from the Secretary of State[1]. This is usually as a result of a request from the representative of a foreign state, or from a police force, as a matter of urgency, and requires there to be such evidence or proceedings as would justify issue of a warrant had the crime been committed where the sheriff, justice (or magistrate) exercises jurisdiction[2]. What this means in Scotland is not clear[3]. It was clearly intended that this process be speedy[4].

Such warrants are referred to as 'provisional'. The evidence required for the issue of a provisional warrant is the same as that for issue of a warrant after 'authority to proceed' has been received from the Secretary of State[5], and is that which would in his opinion justify the issue of a warrant for the arrest of a person accused (or convicted) within his jurisdiction[6].

When such a warrant is issued, a report, together with the evidence, information or complaint, or certified copies of them, must be sent to the Secretary of State, who may cancel the warrant and discharge the person[7]. The warrant requires the person to be brought before any person with the power to issue such a warrant, who is required to order him to be brought before the metropolitan magistrate[8].

The metropolitan magistrate may[9] fix a reasonable time, with reference to the circumstances of the case, within which the Secretary of State may make a normal order signifying that a requisition has been received[10]. If the Secretary of State fails to do this, the metropolitan magistrate must discharge the person[10]. Some Orders in Council embodying extradition 'arrangements' require release after a specified period in any case[11].

Neither delay as such, nor unlawful arrest, are necessarily grounds to set aside subsequent proceedings[12].

1 Extradition Act 1989 (c 33), s 1(3), Sch 1, paras 5(1)(b), 20 (re-enacting the Extradition Act 1870 (c 52), ss 8, 26 (repealed)).
2 Extradition Act 1989, Sch 1, paras 5(1)(b), 20. See also *Government of the Federal Republic of Germany v Sotiriadis* [1975] AC 1 at 25, [1974] 1 All ER 692 at 702, HL, per Lord Diplock.
3 See *Wan Ping Nam v Federal German Republic Minister of Justice* 1972 JC 43, 1972 SLT 220.
4 However, as to delay in execution, see text and note 10, below and para 562, text and note 18, below. See also *R v Bow Street Magistrates Court, ex parte Van der Holst* (1986) 83 Cr App Rep 114, DC; and *Re Rees* [1986] AC 937, [1986] 2 All ER 321, HL. See further para 574, especially text to note 5, below.
5 See para 553 above.
6 See the Extradition Act 1989, Sch 1, para 5(1)(b), and para 553, text and note 7, above.
7 Extradition Act 1989, Sch 1, para 5(2) (re-enacting the Extradition Act 1870, s 8 (repealed)).
8 Extradition Act 1989, Sch 1, para 5(3) (re-enacting with changes the Extradition Act 1870, s 8 (repealed)).
9 He does not appear to be required to do so.
10 Extradition Act 1989, Sch 1, para 5(4) (re-enacting with changes the Extradition Act 1870, s 8 (repealed)). See also *Government of the Federal Republic of Germany v Sotiriadis* [1975] AC 1 at 26, 29, [1974] 1 All ER 692 at 703, 705, HL, per Lord Diplock.
11 Eg fourteen days (France and Luxembourg (the relevant Order in Council has been revoked with savings)), thirty days (Guatemala, Poland and others); ninety days (Chile and Peru). As to the relevant treaties, see para 507 above. See also *Government of the Federal Republic of Germany v Sotiriadis* [1975] AC 1 at 29, [1974] 1 All ER 692 at 705, HL, per Lord Diplock. As to arrangements, see para 511 above.
12 *R v Bow Street Magistrates Court, ex parte Van der Holst* (1986) 83 Cr App Rep 114, DC, where a provisional warrant was issued, the person was arrested but was then charged with a municipal offence and convicted. Upon release after brief imprisonment he was re-arrested under the provisional warrant. Although the procedure was unlawful, the consequent delay was found neither oppressive nor inordinate, and no bad faith or deliberate misconduct, or manipulation of procedures amounting to abuse of process occurred. An application for judicial review was refused for lack of 'serious irregularity'. See also *Re Rees* [1986] AC 937, [1986] 2 All ER 321, HL.

557. Provisional warrants under the 1989 procedure. A sheriff, a justice of the peace or a metropolitan magistrate[1] may issue a provisional warrant upon information that the person is, or is believed to be, in or on his way to the United Kingdom[2]. The circumstances in which this is likely to occur are referred to above[3].

The evidence required for the issue of a provisional warrant is the same as that required for the issue of a warrant after authority to proceed has been issued by the Secretary of State[4], that is, that which would in the magistrate's opinion justify issue of the warrant for the arrest of a person accused (or convicted) within his jurisdiction[5], and it must appear to him that the conduct alleged would constitute an extradition crime[6].

Where a person has been arrested on a provisional warrant, the court of committal[7] may[8] fix a reasonable period[9] (having regard to any such period fixed in the Order in Council, where the request is under 'general extradition arrangements'[10]) and provided the Secretary of State is informed of such period, after which the person will be discharged unless authority to proceed[11] has been received from the Secretary of State[12].

Where a provisional warrant has been issued, the authority issuing it must immediately give notice to the Secretary of State and send him the information or evidence upon which it was issued, or certified copies of it[13]. The Secretary of State may decide not to issue authority to proceed, and whether he does so or not, he may by order cancel the provisional warrant, and discharge the person if he has been arrested under it[13].

1　Ie the chief metropolitan magistrate or one designated by the Lord Chancellor for this purpose: Extradition Act 1989 (c 33), s 8(2).

2　Ibid, s 8(1)(b).

3　See para 556, text to note 2, above.

4　See para 554 above.

5　This is clearly less than is required to make out a prima facie case, since that is no longer always necessary in an extradition: see para 546 above. Also, the case law on the earlier provisions make this clear: see para 553, note 7, above.

6　Extradition Act 1989, s 8(3). The 'double criminality' rule is applied: see para 548 above.

7　Ie the Sheriff of Lothian and Borders or, in England and Wales, a metropolitan magistrate: ibid, s 9(1).

8　The court does not appear to be obliged to do so.

9　Ie where the extradition request is made under general extradition arrangements but no period is so specified, or the application is made under special extradition arrangements: Extradition Act 1989, s 9(7). As to arrangements, see para 511 above.

10　Ibid, s 9(6).

11　See para 554 above.

12　Extradition Act 1989, s 9(5).

13　Ibid, s 8(4).

558. Provisional warrants in relation to the Republic of Ireland. Any sheriff or justice of the peace anywhere in the United Kingdom may issue a provisional warrant to a constable who states on oath that he has reason to believe that an Irish warrant for an indictable offence[1] has been issued, that a senior Irish police officer has made a request on grounds of urgency for issue of a United Kingdom warrant, and that the person is within the sheriff's or magistrate's jurisdiction[2].

No evidence is required. No return to the Secretary of State has to be made, and he cannot cancel the provisional warrant. However, the provisional warrant is valid for only five days[3].

1　Provisional warrants are therefore not available for summary offences, although they may be 'extradition offences': see para 514 above.

2　Backing of Warrants (Republic of Ireland) Act 1965 (c 45), ss 4(1), 10(3). For the form of warrant, see the Act of Adjournal (Consolidation) 1988, SI 1988/110, r 149(2), Sch 1, Form 82. As to England, see the Magistrates' Courts (Backing of Warrants) Rules 1965, SI 1965/1906.

3　Backing of Warrants (Republic of Ireland) Act 1965, s 4(2).

(d) Executing the Warrant

559. Executing the warrant under the 1870 procedure. Ordinary warrants and provisional warrants issued by the metropolitan magistrate may be executed anywhere in the United Kingdom and Isle of Man as if issued or indorsed by a justice of the peace having jurisdiction there[1]. Those provisional warrants issued by a justice of the peace (which includes a sheriff[2]) presumably do require indorsement if executed outside the jurisdiction of the issuing justice (or sheriff)[3].

1　Extradition Act 1989 (c 33), s 1(3), Sch 1, paras 11, 18 (re-enacting the Extradition Act 1870 (c 52), ss 13, 22 (repealed)). As to the effect of irregularities and unjustifiable delay in execution, see *R v Bow Street Magistrates Court, ex parte Van der Holst* (1986) 83 Cr App Rep 114, DC.

2　Extradition Act 1989, Sch 1, para 20 ('justice of the peace').

3 In respect of crimes committed on the high seas, a justice of the peace or a sheriff have the same powers as a metropolitan magistrate, except for the purpose of executing a warrant: ibid, Sch 1, para 13(1)(a).

560. Execution of a warrant under the 1989 procedure.

Both ordinary and provisional warrants may be executed by any person to whom they are directed, or by any constable, in any part of the United Kingdom without being backed[1].

A person arrested under such a warrant is to be brought before a court of committal[2] as soon as practicable[3].

1 Extradition Act 1989 (c 33), s 8(5).
2 Ie a metropolitan magistrate or the sheriff of Lothian and Borders: ibid, s 9(1).
3 Ibid, s 9(1). See also *R v Bow Street Magistrates Court, ex parte Van der Holst* (1986) 83 Cr App Rep 114, DC.

561. Execution of the warrant in relation to the Republic of Ireland.

The procedure for extradition to the Republic of Ireland requires an Irish warrant to be indorsed by a justice of the peace[1] in the United Kingdom[2]. Such indorsement renders the Irish warrant, ordinary or provisional, as valid as one issued by the justice, and so many be executed as such[3]. A provisional warrant is valid only for five days[4].

Whether on a provisional warrant or an ordinary warrant, the person is to be brought as soon as practicable before a sheriff court[5].

1 In Scotland justice of the peace includes a sheriff: Backing of Warrants (Republic of Ireland) Act 1965 (c 45), s 10(3).
2 Ibid, s 1(1)(b): see para 555 above.
3 Ibid, ss 1(4), 4(2).
4 Ibid, s 4(2).
5 See ibid, ss 2(1), 4(3), 10(3), and para 564 below.

(e) Hearing and Committal

562. Hearing and committal under the 1870 procedure.

The hearing is before the metropolitan magistrate[1], unless the crime alleged occurred on the high seas in a vessel or hovercraft which is in a United Kingdom port, in which case any sheriff[2] also has jurisdiction[3].

The metropolitan magistrate (or in the exceptional case where a sheriff has jurisdiction, the sheriff) hears the case in the same manner and has the same jurisdiction and powers, as near as may be, as if the person were before him for committal for trial on an indictable offence[4]. He is not concerned with the requisition from the foreign state, nor can he consider whether the evidence produced by it would be admitted at trial there[5]. Where a sheriff has jurisdiction it is not clear how he should proceed as there is in Scotland no committal for trial procedure[6]. The metropolitan magistrate or sheriff is, however, required to receive any evidence which the person tenders to show that the relevant crime is a political offence, or not an extradition crime[7].

The burden of proof is upon the requisitioning government. It must, in the case of a person accused of an extradition crime, produce an authenticated foreign warrant and such evidence as would, according to the law of England and Wales (sic), justify committal for trial[8]. In the case of a person alleged to have been convicted, it must produce evidence as would, according to the law of England and Wales (sic), prove that the person had been convicted[9].

The person in question may attempt to controvert any such evidence, and raise any other defence, including:

(1) that the offence is not an 'extradition crime'[10], or not an extradition crime in respect of the requisitioning foreign state, not being included in the relevant Order in Council[11];
(2) that the relevant Order in Council debars his surrender on the ground of delay or otherwise[12];
(3) that the political offence exemption and any variation of it applies[13];
(4) that the conviction was obtained 'in contumacy' or *in absentia*[14];
(5) that he has already tholed his assize[15];
(6) that the speciality principle prevents surrender[16];
(7) that he is an 'own national' (where this defence is available)[17]; or
(8) any other defence, including, possibly, that there has been inordinate delay or abuse of process[18].

Also, a person accused of a separate offence within the United Kingdom, or undergoing sentence under any conviction, may not be surrendered until discharged by acquittal, completion of sentence or otherwise, or unless an order is made for the charge in respect of the offence to lie on the file[19].

In any case, if sufficient evidence is produced by the requisitioning state, the metropolitan magistrate (or, in the exceptional case, the sheriff) is required to commit the person to prison to await the Secretary of State's warrant for the person's surrender, and to send to the Secretary of State a certificate of committal forthwith, together with any such report as he thinks fit[20]. If sufficient evidence is not produced, he is required to discharge the person[21]. However, no surrender may take place until fifteen days after the order to commit has expired, and the metropolitan magistrate (or, in the exceptional case, the sheriff) is required to inform the person committed of this, and that he has a right to apply for a writ of *habeas corpus* (sic)[22].

1 Extradition Act 1989 (c 33), s 1(3), Sch 1, para 5(3) (re-enacting the Extradition Act 1870 (c 52), s 8 (repealed)).
2 Or a stipendiary magistrate in England and Wales and a resident magistrate in Northern Ireland: Extradition Act 1989, Sch 1, para 13(1)(a).
3 Ibid, Sch 1, paras 5(3), 13(1)(a), (2) (re-enacting the Extradition Act 1870, ss 8, 16(1) (repealed)).
4 Extradition Act 1989, Sch 1, paras 6(1), 13(1)(a). See also *R v Governor of Brixton Prison, ex parte Kolczynski* [1955] 1 QB 540 at 552, 553, [1955] 1 All ER 31 at 37, 38, DC, per Lord Goddard CJ; *Government of the Federal Republic of Germany v Sotiriadis* [1975] AC 1 at 24, [1974] 1 All ER 692 at 701, HL, per Lord Diplock; *R v Governor of Pentonville Prison, ex parte Singh* [1981] 3 All ER 23, [1981] 1 WLR 1031, DC; *R v Governor of Pentonville Prison, ex parte Passingham* [1983] 2 AC 464, [1983] 2 All ER 123, HL; *Re Nielsen* [1984] AC 606, [1984] 2 All ER 81, HL.
5 *United States Government v Bowe* [1990] 1 AC 500, [1989] 3 All ER 315, PC.
6 English magisterial law appears to be imported lock, stock and barrel: see *Wan Ping Nam v Federal German Republic Minister of Justice* 1972 JC 43, 1972 SLT 220.
7 Extradition Act 1989, Sch 1, paras 6(2), 13(1)(a) (re-enacting the Extradition Act 1870, ss 9, 16(1) (repealed)).
8 Extradition Act 1989, Sch 1, para 7(1) (re-enacting the Extradition Act 1870, s 10 (repealed)). Again, it is unclear how this is thought to apply in Scotland.
9 Extradition Act 1989, Sch 1, para 7(2) (as so re-enacted). Once more, it is unclear how this is thought to apply in Scotland.
10 See para 514 above.
11 Thus fulfilling the 'double criminality' requirement: see para 548 above. As to arrangements under Orders in Council, see para 511 above.
12 See para 511 above.
13 See paras 531, 532, above.
14 See para 536 above.
15 See para 538 above.
16 See paras 540, 541, above.
17 See para 549 above.
18 *R v Bow Street Magistrates Court, ex parte Van der Holst* (1986) 83 Cr App Rep 114, DC.
19 Extradition Act 1989, Sch 1, para 1(4) (re-enacting with changes the Extradition Act 1870, s 3(3) (repealed)).

20 Extradition Act 1989, Sch 1, paras 7(1)–(3), 13(1)(a), (b).
21 Ibid, Sch 1, paras 7(1)–(3), 13(1)(a). As to the effects of irregularity in execution of the metropolitan magistrate's decision to commit or discharge, see *R v Bow Street Magistrates Court, ex parte Van der Holst* (1986) 83 Cr App Rep 114, DC.
22 Extradition Act 1989, Sch 1, paras 1(5), 8(1), 13(1)(a) (re-enacting the Extradition Act 1870, ss 3(4), 11, 16(1) (repealed)). As to the meaning in Scotland of the right to apply for a writ of *habeas corpus*, see *Wan Ping Nam v Federal German Republic Minister of Justice* 1972 JC 43, 1972 SLT 220.

563. Hearing and committal under the 1989 procedure. Before the hearing, copies of the particulars sent by the requesting territory to the Secretary of State must be supplied to the person whose extradition is sought[1]. The hearing is before either the Sheriff of Lothian and Borders or (in respect of England and Wales) the metropolitan magistrate[2] (referred to as the 'court of committal'), as the warrant[3] directs[4]. Proceedings before the Sheriff of Lothian and Borders acting as a court of committal are as nearly as possible as if for trial for a summary offence, and he has the same powers as in such proceedings, including the power to adjourn and meanwhile remand the person in custody or on bail[5].

Authority to proceed[6] having been issued[7], the Sheriff of Lothian and Borders acting as a court of committal must hear any representations in support of the extradition request or on behalf of the relevant person[8]. Where he is satisfied on two issues, and is not prohibited by any other provision of the Extradition Act 1989[9], he is required to commit the person to custody or on bail[10] to await the Secretary of State's decision as to whether to return him, and (if the Secretary of State so decides) the actual return[11]. If he so commits a person, the Sheriff of Lothian and Borders (or in England and Wales, the metropolitan magistrate) is required to issue a certificate identifying the offence against the law of the United Kingdom which the conduct would constitute[12]. If the sheriff acting as a court of committal is not satisfied on these issues, or committal is prohibited by a provision of the Extradition Act 1989, he is required to discharge the person[13].

The first issue on which the sheriff has to be satisfied is that the offence to which the authority to proceed[14] relates is an extradition crime[15]. The second issue is, subject to an exception, that either, in the case of a person accused of an offence, the evidence would be sufficient to warrant his trial had the conduct taken place within the court's jurisdiction[16], or, in the case of a person alleged to have been convicted of the offence, that he appears to have been so convicted and to be unlawfully at large[17]. The exceptional case is where the person is accused of an offence, and the prima facie requirement[18] is dispensed with. Where the request for extradition is from a foreign state, and an Order in Council is in force providing 'general extradition arrangements'[19] covering extradition to that state without requiring a prima facie case to be made out, then there is no need to produce to the sheriff evidence sufficient to warrant trial of the person, had the alleged offence been committed within his jurisdiction[20]. In all other cases, then, the requesting state, country or colony must make out a prima facie case.

The person whose extradition is sought may therefore offer evidence and argument whether the offence is an extradition crime, and on either of the two issues upon which the sheriff must satisfy himself, but it is not clear whether he may offer them upon other matters such as the adequacy of the evidence offered against him.

1 Extradition Act 1989 (c 33), s 7(2). As to the particulars, see para 551 above.
2 Ie the chief metropolitan magistrate or another metropolitan magistrate designated for the purpose by the Lord Chancellor: ibid, s 8(2). Cf the Fugitive Offenders Act 1967 (c 68), s 6(1) (repealed).
3 Ie under the Extradition Act 1989, s 8: see paras 554, 557, 560, above.
4 Ibid, s 9(1). Cf the Fugitive Offenders Act 1967, s 7(1) (repealed).

5 Extradition Act 1989, s 9(3). Cf the Fugitive Offenders Act 1967, s 7(3) (repealed), and the equivalent proceedings under the 1870 procedure, as to which, see para 562 above. In England and Wales, the metropolitan magistrate has the same jurisdiction and powers, as nearly as may be, as examining magistrates, including the power to remand in custody or on bail, ie he acts like a court of committal for an indictable offence: Extradition Act 1989, s 9(2). Cf the Fugitive Offenders Act 1967, s 7(2) (repealed).

6 See para 554 above.

7 Thus the hearing cannot proceed upon the basis of a provisional warrant: see para 557 above.

8 Extradition Act 1989, s 9(8). Cf the Fugitive Offenders Act 1967, s 7(5) (repealed).

9 Eg by the provisions relating to the political offence exemption (see paras 531–534 above); to the person having already tholed his assize (see para 538 above); to speciality (see para 542 above); to the 'own nationals' exemption (if this applies) (see para 549 above).

10 Committal to custody does not preclude bail at a later date if the sheriff considers it appropriate: Extradition Act 1989, s 9(10).

11 Ibid, s 9(8)(i), (ii). Cf the Fugitive Offenders Act 1967, s 7(5) (repealed).

12 Extradition Act 1989, s 9(9).

13 Ibid, s 9(11). Cf the Fugitive Offenders Act 1967, s 7(5) (repealed).

14 See para 554 above.

15 Extradition Act 1989, s 9(8). Cf the Fugitive Offenders Act 1967, s 7(5) (repealed), under which Lord Goddard CJ considered that any special intent or the like necessary to constitute the offence was to be ignored: *R v Governor of Pentonville Prison, ex parte Teja* [1971] 2 QB 274, [1971] 2 All ER 11, DC. As already noted, the sheriff is required to issue a certificate identifying the crime against United Kingdom law which the conduct would constitute: see the text to note 12 above. Thus, the requesting state, Commonwealth country or colony must also detail what the conduct on which the request is based actually is.

16 Thus fulfilling the 'double criminality' requirement: see para 548 above.

17 Extradition Act 1989, s 9(8)(a), (b). Cf the Fugitive Offenders Act 1967, s 7(5) (repealed). The question is whether the evidence would be sufficient to warrant trial in the United Kingdom for what was done in the requesting state: *Government of Canada v Aronson* [1990] 1 AC 579, [1989] 2 All ER 1025, HL.

18 See paras 544, 546, above.

19 See para 511 above.

20 Extradition Act 1989, s 9(4), (8).

564. Hearing and committal in relation to the Republic of Ireland.

Where extradition to the Republic of Ireland is sought the hearing is to take place before a sheriff[1]. Where only a provisional warrant is produced, the court may remand in custody or on bail for not more than three days, after which the person is to be discharged if no ordinary warrant is produced[2]. Where an ordinary warrant is produced within three days, the person is detained under its authority, and the court proceeds with the same powers as for summary proceedings[3] save that no prima facie case need be made out[4]. The applicant need only produce a valid and verified warrant and evidence of the laws of Ireland.

The court may not make an order to surrender the person if the offence does not correspond with one in the law of Scotland, or has a penalty less than required for such surrender[5], or if the offence is political or of a related type[6]. If the court does not discharge the person, it orders him to be delivered to the Garda Síochána[7]. The Secretary of State is not involved.

The person may be remanded in custody or on bail meantime, but any bail bond must be conditional upon reporting at a time fixed by the police, who may extend bail if there is exceptional delay in removal[8].

There may be no delivery to the Garda Síochána until at least fifteen days have elapsed, unless the person consents[9]. If he applies for review, he must not be delivered while the proceedings are pending[10]. In either case, the person must be told of the fifteen-day delay and the right to seek review[11].

1 See the Backing of Warrants (Republic of Ireland) Act 1965 (c 45), ss 2(1), 4(3), 10(3). Since the warrant may be indorsed by any justice of the peace, no particular court is indicated.

2 Ibid, s 4(3)(b), (6). If terms of bail are not kept, bail is forfeit and a warrant for arrest may be issued: s 5(5)(c).

3 See ibid, s 2(4), Schedule, paras 5, 6. The drafting is elliptical and while procedure in England is laid down, it is specifically declared not to apply in Scotland: s 4(4), (6). This is because while in England, remand is to a constable, in Scotland it is to a prison, rendering s 4(4) inapplicable in such a case. I am grateful to Mr A C Normand, late of the Crown Office, for the solution to this puzzle.

4 See ibid, ss 2(1), 4(3)(a). See also *Re Arkins*[1966] 3 All ER 651, [1966] 1 WLR 1593, DC.

5 Backing of Warrants (Republic of Ireland) Act 1965, s 2(2) expressing the principle of 'double criminality', see para 548 above.

6 Ibid, s 2(2)(a). See paras 531, 535, above.

7 Ibid, s 2(1).

8 Ibid, s 5(5)(a), (b). As to breach of bail, see s 5(5)(c), and note 2 above.

9 Ibid, s 3(1)(a). A form is provided for consent to early removal, and it is to be delivered to the governor of the prison or the clerk of court: Act of Adjournal (Consolidation) 1988, SI 1988/110, r 150, Sch 1, Form 83. The governor or clerk is required to deliver the indorsed warrant to a member of the Garda Síochána and a copy of the bail bond (if any) to the police station at which the person is to surrender: r 151.

10 Backing of Warrants (Republic of Ireland) Act 1965, s 3(1)(b).

11 Ibid, s 3(1).

(f) Authentication of Documents

565. Authentication of documents under the 1870 procedure. Depositions and statements on oath taken in a foreign state, copies of such documents, and foreign certificates of or judicial documents stating the facts of conviction may be received in evidence in proceedings under the 1870 procedure if duly authenticated[1].

The rule on admissibility of authenticated documents is not limited to writs from the requisitioning state only, and it is not the concern of the metropolitan magistrate whether they would be available at any trial in the requisitioning state[2]. Photographs of the accused, by which victims identified them, are admissible even though they might tend to show the accused had a criminal record[3].

1 Extradition Act 1989 (c 33), s 1(3), Sch 1, para 12 (re-enacting the Extradition Act 1870 (c 52), s 14 (repealed)). The 1870 Act, s 15 (repealed), indicating what constitutes due authentication, is not re-enacted, but the Extradition Act 1989, s 26 (see para 566 below), now stipulates what is authentication for this purpose. As to the '1870 procedure', see para 510 above.

2 *Re Rees* [1986] AC 937, [1986] 2 All ER 321, HL.

3 *R v Governor of Pentonville Prison, ex parte Voets* [1986] 2 All ER 630, [1986] 1 WLR 470, DC.

566. Authentication of documents under the 1989 procedure. Documents in extradition proceedings from foreign states[1] may be authenticated by the oath of a witness[2]. However, they are deemed to be duly authenticated if purporting to be signed by a judge, magistrate or officer of the foreign state, or if purporting to be certified by being sealed with the official seal of the Minister of Justice or other minister of the foreign state[3]. In the latter case judicial notice is to be taken of such documents, and they are to be received in evidence without further proof[4].

Documents in extradition proceedings from designated Commonwealth countries and colonies[5] are deemed authenticated and sufficient evidence if certified by a judge or magistrate or officer in or of the country or colony to be the original or a true copy, in which case it is sufficient evidence of the matters stated in it, and either sworn to by a witness, or bearing the seal of a minister (in the case of a designated Commonwealth country) or the governor, a minister, secretary or other officer administering a department of the government (in the case of a colony)[6]. This method of authentication applies to a document:

(1) purporting to set out evidence given on oath in a designated Commonwealth country or a colony;
(2) purporting to have been received in evidence in any proceedings in a designated Commonwealth country or a colony, or to be a copy of such a document; and
(3) which certifies that a person was convicted on a specified date of an offence against the law of such country or colony[7].

1 See para 512 above.
2 Extradition Act 1989 (c 33), s 26(1).
3 Ibid, s 26(1)(a), (b). Under the similar law under the Extradition Act 1870 (c 52), it was held in that regard must be had to the relevant treaty: *R v Bow Street Magistrates Court, ex parte Van der Holst* (1986) 83 Cr App Rep 114, DC.
4 Extradition Act 1989, s 26(2).
5 See para 520 above.
6 Extradition Act 1989, s 27(2)–(4). Cf the Fugitive Offenders Act 1967 (c 68), s 11 (repealed), and *Oskar v Government of Australia* [1988] AC 366, [1988] 1 All ER 183, HL.
7 Extradition Act 1989, s 27(1)(a)–(c). Cf the Fugitive Offenders Act 1967, s 11 (repealed).

567. Authentication of documents in relation to the Republic of Ireland. In relation to the Republic of Ireland, a document purporting to be a warrant issued by a judicial authority in the Republic, or a copy of a summons issued by or on behalf of a court in the Republic may be taken to be such a warrant or summons duly issued, if verified in the prescribed manner[1].

Evidence with respect to the laws of the Republic may be given by affidavit or other written statement on oath[2]. However, a certificate purporting to be issued by a judicial authority in the Republic certifying that the offence specified in the warrant can be dealt with in the way described in the certificate is sufficient evidence of that matter[2].

A deposition purporting to have been made in the Republic, or an affidavit or other statement on oath purporting to have been sworn there may be admitted if verified in the prescribed manner[3].

1 See the Backing of Warrants (Republic of Ireland) Act 1965 (c 45), s 7(a), and the Act of Adjournal (Consolidation) 1988, SI 1988/110, r 152(1), (2).
2 Backing of Warrants (Republic of Ireland) Act 1965, s 7(b).
3 See ibid, s 7(c), and the Act of Adjournal (Consolidation) 1988, r 152(3).

(g) Review

568. Review under the 1870 procedure at the instance of the person whose extradition is sought. The decision of the metropolitan magistrate (or in the exceptional case of a crime on the high seas or in a vessel or hovercraft which is in a United Kingdom port, where a sheriff has jurisdiction, the sheriff) is not appealable by the person whose extradition is sought[1]. The decision is subject to judicial review, and the magistrate (or sheriff) is required to inform the person that he has a right to apply for *habeas corpus* and will not be surrendered for at least fifteen days[2]. Normally, all evidence should have been presented in the hearing before *habeas corpus* or judicial review are sought[3].

No Scottish remedy is referred to as such. *Habeas corpus* was sought in one Scottish case and the High Court held the remedy unknown to Scots law, but looking at the intention of the legislation then in force, exercised the *nobile officium* and required the respondent to lodge answers to the petitioner's averments within seven days[4]. There is no appeal from an exercise of the *nobile officium* or refusal to exercise it.

A person may waive the rights of review, if he gives notice in the form prescribed by an Act of Adjournal[5]. If such consent is given, the sheriff[6] may order committal of the person for return at any time thereafter[7].

If there has been no surrender one month after an order following waiver of review rights, or in other cases two months after a *habeas corpus* application, or after committal if there is no such application, the person may apply to a judge of the High Court[8] to order discharge, provided reasonable notice has been given to the Secretary of State[9].

1 See *Atkinson v United States of America Government* [1971] AC 197, [1969] 3 All ER 1317, HL, in relation to a stated case and *Government of the Federal Republic of Germany v Sotiriadis* [1975] AC 1, [1974] 1 All ER 692, HL, in relation to *habeas corpus*.

2 Extradition Act 1989 (c 33), s 1(3), Sch 1, paras 8(1), 13 (re-enacting the Extradition Act 1870 (c 52), ss 11, 16 (repealed)). As to the test for review on the ground of abuse of process, see *Re Parekh* [1988] Crim LR 832, DC, and *R v Governor of Pentonville Prison, ex parte Sinclair* [1990] 2 QB 112, [1990] 2 All ER 789, DC.

3 *United States Government v Bowe* [1990] 1 AC 500, [1989] 3 All ER 315, PC.

4 *Wan Ping Nam v Federal German Republic Minister of Justice* 1972 JC 43, 1972 SLT 220, where a person committed to prison by a sheriff under the Extradition Act 1870, ss 10, 16 (repealed) (ie the 'high seas' jurisdiction: see para 553, note 5, above) was told in the strict terms of s 11 that he might apply for *habeas corpus*. He sought review of the proceedings on the ground that he was a 'citizen of Hong Kong' (sic) and thus a British subject, and that the relevant treaty excluded the surrender of 'own nationals' (see para 549 above). He petitioned the High Court of Justiciary for *habeas corpus* and suspension *ad interim* of the warrant for committal. None of the parties before the court (who included the Secretary of State for Scotland and the Lord Advocate) argued that *habeas corpus* had been introduced into the law of Scotland by the sidewind of s 11. The High Court held the remedy to be unknown to Scots law but, looking at the intention of the 1870 Act (and presuming that a person committed by a sheriff should be in no worse position than one committed by a magistrate in England), it exercised the *nobile officium* and required the respondent to lodge answers to the petitioner's averments within seven days. The answers were in fact adequate, so the petition was refused. It may be inferred that, had they been inadequate, the petitioner would have been liberated.

5 Extradition Act 1989, Sch 1, para 9(1), (3) (re-enacting the Extradition Act 1870, s 11A (added by the Criminal Justice Act 1988 (c 33), s 1, Sch 1, para 2) (repealed)).

6 Ie the sheriff who held the hearing: see para 562 above.

7 Extradition Act 1989, Sch 1, para 9(3) (re-enacting the Extradition Act 1870, s 11A (as added: see note 5 above) (repealed)).

8 Ie the English High Court, not the High Court of Justiciary. However, a case might be founded upon the ambiguity.

9 Extradition Act 1989, Sch 1, paras 9(4), 10 (re-enacting the Extradition Act 1870, s 11A (as added: see note 5 above), s 12 (repealed)). See also *Re Nuland* [1988] Crim LR 690, DC.

569. Review under the 1870 procedure at the instance of the requisitioning state. The decision of the metropolitan magistrate (or sheriff in respect of crimes committed at sea) is not appealable by the requisitioning state[1]. It is subject to judicial review[2].

1 See the authorities cited in para 568, note 1, above.

2 *Re Nielsen* [1984] AC 606, [1984] 2 All ER 81, HL.

570. Review under the 1989 procedure at the instance of the person whose extradition is sought. A person whose extradition is sought under the 1989 procedure, and who has been committed by the Sheriff of Lothian and Borders acting as a 'court of committal' (or the metropolitan magistrate in England) awaiting return by the Secretary of State[1] has no right of appeal. He does have a right to seek review of the committal order, and the sheriff (or metropolitan magistrate) is required to inform him, in ordinary language, of his right to make such an application[2], and such a person is not to be returned until at least fifteen days have elapsed, and not at all while proceedings are pending on an application for review[3].

The High Court of Justiciary may order the person's discharge on any grounds generally available in case of judicial review, and on the grounds that it appears to the court that:

(1) because the offence is trivial, or

(2) because of the passage of time since the offence is alleged to have been committed, or the person became unlawfully at large[4], or

(3) because the accusation was not made in good faith in the interests of justice, having regard to all the circumstances, it would be unjust and oppressive to return the person[5]. The court may receive relevant additional evidence[6].

A person may waive his rights to review by giving notice in a form prescribed by an Act of Adjournal, and the sheriff[7] may order his return at any time thereafter[8].

A person awaiting return may apply to the High Court of Justiciary for his discharge on the grounds of delay if he has not been returned, and the court may direct that he be discharged and quash any warrant ordering his return, if satisfied that reasonable notice of the proposed application has been given to the Secretary of State, and unless sufficient cause is shown to the contrary[9]. The sufficient delay is:

(a) one month from the waiver, if he has waived his rights to review[10];

(b) one month from the end of review proceedings, if he has not waived them and has used them[11];

(c) one month from the Secretary of State's issue of the warrant[12] ordering his return, if there has been such a warrant but it has not been carried out[13]; and

(d) two months from the expiry of the period of fifteen days which must elapse before return can be ordered[14], if he has not waived his rights to review, but has not in fact used them[15].

1 See para 563 above.
2 Extradition Act 1989 (c 33), s 11(1), (6).
3 Ibid, s 11(2), (5), (6).
4 As to the equivalent provisions of the older law, see *Oskar v Government of Australia* [1988] AC 366, [1988] 1 All ER 183, HL; *R v Governor of Pentonville Prison, ex parte Sinclair* [1990] 2 QB 112, [1990] 2 All ER 789, DC.
5 Extradition Act 1989, s 11(3), (6). Cf the Fugitive Offenders Act 1967 (c 68), s 8(3) (repealed). This does not allow review of the facts: *Government of the Federal Republic of Germany v Sotiriadis* [1975] AC 1, [1974] 1 All ER 692, HL.
6 Extradition Act 1989, s 11(4), (6).
7 Ie of Lothian and Borders.
8 Extradition Act 1989, s 14(1), (3).
9 Ibid, s 16(1), (5). See also *Re Soering* Guardian, 22 November 1989, DC, [1989] CLY 1719.
10 Extradition Act 1989, s 14(4).
11 Ibid, s 16(3). Proceedings for judicial review end if they are discontinued, on the day of discontinuance, and if they are determined, on the day on which, disregarding any power of a court to grant leave to appeal out of time, there is no further possibility of an appeal: s 16(4).
12 Ie under ibid, s 12: see para 575 below.
13 Ibid, s 16(2)(b).
14 Ie under ibid, s 11(2).
15 Ibid, s 16(2)(a).

571. Review under the 1989 procedure at the instance of the requesting foreign state, Commonwealth country or colony. The requesting state, Commonwealth country or colony may, on the ground that the decision is wrong in law, question the proceedings by requiring a stated case for the opinion of the High Court of Justiciary (or High Court in England) if the Sheriff of Lothian and Borders (or metropolitan magistrate) has refused to make an order[1] committing a person whose extradition has been sought[2]. The High Court of Justiciary has the power either to remit the case to the court of committal to decide in accordance with the decision of the High Court of

Justiciary on a question of law or dismiss the appeal[3]. Where the High Court of Justiciary dismisses such an appeal, it is required to declare, by order, that the offence in question is not an offence in respect of which the Secretary of State has power to return the person[4].

Rules of court may be made specifying time limits for applications for stated cases, and for the stating of such cases, and where a case is not stated within such limit, the High Court of Justiciary (or in England the High Court) may, on the application of the requesting state, country or colony, require the case to be stated[5].

The sheriff, acting as a court of committal, must make an order detaining the person, or directing that he may be released only upon bail, if the state, country or colony informs him immediately that it is seeking a stated case, and such order continues while the case is pending[6]. Appeal against such an order is possible[7], and it ceases to have effect if the High Court of Justiciary dismisses the appeal[8]. That court may order the person's detention or bail[9].

1 Ie under the Extradition Act 1989 (c 33), s 9: see para 563 above.
2 Ibid, s 10(1). Judicial review is still presumably competent.
3 Ibid, s 10(5).
4 Ibid, s 10(6).
5 Ibid, s 10(3), (4).
6 Ibid, s 10(2), (11). For these purposes a case is pending (unless proceedings are discontinued) until (disregarding any power of a court to grant leave to take any step out of time) there is no step that the state, country or colony can take: s 10(12).
7 See ibid, s 10(13).
8 Ibid, s 10(8). In respect of appeals against the metropolitan magistrate in England, the cessation is subject to the possibility of appeal to the House of Lords: see s 10(7), (9), (10).
9 Ibid, s 10(13).

572. Review at the instance of the person whose extradition is sought in relation to the Republic of Ireland. In relation to extradition to the Republic of Ireland, the High Court of Justiciary may review an order for return as if on appeal from summary conviction, and return is delayed pending such review[1]. A person not surrendered within one month of the order for return may be discharged by the High Court of Justiciary, unless reasonable cause for delay is shown[2]. If it appears to a sheriff of the court making the order[3] that the Garda Síochána no longer requires the person, he must discharge him[4].

1 Backing of Warrants (Republic of Ireland) Act 1965 (c 45), s 3(2).
2 Ibid, s 6(1).
3 For these purposes the sheriff is not necessarily the Sheriff of Lothian and Borders: see para 555 above.
4 Backing of Warrants (Republic of Ireland) Act 1965, s 6(2).

573. Review at the instance of the requesting state in relation to the Republic of Ireland. In respect of appeal against a refusal to commit a person pending return by the Secretary of State, the position is the same as in relation to states, countries and colonies under the 1989 procedure[1], save for two things. The request for a stated case comes from the procurator fiscal of the area to which the constable presenting the application belongs[2]; and there is no requirement that the court dismissing such appeal declare the offence not to be one in respect of which the Secretary of State has power to make an order for return[3]. Also, the sheriff involved need not be the Sheriff of Lothian and Borders[4].

1 See the Backing of Warrants (Republic of Ireland) Act 1965 (c 45), s 2A(2)–(5), (7), (10)–(12) (added by the Criminal Justice Act 1988 (c 33), Sch 1, para 5, and saved by the Extradition Act 1989 (c 33), s 37(5)). See also para 571 above.

2 Backing of Warrants (Republic of Ireland) Act 1965 (c 45), s 2A(1), (12)(a) (as so added and saved). Judicial review is also no doubt competent: *Re Nielsen* [1984] AC 606, [1984] 2 All ER 81, HL.
3 The Secretary of State has no role in proceedings for extradition to the Republic of Ireland.
4 See para 555 above.

(h) Secretary of State's Order to surrender or return

574. Order to surrender under the 1870 procedure. Under the 1870 procedure, after fifteen days from the committal of a person to prison by the metropolitan magistrate (or, in the exceptional case of a crime committed on the high seas in a vessel or hovercraft which is in a United Kingdom port[1], by the sheriff), or fifteen days after the refusal of the remedy of *habeas corpus*, the Secretary of State may (but need not[2]), by warrant, order a person to be surrendered to such a person as may in his opinion be duly authorised to receive that person, provided the required procedures are exhausted, and (presumably subject to the power of a judge to order his discharge if not surrendered after two months[3]), after such further delay as he may allow[4].

This warrant entitles the person to whom the warrant is directed to detain the extraditable person, retake him if he escapes, and convey him into the jurisdiction of the relevant foreign state[5].

1 See para 565 above.
2 Refusal to do so might breach the relevant treaty, as to which see para 507 above.
3 Ie under the Extradition Act 1989 (c 33), s 1(3), Sch 1, para 10: see para 568 above.
4 Ibid, Sch 1, para 8(2), re-enacting the Extradition Act 1870 (c 52), s 11 (repealed).
5 Extradition Act 1989, Sch 1, para 8(3) (as so re-enacted).

575. Order to return under the 1989 procedure. A person may not be returned until fifteen days have elapsed from his committal under the 1989 procedure, or while *habeas corpus* proceedings are pending[1]. Thereafter, if a person has not been discharged as a result of the review procedures[2], the Secretary of State may (but need not[3]), by warrant, order his return, unless such return is prohibited by the Extradition Act 1989[4]. Such prohibitions include the general restrictions upon return[5]. They also include further general grounds not specifically made available to the court of committal.

First, the Secretary of State must not order the return of a person where, having regard to all the circumstances, it would be unjust or oppressive to do so because of the trivial nature of the offence, or because of the passage of time since the alleged offence, or because the accusation was not made in good faith[6]. Secondly, the Secretary of State must not order the return of a person who is charged with an offence, or is serving a sentence of imprisonment or detention in the United Kingdom, until the charge is disposed of, the diet is deserted *pro loco et tempore*, or the sentence is served[7]. Thirdly, the Secretary of State may decide not to order the return of a person accused or convicted of an offence for which he could be or has been sentenced to death, if that offence is not so punishable in Great Britain[8]. Fourthly, the Secretary of State may decide not to order the return of a person if another extradition request has been received in respect of him, and it appears to him that it should be preferred, having regard to all the circumstances of the case, and in particular the relative seriousness of the offences, the relative dates of the two requests, and the nationality or citizenship, and ordinary residence, of the person[9].

When a person is ordered to be returned by the Secretary of State to a Commonwealth country or a colony, he must be given notice forthwith[10].

Where the Secretary of State is contemplating issuing a warrant ordering a person to be returned to a foreign state[11] that person must be given notice of this in writing and in ordinary language[12]. That person has a right to make representations within fifteen days as to why he should not be returned, and he may not be returned during that period unless he has waived that right, and the Secretary of State must consider any such representations[13]. The entitlement to this period of fifteen days exists independently of, and in addition to, the entitlement not to be returned within fifteen days of the order by the court of committal to await the warrant issued by the Secretary of State ordering the person's return.

1 See the Extradition Act 1989 (c 33), s 11(2), (5), and para 570 above. Cf the Fugitive Offenders Act 1967 (c 68), s 8(2) (repealed).
2 See para 570 above.
3 Refusal to return might breach the relevant treaty.
4 Extradition Act 1989, s 12(1). Cf the Fugitive Offenders Act 1967, s 9(1) (repealed).
5 See paras 531 ff below. These bind the Secretary of State as well as the court of committal (for which see para 563 above).
6 Extradition Act 1989, s 12(2)(a). Cf the Fugitive Offenders Act 1967, s 9(3) (repealed). This repeats the grounds available to be argued before the court of committal (see para 570 above), so the same grounds may be argued twice.
7 Extradition Act 1989, s 12(3), (4). Cf the Fugitive Offenders Act 1967, s 9(2) (repealed). Desertion of the diet *simpliciter* no doubt is included within the charge being 'disposed of'. The House of Lords held that the provision requires the Secretary of State to keep in mind such bars and impediments, but does not prevent him from issuing an order to return a person: *Oskar v Government of Australia* [1988] AC 366, [1988] 1 All ER 183, HL.
8 Extradition Act 1989, s 12(2)(b). Cf the Fugitive Offenders Act 1967, s 9(4) (repealed). Treaties have provided for this: see *R v Secretary of State for the Home Department, ex parte Kirkwood* [1984] 2 All ER 390, [1984] 1 WLR 913. The issue also arose in *Soering v United Kingdom* (Ser A No 161, Judgment 7 July 1989) 11 EHRR 439, E Ct HR (cf the English proceedings *Re Soering* [1988] Crim LR 307, DC) in which Soering argued that he should not be extradited to face lengthy delays between sentence and execution, which constituted a breach of the European Convention on Human Rights, art 3, before the European Court of Human Rights, which decided that the law permitted him to raise such issues. The Extradition Act 1989, s 12(2)(b), does not apply if the offence carries the death penalty in Northern Ireland, nor does it require the imposition of the death penalty to be likely. For a discussion of the *Soering* case, see W Finnie 'Extradition and the Death Penalty' 1990 SLT (News) 53. As to the European Convention on Human Rights, see the Convention for the Protection of Human Rights and Fundamental Freedoms (Rome, 4 November 1950; TS 71 (1953); Cmd 8969), and HUMAN RIGHTS IN EUROPE, vol 12, para 26.
9 Extradition Act 1989, s 12(5). Cf the Fugitive Offenders Act 1967, s 9(5) (repealed). See eg *Oskar v Government of Australia* [1988] AC 366, [1988] 1 All ER 183, HL.
10 Extradition Act 1989, s 12(6). Cf the Fugitive Offenders Act 1967, s 9(6) (repealed). As to designated Commonwealth countries and colonies, see para 520 above.
11 See para 512 above.
12 Extradition Act 1989, s 13(1), (3).
13 Ibid, s 13(2), (4).

576. Return to the Republic of Ireland. There is no requirement for an order by the Secretary of State, nor any power for him to issue one[1].

1 See paras 552, 555, 558, above.

(7) EXTRADITION TO THE UNITED KINGDOM

(a) Foreign States

577. Authority and jurisdiction. All United Kingdom extradition treaties are reciprocal or multilateral, and usually extradition to the United Kingdom can be expected to conform to them[1]. They therefore fall under either 'the 1870 procedure' or 'the 1989 procedure'[2]. Their terms are, in so far as they are embodied in an Order in Council under the Extradition Act 1989[3], part of municipal law, but are not drafted so as to create rights which might be vindicated in the United Kingdom.

Nevertheless, under the 1870 procedure, only a single provision applies to extradition to the United Kingdom. This relates to speciality, that is, the principle that an extradited person can be tried only for the crime or offence for which he has been extradited (or possibly some others)[4]. Also, under the 1989 procedure there are only three provisions so applying. Two of these relate to speciality, but one permits a person extradited to the United Kingdom and against whom proceedings are not commenced within a reasonable time to be returned whence he came without delay and at no cost to himself[5].

Thus, subject to these limitations, no particular procedure is required or controls applied. Since the fundamental principle of criminal jurisdiction throughout the United Kingdom is territorial, mere presence of the person is generally regarded as sufficient. In the past, illegality involved in bringing him into the jurisdiction has not tainted the proceedings, and has neither been a defence nor entitled the person to judicial review[6]. It might be taken into account in sentence, and a civil action or even prosecution against a foreign government, or those detaining the person, might be possible either in the United Kingdom or abroad[7].

'Ad hoc' extradition, without benefit of treaty, is also competent in certain circumstances under the 1989 procedure[8]. However, this is an innovation only in respect of extradition from the United Kingdom. Given the cavalier attitude to controls upon extradition to the United Kingdom where there is a treaty in force, controls upon such extradition where there is no treaty are not likely to be more substantial. It is believed that extradition to England without benefit of treaty happened on occasion before the Extradition Act 1989.

This rigorous exclusion of control has been relaxed on occasion. An English court held that the jurisdiction of the trial court was not ousted by the use of unlawful means in bringing the person into the United Kingdom, but the remedy of prohibition would be granted to prevent committal[9]. However, that decision was held by a later court to have been decided *per incuriam*, and that not only did a court have no power to refuse to try such a case, but that also it had no power to inquire into the circumstances in which the person had been brought into the United Kingdom, which was a matter for the surrendering state[10].

The speciality limit itself is not in general a major limitation. Under the 1870 procedure, a person may be tried for the extradition crime for which he was surrendered, and any other extradition crime as may be proved by the facts on which the surrender is grounded[11]. Under the 1989 procedure, a person may be tried for the offence for which he was surrendered, any offence (*semble* whether an extradition crime or not) disclosed by the particulars furnished to the foreign state on which his surrender is grounded, and for any offence (again, *semble*, whether an extradition crime or not) in respect of which the foreign state may consent to his being tried[12]. Nevertheless, it is a rule which can be infringed[13].

1 As to the treaties, see paras 507, 508, above.
2 As to the '1870 procedure', and the '1989 procedure', see paras 510, 511, above.
3 See paras 510, 511, above.
4 Extradition Act 1989 (c 33), s 1(3), Sch 1, para 17 (re-enacting the Extradition Act 1870 (c 52), s 19 (repealed)).
5 Extradition Act 1989, s 20.
6 In the past, people have been, in effect, kidnapped by United Kingdom police officers or others abroad in countries with which an extradition treaty has been in force. This may have occurred with or without the assistance of the foreign authorities, and has not tainted the United Kingdom proceedings: see eg *Sinclair v HM Advocate* (1890) 17 R (J) 38 and *R v Officer Commanding Depot*

Battalion RASC Colchester, ex parte Elliott [1949] 1 All ER 373, DC. See also *R v Bennett* [1978] Crim LR 44 (NZ CA); *Somchai Liangsiriprasert v United States Government* [1991] 1 AC 225, [1990] 2 All ER 866, PC.

In the *Sinclair* case, a person was arrested and handed over by Portuguese authorities in Lisbon without any inquiry (nor any extradition treaty, as none was signed with Portugal until 1892) to a Glasgow detective with a warrant for arrest from the Sheriff Court of Lanarkshire which was not produced to the Portuguese authorities. He was detained in Lisbon for some days, taken onto a ship, refused permission to land at Vigo in Spain, landed at London (where no warrant for his arrest existed) and brought by train to Glasgow.

Lord Justice-Clerk Macdonald observed (at 41) '. . . we cannot be the judges of the wrong-doing of the Government of Portugal. What we have here is that a person has been delivered to a properly authorised officer of this country. He is therefore properly before the Court of a competent jurisdiction on a proper warrant. I do not think we can go behind this', and (at 42) '. . . even if the proceedings here were irregular I am of the opinion that where a Court of competent jurisdiction has a prisoner before it upon a competent complaint they must proceed to try him, no matter what happened before, even although he may have been harshly treated by a foreign Government, and irregularly dealt with by a subordinate officer'.

7 See eg *R v Officer Commanding Depot Battalion RASC Colchester, ex parte Elliott* [1949] 1 All ER 373 at 379, DC.

8 See paras 511, 517, above.

9 *R v Bow Street Magistrates, ex parte Mackeson* (1982) 75 Cr App Rep 24, DC. The authorities in Rhodesia/Zimbabwe were asked, as a disguised form of extradition, to deport Mackeson under the Fugitive Offenders Act 1967 (c 68) (repealed), the relevant legislation then in force (see para 519 above) not applying because the government of that territory was not at the time recognised by Her Majesty's government.

10 *R v Plymouth Justices, ex parte Driver* [1986] QB 95, [1985] 2 All ER 681, DC.

11 Extradition Act 1989, Sch 1, para 17 (re-enacting the Extradition Act 1870, s 19 (repealed)). For the meaning of 'extradition crime' under the 1870 procedure, see para 514 above.

12 Extradition Act 1989, s 18. For the meaning of 'extradition crime' under the 1989 procedure, see para 515 above.

13 See *R v Davies* (1983) 76 Cr App Rep 120, CA. Here a person was extradited to England from the United States. He purported to waive his entitlement under the Extradition Act 1870, s 19 (repealed) (now re-enacted as the Extradition Act 1989, Sch 1, para 17), and pleaded guilty to an offence for which he was not extradited. The Court of Criminal Appeal quashed these proceedings on the ground that the entitlement could not be waived. It was also the case that the offence to which he pleaded guilty was not extraditable in respect of the United States, that during the proceedings in the United States the authorities had been assured that he would not be tried for offences other than those for which he was being extradited, and that the guilty plea resulted from a plea bargain, because trial for the offences for which he had been extradited would have been lengthy, and concerned events some years earlier. Their Lordships did not purport to decide the matter on the basis of those facts, though.

578. Procedure in practice. In practice[1], in the case of an accused person, procurators fiscal are required to report to the Crown Office any case in which they seek extradition. Crown Office legal staff advise Crown counsel as to the existence or otherwise of a relevant treaty. The latter considers the whole evidence and decides if extradition should be sought, taking into account the seriousness and the date of the alleged offence, the strength and availability of evidence having regard to the treaty requirements, the competency and likely success of extradition procedures in the foreign state in question, and the public interest (bearing in mind the time and expense involved). A law officer is not normally involved in the decision.

If extradition is sought, the procurator fiscal obtains depositions of witnesses to the extent required under the relevant treaty and in particular a deposition of an investigating officer summarising the evidence (a statement of facts) and swears a deposition as to the law in Scotland (statement of law). In practice the statements of fact and law are first approved in draft by Crown counsel.

Unless an arrest warrant is already in existence, the procurator fiscal obtains one. The sheriff certifies the taking of depositions and the productions to be transmitted, including a warrant or certified copy, and the procurator fiscal

transmits all the papers to the Crown Office which obtains necessary trans-
lations and passes the papers to the Scottish Office. There, the Home and Health
Department authenticates the signature on the sheriff's certificate accompanying the depositions and transmits the papers to the Foreign and Commonwealth
Office for onward transmission through diplomatic channels, with a formal
request for arrest and surrender in terms of the relevant treaty. Difficulties
thereafter are dealt with by communication through diplomatic channels or
informally between the Crown Office and the relevant prosecuting or judicial
authority.

In the case of those alleged already to have been convicted, the procedure is
essentially the same, except that depositions can generally be confined to statements of facts and law with evidence of identification.

In the case of requests to foreign states with which extradition is possible
without the need to show a *prima facie* case,[2] depositions on evidence going
beyond statements of fact and law should not be necessary.

1 I am grateful to Mr N McFadyen of the Crown Office and Mr A C Normand, late of the Crown
   Office, for the information upon which the following account of procedure, which is otherwise
   unpublished, is based, as well as for comments upon other parts of this section. Neither is
   responsible for what appears here. Procedure in England followed a Home Office Memorandum
   of 1913 which is also unpublished, but is discussed in V E Hartley-Booth *British Extradition Law
   and Procedure* (1980). This may now be out of date.
2 See the Extradition Act 1989 (c 33), s 9(4), (8)(a). For the meaning of 'the prima facie requirement', see paras 545, 546, 554, above. For the meaning of 'general extradition arrangements', see
   para 511 above.

(b) Commonwealth Countries

579. Authority and jurisdiction. There are no intra-Commonwealth treaties on extradition[1], and surrender may be sought from dependencies in any case.
Thus no limit can be imposed from any treaty obligation embodied in an Order
in Council[2] or otherwise.

Only two legislative provisions apply to extradition from designated Commonwealth countries or colonies to the United Kingdom, and they apply in
such cases in the same way as they do to persons extradited from foreign states[3].

1 There is the Agreement following the Commonwealth Law Officers Conference of 1966: see
   Scheme relating to the Rendition of Fugitive Offenders within the Commonwealth (Cmnd 3008) (1966).
   This has no legal effect.
2 See paras 510, 511, above.
3 See the Extradition Act 1989 (c 33), ss 19, 20. As to the application to persons extradited from
   foreign states, see para 577 above. As to designated Commonwealth countries and colonies, see
   para 520 above.

580. Procedure in practice. Procedure in practice in relation to extradition
from Commonwealth countries or colonies is, *mutatis mutandis*, the same as in
relation to extradition from foreign states, save that in no case may the prima
facie requirement be dispensed with[1].

1 See para 578 above. The prima facie requirement (for which, see paras 544–546, 554, above)
   may, by virtue of the Extradition Act 1989 (c 33), s 9(4), (8)(a), be dispensed with only where

there are in force 'general extradition agreements' (see para 510 above) so permitting. By virtue of s 3, 'general extradition agreements' cannot exist with Commonwealth countries or colonies: as to which see para 520 above.

(c) Republic of Ireland

581. Authority and jurisdiction. No extradition treaty exists with the Republic of Ireland, and no part of the legislation covering extradition to the Republic applies to extradition from it[1]. Thus, questions of procedure and illegality in apprehension are in the same position as they are with foreign states, save that the speciality rule, and release and assisted return provisions, do not apply[2].

1 Ie the Backing of Warrants (Republic of Ireland) Act 1965 (c 45).
2 See para 577, especially the text and notes 5, 6, above.

582–600. Procedure in practice. In practice[1], the procurator fiscal, after obtaining instructions from Crown counsel, causes a warrant to be sent to the Deputy Commissioner of the Garda Síochána, together with an affidavit verifying the signature on the warrant and a certificate given by the procurator fiscal either that the relevant offence is indictable and punishable by a maximum period of at least six months' imprisonment and will not be prosecuted summarily, or that it is an offence which will be prosecuted summarily and is so punishable.

The Irish legislation[2] provides that in the case of a warrant for arrest it must not be indorsed by the Garda Síochána (thereby permitting extradition) if the Attorney General of Ireland so directs. He is required to give such a direction unless, having considered such information as he deems appropriate, he is of the opinion that there is a clear intention to prosecute, founded on the existence of sufficient evidence. This does not, however, apply to a warrant following upon conviction.

The Lord Advocate will submit a note confirming the intention to prosecute, and providing statements of fact and law to assist the Attorney General.

1 See para 578, note 1, above.
2 Ie the Extradition Act 1965, as amended by the Extradition (Amendment) Act 1987. The Irish procedure under the 1965 Act was similar to that under the United Kingdom's Backing of Warrants (Republic of Ireland) Act 1965 (c 45). The 1987 Act has introduced a number of significant changes.

INDUSTRIAL AND PROVIDENT SOCIETIES, CREDIT UNIONS AND FRIENDLY SOCIETIES

		PARA
1. INTRODUCTION	. . . .	601
2. INDUSTRIAL AND PROVIDENT SOCIETIES	. .	606
(1) Introduction	. . . . . .	606
(2) Registration	. . . . .	610
(3) Rules	. . . .	612
(4) Membership and Committee of Management	.	618
(5) Finance	. . . .	621
(6) Nominations	. . . . .	626
(7) Accounts	. . . . . .	630
(8) Audit	. . . .	636
(9) Floating Charges	. . . . .	641
(10) Inspection of Books	. . . .	642
(11) Examination of Affairs by Inspectors: Special Meetings	.	646
(12) Disputes	. . . . . .	647
(13) Amalgamations, Transfer and Conversions	.	648
(14) Dissolution and Liquidation	. . .	652
(15) Offences	. . . . . .	654
3. CREDIT UNIONS	. . . . . .	656
(1) Introduction	. . . . . .	656
(2) Registration	. . . . .	661
(3) Rules and Membership	. . . .	663
(4) Operation of Credit Unions	. . .	665
(5) Amalgamations, Transfers and Conversions	.	672
(6) Powers of the Registrar	. . . .	674
(7) Offences	. . . . . .	678
4. FRIENDLY SOCIETIES	. . . . .	679
(1) Introduction	. . . . . .	679
(2) Registration	. . . . .	685
(a) Classes of Friendly Societies	. .	685
(b) Friendly Societies	. . . .	686
(c) Other Societies	. . . .	693
(d) Registration Procedure	. . .	695
(3) Rules	. . . .	698
(4) Membership	. . . . .	704
(5) Trustees and Officers	. . . .	707
(6) Meetings	. . . . . .	713
(7) Accounts and Audit	. . . .	714
(8) Finance	. . . . . .	719
(9) Nominations	. . . . .	722
(10) Disputes	. . . . . .	725
(11) Amalgamations, Transfers and Conversions	.	726
(12) Inspection and Production of Documents	.	732
(13) Suspension and Cancellation	. . .	735
(14) Dissolution and Liquidation	. . .	737
(15) Enforcement	. . . . .	741

1. INTRODUCTION

601. Purposes. As industrial and provident societies, credit unions and friendly societies are comparatively little known, a brief explanation of their purpose may be useful[1]. Friendly societies can be described as voluntary unincorporated associations for the purpose of the mutual relief and maintenance of their members in sickness and old age, or for similar purposes. The friendly societies legislation regulates not only friendly (insurance) societies but also benevolent societies, cattle insurance societies, working men's clubs, old people's homes and other specially authorised societies[2]. Industrial and provident societies were originally intended to be co-operative societies, but the industrial and provident societies legislation allows registration by both co-operative societies and societies whose business is intended to benefit the community[3]. Credit unions were permitted to register by the Credit Unions Act 1979 (c 34) and can be described as credit and thrift co-operative societies, or more instructively, savings and loan co-operative societies, whose members are linked by some common bond[4]. Such societies are incorporated with limited liability.

1 The only other up-to-date detailed text on industrial and provident societies, credit unions and friendly societies is contained in 19 *Halsbury's Laws of England* (4th edn), paras 101 ff, and 24 *Halsbury's Laws of England* (4th edn) paras 1 ff.
2 See paras 679 ff below.
3 See paras 606 ff below.
4 See paras 656 ff below.

602. Historical development. Although the first record of a friendly society dates from 1634 and the first friendly societies legislation was passed in 1793[1], a discussion of the development of the law in the period before 1870 is more appropriate to a historical study[2]. For the present purposes, it is sufficient to say that at the beginning of the nineteenth century the distinction now made between friendly societies, co-operative or industrial and provident societies, building societies and credit unions was by no means apparent; members might use their society for more than one of these purposes. Use was also made of friendly society registration by the early co-operative and building societies to obtain legal recognition and protection. This led to the existing friendly societies legislation being adapted by the Benefit Building Societies Act 1836 and the Industrial and Provident Societies Act 1852 for these types of society[3]. Also, in an attempt to make the registration system more efficient, the Friendly Societies Act 1834 appointed, for the first time in Scotland, the Lord Advocate or one of his deputies to certify a society's rules — which was the expression used for the registration process[4]. The Lord Advocate was made registrar by the Friendly Societies Act 1846, which also appointed English and Irish registrars[5].

On the death of the first English registrar, John Tidd Pratt, in 1870, political manoeuvrings led finally to the appointment of the Royal Commission on Friendly Societies and Benefit Building Societies of 1870–74. Most of its recommendations were adopted, and led to the Building Societies Act 1874 (c 42), the Friendly Societies Act 1875 and the Industrial and Provident Societies Act 1876[6]. These Acts were the foundation of the modern legislation regulating these societies.

1 Ie the Friendly Societies Act 1793 (c 54) (repealed).
2 The standard historical texts are both by P H J H Gosden: see *Friendly Societies in England 1815–1874* (1961) and *Self-Help Voluntary Associations in 19th Century Britain* (1973).
3 The Benefit Building Societies Act 1836 (c 32) and the Industrial and Provident Societies Act 1852 (c 31) are both repealed.
4 See the Friendly Societies Act 1834 (c 40), s 4 (repealed).

5 See the Friendly Societies Act 1846 (c 27), s 10 (repealed).
6 The building societies legislation will not be further dealt with in this title: see BUILDING SOCIETIES. The Friendly Societies Act 1875 (c 60) and the Industrial and Provident Societies Act 1876 (c 45) are both repealed.

603. Current legislation. After a series of amendments and consolidations the current legislation is as follows:
(1) Industrial and provident societies including credit unions:
     the Industrial and Provident Societies Act 1965 (c 12);
     the Industrial and Provident Societies Act 1967 (c 48);
     the Friendly and Industrial and Provident Societies Act 1968 (c 55);
     the Industrial and Provident Societies Act 1975 (c 41);
     the Industrial and Provident Societies Act 1978 (c 34); and
     the Credit Unions Act 1979 (c 34);
(2) Friendly societies:
     the Friendly Societies Act 1974 (c 46);
     the Friendly Societies Act 1981 (c 50); and
     the Friendly Societies Act 1984 (c 62).
There are regulations made under both sets of legislation[1].

1 For the details of the regulations, see para 606, note 3, below (industrial and provident societies); para 656, note 8, below (credit unions); and para 683, note 1, below (friendly societies).

604. The Registry of Friendly Societies. The Friendly Societies Act 1974 provides for the officials necessary to carry out the registration and supervisory functions of the industrial and provident societies and the friendly societies legislation[1]. There is a Chief Registrar of Friendly Societies with assistant registrars based in two offices[2], the Treasury being the relevant ministry. The chief registrar is based in the central office serving the central registration area of England and Wales, the Channel Islands and the Isle of Man through an assistant registrar[3].

There is a separate Scottish area with its own assistant registrar, known as the Assistant Registrar for Scotland[4], who must be a solicitor, advocate or writer to the signet of at least seven years' standing[5]. His duties derive from three sources: his position as registrar for Scotland; possible delegation from the chief registrar; and particular duties under the Friendly Societies Act 1974. First, the legislation confers registration and supervisory functions on the Assistant Registrar for Scotland[6]. Secondly, functions are also conferred on the chief registrar which may be delegated to an assistant registrar[7]. These include, for example, the appointment of inspectors, calling special meetings of societies, the suspension or cancellation of a society's registration or making orders suspending a society's business or ordering a society's dissolution. Thirdly, the Assistant Registrar for Scotland is required to:
(1) send copies of specified documents registered or recorded by him to the central office[8];
(2) record documents sent to him by central office for that purpose, and he has no power to refuse to record rules or their amendments which have already been registered by the central office[9];
(3) distribute to societies any documents etc sent to him by the central office for that purpose or vice versa[10]; and
(4) report to the chief registrar as he may direct[11].

1 For the legislation, see para 603 above.
2 Friendly Societies Act 1974 (c 46), ss 1(2), 4(1).
3 Ibid, s 4(1)(a). The address of the central registration area is: The Chief Registrar of Friendly Societies, 15/17 Great Marlborough Street, London W1V 2AX, tel: 071 437 9992. The central

registration area for friendly societies includes both the Channel Islands and the Isle of Man (s 4(1)(a)), but for industrial and provident societies includes only the Channel Islands (Industrial and Provident Societies Act 1965 (c 12), s 78).

4 Friendly Societies Act 1974, ss 1(3), 4(1)(b). The address of the Assistant Registrar for Scotland is: Assistant Registrar of Friendly Societies, 58 Frederick Street, Edinburgh EH2 1NB, tel: 031 226 3224.

5 Ibid, s 2(3).

6 See the Industrial and Provident Societies Act 1965, s 73, and the Friendly Societies Act 1974, s 111(3).

7 Ibid, s 4(3).

8 Ibid, s 5(1)(a).

9 Ibid, s 5(1)(b), (2).

10 Ibid, s 5(1)(c).

11 Ibid, s 5(1)(d).

605. Registration area. The relevant registration area for a society, or in the case of a friendly society with branches for a branch, is that in which its registered office is situated[1]. One speciality of the industrial and provident societies and the friendly societies legislation[2] is that where a society is registered in one registration area and also carries on business in the other registration area, it must also record its rules in the other area if it is to obtain the privileges of the relevant Acts[3]. In the same way any amendment to the rules must be both registered in the principal area and recorded in the other area to be fully effective[3].

1 Industrial and Provident Societies Act 1965 (c 12), s 73(1)(c); Friendly Societies Act 1974 (c 46), s 111(3).

2 For the legislation, see para 603 above.

3 See the Industrial and Provident Societies Act 1965, s 8, and the Friendly Societies Act 1974, s 10.

2. INDUSTRIAL AND PROVIDENT SOCIETIES

(1) INTRODUCTION

606. Industrial and provident societies generally. The industrial and provident societies legislation[1] provides for the registration and supervision of industrial and provident societies[2], which must be either co-operative societies or public benefit societies[3]. Credit unions are a special type of society, and the particular provisions regulating them are dealt with below[4].

An industrial and provident society is a body corporate with a share capital, share holding being a prerequisite of membership. Shares may or may not be redeemable or transferable. The minimum membership is seven people. A society can also be formed by several societies joining together in which case minimum membership is two societies.

1 Bibliography: 24 *Halsbury's Laws of England* (4th edn) paras 1 ff; Guide to the Law relating to Industrial and Provident Societies (Registry of Friendly Societies); W J Chappenden *Handbook to the Industrial and Provident Societies Act 1965* (including supplements). Still useful even though out of date and out of print are F B Fuller *The Law Relating to Friendly Societies and Industrial and Provident Societies* (4th edn, 1926); M Mackinnon *Pratts Friendly and Industrial and Provident Societies* (15th edn, 1931); I Snaith *The Law of Cooperatives*.

2 The source and meaning of the title 'industrial and provident society' is really unknown. Chief Registrar Brabrook stated it was 'intended to intimate the design that such societies should be industrial as making their profits by the mutual personal exertions of the members and provident as distributing their profits by way of a provision for the future'. On the other hand I Swinney has suggested in *UK Cooperative Law — Freedom of Choice or Confusion* (Plunkett Foundation

Year Book 1981) p 23 that the name was chosen to distinguish an industrial friendly society from the existing provident or mutual insurance/self-help friendly societies and charitable friendly societies.

3 For the legislation, see para 603 above. Various regulations have been made under the legislation: see the Industrial and Provident Societies Regulations 1965, SI 1965/1995 (amended by SI 1967/1310, SI 1988/450, and SI 1989/357); the Industrial and Provident Societies Regulations 1967, SI 1967/1310 (amended by SI 1976/355, SI 1980/1833, SI 1981/1833, SI 1983/350, SI 1984/307, SI 1985/344, SI 1986/621, SI 1987/394, SI 1988/450, and SI 1989/357); the Industrial and Provident Societies (Group Accounts) Rules 1969, SI 1969/1037; the Credit Unions (Authorised Investments) Order 1979, SI 1979/866; the Industrial and Provident Societies (Credit Unions) Regulations 1979, SI 1979/937 (amended by SI 1988/1598 and SI 1989/358); the Industrial and Provident Societies (Increase in Deposit-taking Limits) Order 1981, SI 1981/394; and the Industrial and Provident Societies (Increase in Shareholding Limit) Order 1981, SI 1981/395.

4 See paras 656 ff below.

607. Registrable societies. The Industrial and Provident Societies Act 1965 allows the registration of any society with a registered office in Great Britain or the Channel Islands which will carry on a business[1] and which meets two conditions:

(1) its rules provide for the matters specified[2] in the 1965 Act; and

(2) it is either a co-operative or a community benefit society[3].

Societies which were registered, or deemed registered, under the Industrial and Provident Societies Act 1893 are deemed to be registered under the 1965 Act[4]. A special provision allows a society which was a registered society under the 1893 Act on 1 January 1894 to use any power of the 1965 Act even though its own rules are silent or even exclude the power, unless the exclusion was introduced after 12 September 1893[5].

The Co-operative Development Agency was a co-operative promotional and assistance organisation set up under its own Act[6] and was, therefore, not connected with the Registry of Friendly Societies at all.

1 Ie any industry, business or trade (including dealings of any description with land), whether wholesale or retail: Industrial and Provident Societies Act 1965 (c 12), s 1(1). However, in respect of co-operative societies, this does not include the business of seeking profit to pay interest etc on invested funds: s 1(3).

2 Ie under ibid, s 1(1)(b), Sch 1: see para 613 below.

3 Ibid, s 1(1), (2).

4 See ibid, s 4.

5 Ibid, s 14(3). The Industrial and Provident Societies Act 1893 (c 39) (repealed) was passed on 12 September 1893 and came into force on 1 January 1894, hence the dates in the text.

6 Ie under the Co-operative Development Agency Act 1978 (c 21) (repealed by the Co-operative Development Agency and Industrial Development Act 1984 (c 57), s 6, Sch 2, Pt II: see the Co-operative Development Agency (Winding Up and Dissolution) Order 1990, SI 1990/279). The Co-operative Development Agency was dissolved on 31 December 1990: art 4.

608. Co-operative societies. There is no definition in the Industrial and Provident Societies Act 1965 of a 'co-operative', and it is probably easier to recognise a co-operative than to define one! It should be remembered that there is no general legal definition or status of 'co-operative society'; it may adopt any legal form suitable to its commercial, business or other activities. It is only if it seeks registration under the legislation that its co-operative credentials must be shown. By an express exclusion an organisation whose business is the earning of profit to pay interest, dividends or bonus on money invested or deposited with, or lent to, it cannot be a co-operative[1]. The Registrar of Friendly Societies has issued Notes of Guidance for the Registration of Societies, Form F617, which gives his interpretation of the condition that the society be 'a bona fide co-operative society'[2]. The relevant passage is as follows:

'such a society will normally be expected to satisfy the following conditions:

(a) Conduct of business. The business of the society will be conducted for the mutual benefit of its members in such a way that the benefit which members obtain will stem from their participation in its business. Such participation may vary in accordance with the nature of the society. It may consist of purchasing from or selling to the society, of using the services or amenities provided by it, or supplying services to carry out its business.

(b) Control. Control of the society will under its rules be vested in the members equally and not in accordance with their financial interest in the society. In general the principle of one man one vote must obtain.

(c) Interest on share and loan capital. Interest payable on share and loan capital will under its rules not exceed a rate necessary to obtain and retain the capital required to carry out the objects of the society. The appropriate rate may vary from time to time between societies of different classes and according to the term and security of loans[3].

(d) Profits. The profits of the society's business after payment of interest on share capital if distributable amongst the members, will under the rules, be distributable amongst them in relation to the extent to which they have traded with or taken part in the business of the society. Thus in a retail trading society or an agricultural marketing society profits will be distributable amongst the members as a dividend on purchases from or sales to the society. In some societies (as for example social clubs) profits are not usually distributable amongst members but are ploughed back to cheapen and improve the amenities available to members.

(e) Restriction on membership. There should be no artificial restriction of membership with the object of increasing the value of proprietary rights and interests. There may of course be grounds for restricting membership that do not offend the cooperative principle; for example the membership of a club may be limited by the size of its premises and of a selfbuild housing society by the number of houses that can be erected on a particular site'.

From that it will be seen that the registrar is looking for particular characteristics which will control the way in which the rules will be framed, so ensuring that they conform to co-operative principles generally defined. This gives considerable flexibility in meeting the needs of particular types of co-operative and particular interpretations of co-operative philosophy.

Co-operative principles are, of course, not exclusive to the registrar, and there have been many different formulations over the years. Although not the earliest, probably the most well-known society deriving from the principles underlying the operation of a consumer co-operative is the Rochdale Society of Equitable Pioneers[4]. The ideals of the Rochdale Pioneers influenced the whole British co-operative movement through the spread of local consumer co-operatives formed on the Rochdale pattern. And although that pattern is only one element in international co-operation its very success has ensured its influence in modern statements of co-operative principles. Within the co-operative movement the restatement of co-operative principles by the International Co-operative Alliance[5] is the most generally accepted. They may be summarised as follows:

(1) membership is open, voluntary and free from artificial discrimination;

(2) co-operatives are democratically controlled by their members on a one-member-one-vote basis;

(3) share capital should receive a strictly limited rate of interest, if any;

(4) the economic results belong to the members and should be distributed in an equitable manner, such as for the development of the co-operative or to provide common services or to provide for the patronage refund to the members;

(5) co-operatives should provide for education of members, staff and the public in the principles of co-operation;

(6) co-operatives should co-operate between themselves on a local, national and international basis.

This list of conditions is virtually the same as the criteria used by the registrar, and this is probably why there has been no challenge to the registrar's guidance note and why British co-operatives have been able to register under the 1965 Act without difficulty, regardless of the particular type of co-operative.

Since an organisation that does not conform to co-operative principles in its operation cannot be a co-operative, these principles are not a passive statement of ideals, but dictate the form of the constitution and the manner in which the co-operative is operated[6]. This is also one reason why, in contrast with the Registrar of Companies, the registrar is an interventionist! The registrar is concerned with the actual contents of a society's rules as distinct from their form, and will give assistance in the preparation of rules and the operation of the industrial and provident societies legislation.

The registrar has, with Treasury consent, power to cancel a society's registration if he considers that none of the conditions quoted above is met with respect to that society[7].

1 Industrial and Provident Societies Act 1965 (c 12), s 1(3).

2 Ibid, s 1(2)(a).

3 See ibid, s 1(3).

4 The ideas of the Rochdale Society of Equitable Pioneers can be traced back to the writings of Robert Owen and 'The Cooperator' newspaper of Dr King of Brighton. A similar model to that of the Rochdale system developed in Scotland at an earlier date. Details of the Fenwick Weavers Society which may have done so in 1769, the Lennoxtown Friendly Victualling Society founded in 1812 which certainly did — and does so — and the work of A Campbell in the 1820s is to be found in J A Flanagan *Wholesale Cooperation in Scotland 1868–1918* pp 22–25, 32, 33. That, however, is not a claim for priority, but rather evidence of the widespread interest in different aspects of the self-help movement at that time.

5 *Report of the ICA Commission on Cooperative Principles* (adopted at the ICA 23rd Congress 1966, ICA 1967).

6 For a discussion of the nature and application of co-operative principles, see W P Watkins *Cooperative Principles Today and Tomorrow* (1986).

7 See the Industrial and Provident Societies Act 1965, s 16, and para 611 below.

609. Community benefit societies. The provisions of the Industrial and Provident Societies Act 1965 require both that the business of the society is intended to benefit the community and that there are special reasons why the society should be registered as an industrial and provident society rather than under the Companies Act 1985 (c 6)[1]. Notes of Guidance for the Registration of Societies, Form F617, gives guidance here, stating that a society claiming community benefit:

'must be able to show amongst other things that it will benefit persons other than its own members, and that its business will be in the interests of the community. Typical societies which qualify for registration in this category are those which provide housing for various groups within the community, some (although not all) being charitable or philanthropic in character. In considering whether a society is in this category regard is also to be had to whether it is non-profit making and is prohibited by its rules from distributing its assets among members, and to the matters referred to at (b), (c) and (e) in the section on bona fide cooperatives'[2].

The example within the quotation relates to housing associations, but certain clubs, party political associations, women's institutes and allotment societies also register.

The registrar has, with Treasury consent, power to cancel a society's registration if he considers that neither of the conditions is met with respect to that society[3].

1　Industrial and Provident Societies Act 1965 (c 12), s 1(2)(b) (amended by the Companies Consolidation (Consequential Provisions) Act 1985 (c 9), s 30, Sch 2). It was only by the Prevention of Fraud (Investments) Act 1939 (c 16), s 10 (repealed), that the limitation to co-operative societies was introduced by which time the practice of registering non-co-operatives was well established hence the need for the Industrial and Provident Societies Act 1965, s 1(2)(b), as a strict exclusion of all non-co-operative societies would have been impractical.
2　Ie control, interest on share and loan capital, and membership restriction: see the Notes of Guidance for the Registration of Societies, Form F617, heads (b), (c) and (e) set out in the text in para 608 above.
3　See the Industrial and Provident Societies Act 1965, s 16, and para 611 below.

(2) REGISTRATION

610. Procedure for registration. Provided the registered office of the intended society is in Scotland the Assistant Registrar for Scotland will have jurisdiction as the 'appropriate registrar'[1]. The following documents are lodged with him:

(1)　the application for registration of a society signed by seven members and the secretary, who may be also one of the subscribing members;
(2)　two printed copies of the rules, also signed by the seven members and the secretary; and
(3)　the prescribed fee[2].

The number of signatories is reduced to two committee members and the secretary of each of the two societies where the new society is to be formed by two societies; and to two committee members and the secretary from any three societies where the new society is to be formed from three or more societies[3].

When the registrar is satisfied that the provisions of the Industrial and Provident Societies Act 1965 has been complied with he will issue the acknowledgment of registration[4]. Apart from the minimum number of members noted above the requirements are that the society meets the conditions of the 1965 Act[5] and that its rules are satisfactory and comply with the Act[6]. Unless registration has been cancelled or suspended, the acknowledgment is conclusive of the incorporation of the society with limited liability[7]. Registration also vests any property held in trust for the society in the society, and all legal proceedings pending by or against the trustees may be brought or continued by or against the society's trustees[8].

If the registrar refuses to register a society, an appeal lies in Scotland to the chief registrar and from him to the Court of Session, but if the ground of refusal is non-compliance with section 1(2) of the Act there is no appeal from the initial decision[9]. Abuse by the registrar of his discretion over the application of section 1(2) would appear to be an appropriate case for judicial review[10].

The recording requirements under the Act must be observed if the society intends to carry on business in the central registration area[11].

1　Industrial and Provident Societies Act 1965 (c 12), s 73(1)(c)(ii).
2　Ibid, s 2(1). For the fees, see the Industrial and Provident Societies Regulations 1965, SI 1965/1995, reg 13, Sch 2 (substituted by SI 1991/520).
3　Industrial and Provident Societies Act 1965, s 2(2). Housing societies must also register with the Housing Corporation which in turn notifies the registrar: see the Housing Associations Act 1985 (c 69), s 5(3)(b).
4　Ibid, s 2(3).
5　Ie the requirements of ibid, s 1(2): see paras 608, 609, above.

6 Ie comply with ibid, Sch 1: see paras 612–614 below.
7 Ibid, s 2(3).
8 Ibid, s 3.
9 See ibid, s 18.
10 Ibid, s 18(1)(a) merely excludes the right of appeal given by s 18; there is no drafting device which might be interpreted as an attempt to exclude judicial review. As to applications for judicial review, see ADMINISTRATIVE LAW, vol 1, paras 345 ff.
11 Ie under ibid, s 8: see para 605 above.

611. Cancellation and suspension. Cancellation of registration is provided for in the Industrial and Provident Societies Act 1965 in several cases, some with and some without the consent of the Treasury[1]. The Assistant Registrar for Scotland may cancel registration without Treasury consent:

(1) if membership falls below the statutory minimum of seven members or two societies;
(2) if registration was obtained by fraud or mistake;
(3) if the society no longer exists; or
(4) at the society's request[2].

The last head is at the registrar's discretion and is only likely to be used if the society has ceased trading and has unremaining property.

Treasury consent is required for cancellation if:

(a) the society exists for an illegal purpose;
(b) the society does not comply with the legislation even after notice from the registrar;
(c) the society is no longer qualified for registration[3];
(d) the society was formed to lend money to its members consisting mainly of agricultural etc producers[4] and no longer meets that description[5].

Suspension of registration is available to the registrar when he could otherwise cancel registration with Treasury consent[6]. When an appeal is lodged by a society after notice of cancellation is served, suspension is also imposed until the appeal is decided[7]. The registrar may himself impose suspension for up to three months, but if it is renewed beyond three months Treasury consent is required[8]. The effect of suspension is to deprive the society of the privileges of the legislation.

A society has a right of appeal from cancellation or from renewal of suspension beyond three months to the chief registrar and from his decision to the Court of Session[9].

1 Detailed procedures are set out in the Industrial and Provident Societies Act 1965 (c 12), s 16.
2 Ibid, s 16(1)(a)(i)–(iii), (b)
3 Ie under ibid, s 1(2)(a), (b) (see para 607 above): s 16(1)(c)(ii). There is a saving provision for pre-1938 societies: see s 16(2). The registrar has power to obtain books etc to establish non-compliance: see s 48, and para 645 below.
4 Ie under ibid, s 12: s 16(1)(c)(iii).
5 Ibid, s 16(1)(c)(i)–(iii).
6 Ibid, s 17(1), (3)–(6).
7 Ibid, s 17(2), (4)–(6).
8 Ibid, s 17(1)(a), (b), (6).
9 See ibid, s 18.

(3) RULES

612. Introduction. The rules of a society are its constitution and byelaws contained in one document. Unlike the companies legislation, the industrial and provident societies legislation does not provide an equivalent to the companies Tables A to F[1], nor is there any official pro forma. Instead, the Industrial and

Provident Societies Act 1965 lists fourteen points which must be provided for in the rules[2]. Certain of the points are controlled by the legislation, others by the status of the society as a co-operative or a community benefit society. The registrar has accepted rules that are short, containing the bare minimum to comply with the Act, but usually the rules are longer and more reminiscent of a combined memorandum and articles of association. When preparing the rules for a new society the registrar should be consulted at an early stage and the rules submitted in draft form. The actual contents are negotiated with him as he is concerned not just with a literal, formal compliance with the legislation but with ensuring that the society will operate as a co-operative or a community benefit society as the case may be.

Since the legislation does not contain provisions regulating or setting a minimum acceptable standard for many matters, the registrar's discretion is the mechanism setting the appropriate standard. In most cases rules are not drafted from scratch, but the model rules prepared by a sponsoring organisation are adopted, leaving little more than the name to be chosen. Where suitable model rules are available it is best to adopt them, since not only is the registrar's registration fee reduced[3] but the whole process is very much quicker.

There are several sponsoring organisations[4], some with similar objectives, and certain of them have more than one model available and so a proposed society is not unduly restricted in its choice. Some of the sponsoring organisations are in fact apex bodies representing particular types of co-operative or community activity; others are promotional bodies for a particular activity[5]. That means that by joining the apex organisation the new society is able to benefit from its particular relevant expertise. It should be noted that where model rules are used, the registration procedure is channelled through the sponsoring organisation, and not directly, to the registrar. Full guidance is, of course, given by the sponsoring organisation, for that is one of the advantages of using it.

1 See the Companies (Tables A to F) Regulations 1985, SI 1985/805 (amended by SI 1985/1052).
2 See the Industrial and Provident Societies Act 1965 (c 12), s 1, Sch 1, and para 613 below.
3 Currently the fee of £460 is reduced to £180: see the Industrial and Provident Societies Regulations 1965, SI 1965/1995, reg 13, Sch 2 (substituted by SI 1991/520).
4 The approved sponsors are listed in Form F280.
5 Eg ICOM Ltd (representing the common ownership movement), the National Federation of Housing Associations or the Cooperative Union Ltd (sponsoring inter alia retail co-operative society rules).

613. The fourteen points. The fourteen points in the Industrial and Provident Societies Act 1965 are, in abbreviated form, as follows:
(1) *The name*[1]. The name must end in 'limited'[2]; it must not be undesirable[3] (for example, neither be the same as that of another society nor mislead the public as to its size, status or connections), and must be displayed outside all business premises, on all official documents such as business letters, bills and receipts, cheques etc, and its seal[4]. The name can be changed by resolution of a general meeting[5] with the written approval of the Assistant Registrar for Scotland[6].
(2) *The objects*[7]. The objects clause of a society is normally a single paragraph, for the multi-purpose clause covering objects and powers familiar to company lawyers has never been adopted. Section 9 of the European Communities Act 1972 (c 68)[8] did not extend to societies, and so the common law *ultra vires* rule[9] applies to them in its full rigour[10], restricting its activities to those specified in this clause combined with an implied power to do any other acts needed to carry out its business.

(3) *The place*, which is to be the registered office of the society to which all communications and notices to the society may be addressed[11]. A change in the situation of the registered office amounts to a change in the rules, for which a fee, albeit a reduced one, is chargeable by the registrar[12].

(4) *The terms of admission of the members*, including any society or company investing funds in the society under the provisions of the including societies or companies investing in the society under the provisions of the 1965 Act[13].

(5) *The procedure* of holding meetings, the scale and right of voting, and the mode of making, altering or rescinding rules[14]. The legislation does not expressly provide for most of the necessary procedures. Indeed there is no requirement for an annual general meeting. However, the registrar will not accept rules[15] that do not require regular meetings, conducted in a democratic manner — and where a co-operative is concerned, co-operative principles require the members' democratic control of their society. Voting must be on a one-member-one-vote basis. The only statutory provision on amendment is that no amendment is effective until registered and sets out the procedure, including the registrar's consent[16]. An increased majority for the passing of an amendment is often called for, and is often two-thirds rather than three-quarters.

(6) *The committee, managers and officers*, their appointment, removal, powers and remuneration[17]. Co-operative principles require that the committee should be elected by the members from the members, but this is not necessarily so crucial for a community benefit society. There must be a committee whose members must be at least eighteen years old, as must any trustee, manager or treasurer[18]. By necessary implication there must be a secretary, who is not subject to the age requirement.

(7) *Members' maximum shareholding*[19]. Currently there is a £10,000 maximum on an individual's shareholding[20].

(8) *Borrowing powers*, covering both loans and deposits[21]. The form of the borrowing clause will dictate the extent — in every sense of the word — of the society's ability to borrow. A society may take power to accept deposits even from non-members subject to strict limits without 'carrying on the business of banking'[22].

(9) *The shares*, whether transferable or withdrawable, and if necessary the procedures and forms for transfer or withdrawal[23]. A society can decide whether to have transferable or withdrawable (that is, repayable at par) shares or not. It is not uncommon to have a membership requirement of a single nominal share that is neither repayable nor transferable.

(10) *Audit*[24].

(11) *The termination of membership* and the settlement of the claims of deceased or sequestrated members, and nominees[25]. Termination of membership can be both voluntary or compulsory, either by disqualification or expulsion. The registrar is concerned to ensure that justice is done in compulsory termination rules. Nominations are a privilege of a society's members, allowing them to bequeath their interest in the society to the nominee, and the nominee will succeed without the need for confirmation[26]. A society's management committee may distribute a member's interest in the society, not exceeding £5,000, without confirmation[27].

(12) *The application of profit*[28]. Co-operative principles will dictate how a co-operative may distribute its surplus, as for example through patronage refund, and a community benefit society will normally be prevented from making a distribution to its members. A co-operative may have a political fund established by its rules.

(13) *The use of the seal*[29]. A society is exempted from the need to have witnesses to its seal provided it is accompanied by the signatures of two committee members and the secretary[30]. This applies not only to Scottish societies but also to any writ sealed by a society in Scotland.

(14) *The conditions for the investment of funds*[31]. The 1965 Act allows any investment permitted by the rules as well as local authority loans, in any body corporate with limited liability (companies, building societies), and trustee investments unless expressly excluded[32].

1 The name of the society must comply with the requirements of the Industrial and Provident Societies Act 1965 (c 12), s 5: s 1(1)(b), Sch 1, para 1.
2 Ibid, s 5(2). However, the registrar is permitted to authorise the omission of 'limited' from the name of a wholly charitable or benevolent society: s 5(5).
3 Ibid, s 5(1).
4 Ibid, s 5(6).
5 Ibid, s 5(3)(a). The notice to be given of a meeting to change the name is the same as is required by the rules for an amendment thereof unless the rules themselves make other provisions, but there is no special majority requirement: s 5(3)(a). Where a change in the name is made in accordance with s 5(3), the change of name is registered by the registrar as an amendment of the society's rules: s 10(2)(b). As to amendment of rules, see para 616 below.
6 Ibid, s 5(3)(b). See also s 10(2)(b), and note 5 above. The Act provides for continuity of the society from the old to the new name: s 5(4).
7 Ibid, Sch 1, para 2.
8 See now the Companies Act 1985 (c 6), s 35 (substituted by the Companies Act 1989 (c 40), s 108).
9 *Lafferty v Barrhead Co-operative Society Ltd* 1919 1 SLT 257, OH, confirms the application of the rule in *Ashbury Railway Carriage and Iron Co v Riche* (1875) LR 7 HL 653. See also *Burnley Equitable Co-operative and Industrial Society Ltd* [1891] 1 QB 75; *Warburton v Huddersfield Industrial Society* [1892] 1 QB 817; *Hampton v Toxteth Co-operative Provident Society Ltd* [1915] 1 Ch 721.
10 The DTI Consultative Document *Reform of the Ultra Vires Rule* (1985) does not extend to industrial and provident societies.
11 Industrial and Provident Societies Act 1965, Sch 1, para 3. By s 73(1)(c)(ii) this must be in Scotland.
12 See ibid, s 10(2), and para 616 below.
13 Ibid, Sch 1, para 4.
14 Ibid, Sch 1, para 5.
15 If only because of the Notes of Guidance for the Registration of Societies, Form F617.
16 See the Industrial and Provident Societies Act 1965, s 10, and para 616 below.
17 Ibid, Sch 1, para 6.
18 Ibid, s 20 (amended by the Age of Majority (Scotland) Act 1969 (c 39), s 1(3), Sch 1, Pt I).
19 Industrial and Provident Societies Act 1965, Sch 1, para 7.
20 See ibid, s 6, and para 621 below.
21 Ibid, Sch 1, para 8. See also *Re Airedale Co-operative Worsted Manufacturing Society Ltd* [1933] Ch 639.
22 See the Industrial and Provident Societies Act 1965, s 7, and para 622 below.
23 See ibid, Sch 1, para 9.
24 Ibid, Sch 1, para 10. As to audit, see the Friendly and Industrial and Provident Societies Act 1968 (c 55), ss 4–10, and paras 636–640 below.
25 Industrial and Provident Societies Act 1965, Sch 1, para 11.
26 As to nominations, see ibid, ss 23, 24, and paras 626–628 below.
27 See ibid, s 25, and para 628 below.
28 Ibid, Sch 1, para 12.
29 Ibid, Sch 1, para 13.
30 Ibid, s 36.
31 Ibid, Sch 1, para 14.
32 See ibid, s 31, and para 624 below.

614. Specific points. Once registered, the rules bind both the society and its members as well as those claiming through its members 'to the same extent as if each member has subscribed his name' to an undertaking to comply with the rules[1]. A copy of the rules must be given to any person requesting them, for which service a charge of up to 10p may be made.

The rules of a co-operative may include a provision that would otherwise be in restraint of trade and covered by the Restrictive Trade Practices Act 1976. There are two exemptions to note, one in favour of wholesale co-operative societies the other in favour of agricultural, forestry or fishing associations[2].

1 Industrial and Provident Societies Act 1965 (c 12), s 14(1).
2 See the Restrictive Trade Practices Act 1976 (c 34), s 32 and s 33 (amended by the Companies Consolidation (Consequential Provisions) Act 1985 (c 9), s 30, Sch 2).

615. Additional rules. In addition to the rules required by the Industrial and Provident Societies Act 1965[1], a society may make provision for anything else its promoters/members see as necessary. This is expressly authorised in the Act, the only restriction being illegality[2]. A number of provisions cover specific options:

(1) the forms of instrument needed to carry out the society's objects may be provided in the rules or in a schedule to them[3];

(2) reasonable fines may be imposed on persons contravening the rules and are recoverable on summary conviction[4];

(3) membership may be restricted to those over eighteen[5];

(4) advances to members may be permitted[6];

(5) the ownership or tenancy of land may be prohibited[7];

(6) officers may be required to provide security for the society's funds in their possession[8];

(7) members may have rights of inspection of the books additional to those given by section 46 of the Act[9];

(8) the settlement of disputes may be regulated[10].

1 Ie under Industrial and Provident Societies Act 1965 (c 12), s 1(1), Sch 1; see para 613 above.
2 Ibid, s 13(4).
3 Ibid, s 13(1).
4 Ibid, s 13(2).
5 Ibid, s 20 (amended by the Age of Majority (Scotland) Act 1969 (c 39), s 1(3), Sch 1, Pt I).
6 Industrial and Provident Societies Act 1965, s 21. This is without prejudice to any provision included by virtue of s 12 in respect of agricultural, horticultural and forestry societies.
7 See ibid, s 30.
8 See ibid, s 41, Sch 4, Pt II.
9 As to inspection of books, see paras 642–644 below.
10 See the Industrial and Provident Societies Act 1965, s 60, and para 647 below.

616. Amendment of rules. An amendment[1] can be either a partial alteration of the existing rules or a substitution of a completely new set[2]. In either case, however, the procedure is essentially the same. The society must approve the amendment in the way prescribed by its rules[3]. Thereafter the amendment must be submitted to the Assistant Registrar for Scotland for registration, without which the change is ineffective[4]. Completed prescribed forms[5] accompanied by two copies of the new rules signed by three members and the secretary are forwarded to the registrar[6]. Where the society is formed of other societies, then the new rules are signed by the secretary of the federal society and two committee members and the secretary of the member societies up to a maximum of three societies[7]. The registrar will vet the amendment to ensure compliance with the legislation and may refuse to register the change. In that case there is a right of appeal to the chief registrar and from him to the Court of Session[8]. It is therefore wise to clear a change with the registrar in advance. A fee, varying with the extent of the change, is required[9]. The registrar's official acknowledgment is conclusive of the validity of the amendment[10].

An amendment of rules is binding on all the members, except that the written consent of each member is required to a change requiring them to take and pay for more shares or otherwise increase their obligations to the society[11].

Where the rules of a Scottish society are recorded in the central registration area, any amendment of them must also be recorded to be effective in the central area[12].

1 Amendment procedures are required by the Industrial and Provident Societies Act 1965 (c 12), s 1(1), Sch 1, para 5.
2 The provisions of ibid, s 5 or s 10, apply to change of name or registered office respectively, even though this involves a change in the printed rules: these two cases are not technically regarded as amendments in the strict sense. The Housing Associations Act 1985 (c 69), s 19, applies the Industrial and Provident Societies Act 1965, s 10, so that in the case of a registered housing society the Housing Corporation must be notified of any change in name or registered office and must consent to any other change of rule, the consent being lodged with the registrar along with the new rules. For the prescribed forms, see the Industrial and Provident Societies Regulations 1965, SI 1965/1995, regs 2, 4, Sch 1, Forms E–G.
3 For the declaration in support of an amendment of rules, see ibid, reg 4, Sch 1. Form G, providing for verification by an officer of the society.
4 Industrial and Provident Societies Act 1965, s 10.
5 For the prescribed forms, see the Industrial and Provident Societies Regulations 1965, Sch 1, Form E (complete amendment) and Form F (partial amendment), verified by an officer on Form G. The regulations also set out the required formalities.
6 Industrial and Provident Societies Act 1965, s 10(1)(b).
7 Ibid, s 10(1)(a).
8 See ibid, s 18.
9 For the fees, see the Industrial and Provident Societies Regulations 1965, reg 13, Sch 2 (substituted by SI 1991/520).
10 Industrial and Provident Societies Act 1965, s 10(3). See also *Butler v Springmount Dairy Society* [1906] 2 IR 193.
11 See the Industrial and Provident Societies Act 1965, s 14(1), (2).
12 Ibid, s 8. For the prescribed form, see the Industrial and Provident Societies Regulations 1965, Sch 1, Form D.

617. Other relevant statutes. There are a number of statutes that may affect the form which the rules of a society may take. Housing co-operatives and associations will probably wish to acquire status as a housing society registered by Scottish Homes under the Housing Associations Act 1985 (c 69)[1]. Agricultural or horticultural co-operatives concerned with marketing may use the Agricultural and Horticultural Co-operation Scheme administered by Food From Britain[2]. The Restrictive Trade Practices Act 1976 is also relevant for these co-operatives as well as fisheries and forestry co-operatives[3].

The Industrial Common Ownership Act 1976[4] provided funding for common ownership co-operatives until 1981 but its definitions are still relevant to certain tax reliefs and grants[5].

A society can also qualify as a charity in the usual way[6].

1 See HOUSING, vol 11, paras 1924 ff.
2 See the Agricultural and Horticultural Co-operation Scheme 1971, SI 1971/415 (amended by SI 1980/1382 and SI 1983/1949), made under the Agriculture Act 1967 (c 22).
3 Restrictive Trade Practices Act 1976 (c 34), s 33 (amended by the Companies Consolidation (Consequential Provisions) Act 1985 (c 9), s 30, Sch 2).
4 As to the Industrial Common Ownership Act 1976 (c 78) generally, see LOCAL GOVERNMENT, vol 14, para 651. See also the Inner Urban Areas Act 1978 (c 50) and vol 14, paras 648 ff.
5 See the Income and Corporation Taxes Act 1988 (c 1), ss 360–363, and the Enterprise and New Towns (Scotland) Act 1990 (c 35), s 4(3).
6 See CHARITIES.

(4) MEMBERSHIP AND COMMITTEE OF MANAGEMENT

618. Membership. Agreement by the (prospective) member to take the necessary qualifying shares coupled with acceptance by the society — in the manner prescribed by the rules — is necessary for membership. Societies are required to keep a register of members and officers; for members it must include the details of their shareholdings[1]. The register is prima facie evidence of its contents[2], and so it is the ultimate record of membership. Whilst there is nothing to prevent a society from providing for the issue of share certificates, this appears never to be done in practice. Unless excluded by the rules, a society may admit to membership:

(1) any natural person over the age of sixteen but under eighteen[3]; and

(2) any corporation permitted to join by its own constitution[4].

Unless excluded by the rules, joint membership is possible but is subject to the same limit as any other personal shareholding[5].

The rights of members are those conferred by the legislation or by the rules, and it is the latter that will be the more extensive. The legislation only offers a right:

(a) to a copy of the rules;

(b) to make a nomination;

(c) to apply for a copy of the annual return;

(d) to inspect his share or investment account;

(e) to apply to the Assistant Registrar for Scotland for an inspection of books, of affairs or to hold a special meeting;

(f) to petition to set aside an instrument of dissolution; or

(g) to petition for winding up[6].

Membership is terminated in accordance with the rules[7]. Apart from the necessary implication of death, section 26 of the Industrial and Provident Societies Act 1965, dealing with the permanent insanity of a member, is the only section dealing with termination of membership. Even here it is indirect, as the main purpose of the section is the safe disposal of the insane member's property in the society. The terms of the shareholding will determine if there is to be any repayment of capital.

1 Industrial and Provident Societies Act 1965 (c 12), s 44(1).

2 Ibid, s 44(5).

3 See ibid, s 20 (amended by the Age of Majority (Scotland) Act 1969 (c 39), s 1(3), Sch 1, Pt I).

4 Industrial and Provident Societies Act 1965, s 19(1). A society which is a member of another society will sign any relevant document by means of two committee members and its secretary: s 19(2).

5 See ibid, s 6, and para 621 below.

6 See ibid, ss 15, 23, 39, 46, 47, 55, 58, and paras 614, 626, 634, 643, 644, 652, 653, below.

7 See ibid, Sch 1, para 11, and paras 613, 629, above.

619. Committee of management and officers of a society. Since duties are imposed upon the secretary and the Industrial and Provident Societies Act 1965 requires rules for the appointment and powers of a committee of management and officers or managers[1], a society must have such a committee and a secretary. The rules will make the necessary provision for their qualification, appointment and dismissal[2], and their powers. It is usual to give management functions to the committee and to reserve appointment, removal, final supervision etc to the members in general meeting. Even if the rules open membership to those over sixteen and under eighteen, such a member cannot be appointed as a committee member, trustee, manager or treasurer[3]. There is no bar on appointment as secretary. However, for these purposes, 'officer' is defined as inter alia including a manager or servant of the society, but servants appointed by the committee are expressly excluded[4]. From that it seems correct to conclude that a person between sixteen and eighteen could be employed as manager by the committee but could not be elected manager by the general meeting.

Where an officer is appointed to a post involving custody of the society's money, the rules may require him to give security for that money before undertaking the post[5]. This may be by personal surety with or without a cautioner[6]. Additionally, any such officer or other servant of the society in charge of money may be required to account for or to hand over, in accordance with the society's instructions, all money or other property in his possession[7]. That instruction can be given by the rules on a periodical basis, by written notice left at the home of the officer or servant or by demand[8]. Failure to comply with this will allow the society to enforce any surety or bond of caution and also to apply for enforcement of the duty to account or deliver to the sheriff, whose decision is declared[9] final[10]. The duty to account for or hand over money is extended to the executors of such officers or servant who has died[11].

1 Ie under the Industrial and Provident Societies Act 1965 (c 12), s 1(1), Sch 1, para 6.
2 Scottish Homes has power to remove and appoint committee members under the Housing Associations Act 1985 (c 69), ss 16, 17: see HOUSING, vol 11, para 1928.
3 See the Industrial and Provident Societies Act 1965, s 20, and para 613 above.
4 Ibid, s 74.
5 Ibid, s 41(1).
6 Ibid, s 41(2), (3), Sch 4, Pt II.
7 Ibid, s 42(1).
8 Ibid, s 42(1)(a)–(c).
9 Ie notwithstanding anything in the Summary Jurisdiction (Scotland) Act 1954 (c 48), s 62 (repealed): see now the Criminal Procedure (Scotland) Act 1975 (c 21), s 442 (substituted by the Criminal Justice (Scotland) Act 1980 (c 62), s 34, Sch 3, para 1).
10 Industrial and Provident Societies Act 1965, s 42(3), (4).
11 Ibid, s 42(2).

620. Obligations of the committee of management. The legislation imposes certain obligations on the committee in relation to:
(1) nominations by members[1];
(2) intestate or mentally incapable members[2];
(3) security from officers and recovery of property from them[3];
(4) taking proceedings in cases of fraud etc[4].
Committee members may be liable for offences committed by their society in contravention of the legislation[5].

In carrying out these statutory obligations the committee will be subject to the normal duties of good faith and care and skill deriving from agency expected from those in the position of committee members/directors[6].

1 See the Industrial and Provident Societies Act 1965 (c 12), s 23, 24, and paras 626, 627, below.
2 See ibid, 25, 26, and paras 628, 629, below.
3 See ibid, ss 41, 42, and para 619 above.
4 See ibid, s 66, and para 654 below.
5 See ibid, s 62, and para 654 below.
6 As to offences, see paras 654, 655, below.

(5) FINANCE

621. Share capital. There is no set pattern of shareholding in societies: some have a sizeable share capital rather like companies limited by shares; others have a nominal capital of one share per member rather like companies limited by guarantee. Shares have a fixed nominal value and whilst a strictly limited rate of interest may be paid if the rules permit there can be no distribution of profit by way of dividend as a return on capital[1]. There are no statutory constraints on the rules dealing with the transfer or withdrawal of shares[2], but prudence dictates that rules regulating withdrawal should pay due regard to the continued financial stability of the society. If share capital is purely nominal the shares are neither transferable nor withdrawable and a member's share is cancelled on leaving the society. A member's liability to his or her society is limited to payment for the shares for which the member has subscribed[3].

The minimum shareholding forming the membership qualification is set by the society's rules. A ceiling is set on a member's shareholding in two ways: a statutory maximum of £10,000 which is subject to exceptions[4], and a maximum set by the rules[5], which could possibly be increased by a resolution of the committee taking advantage of the Industrial and Provident Societies Act 1952, 1961 or 1975 (c 41)[6]. First, no member other than:

(1) another registered society,
(2) a local authority holding shares in a registered housing association, and
(3) a member of an agricultural credit society,

may invest more than the statutory maximum[7]. Secondly, the rules must set a maximum figure which can be less than but cannot exceed the statutory maximum. In the past when the maximum has from time to time been increased by statute and statutory instrument, the opportunity has been given for societies to take immediate advantage of the new figure[8]. Provided the society's maximum was that then permitted by the Acts and the committee passed a written resolution within eighteen months of the authorisation of the increase, the new maximum applied to the society without any amendment of the rules. However, the committee does not have power to vary or revoke a resolution once made[9]. The concession was lost if the rules were changed during the eighteen months. Moreover, the effect of the resolution is negatived if, on the next occasion when the rules are changed, the members do not also adopt the maximum set by the committee's resolution. Those members who have increased their shareholding under a resolution that later falls are not affected[9].

1 Ie as to whether the society falls within the definition by the Chief Registrar of Friendly Societies of a co-operative or community benefit society: see Form F617, and paras 608, 609, above.
2 See the Industrial and Provident Societies Act 1965 (c 12), s 1(1), Sch 1, para 9, and para 613 above.
3 Ie under ibid, s 57: see para 653 below.
4 See ibid, s 6(1) (amended by the Industrial and Provident Societies (Increase in Shareholding Limit) Order 1981, SI 1981/395, art 3, and the Housing (Consequential Provisions) Act 1985 (c 71), s 4, Sch 2, para 8).
5 See the Industrial and Provident Societies Act 1965, Sch 1, para 7, and para 613 above.
6 The Industrial and Provident Societies Act 1952 (c 17) and the Industrial and Provident Societies Act 1961 (c 28) are repealed; however, as to pre-1965 societies, see the Industrial and Provident Societies Act 1965, s 6(2)–(4).
7 Ibid, s 6(1)(a)–(c) (as amended: see note 4 above).
8 The stages of change in the maximum figure were: (1) 1952 from £200 to £500; (2) 1961 from £500 to £1,000; (3) 1975 from £1,000 to £5,000; (4) 1981 from £5,000 to £10,000.
9 Industrial and Provident Societies Act 1965, s 6(4).

622. Loans and banking. The rules must provide for:
(1) borrowing, either in loans or deposits from members or third parties;
(2) the conditions and security applicable; and
(3) the maximum amount[1].

A society with withdrawable capital cannot carry on banking business[2]. However, small deposits can be accepted — the maximum is currently £400 — without a society being treated as carrying on banking business[3].

A society carrying on banking business is subject to two specific obligations imposed by the legislation under which an infringing society is liable on summary conviction to a fine not exceeding level 1 of the standard scale[4]. A society cannot have any class of withdrawable capital whilst carrying on its banking business[5]. However, a society may take deposits within the prescribed limits without infringing that prohibition, but must not make any repayment of withdrawable capital whilst deposits are outstanding[6].

Every society which carries on banking business must on the first Monday in February and August complete and conspicuously display a statement of capital, assets and liabilities at its registered office and all banking premises[7].

1 Industrial and Provident Societies Act 1965 (c 12), s 1(1), Sch 1, para 8. See also *Re Airedale Co-operative Worsted Manufacturing Society Ltd* [1933] Ch 639.
2 Industrial and Provident Societies Act 1965, s 7(1).
3 Ibid, s 7(3) (amended by Industrial and Provident Societies (Increase in Deposit-taking Limits) Order 1981, SI 1981/394, art 3). The stages of change in the maximum taking of deposits in any one payment and for any one depositor, payable on not less than two clear days' notice, were respectively: (1) 1952 from 10s to £2 and from £20 to £50; (2) 1978 from £2 to £10 and from £50 to £250; (3) 1981 from £10 and £250 to £400. A society which both has withdrawable capital and accepts deposits cannot allow withdrawal whilst deposits are outstanding: s 7(3).
4 Industrial and Provident Societies Act 1965, s 7(6). As to level 1 on the standard scale, see the Criminal Procedure (Scotland) Act 1975 (c 21), ss 289F, 289G (added by the Criminal Justice Act 1982 (c 48), s 54). At the date at which this volume states the law, level 1 is £50: Increase of Criminal Penalties etc (Scotland) Order 1984, SI 1984/526, art 4.
5 See the Industrial and Provident Societies Act 1965, s 7(1), (6)(a).
6 Ibid, s 7(3), (6)(c).
7 Ibid, s 7(2), (6)(b), Sch 2.

623. Advances to members. The rules may allow advances to members but, unless the society is authorised to carry on banking or is an agricultural, horticultural or forestry credit society, it must have some heritable or moveable property as security[1].

Where a society has a security over a member's property it may discharge the security by indorsed receipt[2]. If the security is over heritage forms are provided for heritable securities[3] and for *ex facie* absolute dispositions[4]. A form is also provided for securities over movables[5]. Such receipts have a maximum registration fee of 25p[6].

1 Industrial and Provident Societies Act 1965 (c 12), s 21. As to agricultural, horticultural or forestry credit societies, see s 12.
2 'Receipt', in relation to any security, means a receipt signed by two members of the committee and countersigned by the secretary, or, if the society is in liquidation, signed by the liquidator or liquidators for the time being, described as such, for all money advanced by the society on the security of the property comprised in that security: s 34(5)(a).
3 See ibid, s 34(2), Sch 3, Pt II, Form D.
4 See ibid, s 34(1), Sch 3, Pt II, Form C. In view of the reduced recording fees, Form C should be used in preference to the forms provided by the Conveyancing and Feudal Reform (Scotland) Act 1970 (c 35). There is no special provision for standard securities in favour of industrial and provident societies in the 1970 Act.
5 See the Industrial and Provident Societies Act 1965, s 34(3), Sch 3, Pt II, Form E.
6 Ibid, s 34(4) (amended by the Finance Act 1971 (c 68), s 69(7), Sch 14, Pt VI).

624. Investments by societies. The investment of a society's funds is covered by the rules[1] and, in addition, the society may invest in:
(1) local authority loans;
(2) securities of bodies corporate; and
(3) investments authorised by the Trustee Investments Act 1961[2].
The Director of Savings may permit unlimited deposits in the National Savings Bank if the rules allow the society such deposits[3]. If consent is refused the limit is £10,000, provided, of course, that the deposit is accepted[3].

1 See the Industrial and Provident Societies Act 1965 (c 12), s 1(1), Sch 1, para 14, and para 613 above.

2 Industrial and Provident Societies Act 1965, s 31 (amended by the Building Societies Act 1986 (c 53), s 120(1), Sch 18, Pt I, para 6). As to the appointment of a society member as proxy, see the Industrial and Provident Societies Act 1965, s 32. As to the authorised investments under the Trustee Investment Act 1961 (c 62), see TRUSTS, TRUSTEES AND JUDICIAL FACTORS, vol 24, para 207.

3 See the Savings Banks (Ordinary Deposits) (Limits) Order 1969, SI 1969/939 (amended by SI 1969/1699 and SI 1987/330), which only applies to the National Savings Bank due to the repeal of the Trustee Savings Bank Act 1969 (c 50), s 14(1). As to savings banks generally, see BANKING AND FINANCIAL INSTITUTIONS, vol 2, paras 1156 ff.

625. Recovery of debts. Where a debt is due by a member to his or her society, the society has two privileges:

(1) the society may sue for the recovery of the debt in the sheriff court with jurisdiction over the society or the member at its option, all money payable being a debt for this purpose; and

(2) an indebted member's shares are subject to a lien in favour of the society, and any sums credited to the member's share capital account may be used to satisfy the debt[1].

1 Industrial and Provident Societies Act 1965 (c 12), s 22(1), (2). See also *Re Gwawr-y-Gweithyr Industrial and Provident Society Ltd, Dovey v Morgan* [1901] 2 KB 477, DC.

(6) NOMINATIONS

626. Introduction. A nomination is a written statement signed by a member of a society naming the person or persons to whom the property in the society is to be transferred after that member's death[1]. A society must keep a register of nominations in which it must record nominations as well as any variation or revocation deposited with it[2]. The nomination must be in writing, signed by the member[3] and either delivered to the society's registered office or made in a book kept there for that purpose during the nominator's lifetime[4]. A nomination may cover all or part of the member's property[5]. An officer or employee of the society cannot be nominated unless he or she is also the husband, wife, father, mother, child, brother, sister, nephew or niece of the nominator[6].

There are two categories of nomination:

(1) *Nominations made before 1 January 1914.* The nomination will pass either all the property credited on the date of the nomination or the amount specified in the nomination, whichever is the lower, provided the total value of the account was £100 or less; if there was more than £100 in the account when the nomination was made it is invalid[7].

(2) *Nominations made after 31 December 1913.* Nominations made after that date will pass either the amount standing to the member's credit at the date of death or the amount specified in the nomination, whichever is the lower[8]. In no case can the nomination transfer more than the statutory maximum relevant to the date on which the nomination was made[9].

The nomination is revoked automatically by the subsequent marriage of the nominator[10]. However, if the society pays the nominee in ignorance of the subsequent marriage, the nominee's receipt is a valid discharge for the society[10].

A nomination may be varied or revoked in the same way as it was made — in writing, signed by the member and delivered at or sent to the society's registered office[11]. That can also be done by a subsequent nomination[11]. It is not affected by any will or codicil made by the member[11].

1 Industrial and Provident Societies Act 1965 (c 12), s 23(1). The rules must provide for the payment of nominees: see s 1(1), Sch 1, para 11, and para 613 above.

2 Ibid, s 23(5).
3 Ibid, s 23(1). In *Morton v French* 1908 SC 171, 15 SLT 517, dealing with the repealed Industrial and Provident Societies Act 1893 (c 39), the words 'writing under his hand' were held to exclude authentication by the member's mark even when witnessed.
4 Industrial and Provident Societies Act 1965, s 23(5). Other than that there are no prescribed formalities. Delivery of the nomination to the secretary is sufficient: *Hughes v Hardy* [1885] FS Cases 402.
5 'Property' means shares, loans or deposits or otherwise: Industrial and Provident Societies Act 1965, s 23(1).
6 Ibid, s 23(2).
7 Ibid, s 23(1)(a), (3)(a).
8 Ibid, s 23(1)(b), (3)(b), (c).
9 The various statutory limits are: (1) nominations made from 1 January 1914 but before 5 August 1954, £100 (s 23(3)(b)); (2) nominations made from 5 August 1954 but before 5 September 1965, £200 (s 23(3)(c) (as originally enacted)); (3) nominations made from 5 September 1965 but before 10 August 1975, £500 (see the Administration of Estates (Small Payments) Act 1965 (c 32), s 2, Sch 2); (3) nominations made from 10 August 1975 but before 11 April 1984, £1,500 (see the Administration of Estates (Small Payments) (Increase of Limit) Order 1975, SI 1975/1137, art 3(a) (revoked)); and (4) nominations made on or after 11 April 1984, £5,000 (see the Administration of Estates (Small Payments) (Increase of Limit) Order 1984, SI 1984/539, art 2(a)).
10 See the Industrial and Provident Societies Act 1965, s 23(6).
11 Ibid, s 23(4).

627. Procedure on death with a nomination.

Where there is a valid nomination, the committee of the society, after receiving satisfactory proof of death, will comply with the nomination either by paying the nominee or transferring the appropriate sum to his or her share account or partly one and partly the other[1]. Shares may be transferred even where the rules declare them to be non-transferable, but no transfer may be made which would make the nominee's share exceed the statutory limit of £10,000[2].

If the nominee is under sixteen the society may pay the sum due to either parent, to any guardian of the nominee or to any other person of full age who will hold it in trust or apply it for the benefit of the nominee and whom the society thinks is a fit person for the purpose[3]. The parent, guardian or other person has power to give a valid discharge for the sum to the society[3].

1 Industrial and Provident Societies Act 1965 (c 12), s 24(1). As to the position where the beneficiary suffers from a mental disorder, see para 629 below.
2 Ibid, s 24(2).
3 Ibid, s 24(3).

628. Procedure on death without a nomination.

Societies have the discretionary privilege[1] of transferring the property[2] of a member who has died to those legally entitled to it without confirmation, the committee having the duty to require satisfactory evidence of that entitlement[3]. This privilege also applies where a nomination is partial and leaves property undisposed[4]. The only restriction is that the total value of the property must not exceed (currently) £5,000[5]. The receipt given to the society by those appearing to the committee to be entitled to succeed is final[6].

If the member was illegitimate and is not survived by a widow, widower, parent or issue legitimate or illegitimate[7], the committee may only deal with his or her property as the Treasury directs[8].

1 Ie under the Industrial and Provident Societies Act 1965 (c 12), s 25. As to the position where the beneficiary suffers from a mental disorder, see para 629 below. As to confirmation of the discretion, see *Escritt v Todmorden Co-operative Society* [1896] 1 QB 461, DC. Prior to 5 September 1965, the Industrial and Provident Societies Act 1965, s 25 only applied in cases of intestacy: see s 25(1) (as originally enacted).

2 'Property' means shares, loans or deposits: ibid, s 25(1).
3 Ibid, s 25(1) (amended by the Administration of Estates (Small Payments) Act 1965 (c 32), ss 3, 7(5), Schs 3, 4).
4 *Escritt v Todmorden Co-operative Society* [1896] 1 QB 461, DC.
5 Industrial and Provident Societies Act 1965, s 25(1) (amended by the Administration of Estates (Small Payments) (Increase of Limit) Order 1984, SI 1984/539, for deaths on or after 11 May 1984). For deaths (1) prior to 5 September 1965 the limit is £100 (see the Industrial and Provident Societies Act 1965, s 25(1) (as originally enacted); (2) on or after 5 September 1965 the limit is £500 (see the Administration of Estates (Small Payments) Act 1965 (c 32), s 1(1), Sch 1, Pt I); (3) on or after 10 August 1975 the limit is £1,500 (see the Administration of Estates (Small Payments) (Increase of Limit) Order 1975, SI 1975/1137).
6 Industrial and Provident Societies Act 1965, s 27.
7 The Law Reform (Parent and Child) (Scotland) Act 1986 (c 9), s 1(4)(a), Sch 1, makes no reference to the Industrial and Provident Societies Act 1965, s 26, which is, therefore, unaffected by the 1986 Act.
8 Industrial and Provident Societies Act 1965, s 25(2) (amended by the Family Law Reform Act 1969 (c 46), ss 19(2), 28(4)(g)).

629. Mental disorder of a member. Where a member is unable to look after his or her affairs because of mental disorder the committee may pay that member's shares, loans or deposits to a suitable person whose receipt will discharge the society[1]. The committee must have suitable medical evidence of the member's mental disorder[2] and be satisfied that the person chosen will use the property for the benefit of the member. This procedure is also available where a person claiming through a member (for example as beneficiary[3]) suffers from mental disorder[4].

1 See the Industrial and Provident Societies Act 1965 (c 12), ss 26(1), 27.
2 This power is excluded if the member is a patient under the (English) Mental Health Act 1959 (c 72), Part VIII (ss 100–121) or if a judge has exercised emergency powers under s 104 (all repealed); Industrial and Provident Societies Act 1965, s 26(2). See now respectively the consolidating Mental Health Act 1983 (c 20), Pt VII (ss 93–113) and s 98, which Act makes no consequential amendments to the 1965 Act. There is no equivalent provision applicable to the appointment of a *curator bonis* or a guardian under the Mental Health (Scotland) Act 1984 (c 36). As to the curatory of persons under mental disability, see GUARDIANSHIP, vol 11, paras 1232 ff.
3 Ie under the Industrial and Provident Societies Act 1965, ss 24, 25: see paras 627, 628, above.
4 Ibid, s 26(1).

(7) ACCOUNTS

630. Introduction. All societies must keep books of account[1] — or accounting records other than traditional bound books — adequate to record its transactions, assets and liabilities, to explain its transactions and to allow the preparation of an annual revenue account and balance sheet showing a true and fair view of the society's affairs[2]. A proper system for the control and security of account books or records, cash holdings, receipts and payments must be maintained[3]. These duties are imposed on the committee of management, which must take reasonable steps to discharge it, under a penalty on summary conviction of a fine not exceeding level 5 on the standard scale[4]. A defaulting committee member has the defence that he reasonably believed that the duty had been placed on a reliable, competent person in a position to discharge it[5].

The accounts are prepared by reference to the 'year of account', which is the period covered in the relevant annual return[6].

1 Accounts are regulated by the Friendly and Industrial and Provident Societies Act 1968 (c 55), which repealed the accounts provisions of the Industrial and Provident Societies Act 1965 (c 12) (ss 37, 38): see the Friendly and Industrial and Provident Societies Act 1968, s 20(1)(b), Sch 2. The

Friendly Societies Act 1974 (c 46) in turn repealed all references to friendly societies in the 1968 Act. Additional provisions apply to registered housing societies: see HOUSING, vol 11, para 1929.
2 Friendly and Industrial and Provident Societies Act 1968, ss 1(1)(a), (2), 2(1).
3 Ibid, ss 1(1)(b), 2(2).
4 Ibid, s 3(7) (amended by the Friendly Societies Act 1971 (c 66), s 11(5)). As to level 5 on the standard scale, see the Criminal Procedure (Scotland) Act 1975 (c 21), ss 289F, 289G (added by the Criminal Justice Act 1982 (c 48), s 54). At the date at which this volume states the law, level 5 is £2,000: Increase of Criminal Penalties etc (Scotland) Order 1984, SI 1984/526, art 4.
5 Friendly and Industrial and Provident Societies Act 1968, s 3(7).
6 Ibid, s 21(1)(b). As to annual returns, see the Industrial and Provident Societies Act 1965, s 39, and para 634 below.

631. Revenue account. Each year a society must prepare either a revenue account relating to the whole business of the society or two or more revenue accounts each relating to a particular business of the society for the year in question[1]. A single account must give a true and fair view of the affairs of the society, and where two or more accounts are prepared each must give such a view of the affairs of the society to which it relates and together they must give such a view of the affairs of the society as a whole[2].

1 Friendly and Industrial and Provident Societies Act 1968 (c 55), s 3(2)(a), (b). For the penalty in respect of non-compliance with the provisions of s 3, see s 3(7), and para 630 above.
2 See ibid, s 3(1), (3).

632. Balance sheet. The annual balance sheet must give a true and fair view of the society's affairs at its date[1]. A copy of the relevant balance sheet must accompany each annual return[2].

1 Friendly and Industrial and Provident Societies Act 1968 (c 55), s 3(4) (amended by the Friendly Societies Act 1974 (c 46), s 116(4), Sch 11).
2 See the Industrial and Provident Societies Act 1965 (c 12), s 39(1)(b), and the Friendly and Industrial and Provident Societies Act 1968, s 11(2)(a).

633. Group accounts. Where a society has subsidiaries it must prepare group accounts showing a true and fair view of the affairs of the group[1]. There are exemptions from this requirement:
(1) if the society is a wholly owned subsidiary of another body corporate incorporated in Great Britain[2];
(2) if the committee obtains the approval of the Chief Registrar of Friendly Societies because either:
  (a) it would be impractical, or be of no real value to members because of the insignificant amounts involved, or would involve expense or delay out of proportion to the value to the members; or
  (b) the result would be misleading or harmful to the society or its subsidiaries; or
  (c) it would be unreasonable to treat the society and its subsidiary as a single undertaking because their respective businesses are so different[3].
The chief registrar has issued regulations prescribing the required contents of group accounts[4]. The group accounts must be audited by the society's auditors and be submitted to the registrar along with the annual return[5].
If the financial years of the society and the subsidiary do not coincide, the accounts of the subsidiary for the year ending immediately before that of the society must be used for the preparation of the group accounts[6]. With the consent of or on the application of the committee the registrar may direct otherwise[6].
Detailed definitions of 'subsidiary company' and 'subsidiary society' are given[7]. A company is deemed to be the subsidiary of the society if either the

society is a member of the company controlling the composition of its board or holds more than half of the equity share capital[8]. A society is deemed to be the subsidiary of another society if it either is a member of the first society controlling the composition of its committee or has a majority of the members' votes[9].

1 Friendly and Industrial and Provident Societies Act 1968 (c 55), s 13(1), (2).
2 Ibid, s 14(1). An industrial and provident society is deemed to be the wholly owned subsidiary of another body corporate if it has no members except that other body corporate and the wholly owned subsidiaries of that body and its or their nominees: s 14(4).
3 Ibid, s 14(2)(a)–(c).
4 See ibid, s 13(3), and the Industrial and Provident Societies (Group Accounts) Regulations 1969, SI 1969/1307.
5 Friendly and Industrial and Provident Societies Act 1968, s 13(5).
6 Ibid, s 13(4).
7 Ie under ibid, s 15.
8 Ibid, s 15(1)(a), (b). See also s 15(2)–(4). For the purposes of s 15 'company' includes any body corporate other than an industrial and provident society, and 'equity share capital' means, in relation to a company, its issued share capital excluding any part thereof which, neither as respects dividends nor as respects capital, carries any right to participate beyond a specified amount in a distribution: s 15(9).
9 Ibid, s 15(1)(a), (b). See also s 15(6), (7). Section 15(4) applies with the necessary modifications in determining whether a society is a subsidiary of another such society as it applies in determining whether a company is a subsidiary of such a society: s 15(8).

634. Annual return. Every society must lodge an annual return with the appropriate registrar not later than 31 March each year[1]. The period for the annual return begins originally with the date of the society's registration and thereafter with the date of the previous annual return[2]. The closing date for each year's annual return is calculated by reference to the 'appropriate date', which is either 31 March of the particular year or the date on which the return is sent, whichever is the earlier[3]. The closing date is the date of the last balance sheet published by the society before the appropriate date[4]. Alternatively the closing date is 31 December of the year immediately preceding the appropriate date in two cases:

(1) if the date of the last balance sheet is before 31 August of the year preceding the appropriate date; or

(2) if the date of the last balance sheet is after 31 January of the year in which the appropriate date falls[5].

Where there are special circumstances the registrar may allow a society to use a different date for the compilation of its return, which must be lodged within three months of that date[6].

The annual return is made on the prescribed form issued by the registrar, includes a revenue or income and expenditure account and must be accompanied by a copy of the balance sheet for the period of the return along with the auditor's report on the accounts and balance sheet[7].

If a society is dissolved by instrument of dissolution a final annual return is required up to the date of that instrument[8].

1 Industrial and Provident Societies Act 1965 (c 12), s 39(1) (amended by the Friendly and Industrial and Provident Societies Act 1968 (c 55), s 11(1)).
2 See the Industrial and Provident Societies Act 1965, s 39(2)(c) (amended by the Friendly and Industrial and Provident Societies Act 1968, s 20(1)(a), Sch 1, para 10).
3 Industrial and Provident Societies Act 1965, s 39(2A) (added by the Friendly and Industrial and Provident Societies Act 1968, Sch 1, para 10).
4 Industrial and Provident Societies Act 1965, s 39(2)(c)(i) (as amended: see note 2 above).
5 Ibid, s 39(2)(c)(ii) (as so amended).
6 Ibid, s 39(3).
7 Ibid, s 39(1)(a), (b).

8 Ibid, s 39(4). As to the instrument of dissolution, see s 55(b), and para 652 below.

635. Publication. In addition to lodging the annual return and accounts with the registrar, a society must display in a conspicuous place a copy of the latest balance sheet and auditors' report at its registered office[1]. A revenue account or balance sheet may only be published by a society if it has been signed by two committee members and the secretary and is accompanied by the auditors' report that it shows a true and fair view of the affairs of the society[2].

Any member or other person interested in the funds of the society may apply for, and must be supplied with, a copy of the latest annual return and the related balance sheet and auditors' report[3].

1 Industrial and Provident Societies Act 1965 (c 12), s 40.
2 Friendly and Industrial and Provident Societies Act 1968 (c 55), s 3(5)(a)–(c).
3 See the Industrial and Provident Societies Act 1965, s 39(5), and the Friendly and Industrial and Provident Societies Act 1968, s 11(5) (amended by the Friendly Societies Act 1974 (c 46), s 116(4), Sch 11).

(8) AUDIT

636. Introduction. Unless a society is exempt, every society must have its accounts audited each year by qualified auditors[1]. An exempt society is one which either:

(1) has receipts and payments for the preceding year of account that do not exceed £5,000; or
(2) has not more than 500 members at the end of the year; or
(3) does not have assets worth more than £5,000 at the end of the year[2].

The registrar may order an exempt society to appoint qualified auditors to audit its accounts and balance sheet for the current year and for any previous year in which it was also exempt[3]. If an annual return was accompanied by an auditors' report by unqualified auditors and the registrar has required the appointment of qualified auditors, the registrar may require a further annual return[4] — thus ensuring the reviewed accounts and balance sheet are placed on the record.

1 Ie under the Industrial and Provident Societies Act 1965 (c 12), s 1(1), Sch 1, para 10 (see para 613 above) (prior to 1 November 1969), and the Friendly and Industrial and Provident Societies Act 1968 (c 55), s 4 (after 1 November 1969).
2 Ibid, s 4(2)(a)–(c) (amended by the Friendly Societies Act 1974 (c 46), s 116(4), Sch 11). Registered housing societies are prohibited from appointing unqualified auditors: see the Housing Associations Act 1985 (c 69), s 25.
3 Friendly and Industrial and Provident Societies Act 1968, s 4(6), (7)(a).
4 Ibid, s 4(7)(b) (as amended: see note 2 above).

637. Qualified auditors. Before 1 October 1991 a qualified auditor[1] had to belong to one of the following organisations:

(1) the Institute of Chartered Accountants of Scotland;
(2) the Institute of Chartered Accountants in England and Wales;
(3) the Association of Certified and Corporate Accountants;
(4) the Institute of Chartered Accountants in Ireland; and
(5) any other body of accountants in the United Kingdom recognised[2] by the Secretary of State[3].

A person specially authorised[4] to audit companies as having similar overseas qualifications may also audit a society[5].

After 1 October 1991 no person is a qualified auditor unless he is eligible[6] for appointment as a company auditor[7].

1 There are transitional provisions in favour of approved auditors under the Industrial and Provident Societies Act 1965 (c 12) who have held office continuously since 26 July 1968 but are not qualified under the Friendly and Industrial and Provident Societies Act 1968 (c 55): see s 7(2), (3) (amended by the Friendly Societies Act 1974 (c 46), s 116(4), Sch 11). Registered housing societies are prohibited from appointing unqualified auditors: see the Housing Associations Act 1985 (c 69), s 25.

2 Ie for the purposes of the Companies Act 1985 (c 6), s 389(1)(a): Friendly and Industrial and Provident Societies Act 1968, s 7(1)(e) (amended by the Companies Consolidation (Consequential Provisions) Act 1985 (c 9), s 30, Sch 2).

3 Friendly and Industrial and Provident Societies Act 1968, s 7(1)(a)–(e) (as so amended).

4 Ie by the Secretary of State under the Companies Act 1985, s 389(1)(b): Friendly and Industrial and Provident Societies Act 1968, s 7(1) (as so amended).

5 Ibid, s 7(1) (as so amended).

6 Ie under the Companies Act 1989 (c 40), s 25: see COMPANIES, vol 4, para 456.

7 Friendly and Industrial Provident Societies Act 1968, s 7(1) (amended by the Companies Act 1989 (Eligibility for Appointment as Company Auditor) (Consequential Amendments) Regulations 1991, SI 1991/1997, regs 2, 4, Schedule, para 20(2), made under the Companies Act 1989, s 50, so that the requirements for the qualifications of auditors mirrors the Companies Act 1985 (c 6), Pt XI, Ch V (ss 384–394A): see COMPANIES, vol 4, paras 456–459.

638. Disqualification of auditor. A person is disqualified from appointment as auditor in any of the following cases:

(1) if he is an officer or employee of the society[1];

(2) if he is a partner of, employed by, or employs, an officer or employee of the society[2];

(3) if it is a body corporate[3].

Disqualification also extends throughout a group: disqualification from auditing one society will disqualify from auditing any constituent society in the group[4]. A society may not appoint as auditor a person disqualifed from auditing any company subsidiary it may have[5]. However, these provisions do not prevent the appointment of a Scottish firm provided none of the partners is disqualified[6].

1 Friendly and Industrial and Provident Societies Act 1968 (c 55), s 8(1)(a). 'Officer or employee' is construed as not including an auditor: s 8(5).

2 Ibid, s 8(1)(b).

3 Ibid, s 8(1)(c) (repealed by the Companies Act 1989 (Eligibility for Appointment as Company Auditor) (Consequential Amendments) Regulations 1991, SI 1991/1997, regs 2, 4, Schedule, para 20(3), as from 1 October 1991).

4 Friendly and Industrial and Provident Societies Act 1968, s 8(2)(a).

5 Ibid, s 8(2)(b) (amended by the Companies Consolidation (Consequential Provisions) Act 1985 (c 9), s 30, Sch 2; and substituted by the Companies Act 1989 (Eligibility for Appointment as Company Auditor) (Consequential Amendments) Regulations 1991, Schedule, para 20(3), as from 1 October 1991). 'Company' has the same meaning as in the Friendly and Industrial and Provident Societies Act 1968, s 15 (see para 633 above): s 8(5).

6 Ibid, s 8(3) (as repealed: see note 3 above).

639. Appointment and removal of auditors. Under the legislation and a society's rules either a qualified auditor or auditors or two or more unqualified auditors must be appointed[1]. If the person is disqualified any attempted appointment is ineffective[2].

A qualified auditor is automatically reappointed for the next year of account unless either:

(1) the general meeting passes a resolution not to appoint him or to appoint someone else in his place[3]; or

(2) he has declined reappointment in writing; or

(3) he is ineligible (that is, disqualified) for reappointment; or

(4) he has ceased to act as auditor through incapacity[4].

If an intended resolution to appoint another person as auditor does not proceed because the other person cannot be appointed through death, incapacity or ineligibility, the retiring auditor is not automatically reappointed[5]. The general meeting may reappoint him, and the resolution is valid even though the notice required by the rules was not given[6].

1 Friendly and Industrial and Provident Societies Act 1968 (c 55), s 4(1), (5). Registered housing societies are prohibited from appointing unqualified auditors: see the Housing Associations Act 1985 (c 69), s 25.
2 Friendly and Industrial and Provident Societies Act 1968, s 8(4).
3 The resolution is ineffective unless notice of it is given to the society at least twenty-eight days before the meeting: ibid, s 6(1) (amended by the Friendly Societies Act 1971 (c 66), s 14, Sch 2, para 49). Thereafter if the society is required by its rules to give notice of the meeting to its members, or of their delegates, it must give them the same notice of the resolution: Friendly and Industrial and Provident Societies Act 1968, s 6(2). If that does not apply, it must give notice in an appropriate newspaper or in the way provided for in its rules at least fourteen days before the meeting: s 6(3). The retiring auditor must be given immediate notice of the resolution by the society: s 6(5). He has the right to submit representations, to have them circulated and to have them read out to the meeting: s 6(6), (7). There are safeguards against disseminating defamatory material by application to the Court of Session: s 6(8), (9).
4 Ibid, s 5(1)(a)–(d).
5 Ibid, s 5(1) proviso. A person is ineligible for appointment for the current year of account, if, but only if, (1) his appointment in relation to the society is prohibited by s 8 (see para 638 above); or (2) in the case of a society which is not exempt in respect of that year, he is not a qualified auditor at the time when the question of his appointment falls to be considered: s 5(2)(a), (b).
6 Ibid, s 6(4).

640. Auditors' reports. The auditors must report to the members on the accounts, revenue account/income and expenditure account and balance sheet of their society for the appropriate year of account[1]. The report must state if the revenue account/income and expenditure account and balance sheet comply with the legislation and show the required true and fair view[2]. In addition the auditors have the statutory duty of checking that the society has kept proper books of account and proper control over its transactions as well as confirming that the revenue account/income and expenditure account and balance sheet agree with those accounts[3]. If they are not satisfied their report must reflect that conclusion[4].

The auditors have a right of access at all times to the society's books of account and to all other necessary documents[5]. They may require any necessary information or explanation from the society's officers[6]. Their report must state if they fail to get the information they believe they require[7]. They are entitled to get the same notices (and related papers) of general meetings that are sent to the members, to attend general meetings and to speak on any business concerning them[8].

The Chief Registrar of Friendly Societies has a power by regulation, which has not yet been exercised, to fix the maximum audit fee payable to qualified auditors[9].

1 Friendly and Industrial and Provident Societies Act 1968 (c 55), s 9(1).
2 See ibid, s 9(2). If other accounts are involved the same reporting requirements apply to them: s 9(3).
3 Ibid, s 9(4)(a)–(c). As to the requirements in respect of books of account, see ss 1–3, and paras 630–632, above.
4 Ibid, s 9(4).
5 Ibid, s 9(5)(a).
6 Ibid, s 9(5)(b).
7 Ibid, s 9(6).
8 Ibid, s 9(7)(a), (b).
9 See ibid, s 10. The registrar has said he hopes never to use this power: Memorandum to Societies F747.

(9) FLOATING CHARGES

641. Agricultural and floating charges. An agricultural supply or marketing society may grant an agricultural charge[1] over its stocks in favour of a bank[2]. Registration of a charge must be made within seven days of execution[3]. It does not confer any security against a landlord or superior's hypothec or the recovery of rates or taxes[4]. Unless the charge provides otherwise the society must pay to the bank the proceeds of sale of any property affected by the charge, the purchaser taking the property free of the charge[5]. Charges rank in order of time of registration[6]. It is enforced in the same way as a landlord's hypothec[7].

Apart from agricultural charges, prior to the Industrial and Provident Societies Act 1967 no society could grant a floating charge. Now, however, a society can grant a floating charge over all or any of its assets[8].

When a floating charge is created by a society the following registration provisions apply. Within twenty-one days of the creation of a floating charge a copy of the charge, certified as a true copy by an officer of the society, or by a person interested in the charge, or by a solicitor acting for either of these, along with the prescribed fee, must be delivered to the registrar[9]. If this is not done the charge is void against everyone except the society[10]. The Court of Session may extend the time limit where non-compliance was due to inadvertence or other sufficient cause[11].

The registrar will issue an acknowledgment detailing the date and time on which the copy of the charge was delivered to him[12]. The acknowledgment is conclusive proof of these facts[13]. The copy of the charge and one of the acknowledgment is to be placed on the society's file, which is open to public inspection[14]. Notices may be given in respect of any release relating to or of any partial or complete satisfaction of the charge[15].

If an agricultural society has granted both agricultural charges and floating charges over the same property, the charges will rank in order of registration, treating the agricultural charges as if they were floating charges registered under the 1967 Act[16].

Receivership is not available to societies[17].

1 Ie under the Agricultural Credits (Scotland) Act 1929 (c 13), ss 5–9, and the Agricultural Credits (Scotland) Regulations 1929, SR & O 1929/495. See further AGRICULTURE, vol 1, paras 709, 713.
2 Agricultural Credits (Scotland) Act 1929, s 5(1).
3 Ibid, s 8(1).
4 Ibid, s 6(2), (3).
5 Ibid, s 6(4).
6 Ibid, s 7(1).
7 Ibid, s 6(1).
8 See the Industrial and Provident Societies Act 1967 (c 48), s 3 (substituted by the Companies Consolidation (Consequential Provisions) Act 1985 (c 9), s 26(2)), which applies to registered societies provisions relating to floating charges: see the Companies Act 1985 (c 6), Pt XVIII, ch I (ss 462–466), ss 517(2), 617(3), and COMPANIES, vol 4, paras 651 ff.
9 See the Industrial and Provident Societies Act 1967, s 4(1)(a), (c) (amended by the Companies (Floating Charges and Receivers) (Scotland) Act 1972 (c 67), s 10, and the Companies Consolidation (Consequential Provisions) Act 1985, s 26(3), (4)), and the Industrial and Provident Societies Regulations 1967, SI 1967/1310, reg 4. The Industrial and Provident Societies Act 1967, s 4(1)(b), provides for a note of prescribed particulars, but the Industrial and Provident Societies Regulations 1967 do not make any requirement or give any Scottish form. At the date at which this volume states the law, the fee is £18: reg 5 (amended by SI 1989/357).
10 Industrial and Provident Societies Act 1967, s 4(1).
11 Ibid, s 4(2)(a) (amended by the Companies (Floating Charges and Receivers) (Scotland) Act 1972, s 10, and the Companies Consolidation (Consequential Provisions) Act 1985, s 26(3)). The Court of Session has power also to correct any note of particulars which may be prescribed: Industrial and Provident Societies Act 1967, s 4(2)(b).

12 See ibid, s 4(3)(a), and the Industrial and Provident Societies Regulations 1967, reg 6, Schedule, Form AK.
13 Industrial and Provident Societies Act 1967, s 4(4).
14 Ibid, s 4(3)(b), (c).
15 Industrial and Provident Societies Regulations 1967, reg 8, Schedule, Forms AN, AO. A statutory declaration must be annexed to every notice: reg 9, Schedule, Form AP.
16 Industrial and Provident Societies Act 1967, s 3(3) (as substituted: see note 8 above).
17 The Scottish Law Commission has recommended that that omission be corrected: see *Floating Charges and Receivers* (Scot Law Com Consultative Memorandum no. 72) (1986).

(10) INSPECTION OF BOOKS

642. Restriction on inspection of books. No one, member or otherwise, has any right to inspect the books of a society except as given by the legislation[1]. Any rule of a society made before 12 September 1893 which confers a wider right of inspection than that given by statute is ineffective — only the statutory rights are available[2].

1 Industrial and Provident Societies Act 1965 (c 12), s 45(1). As to the right of inspection, see paras 643–645 below.
2 Ibid, s 45(2).

643. Inspection of books by members. Any member, or person having an interest in the funds of the society, has a right at all reasonable hours to inspect his or her own account in the society and the register of members and officers[1]. He or she has no right to inspect details of other members' shareholdings or other property in the society[2].

The society may extend the right of inspection by its rules, but without the written agreement of the person concerned no one other than an officer of the society may inspect that person's loan or deposit account[3].

1 Industrial and Provident Societies Act 1965 (c 12), s 46(1)(a), (b). The general meeting has power to make regulations on the time and manner of inspection: s 46(1). 'Persons interested in the funds' is not defined, but it has been suggested that it includes lenders or depositors with the society (W J Chappenden *Handbook to the Industrial and Provident Societies Act 1965* (including supplements) p 71), but does not include creditors (24 *Halsbury's Laws of England* (4th edn) para 123).
2 Ie the particulars required under the Industrial and Provident Societies Act 1965, s 44(1)(b), (c): s 46(1)(b).
3 Ibid, s 46(2). Rules must be made after 12 September 1893: s 46(2).

644. Inspection of books by order. The registrar has a discretion to appoint an accountant or actuary to inspect the books of a society on the application of ten members of at least twelve months' standing[1]. The person appointed has power to make copies or take extracts from any of the society's books[2]. The registrar will communicate the results to both the society and the applicant members[3].

The registrar may require that the applicants give a deposit as security to cover the costs of the inspection[4]. He will apportion the final costs between the society, its present or former officers or members, or the applicants[4].

1 Industrial and Provident Societies Act 1965 (c 12), s 47(1).
2 Ibid, s 47(3). The copies or extracts have to be made during reasonable hours at the society's registered office or at any other place where those books are kept: s 47(3).
3 Ibid, s 47(4).
4 Ibid, s 47(2).

645. Production of documents. The registrar may serve a written notice on a society, or any officer or former officer, to require the production to the registrar of books and other documents relating to the society's business and to give any other information required by the registrar in support of his powers of cancellation of the registration[1] or to apply for liquidation[2] under the legislation[3]. The registrar may order that the costs be met by the society, or its officers or former officers[4].

1 Ie under the Industrial and Provident Societies Act 1965 (c 12), s 16(1)(c)(ii) (see para 611 above), s 16(4) (see para 645 below).
2 Ie under ibid, s 56: see para 653 below.
3 Ibid, s 48(1). The information may be verified by statutory declaration: s 48(1). Failure to comply is an offence punishable on summary conviction to a fine not exceeding level 3 on the standard scale or to imprisonment not exceeding three months, or both: s 48(2). As to level 3 on the standard scale, see the Criminal Procedure (Scotland) Act 1975 (c 21), ss 289F, 289G (added by the Criminal Justice Act 1982 (c 48), s 54). At the date at which this volume states the law, level 3 is £400: Increase of Criminal Penalties etc (Scotland) Order 1984, SI 1984/526, art 4.
4 See the Industrial and Provident Societies Act 1965, s 48(3).

(11) EXAMINATION OF AFFAIRS BY INSPECTORS: SPECIAL MEETINGS

646. Inspection of affairs by inspectors and calling special meeting. One-tenth or one hundred of the members, whichever is the lesser, can apply to the Assistant Registrar for Scotland for either the appointment of inspectors or the calling of a special meeting of the society[1]. The applicants must show that they have good reason for the request and are not actuated by malicious motives, and may be required to give security for the costs involved[2]. The society must be given notice of the application[3]. The registrar has a discretion, but if he grants the request he must have Treasury consent[4]. The registrar may apportion the costs between the applicants, the society, its present or past members or officers[5].

Where an inspector is appointed he has power to examine all books or other documents of any kind belonging to the society and may examine on oath the present or former officers, members, agents or employees of the society[6].

If a special meeting is called, the registrar will determine the time, place and business of the meeting[7]. The meeting has all the powers of one convened under the society's rules in the usual way and can appoint its own chairman even if there are rules to the contrary[7].

1 Industrial and Provident Societies Act 1965 (c 12), s 49(1), (7).
2 Ibid, s 49(2), (3).
3 Ibid, s 49(2).
4 Ibid, s 49(1).
5 Ibid, s 49(4).
6 Ibid, s 49(5). For these purposes he may administer oaths: s 49(5).
7 Ibid, s 49(6).

(12) DISPUTES

647. Settlement of disputes. If there is a dispute[1] between the society or one of its officers and either:

(1) a member, or

(2) any person aggrieved who ceased to be a member within the previous six months, or

(3) a person claiming through such a member or ex-member, or

(4) any person claiming under the rules of the society[2],

the Industrial and Provident Societies Act 1965 makes provision for its settlement in two ways. First, if the society's rules provide a settlement procedure, it must be followed[3]. Secondly, unless excluded by the rules, the parties may by consent refer their dispute to the Assistant Registrar for Scotland[4]. These procedures are limited to disputes arising out of the society/member relationship: they do not apply to disputes arising from member/status, or some other relationship such as customer or employee[5].

Where the rules contain a settlement procedure, it must be followed. If the rules require reference to justices of the peace or their court, or a court of summary jurisdiction, the reference is to be to the sheriff[6].

If the parties agree, the dispute may be referred to the registrar, who may either decide it himself or refer it to some other registrar for decision[7]. The registrar has power to administer oaths, to require the attendance of parties and witnesses and production of documents, and to make an award of expenses against the society or the parties[8].

In either of the above cases the court or the registrar may, on the request of either party, state a case on any question of law for the opinion of the Court of Session[9]. If the rules contain no provision for the settlement of a dispute or no decision is made forty days after it has been referred to the society under its rules, any qualified party to the dispute may refer it to the sheriff for decision[10]. Apart from that exception, the decision is final and is not subject to further judicial review[11]. Jurisdiction is conferred on the sheriff to enforce the decision[12].

1 The provisions in respect of disputes under the Industrial and Provident Societies Act 1965 (c 12), s 60, which apply to Scotland are s 60(1), (2), (3)(b), (7), (8)(a), (c), (9).

2 Ibid, s 60(1)(a)–(c). 'Person claiming through a member', in relation to a registered society, includes executors or heirs, and, where nomination is allowed, his nominee: s 74. 'Person claiming though the rules' has no definition, but Somervell LJ said that it might cover persons 'who though not members would or might have rights or obligations vis-a-vis the society which were dealt with in the rules. The provisions of the present rules as to loans might I think give rise to disputes covered by these words': *Judson v Ellesmere Port Ex-Servicemen's Club Ltd* [1948] 2 KB 52 at 60, [1948] 1 All ER 844 at 848, 849, CA. There is no mention of the loans rule in the opinion, which is necessarily concerned only with what is now the Industrial and Provident Societies Act 1965, s 60(1). Might it include a person who qualified for membership under the rules but was wrongfully refused membership?

3 Ibid, s 60(1).

4 Ibid, s 60(2). For the form of reference of a dispute to the registrar, see the Industrial and Provident Societies Regulations 1965, SI 1965/1995, reg 2, Sch 1, Form AH.

5 *Symington's Executor v Galashiels Co-operative Store Co* (1894) 21 R 371, 1 SLT 400; *Melrose v Adams (Edinburgh Savings Bank)* (1897) 24 R 483, 34 SLR 346; *Judson v Ellesmere Port Ex-Servicemen's Club Ltd* [1948] 2 KB 52, [1948] 1 All ER 844, CA.

6 Industrial and Provident Societies Act 1965, s 60(7)(b)(i).

7 Ibid, s 60(2).

8 Ibid, s 60(8)(a). Any person refusing to attend, or to produce any documents, or to give evidence, is liable on summary conviction to a fine not exceeding level 1 on the standard scale: s 60(8)(a). As to level 1, see para 622, note 4, above. The registrar may grant such warrant for the recovery of documents and examination of havers as might be granted by the sheriff: s 60(8)(c).

9 Ibid, s 60(9).

10 Ibid, s 60(7)(b)(ii). For the qualified parties, see the text, heads (1)–(4).

11 Ibid, s 60(3).

12 Ibid, s 60(3)(b), (7)(a).

(13) AMALGAMATIONS, TRANSFER AND CONVERSIONS

648. Amalgamations. The amalgamation of two or more societies is a fusion, that is, a new society is created[1]. Special resolution procedure is to be followed[2], and the resolution may provide for dissolution or division of funds with respect to the society passing it[3]. Amalgamation takes effect from the date of registration by the registrar of the last of the resolutions. The property of the amalgamating societies is transferred by the resolutions: no form of additional conveyance is required[3]. The rights of creditors of the societies concerned are unaffected[4].

1 Industrial and Provident Societies Act 1965 (c 12), s 50(1).
2 The procedure requires a special resolution by each participating society which will set out the details of the scheme. 'Special resolution' means a resolution passed by at least two-thirds of the members voting in person, or by proxy if proxies are allowed, at a meeting at which notice of the intention to propose the special resolution was given according to the rules (s 50(2)(a)), and the resolution must be confirmed by a simple majority at a general meeting held not less than fourteen clear days nor more than one month from the date of the first (s 50(2)(b)). The chairman's declaration of the passing of the resolution is conclusive: s 50(3). A copy of the resolution, signed by the chairman and secretary, must be sent to the appropriate registrar (see para 610 above) within fourteen days of the confirming resolution and registered by the registrar, when it will take effect: s 50(4), (5). For the forms, see the Industrial and Provident Societies Regulations 1965, SI 1965/1995, regs 2, 6, Sch 1, Form T (in duplicate) and Form V. Annual returns will be required from the amalgamating societies to the date of registration of the society's resolution. If the society is a registered housing society, the consent of the Housing Corporation is needed and must be lodged with the resolution for registration: Housing Associations Act 1985 (c 69), s 21(1), (2) (amended by the Housing Act 1988 (c 50), s 59, Sch 6, para 2).
3 Industrial and Provident Societies Act 1965, s 50(1).
4 Ibid, s 54.

649. Transfer of engagements. A society may transfer its engagements to another society by following the special resolution procedure[1]. The transfer takes effect from the date of registration of the special resolution. The receiving society need pass only an ordinary resolution, but if its rules authorise the society to receive transfers, a resolution of the committee of management is sufficient. The transfer may be of the whole or part of the transferring society's property and is effective without any other conveyance or assignation[2]. The rights of creditors of the transferring society are unaffected[3].

1 Industrial and Provident Societies Act 1965 (c 12), s 51(1). For the procedure, see s 50(2)–(5) (see para 648, note 2, above), which have effect for the purposes of transfer of engagements: s 51(2). The transferring society only lodges its final annual return and its dissolution only takes place when a certificate of transfer is lodged: s 59. For the forms, see the Industrial and Provident Societies Regulations 1965, SI 1965/1995, regs 2, 6, Sch 1, Forms U, V, W, AG. If the society is a registered housing society, the consent of the Housing Corporation is needed and must be lodged with the resolution for registration: Housing Associations Act 1985 (c 69), s 21(1), (2) (amended by the Housing Act 1988 (c 50), s 59, Sch 6, para 2).
2 Industrial and Provident Societies Act 1965, s 51(1), (3).
3 Ibid, s 54.

650. Conversion into a company. A society may convert itself into, amalgamate with, or transfer its engagements to a company by following a modified special resolution procedure[1]. The only provisions made in the legislation, however, are for conversion into a company. If the resolution contains the requirements of a memorandum of association of a company a copy of the registered resolution signed by the Assistant Registrar for Scotland will have the same effect as a signed and witnessed memorandum under the Companies Act

1985 (c 6)[2]. The rights of creditors of the society are unaffected, as is any civil or criminal liability of the society[3].

1   Industrial and Provident Societies Act 1965 (c 12), s 52(1). For the procedure, see s 50(2)–(5) (see para 648 above), but with a three-quarters majority not two-thirds: s 52(3). For the forms, see the Industrial and Provident Societies Regulations 1965, SI 1965/1995, regs 2, 8, 9, Sch 1, Forms v, x (in triplicate), or as the case may be, Forms T or U (both in duplicate), and Form Y. The society's registration becomes void and is cancelled by the Assistant Registrar for Scotland under direction of the chief registrar, but only after a certificate of transfer is lodged: Industrial and Provident Societies Act 1965, ss 54(4), 59. For the form, see the Industrial and Provident Societies Regulations 1965, Sch 1, Form AG. This procedure is not available to a registered housing society: Housing Associations Act 1985 (c 69), s 21(3).

2   Industrial and Provident Societies Act 1965, s 52(2) (amended by the Companies Consolidation (Consequential Provisions) Act 1985 (c 9), s 30, Sch 2). See further COMPANIES.

3   Industrial and Provident Societies Act 1965, ss 52(5), 54.

651. Conversion of a company into a society. A company may convert itself into a society by passing a special resolution[1]. If the nominal value of any shares belonging to a member (other than a society member) exceeds £10,000, the resolution may convert the excess shares into interest-bearing transferable loan stock[2]. A copy of the resolution along with a copy of the proposed rules must be sent to the appropriate registrar who will, if they are in order, acknowledge registration[3]. A copy of the resolution and certificate of registration of the rules must be sent to the Registrar of Companies for registration[4]. Registration both makes the conversion effective and cancels the company registration[5]. Any civil or criminal liability of the company is unaffected[6].

1   Industrial and Provident Societies Act 1965 (c 12), s 53(1) (amended by the Companies Consolidation (Consequential Provisions) Act 1985 (c 9), s 30, Sch 2). For the meaning of 'special resolution', see the Companies Act 1985 (c 6), s 378, and COMPANIES.

2   Industrial and Provident Societies Act 1965, s 53(1) (amended by the Industrial and Provident Societies Act 1975 (c 41), s 3(3)).

3   Industrial and Provident Societies Act 1965, s 53(2). The resolution must appoint seven company members who with the secretary are to sign the rules: s 53(2). It will also either authorise them to accept any changes to the rules required by the registrar, or refer such changes back to a general meeting for adoption: s 53(2)(a), (b). The resolution along with a copy of the rules is lodged with the appropriate registrar who, when registering the society, will issue both an acknowledgment of registration and a certificate of registration of the rules: s 53(3). The name of the new society must not include the word 'company': s 53(5).

4   Ibid, s 53(4) (as amended: see note 1 above).

5   Ibid, s 53(6).

6   Ibid, s 53(7).

(14) DISSOLUTION AND LIQUIDATION

652. Dissolution. Dissolution[1] is the simpler method of dissolving a society, but because of the procedural requirements is only practical for small societies with uncomplicated financial affairs. Additionally, the three-month period during which the dissolution can be set aside means that no distribution should be attempted until it is clear there is no possibility of challenge[2]. The procedure requires the adoption of an instrument of dissolution signed by at least three-quarters of the society's membership[3]. The instrument sets out the financial position of the society, its membership, provision for payment of creditors, and the division of funds[4]. Any alterations in the instrument must be adopted by three-quarters of the members[5].

The instrument of dissolution is sent to the registrar accompanied by:
(1) a statutory declaration;

(2) the final annual return; and

(3) *Gazette* and newspaper advertisement fees[6].

The registrar registers the instrument, whereupon it becomes binding on all members of the society[7]. The registrar must advertise the dissolution in the *Edinburgh Gazette* and a local newspaper[8].

Unless proceedings are commenced in the sheriff court within three months of the *Gazette* notice by persons with a claim on the society's funds which conclude in the setting aside of the dissolution[9], the society is dissolved either from the date of the advertisement in the *Gazette* or, if the certificate of transfer has not been lodged by then, from the date of lodging of that certificate[10].

1 Ie under the Industrial and Provident Societies Act 1965 (c 12), ss 55(b), 58.

2 See ibid, s 58(6). Housing associations may not dispose of net assets of a registered housing society without the consent of Scottish Homes unless it is to Scottish Homes: see the Housing Associations Act 1985 (c 69), s 23, and HOUSING, vol 11, para 1928.

3 Industrial and Provident Societies Act 1965, s 55(b). For the form, see the Industrial and Provident Societies Regulations 1965, SI 1965/1995, regs 2, 10, Sch 1. Form AA, in which has to be declared the liabilities and assets of the society, the number of members and the interest of each in the society, the provision made for payment of creditors, and a statement of the division of the property, unless that is left to the registrar.

4 Industrial and Provident Societies Act 1965, s 58(2)(a)–(d). The instrument has to be signed by three-quarters of the members and accompanied by a statutory declaration made by three members and the secretary that all relevant provisions have been complied with: see ss 55(b), 58(4), and the Industrial and Provident Societies Regulations 1965, Sch 1, Form AB. Where the application relates to a society which consists solely of two registered societies, the statutory declaration must be signed by both members: s 58(9).

5 Industrial and Provident Societies Act 1965, s 58(3).

6 See ibid, s 58(4), and the Industrial and Provident Societies Regulations 1965, reg 10, Sch 1, Forms AA, AB. The final annual return must be prepared to the date of dissolution (Industrial and Provident Societies Act 1965, s 39(4)), and the registrar is prevented from registering the instrument until he receives the final return (s 58(5)).

7 Industrial and Provident Societies Act 1965, s 58(5). If the society is a registered housing society, the lodging of the consent of the Housing Corporation is a precondition to the registration of the resolution: Housing Associations Act 1985, s 21(5).

8 Industrial and Provident Societies Act 1965, s 58(6).

9 Ibid, s 58(6). Notice of such proceedings must be given to the registrar within seven days of the commencement and not later than three months of the date of the advertisement in the *Gazette* whichever is the earlier, and also notice of any order setting aside the dissolution within seven days of its date: s 58(8). For the forms, see the Industrial and Provident Societies Regulations 1965, Sch 1, Forms AE, AF.

10 See the Industrial and Provident Societies Act 1965, s 58(6), (7). As to the certificate of transfer, see s 59. For the form, see the Industrial and Provident Societies Regulations 1965, Sch 1, Form AG.

653. Liquidation. A society can be wound up by either an order or a resolution under the Insolvency Act 1986[1]. Additionally, the appropriate registrar may petition for winding up a society originally registered under the Industrial and Provident Societies Act 1893 (c 39)[2] before 26 July 1938 if the society is neither a bona fide co-operative society nor a community benefit society and it is in the interests of members, depositors or others to wind it up[3]. Specific provision is made for the liability of the past and present members[4]. The society cannot be dissolved until the certificate of transfer of assets has been lodged with the registrar[5].

1 Industrial and Provident Societies Act 1965 (c 12), s 55(a) (amended by the Insolvency Act 1986 (c 45), s 439(2), Sch 14). The provisions of the 1986 Act are applied to that order or resolution as if the society were a company, subject to the following modifications: any reference to the registrar for the purposes of the society's winding up is construed as a reference to the appropriate registrar, and the court having jurisdiction is the sheriff court within whose jurisdiction the society's registered office is situated: Industrial and Provident Societies Act 1965, s 55(a)(i), (ii). If

the society is a registered housing society, a winding up petition or resolution has no effect without the consent of Scottish Homes: Housing Associations Act 1985 (c 69), s 21(4).

2 See the Industrial and Provident Societies Act 1965, s 4, and para 607 above.

3 Ibid, s 56. If it is a registered housing society a winding up petition may be presented by Scottish Homes on the ground that the society is failing to carry out its objects: see the Housing Associations Act 1985, s 22(1), and HOUSING, vol 11, para 1928. The Industrial and Provident Societies Act 1965, s 55, applies only the provisions relating to the winding-up order and its implementation and so only the Insolvency Act 1986, Pt IV (ss 73–219) and Pt VI (ss 230–246) would be relevant: see further COMPANIES, vol 4, paras 716 ff. That does not include Pt IV, Ch X (ss 206–219), in respect of fraudulent and wrongful trading affecting directors. Part II (ss 8–27) would not apply, so a society cannot use an administration order.

4 The liability of members is qualified as follows: (1) liability to contribute to the assets is restricted to present members and those who were members during the year preceding liquidation; (2) those ex-members are only liable for debts incurred during membership and then only if it appears to the court that the contributions of the existing members will be insufficient: see the Industrial and Provident Societies Act 1965, s 57(a)–(d). If a member has withdrawn a share, membership in respect of that share ceases from the date of the application or notice of withdrawal: s 57(e).

5 Ibid, s 59. For the form, see the Industrial and Provident Societies Regulations 1965, SI 1965/1995, reg 2, Sch 1. Form AG. The disposal of the net assets of a registered housing society without the consent of Scottish Homes is prohibited unless it is to Scottish Homes: see the Housing Associations Act 1985, s 23, and HOUSING, vol 11, para 1928.

(15) OFFENCES

654. Introduction. The Industrial and Provident Societies Act 1965 creates a number of offences intended to secure compliance with the legislation. There are two points of general application. An offence caused by act or default is a new offence in each week in which it continues[1]. Where a duty is imposed upon a society and an officer is made responsible for its execution by the society's rules, that officer is responsible for any offence incurred by the society's failure to comply[2]. If there is no such officer, the offence is committed by every committee member who cannot prove either ignorance of, or an attempt to prevent, the commission of the offence[3]. In addition to the relevant procurator fiscal, proceedings for the recovery of any fine are to be instituted by the registrar or any person aggrieved[4]. Where proceedings are taken for the recovery of any fine, service on the society is sufficient by leaving a copy of the summons at its registered office, or, if closed, by posting the copy on the outer door[5].

Regulations made under the Act may provide for the imposition of reasonable fines recoverable on summary conviction for failure to comply with the regulations[6]. Costs and expenses ordered by the registrar to be paid are recoverable in civil proceedings[7].

1 Industrial and Provident Societies Act 1965 (c 12), s 63.

2 Ibid, s 62. 'Officer' is defined in terms which appear to exclude a person appointed by the committee, as distinct from a person elected by the members: s 74 (amended by the Friendly and Industrial and Provident Societies Act 1968 (c 55), s 20(1)(a), Sch 1, para 11).

3 Industrial and Provident Societies Act 1965, s 62.

4 Ibid, s 66(1)(c). However, there are two exceptions. In the case of (1) proceedings under s 64 (1) (see para 655 below), when the society or any specially authorised member or the registrar are authorised to act (s 66(1)(a)(i)–(iii)); and (2) proceedings under s 13(3), when the society only is authorised to act (s 66(1)(b)). Proceedings may be brought by the procurator fiscal or the registrar within one year of the first discovery of the offence by the registrar but not more than three years of its commission: s 66(2).

5 Ibid, s 68.

6 Ibid, s 71(2).

7 Ibid, s 67.

655. Offences. There are a number of general offences which may be committed by a society, officer or member, or any other person, as the case may be:
(1) failure to do anything, including the giving of notice or sending any document or return, which is required of a society;
(2) wilful refusal or neglect in complying with the requirements of the legislation or the registrar, or the doing of a forbidden act;
(3) wilful making of a false return or the provision of inadequate information[1].

There are three offences relating to the dissolution of a society. A person commits an offence who:
(a) makes any false or fraudulent statement in an instrument of dissolution[2];
(b) contravenes the appropriate registrar's directions during the procedure for the cancellation of a society's registration[3]; or
(c) fails to produce books etc or to give information to the registrar[4].

To ensure that the society's name is properly disclosed, a fine of up to level 3 on the standard scale may be imposed on the summary conviction of any officer or other authorised person who uses a seal, issues any official document or bill of exchange or order on which the society's name is not legibly written[5]. In the case of a bill of exchange or order the convicted person is also personally liable if the society defaults[6].

There are other offences. The deliberate falsification of a balance sheet, contribution or collecting book, return or other document is punishable on summary conviction by a fine not exceeding level 3 on the standard scale[7]. The fraudulent issue of rules other than the current rules of a society, or passing off an unregistered society's rules as those of a registered society is punishable on summary conviction by a fine not exceeding level 1 on the standard scale[8]. Anyone who falsely obtains any property of a society or withholds or misapplies such property is liable on summary conviction to a fine not exceeding level 2 on the standard scale and to be ordered to restore the property or repay any money, with a further sanction of up to three months' imprisonment for default[9]. If fraudulent intention is not proved, the order for restoration or repayment with costs is competent though the conviction is not[10].

1 Industrial and Provident Societies Act 1965 (c 12), s 61(a)–(c). On summary conviction the penalty is a fine not exceeding level 3 on the standard scale: s 61 (amended by the Criminal Justice Act 1967 (c 80), ss 92, 106(2), Sch 3, Pt I, and the Criminal Procedure (Scotland) Act 1975 (c 21), s 289H, Sch 7D (added by the Criminal Justice Act 1982 (c 48), s 56, Sch 6, para 20)). At the date at which this volume states the law, level 3 on the standard scale is £400: see the Increase of Criminal Penalties etc (Scotland) Order 1984, SI 1984/526, art 4.

2 Industrial and Provident Societies Act 1965, s 58(4), which provides no set penalty. As to the instrument of dissolution, see para 652 above.

3 Ibid, s 16(5). On summary conviction, a person is liable to a fine not exceeding level 3 on the standard scale or to imprisonment for a term not exceeding three months or to both: s 16(5). As to level 3, see para 645, note 3, above.

4 Ibid, s 48(2). For the penalty, see para 645, note 3, above.

5 Ibid, s 5(6), (7). As to level 3, see para 645, note 3, above.

6 Ibid, s 5(7).

7 Ibid, s 65.

8 Ibid, s 15(2). As to level 1, see the Criminal Procedure (Scotland) Act 1975 (c 21), s 289C (added by the Criminal Law Act 1977 (c 45), s 63(1), Sch 11, para 5; and amended by the Criminal Justice Act 1982 (c 48), s 55(3)(a)), the Criminal Procedure (Scotland) Act 1975, s 289G (added by the Criminal Justice Act 1982, s 54). At the date at which this volume states the law, level 1 on the standard scale is £50: see the Increase of Criminal Penalties etc (Scotland) Order 1984, art 4.

9 Industrial and Provident Societies Act 1965, s 64(1). As to level 2, see the Criminal Procedure (Scotland) Act 1975, s 289C, and the statutes cited in note 8 above. At the date at which this volume states the law, level 2 on the standard scale is £100: see the Increase of Criminal Penalties etc (Scotland) Order 1984, art 4. Prosecution on indictment is allowed unless there has been a prior conviction: Industrial and Provident Societies Act 1965, s 64(1).

10 Ibid, s 64(2).

3. CREDIT UNIONS

(1) INTRODUCTION

656. Historical development. At its simplest, a credit union is a financial co-operative. The first credit union was set up by Wilhelm Raffeisen at Heddes-dorf in 1864. It and its successor societies operated on the principle that only members could borrow and then only for a sound purpose. The security of a member/borrower was his character as known to his fellow members. It is probable that the first credit union in Britain was formed in 1964[1] and though much expanded since that date the numbers are still small when compared to building societies and trustee savings banks[2].

The British credit union movement is largely unified and has affiliations with the United Kingdom co-operative movement and the international credit union movement. This means that all credit unions share a common structure of internal checks and balances designed to keep democratic control, with proper security for the unions and the members' funds.

In 1979 the Credit Unions Act was passed giving credit unions a formal legal structure under the Industrial and Provident Societies Act 1965 suitably adapted. Were it not for specific exemption[3], the effect of the Banking Act 1979 would be to prevent an unregistered credit union from taking deposits and so prevent its operation. Similarly exemption was also necessary from the provisions of the Consumer Credit Act 1974[4]. Since the term 'credit union' is restricted to a registered society[5], an unregistered credit union is only theoretically possible. The relevant legislation is the Industrial and Provident Societies Acts 1965 to 1978[6] and related regulations[7] and the Credit Unions Act 1979 supported by regulations[8].

1 K Brading 'Journal of Co-operative Studies' 1986 No 56 p 10. The contribution of Schulze-Delitzsch to the original concept and Desjardins and Filene to the North American movement should not be forgotten.
2 It is probable that the existence of building societies, trustee savings banks and friendly societies prevented the growth of savings and loan societies. The Loan Societies Act 1840 (c 110) applied only to societies in England and Wales and they were and are insignificant.
3 Ie under the Banking Act 1979 (c 37), s 2(1), Sch 1, para 11 (repealed).
4 Hence the necessity for the Credit Unions Act 1979 (c 34), s 11: see 1979 Official Report, SC A, cols 64, 65. See also para 669, note 8, below. There are no applicable provisions in the Financial Services Act 1986 (c 60).
5 Ie under the Credit Unions Act 1979 (c 34), s 3: see para 658 below.
6 See para 603 above.
7 See para 606, note 3, above.
8 See the Credit Unions (Authorised Investments) Order 1979, SI 1979/866; the Industrial and Provident Societies (Credit Unions) Regulations 1979, SI 1979/937 (amended by SI 1988/451, SI 1989/358); and the Credit Unions (Authorised Banks) (Termination of Powers of Chief Registrar) Order 1980, SI 1980/736.

657. Application of the Industrial and Provident Societies Act 1965. The Industrial and Provident Societies Act 1965 (c 12) applies to the Credit Unions Act 1979 (c 34), subject to the following exclusions and modifications:

1965 Act Section No	1979 Act Section No
1	excluded by 2(1)
2(1)	modified by 6
2(2)	modified by 2
3	excluded by 2(5)
5	modified by 3(4)

6	excluded by 31
7	excluded by 9(1)
10(3)	modified by 4(3)
11	excluded by 4(5)
12	excluded by 31(3)
16(1)(a)(i)	modified by 6(1)
16(1)(a)(i), (ii)	modified by 20(1)
17	modified by 2(6), 20
19, 21, 30, 31	excluded by 31
39(1)	excluded by 24(2)
48(1)	modified by 17(1)
50, 51	modified by 21
52	excluded by 22
53(1)	modified by 23
53(2)	modified by 6(1)
61–66, 68	modified by 28
Sch 1	replaced by Sch 1

658. Transitional provisions. There are two transitional provisions in the Credit Unions Act 1979. A society registered before the Act came into force[1] with the objects of a credit union must take all reasonable steps to re-register as a credit union[2]. If the society does not do so, the registrar has power to cancel or suspend[3] its registration[4].

1 Ie 20 August 1979: see the Credit Unions Act 1979 (Commencement No 1) Order 1979, SI 1979/936 (bringing the Credit Unions Act 1979 (c 34), ss 1, 2, 3(1), (4), 4–14, and 16–31, Schs 1–3 in force). See also the Credit Unions Act 1979 (Commencement No 2) Order 1980, SI 1980/481 (bringing the Credit Unions Act 1979, s 15, into force on 1 October 1989). The Credit Unions Act 1979, ss 32, 33, were brought into force on the passing of the Act (ie 4 April 1979): s 33(2). At the date at which this volume states the law, no order has been made bringing s 3(2), (3), into force.
2 Ibid, s 2(4). As to the continuity of a society so converting to a credit union, see s 2(5).
3 Ie under the Industrial and Provident Societies Act 1965 (c 12), ss 16, 17: see paras 611, 657, above.
4 Credit Unions Act 1979, s 2(6).

659. Taxation. Tax concessions were made available to credit unions by exempting internal profits earned by a credit union from corporation tax[1]. Interest earned from loans made to members is also exempt[1]. Dividends paid to members up to and including the year 1984–1985 are free from tax[1].

1 See the Income and Corporation Taxes Act 1970 (c 10), s 340A (added by the Credit Unions Act 1979 (c 34), s 25) (repealed). See now the Income and Corporation Taxes Act 1988 (c 1), s 487.

660. Scope. In the following treatment the author is concerned only with the legal differences between credit unions and industrial and provident societies. In so far as the same legal rules apply, the reader is referred to the section in this title on Industrial and Provident Societies[1].

1 See paras 606 ff above. As to modifications and exclusions, see para 657 above.

(2) REGISTRATION

661. Meaning of 'credit union'. A credit union is a self-help savings and loan society, run on mutual lines, where the members pool their savings to provide a fund which will give them a source of low cost credit. In more formal terms it is a society which has the following statutory objects of a credit union:

(1) the promotion of thrift through members' savings;
(2) the provision of a source of credit for the members at a reasonable interest rate;
(3) the use of members' savings for the members' mutual benefit;
(4) the education of members in sound financial management[1].

Membership will be limited to those within the common bond set out in the membership qualification in its rules, or qualified relatives of those individuals, so ensuring that the members are known to each other[2].

1 Credit Unions Act 1979 (c 34), s 1(3)(a)–(d).
2 See ibid, s 1(2)(b), (4)–(6).

662. Registration. To qualify for registration[1], a credit union must meet the following conditions:

(1) its objects are only those of a credit union[2];
(2) membership is restricted to those within the common bond[3];
(3) the rules comply with the Credit Unions Act 1979[4];
(4) the registered office is in Scotland[5];
(5) the fidelity insurance requirement will be met[6].

The credit union must satisfy the registrar that it meets these conditions, and the crucial test as set out in a guidance note[7] is 'are the particular features of the proposed union such that there is a reasonable expectation that it will be able and willing to safeguard properly the money of members placed with it?'. If it does so, the registrar will issue an acknowledgment of registration[8] which incorporates the credit union with limited liability[9].

1 For the procedure, see paras 610, 657, above.
2 Credit Unions Act 1979 (c 34), s 1(1)(a), (2)(a), (3).
3 Ibid, s 1(2)(b), (4).
4 Ibid, ss 1(1)(b), 4(1).
5 Ibid, s 1(1)(c).
6 See ibid, s 15, and para 668 below.
7 Guidance Note of 21 April 1986, which is also annexed to the report of the Chief Registrar 1986, vol 2, p 10. This Note is particularly concerned with the common bond and its relationship to the membership requirements as together contributing to the safety of members' funds. The following heavily edited extract is relevant: 'In relation to the common bond there is a three stage consideration
(1) does the membership qualification satisfy s 1(4);
(2) does that establish a common bond, for which the cohesiveness of the membership and the extent one person is known to the others, the frequency of contact between members, the ability of a member in difficulty over repayment to opt out, the existence of backing from an employer, geographical spread and the anticipated significance of the credit union in relation to the community from which the members will come are relevant factors for consideration; and
(3) does this establish a reasonable expectation of the safety of members' funds which is achieved by (1) helping establish the credit worthiness of applicants for loans...; (2) increasing the probability of continuous effective management of the union, its books and papers...; (3) helping ensure the repayment of loans by members...; (4) helping the committee and officers bring pressure for repayment on a member who is late with repayments...'.
8 See the Industrial and Provident Societies Act 1965 (c 12), s 2(3), and para 610 above.
9 Two printed copies of the rules signed by three members and the secretary, the application form, signed by twenty-one members, and the prescribed fee are to be lodged: Industrial and Provident Societies (Credit Unions) Regulations 1979, SI 1979/937, reg 4, Sch 1, Form CU 1. A member is disqualified from signing Form CU 1 if convicted on indictment for dishonesty: Credit Unions Act 1979, s 27. Details of all requirements are given in Form F 836 and the additional Guidance Note of 21 April 1986. For the fees, see the Industrial and Provident Societies (Credit Unions) Regulations 1979, reg 17, Sch 2 (substituted by SI 1991/521).

(3) RULES AND MEMBERSHIP

663. Rules. The Credit Unions Act 1979 requires that the rules provide for the matters detailed in the Act[1]. In particular, additional requirements are included which are necessary to a credit union, such as the making of loans[2] and the provision of protective insurance[3], the limitation and disqualification of members[4] and the transfer of free assets on dissolution to other credit unions or to charity[5]. The appropriate registrar may require additional provisions[6]. The procedure for amendment of the rules requires a two-thirds' majority vote of the members present at a general meeting[7].

The name of a credit union must include the words 'credit union' and end with 'limited'[8].

1 Credit Unions Act 1979 (c 34), s 4(1), Sch 1. For the rules in respect of industrial and provident society, see paras 612–616, 657, above.
2 See ibid, s 11, and para 669 below.
3 See ibid, s 15, and para 668 below.
4 See ibid, ss 5, 6, and para 664 below.
5 See ibid, s 4(1), Sch 1, particularly paras 4, 8, 9, 12–14.
6 Ibid, s 4(1)(b).
7 Ibid, s 4(2). For the forms, see the Industrial and Provident Societies (Credit Unions) Regulations 1979, SI 1979/ 937, reg 6, Sch 1, Form cu 5 (complete amendment) or Form cu 6 (partial amendment) and statutory declaration Form cu 7, together with the fee, two printed copies of the amendments and marked rules, or of the new rules.
8 Credit Unions Act 1979, s 3, reserving the name for such societies. 'Limited' cannot be dispensed with.

664. Membership. Only individuals may be members, and they must both hold at least one fully paid-up share and satisfy the membership qualification set by the common bond requirement[1]. This may be based on occupation, residence or employment in a locality and a common employer or association other than one set up specifically for the formation of a credit union[2].

A person who loses his membership qualification may retain membership provided:
(1) the rules do not exclude this right[3]; and
(2) the total number of non-qualifying members does not exceed 10 per cent of the total[4].
Additionally, a person who is both a relative of, and a member of the same household, as a member by direct qualification, may become a member[5].

The minimum number of members is twenty-one, and the maximum is 5,000[6].

1 Credit Unions Act 1979 (c 34), s 5(1), (2). As to membership of industrial and provident societies, see paras 618, 657, above.
2 Ibid, s 1(4)(a)–(e). The registrar has power to recognise other common bond qualifications: s 1(4). In any case the common bond must be a real one; if it was so wide as to lack any real element of community it would not provide the necessary foundation of trust and co-operation. See also the Registry of Friendly Societies' Guidance Note, and para 662, note 7, above.
3 Credit Unions Act 1979, s 5(5).
4 Ibid, s 5(6).
5 Ibid, s 1(6).
6 Ibid, s 6(1), (2). For exemptions, see s 6(5), (6).

(4) OPERATION OF CREDIT UNIONS

665. Shares. A credit union's shares are of £1 denomination and are withdrawable but not transferable save by nomination[1]. The minimum membership qualification is at least one share, but the rules may require up to five as the minimum holding[2]. The maximum holding is 5,000[3]. Shares cannot be alloted until fully paid and no share certificate is issued[4]. The following restrictions apply to withdrawals:

(1) the rules must require at least sixty days' notice of withdrawal[5];
(2) if the member is a borrower or guarantor and the withdrawal would reduce the shareholding to below the member's liability to the credit union, it is only permitted at the committee's discretion, unless the member is a non-qualifying member, when it is not permitted[6].

1 Credit Unions Act 1979 (c 34), s 7(1)–(4). For the provisions dealing with nominations, see paras 626–629, 657, above.
2 Ibid, s 5(2).
3 Ibid, s 5(3) (amended by the Credit Unions (Increase of Limits of Shareholding of Deposits by persons too young to be members and of Loans) Order 1989, SI 1989/2423, art 3, as from 1 February 1990). The original maximum was 2,000: Credit Unions Act 1979, s 5(3) (as originally enacted).
4 Ibid, s 7(1), (2).
5 Ibid, s 7(4).
6 Ibid, s 7(5)(a), (b).

666. Deposits, borrowings and investments. A credit union may only accept deposits[1] from people too young[2] to be members[3]. The maximum sum taken from such depositor may not exceed £750[4] and must be invested separately in narrower-range investments in the manner specified in the Trustee Investments Act 1961[5], the annual income from which, after deduction of expenses, is to be distributed as interest to the depositors[6].

A credit union may borrow, up to a limit of one-half the paid-up capital, from an authorised bank[7] (and temporarily from another credit union or association of credit unions)[8]. If the registrar agrees in writing, temporary loans from an authorised bank may be disregarded in calculating the limit[9]. A lender is not required to check that the credit union is complying with the limit, but if he has notice of non-compliance when the loan is made (or security taken) the debt (or security) is unenforceable[10]. If the money borrowed is not repaid when due, the credit union may not make loans or permit withdrawal of shares by its members[11].

Surplus funds are to be either kept in cash by an officer, banked with an authorised bank or invested in authorised government or local authority bonds or marketable securities[12]. There is an express waiver allowing temporary loans to other credit unions[13].

1 'Deposit' means a sum of money paid on terms under which it will be repaid, with or without interest or at a premium, and either on demand or as agreed between the parties: see the Banking Act 1987 (c 22), s 5(1)(a), applied by the Credit Unions Act 1979 (c 34), s 8(2) (substituted by the Banking Act 1987, s 108(1), Sch 6, para 7(1)). A deposit is not connected with the provision of property, services or security: s 5(1)(b), (2). As to what does not constitute a deposit, see s 5(3)–(5). Civil liability is not affected if the deposit is otherwise unlawful: Credit Unions Act 1979, s 8(5).
2 Ie under the Industrial and Provident Societies Act 1965 (c 12), s 20: see para 618 above.
3 Credit Unions Act 1979, s 9(1).
4 Ibid, s 9(1) (amended by the Credit Unions (Increase of Limits of Shareholding of Deposits by persons too young to be members and of Loans) Order 1989, SI 1989/2423, art 4, as from 1 February 1990). The chief registrar has power to increase the financial limit: Credit Unions Act 1979, s 9(4), (5). The original maximum limit was £250: see s 9(1) (as originally enacted).
5 Ie under the Trustee Investments Act 1961 (c 62), Sch 1, Pts I, II (see TRUSTS, TRUSTEES AND JUDICIAL FACTORS, vol 24, para 207): Credit Unions Act 1979, s 9(2).
6 Ibid, s 9(3).
7 'Authorised bank' means an institution authorised under the Banking Act 1987 or a municipal bank within the meaning of that Act, the National Savings Bank, and the Post Office in the

exercise of its powers to provide banking services: Credit Unions Act 1979, s 31(1) (amended by the Banking Act 1987, s 108, Sch 6, para 7(2), Sch 7, Pt I, and the Trustee Savings Banks Act 1985 (c 58), ss 4(3), 7(3), Sch 4).

8 Credit Unions Act 1979, s 10(1). Breach of the borrowing limit by a credit union is an offence liable on prosecution on indictment or summarily to a fine which on summary conviction must not exceed the statutory maximum: s 10(6). 'Statutory maximum' means the prescribed sum within the meaning of the Criminal Procedure (Scotland) Act 1975 (c 21), s 289B(6) (added by the Criminal Law Act 1977 (c 45), s 63(1), Sch 11, para 5; substituted by the Criminal Justice Act 1982 (c 48), s 55(2); and amended by the Increase of Criminal Penalties etc (Scotland) Order 1984, SI 1984/526, art 3): Interpretation Act 1978 (c 30), s 5, Sch 1 (added by the Criminal Justice Act 1988 (c 33), s 170(1), Sch 15, para 58(b)). At the date at which this volume states the law, the prescribed sum is £2,000.

9 Credit Unions Act 1979, s 10(2).

10 Ibid, s 10(3). However, no transaction with a credit union is invalid or ineffectual solely by reason of the fact that the limit on borrowing by the credit union has been or is thereby exceeded: s 10(4).

11 Ibid, s 10(5). As to the penalty, see note 8 above.

12 Ibid, s 13(1), (2). 'Surplus funds' means funds not immediately required for its purposes (ie loans to members): s 13(4). See also the Credit Unions (Authorised Investments) Order 1979, SI 1979/866. As to when a bank ceases to be an authorised bank, see the Credit Unions Act 1979, s 13(3). The penalty for breach of the provisions of s 13 on conviction on indictment or summarily is a fine which on summary conviction must not exceed the statutory maximum: see s 13(6), and note 8 above.

13 Ibid, s 13(5)(a). There is also the exclusion of trust deposits under s 9(2): s 13(5)(b).

667. Heritable property.

667. Heritable property. A credit union has full power to own, lease or dispose of heritage, but only for two purposes:

(1) as its own business premises; and

(2) as security for a loan to a member on the security of that land[1].

If the credit union acquires an interest in land through the exercise of its rights as a secured creditor, it must dispose of the interest as soon as reasonably practicable[2].

1 Credit Unions Act 1979 (c 34), s 12(1)–(3). No person is bound to inquire as to the authority for any dealing with land: s 12(6). The receipt of a credit union is a discharge for all money arising from or in connection with any dealing with land by it: s 12(6).

2 Ibid, s 12(4)(b). Breach of the prompt sale requirement is an offence and punishable on conviction on indictment or on summary conviction to a fine which on summary conviction must not exceed the statutory maximum: see s 12(5), and para 666, note 8, above.

668. Committee members and officers.

668. Committee members and officers. Apart from the provisions applying to all industrial and provident societies in respect of the committee of management and officers[1], there are two express provisions to note in respect of credit unions. An undischarged bankrupt or any person who has been convicted on indictment of an offence involving fraud or dishonesty is disqualified from committee membership, from direct or indirect participation in management, or from holding any office in a credit union[2]. It is a precondition for registration that a credit union has in force at all times from its first registration insurance against any loss attributable to the fraud or dishonesty of its officers or employees[3]. The insurance must be for not less than £20,000 for any one claim, although there may be a ceiling on claims of not less than £100,000 in any one year[4]. There can be no excess on any one claim greater than 1 per cent borne by the credit union except with the written consent of the registrar[5].

Credit unions, either singly or together, may enter into guarantee arrangements to protect their members from any loss with any insurer[6]. Two or more credit unions may make other similar arrangements[6]. In either case the credit unions concerned have power to make contributions and to set up any necessary trust[7]. The appropriate registrar must give prior consent both to the initial scheme and to any variation of it[8].

1 See paras 619, 620, 657, above.
2 Credit Unions Act 1979 (c 34), s 27(b)–(d).
3 Ibid, s 15(1), (2)(a). The insurer must be authorised by the Insurance Companies Act 1982 (c 50) for that class of business in Great Britain, Northern Ireland or another member state: Credit Unions Act 1979, s 15(2)(d) (amended by the Insurance Companies Act 1982, s 99(2), Sch 5, para 20).
4 Credit Unions Act 1979, s 15(2)(b). The chief registrar has power to increase the limits with Treasury consent: s 15(3), (4).
5 Ibid, s 15(2)(c).
6 Ibid, s 16(1).
7 Ibid, s 16(2).
8 Ibid, s 16(3).

669. Loans to members. A credit union may make a loan to a member of full age (that is over eighteen) for a provident or productive purpose[1]. The conditions and any security requirement will be contained in the rules[2]. There are a number of conditions affecting the borrowing member and the credit union. The maximum sum that a full member may borrow is the total paid-up share holding plus £5,000[3]. If the member is non-qualifying the total limit (as borrower, guarantor or otherwise) may not exceed the total paid-up capital[4]. A loan must be repaid within five years if secured but within two years if unsecured[5].

A credit union may not lend more than the maximum set by the chief registrar, and any loan that would make the credit unions outstanding loans exceed that limit is unlawful[6]. Interest at a rate not exceeding 1 per cent per month on the reducing monthly balance may be charged on loans to be inclusive of all administrative charges incurred by the credit union[7]. That rate if converted to an annual rate is 12.6825 per cent, which is below the 13 per cent qualifying ceiling for an exempt transaction. This means that a credit union should be entitled to the low cost credit exemption under the Consumer Credit Act 1974[8].

1 Credit Unions Act 1979 (c 34), s 11(1). The words 'provident or productive' are not defined; 'or' requires them to be interpreted separately. The phrase is traditional, dating to the beginning of the movement and frequently occurring in credit union laws but without definition. During the second reading of the Credit Unions Bill the purposes of loans were said to be for everyday requirements, whether for goods or services, for household goods, season tickets and so on. During the committee stage of the Bill, Christmas or holiday expenses (even weddings) were added: (1979) 962 HC Official Report (5th series) cols 799, 800; HC Official Report, SC A, cols 58, 59, 69. The credit union movement itself states that the loan must benefit the member or his or her family.
2 Credit Unions Act 1979, s 11(1).
3 Ibid, s 11(2) (amended by the Credit Unions (Increase of Limits of Shareholding of Deposits by persons too young to be members and of Loans) Order 1989, SI 1989/2423, art 5, as from 1 February 1990). The original limit was £2,000: Credit Unions Act 1979, s 11(2) (as originally enacted).
4 Ibid, s 11(3). 'Liability' includes contingent liabilities: s 11(3).
5 Ibid, s 11(4). The limit can be altered by order: s 11(4).
6 Ibid, s 11(6). The limit is to be specified by order made by the chief registrar with the consent of the Treasury: s 11(7). At the date at which this volume states the law, no such order had been made.
7 Ibid, s 11(5).
8 Ie 13 per cent or the minimum lending rate plus 1 per cent whichever is higher, which qualifies a transaction for the low cost credit exemption under the Consumer Credit Act 1974 (c 39), s 16(5)(b): see CONSUMER CREDIT, vol 5, para 823. However, credit unions are still subject to that Act, and the terms of a loan will need to be considered to obtain the exemption: see generally, vol 5, paras 801 ff.

670. Application of profits. In each year of account, in calculating its profit or loss a credit union must provide for the following items:
(1) all expenses, including interest payments;

(2) depreciation of assets;
(3) tax liabilities; and
(4) bad debts[1].
No provision can be made for dividend payments to the members[1].

The first charge on profits in any year is the general reserve fund, which is to be maintained at between 10 and 20 per cent of total assets[2]. The credit union is free to transfer to and from the general reserve provided these limits are not exceeded[3]. If the general reserve at the year end is less than 10 per cent of the credit union's total assets, then either not less than 20 per cent of profit or the sum needed to increase the reserve to 10 per cent of total assets whichever is the less is to be transferred to the fund[4]. If the general reserve at the year end is more than 20 per cent of the credit union's total assets, then the reserve is to be reduced to at most 20 per cent by a transfer of the excess to the revenue account[5].

After the necessary general reserve adjustments have been made any surplus is the amount available for distribution[6]. Not less than 90 per cent is to be distributed in any of the following ways:
(a) payment of dividend on the members' paid-up share capital at a rate not exceeding 8 per cent per annum[7];
(b) giving a rebate of interest on members' loans, proportional to the interest paid in that year[8];
(c) for social, cultural or charitable purposes[9].
A credit union may accumulate profit for future distribution, because although 90 per cent of profit must be allocated for one of these three purposes immediate payment is not required[10]. The general meeting may resolve to postpone payment, and unless the resolution otherwise provides future payment will be at the committee's discretion[10].

1 Credit Unions Act 1979 (c 34), s 14(1). Nothing in s 14 applies to income arising from, or to expenses incurred by a credit union in operating, a trust fund under s 9(2) (see para 666 above): s 14(7). For the provisions under the Industrial and Provident Societies Act 1965 (c 12), see paras 630 ff above. As to the application of the 1965 Act, see para 657 above.
2 See the Credit Unions Act 1979, s 14(2).
3 Ibid, s 14(2)(c)(i), (ii). This requires a resolution of the general meeting: s 14(2)(c).
4 Ibid, s 14(2)(a).
5 Ibid, s 14(2)(b).
6 Ibid, s 14(3).
7 Ibid, s 14(3)(a), (4). The rate may be varied by order: s 14(4). At the date at which this volume states the law no such order had been made.
8 Ibid, s 14(3)(b).
9 Ibid, s 14(3)(c). Before any such payments may be made a dividend of at least 3 per cent per annum must have been paid to the members: s 14(5). No more than ten per cent of distributable profit may be allocated to these purposes in any one year: s 14(5). 'Charitable' is construed in the same way as in the Income Tax Acts: see CHARITIES.
10 Credit Unions Act 1979, s 14(6).

671. Display of accounts. In addition to the duty to display the most recent balance sheet and auditors' report[1], a credit union may display at its registered office an unaudited interim revenue account or balance sheet[2]. It must be conspicuously marked in block capitals with the words 'unaudited revenue account/balance sheet'[3]. A credit union availing itself of this concession is exempted from the prohibitions against display of unaudited accounts and balance sheets[4] and need not include such interim accounts or balance sheet in the next annual return[5] submitted to the appropriate registrar[6].

1 Ie under the Industrial and Provident Societies Act 1965 (c 12), s 40: see para 635 above.
2 Credit Unions Act 1979 (c 34), s 24(1). The interim revenue account or balance sheet may not be displayed at any other office (s 24(1)), and must be displayed side by side with the latest audited revenue account and balance sheet (s 24(1)(a)).

3 Ibid, s 24(1)(b).
4 Ie under the Friendly and Industrial and Provident Societies Act 1968 (c 55), s 3(5)(a), (b): see para 635 above.
5 Ie under the Industrial and Provident Societies Act 1965, s 39(1).
6 Credit Unions Act 1979, s 24(2).

(5) AMALGAMATIONS, TRANSFERS AND CONVERSIONS

672. Amalgamations and transfer of engagements. The general provisions regulating the procedures in respect of amalgamations and transfers are modified for credit unions[1]. Firstly, a credit union cannot amalgamate with or transfer to any society which is not a credit union[2], nor can it amalgamate with or transfer to a company[3]. Secondly, the registrar must be satisfied that the common bond will continue in the new arrangement, and that the Industrial and Provident Societies Acts 1965 to 1978 and the Credit Unions Act 1979 have been complied with[4]. For these purposes 'non-qualifying member' is defined as including both a person who was such a member of either of the original credit unions and also a person who no longer fulfils the membership qualifications of the credit union established by the amalgamation or transfer[5].

1 Ie under the Credit Unions Act 1979 (c 34), s 21, modifying the Industrial and Provident Societies Act 1965 (c 12), ss 50, 51 (see paras 648, 649, above): Credit Unions Act 1979, s 21(1).
2 Ibid, s 21(2).
3 Ibid, s 22.
4 Credit Unions Act 1979, s 21(3)(a), (b). Unless these points are complied with, the special resolution cannot be registered.
5 Ibid, s 21(4).

673. Company conversions. A credit union cannot convert into a company[1].
A company may convert to a credit union[2] provided that the registrar is satisfied that:
(1) there are either no outstanding deposits owed by the company, or if there are any they will be converted into shares in the new credit union and the members concerned have agreed to this in writing[3];
(2) the members' shareholdings will not exceed the current statutory maximum[4];
(3) the statutory maximum number of members will not be exceeded[5].

1 Credit Unions Act 1979 (c 34), s 22, excluding the provisions of the Industrial and Provident Societies Act 1965 (c 12), s 52.
2 Credit Unions Act 1979, s 23(1), (2), applying with modifications the Industrial and Provident Societies Act 1965, s 53: see para 651 above.
3 Credit Unions Act 1979, s 23(3)(a).
4 Ibid, s 23(3)(b). The shareholding is to include any deposits converted under s 23(3)(a): s 23(3)(b). As to the maximum, see s 5(3), and para 665 above.
5 Ibid, s 23(3)(c). As to the maximum, see s 6(2), and para 664 above. The registrar can grant an exemption (see s 6(5), and para 664 above): s 23(3)(c).

(6) POWERS OF THE REGISTRAR

674. Power to require information. The appropriate registrar may serve written notice on a credit union requiring it to supply a financial statement within a set time limit or to supply regular financial statements to him in addition to the annual return[1]. Failure to comply with such a notice is an offence[2]. This power is without prejudice to the registrar's power[3] to require the production of books, accounts etc[4].

1 Credit Unions Act 1979 (c 34), s 17(2). The notice will give the details and form of the financial statement: s 17(2). The registrar has in fact required quarterly returns: *Report of the Chief Registrar of Friendly Societies 1981–82*, p 32.
2 Credit Unions Act 1979, s 17(3). On summary conviction a credit union is liable to a fine not exceeding level 3 on the standard scale (as to which see para 645, note 3, above): s 17(3).
3 Ie under the Industrial and Provident Societies Act 1965 (c 12), s 48: see para 645 above.
4 Credit Unions Act 1979, s 17(1).

675. Power to appoint inspectors and call meeting. If the chief registrar considers that the affairs of a credit union require investigation he may appoint an inspector to investigate and report on its affairs[1]. The consent of the Treasury is required[2]. He has a similar power to call a meeting of the members or both to appoint an inspector and to call a meeting[3]. This gives the registrar power to initiate such procedures without the requisition of the members.

The expenses of the investigation or meeting are to be paid by the credit union, its present or past members or officers, as the registrar may decide[4].

1 Credit Unions Act 1979 (c 34), s 18(1), which does not affect the Industrial and Provident Societies Act 1965 (c 12), s 49, and a member's requisition: see paras 644, 646, above.
2 Credit Unions Act 1979, s 18(1).
3 Ibid, s 18(1). The procedures of the Industrial and Provident Societies Act 1965, s 49(5), (6) (see para 646 above) apply: Credit Unions Act 1979, s 18(3).
4 Ibid, s 18(2).

676. Power to suspend operations. If the chief registrar considers it expedient in the interests of the members, present or future, he may suspend one or more specified activities of a credit union[1]. The activities affected are borrowing money, lending money, accepting share subscriptions and repaying share capital[2]. Notwithstanding suspension, a credit union may borrow from an authorised bank with the written consent of the registrar[3].

The consent of the Treasury is required for the recall of a suspension notice, and the same publicity of the recall is to be given as was given of the original suspension[4].

If the suspension prevented the credit union from accepting a payment which fell due during that time, recall of the suspension reinstates the obligation but temporarily suspends it for a period equivalent to the original suspension[5]. Subject to that, the suspension rescinds any obligation to make a payment which the credit union is prevented from accepting[6].

1 Credit Unions Act 1979 (c 34), s 19(1). Precise details will be in the notice. Some guidance as to the meaning of the chief registrar's interpretation of the word 'expedient' can be taken from the occasions on which he has exercised this power as recorded in his annual reports: failure to submit annual (and quarterly) returns, to keep adequate accounts, control systems and management, the ability of the credit union to comply fully with the legislation, questions over the financial position and possible insolvency are all relevant. For example, in one case, there had been discrepancies in a credit union's accounts for 1981–82; in the following year it had lost all its records in a car theft and there were doubts as to solvency; however, the registrar was prepared to consider lifting the suspension if the credit union's solvency were proved, its records recreated and adequate managerial control established: see the *Reports of the Chief Registrar of Friendly Societies* 1981–82, p 31, 1983–84, p 32, 1985, p 9.
2 Credit Unions Act 1979, s 19(1)(a)–(d). Treasury consent is required: s 19(1). For the full procedure, see s 19(1), Sch 2. The setting off of a member's debt to the credit union against share capital is treated as a repayment of share capital: s 19(3).
3 Ibid, s 19(2).
4 Ibid, s 19(4). As to notice requirements, see Sch 2, para 6.

5 Ibid, s 19(5).
6 Ibid, s 19(6).

677. Cancellation, suspension and winding up. In addition to the powers of the registrar under the Industrial and Provident Societies Act 1965 to cancel a credit union's registration[1], he may also do so either for failure to comply with the Credit Unions Act 1979[2], or where the common bond has broken down[3]. Suspension of registration on grounds which would justify cancellation[4] and the appeals procedure[5] apply[6].

The registrar may petition for winding up on the following specific grounds:

(1) a credit union either cannot pay sums due to its members, or can only do so by raising fresh share subscriptions or defaulting on its debtors;

(2) a credit union has failed to comply with the Industrial and Provident Societies Acts 1965 to 1978 or the Credit Unions Act 1979 or any direction given under those Acts;

(3) there is no longer a common bond between the members[7].

Additionally a petition may be presented where liquidation is in the public interest, or is just and equitable in the interests of all the members of the credit union[8].

1 Ie under the Industrial and Provident Societies Act 1965 (c 12), s 16(1): see para 611 above.
2 Ie under ibid, s 16(1)(c), applied by the Credit Unions Act 1979 (c 34), s 20(1)(a).
3 Ie under the Industrial and Provident Societies Act 1965, s 16(1)(c)(ii), applied by the Credit Unions Act 1979, s 20(1)(b).
4 Ie under the Industrial and Provident Societies Act 1965, s 17(1): see para 611 above.
5 Ie under ibid, s 18: see para 610 above.
6 Credit Unions Act 1979, s 20(1).
7 Credit Unions Act 1979, s 20(2)(a)–(c).
8 Ibid, s 20(2). As to dissolution and liquidation, see paras 652, 653, above.

(7) OFFENCES

678. Offences. Subject to four qualifications the general provisions for offences in the Industrial and Provident Societies Act 1965 apply to credit unions[1]. A defence that reasonable precautions were taken to avoid the offence is available[2]. The qualifications are:

(1) where a credit union continues to hold land in violation of the Credit Unions Act 1979[3] there is not a new offence committed each week[4];

(2) the extension of the time limit for prosecutions brought by the procurator fiscal or the registrar[5] does not apply to prosecutions brought under the 1979 Act[6];

(3) an offence committed by a credit union is also an offence committed by its officers or committee members[7] who, when convicted on indictment, are liable to up to two years' imprisonment and/or the prescribed fine[8];

(4) where an offence under the 1979 Act has been committed by a body corporate (other than a credit union) its officers are also guilty of the offence[9].

1 Ie under the Credit Unions Act 1979 (c 34), s 28(1), applying with modifications the Industrial and Provident Societies Act 1965 (c 12), ss 61–66, 68: see paras 654, 655, above.
2 Credit Unions Act 1979, s 28(6).
3 Ie under ibid, s 12(5): see para 667 above.
4 Ibid, s 28(3), modifying the Industrial and Provident Societies Act 1965, s 63: see para 654 above.
5 Ie under ibid, s 66(2): see para 654 above.
6 Credit Unions Act 1979, s 28(3).

7 Ie under the Industrial and Provident Societies Act 1965, s 62: see para 654 above.
8 Credit Unions Act 1979, s 28(4).
9 Ibid, s 28(5).

4. FRIENDLY SOCIETIES

(1) INTRODUCTION

679. Introduction. There are various explanatory definitions of 'friendly society', such as 'a voluntary association formed to raise by subscription from the members' funds from which payments may be made for the mutual relief and maintenance of the members, their wives or children in sickness, infancy or old age, infirmity or other related purposes'. Such societies, even when registered, are unincorporated. The early societies were mutual insurance societies for the 'labouring classes' providing sickness and death — even in some cases a form of unemployment — benefit. They were also local societies, but in the early nineteenth century the affiliated orders such as the Oddfellows[1] were established nationally around local lodges, and these two types of friendly societies are provided for in the Friendly Societies Act 1974 along with the other five categories of registrable society[2].

More recently after 1911, when the government first introduced the state old-age pension and health insurance, friendly societies played a major role in administering the schemes on behalf of the government through approved societies. After 1948 the approved societies were taken over by the Ministry of National Insurance[3] when national insurance was introduced.

In the post-war period, too, use has been made of the tax-exempt status of friendly societies, and some have extended their operations to non-traditional areas of business, coupled with much more aggressive marketing. The response of the Inland Revenue has been a tightening up of controls and limits on tax-exempt investment, an example being found in an old society/new society classification disentitling the new societies from the benefits of certain exemptions[4]. The current provisions are now consolidated in the Income and Corporation Taxes Act 1988.

Over the last few years many traditional friendly societies have stopped taking new business and become closed societies, which has meant that, apart from the specialised use of friendly societies for providing pensions for partners in professional firms, the majority of new registrations have been in the working men's clubs category.

1 The full title of the Oddfellows is The Independent Order of Odd Fellows Manchester Unity Friendly Society. It is one of the oldest of the affiliated orders. Others are the Loyal Order of Ancient Shepherds and the Ancient Order of Forresters. Branch registration is dealt with in para 697 below.
2 The five categories are: benevolent societies, cattle insurance societies, working men's clubs, old people's home societies, and specially authorised societies: see para 685 below.
3 The Ministry of National Insurance was amalgamated with the Ministries of Pensions and Health and ultimately renamed the Department of Health and Social Security. At the date at which this volume states the law, the Departments of Social Security and Health have been recreated, but the exact allocation of functions between them is still being finalised. See also SOCIAL SECURITY.
4 As to tax-exempt business, see para 689 below.

680. Unregistered societies. Unregistered friendly societies[1] can and do exist; their existence is recognised and certain statutory privileges granted[2]. An unregistered society is probably an association carrying out the same functions as are carried out by registered friendly societies, but there is no statutory definition. Such a society is not an illegal association under the Companies Act 1985[3] and can be liquidated under the Insolvency Act 1986[4].

By definition there is no record of their existence or numbers and all commentaries on them end with a recognition of their anomalous and uncertain legal position and a recommendation that any such society should regularise its position by registration[5].

1　Unregistered societies will not be further dealt with in this title. For details, see 19 *Halsbury's Laws of England* (4th edn) paras 135–142; F B Fuller *The Law Relating to Friendly Societies and Industrial and Provident Societies* (4th edn, 1926) p 35; and *Pratt's Friendly Societies and Industrial and Provident Societies* (15th edn, 1931, ed M Mackinnon) p 17.

2　Ie under the Reserve and Auxiliary Forces (Protection of Civil Interests) Act 1951 (c 65), ss 55–57 (as amended); the Medical Act 1956 (c 76), ss 28(1), 52(2), 54(1) (repealed: see now the Medical Act 1983 (c 54), ss 47, 56(1), Sch 6, paras 11, 20); the Friendly Societies Act 1974 (c 46), s 71(3); Insurance Companies Act 1982 (c 50), s 2(2) (read with the Industrial Assurance Act 1923 (c 8), s 1(2)); and the Income and Corporation Taxes Act 1988 (c 1), s 459.

3　See the Companies Act 1985 (c 6), s 716; *Oldham Our Ladies Sick and Burial Society v Taylor* (1887) 3 TLR 472, CA; *Re Lead Co's Workmen's Fund Society, Lowes v Governor & Co for Smelting Down Lead with Pit and Sea Coal* [1904] 2 Ch 196.

4　See the Insolvency Act 1986 (c 45), s 220(1); *Oldham Our Ladies Sick and Burial Society v Taylor* (1887) 3 TLR 472, CA; *Re Lead Co's Workmen's Fund Society, Lowes v Governor & Co for Smelting Down Lead with Pit and Sea Coal* [1904] 2 Ch 196.

5　Eg see 7 *Encyclopaedia of the Laws of Scotland* (ed Lord Dunedin and J Wark 1929) para 979; *Fuller* p 39; and *Pratt's* p 18. If a society is a collecting society or a shop (or thrift) club, registration is compulsory under the Industrial Assurance Acts 1923 to 1968. As to collecting societies, see para 682 below. The Industrial Assurance Acts 1923 to 1968 comprise the Industrial Assurance Act 1923, the Industrial Assurance (Juvenile Societies) Act 1926 (c 35), the Industrial Assurance and Friendly Societies Acts 1929 (c 28) and 1948 (c 39), the Industrial Assurance and Friendly Societies Act 1948 (Amendment) Act 1958 (c 27), and the Friendly and Industrial and Provident Societies Act 1968 (c 55).

681. Qualification as a charity. As one of the permitted categories of friendly society is 'benevolent', it is possible for a friendly society to qualify as a charity[1]. If that is the case, the normal controls of charity law will apply in addition to the requirements of the friendly societies legislation which do not separately regulate charity-friendly societies.

1　The benevolent category may include purposes that are not charitable, but if a benevolent society requires poverty as a qualification for the receipt of benefit then it may qualify as a charity: see CHARITIES.

682. Dividing and collecting societies. Dividing societies are those which at regular intervals divide amongst their members any surplus remaining after all claims and debts have been satisfied. This is normally done at yearly intervals. The rules of such societies must ensure that all claims are met before the division is made.

Collecting societies are friendly societies, carrying on industrial assurance business[1], which employ collectors who visit the members to collect their subscriptions (as opposed to the member delivering his subscription to the society directly). They are subject to the industrial assurance legislation[2] which additionally modify the friendly societies legislation in its application to collecting societies.

1　'Industrial assurance business' means the business of effecting assurances on human lives where the premiums are received by means of collectors, however remunerated, at the homes of members or persons assured at intervals of less than two months: Industrial Assurance Act 1923 (c 8), s 1(2). A friendly society carrying on such business is a collecting society.

2 Ie the Industrial and Assurance Acts 1923–1968: see para 680, note 5, above.

683. Current legislation. The current legislation is found in the Friendly Societies Act 1974 and its supporting regulations[1]. This legislation regulates the registration and operation of registered friendly societies, including those certified or registered under the earlier legislation, but does not make registration compulsory. The 1974 Act is the successor to the Friendly Societies Act 1875[2], passed after the Royal Commission of 1870–1874, and the consolidating Friendly Societies Act 1896[3] which with its amending legislation is consolidated into the 1974 Act.

1 Ie under the Friendly Societies Act 1974 (c 46); the Friendly Societies Act 1981 (c 50); the Friendly Societies Act 1984 (c 62); the Income and Corporation Taxes Act 1988 (c 1); and, excluding the territorial regulations that do not extend to Scotland, the Friendly Societies (Qualifications of Actuaries) Regulations 1968, SI 1968/1481; the Friendly Societies (Valuation) Regulations 1969, SI 1969/201 (repealed with saving by SI 1985/1919); the Friendly Societies (Proxy Voting) Regulations 1971, SI 1971/1946; the Friendly Societies Regulations 1975, SI 1975/205 (amended by SI 1988/449 and SI 1989/356); the Friendly Societies (Limits of Benefits) Order 1982, SI 1982/1353; the Friendly Societies (Limits of Benefits) Order 1984, SI 1984/513; the Friendly Societies (Valuation) Regulations 1985, SI 1985/1919 (amended by SI 1988/1959); the Financial Services (Transfer of Functions Relating to Friendly Societies) Order 1987, SI 1987/925; the Friendly Societies (Long Term Insurance Business) Regulations 1987, SI 1987/2132; and the Financial Services Act 1986 (Transfer of Functions Relating to Friendly Societies) (Transitional Provisions) Order 1987, SI 1987/2069, together with the current fees regulations. 19 *Halsbury's Laws of England* (4th edn) is the only modern text on friendly societies. Still useful, though out of date in that they refer to the Friendly Societies Act 1896 (c 25) (partially repealed: see note 3 below), are F B Fuller *The Law Relating to Friendly Societies and Industrial and Provident Societies* (4th edn, 1926) and *Pratt's Friendly Societies and Industrial and Provident Societies* (15th edn, 1931, ed M Mackinnon).

2 Friendly Societies Act 1875 (c 60) (repealed).

3 The Friendly Societies Act 1896 (c 25), except ss 22, 62, 64–67, with saving for ss 2, 8, 56, 101, 103, 104, Sch 2, Pts I, II, is repealed: see the Friendly Societies Act 1974, s 116(2), (4), Sch 10, paras 7–13, Sch 11.

684. Proposed reform. In January 1990 the Treasury issued a Green Paper[1] proposing changes in the powers available to friendly societies to provide a new basis for growth in the modern world and to allow them to compete on an equal footing with other organisations in the financial services sector. The suggestions have been based on ideas put forward in response to lobbying from the friendly society movement and include giving power to manage unit trusts and personal equity plans, to offer all forms of long-term insurance, and to arrange loans, both secured and unsecured. The price of these new powers would be tighter regulation to secure, so far as is possible, the protection of members' investments and the appointment of the now obligatory ombudsman.

Friendly societies seeking to take advantage of the new powers would need to incorporate as industrial and provident societies, and the Green Paper envisages a new friendly society category of industrial and provident society with updated powers replacing those currently contained in the Friendly Societies Act 1974[2].

To comply with the European Economic Community directives controlling the life insurance industry the newly incorporated societies will have to offer the new services through a subsidiary which would be incorporated under the companies legislation[3].

1 *Friendly Societies: A New Framework* (Cm 919) (1990). The period for comment expired in March 1990. It is understood that since the proposals are largely in line with suggestions from the friendly society movement itself, have all party support and are uncontroversial, their implementation is dependent on the government's legislative timetable. The Treasury is in favour of the earliest practical date for the introduction of the legislation.

2 Ie under the Friendly Societies Act 1974 (c 46), s 7(1), Sch 1: see para 686 below.

(2) REGISTRATION

(a) Classes of Friendly Societies

685. Registrable societies. The Friendly Societies Act 1974 sets out the permitted classes of friendly society and the conditions on which they may apply for registration. The classes are:
(1) friendly societies[1];
(2) cattle insurance societies[2];
(3) benevolent societies[3];
(4) working men's clubs[3];
(5) old people's home societies[3]; and
(6) specially authorised societies[3].

1 See the Friendly Societies Act 1974 (c 46), s 7(1)(a), and paras 686 ff below.
2 See ibid, s 7(1)(b), and para 693 below.
3 See ibid, s 7(1)(c)–(f), and para 694 below.

(b) Friendly Societies

686. Meaning of 'friendly societies'. Friendly societies in the strict sense are defined in the Friendly Societies Act 1974, and can be summarised as societies formed to provide by voluntary subscription from the members (with or without additional donations) for any of the following purposes[1]:
(1) the relief or maintenance of the members and specified relations[2] during physical or mental illness, at any age over fifty, or in widowhood, or when unemployed, in distressed circumstances which includes shipwreck or loss or damage to boats or nets[3]; or
(2) insuring money to be paid on the birth of a member's child, or on the death of a member or of a member's husband or wife, parents or grandparents resident in the United Kingdom[4] at the time of the proposal, or during Jewish confined mourning[5]; or
(3) the endowment of members or their nominees at any age or on marriage[6]; or
(4) endowment life assurance of the member or his or her spouse[7]; or
(5) fire insurance (limited to £15) of the tools of trade of a member[8]; or
(6) guaranteeing the performance of their duties by officers or employees of the society or its branches[9].
A friendly society may also issue policies which insure the reasonable funeral expenses of the husband, wife or widow, or child[10] of the member, or which are endowment policies (which may include payment in the event of death before the set term) on the life of the member's parent, grandparent, child[10], grandchild[10], brother or sister where the person insured is resident outside the United Kingdom[11].

1 Friendly Societies Act 1974 (c 46), s 7(1)(a).
2 Ie husbands, wives, children, including adopted and step children, fathers, mothers, brothers, sisters, nephews, nieces, or wards being orphans, or the orphan children, including stepchildren, of members during minority or at any later time whilst they are receiving full-time education: ibid, s 7(1)(a), Sch 1, para (1).
3 Ibid, Sch 1, para (1), (3).

4 Ie the United Kingdom includes the Isle of Man. As to the exemption in respect of certain insurances where a person is resident outside the United Kingdom and the Isle of Man, see ibid, s 74, Sch 6.

5 Ibid, Sch 1, para (2)(a)–(e). There is a limit of £30 (excluding bonus other than guaranteed bonus and repayment of premium, or under a free paid-up policy in force, applied for or claimed before 30 June 1948, or any increase due to an approved scheme under the Decimal Currency Act 1969 (c 19)) on any sum insured on the life of a parent or grandparent under all 'relevant insurance', ie by a registered friendly society: see the Friendly Societies Act 1974, s 72. Any assignation of the rights conferred by such a policy is void unless made for the purpose of keeping the policy in being or restoring it; and on bankruptcy no rights under it pass to the trustee: s 73(2).

6 Ibid, Sch 1, para (4).

7 Ibid, Sch 1, para (5).

8 Ibid, Sch 1, para (6).

9 Ibid, Sch 1, para (7).

10 Limits are placed on the sums insurable in respect of a child's death varying with its age: (1) under 3, £6; (2) under 6, £10; (3) under 10, £15: ibid, s 74, Sch 6, para 3. As to the special rules in respect of a death certificate of a child, see Sch 6, paras 5–7. As to payment on death, see para 723 above.

11 See ibid, s 74, Sch 6. The residence is that applying when the proposal is made.

687. Restrictions on insurance. Friendly societies may not be registered if the insurance benefits they offer exceed specified limits[1]. These restrictions are imposed because qualifying friendly societies have income and corporation tax exemptions which could result in the accumulation of large amounts of tax-free income for the members of societies which, in the Treasury's view, would be a misuse of the friendly society format. In 1984 it was also discovered that, due to misinterpretation of these provisions, particular types of policy had been authorised which were in fact unlawful, and retrospective validating measures, covering policies issued between 3 May 1966 and 1 June 1984, were enacted in the Friendly Societies Act 1984, which also made prospective amendments. The provisions restricting registration, imposing maximum limits on benefits and the qualifications for tax exemption[2] are, as might be expected, interrelated.

Relevant restrictions in some form have been in force since 1966 and have been recast by successive Finance Acts, most recently in 1987, and are now to be found in the latest version of section 7 of the Friendly Societies Act 1974 and the consolidating provisions of the Income and Corporation Taxes Act 1988[3].

1 Ie under the Friendly Societies Act 1974 (c 46), s 7(3), (3A), (5) (which were substituted and added by the Finance (No 2) Act 1975 (c 45), s 52(4), Sch 9, paras 1–3), repealed, with a saving, in respect of insurance policies made on or after 19 March 1985 and insurance policies made before that date which are varied on or after that date: see the Finance Act 1985 (c 54), ss 41(4), 98(6), Sch 27, Pt V, Note 5. Section 41(4) was repealed by the Income and Corporation Taxes Act 1988 (c 1), s 844(4), Sch 31, and re-enacted in s 844(1), Sch 29, para 13. The Friendly Societies Act 1974, s 7(5), was further amended by the Income and Corporation Taxes Act 1988, Sch 29, para 32.

2 As to tax-exempt business, see para 689 below.

3 Ie the Income and Corporation Taxes Act 1988, Pt XII, Ch II (ss 459–467), and Sch 15. See further paras 688–690 below.

688. Restrictions on registration. A friendly society cannot be registered if it does not comply with the following conditions:

(1) it must not issue tax-exempt life or endowment policies giving a benefit of more than £104 a year as an annuity, or £500 as a gross sum[1] (if the society's rules do not allow it to carry on life or endowment business[2] assuring gross sums in excess of £2,000, or to grant annuities exceeding £416 a year, then these figures are to be increased to £208 and £1,000 respectively[3]);

(2) it must not issue policies whose gross value or yearly annuity exceed prescribed[4] limits[5].

Heads (1) and (2) do not apply to policies issued on or after 19 March 1985 or which were issued before that date and varied on or after it[6].

1 Friendly Societies Act 1974 (c 46), s 7(3)(a) (repealed with saving: see para 687, note 1, above).
2 'Life or endowment business' is any business within the Friendly Societies Act 1974, Sch 1, paras (1), (2), (4), (5) (see para 686 above), any pension business and any other life assurance business, but excluding sickness insurance unless at least 60 per cent of the premium is for the sickness insurance and no bonus can be declared on the life assurance element: see the Income and Corporation Taxes Act 1988 (c 1), s 466(1).
3 Friendly Societies Act 1974, s 7(3A) (as repealed with saving (see note 1 above) and amended by the Finance Act 1980 (c 48), s 57(2)(a)).
4 Ie prescribed under the Income and Corporation Taxes Act 1988, s 464 (amended by the Finance Act 1990 (c 29), s 49(3), (4)) (formerly the Friendly Societies Act 1974, s 64 (repealed)).
5 Ibid, s 7(3)(b) (as repealed with saving: see note 1 above).
6 Ibid, s 7(3)(a), (b) (amended by the Income and Corporation Taxes Act 1988, s 844, Sch 29, para 13). This is not a relaxation but caters for new tax rules allowing tax exemption if under the set limits and disallowing it only on the policy which exceeds that limit.

689. Tax-exempt business. Certain friendly societies may claim exemption from income and corporation tax (including capital gains) on their profits on life or endowment business[1]. All societies other than those societies registered after 31 December 1957 which entered into any single premium life or endowment policy during the three months ending 3 May 1966 are eligible[2]. The society's rules must prohibit the issuing of any life or endowment policies assuring gross sums exceeding £2,000 or to grant annuities exceeding £416 a year[3]. Pension business is excluded[4]. Also excluded is so much of the profits arising from life or endowment business as is attributable to contracts for the assurance of gross sums made on or after 20 March 1991 and expressed at the outset not to be made in the course of tax-exempt life or endowment business[5].

The exemption is restricted to profits on qualifying life or endowment policies meeting specified limits[6]. These are:
(1) contracts made on or after the day on which the Finance Act 1991 was passed: the premium for the gross sum assured must not exceed £200 in any twelve months, or for an annual annuity exceed £156[7];
(2) contracts made after 31 August 1990 but before the day on which the Finance Act 1991 was passed: the premium for the gross sum assured must not exceed £150 in any twelve months, or for an annual annuity exceed £156[8];
(3) contracts made after 31 August 1987 but before 1 September 1990: the premium for the gross sum assured must not exceed £100 in any twelve month period or for an annual annuity exceed £156[9];
(4) contracts after 13 March 1984 but before 1 September 1987: the gross sum assured must not exceed £750 or if an annuity £156 annually[10];
(5) contracts made before 14 March 1984: the gross sum assured must not exceed £500 or if an annuity £104 annually[11].
There is a relaxation given to friendly societies whose rules prohibit the issuing of any life or endowment policies assuring gross sums exceeding £2,000 or to grant annuities exceeding £416 a year for policies issued before 14 March 1984, in which case £2,000 and £416 are substituted for £500 and £104[12].

The returns on a friendly society's policies must not only be within these limits but the terms of the policy itself must be those of a qualifying policy[13]. Friendly society policies issued in the course of tax-exempt life or endowment business before 19 March 1985 are qualifying policies provided they have not been varied after that date[14]. Policies issued on or after 19 March 1985 must meet the following conditions:
(a) in the case of a policy for the assurance of a gross sum or annuity, it must comply with the prescribed terms[15]; and
(b) in the case of a policy for the assurance of a gross sum, it must fulfil prescribed terms[16]; and

(c) in the case of a policy issued by a new society, it must be restricted to members over the age of eighteen[17].

1 The tax treatment in this paragraph is restricted to giving sufficient information to explain the relationship between the restrictions on registration and maximum benefits which were imposed principally as anti-avoidance measures. For a commentary, see *Simon's Taxes* vol D.

2 Income and Corporation Taxes Act 1988 (c 1), s 460(1), (2)(a).

3 Ibid, s 460(5). There is provision for the maintenance of the pre-alteration position for existing policies when a society changes its rules or registration by amalgamation or conversion: s 460(8)–(10), (10A), (11), (12) (s 460(10A) added by the Finance Act 1990 (c 29), s 48, Sch 9, paras 6, 7, in relation to transfers of business taking place after 31 December 1989).

4 Income and Corporation Taxes Act 1988, s 460(2)(b).

5 Ibid, s 460(2)(ca) (added by the Finance Act 1991 (c 31), s 50, Sch 9, para 1).

6 Income and Corporation Taxes Act 1988, s 460(2)(c). For the purposes of s 460(2)(c), in respect of contracts for the assurance of gross sums under tax exempt life or endowment business made after 31 August 1987 and before the day on which the Finance Act 1991 was passed, where the amount payable by way of premium under a contract is increased by virtue of a variation made in the period beginning with the day on which the 1991 Act was passed and ending with 31 July 1992, the contract is to be treated as made at the time of the variation: Income and Corporation Taxes Act 1988, s 460(4A), (4B) (as so added). The Finance Act 1991 was passed on 25 July 1991.

7 Income and Corporation Taxes Act 1988, s 460(2)(c)(ai) (as so added). As to the calculation of the premiums payable in a twelve-month period for the purposes of s 460(2)(c)(ai), (i), (ia), see s 460(3) (amended by the Finance Act 1990, s 49, and the Finance Act 1991, Sch 9, para 1).

8 Income and Corporation Taxes Act 1988, s 460(2)(c)(i) (as so amended). See also note 7 above.

9 Ibid, s 460(2)(c)(ia) (added by the Finance Act 1990, s 49, and amended by the Finance Act 1991, Sch 9, para 1). See also note 7 above.

10 Income and Corporation Taxes Act 1988, s 460(2)(c)(ii). Any bonus is to be disregarded in calculating the gross sums assured for the purposes of s 460(2)(c)(ii), (iii): s 460(4).

11 Ibid, s 460(2)(c)(iii). See also note 10 above.

12 See ibid, s 460(2)(c)(iii), (6).

13 As to the conditions for the tax exemption of life and endowment assurance business, see ibid, s 267, Sch 15, para 3.

14 Ibid, Sch 15, para 3(1).

15 Ibid, Sch 15, para 3(1)(a). The conditions can be summarised as follows: (1) the policy cannot be antedated by more than three months; (2) its term must be at least ten years; (3) premiums are to be payable by equal instalments at not more than yearly intervals; (4) surrender before the passing of the shorter of three-quarters of the term or ten years can only secure the return of the premiums paid: Sch 15, para 3(2).

16 Ibid, Sch 15, para 3(1)(b). For the conditions, see Sch 15, para 3(5)–(11) (amended by the Finance Act 1990, s 49(5)), which contain details of conditions on payments, capital sums term, age of insured etc with which the policy must comply.

17 Income and Corporation Taxes Act 1988, Sch 15, para 3(1)(c). 'New society' means a friendly society registered after, or in the three months before, 3 May 1966 which did not carry on any life or endowment business before that date: s 466(2). The Inland Revenue is authorised, with appropriate safeguards, to classify an old society (ie any society that is not a new one) as a new society if it begins to carry on any tax-exempt life or endowment business after 19 March 1985, or carries on any such existing business on an enlarged scale or of a new character after that date: see s 465. The restriction on policies sold to children is removed in respect of policies issued in pursuance of contracts made on or after the day the Finance Act 1991 is passed (see note 6 above): Income and Corporation Taxes Act 1988, Sch 15, para 3(1)(c) (repealed by the Finance Act 1991, Sch 9, para 4).

690. Maximum benefits. No member of a friendly society is entitled to claim benefits in excess of the limits originally imposed by the Friendly Societies Act 1974[1] and now, in their latest form, by the Income and Corporation Taxes Act 1988[2]. The limits are imposed on the aggregate of all friendly society policies held by the member[3]. As an enforcement measure any friendly society may require a member to make a statutory declaration of compliance with both the benefit and premium limits[4].

Policies insuring gross sums under tax-exempt life or endowment business are controlled as follows. A member cannot have outstanding policies issued after 31 August 1987 in respect of:

(1) contracts under which the total premiums payable in any period of twelve months exceed £200;

(2) contracts made before the day on which the Finance Act 1991 was passed and under which the total premiums payable in any period of twelve months exceed £150; or

(3) contracts made before 1 September 1990 under which the total premiums payable in any period of twelve months exceed £100[5].

For policies all of which were issued before that date the limit is imposed by restricting the maximum sum insured. For policies issued before 1 September 1987 the limit is a gross sum of £750[6]. For policies all of which were issued before 14 March 1984 the limit is a gross sum of £2,000[7].

Tax-exempt annuities have the following annual limits. A member cannot have such contracts in excess of £156 where the policies were all issued after 14 March 1984[8]. If the policies were all issued before that date the limit is £416[9].

Where a member has several contracts in force and one was made on or before 13 March 1984 and one after that date and has also an annuity contract with a new society entered into before 1 June 1984, then the annuity contract is to be treated in the calculation of the limits as both an annuity and a gross sum insurance[10].

1 Ie under the Friendly Societies Act 1974 (c 46), s 64 (repealed).

2 Ie under the Income and Corporation Taxes Act 1988 (c 1), s 464.

3 Ibid, s 464(1).

4 Ibid, s 464(7).

5 Ibid, s 464(2), (3) (amended by the Finance Act 1990 (c 29), s 49, and the Finance Act 1991 (c 31), s 50, Sch 9, para 3). The Finance Act 1991 was passed on 25 July 1991. In calculating the limits for the purposes of the Income and Corporation Taxes Act 1988, s 464(3), for new societies only, an annuity contract entered into before 1 June 1984 is to be dealt with as if it were a gross sum contract and included in the calculation: s 464(4) (amended by the Finance Act 1990, s 49). This provision is derived from the Friendly Societies Act 1974, s 64(1B) (added by the Finance Act 1987 (c 16), s 30(4)) (repealed) and appears to be unrelated to the Income and Corporation Taxes Act 1988, s 464(6): see note 10 below.

In calculating the limits in s 464 the following are disregarded: (1) 10 per cent of any premium payable more frequently than annually (s 464(5)(d)(i)); (2) the proportion, if any, due for exceptional risk of death (s 464(5)(d)(iii)); (3) if the society is not a new society (defined in para 689, note 15, above) and the contract was made before 1 September 1987, £10 of the premium (s 464(5)(d)(ii)); (4) all bonuses deriving from increase in value of investments (s 464(5)(a)); and (5) approved annuities under s 620(9), or any annuity or insurances providing an occupational pension scheme (see s 464(5)(b)). For the meaning of 'occupational pension scheme', see the Social Security Act 1973 (c 38), s 51(3)(a), and SOCIAL SECURITY. There is an exclusion for increases in benefit due to the adoption of decimal currency: see the Income and Corporation Taxes Act 1988, s 464(5)(c), and the Decimal Currency Act 1969 (c 19), s 6.

For the purposes of the Income and Corporation Taxes Act 1988, s 464(3), in respect of contracts for the assurance of gross sums under tax exempt life or endowment business made after 31 August 1987 and before the day on which the Finance Act 1991 was passed, where the amount payable by way of premium under a contract is increased by virtue of a variation made in the period beginning with the day on which the 1991 Act was passed and ending with 31 July 1992, the contract is to be treated as made at the time of the variation: Income and Corporation Taxes Act 1988, s 464(4A), (4B) (added by the Finance Act 1991, Sch 9, para 3).

6 Income and Corporation Taxes Act 1988, s 464(1)(a). As to the calculation of the limits, see s 464(5), and note 5 above.

7 Ibid, s 464(1). As to the calculation of the limits, see s 464(5), and note 5 above.

8 Ibid, s 464(1)(b). As to the calculation of the limits, see s 464(5), and note 5 above.

9 Ibid, s 464(1). As to the calculation of the limits, see s 464(5), and note 5 above.

10 Ibid, s 464(6). The annuity contract is considered as not only being an annuity for its contractual annual sum but also for the insurance of a gross sum equivalent to 75 per cent of the total premiums payable under the contract if it were to run for the full term, or if the member were to die at seventy-five: s 464(6). The effect is therefore that the annuity and its special gross sum equivalent not only applies to the limit of £156 of annual annuity under s 464(1)(b) but also to the gross sum insurance of £750 under s 464(1)(a).

691. The Financial Services Act 1986. The Financial Services Act 1986[1] applies to friendly societies but exempts them from the registration requirements imposed on other sellers of insurance and insurance-related products. A registered friendly society, but not a branch, is an 'authorised person', but only in respect of business permitted[2] under the Friendly Societies Act 1974[3]. A friendly society, of course, cannot be registered with objects other than those permitted by the 1974 Act. Friendly societies are subject to the regulations set out in the 1986 Act[4]; these regulations are principally concerned with the powers of the registrar, the control of the Department of Trade and Industry, the position of the Securities and Investment Board and any recognised self-regulating organisation for friendly societies and not with the manner in which friendly societies conduct their business. Certain points which are worth noting are set out below.

Friendly societies apparently are exempted from the conduct of business rules applicable to other authorised persons, but the chief registrar is given power with the consent of the Secretary of State to prescribe conduct of business rules for friendly societies which are not members of a recognised self-regulating organisation for friendly societies[5]. Friendly societies which are members of a recognised self-regulating organisation for friendly societies will be subject to its conduct of business rules.

The registrar is given the necessary powers of investigation and enforcement to the exclusion of the Department of Trade and Industry[6]. The Department of Trade and Industry is required either itself or through the registrar to eliminate non-competitive restrictive practices by friendly societies[7].

A self-regulating organisation for friendly societies may apply to the registrar to be recognised as a self-regulating organisation for friendly societies[8]. The consent of the Secretary of State is required to any recognition given[8]. The registrar is given all necessary powers of control over the organisation[8].

The registrar has been given power to transfer all or any of his supervisory functions to a body corporate set up for that purpose[9]. The consent of the Secretary of State is required[10]. The registrar has used these powers. The first such order made must designate the Securities and Investments Board as the body to which the functions are to be transferred[11].

1 As the Financial Services Act 1986 (c 60) is concerned with the regulation of the financial services industry and not the formation and regulation of friendly societies it is only referred to in passing and points of interest noted.
2 Ie under the Friendly Societies Act 1974 (c 46), Sch 1: see para 686 above.
3 Financial Services Act 1986, s 23(1).
4 Ie under ibid, s 140, Sch 11.
5 Ibid, Sch 11, para 14. Such regulations will prescribe the same standards and protections as would be imposed under s 48 (which does not apply to friendly societies). As the registrar has nominated the Securities and Investments Board to exercise his powers he has not made any such rules. A friendly society which is not a member of a self-regulatory organisation (and so subject to its rules) will be subject to the conduct of business rules made by the board.
6 Ibid, Sch 11, para 23(1).
7 Ibid, Sch 11, para 10.
8 See ibid, Sch 11, Pt II (paras 2–12).
9 See ibid, Sch 11, Pt IV (paras 28–37).
10 Ibid, s 28(1).
11 Ibid, s 28(2). On 19 May 1987 the registrar's functions were transferred to the Securities and Investments Board except those under Sch 11, paras 4(2), 17: Financial Services (Transfer of Functions Relating to Friendly Societies) Order 1987, SI 1987/925. See also the Financial Services Act 1986 (Transfer of Functions Relating to Friendly Societies) (Transitional Provisions) Order 1987, SI 1987/2069.

692. Prohibition on insurance relating to the death of a child under ten. No society may issue a policy making any sum payable on the death of a child under ten, other than a return of premiums paid[1]. This does not apply if the child is ordinarily resident outside the United Kingdom and the Isle of Man[2] nor if the payment is to be made to a person with an insurable interest in the child's life[3].

1 Friendly Societies Act 1974 (c 46), s 71(1).
2 Ibid, s 71(4). Non-resident children are subject to restrictions in respect of the sums insurable: see Sch 6, para 3, and para 686, note 10, below.
3 Ibid, s 71(2). In *Carmichael v Carmichael's Executrix* 1919 SC 636, 1919 2 SLT 89 (revsd 1920 SC (HL) 195, 1920 2 SLT 285) it was suggested that parents probably have an insurable interest in their children's lives: see INSURANCE.

(c) Other Societies

693. Cattle insurance societies. 'Cattle insurance societies' provide insurance to any amount against loss of cattle, sheep, lambs, swine, horses and other animals by death from disease or otherwise[1]. Two points can be made, first that 'other animals' is to be construed *ejusdem generis*, and only other farm(ed) animals of a similar quality to those already listed can be included. Donkeys and mules as well as goats would seem to be safely included, but deer on a venison farm are more contentious. Secondly, the only risk insured against is death, as 'otherwise' is an alternative to disease.

1 Friendly Societies Act 1974 (c 46), s 7(1)(b).

694. Other societies. Benevolent societies are established for any benevolent or charitable purpose[1]. Benevolence implies that the society has been formed to provide benefits for people other than the members or members' relatives, and the form of the benevolence should be specified since a general benevolent purpose is unacceptable[2].

Working men's clubs are formed for social intercourse, mutual helpfulness, mental and moral improvement and rational recreation[3], and any one of these purposes specified in the rules will be sufficient provided also that it is intended to benefit working men.

Old people's home societies are formed to provide homes for the members and others at any age after fifty[4].

'Specially authorised societies' are societies whose objects are any purpose which the Treasury may authorise as a purpose to which the provisions of the Friendly Societies Act 1974, or such of them as are specified in the authority, ought to be extended[5]. Five special authorities are currently in force covering seventeen different purposes[6] which also exempt the society from any need to register under the companies legislation[7].

1 Friendly Societies Act 1974 (c 46), s 7(1)(c). See also *The Chief Registrar's Report* 1879, p 5.
2 However, this has never been judicially decided: see 19 *Halsbury's Laws of England* (4th edn) para 122, note 2.
3 Friendly Societies Act 1974, s 7(1)(d).
4 Ibid, s 7(1)(e).
5 Ibid, s 7(1)(f).
6 Special authorities are not statutory instruments. Full details can be obtained from the registrar. The list is also contained in 19 *Halsbury's Laws of England* (4th edn) para 122, note 5. In summary the special authorities permit the following additional activities: (1) provision of rest centres (Special Authority No 1, 10 June 1976); (2) promotion of agriculture etc, specially authorised loan societies registered before 15 August 1917, provision of funds for the repair or decoration of member-owned premises, miners' welfare and recreational organisations (Special Authority No 2, 10 June 1976); (3) Jewish burial societies, thrift and savings societies registered before 1

January 1968 (Special Authority No 3, 10 June 1976); (4) promotion of sport or science or literature or art or music or education or cookery, fidelity bonding for friendly societies officers, assisting unemployed members if the society was registered before 21 December 1955 (only relevant if the society in question also has other non-friendly society objects) (Special Authority No 4, 10 June 1976); (5) promotion and protection of friendly societies, providing for the investment of the funds of societies registered before 14 November 1898 (Special Authority No 5, 10 June 1976).

7 *Peat v Fowler* (1886) 55 LJQB 271, DC.

(d) Registration Procedure

695. Registration of societies. In order to register a society whose registered office will be in Scotland[1] the following documents must be sent to the Assistant Registrar for Scotland in Edinburgh[2]: the application for registration, signed by seven members and the secretary of the society, two printed copies of the rules, and a list of names of the secretary and every trustee or other officer who is to be authorised to sue on behalf of the society[3]. If the society intends to insure a certain[4] annuity, the contribution tables, certified by a qualified actuary, must accompany the application[5]. The prescribed fee must also be paid[6].

If the registrar is satisfied that the applicant society has complied with the Friendly Societies Act 1974 he will issue the acknowledgment of registration specifying the classification of the society, and giving conclusive evidence of the society's registration[7]. If the society is specially authorised and only certain of the provisions of the Act are to apply, those provisions will be set out in the acknowledgment[8]. The registration of a society does not incorporate it.

If registration is refused, appeal lies from the Assistant Registrar for Scotland to the chief registrar, and from his refusal to grant the appeal to the Court of Session[9]. If the appeal is allowed, an acknowledgment of registration is issued in the normal way[10].

1 As to the Assistant Registrar for Scotland, see para 604 above.
2 If the office of the friendly society is in the central registration area, the application has to be made to the Central Office in London: see para 604 above.
3 Friendly Societies Act 1974 (c 46), s 8(1), (2). For the forms, see the Friendly Societies Regulations 1975, SI 1975/205, reg 2, Sch 1, Form A (application), Forms B, C (acknowledgment of registration).
4 'Certain' implies that the annuity is both certain — as opposed to being dependent on discretionary bonuses, final salary or other variable — in amount and in its nature: see F B Fuller *The Law Relating to Friendly Societies and Industrial and Provident Societies* (4th edn, 1926) p 58.
5 Friendly Societies Act 1974, s 9(2). 'Qualified actuary' means an actuary having such qualifications as the chief registrar may prescribe: s 9(3). See also the Friendly Societies (Qualifications of Actuaries) Regulations 1968, SI 1968/1481, which require fellowship of the Institute of Actuaries or of the Faculty of Actuaries. Additionally the chief registrar may approve actuarially experienced persons on the application of a registered society: reg 2.
6 See the Friendly Societies Regulations 1975, reg 16, Sch 2 (substituted by SI 1991/519).
7 Friendly Societies Act 1974, s 15. For the form, see the Friendly Societies Regulations 1975, Sch 1, Form B. Conclusive relates only to the fact and date of registration of particular rules, not of legality of the rules (*Davie v Colinton Friendly Society* (1870) 9 M 96), nor that the society has been properly registered as a society within the Friendly Societies Act 1974 (*R v Davis* (1866) WN 24).
8 Friendly Societies Regulations 1975, Sch 1, Form C.
9 Friendly Societies Act 1974, s 16(1)(b).
10 Ibid, s 16(2).

696. Recording rules. If a Scottish registered society carries on business in the Central Area[1], or a society registered in that area carries on business in Scotland, it is not entitled to the privileges of registration in that area unless the rules have been recorded by the registrar of the Central Area or, as the case may be, the Assistant Registrar for Scotland[2]. Any amendment of the rules must be similarly recorded.

1 As to the registration areas, see paras 604, 605, above.
2 See the Friendly Societies Act 1974 (c 46), s 10. For the form, see the Friendly Societies Regulations 1975, SI 1975/205, regs 2, 4, Sch 1, Form D.

697. Societies with branches. 'Branch' means any number of the members of a society, under the control of a central body, having a separate fund administered by themselves or by a committee or officers appointed by themselves, and bound to contribute to a fund under the control of a central body[1]. If a society is to have such branches, each branch must be separately registered and the branches are treated in many cases as separate societies. Special provisions apply to registration and secession etc.

If the central society and its branches are to be registered at the same time, the usual registration documents are accompanied by a list of all the branches and the registered office of each, a list of all branch trustees and officers (if any) authorised to sue on behalf of the branch in question, and two copies of the branch rules[2]. The registrar will additionally issue a separate acknowledgment of registration for each branch[3].

If a new branch is to be registered, the secretary of the society must send the required branch particulars to the registrar along with an application form signed by three members and the secretary of the branch and the secretary of the society, and an acknowledgment of registration is issued in the usual way[4].

A society having a fund under the control of a central body to which every branch is bound to contribute may be registered as a single society, and if such a society has branches in the other registration area the rules recording requirement[5] apply[6].

The rules of a society registered with branches must include provisions for the secession of branches[7], and it is usual to include an expulsion provision. The registrar may not register a branch as a new separate society unless a certificate is produced confirming the secession or expulsion of the branch signed by the chief secretary or principal officer of the central society[8]. A branch may not use the name of the central society, or a name implying branch status, after secession or expulsion[9].

The provisions of the Friendly Societies Act 1974 apply to both societies and branches, and so separate mention of both bodies is made only where there is some difference or speciality to be noted.

1 Friendly Societies Act 1974 (c 46), s 111(1). The relationship between branch and the central society is one of federation or affiliation. It originated in the structure adopted by the affiliated Orders prior to the Friendly Societies Act 1875 (c 60) (repealed), when it was unlawful to have branches and separate independent registered societies were affiliated under a central society to create for example the Independent Order of Oddfellows Manchester Unity.
2 Friendly Societies Act 1974, s 11(1). For the form, see the Friendly Societies Regulations 1975, SI 1975/205, reg 2, Sch 1, Form E. Two copies of the rules suffice where all branches have the same rules, but if branch rules differ then two copies of each set of rules is required. As to the registration of the central society, see para 695 above.
3 As to acknowledgment, see para 695 above. For the form, see the Friendly Societies Regulations 1975, Sch 1, Form F.
4 See the Friendly Societies Act 1974, s 12. For the forms, see the Friendly Societies Regulations 1975, Sch 1, Form E (application), Form F (acknowledgment).
5 Ie under the Friendly Societies Act 1974, s 10: see para 696 above.
6 Ibid, s 11(2). It is suggested that s 11(2) regularises the practice of registering a society with branches as a single society first, and then registering the branches as 'new branches' under s 12: *Pratt's Friendly Societies and Industrial and Provident Societies* (15th edn, 1931, ed M Mackinnon) p 27. This procedure is also recommended in F B Fuller *The Law Relating to Friendly Societies and*

Industrial and Provident Societies (4th edn, 1926) p 59. It is possible that this permits a centrally/
locally organised society to elect to register if within the definition of the Friendly Societies Act
1974, s 11(2) either as a society with branches or as a single society with local area offices. In the
latter case the secession/expulsion provisions would not be available.
7 See ibid, s 7(2), Sch 2, para 5.
8 Ibid, s 13. The certificate (see the Friendly Societies Regulations 1975, Sch 1, Form G), must be
given if the rules are complied with: _Green v Hendry_ (1890) Times, 19 May, CA (affg (1890) 25 L
Jo 93); _Re Sheffield Order of Druids Society_ (1892) 8 TLR 389. See also _Scholfield v Vause_ (1886) 36
WR 170n, CA, and _Bolton District National Independent Order of Oddfellows v National Independent
Order of Oddfellows_ (1895) FS Cases 55. There is a right of appeal to the Court of Session against
refusal to issue the certificate: see para 695 above. If the branch is a Scottish branch of an English
registered central society the Court of Session still is the appropriate forum: _Sons of Temperance
Friendly Society_ 1926 SC 418, 1926 SLT 273.
9 Friendly Societies Act 1974, s 14, which extends also to any identifying branch number.

(3) RULES

698. Introduction. The rules of a friendly society form its constitution, and
although there are matters which must be provided for in the rules of societies,
there is no equivalent to the recommended Tables available to registered companies[1]. There are model rules prepared by the registrar. These are, however, so
out of date as to be quite unsuitable for use other than as drafting guides — the
registrar will not issue them[2].

The acknowledgment of registration also conclusively confirms the registration of the rules of the society or branch[3].

The rules must provide for prescribed matters[4]. There are certain requirements applicable only to friendly societies and cattle insurance societies[5].

1 See the Companies Act 1985 (c 6), s 8, and COMPANIES.
2 The model rules are set out in F B Fuller _The Law Relating to Friendly Societies and Industrial and
Provident Societies_ (4th edn, 1926) and _Pratt's Friendly Societies and Industrial and Provident Societies_
(15th edn, 1931, ed M Mackinnon).
3 Friendly Societies Act 1974 (c 46), s 17.
4 Ie under ibid, s 7(2)(a), Sch 2, Pt I (paras 1–11): see para 699 below.
5 Ie under ibid, Sch 2, Pt II (paras 12–15): see para 700 below.

699. Rules applicable to all societies. The rules which apply to all societies
are as follows:
(1) _The name of the society_[1]: A society must not be registered with a name which
    is the same as that of an existing society or so similar to such a name as to
    cause confusion[2]. Similarity is not a disqualification for branch names
    which normally reflect that of the central society by the inclusion of
    common words[3]. The registrar may reject names which are likely to
    confuse the public as to its nature or identity, or are undesirable. If the
    society is a 'collecting society', those words must be the last words of its
    name[4]. A society may apply to the registrar for approval of a change of
    name, and some justification for the application should be given to secure
    the necessary written consent of the registrar[5]. The change is made by an
    amendment of rules[6]. The registration of a change of name does not affect
    any right or obligation of the society or its members nor any legal proceed-
    ings[7].
(2) _The address of the registered office_[8]: The registered office of a Scottish society
    must be in Scotland, and it serves as the official address of the society at
    which specified copy documents must be displayed or kept[9]. The rules will
    themselves provide the procedure for its change and it must be registered as
    an amendment of rules[10].

(3) *The objects of the society*, and the purposes for which the funds are applicable[11]. The objects and purposes must be those, and only those, permitted to the relevant class of society. A society may not use its funds other than for the purposes set out in its objects[12].

(4) *The terms of admission of members*[13]: These will cover any qualifications, age limits[14], religious or occupational conditions required of members and will vary with the class of society.

(5) *The benefit conditions*, that is, the conditions under which any member may become entitled to any benefit assured by the society[15]. These include the contributions or premiums and their payment, the time or event when it may be claimed, including time limits and the procedure for claims. If the society or branch intends to carry on long-term business then the required tables must be certified by a qualified actuary[16]. Tables relating to benefits under approved group assurance business need not be included[17], nor need superseded tables relating to a class of policies or obligations when no new policies are to be issued[18].

(6) *Penalties*: The fines and forfeitures to be imposed on any member and the consequences of non-payment of any subscription or fine[19].

(7) *Meetings*: The method of holding meetings, voting rights, and the manner of making, altering, and rescinding the rules[20]. There are few statutory provisions relating to meetings. Collecting societies must hold at least one meeting annually[21], otherwise there is no statutory requirement for any formal annual meeting. Meetings may be held by delegates appointed by the members[22]. A special resolution[23] is required for the following actions: amalgamations of societies, transfers of engagements to societies or companies, and conversion into a company[24]. That apart, the registrar will require the rules to provide for the holding of sufficient meetings to ensure the effective running of the society in an open and democratic manner. Thus it would be usual to provide for meetings as frequently as each week for payment of subscriptions and premiums, with business meetings quarterly, half-yearly and annually. Provision for special meetings when required is also necessary. If the rules dictate a specific place for the holding of a meeting it must be held there to be legally convened[25]. The registrar will require that the rules provide for the requisitioning of meetings by the committee and a set proportion of members, notice, quorum, voting and proxy rights if required, casting vote to the convener etc so that the meetings are properly conducted. The Friendly Societies Act 1974 provides for the registration of amendments to the rules but does not control the manner of the society's adoption of the change[26].

(8) *Committee and officers*: The appointment and removal of the management committee, treasurer and other officers (who must include the secretary) and trustees[27].

(9) *Central body*: For a society with branches, the composition and powers of the central body (which by definition must have power to operate a central fund to which the branches contribute[28]) and the conditions under which a branch may secede from the society[29].

(10) *Accounts*: The investments of funds, keeping accounts and at least an annual audit[30].

(11) *Returns*: The submission of annual returns to the registrar[31].

(12) *Inspection of books* by those interested in the society's funds[32].

(13) *Settlement of disputes*[33].

1 Friendly Societies Act 1974 (c 46), s 7(2), Sch 2, para 1.
2 Ibid, s 8(3).
3 As to seceded or expelled societies, see ibid, s 14, and para 697 above.

4 Ie if the society was registered as such after 31 December 1895, or became one after 7 June 1923: Industrial Assurance Act 1923 (c 8), s 6.

5 Friendly Societies Act 1974, s 81(1). For societies carrying business exclusively in Scotland, the consent is that of the Assistant Registrar for Scotland, otherwise that of the chief registrar.

6 Ibid, s 81(1).

7 Ibid, s 81(2).

8 Ibid, Sch 2, para 2.

9 Ibid, s 7(2)(b). Business relating to the registered office includes the display of the last annual balance sheet and auditors' report, and valuation, nominations etc delivered and kept, service on the society for legal proceedings: see paras 714 ff below.

10 Ibid, s 18(2). For the forms, see the Friendly Societies Regulations 1975, SI 1975/205, reg 2, Sch 1, Forms P, Q, R.

11 Friendly Societies Act 1974, Sch 2, para 3(1).

12 See *Oram v Hutt* [1914] 1 Ch 98, CA, which involved the *vires* of an unincorporated trade union, and so Lord Sumner's remarks recognising that a society has express and implied powers is valuable in confirming that point. They are less useful in that no indication of what might be embraced by implied powers is given.

13 Friendly Societies Act 1974, Sch 2, para 3(1). As to termination of membership, see para 705 below.

14 Minors of any age may become members: ibid, s 60(1). The age of fifty is relevant in respect of the purposes for which friendly societies may provide (see s 7(1), Sch 1, and para 686 above), and for old people's home societies (see s 7(1)(e), and para 694 above). See further para 704 below.

15 Ibid, Sch 2, para 3(1).

16 Ibid, Sch 2, para 11(2). As to the classes of long-term business, see the Insurance Companies Act 1982 (c 50), s 1, Sch 1.

17 Friendly Societies Act 1974, Sch 2, para 3(2). For the meaning of 'approved group assurance business', see s 65(2).

18 Ibid, Sch 2, para 11(1).

19 Ibid, Sch 2, para 3(1). A society is prohibited from suing for payment of subscriptions: s 61. Any fine must be reasonable otherwise it cannot be recovered: *Lovejoy v Mulkern* (1877) 46 LJ Ch 630, CA.

20 Friendly Societies Act 1974, Sch 2, para 4.

21 Industrial Assurance Act 1923, s 19(1), which requires a general meeting each year. The rules must specify either the day, hour and place of the meeting, or that notice be given either by notice to every member or twice in two county (ie local) newspapers, such notice to contain the day, hour and place of the meeting together with the objects of the meeting and if an amendment of the rules is proposed: s 19(2), (3) (amended by the Friendly and Industrial and Provident Societies Act 1968 (c 55), s 17(5)).

22 Friendly Societies Act 1974, s 111(1).

23 'Special resolution' is a resolution passed at a general meeting of which notice has been given in accordance with the society's rules detailing the intention to propose that resolution by not less than three-quarters of the members voting in person or by proxy, or where delegates vote, by three-quarters of the delegates: s 86(1).

24 See paras 726 ff below.

25 *R v Tidd Pratt* (1865) 6 B & S 672.

26 Friendly Societies Act 1974, s 18. 'Amendment of rule' includes a new rule and a resolution rescinding a rule: see s 111(1), and para 703 below.

27 Ibid, Sch 2, para 5. As to the committee of management, officers, treasurer, secretary and trustees, see paras 709 ff below.

28 Ibid, s 111(1). See also para 697 above.

29 Ibid, Sch 2, para 5.

30 Ibid, Sch 2, para 6. See also paras 714 ff below.

31 Ibid, Sch 2, para 7. See further para 718 below.

32 Ibid, Sch 2, para 8. See further para 732 below.

33 Ibid, Sch 2, para 9. See further para 725 below.

700. Rules applicable to particular classes of society. The rules which apply to particular classes of society[1] are as follows:

(1) dividing societies must provide for the settlement of all claims on the society at the time of division before the division takes place[2];

(2) cattle insurance societies must not only provide for the keeping of accounts

in the usual way[3] but also separate accounts for management expenses and the contributions used to defray them[4];

(3) friendly societies must provide for the periodic valuations[5] required by the Friendly Societies Act 1974[6];

(4) friendly societies and cattle insurance societies must allow voluntary dissolution by three-quarters in number of the members[7];

(5) a proportion of the members of a friendly society or a cattle insurance society may requisition an investigation of the affairs of their society by the registrar or for winding up[8].

1 Ie as defined in the Friendly Societies Act 1974 (c 46), s 7(1): see paras 693, 694, above.
2 Ibid, s 7(2), Sch 2, para 10. As to dividing societies, see para 682 above.
3 Ie under ibid, s 29, which details the books to be kept under Sch 2, para 6. See further paras 719–721 below.
4 Ibid, Sch 2, para 12.
5 Ie under ibid, ss 41, 42: see para 717 below.
6 Ibid, Sch 2, para 13.
7 Ibid, Sch 2, para 14.
8 Ibid, Sch 2, para 15. The registrar has the power to call a special meeting or appoint inspectors on the requisition of one-fifth of the members or 100 members in the case of a society of not less than 1,000 and not more than 10,000 members, or 500 members in the case of a society of more than 10,000 members: see s 90, and para 732 below.

701. Provisions relevant to the preparation of rules. There are provisions relevant to the preparation of rules apart from the matters to be provided for by the rules[1].

If a society intends to issue endowment policies on the life of a parent, grandparent, grandchild, brother or sister of a member or life policies on children under ten[2], it must include in its rules the free policy and surrender value[3].

A society carrying on approved group insurance business is exempt from the requirement of including benefit tables in the rules but is prevented by the terms of the approval from amending its rules so as to change the benefits secured by the policies[4].

The rules may permit the establishment of a fund for the purchase, on behalf of contributing members, of government securities. The rules may allow people to join as members only for the purpose of contributing to this fund, with no other membership rights[5].

Branch rules must be drafted to be consistent with the rules of the central society, making provision for the consequences of subsequent alterations to the rules of the central society[6]. They must provide for the operation of the branch funds, the contribution to the central society's fund and the secession provisions[7].

Collecting societies are additionally required by the Industrial Assurance Act 1923 to provide for separate accounts for industrial assurance business and other policy matters[8].

1 Ie under the Friendly Societies Act 1974 (c 46), s 7(2), Sch 2: see paras 699, 700, above.
2 As to the prohibition on insurance relating to the death of a child under ten, see para 686 above.
3 Ie under the Friendly Societies Act 1974, s 75, which permits an assured who has paid at least one year's premiums during the following year to claim a free paid-up policy or a surrender payment of 90 per cent of the free paid-up policy value. As to the rules for the calculations, see the Industrial Assurance Act 1923 (c 8), Sch 4, and the Industrial Assurance and Friendly Societies Act 1929 (c 28), Schedule.
4 See the Friendly Societies Act 1974, Sch 2, para 3(2), and the Occupational Pension Schemes (Friendly Society) Regulations 1976, SI 1976/598, reg 6. 'Group insurance business' means the business of providing for employees of a specified employer or some other approved group: see the Friendly Societies Act 1974, s 65(2).

5 See ibid, s 47, allowing the adoption of such powers, and for societies existing on 25 April 1940 the registrar may prescribe the necessary rules which may be adopted on the request of the committee, which, after registration, are as effective as if passed by the society itself.

6 The branch is bound to conform to the rules of the central society, and also to any alteration of those rules, even if the effect is to affect benefits etc otherwise available under the branch rules: *Dixon v Thompson* (1891) FS Cases 46.

7 As to branches, see para 697 above. As to the secession provisions, see the Friendly Societies Act 1974, Sch 2, para 5.

8 See the Industrial Assurance Act 1923, s 8, Sch 1.

702. Powers under the rules. A society may only exercise the following powers if its rules so permit:

(1) power to hold land either by purchase or on lease with power to sell, excamb or grant standard securities or leases over it as well as to erect or demolish buildings[1];

(2) power to establish a loan fund for its members[2] (the loan fund must be kept separate and formed from the members' contributions, which must not exceed £200 per member[3]; loans may be made on personal security or with supporting cautioners as the rule provides[4]; and the maximum loan without security will be set by the rule but no member may owe to the society more than £50 in total at any time[5]);

(3) power to accumulate at interest for the members' use any surplus of contributions after paying for the relevant insurance and to provide for withdrawal[6];

(4) power to require the officers to give security[7];

(5) power to reinsure the society's risks to the extent authorised by a qualified actuary[8];

(6) power to contribute to the funds of, or take part in the government of, another society or branch[9] (this provides for the investment of funds in other societies with different objects, in housing associations, in hospitals, charitable, benevolent, or provident institutions[9]);

(7) for specially authorised societies only, power to receive deposits and borrow money at interest from members or others to establish a loan fund for making advances to members for approved purposes[10] (the society's rules must also prohibit the distribution of its funds as dividend or bonus among its members[10]).

1 See the Friendly Societies Act 1974 (c 46), s 53. Title is taken in the name of the trustees of the society or branch, whose receipt discharges any sum paid: s 53(1)(b).

2 Ie under ibid, s 49.

3 Ibid, s 49(b).

4 Ibid, s 49(c).

5 Ibid, s 49(c). This does not apply to branches. The maximum deposit held by the society is fixed in the rules and must not exceed two-thirds of the sums owed by borrowers from the fund: s 49(d). Deposits can be subject to members' nomination: see para 722 below.

6 Ie under ibid, s 63.

7 Ie under ibid, s 27: see para 707, note 11, below.

8 Ie under ibid, s 23(1): see para 121 below.

9 Ie under ibid, ss 50–52: see paras 719, 720, below.

10 Ie under s 23: see para 721 below.

703. Amendment of rules. The only statutory provisions relating to the amendment of rules are concerned with registration and acknowledgment[1], not with the procedure, and apply equally to societies and branches. The rules themselves are required to provide for their own amendment[2], and the accepted view is that amendment covers alteration, addition, substitution or revocation of any rule (partial amendment) and the replacement of the existing rules by a new set (complete amendment). Application for an amendment of rules is made to the registrar[3] on the prescribed form[4]. If the amendment is in accordance with the Friendly Societies Act 1974 and the registrar is satisfied that it has been properly made[5], he will issue an acknowledgment of registration[6]. If he refuses to register the amendment, appeal lies to the chief registrar and from him to the Court of Session[7]. No amendment can have effect until it has been registered[8] and once registered, if the rules are recorded in the central registration area, the amendment must also be recorded there[9].

The following applies in an issue between a member and his society, or between the society and a branch, as to the effect of amendment of rules on rights which may be enjoyed under the unamended rules when no consent has been given to the change. In the usual case there will be an express power to amend the rules, and if there is no separate contract between the society and member he will be bound by any changes made to the rules, whether or not he agreed the change[10]. Alternatively, if there is an additional contract, the alteration of the rules alone without the agreement of the member will not be effective in altering the contract[11] unless the contract itself makes provision for the binding force of subsequent amendments[12].

1 Ie under the Friendly Societies Act 1974 (c 46), ss 18–20, and the Friendly Societies Regulations 1975, SI 1975/205.

2 Ie required under the Friendly Societies Act 1974, s 7(2), Sch 2, para 4: see para 699 above. Prior to the Friendly Societies Act 1875 (c 60) (repealed), societies did not require to include amendment procedures (there was a statutory one, repealed in 1875) and so there could be pre-1875 societies with no alteration procedure, in which case the consent of all members is required.

3 Collecting societies register amendments with the Industrial Assurance Commissioner (the registrar under another name).

4 Friendly Societies Act 1974, s 18(1). The Friendly Societies Regulations 1975, regs 5–7, set out the detailed requirements for registration and provide the necessary forms: see regs 2, 5, Sch 1, Forms I and J, along with a marked up copy of the rules and two copies of the amendment all signed as detailed in Form I (partial amendment), and Forms H and J along with two printed copies of the new rules headed 'all previous rules rescinded' signed as detailed in Form H (for complete amendment). For branch amendments, see regs 2, 6, Sch 1, Forms L and M (partial amendment), Sch 1, Forms K and M along with the copies of rules and amendments required for a society (complete amendment). At the registrar's option Form N may be substituted for Form M: see reg 7. All forms and advice are obtained from the registrar, with whom it is wise to clear all amendments in advance to ensure that the administrative procedures after the society adopts the amendment are a formality.

5 *R v Tidd Pratt* (1865) 6 B & S 672; *Orton v Bristow* (1916) 32 TLR 352, CA (affg (1915) 32 TLR 129). The registrar's obligation is restricted to formal compliance, objectionable rules cannot be challenged on that ground: *R v Brabrook* (1893) 69 LT 718, DC.

6 Friendly Societies Act 1974, s 19. The effect of the acknowledgment is to place beyond challenge all matters prior to the registration, but not its legality nor the power to make amendments: *Davie v Colinton Friendly Society* (1870) 9 M 96; *Laing v Reed* (1869) 5 Ch App 4.

7 Friendly Societies Act 1974, s 20(1)(b).

8 Ibid, s 18(1).

9 See ibid, s 10, and paras 605, 696, above.

10 *Smith v Galloway* [1898] 1 QB 71, DC; *Burke v Amalgamated Society of Dyers* [1906] 2 KB 583. See also the Occupational Pension Schemes (Friendly Societies) Regulations 1976, SI 1976/598, reg 6, which prohibits a society carrying on approved group insurance business from amending its rules so as to alter the terms of issued policies.

11 *Powell v Tokeley* (1906) CR Rep, Part A, 134 (Parliamentary Papers for 1907, vol 78), DC.

12 *Stooke v Mutual Provident Alliance* (1891) FS Cases 195, DC.

(4) MEMBERSHIP

704. Eligibility for membership. The conditions and procedure for joining a society and acquiring membership will be set out in the rules[1]. The minimum number of members to form a society is seven, and unless set by the rules there is no maximum[2]. The following are general points on eligibility for membership.

Minors can be permitted by the rules to become members[3], and the Friendly Societies Act 1974 allows minors over sixteen to execute all documents themselves and confers the necessary power on the parent or guardian of minor members under that age[4].

Honorary membership is permitted, although the statutory recognition of that status has disappeared[5]. The rights (and obligations if any) will be contained in the rules, and these could confer voting rights either in all general meetings or on specified occasions, such as dissolution, which may still be reflected in the rules of earlier societies.

Corporations appear to be eligible for membership; they are certainly not excluded. The particular class of friendly society may well create the necessary implication that corporate membership is impossible[6] — for example old people's home societies — and of course, the reverse is equally true — for example cattle insurance societies[7] or societies offering group insurance business which do not require human personality. It has always been accepted that honorary membership would be available to a corporation without infringing the human element of so many of the permitted purposes[8] of friendly societies[9].

1 Ie under the Friendly Societies Act 1974 (c 46), s 7(2), Sch 2, para 3(1); see para 699 above.
2 Ibid, s 8(1). There is no provision for the deregistration of a society if the number falls below seven, but the registrar, (echoing F B Fuller *The Law Relating to Friendly Societies and Industrial and Provident Societies* (4th edn, 1926) p 40 and 19 *Halsbury's Laws of England* (4th edn) para 194) suggests that three is the minimum below which a society cannot exist. This is based on the number required to sign an amendment of rules. However, since the rules themselves could set a quorum for the necessary general meeting to pass the resolution amending the rules which is greater than three, surely that is the crucial number if it is less than seven.
3 Friendly Societies Act 1974, s 60(1). However, if the rules of a society which were in force on 1 April 1975 were also in force on 1 January 1909 and permit minors to be admitted as members from the age authorised by the Friendly Societies Act 1896 (c 25) (see s 36 (repealed)), they are interpreted as allowing admission at any age without a lower limit: Friendly Societies Act 1974, s 116(2), Sch 10, para 5.
4 Ibid, s 60(2).
5 See the Friendly Societies Act 1896 (c 25), s 78 (repealed).
6 Ie such as working men's clubs and old people's home societies and other specially authorised societies in accordance with the Friendly Societies Act 1974, s 7(2).
7 Or possibly friendly societies in relation to the relief or maintenance of members in respect of the loss or damage to fishing boats or nets: ibid, s 7(1), Sch 1, para (3).
8 See paras 686 above.
9 *Dobinson v Hawks* (1848) 10 Sim 407.

705. Termination of membership. Just as joining a society is regulated by the rules, so also is termination of membership. However, certain general propositions are established.

The procedure for voluntary resignation should be set out in the rules[1], but if these are silent the member appears to be able to withdraw at will, and, once given, the resignation is immediately operative without further acceptance and cannot be revoked by an (ex-)member[2].

It is often a precondition of membership that the member should also be employed by a particular employer or industry, or be also a member of some other specified organisation. If that precondition can no longer be complied with, the terms of the rules will be crucial. If the precondition requires both initial and continued membership, then the loss of one must also mean the loss of the other, but if there is no such automatic termination or other related power of expulsion then membership can continue[3].

It is permissible to provide for automatic termination of membership when contributions are in arrears, normally for a specified period. In such a case the rules themselves must be examined to determine the regularity of any subsequent action by the society[4]. The Friendly Societies Act 1974 confers no protection, but collecting societies must give twenty-eight days' written notice of forfeiture of benefit[5], and the Reserve and Auxilliary Forces (Protection of Civil Interests) Act 1951 applies to specified classes of serviceman[6].

Expulsion of members can only occur if a power to expel is contained in the rules, which in any relevant case must be strictly complied with — there is no opportunity for irregularity or failure to follow the rules of natural justice. The rules must contain provision for the settlement of disputes, and challenge to the operation of an expulsion rule by an aggrieved member would be to the nominated body. Damages would be available for irregular or unjustified expulsion.

1 The Friendly Societies Act 1974 (c 46), does not require inclusion of a termination rule, but does require a rule to provide for the consequences of non-payment of any subscription or fine: see s 7(2), Sch 2, para 3(1), and para 699 above.
2 *Finch v Oake* (1896) 1 Ch 409, CA.
3 *Sargeant v Butterworth* (1907) 51 Sol Jo 429.
4 *Colquhoun v Society of Contributors to the Widows' Fund of the Faculty of Procurators in Glasgow* 1908 SC (HL) 10, 15 SLT 1049; *Milner v Bradford Warehousemans Society* (1909) RCR 12; *Groves v Cardiff Coal Trimmers Superannuation Society* (1922) RCR 12.
5 See the Industrial Assurance Act 1923 (c 8), s 23.
6 Ie under the Reserve and Auxilliary Forces (Protection of Civil Interests) Act 1951 (c 65), Pt VI (ss 54–59). In relation to friendly societies the Act renders null any rule depriving a friendly society member of his or her rights as a result of military service: see s 58. It also protects them from forfeiture of life assurance policies because of non-payment of subscriptions or premiums by allowing reinstatement of the policy on complying with the conditions set out in the Act which also includes an appeal to the chief registrar and provision for the adjustment of the policy rights: see ss 54–57 (amended by the Friendly Societies Act 1955 (4 Eliz 2 c 19), s 3(3), and the Companies Act 1967 (c 81), s 130(4)(e), Sch 8, Pt V (in respect of industrial assurance companies)).

706. Members' liabilities. Registered societies are unincorporated with no form of limited liability for their members, and so on principle a member is only liable to contribute subscriptions provided for in the rules and any other sums contractually due to the society[1].

The rules will contain provision for the consequences of the non-payment of subscriptions or any fines imposed on a member[2]. Those consequences cannot include power to sue the defaulting member to recover unpaid subscriptions, and fines can only be recovered if reasonable and in conformity with the rules[3]. Cattle insurance societies and those specially authorised societies whose authorisation includes this privilege are permitted to sue to recover subscriptions and all sums of money payable by a member to the society or branch provided the obligation in question is derived from the rules[4].

1 See ASSOCIATIONS AND CLUBS, vol 2, paras 812–815.
2 See the Friendly Societies Act 1974 (c 46), s 7(2), Sch 2, para 3(1), and para 699 above.
3 *Lovejoy v Mulkern* (1877) 46 LJ Ch 630, CA.
4 Friendly Societies Act 1974, s 22(2).

(5) TRUSTEES AND OFFICERS

707. General provisions. Each society must make provision in its rules for ordinary management by the officers[1] of the society, as must each friendly society branch. There is specific mention of officers, committee of management, treasurer and trustees, for whom provision must be made in the rules[2]. The Friendly Societies Act 1974 requires a secretary to perform specified functions, and although the provision does not mention the secretary by name, that office must be included in the phrase 'other officers' for whom provision must be made[2]. The 1974 Act makes mention of managers[3] and 'persons authorised to sue and be sued on behalf of the society or branch other than the trustees'[4]. The rules would normally provide for a presiding officer to take the chair at committee and general meetings as well as other officers to provide for a society's own particular needs[5]. There is a prohibition against the appointment of a minor as committee member, trustee, manager or treasurer of a society or branch[6].

The rules will provide for the election or appointment of the officer. If the first officers of a society or branch including the secretary all sign the required list lodged with the application for registration[7], then that list is evidence of their appointment after the registration of the society or branch[8].

Every officer having the receipt or charge of money is obliged to give an account of his intromissions and to pay over all money or other property in his possession in accordance with the society's instructions[9]. This obligation is to be carried out either when required by the rules, or on demand (which can be verbal), or on written notice given to the officer in person or left at his last or usual address[10]. There is the supporting sanction either of the enforcement of any bond of caution required under the rules from such officers[11] or of proceedings in the sheriff court[12].

The rules must contain provision for the removal of officers[13], and such rules should embrace not merely their removal but also make provision for resignation. When an officer is dismissed he must retain any books etc of the society in his possession, delivering them only to the person authorised to receive them by the society[14].

Societies have the privilege of a prior claim both on the death of an officer who has money or other property belonging to the society or branch and also if any diligence is raised against such an officer[15]. At least two of the trustees must serve written notice on the executors, sheriff officers, trustee in bankruptcy or other relevant person, who is then obliged to deliver the property in question to the society in priority to any other creditor or claim against that officer[16].

As the legislation only provides a framework which leaves the obligation to provide the essential detail to the rules, there are only a few provisions dealing with the specific functions and duties of the various officers which a society requires for its smooth operation[17].

1 'Officer' includes any trustee, treasurer, secretary, committee member or person appointed to sue or be sued on behalf of the society or branch: Friendly Societies Act 1974 (c 46), s 111(1).
2 See ibid, s 7(2), Sch 2, para 5, and para 699 above. See also paras 708 ff below.
3 See ibid, s 25. Manager is not included in the definition of 'officer': see note 1 above.
4 See note 1 above.
5 The older affiliated Orders have titles reflecting their origins, eg the Independent Order of Oddfellows (Manchester Unity) has a Grand Master and the Ancient Order of Foresters a Chief Ranger, as well as the earlier social conditions from which they arose, eg medical officer or sick visitor.
6 Friendly Societies Act 1974, s 25. This is the only section to mention managers. From the form of the prohibition it would appear that it would not extend to other officers — even the secretary.
7 Ie under ibid, ss 8(2), 11(1)(b), 12(1)(c). See paras 695, 697, above.
8 Ibid, s 26.
9 Ibid, s 28(1). 'Officer having the receipt or charge of money' would cover eg collectors as well as the treasurer.
10 Ibid, s 28(1)(a)–(c).
11 It is optional for the rules to require any officer having the receipt or charge of money before taking up office to supply caution either by at least one cautioner or that of a guarantee society: see ibid, s 27. For the form of bond of caution, see s 27(2)(a), Sch 3.
12 Ibid, s 28(2), (3). The sheriff's judgment is final, right of appeal under the Criminal Procedure (Scotland) Act 1975 (c 21), s 442 (substituted by the Criminal Justice (Scotland) Act 1980 (c 62), s 34, Sch 3, para 1), being excluded: Friendly Societies Act 1974, s 28(3). By not excluding the jurisdiction of the Court of Session, s 28 leaves proceedings in that court optionally available to a society: *Re Royal Liver Friendly Society* (1887) 35 Ch D 332.

13 Friendly Societies Act 1974, Sch 2, para 5.
14 *Glasgow District of Ancient Order of Foresters v Stevenson* (1899) 2 F 14, 7 SLT 163, which referred to the secretary, but on principle must refer also to all other officers in the like position. It should also apply to a resigning officer to require him to deliver any records in accordance with the society's directions.
15 Friendly Societies Act 1974, s 59(1)(a), (b).
16 Ibid, s 59(2). This priority is narrowly applied. The officer must be properly appointed and in possession of the property by virtue of that office, it is not lost by lack of care in examining accounts but is by failure to secure the cautioner that s 27 may require: *Re Aberdein* [1896] WN 154; *Re Welch, ex parte Trustees of Oddfellows Society* (1894) 63 LJQB 524; *John O'Gaunt Lodge of Oddfellows v Bell* (1883) FS Cases 67; *Re West of England and South Wales District Bank, ex parte Swansea Friendly Society* (1879) 11 Ch D 768; *Ex parte Ross* (1802) 6 Ves 802; *Ex parte Ashley, ex parte Corser* (1801) 6 Ves 441; *Ex parte Amicable Society of Lancaster* (1801) 6 Ves 98.
17 See paras 708 ff below.

708. Trustees. As societies are unincorporated, trustees are required to own the societies' property on behalf of the members. All property belonging to a society is vested in the trustees for the time being for the benefit of the society, its members and persons claiming through the members[1]. A trustee is only liable for money actually received by him[2].

A registered society and branch must have at least one trustee[3]. The rules must provide for appointment, which must be by resolution of a majority of the members present at and entitled to vote at a general meeting, and removal of the trustees[4]. The same person cannot be trustee and secretary or treasurer of the same society or branch[5], but a corporation can be a trustee[6].

The trustees' duties are to hold the society's property and to invest it, with the consent of the committee or of the general meeting, in authorised investments[7]. They also have a variety of statutory duties connected with the protection of the society's property[8] and signing various returns to the registrar[9]. The trustees are also the proper persons to sue and be sued on behalf of the society[10].

The Friendly Societies Act 1974 provides for the automatic vesting of the society's property in the surviving or succeeding trustees (or the executor of the last survivor) without the need for any conveyance or assignation on the death, resignation or removal of a trustee[11].

It will be appreciated that the trustees of a society are rather peculiar trustees as their powers of investment are restricted to carrying out the instructions of the committee or general meeting[12].

1 Friendly Societies Act 1974 (c 46), s 54(1).
2 Ibid, s 54(3). As to investments, see para 719 below.
3 Ibid, s 24(1).
4 See ibid, s 7(2), Sch 2, para 5, and s 24(2). Notice of appointment is to be signed by the new trustee and the secretary: s 24(3). For the form, see the Friendly Societies Regulations 1975, SI 1975/205, reg 2, Sch 1, Form S. For a branch trustee it is sent through the central society's secretary: Friendly Societies Act 1974, s 24(4). There is no requirement affecting removal. As to proof of appointment of trustees for a newly registered society, see s 26, and para 707, above. As to registration of societies and branches, see paras 695, 697, above.
5 Ibid, s 24(5).
6 *Re Pilkington Bros Ltd Workmen's Pension Fund* [1953] 2 All ER 816, [1953] 1 WLR 1084.
7 See the Friendly Societies Act 1974, s 46, and para 719 below.
8 Ie presentation of accounts and accounting for money and recovery of the society's property from a dead or bankrupt officer (see ibid, ss 28, 59, and para 707 above); and the recovery of property acquired from it by fraud (see s 99(2), (6)(a), and para 745 below).
9 Ie notice of appointment (see ibid, s 24, and above); statutory declaration on dissolution (see s 94, and para 738 below); and references by consent to the registrar (see s 77, and para 725 below).
10 Ibid, s 103(1). Other officers can be nominated in place of the trustees by the rules; s 103(1). The trustees' position is nominal; control remains with the committee.
11 Ibid, s 58.

12 See para 719 below.

709. Committee of management. The function of the committee is that of management, as it is the equivalent of the board of directors of a company, and presumably the committee members are subject to the same duties to the society as are other agents[1]. The committee has power to sue to recover any of the society's property that has been fraudulently taken[2], to adjudicate on the entitlement to sums due to the heirs of a dead member when there is no nomination[3], and to consent to investments if the rules so provide[4].

1 Ie the fiduciary duties and duties of care and skill: see AGENCY AND MANDATE, vol I, paras 630 ff. As to offences, see para 744, below.
2 See the Friendly Societies Act 1974 (c 46), s 99(2), (6), and para 745 below.
3 See ibid, s 68(1), and para 723 below.
4 See ibid, s 46(1), and para 719 below.

710. Treasurer. Minors and trustees cannot hold the office of treasurer[1]. Thereafter the Friendly Societies Act 1974 is silent in relation to the treasurer. However, he is primarily the person responsible for ensuring that the society complies with the accounting requirements of the Act and that its financial affairs are conducted in a regular manner[2].

1 Friendly Societies Act 1974 (c 46), ss 24(5), 25. The registrar will not approve a rule that permits the secretary and treasurer to be the same person.
2 Ie under ibid, ss 29–40: see paras 714 ff below. The accounting obligations are imposed on all committee members: see s 30(8), and para 714 below.

711. Secretary. The secretary, in terms of the Friendly Societies Act 1974, is essentially a signing officer, for the duties appropriated to him by the Act are to sign or countersign various documents and supporting statutory declarations which the society must lodge with the registrar in connection with its activities[1]. The rules should deal with the other administrative duties which are necessary for the efficient operation of the society and place responsibility for them on the secretary. These duties could include keeping membership records[2], minutes of general and committee meetings and recording nominations[3] as well as attending to the procedural aspects of the society's affairs.

1 These range from the initial application for registration (see the Friendly Societies Act 1974 (c 46), s 8, and para 695 above) to amendment of rules or notice of change in the registered office (see s 18, and paras 699, 703, above) and cancellation of registration (see s 91, and para 736 below).
2 There is no statutory requirement for a register or other record of membership.
3 Nominations are lodged with the society or branch: see the Friendly Societies Act 1974, s 66, and para 722 below.

712. Manager. There is only one mention of the post of manager, which is not brought within the definition of 'officer'[1], and that is the prohibition against appointing a minor as manager[2]. From its omission from the definition it seems clear that this is a subordinate position of limited authority distinct from and operating under the direction of the committee of management.

1 See para 707, note 1, above.
2 Friendly Societies Act 1974 (c 46), s 25.

(6) MEETINGS

713. General and special meetings. Friendly societies have two types of meeting, of the committee of management and of the members — the general meeting. In earlier days management committee meetings were often fixed by the rules, being held at regular intervals throughout the year on a fixed day and time and place[1]. Prudence requires the management committee to meet regularly, and the rules should make appropriate provision for this without necessarily fixing the time and place of the meetings.

General meetings are equally necessary, and again the rules will make the necessary provision[2], for there is no statutory procedure provided; indeed, there is not even a requirement to hold an annual general meeting. Collecting societies, however, are more strictly regulated by the industrial assurance legislation[3]. Special resolutions are also defined, for which proxy voting is permitted[4]. The registrar is likely to require rules for the convening of annual and extraordinary general meetings on proper notice with voting rights securing democratic procedures at these meetings. However, the absence of statutory requirements means that the rules can cater for the differing needs of a relatively small social club or other specially authorised society or of the insurance friendly societies and the affiliated orders with huge memberships and a quite different member/society relationship.

A specified minority of members[5] may apply to the registrar for the holding of a special meeting of the society[6]. The application must show both good reasons for holding the meeting and an absence of malice in the requisitionists[7]. The registrar will specify the form of the necessary notice of the application served on the society, and security for expenses may be called for[8]. The registrar has a discretion whether to grant the application and if he does, he will fix the time, place and agenda of the meeting, which has all the powers of a meeting called under the rules and can appoint its own chairman[9]. If the members of a branch wish to apply for such a meeting, the consent of the central society is a precondition[10].

1 See eg the registrar's model rules (of 1916), printed in both F B Fuller *The Law Relating to Friendly Societies and Industrial and Provident Societies* (4th edn, 1926) p 477 and *Pratt's Friendly Societies and Industrial and Provident Societies* (15th edn, 1931, ed M Mackinnon) p 115.
2 Ie required by the Friendly Societies Act 1974 (c 46), s 7(2), Sch 2, para 4: see para 699 above.
3 Ie under the Industrial Assurance Act 1923 (c 8), s 19 (see para 699 above), and the Friendly and Industrial and Provident Societies Act 1968 (c 55), s 17(5).
4 'Special resolution' is a resolution passed at a general meeting of which notice, specifying the intention to propose that resolution, has been given in accordance with the society's rules: Friendly Societies Act 1974, s 86(1)(a). The majority is three-quarters of those members for the time being entitled to vote, who vote in person or by proxy: s 86(1)(b). Proxy voting is permitted for special resolutions notwithstanding the rules, provided the Friendly Societies (Proxy Voting) Regulations 1971, SI 1971/1946, are complied with: Friendly Societies Act 1974. s 86(2). If the meeting is a delegates' meeting, then three-quarters of the delegates attending and voting must pass the resolution.
5 Ie one-fifth in the case of a society with less than 1,000 members; 100 in the case of a society with not less than 1,000 members and not more than 10,000 members; and 500 in the case of a society with more than 10,000 members: ibid s 90(1), (2).
6 Ibid, s 90(1). For these purposes the registrar is the chief registrar, unless the society does its business exclusively in Scotland where he is the Assistant Registrar for Scotland: s 90(1).
7 Ibid, s 90(3). For the form, see the Friendly Societies Regulations 1975, SI 1975/205, reg 2, Sch 1, Form AC.
8 Friendly Societies Act 1974, s 90(3), (4).
9 Ibid, s 90(7).
10 Ibid, s 90(2).

(7) ACCOUNTS AND AUDIT

714. Accounts. All societies must keep proper books of account recording their transactions, assets and liabilities, supported by a satisfactory system of control over the books, cash holding, receipts and payments[1]. 'Proper' accounts will be adequate to explain the society's transactions and show a true and fair view of the affairs of the society[2].

The accounting year for societies is the year to 31 December[3], and for each year a society must prepare audited annual accounts consisting of either one revenue acocunt or two or more revenue accounts, each dealing with part of the business of the society, and a balance sheet[4]. The single revenue account must give a true and fair view of the society's income and expenditure for the year in question, and where two or more accounts are prepared a similar requirement is imposed on the accounts when taken as a whole[5]. The balance sheet must also give a true and fair view of the society's affairs at its date[6]. However, if a society[7] is subject to valuation[8], its balance sheet must show a true and fair view of the current assets and liabilities and the resulting balances of its funds[9].

A society must not publish any revenue account or balance sheet unless it has been audited[10] and contains the auditors' report along with, if the society is subject to valuation, the latest valuer's report signed by the secretary and two committee members[11]. All societies must display a copy of the latest balance sheet and auditors' (and if applicable the valuer's) report at the registered office[12]. A copy of the latest annual return or accounts and accompanying auditors' report must be supplied to any member or person interested in the funds requesting them[13].

The duty of compliance with the obligations relating to the preparation and auditing of annual accounts and the requirement that they be signed and accompanied by the auditors' report is imposed on the committee members[14]. Failure can result on summary conviction to a fine not exceeding level 5 on the standard scale[15].

1　Friendly Societies Act 1974 (c 46), s 29(1). Any book of account may be kept other than in bound books provided due security precautions are taken: s 29(3), (4).

2　Ibid, s 29(2).

3　Ie called the 'year of account': ibid, s 111(4). The first year of account begins on the date of registration and ends on the next 31 December; and from 1 January to 31 December thereafter: s 111(4). 'The current year of account' for auditors is that to which the question of appointment arises (s 111(4)(a)), and 'the preceding year' is that immediately preceding the current year of account (s 111(4)(b)).

4　Ibid, s 30(2).

5　Ibid, s 30(1), (3).

6　Ibid, s 30(4).

7　Ie friendly societies and certain specially authorised societies: ibid, s 30(5)(a), (b).

8　Ie for the purposes of a specially authorised society a valuation under ibid, s 41: s 30(5)(b). See also para 717 below.

9　Ibid, s 30(5).

10　Ibid, s 30(6)(a), (7). As to audit, see para 715 below.

11　Ibid, s 30(6)(b), (c), (7).

12　Ibid, s 45.

13　Ibid, s 44. Section 44(1)(b) refers to a balance sheet containing the same particulars as the annual return, which means therefore revenue accounts and balance sheet, not just a balance sheet in the strict sense of the term.

14　Ibid, s 30(8).

15　Ibid, s 30(8). As to level 5 on the standard scale, see para 630, note 4, above. There is a defence that the committee member had reasonable grounds to believe that the duty was the responsibility of a competent and reliable person: s 30(8).

715. Audit. All societies must appoint auditors, but not all need appoint qualified auditors[1]. A society or branch must appoint qualified auditors unless it can qualify for that year of account as an exempt society[2]. To be exempt requires for the preceding year that:

(1) the receipts and payments did not in aggregate exceed £5,000; and

(2) at the end of that year the number of members did not exceed 500; and

(3) at the end of that year its assets in aggregate did not exceed £5,000[3]. Additionally a branch qualifying as exempt under the requirements of heads (1) and (2) may substitute the following for head (3) to obtain exempt status: at the end of the preceding year its assets in aggregate did not exceed £5,000 after at least 75 per cent of its assets had been transferred to the central society or another branch for investment[4] and provided the society or receiving branch was not itself exempt[5].

An exempt society or branch may either appoint a qualified auditor or two or more unqualified people to act as auditors[6]. Notwithstanding a society's possession of exempt status, the registrar may direct that it appoint a qualified auditor for the current year[7]. This direction can be retrospective, applying to preceding years, and a fresh annual return for the years in question must be lodged within three months of the direction[8]. A collecting society or branch cannot be exempt[9].

The rules will provide for the mechanism of appointment[10] and, once appointed, continuity of office is ensured, as removal of an established (or retiring) auditor is subject to procedural safeguards[11]. That auditor continues in office unless:

(a) the general meeting by resolution[12] either appoints another person as auditor or expressly provides that he is not to be reappointed; or
(b) he resigns in writing; or
(c) he is now ineligible[13] for reappointment for the current year of account; or
(d) incapacity or death supervenes[14].

If a person other than the retiring auditor is proposed for appointment but the resolution cannot be implemented because either he is ineligible for appointment or has died in the interim, then the retiring auditor is not automatically reappointed[15].

1 Before 1 October 1991 qualified auditors had to be members of the Institute of Chartered Accountants of Scotland, Ireland, and England and Wales or of any other United Kingdom accountancy body authorised under the Companies Act 1985 (c 6), s 389(1): Friendly Societies Act 1974 (c 46), s 36(1) (amended by the Companies Consolidation (Consequential Provisions) Act 1985 (c 9), s 30, Sch 2). After 1 October 1991 no person is a qualified auditor unless he is eligible for appointment as a company auditor under the Companies Act 1989 (c 40), s 25 (see COMPANIES, vol 4, para 456): see the Friendly Societies Act 1974 (c 46), s 36(1) (amended by the Companies Act 1989 (Eligibility for Appointment as Company Auditor) (Consequential Amendments) Regulations 1991, SI 1991/1997, regs 2, 4, Schedule, para 24 (2), made under the Companies Act 1989, s 50, so that the requirements for the qualification of auditors mirrors the Companies Act 1985 (c 6), Pt XI, Ch V (ss 384–394A): see COMPANIES, vol 4, paras 456–459. Any officer or servant of the society and any partner, employer or employee of such an officer or servant are disqualified from being appointed auditor: Friendly Societies Act 1974, s 37(1). A body corporate, other than a Scottish firm none of whose partners is otherwise ineligible for appointment, is also disqualified: s 37(1)(c),(2) (repealed by the Companies Act 1989 (Eligibility for Appointment as Company Auditor) (Consequential Amendments) Regulations 1991, Schedule, para 24(3), as from 1 October 1991).
2 Ibid, s 31(1).
3 Ibid, s 31(2). An exempt society is one which meets the requirements of s 31(2): s 31(4). See further para 714, note 3, above. The chief registrar has power to make regulations altering any sum or number: see s 31(5). At the date at which this volume states the law, no such regulations had been made.
4 Ie under ibid, s 46: see para 719 below.
5 Ibid, s 31(3)(a)–(c). An exempt branch is one which meets the requirements of s 31(3): s 31(4). The chief registrar has power to make regulations altering any sum or number: see s 31(5). At the date at which this volume states the law, no such regulations had been made.
6 Ibid, s 32(1).
7 Ibid, s 32(2).
8 Ibid, s 32(3).
9 Ibid, s 31(2).
10 Ibid, s 7(2), Sch 2, para 6.

11 Ie under ibid, s 33. From the terms of s 33 it appears that there is an automatic reappointment from year to year and that any vote of a general meeting is at most confirmatory. The auditor appointed for the preceding year of account is reappointed for the current year of account: s 33(1). For the meaning of 'year of account', see para 714, note 3, above.

12 The procedure, in brief, is as follows: (1) a resolution with either proposes appointing a new auditor or not appointing the existing auditor must be notified to the society at least twenty-eight days before the relevant general meeting (ibid, s 34(1)); (2) the society must give notice to its members in accordance with its rules, either to the members or, if that is not done or required, by local newspaper advertisement at least fourteen days before the general meeting or in any other way permitted by the rules (s 34(2), (3)); (3) there is a saving provision allowing the statutory procedure to override the rules (s 34(4)); (4) the society must forthwith give notice of the resolution to the retiring auditor, who has a right to make representations (s 35(1)); (5) if the auditor so requires, notice of his intention to speak at the meeting and notice of the representations themselves must be given to the members (s 35(2)); (6) if the representations are lodged with the society in time, any notice sent to the members must refer to the representations, and intimate that any member can receive a copy on request (the society has an express obligation to comply with that request) (s 35(3)(a)–(c)); (7) the auditor may require his representations to be read to the meeting (s 35(3)); (8) the auditor may speak to the meeting (s 35(3)); (9) an application may be made to the Court of Session to have publication of any such representations restrained if they are defamatory, the expenses of such an action may be awarded against the auditor (s 35(4), (5)). Provision is also made in respect of delegate meetings: ss 34(5), 35(6).

13 A person is ineligible for appointment for the current year of account if, but only if, (1) his appointment is prohibited under ibid, s 37 (see note 2 above), or (2) in respect of a society or branch which is not exempt, he is not a qualified auditor: s 33(3)(a), (b).

14 Ibid, s 33(1)(a)–(d).

15 Ibid, s 33(2).

716. Auditors' rights and duties. The auditors have a statutory right of access to all the society's records and may require any necessary explanation or further information needed to carry out the audit[1]. They must also receive all the notices and related communications sent to the members in connection with any general meeting of the society and may attend and speak at any general meeting, but only in connection with audit business[2].

The auditors' duty is to present a report to the society on the revenue account and balance sheet of the year of appointment[3]. That report is to state whether or not the revenue account (or where more than one account is prepared, accounts) and balance sheet show a true and fair view of the income and expenditure and resulting balances of the society's funds respectively for that year of account[4].

Additionally, the audit itself must be carried out in such a way as to allow the auditor to check that the society has kept proper accounting records[5] and has maintained a satisfactory system of control over its financial affairs[6], and that the revenue and other accounts and balance sheet agree with the accounting records themselves[7]. If the auditor considers that the society has not properly carried out these obligations, or has failed to get adequate information from the society, he must qualify his report accordingly[8].

The registrar has power to prescribe the maximum fees chargeable by the auditors of friendly societies[9].

1 Friendly Societies Act 1974 (c 46), s 39(1).

2 Ibid, s 39(2).

3 Ibid, s 38(1).

4 Ibid, s 38(2). Any other accounts referred to in the report must also show a true and fair view of the matters to which they relate: s 38(3).

5 Ie in accordance with ibid, s 29(1)(a): see para 714 above.

6 Ie in accordance with ibid, s 29(1)(b): see para 714 above.

7 Ibid, s 38(4)(a)–(c).

8 Ibid, s 38(4), (5).

9 See ibid, s 40. At the date at which this volume states the law no regulations had been made.

717. Valuations. The Friendly Societies Act 1974 requires all societies to carry out periodic valuation, but exempts certain classes of society[1]. Exemption is given to societies which are not involved in life assurance: cattle insurance societies, benevolent societies, working men's clubs, old people's home societies, and certain specially authorised societies[2], with an additional power of dispensation vested in the chief registrar when he considers it to be inapplicable to the purposes or nature of the business of the society or the way in which it is conducted[3]. The societies which must carry out valuation are friendly societies and those specially authorised societies which are directed to do so in their authorisation[4].

Valuation is the periodic valuation of assets and liabilities carried out by qualified actuaries or public valuers appointed by the society in question[5]. The actuary must make a report in the prescribed form, which is sent to the registrar and must be displayed at the registered office[6].

Valuation must be carried out at least once in every five years[7]. The registrar may make regulations reducing that period to three years[8]. Societies so affected are those which either:

(1) are registered before 26 July 1968 and have either life or endowment funds exceeding £1,000,000, or contribution income to such funds exceeding £150,000 based on the figures shown in the last valuation return, or have in force, at the end of any year of account, life insurance contracts by the society on any one life securing either singly or in aggregate a sum exceeding £5,000[9]; or

(2) are registered on or after 26 July 1968 and carry on long-term business[10].

In addition, the registrar may direct that a particular society should carry out a three-yearly valuation[11]. The direction can require a three-yearly valuation in respect of specified business and the usual five-yearly valuation for the remaining business[12]. Before issuing a direction the registrar must be satisfied that it is expedient in the interests of the members[13]. A direction can be revoked at any time[14].

An authorised society[15] is, as part of the authorisation requirements relating to the control of insurers undertaking long-term business, subject to annual valuation[16]. The regular annual valuation returns are recognised as being sufficient, and the society does not also have to supply the three-yearly valuations[17]. To qualify for the exemption the society must:

(a) be an authorised society;

(b) have complied with the valuation requirement[18]; and

(c) have submitted an annual valuation[19] or supplied equivalent information in its application for authorisation[20].

1 Ie under the Friendly Societies Act 1974 (c 46), s 41. Periodic valuations have to be provided for in the rules: see the Friendly Societies Regulations 1975, SI 1975/205, reg 2, Forms A, E. See also the Friendly Societies (Valuation) Regulations 1985, SI 1985/1919 (amended by SI 1988/1959). The Friendly Societies (Valuation) Regulations 1969, SI 1969/201, regs 2, 3, remain in force but are otherwise replaced by the 1985 Regulations.

2 Friendly Societies Act 1974, s 41(4).

3 See ibid, s 41(5), (6). Provision is made for partial exemption, and the valuation of the non-exempt part in the usual way: see s 41(6)(a), (b).

4 Ibid, s 41(4)(b).

5 Ibid, s 41(1)(a). The Treasury appoints qualified actuaries as public valuers and fixes their fees: s 41(2)(a), (b). Public valuers must undertake all valuations submitted to them at the fixed fee rate. Details of public valuers, whose appointment is not compulsory, can be obtained from the registrar. 'Qualified actuary' means an actuary having such qualifications as the chief registrar may by regulations prescribe: s 9(3).

6 Ibid, ss 41(1)(b), (3)(a), 45(b). The abstract of the results of the valuation is made by the actuary and is accompanied by any required information on the benefits insured, contributions received and funds, debtors and creditors: s 41(3)(b).

7 Ibid, s 41(1), (4). The registrar has power to require the first valuation of a society which was registered after 25 July 1968 under the Friendly Societies Act 1896 (c 25) or under the Friendly Societies Act 1974, to be made at a specified date.

8 Ie under ibid, s 42.

9 See the Friendly Societies (Valuation) Regulations 1985, reg 3 (amended by SI 1988/1959).

10 Ibid, reg 4 (amended by SI 1988/1959). For the meaning of 'long-term business', see reg 4(6)(a), and the Insurance Companies Act 1982 (c 50), s 1, Sch 1.

11 Friendly Societies Act 1974, s 42(4)(a).

12 Ibid, s 42(4)(b).

13 Ibid, s 42(4).

14 Ibid, s 42(5).

15 In essence an authorised society is one which carries on long-term business and has an annual contribution income exceeding 500,000 units of account, and a society must be specially authorised if it is to carry on long-term business unless it is exempted: see the Friendly Societies (Long Term Insurance Business) Regulations 1987, SI 1987/2132, regs 3–6.

16 See ibid, reg 11.

17 Ie under the Friendly Societies (Valuation) Regulations 1985.

18 Ie under the Friendly Societies Act 1974, s 41 and the Friendly Societies (Valuation) Regulations 1985, if applicable.

19 Ie in accordance with the Friendly Societies (Long Term Insurance Business) Regulations 1987.

20 See the Friendly Societies (Valuation) Regulations 1985, reg 4A (added by SI 1988/1959).

718. Annual return. No later than 31 May each year every society and branch must send its annual return, made up to the year of account, that is 31 December, to the registrar (in the case of a branch through the officer appointed for that purpose by the central society)[1]. The form of the annual return is prescribed, varying with the class of society[2]. The annual return must contain the revenue account or accounts, balance sheet and related auditors' report[3]. Additionally those societies which are required to carry out valuations must include either:

(1) the date of the last actuary's report (or reports where there are more than one) and an address at which the report can be inspected; or

(2) where exemption[4] has been given by the registrar, a statement of the reasons for the exemption; or

(3) where the registrar has given partial exemption[4], the information (a) in respect of non-exempt business, and (b) in respect of the exempt business[5].

1 Friendly Societies Act 1974 (c 46), s 43(1), (2), (3)(a).

2 Ie prescribed by virtue of ibid, s 43(6). Copies of the appropriate style are supplied annually to societies by the registrar.

3 Ibid, s 43(3)(b), (c), (4).

4 Ie under ibid, s 41: see para 717 above.

5 Ibid, s 43(5)(a)–(c).

(8) FINANCE

719. Investments. All property belonging to a friendly society is vested in its trustees for the time being in trust for the members and others entitled to it[1], and it is the trustees who are responsible for its investment subject to the friendly societies legislation and the society's rules, which must provide for the investment of its funds[2]. The investment decision is not that of the trustees alone; by the Friendly Societies Act 1974 the consent of either the committee or the general meeting is required[3]. In the case of a society with branches, the rules may provide for collective investment by either the central society or one of the branches on behalf of all the combined society and branches, any consent required being that of the investing central society or branch[4].

The permitted investment options are as follows:

(1) the National Savings Bank[5] (it should be emphasised that this is for investment funds and not money paid to account for the society's use, when the choice of bank is unrestricted);

(2) in the public funds[6], that is to say in any of the United Kingdom government securities;

(3) in the purchase of land or in the erection or alteration of offices or other buildings thereon[7] (it should be noted that a society's powers of land ownership are extended, subject to its rules[8]. From the terms of the Act it appears that land ownership for whatever purpose requires express authorisation in the rules);

(4) in authorised trustee investments[9], which means investment in the manner required by, and in those securities permitted by, the Trustee Investments Act 1961 (c 62)[10];

(5) in any other security, other than personal security, expressly authorised by the rules[11] (it has long been accepted that security here means money secured on property as opposed to personal guarantee[12], and that meaning is not extended by the accepted use of securities as including company shares, stocks and debentures[13]; it follows that the only company shares permitted for investment are those authorised as trustee investments under head (4));

(6) the rules may expressly permit investment in the share or loan capital of a housing association (but not a development corporation)[14] (such investment can be made only from any unapplied surplus of assets over liabilities shown at the last valuation[15]);

(7) a friendly society may provide funds to a hopsital or other charitable or provident institution to secure the benefits of that institution for its members and their families[16].

Societies may adopt rules for a fund to purchase government securities for members[17]. This is, of course, not investment of the societies' funds.

---

1 See the Friendly Societies Act 1974 (c 456), s 54. 'Property' extends to all heritable and moveable estate: s 111(1).

2 Ie under ibid, s 7(2), Sch 2, para 6: see para 699 above.

3 Ibid, s 46(1). In respect of the power to invest in a housing association, the consent required is of the committee or of a majority of the members present and entitled to vote at the general meeting: s 51(1).

4 Ibid, s 46(2).

5 Ibid, s 46(1)(a) (amended by the Trustee Savings Banks Act 1985 (c 58), ss 4(3), 7(3), Sch 4. For the procedure, see the National Savings Bank Regulations 1972, SI 1972/764, reg 10.

6 Friendly Societies Act 1974, s 46(1)(b).

7 Ibid, s 46(1)(c).

8 Ie under ibid, s 53, permitting the holding, purchasing, leasing, selling, excambion and granting standard securities over land or buildings or to erect buildings on land: see para 702 above.

9 Ibid, s 46(1)(e).

10 See TRUSTS, TRUSTEES AND JUDICIAL FACTORS, vol 24, para 207.

11 Friendly Societies Act 1974, s 46(1)(d). It is suggested that this covers local authority loans secured over rates and mortgages on freehold and leasehold property: 19 *Halsbury's Laws of England* (4th edn) para 245. It should also cover the security of a company's floating charge.

12 *Re Coltman, Coltman v Coltman* (1881) 19 Ch D 64, CA, which declares loans to other than members unauthorised and not illegal, and so recoverable from the recipient.

13 *Re United Law Clerks Society* [1947] Ch 150, [1946] 2 All ER 674, where preference stock or shares were disallowed as an investment medium, but debenture and guarantee stocks were permitted by the registrar.

14 Friendly Societies Act 1974, s 51. 'Housing association' has the same meaning as in the Housing Associations Act 1985 (c 69) (see s 1, and HOUSING, vol 11, para 1924): Friendly Societies Act 1974, s 51(4) (amended by the Housing (Consequential Provisions) Act 1985 (c 71), s 4, Sch 2, para 26).

15 See the Friendly Societies Act 1974, s 51(2), (3), applying s 50, which relates to loans of surplus funds, and defines the calculation of the relevant surplus: see para 720 below.

16 See ibid, s 52. The subscription is limited to that necessary to purchase the benefits in question: s 52(1).

17 See ibid, s 47, and para 701 above.

720. Lending. Societies have only the most limited lending powers, restricted to loans to the members or to certain other societies, and apart from this there is no other power to lend[1].

Loans to members are permitted, when authorised by the rules, in two cases. First, a society may lend to an assured member of at least one year's standing any sum up to one-half the sum assured[2]. The only security required is the written bond of the member together with two cautioners; such security is not affected by the society deducting the advance (with interest) from the sum assured[3]. Secondly, the rules may permit a separate loan fund formed from the members' deposits from which loans can be made to the members; no other source may be used[4]. The maximum loan is £50[5]. In calculating that limit any other sum owed by the member to the society must be included[5]. The loans may be unsecured or supported by cautioners as the rules provide, and the society must impose an upper limit on unsecured loans in its rules. No member may subscribe more than £200 to the loan fund[6]. The society may not hold on deposit more than the maximum permitted by the rules; that maximum may not exceed two-thirds of the total sum owed to the society by the members who have borrowed from the loan fund[7].

The rules may allow a society which is not a benevolent society to lend from its surplus to another society or branch of a different description[8]. The lending society is entitled to take part in the management of the receiving society or branch to the extent permitted by its rules[9]. The surplus, without which such loans cannot be made, is defined as the surplus of assets over liabilities shown by its last valuation (if the society is exempt from valuation reference is to be made to the last annual return)[10]. All previous outstanding loans must be totalled and deducted from the current surplus when calculating the amount available for lending[11].

1 See the Friendly Societies Act 1974 (c 46), ss 48–50, and the societies' rules. See also *Re Coltman, Coltman v Coltman* (1881) 19 Ch D 64, CA.

2 Friendly Societies Act 1974, s 48.

3 Ibid, s 48(2).

4 Ibid, s 49(a). No one other than an officer of the society, a person specially authorised by resolution of the society, or a person authorised in writing by the member concerned may inspect a member's loan account.

5 Ibid, s 49(c).

6 Ibid, s 49(b).

7 Ibid, s 49(d).

8 Ibid, s 50(1). For the purposes of s 50 a society or branch is deemed to be of the same description if, but only if, they are both registered by virtue of the same paragraph of s 7(1) (see para 685 above), and where each of them is a specially authorised society or branch, they are both established for the same purpose or purposes: s 50(5). An advance under s 50 may be interest free: s 50(3).

9 Ibid, s 50(1).

10 See ibid, s 50(2). As to valuation, see para 717 above, and as to annual return, see para 718 above.

11 Ibid, s 50(2)(a). Outstanding advances made after the date to which the valuation or annual return relates are to be deducted in calculating the surplus for all purposes other than that of s 50(2)(a): s 50(2)(b).

721. Borrowing. The only borrowing permitted by societies is on the security of land or buildings and the receipt of loans from the surplus of other 'different description' societies. The first right follows from the terms of section

53 of the Friendly Societies Act 1974, which allows a society whose rules authorise it to hold land to grant standard securities[1]. The second right arises of necessity, as the counterpart of the lending power of section 50 of the Act[2].

Specially authorised societies which create funds to be lent to the members or for their benefit may, provided the rules permit[3], borrow money from their members and others[4]. It is a statutory condition that no part of the society's funds may be distributed among the members, but only lent to them for approved purposes[5].

1 See para 702 above.
2 See para 720 above.
3 Friendly Societies Act 1974 (c 46), s 23(3). This applies only to specially authorised loan societies under Special Authority No 2 of 10 June 1976, which alone meet the definition of s 23. Such loan societies can only have been registered before 15 August 1917. The precursor of this somewhat odd section is the Societies Borrowing Powers Act 1898 (c 15) (repealed), which was required to solve difficulties in *Congested Districts (Ireland) Board* (1895) RCR 3.
4 See the Friendly Societies Act 1974, s 23(1), (2).
5 Ibid, s 23(3)(a), (b).

(9) NOMINATIONS

722. Power to nominate. There is a right of nomination available to the members of all societies except benevolent and old people's home societies and working men's clubs[1]. Any member sixteen years old or older may nominate any person or persons to receive the money payable on his death[2]. If the member is the member of a branch, a valid nomination carries all sums due on his death even if all or part is in fact paid by the society or another branch[3].

A valid nomination is in writing and either delivered to the registered office of the society or branch or made in a book kept there[4]. It must be signed by the grantor[5]. Nomination cannot be made to any person who is at that time an officer or servant of the society unless the person is also the husband, wife, father, mother, child, brother, sister, nephew or niece of the grantor[6]. There is a ceiling set on nominations, which cannot be made for sums in excess of £5,000[7].

A nomination can be revoked or varied in the same way as it was made[8]. It is also automatically revoked on marriage[9].

1 Friendly Societies Act 1974 (c 46), s 66(4).
2 Ibid, s 66(1). The sums will include policy proceeds as well as any loan fund contribution or other sums accumulated for the member: s 66(3).
3 Ibid, s 66(8).
4 Ibid, s 66(1).
5 Ibid, s 66(1). A printed form is acceptable. Signature is essential; an attested mark was rejected in *Morton v French* 1908 SC 171, 15 SLT 517. Delivery, which must be made in the grantor's lifetime, is effective where it is given to and kept by the secretary immediately after execution: *Thorogate and Royal Co-operative Collecting Society* (1947) Reports of Selected Disputes referred to the Industrial Assurance Commissioner 1938–1949, 67; *Hughes v Hardy* [1885] FS Cases 402.
6 Friendly Societies Act 1974, s 66(5).
7 Ibid, s 66(2) (amended by the Administration of Estates (Small Payments) (Increase of Limits) Order 1984, SI 1984/539, art 2, in relation to deaths occurring after 11 May 1984). Earlier limits were as follows: (1) nominations made before 21 December 1955, £100; (2) nominations made after 21 December 1955 and before 5 September 1965, £200; (3) nominations made after 5 September 1965 and before 10 August 1975, £500; (4) nominations made after 10 August 1975 and before 11 May 1984, £1,500. Nomination for an unspecified sum is valid up to the relevant limit which will include any excess attributable to the conversion to decimal currency: see the Friendly Societies Act 1974, ss 64(2)(c), 66(2) (as so amended) (s 64 being repealed by the Income and Corporation Taxes Act 1988 (c 1), s 844(4), Sch 31 as from 9 February 1988).
8 Friendly Societies Act 1974, s 66(6).

9 Ibid, s 66(7). A society honouring a nomination paid in ignorance of the member's subsequent marriage is protected: s 69(2).

723. Payment on death. On a member's death the society must honour a nomination and pay the nominee the sums due in accordance with the nomination up to the relevant limit[1]. A nominee under the age of sixteen cannot give a valid discharge[2].

If a member dies without making a nomination the society may distribute the money due to the member and which might have been nominated between those who are, in the opinion of the committee, entitled to it without confirmation[3]. This right is only available if the total sum due to the member does not exceed £5,000[4]. If the member is illegitimate, the society may pay that money to those persons who would have been entitled to it had the member been legitimate or, if there are no such persons, as the Treasury may direct[5].

The society is protected against any other claim made by the executors or personal representatives of the dead member, who instead are entitled to recover the money so paid from its recipient[6].

1 See the Friendly Societies Act 1974 (c 46), s 67(1), (2) (amended by the Administration of Estates (Small Payments) (Increase of Limits) Order 1984, SI 1984/539, art 2, in relation to deaths occurring after 11 May 1984). In applying the limit, any increase due to the adoption of decimal currency are ignored: Friendly Societies Act 1974, s 67(2) (as so amended). For the limits and the provisions in respect of decimal currency, see para 722, note 7, above.
2 Ibid, s 67(3).
3 Ibid, s 68(1).
4 Ibid, s 68(1) (as amended: see note 1 above). In applying the limit any excess over that sum caused by the adoption of decimal currency is ignored: s 68(3) (as so amended). For the limits and the provisions in respect of decimal currency, see para 722, note 7, above.
5 Ibid, s 68(2). The Law Reform (Parent and Child) (Scotland) Act 1986 (c 9) does not apply: see s 1(4), Sch 1.
6 Friendly Societies Act 1974, s 69(1).

724. Certification. A society may not pay any sum due on the death of a member except on the production of a death certificate[1] or a grant of confirmation[2]. This applies only where the death is one requiring entry in any register of deaths and does not apply to deaths at sea or in colliery accidents, accidents where no body can be found nor where the procurator fiscal certifies that an inquiry is to be held[3].

A special form of death certificate is required when money is payable on the death of a member's parents or grandparents[4], which is obtained on special application to the Registrar of Births, Deaths and Marriages. Only one such certificate can be obtained, although provision is made for the issue of a duplicate in the event of loss or destruction of the first certificate[5]. The society must indorse full details of the payment made on the certificate when making it[6].

A society is permitted to pay sums due on the death of a child under the age of ten[7] only after a special death certificate is produced. The application must be made to the Registrar of Births, Deaths and Marriages who can issue the certificate only after making the entry on the certificate of a registered medical practitioner who either was in attendance at the child's last illness, or can certify the probable cause of death or other satisfactory evidence of death[8]. The society in turn must inquire into any other sums paid on the child's death by any other society, and the total payments made by all societies or branches involved must not exceed (1) £6 for a child under 3; (2) £10 for a child under 6; and (3) £15 for a child under 10[9]. This does not apply where the payment is to be made to a person who has an insurable interest in the child's life[10].

1 Certificates of birth or death required for the purposes of the Friendly Societies Act 1974 (c 46) are to be given on special application at a reduced fee of £3: see s 106 (amended by the Registration of Births, Deaths and Marriages (Fees) (Scotland) Order 1989, SI 1989/2370, art 2, Sch 1, as from 1 April 1990, made under the Public Expenditure and Receipts Act 1968 (c 14), s 5, Sch 3).

2 Friendly Societies Act 1974, s 70(1)(a), (b).

3 Ibid, s 70(2). The use of a Military Record Office note that a soldier had died in action was permitted, as the section did not apply to a death on active service: *Liverpool Victoria Legal Friendly Society v Head* (1915) 50 LJCC 75. 'Inquiry' presumably means fatal accident inquiry, though it is not defined.

4 Ie the insurances permitted by the Friendly Societies Act 1974, Sch 1, para (2)(d), and limited to £30: see para 686, note 5, above.

5 See ibid, ss 72(1), 73, and Sch 5 (as amended: see note 1 above), and the Industrial Assurance and Friendly Societies (Death Certificates) (Scotland) Regulations 1949, SI 1949/1066.

6 Friendly Societies Act 1974, Sch 5, para 2.

7 In view of the prohibition in ibid, s 71, such payments can only be made when the child is ordinarily resident outside the United Kingdom and the Isle of Man: see para 692 above.

8 See ibid, s 74, Sch 6, para 6.

9 Ibid, s 70, and Sch 6, paras 3, 5, which prescribe the procedure in detail, the information to be disclosed in making the application, the indorsements on the certificate(s) by the registrar of deaths and those by the society concerned.

10 Ibid, Sch 6, para 8. However, the comments of Lord Dundas and Lord Guthrie in *Carmichael v Carmichael's Executrix* 1919 SC 636, 1919 2 SLT 89, should be noted.

(10) DISPUTES

725. Disputes. The manner in which disputes are to be settled is one of the mandatory provisions to be included in the rules[1], and there are a number of other dispute-related provisions which supplement that requirement. The cumulative effect of these provisions is virtually to exclude the courts from making any decision on a disputed issue relating to the internal affairs of a society. First, all disputes[2] between:

(1) a member, an aggrieved ex-member, or a person claiming through a member or ex-member, or under the rules, and the society or branch or any officer[3], or

(2) a branch or any officer of a branch and the central society (or branch) to which the branch in question is affiliated[4], or

(3) two or more branches[5] or their officers[6],

must be referred to, and resolved under, the disputes procedure set out in the society's rules[7]. A dispute within the specified categories must be settled in accordance with the rules procedure; all other jurisdictions are excluded[8] unless one of the exceptions noted below applies. The rules may direct that disputes are to be referred to the sheriff court for settlement[9]. An application can be made to the sheriff for the enforcement of the decision reached under the disputes procedure[10].

Special provision is made for a society electing to invest surplus funds in another society or branch and which is entitled to take part in the management of the borrower society or branch to have any dispute arising between them to be decided in accordance with the disputes procedure of that borrower[11]. In this case the sheriff's jurisdiction is excluded only if an application under the borrowers' disputes procedure has been made before the commencement of any court proceedings[12].

Secondly, the sheriff court may decide disputes otherwise reserved to the disputes procedure if no decision is made within forty days of any application under the disputes procedure[13]. Societies with branches may have a more complicated procedure which has its own appeals system from branch to society, and in that case, provided the rules do not allow more than three months to elapse between each successive decision, application must be made to all of the bodies appointed under the rules at each stage of the procedure before the forty-day time limit begins to run[14]. Jurisdiction is also given to the sheriff in those cases where the rules do not contain a disputes procedure[15].

Thirdly, and unless the rules expressly exclude this right, the parties may agree to refer the dispute to the registrar for decision[16]. The registrar is to decide the dispute and to do that is given power to administer oaths, to require the attendance of the parties and witnesses and the production of documents and to award expenses either from the society or from any party to the dispute[17].

Fourthly, any person to whom a dispute is referred has a discretion, following an application from either party, to state a case for the opinion of the Court of Session on any question of law[18]. He cannot be compelled to state a case, notwithstanding anything in any enactment[19].

Finally, these provisions apply only to disputes as defined in section 76 of the Friendly Societies Act 1974, and in any other case there is no restriction on the rights of either party to a dispute to take appropriate legal proceedings in the usual manner[20].

1 See the Friendly Societies Act 1974 (c 46), s 7(2), Sch 2, para 9, and para 699 above.
2 'Dispute' includes questions of membership and its availability, continuation or reinstatement, and is restricted for ex-members to matters arising during membership: ibid, s 76(4). The dispute must also relate to membership as opposed to a dispute not centred on the member's capacity as such: cf the expulsion of an officer from the society (*Glasgow District of Ancient Order of Foresters v Stevenson* (1899) 2 F 14, 7 SLT 163); the repayment of money deposited by a member (*Melrose v Adams (Edinburgh Savings Bank)* (1897) 24 R 483); dispute between two people claiming through a member (*Lewis v Paulton* (1907) 14 SLT 818, OH); dispute over the executor's right to represent a deceased member (*Symington's Executor v Galashiels Co-operative Store Co* (1894) 21 R 371, 1 SLT 400); the allegation that the election of a board member was in breach of the rules (*M'Gowan v Glasgow Friendly Society* 1913 SC 991, 1913 2 SLT 40); whether the society's rules were *ultra vires* or not (*McEllistrim v Ballymacelliogott Co-operative Agricultural and Dairy Sociey* [1919] AC 548, HL); and a claim by a member for damages for breach of contract (*Carroll v Piling* [1939] LJNCCR 148).
3 Friendly Societies Act 1974, s 76(1)(a), (b).
4 Ibid, s 76(1)(c), (d).
5 Ie where the branches are those of a single society: ibid, s 76(1)(e).
6 Ibid, s 76(1)(e).
7 Ibid, s 76(1). For the purposes of the Tribunals and Inquiries Act 1971 (c 62), s 14, the Friendly Societies Act 1974, s 76(1), is deemed to have been contained in an Act passed before 1 August 1958 (s 76(1)), which has the effect of ensuring that judicial review of such judicial/administrative determinations is not excluded.
8 Ibid, s 76(1), (5).
9 Ibid, s 76(3), (5). The rules may refer to justices for whom, in Scotland, is substituted the sheriff.
10 Ibid, s 76(2), (5).
11 Ibid, s 80(1). As to the investing of surplus funds, see para 720 above.
12 Ibid, s 80(2)(a), (b).
13 Ibid, s 79(1). For the purposes of s 79, 'dispute' means a dispute falling within s 76: s 79(4).
14 Ibid, s 79(2). See also *Gall v Loyal Glenbogie Lodge of the Oddfellows Friendly Society* (1900) 2 F 1187, 8 SLT 140; *Collins v Barrowfield United Oddfellows* 1915 SC 190, 1914 2 SLT 401.
15 Friendly Societies Act 1974, s 79(3) (of particular relevance to societies with rules certified or recorded under the repealed Friendly Societies Acts which are deemed to be registered under the Friendly Societies Act 1974).
16 Ibid, s 77(1). For the purposes of s 77 'dispute' means a dispute falling within s 76: s 77(4). For the form of application, see the Friendly Societies Regulations 1975, SI 1975/205, reg 2, Sch 1, Form T.
17 Friendly Societies Act 1974, s 77(2), (3). The registrar has the powers of a sheriff to grant warrants for the production of documents and the examination of havers: s 78(3). The forms were provided in the now revoked Treasury Regulations (Friendly Societies) issued under the Friendly Societies Act 1896 (c 25) and are to be found in F B Fuller *The Law Relating to Friendly Societies and Industrial and Provident Societies* (4th edn, 1926) p 525. The registrar's decision can be enforced by the sheriff: see the Friendly Societies Act 1974, s 76(2), (5).
18 Ibid, s 78(1).

19 Ibid, s 78(1). Although s 78(1) refers expressly only to the Arbitration Act 1950 (c 27), s 21 (repealed), it will also exclude the otherwise overriding terms of the Administration of Justice (Scotland) Act 1972 (c 59), s 3: see generally ARBITRATION, vol 2, para 451.

20 See the cases cited in note 2 above, which illustrate the type of dispute allocated to the disputes procedure or to the regular judicial system.

(11) AMALGAMATIONS, TRANSFERS AND CONVERSIONS

726. Introduction. The Friendly Societies Act 1974 provides for the amalgamation and transfer of engagements of societies, as well as for conversion into a company. An amalgamation is a fusion of societies, creating a single new society from the amalgamating societies, whereas a transfer of engagements enlarges the receiving society which, save in so far as it may choose to alter its own constitution, remains legally unaltered. These procedures are restricted to societies of the same class; where they differ, cancellation followed by re-registration should be adopted.

727. Amalgamations. Two or more societies may amalgamate[1] with or without dissolution or division of funds[2] and without affecting the rights of any creditor of the participating society[3]. Each society must pass a special resolution[4] authorising the amalgamation[5]. The special resolutions do not become effective until registration, which is effected six weeks after the prescribed forms are submitted to the registrar for that purpose[6]; the scheme requires all special resolutions to be lodged before the amalgamated society is established.

If the amalgamating societies are friendly societies, the following additional provisions apply. At least fourteen days before the general meeting the society must send each member a notice giving details of the proposal in terms approved by the chief registrar[7]. Alternatively the chief registrar may authorise the substitution of advertisements in a local newspaper[8]. A right of objection is given to the members and to any other person who would be adversely affected to a significant extent by the amalgamation[9]. The objection is lodged with the chief registrar[10], and cannot be made outside the six-week period after the resolution is lodged with the registrar[11]. The only grounds of objection are that the rules of the society or the statutory procedure has not been complied with[12].

The procedure to be followed by the registrar is set out[13], and the registrar may dismiss the objection, accept it without further declaration, modify or cancel the special resolution, or stipulate additional procedures to be carried out before registration of the resolution[14]. Additionally and in the case of the amalgamation of friendly societies only, any person who is entitled to a benefit from the friendly society in question and is dissatisfied with the arrangements made to secure that benefit may appeal within three months of the passing of the special resolution to the sheriff[15], who may exercise the unlimited powers conferred for the settlement of diputes[16].

1 The effect of an amalgamation and the explanation of the effects of amalgamation in the text are supported by the tax case *Northern Rock Building Society v Davies* [1969] 3 All ER 1310, [1969] 1 WLR 1742.

2 Friendly Societies Act 1974 (c 46), s 82(1). There is no statutory procedure for the amalgamation of branches, which is, therefore, left to the regulation of the rules of the participating branches.

3 Ibid, s 82(7).

4 A special resolution requires notice of the meeting and of the intention to propose that resolution in terms of the rules, the passing of the resolution by a three-quarters majority of members, voting in person or proxy (or of delegates if it is a delegate meeting) and registration with the registrar: see ibid, s 86(1)–(3), and para 713 above. The resolution cannot be challenged for irregularity save under the statutory procedure of s 83(1), (6), (8).

5 Ibid, s 82(1).
6 Ibid, s 86(4). The copy resolution is signed in duplicate by the chairman and the secretary and
   supported by statutory declarations: s 86(3). For the forms, see the Friendly Societies Regulations 1975, SI 1975/205, regs 2, 8, Sch 1, Forms U, V.
7 Friendly Societies Act 1974, s 82(4)(a).
8 Ibid, s 82(4)(b). The form and frequency of the advertisements will be fixed by the registrar:
   s 82(4)(b).
9 Ibid, s 83(1).
10 For Scottish friendly societies, the decision would be that of the Assistant Registrar for Scotland,
   and may delegate the decision to an assistant registrar: ibid, s 88(3), applying the provisions of
   s 77(2), (3) to objections to amalgamations.
11 Ibid, s 83(2). If a complaint is made the resolution is not registered until the complaint is
   withdrawn or settled: s 83(2).
12 Ibid, s 83(1)(a), (b).
13 Ie under ibid, s 83.
14 The registrar may dismiss the complaint or (after giving both sides a hearing) make his decision
   (s 83(4)); he has power to administer oaths, to compel the attendance of parties and witnesses and
   productions, and to award expenses (s 83(3), applying s 77(2), (3)); and to state a case on any legal
   question for the opinion of the Court of Session (s 83(7)). Where a conditional validity is granted,
   the resolution cannot be registered until the conditions are met: s 83(5).
15 Ibid, s 83(8). If the amalgamation has proceeded, the sheriff court appropriate to the amalgamated society has jurisdiction: s 83(8).
16 Ie under s 79(1): see para 725 above.

728. Transfer of engagements.

A society may transfer its engagements to
either another society or to a company[1]. From the terms of section 82 of the
Friendly Societies Act 1974 it is to be inferred, for it is not expressly stated, that a
transfer need not only be complete, but can also be partial. The same procedures
and safeguards as apply to amalgamations apply also to a transfer of engagements[2]. However, the following should be noted:

(1) the transferee or receiving society need only authorise the scheme in the way
    permitted by its rules and need not pass a special resolution[3]; and
(2) if the whole of a society's obligations are transferred to a company, the
    registrar must cancel its registration which has become void[4].

1 Friendly Societies Act 1974 (c 46), s 82(2), (3).
2 See para 727 above. For the forms in respect of transfers to another society, see the Friendly
   Societies Regulations 1975, SI 1975/205, regs 2, 9, 10, Sch 1, Forms V, W, X, Y, signed as
   appropriate and in duplicate by the chairman of the transferee society and the secretaries of both
   societies, and supporting statutory declarations. For the forms in respect of a transfer to a
   company, see reg 12, Sch 1, Forms V, W, AA.
3 Friendly Societies Act 1974, s 82(2).
4 Ibid, s 82(5).

729. Juvenile societies.

A juvenile society is one in which the age of all its
members is below twenty-one; and it may amalgamate with a society or branch
whose members are over that age by following the procedure for amendment of
rules[1]. The scheme may be either for a simple amalgamation of the societies or
branches concerned, or for a distribution of the members of the juvenile society
between several branches[2]. The normal procedure for amalgamation does not
apply[2].

1 Friendly Societies Act 1974 (c 46), s 82(6). The rules will give the amendment procedure: see
   para 703 above.
2 Ibid, s 82(6).

730. Conversion of a society into a branch.

A society may affiliate to
another (central) society and become a branch of it, or of an existing branch of
the society[1]. The converting society passes an ordinary resolution, and that

resolution when approved by the registrar operates to cancel the registration of the society and re-register it as a branch[2]. The registrar's approval is dependent on the suitability of the rules of the converting society as branch rules, and the society, when converting, may adopt appropriate amendments to its rules in the conversion resolution[3], which are registered without further procedure[4].

1 Friendly Societies Act 1974 (c46), s 85(1).
2 Ibid, s 85(1), (4)(a), (b). Two copies of the resolution (and any amendment of rules) signed by the chairman and secretary of the converting society and countersigned by the secretary of the receiving society and a marked-up copy of the rules must be lodged with the registrar, and take effect only on this registration: s 85(3), (4).
3 Ibid, s 85(2). The rules automatically become the rules of the new branch in so far as they are not contrary to the express terms of the Act: s 85(6).
4 Ibid, s 85(5).

731. Conversion of a society into a company. If the members of a society pass the necessary special resolution the society may convert into a company registered under the Companies Act 1985[1]. The registration of the (former) society becomes void and is cancelled after registration of the resolution[2]. If the special resolution contains the necessary clauses required of a company's memorandum and articles of association[3], a copy of the resolution sealed and stamped by the registrar after registration has the same effect as a signed and witnessed memorandum and articles of association[4]. The conversion does not affect any right or penalty which exists against the society and the conversion is to be disregarded in proceedings for enforcement[5]. Such rights and penalties are given priority against the company's property over all other claims against the company[6].

1 Friendly Societies Act 1974 (c46), s 84(1). For the meaning of 'special resolution', see para 713, note 4, above.
2 Ibid, s 84(3). The application is completed in triplicate signed by the chairman and secretary together with the statutory declaration, and lodged with the registrar: Friendly Societies Regulations 1975, SI 1975/205, regs 2, 11, Sch 1, Forms v, z.
3 The new company cannot adopt objects more extensive than those available to it as a society (*Blythe v Birtley* [1910] 1 Ch 228, CA), but as a company it is free to adopt more extensive objects in so far as it is permitted by Companies Act 1985 (c6), ss 4–6 (*McGlade v Royal London Mutual Insurance Society Ltd* [1910] 2 Ch 169, CA). See further COMPANIES.
4 Friendly Societies Act 1974, s 84(2). The resolution will still require registration with the Registrar of Companies to comply with the Companies Act 1985, Pt I, Ch I (ss 1–24): see COMPANIES. The conversion does not make the society's members into company members; allotment/subscription of shares or application for membership as the case may be is required to produce a register of members: *Re Blackburn Philanthropic Assurance Co Ltd* [1914] 2 Ch 430.
5 Friendly Societies Act 1974, s 84(4)(a).
6 Ibid, s 84(4)(b).

(12) INSPECTION AND PRODUCTION OF DOCUMENTS

732. Inspection by members' requisition. A specified minority of the members[1] may apply to the registrar for the appointment of an inspector to investigate and report on the affairs of the society[2]. The application must be supported by proof that there are good reasons for the appointment and that it is not malicious[3]. Some security to cover future costs may be required before appointment, and notice must be served on the society[4].

The inspector is given all necessary powers to require the production of books and papers and to examine on oath all officers, members, agents and employees[5]. The registrar will award expenses as he sees fit against the requisitionists, the society itself or its present or former members or officers[6].

These provisions do not apply to a society with branches save with the consent of the central society[7].

1 Ie (1) one-fifth for a society of not less than 1,000 members; (2) 100 in the case of a society of not less than 1,000 and not more than 10,000 members; and (3) 500 if there are more than 10,000 members. Friendly Societies Act 1974 (c 46), s 90(1), (2)(a), (b).
2 Ibid, s 90(1)(a).
3 Ibid, s 90(3). For the form, see the Friendly Societies Regulations 1975, SI 1975/205, reg 2, Sch 1, Form AC.
4 Friendly Societies Act 1974, s 90(3), (4).
5 Ibid, s 90(6). As to guidance on the way in which an inspection is to be conducted, see *Hearts of Oak Assurance Co Ltd v Attorney-General* [1932] AC 392, HL.
6 Friendly Societies Act 1974, s 90(5).
7 Ibid, s 90(2).

733. Inspection by the registrar. The chief registrar may appoint an inspector to investigate the affairs of a society[1]. He is given all necessary powers to require the production of books and papers and to examine on oath all officers, members, agents and employees[1]. The registrar must be satisfied the appointment is expedient in the interests of the members or of the public[1]. The society or its present or former members may be required to meet the expenses of the investigation[2].

If after receiving the inspector's report the registrar considers that it is in the interests of the members or of the public he may apply to the Court of Session for a winding up order under the Insolvency Act 1986[3].

1 Friendly Societies Act 1974 (c 46), s 87(1). Section 87 applies in relation to a registered branch of a registered friendly society as it applies in relation to the society: s 87(4).
2 Ibid, s 87(3).
3 Friendly Societies Act 1974, s 87(2) (amended by the Companies Consolidation (Consequential Provisions) Act 1985 (c 9), s 30, Sch 2, and the Insolvency Act 1986 (c 45), ss 439(2), 440, Sch 14). As to winding up by the court, see the Insolvency Act 1986, Pt IV, Ch VI (ss 117–162), and COMPANIES.

734. Production of documents. If the chief registrar thinks he has good reasons to do so he may either order a society to produce specified documents[1] or authorise an official personally to require the immediate production of specified documents[2]. This power is extended:
(1) to cover any person who may have possession of the documents subject to the preservation of any right of lien[3];
(2) to allow copies to be made and explanations required from any person including the custodier, present or former officers and employees[4];
(3) if the documents cannot be produced, to require the person under the order to state where he believes them to be[5].
Any person who fails to comply with these provisions commits an offence, and is liable on summary conviction to a fine not exceeding level 5 on the standard scale[6].

1 The time and place along with the documents will be specified in the direction: Friendly Societies Act 1974 (c 46), s 89(1)(a).
2 Ibid, s 89(1)(a), (b). Section 89 applies in relation to a registered branch of a registered friendly society as it applies in relation to the society: s 89(7).
3 Ibid, s 89(2).
4 Ibid, s 89(3)(a).
5 Ibid, s 89(3)(b).
6 Ibid, s 89(4). As to level 5 of the standard scale, see para 630, note 4, above. There is a defence that the documents were not in the person's possession or compliance was not reasonably possible: s 89(5). A statement made by a person in compliance with a requirement imposed by s 89, including any explanation, may be used in evidence against him: s 89(6).

(13) SUSPENSION AND CANCELLATION

735. Power to suspend business. The chief registrar has power to make an order forbidding a society from admitting new members or making new contracts with its existing members[1]. The registrar must conclude that such an order is in the interests of the members or of the public, and he must give one month's notice of his intention to make such an order to the society, stating the reasons justifying his intention[2]. The society in turn may make representations to the registrar, which he is bound to consider before reaching his decision[3]. If, after this procedure, the registrar adheres to his decision to make a suspension order, he must serve notice on the society to that effect and also publish a notice in the *Edinburgh Gazette* and issue such other publicity as he sees necessary to inform the public[4]. The notice served on the society must again include the reasons justifying the order, which must all have been included in the original notice of intention[5].

1 Friendly Societies Act 1974 (c 46), s 88(1). The order may be revoked: s 88(8). Section 88 applies in relation to a registered branch of a registered friendly society as it applies in relation to the society: s 88(9).
2 Ibid, s 88(1), (2), (3).
3 Ibid, s 88(4). The society must make its reply within the time (not less than one month) set by the registrar, who must also allow the society to be heard if it so requests: s 88(4).
4 Ibid, s 88(5), (6). Non-compliance by a society is an offence and punishable on conviction on indictment or on summary conviction by a fine which, on summary conviction, must not exceed the prescribed sum; and non-compliance by every officer who knowingly and wilfully author-ises or permits the contravention is liable (1) on conviction on indictment, to a fine or to imprisonment for a term not exceeding two years, or both, or (2) on summary conviction, to a fine not exceeding the prescribed sum: s 88(7). At the date at which this volume states the law, the prescribed sum is £2,000: see the Criminal Procedure (Scotland) Act 1975 (c 21), s 289B (added by the Criminal Law Act 1977 (c 45), s 63(1), Sch 11, para 5, substituted by the Criminal Justice Act 1982 (c 48), s 55(2), and amended by the Increase of Criminal Penalties etc (Scotland) Order 1984, SI 1984/526, art 3).
5 Friendly Societies Act 1974, s 88(5).

736. Cancellation and suspension of registration. There are five cases in which the registration of a society may be either cancelled or, in the non-voluntary case, suspended by the registrar — the Assistant Registrar for Scot-land if its business is wholly within Scotland, otherwise the chief registrar[1]. The cases, which must be proved to the registrar's satisfaction, are:
(1) where the society so requests;
(2) where registration has been obtained by fraud;
(3) where the society exists for an unlawful purpose;
(4) where it has ceased to exist; or
(5) where it has wilfully and after notice from the registrar violated any pro-vision of the Friendly Societies Act 1974[2].
In the case of voluntary application for cancellation the registrar has a discretion to grant the application and will require some good reason to justify it. Sugges-ted reasons might include a need to re-register under another category of friendly society, or the society having no members, assets or liabilities. Notice of cancellation must be published both in the *Edinburgh Gazette* and in a local newspaper[3]. In the other compulsory cases, the registrar has the option of either cancelling the registration or of suspending registration for not more than three months and of renewing the suspension for further three-month periods[4].

Once he is satisfied that the grounds are established, the registrar must give the society at least two months' written notice of his intention, specifying the grounds justifying the proposed action[5]. During the period of notice the society may lodge an appeal against the proposed decision from the Assistant Registrar for Scotland to the chief registrar, and from his confirmation of the decision to the Court of Session[6]. Lodging of an appeal against a proposed cancellation prevents implementation of the cancellation until the appeal is terminated, but instead the registrar may suspend registration[7]. Notice of the cancellation or suspension is to be given in the *Gazette* and a local newspaper[8].

Cancellation or suspension of registration removes from the society all entitlement to the privileges of the 1974 Act but without prejudice to liabilities incurred by it[9]. In short, it becomes an unregistered society, not an illegal one, nor does it cease to exist[10].

1 Ie under the Friendly Societies Act 1974 (c 46), s 91(1), (2).
2 Ibid, s 91(1)(a)–(c). For the form of application, see the Friendly Societies Regulations 1975, SI 1975/205, regs 2, 13, Sch 1, Form AD.
3 Friendly Societies Act 1974, s 91(6). For the form of notice, see the Friendly Societies Regulations 1975, reg 2, Sch 1, Form AH. The application (see note 2 above) requires the nomination of the appropriate local newspaper and that the costs of these advertisements accompanies the form.
4 Friendly Societies Act 1974, s 91(2)(a), (b).
5 Ibid, s 91(3). This does not apply in the case of cancellation at the request of the society, following transfer of engagements to a company (see s 82(5), and para 728 above), re-registration as a company (see s 84(3), and para 731 above), conversion to a branch (see s 85(4), and para 730 above), or if any appeal is dismissed within the two-month period (see s 92): s 91(4).
6 Ie under ibid, s 92: s 91(5). If the chief registrar makes the decision, appeal lies to the High Court even for a Scottish society if that society does business in England: s 92(2)(b).
7 Ibid, s 91(4), (5).
8 Ibid, s 91(6).
9 Ibid, s 91(7).
10 As to unregistered societies, see para 680 above.

(14) DISSOLUTION AND LIQUIDATION

737. Dissolution generally. There are three methods of dissolving a society:
(1) the occurrence of the event declared by the rules to mark the termination of the society;
(2) by the consent of the members; and
(3) by the award of the registrar[1].
Additionally, a society which has branches cannot be dissolved except with the consent of the central society[2].

As with any other organisation, a friendly society may be formed for a specified purpose with the intention of ending its activities when the purpose is achieved. Accordingly the Friendly Societies Act 1974 authorises the rules specifying an event the happening of which will trigger the dissolution of the society. The Act, whilst permitting this practice, does not make any further provision or supply any procedure. It is, therefore, necessary for the rules to supply the procedure to give effect to a stipulated dissolution event, and how the registrar will ensure that the registered rules are adequate in this respect[3]. If the rules do not provide for the distribution of funds, they are to be divided between the members at the date of dissolution in proportion to the admission fees and subscriptions or other contributions of each[4].

1 Friendly Societies Act 1974 (c 46), s 93(1)(a)–(c).
2 Ibid, s 93(2).
3 Friendly societies and cattle insurance societies are required to include the statutory voluntary dissolution procedure in their rules (s 7(2), Sch 2, para 14), but this would appear to be in addition to any option chosen by virtue of s 93(1)(a). Any such procedure must include a setting out of the division of funds to ensure a final settlement of the society's affairs.
4 *Re Printers and Transferrers Amalgamated Trades Protection Society* [1899] 2 Ch 184; *Re Customs and Excise Officers' Mutual Guarantee Fund, Robson v Attorney-General* [1917] 2 Ch 18.

738. Voluntary dissolution. Voluntary dissolution is possible following the consent of three-quarters of the members of the society[1]. The Friendly Societies Act 1974 does not require a general meeting[2]. Instead, the agreement of the members has to be shown by their signatures to an instrument of dissolution[3]. The instrument of dissolution[4] must include:

(1) details of the assets and liabilities of the society;
(2) the number of its members and their interest in the society;
(3) creditors' claims and the provision for their settlement; and
(4) either the intended division of funds or a statement that this is left to the award of the registrar[5].

If the society is a friendly society, two restrictions apply. First, the division of funds must be so organised as to carry out the objects of the society and satisfy the claims of those receiving annuities or other benefits from the society before any other distribution may be made[6]. Secondly, if the effect of the dissolution is to stop the payment of approved annuities[7], no compensatory payment is to be made from the society's funds, but that sum is to be applied in the purchase of an annuity on similar terms for the persons entitled to the discontinued annuities[8].

The instrument of dissolution is completed in duplicate[9] and registered in the same way as an amendment of rules[10] which provides for the return to the society of an acknowledgment of registration[11]. The instrument of dissolution may be varied by following the same procedure as is required for the initial instrument[12]. The registrar must place notices of the dissolution in the *Edinburgh Gazette* and a local newspaper, and the society will be dissolved from the date of the *Gazette* notice[13]. The dissolution is not final, however, until after three months from that date as any person interested in or having a claim on the funds of the society may bring proceedings in the sheriff court to set aside the dissolution within that time[14]. The instrument of dissolution and any variations are binding on all the members in the same way as are the rules[15].

If a branch elects voluntary dissolution, the consent of the central society must be obtained or the general rules of the society complied with; and a society with branches cannot be dissolved without the consent of the central body[16].

1 Friendly Societies Act 1974 (c 46), s 93(1)(b).
2 *Re Eclipse Mutual Benefit Association* (1854) Kay App 30.
3 Friendly Societies Act 1974, s 93(1)(b). In *Second Edinburgh and Leith Building Society v Aitken* (1892) 19 R 603, the Court of Session required that each member sign personally, although in England the signature of an agent has been accepted: *Dennison v Jeffs* [1896] 1 Ch 611. Minors over sixteen have power to sign for themselves and the parents of those under that age have power to act: Friendly Societies Act 1974, s 60(2).
4 For the forms, see the Friendly Societies Regulations 1975, SI 1975/205, regs 2, 14, Sch 1, Forms A1, A1b, AJ. The instrument itself is in duplicate and accompanied by a statutory declaration by either a trustee or three committee members and the secretary: Friendly Societies Act 1974, s 94(4).
5 Ibid, s 94(2)(a)–(d).
6 Ibid, s 94(5).
7 Ie as defined in the Income and Corporation Taxes Act 1988 (c 1), s 620(9).
8 Friendly Societies Act 1974, s 93(4).
9 See note 4 above.
10 Friendly Societies Act 1974, s 94(6). As to the registration of the amendment of rules, see para 703 above.
11 For the form, see the Friendly Societies Regulations 1975, Sch 1, Form AK.
12 Friendly Societies Act 1974, s 94(3).
13 Ibid, s 94(7). For the form, see the Friendly Societies Regulations 1975, Sch 1, Form AL. The local newspaper must be nominated and the expenses of the advertisements defrayed.
14 Friendly Societies Act 1974, s 93(3). The application is made to the sheriff court of any district in which the society has a place of business (s 93(3)), and notice of the proceedings must be given to the registrar within seven days or the three-month period, whichever expires first, and of any order setting aside the dissolution within seven days (s 97).

15 Ibid, s 94(6). The registrar has decided that the instrument of dissolution supersedes any death benefit otherwise due under the rules where a member dies after its date: *Fortune v Orr* [1894] FS Cases 539; *Russell v Hereford Friendly Society* (1899) CR Rep, Part A, 21 (Parliamentary Papers for 1900, vol 91).

16 Friendly Societies Act 1974, s 93(1)(b), (2).

739. Dissolution by award. The discretion of the chief registrar to award dissolution by award cannot be invoked by the chief registrar himself. The procedure must be initiated by an application from the members. The application is made in writing and must allege, with supporting evidence, an insufficiency either(1) in the society's funds and an inability to meet its claims, or (2) in the contribution rates with inadequate cover for the benefits assured: it then requests an investigation into the allegations with a view to the dissolution of the society[1]. The application must be supported by the same proportion of the membership as is required for an ordinary inspection, and in the case of a branch with the consent of the central society[2]. The chief registrar may grant the application and have the affairs of the society investigated either by the registrar himself, an assistant registrar, an actuary or auditor, the expenses being met by the society itself[3]. At least one month's written notice of the investigation is served on the society by the registrar[4].

If the investigation finds that the alleged insufficiency of funds or contributions is established and if the chief registrar considers it expedient, he may award dissolution of the society and decide on the necessary division of funds[5]. Within twenty-one days of the award notice must be given in the *Edinburgh Gazette* and a local newspaper, the date of the notice being the date of dissolution[6]. The dissolution is subject to there being no (successful) application by a member or other person interested in the funds of the society for the setting aside of the award within three months of the publication of the notice[7]; otherwise it is final, there being no other appeal[8].

If the chief registrar elects to award dissolution, he may further choose to suspend its operation for a specified period sufficient to allow the society to review its affairs and alter its contributions or benefits so as to avoid the insufficiency justifying the award[9]. If the chief registrar is satisfied that changes in contributions or benefits have been made within the specified period and are sufficient to prevent the need for dissolution, he may cancel the award[9].

1 Friendly Societies Act 1974 (c 46), s 95(2)(a)–(c). For the form, see the Friendly Societies Regulations 1975, SI 1975/205, reg 2, Sch 1, Form AM.

2 Friendly Societies Act 1974, s 95(2). For the proportion of membership required for an investigation, see s 90, and para 732, note 1, above.

3 Ibid, s 95(1), (7). Any registrar acting has all the powers as in the settlement of disputes: s 95(5). As to the powers, see ss 77(3), 78(3), and para 725 above.

4 Ibid, s 95(1).

5 Ibid, s 95(3). As to the holders of any discontinued annuities, see s 93(3), and para 738 above. For the form of award, see the Friendly Societies Regulations 1975, Sch 1, Form AN.

6 Friendly Societies Act 1974, s 95(6). For the form, see the Friendly Societies Regulations 1975, Sch 1, Form AO. The application form provides for the selection of the local newspaper.

7 Friendly Societies Act 1974, ss 95(6)(a), (b), 97. Section 93(3) does not apply, consequently it appears from *Wilmot v Grace* [1892] 1 QB 812 that (converting to Scottish courts) only the Court of Session would have jurisdiction.

8 See the Friendly Societies Act 1974, s 96. The award is enforceable by an application to the sheriff through his power to enforce the settlement of disputes under s 76(2): see para 725 above. It is binding on all parties having any claim on the funds of the society, but the doubts expressed in *R v Chief Registrar of Friendly Societies, ex parte Evans* (1900) CR Rep, Part A, 89 (Parliamentary Papers for 1901, vol 72), 16 TLR 346, CA, that this does not include creditors who are not otherwise connected with the society should be noted.

9 Friendly Societies Act 1974, s 95(4).

740. Liquidation. A friendly society is an unregistered company as defined by section 220 of the Insolvency Act 1986 and so falls within Parts IV and V of that Act[1], which gives the court power to appoint a liquidator[2]. In such a case all the provisions applying in a compulsory company liquidation apply to the society[3].

1 Ie under the Insolvency Act 1986 (c 45), Pt IV (ss 73–219), Pt V (ss 220–229): see COMPANIES, vol 4, paras 716 ff.
2 *Canavan* 1929 SLT 636, OH; *Re Twentieth Century Equitable Friendly Society* [1910] WN 236. As to the appointment of a liquidator, see COMPANIES, vol 4, para 753.
3 See the Insolvency Act 1986, Pt IV, Chs VI–X (ss 117–219), Pt V, and COMPANIES, vol 4, paras 720 ff.

(15) ENFORCEMENT

741. Legal proceedings. The Friendly Societies Act 1974 makes the provision necessary for legal proceedings to be taken by or against a society, which is of course unincorporated. The trustees have the power to bring or defend any proceedings concerning any property or claim affecting the society and additionally the rules may nominate any other officer to exercise the same power[1]. Proceedings once begun are not affected by any change in the office holders[2], and if it is necessary to proceed against a trustee the other trustees have the power to act[3]. In the case of proceedings brought against a society by either a member or a person claiming through a member, the defender can be either the official defenders — the trustees or any officer nominated by the rules — or any other officer or any person receiving contributions or issuing policies for the society[4].

Service in proceedings against a society can be effected in several ways:
(1) by personal service on the relevant officer;
(2) by leaving a copy at the registered office or any other place of business of the society which is within the jurisdiction of the particular court;
(3) if that office is closed, the copy may be fixed to the outer door;
(4) by registered or recorded delivery letter addressed to the committee of the society at its registered office and posted at least six days before any further step in the proceedings are taken[5].

However, if the proceedings are for the recovery of a fine imposed under the Act service can be made either by leaving a copy at the registered office or any other place of business of the society which is within the jurisdiction of the particular court, or, if that office is closed, the copy may be fixed to the outer door[6].

1 Friendly Societies Act 1974 (c 46), s 103(1). The appointment of an officer by the rules alternative to the trustees does not supersede the trustees' power to bring or defend proceedings: *General Railway Workers Union v Macdonald* (1900) 37 SLR 721.
2 Ie by death, resignation or removal: Friendly Societies Act 1974, s 103(3).
3 Ibid, s 103(3), (7).
4 Ibid, s 103(2). The defender is to be designated by his or her name followed by 'on behalf of the (named) society or branch': s 103(2).
5 Ibid, s 103(4), (5). In *Gatehouse v Shaw* (1919) CR Rep, Part A, 58 (Parliamentary Papers for 1920, vol 37), the English Court of Appeal decided that (converting the sections to those of the 1974 Act) these special methods of service were only available to proceedings brought under s 103(2), ie by members or those claiming through a member, and that all other proceedings regulated therfore by s 103(1) were to conform to the normal procedure of the court in question.
6 Friendly Societies Act 1974, s 103(6).

742. Recovery of costs. If the registrar directs that costs or expenses are to be recovered from any person, which will include a society, those costs are recoverable in civil proceedings as a debt[1]. This provides a procedure for the recovery of costs or expenses incurred in for example inspections, investigations or special meetings.

1 Friendly Societies Act 1974 (c 46), s 101(2), (3).

743. Prosecution of offences. There are a number of offences[1] detailed in the Friendly Societies Act 1974 which are the subject of summary prosecution, that is in the relevant sheriff court. The chief registrar, any assistant registrar or any person aggrieved[2] is given power to bring such a prosecution[3]. If a society is guilty of a breach of the Act which is an offence, any officer who is required by its rules to discharge that duty is liable to the same penalty as the society[4]. If there is no such officer, all committee members are liable to that penalty unless they can prove they were ignorant of or attempted to prevent the commission of the offence[4]. For each week that a default continues a new offence is committed[5].

Summary proceedings brought by the registrar or by the procurator fiscal for offences under the Act must be brought within one year of its first discovery by the registrar, but may not be brought more than three years from its actual commission[6].

1 The particular offences are recorded in para 744 below.
2 'Person aggrieved' is to be given its ordinary meaning, as someone who has not got a sentimental grievance but has sustained a legal loss or liability: *Robinson v Currey* (1881) 7 QBD 465, CA; *Re Rivière's Trade Mark* (1884) 26 Ch D 48.
3 Friendly Societies Act 1974 (c 46), s 101(1). The concurrence of the procurator fiscal is not required: *Scott v McIntosh* 1876 Guthries Sh Ct Cases (1st series) 211.
4 Friendly Societies Act 1974, s 98(5).
5 Ibid, s 98(6).
6 Ibid, s 98(7). This does not apply if the society is a collecting society: see s 98(8), and the Industrial Assurance Act 1923 (c 8), s 39(5).

744. Offences. The Friendly Societies Act 1974 provides for the following offences and penalties. Unless the Act provides an alternative penalty any society, branch, officer or member found guilty of an offence is liable to a fine on summary conviction not exceeding level 3 on the standard scale[1].

An offence is committed by any society, branch, officer or member who:
(1) fails to give any notice or send any return etc;
(2) wilfully fails to supply any information required by the registrar or other authorised person, or does anything forbidden by the Act;
(3) wilfully supplies false or inadequate information in any return[2].

If a branch has either seceded from or been expelled by its central society, any officer or member of the former branch using the name of that society or its former branch number commits an offence[3]. Any person refusing to attend, produce documents or give evidence to the registrar after a dispute or complaint following an amalgamation or transfer of engagements has been referred to him commits an offence[4]. Where money is payable on the death of a child under ten it may only be paid in accordance with the provisions of the Act otherwise the society commits an offence, as does a parent or personal representative of any child either using an unauthorised or false death certificate or otherwise attempting to evade the controls on such death payments[5].

If a particular breach would otherwise be caught by the general offences but a provision provides its own penalty that will apply in place of the general offence[6].

In the amalgamation, transfer of engagements or dissolution of a friendly society any officer or other person who does not comply with the provisions of the Act is liable on summary conviction to a fine not exceeding level 4 on the standard scale[7].

A person, with intent to mislead or defraud, who falsely supplies another:

(1) with rules which are not, as is claimed, the rules of the society, or

(2) with rules of a registered society or branch when the society or branch is not registered,

is liable, on summary conviction, to a fine not exceeding the prescribed sum or, on conviction on indictment, to a fine or to imprisonment not exceeding two years, or both[8]. Prosecution on indictment is permitted where the offence has been committed by a friendly society or one of its officers but not if there have been prior proceedings[9].

Any person wilfully falsifying a balance sheet or any return or other document prepared for the purposes of the Act is liable on summary conviction to a fine not exceeding level 5 on the standard scale[10].

Any committee member failing to ensure that the society complies with the provisions requiring the revenue account and balance sheet to show a true and fair view of its affairs is liable on summary conviction to a fine not exceeding level 5 on the standard scale[11]. A defence that there were reasonable grounds for his belief that a proper person was responsible for compliance is available[12].

Any person failing to comply with a direction from the chief registrar to produce books or papers or provide any explanation is liable on summary conviction to a fine not exceeding level 5 on the standard scale[13].

A society which fails to comply with the restrictions on limits on insurances on the life of a parent or grandparent is liable on summary conviction to a fine not exceeding level 3 on the standard scale[14]. A society which fails to comply with the restrictions on insuring the life of a child under ten is liable on summary conviction to a fine not exceeding level 3 on the standard scale[15].

A society, exempt from appointing a qualified auditor, failing to comply with the registrar's direction to appoint a qualified auditor is guilty of an offence for which no express penalty is provided[16].

1 Friendly Societies Act 1974 (c 46), s 98(3). As to level 3, see para 645, note 3, above.
2 Ibid, s 98(1)(a)–(c).
3 Ibid, s 98(1)(d).
4 Ibid, s 98(1)(e).
5 Ibid, s 98(1)(f), (g).
6 Ibid, s 98(2).
7 Ibid, s 98(4). As to level 4, see the Criminal Procedure (Scotland) Act 1975 (c 21), ss 289F, 289G (added by the Criminal Justice Act 1982 (c 48), s 54). At the date at which this volume states the law, level 4 is £1,000: Increase of Criminal Penalties etc (Scotland) Order 1984, SI 1984/526, art 4. As to the amalgamation, transfer of engagements or dissolution of societies, see paras 726 ff, and paras 737 ff above.
8 Friendly Societies Act 1974, s 99(1). As to the prescribed sum, see para 735, note 4, above.
9 Ibid, s 99(7).
10 Ibid, s 100. As to level 5, see para 630, note 4, above.
11 Ibid, s 30(8)(a), (b). As to the general provisions in respect of accounts and balance sheets, see para 714 above.
12 Ibid, s 30(8).
13 See ibid, s 89(4), and para 734 above.
14 Ibid, s 73(5). As to the restrictions on limits on insurances on the life of a parent or grandparent, see para 686 above.
15 Ibid, s 71(5). As to the restrictions on insuring the life of a child under ten, see para 692 above.
16 Ibid, s 32(4). As to the audit of exempt societies and branches, see para 715 above. The penalty for contravention is level 3 on the standard scale: see s 98(3) above.

745–800. Recovery of property. If a person either uses false representations to obtain any property from a society or fraudulently withholds property or misapplies it in a manner unauthorised by the rules of the society he is liable on summary conviction to a fine not exceeding level 5 on the standard scale[1]. In addition the court may order the restoration of the property in question to the society[2]. Failure to comply with this order renders the person liable on summary conviction to imprisonment for up to two months[2].

Such proceedings may be instituted by the chief registrar or any assistant registrar to whom he delegates his authority, or any member authorised by the central office[3]. If a society is involved, proceedings may be instituted by the society itself, by any member authorised by it or by its trustees or committee[4]. If a branch is involved, those authorised are the branch, any authorised member, its trustees or committee and in addition the central society or any member of the society or branch authorised by the central society[5].

Alternatively if these criminal proceedings do not result in a conviction and if the sheriff is satisfied that a person has possession of the society's property which he has failed to restore after a request, he may order its restoration[6]. Failure to comply with this order renders the person liable on summary conviction to imprisonment for up to two months[6]. If the person has instead applied the society's money for purposes other than those permitted by the society's rules or the Friendly Societies Act 1974, the sheriff may order repayment of the money so misapplied[7]. If the order is not complied with, it is to be enforced by civil diligence[7]. Appeal against either of these orders is provided for, as if it was made on the conviction of the person against whom it is directed[8], and so any appeal will lie to the High Court of Justiciary as an appeal in a summary cause under the Criminal Procedure (Scotland) Act 1975 (c 21).

There is provision, however, for prosecution on indictment in the normal way where the offence has been committed by a friendly society or one of its officers, whether or not it is one also covered by section 99 of the 1974 Act[9]. Prosecution on indictment is not permitted if there have been prior proceedings[9].

---

1 Friendly Societies Act 1974 (c 46), s 99(2). As to level 5, see para 630, note 4, above. Fraud in the sense adopted by the criminal law is required for conviction; inability to pay, an honest but mistaken misapplication, or a genuine dispute over ownership will not amount to fraud: *Barrett v Markham* (1872) LR 7 CP 405; *Scott v Wilson* (1893) 9 TLR 492; *Madden v Rhodes* [1906] 1 KB 534, DC.

2 Friendly Societies Act 1974, s 99(2).

3 Ibid, s 99(6)(c).

4 Ibid, s 99(6)(a).

5 Ibid, s 99(6)(b).

6 Ibid, s 99(3). It seems this provision was added by the Friendly Societies Act 1908 (c 32) (see s 9 (repealed)) to provide a remedy when the strict requirements of criminal fraud could not be met.

7 Friendly Societies Act 1974, s 99(4).

8 Ibid, s 99(5).

9 Ibid, s 99(7).

INSURANCE

	PARA
1. **INTRODUCTION**	801
2. **CLASSIFICATION OF INSURANCE**	803
3. **THE PROVISION OF INSURANCE AND INSURANCE SERVICES**	806
(1) Introduction	806
(2) Regulation of Insurance Contracts	807
(3) Promotion and Marketing of Insurance Products	809
(4) Regulation of Insurance Intermediaries	811
(5) Miscellaneous Consumer Protection Measures	814
4. **FORMATION OF INSURANCE CONTRACTS**	818
(1) General	818
(2) Statutory Notices and Cooling-Off Periods	819
(3) The Proposal Form	822
(4) The Cover Note	825
5. **THE INSURANCE POLICY**	826
(1) Introduction	826
(2) Premiums	832
(3) Construction of Insurance Policies	837
6. **ASSIGNATION**	845
7. **INSURABLE INTEREST**	848
(1) Introduction	848
(2) The Nature of Insurable Interest	849
(3) Time and Insurable Interest	854
8. **MISREPRESENTATION AND NON-DISCLOSURE**	858
(1) Introduction	858
(2) Misrepresentation	859
(3) Non-disclosure	860
(a) Ambit and Duration of the Positive Duty of Disclosure	860
(b) Materiality	864
9. **WARRANTIES**	873
10. **CAUSATION**	879

11. **CLAIMS** 880
(1) Procedure 880
(2) The Loss Recoverable 885
(3) Subrogation 894
    (a) Introduction 894
    (b) Subrogation as a Measure of Indemnity . . . 900
    (c) Statutory Subrogation 904
(4) Contribution 912

1. INTRODUCTION

801. Historical development of insurance in Scotland. Stair is the first Scottish writer on the law to mention insurance[1]. The reference is brief and is confined to a description of insurance as a form of exchange[2]. The second edition of Erskine's *An Institute of the Law of Scotland* also makes brief reference to insurance. It is only with Bell and Hume that the subject is explored in some detail by writers of status[3]. In 1787, however, two monographs on marine insurance written by Scots appeared[4]. Although not the first treatises on insurance written in English, they are the first to be written by lawyers. The earliest reference to marine insurance found so far in Scotland is an entry in the Edinburgh Dean of Guild Court records for 7 March 1621[5]. The historical evidence available[6] points to a growth in the use of marine insurance in Scotland towards the end of the seventeenth and beginning of the eighteenth centuries. Until the 1830s, there is no doubt that English law and practice was the most important influence on the development of the law relating to insurance. Indeed, in a number of cases, the Court of Session adopted the practice of requiring litigants to obtain the opinions of English counsel and Lloyd's underwriters, and were guided by them[7]. Some assertion of independence can be seen in non-marine cases decided in the mid-nineteenth century, but today, for the most part, the general principles of insurance law are the same in both England and Scotland[8].

1 Stair *Institutions* I, 10, 12.

2 Stair's classification is interesting because the Dutch jurist Grotius also treats insurance as a type of exchange: *De Jure Bellis ac Pacis* (1625) 2, 12, 5. The classification is explicable by reference to the development of forms of marine risk allocation in mediaeval, Mediterranean, Europe. Starting with the *foenus nauticum* (sea loan), in which money loaned was repayable (with interest) on safe completion of the voyage, progression was through the *cambium nauticum* (maritime exchange contract), in which goods were pledged in security in exhange for borrowed money, to the simple *cambium* and thence to premium insurance. For an account of the development of marine insurance, see Florence Edler de Roover 'Early Examples of Marine Insurance' *Journal of Economic History* (1945) V, 172.

3 Bell *Commentaries* I, 598–631; Hume *Lectures on the Law of Scotland* (Stair Soc vol 15, 1952 ed GCH Paton) pp 310–402.

4 John Millar (Junior) *Elements of the Law Relating to Insurances* (1787); James Alan Park *A System of the Law of Marine Insurance* (1787). Park was an expatriate Scot who made his career at the English Bar.

5 Dean of Guild Court records, Edinburgh City Archive, vol 3.

6 Balfour *Practicks* makes no mention of premium insurance, nor does William Welwod in either *The Sea Laws of Scotland* (1590) or *An Abridgement of all Sea-Lawes* (1613): see T Callendar Wade *The Sea Law of Scotland* (Scottish Text Society, 3rd series, iv Miscellany Volume, 1933). Note also the omission of material relevant to insurance in sixteenth and seventeenth century style books and protocol books.

7 Eg *Addison v Duguid* (1793) Mor 7077; *Selkrig v Pitcairn and Scott* (1808) Mor 'Insurance' Appendix no. 10.

8 For an account of the history of marine insurance in Scotland, see ADM Forte 'Marine Insurance and Risk Distribution in Scotland Before 1800' (1987) 5 Law and History Review 393.

802. Purpose and definition of insurance. Insurance is a contract concerned with the allocation of risks and losses. But cautionary obligations, maintenance agreements and manufacturers' guarantees also perform this function. It is necessary to distinguish between insurance and other forms of risk allocation since there are important substantive differences between them. Insurance, for example, is a contract *uberrimae fidei* (of the utmost good faith) and imposes a positive duty of disclosure on both insurer and insured. With the exception of fidelity guarantees, the other forms of risk allocation do not impose any such duty. Insurance, unlike caution, is also a 'direct, not an accessory obligation'[1]. Insurance contracts are specifically excluded from the application of the Unfair Contract Terms Act 1977, but manufacturers' guarantees are not[2]. Moreover, in order to carry on 'insurance business' a company must be authorised by, and comply with the requirements of, the Insurance Companies Act 1982 (c 50) and, in some cases, comply with the requirements of the Financial Services Act 1986 (c 60). 'Insurance business' includes making contracts 'for fidelity bonds, performance bonds . . . or similar contracts of guarantee effected by way of business'[3]. Consequently, the Department of Trade and Industry is watchful to see if schemes intended to confer a benefit on others in return for regular payments constitute insurance business.

Insurance has been defined as being a contract in which 'the insurer undertakes, in consideration of the payment of an estimated equivalent beforehand, to make up to the assured any loss he may sustain by the occurrence of an uncertain contingency'[4]. Bell defines insurance as follows: 'It is essential to the contract of insurance that there shall be a subject in which the insured has an interest, a premium given or engaged for and a risk run'[5]. More recently, it has been decided that it is not a *sine qua non* of insurance that the loss to be made up must take the form of payment of monetary compensation. An obligation to confer a benefit corresponding to money (that is, money's worth) in the event of risk attaching will be treated as a contract of insurance, but an agreement merely to consider conferring a benefit if risk attaches is not so treated[6]. The event insured against must be outwith the insurer's control[7]. The essentials of the modern contract of insurance may be summarised as follows: (1) the benefit received is money or money's worth; (2) the event insured against must involve some element of uncertainty; (3) there must be an insurable interest; and (4) the event insured against must be outwith the insurer's control.

1 *Scottish Amicable Heritable Securities Association Ltd v Northern Assurance Co* (1883) 11 R 287 at 303, per Lord Justice-Clerk Moncreiff.
2 Unfair Contract Terms Act 1977 (c 50), s 15(3)(a).
3 Insurance Companies Act 1982 (c 50), s 95(a).
4 *Scottish Amicable Heritable Securities Association Ltd v Northern Assurance Co* (1883) 11 R 287 at 303, per Lord Justice-Clerk Moncreiff.
5 Bell *Principles* s 457.
6 *Prudential Insurance Co v Inland Revenue Comrs* [1904] 2 KB 658 at 663, per Channell J. In *Department of Trade and Industry v St Christopher Motorists Association Ltd* [1974] 1 All ER 395, [1974] 1 WLR 99, it was held that no distinction should be drawn between paying a disabled driver a monetary sum, representing the cost to him of hiring a chauffeur, and the association itself paying for the chauffeur. Cf *Medical Defence Union Ltd v Department of Trade* [1980] Ch 82, [1979] 2 All ER 421, where it was claimed that the right of union members to request assistance in litigation or to be indemnified in respect of claims made against them was of value to them, and was, therefore, a benefit. The court held against the Department of Trade and Industry on the ground that a purely discretionary right could not be a benefit. For a criticism of this decision, see

OT Roberts 'Contracts of Insurance' (1980) 43 MLR 85. See also ADM Forte 'Defining a Contract of Insurance' (1979) 24 JLSS 517.
7 See J Birds *Modern Insurance Law* (1988) pp 9, 10.

2. CLASSIFICATION OF INSURANCE

803. General. Insurance can be classified in many, different, ways. It is important to understand into which category a contract falls, since insurances of that type may attract the application of principles which are not relevant to other classes of insurance.

804. Indemnity and life cover. The most important distinction to be drawn between types of insurance is that between life assurance and indemnity insurance. Examples of life assurance are 'whole' life policies and endowment policies. Whole life policies simply contain an obligation to pay a specified sum on the death of the insured. Endowment policies involve the paying of money to the insured when an agreed age is reached. In addition to the foregoing, there are many types of investments which are linked to life policies and to which the regulatory provisions of the Financial Services Act 1986 (c 60) apply. Indemnity insurance includes marine cover, household and property cover, fire insurance, motor cover and the like. Indemnity policies contain no investment element and are not affected by the Financial Services Act 1986. The 1986 Association of British Insurers' (ABI) *Statement of Long-Term Insurance Practice* applies to life contracts, and its *Statement of General Insurance Practice* applies to indemnity contracts[1]. The indemnity principle and the doctrine of subrogation apply to indemnity contracts but have no place in life cover[2].

It has been noted that in insurance there must be an element of uncertainty regarding the event insured against. In both life and indemnity contracts there is uncertainty surrounding the event insured against. In a contract for motor insurance one's car may never be involved in an accident but, if it is, one can make a claim under the policy. In the case of indemnity cover, therefore, the uncertainty relates to the occurrence of the event insured against. If one insures one's life, there is also uncertainty but it is of a different nature. It is certain that the insured will die but uncertain when he will die. It is for this reason that life cover is sometimes termed 'contingency' insurance: that is, the proceeds of the policy will be paid on the occurrence of an event certain to take place.

1 For a more detailed discussion of these codes, see para 824 below.
2 See paras 894–911 below.

805. First-party and third-party cover. In first-party insurance, the risk insured against is the risk of loss or harm to the insured. In third-party insurance, the risk insured against is the risk of loss or harm to some third party which is caused by the insured. While there is nothing to compel a person to insure against personal mishap, third-party insurance is frequently compulsory[1] and often highly desirable[2].

1 Examples of compulsory third-party insurance are motor vehicle insurance and employers' liability insurance. See the Road Traffic Act 1988 (c 52), Pt VI, (ss 143–162), and the Employers' Liability (Compulsory Insurance) Act 1969 (c 57).
2 An example of the type of cover which it might be prudent to have is occupiers' liability insurance or medical expenses insurance.

3. THE PROVISION OF INSURANCE AND INSURANCE SERVICES

(1) INTRODUCTION

806. General. Insurance cover may be obtained directly from the insurer or through an intermediary who is either a 'tied agent' (that is, an agent of the insurance company) or an independent intermediary or broker (that is, an agent of the insured). The provision of insurance services is governed partly by statute and partly by self-regulation. Viewed from the perspective of the insured, the purpose of the legislation is that of consumer and investor protection. Insurance cover should be marketed properly, advisers should be properly qualified, and consumers or investors protected against the consequences of financial failure of the insurer. The reason for this is not hard to find. In 1971 an insurer, Vehicle and General, collapsed, leaving about one million motorists without proper cover. The collapse of an insurer providing whole life and investment products would be catastrophic in its effect on policyholders. The most important statutory controls over the insurance industry are (1) the Insurance Companies Act 1982 (c 50); (2) the Financial Services Act 1986 (c 60); (3) the Policyholders Protection Act 1975 (c 75); and (4) the Insurance Brokers (Registration) Act 1977 (c 46). Non-statutory protection is to be found in the Association of British Insurers' (ABI) codes of practice[1] and in schemes such as the Insurance Ombudsman Bureau[2] and the Personal Insurance Arbitration Service[3].

1 See para 815 below.
2 See para 816 below.
3 See para 817 below.

(2) REGULATION OF INSURANCE COMPANIES

807. Authorisation. Under the Insurance Companies Act 1982, in order to carry on either 'long-term business' or 'general business', an insurance company must be authorised to do so by the Department of Trade and Industry[1]. This authorisation relates to the classes of insurance business specified in Schedule 1 or Schedule 2 of the Act, and it may be restricted to certain classes or parts of classes of business[2]. Unless an insurance company has already combined long-term and general insurance business when it receives its authorisation, such combined business will not be authorised except where the long-term business is restricted to reinsurance[3]. Where a company pursues both long-term and general business, it is required to keep the finances of both separate from each other. In the event of liquidation, liabilities relating to long-term business may only be met from the funds in the long-term account[4]. Should liabilities exceed assets, the company may not declare any dividend[5].

An insurer authorised under sections 3 and 4 of the Insurance Companies Act 1982 to carry on insurance business which is 'investment business' is an authorised person under the Financial Services Act 1986 in respect not only of insurance business which is investment business but also regarding any other investment business which the insurer can carry out under section 16 of the 1982 Act[6]. The Financial Services Act 1986 is concerned with investments and investor protection and, therefore, has no real application to companies carrying on general business under the 1982 Act. It is concerned with long-term business which comprehends, broadly, life assurance where there is a clear investment dimension, for example annuity contracts or capital redemption contracts. Whole life policies with no special savings element are excluded from the ambit of the Financial Services Act 1986[7].

Some insurers do not require to be authorised to carry out business other than industrial insurance. These are Lloyd's members[8], friendly societies, and trade unions or employers' associations providing only provident or strike benefits[9]. Bodies providing vehicle repair or recovery services do not have to be authorised[10].

An insurance company will be authorised only where its issued share capital is fully paid up and the Department of Trade and Industry is satisfied that its managing director and chief executive (that is, its 'controllers'), directors, managers or main agent are fit and proper persons to hold their positions[11]. Where authorisation to conduct investment business is sought for a company, the Department of Trade and Industry must take notice of the Securities and Investment Board's views on the application. Insurance companies must also demonstrate that they possess sufficient assets to meet liabilities and are obliged to maintain a 'margin of solvency'[12]. The manner in which the relevant margin of solvency is determined is prescribed by the Insurance Companies Regulations 1981[13]. An insurance company whose head office is not situated in an EEC member state and which wishes to do business in the United Kingdom and the EEC member states must make a deposit as prescribed by the 1981 regulations[14] and satisfy both a margin of solvency and a Community margin of solvency[15].

Authorisation may be revoked either by the insurer's asking for this to be done or for any of the following reasons:

(1) for failure to commence authorised business within one year of authorisation being granted;

(2) if authorisation, had this been requested at a particular time, would have been refused (for example if someone is not considered to be a fit and proper person to exercise control over the insurer);

(3) if the insurer is authorised by another EEC member state and that state has revoked its authorisation[16].

A new ground for the withdrawal of a company's authorisation has been added by the Financial Services Act 1986, namely failure to comply with an obligation imposed by that Act or by the rules of any self-regulating organisation (SRO) of which it is a member[17].

Insurers may also have their authorisation withdrawn, inter alia, on the ground that they have failed to comply with a requirement imposed by the 1982 Act[17]. It is a criminal offence to conduct unauthorised insurance business[18]. Since an insurer may change or add to the class or classes of insurance business which he wishes to conduct and since there are seven classes of long-term insurance and seventeen classes of general business, a mistake may easily be made. If this happens the repercussions for the person insured with the unauthorised insurer may be grave. In *Bedford Insurance Co Ltd v Instituto de Resseguros do Brasil*[19], the view was taken that contracts made in respect of unauthorised business must be tainted by illegality and, therefore, be unenforceable. Accordingly, neither party to the contract could enforce it and the reinsurer was justified in refusing to indemnify the original insurer[20]. The problem concerning the unenforceability of reinsurance contracts is resolved by the second part of section 132(6) of the Financial Services Act 1986. A reinsurance contract is not invalid simply because the original contract was in contravention of section 2 of the 1982 Act. As regards the original contract, the insured may either affirm it as valid or treat it as invalid and reclaim premiums paid and is entitled to damages for any loss suffered in consequence of such payment[21]. The insurer, however, enjoys the right to enforce an unauthorised contract subject to the satisfaction of two conditions: (a) the insurer must have had reasonable grounds for believing that he was authorised; and (b) enforcement of the contract must be considered to be just and equitable[22].

1 Insurance Companies Act 1982 (c 50), ss 2(1), 3(1).
2 Ibid, s 3(3).
3 Ibid, s 6.
4 Ibid, ss 28, 55(3).
5 Ibid, s 29(7).
6 Financial Services Act 1986 (c 60), s 22.
7 Ibid, s 1(1), Sch 1, para 10. Examples include policies which do not have a surrender value and policies whose benefits are payable only on death. However, under LAUTRO rules (see para 809 below) pure risk contracts (which do not constitute 'investments' under the legislation) are also regulated.
8 An account of the workings of Lloyd's of London goes far beyond a work on the general principles of insurance law. For a more detailed treatment, see RW Hodgin *Protection of the Insured* (1989) Ch 2.
9 Insurance Companies Act 1982, s 2(2).
10 Ibid, s 2(5); Insurance Companies Regulations 1981, SI 1981/1654, reg 23 (amended by SI 1987/2130).
11 Insurance Companies Act 1982, s 7. The Rehabilitation of Offenders Act 1974 (c 53) (discussed in para 865 below) does not apply in these cases and previous convictions must be disclosed: see the Rehabilitation of Offenders Act 1974 (Exceptions) Order 1975, SI 1975/1023.
12 Insurance Companies Act 1982, s 32.
13 Insurance Companies Regulations 1981, SI 1981/1654, regs 3–13 (amended by SI 1985/1419).
14 Insurance Companies Regulations 1981, regs 14–21 (as so amended). See also the Insurance Companies Act 1982, s 9(2)(b).
15 Ibid, s 32(3).
16 Ibid, s 11(2)(a)–(c) (amended by the Financial Services Act 1986, s 129, Sch 10, para 7(1)).
17 Insurance Companies Act 1982, s 11(2)(a) (as so amended).
18 Ibid, s 14(1).
19 *Bedford Insurance Co Ltd v Instituto de Resseguros do Brasil* [1985] QB 966, [1984] 3 All ER 766.
20 This approach was not followed in *Stewart v Oriental Fire and Marine Insurance Co Ltd* [1985] QB 988, [1984] 3 All ER 777, and *Phoenix General Insurance Co of Greece SA v Halvanon Insurance Co Ltd* [1988] QB 216, [1987] 2 All ER 152, CA.
21 Financial Services Act 1986, s 132(1).
22 Ibid, s 132(3).

808. Intervention. The Department of Trade and Industry has extensive powers of intervention in the business of an authorised insurer[1]. The most draconian of these powers is the ability to petition for the winding up of the company[2]. Less draconian is the power to require a company to take whatever steps are deemed necessary to protect existing or future policyholders 'against the risk that the company may be unable to meet its liabilities or, in the case of long-term business, to fulfil the reasonable expectations of policyholders or potential policyholders'[3]. The least drastic course open to the Department is to order the insurer to do or to refrain from doing something: for example to maintain the appropriate level of assets in the United Kingdom. Intervention is triggered by any of the following:

(1) the need to protect policyholders against the company being unable to meet its liabilities;
(2) the margin of solvency no longer being satisfied;
(3) false or misleading information having been supplied by the company; or
(4) an unfit person having been appointed to a position of control over the company[4].

Although the reason for intervention must be stated to the company, it is only where the fitness of a person for office is the issue that the company and the individual have the right to put forward their case[5].

1 Insurance Companies Act 1982 (c 50), s 37.

2 Ibid, s 54 (amended by the Companies Consolidation (Consequential Provisions) Act 1985 (c 9), s 30, Sch 2; and the Companies Consolidation (Consequential Provisions) (Northern Ireland) Order 1986, SI 1986/1035, art 23, Sch 1, Pt II).

3 Insurance Companies Act 1982, s 45(1).

4 Ibid, s 37.

5 Ibid, s 46. The Parliamentary Commissioner for Administration had criticised the Department of Trade for failing to allow an individual who was alleged to be unfit from putting forward his case: *Second Report of the Parliamentary Commissioner for Administration* (HC Paper (1976–77) no. 116).

(3) PROMOTION AND MARKETING OF INSURANCE PRODUCTS

809. General. Whereas the authorisation of insurance companies is the function of the Department of Trade and Industry, regulating the marketing of insurance containing an investment element is the function of the Securities and Investments Board (SIB). The Board has, in turn, delegated the day-to-day task of supervision to self-regulatory organisations (SROs) and recognised professional bodies (RPBs). So far as insurance is concerned the principal, relevant, SROs are the Financial Intermediaries, Managers and Brokers Regulatory Association (FIMBRA) and the Life Assurance and Unit Trust Regulatory Organisation (LAUTRO). FIMBRA does not include insurance companies but independent intermediaries who advise clients on life assurance, unit trusts, and investments. LAUTRO does cover insurance companies, as well as friendly societies and unit trusts, and regulates the marketing of these investments[1]. The Insurance Brokers Registration Council is a RPB.

1 For fuller consideration of this area, see RW Hodgin *Protection of the Insured* (1989) pp 62–83.

810. Promotion and marketing. Advertisements of annuity policies and linked long-term insurances are permitted by companies authorised under the Insurance Companies Act 1982 (c 50) to provide insurance of the type advertised[1]. Friendly societies may also advertise. There are criminal penalties for a contravention. Also struck at are misleading statements (which are not advertisements) and market manipulation designed to induce someone to purchase investment type insurance[2]. Collectively, both practices constitute 'investment fraud' and are crimes. In the case of misleading statements, the matter equates with fraud. In other words, the maker of the statement commits an offence when he either (1) knows that his statement is misleading, or false, or *dishonestly conceals* a material fact; or (2) makes a statement recklessly. So both actual dishonesty and recklessness are caught by the Financial Services Act 1986[3]. Market manipulation is a course of conduct undertaken in order to present a misleading impression as to the value or worth of an investment[4]. An example of market manipulation is 'market rigging', where false rumours are spread in order to create a market in a product.

1 Financial Services Act 1986 (c 60), s 130(2).

2 Ibid, ss 47, 133.

3 Ibid, s 47(1).

4 Ibid, s 47(2).

(4) REGULATION OF INSURANCE INTERMEDIARIES

811. General. Consumers of insurance products may deal directly with the insurer, but many approach insurance through the medium of an intermediary.

Accountants, bankers, building societies and solicitors have all played a role in advising their clients on insurance matters. In addition there are the professionals who earn their living by selling insurance products and who account for more than half of such sales[1]. Professional intermediaries divide into those who are tied to one insurer and sell only his products (sometimes termed 'tied agents'), and those who are independent intermediaries free to place business with any insurer. The activities of intermediaries are closely regulated by a complex web of statutory and self-regulatory provisions. The Financial Services Act 1986 (c 60) compels intermediaries to choose to be either completely independent or tied: this is termed 'polarisation'[2]. Regulations require tied agents to disclose that fact, in writing, to consumers where either (1) the consumer is ordinarily resident in the United Kingdom; or (2) the insurance will be placed with an insurer not authorised by the Insurance Companies Act 1982 (c 50)[3]. Only those intermediaries registered under the Insurance Brokers (Registration) Act 1977 (c 46) may call themselves 'insurance brokers'.

1 See *Insurance Intermediaries* (Cmnd 6715) (1977).
2 See J Gray 'Insurance Intermediaries and the Financial Services Act' in *New Foundations in Insurance Law* (1987 ed F Rose) p 23.
3 Insurance Companies Regulations 1981, SI 1981/1654, regs 67–69. An example of an insurer falling into the category envisaged by head (2) would be a foreign insurer.

812. Regulation under the Financial Services Act 1986. The Financial Services Act 1986 is concerned with investments and investor protection. Many types of life assurance are linked to or combined with some investment. These are classified by the Act as 'investments'[1], and the giving of advice in relation to these policies constitutes 'investment business'[2]. Intermediaries who perform these functions are brought within the scope of the Act and are subject to the rules made by the self-regulatory organisation to which they belong which will be either the Life Assurance and Unit Trust Regulatory Organisation (LAUTRO) or the Financial Intermediaries, Managers and Brokers Regulatory Association (FIMBRA) or to their recognised professional body (RPB) (that is, the Insurance Brokers Registration Council)[3].

Tied agents do not require to be individually authorised by the Securities and Investments Board. Their employer will be authorised by LAUTRO and they will be 'appointed representatives' of an authorised principal[4]. Since companies are responsible for breaches of the rules by their agents, they will exercise much stricter control over them in order to present a better service to consumers. Independent intermediaries are authorised by virtue of membership of FIMBRA.

The marketing of life products comes within the ambit of the Act because of the desirability of providing consumers with the fullest and best information available about the products. Because so many potential sources for obtaining insurance exist, the consumer may not know if he is getting independent advice. He may, for example, be dealing with a tied agent who is a self-employed representative of an insurance company and paid a commission on the policies he sells. Even if the consumer deals with an independent intermediary, he may not know that the broker or adviser receives a volume commission or bonus from a particular company. In such cases, the intermediary may try to push the products of that company.

The polarisation requirement addresses the problem of knowing what the status of an intermediary is. Intermediaries must elect whether to continue to be independent or to become company representatives instead. An intermediary selling the products of only one insurer, or of a limited group of insurers, is obliged to disclose this fact to consumers[5]. So far as commissions are concerned, these have to be disclosed by independent intermediaries but not by tied agents.

The precise manner in which the amount of commission should be disclosed is as follows: the intermediary must tell the consumer that he will be receiving commission (expressed as a percentage of the premium) on the policy sold.

'Cold-calling' consumers, either by turning up on the doorstep or telephoning them, either at home or at work, is another problem associated with the selling of insurance. The Act prohibits the making of 'unsolicited calls'[6]. But the ban is not total since the Securities and Investments Board or a self-regulatory organisation may relax or exclude it entirely, and this has been done[7]. The cancellation of policies will be dealt with later[8].

1 Financial Services Act 1986 (c 60), ss 1(1), 129, Sch 1, para 10, Sch 10.
2 Ibid, s 1(2), Sch 1, para 15.
3 The authorisation which may be given by the Insurance Brokers Registration Council is more limited in scope than that which is conferred by membership of FIMBRA. Thus, where a broker's income from 'investment business' is regularly more than 25 per cent of his total income authorisation must come from FIMBRA.
4 Financial Services Act 1986, s 44.
5 LAUTRO Rules, Sch 1, Code of Conduct. See also RW Hodgin *Protection of the Insured* (1989) p 77.
6 Financial Services Act 1986, s 56(1).
7 Ibid, s 56(7) (substituted by the Companies Act 1989 (c 40), s 206(1), Sch 23, para 7); LAUTRO Rules, Sch 1, Code of Conduct. See also *Hodgin* p 77.
8 See paras 819–821 below.

813. Regulation under the Insurance Brokers (Registration) Act 1977.

The Insurance Brokers (Registration) Act 1977 created the Insurance Brokers Registration Council[1]. The council maintains a register of brokers[2] and a list of those carrying on business as insurance brokers[3]. Both the register and the list must be published[4]. The council also sets out the qualifications needed for registration as a broker[5] and approves training courses and qualifications for carrying on business as a broker[6]. The council is empowered to draw up a code of conduct giving guidance as to what constitutes professional conduct; and this it has done[7]. There are also financial criteria which have to be satisfied regarding minimum working capital, solvency margins and the keeping of accounts[8]. A compensation fund exists for the benefit of anyone who suffers loss as a result of negligence, fraud or failure to account on the part of the broker[9]. Provision is made for the investigation of complaints made against insurance brokers[10], and there is a disciplinary committee which enjoys power to remove them from the register for misconduct[11].

Only insurance intermediaries registered under the Act are entitled to design themselves as insurance 'brokers': and the Act applies only to those intermediaries who wish to be registered as brokers. An intermediary who styles himself an 'insurance broker' commits an offence if he does this when he is not registered under the Act[12]. There is no compulsion for intermediaries to seek registration under the Act, and they are free to carry on business provided they do not use the word 'broker' in their business names[13].

1 Insurance Brokers (Registration) Act 1977 (c 46), s 1(1). See RW Hodgin *Insurance Intermediaries and the Law* (1987) p 102.
2 Insurance Brokers (Registration) Act 1977, s 2.
3 Ibid, s 4.
4 Ibid, s 9(1).
5 Ibid, s 3. Registration depends on possession of a recognised qualification, a minimum of three years' professional experience, a good character, and independence from any insurers. Unqualified applicants must have a minimum of five years' full-time experience either as an independent intermediary or as a full-time tied agent for at least two insurance companies. See generally *Pickles v Insurance Brokers Registration Council* [1984] 1 All ER 1073, [1984] 1 WLR 748, DC.
6 Insurance Brokers (Registration) Act 1977, ss 6, 7.

7 Ibid, s 10(1). See the Insurance Brokers Registration Council (Code of Conduct) Approval Order 1978, SI 1978/1394.
8 Insurance Brokers (Registration) Act 1977, s 11. See also the Insurance Brokers Registration Council (Accounts and Business Requirements) Rules Approval Order 1979, SI 1979/489 (amended by SI 1981/1630), and the Insurance Brokers Registration Council (Indemnity Insurance and Grants Scheme) Rules Approval Order 1987, SI 1987/1496. The minimum working capital and margin of solvency are both £1,000.
9 Insurance Brokers (Registration) Act 1977, s 12(2).
10 Ibid, s 13.
11 Ibid, s 15. See also the Insurance Brokers Registration Council (Constitution of the Investigating Committee) Rules Approval Order 1978, SI 1978/1456; the Insurance Brokers Registration Council (Constitution of the Disciplinary Committee) Rules Approval Order 1978, SI 1978/1457; and *James v Insurance Brokers Registration Council* (1984) The Times, 16 February.
12 Insurance Brokers (Registration) Act 1977, s 22.
13 Business descriptions such as 'insurance consultant' or 'insurance adviser' are enough to escape from the controls of the Act.

(5) MISCELLANEOUS CONSUMER PROTECTION MEASURES

814. The Policyholders Protection Board. The Policyholders Protection Act 1975[1] established the Policyholders Protection Board[2]. The board is financed by insurance companies to ensure that policyholders do not suffer should an insurer experience financial difficulty or go into insolvent liquidation. The board has power to make arrangements for the transfer of the insolvent company's business or to arrange for the substitution of a new policy in place of the old[3]. As a last resort, and only regarding general business cover, it may satisfy policyholders' claims for up to 90 per cent of the value of the policy, and in cases of compulsory insurance cover, full payment may be made[4]. In the case of life policies, transfer to another insurer will be made[5].

1 The Act was a direct consequence of the collapse, in 1974, of the National Life Insurance Company.
2 See R W Hodgin *Protection of the Insured* (1989) pp 32–38.
3 Policyholders Protection Act 1975 (c 75), ss 16, 17 (amended by the Companies Consolidation (Consequential Provisions) Act 1985 (c 9), s 30, Sch 2; and the Companies (Consequential Provisions) (Northern Ireland) Order 1986, SI 1986/1035, art 23, Sch 1, Pt II).
4 Policyholders Protection Act 1975, ss 6, 7 (amended by the Road Traffic (Consequential Provisions) Act 1988 (c 54), s 4, Sch 3, para 14; and the Road Traffic (Northern Ireland Consequential Amendments) Order 1981, SI 1981/160).
5 Policyholders Protection Act 1975, s 11.

815. The Association of British Insurers code of practice for intermediaries other than registered brokers. The Association of British Insurers (ABI) *Code of Practice for all Intermediaries (Including Employees of Insurance Companies) Other than Registered Brokers* 1989 applies to both company representatives and independent intermediaries who are insurance 'advisers' or 'consultants'[1]: but only in respect of the selling of 'general business' cover. The code aims at keeping the consumer informed and providing him with the best product for his needs. Many of the duties imposed on intermediaries by the code are similar to the duties imposed on intermediaries selling investment policies. The intermediary must disclose whether he is an employee of the company whose products he is trying to sell, or an agent for more than one company, or an independent intermediary. The ABI companies accept responsibility for all intermediaries other than independent ones and the intermediary is obliged to disclose that fact. The intermediary must follow the 'best execution' rule and recommend only the policy best suited to the needs and finances of the consumer. Cold-calling is not banned, but the code does recommend making a prior arrangement to call if possible and, if not, to call at a time likely to be convenient for the consumer. An independent intermediary is obliged to disclose his commission if asked. However, he is not obliged to inform the consumer that he may ask him to make such disclosure.

There is a related ABI Code of Practice dealing with the selling of non-investment life insurance. Its provisions are virtually identical to the 'general business' code but it applies not only to intermediaries but also to 'introducers'[2].

1 The code does not, therefore, apply to insurance 'brokers' registered under the Insurance Brokers (Registration) Act 1977 (c 46).
2 Ie those who merely introduce a prospective policyholder to a life office but take no part in the subsequent selling process: *Life Insurance (Non-Investment Business) Selling Code of Practice*.

816. The Insurance Ombudsman Bureau. The Insurance Ombudsman Bureau deals with policyholders' complaints about treatment they have received from their insurers[1]. A policyholder can complain to the Ombudsman only (1) if he is a private individual[2]; (2) if his insurer is a member of this scheme; and (3) if he has exhausted his insurer's internal system for handling complaints. There is no charge for making use of this scheme, and, although the Ombudsman's decision is binding on the insurer, it is not binding on the insured, and taking his complaint to the bureau does not bar his right to raise, subsequently, an action in the courts. In relation to health insurance, the Ombudsman can make an award up to £10,000. For other types of insurance, the maximum figure is £100,000[3]. If an award exceeds these sums, the Ombudsman's decision no longer binds the insurer[4].

The Ombudsman is bound to 'reach a fair and commonsense conclusion whatever may be the strict legal position'[5]. He is not bound by decisions of his predecessors[5] and will take into account 'good insurance practice'[6]. This last point is most important. The Association of British Insurers (ABI) *Statement of General Insurance Practice* (1986) and *Statement of Long-Term Insurance Practice* (1986), dealing with indemnity and life insurance respectively, are merely codes of practice and are not legally enforceable[7]. Moreover, these statements apply only to insurance effected in a private (not a business) capacity: that is, 'consumer' contracts. Both statements, however, declare that they are to be taken into account in any arbitration or referral procedures arising from a dispute between insurer and insured[8]. Because the contents of these statements are declared to represent 'normal insurance practice', and because they adopt a significantly different approach to non-disclosure and breach of warranty from that found in the common law, it may be better for the insured to ask for a dispute arising on these grounds to be referred to the Ombudsman before seeking redress in the courts. The Ombudsman will have to take the provisions of the statements into account.

1 For a detailed account of the workings of the Bureau, see R W Hodgin *Protection of the Insured* (1989) pp 125–139. See also J Birds 'Self-regulation and Insurance Contracts' in *New Foundations for Insurance Law* (1987 ed F D Rose) pp 12, 13.
2 The scheme does not apply to insurances effected in the course of a business unless the insurer agrees to this: Insurance Ombudsman's Terms of Reference, cl 5(b).
3 These figures may be revised by a general meeting of the bureau. The scheme deals with only some aspects of life assurance: eg surrender value of policies and bonus rates.
4 This does not mean that the policyholder is back to square one. A negotiated settlement is often reached: see *Hodgin* p 126.
5 *The Insurance Ombudsman Annual Report* (1989), para 2.1.
6 *The Insurance Ombudsman Annual Report* (1989), para 1.1.
7 These statements are discussed in their relevant contexts later in this title.
8 ABI *Statement of General Insurance Practice* (1986), para 6; ABI *Statement of Long-Term Insurance Practice* (1986), para 4.

817. Personal Insurance Arbitration Service. The Personal Insurance Arbitration Service was started as an alternative to the Insurance Ombudsman Bureau scheme and has a much smaller membership, although some insurers belong to both schemes[1]. Unlike the Insurance Ombudsman Bureau, a decision of the arbiter binds both insurer and insured. Also unlike the Insurance Ombudsman Bureau, annual reports are not produced.

1 For a detailed account of the service, see R W Hodgin *Protection of the Insured* (1989) pp 139–141. See also J Birds 'Self Regulation and Insurance Contracts' in *New Foundations for Insurance Law* (1987 ed F D Rose) p 14.

4. FORMATION OF INSURANCE CONTRACTS

(1) GENERAL

818. Law of contract. The contract of insurance, like the majority of other contracts, is formed as a result of offer and acceptance. Until there is *consensus in idem* there is no contract[1]. The party seeking cover offers himself to the insurer as a candidate. In many cases he will do this by completing a proposal form, proposing a contract of insurance between himself and the insurer[2]. It follows that where the insurer does not accept the proposal, on the terms contained therein, but adds new ones, that is a rejection of the offer – although the proposer may treat this as a counter-offer and accept it. Mere delivery, per se, of a policy which introduces new terms is not an acceptance[3]. Where, for example, the insurer responds to the proposal by despatching the policy, that constitutes acceptance. However, where the insurer responds that cover is dependent upon receipt of payment of the first premium, that is a counter-offer which the proposer does not have to accept[4]. It is quite usual for insurers to stipulate in the proposal form that cover will not commence until payment of the first premium or until the policy is delivered[5]. If the policy stipulates that the contract of insurance is subject to a suspensive condition, for example that cover will only commence upon payment of the premium, and the proposer's reply promises to send payment but also asks for some aspects of the cover to be altered, that reply, it is submitted, is not an acceptance but a counter-offer[6], and until payment is made the insurer is not on risk. Although there must be agreement as to the premium, there is no requirement that this must be paid before cover will commence[7]. It is probably an implied term in life assurance, however, that cover does not begin until the premium is paid and the policy issued[8]. No such term will be implied in indemnity insurance because the proposer is usually given temporary cover under a cover note which is effective for the period stipulated therein without payment of any premium[9].

Depending on the facts, both insurer and proposer may enjoy *locus poenitentiae*[10]. Where the proposer communicates withdrawal of his proposal before it is accepted by the insurer and then makes a second, different, proposal, the first proposal dies and is no longer available for acceptance by the insurer[11]. Acceptance on behalf of the insurers will bind them only if the person making the acceptance has actual or ostensible authority to do so[12]. If the terms of a policy differ from those requested by the proposer, the latter may, nonetheless, be bound by them. In *Rust v Abbey Life Insurance Co Ltd*[13], the insured said nothing about a policy for several months. It was held that she had accepted the policy on the insurer's terms because she had made no objection to it at the time she received it. As with contracts generally, acceptance may be inferred from conduct. A motorist who on receipt of a cover note drives his car may be held to have accepted the offer of temporary insurance[14]. In the case of long-term policies, the insured enjoys a right of cancellation after the conclusion of the contract[15].

Again, as with contracts generally, there must be agreement as to the material terms. In insurance, the material terms are (1) the risk to be covered; (2) the premium to be paid; (3) the duration of the cover; and (4) the sum insured for[16]. Strictly speaking, insurer and insured must agree on every term of the contract between them[17], but since most proposal forms expressly stipulate that any contract will be concluded on the usual terms and conditions of the insurer, there is no real problem[18].

1 *Star Fire and Burglary Insurance Co Ltd v Davidson & Sons Ltd* (1902) 5 F 83, 10 SLT 282. See also *Rose v Medical Invalid Life Assurance Co* (1848) 11 D 151.

2 *M'Cartney v Laverty* 1968 SC 207, 1968 SLT (Notes) 50, OH. As to proposal forms, see paras 822–824 below.

3 *National Benefit Trust Ltd v Coulter* 1911 SC 544, 1911 1 SLT 190.

4 *Canning v Farquhar* (1886) 16 QBD 727, CA. In *Looker v Law Union and Rock Insurance Co Ltd* [1928] 1 KB 554, the suggestion was that such a reply was not an offer but rather an invitation to treat. See also *Sickness and Accident Assurance Association Ltd v General Accident Assurance Corpn Ltd* (1892) 19 R 977 at 986, per Lord Adam.

5 E J MacGillvray and M Parkington *Insurance Law* (8th edn, 1988) paras 244–250, 254.

6 *Sickness and Accident Assurance Association Ltd v General Accident Assurance Corpn Ltd* (1892) 19 R 977. This is not an easy case to explain. The defenders issued a liability policy for the period 17 November 1888 to 17 November 1889. The policy stated that the cover would commence on payment of the premium. The proposer's secretary replied agreeing to pay the premium but also asking for cover to run from 24 November 1888 to 24 November 1889. The insurer's agent agreed to make the alteration. On 24 November, before either payment had been made or the new policy issued, an accident occurred. At a meeting on 26 November the defenders refused to provide insurance 'except from the twenty-fourth'. Payment of the premium was sent on 26 November and accepted on 29 November in a letter agreeing to provide cover from 24 November. The Inner House took the view that the defenders were not obliged to pay the pursuers under the policy since there was no contract until 29 November. It can be argued that although the pursuers' letter of 19 November was a counter-offer, it too predicted that cover would only commence from 24 November once the premium was paid. The defenders' letter of 29 November was an acceptance of the letter of 19 November, but any obligation to meet claims under the concluded contract did not arise until payment was made. Since no payment had been made on 24 November, the insurers were not obliged to meet a claim arising from an incident two days before payment was made.

7 *Christie v North British Insurance Co* (1825) 3 S 519 (NE 360); *Rose v Medical Invalid Life Assurance Co* (1848) 11 D 151.

8 *Canning v Farquhar* (1886) 16 QBD 727, CA; *Harrington v Pearl Life Assurance Co Ltd* (1914) 30 TLR 613, CA; *Southern Cross Assurance Co Ltd v Australian Provincial Assurance Co* (1939) 39 SR (NSW) 174.

9 *MacGillivray and Parkington* para 213. It is submitted that this is the correct view. Cf *Sickness and Accident Assurance Association v General Accident Assurance Corpn Ltd* (1892) 19 R 977.

10 *Canning v Farquhar* (1886) 16 QBD 727, CA; *Re Yager and Guardian Assurance Co* (1912) 108 LT 38, DC; *Allis-Chalmers Co v Maryland Fidelity and Deposit Co* (1916) 114 LT 433, HL.

11 *Travis v Nederland Life Insurance Co* 104 Fed Rep 486 (1900).

12 *MacGillivray and Parkington* para 225.

13 *Rust v Abbey Life Insurance Co Ltd* [1979] 2 Lloyd's Rep 334, CA.

14 *Taylor v Allon* [1966] 1 QB 304 at 311, [1965] 1 All ER 557 at 559, DC.

15 Insurance Companies Regulations 1981, SI 1981/1654; Financial Services (Cancellation) Rules 1988 (discussed at paras 819–821 below).

16 See generally *Christie v North British Insurance Co* (1825) 3 S 519 (NE 360); *Allis-Chalmers Co v Maryland Fidelity and Deposit Co* (1916) 114 LT 433, HL; *Murfitt v Royal Insurance Co Ltd* (1922) 38 TLR 334; *Beach v Pearl Assurance Co Ltd* [1938] IAC Rep 3.

17 In *Allis-Chalmers Co v Maryland Fidelity and Deposit Co* (1916) 114 LT 433 at 434, HL, it was suggested that there had to be agreement on *all* the contract terms.

18 *General Accident Insurance Corpn v Cronk* (1901) 17 TLR 233. See *Birds* p 54; 'Insurance' in *The Law of South Africa* (1988, ed Joubert) vol 12, para 44.

(2) STATUTORY NOTICES AND COOLING-OFF PERIODS

819. Introduction. Two sets of regulations exist. The Insurance Companies Regulations 1981[1] apply to long-term policies which have no investment element. The Financial Services (Cancellation) Rules 1988[2] apply to long-term policies which do have an investment element[3].

  1 Insurance Companies Regulations 1981, SI 1981/1654.
  2 The Financial Services (Cancellation) Rules 1988 were made under the Financial Services Act 1986 (c 60), s 51, by the Securities and Investment Board under powers delegated by the Secretary of State for Trade and Industry: Financial Services Act 1986 (Delegation) Order 1987, SI 1987/942.
  3 For a detailed treatment of both sets of regulations, see R W Hodgin *Protection of the Insured* (1989) pp 10–15.

820. The Insurance Companies Regulations 1981. Two forms of notice are prescribed for long-term or linked long-term policies as defined in Schedule 1 of the Insurance Companies Act 1982. These notices must be given to the insured no later than the date when the contract is made. Failure to do so is an offence but does not invalidate the contract[1]. The contents of the two forms are very similar[2]. Under the heading 'YOUR RIGHT TO CHANGE YOUR MIND', the insured must be informed that: 'The law gives you 10 days from the date on which you receive this notice (or in some cases longer – [see below]) to consider the matter again and, if you so wish, to withdraw from the transaction.' Later in this notice, the insured is informed that he need do nothing if he wishes to proceed with the contract but that if he wishes to cancel, he must do so 'before the end of the tenth day after the day on which you received this notice; or the earliest day on which you know both that the contract has been entered into and that the first premium has been paid, whichever is the later.' These notices contain a tear-off portion on which the insured may intimate cancellation, but any written cancellation will suffice.

  1 Insurance Companies Act 1982 (c 50), ss 75–78 (restricted by the Financial Services Act 1986 (c 60), s 129, Sch 10, para 5, and amended by s 137).
  2 For the prescribed form of notice to be given in connection with a long-term policy, see the Insurance Companies Regulations 1981, SI 1981/1654, reg 70(1)(a), Sch 10. For linked long-term policies, see reg 70(1)(b), Sch 11.

821. The Financial Services (Cancellation) Rules. The Financial Services (Cancellation) Rules resemble the 1981 Regulations[1] in that they too provide a cooling-off period for the insured and, if breached, do not invalidate the contract. Where there has been a breach, however, this is actionable[2]. A notice similar to those under the 1981 Regulations must be sent to the insured. The cooling-off period in respect of life insurance contracts with an investment element is either fourteen or twenty-eight days from the date of receipt of such notice. Where the insured is reasonably believed by the insurer to be a business or professional investor, the cooling-off period is inapplicable.

  1 Ie the Insurance Companies Regulations 1981, SI 1981/1654.
  2 Financial Services Act 1986 (c 60), s 62(1).

(3) THE PROPOSAL FORM

822. Form and content. In most types of life assurance, property cover, and motor vehicle insurance the person seeking cover completes a proposal form and returns it either to an intermediary or to the insurer[1]. The proposal form[2] is a standard form questionnaire prepared by the insurer. There is, however, no standard form questionnaire employed by all insurers, and proposal forms vary from insurer to insurer and from risk to risk. There may, nonetheless, be a measure of harmony where the insurer is a member of the Association of British Insurers (ABI) and follows the 1986 Statements of Practice[3]. The proposal form will normally state that the offer contained therein is subject to the usual terms and conditions of the insurer[4]. Accordingly, the insured cannot argue that he did not agree to these terms. Where, however, the policy contains some unusual term, a term which one would not normally expect a policy of its type to include, that amounts to a counter-offer which the proposer is not obliged to accept[5].

1 There are cases where insurance may be arranged without completion of a proposal form. Examples include instant life cover provided at airports and insurance arranged over the telephone: see *Mayne Nickless v Pegler* (1974) 1 NSWLR 228. Insurance cover may also be arranged by a building society providing mortgage finance without the insured completing a proposal form: see *Woolcott v Sun Alliance and London Insurance Ltd* [1978] 1 All ER 1253, [1978] 1 WLR 493.

2 For a detailed picture of the contents of proposal forms, see E R H Ivamy *General Principles of Insurance Law* (5th edn, 1986) ch 8.

3 These are discussed in para 824 below. For detailed comment on the 1986 Statements of Practice, see A D M Forte, 'The Revised Statements of Insurance Practice: Cosmetic Change or Major Surgery?' (1986) 49 MLR 754. These are revised versions of statements first promulgated in 1977.

4 Even where it does not, this will probably be implied. See *General Accident Insurance Corpn v Cronk* (1901) 17 TLR 233; *Rust v Abbey Life Insurance Co Ltd* [1979] 2 Lloyd's Rep 334 at 339, CA, per Brandon LJ.

5 *Star Fire and Burglary Insurance Co Ltd v Davidson & Sons Ltd* (1902) 5 F 83, 10 SLT 282. In this case the proposer had applied for fire cover but received a policy containing a term making him a member of the insurance company. This is a clear case of *dissensus* similar to the situation in *Mathieson Gee (Ayrshire) Ltd v Quigley* 1952 SC (HL) 38, 1952 SLT 239.

823. Basis of the contract clauses. A proposal form will often contain a 'basis of the contract' clause. This is a declaration that the answers given in response to the questions asked by the proposal form are correct and will constitute the basis of the contract between insurer and insured. The effect of such a clause is settled: it creates a warranty as to the truth of the answers given[1]. An incorrect answer to a question where the proposal form contains a basis of the contract clause entitles the insurer to avoid the contract[2]. It is not necessary for the application of this clause that it be repeated in the policy also. The clause is an express term of the proposer's offer to make a contract of insurance with the insurer. Once that offer is accepted by the insurer, the clause becomes a term of the insurance contract[3]. If the proposal form does not contain a basis of the contract clause but the policy does[4], this will amount to a counter-offer. If the proposer knows of the new term and pays the premium, his conduct implies that he has accepted the counter-offer.

1 *Standard Life Assurance Co v Weems* (1884) 11 R (HL) 48; *Dawsons Ltd v Bonnin* 1922 SC (HL) 156, 1922 SLT 444.

2 *Standard Life Assurance Co v Weems* (1884) 11 R (HL) 48; *Dawsons Ltd v Bonnin* 1922 SC (HL) 156, 1922 SLT 444; *Zurich General Accident and Liability Insurance Co Ltd v Leven* 1940 SC 406, 1940 SLT 350. See also *Fourth Report of the Law Reform Committee for Scotland* (Cmnd 330) (1957), para 2; and *Insurance Law: Non-disclosure and Breach of Warranty* (Law Com no. 104) (Cmnd 8064) (1980) para 7.1.

3 *M'Cartney v Laverty* 1968 SC 207, 1968 SLT (Notes) 50, OH.

4 *Star Fire and Burglary Insurance Co Ltd v Davidson & Sons Ltd* (1902) 5 F 83, 10 SLT 282; *Came v City of Glasgow Friendly Society* 1933 SC 69, 1933 SLT 90.

824. The Association of British Insurers statements of insurance practice (1986). The Association of British Insurers (ABI) *Statement of General Insurance Practice* (1986) provides that 'The declaration at the foot of the proposal form should be restricted to completion according to the proposer's knowledge and belief'[1]. Where the proposal form complies with the statement, the proposer is not asked to warrant the truth of his answers. Consequently, an innocently incorrect opinion will not justify avoidance of the contract. However, there must be a sound basis for the opinion given, and a recklessly or negligently incorrect answer will justify the insurer avoiding the contract[2]. The ABI *Statement of Long-Term Insurance Practice* (1986) contains no equivalent provision[3].

The *Statement of General Insurance Practice* provides that the proposal forms of ABI members should state that a copy of the completed form is provided for retention by the proposer at the time of its completion. Alternatively, it may state that it is the normal practice of the insurer to supply a copy, or that a copy will be provided on request within three months of completion. The *Statement of General Insurance Practice* also provides that a copy of the proposal form will be made available to the insured should the insurer raise an issue in connection with it[4]. The *Statement of Long-Term Insurance Practice* enjoins the insurer merely to state that a copy of the completed proposal form is available on request[5].

Both Statements of Practice request ABI members to display prominently in their proposal forms a statement that proposers must disclose all 'material' facts and warning them of the consequences of non-disclosure. They should also explain that 'material' facts are 'those facts an insurer would regard as likely to influence the acceptance and assessment of the proposal' and warn proposers that if in doubt as to the materiality of a fact, they should disclose it[6].

1 ABI *Statement of General Insurance Practice* (1986), para 1(a).
2 *M'Phee v Royal Insurance Co Ltd* 1979 SC 304, 1979 SLT (Notes) 54. The pursuer completed a proposal form for insurance of a cabin cruiser. The proposal form contained a declaration that his answers were true to the best of his knowledge and belief. He guessed the vessel's specifications, in response to a question about these, although he could have easily discovered the answer by consulting the manual for the vessel. The defenders were held not to be obliged to meet a claim under the policy. As Lord Robertson said in the course of his judgment, '... it is clear from the evidence that the respondent did not make due inquiry and that he gave material information that was blameably false and recklessly given. He did not exercise due care'.
3 The consequences of this are discussed at para 861 below.
4 ABI *Statement of General Insurance Practice* (1986), para 1(i).
5 Ibid, para 1(f).
6 Ibid, para 1(c); ABI *Statement of Long-Term Insurance Practice* (1986), para 1(a).

(4) THE COVER NOTE

825. Temporary cover. In indemnity insurance, a cover note is usually issued to the proposer on completion of the proposal form. Although cover notes as such are not used in life assurance, temporary protection may still be offered to the proposer, usually subject to a ceiling figure limiting liability[1]. The cover note, as its name implies, is a temporary contract of insurance[2] while the insurer considers the answers given in the proposal form and decides whether to issue a policy or not. Since it is a temporary contract, cover ends on the expiry date stipulated in the cover note or, if the insurer decides to issue a policy, on the issue of that policy. The cover note may state that it can be cancelled by the insurer giving notice of cancellation[3]. If the cover note indicates that it must be cancelled by the giving of notice to the proposer, then, until this is clearly done, the cover note remains in force and the insurer remains liable[4].

The policy may declare that cover is retrospective[5]. Until superseded by the issue of a policy, the terms of the cover note will apply to any claim arising before the policy is issued[6]. The cover note usually provides that temporary cover is subject to the usual terms and conditions found in the policy. This means that a claim made under the cover note will be treated on the same basis as if the policy had been in force at that time. If the cover note does not expressly incorporate by reference the policy's terms, the usual terms will be implied[7]. Where, however, the policy contains some unusual term, there is no implication that such a term is incorporated into the temporary contract[8]. In addition to the non-implication of unusual terms found in the policy, the policy may also contain terms which are not applicable to temporary cover. Thus terms in the policy requiring immediate notification of a claim will be discounted as inapplicable unless specifically mentioned in the cover note[9].

Where an intermediary, such as a broker, is provided with supplies of blank cover notes, he is treated as an agent of the insurer for the purpose of providing temporary cover[10]. Where a broker has authority to give oral cover on behalf of an insurer, an oral assurance that temporary cover has been given will bind the insurer[11].

In the case of renewable indemnity contracts, such as motor vehicle insurance, a renewal notice is often sent to the insured some time before the date of expiry of current cover. The renewal notice will frequently provide that interim cover for fifteen days from the renewal date will be given. Renewal notices for motor vehicle policies usually state that only third-party cover[12] will be given during the fifteen-day period and on condition that the insured has not changed his insurer[13]. The renewal notice may also stipulate that there is no obligation on the insurer to accept a premium tendered after the renewal date. The Association of British Insurers (ABI) *Statement of General Insurance Practice* (1986) provides that renewal notices 'shall contain a warning about the duty of disclosure including the necessity to advise changes affecting the policy which have occurred since the policy's inception or last renewal date whichever was the later'[14]. The statement also provides that a renewal notice should warn the insured to 'keep a record (including copies of letters) of all information supplied to the insurer for the purposes of renewal of this insurance'[15].

1　E J MacGillivray and M Parkington *Insurance Law* (8th edn, 1988) para 282.
2　*Mackie v European Assurance Society* (1869) 21 LT 102; *Julien Praet & Cie SA v H G Poland Ltd* [1960] 1 Lloyd's Rep 416, CA.
3　*Stockton v Mason* [1978] 2 Lloyd's Rep 430, CA.
4　*Mackie v European Assurance Society* (1869) 21 LT 102; *Tough v Provincial Insurance Co of Canada* (1875) 20 LCJ 168; *Hawke v Niagara District Mutual Fire Insurance Co* (1876) 23 Grant 139; *Queen Insurance Co v Parsons* (1881) 7 App Cas 96, PC.
5　Ie backdated either to the date of the cover note or to a date during the running of the cover note: see *Re Coleman's Depositories Ltd and Life and Health Assurance Association* [1907] 2 KB 798, CA.
6　*Neil v South East Lancashire Insurance Co* 1932 SC 35, 1932 SLT 29.
7　*Wyndham Rather Ltd v Eagle, Star and British Dominions Insurance Co* (1925) 21 Ll L Rep 214, CA. Cf *Re Coleman's Depositories Ltd and Life and Health Assurance Association* [1907] 2 KB 798, CA.
8　*Symington & Co v Union Insurance Society of Canton Ltd* (1928) 45 TLR 181, CA.
9　*Re Coleman's Depositories Ltd and Life and Health Assurance Association* [1907] 2 KB 798, CA, followed in *Parker & Co (Sandbank) Ltd v Western Assurance Co* 1925 SLT 131, OH.
10　*Mackie v European Assurance Society* (1869) 21 LT 102. The intermediary has either implied actual authority or ostensible authority to provide temporary cover.
11　*Stockton v Mason* [1978] 2 Lloyd's Rep 430, CA. The broker's authority to provide temporary cover is implied.
12　Ie the minimum cover necessary to comply with the Road Traffic Act 1988 (c 52), Pt VI (ss 143–162).
13　See *Taylor v Allon* [1966] 1 QB 304, [1965] 1 All ER 557, DC, where a motor vehicle policy expired on 5 April. The renewal notice gave the insured fifteen days in which to renew his cover but he decided against this, effecting cover with another insurer to run from 16 April. On 15 April he drove his car and was subsequently convicted of driving while uninsured. The conviction was upheld. The renewal notice was an offer to reinsure which could only be accepted by the insured complying with its terms. One of those terms was that he should not effect

insurance with another insurer. The insured did so and his conduct in driving a car, in respect of which he had arranged insurance cover with another insurer, did not constitute a valid acceptance of the offer contained in the renewal notice.

14 ABI *Statement of General Insurance Practice* (1986), para 3(a).
15 Ibid, para 3(b).

5. THE INSURANCE POLICY

(1) INTRODUCTION

826. General. The policy is the embodiment of the terms upon which cover is provided. This section of the title outlines the contents of an insurance policy; the mode of constituting the contract; the classification of policies; premiums; and the duration of policies.

827. The contents of an insurance policy. Policies are usually standard form documents and vary between insurers. Broadly speaking, however, policies may be divided into constituent parts along the following lines[1]:
(1) *Heading*: The heading contains identification details. Thus specified are the insurer, the policy's reference number, the duration of insurance, the premium payable, and the sum insured.
(2) *Contract details*: The contract details specified are the duration of insurance; the sum insured and the premium payable; the risks insured against and exceptions thereto[2]; and any terms incorporated into the policy from other documents[3]. If there is doubt about any of these points, reference may be made to the 'recitals' of the policy in order to resolve such doubt[4].
(3) *Reverse side of the policy*: Unless expressly referred to, nothing on the reverse side of a policy is binding on the parties[5]. The reverse side of the policy may deal with the intimation of notice of claims, cancellation rights, assignation, double insurance, and alterations to the risk.
(4) *Docket*: The uppermost side of a folded policy may bear a summary of the policy and may draw the insured's attention to important parts of the policy. These may be made part of the contract by express incorporation[6].
Both the Association of British Insurers (ABI) *Statement of General Insurance Practice* (1986) and the *Statement of Long-Term Insurance Practice* (1986) ask insurers to develop 'clearer and more explicit proposal forms and policy documents'.

1 The contents of an insurance policy are discussed in greater detail in E R H Ivamy *General Principles of Insurance Law* (5th edn,) ch 18. The account which follows in the text is based on Ivamy.
2 The exceptions are termed 'excepted perils' and are discussed in para 837 below.
3 Eg from the proposal form or a temperance statement.
4 The recitals form part of the main body of the contract and specify that a proposal has been made and/or that the premium has been paid: Ivamy p 215, n 4, citing *Notman v Anchor Assurance Co* (1858) 4 CBNS 476.
5 Absence of express incorporation may be remedied by evidence of clear intention: Ivamy p 215. See generally *Caledonian Insurance Co v Gilmour* (1892) 20 R (HL) 13, [1983] AC 85.
6 *Scott v Scottish Accident Insurance Co* (1889) 16 R 630.

828. Formalities of constitution and proof. Despite authority to the contrary[1], the better view, and the one which is generally accepted, is that insurance is not an *obligatio literis*[2]. This states the general rule from which it follows that, providing its existence and contents can be established, an oral contract of insurance can be enforced[3]. There are several exceptions to this general rule, but the only one of these applicable in Scotland concerns marine insurance. A contract of marine insurance must be in writing and is 'inadmissible in evidence unless it is embodied' in a marine policy[4]. Such a policy must specify either the name of the insured or his agent[5]; be signed by or on behalf of the insurer[6]; and designate the subject matter to be covered[7].

1 *M'Elroy v London Assurance Corpn* (1897) 24 R 287, 4 SLT 241.
2 Bell *Commentaries* I,653: 'The policy must be subscribed or underwritten with the names of the several insurers. It is not required to be subscribed according to the formalities of the statutes relative to the subscription of deeds in Scotland; but it is effectual signed with the name simply, accompanied by the addition of the sum for which the underwriter is to be liable. No witnesses are required'. See also *Christie v North British Insurance Co* (1825) 3 S 519 (NE 360); *Parker & Co (Sandbank) Ltd v Western Assurance Co* 1925 SLT 131, OH. See also the more recent view to this effect expressed in A G Walker and N M L Walker *The Law of Evidence in Scotland* (1964), para 115(b), and in *Constitution and Proof of Voluntary Obligations and the Authentication of Writs* (1985) Scot Law Com Consultative Memorandum no. 66 para 4.7.
3 *Murfitt v Royal Insurance Co Ltd* (1922) 38 TLR 334; *Stockton v Mason* [1978] 2 Lloyd's Rep 430, CA. The point that an insurance contract does not have to be expressed in writing is particularly important in the case of temporary contracts. Policies are invariably written documents.
4 Marine Insurance Act 1906 (c 41), s 22 (excluded by the Marine and Aviation Insurance (War Risks) Act 1952 (c 57), s 7(1)). The policy need not be issued at the time the contract is concluded, but may be issued afterwards.
5 Marine Insurance Act 1906, s 23 para (1).
6 Ibid, s 24(1).
7 Ibid, s 26(1).

829. The classification of insurance policies.

The division of insurance into life and indemnity cover has already been noted, as has the distinction between long-term and general insurance and between first-party and third-party cover[1]. A further distinction should be made between valued and unvalued policies.

1 See paras 803–813 above.

830. Valued policies.

The Marine Insurance Act 1906 defines a valued policy as being one which specifies the agreed value of the subject-matter insured[1]. There is no peculiarity of marine cover which renders this definition inapplicable to other indemnity contracts[2]. The value must be agreed as such (or be capable of exact calculation)[3], and an agreed value policy must be distinguished from one which specifies the amount of coverage or 'sum insured'. In the latter case, the figure represents a ceiling beyond which the insurer will not indemnify the insured should the loss exceed that figure[4]. If the loss suffered is total, the insured is entitled to the agreed value specified but no more. The insured cannot be heard to argue that his actual loss exceeds the agreed value[5]. Where the loss suffered is partial, and where the contract is not one of marine insurance, the insured will receive only the actual amount of his loss[6]. However, where the contract is one of marine insurance, the insured will receive the amount specified as the agreed value, even though his loss is only partial[7].

1 Marine Insurance Act 1906 (c 41), s 27(2).
2 *City Tailors Ltd v Evans* (1921) 126 LT 439, CA.
3 *Theobald v Railway Passengers Assurance Co* (1854) 10 Exch 45. Personal accident policies are examples of agreed value policies.
4 *Chapman v Pole, PO* (1870) 22 LT 306 at 307, per Cockburn CJ.
5 *Burnand v Rodocanachi Sons & Co* (1882) 7 App Cas 333 at 335, HL, per Lord Selbourne.
6 *City Tailors Ltd v Evans* (1921) 126 LT 439, CA. If the agreed value is stated in the policy to be £200,000, and the actual value at the time of loss is £100,000 and, thereafter, £60,000, the insured will be entitled to recover £80,000. The formula proceeds on the basis that the insurer is bound to

pay only that fraction of the agreed value represented by the difference between the actual values before and after the time of loss. See *Elcock v Thomson* [1949] 2 KB 755, [1949] 2 All ER 381.

7 Marine Insurance Act 1906, s 27(3).

831. Unvalued policies. Where a policy is unvalued, the insured may recover only the amount of his actual loss[1]. An unvalued policy will not stipulate a sum to be paid in the event of total loss. If the actual loss exceeds the 'sum insured', the excess amount is unrecoverable[2].

1 'Unvalued policy' means a policy which does not specify the value of the subject-matter insured, but, subject to the limit of the sum insured, leaves the insurable value to be subsequently ascertained: Marine Insurance Act 1906 (c 41), s 28. A policy which is silent as to agreed value will be treated as an unvalued policy: see *Leppard v Excess Insurance Co Ltd* [1979] 2 All ER 668, [1979] 1 WLR 512, CA.

2 *Chapman v Pole, PO* (1870) 22 LT 306; *Glasgow Provident Investment Society v Westminster Fire Office* (1887) 14 R 947, affd (1888) 15 R (HL) 89.

(2) PREMIUMS

832. General. The obligation of the insurer under an insurance contract is to indemnify the insured against losses caused by one of the perils insured against. In the case of life assurance the obligation is to pay a sum on the occurrence of the contingency insured against. The obligation of the insured is to observe the terms of the policy and to pay the premium or premiums required.

833. Form of premium. Payment of the premium is usually made by cash or cheque[1]. There is nothing to prevent it being agreed that payment is to be made in some other form, for example by promissory note[2]. Payment may be made in instalments[3], and the insurer may agree to payment by direct debit or standing order.

1 In this case it will be conditional upon the cheque being honoured.

2 *Bell Bros v Hudson Bay Insurance Co* (1911) 44 SCR 419 (Can SC).

3 Payment by instalment may fall within the ambit of the Consumer Credit Act 1974 (c 39). Under s 11(1)(a) it may be a restricted-use credit agreement, and under s 12(a), a debtor-creditor-supplier agreement. However, where no more than four instalments are agreed, the 1974 Act does not apply: see s 16(5) and the Consumer Credit (Exempt Agreements) Order 1980, SI 1980/52.

834. Time. Where the insurer expressly provides that cover does not commence until payment of the first premium is received, then commencement of cover is conditional upon this happening. Accordingly, where the insured is injured by a peril covered by the policy, the insurer is not obliged to meet the claim if the loss occurred before payment of the premium was made[1]. In the absence of an express term, suspending the insurer's obligation until payment of the premium has been made, cover begins with the conclusion of a contract for insurance[2]. If the risk alters before the policy is delivered to the insured and before the premium has been paid, the insurer may decline acceptance of the premium and incur no liability under the policy[3]. Where cover is renewable, payment of premiums must be made in accordance with the terms of the policy. These may specify that premiums must be paid by or on a particular date. Equally, they might specify that premiums be paid within a specified period (termed 'days of grace') from the renewal date. It cannot be assumed (though the insured may be tempted to do so) that the insured is covered during the days of grace. In indemnity insurance, the days of grace may amount to no more than an option to renew cover on the old terms. Conversely, it may be provided that full (or restricted[4]) cover will continue if the premium is paid within the days of grace. But reliance placed by the insured on payment before the expiry of the days of grace can be badly misplaced. The insurer has the option to decline renewal of the insurance and if he does so before the insured suffers any loss, he will not be liable[5]. It is otherwise with life assurance. Here cover is granted for life and must continue, subject to the payment of any premiums when due. If the policy stipulates that cover will continue until the expiry of the days of grace, then the assured's death within that period, but before payment has been made, is covered. Conversely, if the policy stipulates that cover will end on a given date, the days of grace merely confer an option on the assured to renew cover within that period; but the assured is no longer covered by the policy until he pays the premium[6].

1 *Sickness and Accident Assurance Association Ltd v General Accident Assurance Corpn Ltd* (1892) 19 R 977.
2 *M'Elroy v London Assurance Corpn* (1897) 24 R 287, 4 SLT 241. It has already been remarked that in life assurance it is probably an implied term of the contract that cover does not begin until the premium has been paid and the policy delivered.
3 *Sickness and Accident Assurance Association Ltd v General Accident Assurance Corpn Ltd* (1892) 19 R 977.
4 This is the case in motor vehicle insurance where cover is restricted to third-party insurance and is limited to fifteen days.
5 E J MacGillivray and M Parkington *Insurance Law* (8th edn, 1988) para 954, citing *Salvin v James* (1805) 6 East 571.
6 *Stuart v Freeman* [1903] 1 KB 47, CA.

835. Return of premiums. The general rule is that the insurer must repay any premiums received where no risk has in fact been run by him[1]. The right to repayment is probably based on the doctrine of unjust enrichment[2]. It follows that where the risk has been run, though not for the entire period of cover, there is no proportional right to repayment of premium for the period when the insurer was not at risk[3]. Where an insurance contract is void *ab initio*, the insured is entitled to repayment of premiums[4]. Where the contract is voidable, as is the case where there has been innocent non-disclosure of a material fact, and is avoided, the insured is also entitled to repayment of premiums[5]. Breach of warranty by the insured entitles the insurer to rescind the contract. If the policy provides for retention of premiums paid where there has been a breach of warranty by the insured, effect will be given to that provision[6]. If the policy makes no such provision, the effect of a breach of warranty will depend on the nature of the warranty given. If the warranty is taken in the proposal form and made part of the basis of the contract between insurer and insured, then its untruth at that time is fatal to the contract. It follows, therefore, that the insured is entitled in this case to repayment of premiums[7]. If the warranty is a promissory one and the breach did not occur until after it was given, no repayment of premiums is necessary: the insurer was on risk for some period of the contract's duration[8]. Where the contract can be divided into periods in respect of which the premium is payable in order to obtain cover against separate risks, the insured is entitled to repayment of that proportion of the premium due after the time of the breach of warranty[9]. The effect of illegality in an insurance contract depends upon whether the contract is to be treated as illegal *stricto sensu* or merely void. Non-marine contracts to which the Life Assurance Act 1774 applies and which are made without an insurable interest are treated as being illegal[10]. A 'ppi'[11] marine policy, however, is merely declared to be void[12]. In the former case, the insured has no right to repayment of premiums[13]. In the latter he has the right to repayment. Where a contract is illegal, the maxims *ex turpi causa non oritur actio* and *in pari delicto potior est conditio defendentis* will apply. If, for example, an insured is fraudulently induced by an agent for the insurer to take out cover on another party in whom he has no insurable interest, the insured is not equally at fault: they are not both *in pari delicto*[14]. Where insurance is effected with an unauthorised insurer[15], it cannot be enforced against the insured and the latter is entitled to repayment of premiums[16]. A contract with an unauthorised insurer is neither illegal nor void[17].

1 *Standard Life Assurance Co v Weems* (1884) 11 R (HL) 48.
2 E J MacGillivray and M Parkington *Insurance Law* (8th edn, 1988) para 1001.
3 *MacGillivray and Parkington* para 1001. See also *Anderson v Fitzgerald* (1853) 4 HL Cas 484.
4 *Anderson v Fitzgerald* (1853) 4 HL Cas 484. This need not presuppose fraud on the part of the insured: insurance effected on subjects which were, at the time of insuring, no longer in existence falls into this category if their loss was unknown to the parties.
5 This is because the contract can only be avoided *ab initio*: see generally *MacGillivray and Parkington* para 1004.
6 This is the case even where the breach is innocent: see *Duckett v Williams* (1834) 2 Cr & M 348; *Standard Life Assurance Co v Weems* (1884) 11 R (HL) 48; *Kumar v Life Insurance Corpn of India* [1974] 1 Lloyd's Rep 147. There is, however, a prima facie argument that a contract term of this kind may fall to be regarded as a penalty clause and be unenforceable as such. This is certainly the position adopted in South Africa under the Conventional Penalties Act 1962, ss 1, 4. See 'Insurance' in *The Law of South Africa* vol 12 (1988), para 196. See also the doubts expressed in *Kumar v Life Assurance Corpn of India* at 154, per Kerr J.
7 *Standard Life Assurance Co v Weems* (1884) 11 R (HL) 48.
8 *MacGillivray and Parkington* para 1005.
9 Marine Insurance Act 1906 (c 41), s 84(2): 'Where the consideration for the payment of the premium is apportionable and there is a total failure of any apportionable part of the consideration, a proportionate part of the premium is, under the like conditions, thereupon returnable to the assured'. This provision is also illustrative of the position in non-marine insurances. See also *MacGillivray and Parkington* paras 1002, 1005.
10 Life Assurance Act 1774 (c 48), s 1; *Harse v Pearl Life Assurance Co* [1904] 1 KB 558.
11 Ie 'policies proof of interest'.
12 Marine Insurance Act 1906, s 4(1), (2).
13 *Re London County Commercial Reinsurance Office Ltd* [1922] 2 Ch 67; *Re National Benefit Assurance Co Ltd* [1931] 1 Ch 46.
14 *Hughes v Liverpool Victoria Legal Friendly Society* [1916] 2 KB 482, CA. Cf *Harse v Pearl Life Assurance Co* [1904] 1 KB 558.
15 See the Insurance Companies Act 1982 (c 50), s 2 (amended by the Insurance Companies (Assistance) Regulations 1987, SI 1987/2130, reg 2(a)).
16 Financial Services Act 1986 (c 60), s 132(1). As already noted, however, the insurer may, exceptionally, be able to retain the premiums or enforce the contract if he can satisfy the court that (1) he had reasonable grounds for believing that he had authorisation; and (2) that it is just and equitable that the contract be enforced or the premiums retained: s 132(3).
17 Ibid, s 132(6).

836. Duration of the policy.

Where cover is provided for a period between two dates which are declared by the policy to be '*inclusive*', then both dates are included in the period covered[1]. However, where the policy merely refers to two dates, the first is excluded from the period of cover[1]. Cover ceases at midnight on the second of these two dates unless the policy prescribes an earlier time during that day[2]. It is open to the parties to a contract of insurance to agree to cancel the policy before the stipulated date of expiry occurs[3]. Payment in full of the sum insured will terminate the contract but where such payment is made under the error that it is due, the insurer is not entitled to cancel the policy but only to repayment of the money paid out[4].

1 *Sickness and Accident Assurance Association Ltd v General Accident Assurance Corpn Ltd* (1892) 19 R 977.
2 *Isaacs v Royal Insurance Co* (1870) LR 5 Exch 296.
3 *Sickness and Accident Assurance Association Ltd v General Accident Assurance Corpn Ltd* (1892) 19 R 977.
4 *North British and Mercantile Insurance Co v Stewart* (1871) 9 M 534.

(3) CONSTRUCTION OF INSURANCE POLICIES

837. General. Because the Unfair Contract Terms Act 1977 specifically excludes insurance contracts from its ambit[1], the rules of construction or interpretation of policies assume real significance. Insurers may try to couch their policies in plain, uncomplicated language, but this is not always done or achieved, and commercial and investment policies are often expressed in a complex and technical manner[2]. Many claims turn on the interpretation put on the wording of the policy, and the rules of construction are an important weapon for the legal practitioner representing a client whose claim has been rejected.

Insurance policies define the risk insured against and frequently define 'exceptions' where the insurer will not be liable. Unlike exclusion clauses, which operate as a defence to a claim under a contract, the effect of an 'excepted perils' clause is to define the scope of the obligation being undertaken[3]. If, for example, section 1 (a)–(c) of a motor vehicle policy sets out the risks insured against and then, under the heading 'Exceptions to section 1 (a)–(c)', excludes liability for mechanical or electrical breakdown, the insured cannot claim under the policy if his car breaks down. The insurer, in this example, did not undertake to provide cover for breakdowns. But construction of the wording of an excepted perils clause may well reveal that rejection of a claim is unjustified[3].

The construction of words, terms or phrases found in an insurance policy does not differ from the construction techniques employed in other contracts[4]. As a general rule, ordinary words will receive their ordinary meaning. However, this rule is displaced where the words have a technical or specialised meaning. Words may also take their meaning from the context in which they appear and so be read *ejusdem generis* or subject to the maxim *noscitur a sociis*. Words will be given their grammatical meaning and ambiguities construed *contra proferentem*.

In addition to those rules of construction which focus narrowly on the meaning of specific words or phrases, there are also broader canons of construction relating to the enforceability of the contract or to the scope of the obligations assumed thereunder.

1 Unfair Contract Terms Act 1977 (c 50), s 15(3)(a).
2 An example culled from a proposal form for property insurance illustrates the point: 'To the best of your knowledge is there, in the area of your home, any history of subsidence, heave, or landslip?' The question is both vague and technically complex. How wide is 'area'? What is 'heave' and how, if at all, does it differ from 'landslip'?
3 *Davidson v Guardian Royal Exchange Assurance* 1979 SC 192, 1981 SLT 81.
4 E J MacGillivray and M Parkington *Insurance Law* (8th edn, 1988) para 1071, citing the relevant cases.

838. The ordinary meaning of a word. The ordinary meaning of a word is the construction which a 'person of ordinary common sense making ordinary use of language' would put on it[1]. The dictionary definition of the word may be looked at, and if that definition represents the interpretation placed on that word by ordinary people, the word will be given its popular meaning[2]. There may be cases where the appropriate dictionary to refer to is not the *Oxford English Dictionary* but the *Concise Scots Dictionary*[3]. Where goods were insured against theft from a 'warehouse', it was held that this meant under cover of a building. Accordingly, the insurers were not liable to meet a claim where the goods were stolen from a lorry parked in a fenced yard[4]. Where a home insurance policy covered damage caused, inter alia, by 'flood', it was held that this did not cover damage caused by natural water seepage[5]. Where one of the insured perils was loss or damage due to 'storm or tempest', and the roof of a building collapsed under a heavy accumulation of snow, it was held that whether this accumulation constituted 'storm' damage was a question of fact and circumstance. The definition of 'storm' as given in the *Oxford English Dictionary* did not always require wind or some element of violence. Taking into account the duration and intensity of the snowfall and the presence of some significant wind, the weather conditions constituted a storm. Accordingly, a heavy snowfall was a 'storm' and, therefore, a risk covered by the policy[6].

1 *Glasgow Training Group (Motor Trade) Ltd v Lombard Continental plc* 1989 SLT 375, OH. See also *Laidlaw v John M Monteath & Co* 1979 SLT 78 at 81, OH, per Lord Allanbridge.
2 *Glasgow Training Group (Motor Trade) Ltd v Lombard Continental plc* 1989 SLT 375, OH.
3 In *Glasgow Training Group (Motor Trade) Ltd v Lombard Continental plc* 1989 SLT 375, OH, the Lord Ordinary declined to adopt the regional definitions of 'storm' found in the *Concise Scots Dictionary*.
4 *Leo Rapp Ltd v McClure* [1955] 1 Lloyd's Rep 292; *Laidlaw v John M Monteath & Co* 1979 SLT 78, OH.
5 'Flood', it was said, connoted violence, suddenness, and largeness: *Young v Sun Alliance and London Insurance Ltd* [1976] 3 All ER 561, [1977] 1 WLR 104, CA.
6 *Glasgow Training Group (Motor Trade) Ltd v Lombard Continental plc* 1989 SLT 375, OH.

839. Technical words. Where a word has a precise technical meaning or a precise legal meaning, the court will give it that specialised meaning and not its ordinary one[1]. However, if the policy contains a glossary of the terms used in it, then the definition given therein must obtain[2]. Context may indicate that a technical meaning be implied in respect of a word and the converse may also hold true[3]. Trade usage or custom may colour the meaning of a term[4]. Litigants may agree not to ascribe a technical meaning to a word which might otherwise merit such a meaning[5].

1 See generally E R H Ivamy *General Principles of Insurance Law* pp 348–350, and the cases cited there. In *London and Lancashire Fire Insurance Co Ltd v Bolands Ltd* [1924] AC 836, HL, eg, the policy excluded liability for loss or damage caused by a 'riot'. This term was given its legal meaning and the insurer was held not obliged to meet a claim arising from a robbery by several, armed, men.
2 *Re George and Goldsmiths and General Burglary Insurance Association Ltd* [1899] QB 595, CA. The problem as to the meaning of 'storm' in *Glasgow Training Group (Motor Trade) Ltd v Lombard Continental plc* 1989 SLT 375, OH, would have been easily resolved if the policy had contained a definition of that word. See A D M Forte 'The Meaning of "Storm" in Property Insurance' [1989] JBL 72.
3 *Algemeene Bankvereeniging v Langton* (1935) 40 Com Cas 247, CA; *Laurence v Davies* [1972] 2 Lloyd's Rep 231.
4 In *Anglo-African Merchants Ltd v Bayley* [1970] 1 QB 311, [1969] 2 All ER 421, the description of government surplus stock as 'new' was upheld, even though the stock had not just been made. In the clothing trade it was the case that 'new' indicated that stock was government surplus.
5 In *Glasgow Training Group (Motor Trade) Ltd v Lombard Continental plc* 1989 SLT 375, OH, the parties agreed that 'storm' was not to be given the meaning prescribed in the Beaufort wind scale.

840. Context. A court faced with the task of ascribing a meaning to a term of the policy may resort to consideration of the context in which the term or word appears and apply the general rules of construction, *ejusdem generis* or *noscitur a sociis*[1]. But there are also cases where this is not done[2]. If a contextual approach is taken, it often reveals that there are two senses in which the word or phrase may be understood. This points to ambiguity and the court may be persuaded to construe the word or phrase *contra proferentem*[3].

1 *Menzies v North British Insurance Co* (1847) 9 D 694; *Sangster's Trustees v General Accident Assurance Corpn Ltd* (1896) 24 R 56, 4 SLT 163. In *Oddy v Phoenix Assurance Co Ltd* [1966] 1 Lloyd's Rep 134, the phrase 'storm or tempest' was examined. The view taken was that a 'tempest' was a more severe or violent storm. The meaning of 'tempest' was, therefore, coloured by its

association with 'storm'. In *Young v Sun Alliance and London Insurance Ltd* [1976] 3 All ER 561, [1977] 1 WLR 104, CA, a home policy covered the insured against loss or damage caused by 'storm, tempest or flood'. The house was damaged by water seepage and a claim was made for 'flood' damage. Taking a contextual approach, the Court of Appeal held that a 'flood' meant a sudden, violent movement of water.

2 In *Glasgow Training Group (Motor Trade) Ltd v Lombard Continental plc* 1989 SLT 375 at 379, OH, Lord Clyde was of the opinion that the word 'or', in the phrase 'storm or tempest', was not epexegetic; and that although wind was an essential ingredient of a tempest, it was not a prerequisite for weather conditions to be described as a 'storm'.

3 In *Glasgow Training Group (Motor Trade) Ltd v Lombard Continental plc* 1989 SLT 375, OH, Lord Clyde was minded to adopt this approach to the word 'storm' on discovering that the dictionary definition gave two meanings for the word. In *Young v Sun Alliance & London Insurance Co* [1976] 3 All ER 561, [1977] 1 WLR 104, CA, the Court of Appeal was similarly minded.

841. Grammar. So far as it is possible, their ordinary grammatical meaning will be attributed to the words of the policy[1]. The courts will treat as *pro non scripto* obvious grammatical mistakes[2]. Words expressed in the present tense will not be given a future meaning[3]. As with commercial contracts generally, the courts will prefer an interpretation which makes the contract workable[4]. However, where the wording of a policy has come, through the passage of time, to acquire a specific (perhaps technical) significance, then that meaning will prevail over the ordinary grammatical meaning[5]. Nor will the grammatical meaning of words prevail where that would clearly be contrary to the parties' actual intentions[6].

1 See generally *Lewis Emanuel & Son Ltd v Hepburn* [1960] 1 Lloyd's Rep 304; *Balfour v Beaumont* [1984] 1 Lloyd's Rep 272, CA.

2 *Glen's Trustees v Lancashire and Yorkshire Accident Insurance Co Ltd* (1906) 8 F 915, 14 SLT 168.

3 *Kennedy v Smith* 1975 SC 266, 1976 SLT 110.

4 *Pearson v Commercial Union Assurance Co* (1876) 1 App Cas 498, HL. In this case, a term in a marine policy gave cover to a ship while berthed at a named dock and at a named dry dock. It was held that by implication the cover would also extend to the vessel's passage from the named dock to the dry dock.

5 *Price & Co v A1 Ships' Small Damage Insurance Association* (1889) 22 QBD 580, CA.

6 Thus words may not always be given their strict, literal meaning: see *Clidero v Scottish Accident Insurance Co* (1892) 19 R 355; *Sangster's Trustees v General Accident Assurance Corpn Ltd* (1896) 24 R 56, 4 SLT 163. In *Fraser v B N Furman (Productions) Ltd, Miller Smith & Partners Third Parties* [1967] 3 All ER 57, [1967] 1 WLR 898, CA, an indemnity liability policy provided that the insured should 'take reasonable precautions'. It was held that this did not mean that all negligent acts by the insured were automatically in breach of this term. Where a policy defines the meaning of certain words, it will be difficult for either party to argue that another interpretation should be ascribed to them. It may be observed that were policies to include, as a matter of course, a glossary of the terms used, much difficulty would be avoided.

842. Ambiguities. If, having applied the rules of construction referred to above, there remains an ambiguity as to the meaning of a word or phrase, then the rule is that the ambiguous word or words must be construed *contra proferentem*. The argument that, as a commercial transaction, an insurance contract should be construed liberally, has been rejected by Scots law[1]. This does not mean, however, that the courts may not keep in mind 'the commercial object'[2] of the policy. When the policy is looked at as a whole, it may be found that a prima facie ambiguity turns out to have a clear meaning[2]. The courts will not put a strained construction on words which are not ambiguous[3].

It is submitted that the law regarding ambiguities is as expressed in *Kennedy v Smith*[4]. In that case the defender completed a proposal form for motor vehicle insurance in 1961 and declared that he did not drink alcohol. That declaration was true at the time. In 1971, for the first time, he consumed a very small quantity of lager. He crashed his car, killing the passengers travelling with him. The insurers, unsuccessfully, denied liability. They argued that they were protected by a declaration in an 'abstinence form' which read: 'I am a total abstainer from alcoholic drinks and have been since birth.' Their argument was that this declaration created a promissory warranty[5]. The defender argued that the wording of the declaration and, particularly, the tenses used only warranted the position at the time when he proposed himself for cover. The basis upon which the *contra proferentem* rule rests is clearly expressed in the judgment of Lord President Emslie:

> 'I content myself now by saying that if insurers seek to limit their liability under a policy by relying upon an alleged undertaking as to the future, prepared by them and accepted by the insured, the language they use must be such that the terms of the alleged undertaking and its scope are clearly and unambiguously expressed or plainly implied and that any such alleged undertaking will be construed, *in dubio, contra proferentem.*[6]'

The wording of the declaration did not ex facie refer to the future conduct of the insured. When the insurers sought to maintain that it did, they were arguing for an inference which was not apparent from the wording actually used. The wording, therefore, was ambiguous.

Since insurers are responsible for the language used in insurance documentation, and since it is they who would stand to profit should any ambiguity be ignored, it is unfair to give them the benefit of the doubt since they had the opportunity to phrase the documentation more clearly[7]. The *contra proferentem* rule of construction applies with equal force to statements made by the insured[8].

1 *Davidson v Guardian Royal Exchange Assurance* 1979 SC 192, 1981 SLT 81.
2 See E J MacGillivray and M Parkington *Insurance Law* (8th edn, 1988) para 1078.
3 *Laidlaw v John M Monteath & Co* 1979 SLT 78 at 81, OH, per Lord Allanbridge: '. . . the contra proferentem rule must not be used "to create the ambiguity – one must find the ambiguity first"'. See also *Cornish v Accident Insurance Co* (1889) 23 QBD 453, CA, and *Jason v British Traders' Insurance Co Ltd* [1969] 1 Lloyd's Rep 281.
4 *Kennedy v Smith* 1975 SC 266, 1976 SLT 110.
5 Warranties are discussed in more detail in paras 873 ff below.
6 *Kennedy v Smith* 1975 SC 266 at 277, 278, 1976 SLT 110 at 116, 117.
7 In *Kennedy v Smith* 1975 SC 266, 1976 SLT 110, the result might have been different had the declaration included, at the appropriate place, the words 'and shall be' or 'and shall remain'.
8 *Condogianis v Guardian Assurance Co Ltd* [1921] 2 AC 125 at 130, PC: '. . . there must also be a fair and reasonable construction of the answer given [by the insured]; and if on such a construction the answer is not true, although upon extreme literalism it may be correct, then the contract is equally avoided'.

843. Construing the policy as a whole. When considering the effect of a policy term, that term should not be looked at in isolation from the rest of the contract, rather the policy should be looked at as a whole in order to ascertain the effect of the term in question. It is submitted that this approach, which is adopted in relation to exception terms found in contracts[1], applies equally to excepted perils clauses found in insurance policies. In *Davidson v Guardian Royal Exchange Assurance*[2], the insurers exercised their option under a motor vehicle policy to have the insured's car repaired. The car was not returned to the insured for almost a year, and he sued the insurers for breach of an implied term of the contract of insurance that repairs should be effected within a reasonable time. The insurers relied on an exception clause to the risks covered which excepted liability for, inter alia, 'loss of use'. The Second Division rejected any equiparation between an exception clause and exemption or indemnity clauses. The claim was for damages arising from breach of contract, and the proper approach was 'to construe the Policy, to ascertain from it the risk or risks covered by section 1 [of the policy], including the Exceptions, and to see how far, if at all, a claim for breach of contract . . . is covered'[3]. When the terms defining the risks covered and setting out the exceptions qualifying the extent to which those risks were covered were examined, it was found that the policy did not deal with loss of use caused by breach of contract. Where a policy excepts liability if there has been 'wilful exposure to needless peril', non-deliberate injury does not justify a rejection of claim. A man may act carelessly or mistakenly and thus cause his injury but neither of these acts can be described as being 'wilful'[4].

1 *Ailsa Craig Fishing Co Ltd v Malvern Fishing Co Ltd* 1982 SC (HL) 14, 1982 SLT 377.
2 *Davidson v Guardian Royal Exchange Assurance* 1979 SC 192, 1981 SLT 81.
3 *Davidson v Guardian Royal Exchange Assurance* 1979 SC 192 at 198, 1981 SLT 81 at 84, per Lord Kissen.
4 *Glenlight Shipping Ltd v Excess Insurance Co Ltd* 1983 SLT 241. In this case the deceased was covered by a policy which excepted liability for wilful exposure to needless peril. Having taken alcohol, he drove off a ferry before it had berthed, mistakenly thinking that it had docked. The insurer's invocation of the above term was unsuccessful. The deceased had certainly exposed himself to peril when he drove off the ferry but he had not done so 'wilfully'. He had done so 'mistakenly'.

844. 'Accident'. The difficulty in placing the correct construction upon a word or term is nowhere more graphically illustrated than by considering, briefly, the meaning of the word 'accident'[1]. Help in so doing may be had from other cases in which the word has been construed and particularly those dealing with issues under the Workmen's Compensation Acts[2]. It is easier to state what is not an accident than to define what is. Thus illness, disease, ageing, and wear and tear are not considered to be accidents[3]. But where disease or illness is caused by an accident sustained during employment, there is no reason why a claim under an accident policy should not be met[4]. Death during surgery necessitated by some accidental injury is regarded as being caused by the accident[5].

It has been held that death was not caused by accident, or, more precisely, by 'accidental means', where an obese insured died as a result of a slipped colon putting too great a strain on his heart. What caused the colon to slip was the act of putting on his socks and that, it was said, could not be described as accidental since it was a deliberate and intentional act by the insured[6]. In contrast, a dislocated knee, caused by stooping to retrieve a marble, has been held to constitute an accident[7]. The better view, it is submitted, is that taken in the second case. This is to the effect that an accident is a fortuitous occurrence which produces an unexpected or unforeseeable consequence, even though the action giving rise to the occurrence was intended. The decision in the first case has been doubted[8].

1 For detailed treatment of the meaning of 'accident', see E J MacGillivray and M Parkington *Insurance Law* (8th edn, 1988) ch 26.
2 See *MacGillivray and Parkinson* ch 26. However, caution against too uncritical a reliance is necessary. See generally *Stewart v Wilsons and Clyde Coal Co* (1902) 5 F 120, 10 SLT 366; *M'Innes v Dunsmuir and Jackson* 1908 SC 1021, 16 SLT 214; and *Aitken v Finlayson, Bousfield & Co Ltd* 1914 SC 770, 1914 2 SLT 27.
3 One may, of course, insure against sickness, and such cover falls within the category of 'General Business' under the Insurance Companies Act 1982 (c 50), Sch 2, Pt I (amended by the Insurance Companies (Assistance) Regulations 1987, SI 1987/2130, reg 2(b), Schedule).
4 *Drylie v Alloa Coal Co Ltd* 1913 SC 549, 1913 1 SLT 167.
5 *Thomson v Mutter, Howey & Co* 1913 SC 619, 1913 1 SLT 213.
6 *Clidero v Scottish Accident Insurance Co* (1892) 19 R 355.
7 *Hamlyn v Crown Accidental Insurance Co Ltd* [1893] 1 QB 750, CA.
8 *Glenlight Shipping Ltd v Excess Insurance Co Ltd* 1983 SLT 241. However, as has been properly observed, *Clidero* was not dissented from: see *MacGillivray and Parkinson*, para 1793, note 13.

6. ASSIGNATION

845. General. In the absence of a contract term forbidding assignation[1], the insured may assign either his rights under his policy or the policy itself. There is a distinction between the two. An assignation by the insured of his right to be indemnified under his policy, does not require the assignee to possess any insurable interest in the subject insured. It is the cedent's right to be indemnified which is transferred. The insurer's consent to the assignation is unnecessary since it does not result in novation[2]. So long as an insurable interest existed when the insurance was effected, it does not matter that the assignee has no such interest. An assignation by the insured of the policy itself requires the insurer's consent because it does amount to novation[3]. Moreover, an assignation of the policy requires a transfer of the subject to the assignee in order that the latter possesses an insurable interest[4].

1 Policies of Assurance Act 1867 (c 144); Marine Insurance Act 1906 (c 41), s 50(1). See also Bell *Principles* ss 516, 520.
2 There is no substitution under the policy of a new insured.
3 *Peters v General Accident Fire and Life Assurance Corpn Ltd* [1938] 2 All ER 267, CA.
4 See generally E J MacGillivray and M Parkington *Insurance Law* (8th edn, 1988) para 1618; J J Gow *The Mercantile and Industrial Law of Scotland* (1964) p 342. In marine insurance it is provided that an assignation by an insured with no insurable interest is inoperative: Marine Insurance Act 1906, s 51. See also *North of England Pure Oil-Cake Co v Archangel Maritime Insurance Co* (1875) LR 10 QB 249, DC.

846. Assignatus utitur jure auctoris. Whether it is the policy itself which is assigned or merely the cedent's rights under it, the maxim *assignatus utitur jure auctoris* applies. Where, for example, a life policy was assigned by the insured as security for a loan, the insurer succeeded in an action for reduction of the policy on the grounds of breach of warranty and fraudulent misrepresentation by the insured regarding his habits and health[1]. The same is true of an assignation of a right of recovery under a marine policy[2]. If the cedent's right to payment under the policy was made conditional upon his observing correct procedures in the event of loss, and he fails to do so, the assignee may not recover under the policy[3].

1 *Scottish Widow's Fund and Life Assurance Society v Buist* (1876) 3 R 1078; *Scottish Equitable Life Assurance Society v Buist* (1877) 4 R 1076; *Buist v Scottish Equitable Life Assurance Society* (1878) 5 R (HL) 64. See also the Policies of Assurance Act 1867 (c 144), s 2: 'In any action on a policy of life assurance, a defence on equitable grounds, or a reply to such a defence on similar grounds, may be respectively pleaded and relied upon in the same manner and to the same extent as in any other personal action'.
2 Marine Insurance Act 1906 (c 41), s 50(2): 'Where a marine policy has been assigned so as to pass the beneficial interest in such policy, ... the defendant is entitled to make any defence arising out of the contract which he would have been entitled to make if the action had been brought in the name of the person by or on behalf of whom the policy was effected'.
3 Eg by providing proof of loss within a specified time: see *Re Carr and Sun Fire Insurance Co* (1897) 13 TLR 186, CA.

847. Prerequisites of valid assignation. An assignation must be in writing[1], but the choice of form and the wording of the assignation is unrestricted[2]. The assignation of life policies may either be indorsed on the policy itself or effected by means of a separate instrument of assignation[3]. The same is true of marine policies[4].

For the assignee to obtain a real right, enforceable against others, the assignation must be intimated to the insurer[5]. Mere physical delivery and possession of the policy or instrument of assignation is not sufficient[6]. Where, for example, a borrower signed a promissory note and sent his life policy to the lender, it was held that, in a competition with the arrestment of the proceeds of the policy by another of the borrower's creditors, the arrestment must prevail over an unintimated assignation[7]. Delivery of a policy or a deposit receipt for a policy, made with the intention that this is to be treated as a gift to take effect on the donor's death, is a *donatio mortis causa*[8].

1 *Scottish Provident Institution v Cohen & Co* (1886) 16 R 112; *Wylie's Executrix v M'Jannet* (1901) 4 F 195, 9 SLT 326.
2 *Brownlee v Robb* 1907 SC 1302, 15 SLT 261. The Schedule to the Policies of Assurance Act 1867 (c 144) provides the following style: 'I *AB* of, &c, in consideration of, &c, do hereby assign unto *CD* of, &c, his executors, administrators, and assigns, the [within] policy of assurance granted, &c, [*here describe the policy*]. In witness, &c.' For other styles of assignation, see the Transmission of Moveable Property (Scotland) Act 1862 (c 85), Schs A–C.
3 Policies of Assurance Act 1867, s 5.
4 Marine Insurance Act 1906 (c 41), s 50(3).
5 *Strachan v M'Dougle* (1835) 13 S 954; *United Kingdom Life Assurance Co v Dixon* (1838) 16 S 1277; *Scottish Provident Institution v Cohen & Co* (1886) 16 R 112.
6 *Strachan v M'Dougle* (1835) 13 S 954; *United Kingdom Life Assurance Co v Dixon* (1838) 16 S 1277; *Scottish Provident Institution v Cohen & Co* (1886) 16 R 112. The same is true of an assignation of a marine policy: see F Templeman *Marine Insurance* (6th edn, 1986 ed R J Lambeth) p 76.
7 *Strachan v M'Dougle* (1835) 13 S 954 at 959, per Lord Mackenzie: 'The question . . . remains whether the right of the arrester was excluded by the prior right of the assignee? I think there is in substance a good assignation in her favour, but it was not intimated, and, by the law of Scotland, an unintimated assignation cannot compete with an arrestment. To obviate this it is pleaded that the delivery of the policy completes the assignee's right without intimation. This is a doctrine of a dangerous tendency. It is an important general principle of our law, and there is none more vital, that the delivery of the corpus of a deed or instrument will not carry the real right that is contained within such deed or instrument.'
8 *Aiken's Executors v Aiken* 1937 SC 678, 1937 SLT 414; *British Linen Bank v Gammie* (1948) 64 Sh Ct Rep 23.

7. INSURABLE INTEREST

(1) INTRODUCTION

848. General. Bell stipulates, as an essential element of contracts of insurance generally, that 'there shall be a subject in which the insured has an interest'[1]. Regarding life assurance, Bell states as a prerequisite for a valid contract that: 'There can be no valid insurance on life without a pecuniary interest'[2]. The Life Assurance Act 1774 requires the insured to have an interest in the life or subject insured and provides that a contract in which no insurable interest exists 'shall be null and void'[3]. The Marine Insurance Act 1906 deems any marine policy where the insured has no insurable interest to be a gaming or wagering contract[4] which is void for that reason[5]. It is submitted, on the basis of the foregoing account, that the requirement of insurable interest is imposed by both common law and statute.

The scope or ambit of statutory provisions regarding insurable interest may arise for consideration[6]. The Life Assurance Act 1774 provides that the Act does not apply 'to insurances . . . made . . . on ships, goods, or merchandises'[7]. It has been suggested that non-marine indemnity contracts in respect of goods do not require that the insured, personally possesses an insurable interest in the goods unless the policy so stipulates[8]. It is submitted that this view is incorrect because it ignores the common law requirement that a valid contract of insurance must be supported by an insurable interest[9]. An agent who insures goods on his principal's behalf, but without disclosing that he is acting only as an agent, is not entitled to payment under the policy in the event of loss[10].

Where insurable interest is required by statute but the insured does not have an interest, the policy will be void. The insurer may, nonetheless, choose to honour a claim made under the policy and the courts will, in this case, entertain an action arising from any dispute as to who is entitled to the proceeds of the policy[11].

Marine insurance policies may sometimes be made 'interest or no interest' or 'ppi' ('policies proof of interest'). Such 'honour' policies contravene section 4(1) of the Marine Insurance Act 1906 but insurers will, nonetheless, pay or honour any claims made under the policy. Honour policies are subject to the normal rules applicable to insurance contracts[12].

1 Bell *Principles* s 457.
2 Bell *Principles* s 520.
3 Life Assurance Act 1774 (c 48), s 1. Despite its title, this Act applies not only to life assurance but also to certain non-marine indemnity contracts, eg insurance in respect of heritable property.
4 Marine Insurance Act 1906 (c 41), s 4(2).
5 Ibid, s 4(1).
6 The Court of Appeal recently expressed the view that the Life Assurance Act 1774 did not apply to the insurance of real property: see *Mark Rowlands Ltd v Berni Inns Ltd* [1986] QB 211, [1985] 3 All ER 473, CA. The correctness of this view has been cogently and persuasively denied by J Birds in 'Self-regulation and Insurance Contracts' in *New Foundations for Insurance Law* (1987 ed F D Rose) pp 36–39. Since, as is noted in the text, there is a common law requirement that an insurable interest must exist, the scope of the 1774 Act with regard to non-life contracts is not unduly problematic.
7 Life Assurance Act 1774, s 4.
8 J J Gow *The Mercantile and Industrial Law of Scotland* (1964) p 335.
9 Bell predicates a valid contract, inter alia, upon the existence of an insurable interest and states that such an interest need not, however, 'be specified in the policy': see Bell *Principles* ss 457, 461. The absurdity of the view expressed in the text to note 8 above can be demonstrated by posing a simple question: 'Can Mr Smith insure Mr Jones's car or his private collection of porcelain china?'
10 *Ferguson v Aberdeen Parish Council* 1916 SC 715, 1916 1 SLT 393.
11 *Hadden v Bryden* (1899) 1 F 710 6 SLT 362; *Carmichael v Carmichael's Executrix* 1919 SC 636, 1919 2 SLT 89 (revsd 1920 SC (HL) 195, 1920 2 SLT 285). The Scottish view is not followed by the English courts, which deny the insurer the right to waive the requirement of insurable interest: see *Gedge v Royal Exchange Assurance Corpn* [1900] 2 QB 214. Where, however, the insurer has already paid out under the policy but there is a dispute amongst the beneficiaries as to entitlement, then the English courts also pay no attention to the contravention of the statute.
12 In *Gunford Ship Co Ltd (in Liquidation) v Thames and Mersey Marine Insurance Co Ltd* 1910 SC 1072, 1910 2 SLT 154 (revsd in part 1911 SC (HL) 84, 1911 SLT 185), non-disclosure of existing honour policies, which over-insured a vessel, was treated as non-disclosure of a material fact which entitled the insurers to avoid the policy.

(2) THE NATURE OF INSURABLE INTEREST

849. Introduction. 'Interest', states Bell, 'it not limited to property but extends to every real and actual advantage and benefit arising out of or depending on the thing to which it refers[1]'. This definition of the nature of insurable interest predicates its existence on either of two bases, namely, 'advantage or benefit' or 'property'. These are not, however, the only bases for the enjoyment of an insurable interest. A possessory right, short of ownership, may constitute an insurable interest. Somewhat different rules apply to life assurance.

1 Bell *Principles* s 461.

850. Advantage or benefit. Where insurable interest is defined in terms of advantage or benefit, the test of whether or not an insurable interest exists depends on the answer to this question: 'Does the insured stand to benefit if the subject insured continues in existence and will he suffer loss if it is damaged or ceases to exist?[1]' Thus the purchaser of heritable subjects has an insurable interest in these on conclusion of the missives and before the disposition has been recorded[2]. The same is true for the purchaser of goods where the passing of risk and of property are not contemporaneous[3]. The mere expectation of some advantage or benefit does not constitute an insurable interest[4]. English law does not appear to predicate the existence of an insurable interest upon this basis[5]. Although modern Scottish cases dealing with the question of insurable interest do not stress this approach, there is no reason to conclude that it is inappropriate[6]. It is arguable that it is English law which is out of step with modern developments[7].

1 See *Lucena v Craufurd* (1806) 2 B & PNR 269 at 302, HL, per Lawrence J: 'A man is interested in a thing to whom advantage may arise or prejudice happen from the circumstances which may attend it and whom it importeth, that its condition as to safety or other quality should continue. . . . To be interested in the preservation of a thing is to be so circumstanced with respect to it as to have benefit from its existence, prejudice from its destruction.' See also *Mark Rowlands Ltd v Berni Inns Ltd* [1986] QB 211 at 228, [1985] 3 All ER 473 at 481, CA, per Kerr LJ.

2 J J Gow *The Mercantile and Industrial Law of Scotland* (1964) p 336. On conclusion of the contract, risk passes to the purchaser who will still have to proceed with the conveyance should the subjects be destroyed before he has acquired a real right to them. As to the passing of risk, see *Sloans Dairies v Glasgow Corpn* 1977 SC 223, 1979 SLT 17.

3 As to the passing of risk in contracts for the sale of goods, see the Sale of Goods Act 1979 (c 54), s 20.

4 Bell *Principles* s 461.

5 See *Lucena v Craufurd* (1806) 2 B & PNR 269, HL, where the House of Lords rejected what has been termed the 'factual expectation test'. See also J Birds *Modern Insurance Law* (1988) p 40. With regard to marine risks, the Marine Insurance Act 1906 (c 41), s 5(2), provides: '. . . a person is interested in a marine adventure where he stands in any legal or equitable relation to the adventure or to any insurable property at risk therein, in consequence of which he may benefit by the safety or due arrival of insurable property, or may be prejudiced by its loss, or by damage thereto, or by the detention thereof, or may incur liability in respect thereof.' It is submitted that this does not predicate the existence of an insurable interest on the benefit/loss expectation. The governing words are 'legal or equitable relation . . . to any insurable property'. See generally F Templeman *Marine Insurance* (6th edn, 1986 ed R J Lambeth) p 66.

6 Indeed, this would seem to be the only basis upon which it can be said that the purchaser of heritable property enjoys an insurable interest prior to acquiring a real right to the property. See note 2 above.

7 The factual expectation test has been applied by the Canadian Supreme Court in *Constitution Insurance Co of Canada v Kosmopoulos* (1987) 34 DLR (4th) 208 (Can SC). This test is also prescribed as being appropriate in Australia by the Insurance Contracts Act 1984, s 17.

851. Property. Ownership of an item gives the proprietor an insurable interest in it[1]. In *Arif v Excess Insurance Group Ltd*[2], a partner in a hotel business insured the hotel in his own name. The building was destroyed by fire and the insured claimed under the policy. The insurers refused to satisfy the claim. In giving judgment against the insured it was said that: '[i]f . . . the position be that the assets of the business were partnership property, it follows that the pursuer as an individual would have no insurable interest in the assets of the . . . Hotel.[3]' Despite the fact that a debtor by diminishing or disposing of his property may become unable to repay his debts, his creditors do not enjoy an insurable interest in his property[4].

1 The seminal authority is *Macaura v Northern Assurance Co Ltd* [1925] AC 619, HL. This case concerned the insurance of a quantity of timber against loss. The timber was the property of a company in which the insured was the sole shareholder. The timber was, however, insured in

the name of the insured. The timber was destroyed by fire and the insured claimed under the policy. It was held that he was not entitled to compensation. The timber was the property of the company which was in law a separate legal person from the insured: 'It is clear that the appellant has no insurable interest in the timber. . . . It was not his.'

2 *Arif v Excess Insurance Group Ltd* 1987 SLT 473, OH. For a cogent criticism of this case, see J Wolffe 'Insurable Interest: Time for Change' 1989 SLT (News) 103.
3 *Arif v Excess Insurance Group Ltd* 1987 SLT 473 at 474, OH, per Lord Sutherland.
4 *Macaura v Northern Assurance Co Ltd* [1925] AC 619, HL.

852. Possession. Possession of property, both moveable and heritable, may give rise to an insurable interest. It is doubtful that mere possession per se is sufficient to confer an insurable interest[1]. Where the possessor of goods or heritage may incur liability should these be lost or damaged, that will be sufficient to constitute an insurable interest[2]. If the possessor has the right to enjoy the property, that too will constitute an insurable interest. Thus the carrier or custodier of goods entrusted to him may insure against liability to the owner for loss or destruction of the goods and also in respect of the profit which it is hoped to make on the contract of carriage or *locatio custodiae*[3]. A tenant under a lease also has an insurable interest in the property leased to him[4]. With regard to leases of property, an obligation to maintain and repair the premises leased does not confer an insurable interest in the full value of the building[4]. An insurable interest in the full value of the building will exist only where the lease expressly provides that either (1) the tenants are obliged to insure the building against damage or destruction, or (2) they are obliged to repair or rebuild in the event of damage or destruction[5]. It is submitted that the hirer of goods under a contract for their hire has an insurable interest since if they are stolen or damaged he will be liable to the owner of those goods.

1 *Macaura v Northern Assurance Co Ltd* [1925] AC 619, HL. Here the insured was not the custodier of the goods and did not personally possess them.
2 *Aberdeen Harbour Board v Heating Enterprises (Aberdeen) Ltd* 1989 SCLR 716 at 729, 1990 SLT 416 at 425, per Lord Kincraig: '. . . it is trite law that a person has no insurable interest in property in which he has no direct interest either as owner or as a result of a liability to the owner to reinstate'.
3 *Dalgleish v John Buchanan & Co* (1854) 16 D 332. See also *Ferguson v Aberdeen Parish Council* 1916 SC 715, 1916 1 SLT 393.
4 *Fehilly v General Accident Fire and Life Assurance Corpn* 1982 SC 163, 1983 SLT 141.
5 *Fehilly v General Accident Fire and Life Assurance Corpn* 1982 SC 163, 1983 SLT 141. In this case, the insurers did not maintain that the tenants under a commercial lease enjoyed no insurable interest. They argued only that the extent of the tenants' interest was limited to the market value of the lease.

853. Life assurance. According to Bell, 'There can be no valid insurance on life without a pecuniary interest'[1]. It is further stated that 'a father has no insurable interest in the life of his son', and that 'In a policy opened by one on his own life, his family has an interest sufficient'[1]. It is submitted that Bell's view, though accurate, must be taken under some qualification. The requirement that there be a pecuniary interest in the life assured holds good where the relationship between the insured and the party whose life he has insured is that of creditor and debtor respectively. In short, a creditor has an insurable interest in the life of his debtor[2]. An employer has been held to have an insurable interest in the life of an employee[3]. A cautioner also has an insurable interest in the life of the principal debtor[4]. Because these are all pecuniary interests, the amount insurable is limited to the extent of the obligation imposed[5]. In certain cases there is no need to demonstrate a pecuniary interest in the life insured. A person is presumed to have an insurable interest in his own life, and spouses have an insurable interest each in the other's life[6]. It should be noted that what the law presumes in such cases is an insurable interest and not a pecuniary one. Accordingly, no restriction is imposed on the amount which may be insured. Bell's statement that a father had no insurable interest in his child's life was, for a time, displaced by certain obiter remarks in *Carmichael v Carmichael's Executrix*[7]. Thereafter it was accepted that parents did have an interest in their children's lives because they enjoyed a right to be alimented by them in certain circumstances and would suffer if their children died. Under the Family Law (Scotland) Act 1985, parents no longer enjoy an insurable interest on this ground. The Act defines, exclusively, the parties who are under an alimentary duty, and children are not included in this definition[8]. This does not mean that a parent cannot have an insurable interest in his children's lives on some other basis: for example *qua* creditor or employer.

1 Bell *Principles* s 520.
2 *Lindsay v Barmcotte* (1851) 13 D 718; *Simcock v Scottish Imperial Insurance Co Ltd* (1902) 10 SLT 286, OH.
3 *Turnbull & Co v Scottish Provident Institution* (1896) 34 SLR 146, OH; *Simcock v Scottish Imperial Insurance Co Ltd* (1902) 10 SLT 286, OH.
4 *White v Cotton* (1846) 8 D 872.
5 Where eg a contract of employment may be determined by the giving of one week's notice, the extent of the insurable interest is limited to one week's salary: *Simcock v Scottish Imperial Insurance Co Ltd* (1902) 10 SLT 286, OH. Where the period of notice is longer than one week, the amount of insurable interest is extended accordingly.
6 *Wight v Brown* (1845) 11 D 459; *Champion v Duncan* (1867) 6 M 17. See also the Married Women's Policies of Assurance (Scotland) Act 1880 (c 26) (amended by the Married Women's Policies of Assurance (Scotland) (Amendment) Act 1980 (c 56), s 1).
7 *Carmichael v Carmichael's Executrix* 1919 SC 636, 1919 2 SLT 89, revsd (without discussion of this point) 1920 SC (HL) 195, 1920 2 SLT 285.
8 Family Law (Scotland) Act 1985 (c 37), s 1(1).

(3) TIME AND INSURABLE INTEREST

854. The time when the policy is effected. It is settled law that, in contracts of life assurance, the insured must possess an insurable interest at the time when the policy is effected[1]. It follows from this that where a creditor has insured his debtor's life, he is still entitled to payment under the policy on the death of the debtor, even though the debt was repaid before death[2]. An insured may assign his rights under a life policy to a third party who has no insurable interest in the life insured[3].

1 *Dalby v India and London Life Assurance Co* (1854) 15 CB 365, Ex Ch; *Turnbull & Co v Scottish Provident Institution* (1896) 34 SLR 146, OH; Life Assurance Act 1774 (c 48), s 1.
2 *Dalby v India and London Assurance Co* (1854) 15 CB 365, Ex Ch. See also *Turnbull & Co v Scottish Provident Institution* (1896) 34 SLR 146, OH: an agent's life was insured but before the policy was issued he gave in his notice. The agency had not terminated when the policy was issued. It was held that the insured could claim under the policy when the agent died.
3 *MacDonald v National Mutual Life Assurance of Australasia Ltd* (1906) 14 SLT 173, OH; 249, OH. Assignation may not be made before the policy is issued.

855. The time of loss. In marine insurance the interest need not exist when the contract is made but it must exist at the time of loss[1]. In liability indemnity insurance, where the risk is a continuing one and cover is in respect of a class of goods, all that is required is that there be an interest at the time of loss[2].

1 Marine Insurance Act 1906 (c 41), s 6(1).
2 See E R H Ivamy *General Principles of Insurance Law* (5th edn, 1986) p 27. The example given there is that of carriers and custodiers of goods.

856. Time of insuring and time of loss. In cases of indemnity insurance, including those indemnity contracts to which the Life Assurance Act 1774 applies, an insurable interest is required not only at the time when insurance is effected but also at the time when loss occurs[1]. It follows, therefore, that in such contracts no claim can be made where no such interest exists at the time of loss. Examples of contracts falling into this category are fire or house insurance[2], and insurance effected on goods which have been sold[3].

1 E J MacGillivray and M Parkington *Insurance Law* (8th edn, 1988) para 26. However, the Life Assurance Act 1774 (c 48), stipulates only that the interest must exist at the time of contracting.
2 As to fire insurance, see *Sadlers' Co v Badcock* (1743) 2 Atk 554.
3 *MacGillivray and Parkington* paras 128–130. Note also *Anderson v Morice* (1875) LR 10 CP 609, Ex Ch; (1876) 1 App Cas 713, HL.

857. Prospective and retrospective cover. In those situations where insurable interest is required at the time when the contract is made, it would be logical to infer that insurance effected before the acquisition of such interest must be void. For example, the prospective purchaser of heritable property has no insurable interest in that property until a contract for its sale to him has been concluded. It might be thought that prospective cover is ratified by the subsequent purchase of the property but this may not be the case[1]. If at the time when insurance is effected, the insured misrepresents himself as possessing an insurable interest in property, subsequent acquisition will be ineffective to prevent avoidance of the policy[2]. A policy of marine insurance is not void because the insured had no insurable interest at the time when cover was effected, provided he had such an interest at the time of the loss[3]. Where a marine policy in respect of a vessel or its cargo states that these are insured 'lost or not lost', the insured can make a valid claim under the policy even though he had no insurable interest at the time of loss but acquired this later[4]. Where, however, the insured knows that the subjects insured have been lost but the insurer does not, there is no valid insurance[4]. Where a vessel or cargo is insured 'lost or not lost', at a time when, unknown to either insurer or insured, these are already in the port of destination, the insurer can keep the premium[5]. If, however, the insurer knows of safe arrival but the insured does not, he is not entitled to retain the premium[5]. There is no reason why retrospective insurance of non-marine risks should not be possible. The validity of such cover would, of course, be dependent on similar conditions to those applying to marine contracts[6].

1 The law cannot be said to be clear on this issue. Contrast E J MacGillivray and M Parkington *Insurance Law* (8th edn, 1988) para 24, where the view expressed in the text is taken, with the view expressed in E R H Ivamy *General Principles of Insurance Law* (5th edn, 1986) p 27. It is true that certain *obiter dicta* in *Williams v Baltic Insurance Association of London Ltd* [1924] 2 KB 282 at 291, per Roche J, do not support the view advanced in the text, but the judge's comments are not above criticism: see *MacGillivray and Parkington* para 25.
2 *Howard v Lancashire Insurance Co* (1885) 11 SCR 92 (Can SC).
3 Marine Insurance Act 1906 (c 41), s 6(1).
4 Ibid, s 6(1). See also ibid, Sch 1, r 1.
5 Ibid, s 84(3)(b).
6 *Giffard v Queens Insurance Co* (1869) 12 NBR 432.

8. MISREPRESENTATION AND NON-DISCLOSURE

(1) INTRODUCTION

858. General. Parties to any contract must not misrepresent the truth. If asked a question they must answer accurately. They are not, however, under an obligation to volunteer information which, though it might influence the decision of the other party, they are not asked about[1]. Although a contract of insurance may also be reduced on the ground of error induced by misrepresentation as to a material fact, it is more usual for insurers to argue that it should be reduced because of non-disclosure of material facts. Insurers may well invoke both misrepresentation and non-disclosure as grounds for avoiding the contract[2]. Where there has been non-disclosure, the appropriate remedy is the reduction of the contract of insurance, but not damages[3]. Where the non-disclosure or misrepresentation is innocent, the insured is entitled to recover any premium paid[4]. Insurance contracts are said to be *uberrimae fidei* (of the utmost good faith) and both parties[5] are under a positive duty to disclose all material (ie relevant) facts, even if they are not specifically requested by the proposal form to do this[6]. Influenced by the judgment of Lord Mansfield in *Carter v Boehm*[7], the Court of Session imported into Scots law the view that insurance was a contract *uberrimae fidei*[8]. It may be observed that the concept of 'utmost good faith' has been questioned by the South African Appellate Division[9] and has been the occasion of much criticism over the years[10]. Whatever the criticisms levelled against the doctrine of utmost good faith may be, it is clear that as Scots law stands at present 'there can be no doubt that a contract of marine insurance is *uberrimae fidei*, and that every material circumstance which is known to the assured[11] must be disclosed to the insurers before the risk is covered[12]'. Although this dictum was stated in the context of marine insurance[13], there is absolutely no doubt that it applies with equal force to non-marine contracts[14].

1 See generally W M Gloag *The Law of Contract* (2nd edn, 1929) p 457. As to the non-disclosure of facts which there is no duty to disclose, see *Broatch v Jenkins* (1866) 4 M 1030 at 1032, per Lord President McNeill. See also *Hartdegen v Fanner* 1980 SLT (Notes) 23, OH.

2 For a recent example, see *The Dora* [1989] 1 Lloyd's Rep 69. Misrepresentation and non-disclosure are not synonymous. Where an incorrect answer is given to a question asked by a proposal form, there is a misrepresentation. Where material information known only to one party is not volunteered, there is non-disclosure. The two concepts may shade into each other, however, making the distinction unimportant where there is *suppressio veri* or *suggestio falsi*. In both cases the misinformation must be as to a material fact. See generally *Craig v Imperial Union Accident Assurance Co* (1894) 1 SLT 646, OH; *Kumar v Life Insurance Corpn of India* [1974] 1 Lloyd's Rep 147; *Highlands Insurance Co v Continental Insurance Co* [1987] 1 Lloyd's Rep 109n.

3 *Banque Financière de la Cité SA v Westgate Insurance Co Ltd* [1990] 2 All ER 947, HL (affg [1989] 2 All ER 952, CA). The law, generally, is as stated in the context of marine insurance: 'A contract of marine insurance is a contract based upon the utmost good faith, and if the utmost good faith be not observed by either party, the contract may be avoided by the other party': Marine Insurance Act 1906 (c 41), s 17. See also *The Good Luck* [1990] 1 QB 818, [1989] 3 All ER 628, CA.

4 *Banque Financière de la Cité SA v Westgate Insurance Co Ltd* [1990] 2 All ER 947, HL, affg [1989] 2 All ER 952, CA.

5 The Marine Insurance Act 1906, s 17, spells out that the requirement of utmost good faith must be observed by both parties. The point is also made in *Life Association of Scotland v Foster* (1873) 11 M 351. In most of the reported cases dealing with the positive duty of disclosure, it is the non-disclosure of the insured which is the issue. A recent case where the non-disclosure was alleged on the part of the insurer is *Banque Financière de la Cité SA v Westgate Insurance Co Ltd* [1990] 2 All ER 947, HL, affg [1989] 2 All ER 952, CA.

6 The *Statement of General Insurance Practice* 1986, para 1(d) requests ABI insurers to ask, in their proposal forms, clear questions on matters which 'insurers have found generally to be material'. An identical provision is found in the *Statement of Long-Term Insurance Practice* 1986, para 1(c). The positive duty of disclosure arises *ex lege* and is not based on an implied term in the contract: see *March Cabaret Club and Casino Ltd v London Assurance* [1975] 1 Lloyd's Rep 169; *Banque Financière de la Cité SA v Westgate Insurance Co Ltd* [1990] 2 All ER 947, HL, affg [1989] 2 All ER 952, CA.

7 *Carter v Boehm* (1766) 3 Burr 1905.

8 *Stewart v Morison* (1779) Mor 7080 at 7081: 'The principles of mercantile law on which this question depends, are stated as follows in [*Carter v Boehm*] "Insurance is a contract upon speculation; the special facts upon which the contingent chance is to be computed, lie most commonly in the knowledge of the insured only. The underwriter trusts to his representation,

and proceeds upon confidence that he does not keep back any circumstances in his knowledge to mislead the underwriters into a belief that the circumstance does not exist, and induce him to estimate the risk, as if it did not exist." The reason of the rule which obliges parties to disclose, is to prevent fraud, and to encourage good faith.'

9 *Mutual and Federal Insurance Co Ltd v Oudtshoorn Municipality* 1985 (1) SA 419 at 433, per Joubert JA: 'By our law all contracts are *bonae fidei* ... Yet the duty of disclosure is not common to all types of contract. It is restricted to those contracts, such as contracts of insurance, where it is required *ex lege*. Moreover, there is no magic in the expression *uberrima fides*. There are no degrees of good faith. It is entirely inconceivable that there could be a little, more or most (utmost) good faith. The distinction is between good and bad faith. There is no room for *uberrima fides* as a third category of faith in our law'.

10 The seminal work is R A Hasson 'The Doctrine of *Uberrima Fides* in Insurance Law' (1969) 32 MLR 615. For judicial criticism of the consequences of this doctrine, see *Anderson v Fitzgerald* (1853) 4 HL Cas 484; *Glicksman v Lancashire and General Assurance Co Ltd* [1927] AC 139, HL; *Mackay v London General Insurance Co* (1935) 51 Ll L Rep 201; *Zurich General Accident and Liability Insurance Co Ltd v Morrison* [1942] 2 KB 53, [1942] 1 All ER 529, CA; *Lambert v Co-operative Insurance Society Ltd* [1975] 2 Lloyd's Rep 485, CA. Criticism of the law has also been made by the Law Commission: *Insurance Law: Non-Disclosure and Breach of Warranty* (Law Com no. 104) (Cmnd 8064) (1980).

11 And, it may be added, 'to the insurer'. As to the reciprocal nature of the positive duty of disclosure, see note 5 above.

12 *The Spathari* 1924 SC 182 at 196, 1924 SLT 126 at 130, per Lord Justice-Clerk Alness, affd 1925 SC (HL) 6, 1925 SLT 322.

13 Marine Insurance Act 1906, s 17: see note 3 above.

14 *Fourth Report of the Law Reform Committee for Scotland* (Cmnd 330) (1957), para 6: 'Although this statement [of Lord Justice-Clerk Alness in *The Spathari*] was made in a case dealing with marine insurance, it is thought that it would be held to apply to contracts of insurance generally'. See also *Life Association of Scotland v Foster* (1873) 11 M 351, and *Zurich General Accident and Liability Insurance Co Ltd v Leven* 1940 SC 406, 1940 SLT 350.

(2) MISREPRESENTATION

859. General. It is always open to the insurer to plead misrepresentation rather than non-disclosure[1]. To be actionable the misrepresentation must be 'material'. It has been said that a material fact is one 'of such a nature as to influence the judgment of a prudent insurer in determining whether he would take the risk, and if so, at what premium and under what conditions'[2]. More recently, however, the view has been expressed, albeit reluctantly, that it is not necessary that the misrepresentation should have influenced the insurer to grant cover, it being sufficient that it relates to some matter which the insurer would have wanted to know the truth about then taking a decision to grant cover[3]. There is no authority to similar effect in Scots law. There has been a fairly strong tendency for the English courts to treat incorrect answers to the questions asked in proposal forms as amounting to non-disclosure[4]. It may be the case that the Scottish courts more closely observe the distinction[5]. Misrepresentation may still be more difficult to plead for insurers. To avoid a contract of motor vehicle insurance on the ground of misrepresentation, the insurer must not only show that material facts were misrepresented but also that the misrepresentation induced the contract[6]. To avoid a contract on the ground of non-disclosure, all that need be shown is that the undisclosed fact was material: unless, again, the contract is one for motor vehicle cover, in which case it must be shown that the non-disclosure induced the contract[7]. It is an offence for an insurance company or its representative to induce the insured to take cover as a result of a fraudulent misrepresentation[8].

1 *Scottish Widow's Fund and Life Assurance Society v Buist* (1876) 3 R 1078; *Scottish Equitable Life Assurance Society v Buist* (1877) 4 R 1076 (fraudulent misrepresentation); *The Spathari* 1924 SC

182, 1924 SLT 126, affd 1925 SC (HL) 6, 1925 SLT 322; *Zurich General Accident and Liability Insurance Co Ltd v Leven* 1940 SC 406, 1940 SLT 350.

2 *Zurich General Accident and Liability Insurance Co Ltd v Leven* 1940 SC 406 at 416, 1940 SLT 350 at 354, per Lord President Normand. The test has until recently also been applied to test the materiality of undisclosed facts in England: see *Container Transport International Inc and Reliance Group Inc v Oceanus Mutual Underwriting Association (Bermuda) Ltd* [1984] 1 Lloyd's Rep 476, CA.

3 *Highlands Insurance Co v Continental Insurance Co* [1987] 1 Lloyd's Rep 109n.

4 Cf *Kumar v Life Insurance Corpn of India* [1974] 1 Lloyd's Rep 147; *Highlands Insurance Co v Continental Insurance Co* [1987] 1 Lloyd's Rep 109n.

5 *Zurich General Accident and Liability Insurance Co Ltd v Leven* 1940 SC 406 at 415, 1940 SLT 350 at 354, per Lord President Normand: 'The next question is whether that statement is a non-disclosure, or whether it is a misrepresentation of fact which was erroneous. It is clearly an erroneous representation or a misrepresentation of a fact. We had some discussion about the difference between non-disclosure and misrepresentation. In general, non-disclosure means that you have failed to disclose something which was not the subject of a question but which was known to you and which you ought to have considered for yourself would be material, whereas a representation is something directly said in answer to a specific question'. In *M'Phee v Royal Insurance Co Ltd* 1979 SC 304 at 319, per Lord President Emslie, there is a suggestion that the Marine Insurance Act 1906 (c 41), s 18(1) (dealing with non-disclosure), may not apply where specific answers are given to specific questions.

6 In motor vehicle insurance, the insurer may avoid the contract where cover was 'obtained' by misrepresentation: Road Traffic Act 1988 (c 52), s 152(2)(a)(i). See also *Zurich General Accident and Liability Insurance Co Ltd v Morrison* [1942] 2 KB 53, [1942] 1 All ER 529, CA.

7 Road Traffic Act 1988, s 152(2)(a)(ii).

8 Financial Services Act 1986 (c 60), s 133.

(3) NON-DISCLOSURE

(a) Ambit and Duration of the Positive Duty of Disclosure

860. Extent of disclosure. The Marine Insurance Act 1906 requires the insured to disclose not only those material facts which are known to him but also facts 'which in the ordinary course of business, ought to be known to him'[1]. Whether an insured ought to know something is a question of fact[2]. The position cannot be stated with such clarity for non-marine contracts. It has been said that the common law only requires that an insured disclose facts which are actually known to him[3]. On the other hand, it can be argued that the common law also requires disclosure of facts deemed to be within the constructive knowledge of the insured[4]. As regards life assurance, the better view is that the assured need only disclose material facts which are actually known to him[5]. With regard to motor vehicle insurance, there is also good authority that actual and not constructive knowledge is what is required[6]. It has been observed that the statutory phrase 'in the course of business'[7] is inappropriate where the insured effects cover in a private capacity[8]. This still leaves open the question of whether the insured may be deemed to have constructive notice when he effects professional indemnity or business interruption cover.

1 Marine Insurance Act 1906 (c 41), s 18(1). See *London General Insurance Co v General Marine Underwriters' Association* [1921] 1 KB 104.

2 *Australia and New Zealand Bank Ltd v Colonial and Eagle Wharves Ltd* [1960] 2 Lloyd's Rep 241.

3 *The Spathari* 1924 SC 182 at 196, 1924 SLT 126 at 130, per Lord Justice-Clerk Alness, affd 1925 SC (HL) 6, 1925 SLT 322. See also *Zurich General Accident and Liability Insurance Co Ltd v Leven* 1940 SC 406 at 415, 1940 SLT 350 at 354, per Lord President Normand.

4 *Cantiere Meccanico Brindisino v Janson* [1912] 3 KB 452, CA; *Locker and Woolf Ltd v Western Australian Insurance Co Ltd* [1936] 1 KB 408, CA; *Highlands Insurance Co v Continental Insurance Co* [1987] 1 Lloyd's Rep 109n. This position is adopted on the view that the Marine Insurance Act 1906, s 18, is merely a codified form of the common law position. In *Australia and New Zealand Bank Ltd v Colonial and Eagle Wharves Ltd* [1960] 2 Lloyd's Rep 241, McNair J assumed (*sed*

dubitante) the relevance of s 18 in non-marine cases. For contrary *dicta*, see *Joel v Law Union and Crown Insurance Co* [1908] 2 KB 863, CA; *Yorke v Yorkshire Insurance Co Ltd* [1918] 1 KB 662; and *Regina Fur Co Ltd v Bossom* [1957] 2 Lloyd's Rep 466, affd [1958] 2 Lloyd's Rep 425, CA.
  5 *Life Association of Scotland v Foster* (1873) 11 M 351; *Joel v Law Union and Crown Insurance Co* [1908] 2 KB 863, CA.
  6 *Zurich General Accident and Liability Co v Leven* 1940 SC 406, 1940 SLT 350.
  7 Marine Insurance Act 1906, s 18(1).
  8 E J MacGillivray and M Parkington *Insurance Law* (8th edn, 1988) para 640.

861. Statements of opinion. The proposal form may contain a basis of the contract clause declaring that the information supplied by the proposer must be true to the best of his knowledge and belief. This requires only a statement of honest opinion in answer to the questions asked and the insurer cannot avoid the contract where an answer is factually incorrect[1]. In order to avoid the contract in this situation, the insurer needs to show that the insured's answers were untrue to the best of his knowledge and belief. Accordingly, if the insured had no reasonable grounds for believing his opinion to be correct, the contract may be avoided[2].

Regardless of whether or not the proposal form contains such a declaration, many statements made by the insured as to the condition of his health will be treated as expressions of opinion only[3]. The Association of British Insurers (ABI) *Statement of General Insurance Practice* provides (1) that proposal forms should be completed according to the proposer's knowledge and belief; and (2) that 'so far as is practicable, insurers will avoid asking questions which would require expert knowledge beyond that which the proposer could reasonably be expected to possess or obtain or which would require a value judgment on the part of the proposer'[4]. The ABI *Statement of Long-Term Insurance Practice* (applicable to life assurance) contains no equivalent provision to that mentioned in head (1) above. However, this omission is not serious, since, as stated already, one cannot expect an answer to a question regarding general good health to be more than a statement of honest belief and opinion. The *Statement of Long-Term Insurance Practice* does, however, exhort insurers to refrain from asking questions which require a degree of knowledge beyond that which the proposer could reasonably be expected to possess[5].

  1 *M'Phee v Royal Insurance Co Ltd* 1979 Sc 304 at 322, per Lord President Emslie. See also *Hutchison v National Loan Fund Life Assurance Society* (1845) 7 D 467.
  2 *M'Phee v Royal Insurance Co Ltd* 1979 SC 304, 1979 SLT (Notes) 54.
  3 *Life Association of Scotland v Foster* (1873) 11 M 351 at 358, per Lord President Inglis: '. . . a person making a statement regarding his own health must be assumed generally to be speaking according to his own personal knowledge, and there are many facts regarding his health of which he cannot be ignorant . . . But there may be many other facts, materially affecting his state of health and prospect of longevity, of which a person without medical skill or medical advice can know nothing.'
  4 ABI *Statement of General Insurance Practice* para 1(a), (e).
  5 ABI *Statement of Long-Term Insurance Practice* para 1(d).

862. Disclosure to intermediaries. It has been said that the law as to the effect of disclosure of facts to an intermediary, which the latter does not pass on to the insurer, is unclear[1]. This is undoubtedly true. In some of the reported cases it is unclear whether the intermediary was acting as an agent for the insurer or for the insured[2]. In others, there was express provision in the contract that the insurers were not liable should information given to an agent not be transmitted to them[3]. The Law Reform Committee for Scotland recommended in 1957 that, were legislation on the matter to be introduced, disclosure to intermediaries who could be described as agents for or employees of the insurer should be treated as tantamount to disclosure to the insurer. Where the intermediary could not be viewed as agent for the insurer, disclosure to them could not be treated as being disclosure to the insurer[4]. It is submitted that assistance may be had from scrutiny of the English cases; though it should be kept in mind that there too the issue is not free from difficulty. It has been held that where insurance is arranged through an intermediary, and that intermediary can be regarded as the insurer's agent, failure by the intermediary to pass on to the insurer material information disclosed to him by the insured will be insufficient to avoid the policy[5]. The general principle is that the agent's knowledge is imputed to his principal[6]. Where the intermediary can be regarded as the insured's agent, his failure to pass on to the insurer material information disclosed to him by the insured will entitle the insurer to avoid the policy but expose the intermediary to a claim for damages[7]. It may be the case that a misrepresentation by an agent for the insured as to facts which were not disclosed to him by the insured will render the intermediary liable in damages to the latter should the insurer avoid the policy[8]. It has been suggested, in both England and Scotland, that the insured has a duty to check that the information in a proposal form, completed on his behalf by an intermediary, is accurate[9]. That a broker 'who is remunerated by the insurance industry and who presents proposal forms and suggested policies on their behalf' should be viewed as an agent for the insured, has been strongly criticised and reform of the law urged[10].

1 *Fourth Report of the Law Reform Committee for Scotland* (Cmnd 330) (1957) para 14.
2 *Life and Health Assurance Association Ltd v Yule* (1904) 6 F 437, 11 SLT 690; *M'Millan v Accident Insurance Co Ltd* 1907 SC 484, 14 SLT 710; *National Farmers' Union Mutual Insurance Society Ltd v Tully* 1935 SLT 574, OH.
3 *M'Millan v Accident Insurance Co Ltd* 1907 SC 484, 14 SLT 710.
4 *Fourth Report of the Law Reform Committee for Scotland* (Cmnd 330) (1957) para 18.
5 See *Stockton v Mason* [1978] 2 Lloyd's Rep 430, CA; *Woolcott v Excess Insurance Co Ltd (No 2)* [1979] 2 Lloyd's Rep 210. This was the view of the court in *Cruikshank v Northern Accident Insurance Co Ltd* (1895) 23 R 147, 3 SLT 167. The Marine Insurance Act 1906 (c 41), s 19, provides that in contracts of marine insurance the agent must not only disclose to the insurer facts provided to him by his principal, but also 'every material circumstance which is known to himself'. If, therefore, the agent has material information about facts unknown to his principal, he must disclose these. Note *The Dora* [1989] 1 Lloyd's Rep 69. See also F Templeman *Marine Insurance* (6th edn, 1986 by R J Lambeth) p 30.
6 *Stockton v Mason* (1978) 2 Lloyd's Rep 430, CA; *Woolcott v Excess Insurance Co Ltd (No 2)* [1979] 2 Lloyd's Rep 210.
7 *McNealy v Pennine Insurance Co Ltd* [1978] 2 Lloyd's Rep 18, CA; *Dunbar v A and B Painters Ltd* [1986] 2 Lloyd's Rep 38, CA.
8 *Warren v Henry Sutton & Co* [1976] 2 Lloyd's Rep 276, CA. The insured arranged through his broker for another driver to be covered under his policy. The latter had a record of bad driving but this was undisclosed. The broker had expressly told the insurer that the friend had a clean driving licence and no accidents.
9 *O'Connor v BHD Kirby & Co* [1972] 1 QB 90, [1971] 2 All ER 1415, CA. See also *Life and Health Assurance Association Ltd v Yule* (1904) 6 F 437, 11 SLT 690.
10 *Roberts v Plaisted* [1989] 2 Lloyd's Rep 341, CA. The critical observations made by the Court of Appeal in this case fit in well with the observations of the Law Reform Committee for Scotland in the *Fourth Report of the Law Reform Committee for Scotland* (Cmnd 330) (1957), para 18.

863. Duration of the duty of disclosure. A distinction can be drawn between non-renewable and renewable contracts of insurance. Where the insurance is non-renewable, as will be the case with life assurance, the positive duty of disclosure subsists until the contract is concluded[1]. Accordingly, if the proposer learns of some new material fact, between completion of the proposal form and the issue of the policy, he is obliged to notify this to the insurer[2]. However, a new and material fact which is learned only after the policy is issued need not be declared[3]. The position changes where the insurer intimates in some way, prior to the conclusion of the contract (eg in the proposal form), that insurance cover will not begin until receipt of payment of the first premium, or until the policy is delivered to the insured[4]. Where, as with indemnity cover, the insurance is renewable, then a new contract is made on each renewal and there is an obligation to disclose any new material facts[5]. Indemnity policies, such as fire policies, may contain a term obliging the insured to notify the insurer of any increase in the risk[6].

There is no obligation on the insurer to notify the insured that a continuing duty of disclosure exists. The *Statement of General Insurance Practice*, however, provides that renewal notices should contain a warning 'about the duty of disclosure including the necessity to advise changes affecting the policy which have occurred since the policy inception or last renewal date whichever was the later'[7]. Should measures concerning insurance contract law planned by the EEC ever come into force, the duty of continuing disclosure will be abolished unless the policy specifically provides for notification of increase in risk[8].

1 *Fourth Report of the Law Reform Committee for Scotland* (Cmnd 330) (1957) para 11; *Re Yager and Guardian Assurance Co* (1912) 108 LT 38, DC; *Banque Financière de la Cité SA v Westgate Insurance Co Ltd* [1990] 2 All ER 947 at 960, HL, per Lord Jauncey.
2 *Looker v Law Union and Rock Insurance Co Ltd* [1928] 1 KB 554.
3 Eg *Whitwell v Autocar Fire and Accident Insurance Co* (1927) 27 Ll L Rep 418.
4 *Harrington v Pearl Life Assurance Co Ltd* (1913) 30 TLR 24, affd (1914) 30 TLR 613, CA; *Allis-Chalmers Co v Maryland Fidelity and Deposit Co* (1916) 114 LT 433, HL.
5 *Law Accident Insurance Society v Boyd* 1942 SC 384, 1942 SLT 207. See also *Lambert v Co-operative Insurance Society Ltd* [1975] 2 Lloyd's Rep 485, CA; *Woolcott v Excess Insurance Co Ltd* [1979] 1 Lloyd's Rep 231, CA; and *Woolcott v Excess Insurance Co Ltd (No 2)* [1979] 2 Lloyd's Rep 210.
6 *Exchange Theatre Ltd v Iron Trades Mutual Insurance Co Ltd* [1984] 1 Lloyd's Rep 149, CA.
7 ABI *Statement of General Insurance Practice* (1986) para 3(a).
8 Proposal for a Council Directive on the Coordination of Laws, Regulations and Administrative Provisions relating to Insurance Contracts (OJ C190, 28.7.79, p 2).

(b) Materiality

864. Material facts. The parties to a contract of insurance are only obliged to disclose 'material' facts[1]. The parties' opinion as to materiality is irrelevant[2]. But where the appropriate test of materiality[3] is that of the reasonable person, the opinion of the particular insured (or insurer) may well be held to have been tenable by a reasonable person in the same circumstances[4]. It is impossible to give a list of facts to be regarded as material[5]. Under English law, the question of whether a fact is material or not is said, itself, to be a question of fact[6], and this is expressly stated to be the case by the Marine Insurance Act 1906[7]. In Scotland it has been stated, in a non-marine context, that this is a question of law[8]. Where the court is uncertain as to the materiality of a fact, expert evidence may be led on the point[9].

1 *Life Association of Scotland v Foster* (1873) 11 M 351. For marine insurance, see the Marine Insurance Act 1906 (c 41), s 18(1). For motor vehicle insurance, see the Road Traffic Act 1988 c(52), s 151(9).
2 *Brownlie v Campbell* (1880) 5 App Cas 925, HL; *Lambert v Co-operative Insurance Society Ltd* [1975] 2 Lloyd's Rep 485, CA.
3 For the 'test of materiality', see paras 868–871 below.
4 *Life Association of Scotland v Foster* (1873) 11 M 351; E J MacGillivray and M Parkington *Insurance Law* (8th edn, 1988) para 661.
5 Broad groupings of material facts are to be found in the leading text books. Thus *MacGillivray and Parkington* list the following: facts indicating exposure to unusual risks; the insured's living conditions and habits; the moral character of the insured; the fact that insurance has been refused the insured by some other insurer. A broadly similar classification is adopted in E R H Ivamy *General Principles of Insurance Law* (5th edn, 1986).
6 *MacGillivray and Parkington* para 664.

7 Marine Insurance Act 1906, s 18(4).

8 *Zurich General Accident and Liability Insurance Co Ltd v Leven* 1940 SC 406 at 419, 1940 SLT 350 at 356, per Lord Moncrieff. If this view is taken to refer to the legal criterion by which materiality is to be trested (see paras 868–871 below), then it is unobjectionable. But if it is taken as the manner in which to determine if the fact in issue in a particular case is material or not, then it is doubtful that it should be regarded as being correct.

9 This need not be the evidence of other insurers: see *MacGillivray and Parkington* paras 666–667.

865. Immaterial facts and facts of doubtful materiality.

There is no liability for non-disclosure of facts which are not material[1]. Facts not requiring to be disclosed on this basis are: (1) those which diminish the risk to the insurer[2]; (2) facts known to the insurer or which he may be presumed to know; (3) facts which the insurer has waived the right to know about; and (4) facts which are already subject to a warranty[3]. Facts which might ordinarily be thought of as being material may not need to be disclosed in some cases. At one time, for example, the race or nationality of the insured was regarded as being material[4]. Now the Race Relations Act 1976 proscribes discrimination in the provision of insurance[5]. Discrimination on the ground of sex is also largely prohibited[6]. Previous convictions which have become 'spent' under the Rehabilitation of Offenders Act 1974 need not be disclosed, even if a question is asked about the criminal record of the proposer or his family[7]. The 1974 Act sets out the rehabilitation periods after which a conviction becomes spent[8]. Some convictions can never become spent under the 1974 Act[9], and the question then arises: must such convictions be disclosed if they are not made the subject of a specific question in the proposal form? It is quite clear that insurers regard a criminal record as being a material fact[10]. It is submitted, however, that the materiality of a criminal conviction cannot be assumed. There is authority for the view that the passage of a substantial period of time between the conviction and the time of insuring, especially where the offence committed is irrelevant to the risk covered[11], should probably render the fact of conviction immaterial[12]. Where the conviction is for a relatively trivial offence and was long ago, a fortiori it may be regarded as being immaterial[13].

1 *Craig v Imperial Union Accident Assurance Co* (1894) 1 SLT 646, OH. See E R H Ivamy *General Principles of Insurance Law* (5th edn, 1986) 137–142.

2 For a recent example of what was held to be an immaterial fact because it diminished the risk (a vessel berthed in a shipyard at the commencement of the risk), see *The Dora* [1989] 1 Lloyd's Rep 69.

3 *Gunford Ship Co Ltd (in liquidation) v Thames and Mersey Marine Insurance Co Ltd* 1910 SC 1072 at 1084, 1910 2 SLT 154 at 155, per Lord President Dunedin: 'There is no duty of disclosure of any facts which go to matters which are covered by warranty.' The warranty is deemed to confer sufficient protection on the insurer. (*Gunford* was reversed in part: 1911 (HL) SC 84, 1911 SLT 185.)

4 This was the case in *The Spathari* 1925 SC (HL) 6, 1925 SLT 322; affg 1924 SC 182, 1924 SLT 126.

5 Race Relations Act 1976 (c 74), s 20(1), (2)(c). Both direct and indirect discrimination are struck at.

6 Sex Discrimination Act 1975 (c 65), s 29(1), (2)(c). In relation to certain matters in annuity, life and accident policies, some discrimination on the basis of the proposer's sex is not unlawful: see s 45.

7 Rehabilitation of Offenders Act 1974 (c 53), ss 1(1), 4(3)(a). See also *Arif v Excess Insurance Group Ltd* 1982 SLT 183, OH.

8 Rehabilitation of Offenders Act 1974, s 5(2), Tables A, B (amended by the Armed Forces Act 1976 (c 52), s 22(5), Sch 9, para 20(4), (5); Criminal Justice (Scotland) Act 1980 (c 62), s 83(2), Sch 7, para 24; Armed Forces Act 1981 (c 55), s 28(1), Sch 4, para 2(2); Criminal Justice Act 1982 (c 48), s 77, Sch 14, paras 36, 37; and the Criminal Justice Act 1988 (c 33), s 123(6), Sch 8, para 9). The periods under the Rehabilitation of Offenders Act 1974, s 5(2), Table A, include:

Imprisonment for less that six months . . . . seven years
Imprisonment for more that six months but less than thirty months . . . . ten years
A fine . . . . five years

Where the offender is under seventeen, the rehabilitation period is halved: s 5(2)(a). The *terminus a quo* is the date of conviction: s 5(2). Table B covers the rehabilitation period for certain sentences for young offenders.

9 Eg sentences of life imprisonment and custodial sentences of more than thirty months: Rehabilitation of Offenders Act 1974, s 5(1)(a), (b) (amended by the Criminal Justice Act 1982, Sch 14, para 36, and the Criminal Justice Act 1988, Sch 8, para 9).

10 It is regarded as constituting a 'moral hazard': see generally *Zurich General Accident and Liability Insurance Co Ltd v Leven* 1940 SC 406, 1940 SLT 350; *Arif v Excess Insurance Group Ltd* 1982 SLT 183, OH. See also *Lambert v Co-operative Insurance Society Ltd* [1975] 2 Lloyd's Rep 485, CA; *Woolcott v Sun Alliance and London Insurance Ltd* [1978] 1 All ER 1253, [1978] 1 WLR 493; *Reynolds v Phoenix Assurance Co Ltd* [1978] 2 Lloyd's Rep 440.

11 *Reynolds v Pheonix Assurance Co Ltd* [1978] 2 Lloyd's Rep 440. A conviction for receiving stolen property was held not to be material in relation to a contract of fire insurance.

12 *Zurich General Accident and Liability Insurance Co Ltd v Leven* 1940 SC 406 at 416, 1940 SLT 350 at 354, per Lord President Normand: 'On one point there was agreement, that all insurance companies would regard a previous conviction of the kind in this case, if of recent date, as most material, but it was said on behalf of the defenders that a conviction which had taken place five and three-quarter years before the date of the signature of the proposal form was stale and would be considered immaterial by a prudent insurer. . . . It is obviously a question of degree when a conviction may become stale. A conviction 20 years old, with an impeccable record between the date of the conviction and the date of the signature of the form, would be by all sensible people regarded as immaterial.'

13 *Reynolds v Phoenix Assurance Co Ltd* [1978] 2 Lloyd's Rep 440.

866. Waiver of disclosure of material facts. If the insurer accepts a proposal form containing a blank response to some of the questions asked and issues a policy, this will normally be construed as a waiver of the need to disclose material facts germane to that question[1]. This will not, however, be the case where a blank response carries the implication that the answer is in the negative, whereas the converse is actually the true case[2]. The wording and layout of the proposal form may also limit the scope of the duty of disclosure of material facts. Where a proposal form asked a number of questions and concluded with the declaration, 'I wish to insure as above. . . and warrant that all the information entered above is true and complete and that nothing materially affecting the risk has been concealed', it was held that failure to declare a closing order in respect of the property insured, did not entitle the insurers to avoid the contract[3].

1 *Sir William Forbes & Co v Edinburgh Life Assurance Co* (1832) 10 S 451. See also *Roberts v Avon Insurance Co* [1956] 2 Lloyd's Rep 240.

2 *Sir William Forbes & Co v Edinburgh Life Assurance Co* (1832) 10 S 451. In this case no answer was given to the question 'Can you give any and what information respecting [the proposer's] habits?' The insured was an opium addict. The point was made that '. . . an implied abandonment, or waiver, does not relieve from a distinct and conscientious obligation to disclose everything material'.

3 *Hair v Prudential Assurance Co Ltd* [1983] 2 Lloyd's Rep 667. Woolf J, at 673, observed that 'It appears to me that it is reasonable to regard the question as requiring the proposer to make it clear that he or she has given a true and complete answer to the questions which appear above, and what is more, that the proposer has not failed to disclose anything materially affecting the risk with regard to matters on which he is being questioned. I am bound to say that, if it was intended that an assured should answer matters even though he is not being questioned about them, I would expect a different form of statement from the one to which I have just made reference. I would have expected something to be said which clearly indicated to a proposer that, although they had not been asked any specific question about the matter, if there was something which was relevant to the risk which they knew of, but which was not covered by the questions, they should deal with it, and leave space for them to do so'. See also *Roberts v Plaisted* [1989] 2 Lloyd's Rep 341, CA.

867. The Association of British Insurers statements of practice and questions in forms. Both the Association of British Insurers (ABI) *Statement of General Insurance Practice* (1986) and the ABI *Statement of Long-Term Insurance Practice* (1986) enjoin insurers specifically to ask clear questions, in proposal forms, about matters which they have, on past experience, generally found to be material[1].

> 1 ABI *Statement of General Insurance Practice* (1986), para 1(d); ABI *Statement of Long-Term Insurance Practice* (1986) para 1(c). The decision in *Hair v Prudential Assurance Co Ltd* [1983] 2 Lloyd's Rep 667 is consonant with para 1(d) of the *Statement of General Insurance Practice*, as is the earlier Scottish case of *Craig v Imperial Union Accident Assurance Co* (1894) 1 SLT 646, OH.

868. The test of materiality. The appropriate test of the materiality of an undisclosed fact cannot be said to be entirely free from doubt. In some types of insurance the test is prescribed by statute, in which case that is the only test which may be applied. Where the insurance is not of a kind to which a statutory test may be applied, there may be a difference in the approach taken by English law and Scots law in some cases.

869. Statutory tests. In contracts of marine insurance, the test of the materiality of a fact is assessed by reference to the view of a prudent or reasonable insurer[1]. The Court of Appeal has recently interpreted section 18(2) of the Marine Insurance Act 1906 as meaning that the undisclosed fact must be one which an insurer would want to know about in reaching a decision as to whether or not to grant cover. It does not have to be shown that an insurer would have refused cover or that cover would only have been provided at an increased premium, but simply that a prudent or reasonable insurer would have required disclosure of the undisclosed fact in order to form an opinion[2]. It is highly probable that this would be the approach of Scots law[3]. In contracts of motor vehicle insurance also, the test of materiality is that of a reasonable insurer[4]. However, in cases of motor vehicle insurance, the statutory wording requires the insurer to prove that the policy was 'obtained' as a direct result of non-disclosure or misrepresentation[5].

> 1 Marine Insurance Act 1906 (c 41), s 18(2): 'Every circumstance is material which would influence the judgment of a prudent insurer in fixing the premium, or determining whether he will take the risk.'
> 2 *Container Transport International Inc and Reliance Group Inc v Oceanus Mutual Underwriting Association (Bermuda) Ltd* [1984] 1 Lloyd's Rep 476, CA. For comment on this case, see H Brooke 'Materiality in Insurance Contracts' [1985] LMCLQ 437; K Khan 'A New Test for Materiality in Insurance Law' [1986] JBL 37. The case was heard by a particularly strong Bench, with Kerr LJ delivering the principal judgment.
> 3 A dictum of Lord President Inglis, though admittedly made in the context of life assurance, may provide some support for this view. See *Life Association of Scotland v Foster* (1873) 11 M 351 at 159, where it is said of the assured that he is under an obligation to reveal information which 'could in any way influence the insurers in considering and deciding whether they will enter into the contract'.
> 4 'Material' means of such a nature as to influence the judgment of a prudent insurer in determining whether he will take the risk and, if so, at what premium and on what conditions: Road Traffic Act 1988 (c 52), s 151(9)(b). See also *Zurich General Accident and Liability Insurance Co Ltd v Leven* 1940 SC 406, 1940 SLT 350.
> 5 Road Traffic Act 1988 (c 52), s 152(2). The word 'obtained' suggests that the non-disclosure or misrepresentation actually induced the insurer to grant cover. See generally *Zurich General Accident and Liability Insurance Co Ltd v Morrison* [1942] 2 KB 53, [1942] 1 All ER 529, CA.

870. The test of the reasonable insurer. So far as non-marine insurance is concerned, the test of materiality now applied by the English courts to indemnity contracts is that of the reasonable insurer[1]. As with marine cases, the correct approach is to ask whether the undisclosed fact is one which a reasonable insurer would have wanted to know of in the process of deciding whether or not to provide insurance cover[2]. The position in Scots law with regard to the application of this test to insurances which are not regulated by statute is not settled[3].

It is submitted, however, that since the appropriate statutory test in indemnity contracts of marine and motor vehicle insurance is that of the reasonable insurer, then this test is the correct one to apply in all indemnity contracts[4].

1 This was finally made clear by the Court of Appeal in *Lambert v Co-operative Insurance Society Ltd* [1975] 2 Lloyd's Rep 485, CA. This was followed in *Woolcott v Excess Insurance Co Ltd* [1979] 1 Lloyd's Rep 231, CA.

2 It seems clear from the judgments in *Container Transport International Inc and Reliance Group Inc v Oceanus Mutual Underwriting Association (Bermuda) Ltd* [1984] 1 Lloyd's Rep 476, CA, that the Court of Appeal did not think it was restricting the new way of determining materiality to marine insurance generally. This approach was adopted as the relevant one when dealing with misrepresentation in a non-marine context in *Highlands Insurance Co v Continental Insurance Co* [1987] 1 Lloyd's Rep 109n.

3 *Fourth Report of the Law Reform Committee for Scotland* (Cmnd 330) (1957) para 7.

4 *Fourth Report* para 9. In *Gifto Fancy Goods Ltd v Ecclesiastical Insurance Office plc* 1991 GWD 2-117, OH, the parties agreed (referring to the *Container Transport International* case cited in note 2 above) that this was the correct test to apply in relation to fire cover.

871. The test of the reasonable insured. Despite some contrary dicta, English law takes the view that the appropriate test to be applied in life contracts is that of the reasonable insurer[1]. There is, however, clear authority that in Scotland the law is different on this point and that the test is that of the reasonable insured[2]. To be more precise, the test is explained in terms of what a 'reasonable man' would have done in the circumstances[3].

1 *Mutual Life Insurance Co of New York v Ontario Metal Products Co Ltd* [1925] AC 344, PC. Cf *Joel v Law Union and Crown Insurance Co* [1908] 2 KB 863, CA.

2 *Life Association of Scotland v Foster* (1873) 11 M 351.

3 (1873) 11 M 351 at 359, per Lord President Inglis: '. . . without any fraudulent intent, and even in bona fide, the insured may fail in the duty of disclosure. His duty is carefully and diligently to review all the facts known to himself and bearing on the risk proposed to the insurers, and to state every circumstance which *any reasonable man* might suppose could in any way influence the insurers in considering and deciding whether they will enter into the contract' (emphasis added).

872. The position under the Association of British Insurers Statements of Practice (1986). Where the Association of British Insurers (ABI) *Statement of General Insurance Practice* (1986) and the ABI *Statement of Long-Term Insurance Practice* (1986) apply, it is thought that they adopt the reasonable insured test[1].

1 The ABI *Statement of General Insurance Practice* (1986), para 1(c)(i) reads: 'If not included in the declaration, prominently displayed on the proposal form should be a statement drawing the attention of the proposer to the consequences of the failure to disclose all material facts, explained as those facts an insurer would regard as likely to influence the acceptance and assessment of the proposal.' Read in isolation, this appears to be declaratory of the reasonable insurer test, but when read in conjunction with para 2(b)(i) it seems that that is not truly the case. Para 2(b)(i) reads: 'An insurer will not repudiate liability to indemnify a policyholder on grounds of non-disclosure of a material fact which a policyholder could not reasonably be expected to have disclosed'. For a fuller discussion of this point, see A D M Forte 'The Revised Statements of Insurance Practice: Cosmetic Change or Major Surgery?' [1986] 49 MLR 754.

9. WARRANTIES

873. General. As the positive duty of disclosure extends only to material facts and the policy may be avoided only for non-disclosure of material facts, the insurer runs the risk of having to honour claims where there has been non-disclosure of facts which the court has deemed to be immaterial. It is open to the insurer to decrease the risk of having to meet claims arising from non-disclosure of immaterial facts. This may be achieved by requiring the insured to warrant the truth of the information which he has given in his answers to the questions asked by the proposal form. Both the Association of British Insurers (ABI) *Statement of General Insurance Practice* (1986) and the ABI *Statement of Long-Term Insurance Practice* (1986) apply to warranties.

874. Creation. Unlike *uberrima fides*, which arises *ex lege*, a warranty depends for its existence upon contract. Normally, there will be some term in the proposal form which will have the effect of warranting the truth of the answers given: for example, a basis of the contract clause or an express warranty as to the truth of particular answers. Alternatively, the warranty may be created by the policy itself[1]. The existence of a warranty is a question of the parties' intention and not of the language used. Thus the words 'the insured warrants' found in the policy, though prima facie evidence of the intention to create a warranty, cannot be regarded as conclusive of the existence of a warranty[2]. With regard to non-marine insurance, it is the law that a basis of the contract clause in a proposal form has the effect of converting the information contained in the proposer's answers into warranties. This will be so even though the wording of the basis of the contract clause never uses the word 'warranty' and even where the policy makes no reference to the clause[3]. It is otherwise with marine insurance, where it is required that 'an express warranty must be included in, or written upon, the policy, or must be contained in some document incorporated by reference into the policy'[4]. Certain warranties arise by virtue of implication[5].

1 See para 823 above. See generally *Standard Life Assurance Co v Weems* (1884) 11 R (HL) 48; *Dawsons Ltd v Bonnin* 1922 SC (HL) 156, 1922 SLT 444; *M'Cartney v Laverty* 1968 SC 207, 1968 SLT (Notes) 50, OH. The following clause adapted from a proposal form for indemnity cover is sufficient in law to create warranties of the answers given: 'I declare that the information given in this proposal form is to the best of my knowledge and belief correct and complete in every detail and will be the basis of the contract between me and the [insurer]'. Here, however, the warranty is one of opinion only.
2 *De Maurier (Jewels) Ltd v Bastion Insurance Co Ltd* [1967] 2 Lloyd's Rep 550.
3 See the cases cited in note 1 above.
4 Marine Insurance Act 1906 (c 41), s 35(2).
5 Ie as implied terms of the contract. The Marine Insurance Act 1906, s 35(3), provides that an express warranty will not negative an implied one unless inconsistent therewith. Examples of implied warranties are (1) that the subject of the risk is in existence when cover is effected; (2) that the insured possesses an insurable interest in the subject insured; and (3) that a vessel is seaworthy at the start of a voyage.

875. Effect. A warranty renders the materiality of the information warranted irrelevant and makes the truthfulness of the fact warranted 'a condition upon which the validity of the contract depends'[1]. The presence of a warranty may be thought to have three consequences. First, it relieves the insurer from having to show that the undisclosed or incorrect information relates to a material fact[2]. Secondly, it does not matter that the breach of warranty was not relevant to the type of loss suffered[3]. Thirdly, it is irrelevant that the incorrect answer was innocently or honestly given[4]. However, this last consequence may not be fatal, if, despite the error, the answer is 'in substance true and unambiguous'[5].

A breach of warranty entitles the insurer to avoid the contract of insurance from the time of breach but claims in respect of losses incurred prior to that time are unaffected by the breach[6]. The insurer's choice is between waiving the breach or avoiding the entire contract. He may not reject a claim on the grounds of the insured's breach of warranty, while simultaneously relying on, for example, a term of the policy submitting disputes to arbitration[7].

1 *Standard Life Assurance Co v Weems* (1884) 11 R (HL) 48 at 51, per Lord Blackburn: 'It is competent to the contracting parties ... to make the actual existence of anything a condition

precedent to the inception of any contract; and, if they do so, the non-existence of that thing is a good defence. And it is not of any importance whether the existence of that thing was or was not material; the parties . . . have a right to determine for themselves what they shall deem material'. See also *Dawsons Ltd v Bonnin* 1922 SC (HL) 156, 1922 SLT 444; *Neil v South East Lancashire Insurance Co* 1932 SC 35, 1932 SLT 29; *Zurich General Accident and Liability Insurance Co Ltd v Leven* 1940 SC 406, 1940 SLT 350.

2 *Standard Life Assurance Co v Weems* (1884) 11 R (HL) 48; *Dawsons Ltd v Bonnin* 1922 SC (HL) 156, 1922 SLT 444.

3 *Yorkshire Insurance Co Ltd v Campbell* [1917] AC 218, PC. Cf *De Maurier (Jewels) Ltd v Bastion Insurance Co Ltd* [1967] 2 Lloyd's Rep 550. For marine insurance, see the Marine Insurance Act 1906 (c 41), s 33(3).

4 *Standard Life Assurance Co v Weems* (1884) 11 R (HL) 48; *Dawsons Ltd v Bonnin* 1922 SC (HL) 156, 1922 SLT 444. In *Dawsons Ltd v Bonnin* a proposal form for motor vehicle insurance, after asking the proposer to state his address, then asked for the address where the vehicle would normally be garaged. The answer, inadvertently given, was 'Above address'. The House of Lords determined that the insurer could avoid the policy. The result in this case illustrates how harsh the effect of a basis of the contract clause may be. The lorry was, in fact, garaged outside Glasgow: a fact which did not need to be disclosed since it was accepted that it would diminish the risk to the insurer. Moreover, the policy contained, *in gremio*, a term that material misstatements would render it void. Perhaps the proper approach would have been to interpret the effect of the basis clause as qualified by the term in the contract. For a criticism of this case and of the law on warranties generally, see R A Hasson 'The "Basis of the Contract Clause" in Insurance Law' (1971) 34 MLR 29. See also J Birds 'Warranties in Insurance Proposal Forms' [1977] JBL 231.

5 *Dawsons Ltd v Bonnin* 1922 SC (HL) 156, 1922 SLT 444.

6 1922 SC (HL) 156, 1922 SLT 444. The insurer may elect not to avoid the contract: see *The Good Luck* [1990] 1 QB 818, [1989] 3 All ER 628, CA; *Eagle Star Insurance Co v Renton & Son* 1941 SLT 61, OH. The insurer's conduct after the breach may personally bar him from pleading the breach: *Cruikshank v Northern Accident Insurance Co Ltd* (1895) 23 R 147, 3 SLT 167; *Donnison v Employers' Accident and Live Stock Insurance Co* (1897) 24 R 681. See also *Shiells v Scottish Assurance Corpn Ltd* (1889) 16 R 1014.

7 *West v National Motor and Accident Insurance Union Ltd* [1955] 1 All ER 800, [1955] 1 WLR 343, CA.

876. Categories of warranty.
Warranties fall into three basic categories, namely: (1) warranties as to past or present facts; (2) warranties about the future; and (3) warranties of opinion.

(1) *Past or present facts.* Here the truth of the information given at the date of completion of the proposal form is warranted. Thus a declaration made at the time of the completion of the proposal form which reads 'I am a total abstainer from alcoholic drinks and have been since birth' is treated as a warranty of past and present fact[1].

(2) *Future facts.* Warranties of future facts are sometimes termed 'promissory' or 'continuing' warranties. Here the insured warrants the continuing existence (or non-existence) of facts declared to be true when the proposal form was completed[2].

(3) *Opinion.* A warranty of opinion merely warrants that in the opinion of the insured, his answers are true to the best of his knowledge and belief. The fact that a proposal form states that the proposer's answers must be true to the best of his knowledge and belief will not always excuse inaccuracies or relieve the proposer of a duty of inquiry. If, for example, the answer to a question is easily to hand, the proposer who merely guesses (inaccurately) at it will not have satisfied the requirement that the answer is true to the best of his knowledge and belief[3].

1 *Kennedy v Smith* 1975 SC 266, 1976 SLT 110. Further examples of warranties as to past and present facts are to be found in *Life Association of Scotland v Foster* (1873) 11 M 351, and *Zurich General Accident and Liability Insurance Co Ltd v Leven* 1940 SC 406, 1940 SLT 350.

2 'Promissory warranty' in marine insurance means a warranty by which the assured undertakes that some particular thing shall or shall not be done, or that some condition shall be fulfilled, or whereby the insured affirms or negatives the existence of a particular state of facts: Marine

Insurance Act 1906 (c 41), s 33(1). In *Stephen v Scottish Boatowners Mutual Insurance Association* 1986 SLT 234 OH (revsd 1989 SLT 52, 2nd Div; 2nd Div upheld 1989 SLT 283, HL), a term in a marine policy read as follows: 'The insured shall take all reasonable care and precaution to see that the vessel is maintained and kept during the currency of the policy in a seaworthy condition'. This is a promissory warranty. When this case came before the House of Lords, argument centred on a second part to the above clause, requiring the insured to 'take all prompt and reasonable means of saving the vessel'. Leaving the vessel's seacocks open as she was sinking was not treated as failure to comply with this condition of the policy: 'while a more knowledgeable individual, viewing the situation dispassionately, might have assessed the likely source of the ingress of water, and decided that a seacock was one of the probable sources, and acted accordingly, I do not. . . find it possible to hold firmly that any ordinarily competent skipper would have acted differently from the pursuer[1]: see 1989 SLT 283 at 288, HL, per Lord Keith.

3   *M'Phee v Royal Insurance Co Ltd* 1979 SC 304, 1979 SLT (Notes) 54. The requirement to take reasonable care was considered in *Sofi v Prudential Insurance Co Ltd* (1990), CA (unreported).

877. Warranties and the Association of British Insurers Statements of Insurance Practice (1986).

The Association of British Insurers (ABI) *Statement of General Insurance Practice* (1986) and *Statement of Long-Term Insurance Practice* (1986) make some important changes regarding warranties. It has to be emphasised that these codes of practice are voluntary. The *Statement of General Insurance Practice* asks insurers to employ a declaration at the foot of their proposal forms which states that the answers given are true to the proposer's knowledge and belief[1]. This statement also enjoins ABI insurers not to use a basis of the contract clause to create warranties as to past and present facts[2]. Insurers may, however, create warranties as to past and present material facts where they do this by means of individual, specific, warranties[3].

1   ABI *Statement of General Insurance Practice* (1986), s 1(a). There is no similar provision in the ABI *Statement of Long-Term Insurance Practice* (1986), since one is only required in life contracts to give an honest opinion on the state of one's general health.
2   ABI *Statement of General Insurance Practice* (1986), s 1(b). Since no mention is made in this context of future facts, insurers can still use a basis of the contract clause to create warranties as to future facts. There is no rational reason why this exception should exist.
3   ABI *Statement of General Insurance Practice* (1986), s 1(b). See also the ABI *Statement of Long-Term Insurance Practice* (1986), s 1(b).

878. Terms descriptive of risk.

A distinction must be made between a term of the contract of insurance which is a warranty and a term which is merely descriptive of the risk being undertaken. This is not simply a question of the language used. The constitution of a warranty does not require the use of the word 'warranty'[1]. Conversely, where the word 'warranty' is used, it does not follow that a warranty is created[2]. It has been truly said: 'Only such words are necessary from which an intention to warrant can be inferred'[3]. A term descriptive of the risk specifies the period when the insurer will be on risk. Consequently, a breach of such a term does not entitle the insurer to avoid the contract but means, rather, that the insurer is not liable under the policy for as long as the term is not complied with. Terms descriptive of risk are analogous to excepted perils clauses. Where a term is not clearly couched in the language of a promissory warranty, it may still amount to a clause descriptive of risk[4]. It is unclear as to whether a term may be both a promissory warranty and a clause descriptive of risk[5].

1   *Stephen v Scottish Boatowners Mutual Insurance Association* 1986 SLT 234, OH; revsd 1989 SLT 52, 2nd Div; 2nd Div upheld 1989 SLT 283, HL (discussed in para 876 above).
2   *De Maurier (Jewels) Ltd v Bastion Insurance Co Ltd* [1967] 2 Lloyd's Rep 550.
3   *Stephen v Scottish Boatowners Mutual Insurance Association* 1986 SLT 234 at 242, OH, per Lord Mayfield. Any difficulty in preserving the distinction in mind is not made easier by judicial descriptions which refer to 'warranties describing the risk'. See *De Maurier (Jewels) Ltd v Bastion Insurance Co Ltd* [1967] 2 Lloyd's Rep 550.

4 *De Maurier (Jewels) Ltd v Bastion Insurance Co Ltd* [1967] 2 Lloyd's Rep 550.
5 *Provincial Insurance Co Ltd v Morgan* [1933] AC 240, HL.

10. CAUSATION

879. Proximate cause. Where the insured suffers loss or injury caused by one of the perils insured against, he will be entitled to recover under the policy. Recovery is dependent on the insured peril being the proximate cause of the loss. In marine insurance the matter is expressed thus: '. . . the insurer is liable for any loss proximately caused by a peril insured against, but. . . he is not liable for any loss which is not proximately caused by a peril insured against'[1]. This rule also encapsulates the position in non-marine contracts. 'Proximate cause' means the 'dominant or effective or operative cause'[2]. The rule may be excluded by express provision in the policy[3]. It may also be modified in this manner[4]. Problems may arise where there are two or more competing causes of loss or injury. If the later of two competing causes amounts to a *novus actus interveniens*, it must be regarded as the proximate cause. Accordingly, if the loss caused thereby is not covered by the policy the insured has no claim[5]. Whether the later cause amounts to a *novus actus interveniens* is a question of fact. If the later of two competing causes is a direct consequence of the first, and loss caused by the first is an insured peril, the insured will be entitled to recover under his policy[6]. There is no doubt that there can be two or more proximate causes of loss[7]. In such cases a distinction has appeared between (1) those cases where the policy covers losses arising from one proximate cause but specifically excepts liability for losses stemming from the other proximate cause, and (2) those cases where the policy covers losses flowing from one proximate cause but makes no mention of losses caused by the other. In the former case, it has been held that the insurer is not liable to meet claims[8]. In the latter case, it has been held that the insurer is bound to meet claims[9]. It is always possible for the insurer to stipulate in the policy that claims will be met only if the loss covered by the policy is caused 'independently of all other causes'. If this is done, the insurer will be liable only if the loss suffered is caused solely by a peril insured against and nothing else[10].

1 Marine Insurance Act 1906 (c 41), s 55(1).
2 Ie *causa causans*: see *Incorporated General Insurances Ltd v Shooter t/a Shooter's Fisheries* 1987 (1) SA 842. See also E J MacGillivray and M Parkington *Insurance Law* (8th edn, 1988) para 1551; *Leyland Shipping Co Ltd v Norwich Union Fire Insurance Society Ltd* [1918] AC 350, HL; *Yorkshire Dale Steamship Co Ltd v Minister of War Transport* [1942] AC 691, [1942] 2 All ER 6, HL.
3 Marine Insurance Act 1906, s 55(1). Where the policy states that the insurer is to be liable for loss 'directly or indirectly' caused by an insured peril, the rule is excluded: see *Oei v Foster* [1982] 2 Lloyd's Rep 170.
4 *The Miss Jay Jay* [1987] 1 Lloyd's Rep 32, CA.
5 *Scottish Marine Insurance Co v Turner* (1853) 1 Macq 334, HL. This is clearly the position in South Africa: see 'Insurance' in *The Law of South Africa* (1988, ed Joubert) vol 12, para 185. See also 'New cause' in *MacGillivray and Parkington* para 1553.
6 The rule is far easier to state than to apply. There is very little consistency among the reported cases. See generally *MacGillivray and Parkington* para 1552; J Birds *Modern Insurance Law* (1988) pp 186, 187.
7 *The Miss Jay Jay* [1987] 1 Lloyd's Rep 32, CA.
8 *Wayne Tank and Pump Co Ltd v Employers' Liability Assurance Corpn Ltd* [1974] QB 57, [1973] 3 All ER 825, CA.
9 *The Miss Jay Jay* [1987] 1 Lloyd's Rep 32, CA.
10 This was the result achieved by such a clause in *Jason v British Traders' Insurance Co Ltd* [1969] 1 Lloyd's Rep 281.

11. CLAIMS

(1) PROCEDURE

880. General. Where the insured suffers a loss which is caused by one of the perils insured against, he may lodge a claim for compensation with his insurers. If there has been no misrepresentation or non-disclosure of material facts[1], and provided that the claims procedure stipulated in the contract has been observed, then the only remaining question will be the amount to which the insured is entitled.

  1 Where eg the policy is a valued one, a grossly excessive valuation of the property represents a material fact which must be disclosed to the insurer: *Ionides v Pender* (1874) LR 9 QB 531. A grossly excessive valuation takes the contract out of the realm of a bona fide risk and into the realm of a wager: *Ionides v Pender; City Tailors Ltd v Evans* (1921) 126 LT 439, CA.

881. Notification of loss: time. Where the insurance is not of a kind to which the Association of British Insurers (ABI) *Statements of Insurance Practice* (1986) apply, a time limit will be stipulated within which notice of loss must be given. The reported decisions convey, most strongly, the message that such notification of loss clauses are strictly adhered to. Thus where an accident policy required notice of any accident to be given within fourteen days of the date of such accident, and the insured's injury did not manifest itself until some eight months from the date of his accident, it was held that he could not enforce a claim under the policy[1]. If the insurer follows the ABI *Statement of General Insurance Practice* and *Statement of Long-Term Insurance Practice* (1986), the policy should state that claims need only be notified 'as soon as reasonably possible'[2]. Under both statements, ABI insurers have agreed to make payment 'without avoidable delay' once liability under the policy has been established and the amount payable agreed[3]. Under the *Statement of Long-Term Insurance Practice*, when payment of a claim is delayed for longer than two months from the date of death or the date on which the policy matures, the insurer will pay interest on the sum due from the end of the two-month period unless the amount of interest is trivial[4].

  1 See *Cassel v Lancashire and Yorkshire Accident Insurance Co Ltd* (1885) 1 TLR 495. See also *T H Adamson & Sons v Liverpool and London and Globe Insurance Co Ltd* [1953] 2 Lloyd's Rep 355. Where the wording of the policy permits, however, a construction less favourable to the insurer will be preferred: see *Verelst's Administratrix v Motor Union Insurance Co Ltd* [1925] 2 KB 137.
  2 ABI *Statement of General Insurance Practice* (1986), s 2(a); ABI *Statement of Long-Term Insurance Practice* (1986), s 3(c).
  3 ABI *Statement of General Insurance Practice* (1986), s 2(c); ABI *Statement of Long-Term Insurance Practice* (1986), s 3(d).
  4 ABI *Statement of Long-Term Insurance Practice* (1986), 3(e). There is no equivalent provision in the *Statement of General Insurance Practice,* but the Insurance Ombudsman has declared that 'sauce for the goose is sauce for the gander'. Accordingly, in any case of indemnity insurance where the Ombudsman finds for the insured, interest is awarded: *The Insurance Ombudsman: Annual Report 1989* para 2.47. The Ombudsman's practice is similar to that prescribed in the *Statement of Long-Term Insurance Practice* in that interest will not be awarded where the amount would be trivial. But unlike the *Statement of Long-Term Insurance Practice*, where interest is awarded, it runs from the date when the claim could have been settled, which may be earlier than two months.

882. Notification of loss: place. Where the policy specifies that notification of loss be given to the insurer's head office, that is what should be done. Accordingly, notification made to the insurer's local agent is insufficient[1]. This requirement may be relaxed, however, where such an agent communicates the notice of loss to his head office[2].

1 *Brook v Trafalgar Insurance Co Ltd* (1947) 79 Ll L Rep 365, CA.
2 *Shiells v Scottish Assurance Corpn Ltd* (1889) 16 R 1014.

883. Notification of loss: by whom.

Where the insurers are notified of the loss by the insured's agent, or their own[1], that will be sufficient. Where the policy provides 'that the insured shall' give notice to the insurer, then, strictly speaking, notification by anyone unconnected with either insurer or insured will be insufficient. That said, however, it appears as though the courts place more emphasis on the fact that the insurer has actually been informed, rather than on the standing of the party who did the informing[2].

1 *Shiells v Scottish Assurance Corpn Ltd* (1889) 16 R 1014.
2 *Lickiss v Milestone Motor Policies at Lloyds* [1966] 2 All ER 972, *sub nom Barrett Bros (Taxis) Ltd v Davies* [1966] 1 WLR 1334, CA. Here the insurers were notified by the police and not by the insured. For a contrary view see *The Vainqueur José* [1979] 1 Lloyd's Rep 557.

884. Particulars and proof of loss.

Particulars of the loss suffered by the insured are usually stipulated for in the policy and are given by the completion of a claim form. A requirement that 'full particulars' of loss be given has been judicially interpreted to mean 'the best particulars the assured can reasonably give'[1]. Where the policy requires the insured to adduce proof of loss, this will not be satisfied by giving particulars thereof[2]. Where the policy requires that the insured shall furnish such evidence as is required by the insurer, the insurers must not make unreasonable demands of the insured[3]. The nature of a deceased's injuries may constitute prima facie evidence of accidental death[4].

1 *Mason v Harvey* (1853) 8 Exch 819.
2 'Proof' means documentary evidence. 'Particulars' means providing a description of the loss.
3 *A B v Northern Accident Insurance Co Ltd* (1896) 24 R 258, 4 SLT 213. As to the reasonableness of a post-mortem examination, see *Ballantine v Employers' Insurance Co of Great Britain Ltd* (1893) 21 R 305.
4 *Macdonald v Refuge Assurance Co Ltd* (1890) 17 R 955; *Ballantine v Employers' Insurance Co of Great Britain Ltd* (1893) 21 R 305. Death by violent injury is presumed to be accidental unless there is evidence to the contrary: see *Macdonald v Refuge Assurance Co Ltd*.

(2) THE LOSS RECOVERABLE

885. General.

There is an important distinction to be drawn between life assurance and personal accident insurance on the one hand, and indemnity contracts on the other. The indemnity principle applies only to indemnity contracts[1].

1 Personal accident insurance may well be thought of as a type of indemnity contract, but since such policies usually stipulate the amount to be paid, the indemnity principle has no application.

886. The basic principle.

The indemnity principle has been judicially described in the following terms: 'The rule is, that you can get nothing but indemnification for the thing lost, and that you can get nothing more than the value of the thing lost'[1]. Accordingly, by virtue of the indemnity principle, where there has been total loss the insured will be entitled only to the value of the thing lost at the time of loss[2]. Where the policy specifies 'the sum insured' it imposes a ceiling (that is, a limit) on the amount of loss recoverable by the insured[3]. If the value of an item lost is higher at the date of loss than the sum specified as the ceiling, the insured cannot recover more than the ceiling[4]. Where loss is only partial, the insured is entitled to recover the difference between value at time of loss and value after time of loss[5]. There is, however, some quite persuasive authority for the view that the insured's loss should be measured by the cost to him of repairing the item[5]. Where the cost of repairs is the correct measure of indemnity, allowance must be made for betterment and deducted from the sum to be paid[6].

1 *Hercules Insurance Co v Hunter* (1836) 14 S 1137 at 1142, per Lord Moncreiff; *Carrick Furniture House Ltd v General Accident, Fire and Life Assurance Corpn Ltd* 1977 SC 308, 1978 SLT 65. See also *Burnand v Rodocanachi Sons & Co* (1882) 7 App Cas 333, HL, and *Castellain v Preston* (1883) 11 QBD 380 at 386, CA, per Brett LJ: 'the contract of insurance contained in a... fire policy is a contract of indemnity only and... this... means that the assured in a case of loss against which the policy has been made, shall be fully indemnified, but shall never be more than fully indemnified'.

2 *Hercules Insurance Co v Hunter* (1836) 14 S 1137.

3 *Glasgow Provident Investment Society v Westminster Fire Office* (1887) 14 R 947 at 988, per Lord Young, affd (1888) 15 R (HL) 89.

4 In this case there may well be under-insurance which falls foul of an average clause. As to average clauses, see para 893 below.

5 *Glasgow Provident Investment Society v Westminster Fire Office* (1887) 14 R 947, affd (1888) 15 R (HL) 89.

6 In marine insurance this is specifically provided for by the Marine Insurance Act 1906 (c 41), s 69 para (1): 'Where the ship has been repaired, the assured is entitled to the reasonable cost of the repairs, less the customary deductions, but not exceeding the sum insured in respect of any one casualty'. For non-marine insurance, see *Reynolds v Phoenix Assurance Co Ltd* [1978] 2 Lloyd's Rep 440.

887. Contractual variations. The indemnity principle may be varied by express provision in the contract. Some contractual variations benefit the insured; others work to the advantage of the insurer. The following paragraphs describe the most important contractual variations[1].

1 See paras 888–893 below.

888. Agreed value policies. Agreed value, or valued, policies are commonly found in marine insurance[1]. Under such a policy, the insured is entitled on proof of total loss to the sum agreed in or fixed by the policy. The insurer may not argue that the actual value of the item lost or damaged is less than its agreed value. Such policies are clearly to the advantage of the insured[2]. Where the loss is only partial, the insured will obtain the relevant fraction of the agreed value[3].

1 Marine Insurance Act 1906 (c 41), s 27(2): 'A valued policy is a policy which specifies the agreed value of the subject matter insured'.

2 Agreed value policies are also considered in para 830 above.

3 *Elcock v Thomson* [1949] 2 KB 755, [1949] 2 All ER 381. See also para 830 above.

889. Replacement value policies. As the term suggests, a replacement value policy is one which entitles the insured to receive the replacement value of the thing destroyed, rather than its market value at the time of loss. If there is a ceiling clause, that will place a limit on the amount which the insurer will have to pay.

890. Reinstatement clauses. A reinstatement clause confers an option on the insurer either to repair a damaged item or to replace it if lost. These clauses are commonly encountered in fire[1] and heritable property insurance and may also appear in motor vehicle policies[2] and in insurances effected over corporeal moveables generally. Where the policy contains a reinstatement clause, the insurer has the right to choose to reinstate the insured rather than provide him with monetary compensation[3]. Failing express provision in the policy, the insurer must notify the insured of his choice within a reasonable time[4]. If the insurer chooses to reinstate, then he must do so within a reasonable time and completely: consequently, his liability will not be limited by any ceiling clause in the policy[5]. If the policy is silent on the matter of reinstatement the insured will be entitled to insist on monetary compensation[6]. If the insured disputes the right of the insurer to reinstate, the insurer may still press on with the task of reinstatement and it has been held that no interdict to prevent him from so doing will be granted[7]. Under Scots law, insurers enjoy no statutory right to reinstate the insured[8]. It can be stated with certainty that once the insurer makes his choice, either to reinstate or make payment, that choice is irrevocable and the insurer is barred from changing his mind[9]. The question of which of the two courses open to him he has chosen, can be answered only by looking to the facts of the case. It has been opined that the insurer's conduct will not bind him until he is in possession of sufficient information to make a choice[10]. It is unfortunate, however, that the two leading cases on the effect of the insurer's choice appear to be contradictory. In *Sutherland v Society of the Sun Fire Office*[11], the insurer first offered to settle the claim with cash. When this was refused, the insurer offered to go to arbitration as to the amount of money due. This offer also was refused. The insurer then exercised his right to reinstate the insured. The insured raised an action for payment in settlement of the claim. The court held that the insurer was entitled to exercise the option to reinstate. In *Scottish Amicable Heritable Securities Association Ltd v Northern Assurance Co*[12], the insured wished either to be reinstated or compensated financially. The insurer ignored the claim for reinstatement but disputed the amount of the sum claimed and made preparations to submit the matter to arbitration. Subsequently, it offered to reinstate the insured. This time the court held that the offer to reinstate came too late to be effective. One solution to the apparently contradictory results in these cases, though not free from doubt, may be ventured. It is said that once the choice to reinstate has been made, the contract mutates from one of indemnity to one of reinstatement[13]. Indeed, in relation to property cover, it is said to become a building contract[14]. If one continues with the language of contract, the two decisions become capable of reconciliation. In the *Sutherland* case, the insurer offered to make payment. This was refused and so that offer lapsed. The insurer made a second offer, to submit to arbitration. This too was rejected and lapsed accordingly. The insurer then exercised a unilateral right to reinstate. By this time, however, it was too late for the insured to accept the first offer since his rejection had killed it off. All that remained was the right to reinstate and that did not depend on the acceptance of the insured. In the *Scottish Amicable* case, the insured made an offer to settle on either a cash or a reinstatement basis. The insurer, by his conduct, accepted the first option. True, the parties were in dispute as to the amount of compensation, but they were not in dispute as to the method[15].

1 *Glasgow Provident Investment Society v Westminster Fire Office* (1888) 15 R (HL) 89.
2 *Davidson v Guardian Royal Exchange Assurance* 1979 SC 192, 1981 SLT 81.
3 The choice is that of the insurer only and not of the insured: see *Anderson v Commercial Union Assurance Co* (1885) 55 LJQB 146, CA.
4 *Sutherland v Society of the Sun Fire Office* (1852) 14 D 775.
5 *Davidson v Guardian Royal Exchange Assurance* 1979 SC 192, 1981 SLT 81; *Argy Trading Development Co Ltd v Lapid Developments Ltd* [1977] 1 Lloyd's Rep 67, [1977] 1 WLR 444.
6 *Rayner v Preston* (1881) 18 Ch D 1, CA; *Anderson v Commercial Union Assurance Co* (1885) 55 LJQB 146, CA.
7 *Bisset v Royal Exchange Assurance Co* (1822) 1 S 174 (NE 165). The insurer takes the risk, of course, of losing the action which will be raised by the pursuer for payment rather than reinstatement.

8 *Glasgow Provident Investment Society v Westminster Fire Office* (1888) 15 R (HL) 89. This is not so in England: see eg the Fires Prevention (Metropolis) Act 1774 (c 78), s 83.
9 *Sutherland v Society of the Sun Fire Office* (1852) 14 D 775; *Scottish Amicable Heritable Securities Association Ltd v Northern Assurance Co* (1883) 11 R 287.
10 *Sutherland v Society of the Sun Fire Office* (1852) 14 D 775 at 778, per Lord President McNeill.
11 *Sutherland v Society of the Sun Fire Office* (1852) 14 D 775.
12 *Scottish Amicable Heritable Securities Association Ltd v Northern Assurance Co* (1883) 11 R 287.
13 *Brown v Royal Insurance Co* (1859) 1 E & E 853.
14 *Brown v Royal Insurance Co* (1859) 1 E & E 853; E J MacGillivray and M Parkington *Insurance Law* (8th edn, 1988) para 1676.
15 The relevant principles of contract formation are most recently found in *Wolf and Wolf v Forfar Potato Co* 1984 SLT 100; *Rutterford Ltd v Allied Breweries Ltd* 1990 SCLR 186, 1990 SLT 249, OH; and *Findlater v Maan* 1990 SLT 465.

891. Excess clause. Excess clauses are commonly found in motor vehicle and household policies. Such clauses render the insurer liable only for the excess amount of the loss suffered after a previously agreed figure (which may also be stated as a fraction or percentage of the loss) has been deducted. For example, an excess clause of £50 in a motor policy means that if the car should suffer £250's worth of damage, the insurer is only obliged to pay £200 to the insured: ie the excess over £50. Whether the insured can obtain further coverage of the uninsured balance depends on the wording of the excess clause. If, for example, the clause is worded in such a way as to prevent the insured from taking out insurance elsewhere in order to cover the sum not insured by the first insurer, the latter will be entitled to avoid the contract if the insured does so[1]. Where, however, the wording of the clause merely states that the insurer will not be liable for any loss under the stipulated sum, the insured is free to arrange cover of this figure elsewhere[2].

1 *Muirhead v Forth and North Sea Steamboat Mutual Insurance Association* (1893) 21 R (HL) 1, 1 SLT 325.
2 E R H Ivamy *General Principles of Insurance Law* (5th edn, 1986) p 933.

892. Franchise clause. A franchise clause puts the full burden of any loss incurred on the insured where the amount of loss is less than a stated percentage of the total value of the thing insured. However, if the loss suffered exceeds this figure, the full amount of the loss may then be claimed from the insured. Where, for example, the policy provides that losses under 5 per cent of the value of items are not covered, the loss must be 6 per cent before the insurer will be liable, but once that base percentage is reached, the insurer is liable for the full amount of loss.

893. Average clause. Average clauses deal with the problem of under-insurance. Apart from marine insurance, where the average principle is an implied term[1], the insurer will not be able to invoke this principle unless there is an express average clause[2]. Suppose for example, that goods are insured for £100,000 but their actual value is £150,000. If they are completely destroyed by a fire (that is, become a total loss) the insured will be entitled to £100,000 and the average clause will not come into play. If, however, the goods are only partially damaged by the fire, causing a loss of £30,000, the average clause will operate and the insured will be entitled to £20,000: that is, two-thirds of the actual amount of loss[3].

1 Marine Insurance Act 1906 (c 41), s 81: 'Where the assured is insured for an amount less than the insurable value or, in the case of a valued policy, for an amount less than the policy valuation, he is deemed to be his own insurer in respect of the uninsured balance.'
2 See E R H Ivamy *General Principles of Insurance Law* (5th edn, 1986) p 432 and the cases cited there. There are, however, contrary views: see *Carreras v Cunard Steamship Co* [1918] 1 KB 118.

3 It appears to be the general view that average clauses are not yet commonplace in home and household insurance policies, with the exception of Lloyd's policies. See generally, J Birds _Modern Insurance Law_ (1988) p 227.

(3) SUBROGATION

(a) Introduction

894. General. Subrogation is a corollary of the indemnity principle[1]. Accordingly, it has no application to life insurance[2]. The right of the insurer to be subrogated to the position of the insured, vis-à-vis any rights and remedies[3] which the latter may enjoy against the third party who actually caused the insured's loss, is not to be confused with an assignation of a right of action. Both represent means whereby the insurer can recoup the money expended in settling the insured's claim. Assignation requires the insured's express agreement[4]. The right of subrogation, however, has been described as _a naturale_[5] of an insurance contract. In other words, the right of subrogation is an implied term of an insurance contract[6]. The right of subrogation arises automatically once the insurer has paid out on a claim[7]. Assignation requires the insured's consent. Where the insurer is subrogated to the rights and remedies of the insured, he must assert the right of action, not in his own name, but in the name of the insured[8]. If, however, the insured is also the party who has caused the loss to himself, the insurer cannot exercise a right of subrogation: the insurer can only pursue the action in the name of the insured and the insured cannot sue himself[9]. Since subrogation requires to be exercised in the name of the insured it has a certain cosmetic value, making it seem as though the action is an ordinary one between two individual litigants[10]. As subrogation is a corollary of the indemnity principle, the insurer may not (subject to express contractual variation) retain more than the sum he has paid out under the policy. Where he recovers more than the measure of the indemnity paid out, he must account for the surplus to the insured. If, however, the insurer takes an assignation of the insured's rights, he may retain any such surplus[11]. The insurer may not demand that the insured must first pursue his claim against the party who actually caused him loss before claiming under the policy[12]. The party who caused the loss cannot plead the existence of an insurance against either insured or insurer[13].

1 _Castellain v Preston_ (1883) 11 QBD 380, CA; _Morris v Ford Motor Co Ltd_ [1973] QB 792, [1973] 2 All ER 1084, CA.
2 _Simpson & Co v Thomson_ (1877) 5 R (HL) 40.
3 _Esso Petroleum Co Ltd v Hall Russell & Co Ltd_ [1989] AC 643, 1988 SLT 874, HL.
4 The policy may stipulate that the insured must assign his right of action as a precondition of payment: see _L Lucas Ltd v Export Credits Guarantee Department_ [1973] 2 All ER 984, [1973] 1 WLR 914, CA, revsd [1974] 2 All ER 889, [1974] 1 WLR 909, HL.
5 'Insurance' in _The Law of South Africa_ (1988, ed Joubert) vol 12, para 225.
6 _Yorkshire Insurance Co Ltd v Nisbet Shipping Co Ltd_ [1962] 2 QB 330, [1961] 2 All ER 487. It is submitted that the debate in English law as to whether subrogation is an equitable or legal doctrine is irrelevant in Scots law. For this debate, see E J MacGillivray and M Parkington _Insurance Law_ (8th edn, 1988) paras 1163–1170. In _Simpson & Co v Thomson_ (1877) 5 R (HL) 40, subrogation was described as a 'principle of law'.
7 _Simpson & Co v Thomson_ (1877) 5 R (HL) 40. See also _Page v Scottish Insurance Corpn Ltd_ (1929) 98 LJKB 308, CA. In marine insurance, the Marine Insurance Act 1906 (c 41), s 79(1), provides that 'Where the insurer pays for a total loss, either of the whole, or in the case of goods of any apportionable part, of the subject-matter insured, he thereupon becomes entitled to take over the interest of the assured in whatever may remain of the subject-matter so paid for, and he is thereby subrogated to all the rights and remedies of the assured in and in respect of that subject-matter as from the time of the casualty causing the loss'.

8 *Simpson & Co v Thomson* (1877) 5 R (HL) 40; *Esso Petroleum Co Ltd v Hall Russell & Co Ltd* [1989] AC 643 at 674, 1988 SLT 874 at 883, HL, per Lord Jauncey of Tullichettle.
9 *Simpson & Co v Thomson* (1877) 5 R (HL) 40.
10 See eg *Lister v Romford Ice and Cold Storage Co Ltd* [1957] AC 555, [1957] 1 All ER 125, HL.
11 This matter is discussed in detail in paras 901, 902 below.
12 *Collingridge v Royal Exchange Assurance Corpn* (1877) 3 QBD 173.
13 *Port-Glasgow and Newark Sailcloth Co v Caledonian Rly Co* (1892) 19 R 608.

895. The different facets of subrogation.

Subrogation has two distinct facets. Firstly, it refers to the right of the insurer to be 'entitled to succeed to all the ways and means by which the person indemnified might have protected himself or reimbursed himself for the loss'[1]. Secondly, it ensures that the insured does not profit by his loss at the insurer's expense[2].

1 *Simpson & Co v Thomson* (1877) 5 R (HL) 40 at 42, per Lord Cairns LC. See also *Castellain v Preston* (1883) 11 QBD 380 at 388, 389, CA, and *Yorkshire Insurance Co Ltd v Nisbet Shipping Co Ltd* [1962] 2 QB 330, [1961] 2 All ER 487.
2 *Burnand v Rodocanachi Sons & Co* (1882) 7 App Cas 333, HL; *Castellain v Preston* (1883) 11 QBD 380, CA; *Yorkshire Insurance Co Ltd v Nisbet Shipping Co Ltd* [1962] 2 QB 330, [1961] 2 All ER 487.

896. The right of subrogation dependent on settlement of claim.

The right of subrogation does not arise until the insurer has paid out on a claim. Once the insurer has indemnified the insured in accordance with the contract between them, he acquires the right to raise an action in the insured's name[1]. Accordingly, the right to control litigation belongs to the insurer once the insured is fully indemnified, even though the latter may still not be fully compensated for his loss[2].

1 This, it is submitted, is the better view of a somewhat vexed question. In support of the statement in the text is E J MacGillivray and M Parkington *Insurance Law* (8th edn, 1988) para 1181; E R H Ivamy *General Principles of Insurance Law* (5th edn, 1986) p 478; J Birds *Modern Insurance Law* (1988) p 245. This also seems to be the position in marine insurance: see F Templeman *Marine Insurance* (6th edn, 1986 ed R J Lambert) p 452, discussing the Marine Insurance Act 1906 (c 41), s 79. In *Page v Scottish Insurance Corpn Ltd* (1929) 98 LJKB 308, CA, the issue was reserved. Against the statement in the text is 25 Halsbury's Laws (4th edn) para 333(3), and the decision in *Commercial Union Assurance Co v Lister* (1874) 9 Ch App 483. Perhaps the reason why the point does not appear to have given rise to any recent litigation, is because of the practice of making it a term of the contract that the insurer is to control any action raised.
2 *MacGillivray and Parkington* para 1198. If eg the sum insured is £30,000 and the insured suffers a loss of £40,000, then payment by the insurer of £30,000 is full indemnification in terms of the contract. The insured, however, has not been fully compensated.

897. The right of subrogation is not always enforceable.

In *Lister v Romford Ice and Cold Storage Co Ltd*[1], an employee of the insured was injured, negligently, by a co-employee. The insured paid compensation, claimed under his indemnity liability policy and was paid. The insurer then sued the negligent employee under the insured's name. The real pursuer, therefore, was the insurer subrogated to the rights of the insured. The House of Lords held in favour of the insurer. The adverse consequences of this decision for harmonious industrial relations were noted at the time and BIA (now the Association of British Insurers (ABI)) insurers entered into a 'gentleman's agreement' not to enforce their legal right unless collusion or wilful misconduct on the part of the employee was suspected[2]. This agreement should not be regarded as exceptional; it is simply an example of the type of case in which insurers agree to waive their entitlement to be subrogated[3]. 'Knock for knock' agreements are commonplace with regard to motor vehicle insurance[4]. There is no direct authority as to what would happen were an insurer to disregard this gentleman's agreement and sue an employee. However, *Morris v Ford Motor Co*[5] is instructive. A contract for the provision of cleaning services between Ford and Cameron Industrial Services Ltd provided that the latter would indemnify Ford against liability to either's employees, even if Ford's employees were at fault. One of Cameron's employees was injured by a Ford employee. The injured workman sued Ford, Ford claimed under the indemnity against Cameron, and Cameron claimed to be subrogated to Ford's right to sue their negligent employee. In short, the situation was exactly like that in the *Lister* case. The Court of Appeal denied that Cameron was entitled to be subrogated. None of the reasons expressed by the court may be described as convincing, but the least unconvincing view was that of James LJ, who adopted an approach based on the implied term. In his opinion, it was an implied term of the contract between Ford and Cameron that, in the light of *Lister* and the reaction produced by that case, no right of subrogation would exist. The decision in this case is, frankly, suspect. However, since there appears to have been no case since *Lister* in which an insurer has sought to breach the gentleman's agreement, it must be concluded that insurers take their responsibilities seriously.

1 *Lister v Romford Ice and Cold Storage Co Ltd* [1957] AC 555, [1957] 1 All ER 125, HL.
2 G Gardner 'Reports of Committees: Lister v The Romford Ice and Cold Storage Company Ltd' (1959) 22 MLR 652.
3 On the various agreements made by insurers, see R Lewis 'Insurers' agreements not to enforce strict legal rights: bargaining with government in the shadow of the law' [1985] 48 MLR 275.
4 Under the 'knock for knock' system, each insurer indemnifies his own insured and does not seek to recover from the drivers. It still remains open to the innocent driver to sue the other driver. He might eg do this in order to recover the uninsured amount under an excess clause. The defender (most likely to be his insurer) cannot be heard to argue that the knock for knock agreement has deprived the pursuer of his right to sue. See *Hobbs v Marlowe* [1978] AC 16, [1977] 2 All ER 241, HL.
5 *Morris v Ford Motor Co Ltd* [1973] QB 792, [1973] 2 All ER 1084, CA.

898. The insured must not prejudice the right of subrogation. It is settled law that the insured must not do anything to prejudice the insurer's right of subrogation[1]. This does not mean that the insured cannot waive his right to sue the third party who has caused him loss or grant him a discharge. It does mean, however, that the insured is in breach of his duty not to prejudice his insurer's right of subrogation[2]. Where the insured acts in a manner prejudicial to the right of subrogation before the insurer has settled the former's claim under the policy, the insurer can counterclaim for damages in any action raised by the insured for payment. The measure of damages will be the extent to which the insured's conduct has caused him loss. If the policy expressly provides that the insured must not do anything prejudicial to the insurer's right of subrogation, the latter may repudiate liability completely[3]. Where the insured acts in a prejudicial fashion after the insurer has met his claim, the measure of the latter's damages is the extent to which the value of the right of subrogation has been diminished[4]. As the insured's duty is not to prejudice his insurer's right of subrogation, it follows that where the insured's conduct does not prejudice his insurer, the latter has no right of action against the insured[5].

1 The leading cases are *West of England Fire Insurance Co v Isaacs* [1897] 1 QB 226, CA; *Phoenix Assurance Co v Spooner* [1905] 2 KB 753; *Horse, Carriage and General Insurance Co Ltd v Petch* (1916) 33 TLR 131; and *Boag v Standard Marine Insurance Co Ltd* [1937] 2 KB 113, [1937] 1 All ER 714, CA.
2 See the cases cited in note 1 above.
3 E J MacGillivray and M Parkington *Insurance Law* (8th edn, 1988) para 1203.

4 See the cases cited in note 1 above.
5 J Birds *Modern Insurance Law* (1988) p 246.

899. Control of litigation. Strictly speaking, the insurer cannot have control of any action unless and until he has indemnified the insured in terms of the policy[1]. If, however, the policy contains a subrogation clause, this may give control of any litigation to the insurer and also stipulate that the insurer will indemnify the insured against expenses[2]. There may be cases where the insurer does not wish to proceed against the party who caused the loss. However, if the insured does raise an action in his own right, he is obliged to sue for the full extent of his loss[3]. This raises a question which follows from the second facet of subrogation. If the insured's action is successful, he will have to repay to the insurer the money received from him in settlement of his claim[4]. Does this mean, therefore, that the insurer is liable for the expenses of the action? It is submitted that the answer is no[5].

1 E J MacGillivray and M Parkington *Insurance Law* (8th edn, 1988) para 1192.
2 *Netherlands Insurance Co Est 1845 Ltd v Karl Ljungberg & Co AB* [1986] 3 All ER 767, [1986] 2 Lloyd's Rep 19, PC.
3 *Commercial Union Assurance Co v Lister* (1874) 9 Ch App 483.
4 *Burnand v Rodocanachi Sons & Co* (1882) 7 App Cas 333, HL. This aspect of subrogation is discussed in paras 900–903 below.
5 This was expressly stated in *Arthur Barnett Ltd v National Insurance Co of New Zealand Ltd* [1965] NZLR 874 (NZ SC). It appears to be implied in *Hobbs v Marlowe* [1978] AC 16, [1977] 2 All ER 241, HL.

(b) Subrogation as a Measure of Indemnity

900. The basic principle. In *Castellain v Preston*[1], a house burned down after the conclusion of a contract for its sale but before the conveyance had been completed. The seller obtained the insurance money and also payment of the purchase price because the buyer was still obliged to continue with the contract. It was held that the seller was liable to repay to his insurers the sum expended by them. The law is as expounded by Brett LJ:

'The contract of insurance contained in a marine or fire policy is a contract of indemnity only and . . . this contract means that the assured in a case of loss, against which the policy has been made, shall be fully indemnified, but shall never be more than fully indemnified. That is a fundamental principle of [indemnity] insurance'[2].

The insured must, therefore, account to the insurer for any money received from any other source which diminishes his loss[3]. It is possible that the insured may recover from the third party more than was paid to him by his insurer. Clearly, in this case, the insured must account to the insurer for the measure of his indemnity. But what happens to the windfall profit? Is the insured entitled to keep it (even though he will now be bettter off than before the loss), or can the insurer insist that the windfall be paid to him? Both the point and the solution are well illustrated in *Yorkshire Insurance Co Ltd v Nisbet Shipping Co Ltd*[4]. In that case, a ship was insured for £72,000 under an agreed value policy. When the vessel was lost, the insurer paid out that sum. The insured subsequently recovered damages from the Canadian government of £75,514, the dollar equivalent being $336,000. Sterling then devalued, and when the dollars were converted into sterling the insured was paid £126, 971. The insurer claimed this sum but was held to be entitled to recover only the amount it had paid out in settlement of the claim. It is submitted that this decision is clearly correct and consistent with the principle expressed in *Castellain v Preston*[5]. In that case,

Cotton LJ, describing the measure of the insurer's right of subrogation, stated that 'if the purchase money has been paid in full, the insurance office will get back that which they have paid'[6]. In another case it was also stated that where money has been recovered by the insured: 'it becomes an equity that the person who has already paid the full indemnity is entitled to be recouped by having that amount back'[7]. Accordingly, the proposition that the insured cannot recover more than the amount of his loss is too general. It would be more accurate to state that the insured may not profit at the insurer's expense.

1 *Castellain v Preston* (1883) 11 QBD 380, CA.
2 (1883) 11 QBD 380 at 386, CA. This has been referred to as the 'classic' definition of subrogation. See *Esso Petroleum Co Ltd v Hall Russell & Co Ltd* [1989] AC 643 at 671, 672, 1988 SLT 874 at 882, HL, per Lord Jauncey.
3 See also *Darrell v Tibbits* (1880) 5 QBD 560, CA; *Burnand v Rodocanachi Sons & Co* (1882) 7 App Cas 333, HL; and *Yorkshire Insurance Co Ltd v Nisbet Shipping Co Ltd* [1962] 2 QB 330, [1961] 2 All ER 487. It is sometimes said that the insured cannot 'profit' from his loss. This can be dangerously misleading.
4 *Yorkshire Insurance Co Ltd v Nisbet Shipping Co Ltd* [1962] 2 QB 330, [1961] 2 All ER 487.
5 *Castellain v Preston* (1883) 11 QBD 380, CA.
6 (1883) 11 QBD 380 at 396, CA.
7 *Burnand v Rodocanachi Sons & Co* (1882) 7 App Cas 333 at 339, HL, per Lord Blackburn.

901. Contractual variation of the principle. Subrogation has been described as a 'well known principle of law'[1]. However, the ambit of this principle may be varied by the terms of the contract between insurer and insured[2]. It is for the court to construe the contract as a whole, paying due regard to the content of any express terms dealing with subrogation[3]. It is only where the contract is silent as to subrogation, or where a subrogation clause is ambiguous, that reference to the basic legal principle is justified[3]. Consequently, a suitably worded subrogation clause may entitle the insurer to claim any windfall profit[4].

1 *Simpson & Co v Thomson* (1877) 5 R (HL) 40.
2 See J Birds 'Contractual Subrogation in Insurance' [1979] JBL 124.
3 *L Lucas Ltd v Export Credits Guarantee Department* [1973] 2 All ER 984, [1973] 1 WLR 914, CA. The House of Lords reversed the Court of Appeal, but this was done only by putting a different construction on the relevant contract term: [1974] 2 All ER 889, [1974] 1 WLR 909, HL.
4 [1973] 2 All ER 984, [1973] 1 WLR 914, CA, revsd [1974] 2 All ER 889, [1974] 1 WLR 909, HL. Goods were sold to a buyer in the United Arab Republic. The contract price was payable in US dollars and the transaction was covered by the Export Credits Guarantee Department, which undertook to indemnify the exporter against non-payment or delay in payment due to circumstances outwith the buyer's control. Exchange control restrictions were imposed by the United Arab Republic, so payment was delayed, and the exporters received the sterling equivalent of 90 per cent of the value of the goods. When these restrictions were lifted, the exporters were paid by the buyers. But when the contract price was converted into sterling, which had by then devalued, the exporters acquired a surplus of £26,000 more than the original contract price. The exporters argued that under the subrogation principle they were obliged to repay only the sum actually received from the Export Credits Guarantee Department. The Department, however, pointed to a term of the agreement with the exporters stating that they were entitled to recover 90 per cent of any sum received by the exporters. The Court of Appeal held that one had to place the terms of the subrogation clause before any general legal principle and found for the Department. As noted above, although the House of Lords reversed this decision, this was only because it interpreted the term to contrary effect.

902. Gifts. It is easier to state the rules regarding the giving of a gift to the insured than to decide on their application. Two situations fall to be distinguished. If the party responsible for the loss gives a gift to the insured for the purpose of reducing that loss, the insurer is entitled to treat that gift as indemnifying the insured. Accordingly, the loss suffered by the insured is diminished by the amount of the gift, and he must account to the insurer for that amount[1]. If the gift was given in recognition of the harm done to the insured and with the intention of benefiting him personally, rather than reducing the loss he has suffered, he may retain it without liability to account to the insurer[2]. Ascertaining the purpose or intention underlying the gift is all important.

1 *Stearns v Village Main Reef Gold Mining Co Ltd* (1905) 21 TLR 236, CA.
2 *Burnand v Rodocanachi Sons & Co* (1882) 7 App Cas 333, HL.

903. When does the insured's duty to account arise? A distinction may be drawn between indemnification for and compensation of loss[1]. Where, for example, the loss is greater than the sum insured for, the insured may be indemnified under the policy, by receiving that sum, but he has not been fully compensated. If the insured then proceeds directly against the third party who has caused him the loss, and recovers the balance, must he then account to the insurer for that balance? It is submitted that the general rule is that the insured only becomes liable to account to the insurer when he has been fully compensated for the loss he has sustained[2]. This rule, however, may not apply where there is under-insurance and the average rule applies[3], nor where the policy is an agreed value one and there has been undervaluation[4].

1 J Birds *Modern Insurance Law* (1988) p 240.
2 *Birds* p 241; E J MacGillivray and M Parkington *Insurance Law* (8th edn, 1988) para 1220. See also *Re Driscoll, Driscoll v Driscoll* (1918) 1 IR 152; *Scottish Union and National Insurance Co v Davis* [1970] 1 Lloyd's Rep 1, CA; and *Ledingham v Ontario Hospital Services Commission* (1974) 46 DLR (3d) 699 (Can SC).
3 Ie either by implication, as in the case of marine insurance, or expressly, in other indemnity contracts: see *The Commonwealth* [1907] P 216, CA.
4 *MacGillivray and Parkington* para 1222.

(c) Statutory Subrogation

904. General. The Third Parties (Rights against Insurers) Act 1930 is a statutory embodiment of the doctrine of subrogation. The object of statutory subrogation is the same as the common law doctrine (that is, the transfer of rights and remedies), but the focus alters. Where the legislation applies, a third party who has suffered loss is subrogated to the position of the insured in respect of any claim the latter may have had against his insurer under his policy. Consequently, the third party can claim under the insured's policy[1]. The basic right is set out in the Act as follows:

'Where under any contract of insurance a person (hereinafter referred to as the insured) is insured against liabilities to third parties which he may incur, then—
   (a) in the event of the insured becoming bankrupt or making a composition or arrangement with his creditors; or
   (b) in the case of the insured being a company, in the event of a winding-up order or an administration order being made, or a resolution for a voluntary winding-up being passed, with respect to the company, or of a receiver or manager of the company's business or undertaking being duly appointed, or of possession being taken by, or on behalf, of the holders of any debenture secured by a floating charge, of any property comprised in or subject to the charge or of a voluntary arrangement proposed for the purpose of Part I of the Insolvency Act 1986[2] being approved under that Part;
   if, either before or after that event, any such liability as aforesaid is incurred by the insured, his rights against the insurer under the contract in respect of the liability

shall, notwithstanding anything in any Act or rule of law to the contrary, be transferred to and vest in the third party to whom the liability was so incurred[3].'

1 On statutory subrogation, see J Birds *Modern Insurance Law* (1988) pp 280–284; E J MacGillivray and M Parkington *Insurance Law* (8th edn, 1988) paras 1988–1996. See also A J Gamble 'Employers Liability Insurance' (1980) 25 JLSS 173, and A D M Forte 'Statutory Subrogation: A Pyrrhic Victory' (1989) JR 198.
2 The Insolvency Act 1986 (c 45), Pt I, comprises ss 1–7: see COMPANIES, vol 4, paras 579 ff.
3 Third Parties (Rights against Insurers) Act 1930 (c 25), s 1(1) (amended by the Insolvency Act 1985 (c 65), s 235(1), Sch 8, para 7(2), and the Insolvency Act 1986, s 439(2), Sch 14).

905. Application of the Third Parties (Rights against Insurers) Act 1930. Where the insured is a company, the triggers which activate the Third Parties (Rights against Insurers) Act 1930 are (1) its descent into insolvent liquidation or receivership[1], and (2) the existence of a judgment, arbitration award or agreement fixing damages. Where the insured is an individual, the triggers are (a) his bankruptcy or making a composition or arrangement with his creditors[1], and (b) the existence of a judgment, arbitration award or agreement fixing damages. The requirement under head (b), that the insured's liability to the third party must exist and be quantified, was declared to be the law in *Post Office v Norwich Union Fire Insurance Society Ltd*[2]. This requirement is clearly necessary. The insured is entitled to be indemnified under his policy only if his liability to the third party has been established (or agreed) and quantum ascertained. For the third party to be subrogated to the insured's right to claim an indemnity from the insurer, he must be able to point to a sum in respect of which the insured may actually claim under his policy[3].

1 Third Parties (Rights against Insurers) Act 1930 (c 25), s 1(1) (amended by the Insolvency Act 1985 (c 65), s 235(1), Sch 8, para 7(2), and the Insolvency Act 1986 (c 45), s 439(2), Sch 14)).
2 *Post Office v Norwich Union Fire Insurance Society Ltd* [1967] 2 QB 363, [1967] 1 All ER 577, CA, approved in *Bradley v Eagle Star Insurance Co Ltd* [1989] AC 957, [1989] 1 All ER 961, HL.
3 *Post Office v Norwich Union Fire Insurance Society Ltd* [1967] 2 QB 363, [1967] 1 All ER 577, CA; *Bradley v Eagle Star Insurance Co Ltd* [1989] AC 957, [1989] 1 All ER 961, HL.

906. The existence of the insured. A problem may arise where the insured is a company which has been dissolved and removed from the register of companies before the third party's loss or injury becomes manifest[1]. Under the Companies Act 1985, a company may be restored to the register, within twenty years of dissolution, for the purpose of raising an action for damages for personal injuries against it[2]. There is no question of the company having assets to satisfy any judgment against it; it will simply act as a conduit through which a third party's claim will be channelled to the insurer.

1 Eg, where an employee contracts an industrial disease during the course of his employment with the insured but does not display the symptoms of his ill health until many years later. In the case of certain respiratory diseases, there may be an entitlement to lump sum compensation under the Pneumoconiosis etc (Workers' Compensation) Act 1979 (c 41).
2 Companies Act 1985 (c 6), s 651 (amended by the Insolvency Act 1985 (c 65), s 109(1), Sch 6, para 45, Sch 9, para 9, and the Companies Act 1989 (c 40), s 141(2), (3), 212, Sch 24). This measure was introduced as a direct response to the decision of the House of Lords in *Bradley v Eagle Star Insurance Co Ltd* [1989] AC 957, [1989] 1 All ER 961, HL. It effectively reverses this decision.

907. Contracting out. Any attempt to contract out of or alter the parties' rights under the Third Parties (Rights against Insurers) Act 1930 is unenforceable[1]. This has given rise to particular difficulty in relation to the use of the 'pay to be paid' clause found in the rules of P & I clubs relating to marine indemnities[2]. The effect of this clause is to make the benefit of an indemnity to a club member contingent upon his having paid out in settlement of a third party's claim against him. However, where the P & I club member, unable to meet a judgment for payment, is wound up, the third party who claims to be subrogated to the rights of that member will also be bound by the 'pay to be paid' clause. Recently the Court of Appeal determined that since this would require the third party to pay himself before seeking an indemnity from the P & I club, and that since this would be pointless, the clause would be denied effect[3]. The House of Lords reversed this decision, holding that a 'pay to be paid' clause rendered payment to a third party a precondition of a club member's right to be indemnified by his P & I club[4]. A 'pay to be paid' clause does not contravene section 1(3) of the 1930 Act. It neither attempts to avoid the contract, should the insured be wound up, nor does it alter the parties' rights under the contract. Before winding up takes place the insured has a right to be indemnified on settling a claim with a third party. After winding up the position is unaltered. It has been determined that a 'pay to be paid' clause does not alter rights, it merely affects the ability to enforce them[5].

1 The Third Parties (Rights against Insurers) Act 1930 (c 25), s 1(3) (amended by the Insolvency Act 1985 (c 65), s 235(1), Sch 8, para 7(2), and the Insolvency Act 1986 (c 45), s 439(2), Sch 14), provides that 'In so far as any contract of insurance . . . in respect of any liability of the insured to third parties purports, whether directly or indirectly, to avoid the contract or to alter the rights of the parties thereunder upon the happening to the insured of any of the events specified in paragraph (a) or paragraph (b) of subsection (1) [see para 904 above] . . ., the contract shall be of no effect'.

2 'P & I' stands for 'protection and indemnity'. On P & I insurance, see S J Hazlewood *P & I Clubs: Law and Practice* (1989).

3 *The Fanti, The Padre Island (No 2)* [1989] 1 Lloyd's Rep 239, CA.

4 *The Fanti, The Padre Island* [1990] 2 All ER 705, HL.

5 [1990] 2 All ER 705 at 712, HL, per Lord Brandon, and at 718, per Lord Goff.

908. Arrangements between insurer and insured. Once liability has been incurred, no agreement between insurer and insured made after the commencement of bankruptcy or liquidation is effective against the third party[1]. A compromise agreed between insurer and insured before the commencement of such proceedings is not prohibited, and the third party cannot prevent this happening[2]. This is because it is insolvency which triggers the right to be subrogated and until this happens the third party has no rights under the Third Parties (Rights against Insurers) Act 1930.

1 Third Parties (Rights against Insurers) Act 1930 (c 25), s 3 (amended by the Insolvency Act 1985 (c 65), s 235(1), Sch 8, para 7(4)).

2 *Normid Housing Association Ltd v Ralphs* [1989] 1 Lloyd's Rep 265, CA.

909. Defences available to insurers. Since the third party is subrogated to the position of the insured, it follows that the terms and conditions of the policy apply to him and that any defences available against the insured are also available against him. If the insurer is entitled to avoid the policy against the insured, he may avoid it against the third party[1]. An excepted perils clause, excepting liability for loss or injury in defined circumstances, may be invoked against the third party[2]. If the insured was obliged to arbitrate, the third party is also obliged to do so[3]. Where the insured is required to give written notification of an accident or claim, and does not do so, that omission is fatal to the third party[4].

1 *Greenlees v Port of Manchester Insurance Co* 1933 SC 383, 1933 SLT 319.

2 *Kearney v General Accident Fire and Life Assurance Corpn Ltd* [1968] 2 Lloyd's Rep 240.

3 *Freshwater v Western Australian Assurance Co Ltd* [1933] 1 KB 515, CA; *Cunningham v Anglian Insurance Co Ltd* 1934 SLT 273, OH; *Smith v Pearl Assurance Co* [1939] 1 All ER 95, CA.

4 *Pioneer Concrete (UK) Ltd v National Employers Mutual General Insurance Association Ltd* [1985] 1 Lloyd's Rep 274; *Dunbar v A and B Painters Ltd* [1986] 2 Lloyd's Rep 38, CA.

910. Restrictions on available defences. A right of set-off for unpaid premiums cannot be relied upon in claims under the Third Parties (Rights against Insurers) Act 1930[1]. In the case of compulsory employers' liability insurance[2], there is a requirement that policies are not 'subject to any conditions or exceptions prohibited . . . by regulations'[3]. Under the relevant regulations[4] it is provided that policies should not make liability contingent upon notification of accident or loss within a specified time after the occurrence of an event giving rise to a claim[5], or excluding liability because an admission of liability has been made[6]. Also prohibited are 'reasonable precautions' clauses which make liability contingent on the insured taking 'reasonable care to protect his employees against the risk of bodily injury or disease in the course of employment'[7]. Furthermore, liability may not be declared to be contingent on compliance with legislation pertaining to the health and safety at work of employees[8]. Finally, liability is not to be made contingent upon the insured maintaining and keeping such records as are required by the insurer[9].

1 *Murray v Legal and General Assurance Society Ltd* [1970] 2 QB 495, [1969] 3 All ER 794. The observation was made that an insurer may rely only on defences relevant to liability under the policy.
2 Ie under the Employers' Liability (Compulsory Insurance) Act 1969 (c 57).
3 Employers' Liability (Compulsory Insurance) Act 1969, s 1(3)(a).
4 Ie the Employers' Liability (Compulsory Insurance) General Regulations 1971, SI 1971/1117.
5 This effectively reverses the decision in *Farrell v Federated Employers' Insurance Association Ltd* [1970] 3 All ER 632, [1970] 1 WLR 1400, CA. *Sed quaere* where the policy requires something to be done before the risk attaches?
6 Employers' Liability (Compulsory Insurance) General Regulations 1971, reg 2(1)(a).
7 Ibid, reg 2(1)(b).
8 Ibid, reg 2(1)(c).
9 Ibid, reg 2(1)(d).

911. Third party rights in motor vehicle insurance. Where a third party injured by an insured driver has obtained decree in his favour, he is subrogated to the position of the insured where the latter becomes bankrupt or, if a company, goes into liquidation, or, where the insured dies, a judicial factor is appointed to administer his estate under section 11A of the Judicial Factors (Scotland) Act 1989[1]. Unlike subrogation under the Third Parties (Rights against Insurers) Act 1930 (c 25), where the insurer may take the same objections vis-à-vis the third party as against the insured, a motor vehicle insurer cannot plead against a third party any provisions in the policy relating to the matters listed in the Road Traffic Act 1988[2]. Similarly, admissions of liability made by the insured or his failure to notify his loss, in breach of the terms of the policy, do not affect the third party[3]. An insurer who is obliged under the 1988 Act[4] to satisfy the claim of a third party may recover his expenditure from the insured[5].

The right of a third party to be subrogated under the 1988 Act is subject to qualification:

(1) the insurer must be notified within seven days of an action being raised or a counterclaim being lodged[6];
(2) no sum is payable pending an appeal against judgment[7];
(3) the insurer will not be liable if (a) the policy was cancelled before the accident giving rise to liability occurred, and (b) the insured has either surrendered the certificate of insurance or made a statutory declaration that it has been lost or destroyed or the insurer has commenced proceedings for failure to surrender the certificate within fourteen days from cancellation[8];

(4) the insurer will not be liable under a policy where he obtains a judicial declaration that it was obtained as a result of non-disclosure or misrepresentation and provided that (a) this declaration was obtained in an action raised within three months of the commencement of proceedings by the third party against the insured[9] and (b) the third party was given notice within seven days of the commencement of the action for such a declaration specifying the non-disclosure or misrepresentation on which the insurer relies[10].

The insurer's right to rescind the contract for breach of warranty in respect of a matter not covered by the 1988 Act remains unfettered by the 1988 Act.

1 Road Traffic Act 1988 (c 52), s 153(1), (2). For the Judicial Factors (Scotland) Act 1889 (c 39), s 11A (added by the Bankruptcy (Scotland) Act 1985 (c 66), s 75(1), Sch 7 para 4), see BANK-RUPTCY, vol 2, para 1451.
2 Road Traffic Act 1988, s 148(1). The matters are found in s 148(2)(a)–(h), and are as follows: (1) the age or physical or mental condition of the driver; (2) the condition of the vehicle; (3) the number of persons that the vehicle carries; (4) the weight or physical characteristics of the goods carried; (5) the time at which or the areas within which the vehicle is used; (6) the horsepower or cylinder capacity or value of the vehicle; (7) the carrying on the vehicle of any particular apparatus; (8) the carrying on the vehicle of any particular means of identification other than any means of identification required by the Vehicles (Excise) Act 1971 (c 10).
3 Road Traffic Act 1988, s 148(5).
4 Ibid, s 148(1).
5 *National Farmers Union Mutual Insurance Society Ltd v Dawson* [1941] 2 KB 424.
6 Road Traffic Act 1988, s 152(1)(a).
7 Ibid, s 152(1)(b).
8 Ibid, s 152(1)(c).
9 Ibid, s 152(2).
10 Ibid, s 152(3).
11 Ie ibid, s 148(2): see note 2 above.

(4) CONTRIBUTION

912. General. Contribution and subrogation share a common feature: both principles are intended to ensure that the insured is not over-indemnified for his loss. Further, as with subrogation, contribution is a principle relevant only to indemnity insurance. But whereas subrogation is an issue between the insurer and the insured, or between the insurer and a third party subrogated to the rights of the insured, contribution is an issue between two or more insurers[1]. The effect of contribution has been described, judicially, in the following terms:

'a man who insures his interest in property against loss by fire, whether that interest is that of a proprietor or that of a creditor, cannot recover from the insurers a greater amount than he has lost by the contingency insured against. So in the case of double insurances of the same interest with different insurance companies, the assured will not be entitled to recover more than the full amount of the loss which he has suffered'[2].

1 For a detailed treatment of the arithmetic of contribution, see E J MacGillivray and M Parkington *Insurance Law* (8th edn, 1988) paras 1732–1744.
2 *Scottish Amicable Heritable Securities Association Ltd v Northern Assurance Co* (1883) 11 R 287 at 303, per Lord Moncreiff.

913. Double insurance. There is nothing to prevent the insured taking out more than one policy in respect of the same risk[1], but if this means that he is overinsured, he cannot claim the full amount from both of the insurers[2]. In theory, the insured can claim in full from one of his insurers and that insurer can claim a contribution from the co-insurers[3]. In practice, however, it is normal for policies to contain a term dealing with double insurance. This will provide that in the event of double insurance, the insured is not entitled to claim in full from the insurer but may only claim a rateable proportion of the loss[4].

1 For marine insurance, see the Marine Insurance Act 1906 (c 41), s 32(1): 'Where two or more policies are effected by or on behalf of the assured on the same adventure and interest or any part thereof, and the sums insured exceed the indemnity allowed by this Act, the assured is said to be over-insured by double insurance.'

2 For marine insurance, see the Marine Insurance Act 1906, s 32(2): 'Where the assured is over-insured by double insurance — (a) the assured, unless the policy otherwise provides, may claim payment from the insurers in such order as he may think fit, provided that he is not entitled to receive any sum in excess of the indemnity allowed by this Act. . .'

3 *Sickness and Accident Assurance Association Ltd v General Accident Assurance Corpn Ltd* (1892) 19 R 977.

4 There is a dearth of cases dealing with the arithmetical dimension to contribution. See E J MacGillivray and M Parkington *Insurance Law* (8th edn, 1988) paras 1732–1744.

914. Prerequisites for contribution. There are several prerequisites for the operation of the right of contribution which may be subsumed under two broad headings, namely: (1) cover under each policy must be in respect of the same risk and cover the same interest; and (2) each policy must be valid and enforceable at the time of loss.

(1) *The same risk and interest*: If two or more insureds enjoy separate interests in the same property, then even though the policies refer to the same risk and the same subject matter, and even though the combined total of the sums insured exceeds its value, there is no double insurance and no right of contribution. A disposition of heritable property in security to successive incumbrancers each in respect of the loans advanced by each, does not constitute double insurance[1].

Although several policies may be effected, each in respect of a number of different risks, nonetheless, where those policies have at least one risk in common, there will be double insurance in relation to that common risk[2]. Many insurers are party to an agreement, sponsored by the Fire Offices Committee, and applicable to insurance of heritable property only. Under this agreement, insurers ignore the fact that each policy insures different interests and treat the matter as if it were a genuine case of double insurance[3].

(2) *Valid and enforceable policies*: It is axiomatic that there cannot be double insurance, and consequently no right of contribution, where one of the policies was not in force at the time of loss[4]. Equally, there is no entitlement to contribution from an insurer who can show that the insured's right to be indemnified has been forfeited[5].

1 *Scottish Amicable Heritable Securities Association Ltd v Northern Assurance Co* (1883) 11 R 287; *Glasgow Provident Investment Society v Westminster Fire Office* (1887) 14 R 947, affd (1888) 15 R (HL) 89. Cf *Nichols & Co v Scottish Union and National Insurance Co* (1885) 14 R 1094, which was probably wrongly decided.

2 *North British and Mercantile Insurance Co v London, Liverpool and Globe Insurance Co* (1877) 5 Ch D 569, CA.

3 See E J MacGillivray and M Parkington *Insurance Law* (8th edn, 1988) para 1750.

4 *Sickness and Accident Assurance Association Ltd v General Accident Assurance Corpn Ltd* (1892) 19 R 977. See also *National Employers Mutual General Insurance Association Ltd v Haydon* [1980] 2 Lloyd's Rep 149, CA.

5 *Woods v Co-operative Insurance Society* 1924 SC 692, 1924 SLT 529.

915. Contract terms requiring notification of double insurance. A term in the policy may declare it to be void should the insured take out another policy in respect of the same interest and risk[1]. Where the policy provides that it will be void unless the insurer gives his written consent to the second policy, then this must be done if the first policy is to remain valid[2]. Where a clause requires notification to be made but does not specify any time within which this must be done, notification should be given within a reasonable time[3]. A brief and unintentional period of overlap between two policies will not affect the first insurance[4].

A problem may arise where both the first and the second policies provide that notification must be given of other insurances. Strictly speaking, both insurers will be entitled to avoid the contracts made with them if the insured does not comply with this requirement[5]. The burden of proving that there is truly double insurance rests upon the insurer who so alleges[6] and may not be an easy one to discharge. Where an insured, under a policy requiring notice of other insurances, subsequently obtained cover under a cover note requiring the same notice, it was held that the cover note was automatically void and the first policy remained valid. This was said to be so because the insured had failed to intimate the first policy to the second insurer; consequently there was no other insurance to be notified to the first insurer[7]. Where the first policy requires notice of other insurances made subsequently, it has been held that where the second policy expressly declared that cover would not commence until receipt of the first premium, and no premium was ever paid, the second insurance was never effective and did not need to be disclosed[8]. It may be conjectured that where for any reason the second policy is void, then failure to notify the first insurer of its existence will not invalidate the earlier insurance. It would follow from this, however, that where the second insurance is merely voidable, failure to notify the first insurer in the required manner would entitle him to treat the contract as repudiated.

1 Re Marshall and Scottish Employers' Liability and General Insurance Co Ltd (1901) 85 LT 757.
2 Australian Agricultural Co v Saunders (1875) LR 10 CP 668, Ex Ch.
3 O'Flynn v Equitable Fire Insurance and Trust Co and Commercial Assurance Co (1866) 1 Roscoe's Rep 372 (Cape SC); Commercial Union Assurance Co v Temple (1898) 29 SCR 206 (Can SC).
4 Australian Agricultural Co v Saunders (1875) LR 10 CP 668, Ex Ch.
5 E J MacGillivray and M Parkington Insurance Law (8th edn, 1988) para 1716–1717.
6 Jenkins v Deane (1933) 47 Ll L R 342.
7 Steadfast Insurance Co Ltd v F and B Trading Co Pty Ltd (1972) 46 ALJR 10 (Aust HC).
8 Equitable Fire and Accident Office Ltd v Ching Wo Hong [1907] AC 96, PC.

916–1000. Contract terms or limiting liability in cases of double insurance. Contract terms excluding or limiting liability where there is double insurance should not be confused with terms requiring notification of double insurance. The latter do not normally rule out double insurance but make its existence contingent on disclosure of the other contract. The former can exclude liability completely or limit the insurer's liability to a proportion of the loss[1].

Where there is double insurance and one policy excludes liability but the other does not, there should not be a problem. The insured will be entitled to claim under the policy which does not provide for the double insurance situation. Where both policies exclude or limit liability in the event of double insurance, each term cancels out the other[2]. It is clear that the courts will 'try to avoid the absurdity and injustice of holding that a person who has paid premiums for cover by two insurers should be left without insurance cover because each insurer has excluded liability for the risk against which the other has indemnified him'[3].

1 Complete exclusion of liability will follow from a term of this sort: 'There shall be no liability hereunder in respect of any claim for which the insured are entitled to any indemnity under any other policy.' See J Birds Modern Insurance Law (1988) p 265. Proportionate compensation only will follow from a term of this sort: 'If at the time of any claim there shall be any other insurance

covering the same risk or any part thereof, the Company shall not be liable for more than its rateable proportion thereof.' See E J MacGillivray and M Parkington *Insurance Law* (8th edn, 1988) para 1722.

2 *Weddell v Road Transport and General Insurance Co Ltd* [1932] 2 KB 563; *Steelclad Ltd v Iron Trades Mutual Insurance Co Ltd* 1984 SC 71, 1984 SLT 304, following the approach in *Weddell*.

3 *National Employers Mutual General Insurance Association Ltd v Haydon* [1980] 2 Lloyd's Rep 149, CA.

INTEREST

	PARA
1. INTRODUCTION	1001
2. INTEREST DUE BY CONTRACTUAL STIPULATION	1002
3. WRONGFUL WITHHOLDING OF SUMS DUE	1012
4. INTEREST ON TRUST AND EXECUTRY FUNDS	1022
5. INTEREST ON DAMAGES AND DECREES	1032
6. INTEREST ON ARBITRATION AWARDS	1035
7. INTEREST ON TRIBUNAL AWARDS	1036
8. RATE OF INTEREST	1037
9. COMPOUND INTEREST	1038

The General Editors acknowledge with warm appreciation materials and advice received from Mr T Gordon Coutts QC, and assistance on particular topics from the Lord Chancellor, Lord Mackay of Clashfern, Professor John Murray QC, and Ms Sandra Eden ATII. Nicolas Lockhart expresses his appreciation for assistance from Dr H L MacQueen, Mr Niall Whitty, Mr James Cormack, and Ms Gail Ferguson.

1. INTRODUCTION

1001. Background and general principles. The crave for interest is one of the most common claims to come before the civil courts. Since the legalisation of usury following the Reformation, interest has played an increasingly import-ant role as part of our credit economy. Interest is essentially a sum representing compensation paid by a debtor to a creditor for the use of the latter's money[1]. The claim can arise across a broad spectrum of civil actions, being potentially exigible wherever one party demands payment of money from another. The crave for interest will arise almost exclusively as a claim ancillary to and dependent upon a claim for another principal sum. The pursuer is seeking interest on a particular sum for a period when the defender enjoyed the use of it: the interest claim is parasitic upon this claim for the principal[2]. If the defender was not using money belonging and owing to the pursuer, no interest is due[3].

The situations in which interest has been awarded are extensive. Interest has been held due where it is expressly provided for by contract[4]; it has been awarded on sums due on a *quantum meruit* basis[5]; it is generally due as an implied term of a loan[6]; interest may also be due on accounts rendered by tradesmen or professionals[7]. The courts are also empowered under various statutes to award interest: for instance, it may be due by statute on damages[8].

It is usually said that interest is due either *ex lege, ex pacto* or *ex mora*[9], that is, respectively, by operation of a rule of law, or by application of contract terms, or as a result of delayed payment of sums due. This tripartite classification enjoys the merit of being apparently simple, and it undoubtedly embraces every situation in which interest may be due.

The inclusion of interest due *ex mora* as an independent ground of obligation is misleading. The entitlement to interest *ex mora* and the development of the rules associated with it have taken place under the aegis of the common law[10]. Interest *ex mora* should, therefore, properly be regarded as an aspect of interest *ex lege*, and not as an independent ground of claim.

Therefore a debtor may be obliged to pay interest:

(1) by virtue of the general law, whether by statute or at common law (that is, interest due *ex lege*), or

(2) as a result of a voluntary engagement, undertaken either expressly or impliedly (that is, interest due *ex pacto*).

Yet even this general categorisation is somewhat trite and of little real assistance in establishing if a debtor is due to pay interest. It amounts to no more than saying this type of debt, as with all other debts, may arise under the general law or by agreement. It gives no indication of the grounds on which interest may actually be claimed, or the rate of interest which may be awarded, or from whence the interest runs.

Although the courts have often referred to this classification in general terms[11] as being the grounds on which interest may be awarded, the cases reveal that a more efficacious sub-categorisation has evolved. Thus, interest may be due:

(a) by an express or implied contractual stipulation for it; or

(b) as a result of the wrongful withholding of a sum, payment of which is due; or

(c) on sums payable in satisfaction of legal rights in succession; or

(d) on trust funds; or

(e) by the operation of a statute.

Generally, a claim for interest will succeed only if it can be brought within the rules of one of these categories. Though not always free from anomaly, these categories are of assistance in that they indicate with greater clarity the situations in which a claim will be successful.

Although the claim is extremely commonplace, uncertainty is still often expressed as to whether, and if so at what rate, and from what date, interest may be awarded. The assertion by Lord Craighill in *Blair's Trustees v Payne* that 'Nothing can be conceived less amenable to a settled general principle than our law upon a creditor's right to interest'[12] continues to hold credence, influencing the belief that there are few, if any, rules or principles in this area of the law. Over one hundred years after *Blair's Trustees,* in *Shetland Islands Council v BP Petroleum Development Ltd,* Lord Cullen, referring to Lord Craighill's remarks, echoed his sentiments when he said: 'In this field it is somewhat hazardous to make any general statement'[13]. It would be easy to conclude from such remarks that there are indeed no principles or rules which guide the courts where interest is claimed. Most commentaries on interest seem to accept this view, deducing from the cases little more than an enumeration of situations where interest has been held due[14]. However, these views now provide a misleading impression of the law. Although Lord Craighill may have been accurate in so far as he intended to say that there is no *single* principle or rule which governs *every* claim for interest, it is possible to discern in the cases identifiable categories of claim, and rules pertaining thereto. Although the categories and rules may undergo further evolution, and are not always logical, they are nonetheless rules. As Lord Caplan has said:

'The rules of Scots law relating to entitlement to interest are not always easy to explicate because decisions which were based on pragmatic considerations are sometimes difficult to reconcile with principle. However, in general it is now fairly clear what the rules are'[15].

The application of these rules indicates not only if interest will be due, but also dictates from when it runs and the rate at which it runs. Much of the confusion surrounding the claim for interest is resolved by these rules, and the cases become considerably more predictable.

1 See eg Erskine *Institute* III,3,75.
2 Erskine *Institute* III,3,82, notes an obligation for interest 'cannot subsist without a principal to which the interest corresponds . . .'. Bell *Commentaries* I,690, also deals with interest as a claim of an 'accessory nature'.
3 In the case of breach of trust, it suffices that the defender was misusing in an ultra vires manner trust funds in which the pursuer had a beneficial interest, even though the defender was not using the money for his own purposes: see eg *Boyd v Greig* 1913 1 SLT 398, OH.
4 *Bank of Scotland v Davis* 1982 SLT 20.
5 *Keir Ltd v East of Scotland Water Board* 1976 SLT (Notes) 72, OH.
6 *Garthland's Trustees v M'Dowall*, 26 May 1820 FC.
7 *Somervell's Trustee v Edinburgh Life Assurance Co* 1911 SC 1069, 1911 2 SLT 87.
8 Interest on Damages (Scotland) Acts 1958 (c 61) and 1971 (c 31): see para 1032 below.
9 Eg *Blair's Trustees v Payne* (1884) 12 R 104 at 109, per Lord Fraser. This classification derives from Bell I,690 ff, and Erskine *Principles* III,1,76 ff.
10 The modern rules on interest *ex mora* have developed from *Carmichael v Caledonian Rly Co* (1870) 8 M (HL) 119, and are discussed in paras 1012 ff below as 'wrongful withholding' of money.
11 Eg *Blair's Trustees v Payne* (1884) 12 R 104 at 109, per Lord Fraser.
12 (1884) 12 R 104 at 108.
13 *Shetland Islands Council v BP Petroleum Development Ltd* 1989 SCLR 48, 1990 SLT 82 at 97, OH.
14 D M Walker *The Law of Civil Remedies in Scotland* (1974) ch 23 (pp 350 ff), provides an extensive list of situations where interest has been held due, and W W McBryde *The Law of Contract in Scotland* (1987) para 20-108 ff lists situations where interest runs from a particular date. Neither author attempts to expound guiding rules or principles.
15 *Robertson Construction Co (Denny) Ltd v Taylor* 1990 SCLR 304 at 306, 1990 SLT 698 at 700, OH.

2. INTEREST DUE BY CONTRACTUAL STIPULATION

1002. Interest due by express contract. As a matter of basic contract principle, an agreement to pay interest on a particular sum will be enforced by the courts[1]. However, this is subject to statutory and common law rules limiting the rate at which interest may be charged[2]. The terms of the stipulation agreed must, however, be sufficiently clear and precise to enable enforcement[3]. The clause should include provisions on:
(1) the date from which, and the period during which, interest is to run;
(2) the rate at which interest is to be charged, and whether the rate is to be fixed or fluctuating;
(3) the method of calculating the principal sum on which interest is to run; and
(4) whether the interest is to be compounded with the principal; if so, this must be expressly provided for, with the period of compounding stipulated[4].
   If a creditor wishes to ensure that he has a right to interest on a principal sum from the time payment of the sum becomes due, then he must make express provision for the payment of that interest. Generally, where there is no express provision for interest, the mere non-timeous payment of sums due gives no right to interest on the debt in the absence of wrongful withholding of the sum. The application of the rules on wrongful withholding, coupled with the court's reluctance to award interest as damages for breach of contract, make it unwise for a creditor to rely on a claim for interest from the time payment fell due being successful without express stipulation for that interest[5].
   Express stipulations for interest are particularly common in the case of bank and building society loans. However, interest on loans is generally implied,

though this is usually at the legal rate[6]. The benefit of an express stipulation for interest in that case, therefore, lies in the creditor obtaining a more favourable rate; he may also provide for the compounding of the interest with the principal.

1 *Bank of Scotland v Davis* 1982 SLT 20.
2 For statutory rules, see eg the Consumer Credit Act 1974 (c 39), s 139. Under the common law, a stipulation to pay interest in the event of a breach of contract may be a 'penalty' clause: *Dunlop Pneumatic Tyre Co Ltd v New Garage and Motor Co Ltd* [1915] AC 79, HL. See also W W McBryde *The Law of Contract in Scotland* (1987) para 20-124.
3 *Royal Bank of Scotland plc v Geddes* 1983 SLT (Sh Ct) 32.
4 Compound interest is discussed more fully in para 1038 below.
5 *Hunter v Livingston Development Corpn* 1984 SLT 10, OH, illustrates the problems faced by creditors in the absence of an express stipulation for interest. Both wrongful withholding and interest as damages are discussed fully in paras 1012 ff and 1018 ff below.
6 See para 1008 below.

1003. Contract rate or legal rate after decree has been awarded? For some time there was doubt as to whether after decree for payment had been granted the court was entitled to ordain the defender to pay interest at the legal rate until payment if this rate was different from the contract rate, or whether it was obliged to ordain payment at the contractual rate[1]. In both *Avco Financial Services Ltd v McQuire*[2] and *Bank of Scotland v Bruce*[3] the practice of allowing only the legal rate of interest from the date of the decree until payment was described as being 'invariable'. However, in *Bank of Scotland v Davis*[4] the Second Division, recognising that the decree for payment was enforcing the parties' contract, held that as a matter of principle the court could not simultaneously alter the contract terms as to the rate of interest. Thus, where a particular rate of interest is stipulated, that rate cannot be varied or substituted by the decree for payment of the principal sum.

1 For a discussion of this issue, see R Black *An Introduction to Written Pleading* (1982) p 10 and S A Bennett 'Bank Debts: A Matter of Interest' 1983 SLT (News) 85.
2 *Avco Financial Services Ltd v McQuire* 1976 SLT (Sh Ct) 33, per Sheriff Paterson.
3 *Bank of Scotland v Bruce* 1968 SLT (Sh Ct) 58, per Sheriff Murray.
4 *Bank of Scotland v Davis* 1982 SLT 20.

1004. Fluctuating rates of interest. Where the rate of interest which is stipulated is not fixed, but is fluctuating, are the terms of the agreement sufficiently precise to be enforced? Several cases have come before the sheriff courts where interest has been craved pursuant to contract terms stipulating for interest to be paid at a fluctuating rate. Thus, in *Bank of Scotland v Logie* interest was craved 'at five per centum over the pursuers' base rate from time to time from 20th January 1986 until payment'[1]. Doubts had been cast on the competency of such a crave by Sheriff Nicholson in *Royal Bank of Scotland plc v Geddes*[2]. The sheriff's concerns were that such a crave lacked sufficient precision and specificity to be enforced. In *Logie* Sheriff Principal Bell considered these objections, but concluded that since the bank's fluctuating base rate is 'immediately verifiable', and since the specified rate is fixed above this base rate, it is 'sufficiently precise as to leave the defender in no doubt as to the obligation she has to discharge'[3]. The crave for a fluctuating rate until payment therefore appears to be competent, though it is open to question how a decree framed in such terms could be extracted.

1 *Bank of Scotland v Logie* 1986 SLT (Sh Ct) 47.
2 *Royal Bank of Scotland plc v Geddes* 1983 SLT (Sh Ct) 32. The crave was allowed following an amendment to it which provided for the rate to be fixed at an identifiable time.
3 *Bank of Scotland v Logie* 1986 SLT (Sh Ct) 47 at 48.

1005. Interest due by an implied contract term. The obligation to pay interest arises in some cases by implication 'from the nature of the transaction' itself, with no further justification for the claim being necessary[1]. Implied terms are generally of two types[2]:

(1) those which are implied into a specific contract on the basis of its particular facts, and

(2) those which are implied into every contract of a nominate type unless the contrary intention is manifest.

1 Bell *Commentaries* I,692. Bell collects nine examples of implied obligations to pay interest. However, his fourth and seventh examples suggest that interest is due wherever one has had use of another's money. The rules which apply today call for more than just use: without contractual stipulation interest is only due if there is wrongful withholding.

2 As to implied terms in contracts generally, see W W McBryde *The Law of Contract in Scotland* (1987) ch 6.

1006. Implication on the basis of the particular facts. To determine whether a term should be implied into a specific agreement, the courts will consider whether 'business efficacy' necessitates its insertion[1]. There is a dearth of cases where interest has been read into a particular contract, but one case which involved such an implication is *Glasgow Gas-Light Co v Barony Parochial Board of Glasgow*[2]. By contract money was paid over to the defenders, but under reservation. In an action, contemplated by the contract, for the repetition of the sums paid the pursuers craved interest on the principal from the time payment was originally made. The relevant facts giving rise to the implication were summarised by Lord President Inglis:

'. . . here the party . . . says [by contract], "I am not due you this money; I pay only under the compulsion of diligence. I intend to have it back from you, and I am going to litigate the matter for that purpose" '[3].

It was held that where money was paid under such conditions, which had been set out in a minute of agreement, 'the natural result is that interest runs'[4]. The court, therefore, implied into the agreement an obligation for the payment of interest. The interest can only be considered due on this basis as there was no express stipulation for it, and nor was there wrongful withholding from the time of payment.

It is, therefore, open to the court to conclude that in the circumstances of any given case it was intended by the parties that interest should be payable.

1 *The Moorcock* (1889) 14 PD 64, CA.
2 *Glasgow Gas-Light Co v Barony Parochial Board of Glasgow* (1868) 6 M 406.
3 (1868) 6 M 406 at 414, per Lord President Inglis.
4 (1868) 6 M 406 at 415, per Lord Deas.

1007. Implication by general law. There are a number of situations where an obligation for the payment of interest will be imported into an agreement unless a contrary intention is manifested by the parties[1]. Thus, interest is rebuttably due until payment of the principal is made:

(1) on loans, from the date of the loan[2];

(2) on the purchase price in a contract of sale where the buyer is enjoying possession of the property, from the date such possession was taken[3]; and

(3) where there is, by commercial usage, an implied period of credit in a contract, from the expiration of that period[4].

1 For examples of situations where interest is implicitly due, see Bell *Commentaries* I,692. However, as to the reservation regarding this section in *Bell,* see para 1005, note 1, above.

2 *Thomson v Geekie* (1861) 23 D 693 especially at 701, per Lord Justice-Clerk Inglis; approved in *Neilson v Stewart* 1991 SLT 523 at 527, HL, by Lord Jauncey of Tullichettle.
3 *Greenock Harbour Trustees v Glasgow and South-Western Rly Co* 1909 SC (HL) 49, 1909 2 SLT 53.
4 *Blair's Trustees v Payne* (1884) 12 R 104 at 111, 112, per Lord Fraser.

1008. Loans. In *Smellie's Executrix v Smellie,* Lord Hunter declared unequivocally:

'It is not doubtful that, as a general rule, if a loan of money is vouched by a document, then the obligation upon the debtor implies repayment, not only of what he has received on loan, but of interest during the period he has enjoyed the money'[1].

The concept of a 'loan' encompasses all 'cash advances' made to another person, or certain payments made on their behalf; it does not include business charges 'incurred where the debt arises from the provision of goods or services'[2]. The difference between 'cash advances' and 'business charges' is made clearer by considering Lord Fraser's remarks in *Blair's Trustees v Payne* where his Lordship enumerates a variety of 'cash advances' made by agents on behalf of their principals on which interest runs from the time of outlay. These included:

'... advances incurred for the repair of property, payments for premiums of assurance, payments of debts due, counsel's and accountant's fees, stamps and such like'[2].

Had these debts remained unpaid by the agent, the principal would have incurred no interest upon them[3]. They would still be 'business charges' owed to the provider of the services. However, interest is owed on the debts by the principal to the agent since the agent has not provided the service, but, by paying the debt, has made a 'cash advance' on behalf of the principal[4].

Where the agent has himself provided a service for the debt due to him by the principal, such as his professional fees, these are 'business charges' on which no interest runs.

Where a sum of money is given subject to the condition that it need be repaid only in the event of certain contingencies arising, interest cannot run unless and until these conditions are satisfied[5]. Prior to the satisfaction of the conditions, the debt is not exigible and the debtor cannot be considered to be using money owed to the creditor.

IOUs are treated in a similar way. The IOU is considered merely as an acknowledgment that a debt of some type is subsisting[6]. As Lord Justice-Clerk Macdonald noted in *Thiem's Trustees v Collie*[7], the IOU need not imply a loan; it may have been granted to close an account; it may settle a claim for damages; or it may constitute a credit facility. Repayment of the debt is not due until it is demanded. In these circumstances, the court considers that no interest is to be implied. Interest will, therefore, arise only if it can be successfully craved on one of the other specified categories, such as express stipulation for it[8] or wrongful withholding. Interest may also be implied. Thus if the terms of a particular IOU not only acknowledge indebtedness but furthermore acknowledge the receipt of money the transaction will be considered to be a loan, with interest being implied from the time the IOU was granted[9].

In implying an obligation to pay interest on loans, the courts are seeking to give effect to the presumed intention of the parties. Where it is clear that such an intention is lacking, the presumption that interest is due is rebutted. In *Christie v Matheson,* where 'the pursuer had no intention that any interest should be paid by the defender', no interest was held to be due[10].

The court will consider the circumstances of the case to see if they justify the inference that no interest was intended to be due[11]. In *Neilson v Stewart* it was said:

'As for the question of interest on a loan, the law implies that interest shall be paid although this is a presumption which is capable of being displaced by circumstances and, of course, by agreement to the contrary'[12].

Where the loan is between parties who are closely related, that relationship on its own may be sufficient to displace the implication for interest[13].

However, the mere fact that there is a close relationship between the parties may not displace the presumption for interest if other relevant circumstances indicate that interest was due from a particular time[14].

1 *Smellie's Executrix v Smellie* 1933 SC 725 at 727, 1933 SLT 623 at 624, per Lord Hunter.
2 *Blair's Trustees v Payne* (1884) 12 R 104 at 109, per Lord Fraser. For other 'cash advances', see W W McBryde *The Law of Contract in Scotland* (1987) para 20-07.
3 This would be subject to wrongful withholding of the debt.
4 It has been held that interest is not due where an agent pays judicial expenses on behalf of his principal (*Macpherson v Tytler* (1853) 15 D 706) or where he incurs outlays for printing (*Barclay v Barclay* (1850) 22 SJ 354).
5 *Forbes v Forbes* (1869) 8 M 85.
6 *Thiem's Trustees v Collie* (1899) 1 F 764, 7 SLT 4; *Winestone v Wolifson* 1954 SC 77, 1954 SLT 153.
7 *Thiem's Trustees v Collie* (1899) 1 F 764, 7 SLT 4.
8 In *Thiem's Trustees v Collie* (1899) 1 F 764, 7 SLT 4, the IOU expressly carried interest at 4 per cent, and this was awarded by the court.
9 *Haldane v Speirs* (1872) 10 M 537 at 541, per Lord President Inglis.
10 *Christie v Matheson* (1871) 10 M 9 at 10, per Lord President Inglis.
11 *Smellie's Executrix v Smellie* 1933 SC 725, 1933 SLT 623.
12 *Neilson v Stewart* 1990 SLT 346 at 350, affd 1991 SLT 523, HL.
13 1933 SC 725 at 727, 1933 SLT 623 at 624, per Lord Hunter *Smellie's Executrix v Smellie*. See also *Forbes v Forbes* (1869) 8 M 85 (loan between brothers); *Christie v Matheson* (1871) 10 M 9 (loan between brothers); *Williamson v Williamson's Trustee* 1948 SLT (Notes) 72, OH (loan from father to son).
14 *Garthland's Trustees v M'Dowall* 26 May 1820 FC; *Forbes v Forbes* (1869) 8 M 85.

1009. Contracts of sale. According to Bell, in a contract of sale:

'By implied contract, interest is due on the price or value of *any* property, to the use and benefit of which the buyer enters, to the deprivation of the seller'[1].

Thus, irrespective of the nature of the property, as either heritable or moveable, an obligation to pay interest is inferred by the general law in every contract of sale, unless of course the parties indicate a contrary intention. The rationale underlying the implication lies in principles of equity, and is stated by Erskine:

'... from whatever cause the non-payment may proceed, good conscience will not suffer the purchaser, at the same time that he enjoys the fruits of the ... property ... whereof he had bought, to enjoy also the profits or interest of the price'[2].

Although both Bell and Erskine consider that this implication applies to contracts for the sale of *any* property, the authorities cited by them only support the existence of such a term in the context of sales of heritage. There is no case in which a term implying an obligation for payment of interest has been upheld in a sale of moveables. The lack of any such authority led Sheriff Principal O'Brien in *Morton v Cameron & Co* to conclude:

'When heritable property is not involved it is my understanding that the courts have adopted a different standpoint in considering whether interest is payable. "Interest can be demanded only in virtue of a contract, express or implied, or by virtue of the principal sum of money having been wrongfully withheld, and not paid on the date when it ought to have been paid"'[3].

Just as there is no case where such an implied term has been upheld, there is also, with the exception of *Morton,* no case where it has been rejected. It cannot therefore be said that the courts have adopted any 'standpoint' on the matter, least of all one which is 'different' from that in sales of heritage. The implied term claimed by Bell to apply in sales of heritage[4] is, in any event, consistent with the so-called 'different standpoint' Sheriff Principal O'Brien identified when quoting from _Carmichael v Caledonian Rly Co_[5]: interest is due in sales of heritage by virtue of implied contract. The term is an operation of Lord Westbury's dictum in that case, and not an exception to it. Notwithstanding the decision in _Morton,_ it is still open to the courts to hold that in a contract for the sale of moveables the same implied term applies as that in contracts for the sale of heritage. The rationale for the rule is equally applicable to both types of property. Indeed, it would be difficult to justify logically the inconsistency which would arise by implication of the term in sales of heritage but not in sales of moveables — the 'good conscience' which leads Erskine and Bell to apply the rule to the seller of any property must surely still pertain to sellers of moveables.

A case which did involve interest on the purchase price of moveables was _Forrest and Barr v Henderson_[6]. Payment for a derrick crane was to be by 'a bill at four months, when the crane was proved and accepted'. The crane was not formally accepted until nearly four years after it was first used. Interest was, however, awarded by a jury from four months after the buyers actually began to use the crane. The First Division declined to disturb the award made by the jury. Only Lord President Inglis considered the matter of interest, and the grounds on which he considered it to be due are not obvious[7]. He noted that the contract did not contemplate the payment of interest on the price prior to four months after the crane had been proved and accepted, but that in the circumstances the crane was not formally accepted until some time after it was actually used. He did not consider the award made to be contrary to the contract terms, but did not actually state that interest was implied either generally or on the facts. The case may be explicable on the basis that interest was to be implied from the time it was anticipated by the parties that payment of the bill was due, because interest runs on dishonoured bills from maturity[8]. No reference was made to the rule in Erskine or Bell; there is no discussion of interest being implied into all contracts of sale. It is, therefore, stretching the decision in _Forrest and Barr_ to an unacceptable length to rely on it for such a general implication.

An opportunity to clarify the law in the sale of goods was passed over when the Sale of Goods Act 1979 was enacted. Section 49(3) merely states that the seller's right to receive payment of the price under that section is without prejudice to his rights (at common law) to receive interest thereon. The subsection would, therefore, appear to be premised upon the misconception that the common law is clear. It may also be suggested that the section presumes that a common law right to interest on the price does exist[9]. Unfortunately, the position on interest at common law in sales of goods is not as clear as section 49(3) supposes.

1 Bell _Commentaries_ I,693 (emphasis added).
2 Erskine _Institute_ III,3,79.
3 _Morton v Cameron & Co_ 1987 SLT (Sh Ct) 44 at 47, quoting from Lord Westbury in _Carmichael v Caledonian Rly Co_ (1870) 8 M (HL) 119 at 131.
4 See the text to note 1 above.
5 _Carmichael v Caledonian Rly Co_ (1870) 8 M (HL) 119.
6 _Forrest and Barr v Henderson_ (1869) 8 M 187.
7 (1869) 8 M 187 at 196, per Lord President Inglis.
8 See Bell _Commentaries_ I,692.
9 W W McBryde _The Law of Contract in Scotland_ (1987) p 487, n 45, considers that the Sale of Goods Act 1979 (c 54), s 49(3), preserves a common law right to interest and that this 'may reflect a misunderstanding of the common law'.

1010. The application of the implied term in sales of heritage. Aside from Bell there is clear authority that an offer to purchase land necessarily includes an offer of interest on the price of the subjects from the date the buyer enters possession until the price is paid[1].

Although the implication is equitable in origin, it has been held to apply even where one would have thought that its equitable foundation would allow an exception. In *Grandison's Trustees v Jardine* interest was held due on the purchase price notwithstanding that the buyer in possession was refusing to make payment because the seller was unable to confer good title[2].

The content of the term implied is such that the buyer must enjoy not only the fruits of the purchase price, but must also be in possession of the subjects. As Sheriff Kermack said in *Thomson v Vernon,* the term 'cannot be applied if [the buyer] only enjoys one-half of the equation, even if [he] has an unexercised right to the other'[3]. Thus, where the buyer is offered vacant possession but does not take it up, interest cannot run on the ground of this implied term notwithstanding failure to pay the price[4].

It remains open to the parties to reach their own agreement concerning payment of interest on the purchase price. The implied term will give way to a clear expression of intention that it should not apply. The parties may therefore stipulate for interest from the due date of payment with or without possession being taken.

1   *Spiers v Ardrossan Canal Co* (1827) 5 S 764 (NE 714); *Prestwick Cinema Co Ltd v Gardiner* 1951 SC 98, 1951 SLT 69. The rule applies to sums due in contracts of excambion: *Greenock Harbour Trustees v Glasgow and South-Western Rly Co* 1909 SC (HL) 49, 1909 2 SLT 53.

2   *Grandison's Trustees v Jardine* (1895) 22 R 925, 3 SLT 54. This decision conflicts with the contract rules on mutuality which are accepted as relevant to interest and sales of heritage in *Bowie v Semple's Executors* 1978 SLT (Sh Ct) 9. Mutuality is also discussed as a ground for withholding payment of sums due in *Farrans (Construction) Ltd v Dunfermline District Council* 1988 SCLR 272, 1988 SLT 466: see the text to para 1013, note 2, below. Why the buyer should not be entitled to withhold payment until the seller can perform one of his primary obligations is unclear. Referring to *Grandison's Trustees* in similar terms and relying also on *Farrans (Construction) Ltd,* Professor J Murray (who had sight of this title before publication) advances an analogous argument on mutuality in 'Interest on Debt' 1991 SLT (News) 305.

3   *Thomson v Vernon* 1983 SLT (Sh Ct) 17.

4   1983 SLT (Sh Ct) 17; *Bowie v Semple's Executors* 1978 SLT (Sh Ct) 9. However, if the price is wrongfully withheld, interest will run on those grounds.

1011. Implied terms as to credit.

As was noted in considering the nature of a 'loan', a distinction is drawn between 'cash advances' and 'business charges'[1], a business charge being that which arises when the debtor receives goods or services from the creditor and comes under an obligation to pay for them. Such a debt is often described as an 'open account'. Generally, the mere incidence of such a debt carries with it no obligation to pay interest while the debt remains unpaid and is not wrongfully withheld:

'. . . it is not correct to say that interest is claimable upon all debts, either from the date that the account was closed, or from the date that it was rendered'[2].

This general rule is subject to the exception that 'if there be a certain express or *implied* period of credit, interest is claimable if the debt be not paid at the end of that period'[3]. An express period of credit presents no difficulties provided the stipulation is clear[4]. However, there is more difficulty in determining the nature of any implied period of credit. An implied period of credit may arise by mercantile usage or by a prior course of dealing[5]. The implied term must import not only an obligation for payment at a certain time, but — more importantly — must oblige payment of interest from that time where the debt remains unpaid (since the mere fact of non-timeous payment of a debt does not attract an obligation of interest)[6].

A law agent has been held entitled to interest one year from the last entry in the account[7]. Similarly, where an insurance underwriter failed to make payment at the end of the established four-month period of credit, interest was held due[8]. These periods of credit, although established by usage at the time of the decisions, cannot be considered absolute, and may be changed by subsequent usage[9].

Quite separately, interest may be due upon an open account from the time when the principal sums due may be said to have been wrongfully withheld.

1 See para 1008 above.
2 *Blair's Trustees v Payne* (1884) 12 R 104 at 110, per Lord Fraser.
3 (1884) 12 R 104 at 111, per Lord Fraser (emphasis added).
4 See para 1002 above.
5 *Blair's Trustees v Payne* (1884) 12 R 104 at 108, per Lord Craighill, and at 112, per Lord Fraser.
6 *Carmichael v Caledonian Rly Co* (1870) 8 M (HL) 119.
7 *Henry v Sutherland* (1801) Mor 'Annual-Rent' App p 1; *Young v Baillie* (1830) 8 S 624.
8 *Crawford and Stark v Bertram* 15 May 1812, FC.
9 *Blair's Trustees v Payne* (1884) 12 R 104 at 111, per Lord Fraser.

3. WRONGFUL WITHHOLDING OF SUMS DUE

1012. General. Wrongful withholding operates as a residual category under which a creditor may accrue a right to interest. While not all debts will carry an express or implied right to interest by agreement, every debt may, on the facts of the case, be wrongfully withheld, thereby conferring a right of interest. Although wrongful withholding is the residual of the categories conferring a right to interest, it is frequently the only category under which the creditor can claim interest[1]. The rules governing its application are therefore extremely significant. These rules determine not only whether a creditor is entitled to interest, but also, if he is so entitled, from when it runs. If a creditor proves that the principal sum has been wrongfully withheld, interest will run from the date the wrongful withholding commenced.

Lord Westbury's classic statement of the law in *Carmichael v Caledonian Railway Co* identifies the principle of wrongful withholding as a residual category in relation to interest due under contract:

'Interest can be demanded only in virtue of a contract, express or implied, or by virtue of the principal sum of money having been wrongfully withheld and not paid on the day when it *ought* to have been paid'[2].

As Lord Fraser later emphasised in *Blair's Trustees v Payne*:

'The mere fact . . . of delay in payment after payment could have been, or has been, demanded, will not necessarily ground a claim for interest . . . [The money] must be "wrongfully withheld"'[3].

The rules on wrongful withholding have been held to apply to debts due under contract[4]; debts due under statute[5]; sums due *quantum meruit*[6]; sums due as reasonable rent for occupation of heritable subjects[7]; and sums liable to be paid under the principle *causa data causa non secuta*[8]. The rules have allowed interest to be paid on sums from a time prior to their being liquidated by process[9].

1 See eg *Hunter v Livingston Development Corpn* 1984 SLT 10, OH.
2 *Carmichael v Caledonian Rly Co* (1870) 8 M (HL) 119 at 131, per Lord Westbury (emphasis added). Lord Westbury was not considering the liability for interest which arises under statute or which may fall on trustees, and the 'only' must be considered in this context. This dictum has been cited approvingly on numerous occasions and is accepted as stating the principle of Scots law in this area; see eg *Blair's Trustees v Payne* (1884) 12 R 104 at 110, per Lord Fraser; *F W Green & Co Ltd v Brown and Gracie Ltd* 1960 SLT (Notes) 43 at 44, HL, per Lord Keith; *Dean Warwick Ltd v Borthwick* 1983 SLT 533 at 535, per Lord Cameron; *Farrans (Construction) Ltd v Dunfermline*

District Council 1988 SCLR 272 at 277, 1988 SLT 466 at 470, per Lord Justice-Clerk Ross; *Hunter v Livingston Development Corpn* 1984 SLT 10 at 12, 13, OH, per Lord Cowie.

3 *Blair's Trustees v Payne* (1884) 12 R 104 at 110.
4 *Somervell's Trustee v Edinburgh Life Assurance Co* 1911 SC 1069, 1911 2 SLT 87.
5 *Drummond v Law Society of Scotland* 1980 SC 175, OH.
6 *Keir Ltd v East of Scotland Water Board* 1976 SLT (Notes) 72, OH.
7 *HMV Fields Properties Ltd v Skirt 'n' Slack Centre of London Ltd* 1987 SLT 2, OH.
8 *Connelly v Simpson* 1991 SCLR 295, OH, per Lord Cowie. It should be noted that the award of interest was made without discussion of the principles appropriate to either such claims in unjust enrichment actions generally or such claims under this particular principle of unjust enrichment. In the case of repetition of such sums paid in error — the *condictio indebiti* — there is also doubt as to the rules appropriate to an award of interest. In *Countess of Cromertie v Lord Advocate* (1871) 9 M 988, the First Division (Lord Deas dissenting) awarded interest according to the rules on wrongful withholding. However, the Lord Ordinary (Gifford) (with whom Lord Deas agreed) allowed interest from the time of the mistaken payment according to the view that full restitution required restoration of all profit and advantage which had accrued to the possessor. This view is also apparently shared by Lord Kyllachy in *Gwydyr v Lord Advocate* (1894) 2 SLT 280, OH. In *Duncan, Galloway & Co Ltd v Duncan, Falconer & Co* 1913 SC 265, 1912 2 SLT 420, interest was also allowed on sums paid in error from the time of payment. In this case the Lord Ordinary (Hunter), with whom the Second Division generally agreed, allowed interest on the sum by analogy with loan: the sum therefore carried interest from the time of payment. A claim for interest in a restitution action may be met by the defence of bona fide perception and consumption (More *Notes to Stair's Institutions* (5th Edn), Note F, para 7). This defence may, however, not apply to restitution of money. Erskine was clear that it did (Erskine *Institutes* II, 1, 26); there is though, a line of cases which holds that the defence does not apply to money: see eg *Haldane v Ogilvy* (1871) 10 M 62.
9 In *Dean Warwick Ltd v Borthwick* 1983 SLT 533, interest was allowed from citation on a decree where the sum awarded was different from that craved. The rule in *Dean Warwick* might be thought to be in conflict with observations made by Lord Keith in *F W Green & Co Ltd v Brown and Gracie Ltd* 1960 SLT (Notes) 43 at 44, HL (and with the decision in *R and J Dempster Ltd v Motherwell Bridge and Engineering Co Ltd* 1964 SC 308, 1964 SLT 353), that interest could not run on a sum prior to quantification. The critical distinction between the cases is that *F W Green* was an application of the former common law rules on interest on damages, (now covered by statute: see para 1032 ff) whereas *Dean Warwick* concerned payment of a contract debt with interest thereon.

1013. When can wrongful withholding arise? A sum will only be held to have been wrongfully withheld where the debtor's payment of the sum was in fact due, as:

> '. . . money cannot be regarded as having been wrongfully withheld if the debtor has been under no legal obligation to make payment of the money'[1].

Thus, if the time for payment has not passed, there can be no withholding which will be regarded as wrongful. The debtor may also have justifiable grounds for withholding payment other than that the debt was not due, for instance:

> '[If] the creditor has not been performing his obligations under contract, then in my opinion the debtor cannot at the same time be held to have been withholding the money wrongfully'[2].

This is clear recognition of the relevance of the rules regarding mutuality of contract stipulations: where the creditor is failing to fulfil his obligations the debtor has a right to retain payment pending such fulfilment and that retention is not, in those circumstances, wrongful. However, where the debtor disputes the creditor's right to receive payment, and does not merely seek temporarily to withhold payment under mutuality principles, he does not have a justifiable ground for withholding payment if the sum is later found to be due[3]. To avoid the charge of wrongfully withholding the sum, the debtor could agree to make payment on the condition that, if as a result of litigation it is held that no sum was due, repetition will be made to the debtor with interest thereon from the time the disputed payment was made[4]. The debtor will then incur no liability whatsoever for interest, but will himself receive the fruits of his money if he is not found liable to pay. Alternatively, the debtor might consign the disputed money in joint names[5].

1 *Farrans (Construction) Ltd v Dunfermline District Council* 1988 SCLR 272 at 278, 1988 SLT 466 at 470, per Lord Justice-Clerk Ross.
2 1988 SCLR 272 at 278, 1988 SLT 466 at 471, per Lord Justice-Clerk Ross. See also *Bowie v Semple's Executors* 1978 SLT (Sh Ct) 9.
3 *Dean Warwick Ltd v Borthwick* 1983 SLT 533; *Trans Barwil Agencies (UK) Ltd v John S Braid & Co Ltd* 1989 SCLR 647, 1990 SLT 182, OH.
4 Cf *Glasgow Gas-Light Co v Barony Parochial Board of Glasgow* (1868) 6 M 406: see para 1006 above.
5 *Prestwick Cinema Co Ltd v Gardiner* 1945 SC 645, 1950 SLT 13, OH; affd 1951 SC 98, 1951 SLT 69.

1014. What constitutes wrongful withholding? Whether a debt has been wrongfully withheld depends upon all the circumstances of the case[1]. In order for a debt to be regarded as having been withheld wrongfully the debtor must have been aware that payment by him was due:

> 'A demand for payment more or less urgent, seems to me, apart from contract, to be a condition-precedent to liability for interest'[2].

Thus, a court will not regard failure to pay as wrongful until such time as the debtor knew, or could at least be taken to know, that the principal was due.

Generally failure to pay will be regarded as wrongful from the time payment ought to have been made[3]. In the usual case the court considers that payment of the principal ought to have been made when there is a formal judicial demand for that sum.

Indeed it has even been suggested that the rule that interest runs on unpaid debts from the time of formal judicial demand is a rule 'which does not admit of modification'[4]. There is, however, clear authority which supports an award of interest at common law from a time other than that of judicial demand. Thus, in *Somervell's Trustee,* Lord Salvesen, following Lord Fraser's opinion in *Blair's Trustees v Payne*[5], opined:

> 'I think it is a wholesome general rule that interest shall not be allowed on open accounts until there has been either a judicial demand made for payment or an intimation that after a certain date interest will be charged on the account if not paid by that date'[6].

Therefore, certainly in the case of 'open accounts', the formal demand necessary to enable interest to run may be a demand by the creditor for payment at a particular time coupled with an intimation that interest will be charged from that time until payment is tendered.

Furthermore it may be suggested that interest may be awarded from a time independent of either of the formal demands described above, if it can be said that the debtor ought to have rendered payment at such a different time.

1 *M'Phail v Lothian Regional Council* 1981 SLT 173 at 176, OH, per Lord Grieve (not reported on this point in 1981 SC 119).
2 *Blair's Trustees v Payne* (1884) 12 R 104 at 108, per Lord Craighill. The exception made in this dictum to 'contract' cases is ambiguous, and it is not clear exactly what Lord Craighill meant by the reference. He may have meant a demand for payment was unnecessary either where there was a contractually agreed time for payment, or where there was a stipulation for the payment of interest. The reference may also mean that where there is knowledge acquired by contract that payment ought to be made a demand is unnecessary: see the text at para 1017, note 2.
3 See para 1012, text to note 2, above.
4 *Dean Warwick Ltd v Borthwick* 1983 SLT 533 at 535, per Lord Cameron.
5 *Blair's Trustee v Payne* (1884) 12 R 104 at 112.
6 *Somervell's Trustee v Edinburgh Life Assurance Co* 1911 SC 1069 at 1071, 1911 2 SLT 87 at 88. For similar statements, see also *Bunten v Hart* (1902) 9 SLT 476, OH, per Lord Kyllachy; and *Hunter v*

Livingston Development Corpn 1984 SLT 10 at 13, OH, per Lord Cowie. In Lord Fraser's opinion in *Blair's Trustees v Payne* (1884) 12 R 104 at 112, the demand for payment and the intimation that interest would be charged had to be in writing.

1015. Judicial demand. Lord Cameron explained in *Dean Warwick Ltd v Borthwick* that from the time of the judicial demand the creditor was wrongfully deprived of his money and the debtor was wrongfully enjoying the use of it[1]. The deprivation is wrongful because by reason of the demand the party has been called upon to pay and thereafter ought to pay[2].

Generally, the date of judicial demand will be the date of the defender's original citation in the action which calls for payment of the principal: '. . . a [judicial] demand is constituted by citation in [judicial] process'[3]. Where the citation in the original summons contains no conclusion for payment of the principal on which interest is craved, interest will not run from that date. In that situation the citation contains no judicial demand for payment, and so there can be no wrongful withholding. In *H M V Fields Properties Ltd v Skirt 'n' Slack Centre of London Ltd*[4] it was held that there was a judicial demand only when a claim for payment of the principal was incorporated in the record. Interest could run only from the date of that amendment to the record being made.

1 *Dean Warwick Ltd v Borthwick* 1983 SLT 533 at 535.
2 *Napier v Gordon* (1831) 5 W & S 745, HL.
3 *Dean Warwick Ltd v Borthwick* 1983 SLT 533 at 535.
4 *H M V Fields Properties Ltd v Skirt 'n' Slack Centre of London Ltd* 1987 SLT 2 at 6, OH.

1016. Intimation to debtor. It was noted above that in the case of 'open accounts' a court may ordain the debtor to pay interest from the time when he is called upon, in writing by the creditor, to settle the account, provided that the demand for payment contains an intimation that interest will be charged on the unpaid balance from the time payment is demanded until the account is settled[1]. This rule is subject to equitable exception in special circumstances[2]. It is not immediately clear why this rule should operate solely in the context of open accounts; furthermore the operation of the rule exclusively in the context of open accounts may itself be objectionable.

An open account 'is an "account current", not signed, not settled; an open or current account is used in opposition to a fitted or settled account'[3].

The case of *Linlithgow Oil Co Liquidators v North British Rly Co*[4] provides an illustration of the manner in which the rule laid down by Lord Fraser in *Blair's Trustees*[5] operates. The case involved a claim for payment of sums due to account under contract, with interest being claimed on the principal. Under the agreement in question accounts were rendered monthly and it was expected payments would also be made on a monthly basis. There was no contractual stipulation for the payment of interest. However, the creditor, by letter, made a demand for payment to account and intimated that from a stipulated date interest at 4 per cent would be charged on the large unpaid balance. In these circumstances Lord Low considered interest to be due at the specified rate from the stipulated date. He considered the principle applicable to be 'similar'[6] to contractual stipulation for interest. In addition his Lordship upheld the creditor's right to interest on unpaid future accounts — presumably debts, not yet extant, for services to be rendered. The basis of Lord Low's decision seems to have been that since the debtor had failed to make payment when he ought to have paid, interest was to be allowed[7]. This is an expression of the rule on wrongful withholding: interest runs from the time the debtor failed to pay when he ought to have paid[8].

The principal objection to this rule is that it amounts to a unilateral variation of the terms of the contract. In the *Linlithgow Oil Co* case there was no contractual right to interest. The creditor, by written intimation that interest would be charged, acquired a right to interest which the debtor never consented to[9]. Furthermore the intimation was also held to vary the agreement as to future debts.

This objection may, on the one hand, be met since the rule may be said to be an aspect of the wrongful withholding principle. There is a formal demand for payment and the debtor ought to pay when payment is demanded. This was apparently the basis of Lord Low's decision in the *Linlithgow Oil Co* case, and this is consistent with Lord Westbury's *locus classicus* dictum[10]. The rule is merely a common law rule operating in the context of contractual agreements, but not modifying them, in the same way as a formal judicial demand operates.

This, however, raises a second objection. If the rule is a general rule of the common law why does it apply exclusively to open accounts and not to unpaid debts generally? The wrongful withholding principle does, after all, apply to all unpaid debts. There are no grounds for distinguishing open accounts from other debts. In the *Linlithgow Oil Co* case the account was already overdue. It cannot be suggested therefore that it is the fact that an open account has no time for payment which distinguishes these debts. Indeed the fact that the debt is not fitted or settled makes it more uncertain than other debts, and it may be argued presents a weaker case for favourable treatment to the creditor. By restricting the scope of the rule to open accounts its generality as a principle of the common law is undermined, and it appears rather to be a unilateral variation of a particular type of bargain.

The underlying principle — that the debtor ought to pay following a formal demand — as an instance of wrongful withholding is valid. The principle should, however, apply to all unpaid debts.

1 See para 1014, text to note 6, above.
2 *Somervell's Trustee v Edinburgh Life Assurance Co* 1911 SC 1069 at 1071, 1072, 1911 2 SLT 87 at 89, per Lord Salvesen and Lord Mackenzie.
3 *Commercial Bank of Scotland v Rhind* (1860) 3 Macq 643 at 650, HL, per Lord Campbell.
4 *Linlithgow Oil Co Liquidators v North British Rly Co* (1904) 12 SLT 421, OH.
5 *Blair's Trustees v Payne* (1884) 12 R 104 at 112, per Lord Fraser.
6 *Linlithgow Oil Co Liquidators v North British Rly Co* (1904) 12 SLT 421 at 422, OH, per Lord Low.
7 (1904) 12 SLT 421 at 423, OH, per Lord Low.
8 *Carmichael v Caledonian Rly Co* (1870) 8 M (HL) 119 at 131, per Lord Westbury. For the appropriate dictum, see para 1012, text to note 2, above.
9 By upholding the creditor's stipulation as to the rate of interest, Lord Low appears, perhaps inadvertently, to be to an even greater extent enforcing terms laid down by one party only. It may be that this was because the stipulated rate (4 per cent) was lower than the legal rate of the time (5 per cent). If a creditor should demand a rate in excess of the legal rate, the courts should be wary of upholding the demanded rate: where money is wrongfully withheld the legal rate applies.
10 See para 1012, text to note 2, above.

1017. Wrongful withholding as an equitable principle. From the time the debtor ought to have rendered payment he is regarded as wrongfully withholding the debt[1]. While this time will usually be the time of formal judicial demand, or, in the case of an open account, the time of intimation to the debtor that interest will be charged, it is consistent with both authority and principle that the time of wrongful withholding is not absolutely fixed by reference to one or other of these times. Determining when the debtor ought to pay is truly a question of circumstance, decided according to the facts of the case.

In *Trans Barwil Agencies (UK) Ltd v John S Braid & Co Ltd*[2] the pursuers mistakenly invoiced the defenders for sums less than the defenders' true liability to them. The defenders initially drew the pursuers' attention to the error, but the pursuers insisted the invoices were correct. The pursuers later discovered their error and sought payment of the shortfall with interest. An action was first raised in England, but because of jurisdictional difficulties the action failed, and had to be raised before the Scottish courts. Placing great stress on the relationship of the parties as principal (pursuers) and agent (defenders), and the fact that this gave rise to obligations *uberrimae fidei,* Lord McCluskey allowed interest on the principal sum from the time of judicial demand in England. It was conceded at the bar that it was competent to award interest from a time earlier than that of formal judicial demand. Lord McCluskey considered that the appropriate time from when interest should run was to be determined by looking at all the circumstances and applying equitable principles[3]. It may be suggested that this is exactly what is required in every case of wrongful withholding[4]. Determining when the debtor ought to pay is always a question of equity dependent upon the facts of the case. Lord McCluskey concluded that the sum was wrongfully withheld from the time of judicial demand in England, even though this demand was not a judicial demand of the appropriate forum (that is, the Scottish court). The right to interest from that time was therefore not dependent upon the demand being strictly judicial, but rather arose because the demand was sufficiently formal for the court to conclude that in the circumstances, the debtor ought to have appreciated that payment should be made[5].

This case illustrates well the equitable basis of the principle of wrongful withholding. It demonstrates that the time from when it may be said that the debtor ought to have paid is wholly dependent upon the circumstances of the case. While this time will generally be the time of judicial demand in the successful action, it need not invariably be so. Furthermore it may even be that so long as the debtor knew he ought to make payment a formal demand is unnecessary to ground a claim for interest. In Lord Craighill's dictum on demands for payment there is an ambiguous exception made to the requirement for a demand in cases of contract[6]. Lord Craighill may have meant that where by contractual relationship the debtor knew he ought to pay at a particular time a further demand is unnecessary: the debt may be regarded as wrongfully withheld by virtue of knowledge acquired through the contract[7].

Although it will be rare for the time of wrongful withholding to be other than the time of judicial demand, it is certainly the case that the principle underpinning wrongful withholding will admit such variation in appropriate circumstances. As Lord Westbury states in *Carmichael v Caledonian Railway Co,* wrongful withholding arises when a debt is 'not paid on the day when it ought to have been paid'[8]. This may well be a time other than judicial demand.

---

1 *Carmichael v Caledonian Rly Co* (1870) 8 M (HL) 119 at 131, per Lord Westbury. For the appropriate dictum, see para 1012, text to note 2, above, and see the cases there cited. For dicta which relate the time of wrongful withholding to the time when the debtor ought to have paid, see also *Napier v Gordon* (1831) 5 W & S 745 at 758, HL, per Lord Brougham; *Linlithgow Oil Co Liquidators v North British Rly Co* (1904) 12 SLT 421, OH.
2 *Trans Barwil Agencies (UK) Ltd v John S Braid & Co Ltd* 1989 SCLR 647, 1990 SLT 182, OH.
3 1989 SCLR 647 at 650, 1990 SLT 182 at 185, OH.
4 See para 1014, text to note 2, and para 1016, text to note 2, above.
5 *Trans Barwil Agencies (UK) Ltd v John S Braid & Co Ltd* 1989 SCLR 647 at 651, 1990 SLT 182 at 186, OH.
6 See para 1014, text to note 2, above.
7 See further para 1020 below.
8 *Carmichael v Caledonian Rly Co* (1870) 8 M (HL) 119 at 131.

1018. Wrongful withholding and interest as damages for breach of contract. Bell considered the 'most obvious ground of a claim for interest' to be in the case of breach of contract[1]. He felt confident enough to state:

'. . . the law of Scotland has been settled, that breach of contract . . . raises this claim [for interest] without any inquiry into actual damage, and estimating all losses arising from this cause by the same rule, viz. according to the legal rate of interest'[2].

The inevitable consequence of this rule is that whenever there is breach of contract by non-timeous payment of sums due, interest will run from the time payment should have been made:

'In the ordinary case the damage due for delay in payment of money is nothing but interest'[3].

It is difficult to reconcile these rules with those on wrongful withholding, which require more than mere non-payment of sums due. On the one hand, it is said, a delay in payment gives a right to interest as damages, whereas on the other, it is said, the delay must be wrongful before interest is due. Lord Fraser recognising these incompatibilities was categoric in his assertion of the correct position:

'It is sometimes said that interest is due as damages, for the undue detention of money, when a debt clearly ascertained remains unpaid . . . This is plainly not good law. There are many illustrations to the contrary'[4].

There are indeed a number of illustrations to the contrary. Lord Fraser cites payment of feu–duties which are both certain in amount and certain as to time of payment, and yet interest has been held not to be due without a contractual stipulation for it or wrongful withholding[5]. In *M'Phail v Lothian Regional Council* the mere delay in payment of an agreed contract debt gave no right to interest prior to wrongful withholding being established[6]. Is Lord Fraser's assertion therefore correct?

Damages are recoverable for breach of contract under the principle laid down in *Hadley v Baxendale*[7]. A loss will be recoverable if it is:

'such as may fairly and reasonably be considered either arising [1] according to the usual course of things, from such breach of contract itself, or [2] such as may reasonably be supposed to have been in the contemplation of both parties, at the time they made the contract, as the probable result of breach of it'.

Is not interest a loss which could arise under this principle? Would it not be in the 'usual course of things' for a creditor either to have to borrow money, on which he would have to pay interest, or to divert funds from other sources, on which he would lose interest? If so, the creditor would seem to be entitled to pursue a claim for this interest as damages for breach of contract within the first rule in the *Hadley v Baxendale* principle. Furthermore, where it is specifically contemplated by the contractors that interest costs would be lost or incurred, a claim for that interest would seem to lie under the second rule in *Hadley v Baxendale*[8].

The English case of *F G Minter v Welsh Health Technical Services Organisation* explored these issues in the context of the JCT Form of Building Contract (1963 edition)[9]. The interest loss claimed could be recovered only on the basis of the principle laid down in *Hadley v Baxendale*. It was, therefore, incumbent upon the plaintiff to show that the 'financing charges' which he claimed were within the contemplation of the parties. This point was in fact conceded by the defendant during proceedings. Stephenson LJ put the matter thus:

'The loss of the interest which [the creditor] has to pay on the capital he is forced to borrow and on the capital he is not free to invest would be recoverable for the employer's breach of contract within the first rule in *Hadley v Baxendale* without resorting to the second'[10].

Financing charges were therefore awarded on the ground that the interest which comprised them was a loss arising in the usual course of things where a contractor was deprived by delayed payment of vital cash flow. Ackner LJ emphasised this was not a claim for interest on a debt, 'but a debt which has as one of its constituent parts interest charges'[11].

Notwithstanding this semantic distinction, interest was considered to fall within the first rule in *Hadley v Baxendale*. The decision has been followed in England in *Rees and Kirby Ltd v Swansea City Council*[12], but perhaps largely on the ground that *Minter* was accepted as binding.

1 Bell *Commentaries* I,690.
2 *Bell* I,691.
3 *Roissard v Scott's Trustees* (1897) 24 R 861 at 865, 4 SLT 322 at 323, OH, per Lord Kincairney, with whom the Second Division fully agreed.
4 *Blair's Trustees v Payne* (1884) 12 R 104 at 110.
5 *Napier v Spiers' Trustees* (1831) 9 S 655; *Wallace v Earl of Eglinton* (1835) 13 S 564; *Marquis of Tweeddale v Aytoun* (1842) 4 D 862.
6 *M'Phail v Lothian Regional Council* 1981 SC 119, 1981 SLT 173, OH.
7 *Hadley v Baxendale* (1854) 9 Exch 341 at 354, 355.
8 This argument is advanced in similar terms by Professor J Murray (who had sight of this title before publication) in 'Interest on Debt' 1991 SLT (News) 305.
9 *F G Minter Ltd v Welsh Health Technical Services Organisation* (1980) 13 Build LR 1, CA.
10 13 Build LR 1 at 14, CA.
11 13 Build LR 1, CA.
12 *Rees and Kirby Ltd v Swansea City Council* (1985) 30 Build LR 1, CA.

1019. Interest as damages: Scottish decisions. Is it possible then that a similar claim in Scotland for finance charges, that is, interest, could also be brought within the rules of *Hadley v Baxendale*[1] without regard being had to wrongful delay in payment? Lord Kincairney in *Roissard v Scott's Trustees* clearly thought so:

'... the pursuer's claim ... is nothing but a claim of damages for failure to fulfil in due time an obligation to pay money, and it can only, apart from special circumstances, be for such damages as might fairly and naturally be held to flow, according to the usual course of things, from failure to implement the obligation, and that, when the obligation is to pay money, can only be for interest (besides the principal). Nor will a debtor in such a case be subjected to additional liability for damage arising on account of special circumstances unless these special circumstances are fully disclosed to him — See *Hadley v Baxendale* ...'[2].

In *Hunter v Livingston Development Corporation*, Lord Cowie accepted as well-founded arguments:

'... that standing the decision in the case of *F G Minter Ltd v Welsh Health Technical Services Organisation*[3], it was conceivable that a claim for interest, such as that made by the pursuers in the present case, could be justified in certain circumstances'[4].

It seems, therefore, that the Scottish courts would uphold the reasoning of *F G Minter*, that interest loss can arise in the usual course of things, but only 'in certain circumstances'. When though will these circumstances arise?

They did not arise in *Hunter*, as the pursuers failed to make the specific averments to support the claim which Lord Cowie considered to be crucial[5]. These would have included averments as to their financial position and commitments at the time payment should have been received by them.

Interest was also claimed as damages for breach of contract due to non-timeous payment of sums due in *Tiffney v Bachurzewski*[6]. Once again, the circumstances there did not warrant the conclusion that interest expenses were something which arose in the usual course of things. Lord Hunter said:

'Counsel for the pursuer ... attempted an argument that the necessity of the seller obtaining a bridging loan for purchase of an alternative residence when an existing residence was being sold was something which should be within the reasonable contemplation of any purchaser. This, in my opinion, is a somewhat extravagant proposition'[7].

Lord Hunter did not say what would happen in the usual course of things, and how he would expect an alternative residence to be purchased without a bridging loan.

Perhaps predictably, the circumstances of *Inverness Golf Club v James Parr & Associates* did not justify a claim for interest as damages for breach of contract[8]. There was a substantial overspend on a building contract which the pursuers, the employers, had been obliged to cover by using an overdraft. The defenders, the architects for the project, had in breach of contract failed to secure consent for this overspend from the pursuers. The pursuers claimed the interest on this overdraft from the defenders as damages. Lord Jauncey, rejecting the claim under the first rule in *Hadley v Baxendale*, considered:

> '... it cannot be said that borrowing was something which should have been foreseen by the defenders as something likely to happen in the ordinary course of things if there was a substantial overspend'.

He reached this conclusion on the basis that 'there may be options other than borrowing ... which would not involve payment of interest'. These included using other funds available, or raising funds by a levy on members. The defenders could not, therefore, have contemplated that interest costs would be incurred.

A claim under the second rule in *Hadley v Baxendale* was also dismissed. The defenders were aware that the lowest tender received by the pursuers considerably exceeded the amount they had 'available to spend on the project'. It was argued by the pursuers that the defenders should, therefore, have contemplated that to meet any overspend the pursuers would have to borrow, and pay interest. Lord Jauncey, however, emphasising that the pursuers had stated that the sum concerned was the only sum available for *that* project, considered that this did not mean 'that that is the only sum [the pursuer] has available for any project'. Since some of those other funds might be diverted, the defenders could not be taken to contemplate that borrowing would result from an overspend.

It may be thought that these views of Lord Jauncey, and those of Lord Hunter in *Tiffney*, disregard commercial reality, if not the facts of the cases. If a claim for interest is an 'extravagant proposition' in the circumstances of *Tiffney*, and if interest is outwith contemplation in *Inverness Golf Club* because of the outside possibility of the pursuers being able to obtain non-interest bearing funds, then in what circumstances will interest arise in the usual course of things? Perhaps only a decision on all fours with *F G Minter* would give a successful claim for interest as damages from the time of non-payment.

The judicial reluctance to allow such a claim is no doubt a consequence of the general rules on wrongful withholding. To allow interest as damages from the time of non-payment is to depart from the well-established rule that interest can only run in the event of an unpaid debt being wrongfully withheld. The law as it stands, by recognising the possible application of the rules in *Hadley v Baxendale* to a claim for interest as damages, does raise the possibility of such a departure, with the resulting anomalies. However, by severely limiting the operation of the *Hadley v Baxendale* rules on damages where interest is claimed, the courts are obviating difficulties which remain theoretical only[9]. It is to be hoped, though, that the courts will not allow such manifest inconsistency in the law, even if only theoretical, and will give some clear ruling resolving this conflict.

Although it might seem from consideration of the cases that the resolution of this conflict would be to exclude a claim for interest as damages in Scots law, this is not inevitably so. Indeed, there does appear to be a plausible solution to this otherwise intractable conflict. This solution synthesises the rules in *Hadley v*

Baxendale with the rules on wrongful withholding. Both these rules are therefore recognised within a theoretically consistent framework.

1 *Hadley v Baxendale* (1854) 9 Exch 341.
2 *Roissard v Scott's Trustees* (1897) 24 R 861 at 865, 4 SLT 322 at 323, OH. In *James Dunn & Co v Anderston Foundry Co Ltd* (1894) 21 R 880, interest was also awarded as a head of damage in an action for breach of contract.
3 *F G Minter Ltd v Welsh Health Technical Services Organisation* (1980) 13 Build LR 1, CA.
4 *Hunter v Livingston Development Corpn* 1984 SLT 10 at 11, OH.
5 1984 SLT 10 at 12, OH.
6 *Tiffney v Bachurzewski* 1984 SC 108, 1985 SLT 165.
7 1984 SC 108 at 113, 1985 SLT 165 at 167. In *Cochrane v Graham and Sibbald* 1987 SLT 622, the Second Division awarded interest on a bridging loan as a head of damage in a negligence action. Lord Dunpark, at 625, considered that it was within judicial knowledge that in many cases bridging loans are necessary to enable a purchaser to buy his new house pending the sale of his old one. Sellers could not assume that purchasers have sufficient funds to pay the purchase price without borrowing. That being so, interest on a bridging loan was something the wrongdoer ought reasonably to have had in contemplation. In *Grant v Ullah* 1987 SLT 639, OH, Lord Davidson awarded interest as damages for breach of contract. The pursuers were entitled to recover the interest on their building society loan, which would otherwise have been redeemed, from the time the defender ought to have paid the contract price until the pursuer was able to obtain alternative performance in mitigation. Lord Davidson allowed this head of damage on the ground of the defender's knowledge of the loan in question. He must therefore have contemplated the loss: cf para 1020 below.
8 *Inverness Golf Club v James Parr & Associates* 12 Jan 1987 (unreported).
9 In *Hall and Tawse Construction Ltd v Strathclyde Regional Council* 1990 SLT 774 at 780, Lord President Hope discussed a creditor's right to interest in the context of clause 60(6) of the ICE Conditions of Contract. His Lordship considered that since the debtor had had, to the deprivation of the creditor, use of the latter's money it was reasonable that the creditor receive interest. However, the Lord President went on to say that although a right to interest under clause 60(6) was reasonable in the circumstances, those circumstances would not found a claim for interest at common law: express contractual stipulation for interest was necessary. Although obiter, this dictum is indicative of the restrictive approach applied to intererst as damages at common law: notwithstanding the reasonableness of the claim, the breach by failure to certify the sums due under clause 60(2) would not ground a claim for interest as damages.

1020. The possible solution. The essence of the reconciliation involves the attribution of wrongfulness to the withholding of a contractual debt where the debtor contemplates that in consequence of his breach the creditor will incur interest losses 'in the usual course of things'. A number of factors arising from the contractual relationship would seem to justify the conclusion that in failing to perform timeously the debtor has not paid when he ought and that that failure is, in the words of Lord Keith of Avonholm, 'wrongful, improper and unjustifiable'[1].

The first factor is that the debtor made a specific agreement to pay at a particular time and that the creditor will have relied on performance at that time, possibly arranging his financial commitments in the belief that he will receive payment then. More importantly, there is the crucial element of knowledge which the contract confers upon the debtor. Where, as a result of that contractual relationship, the debtor can be taken to have contemplated that his non-timeous payment would in the ordinary course of events cause interest losses, the non-payment is to be considered wrongful. If the necessary degree of knowledge can be attributed to the debtor to enable it to be concluded that he would reasonably have foreseen interest losses by his delayed payment, then it may be concluded that he ought to have made payment when it was due. The prior contemplation of the loss justifies the conclusion that payment ought to have been made when due. It is also this prior contemplation of interest losses that distinguishes contract cases of withholding which is wrongful from other contract cases where it is not.

Furthermore this element ensures the equiparation of the principle in *Hadley v Baxendale*[3] with the rules on wrongful withholding: the conclusion that the withholding is wrongful arises exclusively where under *Hadley v Baxendale* interest loss would be recoverable. The scope of the two claims is, therefore, co-extensive and no divergence or conflict exists.

It should also be noted that in such cases no formal demand is necessary to constitute the withholding as wrongful. The formal demand is generally required so that it can be said that the debtor ought at that time to have made payment[4]. However, in these cases the debtor ought to have paid timeously because he contemplated interest losses to the creditor if he did not. The superfluousness of a demand in such contract cases may have been indicated by Lord Craighill in *Blair's Trustees v Payne*. He considered a demand to be a pre-condition for interest liability in cases '*apart* from contract'[5].

Thus, the court could award interest as damages under *Hadley v Baxendale*, but within the wrongful withholding rule: the non-payment is more than merely a delay, but is a wrongful delay. The theoretical reconciliation of these rules could also encourage the courts, without fear of inconsistency in the law, to adopt a more practical and realistic attitude to when interest losses will arise 'in the usual course of things'. They could apply the first rule in *Hadley v Baxendale*, taking account of the fact that in many situations a creditor deprived of funds will incur interest losses as he will either be forced to incur an interest-bearing loan, or will have to employ other funds which could themselves have earned interest. To that extent the law could once again move back into line with commercial reality[6].

1 *F W Green & Co Ltd v Brown and Gracie Ltd* 1960 SLT (Notes) 43 at 44, HL.
2 See para 1012, text to note 1, and para 1017, above.
3 *Hadley v Baxendale* (1854) 9 Exch 341 at 347.
4 *Trans Barwil Agencies (UK) Ltd v John S Braid & Co Ltd* 1989 SCLR 647, 1990 SLT 182, OH.
5 *Blair's Trustees v Payne* (1884) 12 R 104 at 108 (emphasis added): see para 1017, text to note 7 above.
6 Cf para 1019 above.

1021. A general rule obliging payment of interest for deprivation of moveables?

There is an oft-quoted dictum from Lord Atkin in *Kolbin and Sons v William Kinnear & Co*, which supports a general proposition that a pursuer is entitled to interest where he is deprived of income producing property:

> 'It seems to be established that, by Scots law, a pursuer may recover interest by way of damages where he is deprived of an interest-bearing security or a profit-producing chattel . . .'[1].

Broadly stated, this is an accurate summary of the law. However, despite presenting an integrated appearance, the rule does in fact draw together and intermix principles from different aspects of the law. The rules on interest for deprivation of money become fused with the rules relating to deprivation of property generally.

Where a creditor is deprived of money (the primary example of an interest bearing security), the relevant rules as to his entitlement to interest are those already discussed. The right to interest can arise on a number of grounds, with wrongful withholding (or deprivation) of the money being one of these. That ground of wrongful withholding must have been in the contemplation of Lord Atkin when he made these remarks, given that he cites *Carmichael v Caledonian Rly Co*[2], (where this ground was first established) which establishes it, to support his remarks. In the light of the reliance placed upon *Carmichael*, the deprivation to which Lord Atkin was referring must therefore be taken to mean deprivation which is wrongful, and not any other kind of deprivation.

Besides outlining the rules on interest for wrongful withholding, Lord Atkin takes an uncertain step into the field of deprivation of property generally. Money is treated differently from other types of property where the owner's deprivation of it is concerned. Although in both cases a successful action is predicated upon withholding of the property, which is wrongful, the rules relating to each are different. The conclusion or crave for 'interest' arises exclusively where the debtor has enjoyed use of the creditor's *money*, and is generally charged at the legal interest rate irrespective of the profits actually made on the money. On the other hand, the action for the fruits of property other than money is strictly for the 'income' or 'profits' actually produced during the unlawful possession, or unusually, following spuilzie, the greatest profit the property could have yielded[3]. Interest is not the quantum of damages in this field; rather it is the income the property produced, either actual or its theoretical maximum.

The dictum of Lord Atkin does not, therefore, support any general rule that interest is due for mere deprivation of property. Properly understood it states that a creditor may have a successful claim for interest where he is wrongfully deprived of his money, whilst in the case of property other than money an action for the income which that property actually produced or could have produced lies with the wrongfully deprived owner.

1 *Kolbin & Sons v Kinnear & Co* 1931 SC (HL) 128 at 137, 1931 SLT 464 at 468, HL, cited with approval in *F W Green & Co Ltd v Brown and Gracie Ltd* 1960 SLT (Notes) 43 at 44, HL, per Lord Keith of Avonholm; *Farrans (Construction) Ltd v Dunfermline District Council* 1988 SCLR 272 at 277, 1988 SLT 466 at 470, per Lord Justice-Clerk Ross; *Tiffney v Bachurzewski* 1983 SLT (Sh Ct) 45 at 47, per Sheriff Principal Bennett.
2 *Carmichael v Caledonian Rly Co* (1870) 8 M (HL) 119.
3 These matters on deprivation of property other than money are considered fully in PROPERTY.

4. INTEREST ON TRUST AND EXECUTRY FUNDS

1022. General. Interest may be payable on trust[1] funds in one of three situations:
(1) by the express or implied terms of the trust deed itself calling for the payment of interest;
(2) in the event of a breach of duty, interest may be due to be paid by the trustees on funds; and
(3) where advances are made to beneficiaries, they may be liable to pay interest.

1 Trusts and executries are treated in the same way so far as interest is concerned.

1023. Interest due by the terms of the trust deed. A truster enjoys the same freedom as contractors to stipulate for the payment of interest on funds to be paid to a beneficiary. Generally a truster would stipulate for payment of the income the funds actually earn rather than for payment of a particular rate of interest, thereby avoiding the difficulty which would arise if the income actually earned was insufficient to meet the amount of interest stipulated to be paid. If a rate of interest was specified to be payable which the funds had not actually earned, then, in the absence of a breach of trust, the trustees would not be liable to pay at that rate. Where the trustees through no fault of their own cannot carry out the terms of the trust deed, they will not be liable in interest for the failure of the trust purposes[1]. The right to the stipulated interest would probably be commuted to a right to actual income, if any. The truster may stipulate for payment of the fruits of any income producing property and not merely money.

In addition to express stipulation for interest or income, the courts may also imply into a trust deed a right to interest. Such a stipulation will be imported into the deed in order to give effect to what is considered to be the intention of the truster. In *M'Lean's Trustees v M'Lean* the right to interest on a legacy was implied[2]. The trust disposition obliged payment to the beneficiaries of a specified sum 'payable as at my death' or on the beneficiaries attaining majority. It was held that the beneficial interest included a right to the interest on the sum accruing between death and the time for payment. The right to interest was inferred from the stipulation that the sum due to the beneficiaries was to be a specified sum payable 'as at my death', and that since the legatee cannot get payment of it as at the testator's death unless he gets with it the interest which has accrued on it since the death[3], the interest was due[4]. The court therefore considered that the truster's intention was that the sum to be paid to the beneficiary was the specified sum if it was paid at death, or its equivalent at the time for payment. To give effect to this latter intention, it was necessary that the bequest carry interest. It may be possible to apply the same process of implication to many bequests, so that interest would be due.

1 Cf *Waddell's Trustees v Crawford* 1926 SC 654, 1926 SLT 457.
2 *M'Lean's Trustees v M'Lean* (1891) 18 R 892.
3 (1891) 18 R 892 at 894, per Lord Justice-Clerk Macdonald.
4 An implied right to interest is discussed further in the context of the duty to invest: see para 1025 below.

1024. Trustees' liability for interest. Trustees may incur a personal liability to pay interest on trust funds where they have been in breach of their duties as trustees. This liability may be incurred notwithstanding that the trust deed exonerates them from liability[1]. Normally interest is found due for the defender's use and enjoyment of the pursuer's money. In the case of a trustee's liability to pay interest this is unnecessary. Interest is due in consequence of their breach of duty, and it is not necessary that the trustees used the money for their own purposes. The grounds on which liability for interest may be incurred by a trustee are where he:
(1) fails to properly invest trust funds;
(2) acts *ultra vires* the trust purposes;
(3) uses trust funds for his own purposes;
(4) incurs liability for a co-trustee's breach of duty; or
(5) fails to make timeous payment of the beneficial interest to the beneficiary.

1 *Lord Lynedoch v Ouchterlony* (1832) 11 S 60: the trust deed contained such an exclusion of liability, but the trustee was still liable for his breach of duty.

1025. Duty to invest. It was held in *Melville v Noble's Trustees* that one of the duties incumbent upon a trustee is to properly invest the trust funds so that they 'yield an investment return'[1]. Describing this duty more fully, Lord Trayner said:

'The [trustees] were bound to deal with the trust funds in the same way as a man of ordinary prudence would deal with his own [funds]'[2].

In *Melville* the trustees had in fact placed the trust funds on deposit receipt. However, the court did not consider this to be a proper investment, such as a prudent man would make for his own money. The trustees were, therefore, found liable to pay interest for failing to invest the funds in the requisite manner.

Clearly where there are no trust funds available for investment, the trustees cannot be liable for failing to invest the funds. In such a situation, as with the case of *Waddell's Trustees v Crawford*, where no funds were available to make timeous payment[3], the trustees would not be required to pay interest.

The mere existence of a duty to invest trust funds should not infer that all beneficiaries are entitled to interest on sums due to them. Thus, unless the stipulation for payment of a specified sum carries with it an express or implied right to interest (or income), the interest which accrues in satisfaction of this duty should not be applied thereto, but should be applied to the residual beneficiary. However, in the absence of a residual beneficiary, where the trust fund is divided specifically and payment is postponed, the interest accruing following proper investment should be applied to each beneficiary *pro rata* by necessary inference, since there is no-one else to whom the interest could be applied, and this division must therefore have been intended.

1 *Melville v Noble's Trustees* (1896) 24 R 243 at 249, per Lord Justice-Clerk Macdonald.
2 (1896) 24 R 243 at 253.
3 *Waddell's Trustees v Crawford* 1926 SC 654, 1926 SLT 457.

1026. Loss of trust funds by *ultra vires* actions. The trustees' duty to invest is not merely a duty to make *any* investment. Rather, the duty obliges the trustees to make only those investments which they are entitled to make in terms of the trust deed. In the event of trust funds being lost in the course of an investment which was *ultra vires* the trust deed, the trustees are obliged to make good the lost funds, and in addition to pay interest on the funds from the time they were lost[1]. The rate of interest is that which would have been earned by the funds if an *intra vires* investment had been made. Where through the neglect of a trustee the trust is temporarily deprived of funds (although they are not permanently lost), the negligent trustee is liable to pay interest on the funds during the time his neglect prevented the trust enjoying the fruits of the money[2].

1 *Pollexfen v Stewart* (1841) 3 D 1215; *Boyd v Greig* 1913 1 SLT 398, OH.
2 *Lord Lynedoch v Ouchterlony* (1832) 11 S 60.

1027. Trustees using funds for their own purposes. Unless specifically empowered to do so, trustees may not apply trust funds for their own purposes: they may not be *auctor in rem suam*. Where trustees retain trust funds in their own hands, they are deemed to be *auctor in rem suam*[1]. Where the trustees themselves borrow trust funds, notwithstanding that they provide good security and pay interest, they are considered to be *auctor in rem suam*[2].

Trustees who are *auctor in rem suam* incur a liability to pay interest at the highest legal rate[3], or to pay over the profits which they have actually realised by employing the trust funds[4].

1 *Malcolm's Executors v Malcolm* (1869) 8 M 272.
2 *Templeton v Burgh of Ayr* 1912 1 SLT 421, OH.
3 *Malcolm's Executors v Malcolm* (1869) 8 M 272.
4 *Cochrane v Black* (1855) 17 D 321.

1028. Liability for co-trustees. Where a trustee incurs a liability for a breach of trust by one of his co-trustees, and must therefore make good sums lost by virtue of the co-trustee's actions, that liability incorporates an obligation to pay interest on the sums due from the time they were lost[1].

1 *Millar's Trustees v Polson* (1897) 24 R 1038, 5 SLT 94.

1029. Delay in payment. Interest is payable on trust funds for a delay in payment from the time when payment was due. The rule, which is an application of the principle of wrongful withholding[1], has been frequently considered in cases concerning the delayed payment of legacies:

'The general rule is that legacies bear interest like any other money debt from the date when they are due and payable'[2].

The issue then becomes one of determining when payment was due to be made. Where a date for payment is specified, then the sum must be paid on that date and will be regarded as being wrongfully withheld if it is not. Where no time for payment is specified, then payment is presumed to be due *a morte testatoris*, if there are sufficient funds to make the payment[3].

It was said in *May's Trustees v Paul*:

'However reasonable the trustees' delay was, their delay cannot affect the rights of the legatees [to interest]'[4].

This statement, although indicating that the right to interest is absolute from the time payment was due, must be understood in the context in which it was made and in the light of cases such as *Waddell's Trustees v Crawford*[5], *Ogilvie's Legatees v Hamilton*[6], and *Ewing v Mathieson*[7].

Indeed, it must be emphasised that the rule that interest runs from the date payment should have been made is a general rule, and is neither absolute nor immutable[8].

In *May's Trustees* itself, the issue of delayed payment arose where there were sufficient funds to pay the bequest immediately. The importance of this was stressed in *Waddell's Trustees* where there were no funds available to make payment of the bequests at the time they were due. This insufficiency of funds was the result of a failure of the trust and not a breach of duty by the trustees. In the words of Lord Justice-Clerk Alness:

'If there is no estate available or realisable to pay . . . , no interest is due'[8].

Thus interest will not be due where the non-timeous payment is not caused by the trustees' breach of duty, but is attributable to failure of the trust.

In *Ewing v Mathieson* Lord Stormonth-Darling made remarks similar to those of the Lord Justice-Clerk in *Waddell's Trustees*. He considered that interest will only be due for delayed payment if 'the funds are extant and yielding income . . . in one form or another'. There must, therefore, not only be estate available to make payment but, furthermore, during the time of non-payment, that estate must properly be applied to producing profits. The rationale is that since the bequest ought to have been paid, the income accruing ought to have accrued to the beneficiary, and it is therefore properly attributable to him. These remarks indicate that no interest will be due in the event of delayed payment where the trustees are properly fulfilling their duties, but no income is earned. However, if no income has been earned as a result of a breach of trust, interest would be due.

A good example of the application of these rules and the distinction between a failure to pay due to a failure of the trust and a failure attributable to the trustees, is *Ogilvie's Legatees v Hamilton*[9]. No time was stated for payment of the bequests. They were to be paid from the proceeds of the sale of certain land. The court considered that three years from the testator's death was a reasonable period within which to effectuate the conversion of the estate and pay out the legacies. From the expiration of the three years interest ran on the legacies. Thus, prior to that time the lack of trust funds with which to make payment was not due to a breach of duty by the trustees but was due to the nature of the trust itself. In those circumstances, no interest was due. However, after the three-year period, the failure to pay was due to a breach of duty; any lack of funds was the result of the trustees failing to convert the estate timeously; while if the estate had been converted the legacies should, in proper performance of duty, have been paid. Interest was therefore due.

1 *Waddell's Trustees v Crawford* 1926 SC 654, 1926 SLT 457, where *Carmichael v Caledonian Rly Co* (1870) 8 M (HL) 119 is cited and Lord Westbury's classic dictum on wrongful withholding is stated to be the relevant rule for non-payment of legacies.
2 *May's Trustees v Paul* (1900) 2 F 657 at 660, per Lord Trayner.
3 (1900) 2 F 657.
4 (1900) 2 F 657 at 660, per Lord Adam.
5 *Waddell's Trustees v Crawford* 1926 SC 654, 1926 SLT 457.
6 *Ogilvie's Legatees v Hamilton* (1833) 12 S 189.
7 *Ewing v Mathieson* (1904) 41 SLR 594, OH.
8 *Waddell's Trustees v Crawford* 1926 SC 654, 1926 SLT 457.
9 *Ogilvie's Legatees v Hamilton* (1833) 12 S 189.

1030. Advances to beneficiaries. Beneficiaries may incur a liability to pay interest on advances made to them prior to the date when final payment of their beneficial interest is due. It is necessary to consider separately *intra vires* and *ultra vires* advances.

Where the trustees make an advance to a beneficiary which they have power to make in terms of the trust deed (an *intra vires* advance), interest may be due on that sum. Thus, in calculating the beneficiaries' final entitlement, interest is added to the advance from the time of its payment, and this total sum of capital plus interest is deducted from the stipulated entitlement leaving the residue to be paid. This interest may be expressly provided for by the trust deed, or it may be inferred. In *Matthew's Trustees v Matthew* the court considered whether interest was due on an *intra vires* advance[1]. There was no express stipulation for interest, but, having regard to the truster's 'primary idea' manifested in the scheme of the division of the funds, interest was 'as a matter of impression . . . to be implied'[2].

Where the trustees make an *ultra vires* advance to beneficiaries, then the trustees will incur a primary liability to make good the funds and pay interest on them. This is an application of the rule regarding *ultra vires* acts. However, the trustees are entitled to be relieved of this liability by the beneficiaries: as with *intra vires* advances, the *ultra vires* capital sum paid together with interest thereon from the time of payment, will be deducted from the beneficiaries' remaining entitlement[3]. If the advance plus interest exceeds the beneficiaries' total entitlement, they will be liable in an action for accounting to repay the excess[4].

1 *Matthew's Trustees v Matthew* (1905) 13 SLT 470, OH.
2 (1905) 13 SLT 470 at 472, OH.
3 *Baird's Trustees v Duncanson* (1892) 19 R 1045.
4 *Plaine v Thomson* (1836) 15 S 194. The capital advances made to the beneficiary exceeded her entitlement. She was found liable to repay the excess with interest thereon.

1031. Interest on sums due as legal rights in succession. Where a deceased person is survived by a spouse or any child, then those surviving relations have 'legal rights' in the estate of the deceased[1]. The surviving spouse has a claim for *jus relicti vel relictae*, while the child's claim is for *legitim*. Legal rights arise under the general law and apply to both testate and intestate succession.

Sums of money which are due in satisfaction of legal rights are regarded as ordinary debts against the estate[2]. Interest runs on these sums *a morte testatoris*. This interest may be due on one of two mutually exclusive grounds. The first ground deals with the right to interest prior to the claim for legal rights being made, while the second ground concerns interest due after the claim has been made.

In *Ross v Ross* where this dichotomy originates, Lord McLaren considered that the testamentary representatives were under a duty to invest *a morte testatoris* the funds of the estate from which legal rights were drawn, and that the claimants of the rights were entitled to interest on the sums due as the income which this part of the estate had earned, notwithstanding that no claim or election had yet been made[3]. The rate of interest in this situation is to be calculated with reference to the income 'the money would have produced if safely invested'[4].

The reasoning in *Waddell's Trustees v Crawford*, which prevented interest running *a morte testatoris* on a legacy, seems equally apposite to interest on legal rights[5]. Thus, during any time there was no estate 'available or realisable' from which legal rights could be claimed or paid, no interest could run[6]. The application of the reasoning in *Waddell's Trustees* seems to be perfectly consistent with Lord McLaren's justification for payment of interest. The interest was due as the income the estate would have earned if properly invested; however, if there was no estate there would have been no income, and Lord McLaren would surely not have required the payment of interest. Generally, however, interest runs *a morte testatoris* on legal rights prior to the rights being claimed, pursuant to a duty to invest.

Legal rights are debts which ought to be paid when they are claimed, and interest runs from the time of claim[7]. Where the claimant is obliged to elect between claiming legal rights or testamentary entitlement, the claim is made when the election is made. Where the claimant is not obliged to make any election, it seems the claim will be deemed to have been made *a morte testatoris*[8]. In *Gilchrist v Gilchrist's Trustees* Lord Fraser said:

'If the executor, without justifiable excuse, delays to pay the legitim, he is liable in interest . . .'[9].

The principle underlying this rule is what has now been formulated as wrongful withholding[10]. The fact that legal rights are ordinary debts led Lord McLaren in *Ross v Ross* to conclude that interest is due from the time payment was due (that is, the time of claim) 'as in any other case of the withholding of payment of a just debt'[11]. The claim for the legal rights, being the time payment ought to be made, is equivalent to the demand for payment which gives rise to wrongful withholding[12]. Interest is, therefore, due on this debt, as with all debts, from the time of claim on the ground of wrongful withholding.

Where money has been advanced to a child during the lifetime of the deceased, and it falls to be collated with the part of the estate due in satisfaction of *legitim*, interest on the advance from the date when it was made is not, in the absence of a contrary intention, to be added to the advance in the collation[13].

1 For a fuller discussion of the nature of legal rights and their relationships with a surviving spouse's statutory prior rights and entitlement of the claimant under any testamentary disposition, see WILLS AND SUCCESSION, vol 25.

2 *M'Murray v M'Murray's Trustees* (1852) 14 D 1048.

3 *Ross v Ross* (1896) 23 R 802 (thirteen-year delay in the making of the election).

4 (1896) 23 R 802 at 806, per Lord McLaren.

5 *Waddell's Trustees v Crawford* 1926 SC 654, 1926 SLT 457.

6 1926 SC 654 at 665, 1926 SLT 457 at 464, per Lord Justice-Clerk Alness.

7 *M'Murray v M'Murray's Trustees* (1852) 14 D 1048 at 1053, per Lord President Boyle.

8 *Ross v Ross* (1896) 23 R 802 at 805, per Lord McLaren.

9 *Gilchrist v Gilchrist's Trustees* (1889) 16 R 1118 at 1120.

10 In *Waddell's Trustees v Crawford* 1926 SC 654 at 671, Lord Hunter noted that following *Ross v Ross* (1896) 23 R 802, it was clear that the principle of wrongful withholding applied to *legitim*, and it may be assumed that it also applies to *jus relicti vel relictae*.

11 *Ross v Ross* (1896) 23 R 802.

12 Note that Lord Westbury, in his classic statement in *Carmichael v Caledonian Rly Co* (1870) 8 M (HL) 119 at 131 (see para 1012, text and note 1), said that wrongful withholding arose when a debt was 'not paid on the day when it ought to have been paid'. This applies to legal rights from the time of claim, that being when they ought to be paid.

13 *Gilmour's Trustees v Gilmour* 1922 SC 753, 1922 SLT 596.

5. INTEREST ON DAMAGES AND DECREES

1032. Ordinary litigation. The common law rule with regard to interest on damages and decrees was that interest was normally allowed only from the date of decree, even if that meant that the date was the date of the decree as pronounced after an appeal reasonably taken[1]. However, the Interest on Damages (Scotland) Acts 1958 and 1971 provide for interest to be awarded at the discretion of the court on sums of money decerned for as damages between the date on which the right of action arose and the interlocutor. That discretion extends to allow the whole or part of the sum to bear interest for the whole or part of the period of time and also extends to rates[2].

That discretion is limited in the case of damages which consist of or include damages or *solatium* for personal injuries, in that the court must award interest on such part of the damages and *solatium* as it considers appropriate, unless the court is satisfied that there are reasons special to the case why no interest should be given in respect of these[3].

These provisions might be thought to have replaced the common law rule. They apply to any ground of action[4]. Nevertheless, the common law rule has still some relevance, in that the discretion conferred by the legislation was said by Lord President Clyde to be a remedy applicable in special circumstances. Where there was no undue delay, and no special circumstances present, the court would not vary the normal rules as to the paying of interest[5].

The 1971 Act amending the 1958 Act extended to all actions a power to award interest from the date on which the cause of action arose, instead of from the commencement of the action. However, the court always had power on appeal to award interest if there had been undue delay in prosecuting the appeal[6]; and the House of Lords has an unlimited discretion[7] in the awarding of interest, simple or compound, which, however, it had been observed, should apply to a case which was out of the ordinary[8].

Conversely, where there has been delay on the part of the pursuer, interest may be awarded from the later date, for example the end of the three-year limitation period. Where an accident occurred on 21 August 1978, but the pursuer inexcusably failed to make any progress with his action between November 1982 and October 1985, Lord Davidson indicated that (had he found in favour of the pursuer) he would have allowed interest on part of the *solatium* from 21 August 1981, rather than from the date of the accident[9].

It can reasonably be argued that the 'normal rule' as invoked in *R and J Dempster*[10] is now for a date earlier than that of decree. Not only do the words of the statute make it clear, but also it was judicially stated in relation to the statutory power of the court granted in 1958 that the discretion given was to be exercised on a selective and discriminating basis.

In *Smith v Middleton*[11] Lord Emslie found no indication that the 1971 amendment demanded any different approach in relation to claims for damages for personal injuries and set out his view of the consideration to be applied when awarding interest. A distinction between loss or damage, whether patrimonial loss or *solatium* which was incurred before the decree, and future loss under either head, requires to be made. Issues for the trial of a cause seeking damages for personal injury before a jury require to be so framed as to obtain answers from the jury as to the separate sums to be awarded for past and future patrimonial loss and past and future *solatium*.

The precise approach indicated in *Smith v Middleton* has not been followed to the letter. In that case (a family claim for the death of a husband and father) it was indicated that interest on the loss of support element from death to decree should be awarded at half the then prescribed rate for interest after decree; but at the full rate on *solatium* for the same period. It was said that, since it was unrealistic to treat *solatium* as being computed on a day-to-day basis, there was no reason to reduce the rate. No interest was awarded for the sum awarded for future loss, or future *solatium*.

There appears to be no reason in principle why the *solatium* appropriate when considering the loss occasioned by a death should be computed in any way different from *solatium* for, for example, the loss of a limb. However, the court has rarely awarded the full rate as in *Smith*, and, indeed, in another widow's case, the Second Division, on appeal, awarded half the rate on both loss of society and loss of support[12]. Interest will usually be given at the full rate from any date when the loss can be identified as fully quantified, for example damage to property.

Although the court may refuse interest, if there are reasons special to the case why no interest should be given[13], it has declined to award an increased rate of interest where the circumstances of the case indicated doubtful practice by the defender's insurers, or where liability was not admitted until the eve of the proof[14].

The Interest on Damages (Scotland) Act 1958 expressly provides that it of itself does not authorise the granting of interest upon interest, but also that it does not affect the running of interest which otherwise would run by virtue of any enactment or rule of law[15].

1 *Flensburg Steam Shipping Co v Seligmann* (1871) 9 M 1011. The claim was quantified and made liquid and payable only from the date of the award of damages, or of the interlocutor applying the jury's verdict awarding damages. See the remarks of Lord President Inglis at 1014.

2 Interest on Damages (Scotland) Act 1958 (c 61), s 1(1) (substituted by the Interest on Damages (Scotland) Act 1971 (c 31), s 1(1)).

3 Interest on Damages (Scotland) Act 1958, s 1(1A) (added by the Interest on Damages (Scotland) Act 1971, s 1(1)). For the difficulties encountered, see para 1033 below.

4 Eg breach of contract (*R and J Dempster Ltd v Motherwell Bridge and Engineering Co Ltd* 1964 SC 308, 1964 SLT 353); damage to property (*Fraser v J Morton Wilson Ltd (No 2)* 1966 SLT 22, OH, when the full damage was suffered before the date of citation); interdict and damages (*Roger v J and P Cochrane & Co* 1910 SC 1, 1909 2 SLT 277, when the petitioner should have asked the House of Lords to award interest under the Court of Session Act 1808 (c 151), s 19 (repealed: see now the Court of Session Act 1988 (c 36), s 42)).

5 *R and J Dempster Ltd v Motherwell Bridge and Engineering Co Ltd* 1964 SC 308 at 334, 1964 SLT 353 at 368. For an example of the converse situation, see *Clancy v Dixon's Ironworks Ltd* 1955 SC 17, 1955 SLT 36.

6 *Clancy v Dixon's Ironworks Ltd* 1955 SC 17, 1955 SLT 36, where, following the defenders' 'unjustifiable and improper' delay (throughout a period that included the long vacation) in withdrawing a motion for a new trial, the court awarded interest from the date when the jury's verdict might have been applied on intimation to the vacation judge of their decision not to proceed.

7 Court of Session Act 1808, s 19 (repealed); Court of Session Act 1988, s 42.

8 Where an appellant against a judgment of the Court of Session is dissatisfied with the way in which interest has been dealt with or has not been dealt with in the judgment under appeal he should make clear in the case what his ground of dissatisfaction is and how he would desire the judgment appealed against altered in order to remove his dissatisfaction: see *M'Govern v James Nimmo & Co Ltd* 1938 SC (HL) 18 at 30, 1938 SLT 403 at 408; *F W Green & Co Ltd v Brown and Gracie Ltd* 1960 SLT (Notes) 43 at 44, HL, per Lord Keith of Avonholm.

9 *Buchan v J Marr (Aberdeen) Ltd* 1987 SCLR 96, 1987 SLT (Notes) 521, OH. In *Boots the Chemist Ltd v GA Estates Ltd* (1991) Scotsman, 4 July, OH, the parties had settled an action of damages arising out of flood damage to the pursuers' premises and consequential loss of stock and other expenditure, but five years had elapsed between the event and the pursuers' submission of a full claim, despite reminders. Lord Cameron of Lochbroom, who required to settle only the matter of interest, awarded interest on expenditure from the dates on which it was incurred, at the appropriate judicial rate, but, in regard to the loss of stock, interest was awarded only from the date of citation. The mere fact that the right of action accrued on a particular date (that is, the date of the flood) in respect of an asset lost or destroyed, did not of itself justify an award of interest from that date.

10 *R and J Dempster Ltd v Motherwell Bridge and Engineering Co Ltd* 1964 SC 308, 1964 SLT 353.
11 *Smith v Middleton* 1972 SC 30, 1972 SLT (Notes) 3, OH.
12 *Prentice v Chalmers* 1985 SLT 168 at 177.
13 The wording of the Interest on Damages (Scotland) Act 1958, s 1(1) (as substituted: see note 1 above), is permissive.
14 *Will v Charles Will Ltd* 1980 SLT (Notes) 37, OH.
15 Interest on Damages (Scotland) Act 1958, s 1(2)(a), (c). See also para 1038 below (compound interest).

1033. Lump sum damages. The difficulty of calculating different rates of interest to be applied to the constituent elements of the cumulo damages awarded by a jury was considered by the Second Division in *Ross v British Railways Board*[1]. The apparent alternatives were to award interest either on the whole sum or on such part or parts as the court considered appropriate. The latter option was impracticable. If no evidence is led as to damages, it is impossible to make even an approximate estimate of these elements.

A compromise was sought. Lord Justice-Clerk Grant (with the concurrence of Lord Wheatley and Lord Walker) stated that it was not right that since, in the circumstances of the case under consideration, the pursuer, because of insufficient information, had been awarded what he described as the best of the 'global' world, he should also enjoy interest on the global sum, at the full legal rate of interest over the maximum period. This would be, from the point of view of the defender, 'piling injustice on injustice'. Accordingly, interest was set to run from the date of citation (rather than that of the cause of action — a difference of over fourteen months) at 7 per cent — the rate fixed by the Lord Ordinary[2].

The difficulty was resolved by a change of practice when the First Division in *MacDonald v Glasgow Corporation* approved an amended form of issue setting out clearly the four heads of claim. These are, loss of earnings to date, future loss of earnings, *solatium* to date and future *solatium*. This form was considered to be calculated satisfactorily to avoid in advance the difficulties of applying the new legislation, which would otherwise be insuperable. It has been adopted as the standard practice in appropriate cases[4].

1 *Ross v British Railways Board* 1972 SC 154, 1972 SLT 174.
2 1972 SC 154 at 158, 1972 SLT 174 at 175, per Lord Justice-Clerk Grant.
3 *MacDonald v Glasgow Corpn* 1973 SC 53 at 56, 1973 SLT 107 at 110: '. . . the form of issue is purely a matter of practice, and . . . the Court will, wherever possible and expedient, adapt current practice to meet the demands of new circumstances as they emerge'.
4 D Maxwell *The Practice of the Court of Session* (1980) p 328.

1034. Taxation of interest on damages. Interest on damages is in general taxable[1], except where the interest is payable in respect of damages or *solatium* awards for personal injury or death[2]. The interest is not taxable until it is received[3], and will be taxable under Schedule D, Case III, when paid from a source within the United Kingdom and under Schedule D, Case V, when the source is furth of the United Kingdom.

The question whether income tax should be deducted at source by the payer is determined by reference to the rules relating to deduction of tax in relation to interest payments generally. Interest is paid gross without deduction of tax unless it is interest paid by a company or a local authority in which case it is paid net if it is 'yearly interest'[4]. Whether interest paid as part of an award of damages falls into the category of yearly interest has not been the subject of much judicial consideration, although Lord Denning stated that interest on a debt or damages which had been running for two, three or four years was yearly interest, and thus was payable under deduction of tax at source[5]. This view appears to have been formed without the benefit of argument of counsel and is open to doubt.

The general test as to whether a payment of interest is 'yearly' is whether it was in the contemplation of the parties that the obligation should extend for a year or more[6]. This test is of limited relevance in this context as there is no antecedent contemplation to which the interest can refer. It has been held that interest on a judgment debt is not yearly interest[7], and there is some similarity between this interest and interest on the underlying damages. The point must be regarded as unsettled.

1 *Lee's Trustee v Bensted* 1916 SC 188, 1915 2 SLT 382; *Sweet (Inspector of Taxes) v Henderson* 1921 SC 92, 1920 2 SLT 411; *Riches v Westminster Bank Ltd* 1947 AC 390, [1947] 1 All ER 469, HL.
2 Income and Corporation Taxes Act 1988 (c 1), s 329. 'Personal injuries' include any disease and any impairment of a person's mental or physical condition: s 329(4). In respect of interest on awards paid prior to 6 April 1981, the interest was tax-free only where it was awarded by a court. From that date, interest paid as part of an out-of-court settlement is also tax-free. Although s 329 applies only to awards of courts in Scotland, England and Northern Ireland, by Extra-Statutory Concession A30, awards are also exempt if made by a foreign court, provided that a similar exemption applies in the country where the award was made.
3 *Dewar v Inland Revenue Comrs* [1935] 2 KB 351, (1935) 19 TC 561, CA.
4 Income and Corporation Taxes Act 1988, s 349(2).
5 *Jefford v Gee* [1970] 2 QB 130, [1970] 1 All ER 1202, CA.
6 *Cairns v MacDiarmid (Inspector of Taxes)* (1982) 56 TC 556, [1983] STC 178, CA; *Corinthian Securities v Cato* [1970] 1 QB 377, [1969] 3 All ER 1168, CA.
7 *Re Cooper* [1911] 2 KB 550, CA.

6. INTEREST ON ARBITRATION AWARDS

1035. Award of interest in arbitration. The general rule is that an arbiter's jurisdiction is limited to that conferred in the deed of submission[1]. The question which arises accordingly is what power an arbiter has to consider and deal with matters of interest. In the case of *John G McGregor (Contractors) Ltd v Grampian Regional Council*, Lord Dunpark said:

'I have no doubt that an arbiter has an implied power to award interest on sums found due from the date of his final decree until payment but, in the absence of an express agreement that he shall have power to award interest on principal sums prior to that date, I do not consider that such a power may be implied'[3].

The decision by the court in that case was that interest could not be awarded before the decree arbitral was finally pronounced, that is, after the case stated under consideration had been remitted back to the arbiter and he had arrived at his final decree upon consideration thereof.

It accordingly appears clear that as matters now stand the arbiter has full power or capacity to deal with questions of interest from a date prior to that of his final decree where the parties have, in terms of the deed of submission, expressly given him full power to do so[3]. Where there is no such power expressly conferred on the arbiter by the deed of submission, it seems in the light of the *McGregor* case that the arbiter will have no such power to deal with interest. It will be a matter of construction of the relevant submission to arbitration in each case whether parties have indeed conferred on the arbiter such powers to deal with interest. If such a power to award interest does exist, then the arbiter must apply the general principles upon award of interest. So, in *Farrans (Construction) Ltd v Dunfermline District Council*[4] the court held that an award of interest made by the arbiter had been wrongly made because the sums in question had not been wrongfully withheld at the date from which the arbiter had awarded interest.

It appears to follow that a statement of claim by a party to arbitration will not suffice to constitute the equivalent of a judicial demand from the date of which payment can be described as wrongfully withheld. Indeed, in the *Farrans* case Lord Justice-Clerk Ross stated that normally interest would be due only from the date of the decree arbitral[5]. In the light of these decisions, statements to the effect that an arbiter has an implied power to award interest apparently without qualification, to be found in certain textbook writings, cannot be regarded as sound law[6]. Nevertheless, the view in the textbook writings accords with what is regarded as the implied power of an arbiter under the common law of England, Australia and New Zealand[7].

So far as the rate of interest is concerned, it appears from the *Farrans* case that the arbiter where he has power to award interest has discretion as to the rate of interest to award[8].

1   *Holmes Oil Co Ltd v Pumpherston Oil Co Ltd* (1891) 18 R (HL) 52; see ARBITRATION, vol 2, para 473.
2   *John G McGregor (Contractors) Ltd v Grampian Regional Council* 1991 SLT 136 at 137 (appeal on procedural point refused 1991 GWD 10-569, HL).
3   *Farrans (Construction) Ltd v Dunfermline District Council* 1988 SCLR 272 at 277, 1988 SLT 466 at 469.
4   1988 SCLR 272, 1988 SLT 466.
5   1988 SCLR 272 at 279, 1988 SLT 466 at 471.
6   J C Irons and R D Melville *The Law of Arbitration in Scotland* (1903) p 219; R L C Hunter *The Law of Arbitration in Scotland* (1988) para 15.48.
7   *Angus Group Ltd v Lincoln Industries Ltd* [1990] 3 NZLR 82. See further J Murray 'Interest on Debt' 1991 SLT (News) 305 at 311.
8   *Farrans (Construction) Ltd v Dunfermline District Council* 1988 SCLR 272 at 279, 1988 SLT 466 at 471.

7. INTEREST ON TRIBUNAL AWARDS

1036. Proceedings before tribunals. Awards of compensation made by tribunals, in the absence of statutory authority, should not include awards of interest. Tribunals are not courts, and instituting proceedings before them is not a judicial demand. Thus, even if what was awarded was, for example, a sum by an industrial tribunal for past wage loss, the rule that mere delay in payment does not at common law ground a claim for interest applied[1]. However, a statutory power was given by the Employment Protection (Consolidation) Act 1978 to the Secretary of State to make orders empowering an industrial tribunal to award interest, at such rates and between such times as he prescribed[2]. By order, with effect from 1 April 1990, tribunal awards are to carry interest at a prescribed rate (15 per cent) if unpaid after forty-two days have elapsed from the date of sending the decision to the parties[3].

Interest is due at the prescribed rate on compensation if, in the absence of agreement, it is assessed by the Lands Tribunal for Scotland for the compulsory purchase of land, if the purchaser has taken possession before payment of the compensation[4]. That interest runs from the date of vesting, where it occurs before the date of entry[5].

However, the Lands Tribunal for Scotland has, since 22 December 1980, had a general power to determine that an award of compensation is to carry interest from the date of that award (unless the tribunal rules otherwise as under Rule of Court 66)[6].

1   *Nelson v British Broadcasting Corpn (No 2)* [1980] ICR 110 at 128, [1979] IRLR 346 at paras 78–80, CA. It was held that the tribunal was not a 'court of record' to which the provisions of the Law Reform (Miscellaneous Provisions) Act 1934 (c 41), s 3 (repealed), apply, empowering these courts to include interest in any sums awarded in respect of claims for debt or damages, for any part of the period between the date when the cause of action arose and the date of the judgment.

Cf *Weeks v Thames Water Authority* (1980) 39 P & CR 208, [1979] JPL 774, Lands Trib. This was an English case of compensation for injurious affection. The claimant had been kept out of his money for several years. The authorities are collected in *Thameside Estates Ltd v Greater London Council* (1979) 249 EG 347, 448, Lands Trib. As to injurious affection resulting from the construction of works, see COMPULSORY ACQUISITION AND COMPENSATION, vol 5, paras 174–177.

2 Employment Protection (Consolidation) Act 1978 (c 44), s 128(3), Sch 9, para 6A (added by the Employment Act 1982 (c 46), s 21(2), Sch 3, para 7).

3 Industrial Tribunals (Interest) Order 1990, SI 1990/479.

4 Land Compensation (Scotland) Act 1963 (c 51), s 40. The rate is prescribed from time to time by regulations made by the Treasury: s 40.

5 *Birrell Ltd v City of Edinburgh District Council* 1983 SC (HL) 75, 1982 SLT 363, affg 1982 SLT 111. Here the former owners had been allowed to remain in occupation, paying no rent, but paying rates, with the permission of the purchasing authority, for several months after the date when the land had vested in that authority under the provisions for expedited procedure of the Town and Country Planning (Scotland) Act 1947 (c 53), Sch 11 (repealed). See now 'general vesting declarations' under the Town and Country Planning (Scotland) Act 1972 (c 52), Sch 24, and COMPULSORY ACQUISITION AND COMPENSATION, vol 5, paras 46 ff.

6 Law Reform (Miscellaneous Provisions) (Scotland) Act 1980 (c 55), s 18; AS (Rules of Court, consolidation and amendment) 1965, SI 1965/321, RC 66.

8. RATE OF INTEREST

1037. Rate of interest. The term 'legal interest' has no meaning other than 'that rate of interest allowed by law'. There is no legal rate of interest, as such.

'It is unfortunately only too plain that much confusion was introduced by the use of the ambiguous term "legal interest" — originally applicable to the maximum rate of 5 per cent fixed by a statute of 12 Anne (long since repealed)'[1].

More recently, where a decree arbitral provided that there should be paid:

'[an] amount of recompense appropriately calculated for any loss suffered by the pursuers in consequence of non-payment . . . of any amount or amounts in respect of which the pursuers are entitled to render their account . . .',

it was held that 'appropriately calculated' must mean 'calculated in accordance with the proper principles of law applicable to the loss claimed'[2]. There were no averments justifying the claim for interest in contract (either express or implied) and none from which it could be inferred that the principal sum had been wrongfully withheld. Consequently the claim for interest as calculated by the pursuers was totally irrelevant[2].

In times of widely fluctuating interest rates, whether evidenced by the minimum lending rate of the Bank of England or the base rates of the several clearing banks or expressed and recognised in the appropriate statutory instruments dealing with allowable interest in compensation cases[3], or taxation matters[4], or in the Acts of Sederunt[5] fixing the rates allowed by the court or decrees, it is not useful to rehearse the various figures applied by the court in reported cases, many of which date back to Victorian times. At one time 5 per cent was considered penal, for example, in the Partnership Act 1890[6].

The court will fix a rate if it is given the appropriate material upon which to base its calculation, in the various circumstances of the cases before it. For example, it may have regard to the rate of interest which is paid by or demanded by banks or other financial institutions, which may be earned upon good securities during the period in question[7], or which was actually earned by the funds in the period[8].

Following errors in the calculation for converting a foreign currency into sterling (subsequently corrected), agents wrongfully withheld money due to their principal. The court, having looked at all the circumstances, applied 'equitable principles', and allowed interest on the whole sum at the appropriate (fluctuating) judicial rate prevailing at the material time as fixed by Act of Sederunt[9] from the date when a court action had been raised. This action had been raised in England, but the proceedings had failed for want of jurisdiction[10].

Where the parties have contracted for an agreed rate of interest payable on the principal sum, and provided that it does not breach the provisions of the Consumer Credit Act 1974, for example, as an extortionate credit bargain[11], the Second Division has held that there is no good reason why the court should refuse to grant a decree for payment in terms of the contract. The decree does not terminate the contract[12].

1 *Kearon v Thomson's Trustees* 1949 SC 287 at 293, 1949 SLT 286 at 289, per Lord President Cooper. (The statute of 12 Anne is the Usury Act 1713 (c 15) (repealed by the Usury Laws Repeal Act 1854 (c 90)). See also *Bank of Scotland v Davis* 1982 SLT 20; and cf *Grant v Grant's Trustees* (1898) 25 R 948 at 950.

2 *Hunter v Livingston Development Corpn* 1984 SLT 10 at 13, per Lord Cowie, OH, citing Lord Westbury in *Carmichael v Caledonian Rly Co* (1870) 8 M (HL) 119 at 131.

3 Land Compensation (Scotland) Act 1963 (c 51), s 40; Law Reform (Miscellaneous Provisions) (Scotland) Act 1980 (c 55), s 18.

4 Taxes Management Act 1970 (c 9), s 86 (substituted by the Finance (No 2) Act 1975 (c 45), s 46(1), and amended by the Finance Act 1980 (c 48), ss 61(3), 62(2), and the Finance Act 1989 (c 26), ss 156, 158, 179). Rates of interest are set by regulations made by the Treasury exercisable by statutory instrument subject to annulment in pursuance of a resolution of the House of Commons: Finance Act 1989, s 178.

5 Administration of Justice (Scotland) Act 1933 (c 41), s 16; AS (Rules of Court, consolidation and amendment) 1965, SI 1965/321, RC 66 (amended by SI 1974/2090, SI 1983/398 and SI 1985/ 1178); Sheriff Courts (Scotland) Extracts Act 1892 (c 17), s 9 (substituted by AS (Interest in Sheriff Court Decrees or Extracts) 1975, SI 1975/948, and amended by SI 1983/409 and SI 1985/1179, made under the Administration of Justice (Scotland) Act 1972 (c 59), s 4). Under these provisions the rate at the date at which this volume states the law was 15 per cent, effective from 16 August 1985.

6 Partnership Act 1890 (c 39), s 24(3).

7 *Melville v Noble's Trustees* (1896) 24 R 243, 4 SLT 198. The trustees had been lax in their administration, leaving administration to one of their number, a land agent, who put the money on deposit receipt, earning an average rate of 2³/₈ per cent. The average rate of interest on money invested in Consols was 2⁴/₅ per cent during the same period. The Second Division held that 3 per cent was the proper sum to fix as the return which the trustees should have earned. In the case of privately arranged loans, the rate of interest may be fixed with reference to the rate currently recommended by the Commissioners on the Rate of Interest on Landed Securities in Scotland for the half year following the ensuing term of Whitsunday and Martinmas.

8 *Ross v Ross* (1896) 23 R 802. Where a son, on coming of age, claimed *legitim* out of his father's estate, with interest at 5 per cent, the court held that the 4 per cent earned represented a fair estimate of the actual income of the fund. Five per cent was not a statutory rate of legal interest, only a maximum rate. The court could reduce the rate when there was a permanent fall in the rate of interest obtainable in the country.

9 RC 66 (as amended: see note 5 above); Court of Session Act 1988 (c 36), s 5; cf the Sheriff Courts (Scotland) Extracts Act 1892 (c 17), s 9 (as amended: see note 5 above).

10 *Trans Barwil Agencies (UK) Ltd v John S Braid & Co Ltd* 1989 SCLR 647, 1990 SLT 182, OH.

11 See the Consumer Credit Act 1974 (c 39), ss 137–140, and CONSUMER CREDIT, vol 5, para 932.

12 *Bank of Scotland v Davis* 1982 SLT 20 at 21, followed in *Royal Bank of Scotland v Briggs* 1982 SLT (Sh Ct) 46.

9. COMPOUND INTEREST

1038–1100. Compound interest. The practice of the courts with regard to the awarding of compound interest provides another example of the difficulty of bringing within general principles the rules which the court applies. It has been said that the allowance of compound interest is contrary to principle and unsupported by authority[1]. In Bell's opinion, 'however long arrears of interest may have continued unpaid, they cannot without some voluntary or judicial operation be converted into a principal bearing interest'[2].

If, however, interest is to be regarded as the remedy equivalent to damages for the non-payment of money due, it is difficult to see how a debtor could successfully argue on principle that his creditor should not be put into the position that he would otherwise have been in had he had the use of his money timeously. Yet the courts have been reluctant to make the not unreasonable assumption that interest would compound at least annually.

Nevertheless, compound interest is a necessary feature of commercial life, and the courts have come to recognise this reality.

The circumstances in which compound interest is allowed were set out by Lord Justice-Clerk Patton:

'A claim for compound interest, with annual rests, is a demand which can only be maintained, either in the case of a fixed usage in commercial dealings, or where there has been an abuse in a party trusted with funds, and violating his trust'[3].

Persons in a fiduciary position would be so liable. For example, the estate of a *curator bonis* who had retained his ward's funds in his own hands was held liable to pay compound interest at a rate of 5 per cent on the annual balances, although 4 per cent was the current rate[4]. Advances by a factor for a trust estate do bear compound interest[5].

Parties may agree by contract to compound interest; so interest on a bank overdraft is normally compounded at agreed fixed intervals and the final balance may be sued upon and will bear interest from the date of citation.

Competition between banks and building societies has also led to both offering various interest-paying current accounts and deposit accounts (under a variety of names) paying higher rates of interest. These accounts may be subject to 'penalties', for example for too frequent withdrawals or withdrawals without a specified period of notice, for permitting the balance to fall below a certain sum, or for overdrawing. These 'penalties' may take the form of loss of interest, an enhanced rate of interest on the sum overdrawn or a transaction charge where otherwise there would be none. However, the main attraction of these accounts is that the interest is usually calculated daily and credited on a monthly, quarterly or half-yearly basis, thus consolidating or compounding it with the principal.

The courts have drawn a distinction between allowing interest upon arrears of interest on the one hand, and compound interest on the other hand. So interest upon arrears of interest has been awarded, where the interest due is in the same position as an outstanding principal sum[6].

However, the 'general rule' has been applied to disallow compound interest even on cash advances by a solicitor to a client over a period of years[7], and to interest on expenditure accrued down to the date of citation, where the pursuer sought to add it to the principal — the effect being similar to compound interest[8].

It is very difficult to justify the reluctance to allow compound interest, particularly in cases of damages for personal injuries or fatal accidents. On the other hand, the general view of most legal systems appears to be that the simple rate should be applied, and that view was adopted by the Law Commission for England and Wales[9].

1 *Clyde Navigation Trustees v Kelvin Shipping Co Ltd* 1927 SC 622 at 658, 1927 SLT 436 at 437, per Lord Justice-Clerk Alness.
2 Bell *Commentaries* I,695.
3 *Douglas v Douglas's Trustees* (1867) 5 M 827 at 836, per Lord Justice-Clerk Patton, cited in *Nash Dredging (UK) Ltd v Kestrel Marine Ltd* 1986 SLT 67 at 68, OH.

4 *Blair v Murray* (1843) 5 D 1315.

5 *Scott v Handyside's Trustees* (1868) 6 M 753.

6 *Napier v Gordon* (1831) 5 W & S 745, HL, cited in *Nash Dredging (UK) Ltd v Kestrel Marine Ltd* 1986 SLT 67, OH. *Napier* was an action of multiplepoinding, but the House of Lords held that no doubt existed as to the right to recover interest on the interest which is the subject matter of the action. The party who does not pay is in *mora*; if he consigns the sum claimed into court, he is safe, and from that time he is not chargeable with interest. If he keeps the money mixed with his own funds, he is liable for interest at the legal rate: *Napier v Gordon* (1831) 5 W & S 745 at 758, HL; *Maclean v Campbell* (1856) 18 D 609; *Nash Dredging (UK) Ltd v Kestrel Marine Ltd* 1986 SLT 67, OH.

7 *Bunten v Hart* (1902) 9 SLT 476, OH. Compound interest had been refused by the Auditor of Court following *Douglas v Douglas's Trustees* (1867) 5 M 827. Simple interest on the solicitor's personal account was also refused, since no judicial demand for payment had been made, nor any written intimation (that interest would be claimed from the date of demand) had been given, following *Blair's Trustees v Payne* (1884) 12 R 104.

8 *Clyde Navigation Trustees v Kelvin Shipping Co Ltd* 1927 SC 622, 1927 SLT 436.

9 *Interest* (Law Com Working Paper no. 66) (1976).

INTERPRETATION OF STATUTES, DEEDS AND OTHER INSTRUMENTS

		PARA
1. INTERPRETATION OF STATUTES	. . . . . .	1101
(1) Introduction	. . . .	1101
(2) General Principles of Interpretation	. . . . .	1102
(a) Introduction	. . . .	1102
(b) Construction where the Meaning is Clear	. . .	1103
(A) The Literal Rule	. . . . .	1103
(B) Omissions not to be Inferred	. . .	1107
(C) The Golden Rule	. . . . .	1109
(D) Act not to be Extended beyond its Object	. .	1111
(E) *Contemporanea Expositio*	. . . .	1112
(c) Construction where the Meaning is not Clear	. .	1114
(A) Construction to avoid Injustice	. . .	1114
(B) The Mischief Rule	. . . . .	1115
(C) Construction according to Intent as well as to Words Used	. . . .	1116
(D) Statute to be Read as a Whole	. . .	1119
(E) Construction *ut res Magis Valeat Quam Pereat*	.	1123
(F) Construction to Avoid Absurdity	. . .	1124
(3) Certain Presumptions	. . . . . .	1126
(a) Presumption against Changes in Existing Law and Practice	.	1126
(b) Presumption in Relation to Jurisdiction	. . .	1128
(c) Other Presumptions	. . . . .	1131
(4) Aids to Construction	. . . . . .	1134
(a) Internal Aids	. . . . . .	1134
(b) External Aids	. . . . . .	1143
(A) Introduction	. . . . . .	1143
(B) The Historical Setting	. . . .	1144
(C) Parliamentary History	. . . .	1147
(D) Official Reports Commissioned by Government	.	1149
(E) Textbooks and Dictionaries	. . . .	1151
(F) Conventions	. . . . . .	1152
(G) Other Enactments	. . . . .	1155
(i) Introduction	. . . . .	1155
(ii) Earlier Enactments	. . . .	1156
(iii) Later Enactments	. . . .	1160
(H) Conveyancing and Administrative Practice	.	1161
(I) Uniform Court Decisions and Usage	. .	1163
(J) Statutory Rules made under an Act	. .	1164
(5) Subsidiary Principles of Construction	. . . .	1165
(a) *Expressio Unius est Exclusio Alterius*	. . .	1165
(b) The *Ejusdem Generis* Rule	. . . .	1166
(c) Words of Rank	. . . . . .	1169
(d) *De Minimus Non Curat Praetor*	. . . .	1170
(e) Computation of Time	. . . . .	1171
(6) Mandatory, Directory and Permissive Enactments	. .	1175
(a) Introduction	. . . . . .	1175

(b) Enactments which are Mandatory in Form 1176
(c) Enactments which are Discretionary in Form . . . 1179
(7) Strict and Qualified Duties 1181
(8) Penal, Taxing and Remedial Statutes 1184
(9) Extent and Application of Acts 1187
(10) Retrospection 1189
(11) Repeals 1194
(12) Enactments to which Special Rules of Construction Apply . . 1200
(a) Pre-Union Scots Acts 1200
(b) Private Acts 1202
(c) European Economic Community Legislation . . . 1205
(13) The Interpretation Act 1978 1206

**2. INTERPRETATION OF DEEDS AND OTHER
DOCUMENTS** 1213
(1) Introduction 1213
(2) General Rules of Interpretation 1214
(3) Implications 1235
(4) Particular Deeds 1237
(a) Conveyances 1237
(b) Leases 1251
(c) Heritable Securities 1254
(d) Land Certificates 1259
(e) Miscellaneous Deeds 1260
(5) Wills and Other Testamentary Writings 1263
(a) Principles of Construction 1263
(b) Presumptions 1265
(c) Vesting and Repugnancy 1269
(d) Ineffectual Conditions or Directions 1270

1. INTERPRETATION OF STATUTES

(1) INTRODUCTION

1101. The necessity for rules for the interpretation of statutes. This part of this title is concerned with the principal modern rules for the interpretation of enactments. It may be wondered, at any rate by those who have not been concerned with the making of statute law, why statutes cannot be drafted in simple and unambiguous terms, thereby obviating the need for such rules. It is understandable that rules might be needed for the construction of wills and other documents when these have been drafted, perhaps in non-legal language, by laymen. Most Bills, on the other hand, are drafted by specialist legal draftsmen in implementation of carefully prepared policy instructions. Before they reach the statute book they are systematically examined on a line-by-line basis by both Houses of Parliament, and in the case of the House of Commons by a standing committee sometimes sitting for weeks or even months.

It is, of course, very easy to draft a clear provision that, for instance, all vehicles must be driven on the left hand side of the road, but very few Bills deal with such a simple concept. Enactments have, so far as possible, to be unambiguous, and to achieve this with a complex subject matter often necessitates the sacrifice of each comprehension. As Sir John Rowlatt, a former First Parliamentary Counsel once said, the intelligibility of a complex law is in inverse proportion to its chance of being right[1]. Again, in the drafting of legislation which modifies some existing code of legislation which is already very detailed, for example the Agricultural Holdings Acts, reasonable simplicity and clarity might be achieved by scrapping the existing legislation and starting again, but the impossibility of finding sufficient parliamentary time to consider the much larger Bill produced by proceeding in this way rules out this technique.

So far as Scotland is concerned, often simplicity and reasonable clarity could be achieved if a particular measure could be produced as a Scotland only enactment. Unfortunately lack of parliamentary time may make this impossible, and the only way to proceed is to include Scotland in a Great Britain Bill which may well be drafted in terms which are scarcely suitable for Scotland.

The main reasons, however, for legislation not always being clear and unambiguous appear to be:

(1) that it is not always possible for even the most experienced draftsman to express with complete precision what he intends;

(2) that, particularly with a complex measure, it is not always possible, even with the most thorough consideration, to anticipate every set of facts which may occur, and therefore situations may arise for which the legislation does not cater; and

(3) that, because of the form of instructions to the draftsman, misunderstanding may arise on a point of detail between what the policy maker wants and what the draftsman thinks the policy maker wants, resulting in a provision which the policy maker thinks achieves his purpose when in fact it does not.

1 H S Kent *In on the Act* (1979) p 77.

(2) GENERAL PRINCIPLES OF INTERPRETATION

(a) Introduction

1102. Intention of Parliament. The object of all interpretation is to discover the intention of Parliament. This intention must be deduced from the language used[1]. Statutes should be interpreted in such a way as to carry out the intention of the legislature or, as Lord Radcliffe said in *Attorney-General for Canada v Hallett and Carey*, 'the paramount rule remains that every statute is to be expounded according to its manifest and expressed intention'[2]. In *Westminster Bank v Zang* Lord Reid gave guidance as to how the intention of Parliament is to be ascertained in these words:

'No principle of interpretation of statutes, however, is more firmly settled than the rule that the court must deduce the intention of Parliament from the words used in the Act. If those words are in any way ambiguous — if they are reasonably capable of more than one meaning — or if the provision in question is contradicted by or is incompatible with any other provision in the Act, then the court may depart from the natural meaning of the words in question; but beyond that we cannot go'[3].

Where, then, there are no ambiguities in the provision to be interpreted or no contraditions between that provision and other provisions of the statute concerned, it is not difficult to discover the intention of the provision. In any other circumstances, however, the intention may be uncertain and open to argument. As Lord Watson said in *Salomon v Salomon*:

'"Intention of the Legislature" is a common but very slippery phrase, which, popularly understood, may signify anything from intention embodied in positive enactment to speculative opinion as to what the Legislature probably would have meant, although there has been an omission to enact it'[4].

Various rules and presumptions of construction have therefore been developed over the years to aid the courts in their task of interpretation, but, as will be seen from what follows, these rules and presumptions often appear to conflict and may be cited in support of either a narrow or a wide interpretation in any particular case. No canon of construction has any greater authority in law than any other canon and it is, therefore, very difficult to predict which interpretation the court will favour in any given case. However, the principal rules and presumptions are set out below[5].

1 *Capper v Baldwin* [1965] 2 QB 53 at 61, [1965] 1 All ER 787 at 791, DC, per Lord Parker CJ.
2 *Attorney-General for Canada v Hallet and Carey Ltd* [1952] AC 427 at 429, PC.
3 *Westminster Bank Ltd v Zang* [1966] AC 182 at 222, [1966] 1 All ER 114 at 120, HL.
4 *Salomon v A Salomon & Co Ltd* [1897] AC 22 at 38, HL.
5 See paras 1103 ff below.

(b) Construction where the Meaning is Clear

(A) THE LITERAL RULE

1103. Introduction. The first principle for the construction of Acts of Parliament is that it is to be assumed that words and phrases of technical legislation are used in their technical meaning if they have acquired one and otherwise, if the words of the statute are precise and unambiguous, then these words must be given their ordinary and natural meaning and no further questions of interpretation arise. As Bell put it, 'there is place for interpretation only where the words admit of two different meanings'[1]. Again, Lord Morris of Borth-y-Gest in *Shop and Store Developments v Inland Revenue Comrs* said:

> 'the decision in this case calls for a full and fair application of particular statutory language to particular facts as found. The desirability or the undesirability of one conclusion as compared with another cannot furnish a guide in reaching a decision. The result reached must be that which is directed by that which is enacted'[2].

It is also part of the literal principle that the provisions of a statute are to be construed according to the rules of grammar.

1 W Bell *A Dictionary and Digest of the Law of Scotland* (4th edn, 1838) under 'Statute Law'.
2 *Shop and Store Developments v Inland Revenue Comrs* [1967] 1 AC 472 at 493, [1967] 1 All ER 42 at 47, HL.

1104. Application of the literal rule. The case of *Pawley v Wharldall*[1] provides a simple example of the application of the literal rule. Under what is now section 3 of the Road Traffic Act 1988 (c 52), it is an offence for a person to drive a motor vehicle on a road 'without reasonable consideration for other persons using the road'. In the *Pawley* case the defendant was charged with a contravention of the provision while driving an omnibus from Wetherby to Leeds. Five of his passengers gave evidence against him, but no evidence was offered by the prosecution that anyone outside the vehicle was treated without reasonable consideration. On appeal the court rejected the argument that the words 'other persons using the road' applied to persons outside the vehicle and did not include passengers in the vehicle itself. Lord Parker CJ said other persons using the road:

> 'are clearly persons other than the driver of the motor vehicle in question, and prima facie I should have thought any passenger uses the road just as much as does the driver'[2].

and he went on:

'if one was going to construe those words in the manner contended for by the [defendant]..., one would have to insert some such words as "without reasonable consideration for other persons using the road other than such persons using the road as passengers in the vehicle being driven by the person concerned". There seems to me no warrant for inserting words of that sort or for giving the words other than their natural meaning'[3].

1 *Pawley v Wharldall* [1966] 1 QB 373, [1965] 2 All ER 757, DC.
2 [1966] 1 QB 373 at 376, [1965] 2 All ER 757 at 758, DC.
3 [1966] 1 QB 373 at 378, [1965] 2 All ER 757 at 760, DC.

1105. Unambiguous words. Going one step further, it has been said that where words are unambiguous they must be interpreted in that unambiguous sense 'whatever hardship may be the consequence'[1]. This principle of following the literal meaning of unambiguous words, regardless of harsh consequences, has been accepted even in modern times, for example, in *Cartledge v Jopling*[2], where the House of Lords held that the plaintiffs who had contracted pneumo-coniosis as a result of the defendant's negligence were statute barred by the Limitation Act 1939 before they knew or might reasonably have discovered that they were suffering from the disease[3]. The decision in that case was in fact overturned by the Limitation Act 1963[4].

Again, in *Inland Revenue Comrs v Hinchy* Lord Reid said that even though it is difficult to believe that Parliament ever really intended the consequences of a literal interpretation:

'we can only take the intention of Parliament from the words which they have used in the Act, and therefore the question is whether these words are capable of a more limited construction. If not, then we must apply them as they stand, however unreasonable or unjust the consequences, and however strongly we may suspect that this is not the real intention of Parliament'[5].

In that case the House of Lords held that a penalty, in the now repealed section 25(3) of the Income Tax Act 1952 (c 10) (for making an incorrect return of income) of £20 'and treble the tax which he ought to be charged under this Act', referred not to the tax on the amount which the taxpayer had failed to declare, but to the whole tax which he ought to be charged for the relevant year, notwithstanding that this produced an inequitable result for the taxpayer[6].

1 W Bell *A Dictionary and Digest of the Law of Scotland* (4th edn, 1838) under 'Statute Law'.
2 *Cartledge v E Jopling & Sons Ltd* [1963] AC 758, [1963] 1 All ER 341, HL.
3 The Limitation Act 1939 (c 21) is repealed with savings.
4 Ie the Limitation Act 1963 (c 47) Pt I (ss 1–7) (repealed). For the corresponding provisions applicable to Scotland, see Pt II (ss 8–13) (repealed). See now the Prescription and Limitation (Scotland) Act 1973 (c 52), Pt II (ss 17–23), and PRESCRIPTION AND LIMITATION.
5 *Inland Revenue Comrs v Hinchy* [1960] AC 748 at 767, [1960] 1 All ER 505 at 512, HL.
6 This result was remedied by the Finance Act 1960 (c 44), ss 47, 48 (repealed). See now the Taxes Management Act 1970 (c 9), s 95(1), (2) (amended by the Income and Corporation Taxes Act 1988 (c 1), s 844, Sch 29, para 32).

1106. Literal construction not to prevail if opposed to the legislature; grammar. In *Caledonian Rly Co v North British Rly Co* Lord Chancellor Selbourne observed that:

'The more literal construction ought not to prevail if... it is opposed to the intention of the Legislature as apparent by the statute, and if the words are sufficiently flexible to admit of some other construction by which that intention will be better effectuated'[1].

Moreover, the rule that enactments are to be construed according to the rules of grammar was qualified in *Warburton v Loveland* in these words:

'I apprehend it is a rule in the construction of statutes that in the first instance the grammatical sense of the words is to be adhered to. If that is contrary to, or inconsistent with, any expressed intention or declared purpose of the statutes, or if it would involve any absurdity, repugnance or inconsistency, the grammatical sense must be modified, extended, or abridged, so far as to avoid such an inconvenience, but no further'[2].

1 *Caledonian Rly Co v North British Rly* (1881) 8 R (HL) 23 at 25. See also *Inland Revenue v Luke* 1963 SC (HL) 65 at 80, 1963 SLT 129 at 135, per Lord Reid.
2 *Warburton v Loveland d Ivie* (1828) 1 Hud & B 623 at 648, Ex Ch, per Burton J.

(B) OMISSIONS NOT TO BE INFERRED

1107. *Casus omissus* not to be supplied by the courts. It follows from the literal rule that where the meaning of a statutory provision is plain, the court is not entitled to fill in any gaps disclosed in it, as to do so would be to usurp the functions of the legislature[1]. In *Jones v Smart*[2] the question was whether a doctor of physic in a Scottish university was qualified to kill game under the Game Act 1670 which provided 'that every person . . . other than the son . . . of an esquire, or other person of higher degree . . . are declared to be persons by the laws of this realm not allowed to have . . . any guns . . . for taking game'[3]. Among other arguments for proving that the Scottish doctor was qualified, it was contended that the legislature could not have intended to exclude such a person. However, Buller J rejected this argument, saying:

'we are bound to take the act of parliament, as they have made it; a *casus omissus* can in no case be supplied by a court of law, for that would be to make laws'[4].

A clear modern example of a case where the rule that a *casus omissus* is not to be supplied by the courts is *Fisher v Bell*[5]. In that case a shopkeeper displayed in his shop window a 'flick knife' with a ticket behind it bearing the words 'Ejector knife-4*s*'. The shopkeeper was charged under the Restriction of Offensive Weapons Act 1959 which provides that any person who manufactures, sells or hires or offers for sale or hire, or lends or gives to any other person a 'flick knife' is guilty of an offence[6]. It was argued by the defendant that it is a well-known law that displaying goods in a shop window does not amount to an offer for sale but merely an invitation to treat and therefore the Act did not cover the situation in the case. Lord Parker CJ, giving the leading judgment, reluctantly accepted this argument on the basis that Parliament must be taken to know the general law, and continued:

'At first sight it sounds absurd that knives of this sort cannot be manufactured, sold, hired, lent, or given, but apparently they can be displayed in shop windows; but even if this . . . is a casus omissus it is not for this court to supply the omission'[7].

He then went on to cite Lord Simonds from *Magor and St Mellons Rural District Council v Newport Corpn*[8].

1 *Magor and St Mellons Rural District Council v Newport Corpn* [1952] AC 189 at 191, [1951] 2 All ER 839 at 841, HL, per Lord Simonds.
2 *Jones v Smart* (1875) 1 Term Rep 44.
3 Game Act 1670 (22 & 23 Cha 2 c 25), s 3 (repealed).
4 *Jones v Smart* (1875) 1 Term Rep 44 at 52.
5 *Fisher v Bell* [1961] 1 QB 394, [1960] 3 All ER 731, DC.
6 See the Restriction of Offensive Weapons Act 1959 (c 37), s 1(1) (as originally enacted). See now s 1(1) (amended by the Restriction of Offensive Weapons Act 1961 (c 22), s 1).
7 *Fisher v Bell* [1961] 1 QB 394 at 399, 400, [1960] 3 All ER 731, 733, DC.
8 See note 1 above.

1108. Distinction between inferring omissions and correcting faultiness of expression. In the case of *R v Oakes*[1] a distinction was made between inferring omissions and correcting a faultiness of expression where the literal reading of an Act produced an unintelligible result. In that case the defendant was charged with doing an act preparatory to the commission of an offence under the Official Secrets Act 1920, which provides that any person who aids or abets and does any act preparatory to the commission of an offence is guilty of a felony[2]. The defendant contended that he was not charged with any offence since he was not also accused of aiding or abetting. In his judgment Lord Parker CJ accepted the rule against supplying omissions in these words:

'where the literal reading of a statute, and a penal statute, produces an intelligible result, clearly there is no ground for reading in words or changing words according to what may be the supposed intention of Parliament'[3].

In this case, however, he thought that a literal reading produced an unintelligible result, that what the court was dealing with was a mere faultiness in expression and that, in accordance with the clear intention of the enactment, the court was entitled to substitute 'or' for 'and'[4].

1 *R v Oakes* [1959] 2 QB 350, [1959] 2 All ER 92, CCA.
2 See the Official Secrets Act 1920 (c 75), s 7.
3 *R v Oakes* [1959] 2 QB 350 at 354, [1959] 2 All ER 92 at 94, CCA.
4 [1959] 2 QB 350 at 356, 357, [1959] 2 All ER 92 at 95, 96, CCA.

(C) THE GOLDEN RULE

1109. The golden rule. The golden rule was so named by Jervis CJ[1] and was perhaps best expressed by Lord Wensleydale in *Grey v Pearson*:

'in construing wills and indeed statutes, and all written instruments, the grammatical and ordinary sense of the words is to be adhered to, unless that would lead to some absurdity, or some repugnance or inconsistency with the rest of the instrument, in which case the grammatical and ordinary sense of the words may be modified, so as to avoid that absurdity and inconsistency, but no further'[2].

The rule is clearly illustrated by the English case of *Lee v Knapp*[3]. Under what is now section 170(2) of the Road Traffic Act 1988 (c 52) the driver of a motor vehicle must 'stop' after an accident. Winn LJ agreed with the view expressed in an Australian case[4] that a momentary pause after an accident would not exempt the driver of a car from the necessity of stopping to give particulars, and went on:

'The phrase "the driver of the motor vehicle shall stop" is properly to be construed as meaning the driver of the motor vehicle shall stop it and remain where he has stopped it for such a period of time as in the prevailing circumstances, having regard in particular to the character of the road or place in which the accident happened, will provide a sufficient period to enable persons who have a right so to do, and reasonable ground for so doing, to require of him direct and personally the information which may be required under the section'[5].

1 *Mattison v Hart* (1854) 14 CB 357 at 385.
2 *Grey v Pearson* (1857) 6 HL Cas 61 at 106.
3 *Lee v Knapp* [1967] 2 QB 442, [1966] 3 All ER 961, DC.
4 *Noblet v Condon* [1935] SASR 329.
5 *Lee v Knapp* [1967] 2 QB 442 at 447, 448, [1966] 3 All ER 961 at 963, DC.

1110. Limitations. Lord Blackburn, while accepting the golden rule, drew attention to the limitations:

'I agree in that completely, but unfortunately in the cases in which there is real difficulty it does not help us much, because the cases in which there is real difficulty are those in which there is a controversy as to what the grammatical and ordinary sense of the words used with reference to the subject-matter is. To one mind it may appear that the most that can be said is, that the sense may be what is contended by the one side, and that the inconsistency and repugnancy is very great, that you should make a great stretch to avoid such absurdity, and that what is required to avoid it is a very little stretch or none at all. To another mind it may appear that the meaning of the words is perfectly clear, that they can bear no other meaning at all, and that to substitute any other meaning would be not to interpret the words used, but to make an instrument for the parties, and that the supposed inconsistency or repugnancy is perhaps a hardship — a thing which perhaps it would have been wiser to have avoided, but which we have no power to deal with'[1].

1 *Caledonian Rly Co v North British Rly* (1881) 8 R (HL) 23 at 31.

(D) ACT NOT TO BE EXTENDED BEYOND ITS OBJECT

1111. Object of Act. If a statute has been passed for one particular purpose, a court will not interpret the Act so as to extend its operation to something which is foreign to its object and beyond its scope. *Macbeth v Ashley*[1] was concerned with the power of magistrates under the Public Houses Acts Amendment (Scotland) Act 1862 to close public houses 'in any particular locality' before the statutory hour[2]. It was held (obiter) in that case that, if the magistrates, under the guise of exercising this power, were to order the public houses to be closed earlier, not merely in one particular locality, but in portion after portion of the whole district, not with reference to the particular wants or requirements of each portion, until eventually all the public houses in the whole district had been closed at the earlier hour, this would be as Lord Chancellor Cairns said:

'adopting [a] course for the purpose of doing what I must describe as evading an Act of Parliament, your Lordships would not be prepared to sanction, but would discountenance and prevent the exercise of a power which was used in that way'[3].

1 *Macbeth v Ashley* (1874) 1 R (HL) 14, 2 LR Sc & Div 352.
2 See the Public Houses Acts Amendment (Scotland) Act 1862 (c 35), s 2 (repealed).
3 *Macbeth v Ashley* (1874) 1 R (HL) 14 at 18, 2 LR Sc & Div 352 at 357.

(E) *CONTEMPORANEA EXPOSITIO*

1112. Ancient statutes. It has often been held, and not unwisely or improperly, that the construction of very ancient statutes must be elucidated by what in the language of the courts is called *contemporanea expositio*, that is, seeing how they were understood at the time they were passed[1]. In *Graham v Irving* both Lord McLaren and Lord Kinnear were of the opinion that, in construing the March Dykes Act 1661 (c 284), 'great weight ought to be given to the contemporaneous decisions of the court'[2], for, as Lord McLaren said in *Middleton v Tough*, in considering old Scots Acts relating to Sunday labour:

'we know that it was the practice of the Scottish Legislature to pass statutes which were expressed in very general terms, which were not always workable without the aid of judicial construction, and which were intended to be worked out by the Courts of law applying common-sense principles to their interpretation'[3].

However, in *Walker Trustees v Lord Advocate*[4] it was held that, as the terms of article 20 of the Union with England Act 1707 (c 7) were unambiguous, no consideration could be given to the fact that it had been operated between 1766 and 1904 in a way contrary to these terms.

1 *Earl of Crawford v Duke of Montrose* (1853) 1 Macq 401 at 406, HL, per Lord Cranworth LC.
2 *Graham v Irving* (1899) 2 F 29 at 36.
3 *Middleton v Tough* 1908 SC (J) 32 at 39, 15 SLT 991 at 995.
4 *Walker Trustees v Lord Advocate* 1912 SC (HL) 12, 1911 2 SLT 455.

1113. Modern statutes. The position is less clear cut in relation to the use of *contemporanea expositio* in the interpretation of modern statutes. In *Clyde Navigation Trustees v Laird & Son* Lord Watson said:

> 'When there are ambiguous expressions in an Act passed one or two centuries ago, it may be legitimate to refer to the construction put upon these expressions throughout a long course of years, by the unanimous consent of all parties interested, as evidencing what must presumably have been the intention of the Legislature at that remote period. But I feel bound to construe a recent statute according to its own terms, when these are brought into controversy, and not according to the views which interested parties may have hitherto taken: and in determining the true import of such a statute it appears to me to be quite immaterial to consider whether it was passed in the year 1858 or in 1883'[1].

Lord Watson's dictum was adopted by Cozens-Hardy LJ in *Assheton-Smith v Owen*[2], but Lord Blackburn in the *Clyde Navigation* case, supported by Stirling LJ in the *Assheton-Smith* case, were prepared to admit *contemporanea expositio* as an aid to construction. Again, in *Scottish Cinema and Variety Theatres v Ritchie*[3] it was held that a building which it was proposed to erect for use as a picture house was not a 'theatre' within the meaning of section 251 of the Greenock Corporation Act 1909 (c cxxix) because inter alia, according to *contemporanea expositio*, the expression 'theatre' in section 251 did not include a building devoted to the exhibition of cinematograph films.

1 *Clyde Navigation Trustees v Laird & Son* (1883) 10 R (HL) 77 at 83.
2 *Assheton Smith v Owen* [1906] 1 Ch 179 at 212, 213.
3 *Scottish Cinema and Variety Theatres Ltd v Ritchie* 1929 SC 350, 1929 SLT 323.

(c) Construction where the Meaning is not Clear

(A) CONSTRUCTION TO AVOID INJUSTICE

1114. Duty of courts to avoid injustice. As has already been stated, when the language of a statute is unambiguous and explicit, it must receive full effect, regardless of any harsh consequences. However, if an enactment is open to two possible constructions and if it appears that one of those constructions will do injustice and the other will avoid that injustice 'it is the bounden duty of the Court to adopt the second and not to adopt the first of those constructions'[1]. In the Scottish case of *Heritable Reversionary Co v Millar* where the language of the enactment concerned was capable of two possible constructions, Lord Field cited the above quoted rule[1] and said:

> 'This rule does not depend upon any principle or authority peculiar to the English law, but may safely be applied to the construction of an analogous statute forming part of the law of Scotland'[2].

In another case involving the interpretation of an enactment whose meaning was obscure, the Judge Ordinary said:

'how difficult, not to say impossible, it is to put a perfectly logical construction upon it; but the Court is bound to construe it, and, as far as it can, to make it available for carrying out the objects of the legislature, and for doing justice between the parties'[3].

1 *Hill v East and West India Dock Co* (1884) 9 App Cas 448 at 456, HL, per Lord Cairns.
2 *Heritable Reversionary Co v Millar* (1892) 19 R (HL) 43 at 55.
3 *Phillips v Phillips* (1866) LR 1 P & D 169 at 173.

(B) THE MISCHIEF RULE

1115. *Heydon's Case*. The mischief rule was originally enunciated in 1584 in *Heydon's Case* in the following terms:

'that for the sure and true interpretation of all statutes in general (be they penal or beneficial, restrictive or enlarging of the common law) four things are to be discerned and considered:
1st What was the common law before the making of the Act.
2nd What was the mischief and defect for which the common law did not provide.
3rd What remedy the parliament hath resolved and appointed to cure the disease of the commonwealth. And
4th The true reason of the remedy; and then the office of all the judges is always to make such construction as shall suppress the mischief, and advance the remedy, and to suppress subtle inventions and evasions for the continuance of the mischief, and *pro privato commodo*, and to add force and life to the cure and remedy according to the true intent of the makers of the act, *pro bono publico*'[1].

The so-called rule in *Heydon's Case* is still in effect. As Lindley MR expressed it in *Re Mayfair Property Co*:

'In order properly to interpret any statute it is as necessary now as it was when Lord Coke reported *Heydon's Case* to consider how the law stood when the statute to be construed was passed, what the mischief was for which the old law did not provide, and the remedy provided by the statute to cure that mischief'[2].

Again in the more recent case of *Gartside v Inland Revenue Comrs* Lord Reid said:

'It is always proper to construe an ambiguous word or phrase in the light of the mischief which the provision is obviously designed to prevent, and in light of the reasonableness of the consequences which follow from giving it a particular construction'[3].

The mischief rule is well illustrated by the case of *Smith v Hughes* which concerned the interpretation of the words 'in a street' in section 1(1) of the Street Offences Act 1959 (c 57), which makes it an offence for a prostitute to solicit in a street. In that case prostitutes were attracting the attention of passers-by from balconies or windows. Lord Parker in finding them guilty said:

'I approach the matter by considering what is the mischief aimed at by this Act. Everybody knows that this was an Act intended to clean up the streets, to enable people to walk along the streets without being molested or solicited by common prostitutes. Viewed in that way, it can matter little whether the prostitute is soliciting while in the street or is standing in a doorway or on a balcony, or at a window, or whether the window is shut or open or half open; in each case her solicitation is projected to and addressed to somebody walking in the street'[4].

The rule in *Heydon's Case* has been extended so that now it is necessary to look not only at the state of the common law at the date of the passing of the enactment to be interpreted but also at the state of any relevant statute law and at any judicial interpretation thereof at that date[5].

1 *Heydon's Case* (1584) 2 Co Rep 7a at 7b.
2 *Re Mayfair Property Co, Bartlett v Mayfair Property Co* [1898] 2 Ch 28 at 35, CA.
3 *Gartside v Inland Revenue Comrs* [1968] AC 553 at 612, [1968] 1 All ER 121 at 131, HL.
4 *Smith v Hughes* [1960] 2 All ER 859 at 861, [1960] 1 WLR 830 at 832, DC. For criticism of this
    decision, see Glanville Williams 'Statute Interpretation, Prostitution and the Rule of Law' in
    Crime, Proof and Punishment — Essays in Memory of Sir Rupert Cross (1981, ed C F Tapper).
5 *Macmillan & Co v Dent* [1907] 1 Ch 107 at 120, CA, per Fletcher Moulton LJ.

(C) CONSTRUCTION ACCORDING TO INTENT AS WELL AS TO WORDS USED

1116. Introduction. A very difficult question of construction of statutes
which continually falls to be determined by the courts is whether they are
entitled to look beyond the words actually used to ascertain the spirit and intent
of the legislature; and conflicting views have been held. On the one hand, Lord
Goddard CJ has said that one has to apply a certain amount of common sense in
construing statutes and to bear in mind the object of the Act[1]; and Jessel MR has
said that there is still such a thing as construing an Act according to its intent,
though not according to its words[2]. On the other hand, in *Abel v Lee* Willis J said
that he utterly repudiated the notion that it is competent to a judge to modify the
language of an Act to bring it in accordance with his views of what is right or
reasonable[3]; and in *Magor and St Mellons v Newport Corpn* Lord Simonds said the
duty of the court is to interpret the words the legislature has used; those words
may be ambiguous, but, even if they are, the power and duty of the court to
travel outside them on a voyage of discovery are strictly limited[4].

    In *Heriot's Trust v Caledonian Rly Co* Lord Dunedin took up a position which
perhaps comes somewhere between those conflicting views where he says:

> 'the duty of a Court of law, in my opinion, is, if possible, so to interpret a statute as
> to allow of its spirit being fulfilled, provided only that in order so to do it does not
> read into the statute provisions which are not there'[5].

Again, it has been said that, however inaccurate the terms of the Act, it is the
duty of the court to give effect to its spirit, so long as the words used do not
absolutely preclude the court from so doing[6].

1 *Barnes v Jarvis* [1953] 1 All ER 1061 at 1063, [1953] 1 WLR 649 at 652, DC.
2 *Re Bethlem Hospital* (1875) LR 19 Eq 457 at 459.
3 *Abel v Lee* (1871) LR 6 CP 365 at 371.
4 *Magor and St Mellons Rural District Council v Newport Corpn* [1952] AC 189 at 191, [1951] 2 All ER
    839 at 841, HL.
5 *Heriot's Trust v Caledonian Rly Co* 1915 SC (HL) 52 at 60, 1915 1 SLT 347 at 352.
6 *Campbell's Trustees v O'Neill* 1911 SC 188 at 196, 1910 2 SLT 392 at 397, per Lord President
    Dunedin.

1117. Illustrations of the conflicting approaches. Two Scottish cases illustrate the conflicting approaches. In *Hutchison's Trustees v Downie's Trustees*[1],
trustees of heritable creditors sued the debtor's trustees for the principal sum due
under bonds and dispositions in security. Section 7 of the now repealed Increase
of Rent and Mortgage Interest (Restrictions) Act 1920 (c 17), however, provided that it is not lawful for the creditor in a heritable security, so long as the
debtor 'keeps the property in a proper state of repair', to take any steps before
enforcing his security or for recovering the principal sum thereby secured. Lord
Ashmore rejected the creditors' argument that the language used in the section
ought to be taken according to its plain and ordinary meaning and that, construed in that way, 'proper repair' included structural alterations and the making
good in a permanent way of damage done to the security subjects. Instead he

followed Mr Justice Sargant[2], who had to interpret the same wording in the English case of *Woodifield v Bond*. In that case Mr Justice Sargant said:

> 'it is permissible, and may often be necessary, to consider the general scope of the statute in question and the mischief sought to be remedied, and to give to any general, doubtful or ill-defined terms such a meaning as will best accord with the main object of the measure'[3],

and Lord Ashmore found this principle of construction particularly appropriate for the interpretation of section 7 of the 1920 Act. Having regard to that object, Mr Justice Sargant held that 'proper state of repair' in the sense of the statute must be measured by the general condition of the property at the date of the mortgage, and must not be extended beyond the preservation of the property in a state corresponding with what existed at that date, and Lord Ashmore accepted this interpretation of the intention of section 7[4].

In *Ayrshire Employers Mutual Insurance v Inland Revenue Comrs*[5], a company limited by guarantee, with no share capital and no shareholders, existed for the purpose of insuring its members against claims arising out of accidents to their workmen. The members were the only contributors and the only participators. For the year ending 5 April 1936 the transactions of the company resulted in a surplus which the Inland Revenue claimed was chargeable to income tax under Case I of Schedule D by virtue of section 31(1) of the Finance Act 1933 (c 19). That enactment provided:

> 'In the application to any company or society of any provision or rule relating to profits or gains chargeable under Case I of Schedule D (which relates to trades) . . . any reference to profits or gains shall be deemed to include a reference to a profit or surplus arising from transactions of the company or society with its members which would be included in profits or gains for the purposes of that provision or rule if those transactions were transactions with non-members, . . .'.

There had been a series of cases before 1933 which settled that surpluses arising out of transactions of purely mutual assurance between an association and its members were not assessable to income tax, and the Attorney-General for the Inland Revenue contended that the intention of Parliament in enacting section 31(1) of the 1933 Act was to reverse these decisions, and indeed he could not think of any other effect of the enactment. The House of Lords held that section 31(1) did not make the surplus of the company assessable to income tax. Lord Macmillan was of the opinion that 'The Legislature has plainly misfired'[6] — his reasons for this view being set out in his analysis of section 31(1):

> 'It assumes that a surplus arising from the transactions of an incorporated company with its members is not taxable as profits or gains. To render such a surplus taxable it enacts that the surplus, although in fact arising from transactions of the company with its members, shall be deemed to be something which it is not, namely, a surplus arising from transactions of the company with non-members. The hypothesis is that a surplus arising on the transactions of a mutual insurance company with non-members is taxable as profits or gains of the company. But unfortunately for the Inland Revenue the hypothesis is wrong. It is not membership or non-membership which determines immunity from or liability to tax; it is the nature of the transactions. If the transactions are of the nature of mutual insurance, the resultant surplus is not taxable, whether the transactions are with members or with non-members'[7].

Lord Simonds said that section 31:

> 'is clearly a remedial section, if that is a proper description of a section intended to bring further subject-matter within the ambit of taxation. It is at least clear what is the gap that is intended to be filled and hardly less clear how it is intended to fill that

gap. Yet I can come to no other conclusion than that the language of the section fails to achieve its apparent purpose, and I must decline to insert words or phrases which might succeed where the draftsman failed'[8].

However, in *Inland Revenue Comrs v Bates* Lord Denning MR rejected the argument of counsel that the proper construction of certain tax provisions was to make them meaningless or ridiculous:

'If we gave them his interpretation, it would make nonsense of the statute. But he exhorted us to take heart from the decision of the House of Lords in *Inland Revenue Comrs v Ayrshire Employers Mutual Insurance Association*[9], where the legislature "plainly missed fire". So here we should give the words their literal interpretation heedless of what Parliament intended. I cannot think that this is right. It would reduce the interpretation of statutes to a mere exercise in semantics. Whereas the object, as I have always understood it, is to ascertain the intention of the legislature. This intention must be discovered, of course, from the words which they have used. . . . But the words must be sensibly interpreted. We do not sit here to make nonsense of them'[10].

Russell LJ in the same case, however, did not actually disagree with the decision in the *Ayrshire Employers* case but sought to distinguish it as a case in which 'the language selected could by no possible means be modified by reference to context'[11].

1 *Hutchison's Trustees v Downie's Trustees* 1923 SLT 49, OH.
2 1923 SLT 49 at 51, OH.
3 *Woodifield v Bond* [1922] 2 Ch 40 at 50.
4 *Hutchison's Trustees v Downie's Trustees* 1923 SLT 49 at 51, OH.
5 *Ayrshire Employers Mutual Insurance Association Ltd v Inland Revenue Comrs* 1946 SC (HL) 1, 1946 SLT 235.
6 1946 SC (HL) 1 at 9, 1946 SLT 235 at 237.
7 1946 SC (HL) 1 at 8, 1946 SLT 235 at 236.
8 1946 SC (HL) 1 at 9, 1946 SLT 235 at 237.
9 See note 5 above.
10 *Inland Revenue Comrs v Bates* [1965] 3 All ER 64 at 71, [1965] 1 WLR 1133 at 1147, CA (affd in part [1968] AC 483, [1967] 1 All ER 84, HL).
11 [1965] 3 All ER 64 at 73, [1965] 1 WLR 1133 at 1150, CA.

1118. Object of a section. In *Nimmo v Alexander Cowan*[1] Lord Guest looked to the object of the section in interpreting section 29(1) of the Factories Act 1961 (c 34) which inter alia provides that every place at which any person has at any time to work 'shall, so far as is reasonably practicable, be made and kept safe for any person working there'. The pursuer maintained that, to make a relevant case, it was sufficient for him to aver that the defenders failed to make the place of work safe, whereas the defenders contended that it was also necessary for the pursuer to aver that it was reasonably practicable for the defenders to do so. The Lord Ordinary and the Inner House of the Court of Session found in favour of the defenders, holding that the words 'so far as is reasonably practicable' are in the words of Lord Migdale 'woven into' the verbs 'made safe' and 'kept safe'. In the appeal to the House of Lords, however, Lord Guest was unhappy with the opinion of those courts because it paid:

'little or no regard to the purpose of the section. The object of the section was to provide for a safe working place . . . The question appears to me to depend upon which construction will best achieve the result to be attained, namely, to make and keep the working place safe'[2].

1 *Nimmo v Alexander Cowan & Sons Ltd* 1967 SC (HL) 79, 1967 SLT 277.

2 1967 SC (HL) 79 at 102, 1967 SLT 277 at 281.

(D) STATUTE TO BE READ AS A WHOLE

1119. Rule and principle of construction. Every clause of a statute is to be construed with reference to the context and other clauses of the Act so as, as far as possible, to make a consistent enactment of the whole statute[1]. In *Colquhoun v Brooks* Lord Hershell said:

> 'It is beyond dispute, too, that we are entitled, and indeed bound when construing the terms of any provision found in a statute to consider any other parts of the Act which throw light upon the intention of the legislature and which may serve to shew that the particular provision ought not to be construed as it would be if considered alone and apart from the rest of the Act'[2].

Consideration of this rule of construction arose in *Tennent v Partick Magistrates*[3]. In that case Tennent, a wine and spirit merchant, held a public house certificate for premises granted by the justices of the peace of the lower ward of Lanarkshire. The magistrates of Partick, however, maintained that, by virtue of the now repealed section 38 of the Burgh Police (Scotland) Act 1892 (c 55), those justices of the peace had been divested of the power and duty of granting certificates for licences to sell excisable liquors within the police burgh of Patrick and that that power and duty were now vested in themselves. That section provided that 'the magistrates and commissioners elected in virtue of this Act shall, within the limits of the burgh, *for the purposes of this Act*, possess such and the like rights, powers, authorities and jurisdiction, as are possessed by the magistrates and council of royal and parliamentary burghs in Scotland'. Tennent brought an action for declarator that the magistrates of Partick had no right or title to act as the licensing authority for that burgh. The Lord President, in giving the leading judgment finding in favour of Tennent, said that:

> 'the proper and professed function of a clause like section 38 [that is with the qualifying words "for the purposes of this Act"] is to effectuate the other provisions of the Act; it is executive of the purposes of the Act; . . . Accordingly, section 38 is not a self-contained section, it bids us look outside its own terms for its scope, and points to the other sections of the Act for information as to what its purposes are. . . . On a review of the whole statute I can find no indication that the amendment of the law relating to the licensing of public-houses is one of the purposes of the Act'[4].

1 *Canada Sugar Refining Co Ltd v R* [1898] AC 735 at 741, PC, per Lord Davey.
2 *Colquhoun v Brooks* (1889) 14 App Cas 493 at 506, HL.
3 *Tennent v Partick Magistrates* (1894) 21 R 735 (not reported fully in 1 SLT 594).
4 (1894) 21 R 735 at 741.

1120. Application of principle of construction. The principle of construction expounded above was applied in *Barty v Hill*[1] to the effect that the different parts of a complicated section were to be read as a whole. In that case a licensed grocer was charged with having exposed for sale by weight certain packages of butter, each of which weighed less than as represented by him, in contravention of the now repealed section 430 of the Burgh Police (Scotland) Act 1892 (c 55). The section provides inter alia that any inspector of weights and measures may enter any building in which any article is exposed for sale by weight or in which any article is weighed and require such article to be weighed in his presence; and, if the weight ascertained does not correspond with the weight which has been represented by the person who has exposed the article for sale or who weighed it, the inspector may seize the article and the magistrate may sentence the person who has exposed the article for sale *and* who has incorrectly weighed it to a penalty. The contention in the case was that, in view of the italicised word 'and' in the section, the complaint was irrelevant in that it had failed to charge the grocer with having incorrectly weighed the packages also. It was held on appeal, however, with Lord Stormonth-Darling dissenting, that the complaint was relevant. In upholding the relevancy of the complaint Lord Low said:

'At first sight the meaning of the section is by no means clear, and if it is really ambiguous the person accused of a contravention must have the benefit of the doubt. It seems to me, however, that when once the scheme of the section, or in other words the principle on which it is framed, is grasped, there is really no ambiguity, although the draftsmanship and the grammar are alike open to criticism'[2].

He then went on to analyse the section. He thought that the first part contemplated the possibility of two buildings being involved — the building where the article was exposed for sale and the building where it was weighed. Coming to the next part of the section concerning the seizure of the article where its weight did not correspond with the weight represented by the person who exposed the article for sale or who weighed it, he considered that the two persons were referred to corresponding to the two buildings previously mentioned. Coming to the last part of the section authorising conviction, it was clear to him that the person who has exposed the article for sale is the person who, in the previous part of the section, is referred to as exposing an article for sale in a building in which articles are sold by weight. That being so, the words that follow — 'and who has incorrectly weighed it' — can, in the opinion of Lord Low, only refer to the person described in the previous part of the section as weighing an article in a building in which articles are weighed[3].

The principle is also illustrated by the case of *Butter v Bennett*[4]. In that case the manager of a paper mill employed by a limited company was required by the terms of his employment to live in a house provided by his employer, and the question at issue was whether free coal and electricity and the services of a gardener supplied to him by the employer under the service agreement were supplied to him 'in or in connection with the provision of living accommodation' for the purposes of section 161(3) of the Income Tax Act 1952[5]. Section 161(1) in effect made chargeable to an employee the costs of living or other accommodation, of entertainment, of domestic or other services or of other benefits or facilities of whatsoever nature with which he is provided by the company which employs him. Section 161(3), however, provides that an employee is not to be accountable for expenses incurred by the employer in or in connection with the provision of living accommodation for the employee in part of any of the employer's business premises in which the employee is required to live under a service agreement. The Court of Appeal held that what was supplied under the service agreement did not fall within the exception of section 161(3). Lord Denning interpreted subsection (3) by looking back to subsection (1):

'Parliament there draws a distinction between "living accommodation" and "other accommodation". It draws a distinction between "living accommodation" and "domestic or other services or of other benefits or facilities" whatsoever, so it seems to me in this situation "living accommodation" must be narrowly construed as meaning the premises themselves which the employee occupies'[6].

Lord Donovan says that what was supplied might have been interpreted as falling within the exception of subsection (3) if one construed the expression in that subsection 'out of its context', but:

'the context of subsection (3) requires, I fear, a narrow construction. It is a subsection which exempts a person in the position of the taxpayer from liabilities which would otherwise fall upon him if subsection (1) of section 161 had been left unrestricted'[7].

The same principle has been applied in relation to the application of a defined expression in an interpretation section of an Act where it is not apt for the interpretation of a particular provision of the Act[8].

1 *Barty v Hill* 1907 SC (J) 36, 14 SLT 616.
2 1907 SC (J) 36 at 38, 14 SLT 616 at 618.
3 See 1907 SC (J) 36 at 38, 39, 14 SLT 616 at 618, 619.
4 *Butter v Bennett* [1963] Ch 185, [1962] 3 All ER 204, CA.
5 The Income Tax Act 1952 (c 10) is repealed. See now the Income and Corporation Taxes Act 1988 (c 1), s 154.
6 *Butter v Bennett* [1963] Ch 185 at 195, [1962] 3 All ER 204 at 207, CA.
7 [1963] Ch 185 at 196, [1962] 3 All ER 204 at 209, CA.
8 *Strathern v Padden* 1926 JC 9, 1925 SLT 650.

1121. Limitation of principle of construction. The principle of reading a statute as a whole, however, is not applicable in every case. As was said in *Warburton v Loveland*, no rule of construction can require that when the words of one part of a statute convey a clear meaning it is necessary to introduce another part of a statute for the purpose of controlling or diminishing the efficacy of the first part[1]. In *Cramas Properties v Connaught Fur Trimmings* Lord Guest said:

'Where a statute has used words which prima facie have an unambiguous meaning it is not . . . legitimate to extract a forced and unnatural meaning from a consideration of other provisions in the same statute'[2].

This limitation on the applicability of the principle is well illustrated by *Gardiner v Admiralty Comrs*[3] involving the interpretation of section 26(1) of the Factories Act 1937 which provided that there must, so far as is reasonably practicable, be provided and maintained safe means of access to every place at which any person has at any time to work[4]. In that case a shipwright was employed to caulk the decks of a fishing vessel which was being repaired in a dry dock which it was agreed was a factory within the meaning of the Act. He averred that to reach his work he had to carry buckets of boiling pitch from the ground, up a ladder and on to, and across, the deck to the other side of the vessel, and that he tripped over obstacles in his path on the deck causing him to spill pitch which burned him. He claimed that the accident was caused by the occupiers of the dockyard in that his means of access had been rendered unsafe by the obstructions on the deck. The Court of Session, in holding (by a majority) that the pursuer's case was irrelevant, found that the scope of section 26(1) was restricted to the premises of the dry dock and did not extend to the means of access within insofar as it passed over the ship being repaired. They reached their decision on the basis that all the safety provisions of Part II of the Act[5] were concerned only with the premises and plant of a factory. In giving the leading judgment in the House of Lords reversing the decision of the Court of Session, Lord Guest said:

'I agree that the majority of the provisions in Part II . . . are concerned with the plant and premises, but I do not understand why for this reason section 26 should have a similarly restricted meaning. The provisions of section 26 are perfectly general in their terms. There is no principle which would compel a Court to restrict general words to be found in one section by a limitation to be found in other surrounding sections dealing with different matters'[6].

1 *Warburton v Loveland* (1831) 2 Dow & Cl 480 at 500, HL.
2 *Cramas Properties Ltd v Connaught Fur Trimmings Ltd* [1965] 2 All ER 382 at 387, [1965] 1 WLR 892 at 901, HL.
3 *Gardiner v Admiralty Comrs* 1964 SC (HL) 85, 1964 SLT 194.
4 The Factories Act 1937 (c 67) is repealed. See now the Factories Act 1961 (c 34), s 29(1).

5 The Factories Act 1937, Pt II, comprised ss 12–40 (repealed).
6 *Gardiner v Admiralty Comrs* 1964 SC (HL) 85 at 91, 1964 SLT 194 at 195.

1122. Application of rule of construction to the scheme of an Act. The rule that a statute has to be read as a whole has so far been considered in the context that one provision in a statute may be interpreted by reference to other individual provisions of the Act. The rule has also been applied to the effect that the meaning of a section may be determined by reference to the scheme of the Act regarded in general. In *Re Newspaper Proprietors' Agreement*[1] the question at issue was whether the jurisdiction conferred on the Restrictive Practices Court by the now repealed section 20 of the Restrictive Trade Practices Act 1956 (c 68) 'in respect of any agreement of which particulars are for the time being registered' was limited to existing agreements or applied also to agreements which had already been terminated by the parties. The House of Lords decided that the jurisdiction did extend to the terminated agreement on the ground that section 20, when looking at the whole Act, could be construed as referring to both existing and terminated agreements. Lord Evershed, while accepting that the natural conclusion which the language of section 20 suggested, if read without regard to the rest of the Act, would be to confine the jurisdiction of the court to subsisting agreements, said:

> 'There is, indeed, solid and respectable authority for the rule that you should "begin at the beginning and go on till you come to the end: then stop"[2]; and, in my opinion, the rule is . . . peculiarly proper when construing an Act of Parliament and seeking to discover from the Act the parliamentary intention'[3].

In *Moss Empires Limited v Glasgow Assessor*[4], an entry in the valuation roll was increased in amount but there was a failure to comply with the now repealed section 5 of the Valuation of Lands (Scotland) Act 1854 (c 91) which provided that a copy of every entry in the valuation roll — except where the entry is a mere repetition of the previous years entry — must be transmitted by the assessor to the person affected. The person aggrieved by the entry brought an action for its reduction based on the failure of the assessor to give notice. The defenders argued that the action was incompetent in that the failure to give notice was a want of compliance with the provisions of the Act for making up the roll and section 30 of the Act rendered incompetent challenge of the valuation on the ground of such lack of compliance. The House of Lords rejected the defenders' argument, Lord Haldane saying that:

> 'where the Act as a whole contains a scheme which expressly confers a definite right on the person concerned, then you are not to treat the definitive language of that Act in an earlier section as repealed by language which is not precise, and which occurs in a merely general form, in a later section, only because the later language is capable of that construction. If the language is ambiguous, if a phrase like "making up" is used in two senses, then you ought, in my view of the rule of construction, to interpret the statute, not as destroying the right previously given, or as abrogating it'[5].

1 *Associated Newspapers Ltd v Registrar of Restrictive Trading Agreements* [1964] 1 All ER 55, [1964] 1 WLR 31, HL.
2 L Carroll *Alice's Adventures in Wonderland* ch 12.
3 *Associated Newspapers Ltd v Registrar of Restrictive Trading Agreements* [1964] 1 All ER 55 at 59, [1964] 1 WLR 31 at 39, HL.
4 *Moss' Empires Ltd v Glasgow Assessor* 1917 SC (HL) 1, 1916 2 SLT 215.
5 1917 SC (HL) 1 at 5, 1916 2 SLT 215 at 217.

(E) CONSTRUCTION *UT RES MAGIS VALEAT QUAM PEREAT*

1123. Construction not to make an Act invalid. The rule of construction *ut* *res magis valeat quam pereat* in effect means that a statute is to be interpreted so as to give it effect rather than to render it invalid. As Lord Brougham said in *Auchterarder Presbytery v Earl of Kinnoull*, 'a legislature is never supposed to use words without a meaning'[1]:

> '[I]f the choice is between two interpretations, the narrower of which would fail to achieve the manifest purpose of the legislation, we should avoid a construction which would reduce the legislation to futility and should rather accept the bolder construction based on the view that Parliament would legislate only for the purpose of bringing about an effective result'[2].

Again:

> 'where alternative constructions are equally open, that alternative is to be chosen which will be consistent with the smooth working of the system which the statute purports to be regulating; and that alternative is to be rejected which will introduce uncertainty, friction or confusion into the working of the system'[3].

And in *Curtis v Stovin* Bowen LJ said:

> 'The rules for the construction of statutes are very like those which apply to the construction of other documents, especially as regards one crucial rule, viz. that, if it is possible, the words of a statute must be construed so as to give a sensible meaning to them. The words ought to be construed *ut res magis valeat quam pereat*'[4].

1 *Auchterarder Presbytery v Earl of Kinnoull* (1839) Macl & R 220 at 280, HL.
2 *Nokes v Doncaster Amalgamated Collieries Ltd* [1940] AC 1014 at 1022, [1940] 3 All ER 549 at 554, HL, per Viscount Simon.
3 *Shannon Realties Ltd v Ville de St Michel* [1924] AC 185 at 192, 193, PC, per Lord Shaw.
4 *Curtis v Stovin* (1889) 22 QBD 513 at 519, CA.

(F) CONSTRUCTION TO AVOID ABSURDITY

1124. Introduction. Construction to avoid absurdity is really a sub-division of the wider rule just mentioned that construction should be *ut res magis valeat quam pereat*. The rule appears to be that where there is an ambiguity in the wording of a statutory provision and one interpretation would produce a fair and reasonable result, and the other an absurd result, the former is to be preferred. On the other hand, if there is no ambiguity in the words used, the literal meaning must be given effect to even if this results in an absurdity. The real problem is in determining in any particular case whether or not there is an ambiguity in the language used, and, however well a provision in a statute is drafted, it is usually possible for a lawyer to argue that it contains an ambiguity.

1125. Construction to avoid absurdity. An example of construction to avoid absurdity is the relatively simple case of *Thompson v Thompson*[1], in which a husband presented a petition under the now repealed section 16 of the Matrimonial Causes Act 1950 (c 25) for a decree of presumption of death and dissolution of marriage seven years and seven days after the date on which his wife had last been seen or heard. Section 16(2) provided that in any such proceedings the fact that for a period of seven years or upwards the other party to the marriage has been continually absent from the petitioner, and *the petitioner has no reason to believe that the other party has been living within that time*, is evidence that he or she is dead until the contrary is proved. Sachs J rejected the argument that, because the wife was alive before the seven-year period began, it must reasonably be assumed that she was alive during some part of the period and it was therefore difficult to determine at what stage after the wife had disappeared the seven-year period should start to run. The judge found that such an interpretation would mean in effect that:

'the seven years could not start to run until such date as death could be presumed under the normal common law rules. Such a result would produce inconvenience and hardship to a petitioner contrary to the apparent intentions of the legislature and would indeed reduce subsection (2) to an absurdity'[2].

He therefore held that the italicised words in section 16(2) had to be construed:

'as if the legislature had in substance said "if nothing has happened within that time to give the petitioner reason to believe that the other party was then living"'[3].

Again, in *Adler v George* the court held that the phrase 'in the vicinity of any prohibited place' in section 3 of the Official Secrets Act 1920 (c 75) must mean 'in or in the vicinity' of the place because otherwise an offence in the prohibited place would be exempt, which would be an absurdity[4].

On the other hand what appears to be an absurd result was arrived at in *Attorney-General v Prince of Hanover*[5] on the ground that the language of the enactment concerned was unambiguous. In that case a great-great-grandson of Ernest Augustus (a descendant of the Princess Sophia) brought an action for a declaration that he was a British subject by virtue of a statute of 1705[6] which provided that the Princess Sophia and the issue of her body, and all persons lineally descending from her, born or hereafter to be born, be and is deemed natural born subjects of this Kingdom. The House of Lords rejected the argument of the Attorney-General that the intention was to limit the statute's operation to descendants of the Princess born in Queen Anne's lifetime, Lord Morton saying:

'[We are asked] to perform a surgical operation on the enacting part of the statute by inserting, immediately after the words "born or hereafter to be born" the words "in Your Majesty's life time". Now, if the legislature had intended to limit the class of persons to be naturalized, I can think of no reason why these words should not have been inserted'[7].

And in the Court of Appeal Romer LJ said:

'as to the suggested absurdity of the enactment clause if taken by itself, it appears to me to be a dangerous doctrine that the courts, when confronted by plain and unambiguous legislative language, should reject it as absurd. . . . if such power in fact be vested in the courts, it should only be exercised in cases that imperatively demand its application; for, apart from the fact that its exercise comes perilously close to legislating, that which seems absurd to one mind may not appear so to another'[8].

1 *Thompson v Thompson* [1956] P 414, [1956] 1 All ER 603.
2 [1956] P 414 at 423, [1956] 1 All ER 603 at 607.
3 [1956] P 414 at 425, [1956] 1 All ER 603 at 608.
4 *Adler v George* [1964] 2 QB 7 at 9, [1964] 1 All ER 628 at 629, DC.
5 *Attorney-General v Prince Ernest Augustus of Hanover* [1957] AC 436, [1957] 1 All ER 49, HL.
6 Ie the Princess Sophia Naturalization Act 1705 (c 16) (repealed).
7 *Attorney-General v Prince Ernest Augustus of Hanover* [1957] AC 436 at 469, 470, [1957] 1 All ER 49 at 59, HL.
8 *Prince Ernest Augustus of Hanover v Attorney-General* [1956] Ch 188 at 218, [1955] 3 All ER 647 at 662, CA.

(3) CERTAIN PRESUMPTIONS

(a) Presumption against Changes in Existing Law and Practice

1126. Common law. There is a presumption against the common law being changed by statute, and if a deep seated principle of the common law 'is to be overturned, it must be overturned by a clear, definite and positive enactment, not by an ambiguous one'[1]. If the arguments on a question of interpretation are 'fairly evenly balanced, that interpretation should be chosen which involves the least alteration of the existing law'[2].

In *Hynd's Trustee v Hynd's Trustees*,[3] a testator instructed a firm of solicitors to prepare a settlement, but, before it was ready for signature, he was taken seriously ill. Consequently a solicitor employed by the firm, together with two clerks, attended the testator at his house. The testator being unable to complete his signature, the solicitor signed the settlement in the presence of the testator and the two clerks, leaving a space in which to insert the docquet (stating what had taken place) as required by section 18(1) of the Conveyancing (Scotland) Act 1924 (c 27). Afterwards, in the office of the firm, he inserted the docquet, and the deed was then subscribed by the two clerks as witnesses. The enactment concerned provides that any deed may, after having been read over to the granter, be validly executed on behalf of such granter, if he is blind or unable to write, by a law agent subscribing the same in the presence of the granter and by his authority, all before two witnesses who have heard such deed read over to the granter, and heard and seen such authority given, and a holograph docquet must *precede* the signature of such law agent. The House of Lords rejected the argument that in relation to a docquet, which is something written and not the act of writing, the word 'precede' cannot have a temporal significance and held that section 18(1) had not been complied with because the completion of the docquet, together with the signatures of the solicitor and the two witnesses, had not been made *unico contextu* in the presence of the granter; the deed was accordingly invalid. Lord Reid stated that it was clear that, before the enactment of the 1924 Act, in notarial execution the docquet had to be written in the presence of the granter of the deed[4]. He then went on to consider whether this law has been changed by section 18(1) of the 1924 Act. Of that enactment he said:

> 'The drafting is somewhat confused. If the intention was to enact that the docquet should be written out and subscribed in the presence of the granter, one might have expected this to be stated in plain language. Instead, while the section expressly provides that the law agent ... is to subscribe the deed in the presence of the granter, it does not say that the docquet is to be written out in the presence of the granter or is to be subscribed by the law agent ... It merely says that the docquet is to precede the signature of the law agent ... But I cannot infer from this that the intention was that a space might be left above the signature into which the docquet could be written later. In spite of the confused drafting I am forced to the conclusion that no indication can be found in the section of any intention to alter existing law on this matter and that it is still necessary for the law agent ... to write out and subscribe the docquet in the presence of the granter of the deed. I have reached this conclusion with regret'[5].

In *Nicol's Trustees v Sutherland*[6] the question at issue was whether section 100 of the Bills of Exchange Act 1882 (c 61) overruled the previous common law rule that payment of a written obligation cannot be proved by parole. That section provides that in any judicial proceedings in Scotland, any fact relating to a bill of exchange, bank cheque or promissory note, which is relevant to any question of liability thereon, may be proved by parole evidence. The House of Lords, by a majority, approving the decision in *Robertson v Thomson*[7], held that the language of section 100 was not sufficiently clear to overrule the settled rule of law that parole evidence was incompetent as proof of payment.

---

1 *Leach v R* [1912] AC 305 at 311, HL, per Lord Atkinson.
2 *George Wimpey & Co Ltd v British Overseas Airways Corpn* [1955] AC 169 at 191, [1954] 3 All ER 661 at 672, 673, HL, per Lord Reid.

3 *Hynd's Trustee v Hynd's Trustees* 1955 SC (HL) 1, 1955 SLT 105.
4 1955 SC (HL) 1 at 19, 20, 1955 SLT 105 at 113.
5 1955 SC (HL) 1 at 20, 1955 SLT 105 at 113.
6 *Nicol's Trustees v Sutherland* 1951 SC (HL) 21, 1951 SLT 201.
7 *Robertson v Thomson* (1900) 3 F 5, 8 SLT 202.

1127. Rules of practice and procedure. The position with regard to changes effected by statute to rules of practice and procedure is the same as it is to alterations to the substantive common law. Thus in *Kinnear v Whyte* Lord Ardmillan said:

'When we have an uniform and long continued rule of practice, we must be very careful not to construe a new Act in such a manner as to introduce an alteration not plainly intended by the Legislature'[1].

And in *Portobello Magistrates v Edinburgh Magistrates* the Court of Session rejected an argument that the now repealed Rivers Pollution Prevention Act 1876 (c 75), in providing for appeal from the judge of first instance to the Court of Session by special case, intended that that should be the only competent form of appeal, rendering incompetent appeal from the sheriff substitute to the sheriff principal. Lord Justice-Clerk Moncrieff said:

'that where a well-known and recognised jurisdiction is invoked by the Legislature for the purpose of carrying out a series of provisions which are important for the public without any specific form of process being prescribed, the presumption is that the ordinary forms of that Court are to be observed in carrying out the provisions'[2].

1 *Kinnear and Brymer v Whyte* (1868) 6 M 804 at 807.
2 *Portobello Magistrates v Edinburgh Magistrates* (1882) 10 R 130 at 137.

(b) Presumption in Relation to Jurisdiction

1128. Superior courts. A clear and unambiguous statutory provision is required in order to oust or add to the jurisdiction of a superior court. In *Dunbar v Scottish County Investment*[1] in pursuance of section 5 of the Sheriff Courts (Scotland) Act 1907 (c 51) an action of proving the tenor of a missing document was brought in the sheriff court. That section provides inter alia that the jurisdiction of the sheriff includes 'actions of declarator'. It was held that the action was incompetent because, as Lord Justice-Clerk Scott Dickson said:

'Although the initial conclusion [of the summons] is in form declaratory, the extract of the decree becomes as valid and effectual as the deed which has been lost'[2],

and in any event it had never been regarded as a declaratory action. Lord Salvesen said:

'A general rule applicable to the construction of statutes is that there is not to be presumed, without express words, an authority to deprive the Supreme Court of a jurisdiction which it had previously exercised, or to extend what was once the privative jurisdiction of the Supreme Court to the inferior Courts. Accordingly, if the word "declarator" were to be regarded as ambiguous, the presumption would be against its including an action of proving the tenor'[3].

1 *Dunbar & Co v Scottish County Investment Co Ltd* 1920 SC 210, 1920 1 SLT 136.
2 1920 SC 210 at 213, 1920 1 SLT 136 at 138.
3 1920 SC 210 at 217, 1920 1 SLT 136 at 140.

1129. Sheriff courts. In *Cameron v Macniven*[1] it was held that the now repealed Burgh Police (Scotland) Act 1892 (c 55) did not deprive the sheriff of a county of jurisdiction to try persons for offences committed within a burgh in the county. Lord Justice-Clerk Macdonald said:

> 'It is a fixed rule of our law that the Sheriff of a county has jurisdiction at common law in all manner of offences, whether at common law or created by statute, ... To deprive the Sheriff of this inherent jurisdiction over any new crime created by statute, his jurisdiction must be distinctly excluded by the Act of Parliament creating the new offence. I do not say it must be expressly excluded; the exclusion may be merely by implication, but to be valid it must be distinct and unambiguous'[2].

1 *Cameron v Macniven* (1894) 21 R (J) 31, 1 SLT 467. See also *Tennent v Partick Magistrates* (1894) 21 R 735, 1 SLT 594; *Dunlop v Mundell* 1943 SLT 286, OH.
2 *Cameron v Macniven* (1894) 21 R (J) 31 at 32, 33 (not fully reported in 1 SLT 467).

1130. Extension of supervisory power of superior courts.

By virtue of section 14(2) of the Tribunals and Inquiries Act 1971 (c 62):

> '... any provision in an Act passed before 1 August 1958 that any order or determination shall not be called into question in any court, or any provision in such an Act which by similar words excludes any jurisdiction which the Court of Session would otherwise have to entertain an application for reduction or suspension of any order or determination, or otherwise to consider the validity of any order or determination, shall not have effect so as to prevent the exercise of any such jurisdiction'.

(c) Other Presumptions

1131. Presumption against taking away rights or imposing burdens.

Enactments which take away rights or impose burdens are to be strictly construed, and if there is any ambiguity the construction which is in favour of the freedom of the individual should be adopted[1].

> '[I]f there is any ambiguity about the extent of that derogation [by a statute from common law rights], the principle is clear that it is to be resolved in favour of maintaining common law rights unless they are clearly taken away'[2].

In *James Ross v Lord Advocate* the manufacturers of 'Choco-Puff' brought an action against the Lord Advocate as representing the Minister of Food to have it declared that 'Choco-Puff' was not 'chocolate confectionery' within the meaning of the Chocolate, Sugar Confectionery and Cocoa Products Order 1949, SI 1949/781. On the question of the burden of proof Lord Birnam said that:

> 'if the question of *onus* were important my view would be that the presumption is in favour of freedom and that in cases of doubt the burden is upon the Ministry to show that a particular foodstuff is covered by the terms of the Order'[3].

1 *David v S P A De Silva* [1934] AC 106, PC.
2 *East Coast Amusement Co Ltd v British Transport Board* [1965] AC 58 at 71, [1963] 2 All ER 775 at 778, HL, per Viscount Simonds.
3 *James Ross & Son v Lord Advocate* 1952 SLT (Notes) 77, OH.

1132. Presumption in favour of popular construction.

General statutes are presumed to use words in their popular sense or, as Lord Reid has put it:

> 'Any decision by any court ... whether the words of an Act apply to the facts of a particular case must, unless the matter is concluded by authority, ultimately depend on its knowledge of the usage of the English language in ordinary affairs of the kind with which the particular Act is concerned'[1].

Thus 'five miles square' was interpreted in its popular, rather than in its strict mathematical, sense as meaning an area of twenty-five square miles, irrespective of whether it formed a geometrical figure five miles square[2]. Again, 'accident' has been given its ordinary meaning of an unintended occurrence with an adverse physical result[3]. Sometimes, however, words are given a strict legal interpretation[4]. Moreover, if an

'Act is one passed with reference to a particular trade, business, or transaction, and words are used which everybody conversant with that trade, business, or transaction, knows and understands to have a particular meaning in it, then the words are to be construed as having that particular meaning, though it may differ from the common or ordinary meaning of the words'[5].

1 *Griffiths v J P Harrison (Watford) Ltd* [1963] AC 1 at 15, [1962] 1 All ER 909 at 914, HL.
2 *Robertson v Day* (1879) 5 App Cas 63, PC.
3 *R v Morris* [1972] 1 All ER 384, [1972] 1 WLR 228, CA. Cf *West Midlands Police Chief Constable v Billingham* [1972] 2 All ER 182, [1979] 1 WLR 747, DC.
4 *Adamson v Melbourne and Metropolitan Board of Works* [1929] AC 142, PC.
5 *Unwin v Hanson* [1891] 2 QB 115 at 119, CA.

1133. Presumption that words are used correctly. There is a presumption that 'words are used in an Act of Parliament correctly and exactly, and not loosely and inexactly. Upon those who assert that the rule has been broken the burden of establishing their proposition lies heavily'[1].

1 *New Plymouth Corpn v Taranaki Electric-Power Board* [1933] AC 680 at 682, PC, per Lord Macmillan.

(4) AIDS TO CONSTRUCTION

(a) Internal Aids

1134. Introduction. Consideration is now given to the extent (if any) to which the provisions of a statute may be construed by reference to the following parts of the Act:
(1) the title, short and long;
(2) the preamble;
(3) the rubric or side note of a section;
(4) headings;
(5) provisos;
(6) interpretation sections;
(7) schedules;
(8) punctuation.

1135. The short and long title. Nowadays statutes all have a short title which is generally found in a section near the end of the Act. It appears that the short title, although it is contained in the body of the statute and may be amended by Parliament, may not be utilised in interpreting the Act. As Lord Moulton said in *Vacher & Sons v London Society of Compositors*, the short title is:

'given to the Act solely for the purpose of facility of reference. If I may use the phrase, it is a statutory nickname to obviate the necessity of always referring to the Act under its full and descriptive title . . . Its object is identification and not description'[1].

The long title may be amended by either House of Parliament and, as Lord Moulton said in the *Vacher* case, the long title:

'is part of the Act itself, and it is legitimate to use it for the purpose of interpreting the Act as a whole and ascertaining its scope'[1].

In *R v Bates*, however, Donovan J, while recognising that 'in many cases the long title may supply the key to the meaning', said:

'if its meaning be clear, that meaning is not to be narrowed or restricted by reference to the long title'[2].

1 *Vacher & Sons Ltd v London Society of Compositors* [1913] AC 107 at 128, HL.
2 *R v Bates* [1952] 2 All ER 842 at 844.

1136. The preamble. Many old statutes have preambles, and in a number of cases in the nineteenth century preambles were held to be legitimate aids in construing the enacting parts where the meaning was not clear[1]. Hardly any modern statutes have preambles and therefore their importance as an aid to construction is constantly declining. Lord Normand, however, in the comparatively recent case of *Attorney-General v Prince Ernest Augustus of Hanover*, gave an authoritative statement of their use in construction:

'When there is a preamble it is generally in its recitals that the mischief to be remedied and the scope of the Act are described. It is therefore clearly permissible to have recourse to it as an aid to construing the enacting provisions. The preamble is not, however, of the same weight as an aid to construction of a section of the Act as are other relevant enacting words to be found elsewhere in the Act or even in related Acts. There may be no exact correspondence between preamble and enactment, and the enactment may go beyond, or it may fall short of the indications that may be gathered from the preamble. Again, the preamble cannot be of much or any assistance in construing provisions which embody qualifications or exceptions from the operation of the general purpose of the Act. It is only when it conveys a clear and definite meaning in comparison with relatively obscure or indefinite enacting words that the preamble may legitimately prevail'[2].

1 See eg *Minister of Brydekirk v Minister of Heritors of Hoddam* (1877) 4 R 798; *Tennent v Partick Magistrates* (1894) 21 R 735, 1 SLT 594; *Renfrewshire County Council v Trustees of Orphan Homes of Scotland* (1898) 1 F 186, 6 SLT 229.
2 *Attorney-General v Prince Ernest Augustus of Hanover* [1957] AC 436 at 467, [1957] 1 All ER 49 at 57, 58, HL. See also *Anderson v Jenkins Express Removals Ltd* 1944 reported in *James Kemp (Leslie) Ltd v Robertson* 1967 SC 229 at 231 at 234, 1967 SLT 213 at 215 at 216, OH, per Lord Mackintosh.

1137. The rubric or side note of a section. The side note or, as it is sometimes called, the rubric of a section can afford no aid to the construction of a statute. In *Farquharson v Whyte*[1] the court rejected the argument that, because the rubric of section 4 of the Interpretation of Acts Act 1850 (c 21) read 'Interpretation of certain Words for *future* Acts', the section did not apply to Acts passed before that Act. The relevant part of the section for the purposes of that case read 'in all Acts . . . the Word "month" [shall be deemed] to mean Calendar Month, unless Words be added showing Lunar Month to be intended'. Lord Young expressed the matter in this way:

'I am not moved by any reference to the marginal rubric. I quite agree that it is no part of the statute, although it may suggest an idea to the mind with which you are to read the statute. It is not put to Parliament, not submitted for its consideration. It is only for the convenience of the reader'[2].

The same decision was reached in the more modern case of *Chandler v Director of Public Prosecutions*, Lord Reid saying:

'In my view side notes cannot be used as an aid to construction. They are mere catchwords and I have never heard of it being supposed in recent times that an amendment to alter a side note could be proposed in either House of Parliament. Side notes in the original Bill are inserted by the draftsman. During the passage of the Bill through its various stages amendments to it or other reasons may make it desirable to alter a side note. In that event I have reason to believe that alteration is made by the appropriate officer of the House — no doubt in consultation with the draftsman. So side notes cannot be said to be enacted in the same sense as the long title or any part of the body of the Act'[3].

1 *Farquharson v Whyte* (1886) 13 R (J) 29.
2 (1886) 13 R (J) 29 at 32.
3 *Chandler v Director of Public Prosecutions* [1964] AC 763 at 789, 790, [1962] 3 All ER 142 at 145, 146, HL.

1138. Headings. The extent to which cross-headings may be used in the interpretation of statutes is clearly set out by Lord President Clyde in *Buckie Magistrates v Countess of Seafield's Trustees*[1], and repeated by Lord Elliott in the recent case of *Hill v Orkney Islands Council*[2]:

> 'It seems to me that . . . two propositions may be regarded as well settled. The first is that in construing a statutory enactment — assuming that there is anything in it which fairly raises a question of doubtful construction — the enactment must be interpreted in the light of the context in which it is found; and that, if the Act in which the enactment occurs is divided into parts or compartments with separate headings, the particular enactment under construction must be considered in the light thrown upon it by the description of the heading under which it is placed. . . . The second proposition . . . is that, if one of the enacting sections of a statute contains something which is unambiguous in its own terms and raises no question of doubtful construction, it must be given effect to notwithstanding that it goes beyond its context and beyond the scope of the heading of the part, or fasciculus, in which it is placed'[3].

Lord President Clyde's dictum in the *Buckie Magistrates* case is in line with various earlier decisions[4].

1 *Buckie Magistrates v Dowager Countess of Seafield's Trustees* 1928 SC 525, 1928 SLT 362.
2 *Hill v Orkney Islands Council* 1983 SLT (Lands Tr) 2 at 4.
3 *Buckie Magistrates v Dowager Countess of Seafield's Trustees* 1928 SC 525 at 528, 529, 1928 SLT 362 at 364.
4 See eg *Inglis v Robertson and Baxter* (1898) 25 R (HL) 70; *M'Ewan v Perth Magistrates* (1905) 7 F 714, 12 SLT 846.

1139. Provisos. Provisos are clauses of exception or qualification in an Act, excepting something out of, or qualifying something in, the enactment which, but for the proviso, would be within it. These can generally be identified by the words 'provided that' or 'this section does not apply to' etc. The relationship between a proviso and the enactment to which it applies is stated by Lord Cowan in *Forster v Forster*:

> 'As [a] matter of general construction, it is certain that when an enactment is followed by a *proviso*, the terms of the latter are construed always with due regard to the subject of the enactment. The *proviso* may be held to explain this enactment, and to state the instances or cases to which it is not to be applicable. But unless the contrary be explicitly declared, no *proviso* will enlarge the scope and operation of the enacting words'[1].

A provision, of course, may in form be a proviso, but in reality be a substantive enactment, and in such a case effect will be given to the reality[2].

1 *Forster v Forster* (1871) 9 M 397 at 399.
2 *Davidson v Johnston* (1903) 6 F 239, 11 SLT 503.

1140. Interpretation sections. Most modern statutes of any size contain an interpretation section which provides that certain words and phrases, when used in the statute, are to bear particular meanings. Interpretation provisions take one of two forms. They provide either:

(1) that the word or phrase is to 'mean' such and such; or

(2) that it is to 'include' such and such.

The use of the word 'mean' restricts the scope of the word or phrase to what is indicated in the definition[1]. The word 'include', on the other hand, is used:

> 'in order to enlarge the meaning of words or phrases occurring in the body of the statute; and when it is so used these words or phrases must be construed as comprehending, not only such things as they signify according to their nautral import, but also those things which the interpretation clause declares that they shall include'[2].

Or, as Lord Selbourne said in *Robinson v Barton-Eccles Local Board*, an interpretation clause which extends the meaning of a word:

> 'is not meant to prevent the word receiving its ordinary, popular, and natural sense whenever that would be properly applicable; but to enable the word as used in the Act, when there is nothing in the context or the subject-matter to the contrary, to be applied to some things to which it would not ordinarily be applicable'[3].

The case of *Strathern v Padden*[4] was concerned with the situation where a definition in the interpretation section of the Prevention of Crime Act 1871 (c 112) (section 20) was not apt in the context of the now repealed section 7 of that Act. Section 7 made it an offence under the Act if a person who was convicted of a crime and had a previous conviction proved against him, committed, at any time within seven years after the expiration of his last sentence, certain acts, including 'Thirdly, If he is found in any place, whether public or private, under such circumstances as to satisfy the court before whom he is brought that he was about to commit . . . any offence punishable on indictment or summary conviction . . .'. Section 20, after defining 'crime', defines 'offence' as 'any act or omission which is not a crime as defined by this Act, and is punishable on indictment or summary conviction'. A complaint charged the accused that, having been previously convicted of a crime aggravated by previous convictions, he was, within seven years of the expiry of his sentence, found about to commit theft by housebreaking, 'an offence punishable on indictment or summary conviction' contrary to the said section 7. Objection was taken to the relevancy of the complaint on the ground that, as theft by housebreaking was a 'crime' as defined by section 20, it was not an 'offence' as therein defined; but this objection was rejected by the High Court of Justiciary. Lord Justice-General Clyde analysed the definitions of 'crime' and 'offence' in section 20 and found that, roughly speaking, 'crime' was designed to embrace major criminal offences and 'offence' minor ones. If this were applied to section 7:

> 'it would follow that a statutory offence occurs if the circumstances are that the person accused was about to commit what I have described as a minor criminal offence; but no statutory offence will occur where the evidence shows that the accused was about to commit any of those major criminal offences which the statute defines as a "crime". This is a sufficiently startling result of the strict application of the definition clause to the terms of section 7. It might almost be said that it makes nonsense of the statute'[5].

And the Lord President continued:

> 'A definition clause does not necessarily, in any statute, apply in all possible contexts in which the word may be found therein . . . I have no doubt that it is in accordance

with the law of Scotland in relation to the interpretation of statutes that, if defined expressions are used in a context which the definition will not fit, then the words may be interpreted according to their ordinary meaning'[6].

1 *R v Britton* [1967] 2 QB 51, [1967] 1 All ER 486, CA.
2 *Dilworth v Stamps Comrs* [1899] AC 99 at 105, PC, per Lord Watson.
3 *Robinson v Barton-Eccles Local Board* (1883) 8 App Cas 798 at 801, HL.
4 *Strathern v Padden* 1926 JC 9, 1925 SLT 650.
5 1926 JC 9 at 12, 1925 SLT 650 at 652.
6 1926 JC 9 at 13, 1925 SLT 650 at 652.

1141. Schedules. Schedules to statutes are as much part of an Act as any other, and may be used in construing provisions in the body of the Act[1]. Conversely, provisions in a schedule will be construed in accordance with what is enacted in the sections[2]. However, where 'the words used in a schedule vary from the words used in the enacting clause, the latter must govern'[3]. It has also been held, in construing a private Act, that the words in a schedule to the Act cannot be used to enlarge the scope of a provision in the body of the Act[4].

1 See *Lloyd v Brassey* [1969] 2 QB 98 at 106, [1969] 1 All ER 382 at 386, CA, per Salmon J.
2 See *Inland Revenue Comrs v Littlewoods Mail Order Stores Ltd* [1963] AC 135 at 152, [1962] 2 All ER 279 at 283, HL.
3 *Jacobs v Hart* (1900) 2 F (J) 33 at 38, per Lord Justice-General Balfour (not fully reported in 7 SLT 425).
4 *Laird & Sons v Clyde Navigation Trustees* (1879) 6 R 756 (affd (1883) 10 R (HL) 77).

1142. Punctuation. The use of punctuation in the construction of a statute arose in *Alexander v Mackenzie*[1]. In that case the owner of a kippering factory was charged on a complaint that 'you did cause or permit refuse, namely herring offal, to enter a public sewer which discharges on to the foreshore... contrary to the Burgh Police (Scotland) Act 1892, section 233'[2]. That section provided that 'Any owner... of... works who causes or permits any refuse, refuse water, steam, or other substance fitted to interrupt the free passage of a sewer or to be otherwise injurious thereto, or to be injurious to the health of persons living in the vicinity, to enter a public sewer... from any such works shall be guilty of an offence'. Objection was taken by the accused to the relevancy of the complaint on the ground that it was not an offence to permit refuse to enter a public sewer unless the refuse offended in one of the ways specified in the section. The accused maintained that the argument that the qualifying words in the section applied to 'other substances' only was unsound because punctuation should not be looked at in construing a statute. The accused was convicted but the conviction was quashed on appeal. Lord Jamieson, however, was:

'not prepared to hold that in construing a modern Act of Parliament a Court may not have regard to punctuation. Bills when introduced in Parliament have punctuation, and without such would be unintelligible to the legislators, who pass them into law as punctuated. There appears to me no valid reason why regard should be denied to punctuation in construing a statute so passed'[3].

Lord Jamieson nevertheless went on to say:

'While notice may, therefore, in my view be taken of punctuation in construing a statute, a comma or the absence of a comma must, I think, be disregarded if to give effect to it would so alter the sense as to be contrary to the plain intention of the statute. That is the case here'[3].

Again in the same case Lord Stevenson said:

'the older cases indicate that punctuation formed no part of the Act. In my opinion, our duty is to ascertain the intention of the Legislature as expressed by the Act itself, and that, while we may derive some assistance from punctuation, we are entitled either to disregard it or add commas if it should be necessary so to do in order to give effect to the obvious purpose of the Act'[4].

In *Inland Revenue Comrs v Hendry* Lord Reid took a rather different view from that taken in the *Alexander* case where he said:

'before 1850 there was no punctuation in the manuscript copy of an Act which received the Royal Assent, and it does not appear that the printers had any statutory authority to insert punctuation thereafter. So even if punctuation in more modern Acts can be looked at (which is very doubtful), I do not think that one can have any regard to punctuation in older Acts'[5].

1 *Alexander v Mackenzie* 1947 JC 155, 1948 SLT 68.
2 1947 JC 155 at 167, 1948 SLT 68 at 73. The Burgh Police (Scotland) Act 1892 (c 55) is repealed.
3 *Alexander v Mackenzie* 1947 JC 155 at 166, 1948 SLT 68 at 72.
4 1947 JC 155 at 168, 1948 SLT 68 at 73.
5 *Inland Revenue Comrs v Hinchy* [1960] AC 748 at 765, [1960] 1 All ER 505 at 510, HL. For a critical discussion of the attitude of judges to punctuation in legislation, see F A R Bennion *Statutory Interpretation* (1984) pp 594–600, and the authorities cited therein.

(b) External Aids

(A) INTRODUCTION

1143. The external aids. The previous section of this part of the title dealt with the extent to which a provision of a statute could be construed by reference to other parts of it. In this section consideration is given to the extent to which external matters may be taken into account in construing an Act of Parliament. These matters are:

  (1) the historical setting;
  (2) parliamentary history;
  (3) official reports commissioned by government;
  (4) explanatory memoranda issued by government departments;
  (5) textbooks and dictionaries;
  (6) international conventions;
  (7) *travaux préparatoires*;
  (8) other enactments;
  (9) conveyancing and administrative practice;
(10) uniform court decisions and usage;
(11) statutory rules made under an Act.

(B) THE HISTORICAL SETTING

1144. Introduction. The older cases indicate that the historical setting in which an Act was passed is not relevant to its construction[1]. More recently, however, general history has been admitted in some cases as an aid to interpretation.

1 *Gorham v Bishop of Exeter* (1850) 5 Exch 630 at 667, per Alderson B; *R v West Riding of Yorkshire County Council* [1906] 2 KB 676 at 716, CA, per Farwell LJ.

1145. Older decisions. In *Nairn v St Andrews and Edinburgh University Courts*[1], women who were graduates of Edinburgh University and as such had their names enrolled on the register of the general council of that university claimed the right to vote in the election of the parliamentary representative of Edinburgh and St Andrews Universities. By the now repealed section 27 of the Representation of the People (Scotland) Act 1868 (c 48) '. . . every Person whose Name is for the Time being on the Register . . . of the General Council of such University, shall, if of full Age, and not subject to any legal Incapacity, be entitled to vote in the Election of a Member to serve in any future Parliament for such University'; and by the now repealed section 28(2) of that Act all persons on whom the university to which such general council belongs has conferred certain degrees are to be members of the general council of the university. By virtue of an ordinance made under section 14 of the Universities (Scotland) Act 1889 (c 55), in 1892 women were admitted to graduation in, and their names were placed on the register of the general councils of, the universities of Edinburgh and St Andrews. In giving the leading judgment of the Inner House of the Court of Session against the women graduates, Lord McLaren construed the above enactments against the historical setting when the 1868 Act was passed and said:

> 'All varieties of the Parliamentary franchise had this element in common, that its exercise was confined to men . . . In view of these facts, we must conclude that it was a principle of the unwritten constitutional law of the country that men only were entitled to take part in the election of representatives to Parliament. All ambiguous expressions in modern Acts of Parliament must be construed in the light of this general constitutional principle. We are not to be understood as invoking any merely technical rule of construction in this matter; what is meant is that if Parliament had intended to subvert an existing constitutional law in favour of women graduates, the intention would naturally be expressed in plain language, and therefore if ambiguous language is used it must be construed in accordance with the general constitutional rule'[2].

Lord McLaren then went on to find in the 1868 and 1889 Acts no clear intention to change that constitutional rule. The Inner House decision was upheld by the House of Lords.

In the *Claim of Viscountess Rhondda*[3] the Viscountess, a peeress of the United Kingdom in her own right, petitioned for the issue to her of a writ of summons to the House of Lords. She based her claim to receive the writ of summons on section 1 of the Sex Disqualification (Removal) Act 1919 (c 71), which provided that a person should not be disqualified by sex or marriage from the exercise of any public function or from being appointed to or holding any civil or judicial office or post. The Committee for Privileges by a majority rejected her claim, the reasoning of the majority being most simply expressed by Lord Dunedin in these words:

> 'It is certain that the words of the Act only remove a disability; they do not create a right. Now we find that historically no one has ever been held to have a right to demand . . . a writ of summons to sit as a Lord of Parliament, except a male peer . . . This historical fact in my view turns the scale in the balanced question of construction. Looking at the state of the matter historically, it seems to me that the Legislature, if wishing to confer the right on peeresses, would not have been content to use mere words of removal of disability, but would naturally have passed an enabling clause'[4].

---

1 *Nairn v St Andrews and Edinburgh University Courts* 1908 SC 113, 15 SLT 471 (on appeal 1909 SC (HL) 10, 16 SLT 619).
2 1908 SC 113 at 120, 121, 15 SLT 471 at 473.
3 *Viscountess Rhondda's Claim* [1922] 2 AC 339, HL.
4 [1922] 2 AC 339 at 390, 391, HL.

1146. Modern decisions. More recent examples of history being used as an aid to interpretation are *Chandler v Director of Public Prosecutions*[1] and *Schtraks v Government of Israel*[2]. In the *Chandler* case, the accused were charged with committing a breach of section 1 of the Official Secrets Act 1911 (c 28), namely, for a purpose prejudicial to the safety or interests of the state to enter a Royal Air Force station. The House of Lords rejected an argument by the accused that they were entitled to show by evidence that the policies to which they adhered would be beneficial, and not prejudicial to the state, Lord Reid saying:

'The 1911 Act was passed at a time of grave misgiving about the German menace, and it would be surprising and hardly credible that the Parliament of that date intended that a person who deliberately interfered with vital dispositions of the armed forces should be entitled to submit to a jury that Government policy was wrong and that what he did was really in the best interests of the country, and then perhaps to escape conviction because a unanimous verdict on that question could not be obtained'[3].

And in the *Schtraks* case, Lord Reid, in construing the phrase 'an offence of a political character' in section 3(1) of the Extradition Act 1870 (c 52), said:

'In reading the Act of 1870 one is entitled to look through mid-Victorian spectacles. Many people then regarded insurgents against continental governments as heroes intolerably provoked by tyranny who ought to have asylum here although they might have destroyed life and property in the course of their struggles'[4].

1 *Chandler v Director of Public Prosecutions* [1964] AC 763, [1962] 3 All ER 142, HL.
2 *Schtraks v Government of Israel* [1964] AC 556, [1962] 3 All ER 529, HL.
3 *Chandler v Director of Public Prosecutions* [1964] AC 763 at 791, [1962] 3 All ER 142 at 146, 147, HL.
4 *Schtraks v Government of Israel* [1964] AC 556 at 582, 583, [1962] 3 All ER 529 at 535, HL.

(C) PARLIAMENTARY HISTORY

1147. Legislative history. In *Escoigne Properties v Inland Revenue Comrs* Lord Denning said:

'In this country we do not refer to the legislative history of an enactment as they do in the United States of America. We do not look at the explanatory memoranda which preface the Bills before Parliament. We do not have recourse to the pages of Hansard. All that the courts can do is to take judicial notice of the previous state of the law and of other matters generally known to well-informed people'[1].

So far as the citing of parliamentary debates was concerned, Lord Reid in *Beswick v Beswick* considered that this was not permitted for 'purely practical reasons', and said:

'it would add greatly to the time and expense involved in preparing cases involving the construction of a statute if counsel were expected to read all the debates in Hansard, and it would often be impracticable for counsel to get access to at least the older reports of debates in Select Committees of the House of Commons'[2].

However, in *R v Warner*[3] Lord Reid showed some unhappiness with the absolute rule against the use of parliamentary debates as an aid to construction. That case concerned the interpretation of the now repealed section 1(1) of the Drugs (Prevention of Misuse) Act 1964 (c 64) which provides that it is not lawful for a person to have in his possession certain drugs — the question at issue being whether this was an absolute offence or whether it requires *mens rea*. Lord Reid said:

'in cases of this kind the question is not what the words mean but whether there are sufficient grounds for inferring that Parliament intended to exclude the general rule

that mens rea is an essential element in every offence... The rule is firmly established that we may not look at Hansard and in general I agree with it, for reasons
which I gave last year in *Beswick*... This is not a suitable case in which to reopen the
matter but I am bound to say that this case seems to show that there is room for an
exception where examining the proceedings in Parliament would almost certainly
settle the matter immediately one way or the other[4].

Finally, a clear breach in the rule against looking at Hansard reports for the
interpretation of statutes was made by *Pickstone v Freemans plc*[5]. That case
involved the insertion of a section into the Equal Pay Act 1970 (c 41) to bring it
into line with Community law. The insertion was made by means of regulations. The House of Lords held that it was competent to look at the statement
of the minister in introducing the regulations as reported in Hansard. The
breach made by this case, however, appears to be somewhat limited as it seems
to have been allowed only because (1) the object of the regulations was to
implement Community law, and (2) the section was introduced by regulations
and the regulations, although subject to parliamentary approval, could not be
amended by Parliament.

1 *Escoigne Properties Ltd v Inland Revenue Comrs* [1958] AC 549 at 566, [1958] 1 All ER 406 at 414,
   HL.
2 *Beswick v Beswick* [1968] AC 58 at 74, [1967] 2 All ER 1197 at 1202, HL.
3 *Warner v Metropolitan Police Comr* [1969] 2 AC 256, [1968] 2 All ER 356, HL.
4 [1969] 2 AC 256 at 279, [1968] 2 All ER 356 at 366, 367, HL.
5 *Pickstone v Freemans plc* [1989] AC 66, [1988] 2 All ER 803, HL. See also A I L Campbell 'Hansard
   and the Interpretation of Statutes' 1989 SLT (News) 137.

1148. Consolidating Acts. A small exception has also been made in the case
of consolidation Acts. In the *Beswick* case, Lord Upjohn saw no objection to
considering the proceedings of the Joint Committee of the two Houses of
Parliament on consolidation Bills:

> 'not with a view to construing the Act, that is of course not permissible, but to see
> whether the weight of the presumption as to the effect of consolidation Acts [that is
> that they do not alter the law] is weakened by anything that took place in those
> proceedings'[1].

1 *Beswick v Beswick* [1968] AC 58 at 105, [1967] 2 All ER 1197 at 1223, HL.

(D) OFFICIAL REPORTS COMMISSIONED BY GOVERNMENT

1149. Official reports and explanatory memoranda. The report of a
government commission or committee presented to Parliament which is followed by an Act to implement the report may be looked at for the purpose of
seeing what actually was the mischief which Parliament was seeking to remedy
when passing the Act but not in construing the actual wording of the statute.
The leading case in this matter is *Black-Clawson v Papierwerke*[1]. In that case
section 8(1) of the Foreign Judgments (Reciprocal Enforcement) Act 1933 (c 13)
fell to be construed, and prior to that Act there had been presented to Parliament
the report of the Foreign Judgments (Reciprocal Enforcement) Committee 1932
(Cmd 4213) containing a draft Bill which was substantially adopted in the Act.
Lord Reid said:

> 'It has always been said to be important to consider the "mischief" which the Act
> was apparently intended to remedy. The word "mischief" is traditional. I would
> expand it in this way. In addition to reading the Act you look at the facts presumed to

be known to Parliament when the Bill which became the Act in question was before it, and you consider whether there is disclosed some unsatisfactory state of affairs which Parliament can properly be supposed to have intended to remedy by the Act. There is a presumption which can be stated in various ways. One is that in the absence of any clear indication to the contrary Parliament can be presumed not to have altered the common law further than was necessary to remedy the "mischief". Of course it may and quite often does go further. But the principle is that if the enactment is ambiguous, that meaning which relates the scope of the Act to the mischief should be taken rather than a different or wider meaning which the contemporary situation did not call for. The mischief which this Act was intended to remedy may have been common knowledge 40 years ago. I do not think that it is today. But it so happens that a committee including many eminent and highly skilled members made a full investigation of the matter and reported some months before the Act was passed . . . I think that we can take this report as accurately stating the "mischief" and the law as it was then understood to be, and therefore we are fully entitled to look at those parts of the report which deal with those matters. But the report contains a great deal more than that. It contains recommendations, and draft Bill and other instruments intended to embody those recommendations, and comments on what the committee thought the Bill achieved. The draft Bill corresponds in all material respects with the Act so it is clear that Parliament adopted the recommendations of the committee. But nevertheless I do not think that we are entitled to take any of this into account in construing the Act. Construction of the provisions of an Act is for the court and for no one else. This may seem technical but it is good sense'[2].

In *Keith v Texaco*[3] the Lands Tribunal followed the decision in the *Black-Clawson* case where it held that it was entitled, for the purpose of ascertaining the mischief which section 1 of the Conveyancing and Feudal Reform (Scotland) Act 1970 (c 35) was designed to remedy, to look at the report of the Halliday Committee[4] which had been presented to Parliament and which the Act was intended to implement.

1 *Black-Clawson International Ltd v Papierwerke Waldhof-Aschaffenburg AG* [1975] AC 591, [1975] 1 All ER 810, HL.
2 [1975] AC 591 at 614, [1975] 1 All ER 810 at 814, HL.
3 *Keith v Texaco Ltd* 1977 SLT (Lands Tr) 16.
4 Ie the *Report of the Committee on Conveyancing Legislation and Practice* (the Halliday Report) (Cmnd 3118) (1966).

1150. Explanatory memoranda issued by government departments. An explanatory memorandum issued by a government department to give guidance to public authorities on the scope of an enactment is inadmissible for the purpose of construing it[1]. In the *Inglis* case the Lands Tribunal refused to use a departmental memorandum as an aid to construction of the Land Compensation (Scotland) Act 1973 (c 56). The tribunal said the memorandum:

'cannot provide a gloss on the actual words used by Parliament nor can it be used by a judicial tribunal as an aid to construing the wording of a statute or as a guide to the intentions of Parliament'[2].

Having pointed out that in the *Black-Clawson* case[3] the House of Lords had said that a report of a government committee could not be used in construing the actual words of a statute, the tribunal continued:

'Yet in this case the respondents' solicitor is now asking the tribunal to look for guidance not to a government report laid before Parliament when the legislation was being debated but to an explanatory memorandum subsequently issued by the department which was not before the legislature at all'[4].

1 *Inglis v British Airports Authority* 1978 SLT (Lands Tr) 30.

2 1978 SLT (Lands Tr) 30 at 32.
3 *Black-Clawson International Ltd v Papierwerke Waldhof-Aschaffenburg AG* [1975] AC 591, [1975] 1 All ER 810, HL.
4 *Inglis v British Airports Authority* 1978 SLT (Lands Tr) 30 at 32.

(E) TEXTBOOKS AND DICTIONARIES

1151. Textbooks and dictionaries generally. Textbooks may be used as an aid to construction of a statute. The position was clearly stated by Lord Goddard in *Bastin v Davies*[1] where he considered whether it was appropriate to look at Bell's *Sale of Food and Drugs* in determining the meaning of the word 'substance' in the now repealed section 3(1) of the Food and Drugs Act 1938 (c 56). He said:

'This court would never hesitate to disagree with a statement in a textbook, however authoritative, or however long it had stood, if it thought right to do so. In fact, it has had occasion, I think, in the past to differ from statements in Stone's Justices' Manual, which justices are accustomed to treat with almost the respect paid to the Bible... It would be unfortunate if doubt had to be thrown on a statement which has appeared in a well-known textbook for a great number of years without being judicially doubted and after it has been acted on by justices and their clerks for many years'[2].

Dictionaries:

'are not to be taken as authoritative exponents of the meanings of words used in Acts of Parliament, but it is a well-known rule of courts of law that words should be taken to be used in their ordinary sense, and we are therefore sent for instruction to these books'[3].

Moreover, in interpreting a statute:

'the Court may no doubt assist themselves in the discharge of their duty by any literary help they can find, including of course... reference to well-known and authoritative dictionaries'[4].

1 *Bastin v Davies* [1950] 2 KB 579, [1950] 1 All ER 1095, DC.
2 [1950] 2 KB 579 at 582, 583, [1950] 1 All ER 1095 at 1096, DC.
3 *R v Peters* (1886) 16 QBD 636 at 641, per Lord Coleridge.
4 *Marquis Camden v Inland Revenue Comrs* [1914] 1 KB 641 at 648, CA, per Cozens-Hardy MR.

(F) CONVENTIONS

1152. International conventions. Where the terms of legislation which implements an international convention 'are clear and unambiguous, they must be given effect to, whether or not they carry out Her Majesty's treaty obligations'[1]. If, however, the terms of the legislation are not clear, 'we can refer to the convention to resolve ambiguities or obscurities of language'[2], and the convention can be referred to even although there is no express reference to it in the statute[3].

If the words of the domestic legislation are narrower or wider than the convention which it implements, then the words of the domestic legislation must prevail, and it is those words which have got to be construed[4].

1 *Salomon v Customs and Excise Comrs* [1967] 2 QB 116 at 143, [1966] 3 All ER 871 at 875, CA per Diplock LJ.
2 [1967] 2 QB 116 at 145, [1966] 3 All ER 871 at 876, CA per Diplock LJ.

3 [1967] 2 QB 116 at 144, [1966] 3 All ER 871 at 876, CA, per Diplock LJ.
4 *Post Office v Estuary Radio Ltd* [1967] 3 All ER 663 at 675, [1967] 1 WLR 847 at 865, per O'Connor
   J.

1153. The European Convention on Human Rights. The European Convention on Human Rights[1] came into force in 1953 and has been ratified by the United Kingdom. The United Kingdom has accepted the right of individuals to petition the European Commission of Human Rights, but has not made the convention part of its municipal law[2].

The Scottish and English courts appear to have adopted a different approach in determining whether to have regard to the convention for the purpose of interpreting a United Kingdom statute. The English courts have consistently held that they should take the convention into account whenever interpreting a statute which affects the rights and liberties of the individual[3]. So far as Scotland is concerned, however, Lord Ross has said:

> 'With all respect to the distinguished judges in England who have said that the Courts should look to an International Convention such as the European Convention on Human Rights for the purpose of interpreting a United Kingdom Statute, I find such a concept extremely difficult to comprehend. If the Convention does not form part of the municipal law, I do not see why the Court should have regard to it at all ... For myself, I find myself in agreement with Professor Hood Phillips, ... where he points out that to use the Convention as an aid to construction is "potentially dangerous," because the Court is then challenging the well-settled principle that the Executive by itself cannot make law. As he says "Indeed, one might argue that the fact that Parliament has hitherto refrained from incorporating the European Convention into our law indicates an intention that its provisions should not be taken into account by the Courts, so that the Convention ought not to be cited by counsel or looked at by the judges." ... So far as Scotland is concerned, I am of opinion that the Court is not entitled to have regard to the Convention either as an aid to construction or otherwise'[4].

1 Convention for the Protection of Human Rights and Fundamental Freedoms (Rome, 4 November 1950; 213 UNTS 221; TS 71 (1953); Cmd 8969).
2 As to the relation of the convention to United Kingdom domestic law, see HUMAN RIGHTS, para 8,
   above.
3 *R v Secretary of State for the Home Department, ex parte Bhajan Singh* [1976] QB 198 at 207, [1975] 2
   All ER 1081 at 1083, CA, per Lord Denning MR; *Garland v British Rail Engineering Ltd* [1983] 2
   AC 751 at 771, [1982] 2 All ER 402 at 415, HL, per Lord Diplock; *Attorney General v Guardian
   Newspapers Ltd (No 2)* [1990] 1 AC 109, [1983] 3 All ER 546, HL.
4 *Kaur v Lord Advocate* 1980 SC 319 at 328, 329, 1981 SLT 322 at 329, 330, OH, per Lord Ross.
   Lord Ross's decision was adopted by Lord Justice-Clerk Wheatley in *Moore v Secretary of State for
   Scotland* 1985 SLT 38 at 41. See also the opinion of Lord Milligan in *Hamilton v Secretary of State for
   Scotland* 1991 GWD 10-624, OH.

1154. *Travaux préparatoires*. In *Fothergill v Monarch Airlines*[1] consideration was given to the question whether *travaux préparatoires* as aids to the construction of a convention which has been incorporated into or implemented by statute could be used as an aid to the construction of the Warsaw Convention for the Unification of Certain Rules relating to International Carriage by Air[2] which had been given the force of law in the United Kingdom by section 1(1) of the Carriage by Air Act 1961 (c 27) and was set out in a Schedule to that Act. In holding in that case that the *travaux préparatoires* should be admissible as aids to interpretation Lord Wilberforce said their use should be cautious but:

> 'there may be cases where such travaux préparatoires can profitably be used. These cases should be rare, and only where two conditions are fulfilled, first, that the material involved is public and accessible, and secondly, that the travaux préparatoires clearly and indisputably point to a definite legislative intention'[3];

and Lord Scarman said:

> 'We know that in the great majority of the contracting states . . . the "travaux préparatoires" . . . would be admissible as aids to the interpretation of the Convention. We know also that such sources would be used in the practice of public international law. They should, therefore, also be admissible in our courts: but they are to be used as *aids* only [not as] a substitute for the terms of a convention . . . the court must first look at the terms of the convention as enacted by Parliament. But, if there be ambiguity or doubt, or if a literal construction appears to conflict with the purpose of the convention, the court must then, in my judgment, have recourse to such aids as are admissible'[4],

including *travaux préparatoires*.

Gatoil International v Arkwright-Boston Manufacturers[5] was concerned with the interpretation of an ambiguity in section 47 of the Administration of Justice Act 1956 (c 46) which was enacted to give effect to the obligations of the United Kingdom consequent on its accession to the 1952 Brussels International Convention relating to the Arrest of Sea-going Ships[6]. Lord Wilberforce, adopting his dictum in the *Fothergill* case quoted above, held that the proceedings of the conference which led to the Brussels Convention could legitimately be used as an aid to the construction of section 47 because the proceedings were public and accessible and showed a clear legislative intention[7].

1 *Fothergill v Monarch Airlines Ltd* [1981] AC 251, [1980] 2 All ER 696, HL.
2 Convention for the Unification of Certain Rules relating to International Carriage by Air (Warsaw, 12 October 1929; TS 11 (1933); Cmd 4284).
3 *Fothergill v Monarch Airlines Ltd* [1981] AC 251 at 278, [1980] 2 All ER 696 at 703, HL.
4 [1981] AC 251 at 294, [1980] 2 All ER 696 at 715, HL.
5 *Gatoil International Inc v Arkwright-Boston Manufacturers Mutual Insurance Co* 1985 SC (HL) 1, 1985 SLT 68.
6 International Convention relating to the Arrest of Sea-going Ships (Brussels, 10 May 1952; TS 47 (1960), Cmnd 1128).
7 *Gatoil International Inc v Arkwright-Boston Manufacturers Mutual Insurance Co* 1985 SC (HL) 1 at 10, 11, 1985 SLT 68 at 70, 71.

(G) OTHER ENACTMENTS

(i) Introduction

1155. Use of earlier or later enactments generally. Different rules apply as to the use of earlier[1] or later[2] enactments as an aid in the construction of a statute.

1 See paras 1156 ff below.
2 See para 1160 below.

(ii) Earlier Enactments

1156. Statutes *in pari materia*. A rule was laid down by Lord Mansfield in *R v Loxdale* that:

> 'Where there are different statutes *in pari materia*, though made at different times, or even expired and not referring to each other, they shall be taken and construed together as one system and as explanatory of each other'[1].

The same principle is expressed in different language by Griffiths CJ in *Perth Local Board v Maley*, namely:

'It is usual to credit the legislature with a knowledge of the existing law on the subject dealt with, and when we find that such a meaning has been consistently attributed to the word "necessary" in other Acts dealing with similar matters, they may have reasonably expected that the word would in this Act be construed as having the same meaning. Against that construction no authorities have been cited'[2].

In *Hamilton v National Coal Board*[3] Lord Jenkins considered it appropriate to construe an enactment by reference to an earlier one where the Acts were dealing with different subject matters — the later Act relating to mines and the earlier one to factories — but in precisely similar circumstances. The case was concerned with the interpretation of the expression 'properly maintained' in section 81(1) of the Mines and Quarries Act 1954 (c 70), which was in terms similar to the now repealed corresponding provision (section 24(1)) in the Factories Act 1937 (c 67). Lord Jenkins had this to say:

'The process of construing one statute by reference to another, and treating decisions on the meaning of the latter as determining the construction of the former is a process which should be applied with caution. But in the present case the language, the subject-matter and the intent of... section 24(1) of the Act of 1937 and section 81(1) of the Act of 1954 are so closely allied that... it would, to my mind, be clearly wrong to give the words "properly maintained" in section 81(1) a different meaning from that which has been authoritatively assigned to precisely the same words in comparable provisions of the Act of 1937... It would, as I think, be manifestly absurd if the same statutory language applied to two precisely similar machines, with precisely similar defects contracted in precisely similar circumstances, should give rise to a breach of statutory duty with respect to one of them, but not with respect to the other, merely because the *locus in quo* was, in the one case a mine, and in the other a factory'[4].

It is proper to refer to earlier Acts *in pari materia* only where there is ambiguity[5]. This is clearly illustrated by *Couper v Mackenzie*[6], which was concerned with construing the words 'registered under this Act' in the now repealed section 2(1) of the Merchant Shipping Act 1894 (c 60). That provision, re-enacting an earlier enactment, provides for registration under the Act of all British ships, and section 2(2) states that a ship not so registered is not recognised as a British ship. The now repealed section 503 of the 1894 Act confers a limitation of liability on owners of British ships for loss or damage caused by them. The now repealed section 373 of that Act for the first time required every fishing boat to be registered in the Fishing Boat Register. In that case a fishing boat was registered in the Fishing Boat Register but not under section 2 of the Act, and it was argued that, because under the earlier enactment it was necessary to register under the provision corresponding to section 2, it was not sufficient, for the owner to gain the benefit conferred by section 503, to register only in the Fishing Boat Register. The court rejected this argument, Lord Kyllachy disposing of it in these words:

'I should doubt much whether they [that is courts of law] are at liberty, in construing Acts of Parliament, to do so with reference to the course of previous legislation, or to inferences which they may be disposed to draw from previous statutes, as to the probable intentions of the Legislature. Their duty, I apprehend, is to interpret, in its natural sense, the language of the particular enactment which is before them'[7].

The court was accordingly satisfied that registration in the Fishing Boat Register was as much registration 'under this Act' as registration under section 2.

For the purposes of construction, the Rent Restriction Acts have been held not to be *in pari materia* with the real property legislation of 1925[8], nor with the town and country planning legislation[9], which in turn were not to be *in pari materia* with the rating legislation[10]. And in *Howden v Rocheid* Lord Colonsay rejected an argument that, because two Acts of 1681 and 1685 were contemporaneous, the language of the one Act should be read as uniform with the language of the other even although they dealt with different matters[11].

1 *R v Loxdale* (1758) 1 Burr 445 at 447.
2 *Perth Local Board of Health v Maley* (1904) 1 CLR 702 at 715.
3 *Hamilton v National Coal Board* 1960 SC (HL) 1, 1960 SLT 24.
4 1960 SC (HL) 1 at 17, 1960 SLT 24 at 31.
5 *R v Titterton* [1895] 2 QB 61 at 67, DC, per Lord Russell of Killowen.
6 *Couper v Mackenzie* (1906) 8 F 1202, 13 SLT 870.
7 (1906) 8 F 1202 at 1208, 13 SLT 870 at 872.
8 *Powell v Cleland* [1948] 1 KB 262 at 273, [1947] 2 All ER 672 at 676, CA, per Evershed LJ.
9 *Birmingham Corpn v Minister of Housing and Local Government and Habib Ullah* [1964] 1 QB 178 at 186, [1963] 3 All ER 668 at 674, DC, per Lord Parker CJ.
10 *Caravans and Automobiles v Southall Borough Council* [1963] 2 All ER 533, [1963] 1 WLR 690, DC.
11 *Howden v Rocheid* (1869) 7 M (HL) 110 at 117.

1157. Statutes construed with other statutes. Where a provision in an Act provides that the Act is to be construed as one with another Act, then the court must construe every part of each of the Acts 'as if had been contained in one Act, unless there is some manifest discrepancy making it necessary to hold that the later Act has, to some extent, modified something found in the earlier Act'[1].

> 'For many purposes of construction it may be convenient that a series of statutes should be construed as one Act. But there must be some limit to this convenient rule; because in each statute of the series something in the previous legislation is repealed or altered, and it is not possible to construe two inconsistent provisions as one'[2].

1 *Canada Southern Rly Co v International Bridge Co* (1883) 8 App Cas 723 at 727, PC, per Earl of Selbourne LC. Cf *Phillips v Parnaby* [1934] 2 KB 299 at 303. See also F A R Bennion *Statutory Interpretation* (1984) pp 603–605.
2 *Lord Advocate v Sprot's Trustees* (1901) 3 F 440 at 445, 8 SLT 403 at 404, Lord M'Laren.

1158. Consolidation Acts. Special rules apply to the construction of consolidation Acts, but to understand the basis of these rules it is first necessary to know what these Acts are. They are Acts which bring together in one Act the statutory provisions relating to a particular topic without any changes in the law and are not subject to amendment in their passage through Parliament. However, Parliament has to be assured that no changes have been made in the law. A consolidation Bill is therefore scrutinised by a joint committee of both Houses of Parliament, which has the function of satisfying itself that the law has been correctly produced. If the Bill is approved by the joint committee, it is not open to debate on its details in its subsequent stages through Parliament. The advantages of the consolidation procedure are now available to Bills which consolidate but which incorporate (1) corrections and minor improvements in terms of the Consolidation of Enactments (Procedure) Act 1949 (c 33), or (2) amendments recommended by the Law Commissions. The corrections and minor improvements or the recommended amendments have to be approved by the joint committee. The amendments recommended by the Law Commissions:

> 'should be for the following purposes: to tidy up errors of the past, to remove ambiguities, and generally to introduce common sense on points where the form of drafting in the past appeared to lead to a result which departed from common sense; though not to introduce any substantial change in the law or one that might be controversial — indeed nothing that Parliament as a whole would wish to reserve for its consideration'[1].

In interpreting a consolidating Act it is proper to look at the earlier provisions which it consolidated because there is a very strong presumption that it does not alter the law contained in the consolidated enactments[2]. The reason for this presumption is that:

> 'it is the invariable practice of Parliament to require from those who have prepared a consolidation Bill an assurance that it will make no substantial change in the law and to have that checked by a committee'[3].

In *Boyle v Wilson*[4] the question at issue was the extent of the discretion of a licensing court to refuse an application for renewal of a licence of a public house under the now repealed Licensing (Scotland) Act 1903 (c 25). Lord Loreburn LC said:

> 'the sections operative on that point in the Act of 1903 ... are either echoes or adaptations that do not alter the sense of corresponding sections in earlier Acts ... And the ruling decision of *Lundie v Falkirk Magistrates*[5] decided under the old Acts, applies equally to the new'[6].

1 *Report of the Joint Committee on Consolidation Bills on the Rent Bill 1977* (Report 5: HL Paper (1977) no. 169; HC Paper (1977) no. 387).
2 *Inland Revenue Comrs v Hinchy* [1960] AC 748 at 768, [1960] 1 All ER 505 at 512, HL, per Lord Reid.
3 *Beswick v Beswick* [1968] AC 58 at 73, [1967] 2 All ER 1197 at 1202, HL, per Lord Reid.
4 *Boyle v Wilson* [1907] AC 45, HL.
5 *Lundie v Falkirk Magistrates* (1890) 18 R 60, where it was held that the discretion of the licensing authority was absolute provided that it did not exceed its statutory jurisdiction.
6 *Boyle v Wilson* [1907] AC 45 at 55, HL.

1159. Modifications and re-enactments. In *Barras v Aberdeen Steam Trawling and Fishing Co*[1] the later enactment — the now repealed section 1(1) of the Merchant Shipping (International Labour Conventions) Act 1925 (c 42) — was not a provision consolidating the earlier enactment — section 158 of the Merchant Shipping Act 1894 (c 60) — but a provision modifying it but using the same language. Section 1(1) of the 1925 Act provided that 'Where by reason of the wreck or loss of a ship' a seaman's service terminates before the agreed date, he is entitled to receive wages, if unemployed, for a period of two months from the termination of his service. In this case a seaman was engaged under an agreement to serve as an engineer of a trawler for the period from July to December 1930. In September 1930 the trawler sustained damage in a collision at sea, but managed to reach port where the crew was paid off and the ship was laid up for repairs for fourteen days. On the repairs being completed, the seaman was re-engaged. He claimed wages, under section 1(1) of the 1925 Act, for the fourteen days during which the ship was under repair, on the ground that his service had been terminated by reason of the 'wreck' of the ship. The House of Lords rejected his claim.

In *The Olympic* 'the wreck of the ship' in section 158 of the 1894 Act was held to be:

> 'anything happening to the ship which renders her incapable of carrying out the maritime adventure in respect of which the seaman's contract was entered into'[2],

and Lord Buckmaster in the *Barras* case felt bound by this interpretation:

> 'It has long been a well-established principle to be applied in the consideration of Acts of Parliament that, where a word of doubtful meaning has received a clear judicial interpretation, the subsequent statute which incorporates the same word or the same phrase in a similar context must be construed so that the word or phrase is interpreted according to the meaning that has previously been assigned to it'[3].

However, Lord Macmillan in the same case was of the opinion that the re-enactment of a provision previously judicially interpreted raises no more than a presumption that Parliament intended that the language so used should be given the same meaning as that judicially attributed to it[4]. Moreover, in *Royal Crown Derby Porcelain v Russell* Lord Denning said:

'I do not believe that whenever Parliament re-enacts a provision of a statute it thereby gives statutory authority to every erroneous interpretation which has been put upon it. The true view is that the court will be slow to overrule a previous decision... when it has long been acted on, and it will be more than usually slow to do so when Parliament has, since the decision, re-enacted the statute in the same terms. But if a decision is, in fact, shown to be erroneous, there is no rule of law which prevents it being overruled'[5].

1 *Barras v Aberdeen Steam Trawling and Fishing Co* 1933 SC (HL) 21, 1933 SLT 338.
2 *The Olympic* [1913] P 92 at 107, per Lord Wrenbury.
3 *Barras v Aberdeen Steam Trawling and Fishing Co* 1933 SC (HL) 21 at 27, 1933 SLT 338 at 339.
4 1933 SC (HL) 21 at 50, 1933 SLT 338 at 353.
5 *Royal Crown Derby Porcelain Co v Russell* [1949] 2 KB 417 at 429, [1949] 1 All ER 749 at 755, CA.

(iii) Later Enactments

1160. Construction of an earlier statute. In *Kirkness v John Hudson & Co*[1] Lord Reid referred to *Ormond Investment Co v Betts*[2] and said that it was:

'conclusive and binding authority for the proposition that, in construing a provision of an earlier Act, the provisions of a later Act cannot be taken into account except in a limited class of case, and that that rule applies although the later Act contains a provision that it is to be read as one with the earlier Act. Of course, that does not apply where the later Act amends the earlier Act or purports to declare its meaning: in such cases the later Act operates directly by its own force. But there the provisions of the later Act could only operate indirectly as an aid to the construction of words in the earlier Act those provisions can only be used for that purpose if certain conditions apply to the earlier Act when it is considered by itself'[3].

The conditions applicable to the earlier Act are that it contains some 'phrase fairly and equally open to divers meanings'[4] or something 'obscure or ambiguous, or readily capable of more than one interpretation'[5].

1 *Kirkness v John Hudson & Co Ltd* [1955] AC 696, [1955] 2 All ER 345, HL.
2 *Ormond Investment Co Ltd v Betts* [1928] AC 143, HL.
3 *Kirkness v John Hudson & Co Ltd* [1955] AC 696 at 735, [1955] 2 All ER 345 at 365, 366, HL.
4 *Ormond Investment Co Ltd v Betts* [1928] AC 143 at 156, HL, per Lord Buckmaster.
5 [1928] AC 143 at 164, HL, per Lord Atkinson.

(H) CONVEYANCING AND ADMINISTRATIVE PRACTICE

1161. Conveyancing practice. The uniform opinion and practice of eminent conveyancers has always had regard paid to it by all courts of justice[1]. In *Kirkpatrick's Trustee v Kirkpatrick*[2] a trust disposition and settlement which, without using the word 'dispone', purported to convey heritable estate was executed prior to the enactment of the Titles to Land Consolidation (Scotland) Act 1868 (c 101). Section 20 of that Act provided that no testamentary deed is to be held to be invalid on the ground that the granter of the deed has not used the word 'dispone'. Lord Cairns LC, affirming the judgment of the Court of Session that, in the absence of the words 'dispone' the deed was invalid, said:

'looking to the unanimity prevailing in the Court below... [and] the decisions which from time to time have been arrived at, and the *dicta* which have fallen from

Judges in Scotland . . . [and] the expressions of text writers as indicating the opinion and practice of the profession, it would be impossible now to open or disturb the question as to the necessity for this word "dispone" in a conveyance of heritable property. It may appear to be a very technical view to hold the presence or absence of a single word of this kind to be efficacious or fatal in a deed conveying heritable property, but your Lordships must bear in mind that according to the law of England also there are other words, I apprehend, not of greater importance, the presence or absence of which will be found to have an equal effect on the validity of a deed in this country'[3].

1 *Basset v Basset* (1744) 3 Atk 203 at 208, per Hardwicke LC.
2 *Kirkpatrick's Trustee v Kirkpatrick* (1874) 1 R (HL) 37.
3 (1874) 1 R (HL) 37 at 42.

1162. Administrative practice. The views of a government department as to the meaning of a statute which is administered by it are not admissible as an aid to construction. An exception to this rule has been made in the case of the Income Tax Act because it:

'is not a statute which was passed once for all. It has expired, and been revived, and re-enacted over and over again; every revival and re-enactment is a new Act . . . [and] when you find legislation following a continuous practice and repeating the very words on which that practice was founded, it may perhaps fairly be inferred that the Legislature in re-enacting the statute intended those words to be understood in their received meaning. And perhaps it might be argued that the inference grows stronger with each successive re-enactment'[1].

1 *Income Tax Special Purposes Comrs v Pemsel* [1891] AC 531 at 591, HL, per Lord Macnaghten.

(I) UNIFORM COURT DECISIONS AND USAGE

1163. Uniform decisions and usage. If the meaning of a statute is ambiguous and a certain interpretation has been uniformly put upon it and transactions, such as dealings in property and the making of contracts, have taken place on the faith of that interpretation, the court will not put a different interpretation upon it which would materially affect those transactions[1]. In *Bourne v Keane* Lord Buckmaster said that:

'the construction of a statute of doubtful meaning, once laid down and accepted for a long period of time, ought not to be altered unless your Lordships could say positively that it was wrong and productive of inconvenience'[2].

And Lord Brougham said:

'Where a statute speaking on some points is silent as to others, usage may well supply the defect; for where the statute uses language of doubtful import, the acting under it for a long course of years may well give an interpretation to that obscure meaning and reduce that uncertainty to a fixed rule . . . but it is quite plain that against a plain statutory law no usage is of any avail'[3].

1 *Marquis of Tweeddale Case* (1793) 1 Anst 143.
2 *Bourne v Keane* [1919] AC 815 at 874, HL.
3 *Dunbar Magistrates v Duchess of Roxburghe* (1835) 3 Cl & Fin 335 at 354, HL, per Lord Brougham.

(J) STATUTORY RULES MADE UNDER AN ACT

1164. Use of statutory instruments as to construction of an Act and *vice versa*. There appear to be conflicting views as to whether statutory instruments

made under an Act may be used as an aid in its construction. In *Re Wier* James LJ
and Mellish LJ said:

> 'that, where the construction of the Act is ambiguous and doubtful on any point,
> recourse may be had to the rules which have been made . . . under the authority of
> the Act, and if we find that in the rules any particular construction has been put on
> the Act, that it is our duty to adopt and follow that construction'[1].

In *Stephens v Cuckfield Rural District Council*, however, Upjohn LJ said:

> 'We doubt very much whether it is right to construe the words of the section by
> reference to regulations made under powers therein contained'[2].

In *Britt v Buckinghamshire County Council*[3] the court held that where a statute
gave power to a minister to prescribe by regulations 'exceptions and modifications' to an Act, the regulations (which had come into force at the same time as
the Act) might legitimately be used in construing the Act. Harman LJ did not
disagree with the above quoted dictum of Upjohn LJ but distinguished the
Stephens case from the *Britt* case saying that in *Britt* there was:

> 'a process which I have not seen anywhere else. There is a power given by the Act
> itself to the Minister to modify another section of the Act so that when the Minister
> does produce that modification . . . that regulation becomes in fact part of the Act. It
> is like an amending section of the Act. So that in my judgment that regulation can be
> referred to because it is embodied in the Act itself and, having a quasi-parliamentary
> validity, is a good indication of the wishes of the legislature, just as much as if it were
> enacted in the Act itself . . . It is not a question of construing an Act by subsequent
> regulations, in the ordinary sense of those words'[4].

Statutes may of course be referred to in the interpretation of statutory instruments[5], and where an Act confers power to make subordinate legislation,
expressions used in that legislation have, unless the contrary intention appears,
the meanings which they bear in the Act[6].

1 *Re Wier, ex parte Wier* (1871) 6 Ch App 875 at 879.
2 *Stephens v Cuckfield Rural District Council* [1960] 2 QB 373 at 381, [1960] 2 All ER 716 at 718, CA.
3 *Britt v Buckinghamshire County Council* [1964] 1 QB 77, [1963] 2 All ER 175, CA.
4 [1964] 1 QB 77 at 88, 89, [1963] 2 All ER 175 at 180, CA.
5 *Hargreaves v Alderson* [1964] 2 QB 159 at 167, [1962] 3 All ER 1019 at 1024, DC, per Salmon J.
6 Interpretation Act 1978 (c 30), s 11, re-enacting in substance the Interpretation Act 1889 (c 63),
   s 31 (repealed).

(5) SUBSIDIARY PRINCIPLES OF CONSTRUCTION

(a) *Expressio Unius est Exclusio Alterius*

1165. Meaning of *expressio unius est exclusio alterius*. Lord Dunedin in
Whiteman v Sadler expressed the Latin maxim *expressio unius est exclusio alterius* as
meaning 'express enactment shuts the door to further implication'[1]. In *Inverness
County Council v Inverness Burgh*[2] the burgh of Inverness was extended by the
sheriff, under section 11 of the now repealed Burgh Police (Scotland) Act 1892
(c 55), so as to include an area in the county of Inverness. The Act contained no
provision for the adjustment or transference of liabilities affecting areas brought
within the boundaries of a burgh except in sections 21 and 22 dealing respectively with matters pertaining to public health and the preparation of the parliamentary register. An action brought by the county council against the burgh for
declarator that the burgh was liable in repayment of a proportionate share of all
loans effected by the county council which existed at the date of the extension of
the burgh's boundaries was dismissed. The Lord Ordinary said:

'The Legislature, in 1892, having dealt expressly with the adjustment of certain debts and obligation [that is by sections 21 and 22] and said nothing about any other, must, in my opinion, be held, on the ground of *expressio unius*, to have intended that there should be adjustment only in the two cases expressly dealt with'[3].

In *Colquhoun v Brooks*, however, Lopez LJ said of the maxim *expressio unius*:

'It is often a valuable servant, but a dangerous master to follow in the construction of statutes or documents. The exclusio is often the result of inadvertence or accident, and the maxim ought not to be applied, when its application, having regard to the subject-matter to which it is to be applied, leads to inconsistency or injustice'[4].

Again, in *Stevenson v Hunter* Lord Kyllachy said that:

'it is not I think a sound proposition that where a proviso is attached to an enacting or exegetical section of an Act of Parliament such a proviso falls necessarily to be construed on the principle of *expressio unius est exclusio alterius*'[5].

In support of this dictum Lord Kyllachy quoted the following words from Lord Watson in *West Derby Union v Metropolitan Life Insurance*:

'I am perfectly clear that if the language of the enacting part of the statute does not contain the provisions which are said to occur in it, you cannot derive these provisions by implication from a proviso'[6].

1 *Whiteman v Sadler* [1910] AC 514 at 527, HL.
2 *Inverness County Council v Inverness Magistrates* 1909 SC 386, 15 SLT 966, OH.
3 1909 SC 386 at 391, 15 SLT 966 at 968, OH. The Lord Ordinary was upheld by the Inner House: *Inverness County Council v Inverness Magistrates* 1909 SC 386 at 393, 1909 1 SLT 59 at 60, per Lord Low.
4 *Colquhoun v Brooks* (1888) 21 QBD 52 at 65, CA.
5 *Stevenson v Hunter* (1903) 5 F 761 at 765, 10 SLT 360 at 362, OH.
6 *West Derby Union v Metropolitan Life Assurance Society* [1897] AC 647 at 652, HL.

(b) The *Ejusdem Generis* Rule

1166. The *ejusdem generis* rule. As Viscount Haldane understood the *ejusdem generis* rule:

'it applies when there is an enumeration of particular instances, every one of which illustrates a species which makes up a class. Then when you have general words following the enumeration of the individual cases you confine these general words by the species which is the dominant factor in the enumeration'[1].

Thus in *Duncan v Jackson*[2] it was held that the words 'other building' in the enumeration in the now repealed section 11 of the Representation of the People (Scotland) Act 1832 (c 65) 'of any house, warehouse, counting house, shop or other building' within a burgh were to be construed as including only such buildings as were *ejusdem generis* with the buildings specifically enumerated, that is buildings for residential or for commercial (including agricultural) purposes, and that a gas meter-house, 4 feet 6 inches long and 4 feet high, built of stone and brick, which contained a meter for the supply of gas to a dwelling house outside the burgh, was not a building within the meaning of the Act.

Caledonian Rly Co v Glasgow Corpn[3] was concerned with the interpretation of the now repealed section 28 of the Waterworks Clauses Act 1847 (c 17), which provided that the undertakers may open and break up the soil and pavement of the several streets and bridges within the limits of the special Act, and may open and break up any sewers, drains or tunnels within or under such streets or bridges. It was held in that case that the 'tunnels' referred to in the section must be *ejusdem generis* with sewers or drains, and that it was *ultra vires* of public water commissioners to break open the brickwork forming the arch of the bridge or roof of a railway tunnel.

However, as Lord Kinnear said in *The Admiralty v Burns*:

'if you are to limit general words by holding that they must cover only things that are *ejusdem generis* with preceding specific words, you must find that these specific words themselves are *ejusdem generis* with one another'[4].

In *Crichton Stuart v Ogilvie*[5] the words 'or other purposes' in the now repealed section 18 of the Agricultural Holdings (Scotland) Act 1908 (c 64) fell to be construed. That section provided that in leases from year to year six months' notice of termination must be given, except where there is a stipulation entitling the landlord to resume land for 'building, planting, feuing or other purposes'. Applying Lord Kinnear's dictum quoted above in the *Admiralty* case, the court held that the *ejusdem generis* rule did not apply to the construction of the words 'or other purposes' because 'building, planting and feuing' did not form a genus. Again, in *Prior v Kelvin Shipping Co*[6] Lord Strachan found the *ejusdem generis* rule inapplicable in construing general words following the words 'collision at sea, salvage, towage' in section 2 of the National Assessors (Scotland) Act 1894 (c 40) because the specific words did not constitute any one genus.

1 *Moss' Empires Ltd v Glasgow Assessor* 1917 SC (HL) 1 at 5, 1916 2 SLT 215 at 217.
2 *Duncan v Jackson* (1905) 8 F 323, 13 SLT 932.
3 *Caledonian Rly Co v Glasgow Corpn* (1901) 3 F 526, 8 SLT 457. See also *Walker v Lamb* 1892 19 R (J) 50, *Benzie v Mickel* 1945 JC 47, 1945 SLT 166.
4 *The Admiralty v Burns* 1910 SC 531 at 538, 1910 1 SLT 277 at 280.
5 *Crichton Stuart v Ogilvie* 1914 SC 888, 1914 2 SLT 116.
6 *Prior v Kelvin Shipping Co Ltd* 1954 SLT (Notes) 12, OH. See also *Minister of Pensions v Ballantyne* 1948 SC 176 at 182, 1948 SLT 242 at 245, per Lord Mackay.

1167. Ejusdem generis rule is a rule of construction. It has to be remembered that the *ejusdem generis* rule is a rule of construction and not a rule of law. In *Minister of Pensions v Ballantyne*[1] Lord Mackay noted with approval the dictum of Lord Kinnear in *The Admiralty v Burns* that in relation to the construction of contracts the *ejusdem generis* rule was not to be applied as an abstract rule of law and his words that:

'we are to begin by reading the contract itself, taking it as a whole, considering the true meaning of the particular clause with reference to its language, to its place in the contract, and to the general scope and purpose of the contract itself'[2].

and added 'The same qualification is equally, or even more, applicable in statutory construction'[3]. Again, in *National Association of Local Government Officers v Bolton Corpn* Lord Wright said 'The *ejusdem generis* rule is often useful or convenient, but it is merely a rule of construction, not a rule of law'[4].

1 *Minister of Pensions v Ballantyne* 1948 SC 176, 1948 SLT 242.
2 *The Admiralty v Burns* 1910 SC 531 at 538, 1910 1 SLT 277 at 280.
3 *Minister of Pensions v Ballantyne* 1948 SC 176 at 182, 1948 SLT 242 at 245.
4 *National Association of Local Government Officers v Bolton Corpn* [1943] AC 166 at 185, 186, [1942] 2 All ER 425 at 433, HL.

1168. Inapplicability of the rule. The *ejusdem generis* rule:

'is not applicable when the general expression is antecedent to the particulars. You cannot, as it were, hold in suspense the meaning of the opening words till you have reached the end of the catalogue, although you can interpret the closing words of the catalogue when you reach them by the other items which have preceded them'[1].

Thus, in the *Chernack* case it was held that the *ejusdem generis* rule was not applicable to the definition of 'broker' in the now repealed section 4(2) of the

Burgh Police (Scotland) Act 1892 (c 55), which provided that 'broker' includes any person dealing in second-hand goods or articles, or in yarn or waste, or in other unwrought material, or in old metals, bones, or rags; and that the words 'second-hand goods or articles' occurring in the definition must therefore receive a literal construction.

Gray v The Crofters Commission[2] was concerned with the interpretation of section 16A(2) of the Crofters (Scotland) Act 1955[3] which provides that the Crofters Commission, in determining whether or not to give a direction under section 16(9) that a vacant croft is to cease to be a croft, must have regard to the general interest of the crofting community in the district in which the croft is situated and in particular to the demand, if any, for a tenancy of the croft from persons who might reasonably be expected to obtain that tenancy if the croft were offered for letting on the open market on the date when it is considering the application. In reversing a decision of the Crofters Commission not to grant a direction under section 16(9) of the Act, the Land Court said that the words in section 16A(2):

> 'which follow, prefaced by the phrase "and, in particular", merely indicate a particular aspect of the foregoing general interest, namely, the demand by prospective acceptable tenants for the crofting tenancy in question. In our view the Crofters Commission have wrongly construed words of particularity following words of generality as restricting the operation of the preceding words ... But the ejusdem generis rule cannot be applied in reverse'[4].

and, in support of its view against the reverse application of the rule, the Land Court went on to quote from cases determined by the House of Lords and the Judicial Committee of the Privy Council[5].

1 *Chernack v Mill* 1938 JC 39 at 46, 1938 SLT 10 at 14, per Lord Justice-General Normand.
2 *Gray v Crofters Commission* 1980 SLT (Land Ct) 2.
3 The Crofters (Scotland) Act 1955 (c 21) s 16A(2), was added by the Crofting Reform (Scotland) Act 1976 (c 21), s 13(3).
4 *Gray v Crofters Commission* 1980 SLT (Land Ct) 2 at 7.
5 *Ambatielos v Anton Jurgens Margarine Works* [1923] AC 175 at 183, HL, per Cave LC; *Canadian National Railways v Canada SS Lines Ltd* [1945] AC 204 at 211, PC.

(c) Words of Rank

1169. Words of rank generally. Analogous to the *ejusdem generis* rule is the rule that general words following particular words will not include anything of a class superior to that to which the particular words belong. Thus, in *Casher v Holmes*[1] it was held that the general words 'all other metals' following the particular words 'copper, brass, pewter and tin' in a local Act[2] did not include silver or gold as they were superior to the particular metals mentioned in the Act.

1 *Casher v Holmes* (1831) 2 B & Ad 592.
2 Littlehampton Harbour Act 1825 (6 Geo 4 c clxx).

(d) De Minimis Non Curat Praetor

1170. Meaning of *de minimis non curat praetor*. The maxim *de minimis non curat praetor* means that the praetor does not concern himself about trifles or, as interpreted by Trayner, 'the praetor does not apply his equitable remedies in matters of small amount'[1]. The application of the doctrine arose in three cases before the Lands Valuation Appeal Court[2]. Each of the cases was concerned with the interpretation of section 7(2) and (3) of the Valuation and Rating (Scotland) Act 1956 (c 60) and section 14(1) of the Local Government (Financial Provisions) (Scotland) Act 1963 (c 12), which provided in effect that a building used solely in connection with agricultural operations on any agricultural land is to be treated as agricultural lands and heritages resulting in its exclusion from the valuation roll. In each case the building was used to some extent for a non-agricultural purpose but it was argued that such use was so minimal that the '*de minimis*' maxim fell to be applied. In all three cases the argument was rejected. In the *Rimmer* case Lord Kilbrandon said that the maxim was:

> 'not a rule of law, and that so far as it can be said to embody any principle, its operation can be equitable only. When a statute provides that a result shall follow *only* on the fulfilment of a certain condition, it is hard to formulate a logical proposition which will justify that result following when the condition is very nearly fulfilled'[3].

In the *Angus Assessor* case, Lord Fraser recognised the question of the application of the maxim as:

> 'an important one of principle in relation to the construction of statutes. I fully recognise the logical difficulty of treating a word such as "solely" or "only" in a statute as being open to construction by the application of the de minimis brocard. On the other hand, it is not difficult to figure circumstances where the literal reading of such words would lead to results that might reasonably be described as harsh or even absurd and I am not, as at present advised, satisfied that in such circumstances the Court could not avoid those results by applying the brocard'[4].

Lord Fraser also said that:

> 'it may be that the English doctrine, which I think is generally expressed as de minimis non curat lex, differs in its scope and application from the Scots doctrine, in which the final word is not lex but praetor . . . and it may therefore be that English authorities are not safe guides for us'[5].

1 J Trayner *Latin Maxims and Phrases* (4th edn, 1894) p 143.
2 *W T Rimmer & Co v Perth and Kinross Assessor* 1965 SLT 406; *Angus Assessor v George Ogilvie (Montrose) Ltd* 1968 SLT 348; *Moray and Nairn Assessor v Charles Meldrum & Sons* 1968 SLT 366.
3 *W T Rimmer & Co v Perth and Kinross Assessor* 1965 SLT 406 at 408.
4 *Angus Assessor v George Ogilvie (Montrose) Ltd* 1968 SLT 348 at 352, 353.
5 1968 SLT 348 at 352.

(e) Computation of Time

1171. Financial year, month, week. 'Financial year' means, in respect of matters relating to the Consolidated Fund, the National Loans Fund or money provided by Parliament or relating to the Exchequer or to central taxes or finance, the twelve months ending with 31 March[1]. Likewise the financial year of a local authority is the period of twelve months ending with 31 March[2].

In any statute passed since 1850 'month' means a calendar month unless the contrary intention appears[3]. In a statute passed before 1851 it generally means a period of twenty-eight days.

The interpretation of 'week' seems to depend on the context. Thus in *Aberdeen Magistrates v Watt*[4] it was held that a notice which had been inserted in an Aberdeen daily newspaper on Friday in one week, and on Wednesday in the following week, was a notice which had been inserted 'for two successive weeks' within the meaning of section 145 of the Aberdeen Municipality Extension Act 1871 (c cxli). As Lord Trayner said:

'I take the word "week" in this clause (there being nothing in the context to indicate a different meaning) as signifying a calendar week — *ie*, the period beginning with Sunday and ending with Saturday. I do not think it means a period of seven days beginning on any one day and ending on the seventh day thereafter'[5].

In the context of an Australian Factories Act, however, 'week' was held to mean a week of work[6].

1 Interpretation Act 1978 (c 30), s 5, Sch 1.
2 Local Government (Scotland) Act 1973 (c 65), s 96(5) (substituted by the Local Government (Scotland) Act 1975 (c 30), s 18).
3 Interpretation Act 1978, Sch 1.
4 *Aberdeen Magistrates v Watt* (1901) 3 F 787 (not reported fully in 9 SLT 36).
5 (1901) 3 F 787 at 790 (not reported fully in 9 SLT 36).
6 *Bishop v Hooper* [1905] VLR 220.

1172. Period of time before an event. Where something has to be done so many days or weeks before a particular event, both the day on which the thing is done and the day by which it has to be done are excluded from the computation, so that there is a clear period of so many days or weeks intervening. Thus in *Watson, Gow & Co v Glasgow Assessor*[1] the valuation appeal court construed a provision in the now repealed section 9 of the Valuation of Lands (Scotland) Act 1854 (c 91), which required an appellant to give notice of appeal 'six days at least before such appeal is heard', as requiring six clear days' notice. Lord Dundas put the matter in this way:

'The appellants were thus duly certiorated that, if they meant to appeal, they must give six days' notice before the 10th of September — that is, not later than 3rd September'[2].

In *McMillan v HM Advocate*[3], where the words to be construed were 'not less than seven days before the hearing or trial', the court followed the decision in the *Watson, Gow* case and considered that the qualifying words 'not less than' and 'at least' were synonomous. They also referred to *R v Long*[4] to show that the same rule of construction applied under English law.

For the purposes of a claim for unfair dismissal of persons employed in the business of a company, it was held by the House of Lords (reversing a decision of the Court of Session) that those persons who had been dismissed one hour before the transfer of the business had been employed by the company immediately before the transfer within the meaning of the regulations[5]. The ratio was that the regulations had been enacted in order to comply with a directive of the European Economic Community which provided for the safeguarding of employees' rights on the transfer of a business[5].

1 *Watson, Gow & Co Ltd v Glasgow Assessor* 1910 SC 807, 1910 1 SLT 189.
2 1910 SC 807 at 809, 1910 1 SLT 189 at 190.
3 *McMillan v HM Advocate* 1982 SCCR 309, 1983 SLT 24.
4 *R v Long* [1960] 1 QB 681, [1959] 3 All ER 559, CCA.
5 *Litster v Forth Dry Dock and Engineering Co Ltd (In Receivership)* [1990] 1 AC 546, 1989 SLT 540, HL.

1173. Period of time after, or from, an event within which something has to be done. Where a statute prescribes a period of time after, or from, some event within which some act has to be done, then, unless the context otherwise requires, in the computation of the period the first day of the period is disregarded and the last day is included. Thus in *Stewart v Chapman*[1] where a motorist on 25 January received a notice of intended prosecution of alleged careless driving on 11 January, the court held that the notice had been served within fourteen days after the commission of the offence as required by what is now section 1(1)(c) of the Road Traffic Offenders Act 1988 (c 53). The same rule of construction applies to a statutory period running from a specified date to another specified date.

In modern statutes where the aim is to bring the statute into operation at the end of a specified period after royal assent, the formula generally used is that 'This Act shall come into force at the expiration of a period of ... months beginning with the date on which it is passed'. As Winn J said in *Hare v Gocher*, the reason for this formula is to avoid equivocation and to exclude the application of the general rule that the first day of a period should be excluded from a computation[2]. In the *S* case[3], following the *Hare*[4] case, it was held in construing the words 'within a period of three weeks beginning with the date of any decision of a children's hearing' in section 49(1) of the Social Work (Scotland) Act 1968 (c 49) that the period included the date of the hearing.

1 *Stewart v Chapman* [1951] 2 KB 792, [1951] 2 All ER 613, DC.
2 *Hare v Gocher* [1962] 2 QB 641 at 646, [1962] 2 All ER 763 at 765, DC.
3 *S* 1979 SLT (Sh Ct) 37.
4 See note 2 above.

1174. Meaning of 'forthwith'. In *Brown v Bonnyrigg and Lasswade Magistrates* Lord President Normand said that 'forthwith' is certainly a word open to construction, and must be construed according to the circumstances in which it is used[1]. In that case there fell to be construed the word 'forthwith' in the now repealed section 16 of the Housing (Scotland) Act 1930 (c 40) which required a local authority, after serving notice on the owner of a dwelling house stating that the house was unfit for human habitation and receiving no satisfactory undertaking by the owner regarding the house, to 'forthwith make a demolition order'. The court held that a demolition order made nearly three years after service of the notice was made 'forthwith' on the ground that the delay was not unreasonable in the circumstances and had not caused prejudice to any party.

In a later case[2] the High Court of Justiciary, following Lord Normand's dictum in the *Brown* case that 'forthwith' must be construed according to the circumstances in which it is used, held that a regulation which required an owner of a vehicle to notify forthwith a change in its ownership required notification as soon as possible after the change of ownership or within a day or two thereafter.

1 *Brown v Bonnyrigg and Lasswade Magistrates* 1936 SC 258 at 265, 1936 SLT 304 at 307.
2 *A & C McLennan (Blairgowrie) Ltd v MacMillan* 1964 JC 1, 1964 SLT 2.

(6) MANDATORY, DIRECTORY AND PERMISSIVE ENACTMENTS

(a) Introduction

1175. Mandatory and discretionary enactments generally. A question which frequently comes before the courts is whether, when a statute requires that something must be done, or done in a particular form or manner, without expressly declaring what is to be the consequence of non-compliance, the requirement is to be regarded as mandatory or merely directory or permissive. Another allied question is whether an enactment which is permissive in form may be mandatory in effect. Where the statute is held to be mandatory, failure to comply with it will invalidate the thing done under it, but where the enactment is regarded as merely directory or permissive the thing done will be unaffected, subject to any penalty that may be provided by the statute for breach of it.

'An absolute enactment must be obeyed or fulfilled exactly, but it is sufficient if a directory enactment is obeyed or fulfilled substantially'[1].

Enactments which are mandatory and permissive in form are dealt with in turn.

1   *Woodward v Sarsons* (1875) LR 10 CP 733 at 746, per Coleridge CJ.

(b) Enactments which are Mandatory in Form

1176. Introduction. As to whether an enactment which is mandatory in form is in effect mandatory or merely directory 'no universal rule can be laid down . . . It is the duty of courts of justice to try to get at the real intention of the legislature by attending to the whole scope of the statute to be construed'[1].

'You cannot safely go further than that in each case you must look to the subject-matter, consider the importance of the provision that has been disregarded and the relation of that provision to the general object intended to be secured by the Act, and upon a review of the case in that aspect decide whether the matter is what is called imperative or only directory'[2].

However, some help may be derived from a consideration of the cases set out in the following paragraphs on this topic.

1   *Liverpool Borough Bank v Turner* (1860) 30 LJ Ch 379 at 380, per Campbell CJ.
2   *Howard v Bodington* (1877) 2 PD 203 at 211, per Lord Penzance.

1177. Cases in which statutory requirements have been held to be mandatory. In *London and Clydesdale Estates v Aberdeen District Council*[1] the owners of ground which the council proposed to acquire for educational purposes submitted that an appropriate class of development would be residential with associated commercial purposes. In rejecting the owners' proposal the council omitted to inform the owners in writing, as they were required to do by the now revoked article 3(3) of the Town and Country Planning (General Development) (Scotland) Order 1959, SI 1959/1361, that they had a statutory right of appeal. The House of Lords held that the requirements of article 3(3) were mandatory, Lord Hailsham saying that:

'where Parliament prescribes that an authority with compulsory powers should inform the subject of his right to question those powers, *prima facie* the requirement must be treated as mandatory'[2].

Robertson v Adamson[3] was concerned with the interpretation of the now repealed Ballot Act 1872 (c 33), of which section 2 laid down the method of taking votes at elections. Section 28 provided that 'The schedules to this Act, and the notes thereto, and directions therein, shall be construed and have effect as part of this Act', and Schedule 1 contained rules for the guidance of those taking part in elections. Lord Justice-Clerk Moncrieff observed that, in so far as the rules were mere matters of form such as for example the form of the writs to be used, their words were directory and would be complied with by as exact an adherence as circumstances would permit, but that directions given to the elector or the returning officer were a different class, and were of the nature of injunctions or prohibitions which must be as specifically complied with as if they had been specially provided in the body of the statute[4].

It seems that the following are also mandatory:
(1) rules of procedure[5]; and
(2) negative and prohibitory words[6].

1 *London and Clydesdale Estates Ltd v Aberdeen District Council* 1980 SC (HL) 1, 1980 SLT 81.
2 1980 SC (HL) 1 at 27, 1980 SLT 81 at 84. See also at 42, 43, and at 92, per Lord Keith of Kinkel.
3 *Robertson v Adamson* (1876) 3 R 978.
4 (1876) 3 R 978 at 982.
5 *Public Prosecutor v Oie Hee Koi* [1968] AC 829 at 852, [1968] 1 All ER 419 at 422, PC. See also P B Maxwell *Interpretation of Statutes* (12th edn, 1969) pp 320–322.
6 *Cowper v Callender* (1872) 10 M 353.

1178. Cases in which statutory requirements have been held to be discretionary. It seems that if a statute provides that something is to be done within a certain period of time, that requirement is directory only[1]. Where a statute provides that a notice or a similar document must be in a prescribed form, the precise form of words is usually directory only. Thus a bill of sale need not be a verbal and literal transcript of the statutory form[2]. Again in *Samuel Montagu v Swiss Air Transport*[3] Lord Denning, in construing article 8 of Schedule 1 to the Carriage by Air Act 1932 (c 36), which specified particulars which were to be contained in consignment notes, said that it did not mean:

'that the waybill must contain the statement *verbatim*. It is sufficient if it contains a statement to the like effect'[4].

Kinnear v Whyte[5] was concerned with the interpretation of the now repealed section 18(2) of the Summary Procedure (Scotland) Act 1864 (c 53) which provided that 'In Complaints for the Contravention of any Act of Parliament under which the Accused is or shall be liable on summary Conviction to be imprisoned ... the Sentence of the Court awarding Imprisonment shall be in the Form No. 2' in Schedule K to the Act. The court rejected the argument that the form was mandatory, Lord Deas being of the opinion that the schedule was to be regarded as directory and not imperative in the sense that in every case it 'must be followed *verbatim*, under pain of nullity'[6].

The Dunkeld Bridge Act 1803 (c xxxiii) conferred upon a proprietor a right to erect a bridge and to levy pontage dues provided that he kept accounts and laid them annually before justices of the peace. It was held in *Campbell v Duke of Atholl*[7] that the clause as to the lodging of accounts was not to be construed as an imperative enactment, but that it was merely directory, and that failure to comply with it did not infer a forfeiture of the right to levy pontage dues.

1 *HM Advocate v M'Donald* 1984 JC 94, 1984 SLT 426; *HM Advocate v Graham* 1985 SLT 498; *Dumfries and Galloway Regional Council v M* 1990 SLT 272. However, see also *Simpson v Selkirkshire Assessor* 1948 SC 270, 1948, SLT 221, LVAC.
2 *Thomas v Kelly* (1888) 13 App Cas 506 at 520, HL, per Lord Macnaghten. This case concerned the Bills of Sale Act (1878) Amendment Act 1882 (c 43), which does not apply to Scotland.
3 *Samuel Montagu & Co Ltd v Swiss Air Transport Co Ltd* [1966] 2 QB 306, [1966] 1 All ER 814, CA.
4 [1966] 2 QB 306 at 314, [1966] 1 All ER 814 at 816, CA.
5 *Kinnear and Brymer v Whyte* (1868) 6 M 804.
6 (1868) 6 M 804 at 806.
7 *Campbell v Duke of Atholl* (1869) 8 M 308.

(c) Enactments which are Discretionary in Form

1179. Introduction. In *Gray v St Andrews and Cupar District Committees*[1] it was held that, looking to the context and general scope of the now repealed Highway (Scotland) Act 1771 (c 53), section 1 of that Act which empowered those responsible for the upkeep of statute labour roads to provide 20 feet of clear passage road, though permissive in form, was in effect imperative:

> 'if the object for which the power is conferred is for the purpose of enforcing a right, there may be a duty cast on the donee of the power, to exercise it for the benefit of those who have that right, when required on their behalf. Where there is such a duty, it is not inaccurate to say that the words conferring the power are equivalent to saying that the donee must exercise it'[2].

Moreover:

> 'if the object of giving the power is to enable the donee to effectuate a right, then it is the duty of the donee of the powers to exercise the power when those who have the right call upon him to do so'[3].

> 'when a party can point to having a legal right . . . and the object of the power in question is to bring into effect, to fulfil or to complete that right, . . . he can rely on the words, although permissive in form, being given a compulsive force'[4].

Following these dicta it was held that a section of a private Act which empowered the master of works of Glasgow Corporation to require the proprietor of any land adjoining any street to repair a private footpath along it was mandatory in effect and implied a duty to inspect the footpath[5]. The ratio of the decision was that the object of the section was to secure the fulfilment of the right of members of the public to safe passage over the pavement and to compel frontagers to put their footpath into such a condition that the right of walking on it would be enjoyed in safety.

However, in *Fleming v Paisley Magistrates*[6], also applying the dicta in the *Julius* case[7], it was held that section 12 of the Cart Navigation Act 1885 (c clxxiii), which provided that the undertakers 'may make and maintain' specified works including the deepening of the Cart navigation and maintaining it at a depth of 17 feet below high mark, was not mandatory because the powers were not:

> 'conferred on the trustees for effectuating the legal right of navigation pertaining to the members of the public over this tidal river'[8].

1 *Gray v St Andrews and Cupar District Committees of Fife County Council* 1911 SC 266, 1910 2 SLT 354.
2 *Julius v Lord Bishop of Oxford* (1880) 5 App Cas 214 at 241, HL, per Lord Blackburn.
3 (1880) 5 App Cas 214 at 243, HL, per Lord Blackburn.
4 *Monaghan v Glasgow Corpn* 1955 SC 80 at 89, 1955 SLT 89 at 94, per Lord Carmont.
5 *Black v Glasgow Corpn* 1958 SC 260 at 269, 1959 SLT 219 at 223, per Lord President Clyde.
6 *Fleming and Ferguson Ltd v Paisley Magistrates* 1948 SC 547, 1948 SLT 457.
7 See the text and note 2 above.
8 *Fleming and Ferguson Ltd v Paisley Magistrates* 1948 SC 547 at 553, 1948 SLT 457 at 459, per Lord Mackintosh.

1180. Cases where enactment discretionary in form found not to be mandatory in effect. An argument that an enactment although discretionary in form was mandatory in effect was rejected in two cases. In *Dunlop v Mundell*[1] it was held that an enactment which provided that an arbiter's award 'may be set aside by the sheriff' was discretionary only and did not derogate from the jurisdiction of the Court of Session to entertain an action of reduction of the award. In *Degan v Dundee Corpn*[2] it was held that a statute which provided that 'the corporation may provide and maintain . . . and may run omnibuses within the city' was merely permissive and did not impose any obligation to provide immediate accommodation for every intending traveller.

In two cases under the betting and gaming legislation the court rejected the argument that if the grounds on which a licensing authority 'may refuse' to grant a licence were met, 'may' was imperative[3].

1 *Dunlop v Mundell* 1943 SLT 286, OH.
2 *Degan v Dundee Corpn* 1940 SC 457, 1940 SLT 375.
3 *Mecca Bookmakers (Scotland) Ltd v East Lothian District Licensing Board* 1988 SLT 520, OH; *Patmor Ltd v City of Edinburgh District Licensing Board* 1988 SLT 850.

(7) STRICT AND QUALIFIED DUTIES

1181. Introduction. Sometimes a duty imposed by statute is absolute in its terms, while in other cases the duty is qualified. Where the duty is absolute, although a plea of contributory negligence can competently be taken, it will be a defence for a person bound by the obligation to say that he took all reasonable steps to fulfil it. Indeed, in a case where an absolute statutory duty is laid on an employer, the fact that the obligation has not been performed is in itself evidence of personal negligence on his part[1]. Whether the duty is absolute or qualified will depend on the wording of the enactment concerned. Where the statute requires 'reasonably practicable' steps to be taken the duty is clearly qualified. In other statutes the wording is not so clear cut, and in relation to those statutes the cases discussed in the following paragraphs may be of some assistance.

1 *M'Mullan v Lochgelly Iron and Coal Co* 1933 SC (HL) 64 at 70, 1934 SLT 114 at 117, per Lord Warrington of Clyffe.

1182. Cases in which statutory duties have been held to be absolute. In *Millar v Galashiels Gas Co*[1] a workman was killed through the failure of the brake mechanism of a hoist in his employer's works, the employer having taken every practical step to ensure that the mechanism worked properly and that the hoist was safe for use. An action was brought alleging breach of the now repealed section 22(1) of the Factories Act 1937 (c 67), which provided that every hoist must be properly maintained, 'maintained' being defined in the Act as including 'maintained . . . in efficient order'. It was held that the obligation created by the Act was of an absolute and continuing nature, and that the fact of the failure of the brake was sufficient to establish a breach of the employer's statutory duty.

Again in *Smith v Cammell Laird*[2], it was held that a requirement that 'all staging' in a shipbuilding yard must be maintained in such condition as to ensure the safety of all persons employed could not be satisfied by the taking of all reasonable care to maintain the staging properly. 'The wording is too strong to justify the wider view'[3].

In *Hamilton v National Coal Board*[4] it was held that the statutory requirement that all parts and working gear of all machinery and apparatus used as or forming part of the equipment of a mine must be properly maintained imposed an absolute duty on the mine owners to keep a winch in a proper and efficient state, and did not merely impose on them the duty of servicing it properly.

The cases of *Millar, Smith* and *Hamilton* were all concerned with the liability of an employer to an employee. *Brown v Lord Advocate*[5] was concerned with the liability of one proprietor to another. In that case an action was brought by a proprietor of land against a neighbouring proprietor alleging breach of the now repealed Winter Herding Act 1686 (c 11) in respect of damage done to his property by sheep belonging to the neighbour. That Act required the herding of sheep to prevent them eating or destroying the neighbour's woods or planting. It was held that the Act conferred upon the proprietor whose pastures or woodlands had been invaded an absolute right to recover compensation.

1 *Millar v Galashiels Gas Co Ltd* 1949 SC (HL) 31, 1949 SLT 223.

2 *Smith v Cammell Laird & Co Ltd* [1940] AC 242, [1939] 4 All ER 381, HL.
3 [1940] AC 242 at 263, [1939] 4 All ER 381 at 394, HL, per Lord Russell of Killowen.
4 *Hamilton v National Coal Board* 1960 SC (HL) 1, 1960 SLT 24.
5 *Brown v Lord Advocate* 1973 SLT 205.

1183. Cases in which statutory duties have been held to be qualified. In *Sinclair v National Coal Board*[1], applying the decision of the House of Lords in an English case[2], it was held that the duty imposed on a manager of a mine by section 48(1) of the Mines and Quarries Act 1954 (c 70) 'to take, with respect to every road and working place in the mine, such steps by way of controlling movement of the strata in the mine and supporting the roof and sides of the road or working place as may be necessary for keeping the road or working place secure' was not an absolute duty. A fall of stone from the roof of the working place, however, was prima facie evidence of breach of the statute and the onus then lay on the employer to prove that the manager took the necessary steps, or that it was impracticable, to avoid the contravention.

Again, in an English case[3] it was held that the duty imposed on the manager of a quarry by section 108 of the same Act to ensure that quarrying operations are so carried on as to avoid danger from falls, though high, was not an absolute duty, being qualified by the provision of section 157.

1 *Sinclair v National Coal Board* 1963 SC 586, 1963 SLT 296. See also MINES AND QUARRIES, vol 14, para 1633.
2 *Brown v National Coal Board* [1962] AC 574, [1962] 1 All ER 81, HL.
3 *Brazier v Skipton Rock Co Ltd* [1962] 1 All ER 955, [1962] 1 WLR 471. See also vol 14, para 1620, and para 1702, notes 5–7.

(8) PENAL, TAXING AND REMEDIAL STATUTES

1184. Penal statutes. Where a penal statute is ambiguous, then the benefit of the doubt must be given to the person against whom the penalty is directed. Thus in *Johnston v Robson*[1] the court held that a penal provision for fishing for salmon in contravention of the statute concerned which provided for 'a penalty not exceeding £10, and an additional penalty of 10 shillings for each salmon' had to be construed *in mitiori sensu*; and that the expression ' "not exceeding" here is to be read as qualifying, not the penalty only, but also the 10s for each fish'[2].

However, more recently, Lord Parker CJ, in construing a penal enactment, differentiated between a provision which is ambiguous and one that is merely difficult to interpret:

'It may well be that many sections of Acts are difficult to interpret, but can be interpreted by the proper canons of construction. A provision can only be said to be ambiguous, in the sense that if it be a penal section it would be resolved in a manner most favourable to the citizen, where having applied all the proper canons of interpretation the matter is still left in doubt'[3].

1 *Johnston v Robson* (1868) 6 M 800.
2 (1868) 6 M 800 at 804.
3 *Bowers v Gloucester Corpn* [1963] 1 QB 881 at 886, 887, [1963] 1 All ER 437 at 439, DC.

1185. Taxing statutes. Taxing statutes fall to be strictly construed:

'in a taxing Act it is impossible ... to assume any intention, any governing purpose in the Act ... except to take such tax as the statute imposes ... Cases, therefore, under the Taxing Acts always resolve themselves into a question whether or not the words of the Act have reached the alleged subject of taxation'[1].

Again,

> 'we have no governing principle of the Act to look at, we have simply to go on the Act itself to see whether the duty claimed under it is that which the Legislature has enacted'[2].

In another case Lord Thankerton said:

> 'counsel are apt to use the adjective "penal" in describing the harsh consequences of a taxing provision, but, if the meaning of the provision is reasonably clear, the Courts have no jurisdiction to mitigate such harshness'[3].

Finally, in *Inland Revenue v Saunders* Lord Reid said:

> 'It is sometimes said that we should apply the spirit and not the letter of the law so as to bring in cases which, though not within the letter of the law, are within the mischief at which the law is aimed. But it has long been recognized that our courts cannot so apply taxing Acts'[4].

The courts, in dealing with taxing Acts, will not presume in favour of any special privilege of exemption from taxation. Thus in *Hogg v Auchtermuchty Parochial Board* Lord Young said:

> 'I think it proper to say that *in dubio* I should deem it the duty of the Court to reject any construction of a modern statute which implied the extension of a class privilege of exemption from taxation provided the language reasonably admitted of another interpretation'[5].

Again, in another case Lord Ardmillan said:

> 'We have been told that a taxing statute must be construed liberally and favourably to the subjects. In one sense that is true, and the remark is well founded; but, on the other hand, equality and impartial justice in the incidence of taxation is of greater moment, and the statute should be construed so as to promote that equality and that impartiality of justice. There is no presumption in favour of the exemption of the few from the incidence of the general tax. I think the presumption is for equality, and rather against the partiality which is involved in special exemptions'[6].

1 *Tennant v Smith* (1892) 19 R (HL) 1 at 3, per Lord Halsbury LC.
2 *Lord Advocate v Robertson* (1897) 24 R (HL) 42 at 42, per Lord Halsbury LC.
3 *Ross and Coulter v Inland Revenue* 1948 SC (HL) 1 at 10, 1948 SLT 303 at 306.
4 *Inland Revenue Comrs v Saunders* [1958] AC 285 at 298, [1957] 3 All ER 43 at 49, 50, HL.
5 *Hogg v Auchtermuchty Parochial Board* (1880) 7 R 986 at 996.
6 *Edinburgh Life Assurance Co v Inland Revenue, Scottish Widows' Fund v Inland Revenue* (1875) 2 R 394 at 398.

1186. Remedial statutes. A remedial Act is one that is designed to redress a grievance or to afford relief. Such an Act should be given a benevolent construction. Thus, in *Robb v Logiealmond School Board* Lord President Inglis said:

> 'A remedial statute is not to be strictly construed... A remedial statute ought to receive a benign and favourable construction, and is often applied *ad consimiles casus*'[1].

Further, a remedial statute should be construed by reference to the mischief at which it is directed. So, in construing an enactment which in effect remedied the previously existing situation that where a person who would have had a claim on intestacy has predeceased the intestate, his children could not come in his place in that claim, Lord President Inglis said:

> 'But if the words are not clear in themselves, we are quite entitled to resort to a canon of construction applicable to this case, because this is a remedial statute, and a remedial statute is always to be construed with reference to the mischief intended to be remedied'[2].

1 *Robb v Logiealmond School Board* (1875) 2 R 417 at 422.
2 *Turner* (1869) 8 M 222 at 224.

(9) EXTENT AND APPLICATION OF ACTS

1187. Territorial extent of Acts. Unless the contrary intention appears, Parliament is taken to intend an Act to extend to each territory of the United Kingdom but not to any territory outside the United Kingdom. The reason for this presumption is that Parliament is the only sovereign legislature for the area of the United Kingdom[1]. Where an Act is silent, therefore, it is presumed to extend to Scotland. Despite, however, the presumption of extension to all parts of the United Kingdom, where an Act is to apply to Northern Ireland it is normal modern practice to state expressly that it does so. The reason for this unnecessary provision (unnecessary, that is, from a legal point of view) is to save the government lawyers in Northern Ireland from having to comb through each Act to see whether or not their province is included[2].

The specialist draftsmen in the Lord Advocate's Department are very conscious of the need in the drafting of modern statutes to remove any doubt as to whether an Act or any part or section of an Act extends to Scotland. In earlier times, however, such care was not always taken:

'the statute proclaims its origin, and speaks the language of an English lawyer, with some Scotch legal phrases thrown in rather casually'[3].

In relation to older Acts, then, where English terminology has been used without Scottish adaptation there has sometimes been uncertainty as to whether a particular Act extends to Scotland, bearing in mind the presumption, as explained above, that it does[4]. The sort of difficulty that can arise was well expressed by Lord Moncrieff in relation to one statute in these words:

'The only reason for supposing that it was not meant to extend to Scotland is that it is drawn with such exclusive reference to English legislation and English institutions and procedure that though it would be easy enough to find equivalents in our own usages for these English requisites it would be difficult, if not impossible, to follow out in Scotland the precise injunctions of the Act . . . I incline to the opinion that the statute applies to Scotland, because its object is general, and there are no words to exclude, and no reason for excluding Scotland from its operations, although I see great difficulties in the way of its practical application'[5].

1 F A R Bennion *Statutory Interpretation* (1984) p 462. For a discussion of the application of enactments to the Crown, see THE CROWN.
2 Ibid, p 456.
3 *Income Tax Special Purposes Comrs v Pemsel* [1891] AC 531 at 579, HL, per Lord Macnaghten.
4 For earlier difficulties, see J J Gow *The Mercantile and Industrial Law of Scotland* (1964) p 107; J J Gow 'The Categories of Voluntary Obligations' 1961 SLT (News) 101, especially at 101; and J J Gow 'Humpty Dumpty and the Whole Court' 1961 SLT (News) 105, especially at 106. The earlier Factors Acts were drafted in wholly English terminology. See also *Westminster Fire Office v Glasgow Provident Investment Society* (1888) 15 R (HL) 89; *Calder v Stevens* (1871) 9 M 1074; *Dunlop v Goudie* (1895) 22 R (J) 34; *London and North Eastern Rly Co v Glasgow Assessor* 1937 SC 309, 1937 SLT 167.
5 *Perth Water Comrs v M'Donald* (1879) 6 R 1050 at 1055, 1056.

1188. Uniform application of Acts extending to Great Britain. A statute which extends to more than one part of the United Kingdom is presumed to be intended to have a uniform meaning in all the parts to which it applies. This question of uniform application has arisen most often in relation to taxing Acts[1]. Viscount Simon LC has expressed the matter in these words:

'in construing a taxing statute which applies to England and Scotland alike, it is desirable to adopt a construction of the statutory words which avoids differences of interpretation of a technical character such as are calculated to produce inequalities in taxation as between citizens of the two countries'[2].

In the English case of *Cording v Halse*[3] the principle of uniformity was adopted in relation to a statute creating a criminal offence where the decision in an earlier Scottish case[4] was followed. As Lord Goddard said:

'It is very desirable that with statutes of this nature the same interpretation should be given on either side of the Border. It would be very unfortunate to have, on a similar set of facts, a conviction in England and no conviction in Scotland or vice versa'[5].

1 See eg *Lord Saltoun v HM Advocate-General for Scotland* (1860) 3 Macq 659 at 671, HL, per Lord Campbell; *Income Tax Special Purposes Comrs v Pemsel* [1891] AC 531, HL; *Inland Revenue Comrs v City of Glasgow Police Athletic Association* 1952 SC 102, 1952 SLT 136.
2 *Income Tax General Purposes Comrs for City of London v Gibbs* [1942] AC 402 at 414, [1942] 1 All ER 415 at 422, HL. See also *Winter v Inland Revenue Comrs* [1963] AC 235 at 248, 249, [1961] 3 All ER 855 at 858, 859, HL, per Lord Reid and at 263 and at 868, per Lord Guest.
3 *Cording v Halse* [1955] 1 QB 63, [1954] 3 All ER 287, DC.
4 *M'Cowan v Stewart* 1936 JC 36, 1936 SLT 370.
5 *Cording v Halse* [1955] 1 QB 63 at 70, [1954] 3 All ER 287 at 291, DC.

(10) RETROSPECTION

1189. Introduction. It is obviously competent for the legislature, if it pleases, in its wisdom to make the provision of an Act of Parliament retrospective; but before giving such a construction to an Act of Parliament one would require that it should either appear very clearly in the terms of the Act, or arise by necessary and distinct implication[1]. Where an Act contains no clear and explicit statement of whether it is to be retrospective, or merely to be prospective, it is necessary to examine the subject matter of the enactment which one has to construe, to bear in mind the effect of a construction which would make it retrospective, and to ask oneself whether it is to be supposed that that construction was intended by the legislature to be given to it[2].

1 *Smith v Callander* (1901) 3 F (HL) 28 at 30, 9 SLT 39 at 39, per Lord Ashbourne. See also *Callander v Smith* (1900) 2 F 1140 at 1146, per Lord Trayner (not reported in 8 SLT 132).
2 *Gardner v Beresford's Trustees* (1878) 5 R (HL) 105 at 108, per Lord Cairns LC.

1190. Vested rights and legality of past transactions. Where an Act, if it operated retrospectively, would prejudicially affect vested rights or the legality of past transactions, it must not be construed retrospectively without express provision to that effect[1]. Or, as Lord Brightman expressed the matter, there is a presumption against construing a statute retrospectively where, if so construed:

'it takes away or impairs a vested right acquired under existing law, or creates a new obligation, or imposes a new duty, or attaches a new disability, in regard to events already past'[2].

Thus in the *Gardner* case a deed dated prior to 1874 which was signed by the granter on the last page only, the other pages being initialled by him, and which was consequently invalid under the Deeds Act 1696 (c 15), was held not to be validated by section 39 of the Conveyancing (Scotland) Act 1874 (c 94). That section provides that a deed subscribed by the granter and attested by two witnesses is not to be deemed invalid because of any informality of execution. As Cairns LC said, the consequence of holding that section 39 of the 1874 Act was retrospective in effect would have been to bring:

'again into existence . . . every instrument which had failed of validity, which had failed to come into existence by want of compliance with the formalities of the Act of 1696, and must have the effect of setting up every such instrument, notwithstanding the titles and the arrangements of property which might have been made upon an assumption that those instruments were absolutely invalid'[3].

On the other hand, in a case where there was no ambiguity in the language of the statute concerned, retrospective effect was given to it although the operation of retrospection interfered with existing rights[4].

1 *Urquhart v Urquhart* (1853) 1 Macq 658 at 662, HL, per Cranworth LC; *Gardner v Beresford's Trustees* (1878) 5 R (HL) 105 at 108, per Lord Cairns LC.
2 *Yew Bon Tew v Kenderaan Bas Mara* [1983] 1 AC 553 at 558, [1982] 3 All ER 833 at 836, PC.
3 *Gardner v Beresford's Trustees* (1878) 5 R (HL) 105 at 110, per Lord Cairns LC.
4 *Lord Macdonald v Finlayson* (1884) 12 R 228 at 231, per Lord Shand.

1191. Rebuttal. The rule against the operation of retrospection is only a presumption which may be rebutted:

'In considering in any case whether the presumption has been displaced, regard must be had to the exact language employed by the Legislature, the subject-matter with which the Act deals, whether the object of the legislation is remedial, and, if so, what was the mischief or state of facts to be remedied, and, generally, the whole circumstances of the legislation must be taken into account from which the true intention of the Legislature is to be inferred. It is easier to infer a retrospective intention where to deny it would leave only partially removed the abuses or mischiefs with which in general the main purpose of the Act is concerned'[1].

In the *Wilson* case, following the above quoted dictum, it was held in an action of divorce on the ground of cruelty brought in pursuance of the now repealed Divorce (Scotland) Act 1938 (c 50), which introduced such a ground, that it was competent to libel acts of cruelty which occurred before the Act was passed.

Again in *Taylor v Taylor*[2] it was held that the now repealed section 16 of the Conjugal Rights (Scotland) Act 1861 (c 86), by which a wife was entitled in certain circumstances to a reasonable provision out of property to which she had succeeded, applied to property to which she may have succeeded before the passing of the Act.

Finally, in *Bell v Hay*[3] it was held that section 1 of the Damages (Scotland) Act 1976 (c 13), which provides that where a person dies as a result of a wrongful act of another, certain relatives have a title to sue for losses sustained by them in consequence of the death, conferred a title to sue on a divorced wife in relation to the death of her husband before 1976. Lord Ordinary Brand considered that, in relation to a claim of a divorced wife, the object of the Act was remedial, namely to provide her with a remedy for the loss of a divorced husband, and that to deny retrospective intention would have only partially removed the injustice which the Act was designed to prevent. On the other hand, *Edinburgh Welfare Housing Trust v Assessor for Edinburgh*[4] is an example of a case where the presumption against retrospection was not rebutted.

1 *Wilson v Wilson* 1939 SC 102 at 105, 106, 1939 SLT 97 at 99, per Lord Justice-Clerk Aitchison.
2 *Taylor v Taylor* (1871) 9 M 893.
3 *Bell v Hay* 1979 SC 237, 1980 SLT 110. See also *Sunshine Porcelain Potteries Pty Ltd v Nash* [1961] AC 927 at 938, [1961] 3 All ER 203 at 206, PC, per Lord Reid.
4 *Edinburgh Welfare Housing Trust v Edinburgh Assessor* 1939 SC 279, 1939 SLT 184.

1192. Alterations in procedure. Alterations in the form of procedure are always retrospective, unless there is some good reason or other why they should not be so[1]. However, as Lord Brightman has pointed out:

'an Act which is procedural in one sense may in particular circumstances do far more than regulate the course of proceedings, because it may, on one interpretation, revive or destroy the cause of action itself'[2].

In *Colonial Sugar Refining Co v Irving*[3] the Judicial Committee of the Privy Council held that the power to give leave to appeal to it which had been abrogated by the Australian Commonwealth Judiciary Act 1903 did not prevent such leave being granted in an action commenced before the Act came into force. The decision hinged on the question whether the appeal was 'a right vested in the appellants at the date of the passing of the Act or a mere matter of procedure', and the Judicial Committee had no difficulty in finding that to deprive a suitor in a pending action of an appeal to a superior tribunal which belonged to him as of right is a very different thing from regulating procedure.

A court of appeal dealing with any case:

'cannot take into account a statute which has been passed in the interval since the case was decided at first instance, because the rights of litigants are generally to be determined according to the law in force at the date of the earlier proceedings'[4].

unless the statute is expressly retrospective or is merely procedural.

1 *Gardner v Beresford's Trustees* (1878) 5 R (HL) 105 at 117, per Lord Blackburn.
2 *Yew Bon Tew v Kenderaan Bas Mara* [1983] 1 AC 553 at 558, 559, [1982] 3 All ER 833 at 836, PC.
3 *Colonial Sugar Refining Co Ltd v Irving* [1905] AC 369 at 372, PC, per Lord Macnaghten.
4 *Attorney-General v Vernazza* [1960] AC 965 at 978, [1960] 3 All ER 97 at 101, HL, per Lord Denning.

1193. Declaratory Acts. Where an Act is in its nature a declaratory Act, the presumption against construing it retrospectively is inapplicable. An Act is to be regarded as declaratory even although it is in the form of an amendment to a previous Act where it is in effect enacting how that earlier Act is to be construed[1].

1 *Attorney-General v Theobald* (1890) 24 QBD 557; *Scott v Craig's Representative* (1897) 24 R 462 at 467, OH, per Lord Kincairney (not reported fully in 4 SLT 173); *Murray v Inland Revenue* 1918 SC (HL) 111 at 118, per Lord Salvesen (not fully reported in 1917 2 SLT 115).

(11) REPEALS

1194. Introduction. Section 16(1) of the Interpretation Act 1978, re-enacting section 38(2) of the Interpretation Act 1889 (c 63), provides inter alia that, unless the contrary intention appears, a repealing Act does not:
(1) affect the previous operation of the enactment repealed or anything duly done or suffered under that enactment;
(2) affect any right, privilege, obligation or liability acquired, accrued or incurred under that enactment;
(3) affect any penalty, forfeiture or punishment incurred in respect of any offence committed against that enactment;
(4) affect any investigation, legal proceeding or remedy in respect of any such right, privilege, obligation, liability, penalty, forfeiture or punishment[1].
The effect of section 38(2) of the 1889 Act and in particular the meaning to be given to the words 'right, privilege, obligation or liability acquired, accrued or incurred' in head (2) has been considered in a number of decisions[2] which have been well summarised by Lord Hunter in *Moray County Council v MacLean* and from which he held that the following propositions had been established:
(a) the mere abstract right to take advantage of a statutory enactment is not a 'right acquired' or a 'right accrued';

(b) even if a person has taken steps to put statutory machinery in motion, the statutory proceedings may only by the date of repeal have reached the stage when he has a hope or expectation of acquiring a right. In such a case no right would be 'acquired' or 'accrued';

(c) where statutory machinery has been set in motion before the repeal, there may be a right 'acquired' or 'accrued' although at the date of repeal further steps are still necessary to prove that the right did in fact exist at the date of repeal and even to prove the measure of the obligation incurred;

(d) a right may at any rate in certain circumstances be a 'right acquired' although it may at the date of repeal still be of a contingent nature[3].

1 Interpretation Act 1978 (c 30), s 16(1)(b)–(e).
2 *Director of Public Works v Ho Po Sang* [1961] AC 901, [1961] 2 All ER 721, PC; *Abbott v Minister for Lands* [1895] AC 425, PC; *Hamilton Gell v White* [1922] 2 KB 422, CA; *Heston and Isleworth Urban District Council v Grout* [1897] 2 Ch 306, CA.
3 *Moray County Council v Maclean* 1962 SC 601 at 606, 1962 SLT 236 at 239, 240, OH.

1195. Substituted provisions. An important provision of the Interpretation Act 1978 is in respect of substituted provisions. The Act provides that where an Act repeals a previous enactment and substitutes provisions for the enactment repealed, the repealed enactment remains in force until the substituted provisions come into force[1].

1 Interpretation Act 1978 (c 30), s 17(1), re-enacting the Interpretation Act 1889 (c 63), s 11(2) (repealed).

1196. Re-enactment. Where an Act repeals and re-enacts, with or without modification, a previous enactment then, unless the contrary intention appears:
(1) references in any other Act to the enactment repealed are to be construed as references to the provision re-enacted;
(2) insofar as any subordinate legislation made under the repealed enactment could have been made under the provision re-enacted, it has effect as if made under that provision[1].

Where an Act is repealed without re-enactment, any delegated legislation made under it is impliedly revoked unless it is expressly preserved[2]. Where the delegated legislation is continued in force, its scope is determined according to the repealed enactment under which it was made[3]. However, where subordinate legislation is made under a provision which is subsequently repealed and re-enacted in a narrower form, the subordinate legislation must be cut down so as not to conflict with the narrower statute[4].

1 Interpretation Act 1978 (c 30), s 17(2)(a), (b), re-enacting the Interpretation Act 1889 (c 63), s 38(1).
2 *Watson v Winch* [1916] 1 KB 688.
3 *Miller's Cash Stores Ltd v West Ham Corpn* [1955] 3 All ER 282, [1955] 1 WLR 1121, DC.
4 *Re Simpkin Marshall Ltd* [1959] Ch 229, [1958] 3 All ER 611.

1197. Revival of Acts. Where an Act repeals a repealing enactment, the repeal does not revive any enactment previously repealed unless words are added reviving it[1]. The Interpretation Act 1978 goes beyond the revival of statutes by providing that, unless the contrary intention appears, a repealing enactment does not revive anything not in force or existing at the time at which the repeal takes effect[2]. The effect of this provision is that the repeal does not, for instance, revive a contract which the repealed enactment had rendered illegal or otherwise put an end to[3]. The provision also seems to apply to rules of common law which had been abrogated by the repealed enactment and were therefore 'not in force or existing' at the time the repeal took effect[4].

1 Interpretation Act 1978 (c 30), s 15, re-enacting the Interpretation Act 1889 (c 63), s 11(1) (repealed).
2 Interpretation Act 1978, s 16(1)(a), re-enacting the Interpretation Act 1889, s 38(2)(a) (repealed).
3 *Coates v Diment* [1951] 1 All ER 890.
4 F A R Bennion *Statutory Interpretation* (1984) p 437.

1198. Implied repeal. The repeal, by mere implication, of one statute by another subsequently passed is not easily to be presumed, and, before such repeal can be inferred by implication, repugnancy between the provisions of the two statutes must be proved in whole or in part[1]. So far as the relationship between a special Act and a subsequent general Act is concerned, A L Smith J had this to say in *Kutner v Phillips*:

'special Acts are not repealed by general Acts unless there is some express reference to the previous legislation, or unless there is a necessary inconsistency in the two Act standing together'[2].

The *Kutner* and *Seward* cases were followed in *Aberdeen Suburban Tramways v Aberdeen Magistrates*[3]. In that case Aberdeen Corporation was by a private Act protected from any liability for damage which the tramway company authorised by the Act might sustain through acts of the corporation or exercise of its powers. The corporation was subsequently authorised by another private Act to lay an aqueduct along a main road and was empowered to break up roads and cross under or over them, on making compensation to persons injured thereby. The tramway company sued for damage caused by the construction of the aqueduct, but it was held barred by the provisions of the earlier Act, the special provisions of which had not been impliedly repealed by the general provisions of the later Act.

1 *Bain v Mackay* (1875) 2 R (J) 32 at 36, per Lord Justice-Clerk Moncrieff. See also *Ellen Street Estates Ltd v Minister of Health* [1934] 1 KB 590, CA; *Vauxhall Estates Ltd v Liverpool Corpn* [1932] 1 KB 733.
2 *Kutner v Phillps* [1891] 1 QB 267 at 272. See also *Seward v The 'Vera Cruz'* (1884) 10 App Cas 59 at 68, HL, per Selbourne LC.
3 *Aberdeen Suburban Tramways Co v Aberdeen Magistrates* 1927 SC 683, 1927 SLT 468.

1199. Prevailing practice. It is at the very least doubtful whether a repealing statute can be construed by reference to the practice which prevailed under the statute which it repeals, for, as Lord Kinnear has said, the later Act may have repealed the earlier Act 'just because of the practice that may have followed upon it'[1].

1 *Thomson v Bent Colliery Co Ltd* 1912 SC 242 at 246, 1912 1 SLT 53 at 54.

(12) ENACTMENTS TO WHICH SPECIAL RULES OF CONSTRUCTION APPLY

(a) Pre-Union Scots Acts

1200. Introduction. The general rules applicable to the interpretation of statutes do not apply to the Acts of the Parliaments of Scotland passed before the Union in 1707. In relation to those Acts, the practice of the Scottish legislature was:

'to pass statutes which were expressed in very general terms, which were not always workable without the aid of judicial construction, and which were intended to be worked out by the Courts of law applying commonsense principles to their interpretation'[1].

As Lord Eldon said in *Johnstone v Stott*:

'the Scots do not scruple to enforce their statutes at times as gently as the statutes admit of being interpreted'[2].

Again in *Heriot's Trust v Paton's Trustees* Lord President Normand said that the Scots Acts:

'were passed under a totally different state of affairs, with language that does not always fit modern life. The function of the Court in interpreting them is not that of modification: it is truly interpretation, but necessarily, in such a case, of the spirit and not of the letter'[3].

It has also been said that a pre-Union Scots Act has to be interpreted 'according to the uniform construction which it has received in Scotland from the time of its passing'[4].

1 *Middleton v Tough* 1908 SC (J) 32 at 39, 15 SLT 991 at 995, per Lord M'Laren.
2 *Johnstone v Stott* (1802) 4 Pat App 274 at 285, HL.
3 *George Heriot's Trust Governors v Paton's Trustees* 1912 SC 1123 at 1135, 1912 2 SLT 116 at 122.
4 *Fergusson v Skirving* (1852) 1 Macq 232 at 233, HL, per Lord St Leonards LC.

1201. Desuetude. The pre-Union Scots Acts may be impliedly repealed by falling into desuetude. This rule does not seem to apply to Scots Acts passed since 1707 — at least there is no reported case applying the rule to such an Act — nor does it apply to English Acts which 'of whatever antiquity, remain for ever in force till they be repealed'[1]. Mere age is not a sufficient ground for holding that an old Scots Act has fallen into desuetude. As Lord Mackay expressed the matter in *Brown v Edinburgh Magistrates*:

'desuetude requires for its operation a very considerable period, not merely of neglect, but of contrary usage of such a character as practically to infer such completely established habit of the community as to set up a counter law or establish a *quasi*-repeal'[2].

A statute might be partly in desuetude and partly not, where portions of the statute were separable but it cannot be partially in desuetude in respect of its application[3].

1 Stair, *Institutions* I, 1 16; *Bute v More* (1870) 9 M 180 at 190, per Lord Deas.
2 *Brown v Edinburgh Magistrates* 1931 SLT 456 at 458. See also *MacCormick v Lord Advocate* 1953 SC 396 at 417, 1953 SLT 255 at 265, per Lord Russell.
3 *M'Ara v Edinburgh Magistrates* 1913 SC 1059 at 1975, 1913 2 SLT 110 at 117, per Lord President Dunedin.

(b) Private Acts

1202. Introduction. A private Act is one which affects the interests of particular localities, persons or corporations, and is not of a general public character[1]. Unlike public Acts, private Acts are introduced to Parliament by petition and the proceedings are largely of a judicial nature involving the hearing of objections to the Bill. Every Act passed since 1850 is deemed to be a public Act to be judicially noticed as such, unless the contrary is expressly provided by the Act[2].

1 As to Scottish private legislation, see PROVISIONAL ORDERS AND PRIVATE LEGISLATION, vol 19, paras 1 ff.

2 See the Interpretation Act 1889 (c 63), s 9 (repealed), and the Interpretation Act 1978 (c 30), s 3.

1203. Strict interpretation. The rules and presumptions applicable to the construction of public Acts apply equally to the construction of private Acts except that private Acts are very strictly interpreted[1]. As Lord Esher MR said in *Altrincham Union v Cheshire Lines Committee*:

' In the case of a private Act, which is obtained by persons for their own benefit, you construe more strictly provisions which they allege to be in their favour, because the persons who obtain a private Act ought to take care, that it is so worded that that which they desire to obtain for themselves is plainly stated in it'[2].

Again, in *Scottish Drainage and Improvement Co v Campbell* Lord Hershell said that when a private Act:

'is obtained by a company, incorporated for purposes of profit, to confer upon them rights and powers which they would not have at common law, the provisions of such a statute must be somewhat jealously scrutinized, and I think that they ought not to be held to possess any right unless it be given in plain terms or arises as a necessary inference from the language used'[3],

and in the same case Lord Fitzgerald said that:

'I have always understood, with reference to private Acts as contradistinguished from public Acts of Parliament, that if a charge is imposed upon the person of an individual it must be so imposed in clear and express terms and not left to implication'[4].

And in *Bruce v Whyte* Lord President Balfour considered that section 366 of the Glasgow Police Act 1866 (c cclxxiii):

'should be construed in accordance with the rules applicable to private Acts, in the case of which the benefit of any doubt is given to persons who might be prejudiced by the imposition of exceptional restrictions'[5].

In *Countess of Rothes v Kirkcaldy Waterworks Comrs*[6] the commissioners were authorised by the Kirkcaldy and Dysart Water-Works Act 1867 (c cxxxic) to construct reservoirs in the Lomond Hills and to impound therein the water of a stream which flowed through the lands of R. By section 43 of the Act the Commissioners were bound to make good to R all damages which might be occasioned to her by reason or in consequence of any bursting, or flood, or escape of water from any reservoir, aqueduct, or pipe, or other work connected therewith, which might be constructed or laid by the commissioners. In an action brought by R for compensation for damage caused by an extraordinary discharge of water from one of the reservoirs owing to an extraordinary rainfall, it was held by a majority in the House of Lords that the commissioners were liable for all damage to R's lands from floods from the reservoirs, however caused. Lord Fitzgerald said that if the language of section 43 was:

'not clear, then the rule of interpretation "*contra proferentem*" seems to me to be specially applicable. The language of the section must be taken as that of the promoters of the Act. They ask the Legislature to grant large powers and privileges, and they propose to give in return to the individuals who may be affected certain rights and protection. They should have taken care to define with accuracy the limits of their liability, so that the parties whose rights they interfere with should not be misled. We are bound to put a construction on the section as favourable to the pursuer as the words of the section will fairly and reasonably bear, for the words are not hers, but those of the promoters'[7].

1 As to when strict interpretation has not been applied, see para 1204 below.
2 *Altrincham Union Assessment Committee v Cheshire Lines Committee* (1885) 15 QBD 597 at 603, CA.

3 *Scottish Drainage and Improvement Co v Campbell* (1889) 16 R (HL) 16 at 17.
4 1889 16 R (HL) 16 at 20.
5 *Bruce v Whyte* (1900) 2 F 823 at 829, 7 SLT 436 at 439.
6 *Countess of Rothes v Kirkcaldy Waterworks Comrs* (1882) 9 R (HL) 108.
7 (1882) 9 R (HL) 108 at 115. See also *Holburnhead Salmon Fishing Co v Scrabster Harbour Trustees* 1982 SC 65 at 67, per Lord Ross.

1204. Cases where strict interpretation not applied. In two modern English cases the rule of strict construction of private Acts has not been applied. In *Pyx Granite v Ministry of Housing* the House of Lords construed a private Act in favour of its promoters by construing the ambiguous words 'all lands common or waste' as meaning 'all lands or common or waste' not 'all common or waste lands'[1]. And in *Garland v Wisbech Corpn* Diplock J, by not construing a private Act strictly, held that there was no inconsistency between it and an earlier public Act[2].

1 *Pyx Granite Co Ltd v Ministry of Housing and Local Government* [1960] AC 260 at 288, [1959] 3 All ER 1 at 7, HL, per Viscount Simonds.
2 *Garland and Flexman v Wisbech Corpn* [1962] 1 QB 151, [1961] 3 All ER 342.

(c) European Economic Community Legislation

1205. Principles of interpretation. The principles to be applied in the interpretation of the European Economic Community Treaty and of Community regulations and directives are well set out by Lord Denning in *Bulmer v Bollinger*. In the first place he says that:

'All the courts of all nine countries should interpret the treaty in the same way. They should all apply the same principles. It is enjoined on the English courts by section 3 of the European Communities Act 1972 (c 68)'[1].

He then goes on to contrast the extremely detailed form of United Kingdom statutes with the European Economic Community legislation which merely lays down general principles, this contrast leading to different rules of interpretation. So far as United Kingdom statutes are concerned:

'If the words of the statute do not cover a new situation — which was not foreseen — the judges hold that they have no power to fill the gap . . . The gap must remain open until Parliament finds time to fill it'[1].

In relation to European Economic Community legislation, however, Lord Denning says that the courts must no longer:

'examine the words in meticulous detail. No longer must they argue about the precise grammatical sense. They must look to the purpose or intent . . . They must not confine themselves to the English text. They must consider, if need be, all the authentic texts . . . They must divine the spirit of the treaty and gain inspiration from it. If they find a gap, they must fill it as best they can. They must do what the framers of the instrument would have done if they had thought about it'[1].

1 *H P Bulmer Ltd v J Bollinger SA* [1974] Ch 401 at 425, [1974] 2 All ER 1226 at 1237, CA.

(13) THE INTERPRETATION ACT 1978

1206. Introduction. The general interpretation Act currently in force is the Interpretation Act 1978 (c 30). This replaced the Interpretation Act 1889 (c 63), which in turn replaced the first interpretation Act, known as Lord Brougham's Act 1850[1]. The object of an interpretation Act is to shorten the language used in Acts of Parliament. This is achieved by producing in the interpretation Act what amount to a series of definitions of general application. Relying on such a definition, the draftsman does not need to repeat what it contains every time the point concerned arises in the particular statute. However, the difficulty with an interpretation Act is that the practitioner in reading an individual statute may very easily overlook the fact that the interpretation Act has a bearing on what he is reading. Attention is therefore drawn in this title to the more important provisions of the 1978 Act[2].

1 Ie the Interpretation of Acts Act 1850 (c 21) (repealed).
2 See paras 1207 ff below. For provisions of the Act relating to repeals, see paras 1194 ff above.

1207. Rules as to gender and number. In any Act, unless the contrary intention appears:
(1) words importing the masculine gender include the feminine;
(2) words importing the feminine gender include the masculine;
(3) words in the singular include the plural and words in the plural include the singular[1].
This provision has frequently to be applied by the courts and the problem which arises is when does an Act indicate a 'contrary intention'.

In *Nairn v St Andrews and Edinburgh University*[2] the House of Lords rejected the claim of women members of the General Council of Edinburgh University to vote in parliamentary elections for St Andrews and Edinburgh Universities, although the now repealed section 20 of the Representation of the People (Scotland) Act 1868 (c 48) provided that every person whose name is for the time being on the register of the general council of such university, must, if of full age and not subject to any legal incapacity, be entitled to vote in the election of a member of Parliament for the university. Lord Robertson, while recognising that:

'the avail of the words "male persons" as distinguished from "persons" has been greatly reduced by Lord Brougham's Act[3] so that the choice of the word "person" had of itself the smaller significance in the direction of including women'[4],

considered that 'the one expression like the other needs to be read in the light of the subject-matter'[5]. All the judges in the House of Lords were of the opinion that, as the parliamentary franchise was by constitutional principle and practice confined to men, plain language would be required to change this position, and this change could not be left to be inferred from the use of the word 'person' in the 1868 Act.

In *Floor v Davis*[6] the principal question at issue was whether the word 'person' in paragraph 15(2) of Schedule 7 to the Finance Act 1965 (c 25) was by virtue of the now repealed section 1(1)(b) of the Interpretation Act 1889 (c 63) to be construed as including the plural. The construction of this word affected the application of the definition of 'control' in paragraph 3 of Schedule 18 to the Finance Act 1965. In considering this question Lord Dilhorne said:

'If . . . on examination of the application of the Interpretation Act and construing "control" in accordance with paragraph 3 led to paragraph 15(2) being unworkable, or if not unworkable, to a result that Parliament could not have intended, then it can be concluded that an intention contrary to the application of the Interpretation Act appears and that "control" is not to be so construed'[7].

1 Interpretation Act 1978 (c 30), s 6.
2 *Nairn v St Andrews and Edinburgh University Courts* 1909 SC (HL) 10, 16 SLT 619.

3 Ie the Interpretation of Acts Act 1850 (c 21) (repealed).
4 *Nairn v St Andrews and Edinburgh University Courts* 1909 SC (HL) 10 at 15, 16, 16 SLT 619 at 622.
5 1909 SC (HL) 10 at 16, SLT 619 at 622.
6 *Floor v Davis* [1980] AC 695; [1979] 2 All ER 677, HL. See also *Munro v Dunbartonshire County Council* 1954 SC 126, 1954 SLT 186.
7 *Floor v Davis* [1980] AC 695 at 709, [1979] 2 All ER 677 at 684, HL.

1208. Service by post. Where an Act authorises or requires any document to be served by post (whether the expression 'serve' or the expression 'give' or 'send' or any other expression is used) then, unless the contrary intention appears, the service is deemed to be effected by properly addressing, pre-paying and posting a letter containing the document and, unless the contrary is proved, to have been effected at the time at which the letter would be delivered in the ordinary course of post[1].

1 Interpretation Act 1978 (c 30), s 7.

1209. Measurement of distance. In the measurement of any distance for the purposes of an Act, the distance must, unless the contrary intention appears, be measured in a straight line on a horizontal plane[1].

1 Interpretation Act 1978 (c 30), s 8.

1210. Continuity of powers and duties. Where an Act confers a power or imposes a duty, it is implied, unless the contrary intention appears, that the power may be exercised, or the duty is to be performed, from time to time as occasion requires[1].

1 Interpretation Act 1978 (c 30), s 12(1).

1211. Meaning of 'person'. In any Act passed on or after 1889, unless the contrary intention appears 'person' includes a body of persons corporate or unincorporate[1]. However, 'person', so far as it includes bodies corporate, applies to any provision of an Act whenever passed relating to an offence punishable on indictment or on summary conviction[2].

1 Interpretation Act 1978 (c 30), s 5, Sch 1, Sch 2, para 4(1)(a). For an example of a case where, because of contrary intention appearing in the Act, 'person' was held not to include the corporation of a burgh, see *Colquhoun v Dumbarton Magistrates* 1907 SC (J) 57, 14 SLT 847.
2 Interpretation Act 1978, Sch 2, para 4(5).

1212. References to other enactments. The Interpretation Act 1978 provides that:

'Where an Act refers to an enactment, the reference, unless the contrary intention appears, is a reference to that enactment as amended, and includes a reference thereto as extended or applied, by or under any other enactment, including any other provision of that Act'[1].

It is clear that the effect of this provision is that a reference in an Act to another enactment is a reference to that enactment as amended before the passing of that Act, but it is doubtful whether it would include a reference to the enactment as amended after the passing of that Act[2]. It was held, however, that a provision on similar lines[3] did not apply to future amendments, although it was stressed that the court was dealing with a taxing statute[4].

1 Interpretation Act 1978 (c 30), s 20(2).

2 F A R Bennion *Statutory Interpretation* (1984) pp 427, 428.
3 Ie the Income and Corporation Taxes Act 1970 (c 10), s 540(3).
4 *Willows v Lewis* [1981] TR 437, 125 Sol Jo 792. As to taxing statutes, see para 1185 above.

2. INTERPRETATION OF DEEDS AND OTHER DOCUMENTS

(1) INTRODUCTION

1213. Scope of title. This part of the title is concerned with the interpretation of deeds and other documents. This includes conveyances and wills and to some extent overlaps or duplicates material to be found elsewhere in this work[1]. However, in respect of conveyancing, this part of the title is a guide for the reader to finding his way through the principles of interpretation of conveyancing and other deeds as opposed to the application of conveyancing law and practice. In respect of wills, the material is an integration with the material found elsewhere and is, therefore, set out here in order to be of more convenience for the reader.

1 See generally CONVEYANCING, INCLUDING REGISTRATION OF TITLE, vol 6, paras 401 ff, and WILLS AND SUCCESSION, vol 25, paras 817 ff.

(2) GENERAL RULES OF INTERPRETATION

1214. Purpose of interpretation. In the case of a will or testamentary writing the object of interpretation is to establish the intention of the testator[1]. Deeds of a testamentary nature are more favoured, and therefore receive a more liberal interpretation, than obligations *inter vivos*[2]. In a question of construction of a contract the matter is more complex since the intention of the parties to the contract may be in dispute[3]. The question of interpretation involves determining what the terms of the contract mean in the circumstances, what they require to be done, and whether they have been implemented[4]. Interpretation is a question of law, not of fact, to be determined by the court or, if appropriate, by an arbiter.

1 W M Gloag *The Law of Contract* (2nd edn, 1929) p 398.
2 Erskine *Institute* III,9,14.
3 *Gloag* p 398.
4 D M Walker *The Law of Contracts and Related Obligations in Scotland* (2nd edn, 1985) para 24.1.

1215. General rules. General rules of interpretation of writs are found in the institutional writings, where Stair lays down seven general rules[1] and Bell observes that courts of justice are frequently compelled to make an election between different meanings and sometimes to admit the evidence of usage to qualify the whole[2]. Bell's 'special rules' for the construction of contracts are as follows:
(1) that the popular sense of the words, as known and used at the place and time, is to be followed, unless the words be technical;
(2) that technical words are to be taken technically, if no doubt can be entertained of the meaning and application: and for their meaning usage may be resorted to[3];

(3) that the sense which gives validity and effect to the agreement, is to be preferred to that which invalidates or defeats it[4];

(4) that usage enters into, extends, limits and qualifies contracts, especially in matters of trade;

(5) that words, however general, are to be confined to the subject and matter of the agreement contemplated by the parties;

(6) that in the several contracts, sale, location etc, the *naturalia* of the particular contract are tacitly part of the agreement;

(7) if a series of conversations and communings, or of letters has resulted in a distinct written agreement, all previous correspondence and communings are discharged[5];

(8) the true point of inquiry in all doubtful cases is not (as in a will) the intention of one party, but that meaning of the terms made use of which the adverse party understood, and on which he was entitled to rely[6].

1 Stair *Institutions* IV,42,21.
2 Bell *Principles* s 524.
3 See eg *Tancred, Arrol & Co v Steel Co of Scotland Ltd* (1890) 17 R (HL) 31; *Sutton & Co v Ciceri & Co* (1890) 17 R (HL) 40.
4 See eg *Watson v Neuffert* (1863) 1 M 1110.
5 See eg *Inglis v Buttery & Co* (1878) 5 R (HL) 87; *Lee v Alexander* (1883) 10 R (HL) 91.
6 *Bell* s 524.

1216. How intention is ascertained. It is a general principle that words must be given their plain ordinary meaning[1]. For the lawyer the words of the document are authoritative as words and there is no possibility of obtaining further information from the author, either because the author is dead or because of the rules of evidence precluding reference to him[2]. Where a layman or an ordinary person has been involved in its preparation the words ought to be understood in their ordinary sense[3]. Where the alteration of a single word or two will bring to a document a meaning which was obviously the intention of the contractors the court has presumed that the mistake proceeded from the inaccuracy of the writer and has corrected the clause accordingly[4]. Applications of the ordinary rules of construction may in some cases defeat the intention of the parties.

1 Bell *Principles* s 524. See also *Buchanan v Andrew* (1873) 11 M (HL) 13; *Hunter v Fox* 1964 SC (HL) 95, 1964 SLT 201.
2 G L Williams 'Language and the Law–II' (1945) 61 LQR 179 at 191. See also *Coomber v Ross* 1987 SLT 266 at 268, OH.
3 Stair *Institutions* IV,42,21; Erskine *Institute* III,3,87.
4 *Coutts & Co v Allan & Co* (1758) Mor 11549; *Hunter v Fox* 1964 SC (HL) 95, 1964 SLT 201.

1217. Foreign language and technical terms. Where a language other than English is used in a deed it may be necessary to have a translation from an expert familiar with the language used. So too may evidence be required from persons familiar with technical terms which may indeed be ordinary words with an extraordinary meaning in the technical or business sense used[1].

1 Bell *Principles* s 524; D M Walker *The Law of Contracts and Related Obligations in Scotland* (2nd edn, 1985) ch 24; *Von Mehren & Co v Edinburgh Roperie and Sailcloth Co* (1901) 4 F 232, 9 SLT 335. Cf *P and W MacLellan v Peattie's Trustees* (1903) 5 F 1031, 11 SLT 245. For a list of illustrated cases, see W M Gloag *The Law of Contract* (2nd edn, 1929) p 365, note 4.

1218. Effect of statute. In some instances statute has given a particular interpretation to deeds where such an interpretation either would not or might not otherwise apply.

In a conveyance of lands where no term of entry is specified, entry must be the first term of Whitsunday or Martinmas after the date or last date of the conveyance, unless a contrary intention is apparent from the conveyance[1]. Every holograph writing of a testamentary character is, in the absence of evidence to the contrary, deemed to have been executed or made of the date it bears[2]. However, special rules apply after the making of an adoption order to any deed whereby property is conveyed or under which a succession arises to adopted children and to persons related to adopted children[3].

References to 'minor' or 'majority' in deeds executed prior to 1 January 1970 relate to the age of majority as twenty-one, not as eighteen[4]. This is an important provision bearing in mind the infrequency with which many people renew or alter existing wills.

Overriding interests are an exception to the general rule that a purchaser of heritable property registered in the Land Register of Scotland may rely exclusively on the title sheet of the registered interest in land to disclose all matters relevant to it[5].

1 Conveyancing (Scotland) Act 1874 (c 94), s 28. For the purpose of any enactment or rule of law, and of any lease, agreement or undertaking entered into or given, or any document executed, after 13 July 1991, Whitsunday and Martinmas mean 28 May and 28 November respectively: Term and Quarter Days (Scotland) Act 1990 (c 22), ss 1(1)(a), (2), 3(2). See generally, TIME, vol 22, para 812.
2 Conveyancing (Scotland) Act 1874, s 40.
3 See the Succession (Scotland) Act 1964 (c 41), s 23, and WILLS AND SUCCESSION, vol 25, para 713.
4 Age of Majority (Scotland) Act 1969 (c 39), s 1(2). However, minority extends to twenty-one for the purposes of accumulation periods, irrespective of the date of the deed: see vol 25, para 768, note 5.
5 See generally the Land Registration (Scotland) Act 1979 (c 33), ss 6(4), 9(3), (4), 28(1), and CONVEYANCING, INCLUDING REGISTRATION OF TITLE, vol 6, paras 737 ff.

1219. Construction or interpretation of words. Many individual words have been judicially defined, and lists may be found in the *Faculty Digest* 1868–1922 and the supplementary volumes thereto[1].

> 'If the words are self-contradictory, or so obscure that one has to grope for the meaning, then the provision is ineffective, and it is also ineffective if it is ambiguous or reasonably capable of having more than one meaning... But if the meaning is clearly apparent, that is sufficient to satisfy the test of strict construction. I can find neither reason nor authority for holding that defective drafting which does not obscure the meaning of the provision is enough to invalidate it'[2].

The rule is that in construing all formal deeds the grammatical and ordinary sense of the word is to be adhered to unless that would lead to some absurdity, or some repugnancy or inconsistency with the rest of the deed, in which case the grammatical and ordinary sense of the words may be modified, so as to avoid that absurdity and inconsistency, but no farther[3].

1 Definitions and interpretations of individual words may also be found in 16 *Encyclopaedia of the Laws of Scotland* (eds Lord Dunedin and J Wark, 1934) pp 100–103, and in the Glossary in the *Laws of Scotland* Service.
2 *Hunter v Fox* 1964 SC (HL) 95 at 99, 1964 SLT 201 at 202, per Lord Reid.
3 12 *Halsbury's Laws of England* (4th edn) para 1463.

1220. Local or class usage. Where it is known that a particular word has a local meaning in the district in which it has been used by the granter of a deed, or among the social class to which he belongs, and the implication is clear that he intended to use the word with that local or class meaning, then this meaning should be given effect in construing the deed. Examples are the use of the term 'advocate' in Aberdeen to mean solicitor; or the term 'public school'[1] which has a different meaning according to the class to which the granter belongs, or may think he belongs.

1 The Education (Scotland) Act 1980 (c 44), s 135(1), defines a public school as a school under the management of an education authority, which is comparable with a 'state school' in England and Wales: see 15 *Halsbury's Laws of England* (4th edn) paras 96, 244.

1221. Deed construed as a whole. As a general rule the whole deed may be looked at in order to determine the meaning of a word or phrase[1]. In the case of a conveyance of land the dispositive clause[2] determines the measure of the grant. Only if the dispositive clause is ambiguous may other clauses in the deed be looked at[3]. An exception to this rule is found where there was a reservation in the *tenendas* clause[4].

1 *Taylor v John Lewis Ltd* 1927 SC 891, 1927 SLT 625; *Laing's Trustees v Horsburgh* 1965 SC 339, 1965 SLT 215.
2 See CONVEYANCING, INCLUDING REGISTRATION OF TITLE, vol 6, para 582.
3 *Orr v Mitchell* (1893) 20 R (HL) 27; *Cooper Scott v Gill Scott* 1924 SC 309, 1924 SLT 204.
4 *Largs Hydropathic Ltd v Largs Town Council* 1967 SC 1, 1967 SLT 23; *Bain v Duke of Hamilton* (1865) 3 M 821. As to *tenendas* clauses, see vol 6, para 527.

1222. Prior communications. After completion of a written contract or deed it is not generally competent to seek clarification of its terms by reference to prior communings:

'Now, I think it is quite fixed, and no more wholesome or salutary rule relative to written contracts can be devised, that where parties agree to embody, and do actually embody, their contract in a formal written deed, then in determining what the contract really was and really meant, a Court must look to the formal deed, and to that deed alone. This is only carrying out the will of the parties. The only meaning of adjusting a formal contract is that the formal contract shall supersede all loose and preliminary negotiations, that there shall be no room for misunderstandings, which may often arise, and which do constantly arise, in the course of long, and it may be desultory, conversations, or of correspondence or negotiations, in the course of which the parties are often widely at issue as to what they will insist on and what they will concede. The very purpose of a formal contract is to put an end to the disputes which would inevitably arise if the matter were left upon verbal negotiations or upon mixed communings partly consisting of letters and partly of conversations. The written contract is that which is to be appealed to by both parties, however different it may be from their previous demands or stipulations, whether contained in letters or in verbal conversation. There can be no doubt that this is the general rule'[1].

It is incompetent to supersede a contract of sale instructed by writing by parole proof of an antecedent oral contract of an entirely different character; the alleged agreement could only be proved by the writ or oath of the pursuer as it was an agreement of an innominate and unusual character[2]. If the contract is embodied in writing the court is not entitled to go *dehors* the documents so as to give effect to preliminary negotiations either verbal or in writing, or to what was said or done *unico contextu* with the concluding of the agreement, even though these are expressly referred to therein[3].

Parole evidence is not admissible to explain or contradict unambiguous writs where it is not conceded that they did not truly represent the transactions referred to[4]. However, it is competent to lead parole evidence where it is admitted that the writing does not give a true account of the agreement[5].

1 *Inglis v Buttery & Co* (1878) 5 R (HL) 87 at 102, per Lord Blackburn (approving the dicta of Lord Gifford (1877) 5 R 58 at 69), quoted virtually in extenso in W M Gloag *The Law of Contract* (2nd edn, 1929) p 369.

2 *Müller & Co v Weber and Schaer* (1901) 3 F 401, 8 SLT 401.
3 Erskine *Principles* III, 1, 6F.
4 *Pickards v Pickard* 1963 SC 604, 1963 SLT 56.
5 *Grant's Trustees v Morison* (1875) 2 R 377; *How Group Northern v Sun Ventilating Co* 1979 SLT 277.

1223. Ambiguity. Ambiguities may be self evident or patent on reading the deed, or latent where other information, outwith the deed, gives rise to the ambiguity[1]. Parole evidence is competent to assist the court in determining such a dispute[2]. Doubtful clauses in obligations are to be interpreted against the granter since he did not express his mind more clearly when it was in his power[3]. Doubtful matters in regard to insurance policies, where the insurance company is largely controlling the terminology used, and registration procedures are interpreted favourably to the insured[4].

1 A G Walker and N M L Walker *The Law of Evidence in Scotland* (1964) para 269; W M Gloag and R C Henderson *Introduction to the Law of Scotland* (9th edn, 1987 eds A B Wilkinson and W A Wilson) para 12.16. The distinction between patent and latent ambiguities is said by *Walker and Walker* (para 269) never to have been applied in Scotland, and the heading to this paragraph reads 'Supposed Distinction Between Patent and Latent Ambiguities'. W M Gloag *The Law of Contract* (2nd edn, 1929) p 373, finds the distinction 'not always very satisfactory or easy to apply'. *Gloag and Henderson* seem to agree.
2 *Holdsworth v Gordon Cumming* 1910 SC (HL) 49 at 55, 56, 1910 2 SLT 136 at 139, per Lord Kinnear.
3 Erskine *Institute* III,3,87. See also *Anderson v Dickie* 1915 SC (HL) 79, 1915 1 SLT 393; *Hunter v Fox* 1964 SC (HL) 95, 1964 SLT 201.
4 *Hunter v General Accident Fire and Life Assurance Corpn* 1909 SC (HL) 30, 1909 2 SLT 99, where the claim for benefit arose following completion of a Lett's diary coupon and the subsequent death of the insured in a railway accident.

1224. Construction *ejusdem generis*. Where a list of things is given, to which some provision of the contract applies, and that list concludes with wide general words, the meaning of these general words is so far controlled by the context that they apply only to things of the same class (*ejusdem generis*) as those in the preceding list[1]. The use of the phrase 'all expenses whatever' precluded the application of the *ejusdem generis* principle where a dispute arose concerning payment of local authority rates[2]. The principle was considered but excluded to allow the Admiralty to resume some farm land at Rosyth[3], but applied in the *Abchurch SS Co* case[4].

1 W M Gloag *The Law of Contract* (2nd edn, 1929) p 403.
2 *Glasgow Corpn v Glasgow Tramway and Omnibus Co Ltd* (1898) 25 R (HL) 77, 6 SLT 129.
3 *The Admiralty v Burns* 1910 SC 531, 1910 1 SLT 277.
4 *Abchurch SS Co Ltd v Stinnes* 1911 SC 1010, 1911 2 SLT 72.

1225. Extrinsic evidence. Extrinsic evidence is generally excluded, but as has been noted it is competent in exceptional cases to lead parole evidence to assist the court in determining the intentions of the parties to a contract[1].

'I do not think that the rule of law which excludes parole evidence to qualify a written contract precludes a party from showing that two separate documents, drawn up and signed at the same time, are in effect two parts of the same contract, or, to put [it] in a different way, that there is such an interdependence of the two contracts that fulfilment of the one cannot be insisted on where the party seeking to enforce the one contract is, it may be by no fault of his own, unable to make implement of the other'[2].

Parole evidence was admissible to determine the extent of the estate of Dallas in Morayshire[3], the extent of land tenanted[4], and the terms of a collateral agreement[5].

The general principle remains, however, that where a contract has been entered into in writing, formal or informal, the writing is presumed to express the parties' concluded and settled intentions, and it is not competent to qualify or contradict the terms of the writing by parole evidence[6].

1 See para 1225, text to note 5, above, and D M Walker *The Law of Contracts and Related Obligations in Scotland* (2nd edn, 1985) paras 24.16–24.37.
2 *Claddagh SS Co Ltd v Steven & Co* 1919 SC 184 at 189, 1918 2 SLT 89 at 90, OH (approved 1919 SC (HL) 132 at 135, 1919 2 SLT 170 at 172, per Viscount Finlay).
3 *Holdsworth v Gordon Cumming* 1910 SC (HL) 49, 1910 2 SLT 136. See also *Currie v Campbell's Trustees* (1888) 16 R 237.
4 *Earl of Ancaster v Doig* 1960 SC 203, 1960 SLT 257.
5 *William Masson Ltd v Scottish Brewers Ltd* 1966 SC 9.
6 Walker para 24.26. See also *M'Phersons v Haggarts* (1881) 9 R 306.

1226. Testing clause. Where a testing clause[1] is used to record the particulars of execution of a deed, such a clause may not be used to alter or affect the provisions of the deed itself. Any purported alteration of or addition to the terms of the deed found in the testing clause will be disregarded[2]. This must be so since the testing clause itself is added to the deed after signature by the granter and may contain only particulars of that execution with reference also to any alterations which have been authenticated. In the *Caldwell* case[3] the court permitted the petitioner to obtain access to a testamentary disposition registered in the Books of Council and Session to supply an omission to the testing clause.

1 As to testing clauses, see CONVEYANCING, INCLUDING REGISTRATION OF TITLE, vol 6, paras 427–429.
2 *Smith v Chambers' Trustees* (1878) 5 R 97 (affd (1878) 5 R (HL) 151 (however, Lord Gordon's obiter remarks at 168–170 should be noted, where he expresses the opposite view, which appears to be contrary to the principle)); *Blair v Assets Co* (1896) 25 R (HL) 36, 4 SLT 13.
3 *Caldwell* (1871) 10 M 99.

1227. Alterations in deeds. In formal attested deeds the presumption of law is that all alterations and additions are deemed to have been made after the deed has been completed and delivered, and save for a statutory provision[1], the presumption is irrebuttable[2]. Any alteration or addition not authenticated by the granter of the deed is accordingly regarded as *pro non scripto*. Where erased words cannot be read it is presumed that they were of importance, but an objector is not entitled to read anything he pleases in their place with a view to destroying the deed. The principles of law regarding alterations in attested wills are stated by Lord McLaren in *Pattison's Trustees v Edinburgh University*[3]. There are statutory provisions concerning erasures in notarial instruments and notices of title[4], and erasures in the record of a deed in the Register of Sasines[5].

If marginal notes are not signed by the granter of the deed, one of two things must be presumed, either they have been added unwarrantably, after delivery of the deed, or if at one time communed on, and proposed, that they were in the end departed from[6].

1 See the Conveyancing (Scotland) Act 1874 (c 94), s 39, and CONVEYANCING, INCLUDING REGISTRATION OF TITLE, vol 6, para 430.
2 *Kedder v Reid* (1840) 1 Robin 183 at 211, HL, per Lord Brougham; *Munro v Butler Johnstone (Corehead)* (1868) 7 M 250 at 256, per Lord Neaves.
3 *Pattison's Trustees v University of Edinburgh* (1888) 16 R 73 at 76, 77, OH. As to the authentication of errors, see vol 6, paras 422 ff.
4 Titles to Land Consolidation (Scotland) Act 1868 (c 101), s 144.
5 Conveyancing (Scotland) Act 1874 (c 94), s 54. See also the Land Registration (Scotland) Act 1979 (c 33), s 9, and vol 6, paras 750–752.
6 Hume *Lectures* vol VI (Stair Soc vol 19, 1958 ed G C H Paton) p 8.

1228. Blanks. As a matter of good practice, deeds should be completed before execution and no blank spaces should be left for later completion. The testing clause in a formal deed is an exception[1], and in a disposition of land the date of entry is occasionally left blank at the time of execution because the actual date of entry is not then known. As the date of entry is not an essential part of the deed its validity is unimpaired. In these circumstances, the date of entry is presumed to be the first term of Whitsunday or Martinmas after the date (or the last date) of the conveyance, unless another term of entry appears to be implied[2].

If a blank occurs in a probative deed when it is founded upon, the deed is not probative *quoad* that part of it. The deed is ineffectual if the blank occurs in a material part, but if not material or if the part of the deed including the blank is separable from the remainder, only the defective part is ineffectual[3]. If words are later inserted in blanks left in an executed deed they should be authenticated by the granter and noticed in the testing clause as with an alteration[4]. Where a sum of money borrowed from an insurance company was left blank in a bond of annuity and disposition in security at the time the deed was executed by the borrower and his wife and a figure was subsequently inserted by the lenders or their agents it was presumed by the court that the granter had not consented to the figure, and the onus of proving the contrary rested with the party seeking to uphold the deed[4].

> 'I consider this the same as if there had been an erasure. To say it was blank is as positive an ascertion as to say there was something previously written'[5].

The practical difficulties which could arise by virtue of deeds partly printed and partly typed or handwritten, such as printed forms of wills, or agreements or back letters qualifying security documents, provided that they are properly attested, are obviated by statute[6]. It is nevertheless liable to create problems in the future for beneficiaries where a printed form of will is used by a testator.

Stair and Erskine outline the historical position relating to blanks in writs and bonds which are no longer competent[7]. Hume also considers at some length blanks in deeds and the importance of authentication by the granter if a deed has been signed while as yet blank in material passages[8]. He observes that:

> 'It is only by usage, and from necessity, that a deed is good which is signed blank in the testing clause, which is not of the substance of the deed'[9].

1 See para 1226 above.
2 See the Conveyancing (Scotland) Act 1874 (c 94), s 28, and para 1218, note 1, above.
3 *Abernethy v Forbes* (1835) 13 S 263.
4 *Earl of Buchan v Scottish Widows Fund Society* (1857) 19 D 551.
5 (1857) 19 D 551 at 555, per Lord Murray.
6 See the Titles to Land Consolidation (Scotland) Act 1868 (c 101), s 149, and the Conveyancing (Scotland) Act 1874, s 38.
7 Stair *Institutions* IV,42,19 (Fourthly); Erskine *Institute* III,2,6. See also the Blank Bonds and Trusts Act 1696 (c 25).
8 Hume *Lectures* vol VI (Stair Soc vol 19, 1958 ed G C H Paton) pp 33, 34.
9 *Hume* p 33.

1229. Capacity. Persons in nonage have certain limitations imposed by law upon their capacity to look after their affairs and enter into contracts or to grant deeds. A pupil[1] himself or herself cannot grant deeds and deeds which he or she purports to grant are void. Deeds by a pupil are granted on his or her behalf by a tutor. A tutor has all the powers of a trustee under the Trusts (Scotland) Act 1921[2]. Either father or mother may act as tutor[3]. Deeds granted voluntarily by a tutor are voidable at the instance of the pupil within the *quadriennium utile* on the grounds of nonage and enorm lesion.

A deed by a minor who has a curator without the consent of the curator is void[4]. Exceptions to this rule are:

(1) where the consideration is *in rem versum*[5];
(2) where a minor who is engaged in trade undertakes obligations *in re mercatoria*;
(3) where a minor holds himself or herself out to be of full age and is reasonably believed to be so[6]; and
(4) where the deed makes provision for his wife or children or both, as far as lesion is not proved.

A deed granted by a minor who has no curator, or by a minor with consent of his curator if he or she has one, may be reduced within the *quadriennium utile* on the grounds of minority and enorm lesion. Since 10 September 1964 a minor has had the like capacity to test on heritable property as he or she has on moveable property[7]. Prior to that date a minor could not test on heritable property.

Any deed granted by a person who is incapax is void. A *curator bonis* to look after the affairs of an incapax may be appointed by the Court of Session or the sheriff court. A will made by an incapax during a lucid interval may be sustained[8], but deeds executed by an incapax may be reduced even although the incapacity was temporary[9].

In respect of special relationships:

> 'No doubt cases may be figured where, in view of the relationship of the parties "agree" may be construed as not meaning more than "intend". For example, if a father says to his son who is going to Oxford: "I agree to allow you £300 for three years", it may very well be that this does not constitute a continuous and binding obligation'[10].

Those persons who are incompetent to act as witnesses to the signature of the granter of a deed are:
(a) persons under fourteen years of age;
(b) blind persons;
(c) persons *non compos mentis*;
(d) persons who have signed the same deed as principals;
(e) persons who cannot write.

It is competent for a girl between the ages of twelve and fourteen to attest but not to test[11].

A deed executed on a Sunday is not invalid on that account[12].

---

1 Ie boys under fourteen and girls under twelve.
2 See the Trusts (Scotland) Act 1921 (c 58), s 2 (amended by the Law Reform (Parent and Child) (Scotland) Act 1986 (c 9), s 10(1), Sch 1, para 4 (re-enacting the Guardianship of Infants Act 1925 (c 45), s 10 (repealed)), and TRUSTS, TRUSTEES AND JUDICIAL FACTORS, vol 24, para 128.
3 See GUARDIANSHIP, vol 11, para 1209.
4 *O'Donnell v Brownieside Coal Co Ltd* 1934 SC 534, 1934 SLT 493; *Faulds v British Steel Corpn* 1977 SLT (Notes) 18.
5 Ie used to his or her advantage.
6 *Wilkie v Dunlop & Co* (1834) 12 S 506.
7 See the Succession (Scotland) Act 1964 (c 41), s 28, and WILLS AND SUCCESSION, vol 25, para 761.
8 D M Walker *Principles of Scottish Private Law* (4th edn, 1988) vol 1, p 222. See also *Nisbet's Trustees v Nisbet* (1871) 9 M 937 at 947, where the deceased's 'ailments were aggravated by drink, and mitigated by quiet and restraint in living'. Cf *Muirden v Garden's Executors* 1981 SLT (Notes) 9.
9 *Walker* vol 1, p 222; Erskine *Institute* I,7,51.
10 *Wick Harbour Trustees v The Admiralty* 1921 2 SLT 109 at 110, 111, OH, per Lord Sands.
11 Titles to Land Consolidation (Scotland) Act 1868 (c 101), s 139.
12 *Yeats v Yeats' Trustees* (1833) 11 S 915.

1230. Substance with which deed is written. It is not necessary that deeds should be typewritten or handwritten in ink. It is desirable to use for writing a permanent medium which will remain visible during the likely period of the deed, but deeds written in pencil are not denied effect merely on that account. A deed written in pencil may be open to challenge on the basis that it was not final but deliberative[1].

If a deed is written in ink but been altered in pencil there is a presumption in law not conclusive but rebuttable that the granter did not intend the pencil amendments to be effective[2].

1 *Muir's Trustees* (1869) 8 M 53.
2 *Lamont v Glasgow Magistrates* (1887) 14 R 603; *Munro's Executors v Munro* (1890) 18 R 122; *Currie's Trustees v Currie* (1904) 7 F 364, 12 SLT 613.

1231. Statutory meanings. References to 'full age', 'nonage', 'minor' or 'majority' in deeds executed on or after 1 January 1970 relate to the age of majority as eighteen[1].

On and after 15 February 1971 any reference to an amount of money in the old currency contained in any cheque, bill of exchange, promissory note, money order or postal order, in so far as it refers to an amount in shillings or pence, is to be read as referring to the corresponding amount in the new decimal currency[2]. Where an amount of money in the old currency which is not a whole number of pounds falls to be paid after 31 August 1971[3], the amount payable in respect of so much of it as is in shillings or pence is to be the corresponding amount in the new currency[4].

The estates of persons who died before 13 March 1975 were liable to estate duty, not to capital transfer tax which was introduced by the Finance Act 1975[5]. The estates of persons dying on or after 13 March 1975 became chargeable to capital transfer tax as, to a limited extent, are lifetime gifts since 27 March 1974. So far as any provision in any document, whether executed before or after the passing of the Finance Act 1975, refers to estate duty or death duties it is to have effect, as far as may be, as if the reference included a reference to capital transfer tax chargeable[6] under the Act[7]. This provision obviates the difficulty which could otherwise have arisen in the interpretation of wills or other documents in which there is a reference to estate duty. Similar provisions deal with the renaming of capital transfer tax as inheritance tax[8].

The construction and operation of Acts of Parliament of the United Kingdom is now assisted by the Interpretation Act 1978, which came into force on 1 January 1979 replacing inter alia the Interpretation Act 1889 (c 63)[9]. An Act or provision of an Act comes into force at the beginning of the appropriate day on which it receives the royal assent (and thus may be marginally retrospective) or on the particular day indicated in the Act itself or in a commencement order[10]. In any Act words importing the masculine gender include the feminine and vice versa, words in the plural include the singular and vice versa[11]. It is often advisable in deeds or other documents to make similar provision.

Occupancy rights in a matrimonial home may belong to a non-entitled spouse, a hybrid creation of statute[12] who although non-existent prior to 31 December 1985 involved an unmarried man or woman being deemed to be an entitled spouse for the purposes of making an affidavit that he or she had no non-entitled spouse[13]. An amended form of affidavit to overcome this unhappy use of words has now come into operation[14]. The period during which such occupancy rights may be claimed by a non-entitled spouse who has not occupied the matrimonial home during that period has now been restricted to a continuous period of five years[15].

1 Age of Majority (Scotland) Act 1969 (c 39), s 1(2). However, this does not apply to deeds directing accumulations: see WILLS AND SUCCESSION, vol 25, para 768, note 5.
2 Ie calculated in accordance with the provisions of the Decimal Currency Act 1969 (c 19), s 3, Sch 1.

3 Decimal Currency (End of Transitional Period) Order 1971, SI 1971/1123.
4 Ie calculated in accordance with the Decimal Currency Act 1969, s 9, Sch 1.
5 Ie under the Finance Act 1975 (c 7), s 19(1) (repealed). Capital transfer tax is now inheritance tax: see vol 25, para 1969.
6 Ie chargeable under ibid, s 22 (repealed), or under the Inheritance Tax Act 1984 (c 51), s 4. This Act was formerly the Capital Transfer Tax Act 1984: Finance Act 1986 (c 41), s 100(1)(a).
7 Inheritance Tax Act 1984, s 273, Sch 6, para 1, re-enacting the Finance Act 1975, s 49(5) (repealed).
8 Any reference to capital transfer tax in any document has effect as a reference to inheritance tax: Finance Act 1986, s 100(1)(b).
9 See paras 1206 ff above.
10 Interpretation Act 1978 (c 30), s 4.
11 See ibid, s 6, and para 1207 above.
12 See the Matrimonial Homes (Family Protection) (Scotland) Act 1981 (c 59), s 1, and FAMILY LAW, vol 10, paras 855, 856.
13 See ibid, ss 6(3)(e), 8(2)(a), and vol 10, para 860.
14 Ie by the Law Reform (Miscellaneous Provisions) (Scotland) Act 1985 (c 73), s 13(6): see CONVEYANCING, INCLUDING REGISTRATION OF TITLE, vol 6, paras 747, 783.
15 See the Matrimonial Homes (Family Protection) (Scotland) Act 1981, s 6(3)(f), and vol 6, para 783.

1232. Construction *contra proferentem*. Words are to be interpreted against the person using them — *verba sunt interpretanda contra proferentem*. This is one of the rules observed in the interpretation of writs[1], which applies particularly in the enforcement by a superior against a vassal of real burdens or land obligations[2].

Following the death of the life assured an insurance company attempted to reduce the life policy on the grounds of breach of warranty and concealment of material facts in the proposal form completed by the assured[3]. The court held that there had been no such breach or concealment:

'... such obligations fall to be construed strictly *contra proferentem*. This rule, founded on plain justice, is quite settled in practice. Insurance companies have the framing of their contracts in their own hands. They may make such conditions as they please, but they are bound so to express them as to leave no room for ambiguity'[4].

The maxim applies in the interpretation of writs where the parties are skilful, or are known to have trusted skilful persons in forming of the writs; and therefore the same should be as much extended in favour of the other party as their sense can bear[5].

In *Kennedy v Smith and Ansvar Insurance Co*[6] an insurance company refused to indemnify the insured following a fatal car accident. In finding against the insurers Lord President Emslie said:

'... if insurers seek to limit their liability under a policy by relying upon an alleged undertaking as to the future, prepared by them and accepted by the insured, the language they use must be such that the terms of the alleged undertaking and its scope are clearly and unambiguously expressed or plainly implied and that any such alleged undertaking will be construed, *in dubio, contra proferentem*'[7].

Further cases have been collected by Professor Walker both under this heading and ambiguity[8].

1 J Trayner *Latin Maxims and Phrases* (4th edn, 1894).
2 *Corpn of Tailors of Aberdeen v Coutts* (1834) 2 Sh & Macl 609, HL (further proceedings (1840) 1 Robin 296, HL) (see CONVEYANCING, INCLUDING REGISTRATION OF TITLE, vol 6, paras 497–504); *Bainbridge v Campbell* 1912 SC 92, 1911 2 SLT 373; *Heriot's Hospital Governors v Ferguson* (1774) 3 Pat 674, HL; *Anderson v Valentine* 1957 SLT 57, OH. As to real burdens and conditions, see paras 1245 ff below.
3 *Life Association of Scotland v Foster* (1873) 11 M 351.
4 (1873) 11 M 351 at 358, per Lord President Inglis. See also *Hunter v General Accident Fire and Life Assurance Corpn* 1909 SC (HL) 30, 1909 2 SLT 99.

5 Stair *Institutions* IV,42,21.
6 *Kennedy v Smith* 1975 SC 266, 1976 SLT 110.
7 1975 SC 266 at 277, 278, 1976 SLT 110 at 116, 117.
8 D M Walker The Law of Contracts and Related Obligations in Scotland (2nd edn, 1985) paras 24.12, 24.13.

1233. Clerical error. In the interpretation of deeds it is on occasion apparent that there had been a clerical error as distinct from error in expression or in intention between the parties. If an agreement is embodied in a document intended to be obligatory, such as a bond, lease or policy of insurance, and by some mistake it is drawn up and executed incorrectly, the court has a very wide equitable power to rectify the document and so to give effect to the real intentions of the parties[1]. It is interesting that in making this comment Professor Gloag's view remained unaltered between the first and second editions of *The Law of Contract*.

The matter is well illustrated in *Glen's Trustees v Lancashire and Yorkshire Accident Insurance Co*[2] where the court was asked to construe a deed by correcting a grammatical error which, if allowed to stand, would have nullified the intention of the granters. In granting the plea Lord President Dunedin said:

'In my opinion the Court is entitled to correct such an error. The word "not" was evidently inserted . . . by failing to notice that the conjunction preceding was "unless" and not "if". I think we should read the stipulation as if the word "not" was deleted'[3].

There are some similarities with the decision in *Hunter v Fox*[4], where the House of Lords agreed to treat the words 'at present' as *pro non scripto* in order to give a sensible meaning to part of a disposition of land. However, there was no suggestion of clerical error in the *Hunter* case.

There is more difficulty when the mistake is not admitted by one party but Gloag comments 'it would appear that proof of anything which can be termed a clerical error is competent, and that there is no restriction as to the evidence which may be led'[5].

In *Krupp v Menzies*[6] a clerk who was asked to halve one-tenth in a new contract had by mistake put one-fifth as the half of one-tenth.

1 W M Gloag *The Law of Contract* (2nd edn, 1929) p 435 (repeating (1st edn, 1914) p 475); *Caldwell* (1871) 10 M 99.
2 *Glen's Trustees v Lancashire and Yorkshire Accident Insurance Co Ltd* (1906) 8 F 915, 14 SLT 168.
3 (1906) 8 F 915 at 918, 14 SLT 168 at 168.
4 *Hunter v Fox* 1964 SC (HL) 95, 1964 SLT 201.
5 *Gloag* p 436.
6 *Krupp v John Menzies Ltd* 1907 SC 903, 15 SLT 36.

1234. Rectification of errors. Considerable difficulty is likely where an attempt is made to rectify a clerical error, not admitted by one party, in a deed already recorded in the Register of Sasines[1]. It remains to be seen how the Keeper of the Registers of Scotland or the court or the Lands Tribunal for Scotland will deal with cases which may arise in the future for rectification of an inaccuracy in the Land Register for Scotland[2].

In the leading case of *Anderson v Lambie*[3] it was held that a duly recorded disposition of land fell to be reduced owing to a mistake common to both parties, but not admitted by the purchaser, to be replaced by a disposition giving true effect to the prior missives of sale. In the House of Lords Lord Reid said:

'In my judgment, if two parties both intend their contract to deal with one thing and by mistake the contract or conveyance is so written out that it deals with another, then as a general rule the written document cannot stand if either party attacks it'[4].

It would have been unwise for a conveyancer to presume too much latitude on the part of the court in attempting to resolve such a blunder in the future had it not been for the enactment of the Law Reform (Miscellaneous Provisions) (Scotland) Act 1985. This provides that, subject to section 9 of this Act, where the court is satisfied, on an application made to it, that:

(1) a document intended to express or to give effect to an agreement fails to express accurately the common intention of the parties to the agreement at the date when it was made, or

(2) a document intended to create, transfer, vary or renounce a right, not being a document falling within head (1) above, fails to express accurately the intention of the granter of the document at the date when it was executed,

it may order the document to be rectified in any manner that it may specify in order to give effect to that intention[5]. This wide ranging provision has been in force only since 31 December 1985. The court is entitled to have regard to all relevant evidence, whether written or oral[6] but, in the view of Lord McCluskey, rectification may be ordered only if six points are satisfied, namely:

> '(1) that there is a document to be rectified; (2) that that document was intended to express or give effect to an already existing agreement arrived at between two (or more) parties; (3) that there was, when the document was executed, such a pre-existing agreement — whether or not enforceable; (4) that that agreement itself embodied and was an expression of one or more intentions common to (that is to say, shared by) the parties; (5) that the intentions were actual (not deemed) intentions; (6) that the agreement itself must have been reached at a definite point in time (cf "the date when it was made")'[7].

Documents to which these provisions apply include a document recorded in the Register of Sasines[8], being a register of deeds, but exclude a document of a testamentary nature[9]. Where rectification is ordered by the court the document is to have effect as if it had always been so rectified[10], unless the court specifies a later effective date[11]. Application for such rectification may be made to the Court of Session or to the sheriff court[12].

The proviso that rectification under section 8 is conditional upon section 9 is to allow other interests to be protected. It is evident that regard has been taken of the interests of a person who has relied on the title sheet of an interest in land registered in the Land Register of Scotland which follows a document which might be the subject of an application to rectify[13]. The distinction between the Register of Sasines as a register of deeds and the Land Register of Scotland as a register of interests in land creates an added complication to a statutory provision which will inevitably create an uncertainty in the future interpretation of title deeds. Will it no longer be possible to rely on the faith of the records as hitherto? Not only is it now possible to apply to the court for rectification of a document, it is also possible for the court to grant an application to reduce the rectifying order in certain circumstances[14].

Will a prudent conveyancer now be confident to rely on section 45 of the Conveyancing and Feudal Reform (Scotland) Act 1970 (c 35)[15] in accepting a sasine extract of a duly recorded deed 'for all purposes as sufficient evidence of the contents of the original so recorded'? It may become practice to refuse to accept as a link in title such a sasine extract unless newly obtained for the transaction then current. It is also possible that yet another clause to cover the possibility of rectification or reduction of rectification of a document may become standard in missives for the sale and purchase of heritable property in Scotland.

The benefits of section 8 of the 1985 Act may be outweighed by the disadvantages.

1 *Glasgow Feuing and Building Co v Watson's Trustees* (1887) 14 R 610; *Anderson v Lambie* 1954 SC (HL) 43, 1954 SLT 73.
2 See the Land Registration (Scotland) Act 1979 (c 33), s 9, and CONVEYANCING, INCLUDING REGISTRATION OF TITLE, vol 6, paras 750–752.
3 *Anderson v Lambie* 1954 SC (HL) 43, 1954 SLT 73.
4 1954 SC (HL) 43 at 57, 1954 SLT 73 at 78.
5 Law Reform (Miscellaneous Provisions) (Scotland) Act 1985 (c 73), s 8(1).
6 Ibid, s 8(2).
7 *Shaw v William Grant (Minerals) Ltd* 1989 SLT 121 at 121, OH.
8 Law Reform (Miscellaneous Provisions) (Scotland) Act 1985, s 8(5).
9 See ibid, s 8(6), and vol 6, para 771.
10 Ibid, s 8(4).
11 Ibid, s 9(4), and vol 6, para 752.
12 See ibid, s 8(9), and vol 6, para 771.
13 Ibid, s 9(2).
14 See ibid, s 9(7), (8).
15 See vol 6, para 452.

(3) IMPLICATIONS

1235. Implied terms. Provisions may be implied in a deed without express mention in certain cases. In any deed executed on or after 4 April 1979[1] which conveys an interest in land, unless specially qualified, a clause of assignation of writs, a clause of assignation of rents or a clause of obligation of relief of feuduties and public burdens, is imported without any reference in the deed[2]. Statutory meaning is given to the clauses which are deemed to form part of the conveyance.

A land obligation in a deed of conditions executed on or after 4 April 1979 in accordance with section 32 of the Conveyancing (Scotland) Act 1874 (c 94) must:
(1) on the recording of that deed in the Register of Sasines, or
(2) on the obligation being registered in the Land Register of Scotland,
become a real obligation affecting the land to which it relates unless it is expressly stated in such deed that such a provision is not to apply[3].

It is most unlikely that any lay person would understand the implication of silence on these two matters introduced only in 1979. They run counter to the apparent approach of government towards relaxation of standards in seeking qualification as a conveyancer.

Statutory import had already been given to clauses of assignation of writs, assignation of rents, warrandice and obligation of relief by section 8 of the Titles to Land Consolidation (Scotland) Act 1868[4]. This applied to the formal clauses as they appeared in a disposition of land whether or not held burgage[5].

Absolute warrandice is implied in sales of heritage and moveables, other than assignations of debts, for an adequate consideration[6]. It is also implied in leases for a fair rent[7]. The tenant's title is warranted at the date of entry, absolute warrandice being implied in the absence of express stipulation to the contrary[8].

Warrandice from fact and deed only is implied in assignations of debts for a fair price when it is also implied *debitum subesse*, that is that the debt still exists[9]. There is no implied warrandice that the debtor is solvent and able to pay.

Erskine states that by warrandice the granter becomes obliged that the subject made over is effectual to the vassal, and not evicted from him by any one as having a better or preferable right to it[10]. The obligation of warrandice is, without any special or express clause, implied in all deeds, either in a more extended or a more limited degree, according to the nature of the deed[10]. It is also suggested by Erskine, but now doubted, that where the deed is granted for a cause, onerous indeed, but below the true value of the subject, warrandice is implied not only against the granter's future deeds, but his past deeds[10]. Where the sale is on credit, solvency is an implied condition[11].

However, 'oft-times when warrandice is not expressed, it is implied; as rights are to be warranted, which are granted for an equivalent cause onerous'[12]. Simple warrandice is the least onerous degree and, if not expressed, is implied by law in gratuitous deeds. Whether express or implied it means that the granter will not in the future voluntarily do anything that will prejudice the right given to the grantee in the deed. Warrandice if expressed always displaces the warrandice which would otherwise have been implied[13].

Real warrandice, as distinct from personal warrandice, could also be express or implied as in contracts of excambion, but as from 1 January 1925 real warrandice has been abolished whether express or *ex lege*[14].

The import of the clause of personal obligation contained in Form A of Schedule 2 to the Conveyancing and Feudal Reform (Scotland) Act 1970 (c 35) expressed in any standard security, unless specially qualified, is found in section 10 of the Act[15]. So too is the import of ancillary clauses including the clause of warrandice and the clause of consent to registration for execution in a standard security[16].

The standard conditions set out in Schedule 3 of the 1970 Act must, subject to such variations as have been agreed by the parties, regulate every standard security[17].

The tenant of an agricultural holding[18] may impliedly terminate the tenancy by abandoning possession of the holding[19]. The lease of such a holding may terminate by implied renunciation when the parties enter into a new lease differing in any material respect from the old[20].

1 Ie the date on which the Land Registration (Scotland) Act 1979 (c 33), ss 1, 16–23 came into force: s 30.
2 See ibid, s 16, and CONVEYANCING, INCLUDING REGISTRATION OF TITLE, vol 6, paras 538–540.
3 See ibid, s 17, and vol 6, paras 496 ff.
4 See vol 6, paras 538 ff.
5 See the Titles to Land Consolidation (Scotland) Act 1868 (c 101), s 8, Sch (B), and vol 6, paras 538 ff. See also vol 6, para 586.
6 See vol 6, para 543.
7 J Rankine *The Law of Leases in Scotland* (3rd edn, 1916) pp 213, 214.
8 G C H Paton and J G S Cameron *The Law of Landlord and Tenant in Scotland* (1967) p 128.
9 See vol 6, para 544.
10 Erskine *Institute* II, 3, 25.
11 Bell *Principles* s 100.
12 Stair *Institutions* II, 3, 46.
13 *Coventry v Coventry* (1834) 12 S 895.
14 See the Conveyancing (Scotland) Act 1924 (c 27), s 14(1), and vol 6, para 542.
15 See vol 6, paras 633 ff.
16 See vol 6, para 548.
17 See the Conveyancing and Feudal Reform (Scotland) Act 1970 (c 35), s 11(2), and vol 6, paras 633 ff.
18 Ie land held under a lease for agricultural purposes: see the Agricultural Holdings (Scotland) Act 1949 (c 75), s 1, and AGRICULTURE, vol 1, paras 729 ff.
19 *Paton and Cameron* p 239; B Gill *The Law of Agricultural Holdings in Scotland* (1982) ch 14.
20 *Erskine* II, 6, 64; *Gill* ch 14.

1236. Where implication inappropriate. It has already been noted that express warrandice displaces the level of warrandice which would otherwise have been implied[1]. Conditions must be lawful in order to receive effect. They may be not only express but implied[2].

In relation to the powers of mandate to a factor:
(1) where the terms are express, the limits are absolute;

(2) mercantile mandates are extended, restrained or qualified, and in general are aided by the settled rules and usage of trade[3].

The mandatory must follow the precise rules prescribed by his employer, for as all his power's flow from the mandant's commission, whatever he does *ultra fines mandati* is without authority, and cannot bind his constituent[4].

Expressum facit cessare tacitum — a thing expressed puts an end to tacit implication — is a general rule of application in the construction of deeds and contracts[5].

1 See *Coventry v Coventry* (1834) 12 S 895, and CONVEYANCING, INCLUDING REGISTRATION OF TITLE, vol 6, paras 541 ff.
2 Bell *Principles* s 47. Bell gives as an example an obligation to pay a tocher (dowry), implying marriage as a condition.
3 *Bell* s 225.
4 Erskine *Institute* III, 3, 35.
5 Reference is made and examples are given in J Trayner *Latin Maxims and Phrases* (3rd edn, 1883). Further examples are found in 12 *Halsbury's Laws of England* (4th edn) para 1475.

(4) PARTICULAR DEEDS

(a) Conveyances

1237. Feu writs and dispositions. It is convenient to consider together the interpretation of feu writs and dispositions[1]. So far as feu writs are concerned, these may be by feu contract which is a bilateral deed, or by feu charter or feu disposition both of which are unilateral deeds.

In a feu writ or disposition the dispositive clause is the ruling clause and determines the extent of the grant to which it relates[2]. If the terms of the dispositive clause are clear they cannot be altered or varied by other clauses which indicate a contrary meaning[3]. Only where the dispositive clause is ambiguous may reference be made to other clauses to assist in construing the dispositive clause[4].

The word 'dispone' is normally used in a conveyance of land but it is no longer necessary, provided that other words importing conveyance or transference or present intention to convey or transfer are used[5].

1 As to feu writs and dispositions, see CONVEYANCING, INCLUDING REGISTRATION OR TITLE, vol 6, paras 463, 474, 579 ff.
2 As to dispositive clauses, see vol 6, paras 478–481.
3 *Chancellor v Mosman* (1872) 10 M 995; *Cooper Scott v Gill Scott* 1924 SC 309, 1924 SLT 204; *Graham v Graham* (1816) 1 Ross LC 46; *Largs Hydropathic Ltd v Largs Town Council* 1966 SLT 117, OH (revsd 1967 SC 1, 1967 SLT 23).
4 *Orr v Mitchell* (1893) 20 R (HL) 27; *Lord Advocate v M'Culloch* (1874) 2 R 27; *Dick-Lauder v Leather-Cully* 1920 SC 48, 1919 2 SLT 241.
5 See the Conveyancing (Scotland) Act 1874 (c 94), s 27, and vol 6, para 478.

1238. Descriptions generally. A description of the subjects conveyed is part of the dispositive clause. Professor Montgomerie Bell said:

'Secure that the description shall embrace everything intended to be disponed; that it shall not contain anything not intended to be disponed; and that the subjects disponed shall be capable of clear and absolute identification'[1].

That is the ideal. At common law the requirement is to identify the subjects being conveyed and distinguish them from all other subjects. In *Murray's Trustees v Wood*[2] the First Division upheld the Lord Ordinary in accepting as adequate the description used in a bond and disposition in security over subjects in Baker Street, Aberdeen, described in a feu charter by named persons bearing specified dates and recorded in the register for the county of Aberdeen although the particular subjects were not further identified in relation to other properties in Baker Street and the date of recording the feu charter was omitted. The Lord President considered that the facilities for finding the feu charter were ample.

In a similar case, *Matheson v Gemmell*[3], where a reference to a prior disposition was blundered, it was held on appeal, again upholding the Lord Ordinary, that the misdescription in the prior deed was merely *falsa demonstratio* and not fatal to a valid conveyance.

The Keeper of the Registers of Scotland may refuse to accept a deed for recording[4], or in relation to an application for registration in the Land Register which is map based may refuse to register an interest. In the latter case the land must be sufficiently described to enable the Keeper to identify it by reference to the Ordnance map[5].

Either a general description or a particular description may be used. The former has the benefit of brevity and simplicity; it may prevent the omission of land possessed by the granter of the deed but outwith a particular description. Possession and prescription with such a general description may add to the grantee's acquisition[6]. Salmon fishings still require to be specifically conveyed if the grantee is to acquire title to them, except in the case of a barony title, which may include such regalia.

A general description may, however, inadvertently create problems by including in the conveyance subjects not intended to be sold or omitting from the conveyance subjects which should have been included. In a dispute between purchaser and seller regarding the extent of 'the estate of Dallas' included in a contract for sale Lord Kinnear said:

'... if a question arises as to the description to be inserted in a disposition, the first thing to be settled is what is the exact subject sold; and that is to be determined, not by the existing titles, but by the contract of sale, interpreted, as every document whatsoever must, more or less, be interpreted by reference to the surrounding circumstances'[7].

The House of Lords agreed unanimously that reference to a plan which did not itself form part of the written contract was admissible to prove the external facts to which the contract relates.

1 A M Bell *Lectures on Conveyancing* (3rd edn, 1882) vol 1, p 588. As to descriptions of property, see CONVEYANCING, INCLUDING REGISTRATION OF TITLE, vol 6, paras 482 ff.
2 *Murray's Trustee v Wood* (1887) 14 R 856.
3 *Matheson v Gemmell* (1903) 5 F 448, 10 SLT 625.
4 *Macdonald v Keeper of the General Register of Sasines* 1914 SC 854, 1914 2 SLT 90.
5 See the Land Registration (Scotland) Act 1979 (c 33), s 4(2)(a), and vol 6, para 723.
6 *Young v Carmichael* (1671) Mor 9636; *St Monance Magistrates v Mackie* (1845) 7 D 582; *Lord Advocate v Wemyss* (1899) 2 F (HL) 1, 7 SLT 172.
7 *Houldsworth v Gordon Cumming* 1910 SC (HL) 49 at 55, 1910 2 SLT 136 at 139.

1239. Description of boundaries. A particular description is a bounding title by reference to specific boundaries expressly or by implication. Where a bounding charter is so precise and intelligible in its terms as to enable the court, without further inquiry, to fix the boundaries, no proof of possession will be allowed[1]. If the limits given are ambiguous and unintelligible without extrinsic evidence, a proof will be necessary, in which prescriptive possession by the grantee, or acquiescence by the granter, will be important elements[2].

Particular boundaries which have been judicially construed include the following:

(1) *Sea, lowest low-water mark* mean that the ground extends to the low-water mark of ordinary spring tides[3], including the foreshore (ground between high and low-water marks of ordinary spring tides) subject to the inalienable rights of the public upon it, such as navigation, drying nets and white fishing, and probably walking for recreation[4].

(2) *Full sea, sea flood, flood mark* show the intention to exclude the beach or foreshore and the boundary is the high-water mark of ordinary spring tides[5].

(3) *Sea beach, sea shore* are doubtful terms and the court will look to the intention of the parties in the transaction[6].

(4) *Tidal navigable river*: the same rules apply as for the sea[7].

(5) *Non-tidal river*: the boundary is the *medium filum* or middle line of the river bed[8]. If the line of the river alters naturally, the boundary follows the centre line of the new river bed, so extending or restricting the lands as the case may be.

(6) *Canal* includes both canal and tow path[9].

(7) *Road*: lands stated to be bounded by a road normally do not include the road[10], but where it is a public road[11] or a private road between two estates or feus[12], the presumption is that the *medium filum* is the boundary.

(8) *Wall*: the boundary is the inside of the wall, the wall itself and the solum of it being excluded[13].

(9) *Mutual wall*: the boundary may be the centre line of the wall, each proprietor having a right of property in his own half and a common interest in the other half. Alternatively the boundary may be the inner face of the wall, and the wall and its solum are held *pro indiviso*. Neither party can alter the wall without the other's consent[14].

(10) *Gable wall*: bounded 'by' the gable wall excludes the wall[15].

(11) *Lane*: bounded 'by' a lane excludes the lane[16], but a right of access over it may be implied[17].

(12) *March stones*: the presumption is for a straight line between the stones[18].

(13) *Lateral boundaries*: where contiguous estates are situated on the coast or in a river estuary[19], a perpendicular line is drawn seawards, or in the river estuary to a line which represents the general direction of the *medium filum* of the river at low water, from the end of the land boundary to a straight line drawn parallel to the average or general direction of the coast[20].

It is necessary in framing descriptions of an area of ground formerly part of larger subjects to be specific in referring to boundaries such as a road or wall where the actual boundary may include or exclude or be the centre line of the road or wall[21]. In using these phrases to describe a particular boundary it is essential to know what you mean to describe.

1 *Earl of Dalhousie's Tutors v Lochlee Minister* (1890) 17 R 1060.
2 J Rankine *The Law of Land-ownership in Scotland* (4th edn, 1909) p 102.
3 *Smith v Lerwick Harbour Trustees* (1903) 5 F 680, 10 SLT 742; *Cadell v Allan* (1905) 7 F 606, 13 SLT 10.
4 *Hope v Bennewith* (1904) 6 F 1004, 12 SLT 243, where a member of the public has the right to shoot on the foreshore.
5 *Keiller v Dundee Magistrates, Scott v Dundee Magistrates* (1886) 14 R 191.
6 *Fisherrow Harbour Comrs v Musselburgh Real Estate Co Ltd* (1903) 5 F 367, 10 SLT 512; *Musselburgh Magistrates v Musselburgh Real Estate Co Ltd* (1904) 7 F 308, 12 SLT 636.
7 *Hunter v Lord Advocate* (1869) 7 M 899.
8 *Gibson v Bonnington Sugar Refining Co Ltd* (1869) 7 M 394; *Hamilton Magistrates v Bent Colliery Co* 1929 SC 686, 1929 SLT 569; *Menzies v Marquess of Breadalbane* (1901) 4 F 55; *Fothringham v Passmore* 1984 SC (HL) 96, 1984 SLT 401.
9 *Fleming v Baird* (1841) 3 D 1015.
10 *Houstoun v Barr* 1911 SC 134, 1910 2 SLT 286.
11 *Ayr Magistrates v Dobbie* (1898) 25 R 1184, 6 SLT 110.

12 *Wishart v Wyllie* (1853) 1 Macq 389, HL.
13 *Smyth v Allan* (1813) 4 Pat 699, HL.
14 For commentary, see J Rankine *The Law of Land-ownership in Scotland* (4th edn, 1909) p 620;
     J Burns *Conveyancing Practice* (4th edn, 1957 ed F MacRitchie) p 329; J M Halliday *Conveyancing
     Law and Practice in Scotland* (1986) vol II, 18–11; *Gray v MacLeod* 1979 SLT (Sh Ct) 17. See also
     PROPERTY.
15 *Campbell v Paterson* (1896) 4 SLT 79.
16 *Argyllshire Commissioners of Supply v Campbell* (1885) 12 R 1255 at 1261, per Lord Shand.
17 *Boyd v Hamilton* 1907 SC 912, 15 SLT 57.
18 *Earl of Dalhousie's Tutors v Lochlee Minister* (1890) 17 R 1060.
19 *Burns* p 329.
20 *Halliday* vol II, 18–11; *M'Taggart v M'Douall* (1867) 5 M 534; *Keith v Smyth* (1884) 12 R 66.
21 *Rankine* p 620; *Gray v MacLeod* 1979 SLT (Sh Ct) 17.

1240. Plans. The map-based system now in use for the Land Register of
Scotland will ensure that details of all boundaries appear in each land certificate
as it is issued. This will, however, take many years to cover the whole of
Scotland. Only four of the county areas were operational areas for the purposes
of the Land Register by the end of 1990[1].

It is normal to attach a plan to a deed being recorded in the Register of Sasines
where one or more new boundaries are being created. In the leading case of
North British Rly Co v Hawick Magistrates, the Lord President says:

> 'I can conceive no description more clearly taxative than that which we have
> here... The conveyance describes the ground as consisting of a specific quantity
> specially mentioned, and it makes reference to a plan upon which that ground is
> delineated. All that is conveyed is delineated on the plan by certain lines. That is fully
> as good as any words describing the line of boundary of this property'[2].

The Conveyancing (Scotland) Act 1924 provides for registration of such plans
with a duplicate plan duly docquetted being retained in the register[3].

Since boundaries, plans and ground areas are all used to identify a particular
plot of ground, difficulty in interpretation can arise where one is inconsistent
with another, sometimes because of a draftsman's error. Where such conflict
arises the court attempts to ascertain what was intended by the parties to the
deeds or other documents involved. Subject to that qualification certain presumptions emerge:
(1) where boundaries and plan conflict, and measurements are also given, the
     boundaries or the plan will be preferred according to whichever is supported
     by the measurements[4];
(2) where boundaries and plan, or boundaries and measurements conflict, the
     boundaries if clear will prevail[5];
(3) where there are measurements only, they are taxative[6].

The colours used in original plans are normally of considerable help in
identifying the subjects to which they relate. Sasine extracts with a plan attached
lose the benefit of the colours, as do most photocopied deeds. It is now possible
to have deed plans photographed reproducing the original colours, but this
facility is not yet generally available. To assist in the interpretation of deeds
relating to neighbouring properties it is recommended that deeds to which
coloured plans are attached be retained and not destroyed after registration of
the relevant interest in the Land Register of Scotland, notwithstanding that a
land certificate reflecting the registered interest has been issued without restriction of indemnity.

1 For the areas, see CONVEYANCING, INCLUDING REGISTRATION OF TITLE, vol 6, para 703.
2 *North British Rly Co v Hawick Magistrates* (1862) 1 M 200 at 203.
3 See the Conveyancing (Scotland) Act 1924 (c 27), s 48, and vol 6, paras 486, 729.
4 *North British Rly Co v Moon's Trustee* (1879) 6 R 640.
5 *Ure v Anderson* (1834) 12 S 494; *Currie v Campbell's Trustees* (1888) 16 R 237.

6 *Brown v North British Rly Co* (1906) 8 F 534, 13 SLT 797.

1241. Statutory descriptions. The use of statutory descriptions[1] is wide-spread and effective. The only problem of interpretation arises where such a description is blundered. To overcome this difficulty it is desirable to include a simple common law description such as a postal address as well as the statutory description.

As a practical matter it simplifies interpretation of successive dispositions of the same subjects to follow a previous description by reference if it is sufficient in its terms to satisfy the statutory requirements, even if the style differs from the style normally used by the disponee's solicitor.

1 As to the rules, see the Conveyancing (Scotland) Act 1874 (c 94), s 61, the Conveyancing (Scotland) Act 1924 (c 27), s 8, Sch D, and CONVEYANCING, INCLUDING REGISTRATION OF TITLE, vol 6, para 582. The provisions of the Conveyancing (Scotland) Act 1924, s 8(1), are retrospective.

1242. Pertinents. The phrase 'together with parts, privileges and pertinents thereof' is normally included after the description of the subjects conveyed. The interpretation placed on these words varies considerably from one judicial decision to another[1]. 'Parts and pertinents' are defined as such accessory parts and fixtures and appendages to land, or houses, or such separate possessions, or privileges, as accompany the occupation and use of land[2]. They are carried without being named or described in the charter[2]. Erskine describes them as everything which, from its close coherence or connection with land, goes to the vassal as an accessory of the subject contained in the feudal grant[3]. Woods, trees, orchards, mines and minerals, houses, church seats and servitudes are parts and pertinents listed by Professor Bell[4]. So too is the right of trout fishing in a river passing through the land, but not the right of salmon fishing, which requires an express conveyance[5].

Whether or not a particular substance is a mineral has resulted in much litigation. It is a question of fact depending on the circumstances of each case[6]. It should be something different from the ordinary subsoil of the area[7]. It is helpful to name in a conveyance mineral substances which are to be included or excluded. In construing a mineral reservation clause:

(1) everything is conveyed which is not covered by the reservation;
(2) any reservation is construed strictly *contra proferentem*; and
(3) general terms following a list of particular substances may be restricted by the *ejusdem generis* rule.

1 *Gordon v Grant* (1850) 13 D 1 at 7, per Lord Justice-Clerk Hope; *Cooper's Trustees v Stark's Trustees* (1898) 25 R 1160; *Meacher v Blair-Oliphant* 1913 SC 417, 1913 1 SLT 131. See also *Duke of Argyll v Campbell* 1912 SC 458 at 491, 1912 1 SLT 316 at 335, per Lord Johnston. See further CONVEYANCING, INCLUDING REGISTRATION OF TITLE, vol 6, para 489, and PROPERTY.
2 Bell *Principles* s 739.
3 Erskine *Institute* II,6,4.
4 Bell ss 740–745.
5 Ibid, s 747. A useful list of cases dealing with pertinents is found in 10 *Encyclopaedia of the Laws of Scotland* (ed Lord Dunedin and J Wark 1930) para 1299.
6 *Caledonian Rly Co v Glenboig Union Fireclay Co Ltd* 1911 SC (HL) 72, 1911 1 SLT 416; *Caledonian Rly Co v Symington* 1912 SC (HL) 9, 1911 2 SLT 411.
7 *Caledonian Rly Co v Glenboig Union Fireclay Co Ltd* 1911 SC (HL) 72, 1911 1 SLT 416; *Borthwick-Norton v Gavin Paul & Sons* 1947 SC 659, 1948 SLT 89.

1243. Minerals etc. The principle *a coelo usque ad centrum*, from the heavens to the centre (of the earth), applies to the interest of a proprietor of land. In theory the proprietor has right to the minerals below the surface, unless the conveyance is qualified because of a reservation or separate grant of the minerals, and to the buildings, trees etc on the surface as well as the sky above[1]. These rights have been restricted by statute, notable examples being the Petroleum (Production) Act 1934[2] and the Coal Industry Nationalisation Act 1946[3].

A seller of heritage must, therefore, disclose to the purchaser that the minerals are not included in the sale, otherwise the purchaser will have the right to resile from the contract or missives of sale and purchase[4]. In the absence of a reservation or exclusion of the nationalised and other minerals, the purchaser of heritable property is being offered by the seller an opportunity to resile even although he or she has no interest in acquiring title to the minerals, let alone working the same.

1 See generally CONVEYANCING, INCLUDING REGISTRATION OF TITLE, vol 6, para 491.
2 See the Petroleum (Production) Act 1934 (c 36), s 1, and ENERGY, vol 9, para 724.
3 See the Coal Industry Nationalisation Act 1946 (c 59), s 5. Sch 1, and MINES AND QUARRIES, vol 14, para 1603.
4 *Campbell v McCutcheon* 1963 SC 505, 1963 SLT 290.

1244. Conditions involving incorporeal rights. A number of further qualifications of the grant in favour of the vassal or disponee are possible, but only if expressed in the deed and not affected by statutory limitation. Such qualifications being a restriction on freedom are construed against the granter *contra proferentem*.

It is legal for the granter of a deed to insert a clause of pre-emption in terms of which on a sale by either a vassal or a disponee the subjects of sale must first be offered to the superior or disponer at the same price as is offered by an intending purchaser, or on other pre-agreed terms. Such a right of pre-emption, irrespective of the provisions in the deed itself, is now affected by statute[1]. Where the right is held by a superior, failure to exercise the right on one occasion terminates the right, whether or not the deed provides otherwise. If the superior wishes to exercise the right he must do so within twenty-one days or such shorter period as is specified in the deed. It is important for the purchaser of a subject to which such a right of pre-emption applies to put up with the title deeds evidence of the decision taken by the superior on a previous sale.

Further statutory provision has extended these provisions to rights of pre-emption created in deeds other than feudal grants, but only where such deed or other writing is executed after 1 September 1974[2]. A right of pre-emption created in a deed or writing which is not a feudal grant and is dated 1 September 1974 or earlier is therefore still exercisable on more than one occasion[3].

A clause of redemption (other than the right of a lessor to the reversion of a lease) entitling the holder of the right to re-acquire the subjects at a fixed price or a price to be determined in accordance with an agreed formula is still valid[4] but is now exercisable only within twenty years of its creation if in a deed executed on or after 1 September 1974 and certain other provisions apply[5].

A clause requiring a feu grant to be recorded in the Register of Sasines within sixty days (or another stated period) of its date is still found in some cases. The clause is still valid. The equivalent step for a Land Register transaction would be to register the interest in the Land Register of Scotland, thereby creating a real right[6].

A clause in a feu writ prohibiting subinfeudation is null and void irrespective of the date of the deed creating the right[7].

1 See the Conveyancing Amendment (Scotland) Act 1938 (c 24), s 9(1), and CONVEYANCING, INCLUDING REGISTRATION OF TITLE, vol 6, para 520.
2 See ibid, s 9(3), and vol 6, para 520.
3 *Christie v Jackson* (1898) 6 SLT 245, OH; *Earl of Mar v Ramsay* (1838) 1 D 116.
4 See the Tenures Abolition Act 1746 (c 50), s 10 (amended by the Statute Law Revision Act 1867 (c 59)), and *M'Elroy v Duke of Argyll* (1902) 4 F 885, 10 SLT 156.

5 See the Land Tenure Reform (Scotland) Act 1974 (c 38), s 12, and vol 6, para 521.
6 See the Land Registration (Scotland) Act 1979 (c 33), s 3(1)(b), and vol 6, para 726.
7 See vol 6, para 523.

1245. Real burdens and conditions generally. Real burdens and conditions affect the land and are transmitted with the land when it passes to singular successors of the vassal or the disponee. Such qualifications of the grant may be created by a superior or by the granter of a disposition[1]. They are construed strictly *contra proferentem* since there is a presumption for freedom. A real burden is strictly an obligation to pay money and a real condition or restriction is the correct term for other continuing provisions.

  1 *Braid Hills Hotel Co Ltd v Manuels* 1909 SC 120, 16 SLT 523; *Nicholson v Glasgow Asylum for the Blind* 1911 SC 391, 1911 1 SLT 37; *Scottish Co-operative Wholesale Society Ltd v Finnie* 1937 SC 835, 1938 SLT 78.

1246. Constitution of real burdens and conditions. The principles for constitution of a real burden or condition have remained largely unaltered for 150 years since the leading case of *Tailors of Aberdeen v Coutts*[1]. In order to create a condition which is binding upon singular successors, words must be used in the conveyance which clearly express that the subject itself is to be affected, and not merely the grantee and his heirs and successors, and these words must enter the infeftment and the register, and be repeated or validly referred to in the subsequent transmissions and infeftments[1]. The principles may be summarised as follows:
(1) no *voces signatae* or technical form of words are required;
(2) the burden or condition must not be contrary to law or public policy nor vexatious nor inconsistent with the nature of the property;
(3) the burden or condition must be specific;
(4) if it relates to payment of money it must be definite in amount and payable to an identifiable creditor;
(5) it must appear in the infeftment of the proprietor of the burdened ground and be recorded in the Register of Sasines[2], and must be in the dispositive clause of the deed;
(6) it is not necessary that it should be fenced with an irritant and resolutive clause, although that is usual;
(7) the party seeking to enforce it must have both a title and an interest to do so[3].
The reference to the Register of Sasines must now be supplemented by the alternative of the real burden or condition appearing in the Burdens Section of the title sheet to be made up and maintained by the Keeper of the Registers of Scotland[4]. The 'land certificate' issued by the Keeper to an applicant for registration of an interest in land is a copy of the title sheet authenticated by the seal of the register[5]. A land certificate is accepted for all purposes as sufficient evidence of the contents of the title sheet of which the land certificate is a copy[6].
   To show intention to create an obligation which will affect singular successors it is helpful if the obligation is of a continuing character such as maintaining a building or insuring it against fire and other risks[7]. An obligation to pay a share of the cost of constructing a road was held not to run with the lands[8].

  1 *Corpn of Tailors of Aberdeen v Coutts* (1834) 2 Sh & Macl 609, HL (further proceedings (1840) 1 Robin 296, HL).
  2 This is not applicable to a Land Register transaction.
  3 For a full discussion of these points, see CONVEYANCING, INCLUDING REGISTRATION OF TITLE, vol 6, paras 498–504.
  4 See the Land Registration (Scotland) Act 1979 (c 33), s 6, the Land Registration (Scotland) Rules 1980, SI 1980/1413, rr 3, 7, and vol 6, paras 707, 711.

5 See the Land Registration (Scotland) Act 1979, s 5(2), and vol 6, para 713.
6 See ibid, s 5(4), and vol 6, para 713.
7 *Clark v City of Glasgow Life Assurance Co* (1854) 17 D (HL) 27.
8 *Edinburgh Magistrates v Begg* (1883) 11 R 352.

1247. Interpretation of real burdens and conditions. Judicial decisions which assist practitioner and client alike in trying to interpret the burdens clause in deeds are readily found. A prohibition in a feu contract against the sale of liquor was held not to be inconsistent with the nature of the property nor contrary to public policy[1]. Real conditions prohibiting the sale of alcohol or the use of a building as licensed premises abound, and the Lands Tribunal for Scotland has been called upon to deal with many such applications[2] for discharge or variation of a land obligation under the provisions of Conveyancing and Feudal Reform (Scotland) Act 1970[3].

In *Anderson v Valentine*[4] it was held by Lord Hill Watson that conventional irritancies would be enforced according to their terms without regard to hardship, and that if the irritancy was to be enforced the correct procedure was to obtain from the court an order ordaining the vassal to erect buildings within a specified time. The strict construction *contra proferentem* is illustrated by the decisions that the right to erect a house and garage did not preclude the erection of another garage[5]; where there was an obligation to erect self-contained villas of a certain value on a feu, and that had been done, there was no implied restriction on also building tenements on other parts of the feu[6]; and obligation to use ground at Largs in all time coming for a pier did not infer prohibition of the use of part of it for another purpose[7]; an obligation to build a house does not imply an obligation to maintain it[8]; and an obligation regarding the construction and maintenance of a self-contained lodging did not relate to its use[9].

A contract between magistrates, the superior and the vassal contained building conditions but was not recorded and no instrument of sasine repeating the conditions was recorded; various recorded deeds later referred to the conditions but did not state them *ad longum*; and it was held that they were not real burdens[10]. The words of restriction are peculiarly placed in the disposition. They do not occur in the dispositive clause, the appropriate place for expressing both the extent of the grant and any qualifications of it[11].

1 *Earl of Zetland v Hislop* (1882) 9 R (HL) 40.
2 *Murrayfield Ice Rink Ltd v Scottish Rugby Union* 1972 SLT (Lands Trib) 20 (on appeal 1973 SC 21, 1973 SLT 99); *McVey v Glasgow Corpn* 1973 SLT (Lands Trib) 15; *Manz v Butler's Trustees* 1973 SLT (Lands Trib) 2; *Leney v Craig* 1982 SLT (Lands Trib) 9; *Vic Booth (Joiners) Ltd* (14 January 1986, unreported) Lands Trib, where an obligation prohibiting the sale of alcoholic liquor was discharged notwithstanding the objection of another licence holder.
3 See the Conveyancing and Feudal Reform (Scotland) Act 1970 (c 35), ss 1, 2 and CONVEYANCING, INCLUDING REGISTRATION OF TITLE, vol 6, paras 511 ff.
4 *Anderson v Valentine* 1957 SLT 57, OH.
5 *Carswell v Goldie* 1967 SLT 339.
6 *Fleming v Ure* (1896) 4 SLT 26.
7 *Kemp v Largs Magistrates* 1939 SC (HL) 6, 1939 SLT 228 (see particularly the judgment of Lord Macmillan).
8 *Peter Walker & Son (Edinburgh) Ltd v Church of Scotland General Trustees* 1967 SLT 297.
9 *Porter v Campbell's Trustees* 1923 SC (HL) 94, 1923 SLT 619.
10 *Liddall v Duncan* (1898) 25 R 1119, 6 SLT 77.
11 *Kemp v Largs Magistrates* 1939 SC (HL) 6 at 14, 1939 SLT 228 at 232, per Lord Macmillan.

1248. Enforcement of real burdens and conditions. A person seeking to enforce a real burden must consider:
(1) whether a title to enforce the real burden or condition has been effectively conferred upon him;
(2) whether he then had an interest to do so; and

(3) whether the title or interest has been lost by the subsequent actings of the parties.

The onus on a superior showing that he has an interest to enforce a condition in a feu grant is very light[1]. It is less easy for a co-feuar to establish a *jus quaesitum tertio*. The requirements were defined by Lord Dunedin as:

(a) there must be a benefit intended for the tertius;

(b) it must be conceived in his favour in an irrevocable deed; and

(c) the tertius must have knowledge of its existence and that he can rely on it[2].

The leading case on the title of a co-feuar to enforce real burdens is *Hislop v MacRitchie's Trustees*[3]. It is important to establish some mutuality or community of rights and interests. Such mutuality may be established by express stipulation[4], reasonable implication[5], or mutual agreement among the feuars[6]. Once established, a *jus quaesitum tertio* is an independent right[7]. It has been held that, even where a disponer had disposed of the remainder of the ground which restrictions in his favour were designed to protect, the onus was still on the disponee to show that the disponer no longer had an interest to enforce the restrictions[8].

The right to enforce restrictions may be lost by acquiescence, such as permitting the feuar to contravene a restriction for a long period and to incur expense without taking objection[9], or if a number of feuars have been allowed to depart from the provisions of their feus over a long period, other feuars may also be free of the restriction[10]. In 1965 the superior resisted successfully a plea that the right to object to change of use of a house in Portland Road, Kilmarnock, to an office had been lost because approximately twenty out of sixty houses in the road had already ceased to be used as houses[11]. In that case the superior had no objection in principle to the proposed change of use, but sought a payment of £1,250 to grant a minute of waiver. It was this kind of dispute between superior and vassal which led to the provisions of the Conveyancing and Feudal Reform (Scotland) Act 1970 permitting an application to the Lands Tribunal for Scotland[12] to have a land obligation[13] discharged or varied. The tribunal may vary or discharge the obligation wholly or in part, and subject to payment of such sum, if any, as the tribunal deems to be appropriate to the benefited proprietor as compensation, on being satisfied that in all the circumstances:

(i) by reason of changes in the character of the land affected by the obligation or of the neighbourhood thereof or other circumstances which the tribunal may deem material, the obligation is or has become unreasonable or inappropriate; or

(ii) the obligation is unduly burdensome compared with any benefit resulting or which would result from its performance; or

(iii) the existence of the obligation impedes some reasonable use of the land[14].

These provisions have been in operation since 1 March 1971 and, although few of the tribunal's decisions are reported in the law reports or journals, an impressive number of decisions is now available. It would be helpful if these could be more fully reported.

1 *Menzies v Caledonian Canal Comrs* (1900) 2 F 953, 8 SLT 87; *Earl of Zetland v Hislop* (1882) 9 R (HL) 40; *Macdonald v Douglas* 1963 SC 374, 1963 SLT 191.

2 *Carmichael v Carmichael's Executrix* 1920 SC (HL) 195, 1920 2 SLT 285.

3 *Hislop v MacRitchie's Trustees* (1881) 8 R (HL) 95. See also CONVEYANCING, INCLUDING REGISTRATION OF TITLE, vol 6, paras 506 ff.

4 *Macdonald v Douglas* 1963 SC 374, 1963 SC 191.

5 *Johnstone v The Walker Trustees* (1897) 24 R 1061, 5 SLT 86.

6 *Hislop v MacRitchie's Trustees* (1881) 8 R (HL) 95.

7 *Lawrence v Scott* 1965 SC 403, 1965 SLT 390.

8 *Scottish Co-operative Wholesale Society Ltd v Finnie* 1937 SC 835, 1938 SLT 78.

9 *Ben Challum Ltd v Buchanan* 1955 SC 348, 1955 SLT 294.

10 *Campbell v Clydesdale Banking Co* (1868) 6 M 943.

11 *Howard de Walden Estates Ltd v Bowmaker Ltd* 1965 SC 163, 1965 SLT 254.

12 As to the Lands Tribunal for Scotland, see COURTS AND COMPETENCY, vol 6, paras 1139 ff. See also CONVEYANCING, INCLUDING REGISTRATION OF TITLE, vol 6, para 511, text to notes 9–11, and paras 512, 513.

13 Ie as defined in the Conveyancing and Feudal Reform (Scotland) Act 1970 (c 35), s 1(2): see CONVEYANCING, INCLUDING REGISTRATION OF TITLE, vol 6, paras 496, 511.

14 Ibid, s 1(3)(a)–(c).

1249. Reddendo. Apart from transitional provisions which no longer apply, no deed executed since 1 September 1974[1] may impose:

(1) a feuduty[2];

(2) ground annual, skat or any other periodical payment (other than feuduty) in respect of the tenure or use of land or under a land obligation subject to certain exceptions:

(a) a payment in respect of a lease, liferent or other right of occupancy;

(b) a payment of teind, stipend or standard charge;

(c) a payment in defrayal of or contribution towards some continuing cost related to the land, or a payment under a heritable security[3].

If a deed executed after 1 September 1974 attempts to impose feuduty or one of the other prohibited periodical payments that provision will not apply but the deed is not otherwise void or unenforceable[4].

On a sale for valuable consideration on or after 1 September 1974 any feuduty exigible is deemed to have been redeemed at the date of redemption, that is the date when entry is taken under an obligation to grant a conveyance of the feu[5].

There is a right to redeem feuduty and certain other periodic payments on a voluntary basis[6]. The effect of these provisions is that in many cases, in the interpretation of feu writs executed prior to 1 September 1974, provisions relating to the *reddendo* will not mean what they say. This is, however, one of the situations where reliance on the faith of the records is of no assistance in noting a title. Feuduty redemptions are not recorded in the Register of Sasines, but the Keeper does require a feuduty redemption receipt to be submitted to him with an application for registration of an interest in the Land Register of Scotland. This is, therefore, another instance where the interpretation of a deed requires knowledge extrinsic of the deed itself[7].

It has already become increasingly difficult for the prudent conveyancer to submit to the superior or his agent a notice of change of ownership[8] following a sale of heritable property since the lack of a feuduty notice not only misleads some practitioners into the belief that such a notice is no longer required — when it is — but also makes it increasingly difficult to trace the superior. It would appear necessary for further statutory provision to remedy this state of affairs.

Separate provision is made in the Land Tenure Reform (Scotland) Act 1974 for redemption by law of feuduty, ground annual and other periodic payments on the acquisition of land by an authority possessing compulsory powers[9].

Where a deed provides for payment of an unallocated feuduty it is now possible for the proprietor of part of a feu to serve on the superior a notice of allocation of the proportion of the *cumulo* feuduty which has been apportioned on that part of the feu[10]. Subject to the right of the superior to appeal to the Lands Tribunal of Scotland, if he objects to the proposed allocation and to any adjustment made by the tribunal, a notice of allocation is effective to allocate on the part of the feu the portion of the *cumulo* feuduty stated in the notice[11]. Similar provisions apply to allocation of ground annuals[12]. As the notice of allocation is not recorded in the Register of Sasines, here again is the possibility of an alteration to the meaning of a deed which is not apparent from examination of the deed itself.

1 Ie the date the Land Tenure Reform (Scotland) Act 1974 (c 38) was brought into force: s 24(2).
2 Ibid, s 1(1). See also CONVEYANCING, INCLUDING REGISTRATION OF TITLE, vol 6, para 528.
3 Ibid, s 2(1).
4 Ibid, ss 1(2), 2(2).
5 Ibid, s 5(1). As to the meaning of 'feuduty' for the purpose of s 5, see s 5(7). However, it does not include an unallocated portion of a *cumulo* feuduty: s 5(12).
6 Ie in terms of ibid, s 4. For the meaning of 'feuduty' for the purpose of s 4, see s 4(7). It should be noted that the definition of feuduty for the purposes of voluntary and compulsory redemption differ.
7 As to extrinsic evidence, see para 1225 above.
8 See the Conveyancing (Scotland) Act 1874 (c 94), s 4(2), Sch A.
9 See the Land Tenure Reform (Scotland) Act 1974, s 6, and vol 6, paras 535, 537.
10 See the Conveyancing and Feudal Reform (Scotland) Act 1970 (c 35), s 3, and vol 6, paras 529, 531.
11 Ibid, s 3(5). See also s 4, and vol 6, para 531.
12 See ibid, s 6, and vol 6, para 586.

1250. Other clauses. Reference has already been made to the clauses of assignation of writs, assignation of rents, and relief from feuduties and public burdens. The absence of such clauses in modern deeds has itself a statutory meaning in interpreting the deed[1].

The clause of warrandice, when used in the normal way, has a statutory meaning, as do the clauses of assignation of writs and rents and the clause of obligation of relief, where these clauses are still used[2]. Implied warrandice has already been discussed[3].

1 See the Land Registration (Scotland) Act 1979 (c 33), s 16, and CONVEYANCING, INCLUDING REGISTRATION OF TITLE, vol 6, paras 538–540.
2 See the Titles to Land Consolidation (Scotland) Act 1868 (c 101), s 8, and vol 6, para 543.
3 See para 1235 above.

(b) Leases

1251. Principles of construction. The ordinary principles of construction fall to be applied to a lease[1]. If it relates to land or buildings in Scotland it prima facie falls to be interpreted by Scots law, even if drawn in English form[2] as happens with many full repairing and insuring leases of office or commercial premises. The lease must be construed as a whole, each clause being taken in connection with all the others and with the common and statutory law of the land[3]. In the interpretation of a lease extraneous evidence may in certain cases be competently adduced[4].

Professor Rankine says that the only presumption admissible seems to be the general maxim that a deed must be construed *contra proferentem*, that is against the party who had the drawing up of a deed to which the other only consented[5]. Where an improbative lease was followed by possession, parole proof as to date of entry was held to be competent[6].

It is a condition of every long lease (that is a lease exceeding twenty years)[7] executed after 1 September 1974 that, with a few specified exceptions, no part of the property which is subject to the lease is to be used as or as part of a private dwelling house[8]. A breach of that statutory condition does not, however, render the offending lease void or unenforceable, but the lessor may give to the lessee notice of termination[9]. The tenant could not receive from the court a further period of lease beyond twenty years from the date of the formal notice[10].

The Land Tenure Reform (Scotland) Act 1974 provides that in leases executed after 1 September 1974 it is not competent to stipulate for the payment of any casualty[11]. Casualties do remain exigible in earlier leases, some of which run for

999 years and involve the tenant or lessee in paying a year's rent on a change of tenancy. Interposed leases are now competent, and are deemed always to have been competent for the person in right of the lessor of a lease to grant[12]. The right is, therefore, available by statute, not in terms of the lease itself. It is also possible since 31 December 1985 to create real conditions in assignations of certain long leases, and for this purpose section 17 of the Land Registration (Scotland) Act 1979[13] applies with such modifications as are necessary[14].

A landlord is no longer, for the purpose of treating a lease as terminated or terminating it, entitled to rely on a provision in the lease which purports to terminate it, or to enable him to terminate it, in the event of a failure of the tenant to pay rent or to make any other payment on or before the due date without further notice in writing giving not less than fourteen days' warning, or of an act or omission by the tenant, or of a change in the tenant's circumstances if in all the circumstances of the case a fair and reasonable landlord would not seek so to rely[15]. This relaxation of the conventional irritancy clause with effect from 31 December 1985 follows the recommendation of the Scottish Law Commission[16].

1 See generally, CONVEYANCING, INCLUDING REGISTRATION OF TITLE, vol 6, paras 639, 707, text and note 4, paras 714, 775, and LANDLORD AND TENANT.
2 D M Walker *Principles of Scottish Private Law* (4th edn, 1989) vol 3, p 212; *Mackintosh v May* (1895) 22 R 345, 2 SLT 471.
3 J Rankine *The Law of Leases in Scotland* (3rd edn, 1916) p 98.
4 *Rankine* pp 98, 101. See also *The Admiralty v Burns* 1910 SC 531, 1910 1 SLT 277; *Earl of Ancaster v Doig* 1960 SC 203, 1960 SLT 257. However, for a more restrictive view, see *Campbell v Western Isles Islands Council* 1989 SLT 602 at 604 (affg 1988 SLT (Lands Trib) 4 (see especially at 6)).
5 *Rankine* p 98. See also *Johnston v Gordon* (1805) Hume 822.
6 *Watters v Hunter* 1927 SC 310, 1927 SLT 232.
7 See the Registration of Leases (Scotland) Act 1857 (c 26), s 1, and vol 6, para 707, note 3.
8 See the Land Tenure Reform (Scotland) Act 1974 (c 38), s 8(1), and vol 6, para 639.
9 See ibid, s 9(1).
10 See ibid, s 9(4)(a).
11 See ibid, s 16. For the meaning of 'casualty', see the Glossary in the *Laws of Scotland* Service, and PROPERTY.
12 See ibid, s 17. As to interposition, see LANDLORD AND TENANT.
13 Which provides that certain obligations in deeds of conditions become real obligations upon the recording of the deed or registration of the obligation.
14 See the Registration of Leases (Scotland) Act 1857, s 3(2), and vol 6, para 639.
15 See the Law Reform (Miscellaneous Provisions) (Scotland) Act 1985 (c 73), ss 4–7, and LAND-LORD AND TENANT.
16 *Irritancies in Leases* (Scot Law Com no. 75; Cmnd 8760 (1983)): see SOURCES OF LAW (GENERAL AND HISTORICAL), vol 22, para 681. See also *Dorchester Studios (Glasgow) Ltd v Stone* 1975 SC (HL) 56, 1975 SLT 153; *HMV Fields Properties Ltd v Skirt 'n' Slack Centre of London Ltd* 1982 SLT 477; *What Every Woman Wants (1971) Ltd v Wholesale Paint and Wallpaper Co Ltd* 1984 SLT 133.

1252. Distinction between leases and licences. It is not always easy to differentiate between a lease and a licence, the latter term being little used in Scotland compared with the frequency of its use in England. Paton and Cameron observed in 1967 'the concept of personal licence does not seem to have been accepted until comparatively recently'[1]. The distinction may be important for purposes of rating and valuation[2]. An attempt may also be made to circumvent the restrictions as to rent and security of tenure applicable to the lease of a dwellinghouse by use of what is called a licence agreement[3]. This may also be relevant in questions of a public sector tenant's 'right to buy' under the Housing (Scotland) Act 1987 (c 26)[4].

Without the cardinal elements of a lease (1) *consensus in idem*, (2) heritable subjects, (3) rent, and (4) definite period of let, a lease cannot be sustained by the courts. In an agreement to allow one party the tenancy of a garage in Glasgow on payment of a lump sum for a period of ten years on the basis that a refund would be made for such years not so used, it was held on challenge by a singular successor of the landlord that the arrangement was a personal licence and not a lease as no rent was payable[5].

1 G C H Paton and J G S Cameron *The Law of Landlord and Tenant in Scotland* (1967) p 12.
2 S B Armour *Valuation for Rating* (5th edn, 1985 ed J J Clyde and J A D Hope).
3 *Scottish Residential Estates Development Co Ltd v Henderson* 1989 GWD 22–932 (Sh Ct), where a grant was construed as a licence. See eg dicta in English cases, *Walsh v Griffiths-Jones* [1978] 2 All ER 1002 at 1008; *Aslan v Murphy (No 1) and (No 2), Wynne v Duke* [1989] 3 All ER 130, CA; *Mikeover Ltd v Brady* [1989] 3 All ER 618, CA; *A G Securities v Vaughan, Antoniades v Villiers* [1990] AC 417, [1988] 3 All ER 1058, HL. For a full discussion, see *Errington v Errington and Woods* [1952] 1 KB 290 at 295 ff, [1952] 1 All ER 149 at 153 ff, CA, per Denning LJ.
4 See HOUSING, vol 11, paras 1954 ff.
5 *Mann v Houston* 1957 SLT 89.

1253. The Rent (Scotland) Act 1984. The Rent (Scotland) Act 1984 is a consolidation Act which provides inter alia ten cases where the court may make an order for possession in favour of the landlord of a private dwellinghouse, and a further eleven cases where it is mandatory for the court to order possession[1]. In the interpretation of leases relating to private sector houses, the Rent (Scotland) Act 1984, rather than the lease itself, determines questions regarding regulated tenancies. Irrespective of the terms of a lease no tenant may be evicted without a court order[2].

1 See the Rent (Scotland) Act 1984 (c 58), Pt I (ss 1–10), Pt II (ss 11–21), Sch 2, and LANDLORD AND TENANT.
2 See ibid, s 23, and LANDLORD AND TENANT. This principle was first enacted in the Removings Act 1555 (c 12) and amplified in the Protection from Eviction Act 1964 (c 97) (both repealed).

(c) Heritable Securities

1254. Introduction. Since 29 November 1970[1] a grant of any right over an interest in land for the purpose of securing any debt by way of a heritable security is capable of being effected at law only if it is embodied in a standard security[2]. This new form of heritable security replaced the old forms in use prior to that date, namely the bond and disposition in security for advances of a fixed amount[3], the bond of cash credit and disposition in security for advances of a fluctuating amount[4] and the *ex facie* absolute disposition[5] qualified by an agreement normally unrecorded which could be used for securing advances of fixed or fluctuating amounts.

In the Halliday Report on conveyancing legislation and practice[6] are found criticisms of the old forms of heritable security, but these criticisms related more to procedure than interpretation of the deeds. The report does observe that the value of the Register of Sasines as a public record of ownership of properties was diminished by the use of the security in the form of an absolute conveyance[7]. In this respect the interpretation of such a disposition could and still does on occasion lead to difficulty since the conveyance to the disponee does not mean what it appears to mean and reference to an unrecorded qualifying agreement is necessary to ascertain the true nature of the conveyance. With the passage of time the old forms of security still in existence have steadily decreased, but there are still many of these which the present day conveyancer may have to call up or assign or discharge.

1 Ie the date the provisions of the Conveyancing and Feudal Reform (Scotland) Act 1970 (c 35), Pt II (ss 9–32) came into force: s 54(2)(a).

2 Ibid, s 9(3).
3 See CONVEYANCING, INCLUDING REGISTRATION OF TITLE, vol 6, para 629.
4 See vol 6, para 630.
5 See vol 6, para 631.
6 *Conveyancing Legislation and Practice* (the Halliday Report) (Cmnd 3118) (1966).
7 Ibid, para 105.

1255. The standard security and conditions. The standard security is now familiar to conveyancers. It follows the modern practice of a brief statutory form[1] with an imported meaning[2]. It is, therefore, necessary for the practitioner in interpreting standard securities to be familiar with the statutory provisions which regulate them, in particular with the clauses relating to the personal obligation, to warrandice, which is unchanged from the former position, to registration for execution, to the right to the title deeds[3] and to ranking[4]. The ranking clause and the reference to prior, postponed or *pari passu* standard securities requires particular care on the part of the draftsman if the provision is to receive the interpretation desired[5].

To achieve the aim of brevity and uniformity every standard security is deemed to be regulated by the standard conditions[6], except in so far as those conditions which are variable by agreement between the parties involved have been so varied. It is quite usual to find that the obligation on the debtor to insure the security subjects is varied to give cover on the basis of replacement, but without such a variation insurance cover is only required to the extent of the market value thereof.

Many of the banks and building societies or other institutional lenders have printed forms of the standard conditions which apply to the debtor who borrows from the particular lender. The issue of the printed forms to the debtor is an attempt to ensure that the debtor is fully informed of his obligations and rights.

1 See the Conveyancing and Feudal Reform (Scotland) Act 1970 (c 35), s 9(2), Sch 2, and CONVEY-ANCING, INCLUDING REGISTRATION OF TITLE, vol 6, paras 633 ff.
2 See ibid, s 10.
3 See ibid, s 10(2).
4 See ibid, s 13.
5 For a commentary, see J M Halliday *The Conveyancing and Feudal Reform (Scotland) Act 1970* (2nd edn, 1977) paras 6.20, 6.23, 7.60, 7.61; J M Halliday *Conveyancing Law and Practice in Scotland* (1987) vol III, chs 37–40, 42.
6 See the Conveyancing and Feudal Reform (Scotland) Act 1970, s 11, Sch 3, and vol 6, paras 634 ff.

1256. Charge certificate. Where the security subjects lie within an operational area for the purposes of the Land Registration (Scotland) Act 1979 (c 33), the standard security itself forms part of the charge certificate[1] and in due course on discharge of the security should be destroyed as it no longer affects the subjects. Particulars of any heritable security over the interest in land also appear in the Charges Section of the land certificate[2] which may be held separately because two or more charges exist.

1 See CONVEYANCING, INCLUDING REGISTRATION OF TITLE, vol 6, para 774, text to note 7.
2 See para 1259 below, and vol 6, para 713.

1257. Discharge. The fiction of an *ex facie* absolute disposition being an outright conveyance to the disponee was in general carefully preserved in any reconveyance or subsequent disposition in favour of a purchaser. The true nature of the security disposition remained concealed behind the form of words used. Such pretence ceased with the introduction of the short statutory form of discharge of a heritable security constituted by an ex facie absolute conveyance[1]. The discharge includes the phrase 'although in its terms *ex facie* absolute was truly in security of an advance of . . .'[2].

1 See the Conveyancing and Feudal Reform (Scotland) Act 1970 (c 35), s 40, Sch 9, and CONVEY-ANCING, INCLUDING REGISTRATION OF TITLE, vol 6, paras 615, 632.
2 See ibid, Sch 9.

1258. Savings. Saving and enabling clauses in the Conveyancing and Feudal Reform (Scotland) Act 1970 preserved the efficacy of any heritable security duly recorded prior to 29 November 1970 and ensured that provisions relating to the old bond and disposition or assignation in security apply to standard securities except in so far as inconsistent with the provisions of Part II of the Act[1].

1 See the Conveyancing and Feudal Reform (Scotland) Act 1970 (c 35), ss 31, 32. As to Pt II (ss 9–32), see CONVEYANCING, INCLUDING REGISTRATION OF TITLE, vol 6, paras 629 ff.

(d) Land Certificates

1259. Interpretation. Registration of title is dealt with fully elsewhere in this work[1]. However, it is relevant to the interpretation of deeds to draw attention to two particular matters in relation to land certificates, which although still comparatively rare will within a few years, it may be hoped, be the norm throughout Scotland.

First, registration of title is map based by reference to the Ordnance map[2]. Explanation of the symbols used in the title plan which forms part of the land certificate is prescribed[3]. These are reproduced in each land certificate.

Secondly, it is well known that a right such as a servitude may be acquired by prescription[4] and a positive servitude may be express or implied, but in land register transactions the interest of the proprietor of the dominant tenement in a servitude is only one of eleven such interests, grouped together as overriding interests[5], which affect the interest in land although not appearing in the title sheet and consequently not reproduced in the land certificate. These overriding interests have already been increased since the passing of the Land Registration (Scotland) Act 1979[6] and they will no doubt be added to in the future. Reference is made to such interests in the land certificate. It is unfortunate that there should be rights and liabilities affecting land which it is not practicable to register, but which though not registered, must nevertheless retain their validity, but Rowton Simpson comments that all systems of registration of title make provisions for such exceptions[7]. He refers to overriding interests as a blemish on the principle that the register should be complete[8], and we must hope that in Scotland the list of such interests is kept as short as possible.

1 CONVEYANCING, INCLUDING REGISTRATION OF TITLE, vol 6, paras 701 ff.
2 See the Land Registration (Scotland) Act 1979 (c 33), s 4(2)(a), and vol 6, paras 486, 723.
3 See the Land Registration (Scotland) Rules 1980, SI 1980/1413, r 14, Sch A, Form 6 (substituted by SI 1988/1143).
4 See the Prescription and Limitation (Scotland) Act 1973 (c 52), s 3.
5 For the meaning of 'overriding interests', see the Land Registration (Scotland) Act 1979, s 28, and vol 6, paras 737 ff. See also J M Halliday *Conveyancing Law and Practice in Scotland* (1986) vol II para 24–35.
6 See the Land Registration (Scotland) Act 1979, s 28(1) (amended by the Matrimonial Homes (Family Protection) (Scotland) Act 1981 (c 59), s 6(4), and the Telecommunications Act 1984 (c 12), s 109(1), Sch 4, para 71), and vol 6, paras 744, 747.
7 S R Simpson *Land Law and Registration* (1976) para 2.5.1.
8 *Simpson* para 2.5.3.

(e) Miscellaneous Deeds

1260. Deeds of conditions. Deeds of conditions were introduced over 100 years ago[1], but that name was not used in a statute until much later. Such deeds may be granted by 'any proprietor of lands'. In practice such proprietor would require to be infeft since there is no statutory provision for deduction of title in such a deed, yet by virtue of a subsequent enactment on the recording of such a deed executed after 4 April 1979 in the Register of Sasines or on a land obligation specified in such a deed being registered the land obligation becomes a real obligation affecting the land to which it relates, unless it is expressly stated in such deed that these provisions are not to apply to that obligation[2].

Prior to 4 April 1979 there was some doubt whether conditions specified in a deed of conditions became real on the recording of the deed or only when they were subsequently referred to in a conveyance of part of the subjects to which they applied[3]. The doubt remains in theory for deeds of conditions executed prior to 4 April 1979, but in practice it is unlikely that any of these deeds have not yet been followed by reference to the conditions in a subsequent conveyance.

1 See the Conveyancing (Scotland) Act 1874 (c 94), s 32.
2 See the Land Registration (Scotland) Act 1979 (c 33), ss 17(1), 30(2). For the meaning of 'land obligation', see CONVEYANCING, INCLUDING REGISTRATION OF TITLE, vol 6, para 511. See also J M Halliday *Conveyancing Law and Practice in Scotland* (1986) vol II, paras 19-65–19-67.
3 See *Conveyancing Legislation and Practice* (the Halliday Report) (Cmnd 3118) (1966) para 83. See also Professor Halliday's annotated commentary on the Land Registration (Scotland) Act 1979, s 18, in *Scottish Current Law Statutes*.

1261. Contracts of co-partnership. Where a contract of co-partnership exists, the interpretation of the deed will be subject to the provisions of the Partnership Act 1890, although many of the sections of that Act are subject to any agreement otherwise between or among the parties. Unless there is agreement to the contrary, a continuing guaranty or cautionary obligation given either to a firm or to a third person in respect of the transaction of a firm is revoked as to future transactions by any change in the constitution of the firm to which, or of the firm in respect of the transactions of which, the guaranty or obligation was given[1]. It is usual to contract out of this provision. A partner may not be expelled from the partnership by a majority of the other partners unless there is express agreement to that effect among the partners[2]. The death or bankruptcy of any partner dissolves the firm unless there is agreement otherwise between the partners[3].

1 Partnership Act 1890 (c 39), s 18.
2 Ibid, s 25.
3 Ibid, s 33(1). See also *William S Gordon & Co Ltd v Thomson Partnership* 1985 SLT 122, where it was held that because of the terms of the contract the death of Mrs Thomson did not operate as dissolution of the partnership. For detailed commentary, see J B Miller *The Law of Partnership in Scotland* (1973) pp 444–452, and PARTNERSHIP. See also F W Clark *The Law of Partnership and Joint Stock Companies according to the Law of Scotland* (1866).

1262. Other deeds. The interpretation of other deeds not specially mentioned, for example a factory and commission or power of attorney[1], a minute of waiver or renunciation, an affidavit or statutory declaration[2], contracts of ground annual, servitudes, floating charges, deeds of entail, contracts of marriage[3], voluntary trust deeds for creditors[4], deeds of family arrangements[5] and other *inter vivos* settlements follow the same general rules and principles of construction. If it is intended that the law of Scotland should apply in the interpretation of such deeds specific provision to that effect should be inserted unless the *lex situs* would prima facie apply because land or buildings are involved.

1 See AGENCY AND MANDATE, vol 1, para 604.
2 Ie under the Statutory Declaration Act 1835 (c 62).
3 See CONVEYANCING, INCLUDING REGISTRATION OF TITLE, vol 6 para 466 (deeds of entail), paras 514–517 (servitudes), para 586 (contracts of ground annual), para 638 (floating charges), and para 714, note 8 (contracts of marriage).
4 See BANKRUPTCY, vol 2, paras 1456 ff.
5 See WILLS AND SUCCESSION, vol 25, para 1028.

(5) WILLS AND OTHER TESTAMENTARY WRITINGS

(a) Principles of Construction

1263. Ascertainment of intention. It has already been noted that in the case of a will or testamentary writing the object of interpretation is to establish the intentions of the testator[1]. Deeds of a testamentary nature receive a more liberal interpretation than obligations *inter vivos*[2]. Words in latter-wills, or donations or dispositions in contemplation of imminent death, are more favourably to be interpreted, and to be further extended than in deeds *inter vivos*[3].

In the First Division Lord President Emslie said:

> 'What we have to decide is whether the holograph writing, properly construed in the light of the agreed circumstances only, envinces a present concluded testamentary intention; or whether . . . it falls to be regarded as a mere note or memorandum of points on which she [the testator] wanted her solicitor's advice with a view to his taking instructions for certain changes to be made in her last will and settlement'[4].

The particular holograph writing found in the testator's desk after her death in an envelope addressed to her solicitor was held to be no more than an *aide-memoire*.

A will written in pencil by a friend, then signed by the testator in ink before three witnesses, was held to have valid testamentary effect[5], although two of the witnesses were beneficiaries. Where a printed will form was completed in his own handwriting and signed by the testator without witnesses it was held that, although a borderline case, there was just enough in the holograph parts of the document to embody the essentials of a will.

The word 'to' is not sufficient to indicate testamentary intention, but the word 'residue' had an undoubted testamentary connotation[6]. Subscription is always required[7]. In *Lorimer's Executors v Hird* Lord President Clyde said:

> 'The rigid statutory rules applicable in cases of attestation of deeds, designed to protect parties against fraud, have no place in regard to a holograph document . . . But in regard to holograph documents of a testamentary character subscription by the granter is essential to satisfy the requirements of a completed testamentary act'[8].

Where a testator has made a probative will drawn on his or her behalf by solicitors and subsequently subscribes a holograph testamentary writing it is not always clear whether the deeds are to be read together[9], or the later holograph writing has revoked the earlier probative will[10]. Where two provisions of a will are totally irreconcilable, so that they cannot possibly stand together, the last written, or that which is posterior in local position, must be considered as indicating a subsequent intention, and must prevail, if there is nothing in the context or general scope of the instrument which leads to a different decision[11]. Extrinsic evidence to aid the interpretation of a will is rarely admitted[12].

A useful list of decisions on applications to determine whether a writing is entitled to receive effect as a completed will, or whether it is merely deliberative is found in Currie on *Confirmation*[13]. The decisions have been divided helpfully between those held to be testamentary and those held not to be testamentary. Lord McLaren laid down four propositions regarding the interpretation of unauthenticated interlineations and deletions which are still followed today[14].

1 W M Gloag *The Law of Contract* (2nd edn, 1929) ch XXII. See generally WILLS AND SUCCESSION, vol 25, paras 817 ff.
2 Erskine *Institute* III,9,14.
3 Stair *Institutions* IV,42,21.
4 *Jamieson's Executors* 1982 SC 1 at 3, 1982 SLT 198 at 199. See also vol 25, para 765.
5 *Simson v Simson* (1883) 10 R 1247. For examples of court decisions on testamentary intention, see D M Walker *Principles of Scottish Private Law* (4th edn, 1989) vol 4, pp 150, 151.
6 *Gillies v Glasgow Royal Infirmary* 1960 SC 438, 1961 SLT 93.
7 *Taylor's Executrices v Thom* 1914 SC 79, 1913 2 SLT 337.
8 *Lorimer's Executors v Hird* 1959 SLT (Notes) 8 at 8, OH.
9 *Morton's Executor* 1985 SLT 14.
10 *Macrorie's Executors v McLaren* 1984 SLT 271.
11 J McLaren *Law of Wills and Succession as administered in Scotland* (3rd edn, 1894) I, paras 645 ff. See also vol 25, para 826.
12 The rules for admitting such evidence are found in *McLaren* I, para 680, but originate from Sir James Wigram, Vice Chancellor, and appear in his book, *Rules of Law respecting the Admission of Extrinsic Evidence in Aid of the Interpretation of Wills* (5th edn, 1914). The rules may also be found in W M Gloag and R C Henderson *Introduction to the Law of Scotland* (9th edn, 1987 ed A B Wilkinson and W A Wilson) para 43.11. See also vol 25, paras 827 ff.
13 J G Currie *The Confirmation of Executors in Scotland* (7th edn, 1973 ed A E McRae) pp 61–63.
14 *Pattison's Trustees v University of Edinburgh* (1888) 16 R 73, OH.

1264. Restrictions affecting testamentary writings. The restrictions which affect the right of an individual testator to settle his or her property by *mortis causa* deed may be common law restrictions or statutory restrictions.

Common law restrictions include the legal rights of spouses and children[1]. Irrespective of the terms of a will the legal rights of *jus relicti* or *jus relictae* and legitim are exigible. Prior rights in terms of the Succession (Scotland) Act 1964 (c 41) are exigible only on intestacy and do not affect the interpretation of a will, although they may affect a decision by a surviving spouse as to whether or not to accept the provisions of a will in his or her favour[2]. Claims under legal rights may be discharged prior to the death of the testator[3], and may be restricted in amount if the testator invests his or her wealth in heritage, which for this purpose includes heritable securities[4]. If a testator wishes to create a liferent or annuity provision which is alimentary in favour of a beneficiary named in the will, it is essential that a trust be created[5]. An alimentary liferent may be declined before, but not after, enjoyment of it has commenced[6].

Statutory restrictions on the testator's freedom to test are found in the Accumulations Act 1800 (c 98) (the Thellusson Act), which was repealed and re-enacted with modifications in the Trusts (Scotland) Act 1961, which prohibit the accumulation of income beyond four periods, increased to six periods by section 6 of the Law Reform (Miscellaneous Provisions) (Scotland) Act 1966 (c 19)[7].

A further restriction on the duration of liferents is found in section 18 of the Law Reform (Miscellaneous Provisions) (Scotland) Act 1968 (c 70), which applies only to deeds executed on or after 25 November 1968 and affects the entitlement to a liferent interest of a person who was not living or *in utero* at the date of the deed coming into operation[8].

1 As to legal rights, see WILLS AND SUCCESSION, vol 25, paras 772 ff.
2 *Kerr* 1968 SLT (Sh Ct) 61. See also M C Meston *The Succession (Scotland) Act 1964* (3rd edn, 1982) pp 37, 38, and vol 25, para 693.
3 See vol 25, para 775.
4 See vol 25, para 810. For other devices, see *Buchanan v Buchanan* (1876) 3 R 556 (*inter vivos* trust); *Allan v Stark* (1901) 8 SLT 468, OH (donation to deceased's sister before death).
5 *White's Trustees v Whyte* (1877) 4 R 786; *Forbes's Trustees v Tennant* 1926 SC 294, 1926 SLT 135.
6 *Chrystal's Trustees v Haldane* 1960 SC 127 at 133, 1961 SLT 25 at 27, per Lord President Clyde. See also *Ford v Ford's Trustees* 1961 SC 122, 1961 SLT 128, OH.
7 See the Trusts (Scotland) Act 1961 (c 57), s 5, and vol 25, paras 768, 769. For general comment on accumulations of income, see J McLaren *Law of Wills and Succession as administered in Scotland* (3rd edn, 1894) I, ch XV, section III, and D M Walker *Principles of Scottish Private Law* (4th edn, 1989) vol IV, pp 29, 30 and 190, 191.
8 See vol 25, para 770.

(b) Presumptions

1265. *Conditio si testator sine liberis decesserit* and *conditio si institutus sine liberis decesserit.* *Conditio si testator sine liberis decesserit* is a method of revocation of wills by operation of law[1]. If a man's will does not deal with children it is presumed to have been revoked by the subsequent birth of a child whether legitimate or illegitimate[2].

Conditio si institutus sine liberis decesserit means that where there is a bequest to descendants or to nephews and nieces there is a presumption that their issue, though not mentioned, may take if the parents have predeceased[3].

1 See WILLS AND SUCCESSION, vol 25, paras 751–754.
2 See the Law Reform (Miscellaneous Provisions (Scotland) Act 1968 (c 70), s 6(2), (3) (repealed), and s 22(5), and vol 25, paras 663, 664. A deed executed before 25 November 1968 is not affected by the subsequent birth of an illegitimate child. See also W M Gloag and R C Henderson *Introduction to the Law of Scotland* (9th edn, 1987 ed A B Wilkinson and W A Wilson) para 43.8.
3 *Gloag and Henderson* para 43.28. See also vol 25, paras 894 ff.

1266. Common calamity. Where two persons have died in circumstances indicating that they died simultaneously or rendering it uncertain which, if either, of them survived the other, it is presumed that the younger person survived the elder, with two exceptions:
(1) where the persons were husband and wife, it is presumed that neither survived the other; and
(2) where the presumption would lead to intestacy if the younger survived the elder but not if the elder survived the younger, it is to be presumed that the elder survived the younger[1].
The standard of proof is a balance of probabilities on all the evidence[2].

1 See the Succession (Scotland) Act 1964 (c 41), s 31, and WILLS AND SUCCESSION, vol 25, paras 657, 658. This provision should overcome the problems which arose in *Ross's Judicial Factor v Martin* 1954 SC 18, 1954 SLT 49.
2 *Lamb v Lord Advocate* 1976 SC 110, 1976 SLT 151.

1267. Presumption against intestacy and presumption of legality. There is a general presumption against intestacy, but its force depends on the circumstances of each case. If a testator when he makes a will deals with part only of his estate, the court will not attempt to deal with the residue of his estate. In such a case it must be assumed that the testator wished to deal with part only of his estate. If, on the other hand, the construction of the will is doubtful, the court acts on the presumption that the testator did not intend to die wholly or partially intestate. The court would incline towards a construction of testacy[1].

There is also a presumption of legality and of knowledge on the part of the testator[2].

1 50 *Halsbury's Laws of England* (4th edn) paras 440–442.
2 Ibid, paras 443, 444.

1268. *Falsa demonstratio non nocet.* An erroneous description does not injure or vitiate a document[1]. In describing legatees there are various presumptions in law and terms which have precise meanings in law:

(1) 'issue' includes all descendants in the direct line, unless the context indicates a more restricted interpretation[2];
(2) 'children' excludes grandchildren[3];
(3) if a bequest is to a number of persons or a class the presumption is for equal division *per capita* among all the persons or members of the class[4];
(4) the use of the word 'between' may be interpreted as meaning 'among'[5];
(5) the words 'heirs' is now likely to be construed as the persons who would succeed to the property on intestacy under the Succession (Scotland) Act 1964[6];
(6) 'next of kin' is indefinite and its interpretation may vary according to the context[7];
(7) 'blood relations' is wider than 'next of kin' and includes any person having a traceable relationship by blood with the person referred to[8];
(8) 'dependants' is too vague to receive effect[9].

In the case of deeds executed on or after 25 November 1968, unless the contrary intention appears, any relationship for succession purposes includes one which is illegitimate[10]. The status of illegitimacy is effectively abolished[11], with limited exceptions relating to domicile, adoption and hereditary titles and dignities[12]. Accordingly in the case of deeds executed on or after 8 December 1986, the biological relationship is what counts, unless the contrary intention is demonstrated by the use of the words 'legitimate', 'illegitimate' or others to like effect indicating the granter's intention[13]. In any deed whereby property is conveyed or under which succession arises executed after the making of an adoption order, unless the contrary intention appears, adopted children are regarded as the natural children of the adopting parents and not of the natural parents[14]. In the case of a testamentary deed in which adopted persons might have an interest the date of execution is deemed to be the date of death of the testator[15]. The word 'children' now includes adopted children unless they are specifically excluded[16].

The term 'majority' in deeds executed before 1 January 1970 means twenty-one; in deeds dated on or after 1 January 1970 'majority' means eighteen[17].

1 As to *falsa demonstratio non nocet*, see WILLS AND SUCCESSION, vol 25, para 824.
2 *Stewart's Trustees v Whitelaw* 1926 SC 701, 1926 SLT 400; *Stirling's Trustees v Legal and General Assurance Society Ltd* 1957 SLT 73, OH. See also vol 25, para 877.
3 *Adam's Executrix v Maxwell* 1921 SC 418, 1921 1 SLT 221.
4 See vol 25, para 888.
5 *Bogie's Trustees v Christie* (1882) 9 R 453; *Campbell's Trustee v Welsh* 1952 SC 343, 1952 SLT 352.
6 See vol 25, paras 689 ff. See also para 878.
7 *Borthwick's Trustees v Borthwick* 1955 SC 227. See also vol 25, para 879.
8 *Cunninghame v Cunninghame's Trustees* 1961 SC 32, 1961 SLT 194.
9 *Robertson's Judicial Factor v Robertson* 1968 SLT 32, OH.
10 See vol 25, paras 663, 884.
11 See vol 25, para 664.
12 See FAMILY LAW, vol 10, paras 1185–1187.
13 See generally vol 25, para 886.
14 See the Succession (Scotland) Act 1964 (c 41), s 23(2), and vol 25, paras 713, 714.
15 See vol 25, para 882.

16 *Spencer's Trustees v Ruggles* 1981 SC 289, 1982 SLT 165.
17 See the Age of Majority (Scotland) Act 1969 (c 39), s 1, and vol 25, para 885.

(c) Vesting and Repugnancy

1269. Vesting and repugnancy generally. The principles of vesting are dealt with elsewhere in this work[1]. In respect of repugnancy, as far as possible the court will give effect to the full intention of a testator, but where a condition or limitation attached to a bequest is repugnant to the right of property given in the leading words of the bequest the qualifying condition or limitation will be disregarded. Examples are:

(1) an absolute legacy qualified by a subsequent declaration that it is to be alimentary[2];
(2) an unqualified gift of an annuity followed by a qualifying direction to the trustees[3];
(3) a right to fee given in the will equally among three children followed by a codicil restricting the interest of one son to interest[4].

There is a clear distinction between repugnancy and a gift which is subject to conditions. In the latter case the conditions must apply[5].

1 See WILLS AND SUCCESSION, vol 25, paras 902 ff.
2 *Watson's Trustees v Watson* 1913 SC 1133, 1913 2 SLT 172.
3 *Dow v Kilgour's Trustees* (1877) 4 R 403.
4 *Graham v Graham's Trustees* 1927 SC 388, 1927 SLT 237.
5 *Gore-Browne-Henderson's Trustees v Grenfell* 1968 SC 73, 1968 SLT 237.

(d) Ineffectual Conditions or Directions

1270. Conditions contrary to public policy. In Scotland it is a universal rule that a provision in a will such as a legacy or bequest, subject to a condition or direction which is unlawful or *contra bonos mores* is nevertheless effectual[1], the condition being either held to be *pro non scripto* or regarded as having been satisfied[2]. For example, conditions which attempt to interfere with normal family relationships, a wife should not live with her husband[3], a child should not live with his parents when their character was not open to criticism[4], absolute or total restraints on marriage[5] as distinct from 'reasonable restraints' to marry, or not to marry, a particular person[6]. Such conditions or directions will not be enforced. The *Sturrock* case illustrates in this respect a different approach to restraint on marriage between the English and the Scottish courts. The Lord Justice-Clerk refers particularly to the distinction between conditions precedent and subsequent so far as married status is concerned[7]. It is arguable that the courts today would adopt a more liberal attitude than in the past in the interpretation of such restrictions affecting marriage or cohabitation. Difficulties will continue to arise not necessarily in understanding the meaning of a qualifying condition but in the effectiveness of such a condition.

The court will deny effect to conditions or directions which amount to a waste of money and confer no benefit[8]. In *Sutherland's Trustee v Verschoyle*[9] the Lord Justice-Clerk Grant said 'it is only in the most exceptional circumstances that the courts will interfere with the expressed wishes of a testator', but in a special case it was agreed to set aside a direction by the testatrix to provide a house of a certain size and dignity in St Andrews to display her valuable art collection because it was of insufficient merit.

1 See WILLS AND SUCCESSION, vol 25, para 864.
2 J McLaren *Law of Wills and Succession as administered in Scotland* (3rd edn, 1894) I, para 1094; Bell *Principles* s 1785; *Dunbar v Scott's Trustees* (1872) 10 M 982.
3 *Wilkinson v Wilkinson* (1871) LR 12 Eq 604.
4 *Grant's Trustees v Grant* (1898) 25 R 929.
5 See vol 25, para 866.
6 Stair *Institutions* I, 3, 7; Bell *Principles* s 1785; *Sturrock v Rankin's Trustees* (1875) 2 R 850; *Kidd v Kidd* (1863) 2 M 227.
7 *Sturrock v Rankin's Trustees* (1875) 2 R 850 at 853.
8 *M'Caig v Glasgow University* 1907 SC 231, 14 SLT 600, regarding proposed statutes in Oban; *Aitken's Trustees v Aitken* 1927 SC 374, 1927 SLT 308, regarding the erection of an equestrian bronze statue in Musselburgh.
9 *Sutherland's Trustee v Verschoyle* 1968 SLT 43.

1271. Uncertainty. For a provision in a will to be void for uncertainty, it must be utterly impossible to put a meaning upon it[1]. The courts will if at all possible attempt to favour one construction of an ambiguous gift more than another to avoid intestacy[1]. It is possible that extrinsic evidence might be admitted by the court to resolve an ambiguity in the testamentary writings[2]. If, however, the terms are so vague either as to the subject matter or the intended beneficiary as to be incapable of ascertainment the bequest will fail.

Difficulty arises where trustees are given discretionary powers in such wide terms as to imply delegation of the testator's power to test. In *Anderson v Smoke*[3] a father directed his daughters to dispose of the balance of his estate 'in any way they should think proper'. This direction was held to be void for uncertainty and the sum fell into the residue of the father's estate. The testator may select a particular class of persons or objects from which the beneficiaries are to be selected and thereafter permit his trustees or a particular person to exercise the final choice. Institutions for charitable and benevolent purposes in Glasgow or the neighbourhood thereof were sustained as valid[4], but 'for such charitable or public purposes as my trustees think proper' was held to be too wide[5]. There is only a narrow distinction between these cases.

In the construction of wills where the objects are 'charitable', the courts appear to regard 'charitable' by itself as sufficient, but not so if the word is amplified, for example charitable or other deserving institutions in connection with the City of Glasgow as my trustees shall think fit' was held to be too vague to receive effect as it was interpreted as meaning 'charitable or not charitable'[6]. The words 'public'[7], 'religious'[8] and 'deserving'[9] are too vague.

Where a testator has nominated a particular charity to receive a legacy difficulty can arise through an inaccurate reference to the charity resulting in competing claims from charities with similar names and objects, for example the National Society for the Prevention of Cruelty to Children and the Scottish National Society for the Prevention of Cruelty to Children[10]. It is evident that in these situations the competing claimants are not always charitable in their approach, but the difficulty arises from an inaccurate description of the charity. In a holograph will a testatrix directed that her estate be divided equally between heart diseases and cancer research[11]. The general intention of the testatrix was upheld by the court. Where a charity had been correctly named but had ceased to exist prior to the date of vesting of the bequest it was held that the bequest had lapsed and the successors under a *cy près* scheme were not entitled to the fund[12]. Where a testator directed that his estate be divided equally among the Royal Naval Benevolent Fund, the Army Benevolent Fund and the Royal Air Force Benevolent Fund it was found after his death that while the second and third existed the first did not, it was held that the claims of both the Royal Naval Benevolent Society and the Royal Naval Benevolent Trust be upheld and a *cy près* scheme be prepared[13]. A general charitable intention was also upheld in the case of two incorrectly named charities and a *cy près* scheme allowed[14].

It is an accepted rule of construction in both Scotland and England, which applies to all deeds and not only to wills, that if a description, although blundered, is sufficient to identify the person or property intended, the words which are incorrect or untrue may be disregarded[15]. Lord Justice-Clerk Moncrieff said 'If, as has often been said, there is reasonable certainty there is no uncertainty'[16]. A legacy is valid, although there may be an error in the name or designation of the legatee, if, from the whole deed or circumstances connected with it, it is sufficiently plain who is the person meant[17].

The effect of testamentary dispositions on special destinations is now subject to statutory provision which applies only to deeds executed on or after 10 September 1964[18]. Such testamentary deeds do not have the effect to evacuate a special destination unless they contain a specific reference to the destination and a declared intention on the part of the testator to evacuate it. A strict construction is now placed on attempts to evacuate a special destination[19].

1 50 *Halsbury's Laws of England* (4th edn) para 448.
2 See WILLS AND SUCCESSION, vol 25, para 830. See also *Re Williams, Wiles v Madgin* [1985] 1 All ER 964, [1985] 1 WLR 905; *Rabin v Gerson Berger Association Ltd* [1985] 1 All ER 1041, [1985] 1 WLR 595 (both English decisions).
3 *Anderson v Smoke* (1898) 25 R 493, 5 SLT 309.
4 *Hills v Burns* (1826) 2 W & S 80, HL.
5 *Blair v Duncan* (1901) 4 F (HL) 1, 9 SLT 390.
6 *Campbell's Trustees v Campbell* 1921 SC (HL) 12, 1921 1 SLT 50. See also the minority opinion of Lord Dundas in the earlier hearing, *Campbell's Trustees v Campbell* 1920 SC 297, 1920 1 SLT 188, before the Second Division, overturned by the House of Lords.
7 *Turnbull's Trustees v Lord Advocate* 1918 SC (HL) 88, 1918 1 SLT 112.
8 *Macintyre v Grimond's Trustees* (1905) 7 F (HL) 90, 12 SLT 760.
9 *Campbell's Trustees v Campbell* 1921 SC (HL) 12, 1921 1 SLT 50.
10 See vol 25, para 829.
11 *Ballingall's Judicial Factor v Hamilton* 1973 SLT 236.
12 *Fergusson's Trustees v Buchanan* 1973 SLT 41.
13 *Pomphrey's Trustees v Royal Naval Benevolent Trust* 1967 SLT 61, OH.
14 *Cumming's Executors v Cumming* 1967 SLT 68, OH.
15 See para 1268 above, and vol 25, para 824. See also 50 *Halsbury's Laws of England* (4th edn) paras 455–457; *Macfarlane's Trustees v Henderson* (1878) R 288.
16 *Macfarlane's Trustees v Henderson* (1878) 6 R 288 at 289.
17 Ie *dummodo constet de persona*: J Trayner *Latin Maxims and Phrases* (4th edn, 1894).
18 See the Succession (Scotland) Act 1964 (c 41), s 30, and vol 25, paras 755–758.
19 Ie as illustrated by *Stirling's Trustees* 1977 SC 139, 1977 SLT 229.

1272–1300. Powers of trustees. General powers of trustees are found in the Trusts (Scotland) Act 1921[1]. Unless the contrary be expressed, all trusts are held to include power to any trustee to resign office and to assume new trustees[2]. Provision is also provided for a quorum, and the extent of liability of the trustees[2]. There is a lengthy list of powers held by trustees, where such acts are not at variance with the terms or purposes of the trust[3]. Many of these powers are therefore available to trustees although the trust deed makes no mention of them.

Investment powers were altered separately by the Trustee Investments Act 1961 (c 62), which superimposes further powers regarding supervision of investments held by trustees[4]. If the testator holds shares in private companies there may be conflict between the provisions of his will and the memorandum and articles of association of the company which would prevail.

1 Ie under the Trusts (Scotland) Act 1921 (c 58), ss 3, 4.
2 See ibid, s 3, and TRUSTS, TRUSTEES AND JUDICIAL FACTORS, vol 24, paras 141 ff.
3 See ibid, s 4, and vol 24, para 202.
4 See vol 24, paras 204–208.

INVESTOR PROTECTION

	PARA
1. THE FINANCIAL SERVICES ACT 1986	1301
(1) Introduction	1301
(2) The Regulatory Structure under the Financial Services Act 1986	1306
(a) Introduction	1306
(b) Authorisation	1309
(c) Automatic Authorisation	1315
(d) Exempted Persons	1321
(e) Interdict and Restitution Orders	1324
(3) Collective Investment Schemes	1325
(4) Conduct of Investment Business	1331
(5) The SIB Rules: The New Settlement	1340
(a) Introduction	1340
(b) S I B Statements of Principle	1342
(A) The Principles	1342
(B) The Principles and Fiduciary Duties . .	1353
(c) The Core Conduct of Business Rules . . .	1356
(A) Introduction	1356
(B) Independence	1357
(C) Information and Advice	1363
(D) Advertising	1366
(E) Relationship with Customers . . .	1371
(F) Dealing with Customers	1379
(G) Market Integrity	1387
(H) Administration	1391
(d) The Financial Supervision Rules	1402
(e) The Clients' Money Regulations	1409
(6) Investors' Remedies	1410
(7) The Financial Services Tribunal	1416
(8) Compensation	1420
(9) Conclusion	1423
2. INSIDER DEALING	1501
(1) Introduction	1501
(2) Dealings in Securities of a Company by Individuals who are connected with the Company	1503
(3) Dealings in Securities of another Company by an Individual who is connected with a Company	1511
(4) Dealings by 'Tippees'	1512
(5) Dealings by Individuals contemplating Takeover Offers . .	1514
(6) Dealings by 'Tippees' from Individuals contemplating Takeover Offers	1516
(7) Counselling or procuring Others to deal . . .	1517
(8) Communicating Information	1518
(9) Abuse of Information obtained in an Official Capacity . .	1519
(10) Off-market Deals in Advertised Securities . . .	1523
(11) Actions not prohibited	1526
(12) Price Stabilisation	1531
(13) Trustees and Personal Representatives	1532
(14) Investigations and Legal Proceedings	1533
(15) Proposals for Reform	1536

The General Editors acknowledge with gratitude invaluable advice, assistance and materials given by Lynn Hamilton and R B Ferguson in the preparation of Part 1 of this title.

1. THE FINANCIAL SERVICES ACT 1986

(1) INTRODUCTION

1301. The Financial Services Act 1986. The Financial Services Act 1986 represents the most comprehensive overhaul of investor protection legislation for forty years. The Act provides that no person may carry on, or purport to carry on, investment business[1] in the United Kingdom unless he is either an authorised person[2] or an exempted person[3]. Any person who carries on, or purports to carry on, investment business in contravention of this prohibition is guilty of an offence and liable on conviction on indictment to imprisonment for a term not exceeding two years or to a fine or both, or on summary conviction to imprisonment for a term not exceeding six months or to a fine not exceeding the statutory maximum or both[4].

This title outlines the background to, and the range of persons and products affected by, the Act, explains the various routes to obtaining authorisation and examines the scope and nature of the regulatory framework imposed on authorised persons and the consequent protection given to investors. It also seeks to examine and comment on the development in the form and content of the regime under the Act in the first few years of its life.

This part of the title does not attempt to deal extensively with Parts IV to VII of the Act, which make provision regarding the official listing of securities[5], offers of unlisted securities[6], takeover offers[7] and insider dealing[8]. Nor does the title consider, except where relevant, the various legislative provisions applying in insurance, company or banking law whose underlying purpose is to secure a measure of protection for investors.

1 For the meaning of 'investment business', see para 1307 below.
2 Ie an authorised person under the Financial Services Act 1986 (c 60), Pt I, Ch III (ss 7–34): see paras 1309 ff below.
3 Ibid, s 3. As to exempt persons, see Pt I, Ch IV (ss 35–46), and paras 1321–1323 below.
4 Financial Services Act 1986, s 4(1)(a), (b). The statutory maximum is £2,000: Interpretation Act 1978 (c 30), s 5, Sch 1 (amended by the Criminal Justice Act 1988 (c 33), s 170(1), Sch 15, para 58(b)), by reference to the Criminal Procedure (Scotland) Act 1975 (c 21), s 289B(6) (added by the Criminal Law Act 1977 (c 45), s 63(1), Sch 11, para 5, and substituted by the Criminal Justice Act 1982 (c 48), s 44(2)), and the Increase of Criminal Penalties etc (Scotland) Order 1984, SI 1984/526, art 3. It is a defence for the accused to prove that he took all reasonable precautions and exercised all due diligence to avoid committing the offence: Financial Services Act 1986, s 4(2).
5 Ibid, Pt IV (ss 142–157).
6 Ibid, Pt V (ss 158–171).
7 Ibid, Pt VI (s 172).
8 Ibid, Pt VII (ss 173–178). As to insider dealing, see Part 2 of this title, paras 1501 ff below.

1302. Earlier legislation. The Financial Services Act 1986 replaces the provisions of the Prevention of Fraud (Investments) Act 1958, which itself superseded the Prevention of Fraud (Investments) Act 1939 (c 16). Both these Acts regulated by means of a system of licences and exemptions granted by the then Board or Department of Trade a limited section of the financial services market, namely those persons who dealt in or arranged deals in securities. The 1958 Act also provided for the authorisation of unit trusts[1], but contained only a limited degree of regulation in this area. The regulatory net of the Financial Services Act 1986, however, is far more widely cast, extending to all persons who carry on investment business[2].

1 See the Prevention of Fraud (Investments) Act 1958 (c 45), s 17, Sch 1 (repealed).
2 For the meaning of 'investment business', see para 1307 below.

1303. Development of the law. Despite the exclusion of certain purposes and activities[1], the scope of the Financial Services Act 1986 (c 60) remains far wider than that of the previous legislation, and it is worth considering the background to this radical extension of the previous regime[2].

Whilst the City has always been subject to change, the latter half of the twentieth century has perhaps been the period of most rapid development. The investment world had altered considerably since the passing of the Prevention of Fraud (Investments) Act 1958 (c 45). New markets, such as the Unlisted Securities Market ('USM'), the Over the Counter Market ('OTC') and the new markets for derivative products such as futures and options had emerged, and new players, many of them large international financial conglomerates, had joined the game. The range and complexity of investment vehicles had increased dramatically, with a commensurate increase in the risks (and rewards) presented to investors[3]. As far back as 1974, when the Department of Trade sent out questionnaires to interested parties, it was recognised that the 1958 Act did not provide adequate regulation of the securities market. In 1977 the government published a consultative document[4] containing proposals for a revision of the 1958 Act itself, and in particular its extension to investment advisers and improvements in the licensing and enforcement provisions, as well as amendments to the Licensed Dealers (Conduct of Business) Rules 1960[5], made under the Act.

A change of government in 1979 led to a reduction in priority for this subject. However, following the collapse in the late 1970s and early 1980s of several licensed dealers in securities and a subsequent series of scandals in the commodities and insurance markets[6], there was renewed pressure for a comprehensive regime for the protection of investors, which manifested itself in various ways. The Stock Exchange's 'Big Bang', which from 27 October 1986 saw the abolition of brokers' scale fees and the emergence of dual capacity institutions acting both as stockbrokers and as market makers, took place during the gestation period of the new regulatory regime, as did the reforms, both statutory and self-regulatory, at Lloyd's[7].

1 For these exclusions, see para 1307 below.
2 See R R Pennington *The Law of the Investment Markets* (1990).
3 See generally J Plender and P Wallace *The Square Mile — A Guide to the New City of London* (1985).
4 *Amendment to the Prevention of Fraud (Investments) Act 1958* (Cmnd 6893) (1977).
5 Licensed Dealers (Conduct of Business) Rules 1960, SI 1960/1216 (revoked). See now the Licensed Dealers (Conduct of Business) Rules 1983, SI 1983/585.
6 See M Clarke *Regulating the City: Competition, Scandal and Reform* (1986).
7 See the Lloyd's Act 1982 (c xiv).

1304. The Gower Report. 'Big Bang' and the reforms at Lloyd's were still to crystalise when in July 1981 the government appointed Professor L C B Gower:

'(a) to consider the statutory protection now required by (i) private and (ii) business investors in securities and other property, including investors through unit trusts and open-ended investment companies...; (b) to consider the need for statutory control of dealers in securities, investment consultants and investment managers; and (c) to advise on the need for new legislation'.

Professor Gower speedily prepared and published in January 1982 a discussion document[1] and invited comments. Part 1 of the Gower Report[2] was published two years later. Some of Professor Gower's provisional proposals which had been contained in the discussion document were revised to take account of comments received, but his views regarding the basic structure of a new regulatory regime remained unchanged.

He proposed the introduction of a new regulatory system, replacing the Prevention of Fraud (Investments) Act 1958 (c 45) with a new Investor Protection Act which would make it a criminal offence for a person to carry on any type of investment business (a term which would be widely defined and flexible) unless he was registered[3]. Professor Gower accepted the logic for a self-standing Securities Commission to fulfil the overall regulatory and surveillance function, but, due to practical and political considerations, did not recommend its establishment. Instead he recommended that the government's role be left to the Department of Trade and Industry. However, he proposed that the functions of that department be undertaken by a self-standing commission appointed by the Secretary of State if it became apparent that a substantial volume of day-to-day governmental regulation and supervision would have to be undertaken by the department.

Under the Gower proposals the department (or commission) would have had the power to make rules of conduct binding on those who registered directly with it, and would also have had power to recognise 'self-regulatory agencies' with which those providing financial services could register as an alternative to registering directly with the department. These agencies, which were to be based on existing professional and commercial groupings, would not be recognised unless they satisfied certain conditions, including having rules which would ensure protection to investors at least equivalent to those of the department or commission — the so-called 'equivalence test' — and the ability to monitor their observance.

1 *Review of Investor Protection: A Discussion Document by Prof L C B Gower* (1982).
2 *Review of Investor Protection, Part 1* (the Gower Report) (Cmnd 9125) (1984).
3 Ibid, para 2.11.

1305. The government's White Paper. Before Part 2 of the Gower Report (which was to contain draft legislation) was published, the government in January 1985 issued its White Paper[1]. Overtaken by developments, Professor Gower had to content himself in the second part of his report[2] with commenting on the White Paper which, in the main, followed the recommendations of his first report[3].

In relation to the overall supervisory body, however, the White Paper adopted the recommendations not of Professor Gower but of the two City Advisory Groups which had been set up in mid-1984 under Mr Martin Jacomb and Mr Marshall Field respectively[4]. These recommendations were that governmental powers over the authorisation and regulation of financial services should be delegated to two private sector bodies, provisionally named the Securities and Investments Board ('SIB') and the Marketing of Investments Board ('MIB'). These boards would have the powers which Professor Gower had envisaged would be exercised by the Department of Trade, namely the power to promulgate conduct of business rules to apply to persons who were directly authorised by (rather than registered with) the boards and to recognise self-regulatory agencies (referred to in the White Paper as 'self-regulating organisations' ('SROs')), which would oversee the conduct of certain sections of the financial services market.

Shortly after the publication of the White Paper these two bodies were established, the SIB under the chairmanship of Sir Kenneth Berrill and the other, in the form of an Organising Committee ('MIBOC') under the chairmanship of Sir Mark Weinberg. The two bodies merged in 1986 to form the Securities and Investments Board Limited[5].

It was acknowledged in the White Paper[6] and during the parliamentary passage of the Financial Services Bill that to provide for a statutory power of authorisation and regulation to be given to a private sector body was unprecedented, but stress was laid on the safeguards which would be provided[7]. These safeguards, later incorporated in the Financial Services Act 1986, included provisions giving powers to the Secretary of State in relation to the appointment and dismissal of members of the Securities and Investments Board[8], the imposition of a requirement on the board to report annually to the Secretary of State and hence to Parliament[9], the establishment of a Financial Services Tribunal to hear appeals against decisions of the board[10], and the residual power of control over the board which the Secretary of State would exercise[11].

Although these safeguards were incorporated in the Bill as first presented to Parliament, there was an obvious omission so far as Scotland was concerned. Empowered to determine within the framework given by the Financial Services Act 1986 whether any particular organisation should be recognised as a 'second tier' regulatory body and to prescribe the rules on which all such regulatory bodies' regulations would require to be based, the SIB was obviously a powerful institution. Yet as the board is a limited company incorporated in England, its use or interpretation of its powers could be challenged in legal proceedings only in the English courts. It was due only to strong lobbying, particularly from the Law Society of Scotland, that a provision was introduced into the Bill that proceedings arising out of any act or omission of the SIB — and, for good measure, The Stock Exchange — could be brought in the High Court in England or the Court of Session[12].

1 *Financial Services in the United Kingdom: A new Framework for Investor Protection* (Cmnd 9432) (1985).
2 *Review of Investor Protection, Part 2* (the Gower Report) (1985).
3 *Review of Investor Protection, Part 1* (the Gower Report) (Cmnd 9125) (1984).
4 See *Financial Services in the United Kingdom: A new Framework for Investor Protection*, para 2.18.
5 See ibid, para 5.3, and *Review of Investor Protection, Part 2*, ch 2, para 2.03–5.
6 See *Financial Services in the United Kingdom: A new Framework for Investor Protection*, para 5.7.
7 See ibid, para 5.8, and *Review of Investor Protection, Part 2*, ch 8.
8 See the Financial Services Act 1986 (c 60), s 114(1), Sch 7, para 1.
9 See ibid, s 117(1), (2).
10 See ibid, Pt I, Ch IX (ss 96–101), and paras 1416–1419 below.
11 See ibid, s 115 (amended by the Companies Act 1989 (c 40), s 206(1), Sch 23, para 13(2), (3)), and the Financial Services Act 1986, s 121(2), (3)(a) (amended by the Companies Act 1989, Sch 23, para 15(3)).
12 Financial Services Act 1986, s 188(1) (substituted, so as to extend also to acts or omissions of recognised self-regulating organisations, by the Companies Act 1989, s 200(1)).

(2) THE REGULATORY STRUCTURE UNDER THE FINANCIAL SERVICES ACT 1986

1306. Necessity for authorisation. Any person who carries on or purports to carry on investment business[1] in the United Kingdom must be either an authorised person[2] or an exempted person[3].

1 For the meaning of 'investment business', see para 1307 below.

2 'Authorised person' means a person authorised under the Financial Services Act 1986 (c 60), Pt I,
   Ch III (ss 7–34): s 207(1). For the routes to authorisation, see para 1309 below.
3 Ibid, s 3. 'Exempted person' means a person exempted under Pt I, Ch IV (ss 35–46): s 207(1). As
   to exempted persons, see paras 1321–1323 below.

1307. Meaning of 'investment business'. In the Financial Services Act 1986,
subject to the exclusions mentioned below, 'investment business' means the
business of engaging in one or more of the following activities[1]:
(1) dealing in investments[2] (that is, buying, selling, subscribing for or un-
    derwriting them or offering or agreeing to do so, whether as principal or as
    an agent);
(2) making, or offering or agreeing to make, arrangements with a view to
    another person dealing in a particular investment, or with a view to a person
    who participates in the arrangements dealing in investments;
(3) managing or offering or agreeing to manage assets (being assets which
    include investments) belonging to another person;
(4) giving, or offering or agreeing to give, advice to investors or potential
    investors;
(5) establishing, operating or winding up a collective investment scheme[3],
    including acting as trustee of an authorised unit trust scheme[4].
Due to the exceptionally wide definition of 'investment' and 'investment business', it was thought necessary to restrict the width of the operation of the
Financial Services Act 1986 by excluding certain purposes and activities.
Accordingly there is excluded from 'investment business'[5]:
(a) certain 'own account' dealings[6];
(b) investment transactions arranged and advice given between companies in
    the same group or participating in a joint enterprise[7];
(c) investment transactions arranged and advice given in connection with the
    sale or supply of goods or services by industrial or commercial concerns[8];
(d) investment transactions arranged for the purposes of an employees' share
    scheme[9];
(e) investment transactions designed to secure the acquisition of 75 per cent or
    more of the shares in a body corporate other than an open-ended investment
    company[10];
(f) certain investment transactions arranged and advice given by or for a trustee
    or personal representative[11];
(g) certain dealings by permitted persons in the course of non-investment
    business[12];
(h) advice given or arrangements made in the course of a profession or non-
    investment business[13];
(i) advice given in a newspaper or magazine[14] or in a sound, television or cable
    programme[15];
(j) investment transactions arranged for the purposes of an international securi-
    ties self-regulating organisation[16].
There are further exclusions for persons without a permanent place of business
in the United Kingdom[17]. A number of other exemptions are discussed
below[18].
    The drafting of these exclusions gave rise to considerable debate during the
parliamentary passage of the Bill for the Financial Services Act 1986, and various
refinements were introduced at that stage, including the last-minute introduction of the 'permitted person' exclusion in head (g) to cover the dealing activities
of trading and manufacturing companies, corporate treasurers and others which
did not satisfy the exclusions in heads (b) and (c). However, despite these
changes, it soon became apparent that the exclusions finally incorporated in the
Act were deficient in various respects. Early in 1988, before the main elements

of the Act came into force, the Secretary of State exercised his powers to make orders amending the ambit of the Act[19] and the definition of 'collective investment scheme'[20], and subsequent orders have continued the amendment process[21].

1 Financial Services Act 1986 (c 60), s 1(2).
2 For the meaning of 'investment', see para 1308 below.
3 For the meaning of 'collective investment scheme', see the Financial Services Act 1986, s 75(1), and para 1325 below.
4 Ibid, Sch 1, Pt II (paras 12–16). Schedule 1, para 12, was amended by the Financial Services Act 1986 (Restriction of Scope of Act and Meaning of Collective Investment Scheme) Order 1988, SI 1988/803. The Financial Services Act 1986, Sch 1, para 13, was amended by the Financial Services Act 1986 (Restriction of Scope of Act) Order 1988, SI 1988/318, and by SI 1988/803.
5 Financial Services Act 1986, s 1(2).
6 See ibid, Sch 1, para 17 (amended by SI 1988/318, and by the Financial Services Act 1986 (Restriction of Scope of Act and Meaning of Collective Investment Scheme) Order 1990, SI 1990/349, which provides an exclusion from head (1).
7 See the Financial Services Act 1986, Sch 1, para 18, which provides exclusions from heads (1) to (4).
8 See ibid, Sch 1, para 19 (amended by the Financial Services Act 1986 (Extension of Scope of Act and Meaning of Collective Investment Scheme) Order 1988, SI 1988/496, by SI 1990/349, and by the Financial Services Act 1986 (Restriction of Scope of Act and Meaning of Collective Investment Scheme) (No 2) Order 1990, SI 1990/1493), which provides exclusions from heads (1) to (4).
9 See the Financial Services Act 1986, Sch 1, para 20, which provides exclusions from heads (1) and (2).
10 See ibid, Sch 1, para 21 (amended by SI 1988/318), which provides exclusions from heads (1) and (2). For the meaning of 'open-ended investment company', see s 75(8), and para 1325 below.
11 See ibid, Sch 1, para 22, which provides exclusions from heads (1) to (4).
12 See ibid, Sch 1, para 23, which provides an exclusion from head (1).
13 See ibid, Sch 1, para 24 (amended by SI 1988/803), which provides an exclusion from head (4).
14 See ibid, Sch 1, para 25, which provides an exclusion from head (4).
15 See ibid, Sch 1, para 25A (added by SI 1988/318 and substituted by SI 1990/349), which provides an exclusion from head (4).
16 See ibid, Sch 1, para 25B (added by SI 1988/318), which provides an exclusion from head (2).
17 See ibid, Sch 1, Pt IV (paras 26, 27), which provide exclusions from heads (1) and (2).
18 See ibid, ss 42–46, and paras 1321, 1323, 1361, below.
19 Ibid, s 2.
20 Ibid, s 75(9).
21 See the orders cited in the notes above.

1308. Meaning of 'investment'. In the Financial Services Act 1986, 'investment' means any asset, right or interest falling within the following heads[1]:
  (1) shares and stock in the share capital of a company or other body (but not a building society, industrial and provident society or credit union, although building society deferred shares are included);
  (2) debentures, debenture stock, loan stock, bonds, certificates of deposit and other instruments creating or acknowledging indebtedness (not being instruments within head (3)), but excluding (a) instruments relating to the consideration payable for the supply of goods or services, (b) cheques and other bills of exchange, banker's drafts and letters of credit; (c) banknotes, statements showing the balance in a current, deposit or savings account, leases etc, heritable securities and insurance policies;
  (3) loan stock, bonds and other instruments creating or acknowledging indebtedness issued by or for a government, local authority or public authority, with the same exclusions as in head (2);
  (4) warrants or other instruments entitling the holder to subscribe for investments within heads (1) to (3);

(5) certain certificates or other instruments representing securities, for example those conferring property rights in respect of investments under heads (1) to (4);

(6) units in collective investment schemes, including shares in or securities of an open-ended investment company[2];

(7) options;

(8) futures, excluding rights under contracts made for commercial and not investment purposes;

(9) rights under a contract for differences (for example Stock Exchange index bets);

(10) long-term insurance contracts[3], excluding pure 'protection' policies such as a term assurance with no savings or investment element;

(11) rights to and interests in anything which is an investment under any of heads (1) to (10)[4].

1 Financial Services Act 1986 (c 60), s 1(1).

2 For the meaning of 'collective investment scheme' and 'open-ended investment company', see ibid, ss 75(1), (8), and para 1325 below.

3 'Long-term business' means insurance business of any class specified in the Insurance Companies Act 1982 (c 50), Sch 1 (ie life and annuity, marriage and birth, linked long-term, permanent health, tontines, capital redemption and pension fund management: s 1(1).

4 See the Financial Services Act 1986, Sch 1, Pt I (paras 1–11), which contains many explanatory notes. The note to Sch 1, para 1, was amended, so as to include deferred building society shares within the meaning of the Building Societies Act 1986 (c 53), s 119 (see the Building Societies (Deferred Shares) Order 1991, SI 1991/701), by the Financial Services Act 1986 (Extension of Scope of Act) Order 1991, SI 1991/1104. The Financial Services Act 1986, Sch 1, paras 3, 9, were amended by the Financial Services Act 1986 (Restriction of Scope of Act and Meaning of Collective Investment Scheme) Order 1990, SI 1990/349. The Financial Services Act 1986, Sch 1, para 7, was amended by the Financial Services Act 1986 (Extension of Scope of Act and Meaning of Collective Investment Scheme) Order 1988, SI 1988/496.

(b) Authorisation

1309. Routes to authorisation. Before a person or body may be involved in investment business[1] that person or body must obtain authorisation in one of the ways prescribed by the Financial Services Act 1986. There are three main routes to authorisation.

First, it is possible to obtain direct authorisation from the Securities and Investments Board ('SIB'). Secondly and thirdly, automatic authorisation is conferred on members of self-regulating organisations recognised by the SIB and on members of recognised professional bodies which have been certified by the SIB. These three routes to authorisation are discussed in the paragraphs which follow.

1 For the meaning of 'investment business', see para 1307 above.

1310. Authorisation by the Securities and Investments Board. A person holding an authorisation under the following provisions is an 'authorised person'[1]. An application for authorisation by the Securities and Investments Board ('SIB')[2] may be made by an individual, a body corporate, a partnership or an unincorporated association[3]. The application must be made in such manner as the SIB directs, and must give information as to the investment business which the applicant proposes to carry on and the services he will hold himself out as able to provide, together which such other information as is reasonably required and an address for service in the United Kingdom[4].

The SIB may grant or refuse the application[5], but it must grant the application if it appears that the applicant is a fit and proper person to carry on the investment business and provide the services described in the application[6]. In determining whether to grant or refuse the application the SIB may take into account any matter relating to any person to be employed or concerned in the business, to any business to be carried on in connection with the investment business, and any authorisation to carry on investment business in another member state[7].

The expression 'fit and proper person' is one of the fundamental concepts of the financial services regime. It applies not only to persons authorised by the SIB but also to those authorised by a self-regulating organisation[8]. Although the determination of who is 'fit and proper' will largely be subjective and will vary according to the investment business to be carried on, it is clear that the concept includes considerations of honesty, competence and solvency[9].

1 Financial Services Act 1986 (c 60), s 25. For the meaning of 'authorised person', see para 1306, note 2, above.
2 With certain exceptions the functions of the Secretary of State under ibid, Pt I, Ch II–XII (ss 3–113) are transferred to the SIB: see s 114(1), (4)–(6) (amended by the Companies Act 1989 (c 40), s 193(2)), and the Financial Services Act 1986 (Delegation) Order 1987, SI 1987/942, art 3, Schs 1, 2.
3 Financial Services Act 1986, s 26(1).
4 Ibid, s 26(2). As to withdrawal of the application, see s 30(1).
5 Ibid, s 27(1).
6 Ibid, s 27(2). As to withdrawal of the authorisation, see s 30(1)–(4).
7 See ibid, s 27(3)–(5).
8 As to such organisations, see para 1312 below.
9 See A Whittaker and G Morse *The Financial Services Act 1986: A Guide to the New Law* (1987).

1311. Refusal, withdrawal or suspension of authorisation. The Securities and Investments Board ('SIB') may at any time withdraw or suspend an authorisation granted by it if it appears:
(1) that the holder is not a fit and proper person[1] to carry on the investment business which he is carrying on or proposing to carry on, or
(2) that the holder has contravened any provision of the Financial Services Act 1986 or rules or regulations made under it (including, where the holder is a member of a recognised self-regulating organisation or a person certified by a recognised professional body, the rules etc of that organisation or body)[2].
Suspension is for a specified period or until the occurrence of a specified event or until specified conditions are complied with[3].

Where the SIB proposes to refuse an application for authorisation or for variation of the terms of a suspension, or to withdraw or suspend an authorisation, it must give the applicant or authorised person written notice of its intention, stating the reasons and giving particulars of the right to require the case to be referred to the Financial Services Tribunal[4].

Although when authorisation is suspended the holder is no longer an authorised person, intervention powers and powers to obtain winding up and administration orders are exercisable against the holder.

1 As to the meaning of 'fit and proper person', see para 1310 above.
2 Financial Services Act 1986 (c 60), s 28(1)(a), (b), (3).
3 Ibid, s 28(4). Any specified period, event or condition may be varied by the SIB on the application of the holder: s 28(5).
4 Ibid, s 29(1), (4). As to the tribunal, see paras 1416–1419 below.

1312. Self-regulating organisations. 'Self-regulating organisation' ('SRO') is defined by reference to its function. It means a body corporate or unincorporated association which regulates the carrying on of investment business of any kind by enforcing rules which are binding on persons carrying on business of that kind either because they are members of the SRO or because they are otherwise subject to its control[1]. A member of a recognised SRO[2] is an 'authorised person' by virtue of his membership[3].

An SRO may apply to the Securities and Investments Board ('SIB') for recognition[4]. The SIB may grant or refuse the application[5]. Unless it considers that recognition is unnecessary having regard to the existence of other organisations in the same field[6], the SIB must make a recognition order if it appears that the rules, constitution and practices of the SRO comply with prescribed requirements[7]. However, it may not make such an order without the leave of the Secretary of State, and he must not give leave unless satisfied that the organisation's rules, guidance, statements of principle, regulations and codes of practice do not have and are not intended or likely to have, to any significant extent, the effect of restricting, distorting or preventing competition save to the extent necessary for the protection of investors[8].

The SROs recognised by the SIB are the Financial Intermediaries Managers and Brokers Regulatory Association ('FIMBRA')[9], the Investment Management Regulatory Organisation ('IMRO')[10], the Life Assurance and Unit Trust Regulatory Organisation ('LAUTRO')[11] and the Securities and Futures Association ('SFA')[12] (formerly the Association of Futures Brokers and Dealers ('AFBD') and the Securities Association ('TSA'))[13].

1 Financial Services Act 1986 (c 60), s 8(1). For the meaning of 'investment business', see para 1307 above.

2 References in the Act to members of an SRO are references to persons who, whether or not they are members, are subject to its rules: ibid, s 8(2). 'Recognised self-regulating organisation' means a body declared by order of the Secretary of State to be a recognised self-regulating organisation for the purposes of the Financial Services Act 1986: s 207(1).

3 Ibid, s 7(1). Section 7 does not apply to a member who is an authorised person by virtue of s 22 (authorised insurers: see para 1316 below) or s 23 (friendly societies: see para 1317 below) or an insurance company which is an authorised person by virtue of s 31 (Europersons: see para 1320 below): s 7(2). For the meaning of 'authorised person', see para 1306, note 2, above.

4 Ibid, s 9(1). As to the delegation of functions, see para 1310, note 2, above. The application must be made in such manner as the SIB directs, accompanied by such information as it reasonably requires: s 9(2). The SIB may also call for further information: s 9(3). Directions and requirements under s 9(2) and s 9(3) may differ as between different applications: s 9(4). The information must be furnished in such form as the SIB specifies: s 9(5). The application must be accompanied by a copy of the applicant's rules and of any written guidance issued by it which is intended to have continuing effect: s 9(6).

5 Ibid, s 10(1).

6 See ibid, s 10(4).

7 Ibid, s 10(2). For these requirements, see s 10(3), Sch 2 (amended by the Companies Act 1989 (c 40), ss 203(2), 204(1), 206(1), Sch 23, para 21). Thus the SRO must secure that its members are fit and proper persons to carry on investment business of the kind with which it is concerned (and do not carry on investment business of other kinds unless otherwise authorised to do so); it must have fair and reasonable rules and practices for admission, expulsion and discipline; its rules must safeguard investors; it must be able to monitor and enforce its rules and investigate complaints; and it must be able and willing to promote and maintain high standards of integrity and fair dealing.

8 Financial Services Act 1986, s 120(1), (2), applying s 119(1) (amended by the Companies Act 1989, Sch 23, para 14(2)). As to the necessity for consultation with the Director General of Fair Trading, see the Financial Services Act 1986, ss 122, 123 (amended by the Companies Act 1989, s 153, Sch 20, para 26, Sch 23, para 16).

9 FIMBRA (formerly the National Association of Securities Dealers and Investment Managers ('NASDIM')) regulates all kinds of investment business other than futures contracts and contracts for differences, market making activities or the activities of establishing, operating, acting as trustee for or winding up an authorised unit trust scheme.

10 IMRO is responsible for the regulation of investment management of securities and operators, managers and trustees of authorised unit trusts or recognised collective investment schemes.

11 LAUTRO has three categories of members: insurance companies, managers of collective investment schemes, and friendly societies.

12 SFA is responsible for the regulation of persons who deal, arrange deals or advise on deals in all types of investments as defined in the Financial Services Act 1986, Sch 1, Pt I (paras 1–11) (see para 1308 above), except, for the most part, units in collective investment schemes and long-term insurance contracts which are primarily regulated by other SROs. The range of instruments regulated by SFA include eg domestic and foreign equities, domestic and foreign debt instruments including gilts, treasuries and Eurobonds, financial and commodity options, and futures contracts.

13 The merger took place on 2 April 1990. TSA was formed in 1987 by a merger of the International Securities Regulatory Organisation ('ISRO') and The Stock Exchange.

1313. Authorisation by recognised professional bodies. A person holding an appropriate certificate[1] issued by a recognised professional body is an authorised person[2]. 'Professional body' means a body which regulates the practice of a profession — but references to the practice of a profession do not include references to carrying on a business consisting wholly or mainly of investment business[3]. Thus the members of the professions envisaged may be actively engaged in investment business, but to a more limited extent than the full-time players in the investment market. References to the members of a professional body are references to individuals who, whether or not members of the body, are entitled to practise the profession and, in practising it, are subject to the rules of the body[4]. A professional body may apply to the Securities and Investments Board ('SIB') for a recognition order[5]. The SIB may make or refuse to make the order[6], and may make the order if it appears that the body satisfies prescribed requirements[7].

Nine professional bodies have been recognised: the Law Society, the Law Society of Scotland, the Law Society of Northern Ireland, the Institute of Chartered Accountants in England and Wales, the Institute of Chartered Accountants in Scotland, the Institute of Chartered Accountants in Northern Ireland, the Institute of Actuaries, the Chartered Association of Certified Accountants, and the Insurance Brokers Registration Council.

1 Ie a certificate issued for the purposes of the Financial Services Act 1986 (c 60), Pt I (ss 1–128).
2 Ibid, s 15(1). Such a certificate may be issued to an individual, a body corporate, a partnership or an unincorporated association: s 15(2).
3 Ibid, s 16(1). For the meaning of 'investment business', see para 1307 above.
4 Ibid, s 16(2).
5 Ibid, s 17(1). As to the delegation of functions, see para 1310, note 2, above.
6 Ibid, s 18(1).
7 Ibid, s 18(2). Thus the body must have rules imposing acceptable limits on the kinds of investment business which may be carried on by certified persons and the circumstances in which they may carry it on: s 18(3). The body must have statutory status; it must have rules, practices and arrangements to ensure that no person can be certified unless he is a member or is a person managed and controlled by a member; its rules must provide safeguards for investors; it must have adequate arrangements and resources for monitoring and enforcing compliance with its rules etc and effective arrangements for investigating complaints; and it must be able and willing to promote and maintain high standards of integrity and fair dealing: see Sch 3 (amended by the Companies Act 1989 (c 40), ss 203(2), 206(1), Sch 23, para 21).

1314. Refusal and revocation of recognition; compliance orders. If the Securities and Investments Board ('SIB') refuses an application by a self-regulating organisation ('SRO') or a professional body for a recognition order, it must notify the applicant in writing of the refusal, stating the reasons[1].

The SIB may revoke a recognition order by a further order if it appears that the prerequisites for recognition are not satisfied or that the recognised body has failed to comply with any obligation to which it is subject by virtue of the Financial Services Act 1986, or (in the case of an SRO) that continued recognition is undesirable having regard to the existence of other recognised organis-ations[2]. Before revoking the recognition order the SIB must give the recognised body written notice of its intention, stating the reasons, must take steps to bring the notice to the attention of members and publish it to bring it to the attention of other persons affected[3], although a recognition order may be revoked with-out notice if the SIB considers it essential in the interests of investors[4]. The recognised body, any member of it or any other person affected may within three months of the notice make representations to which the SIB must have regard in determining whether to revoke the recognition order[5].

If at any time it appears to the SIB that the prerequisites for recognition are not satisfied or that the recognised body has failed to comply with any obligation to which it is subject by virtue of the Financial Services Act 1986, it may, instead of revoking the recognition order, apply to the High Court or the Court of Session[6], and the court may order the body to take such steps as the court directs to satisfy the requirements or comply with the obligation[7].

1 See the Financial Services Act 1986 (c 60), ss 10(5), 18(4). As to the delegation of functions, see para 1310, note 2, above.
2 Ibid, ss 11(1)(a)–(c), 19(1)(a), (b). The revocation order must state the date on which it takes effect, which must not be earlier than three months after the making of the recognition order: ss 11(2), 19(2).
3 Ibid, ss 11(3), (4), 19(2).
4 Ibid, ss 11(6), 19(2).
5 Ibid, ss 11(5), 19(2).
6 Ibid, ss 12(1), (3), 20(1), (3).
7 Ibid, ss 12(2), 20(2).

(c) Automatic Authorisation

1315. Introduction. The Financial Services Act 1986 recognises that for vari-ous reasons, such as the United Kingdom's European Community obligations, and the existence of institutions with proven regulatory arrangements, it would not be appropriate for all persons or businesses who carry on investment business to be subjected to the supervision of the Securities and Investments Board or one of the recognised self-regulatory organisations or recognised professional bodies. Provision is therefore made for the automatic authorisation of authorised insurers, registered friendly societies, the operators and trustees of certain collective investment schemes, persons authorised by the Secretary of State and persons authorised in other member states of the European Com-munity[1].

1 See paras 1316 ff below.

1316. Insurance companies. A body which is authorised under the Insurance Companies Act 1982[1] to carry on insurance business which is investment business[2] and carries on such insurance business in the United Kingdom is an authorised person[3] as respects (1) any insurance business which is investment business, and (2) any other investment business which that body may carry on without contravening the prohibition[4] on insurance companies carrying on activities otherwise than in connection with or for the purposes of its insurance business[5].

Such bodies are prohibited from obtaining any further authorisation to carry on investment business[6], although there is nothing to prevent an insurance company being a member of a self-regulating organisation[7]. Authorised insurance companies will therefore remain at least in part subject to the supervision of the Department of Trade and Industry[8].

Regulated insurance companies which are not authorised under the 1982 Act but which are regulated by it are automatically authorised for the purposes of the Financial Services Act 1986 only as respects the management of the investments of a pension fund which is established solely for the benefit of the officers or employees of the company or any company in the same group, and their dependants[9]. However, such companies may seek authorisation from a recognised self-regulating organisation or the Securities and Investments Board. Most regulated insurance companies are supervised, at least in part, by the board or by the Life Assurance and Unit Trust Regulatory Organisation ('LAU-TRO').

The effect of these provisions is that the requirements of the 1982 Act are paramount in respect of solvency matters, whereas the 1986 Act is paramount so far as the marketing of life assurance and pension fund management is concerned.

The Secretary of State may direct that an insurance company is to cease to be authorised to carry on insurance business if it has failed to satisfy an obligation to which it is subject under the 1986 Act or, if it is a member of a self-regulating organisation, an obligation to which it is subject by virtue of the rules of that organisation[10].

1 Ie authorised under the Insurance Companies Act 1982 (c 50), s 3 (authorisation by the Secretary of State) or s 4 (authorisation of existing companies).
2 For the meaning of 'investment business', see para 1307 above.
3 For the meaning of 'authorised person', see para 1306, note 2, above.
4 Ie the prohibition under the Insurance Companies Act 1982, s 16.
5 Financial Services Act 1986 (c 60), s 2(a), (b).
6 Ibid, s 129, Sch 10, para 2(1).
7 However, the rules of a self-regulating organisation with insurance company members must take proper account of the Insurance Companies Act 1982, Pt II (ss 15–71: regulation of insurance business): Financial Services Act 1986, Sch 10, para 3(1).
8 See eg the Insurance Companies Act 1982, ss 37–48.
9 Financial Services Act 1986, Sch 10, para 2(2).
10 Insurance Companies Act 1982, s 13(2A) (added by the Financial Services Act 1986, Sch 10, para 7(2)).

1317. Registered friendly societies. A friendly society[1] which is registered under the Friendly Societies Act 1974 (but not as a branch of a society), which under its rules has its registered office in Great Britain and which carries on investment business[2] in the United Kingdom is an authorised person[3] as respects any investment business which it carries on for or in connection with any of its friendly society purposes[4].

Provision is made for the recognition of self-regulating organisations for friendly societies[5] and for the conduct of investment business by regulated friendly societies[6].

1 Ie within the meaning of the Friendly Societies Act 1974 (c 46), s 7(1)(a).
2 For the meaning of 'investment business', see para 1307 above.
3 For the meaning of 'authorised person', see para 1306, note 2, above.
4 Financial Services Act 1986 (c 60), s 23(1). For the friendly society purposes, see the Friendly Societies Act 1974, Sch 1.
5 See the Financial Services Act 1986, s 140, Sch 11, Pt II (paras 2–12).
6 See ibid, Sch 11, Pt III (paras 13–27).

1318. Collective investment schemes from other member states. The operator or trustee of a recognised collective investment scheme[1] constituted in a member state of the European Community[2] other than the United Kingdom is authorised as respects investment business consisting of operating or acting as trustee in relation to the scheme and as respects any investment business[3] carried on by him in connection with or for the purposes of the scheme[4]. This automatic authorisation is restricted to schemes constituted and authorised in other member states. Operators and trustees of other classes of recognised collective investment schemes who need authorisation must obtain it through one of the other routes[5].

1 For the meaning of 'collective investment scheme', see para 1325 below.
2 As to when a scheme is constituted in a member state, see the Financial Services Act 1986 (c 60), s 86(8), and para 1328, note 3, below.
3 For the meaning of 'investment business', see para 1307 above.
4 Financial Services Act 1986, s 24(a), (b), read with s 86 (amended by the Companies Act 1989 (c 40), s 206(1), Sch 23, para 8), which provides for the recognition of schemes constituted in other member states and sets out the requirements for such recognition: see para 1328 below.
5 A Whittaker and G Morse *The Financial Services Act 1986: A Guide to the New Law* (1987).

1319. Persons authorised by the Secretary of State. The Secretary of State may grant automatic authorisation to any individual, body corporate, partnership or unincorporated association who or which submits an application for such authorisation[1]. This function is, however, capable of delegation to a 'designated agency' (the Securities and Investments Board ('SIB')) to be dealt with accordingly[2].

As is the case where the authority to grant an application is delegated to the SIB, the Secretary of State may grant or refuse the application[3], but must grant an application for direct authorisation made in accordance with the required procedure if it appears to him from the information provided and having regard to any other information in his possession that the applicant is a fit and proper person[4] to carry on investment business[5] and provide the services described in the application[6].

1 See the Financial Services Act 1986 (c 60), ss 25–27, and para 1310 above.
2 See ibid, s 114.
3 Ibid, s 27(1).
4 As to the meaning of 'fit and proper person', see para 1310 above.
5 For the meaning of 'investment business', see para 1307 above.
6 Financial Services Act 1986, s 27(2). See A Whittaker and G Morse *The Financial Services Act 1986: A Guide to the New Law* (1987).

1320. 'Europersons'. In order to give effect to the obligations of the United Kingdom under the EEC Treaty, a person is authorised to carry on investment business[1] in the United Kingdom if he is established in another member state the law of which recognises him as a national of that or another member state, and he is authorised under that law to carry on investment business or investment business of a particular kind[2].

This automatic authorisation applies only if the provisions of the law under which he is authorised to carry on the business (1) afford to investors in the United Kingdom protection, in relation to the carrying on of that business, at least equivalent to that provided for them by the Financial Services Act 1986 relating to members of recognised self-regulating organisations or persons authorised by the Securities and Investments Board; or (2) satisfy the conditions laid down by a Community instrument for the co-ordination or approximation of laws, regulations or administrative provisions of member states relating to the carrying on of investment business or investment business of the relevant kind[3].

The authorisation may be terminated or suspended on contravention of the statutory provisions, rules or regulations[4].

1 For the meaning of 'investment business', see para 1307 above.

2 Financial Services Act 1986 (c 60), s 31(1). To be established in another member state a person must have his head office there and must not transact investment business from a permanent place of business maintained by him in the United Kingdom: s 31(2). He must give prior notice to the Securities and Investments Board of his intention to carry on investment business in the United Kingdom: s 32(1).

3 Ibid, s 31(3)(a), (b). The European element is at present covered by the directive of the Undertakings for Collective Investment in Transferable Securities, but this provision will in due course cover the Investment Services and proposed Capital Adequacy Directives.

4 See ibid, s 33. Termination or suspension is effected by written notice, stating the reasons and the right to require a reference to the Financial Services Tribunal (as to which see paras 1416–1419 below): s 34(1), (4).

(d) Exempted Persons

1321. The Bank of England and Lloyd's. The Financial Services Act 1986 provides for a number of persons to be 'exempted persons'[1]. They may accordingly carry on investment business even though they are not 'authorised persons'[2].

The Bank of England is an exempted person[3]. The Society of Lloyd's and persons permitted by the Council of Lloyd's to act as underwriting agents at Lloyd's are exempted persons as respects investment business carried on in connection with or for the purpose of insurance business at Lloyd's[4].

The Act also exempts, for certain purposes, listed money market institutions, which are, in any case, subject to regulation by the Bank of England[5].

1 For the meaning of 'exempted person', see para 1306, note 3, above.

2 See the Financial Services Act 1986 (c 60), s 3, and para 1306 above. For the meaning of 'investment business', see para 1307 above, and for the meaning of 'authorised person', see para 1306, note 2, above.

3 Ibid, s 35.

4 Ibid, s 42.

5 See ibid, s 43, Sch 5, and the Treasury consultative document *The Future Regulations of the Wholesale Markets in Sterling, Foreign Exchange and Bullion* (December 1986).

1322. Recognised investment exchanges and clearing houses. A recognised investment exchange is an exempted person as respects anything done in its capacity as such which constitutes investment business[1], and a recognised clearing house is an exempted person as respects anything done by it in its capacity as a person providing clearing services for the transaction of investment business[2]. Any body corporate or unincorporated association may apply to the Securities and Investments Board ('SIB') for an order declaring it to be a recognised investment exchange or, as the case may be, a recognised clearing house for these purposes[3]. The SIB may make a recognition order if it appears that the statutory requirements are satisfied[4]. In particular, a clearing house must demonstrate that it has financial resources sufficient for the proper performance of its functions[5]; that it has adequate arrangements and resources for the effective monitoring and enforcement of compliance with its rules[6]; that it can provide clearing services which would enable a recognised investment exchange to make arrangements with it that satisfy the rules for safeguarding investors[7]; and that it is able and willing to promote and maintain high standards of integrity and fair dealing[8].

In the case of a body or association whose head office is outside the United Kingdom, the application (which must be made to the Secretary of State, not the SIB[9]) must include an address for service in the United Kingdom[10]. The requirements for recognition are different in comparison with their United

Kingdom counterparts. In particular such a body or association must demonstrate that it meets the 'equivalence test' in that it must show that in the country of its head office there is sufficient supervision to ensure that United Kingdom investors enjoy the same degree of protection as is afforded by the Financial Services Act 1986[11]; that it is able and willing to co-operate with United Kingdom regulators by way of the sharing of information and other means[12]; and that adequate arrangements exist for such co-operation between the relevant regulating authorities of the investment exchange or clearing house and the United Kingdom regulators[13].

Neither 'investment exchange' nor 'clearing house' is defined. However, in essence the function of an investment exchange, such as The Stock Exchange or the London International Financial Futures Exchange, is to provide an organised market framework for investment trading by, for example, implying terms into the bargains made on the exchange and prescribing settlement periods and procedures[14]. On the other hand, the function of a clearing house, such as the London Options Clearing House, is to provide clearing services by matching transactions and guaranteeing the performance of contracts in respect of investment transactions effected on investment exchanges.

1 Financial Services Act 1986 (c 60), s 36(1). For the meaning of 'exempted person', see para 1306, note 3, above, and for the meaning of 'investment business', see para 1307 above.
2 Ibid, s 38(1).
3 Ibid, ss 37(1), 39(1). As to the delegation of functions, see para 1310, note 2, above. Section 9(2)–(5) (see para 1312 above) has effect in relation to the application, which must be accompanied by a copy of the applicant's rules and any written guidance issued by it which is intended to have continuing effect, and by either (1) particulars of any arrangements which the applicant for recognition as an investment exchange has made or proposes to make for the provision of clearing services, or (2) particulars of any recognised investment exchange with which the applicant for recognition as a clearing house proposes to make clearing arrangements and of any other person (whether or not such an exchange) for whom the applicant provides clearing services: ss 37(2), 39(2).
4 Ibid, ss 37(4), 39(4). For these requirements, see Sch 4 (amended by the Companies Act 1989 (c 40) s 205(1)) (investment exchanges), and the Financial Services Act 1986, s 39(4)(a)–(d) (clearing houses), and, in each case, ss 119, 120 (competition: cf para 1312 above).
5 Ibid, s 39(4)(a).
6 Ibid, s 39(4)(b).
7 Ibid, s 39(4)(c), referring to the requirements of Sch 4.
8 Ibid, s 39(4)(d), by reference to Sch 4, para 5.
9 See ibid, s 114(6).
10 Ibid, s 40(1).
11 Ibid, s 40(2)(a).
12 Ibid, s 40(2)(b).
13 Ibid, s 40(2)(c).
14 See B A K Rider et al *Guide to the Financial Services Act 1986* (1987).

1323. Miscellaneous exemptions. Miscellaneous individuals when acting in their offical capacities are also 'exempted persons'[1]. These include the Accountant of Court and a sheriff clerk when acting (in either case) in the exercise of his functions in connection with the consignation or deposit of sums of money[2].

A special exemption exists for the interim or permanent trustee of an authorised person[3] (or of a person whose direct authorisation or authorisation as a 'Europerson' is suspended) when that person's estate is sequestrated, or for the interim or permanent trustee or liquidator of a partnership which is such a person when a winding up order is made in respect of the partnership[4].

The Secretary of State may by order provide for additional exemptions, or for removing or restricting any of the exemptions referred to above[5]. In three orders made under this power he has provided that the following are exempted persons:

(1) the trustees of the Church of Scotland Trust when acting in the exercise of their powers under the Church of Scotland Trust Orders 1932 to 1985 (which are orders made under private Acts), the Church of Scotland General Trustees when acting in their capacity as such and the General Synod of the Scottish Episcopal Church when acting as trustee of funds held for objects connected with the work of that church[6];

(2) Scottish Enterprise (formerly the Scottish Development Agency) and the Scottish Tourist Board, and judicial factors when acting in their capacity as such[7];

(3) Scottish Nuclear Ltd and any body corporate connected with it as respects certain activities involving arranging deals in investments[8]; and

(4) The European Bank for Reconstruction and Development[8].

A further category of persons exempted from the requirement to obtain authorisation are appointed representatives: an appointed representative is an exempted person as respects investment business carried on by him as such a representative[9].

1 For the meaning of 'exempted person', see para 1306, note 3, above.
2 Financial Services Act 1986 (c 60), s 45(1)(d), (i).
3 For the meaning of 'authorised person', see para 1306, note 2, above.
4 See the Financial Services Act 1986, s 45(2), (3).
5 Ibid, s 46(1).
6 Financial Services Act 1986 (Miscellaneous Exemptions) Order 1988, SI 1988/350.
7 Financial Services Act 1986 (Miscellaneous Exemptions) (No 2) Order 1988, SI 1988/723.
8 Financial Services Act 1986 (Miscellaneous Exemptions) Order 1991, SI 1991/493.
9 See the Financial Services Act 1986, s 44(1), and para 1361 below, where 'appointed representative' is defined.

(e) Interdict and Restitution Orders

1324. Power of the Court of Session to grant interdict and restitution orders. If on the application of the Secretary of State or the Securities and Investments Board ('SIB') the Court of Session is satisfied that there is a reasonable likelihood that a person who is neither an authorised nor an exempted person has contravened the prohibition in section 3 of the Financial Services Act 1986 on carrying on investment business[1], or that any such person has contravened that prohibition and that there is a reasonable likelihood that the contravention will continue or be repeated, the court may grant interdict prohibiting the contravention[2].

If on the application of the Secretary of State or the SIB the court is satisfied that a person has entered into a transaction in contravention of section 3, the court may order that person and any other person who was knowingly concerned to take steps to restore the *status quo*[3]. On a similar application the court, if satisfied that a person has been carrying on investment business in contravention of section 3 and:

(1) that profits have accrued to him as a result, or

(2) that investors have suffered loss or otherwise been adversely affected as a result of his misleading statements or practices[4] or unsolicited calls[5], or his failure to comply with the conduct of business rules,

may order the person concerned to pay to the applicant such sum as appears just having regard to that profit or loss, and the applicant must pay over that sum to such persons as the court may direct[6].

Nothing in these provisions affects the right of any other person to bring proceedings in respect of any of the matters to which these provisions apply[7].

1 Ie the prohibition under the Financial Services Act 1986 (c 60), s 3: see para 1306 above.

2　Ibid, s 6(1), (8); Financial Services Act 1986 (Delegation) Order 1987, SI 1987/942. See *Securities and Investments Board v Pantell SA* [1990] Ch 426, [1989] 2 All ER 673.
3　Financial Services Act 1986, s 6(2).
4　Ie in contravention of ibid, s 47: see para 1332 below.
5　Ie in contravention of ibid, s 56: see paras 1333, 1334, below.
6　Ibid, s 6(3), (5), (6). The court may require the person concerned to furnish it with and verify necessary accounts and information: s 6(7).
7　Ibid, s 6(9).

(3) COLLECTIVE INVESTMENT SCHEMES

1325. Meaning of 'collective investment scheme'. 'A collective investment scheme' means any arrangements with respect to property of any description, including money, the purpose or effect of which is to enable persons taking part in the arrangements (whether by becoming owners of the property or any part of it or otherwise) to participate in or receive profits or income arising from the acquisition, holding, management or disposal of the property or sums paid out of such profits or income[1].

The arrangements must be such that the participants do not have day-to-day control over the management of the property, whether or not they have the right to be consulted or to give directions, and the arrangements must have either or both of these characteristics:

(1)　that the participants' contributions and the profits or income out of which payments are to be made are pooled[2];

(2)　that the property is managed as a whole by or on behalf of the operator of the scheme[3].

However, arrangements are not a collective investment scheme if:

(a)　the property (other than cash awaiting investment) consists of specified investments[4];

(b)　each participant is the owner of a part of the property and entitled to withdraw it at any time;

(c)　the arrangements do not have the characteristic mentioned in head (1) and have those mentioned in head (2) only because the parts of the property belonging to different participants are not bought and sold separately except where a person becomes or ceases to be a participant[5].

The following are not collective investment schemes:

(i)　arrangements operated by a person otherwise than by way of business[6];

(ii)　arrangements where each participant carries on a business other than investment business and enters into the arrangements for commercial purposes related to that business[7];

(iii)　arrangements where each participant is a body corporate in the same group as the operator[8];

(iv)　arrangements where (1) each participant is a bona fide employee or former employee, or the spouse, widow, widower, child or stepchild under eighteen of such employee or former employee, of a body corporate in the same group as the operator, and (2) the property consists of shares or debentures in or of a member of that group[9];

(v)　arrangements where the receipt of the participants' contributions constitutes the acceptance of deposits in a deposit-taking business and does not constitute a prescribed transaction[10];

(vi)　franchise arrangements[11];

(vii)　arrangements the predominant purpose of which is to enable participants to share in the use or enjoyment of particular property or to make its use or enjoyment available gratuitously to others[12];

(viii) arrangements under which the participants' rights or interests are certain certificates representing securities[13];

(ix) arrangements the purpose of which is the provision of clearing services and which are operated by an authorised person, a recognised clearing house or a recognised investment exchange[14];

(x) contracts of insurance[15];

(xi) occupational pension schemes[16].

Further, no body corporate incorporated under the law of, or of any part of, the United Kingdom relating to building societies or industrial and provident societies, or registered under any such law relating to friendly societies, and no body corporate other than an open-ended investment company, may be regarded as constituting a collective investment scheme[17].

These provisions are necessarily complex, but, taking account of the various exclusions (which cover such things as personal equity plans ('PEPs'), employee share schemes, investment clubs, occupational pension schemes and certain partnerships, joint ventures and franchise arrangements), the most common types of collective investment schemes are unit trust schemes and open-ended investment companies.

'Unit trust scheme' means a collective investment scheme under which the property is held on trust for the participants[18], and 'authorised unit trust scheme' means a unit trust scheme declared by an order of the Secretary of State to be authorised for the purposes of the Financial Services Act 1986[19].

'Open-ended investment company' means a collective investment scheme under which:

(A) the property belongs beneficially to, and is managed by or on behalf of, a body corporate having as its purpose the investment of its fund with the aim of spreading investment risk and giving its members the benefit of the results of the management of those funds by or on behalf of that body; and

(B) the participants' rights are represented by shares in or securities of that body which (1) the participants are entitled to have redeemed or repurchased, or which (otherwise than under the provisions of the Companies Act 1985 relating to redeemable shares and the purchase by a company of its own shares[20]) are redeemed or repurchased from them by, or out of funds provided by, that body; or (2) the body ensures can be sold by the participants on an investment exchange at a price related to the value of the property to which they relate[21].

---

1 Financial Services Act 1986 (c 60), s 75(1).

2 Ibid, s 75(2), (3)(a). Where arrangements provide for such pooling in relation to separate parts of the property, the arrangements do not constitute a single collective investment scheme unless the participants are entitled to exchange rights in one part for rights in another: s 75(4).

3 Ibid, s 75(2), (3)(b). 'The operator', in relation to a unit trust scheme with a separate trustee, means the manager, and, in relation to an open-ended investment company, means that company: s 75(9).

4 The specified investments are those falling within ibid, Sch 1, paras 1–5, 6 (so far as relates to units in authorised unit trust schemes and recognised schemes), 10: see para 1308 above.

5 Ibid, s 75(5)(a)–(c).

6 Ibid, s 75(6)(a).

7 Ibid, s 75(6)(b). For the meaning of 'investment business', see para 1307 above.

8 Ibid, s 75(6)(c).

9 Ibid, s 75(6)(d)(i), (ii). 'Shares' and 'debentures' are defined in Sch 1, para 20(4).

10 Ibid, s 75(6)(e) (amended by the Banking Act 1987 (c 22), s 108(1), Sch 6, para 27(1)), referring to a deposit-taking business for the purposes of that 1987 Act and transactions prescribed for the purposes of s 2 of that Act.

11 Financial Services Act 1986, s 75(6)(f), which defines such arrangements as arrangements under which a person earns profits or income by exploiting a right conferred by the arrangements to use a trade name or design or other intellectual property or a goodwill attached to it.

12 Ibid, s 75(6)(g).

13 Ibid, s 75(6)(h), referring to investments falling within Sch 1, para 5.
14 Ibid, s 75(6)(i).
15 Ibid, s 75(6)(j).
16 Ibid, s 75(6)(k).
17 Ibid, s 75(7).
18 Ibid, s 75(8).
19 Ibid, s 207(1). As to such orders, see s 78, and para 1327 below.
20 Ie the Companies Act 1985 (c 6), Pt V, Ch VII (ss 159–181).
21 Financial Services Act 1986, s 75(8).

1326. Promotion of schemes. In general an authorised person may not promote a collective investment scheme unless the scheme is an authorised unit trust scheme or a recognised scheme[1]. A person promotes a scheme if he:

(1) issues or causes to be issued in the United Kingdom any advertisement inviting persons to become or offer to become participants in a scheme or containing information calculated to lead directly or indirectly to persons becoming or offering to become participants, or

(2) advises or procures any person in the United Kingdom to become or offer to become a participant[2].

However, this does not apply if the advertisement is issued to or the person mentioned in head (2) is either an authorised person or a person whose ordinary business involves the acquisition and disposal of property of the same kind as the property, or a substantial part of the property, to which the scheme relates[3]. Nor does it apply to anything done in accordance with regulations made by the Securities and Investments Board ('SIB') for the purpose of exempting from it the promotion otherwise than to the general public of specified descriptions of schemes[4]. The Secretary of State may make regulations exempting 'single property schemes' from the above provision[5].

1 Financial Services Act 1986 (c 60), s 76(1). For the meaning of 'collective investment scheme' and 'authorised unit trust scheme', see para 1325 above. As to recognised schemes, see s 86, and para 1328 below.
2 Ibid, s 76(1)(a), (b).
3 Ibid, s 76(2).
4 Ibid, s 76(3). See the Financial Services (Promotion of Unregulated Collective Investment Schemes) Regulations 1991, made by the SIB, which permit the promotion of schemes to certain categories of non-private customers. Earlier regulations used the phrase 'experienced or professional investors' in place of 'non-private customers'. As to the delegation of functions, see the Financial Services Act 1986 (Delegation) (No 2) Order 1988, SI 1988/738.
5 Financial Services Act 1986, s 76(4). As to such schemes, see s 76(5)–(7), the Financial Services Act 1986 (Single Property Schemes) (Exemption) Regulations 1989, SI 1989/28, and also the Financial Services (Single Property Schemes) (Supplementary) Regulations 1989, made by the SIB.

1327. Authorisation of unit trust schemes. The manager and trustee, or proposed manager and trustee, of a unit trust scheme (who must be different persons) may apply to the Securities and Investments Board ('SIB') for an order declaring the scheme to be an authorised scheme[1]. On such an application, and on being supplied with the necessary information, the SIB may make the order if:

(1) it appears to it that the scheme complies with regulations as to the constitution and management of such schemes[2] and with the statutory provisions as to such schemes[3]; and

(2) it has been furnished with a copy of the trust deed and a solicitor's certificate to the effect that it complies with such of those requirements as relate to its contents[4].

The SIB must inform the applicants of its decision within six months of the receipt of the application[5], and on making the order it may issue a certificate that the scheme complies with the conditions necessary for it to enjoy the rights conferred by any relevant Community instrument[6]. The SIB may revoke the order if it appears that the appropriate requirements are no longer satisfied, that it is undesirable in the interests of participants that the scheme should continue to be authorised, or that the manager or trustee has contravened any of the relevant provisions[7]. It also has power to revoke the order at the request of the manager or trustee[8].

The manager of an authorised unit trust scheme must notify the SIB of any proposed alteration to the scheme and any proposal to replace the trustee; and the trustee must notify the SIB of any proposal to replace the manager[9]. There are restrictions on the activities of the manager of the scheme[10].

The SIB may by regulations require the manager to submit to it and make available to the public on request scheme particulars containing information about the scheme[11].

1 See the Financial Services Act 1986 (c 60), s 77. As to the delegation of functions, see para 1326, note 4, above.
2 Such regulations are made under ibid, s 81. See the Financial Services (Regulated Schemes) Regulations 1991, made by the SIB.
3 Financial Services Act 1986, s 78(1)(a). Thus, for example, the manager and trustee must be independent of each other (s 78(2)), each must be a body corporate incorporated in the United Kingdom or another member state and have a place of business in the United Kingdom (s 78(3)), each must be an authorised person (s 78(4)), the name of the scheme must not be undesirable or misleading and the purposes of the scheme must be reasonably capable of being successfully carried into effect (s 78(5)), and the participants must be entitled to have their units redeemed at a price related to the net value of the property to which the units relate (s 78(6)). The SIB has the ultimate discretion whether or not to authorise the scheme: *Allied Investors Trust Ltd v Board of Trade* [1956] Ch 232, [1956] 1 All ER 162.
4 Financial Services Act 1986, s 78(1)(b).
5 Ibid, s 78(7). If it proposes to refuse the application it must give the applicants notice, stating its reasons, and permit them to make representations: see s 80.
6 Ibid, s 78(8).
7 Ibid, s 79(1). It must first give the applicants notice, stating its reasons and permit them to make representations: see s 80.
8 See ibid, s 79(4).
9 Ibid, s 82(1), (2). Effect may not be given to the proposal unless either the SIB gives its approval or a month passes without it having notified its disapproval: s 82(3).
10 See ibid, s 83.
11 See ibid, s 85, and the Financial Services (Regulated Schemes) Regulations 1991, made by the SIB.

1328. Recognised collective investment schemes. There are three types of collective investment scheme[1] which can be recognised for marketing to the public in the United Kingdom:
(1) schemes authorised in other member states of the European Community, being schemes which comply with the requirements of the appropriate Community directive: such schemes can obtain recognition under section 86 of the Financial Services Act 1986;
(2) schemes authorised in designated countries or territories which are of a class specified by the Secretary of State: such schemes can obtain recognition under section 87;
(3) overseas schemes which do not qualify for recognition under section 86 or section 87: such schemes may seek recognition under section 88[2].
These three types will now be discussed in turn.

Under head (1), a collective investment scheme will be recognised if it is constituted in a member state of the European Community[3] and complies with the requirement of the Community Directive on Undertakings for Collective Investment in Transferable Securities ('UCITS')[4] and satisfies prescribed requirements[5]. However, not less than two months before inviting persons in the United Kingdom to become participants, the operator of the scheme must give the Securities and Investments Board ('SIB') written notice of his intention to do so, specifying the manner in which the invitation is to be made, and the scheme will not be a recognised scheme if the SIB within two months notifies the operator and the authorities of the authorising state that the manner in which the invitation is to be made does not comply with United Kingdom law, giving reasons and stating the right to make representations[6].

Under head (2), a collective investment scheme which is not recognised by virtue of the foregoing provision but is managed in and authorised under the law of a country or territory outside the United Kingdom is a recognised scheme if that country or territory is designated for the purpose by order of the Secretary of State[7], and if the scheme is of a class specified by the order[8]. However, a scheme will not be recognised unless the operator gives the SIB notice that he wishes it to be recognised nor if the SIB notifies the operator that the scheme is not to be recognised[9]. It may also direct on certain grounds that a recognised scheme cease to be recognised[10].

Under head (3), a scheme which is managed in a country or territory outside the United Kingdom but which does not qualify for recognition under any of the foregoing provisions may, on the application of the operator[11], be declared by the SIB to be a recognised scheme if it appears to it that the scheme affords adequate protection to the participants, makes adequate provision for the matters dealt with by regulations as to the constitution and management of authorised unit trust schemes[12], and satisfies certain statutory requirements[13]. The SIB may direct on certain grounds that a recognised scheme cease to be recognised[14].

The SIB may by regulations require operators of recognised schemes to maintain in the United Kingdom such specified facilities as it thinks desirable in the interests of participants[15], and may by notice in writing require the operator of any recognised scheme to include specified explanatory information in any investment advertisement issued in the United Kingdom in which the scheme is named[16].

Furthermore, the secondary legislation relating to the constitution, management and admission to marketing in the United Kingdom of such schemes is provided by the SIB[17]. The SIB regulations are intended to maintain and enhance the product distinctiveness of regulated schemes and to provide flexibility and innovation to ensure that new features and new products are developed.

1 For the meaning of 'collective investment scheme', see para 1325 above.

2 See *Proposed Regulations for Collective Investment Schemes* (Securities and Investments Board, May 1991).

3 A collective investment scheme is constituted in a member state if it is constituted under the law of that state by a contract or under a trust and is managed by a body corporate incorporated under that law, or if it takes the form of an open-ended investment company (defined in para 1325 above) incorporated under that law: Financial Services Act 1986 (c60), s 86(8)(a), (b).

4 EC Council Directive 85/611 (OJ L375, 31.12.85, p 3).

5 Financial Services Act 1986, s 86(1). As to the authorisation of the operator or trustee of such a scheme, see the Financial Services Act 1986, s 24, and para 1318 above.

6 Ibid, s 86(2), (4), (5). As to the operator's notice, see also s 86(3), and the Financial Services (Regulated Schemes) Regulations 1991, made by the SIB.

7 Financial Services Act 1986, s 87(1)(a). As to designation orders, see also s 87(2). Countries and territories have been designated by the Financial Services (Designated Countries and Territories) (Overseas Collective Investment Schemes) Order 1988, SI 1988/2015 (designating the Isle of Man), the Financial Services (Designated Countries and Territories) (Overseas Collective Investment Schemes) (Guernsey) Order 1988, SI 1988/2148, the Financial Services (Designated Countries and Territories) (Overseas Collective Investment Schemes) (Jersey) Order 1988, SI 1988/2149, and the Financial Services (Designated Countries and Territories) (Overseas Collective Investment Schemes) (Bermuda) Order 1988, SI 1988/2284.

8 Financial Services Act 1986, s 87(1)(b). Scheme particulars may be required: see s 85, and para 1327 above, applied by s 87(5).
9 Ibid, s 87(3).
10 See ibid, s 89.
11 The provisions of ibid, s 77(2)–(5), as to applications for authorisation of unit trust schemes are applied by ibid, s 88(8).
12 Ie regulations made under ibid, s 81.
13 Ibid, s 88(1). Thus the operator must be a body corporate or the scheme must take the form of an open-ended investment company (defined in para 1325 above) (s 88(2)); the operator and any trustee must either be fit and proper persons to act as such or must be authorised persons (s 88(3), (4)); the operator, unless he is an authorised person, must have a representative in the United Kingdom who is an authorised person with power to act generally for the operator (s 88(5)); the name of the scheme must not be undesirable or misleading and the purposes of the scheme must be reasonably capable of being successfully carried into effect (s 88(6)), and the participants must be entitled to have their units redeemed at a price related to the net value of the property to which the units relate (s 88(7)). Scheme particulars may be required: see s 85, and para 1327 above, applied by s 88(10).
14 See ibid, s 89.
15 Ibid, s 90(1). See the Financial Services (Regulated Schemes) Regulations 1991, made by the SIB.
16 Financial Services Act 1986, s 90(2).
17 See the Financial Services (Regulated Schemes) Regulations 1991, made by the SIB.

1329. Powers of intervention. The Securities and Investments Board ('SIB'), by delegation from the Secretary of State[1], may by direction require the manager of an authorised unit trust scheme[2] to cease the issue or redemption, or both the issue and redemption, of units under the scheme on a specified date until a further specified date, or require the manager and trustee to wind up the scheme by a specified date or, if no date is specified, as soon as practicable[3]. Such a direction may be given if it appears to the SIB that:

(1) any of the requirements for the making of an order authorising the scheme are no longer satisfied;
(2) the exercise of the power to give the direction is desirable in the interests of participants or potential participants; or
(3) without prejudice to head (2), the manager or trustee has contravened any provision of the Financial Services Act 1986 or rules or regulations made under it, has furnished false, inaccurate or misleading information or has contravened any prohibition or requirement under the Act[4].

There is a corresponding power to direct that a scheme authorised in a designated country or territory[5] or another oveseas scheme[6] is not to be a recognised scheme for a specified period or until the occurrence of a specified event or until specified conditions are complied with[7].

The power to give any such a direction is exercisable by written notice served on the manager and trustee or, as the case may be, on the operator of the scheme[8].

1 Financial Services Act 1986 (Delegation) Order 1987, SI 1987/942.
2 For the meaning of 'authorised unit trust scheme', see para 1325 above.
3 Financial Services Act 1986 (c 60), s 91(2)(a), (b). The SIB may apply to the Court of Session for an order removing either the trustee or manager, or both, and replacing them with a person or persons nominated by the SIB, or appointing an authorised person to wind up the scheme: see s 93(1), (4).
4 Ibid, s 91(1)(a)–(c).
5 Ie a scheme recognised under ibid, s 87.
6 Ie a scheme recognised under ibid, s 88.
7 See ibid, s 91(5).
8 Ibid, s 92(1). The notice must state the reasons for the direction: s 92(3). Public notice of the direction may be given: s 92(4).

1330. Investigations. If it appears to the Securities and Investments Board ('SIB'), by delegation from the Secretary of State[1], that it is in the interests of the participants to do so or that the matter is of public concern, it may appoint one or more competent inspectors to investigate and report on:

(1) the affairs of, or of the manager or trustee of, any authorised unit trust scheme[2];

(2) the affairs of, or of the operator or trustee of, any recognised scheme so far as relating to activities carried on in the United Kingdom; or

(3) the affairs of, or of the operator or trustee of, any other collective investment scheme[3].

The powers of inspectors under the Companies Act 1985 are applied with modifications[4]. There is protection for client and professional legal adviser confidentiality[5] and for banking confidentiality[6]. The investigation may be curtailed if criminal acts come to light and are referred to the appropriate prosecuting authority[7].

1 Financial Services Act 1986 (Delegation) Order 1987, SI 1987/942.
2 For the meaning of 'authorised unit trust scheme', see para 1325 above.
3 Financial Services Act 1986 (c 60), s 94(1)(a)–(c). For the meaning of 'collective investment scheme', see para 1325 above, and as to recognised schemes, see para 1328 above. As to the inspector's powers to investigate other schemes with the same manager, trustee or operator, see s 94(2). As to reports, see s 94(8), (8B), (9), (s 94(8B) being added by the Companies Act 1989 (c 40), s 72(3)).
4 See the Financial Services Act 1986, s 94(3), applying, with modifications set out in s 94(4) (both amended by the Companies Act 1989, s 212, Sch 24), the Companies Act 1985 (c 6), ss 434–436 (for which see COMPANIES, vol 4, para 527).
5 See the Financial Services Act 1986, s 94(5).
6 See ibid, s 94(7), (7A) (substituted and added by the Companies Act 1989, s 72(2)).
7 Financial Services Act 1986, s 94(8A) (as added: see note 3 above).

(4) CONDUCT OF INVESTMENT BUSINESS

1331. Introduction. The Secretary of State has power to make rules regulating the conduct of investment business by authorised persons[1]. This power may be delegated to a 'designated agency' (the Securities and Investments Board). The Conduct of Business Rules are important to the protection of investors as they are the main way of regulating how day-to-day investment business is conducted.

1 See the Financial Services Act 1986 (c 60), s 48, and para 1356 below.
2 See ibid, s 114, and the Financial Services Act 1986 (Delegation) Order 1987, SI 1987/942.

1332. Misleading statements and practices. Any person who (1) makes a statement, promise or forecast which he knows to be misleading, false or deceptive or dishonestly conceals any material facts, or (2) recklessly makes (dishonestly or otherwise) a statement, promise or forecast which is misleading, false or deceptive, is guilty of an offence if he makes the statement, promise or forecast or conceals the facts for the purpose of inducing, or is reckless as to whether it may induce, another person[1] to enter or offer to enter into, or refrain from entering or offering to enter into, any investment agreement[2] or to exercise, or refrain from exercising, any rights conferred by an investment[3]. However, this does not apply unless the statement, promise or forecast is made in or from, or the facts are concealed in or from, the United Kingdom; or the person on whom the inducement is intended to or may have effect is in the United Kingdom; or the agreement is or would be entered into or the rights are or would be exercised in the United Kingdom[4].

Any person who does any act or engages in any course of conduct which creates a false or misleading impression as to the market in or the price or value of any investments is guilty of an offence if he does so for the purpose of creating that impression and of thereby inducing another person to acquire, dispose of, subscribe for or underwrite those investments or to refrain from doing so or to exercise, or refrain from exercising, any rights conferred by them[5]. However, this does not apply unless the act is done or the course of conduct is engaged in in the United Kingdom; or the false or misleading impression is created there[6].

Breach of these provisions carries a severe penalty. A person guilty of any of the above offences is liable on conviction on indictment to imprisonment for a term not exceeding seven years or a fine or both, or on summary conviction to imprisonment for a term not exceeding six months or a fine not exceeding the statutory maximum or both[7].

Attention must be drawn to the fact that these provisions have an extra-territorial effect[8]. If the effect of a breach of the provisions are suffered in the United Kingdom, the person guilty of the breach will be liable as though he had performed the breach in the United Kingdom. Therefore investors in the United Kingdom who suffer loss as a result of actions by an overseas person will have legal recourse[9]. For example, where an investor has suffered loss as a result of misleading statements or practices, the Court of Session may make a restitution order[10].

1 This need not be the person to whom the statement etc was made or from whom the facts were concealed.
2 'Investment agreement' means any agreement the making or performance of which by either party constitutes an activity which falls within any paragraph of the Financial Services Act 1986 (c 60), Sch 1, Pt II (paras 12–16), or would do so apart from Sch 1, Pt III (paras 17–25B) or Pt IV (paras 26, 27) (excluded activities): s 44(9).
3 Financial Services Act 1986 (c 60), s 47(1). For the penalties, see below.
4 Ibid, s 47(4)(a)–(c).
5 Ibid, s 47(2). For the penalties, see below. It is a defence for the accused to prove that he reasonably believed that his act or conduct would not create a false or misleading impression: s 47(3). Section 47(2) is not contravened by anything done for the purpose of stabilising the price of investments if done in conformity with conduct of business rules (see para 1388 below) and (1) in respect of investments within Sch 1, paras 1–5, and specified by the rules, and (2) during such period as is specified by the rules: s 48(7) (which may be amended by the Secretary of State under s 48(8) by restricting or extending the investments to which it applies, or by restricting it so as to apply only to investments issued in specified circumstances, or by extending it so as to apply to things done in respect of a particular kind of investment to things done during a specified period).
6 Ibid, s 47(5)(a), (b).
7 Ibid, s 47(6). As to the statutory maximum, see para 1301, note 4, above.
8 See the Financial Services Act 1986, s 47(4), (5).
9 It was held in *Secretary of State for Trade v Markus* [1976] AC 35, [1975] 1 All ER 958, HL, that the corresponding provisions of the Prevention of Fraud (Investments) Act 1958 (c 45), s 13(1) (repealed), created a 'result' crime. Therefore the provision applied to acts overseas producing results in the United Kingdom, as well as to acts actually performed in the United Kingdom. See also A Whittaker and G Morse *The Financial Services Act 1986: A Guide to the New Law* (1987).
10 See the Financial Services Act 1986, s 6(3), and para 1324 above.

1333. Prohibition on unsolicited calls or 'cold calling'. The Financial Services Act 1986 effectively prohibits unsolicited or 'cold' calling by declaring that unless specifically permitted by regulations[1] no persons may in the course of or in consequence of an unsolicited call[2] made on a person in the United Kingdom, or made from the United Kingdom on a person elsewhere, by way of business enter into an investment agreement with the person on whom the call is made or procure or endeavour to procure that person to enter into such an agreement[3].

The prohibition is not limited to authorised persons or even to those carrying on investment business. It is, however, limited to entering into an investment agreement or procuring or endeavouring to procure a person to do so in the course of or in consequence of an unsolicited call. Hence there is no prohibition on the unsolicited call itself[4].

The prohibition has an extra-territorial application. Unsolicited calls are prohibited if made overseas to persons in the United Kingdom and if made by persons in the United Kingdom to persons overseas.

1 See the Financial Services (Common Unsolicited Calls) Regulations 1991, made by the Securities and Investments Board, and para 1335 below.
2 'Unsolicited call' means a personal visit or oral communication made without express invitation: Financial Services Act 1986 (c 60), s 56(8).
3 Ibid, s 56(1). For the meaning of 'investment agreement', see para 1332, note 2, above. For the application of this provision to members of recognised self-regulating organisations and persons certified by recognised professional bodies, see s 56(7), (7A) (substituted and added by the Companies Act 1989 (c 40), s 206(1), Sch 23, para 7).
4 A Whittaker and G Morse *The Financial Services Act 1986: A Guide to the New Law* (1987).

1334. Effect of agreement entered into after cold calling. A person is not guilty of a criminal offence by contravening the prohibition on unsolicited calls[1]. He is, however, in contravention of the Financial Services Act 1986. Consequently interdict and restitution orders are available[2] and contraventions by authorised persons and their appointed representatives can give rise to disciplinary or intervention action. The most important sanction is, however, that any agreement entered into as a result will not be enforceable against the person on whom the call was made[3]. Furthermore, if that person parts with any money or other property as a result he may recover it, with compensation for any loss[4], although a court may allow such an agreement to be enforced or money or other property to be retained if it is satisfied:

(1) that the person on whom the call was made was not influenced or not influenced to any material extent by anything said or done in the course of or in consequence of the call;

(2) without prejudice to head (1), that the person on whom the call was made entered into the agreement (a) following discussions between the parties of such a nature and over such a period that his entering into the agreement can fairly be regarded as a consequence of those discussions rather than the call; and (b) was aware of the nature of the agreement and any risks involved in entering into it; or

(3) that the call was not made by (a) the person seeking to enforce the agreement or to retain the money or property, or a person acting on his behalf or an appointed representative[5] whose principal he was; or (b) a person who has received or is to receive, or in the case of an appointed representative whose principal has received or is to receive, any commission or other inducement in respect of the agreement from a person mentioned in head (3)(a)[6].

This sanction of unenforceability can apply even where the person who suffers from the unenforceability is not the person in contravention, since a contravention by a caller or intermediate dealer can prevent an ultimate dealer from enforcing the agreement.

Where a person elects not to perform an agreement which is unenforceable under these provisions, or by virtue of these provisions recovers money paid or other property transferred by him under the agreement, he must repay any money and return any other property which he received under the agreement[7].

1 Financial Services Act 1986 (c 60), s 56(2). For the prohibition, see para 1333 above.
2 See para 1324 above.
3 Financial Services Act 1986, s 56(2)(a).
4 Ibid, s 56(2)(b). The compensation is to be such as the parties may agree or the court, on the application of either party, may determine: s 56(3).

5 As to appointed representatives, see para 1361 below.
6 Financial Services Act 1986, s 56(4)(a)–(c).
7 Ibid, s 56(5).

1335. Unsolicited calls regulations. The Secretary of State may make regulations lifting the prohibition on cold calling[1], a power he has delegated to the Securities and Investments Board ('SIB')[2]. The SIB's Financial Services (Common Unsolicited Calls) Regulations 1991 apply to members of all self-regulating organisations. They distinguish between the 'dealing restriction' (that is, the restriction on entering into an investment agreement with the person on whom the unsolicited call is made) and the 'marketing restriction' (that is, the restriction on procuring or endeavouring to procure a person to enter into an investment agreement). The regulations permit 'cold' calls inter alia:

(1) to investors who do not fall within the definition of 'private investors'[3];
(2) to existing customers of the caller or dealer or associate of either;
(3) to certain individuals connected with the authorised firm;
(4) in certain circumstances in the course of a public takeover, acquisition of investment business or corporate acquisition;
(5) for certain purposes connected with employees' share schemes;
(6) made in the course of a profession or non-investment business;
(7) made in the course of non-commercial business;
(8) for the sale of non-geared packaged products[4];
(9) for services provided under a cancellable customer agreement;
(10) for certain purposes connected with occupational pension schemes; and
(11) to exempted persons[5].

There are also a number of limits on permissions provided. Calls prohibited by a telecommunications licence related to unsolicited calls and calls made by persons carrying on business in contravention of section 3 of the Financial Services Act 1986[6] are permissible only where they relate to public takeovers. There are also limits on calls made by unauthorised overseas persons, so that authorisation is required for business solicited by calls on private investors and business solicited by calls on business investors whose business does not include dealing in the products concerned. Authorisation is not, however, required for solicitations within the permission for takeovers subject to the City Code on Takeovers.

The cold calling rules apply only to investment business. Telephone calls inquiring whether the recipient would be interested in receiving advice about investments are not covered[7].

The Office of Fair Trading has issued guidelines on selling by telephone[8]. These provide, in particular, that unsolicited calls should not be made to people at their place of work.

1 Financial Services Act 1986 (c 60), s 57(1), and s 63A (added by the Companies Act 1989 (c 40), s 194).
2 Financial Services Act 1986 (Delegation) Order 1987, SI 1987/942.
3 For the meaning of 'private investor', see para 1412 below.
4 Ie a life policy, a unit in a regulated collective investment scheme or an investment trust savings scheme.
5 For the meaning of 'exempted person', see para 1306, note 3, above.
6 For the Financial Services Act 1986, s 3, see para 1306 above.
7 The present authors have been advised by SIB, with apparent approval, that there now exist wholly unauthorised firms of 'prospectors' who conduct such telephone surveys and sell the contacts so made to authorised providers of investment products and advice.
8 *Selling by Telephone* (October 1984). The guidelines are reprinted in telephone directories.

1336. Cancellation and cooling-off. Closely related to the provisions as to unsolicited calls are provisions as to cancellation and cooling-off. Rules made by the Securities and Investments Board ('SIB') (by delegation from the Secretary of State[1]) may enable a person who has entered or offered to enter into an investment agreement with an authorised person to rescind the agreement or withdraw the offer within a prescribed period and in a prescribed manner[2]. The underlying purpose of the rules which the SIB has made is to provide investors with the opportunity to make well-informed and considered investment decisions by giving a period for reflection, and, by making investors' commitments revocable during the cooling-off period, to reduce the incentive for firms selling investments to adopt 'hard-sell' tactics[3].

The rules specify the cases where a right to cancel arises by reference to the types of product[4] and the types of investor or circumstances of purchase[5]. Where there is a right to cancel, the firm which enters into the agreement with the investor must post to him[6] a prescribed form of notice of the right to cancel[7] within fifteen days of the agreement or, where the agreement was for a lump sum or single payment and the market falls during the cancellation period so that the firm is entitled to charge on cancellation (for 'shortfall'), within eight days of the agreement[8]. A person who receives such a notice may cancel the agreement by giving notice of cancellation before the end of the fourteenth day after the day of receipt of the notice of the right to cancel[9]. If the firm fails to give notice of the right to cancel, the investor may cancel at any time within two years of the agreement[10]. Service of notice of cancellation has the effect of withdrawing any offer by the person giving the notice to enter into the investment agreement and rescinds any such agreement, subject to the transfer back of any property transferred under the agreement, the repayment of any money paid in connection with the agreement or proposed agreement, and the payment to the firm of any sum paid by it under the agreement or due to it by way of 'shortfall'[11].

1 Financial Services Act 1986 (Delegation) Order 1987, SI 1987/942.
2 Financial Services Act 1986 (c 60), s 51(1). The rules may also require certain notices to be served and provide for the restitution of property and the recovery of payments: see s 51(2).
3 SIB Financial Services (Cancellation) Rules 1989, r 2.01, Explanation (b).
4 See ibid, r 2.01, Table CA1.
5 See ibid, r 2.01, Table CA2.
6 In the case of a life policy issued in the course of industrial assurance business the notice may be given rather than posted: ibid, r 2.02(3).
7 Ibid, Schedule, Forms 1A, 1B.
8 Ibid, rr 2.02(1), (2), 2.05.
9 Ibid, r 2.03.
10 Ibid, r 2.02(6).
11 Ibid, r 2.04.

1337. Restrictions on advertising. Subject to certain exceptions[1], no person other than an authorised person may issue or cause to be issued an investment advertisement[2] in the United Kingdom unless its contents have been approved by an authorised person[3].

Contravention of this provision is a criminal offence[4]; any agreement or obligation entered into as a result will not be enforceable, and if a person parts with any money or other property as a result he may recover it, with compensation for any loss[5], although in proper circumstances a court may allow such an agreement or obligation to be enforced or money or other property to be retained[6].

This prohibition has extra-territorial application in that investment advertisements actually issued outside the United Kingdom are to be treated as though they were issued in the United Kingdom if they are directed to persons in the United Kingdom or made available to them otherwise than in a newspaper, journal, magazine or other periodical published and circulating principally outside the United Kingdom or in a sound or television broadcast transmitted principally for reception outside the United Kingdom[7].

1 For the exceptions, see the Financial Services Act 1986 (c 60), s 58. They include appropriate advertisements by the United Kingdom or other governments, local authorities, the Bank of England, international organisations, exempt persons (such as recognised investment exchanges and clearing houses, Lloyd's, listed money market institutions, appointed representatives), or nationals of other member states in the course of lawful investment business; advertisements in connection with listing applications; certain advertisements concerning unlisted securities; and advertisements exempted by order under s 58(3) made by the Secretary of State (see the Financial Services Act 1986 (Investment Advertisements) (Exemptions) Order 1988, SI 1988/316, the Financial Services Act 1986 (Investment Advertisements) (Exemptions) (No 2) Order 1988, SI 1988/716, and the Financial Services Act 1986 (Investment Advertisements) (Exemptions) Order 1990, SI 1990/27).

2 'An investment advertisement' means an advertisement inviting persons to enter or offer to enter into an investment agreement (defined in para 1332, note 7, above) or to exercise any rights conferred by an investment to acquire, dispose of, underwrite or convert an investment or containing information calculated to lead directly or indirectly to persons doing so: Financial Services Act 1986, s 57(2). 'Advertisement' includes every form of advertising, whether in a publication, by the display of notices, signs, labels or showcards, by means of circulars, catalogues, price lists or other documents, by an exhibition of pictures or photographic or cinematographic films, by way of sound broadcasting or television, by the distribution of recordings, or in any other manner, and references to the issue of an advertisement are to be construed accordingly: s 207(2).

3 Ibid, s 57(1). For Core Conduct of Business Rules on advertising, see paras 1366 ff below.

4 See the Financial Services Act 1986, s 57(3). It is a defence for an accused person who in the ordinary course of a business other than investment business issues an advertisement to the order of another person to prove that he believed on reasonable grounds that that other person was an authorised person (defined in para 1306, note 2, above), that the contents of the advertisement were approved by an authorised person or that the advertisement was permitted by or under s 58 (see note 1 above): 57(4).

5 See ibid, s 57(5)–(7).

6 See bid, s 57(8).

7 Ibid, s 207(3).

1338. Employment of prohibited persons. If it appears to the Securities and Investments Board ('SIB'), by delegation from the Secretary of State[1], that any individual is not a fit and proper person to be employed[2] in connection with investment business[3] or investment business of a particular kind, it may by 'a disqualification direction' direct that he is not, without its written consent, to be so employed:

(1) by authorised persons or exempted persons, or

(2) by any specified person or persons, or by persons of any specified description, falling within head (1)[4].

A disqualification direction, which must specify the date on which it takes effect, must be served on the person to whom it relates[5]. Any consent to the employment of a disqualified person may relate to employment generally or employment of a particular kind, may be given subject to conditions and restrictions and may be varied from time to time[6].

Where the SIB proposes to give a disqualification direction or to refuse an application for consent or for the variation of consent it must give the person concerned notice of its intention, stating its reasons and giving particulars of the right to require the case to be referred to the Financial Services Tribunal[7].

A person who accepts or continues in employment in contravention of a disqualification direction is guilty of an offence[8], and it is the duty of an authorised person and an appointed representative to take reasonable care not to employ or continue to employ a person in contravention of such a direction[9].

As the SIB does not publish a list of prohibited persons (although it may publish statements in particular cases[10]), it appears that the only means of ensuring that the duty not to employ or continue to employ a person in contravention of a direction is to contact the SIB with the name of the person concerned to ascertain whether that person has been prohibited.

1 Financial Services Act 1986 (Delegation) Order 1987, SI 1987/942.
2 'Employment' includes employment otherwise than under a contract of service: Financial Services Act 1986 (c 60), s 59(8).
3 For the meaning of 'investment business', see para 1307 above.
4 Financial Services Act 1986, s 59(1)(a), (b). For the meaning of 'authorised person' and 'exempted person', see para 1306, notes 2, 3, above. The SIB may revoke a disqualification direction: s 59(7).
5 Ibid, s 59(2).
6 Ibid, s 59(3).
7 Ibid, s 59(4). As to the tribunal, see paras 1416–1419 below.
8 Ibid, s 59(5).
9 Ibid, s 59(6).
10 See para 1339 below.

1339. Public statement as to misconduct. If it appears to the Securities and Investments Board ('SIB'), by delegation from the Secretary of State[1], that a person who is or was an authorised person of a specified class[2] has contravened any provision of rules or regulations relating to the conduct of investment business[3] or the provisions as to unsolicited calls[4] or the employment of prohibited persons[5], or any condition subject to which conduct of business rules and financial resources rules have been modified[6], it may publish a statement to that effect[7], having first given the person concerned written notice of the proposed statement and its reasons for making it[8].

1 Financial Services Act 1986 (Delegation) Order 1987, SI 1987/942.
2 Ie an authorised person (defined in para 1306, note 2, above) by virtue of the Financial Services Act 1986 (c 60), s 22 (authorised insurers), s 24 (operators and trustees of collective investment schemes), s 25 (persons authorised by the SIB), or s 31 (persons authorised in other member states).
3 Ie rules or regulations made under ibid, Pt I, Ch V (ss 47–63c). These include conduct of business rules, financial resources rules, notification regulations, indemnity rules, and regulations as to client's money.
4 Ie ibid, s 56: see paras 1333, 1334, above.
5 Ie ibid, s 59: see para 1338 above.
6 Ie under ibid, s 50.
7 Ibid, s 60(1).
8 Ibid, s 60(2). The notice must give particulars of the right to have the case referred to the Financial Services Tribunal (as to which see paras 1416–1419 below): s 60(4). Unless the case is so referred, the SIB must notify the person concerned that the statement is or is not to be published, and, if it is published, must send a copy of it to him: s 60(5). Where the reasons stated in the notice of the proposed statement relate specifically to matters which refer to an identified third person and are prejudicial to him in any office or employment, the SIB must serve a copy of the notice on that person if practicable (s 60(3)), and if the statement is subsequently published must send him a copy of it (s 60(5)).

(5) THE SIB RULES: THE NEW SETTLEMENT

(a) Introduction

1340. Rule-making powers of the Securities and Investments Board. The Financial Services Act 1986 bestows on the Securities and Investments Board

('SIB'), by delegation from the Secretary of State[1], wide-ranging powers to make rules and regulations regulating all areas of conduct of investment business by authorised persons[2]. The Act permits the making of:

(1) 'conduct of business rules' regulating the conduct of investment business generally[3];

(2) 'financial resources rules' requiring authorised persons to have and maintain adequate financial resources[4];

(3) 'cancellation rules' enabling a person to rescind an investment agreement[5];

(4) 'notification regulations' obliging an authorised person to notify the SIB of certain events[6];

(5) 'indemnity rules' concerning indemnity against claims raised against authorised persons in connection with investment business[7];

(6) rules establishing a compensation fund[8];

(7) regulations governing the holding of clients' money[9]; and

(8) rules permitting certain unsolicited calls[10].

1 Financial Services Act 1986 (Delegation) Order 1987, SI 1987/942.

2 For the meaning of 'authorised person', see para 1306, note 2, above.

3 See the Financial Services Act 1986 (c 60), s 48 (amended by the Companies Act 1989 (c 40), ss 206(1), 212, Sch 23, para 2, Sch 24), the Core Conduct of Business Rules and the Financial Services (Conduct of Business) Rules 1990, both made by the SIB, and paras 1356 ff below. As to modifications of the Financial Services Act 1986, ss 48, 49, to adapt the rules to the circumstances of a particular applicant, see s 50 (amended by the Companies Act 1989, Sch 23, para 4).

4 See the Financial Services Act 1986, s 49 (amended by the Companies Act 1989, Sch 23, para 3), and the Financial Services (Financial Supervision) Rules 1990 made by the SIB. See paras 1402 ff below. As to modifications, see note 3 above.

5 See the Financial Services Act 1986, s 51, and the Financial Services (Cancellation) Rules 1989 made by the SIB. See para 1336 above.

6 See the Financial Services Act 1986, s 52 (amended by the Companies Act 1989, Sch 23, para 5), and the Financial Services (Notification) Regulations 1988 made by the SIB.

7 See the Financial Services Act 1986, s 53, which is to come into force on a day to be appointed by order under s 211(1).

8 See ibid, s 54, and the Financial Services (Compensation of Investors) Rules 1990 made by the SIB. See para 1421 below.

9 See the Financial Services Act 1986, s 55 (amended by the Companies Act 1989, Sch 23, para 6, Sch 24), and the Financial Services (Clients' Money) Regulations 1987 and the Financial Services (Investment Business Clients' Money) (Chartered Accountants) Regulations 1988, both made by the SIB. See para 1409 below.

10 See the Financial Services Act 1986, s 56(1), the Financial Services (Common Unsolicited Calls) Regulations 1991 made by the SIB, and para 1335 above.

1341. Recent statutory changes. The rules and regulations originally made by the Securities and Investments Board ('SIB') under the provisions listed in the preceding paragraph were many and detailed. Even before the provisions were fully implemented, the form and content of the rule books of the SIB and self-regulating organisations were subject to substantial criticism, from both authorised persons and bodies representing consumer interests, as being too complex, cumbersome and detailed. Criticism grew louder as the volume and complexity of amendments, proposed amendments, transitional provisions and guidance notes issued by the SIB increased[1].

As a result of this pressure the SIB Chairman, Sir David Walker, announced a thorough review of the SIB rules. The results of this review are embodied in the Companies Act 1989[2] and the 'new settlement' approach to rule-making. The amendments to the Financial Services Act 1986 effected by the 1989 Act achieved two main purposes.

First, there is a restriction on the right to raise an action for damages in respect of any contravention of rules made under the 1986 Act. Formerly all investors had the right to sue for damages for loss suffered as a result of such a contravention[3]. Now the right of action is restricted to 'private investors'[4].

Secondly, the previous 'equivalence test' is replaced by an 'adequacy test' which takes account of the costs of compliance for authorised persons and permits the restructuring of the SIB rule book to a three-tier approach involving:

(1) the creation of 'statements of principle' with respect to the conduct and financial standing of persons authorised to carry on investment business[5];

(2) a set of core rules made by the SIB in consultation with the self-regulating organisations ('SROs')[6], which will be common to all such organisations and serve as an enforcement backbone for the regulatory system and as a framework for its more detailed aspects; and

(3) detailed support, made by each SRO in consultation with the SIB, which may take the form of rules or formal guidance[7] which differs between SROs[8].

1 By January 1990 some seventy amendment releases had been issued, together with some thirty consultative papers.
2 See the Companies Act 1989 (c 40), Pt VIII (ss 192–206), with Schs 23, 24, which amend the Financial Services Act 1986 (c 60). Further amendments to the 1986 Act are effected by the Companies Act 1989, ss 72–76, relating particularly to investigations.
3 See the Financial Services Act 1986, s 62, and para 1412 below, where 'private investor' is defined.
4 See ibid, s 62A (added by the Companies Act 1989, s 193(1)), and para 1412 below.
5 See the Financial Services Act 1986, s 47A (added by the Companies Act 1989, s 192), and paras 1342 ff below.
6 See the Financial Services Act 1986, s 63A (added by the Companies Act 1989, s 194), and paras 1356 ff below. The core rules apply also to friendly societies and are designated under the Financial Services Act 1986, Sch 11, para 22B (added by the Companies Act 1989, s 206(1), Sch 23, para 36).
7 'Formal guidance' means guidance which is intended to have continuing effect and is issued generally or to a class of persons and in writing or other legible form: SIB Financial Services Glossary 1991. Generally, compliance with formal guidance will raise a presumption that a firm is in compliance with the relevant rule to which the guidance refers, and failure to comply with formal guidance will raise a presumption that a firm is not in compliance with the relevant rule.
8 See SIB *Regulation of the Conduct of Investment Business: A Proposal* (August 1989).

(b) SIB Statements of Principle

(A) THE PRINCIPLES

1342. Introduction. Under amendments to the Financial Services Act 1986 effected by the Companies Act 1989, the Securities and Investments Board ('SIB'), by delegation from the Secretary of State[1], may issue statements of principle with respect to the conduct and financial standing of persons authorised to carry on investment business[2]. The conduct expected may include compliance with a code or standard issued by another person[3]. Failure to comply with a statement of principle is a ground for taking disciplinary action[4] or the exercise of powers of intervention, but does not of itself give rise to any right of action by investors or other persons affected or affect the validity of any transaction[5]. The relevant regulatory authority may on the application of any person modify a statement of principle to adapt it to his circumstances, or dispense him from compliance with it, if compliance would be unduly burdensome for him and the modification or dispensation will not result in undue risk to investors[6].

The SIB's Statements of Principle were issued on 15 March 1990 and came into effect on 30 April 1990[7]. They are intended to form a universal statement of the standards expected of persons who are involved in investment business[8]. They apply directly to the conduct of such business and financial standing of all authorised persons ('firms'), including members of recognised self-regulating organisations and firms certified by recognised professional bodies[8]. The principles are not exhaustive of the standards expected[9]. Conformity with them does not absolve a failure to observe other requirements, while the observance of other requirements does not necessarily amount to conformity with the principles[9].

1 Companies Act 1989 (Commencement No 3, Transitional Provisions and Transfer of Functions under the Financial Services Act 1986) Order 1990, SI 1990/354.
2 Financial Services Act 1986 (c 60), s 47A(1) (added by the Companies Act 1989 (c 40), s 192). For the meaning of 'investment business', see para 1307 above.
3 Financial Services Act 1986, s 47A(2) (as so added).
4 Ie (1) the withdrawal or suspension of authorisation under ibid, s 28 (see para 1311 above), or the termination or suspension of authorisation under s 33 (see para 1320 above); (2) a disqualification direction under s 59 (see para 1338 above); (3) a public statement under s 60 (see para 1339 above); or (4) an interdict or other order under s 61(1) (see paras 1410, 1411, below): s 47A(4) (as so added).
5 Ibid, s 47A(3) (as so added).
6 Ibid, s 47B(1), (2) (as so added). As to the relevant regulatory authority, see s 47B(4) (as so added).
7 SIB Statements of Principle, Introduction, para (5).
8 Ibid, Introduction, para (1).
9 Ibid, Introduction, para (2).

1343. Integrity. A firm should observe high standards of integrity and fair dealing[1].

1 SIB Statements of Principle, principle 1.

1344. Skill, care and diligence. A firm should act with due skill, care and diligence[1].
'Due skill' implies ensuring that the firm has the requisite competence, acquired by training and experience, to carry on its business and that such competence is properly applied[2]. 'Due care' suggests a variable standard of care reflected in the categorisation of customers or clients by the Securities and Investments Board according to their degree of sophistication in the relevant market. 'Due diligence' calls for the application of the effort required to carry through the action.

1 SIB Statements of Principle, principle 2.
2 See Dr Oonagh McDonald's report to the SIB *Competence in the Financial Services Industry* (1990).

1345. Market practice. A firm should observe high standards of market conduct. It should also, to the extent endorsed for the purpose of this principle, comply with any code or standard as in force from time to time and as it applies to the firm either according to its terms or by rulings made under it[1].
There may be circumstances where compliance with recognised market practice can amount to a custom so as to be recognised as legally binding on the parties[2]. Difficulties may arise in relation to codes or standards 'endorsed for the purpose of this principle'. The endorsement is expected to be made by the appropriate regulator[3], and the extent of the endorsement will depend upon the nature of the regulator. It is probable that the Law Societies will endorse codes only to the extent compatible with their members' professional duties so that, for example, 'cold shoulder' rules requiring the practitioner to withdraw his

services from anyone in breach of a particular code (such as the Takeover Code) would be excluded from the endorsement.

1 SIB Statements of Principle, principle 3.
2 See eg *Clydesdale Bank (Moore Place) Nominees Ltd v Snodgrass* 1939 SC 805, 1940 SLT 46.
3 Ie the Securities and Investments Board, a self-regulating organisation or a recognised professional body.

1346. Information about customers. A firm should seek from customers it advises or for whom it exercises discretion any information about their circumstances and investment objectives which might reasonably be expected to be relevant in enabling the firm to fulfil its responsibilities to them[1].

This is the basis of the 'know your client' rules[2]. It should be noted that the duty is to 'seek' the information. The principle does not require the firm to refrain from advising or exercising discretion in the absence of the information sought. However, a firm in such a position should proceed only with great care if after advising the customer the firm proceeds without full information.

1 SIB Statements of Principle, principle 4.
2 See SIB Core Code of Business Rules, r 16, and para 1373 below.

1347. Information for customers. A firm should take reasonable steps to give a customer it advises, in a comprehensible[1] and timely way, any information needed to enable him to make a balanced and informed decision[2]. A firm should similarly be ready to provide a customer with a full and fair account of the fulfilment of its responsibilities to him[3].

1 As to comprehensibility of information, see SIB Core Conduct of Business Rule 9, and para 1371 below.
2 As to the disclosure of the risks involved in a particular investment, see ibid, r 10, and para 1372 below.
3 SIB Statements of Principle, principle 5. For conduct of business rules concerning information about packaged products and about the firm, see paras 1363, 1364 below.

1348. Conflicts of interest. A firm should either avoid any conflict of interest arising or, where conflicts arise, should ensure fair treatment to all its customers by disclosure, internal rules of confidentiality, declining to act, or otherwise. A firm should not unfairly place its interests above those of its customers and, where a properly informed customer would reasonably expect that the firm would place his interests above its own, the firm should live up to that expectation[1].

In the view of the present authors, this principle illustrates a major flaw in the regime of the Financial Services Act 1986 which fails to distinguish adequately between the agent acting for a client and the salesperson selling a product to a customer. It is notable that the principle itself does not require disclosure of the conflict to the client[2]. The authors are also concerned that the principle implies that in the case of a conflict of interest the firm may 'fairly' place its interests above the client's interests.

1 SIB Statements of Principle, principle 6. See also para 1355 below.
2 However, see the comments on SIB Core Code of Business Rules, r 2, in para 1358 below.

1349. Customer assets. Where a firm has control of or is otherwise responsible for assets belonging to a customer which it is required to safeguard, it should arrange proper protection for them, by way of segregation and identification of those assets or otherwise, in accordance with the responsibility it has accepted[1].

It is difficult to envisage any situation in which a firm would have control of or be responsible for a customer's assets without being under a duty to safeguard them, whether or not that duty has been expressed in a customer agreement. Identification of the customer's assets must be essential, so the inclusion of the words 'or otherwise' is puzzling.

1 SIB Statements of Principle, principle 7. For conduct of business rules as to safeguarding customer investments, see para 1391 below.

1350. Financial resources. A firm should ensure that it maintains adequate financial resources to meet its investment business commitments and to withstand the risks to which its business is subject[1].

While the drafting covers both the agent acting for a client, where the risk is not significant, and the dealer who operates on his own account and sometimes with or for a customer, where the risks can be substantial, this principle offers no guidance as to the adequacy of financial resources. It therefore appears possible that a firm could find itself in breach of the principle and subject to disciplinary or intervention action, but not an action for damages[2] where the firm has complied with the financial resources requirements of its regulator, but it collapses because it cannot meet its investment business commitments. It might have been preferable for the principle to have been expressed the other way about, namely that a firm should not take on investment business commitments or risks beyond its financial resources.

1 SIB Statements of Principle, principle 8. For rules on financial supervision, see paras 1402 ff below.
2 See para 1341 above.

1351. Internal organisation. A firm should organise and control its internal affairs in a responsible manner, keeping proper records, and where the firm employs staff or is responsible for the conduct of investment business by others, should have adequate arrangements to ensure that they are suitable, adequately trained and properly supervised and that it has well-defined compliance procedures[1].

It is possible that the temptation to be brief has distorted the meaning of this principle. The core and third-tier rules make clear that proper records are to be kept in order to demonstrate that the firm has organised and controlled its internal affairs responsibly[2].

1 SIB Statements of Principle, principle 9. For the rules on financial supervision associated with this principle, see para 1402 below, and as to compliance and record keeping, see SIB Core Conduct of Business Rule 34, and para 1393 below.
2 See para 1393 below.

1352. Relations with regulators. A firm should deal with its regulator[1] in an open and co-operative manner and keep the regulator promptly informed of anything concerning the firm which might reasonably be expected to be disclosed to it[2].

1 Ie the Securities and Investments Board, self-regulating organisation or recognised professional body.
2 SIB Statements of Principle, principle 10. The SIB and self-regulating organisations require regular returns from authorised firms as a condition of membership. For the rules on financial supervision associated with this principle, see para 1402 below, and as to the disclosure of information to a firm's regulator, see SIB Core Conduct of Business Rules 31, 34, and paras 1390, 1393, below.

(B) THE PRINCIPLES AND FIDUCIARY DUTIES

1353. Classification of adviser. While most of the SIB Principles are unexceptionable, there are some indications of the compromises required to achieve statements which are tolerable to all participators in the investment business field. The main compromise arises from the failure adequately to distinguish between those who engage in investment business as agents on behalf of clients and those who do so as principals dealing with customers. For the former group it is possible that the standards in principles 1 and 3 (integrity; market practice)[1] are not high enough, and it is certain that the standard in principle 6 (conflicts of interest)[2] is inadequate. The duties enshrined in these principles spring from fiduciary duties of agents which, in the view of the present authors, are not in any way abrogated or reduced by the Financial Services Act 1986. Principals dealing with customers may seek some shelter from the concept of *caveat emptor*, but as many principals represent themselves to the public as people of skill, situations may well arise where it is clear that the 'customer' is placing reliance on that skill.

This area of uncertainty may be clarified when the Law Commissions report on a reference from the Department of Trade and Industry in April 1990 which has been explained thus:

> 'Certain professional and business activities are subject to public law regulation by statutory or self-regulatory control. The Scottish Law Commission is to consider the principles which should govern the effect of such controls on the fiduciary and analogous duties of those carrying on such activities, and to make recommendations. The enquiry will consider examples from differing areas of activity but will be with particular reference to financial services'[3].

1 See paras 1343, 1345, above.
2 See para 1348 above.
3 Scottish Law Commission *25th Annual Report for 1989–90*, para 2.43.

1354. The nature of the fiduciary duties. Fiduciary and analogous duties of authorised persons are at present regulated by the common law and the regulatory framework of the Financial Services Act 1986 (c 60). In the present context it is instructive to take note of the fiduciary duties relevant to investor protection and to consider how far those duties are met by the new regime being developed by the Securities and Investments Board ('SIB'). Professor Gloag provided a useful introduction to the law in this area[1]. On the basis of this, it is suggested that the following duties are relevant to the present discussion:

(1) An agent is bound to account to his principal for any incidental advantage which, without the knowledge of his principal, he has obtained from his position as agent. The agent's liability is measured by the gain he has made and not by the loss, if any, which his principal has sustained.

(2) An agent must not act in such a way as to bring his interests into conflict with those of his principal.

(3) An agent employed to introduce business is not entitled, without the knowledge and consent of his principal, to take any commission from the party with whom he deals. The principal's consent may be presumed if the principal gave no payment and if the agent's work was of a character not generally done gratuitously. A custom of trade not known to the principal is no defence for a secret commission.

(4) An invitation to take shares in a company involves *uberrima fides*.

(5) A director is in a fiduciary relationship to the company of which he is a director. A director is not entitled to make any undisclosed or secret profit from his position.

(6) An agent is in a fiduciary relationship with his principal which requires full disclosure on the basis of *uberrima fides*.

It will be noticed that the SIB Statements of Principle make no reference whatsoever to fiduciary duties or to the common law. Principle 3 requires that a firm should observe 'high standards of market conduct'[2], but if the standards of market conduct are represented by the rules of the SIB, of self-regulating organisations and of recognised professional bodies there is at least one area where those standards are lower than the requirements of the fiduciary duties outlined above[3].

1 W M Gloag *The Law of Contract* (2nd edn, 1929) ch XXXI (pp 508 ff).
2 See para 1345 above.
3 See para 1355 below.

1355. Conflicts of interest. SIB principle 6 deals with conflicts of interest and requires that a firm should avoid any conflicts of interest or ensure fair treatment to all its customers and that a firm should not unfairly place its interests above those of its customers[1]. This is clearly a lower standard than that set out under head (2) in the preceding paragraph. In *Aberdeen Railway Company v Blaikie Brothers* the Lord Chancellor, Lord Cranworth, said:

'... agents have duties to discharge of a fiduciary nature towards their principal. And it is a rule of universal application, that no one, having such duties to discharge, shall be allowed to enter into engagements in which he has, or can have, a personal interest conflicting, or which possibly may conflict, with the interests of those whom he is bound to protect'[2].

It should be noted that solicitors in Scotland have been advised by the Law Society of Scotland that the SIB Principles apply unless some higher duty prevails. In such circumstances solicitors who are involved in investment business must ensure that they also comply with their common law obligations.

1 See para 1348 above.
2 *Aberdeen Rly Co v Blaikie Bros* (1854) 1 Macq 461 at 471, HL.

(c) The Core Conduct of Business Rules

(A) INTRODUCTION

1356. General. After the Statements of Principle, the next tier in the new regime is the Core Conduct of Business Rules of the Securities and Investments Board ('SIB'). The Financial Services Act 1986 empowers the SIB to make rules regulating the conduct of investment business[1] by authorised persons, although the rules do not apply to persons certified by a recognised professional body ('RPB') in respect of such business which they carry on subject to the rules of that body[2]. However, the rules do apply to members of self-regulating organisations ('SROs') in respect of investment business which they carry on subject to the rules of the organisation[3], and also to friendly societies[4].

There are forty core rules, largely condensed from the existing SIB and SRO rule books. The purpose of the core rules is to establish common standards of behaviour throughout the financial services industry in the United Kingdom. They represent an attempt by the SIB to deregulate the industry in respect of dealings with non-private customers (essentially large businesses and professional and experienced investors) and to re-establish the concept of self-regulation by allowing the SROs to impose the detailed and specialised third-tier rules and guidance tailored to fit the particular kind of business carried on by their members. Whilst the rules do not apply to persons certified by RPBs, the SIB expects that RPBs will find it helpful to make use of the core rules in revising their own rule books as the core rules reflect important elements of the SIB's assessment of what constitutes 'adequate' investor protection.

1 For the meaning of 'investment business', see para 1307 above.
2 Financial Services Act 1986 (c 60), s 48(1) (amended by the Companies Act 1989 (c 40), ss 206(1), 212, Sch 23, para 2, Sch 24). For provision which may be made by the rules, see the Financial Services Act 1986, s 48(2)–(5).
3 Ibid, s 63A(1) (added by the Companies Act 1989, s 194).
4 See the Financial Services Act 1986, s 140, Sch 11, para 14 (amended by the Companies Act 1989, Sch 23, para 23, Sch 24).

(B) INDEPENDENCE

1357. Inducements. Core Rule 1 provides that:

'A firm must take reasonable steps to ensure that neither it nor any of its agents:
(a) offers or gives, or
(b) solicits or accepts,
either in the course of regulated business or otherwise any inducement which is likely significantly to conflict with any duties of the recipient (or the recipient's employer) owed to customers in connection with regulated business'[1].

The giving or receipt of gifts or other inducements to place business is caught by this rule, although inducements (such as commission) which are disclosed to the client in advance will be excluded[2]. Also excluded from this requirement are any reasonable arrangements for remuneration between a firm and its employees or appointed or company representatives. This will allow company salespersons, for example, to continue to be remunerated in whole or in part through commissions related to the volume of sales generated. Product companies will still be able to vary commission amounts payable to independent intermediaries according to the size of the individual transactions placed so that the reduction in commercial costs of dealing in large transactions can be reflected. However, the practice of some product companies of paying an independent intermediary commission linked to the total volume of business placed by him (known as 'volume overriders') continues to be outlawed due to the likelihood of such volume overriders conflicting with the intermediary's duties to his customers.

1 SIB Core Code of Business Rules, r 1. 'Regulated business' means investment business (defined in para 1307 above) which is (1) business carried on from a permanent place of business maintained by a firm or its appointed representative in the United Kingdom; and (2) other business carried on with or for customers in the United Kingdom unless it is (a) business carried on from an office of a firm outside the United Kingdom which would not be treated as carried on in the United Kingdom if that office were a separate person, or (b) business of an appointed representative of the firm which is not carried on in the United Kingdom: SIB Financial Services Glossary 1991.
2 The SIB Financial Services Glossary 1991 excludes from the definition of 'inducements' disclosable commission.

1358. Material interest. Core Rule 2 provides as follows:

'Where a firm has a material interest in a transaction to be entered into with or for a customer or a relationship which gives rise to a conflict of interest in relation to such a transaction, the firm must not knowingly either advise, or deal in the exercise of discretion, in relation to that transaction unless it takes reasonable steps to ensure fair treatment for the customer'[1].

It is likely that in the majority of cases 'fair treatment' will be ensured by the third-tier rules requiring disclosure of the precise nature and extent of the material interest, adherence to an 'independence' policy whereby an employee must disregard any material interest when advising or dealing for a customer, and obtaining the customer's express consent, either in the client agreement[2] or separately. Such disclosure, 'independence' and consent is required where, for example, the firm has dealt as principal or as agent for an associated company or in a dual agency capacity and where the firm has been involved in the underwriting or other arrangements for the issuing of securities being purchased by the investor.

Circumstances where 'Chinese wall' arrangements[3] prevent information being transferred between different departments in multi-faceted financial services companies (for example the investment management and corporate finance arms of a financial conglomerate) are not excluded from the requirements of this rule.

'Material interest', in relation to a transaction, does not include (1) disclosable commission on the transaction, or (2) goods or services which can reasonably be expected to assist in the provision of investment services to customers and which are provided or to be provided under a soft commission agreement[4].

1 SIB Core Conduct of Business Rules, r 2. As to conflict of interest, see also SIB Statements of Principle, principle 6, and para 1348 above.
2 See para 1375 below.
3 As to 'Chinese walls', see para 1395 below.
4 SIB Financial Services Glossary 1991. As to soft commission agreements, see para 1359 below.

1359. Soft commission.
Core Rule 3 outlines the circumstances in and the conditions subject to which firms may enter into 'soft commission' arrangements (defined below). It provides that:

'A firm which deals for a customer on an advisory basis or in the exercise of discretion may not so deal through a broker pursuant to a soft commission agreement unless:

(a) the only benefits to be provided under the agreement are goods or services which can reasonably be expected to assist in the provision of investment services to the firm's customers and which are in fact so used;
(b) the broker has agreed to provide best execution to the customer[1];
(c) the firm is satisfied on reasonable grounds that the terms of business and methods by which the relevant broking services will be supplied do not involve any potential for comparative price disadvantage to the customer;
(d) in transactions in which the broker acts as principal, he is not remunerated by spread alone[2]; and
(e) adequate prior and periodic disclosure is made'[3].

'Soft commission agreement' means any agreement, whether oral or written, under which a firm which deals in securities on an advisory basis or in the exercise of discretion receives goods or services in return for an assurance that not less than a certain amount of such business will be put through or in the way of another person[4].

Such arrangements are becoming increasingly common both in the United Kingdom and in other jurisdictions. In purchasing and disposing of equities, investors (in practice only institutional investors such as portfolio managers) have the option of dealing through a market maker where no commission is payable — the market maker making his profit or 'turn' on the spread between the price at which he is prepared to offer stock to the market ('the offer price') and the price at which he is prepared to bid for stock ('the bid price') — or dealing through an agency broker who will himself deal with a market maker (usually guaranteeing to obtain the best price offered by all competing market makers) and will charge a commission for doing this. In addition to providing this execution service, agency brokers also provide stock information, research and analysis. Since agency brokers in general guarantee the best price, the quantity and quality of such additional services influences the investor's choice of agency broker. The provision by brokers of such research and analysis services is obviously economic only if a certain level of commission business can be generated from the investor or investment house to whom the services are provided. Accordingly agency brokers have taken to formalising these arrangements, undertaking to provide specified research, analysis and other services, either supplied by in-house analysts or acquired by the broker from a third party, in return for a firm undertaking from the investor to place a certain amount of business through the broker. In determining the level of commission business required, the broker will apply a 'multiple' to the 'hard' cost of the service.

1　Although under SIB Core Conduct of Business Rules, r 22 (see para 1381 below), best execution does not always have to be provided to non-private customers, this paragraph requires that best execution must always be provided when a transaction is executed which might generate soft commission.

2　This paragraph effectively prohibits 'soft for net' arrangements where the broker deals 'net', ie without commission, making his 'turn' on the 'spread'. Paragraph (c) may also prohibit such arrangements where the multiplier required is too low to be economically viable.

3　SIB Core Conduct of Busiess Rules, r 3.

4　SIB Financial Services Glossary 1991.

1360. Polarisation. Core Rule 4 provides as follows:

'(1)　A firm which advises a private customer[1] on packaged products[2] must either:
(a)　be a product company[3] or its marketing group associate[4]; or
(b)　do so as an independent intermediary.

(2)　A firm which is a product company or its marketing group associate must not advise customers to buy packaged products which are not those of the marketing group.

(3)　A firm which acts as an independent intermediary in advising a private customer on packaged products must act as an independent intermediary whenever it advises private customers on packaged products in the course of regulated business[5].

(4)　But where a firm acts as an investment manager for a customer, the core rule on polarisation does not prevent the firm from advising the customer on any packaged product'[6].

As a result of pressure from financial institutions and the Office of Fair Trading[7], the polarisation principle is somewhat blurred in terms of advice provided by an investment manager. Core rule 4(4) is the manifestation of this blurring in that it allows tied agents to refer clients to independent intermediaries and to participate in 'conduit advice', that is, the channelling of advice from independent intermediaries to clients, provided the tied agent does not comment on the merits of the advice given by the independent intermediary.

It must be noted that Core Rule 4 is intended to be read with Core Rule 17[8], which puts an obligation on the firm to ensure that those advising on packaged products should be fully informed of the products they are able to sell.

1　'Private customer' means (1) a customer who is an individual and is not acting in the course of carrying on investment business (defined in para 1307 above), or (2) unless he is reasonably believed to be an ordinary business investor, a customer who is a small business investor: SIB

Financial Services Glossary 1991, under which 'ordinary business investor' means (a) a government, local authority or public authority within the meaning of the Financial Services Act 1986 (c 60), Sch 1; (b) a company or partnership satisfying certain size requirements; and 'customer' does not include a market counterparty or a trust beneficiary but includes (i) a potential customer; (ii) an indirect customer; and (iii) a customer of an appointed representative of a firm with or for whom the representative acts in the course of business for which the firm has accepted responsibility. As to appointed representatives, see para 1361 below.

2 'Packaged product' means a life policy, a unit in a regulated collective investment scheme, or an investment trust savings scheme: SIB Financial Services Glossary 1991.

3 'Product company' means (1) in relation to a life policy, the issuing life office; (2) in relation to units in a regulated collective investment scheme or an investment trust savings scheme, the operator of the scheme: ibid.

4 'Marketing group' means a group of persons who (1) are allied together, formally or informally, for purposes of marketing packaged products of the group, and (2) each of whom, if it holds itself out in the United Kingdom as marketing any packaged products to private investors, does so only as an investment manager or in relation to those of the marketing group; and 'marketing group associate', in relation to a person in a marketing group, means any other person which is a member of that group: ibid.

5 For the meaning of 'regulated business', see para 1357, note 1, above.

6 SIB Core Conduct of Business Rules, r 4.

7 Office of Fair Trading *Report on the Rules of LAUTRO, Part I* (March 1988) p 2.

8 For SIB Core Conduct of Business Rules, r 17, see para 1365 below.

1361. Appointed representatives. A further category of persons exempted from the requirement to obtain authorisation are appointed representatives: an appointed representative is an exempted person as respects investment business carried on by him as such a representative[1]. This provision enables certain activities by firms to be regulated as if the activities had been performed by employees rather than by a firm carrying on a business. The exemption is of particular use to self-employed agents of life assurance and unit trust companies[2]. 'Appointed representative' means a person:

(1) who is employed by an authorised person (his 'principal') under a contract for services which (a) requires or permits him to carry on investment business of a prescribed kind[3] and (b) complies with prescribed requirements[4]; and

(2) for whose activities in carrying on the whole or part of that investment business his principal has accepted responsibility in writing[5];

and the investment business carried on by the appointed representative as such is the investment business for which the principal has accepted responsibility[6].

These provisions are, however, limited to particular activities in procuring and advising on entering into investment agreements with the principal or, if not prohibited by the contract, with other authorised persons[7].

The principal is responsible, to the same extent as if he had expressly authorised it, for anything said or done or omitted by the representative in carrying on the investment business for which the principal has accepted responsibility[8]. The effect of this provision is that any difficulties which a third party may have had in seeking recourse against the principal because the principal was not a party to the contract is avoided. The provision also means that any need to fulfil the usual conditions for making a principal liable for his agent's actions is alleviated[9].

1 Financial Services Act 1986 (c 60), s 44(1). For the meaning of 'exempted person', see para 1306, note 3, above, and for the meaning of 'investment business', see para 1307 above. See also SIB Core Conduct of Business Rules, r 13, and para 1378 below.

2 See A Whittaker and G Morse *The Financial Services Act 1986: A Guide to the New Law* (1987).

3 Ie investment business consisting of (1) procuring or endeavouring to procure the persons with whom he deals to enter into investment agreements (defined in para 1332, note 2, above) with his principal or (if not prohibited by his contract) with other persons; (2) giving advice to those persons about entering into such agreements; or (3) giving advice as to the sale of investments

issued by his principal or as to the exercise of rights conferred by an investment whether or not so issued: Financial Services Act 1986, s 44(3)(a)–(c).

4 Ibid, s 44(2)(a). The prescribed requirements are (1) that if the contract between the appointed representative and his principal does not prohibit the representative from procuring or endeavouring to procure persons to enter into investment agreements with third persons, it must make provision for enabling the principal either to impose such a prohibition or to restrict the kinds of investment to which those agreements may relate or the persons with whom they may be entered into; and (2) that if that contract does not prohibit the representative from giving advice about entering into such agreements with third persons it must make provision for enabling the principal either to impose such a prohibition or to restrict the kinds of advice which the representative may give by reference to the kinds of investment in relation to which or the persons with whom he may advise that such agreements should be made: ibid, s 44(4), (5).

5 Ibid, s 44(2)(b).
6 Ibid, s 44(2).
7 Ibid, s 44(3).
8 Ibid, s 44(6).
9 *Whittaker and Morse.*

1362. Commentary. As noticed above in relation to the Statements of Principle, it may be useful to consider the adequacy of the Core Rules as investor protection in the light of the fiduciary duties which we have identified. For instance, Core Rule 1[1] deals with inducements and provides that a firm must not offer or give or solicit or accept any gift or inducement of a kind which might reasonably be expected to cause the recipient to act in a manner which would or might conflict with any duties of the recipient (or the recipient's firm) to customers. As it appears to be the common law duty not to accept any inducement whatsoever and to act impartially and never to act in a situation which would conflict with the interests of the principal, this Core Rule does not measure up to the standard set by the common law. Core Rule 3[2], dealing with soft commission, suffers from the same criticism. Core Rule 2[3] deals with material interests, and provides that where a firm has such an interest in the subject matter of a possible transaction it must not advise or deal in the exercise of discretion in relation to that transaction unless it has observed such requirements as may be imposed by its regulator in order to obtain fair treatment for all the firm's customers. The common law would appear to prevent an agent from acting in such circumstances at all.

The present authors consider that the Core Rules suffer from a failure to distinguish between an agent acting for a client and a dealer buying or selling from or to a customer. They also consider that further defects arise in the Core Rules in that a number of the rules make specific provision to protect the 'private investor', and by implication may have the effect of withdrawing protection from the non-private customer. This follows the scheme set out in the Companies Act 1989 amendments to the Financial Services Act 1986, whereby the statutory right of action for damages in respect of a loss sustained by an investor pursuant to a breach of the self-regulating organisation rules is available only to the 'private investor'[4] and not to the corporate and experienced investor. It is possible that in practice such restriction will have little effect, as in most cases where any such action could be raised the aggrieved party could raise an action in delict, and there is nothing in the legislation which suggests that that basic right of action has been withdrawn from anyone, whether a private investor or otherwise. The Securities and Investments Board reports that there has been pressure from firms to disapply the Core Rules for non-private customers. The SIB has, in keeping with a view widely but not universally held in the industry that 'professional' customers do not need protection and burdensome rules, bowed to their requests in a few instances where less protection seemed justified to the SIB.

1 For SIB Core Conduct of Business Rules, r 1, see para 1357 above.

2 For ibid, r 3, see para 1359 above.
3 For ibid, r 2, see para 1358 above.
4 See the Financial Services Act 1986 (c 60), s 62A (added by the Companies Act 1989 (c 40), s 193), and the Financial Services Act 1986 (Restriction of Right of Action) Regulations 1991, SI 1991/489, which defines 'private investor' for these purposes (see para 1412 below) and sets out the circumstances in which a person who is not a private investor retains the right to bring an action under the Financial Services Act 1986, s 62 (for which see para 1412 below).

(C) INFORMATION AND ADVICE

1363. Information about packaged products. Core Rule 12 provides as follows:

'(1) Before or when making a personal recommendation to a private customer[1] to buy a packaged product[2], a firm must give him information about the product which is adequate to enable him to make an informed investment decision.

(2) Before or as soon as practicable after a private customer buys a packaged product in a transaction recommended, effected or arranged by a firm, the firm must provide him with appropriate written product particulars unless:

(a) the firm buys the packaged product as a discretionary investment manager, or

(b) the transaction is effected or arranged on an execution-only basis'[3].

Originally disclosure of product information was required at or before the point of sale. Although the advertising rules[4] still require certain information to be contained in marketing material, particularly 'off-the-page' advertisements[5] and detailed disclosure in relation to packaged products in particular, disclosure in respect of charges and commission is now generally required after the point of sale. The reason for this appears to stem from the 'cancellation' or 'cooling-off' period which applies to such investments[6]. Thus the detailed particulars are provided at the same time as the investor is advised or reminded of his cancellation or cooling-off rights.

Generally the written product particulars envisaged under Core Rule 12(2) and specified in the third-tier rules of the self-regulating organisations reflect the existing requirements, with appropriate modifications to take account of the new investment vehicles being brought within the definition of 'packaged product'. Product particulars in most cases will require to contain[7] inter alia:

(a) a detailed description of the investment product, including investment objectives and policies, minimum investment, pricing mechanism and frequency of pricing and dealing;

(b) details of the payment arrangements and the consequences of an investor's failure to meet payment obligations;

(c) details of taxation consequences;

(d) information regarding charges and commission payments; and

(e) details of how further information may be obtained.

It must be noted that the application of this core rule is restricted to firms advising private customers. Disclosure of product information in compliance with the rule is not required when a firm is advising non-private customers[8].

1 For the meaning of 'private customer', see para 1360, note 1, above.
2 For the meaning of 'packaged product', see para 1360, note 2, above.
3 SIB Core Conduct of Business Rules, r 12. As to information for customers, see SIB Statements of Principle, principle 5, and para 1347 above.
4 See SIB Core Conduct of Business Rules, r 5(1), and para 1367 below. See also the Financial Services Act 1986 (c 60), s 85, and scheme particulars regulations made thereunder, and para 1327 above.
5 Ie advertisements which include an application form.

6 See para 1336 above.
7 Like so many areas of the Financial Services Act regime, the disclosure of information (particularly in relation to charges) is currently under review. The SIB Quality of Information Working Party may yet recommend sweeping changes to the current disclosure of information requirements in all areas of the rule book, not merely product particulars.
8 'Non-private customer' means a customer who is not a private customer as defined in para 1360, note 1, above: SIB Financial Services Glossary 1991.

1364. Information about the firm. Core Rule 11 makes provision for the information about the firm which must be supplied. It provides as follows:

'(1) A firm must take reasonable steps to ensure that a private customer[1] to whom it provides investment services is given adequate information about its identity and business address, the identity and status with the firm of employees and other relevant agents with whom the customer has contact and the identity of the firm's regulator.

(2) Unless a firm is acting as an investment manager, it must take reasonable steps to ensure that a private customer it advises to buy a packaged product is also given adequate information about the firm's polarisation status, the buying process and any limits on the packaged products on which it can advise'[2].

1 For the meaning of 'private customer', see para 1360, note 1, above.
2 SIB Core Conduct of Business Rules, r 11. As to polarisation, see para 1360 above, and as to packaged products, see paras 1360, 1363, above. As to information for customers, see SIB Statements of Principle, principle 5, and para 1347 above.

1365. Standards of advice on packaged products. Core Rule 17 provides standards of advice on packaged products[1] as follows:

'(1) A firm which advises private customers[2] to buy packaged products must take reasonable steps to inform itself and relevant agents:
   (a) where the firm is a product company[3] or its marketing group associate, about packaged products available from the marketing group[4]; or
   (b) where the firm is an independent intermediary, about packaged products which are generally available on the market and on which it can advise.

(2) Where a firm is a product company or its marketing group associate, it must not advise a private customer to buy a packaged product, or buy a packaged product for him in the exercise of discretion, if it is aware of a packaged product of the marketing group which would better meet his needs.

(3) Where a firm is acting as an independent intermediary, it must not advise a private customer to buy a packaged product, or buy a packaged product for him in the exercise of discretion, if it is aware of a generally available packaged product which would better meet his needs.

(4) Where a firm is a product company or its marketing group associate and is acting as an investment manager, it must not advise a private customer to buy a packaged product of a product company outside the marketing group, or buy such a product for him in the exercise of discretion, if it is, or reasonably should be, aware of a generally available packaged product which would better meet his needs.

(5) Where a firm is acting for a private customer as an independent intermediary but not as an investment manager, it must not advise him to buy a packaged product from its extended group[5] if it is aware of a generally available packaged product which is not a product of the extended group and which would meet his needs as well as the extended group product.

(6) In assessing the merits of a packaged product to be held as the plan investment of a personal equity plan, a firm must take into account the characteristics (including charging arrangements) of the plan, as well as those of the product'[6].

These rules were previously subsumed under the general heading 'Best advice' since in essence they required product companies and their representatives to give the best advice about investment business and the range of products generally available on the market. 'Best' is to be judged without the benefit of hindsight.

1 For the meaning of 'packaged product', see para 1360, note 2, above.
2 For the meaning of 'private customer', see para 1360, note 1, above.
3 For the meaning of 'product company', see para 1360, note 3, above.
4 For the meaning of 'marketing group' and 'marketing group associate', see para 1360, note 4, above.
5 'Extended group' means the extended group consisting of the members of a group of undertakings and the marketing group associates of any of them: SIB Financial Services Glossary 1991.
6 SIB Core Conduct of Business Rules, r 17.

(D) ADVERTISING

1366. Introduction. The next group of Core Rules (Rules 5 to 13) deal with advertising and marketing[1]. The Financial Services Act 1986 generally restricts investment advertising to authorised persons[2], although in some circumstances investment advertisements issued by overseas (non-authorised) persons are allowed[3]. However, these circumstances are closely regulated so as to ensure that investors in the United Kingdom are protected from overseas firms which may not deal with them honestly.

1 For the application of these rules, see para 1400 below.
2 See the Financial Services Act 1986 (c 60), s 57, and para 1337 above. For the meaning of 'investment advertisement', see para 1337, note 2, above, and for the meaning of 'authorised person', see para 1306, note 2, above.
3 See SIB Core Conduct of Business Rules, r 6, and para 1368 below.

1367. Issue and approval of advertisements. Core Rule 5 provides for the issue and approval of investment advertisements[1] in these terms:

'(1) Where a firm issues or approves an investment advertisement, it must:
    (a) apply appropriate expertise; and
    (b) be able to show that it believes on reasonable grounds that the advertisement is fair and not misleading.
(2) Where a firm issues or approves a specific investment advertisement[2] it must ensure that the advertisement identifies it as issuer or approver, and also identifies its regulator.
(3) A firm must not approve a specific investment advertisement if it relates to units in an unregulated collective investment scheme.
(4) A firm must take reasonable steps to ensure that it does not issue or approve a direct advertisement[3] for the sale of investments or the provision of investment services to a private customer[4] unless the advertisement:
    (a) gives information about the investments or investment services, the terms of the offer, and the risks involved, which is adequate and fair having regard to the (UK or overseas) regulatory protections which apply and the market to which the advertisement is directed; and
    (b) offers derivatives or warrants only where the firm itself issues the advertisement and does so only to a customer for whom it believes on reasonable grounds the investment or investment services to be suitable'[5].

Core Rules 5 and 6[6] must be read in conjunction with Core Rule 40(2), which limits the types of investment advertisements to which the rules apply[7], and which excludes from the application of Rule 5 and 6 exempt advertisements[8], DIE advertisements[9] and takeover advertisements[10].

The prohibition in Core Rule 5(3) on *approving* specific investment advertisements relating to units in unregulated collective investment schemes mirrors the prohibition on the promotion of such schemes in section 76 of the Financial Services Act 1986[11].

The third-tier rules specify particular risk warnings required under Core Rule 5(4). The level of warnings varies according to the form and content of the advertising material as well as to the audience to which the material is directed.

Advertising material directed solely to non-private customers[12] is subject to few requirements, as are 'short form' or 'image' advertisements which contain only limited information about the firm, the type of product and the services it offers and details of contact points for further information.

Advertisements for private customers are subject to more detailed requirements, including for example specification of:

(a) the risks of fluctuations in the value of and income from shares, together, where relevant, with exchange rate risks;

(b) the fact that past performance is not necessarily a guide to future performance;

(c) the lack of liquidity of and information relating to investments which are not readily realisable;

(d) the source of factual information or status;

(e) taxation implications; and

(f) cancellation rights.

'Direct offer' or 'off-the-page' advertisements are subject to more restrictions. Generally, the third-tier rules limit the investments which may be marketed in this way and the information which may be included in such advertisements. Although Core Rule 5(4)(b) already restricts the categories of investors to whom advertisements relating to warrants and other derivative products (such as futures, options and contracts for differences) may be issued, there is, in addition, a requirement for strong prescribed risk warnings to accompany such advertisements. Certain corporate material which would otherwise be subject to these detailed requirements is excluded as this is already subject to regulation, such as listing particulars and prospectuses.

Core Rule 5 is intended to be read with Core Rule 9[13], which requires communications, including those related to advertising, to be fair and not misleading.

1 For the meaning of 'investment advertisement', see para 1337, note 2, above.

2 'Specific investment advertisement' means an investment advertisement which identifies and promotes a particular investment or particular investment services: SIB Financial Services Glossary 1991.

3 'Direct offer advertisement' means a specific investment advertisement (included a pre-printed or off-the-screen advertisement) which (1) contains (a) an offer by the firm or another offeror to enter into an investment agreement with anyone who responds, or (b) an invitation to anyone to respond by making an offer to the firm or another offeree to enter into an investment agreement; and (2) specifies the manner or indicates a form in which any response is to be made (eg by providing a tear-off slip): ibid.

4 For the meaning of 'private customer', see para 1360, note 1, above.

5 SIB Core Conduct of Business Rules, r 5.

6 For ibid, r 6, see para 1368 below.

7 For ibid, r 40, see para 1400 below.

8 'Exempt advertisement' means an investment advertisement which can lawfully be issued in the United Kingdom by a person who is not an authorised person without approval of its contents by an authorised person: SIB Financial Services Glossary 1991.

9 'DIE advertisement' means an advertisement issued by a designated investment exchange (defined in para 1386, note 2, below) or required or permitted to be published by the rules of such an exchange: ibid.

10 'Takeover advertisement' means an advertisement to which the City Code on Takeovers and Mergers applies (or would apply but for any exemption granted by the Panel on Takeovers and Mergers): ibid.

11 See the Financial Services Act 1986 (c 60), s 76(2), and para 1326 above.

12 For the meaning of 'non-private customer', see para 1363, note 8, above.
13 For SIB Core Conduct of Business Rules, r 9, see para 1371 below.

1368. Issue or approval of advertisements for an overseas person. Core Rules 6 to 8 make provision for the complex (but, with the approach of 1992, increasingly important) area of cross-border investment business. Under Core Rule 6:

'A firm must not issue or approve a specific investment advertisement[1] which is calculated to lead directly or indirectly to an overseas person[2] carrying on investment business[3]:
(a) which is not regulated business[4]; and
(b) with or for a private customer who is in the United Kingdom;
unless both the advertisement contains the prescribed disclosure and the firm has no reason to doubt that the overseas person will deal with investors in the United Kingdom in an honest and reliable way'[5].

Core Rule 6 is intended to be read with Core Rule 40(2), which excludes from Core Rule 6 certain types of advertisements[6].

'The prescribed disclosure' required under this rule involves a written statement which must make clear:
(1) that all or most of the protections provided by the United Kingdom regulatory system[7] do not apply; and
(2) where the business is excluded from the Investors Compensation Scheme by its territorial scope (or would be so excluded if the person carrying it on were a participant firm), that compensation under that scheme will not be available;
and which may also indicate the protections or compensation available under another system of regulation[8].

1 For the meaning of 'specific investment advertisement', see para 1367, note 2, above.
2 'Overseas person' means a person who carries on investment business but who does not do so from a permanent place of business maintained by him in the United Kingdom: SIB Financial Services Glossary 1991.
3 For the meaning of 'investment business', see para 1307 above.
4 For the meaning of 'regulated business', see para 1357, note 1, above.
5 SIB Core Conduct of Business Rules, r 6.
6 For ibid, r 40, see para 1400 below. See also para 1367 above.
7 'Regulatory system' means the arrangements for regulating a firm under the Financial Services Act 1986 (c 60), including the SIB Statements of Principle, the Core Conduct of Business Rules and the rules of its regulator: SIB Financial Services Glossary 1991.
8 Ibid.

1369. Overseas business for United Kingdom private customers. Core Rule 7 provides as follows:

'(1) A firm must not carry on investment business[1]:
(a) which is not regulated business[2]; and
(b) with or for a private customer[3] who is in the United Kingdom;
unless it has made the prescribed disclosure[4] to the customer.
(2) A firm must not give an introduction or advice, or make arrangements, with a view to another person carrying on such business with or for such a customer, unless it has both made the prescribed disclosure and has no reason to doubt that the customer will be dealt with in an honest and reliable way'[5].

1 For the meaning of 'investment business', see para 1307 above.
2 For the meaning of 'regulated business', see para 1357, note 1, above.
3 For the meaning of 'private customer', see para 1360, note 1, above.
4 For the meaning of 'prescribed disclosure', see para 1368 above.

5 SIB Core Conduct of Business Rules, r 7.

1370. Business conducted from an overseas place of business with overseas customers. Under Core Rule 8:

'If, in any communication made or advertisement[1] issued to a private customer[2] outside the United Kingdom in connection with investment business[3] which is not regulated business[4], a firm indicates that it is an authorised person[5], it must also, and with equal prominence, make the prescribed disclosure'[6].

1 For the meaning of 'advertisement', see para 1337, note 2, above.
2 For the meaning of 'private customer', see para 1360, note 1, above.
3 For the meaning of 'investment business', see para 1307 above.
4 For the meaning of 'regulated business', see para 1357, note 1, above.
5 For the meaning of 'authorised person', see para 1306, note 2, above.
6 SIB Core Conduct of Business Rules, r 8. For the meaning of 'prescribed disclosure', see para 1368 above.

(E) RELATIONSHIP WITH CUSTOMERS

1371. Fair and clear communications. Core Rule 9 requires communications between a firm and its customers to be fair and clear. It provides as follows:

'(1) A firm may make a communication with another person which is designed to promote the provision of investment services only if it can show that it believes on reasonable grounds that the communication is fair and not misleading.

(2) A firm must take reasonable steps to ensure that any agreement, written communication, notification or information which it gives or sends to a private customer[1] to whom it provides investment services is presented fairly and clearly'[2].

1 For the meaning of 'private customer', see para 1360, note 1, above.
2 SIB Core Conduct of Business Rules, r 9. As to information for customers, see SIB Statements of Principle, principle 5, and para 1347 above.

1372. Customers' understanding. Core Rule 10 also requires fairness and clarity in the particular area of customers' understanding of risk. It requires that:

'A firm must not recommend a transaction to a private customer[1], or act as a discretionary manager for him, unless it has taken reasonable steps to enable him to understand the nature of the risks involved'[2].

For the most part, in order to demonstrate that it has taken reasonable steps to enable private customers to understand the relevant risks of any particular investment, a firm will at the least require to show that the appropriate risk warnings relevant to advertisements[3] have been made, as well as the inclusion of appropriate warnings and explanations in the customer agreement[4].

1 For the meaning of 'private customer', see para 1360, note 1, above.
2 SIB Core Conduct of Business Rules, r 10. As to information for customers, see SIB Statements of Principle, principle 5, and para 1347 above.
3 See para 1367 above.
4 See para 1375 below.

1373. Suitability. That simply appraising customers of the risks inherent in different investments will not necessarily be sufficient is shown by Core Rule 16, which provides as follows:

'(1) A firm must take reasonable steps to ensure that it does not in the course of regulated business or associated business[1]:

   (a) make any personal recommendation to a private customer[2] of an investment or investment agreement; or

   (b) effect or arrange a discretionary transaction with or for a private customer or, subject to any exceptions contained in the rules of an SRO [self-regulating organisation] of which the firm is a member, any other customer;

unless the recommendation or transaction is suitable for him having regard to the facts disclosed by that customer and other relevant facts about the customer of which the firm is, or reasonably should be, aware.

  (2) But where, with the agreement of the customer, a firm has pooled his funds with those of others with a view to taking common management decisions, the firm must instead take reasonable steps to ensure that the transaction is suitable for the fund, having regard to the stated investment objectives of the fund'[3].

Core Rule 16(1) outlines the standards which these rules impose in relation to the giving of investment advice or the effecting of discretionary investment transactions: the 'know your client' and 'suitability' tests. These requirements are reflected elsewhere[4], and are further refined in relation to packaged products under the polarisation approach[5]. Rule 16(2) makes it clear that the suitability test in relation to pooled investment vehicles such as collective investment schemes or PEPs applies in respect of the vehicle itself rather than the individuals investing in it. In order to discharge their obligations under this rule, authorised persons require to maintain records demonstrating their knowledge of clients' personal and financial circumstances and the features of the investment or transaction recommended or effected for each client.

1 'Associated business' means business which is carried on in connection with investment business (defined in para 1307 above): SIB Financial Services Glossary 1991.
2 For the meaning of 'private customer', see para 1360, note 1, above.
3 SIB Core Conduct of Business Rules, r 16. For the principle that a firm should seek from its customers information about their circumstances and investment objectives, see para 1346 above.
4 See eg ibid, r 5(4)(b), and para 1367 above.
5 See ibid, r 4, and para 1360 above.

1374. Charges and other remuneration. The fairness of the charges made by a firm to its clients is governed by Core Rule 18, which provides:

'(1) The amount of a firm's charges[1] to a private customer[2] for the provision of investment services to him must not be unreasonable in the circumstances.

  (2) Subject to any exceptions contained in the rules of an SRO [self-regulating organisation] of which it is a member, before a firm provides investment services to a private customer (other than an indirect customer[3]), it must disclose to him the basis or amount of its charges for the provision of those services and the nature or amount of any other remuneration receivable by it (or, to its knowledge, by its associate) and attributable to them'[4].

In addition to the exception for indirect customers (who will, it is assumed, be advised by their agents), it is expected that disclosure on a case-by-case basis will not be required where the firm's charges have already been disclosed in the customer agreement[5] or in relation to certain packaged products[6].

'Other remuneration' includes commission from the counterparty to the transaction on any third party, and any mark-up made by the firm or any associate when selling as principal.

1 'Charges' means any charges made to a customer in connection with investment services, including any mark-up or mark-down from the price at which best execution would be achieved: SIB Financial Services Glossary 1991.

2 For the meaning of 'private customer', see para 1360, note 1, above.
3 'Indirect customer' means, where a customer is known to be acting as agent, an identified principal who would be a customer if he were dealt with direct: SIB Financial Services Glossary 1991.
4 SIB Core Conduct of Business Rules, r 18.
5 See para 1375 below.
6 See para 1363 above.

1375. Customer agreements. Core Rule 14 contains one of the basic requirements of the Financial Services Act 1986 regime: the stipulation that there should be a written agreement between a firm and its customer. It provides as follows:

'(1) Where a firm provides investment services to a private customer[1] (other than an indirect customer[2]) on written contractual terms, the agreement must set out in adequate detail the basis on which those services are provided.
(2) Where a firm provides to a private customer (other than an indirect customer) investment services involving:
(a) contingent liability transactions[3]; or
(b) the discretionary management of the customer's assets;
it must do so under a two-way customer agreement[4] unless the customer is ordinarily resident outside the United Kingdom and the firm believes on reasonable grounds that he does not wish a two-way agreement to be used'[5].

The rule does not, therefore, require written contractual terms:
(a) where the only services which the firm will perform for the customer are 'execution only' — this arises where the transactions are executed in accordance with instructions given by the customer, with no advice being offered; or
(b) where the only services which the firm will perform are the purchase or sale of life policies and/or units in regulated collective investment schemes[6];
(c) between the trustee and manager of a recognised collective investment scheme, since this is already governed by the trust deed which will itself be subject to required terms under the unit trust regulations[7];
(d) in relation to services performed in anticipation of an agreement coming into force or in the course of, for example, winding up a portfolio following the termination of a customer agreement.
Generally, where a customer agreement is necessary, it will need to contain:
(i) provisions as to commencement and termination;
(ii) details of the remuneration to be received by the firm under the agreement;
(iii) details of the customer's investment objective and any restrictions imposed in relation to his investments;
(iv) details of which category of customer the customer will be treated as;
(v) details of soft commission arrangements to which the firm is a party[8];
(vi) details of any circumstances in which the firm can effect transactions in which it has a material interest[9];
(vii) details as to how customers' assets are to be held and dealt with;
(viii) whether 'cold calling'[10] is permitted, and, if so, its consequences; and
(ix) appropriate risk warnings regarding the type of services to be provided by the firm and the type of investments to which they relate.

1 For the meaning of 'private customer', see para 1360, note 1, above.
2 For the meaning of 'indirect customer', see para 1374, note 3, above.
3 'Contingent liability transaction' means a derivatives transaction under the terms of which the customer will or may be liable to make further payments (other than charges, and whether or not secured by margin) when the transaction falls to be completed or upon the earlier closing out of his position: SIB Financial Services Glossary 1991. See also para 1386 below.

4 'Two-way customer agreement' means a written agreement to which the customer has signified his assent in writing in circumstances where the firm is satisfied that he has had a proper opportunity to consider its terms: ibid.
5 SIB Core Conduct of Business Rules, r 14.
6 The rationale behind this exception, which was contained in the original Conduct of Business Rules, appears to be that information about these 'polarised products' would be available to the investor prior to and immediately following purchase, and since investors would have the right to cancel investments made in such products within a specified period (see para 1336 above), the requirement to enter into a client agreement would secure no additional benefits.
7 As to collective investment schemes, see paras 1325 ff above.
8 As to soft commission, see para 1359 above.
9 As to material interest, see para 1358 above.
10 As to cold calling, see paras 1333, 1334, above.

1376. Customers' rights. In addition to requiring a written customer agreement[1], the Core Rules also seek to ensure that no attempts are made in the written agreement, and indeed in any other written agreement between a firm and its customers, to exclude any obligations owed under the regime of the Financial Services Act 1986. Core Rule 15, therefore, provides as follows:

'(1) A firm must not, in any written communication or agreement, seek to exclude or restrict any duty or liability to a customer which it has under the Act, or under the regulatory system[2].
(2) Similarly, unless it is reasonable to do so in the circumstances, a firm must not, in any written communication or agreement, seek to exclude or restrict:
(a) any other duty to act with skill, care and diligence which is owed to a private customer[3] in connection with the provision to him of investment services in the course of regulated business[4]; or
(b) any liability owed to a private customer in connection with regulated business for failure to exercise the degree of skill, care and diligence which may reasonably be expected of it in the provision of investment services in the course of that business.
(3) A firm must not seek unreasonably to rely on any provision seeking to exclude or restrict any such duty or liability'[5].

Under the terms of regulations made under the 1986 Act, a breach of this rule may also give a right of action[6] to non-private investors[7].

1 See para 1375 above.
2 For the meaning of 'regulatory system', see para 1368, note 7, above.
3 For the meaning of 'private customer', see para 1360, note 1, above.
4 For the meaning of 'regulated business', see para 1357, note 1, above.
5 SIB Core Conduct of Business Rules, r 15.
6 Ie under the Financial Services Act 1986 (c 60), s 62, for which see para 1412 below.
7 See the Financial Services Act 1986 (Restriction of Right of Action) Regulations 1991, SI 1991/489, made under the Financial Services Act 1986, s 62A (added by the Companies Act 1989 (c 40), s 193(1)), and para 1412 below.

1377. Confirmations and periodic information. Core Rule 19 highlights the necessity under the regime of the Financial Services Act 1986 of firms making adequate and accurate disclosure of information to their customers. It provides:

'(1) Subject to any exceptions contained in the rules of an SRO [self-regulating organisation] of which it is a member, a firm which effects a sale or purchase of an investment (other than a life policy) with or for a customer must ensure that he is sent with due despatch a note containing the essential details of the transaction.
(2) Subject to any exceptions contained in the rules of an SRO of which it is a member, a firm which acts as an investment manager for a customer must

ensure that he is sent at suitable intervals a report stating the value of the portfolio or account at the beginning and end of the period, its composition at the end, and, in the case of a discretionary portfolio or account, changes in its composition between those dates'[1].

Generally, the 'essential details' include:

(a) the parties to the transaction (that is, the customer and the broker);
(b) whether the broker or other firm involved in the transaction was acting as principal or had any other material interest in the transaction;
(c) the date and time of the transaction and settlement details;
(d) the amount and price of the investment bought or sold; and
(e) details of any commission or other payments made by or to third parties in relation to the transaction.

The third-tier rules generally contain exemptions from the obligation to provide contract notes where:

(i) the customer is an overseas customer and has indicated that he does not wish to receive contract notes;
(ii) the transaction is effected under a regulated collective investment scheme or an investment trust saving scheme; or
(iii) the transaction is effected under a personal equity plan (PEP).

In some of these circumstances, however (for example regulated collective investment schemes, investment trust saving schemes and PEPs), the firm may be required to send regular statements which will include all the details which would have been included in contract notes.

Core Rule 19(2) relates to periodic reports. Generally they will be required to be provided at six-monthly intervals at least in relation to managed portfolios and will contain additional information to that specified in the rule. This information will generally include:

(A) details of the basis of valuing assets;
(B) details of any assets lent or charges or securities created over assets[2];
(C) income received from portfolio assets over the period; and
(D) interest paid from the portfolio over the period in respect of sums borrowed.

---

1 SIB Core Conduct of Business Rules, r 19.
2 Additional, more frequent reports are expected to be required where stock lending is carried out, securities are created over portfolio assets or there are uncovered open positions in relation to investment in derivative instruments.

1378. Appointed representatives. As explained above, appointed representatives do not require to obtain authorisation under the Financial Services Act 1986[1] since the firm to which the representative is appointed must accept full responsibility for the investment business carried on by the representative. In the first two years of the Financial Services Act regime a number of problems were experienced with authorised persons failing to exercise adequate control and supervision of their appointed representatives. Accordingly, the Securities and Investments Board took the opportunity within the 'New Framework' to make specific provision reinforcing the provisions of the Act relating to appointed representatives. Core Rule 13 makes provision applying to their initial appointment, continued supervision and termination of employment. It states:

'(1) A firm must satisfy itself on reasonable grounds and on a continuing basis that any appointed representative it appoints is fit and proper to act for it in that capacity.

(2) A firm must also satisfy itself on reasonable grounds and on a continuing basis that it has adequate resources to monitor and enforce compliance by its appointed representatives with high standards of business conduct.

(3) A firm must ensure that any of its appointed representatives carries on regulated business[2] for which the firm has accepted responsibility only:

   (a) in circumstances where the representative does not carry on (or purport to carry on) in the United Kingdom any investment business[3] for which the representative is not an authorised or exempted person; and

   (b) in a way which ensures that the business for which the firm has accepted responsibility is, and is held out as being, clearly distinct from any financial business which the representative carries on which is not investment business, unless that other financial business is covered by authorisation under an enactment as a bank or building society;

but a firm does not break this requirement if it can show it has taken reasonable steps to comply with it.

(4) Subject to any exceptions contained in the rules of an SRO [self-regulating organisation] of which it is a member, a firm must ensure that its employment of any of its appointed representatives can be terminated only with the authority of its regulator'[4].

1 See the Financial Services Act 1986 (c 60), s 44, and para 1361 above (where 'appointed representative' is defined).

2 For the meaning of 'regulated business', see para 1357, note 1, above.

3 For the meaning of 'investment business', see para 1307 above.

4 SIB Core Conduct of Business Rules, r 13.

(F) DEALING WITH CUSTOMERS

1379. Customer order priority. Core Rule 20 provides simply that 'A firm should deal with customer and own account[1] orders[2] fairly and in due turn'[3].

The earlier detailed versions of this rule specified that the customer's order had priority so that the firm could not deal on its own account until the customer's order had been fulfilled or withdrawn. This remains sound advice. The ranking of customer orders should be based on the time of instruction or of the decision to exercise discretion. However, the size of orders (due to volume business generally moving price) or any limit on the price at which the customer is prepared to deal may well affect timing and could change the order of execution quite fairly.

1 'Own account order' includes an 'own account transaction', which means a transaction (1) effected or arranged by the firm in the course of carrying on either investment business (defined in para 1307 above) or associated business (defined in para 1373, note 1, above); and (2) on its own account or on the account of an associate on its own account: SIB Financial Services Glossary 1991.

2 'Order' means (1) an order to a firm from the customer to effect a transaction as agent; (2) any other order to a firm from the customer to effect a transaction in circumstances giving rise to similar duties as those arising on an order to effect a transaction as agent; and (3) a decision by the firm in the exercise of discretion for the customer: ibid.

3 SIB Core Conduct of Business Rules, r 20. As to the aggregation of orders and subsequent allocations, see r 24, and para 1383 below.

1380. Timely execution. Core Rule 21 provides as follows:

'(1) Once a firm has agreed or decided in its discretion to effect or arrange a current customer order[1], it must effect or arrange the execution of the order as soon as reasonably practicable in the circumstances.

(2) But the core rule on timely execution does not preclude a firm from postponing execution of an order where it believes on reasonable grounds that this is in the best interests of the customer'[2].

It is obviously in the firm's interest to be able to demonstrate — as it must through its proper records — that orders are dealt with promptly, but occasionally the customer might be better served by the delay of his order, for example in order to aggregate his order with other orders[3] to achieve a better price.

1 'Current customer order' means both a customer order for immediate execution and, once the condition is fulfilled, a customer order which is to be executed only on fulfilment of a condition: SIB Financial Services Glossary 1991. For the meaning of 'order', see para 1379, note 2, above.
2 SIB Core Conduct of Business Rules, r 21.
3 As to the aggregation of orders, see para 1383 below.

1381. Best execution. Core Rule 22 provides as follows:

'(1) Where a firm deals with or for a private customer[1], it must provide best execution.

(2) A firm must also provide best execution where it fulfils an order[2] from a non-private customer[3].

(3) A firm may rely on another person who executes the transaction to provide best execution, but only if it believes on reasonable grounds that he will do so.

(4) For the purposes of the core rule on best execution, a firm provides best execution if:

(a) it takes reasonable care to ascertain the price which is the best available for the customer in the relevant market at the time for transactions of the kind and size concerned; and

(b) unless the circumstances require it to do otherwise in the interests of the customer, it deals at a price which is no less advantageous to him;

and in applying the core rule on best execution, a firm should leave out of account any charges disclosed to the customer which it or its agent would make.

(5) The core rule on best execution does not require a firm to provide best execution on a purchase of a life policy or on a purchase from the operator of a regulated collective investment scheme[4] of units in the scheme'[5].

There are two legs to achieving best execution: first finding the best available price for the transaction and secondly dealing at a price no less advantageous to the customer than that best available price 'unless the circumstances require [the firm] to do otherwise in the interests of the customer'. Various factors could come into play: a related currency transaction, a series of transactions of which this is only one, or uncertainty about the counterparty.

The fact that Core Rules 22(1) and 22(2) are separately expressed means that in some circumstances a firm dealing for a non-private customer will not owe that customer the duty of best execution. Specifically, when a firm is not fulfilling an 'order', no such duty will be owed.

1 For the meaning of 'private customer', see para 1360, note 1, above.
2 For the meaning of 'order', see para 1379, note 2, above.
3 For the meaning of 'non-private customer', see para 1363, note 8, above.
4 For the meaning of 'collective investment scheme', see para 1325 above. 'Regulated collective investment scheme' means an authorised unit trust scheme (as to which see para 1327 above) or a recognised scheme (as to which see para 1328 above): SIB Financial Services Glossary 1991.
5 SIB Core Conduct of Business Rules, r 22.

1382. Timely allocation. Core Rule 23 provides that:

'A firm must ensure that a transaction it executes is promptly allocated'[1].

The prompt allocation of a transaction which has been duly recorded protects the customer against the potential abuse of the firm waiting to see if the investment rises or falls before allocating the risen price to the firm's own account and the fallen price to the customer.

1 SIB Core Conduct of Business Rules, r 23.

1383. Fair allocation. Core Rule 24 provides as follows:

'Where a firm has aggregated an order for a customer transaction[1] with an order for an own account transaction[2], or with another order for a customer transaction, then in the subsequent allocation:

(a) it must not give unfair preference to itself or to any of those for whom it dealt; and

(b) if all cannot be satisfied, it must give priority to satisfying orders for customer transactions unless it believes on reasonable grounds that, without its own participation, it would not have been able to effect those orders either on such favourable terms or at all'[3].

1 'Customer transaction' does not include an own account transaction: SIB Financial Services Glossary 1991.
2 For the meaning of 'own account transaction', see para 1379, note 1, above.
3 SIB Core Conduct of Business Rules, r 24.

1384. Dealing ahead of publication. Core Rule 25 concerns dealing by a firm in an investment in advance of the publication to and perusal by its customers of information concerning that investment. It provides as follows:

'Subject to any exceptions contained in the rules of an SRO [self-regulating organisation] of which it is a member, where a firm or its associate intends to publish to customers a recommendation or a piece of research or analysis, it must not knowingly effect an own account transaction[1] in the investment concerned or any related investment until the customers for whom the publication was principally intended have had (or are likely to have had) a reasonable opportunity to react to it'[2].

Some third-tier rules create further exceptions. These include circumstances where the firm believes that its customers, on reading the publication, will wish to purchase the investment and the firm may accordingly be permitted to purchase, ahead of publication, a sufficient amount of the investment to meet the expected demand, always provided that such purchases are not likely themselves to affect the price of the investment. Clearly, properly maintained records would demonstrate whether the recommendation was formulated before or after the purchase by the firm. In most firms 'Chinese walls'[3] will be employed to avoid the dealers knowing what the researchers and analysts are about to publish.

1 For the meaning of 'own account transaction', see para 1379, note 1, above.
2 SIB Core Conduct of Business Rules, r 25.
3 As to 'Chinese walls', see ibid, r 36, and para 1395 below.

1385. Churning and switching. 'Churning' is more readily recognised than described. It occurs where the firm is more concerned with its 'turn' or commission than its customer or its relationship with him. 'Switching' occurs most notoriously in connection with life policies associated with mortgage loans. Customers frequently fail to appreciate the loss entailed in surrendering an existing policy — almost invariably for less than the policy could fetch if sold on the open market — and starting a new contract where the commissions which are charged will take the bulk of the early premium. Core Rule 26 deals with these situations. It provides as follows:

'(1) A firm must not:
(a) make a personal recommendation to a private customer[1] to deal; or
(b) deal or arrange a deal in the exercise of discretion for any customer;

if the dealing would reasonably be regarded as too frequent in the circumstances.

(2) A firm must not:
- (a) make a personal recommendation to a private customer to switch within a packaged product[2] or between packaged products; or
- (b) effect such a switch in the exercise of discretion for a private customer;

unless it believes on reasonable grounds that the switch is justified from the customer's viewpoint'[3].

1 For the meaning of 'private customer', see para 1360, note 1, above.
2 For the meaning of 'packaged product', see para 1360, note 2, above.
3 SIB Core Conduct of Business Rules, r 26.

1386. Certain derivative transactions to be on exchange. A contingent liability transaction[1] can involve an obligation to make further payments over and above any amount paid when the transaction was originally entered into. Moreover, a contingent liability transaction which is not traded on or under the rules of a recognised or designated investment exchange[2] may result in exposure to substantially greater risks. Therefore Core Rule 27 is an attempt to protect investors from the greater risk by ensuring that the contract is made on an exchange which meets certain stringent requirements or is designed for protective rather than speculative purposes. It provides as follows:

'A firm must not effect, arrange or recommend a contingent liability transaction with, for or to a private customer[3] unless:
- (a) the transaction is made on a recognised or designated investment exchange; or
- (b) the firm believes on reasonable grounds that the purpose of the transaction is to hedge against currency risk involved in a position which the customer holds'[4].

1 For the meaning of 'contingent liability transaction', see para 1375, note 3, above.
2 'Recognised investment exchange' means a body declared by order of the Secretary of State to be a recognised investment exchange for the purposes of the Financial Services Act 1986 (c 60) (s 207(1)); and 'designated investment exchange' means any investment exchange designated by the Securities and Investments Board as a designated investment exchange for the purposes of the Financial Services (Conduct of Business) Rules 1990 or the Core Conduct of Business Rules (SIB Financial Services Glossary 1991).
3 For the meaning of 'private customer', see para 1360, note 1, above.
4 SIB Core Conduct of Business Rules, r 27.

(G) MARKET INTEGRITY

1387. Insider dealing. Insider dealing is defined and outlawed by the Company Securities (Insider Dealing) Act 1985 (c 8)[1]. The intention of Core Rule 28 is to offer a basis for civil action. It provides as follows:

'(1) A firm must not effect (either in the United Kingdom or elsewhere) an own account transaction[2] when it knows of circumstances which mean that it, its associate, or an employee of either, is prohibited from effecting that transaction by the statutory restrictions on insider dealing.

(2) A firm must use its best endeavours to ensure that it does not knowingly effect (either in the course of regulated business[3] or otherwise) a transaction for a customer it knows is so prohibited.

(3) But the core rule on insider dealing does not apply where:
- (a) the prohibition applies only because of knowledge of the firm's own intentions;
- (b) the firm is a recognised market maker[4] with obligations to deal in the investment; or

(c) the firm is a trustee or personal representative who acts on the advice of a third party appearing to be an appropriate adviser who is not so prohibited'[5].

It is interesting that this rule seeks to impose an extra–territorial impact, and may potentially be challengeable as *ultra vires*, although the Financial Services Act 1986 (c 60) is concerned solely with investment business conducted in the United Kingdom.

This Core Rule has special significance in that a breach of the Company Securities (Insider Dealing) Act 1985 is a criminal offence[6], but does not of itself create a right of civil action[7]. Core Rule 28, however, creates such a right by virtue of section 62 of the Financial Services Act 1986[8] against members of self-regulating authorities who are guilty of insider dealing. Furthermore, under regulations made under that Act, the right of action is specifically not limited to private investors[9].

1 As to insider dealing, see paras 1501 ff below.
2 For the meaning of 'own account transaction', see para 1379, note 1, above.
3 For the meaning of 'regulated business', see para 1357, note 1, above.
4 'Market maker', in relation to an investment of any description, means a person who (otherwise than as the operator of a regulated collective investment scheme (defined in para 1381, note 4, above)) holds himself out as able and willing to enter into transactions of sale and purchase in investments of that description at prices determined by him generally and continuously rather than in respect of each particular transaction; and 'recognised market maker' means a person (whether an individual, partnership or company) who (1) holds himself out at all normal times in compliance with the rules of a recognised investment exchange (defined in para 1386, note 2, above) as willing to buy and sell securities at prices specified by him, and (2) is recognised as doing so by that exchange: SIB Financial Services Glossary 1991.
5 SIB Core Conduct of Business Rules, r 28.
6 See para 1502 below.
7 See para 1535 below.
8 For the Financial Services Act 1986 (c 60), s 62, see para 1412 below.
9 See the Financial Services Act 1986 (Restriction of Right of Action) Regulations 1991, SI 1991/489, made under the Financial Services Act 1986, s 62A (added by the Companies Act 1989 (c 40), s 193(1)), and para 1412 below.

1388. Stabilisation of securities. Stabilisation is the making of bids or effecting of transactions for the purpose of stabilising the price of securities which are the subject of a recent new issue. Core Rule 29 provides that:

'Where a firm takes action (either in the course of regulated business[1] or otherwise) for the purpose of stabilising the price of securities, it must comply with any applicable provisions of the statutory stabilisation rules'[2].

The statutory stabilisation rules contain considerable detail to ensure that appropriate procedures are followed during the stabilisation of securities. They include, for example, stipulations as to who may stabilise, when they may stabilise and how they may do so. The rules also require disclosure that stabilisation of securities will take or has taken place. Stabilised issues entail a higher degree of risk and deals should not be made for a customer in such issues unless the customer has been made fully aware of the risks.

1 For the meaning of 'regulated business', see para 1357, note 1, above.
2 SIB Core Conduct of Business Rules, r 29. 'Statutory stabilisation rules' means the rules found in Part 10 of the Financial Services (Conduct of Business) Rules 1990: SIB Financial Services Glossary 1991. The Financial Services (Conduct of Business) Rules 1990, Pt 10, comprises rr 10.01–10.07.

1389. Off-exchange market makers. Core Rule 30 offers some protection to investors in relation to investments which are not or may not be readily realisable but which might appear to be. The rule provides as follows:

'Where a firm sells to a private customer[1] any securities which are not quoted on a recognised or designated investment exchange[2], whilst giving the customer the impression that the firm is a market maker[3] in the investment concerned, it must;

(a) give notice to the customer that it is required to ensure that a reasonable price for repurchase of the investment is available to him for a specified period which must not be less than three months after the date the notice is given; and

(b) ensure that such a price is available to him for that specified period'[4].

1 For the meaning of 'private customer', see para 1360, note 1, above.
2 For the meaning of 'recognised investment exchange' and 'designated investment exchange', see para 1386, note 2, above.
3 For the meaning of 'market maker', see para 1387, note 4, above.
4 SIB Core Conduct of Business Rules, r 30.

1390. Reportable transactions. Core Rule 31 provides that:

'Unless otherwise provided by the rules of an SRO [self-regulating organisation] of which it is a member, a firm must make available to its regulator details about transactions (including own account transactions[1]) in securities which it effects other than on a recognised investment exchange'[2].

In some situations 'make available' will operate after an inquiry by the regulator.

1 For the meaning of 'own account transaction', see para 1379, note 1, above.
2 SIB Core Conduct of Business Rules, r 31. For the meaning of 'recognised investment exchange', see para 1386, note 2, above. As to relations with regulators, see SIB Statements of Principle, principle 5, and para 1347 above.

(H) ADMINISTRATION

1391. Safeguarding of customer investments. Core Rule 32 imposes on firms the duty to safeguard its customers' investments. It provides that:

'A firm which has custody of a customer's investments in connection with or with a view to regulated business[1] must, subject to any exceptions contained in the rules of an SRO [self-regulating organisation] of which it is a member:

(a) keep safe, or arrange for the safekeeping of, any documents of title relating to them;

(b) ensure that any registrable investments which it buys or holds for a customer in the course of regulated business are properly registered in his name or, with the consent of the customer, in the name of an eligible nominee[2]; and

(c) where title to investments is recorded electronically, ensure that customer entitlements are separately identifiable from those of the firm in the records of the person maintaining records of entitlement'[3].

1 For the meaning of 'regulated business', see para 1357, note 1, above.
2 'Eligible nominee' means (1) an individual chosen by the customer who is not known by the firm to be an associate of the firm; (2) a corporate nominee with no other business; or (3) an institution authorised under the Banking Act 1987 (c 22): SIB Financial Services Glossary 1991.
3 SIB Core Conduct of Business Rules, r 32. As to the protection of customer assets, see SIB Statements of Principle, principle 10, and para 1352 above.

1392. Scope of business. Core Rule 33 provides that:

'A firm must maintain a business profile describing the kind of investment business[1] it carries on in the United Kingdom and may carry on (and hold itself out as carrying on) investment business in the United Kingdom of that kind only'[2].

This rule simply requires that a firm must have a written description of its investment business and must adhere to it.

1 For the meaning of 'investment business', see para 1307 above.
2 SIB Core Conduct of Business Rules, r 33.

1393. Compliance. Core Rule 34 requires firms to ensure compliance with regulatory systems and to keep and retain appropriate records. It provides as follows:

'(1) A firm must take reasonable steps, including the establishment and maintenance of procedures, to ensure that its officers and employees and officers and employees of its appointed representatives[1] act in conformity with:
   (a) their own and their employer's relevant responsibilities under the regulatory system[2];
   (b) where relevant, the requirements of the statutory restrictions on insider dealing[3]; and
   (c) appropriate arrangements on propriety in personal dealings.
(2) A firm must take reasonable steps, including the establishment and maintenance of procedures, to ensure that sufficient information is recorded and retained about its regulated business[4] and compliance with the regulatory system.
(3) Records required to be maintained by the regulatory system may be inspected by a person appointed for the purpose by the firm's regulator'[5].

In order to ensure compliance, the third-tier rules specify that procedures must be documented in a compliance or procedures manual and that they be regularly monitored by the firm itself and reported on to the regulator. Generally, records will require to display an 'audit trail' of advice given to and transactions effected for customers and justifications for them.

The regulatory bodies, in addition to requiring regular compliance reports from firms, will conduct both routine and *ad hoc* inspections of members to monitor adherence to the relevant regulations. Like the Securities and Investments Board itself, the regulatory bodies generally have fairly sweeping investigative and disciplinary powers.

1 As to appointed representatives, see para 1361 above.
2 For the meaning of 'regulatory system', see para 1368, note 7, above.
3 'Statutory restrictions on insider dealing' means the Company Securities (Insider Dealing) Act 1985 (c 8) (see paras 1501 ff below): SIB Financial Services Glossary 1991.
4 For the meaning of 'regulated business', see para 1357, note 1, above.
5 SIB Core Conduct of Business Rules, r 34. As to the reporting to regulators, see SIB Statements of Principle, principle 10, and para 1352 above.

1394. Complaints. A complaints procedure is called for by Core Rule 35, which provides as follows:

'(1) A firm must have procedures to ensure:
   (a) the proper handling of complaints from customers[1] relevant to its compliance with the regulatory system[2];
   (b) that any appropriate remedial action on those complaints is promptly taken; and
   (c) where the complaint is not promptly remedied, that the customer is advised of any further avenue for complaint available to him under the regulatory system.
(2) A firm must cooperate with a person appointed by its regulator to investigate complaints'[3].

1 For the meaning of 'customer', see para 1360, note 1, above.
2 For the meaning of 'regulatory system', see para 1368, note 7, above.
3 SIB Core Conduct of Business Rules, r 35.

1395. 'Chinese walls'. The requirement for introducing a 'Chinese walls' provision stems from the acceptance in Principle 6[1] that a firm can allow itself to enter into a conflict of interest with its customer. Core Rule 36 provides as follows:

'(1) Where a firm maintains an established arrangement which requires information obtained by the firm in the course of carrying on one part of its business of any kind to be withheld in certain circumstances from persons with whom it deals in the course of carrying on another part of its business of any kind, then in those circumstances:

(a) that information may be so withheld; and

(b) for that purpose, persons employed in the first part may withhold information from those employed in the second;

but only to the extent that the business of one of those parts involves investment business[2] or associated business.

(2) Information may also be withheld where this is required by an established arrangement between different parts of the business (of any kind) of a group, but this provision does not affect any requirement to transmit information which may arise apart from the Core Conduct of Business Rules.

(3) Where the Core Conduct of Business Rules apply only if a firm acts with knowledge, the firm is not for the purposes of the Core Conduct of Business Rules to be taken to act with knowledge if none of the relevant individuals involved on behalf of the firm acts with knowledge.

(4) In addition, in order to avoid the attribution of information held within a firm to that firm for the purposes of section 47 of the [Financial Services Act 1986][3], the effect of section 48(6) of the Act[4] is that nothing done in conformity with paragraph (1) of the core rule on Chinese walls is to be regarded as a contravention of section 47 of the Act'[5].

The most common Chinese walls exist between the corporate finance and advisory or management departments of banks and other large institutions.

Core Rule 36(4) clarifies the statutory provisions so that withholding information where required by a Chinese wall will not constitute any of the statutory offences of concealing material facts in the context of misleading statements and practices.

Recent decisions suggest that the courts are not sympathetic to Chinese wall defences without clear proof of their efficacy[6].

1 For SIB Statements of Principle, principle 6, see para 1348 above.
2 For the meaning of 'investment business', see para 1307 above.
3 For the Financial Services Act 1986 (c 60), s 47 (misleading statements and practices), see para 1332 above.
4 Ibid, s 48(6), provides that nothing done in conformity with conduct of business rules made under s 48(2)(h) (which is somewhat similar to Core Rule 36(1)) is to be regarded as a contravention of s 47.
5 SIB Core Conduct of Business Rules, r 36.
6 See *David Lee & Co (Lincoln Ltd) v Coward Chance* [1991] Ch 259, [1991] 1 All ER 668, and *Re a Firm of Solicitors* The Times, 20 June 1991, CA; and A Berg 'Chinese Walls Come Tumbling Down' Int Financial L Rev October 1991 p 23.

1396. Cessation of business. Core Rule 37 provides for the situation where a firm withdraws from business leaving business outstanding or where an individual in the firm dies or is incapacitated in circumstances which might affect the interests of private customers. It states:

'(1) Where a firm or its appointed representative[1] decides to withdraw from providing any investment or related custodian services to private customers[2], the firm must ensure that any such business which is outstanding is properly completed or is transferred to another firm.

(2) Where the interest of private customers of a firm would be significantly affected by the death or incapacity of an individual within the firm, the firm must make arrangements to protect the interests of those customers in that event'[3].

A more significant cessation of investment business arises when a firm loses its authorisation[4]. There is clear need for the powers of regulators to continue so that the regulator may have residual authority over firms after such loss of authorisation so as to ensure the orderly transfer of customers' business and assets, and so as to be enabled, where necessary, to take remedial or disciplinary action. Most recognised professional bodies and self-regulating organisations have provided for the necessary powers.

1 As to appointed representatives, see para 1361 above.
2 For the meaning of 'private customer', see para 1360, note 1, above.
3 SIB Core Conduct of Business Rules, r 37.
4 As to loss of authorisation, see para 1311 above.

1397. Reliance on others. Core Rule 38 has two main purposes: first, to provide a backing for third-tier promulgations which take the form of guidance rather than rules or regulations; and secondly to permit intermediaries, for example, to pass on to clients documents such as contract notes from agency brokers or performance measurement statistics provided by an independent service without fear of being found in breach of a rule and hence exposed to an action for damages[1] due to the error or malfeasance of another. The rule provides as follows:

'(1) A person is to be taken to act in conformity with the Core Conduct of Business Rules to the extent that:
    (a) the relevant regulator has issued formal guidance on compliance with them; and
    (b) in reliance on standards set in that guidance, the person concerned believes on reasonable grounds that he is acting in conformity with the rules.
(2) A person is to be taken to act in conformity with any of the Core Conduct of Business Rules as to information, to the extent that he can show that he reasonably relied on information provided to him in writing by a third party whom he believed on reasonable grounds to be independent and competent to provide the information.
(3) Any communication required under the Core Conduct of Business Rules to be sent to a customer may be sent to the order of the customer, so long as the recipient is independent of the firm; and there is no need for a firm to send a communication itself where it believes on reasonable grounds that this has been or will be supplied direct by another person'[2].

It remains to be determined how far this rule can be reconciled with the common law duties of an agent of a particular type to show the degree of skill and knowledge and to exercise the care expected of a reasonably competent agent of that type.

1 Ie an action under the Financial Services Act 1986 (c 60), s 62, for which see para 1412 below.
2 SIB Core Conduct of Business Rules, r 38.

1398. Classes of customer. Core Rule 39 provides as follows:

'(1) The Core Rules on Conduct of Business apply subject to any exceptions contained in the rules of an SRO [self-regulating organisation] of which the firm is a member which enable it to treat a customer who would otherwise be a private customer[1] as a non-private customer[2] for the purposes of the Core Conduct of Business Rules if:
    (a) it can show that it believes on reasonable grounds that the customer has sufficient experience and understanding to waive the protections provided for private customers;
    (b) it has given a clear written warning to the customer of the protections under the regulatory system[3] which he will lose; and

(c) the customer has given his written consent after a proper opportunity to consider that warning.

(2) But SRO rules need not require written consent where the customer is ordinarily resident outside the United Kingdom and is reasonably believed not to wish to consent in writing'[4].

This rule effectively permits a firm, in certain circumstances, to treat a private customer as a non-private customer for the purpose of the application of the Core Rules. Therefore, even though a private investor retains his right of action under section 62 of the Financial Services Act 1986[5], the firm will not owe him the duties established by the Core Rules for the protection of private customers. For example, if a firm believes that a customer has sufficient experience and understanding to waive the protections provided for private customers, and the private customer agrees to be treated as a non-private customer, the firm dealing with or for him will not be required, under the Core Rules, to provide him with a two-way customer agreement[6], will not be required to ensure that he understands the nature of the risks involved in a particular investment[7], or will not be required to refrain from effecting, arranging or recommending a contingent liability transaction[8] which is not on a recognised or designated investment exchange[9].

1 For the meaning of 'customer' and 'private customer', see para 1360, note 1, above.
2 For the meaning of 'non-private customer', see para 1363, note 8, above.
3 For the meaning of 'regulatory system', see para 1368, note 7, above.
4 SIB Core Conduct of Business Rules, r 39.
5 For the Financial Services Act 1986 (c 60), s 62, see para 1412 below.
6 See SIB Core Conduct of Business Rules, r 5, and para 1375 above. For the meaning of 'two-way customer agreement', see para 1375, note 4, above.
7 See ibid, r 10, and para 1372 above.
8 For the meaning of 'contingent liability transaction', see para 1375, note 3, above.
9 See SIB Core Conduct of Business Rules, r 27, and para 1386 above. For the meaning of 'recognised investment exchange' and 'designated investment exchange', see para 1386, note 2, above.

1399. Application of the Core Conduct of Business Rules to business. Core Rule 40 contains various provisions regarding the application of the rules. Rule 40(1) relates to the application of the rules to business, in these terms:

'(a) The general application of the Core Conduct of Business Rules is that, as far as they relate to business, they relate to business which is regulated business[1], and accordingly, where a rule relating to business applies only in particular circumstances, the rule applies only if those circumstances apply in the course of regulated business.

(b) To the extent indicated, the Core Conduct of Business Rules also apply to the carrying on (whether in the UK or elsewhere) of other business if that other business is investment business[2], associated business or business which is held out as being for the purposes of investment.

(c) The Core Conduct of Business Rules do not apply to authorised persons[3] to the extent that they are acting as authorised persons certified by recognised professional bodies (since these persons are subject to regulation by those bodies) or to the extent that they are acting as exempted persons[4].

(d) The Core Conduct of Business Rules are limited in their application to regulated insurance companies (by paragraph 4 of Schedule 10 to the [Financial Services Act 1986]), to regulated friendly societies (by paragraph 14 of Schedule 11 to the Act) and to certain UCITS[5] operators and trustees (by section 86(7) of the Act).

(e) The Core Conduct of Business Rules apply to an oil market participant subject to exceptions contained in the rules of an SRO [self-regulating organisation] of which the firm is a member.

(f) Where the firm is:
  (i) a journalist, broadcaster, author or publisher;
  (ii) whose only investment business is the provision of investment advice;
  the Core Conduct of Business Rules apply subject to exceptions contained in the rules of an SRO of which the firm is a member'[6].

1 For the meaning of 'regulated business', see para 1357, note 1, above.
2 For the meaning of 'investment business', see para 1307 above.
3 For the meaning of 'authorised person', see para 1306, note 2, above.
4 For the meaning of 'exempted person', see para 1306, note 3, above.
5 Ie Undertakings for Collective Investment in Transferable Securities.
6 SIB Core Conduct of Business Rules, r 40(1).

1400. Application of the Core Conduct of Business Rules to advertisements. Core Rule 40(2) provides as follows:

'(a) Where the Core Conduct of Business Rules govern the issue or approval of an investment advertisement[1] then, except to the extent indicated, they govern issue of an investment advertisement in the United Kingdom and approval (whether in the United Kingdom or elsewhere) of an investment advertisement for issue in the United Kingdom.

(b) The Core Conduct of Business Rules on issue and approval of advertisements[2] and on issue or approval of advertisements for an overseas person[3] do not apply:
  (i) to the issue[5] by an authorised person[4] of an exempt advertisement; or
  (ii) to the issue or approval of a DIE advertisement[6], a takeover advertisement[7], or (unless they constitute a direct offer advertisement[8]) scheme particulars[9].

(c) The Core Conduct of Business Rules do not apply to the reissue of an investment advertisement which has been prepared and issued by another person and which the firm believes on reasonable grounds:
  (i) is an exempt advertisement, a DIE advertisement, a takeover advertisement, or (unless they constitute a direct offer advertisement) scheme particulars; or
  (ii) is already issued or approved by an authorised person and is issued to a market for which it was intended at the time of its issue or approval by the authorised person'[10].

1 For the meaning of 'an investment advertisement', see para 1337, note 2, above. For the Core Rules as to advertisements, see paras 1366 ff above.
2 See SIB Core Conduct of Business Rules, r 5, and para 1367 above.
3 See ibid, r 6, and para 1368 above.
4 For the meaning of 'authorised person', see para 1306, note 2, above.
5 For the meaning of 'exempt advertisement', see para 1367, note 8, above.
6 For the meaning of 'DIE advertisement', see para 1367, note 9, above.
7 For the meaning of 'takeover advertisement', see para 1367, note 10, above.
8 For the meaning of 'direct offer advertisement', see para 1367, note 3, above.
9 'Scheme particulars' means a document containing information about a regulated collective investment scheme (defined in para 1381, note 4, above) and subject to requirements as to the content of scheme particulars made either under the Financial Services Act 1986 (c 60), or, in the case of a scheme recognised under s 86 (see para 1328 above), by the certifying member state: SIB Financial Services Glossary 1991.
10 SIB Core Conduct of Business Rules, r 40(2). This rule must be read in conjunction with Core Rules 5 and 6 (on investment advertising), as it limits the types of investment advertisement to which those rules apply.

1401. Application of the Core Conduct of Business Rules as to time. The application of the Core Conduct of Business Rules as to time is that they apply to a firm from the date specified for firms of the relevant class in a separate commencement instrument made by the Securities and Investments Board (subject to any transitional provisions contained in that instrument)[1].

This means in practice that once a self-regulating organisation ('SRO') completes its third-tier rules and they are ready to be applied to the members of that SRO, the Securities and Investments Board will issue a commencement order so that the Core Rules will apply at the same time to those members. The result is that the Core Rules will begin application to members of each SRO at different times.

1 SIB Core Conduct of Business Rules, r 40(3).

(d) The Financial Supervision Rules

1402. Introduction. In June 1990 the Securities and Investments Board ('SIB') promulgated the Financial Services (Financial Supervision) Rules 1990, which follow the three-tier approach first set down in the proposal document of August 1989[1]. The financial supervision requirements are based on three of the Principles: those relating to financial resources[2], to internal organisation[3] and to relations with regulators[4].

There are five Core Rules, which are discussed in the following paragraphs, in addition to more detailed rules. In general the Core Rules apply to any member of a recognised self-regulating organisation ('SRO') in respect of investment business[5] in the carrying on of which he is subject to the rules of that organisation[6].

The financial supervision rules are disapplied for entities where another supervisor is better placed to monitor prudential supervision[7]. In the United Kingdom this policy extends to banks, building societies, insurance companies and friendly societies. The SIB relies on the supervision of the primary regulators (the Bank of England, the Building Societies Commission, the Department of Trade and Industry Insurance Division and the Registrar of Friendly Societies) through simple information sharing memoranda of understanding.

1 *Regulation of the Conduct of Investment Business: A Proposal* (1989). The rules were made under the Financial Services Act 1986 (c 60), s 49 (amended by the Companies Act 1989 (c 40), s 206(1), Sch 23, para 3(2)).
2 SIB Statement of Principles, principle 8: see para 1350 above.
3 Ibid, principle 9: see para 1351 above.
4 Ibid, principle 10: see para 1352 above.
5 For the meaning of 'investment business', see para 1307 above.
6 SIB Financial Services (Financial Supervision) Rules 1990, r 1.04(1).
7 See ibid, r 1.04(2), (3).

1403. Financial resources. Core Rule A provides that:

'A firm must at all times have available the amount and type of financial resources required by the rules of its regulator'[1].

The rules distinguish between four categories of firm (low risk, medium risk, higher risk, and special) to reflect the vulnerability of different types of firm to various risks undertaken in their investment business activities.

Low risk firms include investment advisers which have chosen not to receive or hold client money or assets and confine themselves to undertaking only low risk investment business (essentially investment advice, arranging transactions in life policies, units in regulated collected investments schemes and PEPs and the submission of applications for shares in new issues, particularly privatisation issues)[2]. Since these firms are not exposed to the same risks as those in higher categories they do not, in turn, expose other market participants or clients with or for whom they deal to substantial risks. Accordingly they are not required to meet a detailed capital or liquidity test but must instead satisfy a basic solvency test: they must be able to meet liabilities as they fall due[3].

Medium risk firms are involved in similar types of activity to low risk firms, but receive and/or hold client's money and/or assets and carry out limited types of investment management[4]. Since the risks for such firms are moderate, the requirements are also more moderate than those applying to higher risk firms. Medium risk firms are required to meet a net liquid assets test and a current liquidity test: they must have sufficient assets which can be realised in the next twelve months to cover liabilities falling due within that period[5].

Higher risk firms include firms broking or dealing in securities and general investment managers[6]. Such firms are subject to a net liquid assets test which is more stringent than the test for medium risk firms and, since the firms involved in securities and commodities dealing and broking are exposed to a much wider range of risks, separate requirements are introduced to cover these[7]. The risks to which higher risk firms are subject are (1) counterparty risk (the risk that a counterparty in the deal will not meet its contractual obligations)[8], (2) position risk (the risk which faces a firm which has its own account positions, namely the risk that the value of the holding could move in an adverse way)[9], and (3) foreign currency exposure risk[10].

The fourth category of authorised persons, 'special firms', are required to have a substantial minimum level of growth capital[11]. This category of special firms is restricted to trustees of authorised unit trusts[12].

1 SIB Financial Services (Financial Supervision) Rules 1990, r 1.03, Core Rule A.
2 Ibid, r 2.01.
3 Ibid, r 3.02.
4 Ibid, r 2.02.
5 Ibid, rr 4.02, 4.03.
6 Ibid, r 2.03.
7 Ibid, rr 5.02, 5.08.
8 Ibid, r 5.09.
9 Ibid, r 5.10.
10 Ibid, r 5.11.
11 Ibid, r 6.02.
12 Ibid, r 2.04.

1404. Records and reporting. Core Rule B requires that:

'A firm must ensure that it maintains adequate accounting records and must prepare and submit such reports as are required by its regulator in a timely manner. A firm's records:
(a) must be up to date and must disclose with reasonable accuracy at any time the firm's financial position at that time;
(b) must enable the firm to demonstrate its continuing compliance with its financial resources requirements; and
(c) must provide the information:
  (i) which the firm needs to prepare such financial statements and periodical reports as may be required by its regulator, and
  (ii) which the firm's auditor (where the regulator requires one to be appointed) needs to form an opinion on any statements of the firm on which the auditor is required to report[1]'.

The reporting requirements imposed under the Financial Services (Financial Supervision) Rules 1990 vary between the different categories of firm[2]. Special firms are required to submit annual financial statements[3]. Low risk firms complete a mid-year and end-year questionnaire with an annual declaration of solvency[4]. Medium risk firms are required to submit annual reports as well as mid-year and end-year questionnaires[5]. Medium risk firms are also required to prepare quarterly statements but need submit these only if requested by the Securities and Investments Board[5]. Higher risk firms are required to submit monthly statements showing their financial resources, as well as more detailed quarterly and end-year statements[6].

1 SIB Financial Services (Financial Supervision) Rules 1990, r 1.03, Core Rule B.
2 As to these categories, see para 1403 above.
3 SIB Financial Services (Financial Supervision) Rules 1990, r 7.01.
4 Ibid, rr 7.02, 7.03.
5 Ibid, rr 7.01, 7.03, 7.04.
6 Ibid, rr 7.01, 7.04, 7.05.

1405. Appointment of auditors. The appointment of auditors referred to in Core Rule B(c)(ii) is also referred to in Core Rule E. This requires that:

'A firm shall appoint an auditor where required to do so by its regulator. A firm shall make available to its auditor the information and explanations he needs to discharge his responsibilities as required by the firm's regulator'[1].

Under the third-tier rules issued by the Securities and Investments Board, medium risk, high risk and special firms require to appoint auditors[2] if they have not already done so under the requirements of the Companies Act 1985 (c 6). Low risk firms need not appoint auditors unless required to do so under that Act.

1 SIB Financial Services (Financial Supervision) Rules 1990, r 1.03, Core Rule E.
2 Ibid, r 10.02.

1406. *Ad hoc* reporting requirements. Core Rule D supplements the reporting requirements contained in Core Rule B. It states that:

'A firm must notify its regulator immediately it becomes aware that it is in breach of, or that it expects shortly to be in breach of, the core rules on financial resources (A), records and reporting (B) or internal controls and systems (C)'[1].

All firms are required to report to the Securities and Investments Board ('SIB') forthwith, in writing (or, if speed prevents writing, then with confirmation in writing)[2], any breach of its duty to have sufficient financial resources[3], any deficiency of net assets in a subsidiary, any change in the information it gave in its application for authorisation, certain failures to comply with the rules, any substantial legal action raised against it, any misleading statement it discovers in financial statements previously supplied, any audited financial statements required under other enactments, any claim it makes under its professional indemnity or related insurance policy, and any serious emergency which arises and how it proposes to deal with it[4]. In addition, medium risk, higher risk and special firms must notify SIB of significant falls in their allowable financial resources, and of certain matters concerned with the auditor's report[5].

1 SIB Financial Services (Financial Supervision) Rules 1990, r 1.03, Core Rule E.
2 Ibid, r 8.01.
3 In this case the initial report must be by telephone or telex: ibid, r 8.02(1).
4 Ibid, r 8.02(1)–(9).
5 Ibid, r 8.03.

1407. Internal controls and systems. Core Rule C provides that:

'A firm must, for the purpose of its compliance with rules on financial supervision, ensure that its internal controls and systems are adequate for the size, nature and complexity of its activities'[1].

1 SIB Financial Services (Financial Supervision) Rules 1990, r 1.03, Core Rule C.

1408. Commentary. The accounting records kept by directly regulated persons must be sufficient to disclose with reasonable accuracy the firm's financial position at any time and to enable any particular transaction of the firm or its investing customers to be identified and traced through the firm's accounting system[1]. The financial regulation section of the Securities and Investments Board ('SIB') rule book is, of course, intended to protect clients against loss of funds and stems in part from the scandals of the late 1970s when investors suffered irrecoverable losses at the hands of under-capitalised investment business. In addition to the primary protection against financial loss, the regulations were designed to allow clients to avoid both the delay and inconvenience of relying on other compensation arrangements (such as insurance) and the cost and inconvenience involved when the firm with which they deal ceases trading through insolvency — the so called 'continuity risk'. Protection is also provided against 'systemic risk' — the danger of the 'domino' effect of the failure of one business on another[2]. In addition, the requirement to maintain financial resources protects the central compensation fund established by SIB[3]. SIB's financial package, however, is not designed to eliminate entirely the risk of insolvency. It aims to achieve the most that can be hoped for, that is, the imposition within the constraints of a competitive market of internal financial discipline on authorised firms alerting SIB, through the regular returns, to problem areas before firms' financial positions becomes such as would be likely to pose a threat to the investing public.

Following some of SIB's earlier failures to recognise the separateness of the Scottish financial and legal system, SIB reacted swiftly to criticisms that certain provisions of the original financial resources requirements were prejudicial to Scottish interests. In particular, the provisions requiring the permitted subordinated loans and bank undertakings (which would be taken into account for financial resources requirements) to be written under and governed exclusively by English law were quickly replaced by provisions which gave equal prominence to the laws of the other jurisdictions in the United Kingdom[4].

The Core Rules referred to above do not deal with all areas within SIB's regulatory ambit. The current rules on clients' money, compensation, unsolicited calls and compensation, which should in due course be amended to fit in with the three-tier approach, are examined below[5].

1 SIB Financial Services (Financial Supervision) Rules 1990, r 9.01(2). This is the so-called 'audit trail'.
2 See Office of Fair Trading Report on the SIB Rule Book 1987, p 8.
3 As to compensation, see para 1420 below.
4 However, not all self-regulating organisations were so quick to react. The original rule book of the Financial Intermediaries, Managers and Brokers Regulatory Association ('FIMBRA'), for example, followed the first draft of the SIB rules and referred only to English law — a particularly unacceptable position for FIMBRA, which is a Scottish registered company.
5 See para 1409 ff below. However, as to unsolicited calls, see paras 1333 ff above.

(12) THE CLIENTS' MONEY REGULATIONS

1409. Custody of clients' money. Allied to the financial requirements[1] are the Financial Services (Clients' Money) Regulations 1987, made by the Securities and Investments Board ('SIB')[2]. The regulations apply generally to all firms authorised to carry on investment business[3], but do not apply to a firm holding a certificate issued by certain professional bodies, including the Law Society of

Scotland[4]. The basic requirements of the regulations are that all client money be held by the authorised firm as agent or trustee for the client[5] in an account at an approved bank which is in the name of the firm and includes in its title the description 'client account'[6], and that interest is paid on such money[7]. The purpose of the regulations is to ensure that the money of one client is not used to discharge the obligations of another or by the firm to finance its business and that in the event of the insolvency of an authorised firm, clients' money is protected from the claims of the firm's general creditors and from rights of set-off by the bank in which the money is held[8].

For the purposes of the regulations, 'client money' means money of any currency which, in the course of carrying on investment business, a firm holds or receives, whether or not in the United Kingdom, in respect of any investment agreement entered into or to be entered into with or for a client and which is not immediately due and payable on demand to the firm for its own account[9]. Money which a firm is due to pay to a client (for example following the purchase of an investment by the firm from the client) also falls within the definition, as does interest on the money described above. There is, however, provision for the authorised person to retain interest on trivial sums held only for short periods (that is, interest amounting to £10 or less)[10]. 'Client money' also includes money of any currency which in the course of carrying on investment business a firm pays into a client bank account in pursuance of an obligation to do so under the regulations or, where applicable, the rules of a recognised self-regulating organisation or recognised professional body governing the operation of that client bank account[11].

Attempting to contract out of the segregation requirement imposed by the regulations is prohibited except in relation to certain categories of sophisticated investor (that is, 'business', 'professional' and 'experienced' investors)[12]. Contracting out of the payment of interest requirements is, however, permitted where appropriate contractual provision to this effect is made[13].

Like many other areas of the SIB rules, the operation of the clients' money regulations is currently being reviewed. It is understood that SIB will propose relaxations to the rules on the payment of interest, which have caused practical problems and resulted in many firms contracting out of the provisions altogether rather than attempting to meet the detailed SIB requirements, thus effectively reducing rather than increasing investor protection.

Amendments to the rules requiring that client accounts hold no less and no more than the precise amount held by the firm for clients at any one time are also expected. The rules as currently drafted effectively prevent a firm from maintaining a 'float'[14] in a client account. It is understood that the current rules were prepared on the basis of the elderly English law which removes trust protection offered by a client account if excess funds are held therein. The new rules should, however, recognise the difference in Scots law which permits excess money to be held in an agent's account without prejudicing the sanctity of that account provided the excess money is clearly identifiable.

1 See paras 1402 ff above.
2 The rules were made under the Financial Services Act 1986 (c 60), s 55 (now amended by the Companies Act 1989 (c 40), ss 206(1), 212, Sch 23, para 6, Sch 24). They have been amended by the Financial Services (Clients' Money) Amendment Regulations 1990.
3 SIB Financial services (Clients' Money) Regulations 1987, reg 1.4(1). For the meaning of 'investment business', see para 1307 above.
4 Ibid, reg 1.4(2)(a). For other firms to which the regulations do not apply, see reg 1.4(2)–(5).
5 Ibid, reg 2.2.
6 Ibid, reg 3.1. For the meaning of 'approved bank', see reg 1.3(1).
7 Ibid, reg 2.3.
8 See the Explanatory Memorandum dated 7 October 1987.

9 SIB Financial Services (Clients' Money) Regulations 1987, reg 2.1(1)(a). For the meaning of 'investment agreement', see para 1332, note 2, above. Money is not immediately due and payable to the firm for its own account to the extent that the firm's obligations in respect of which the money is held or received remain unperformed: reg 2.1(2).

10 Ibid, reg 2.3(6).

11 Ibid, reg 2.1(1)(b).

12 Ibid, reg 2.1(3).

13 Ibid, reg 2.3(7).

14 Ie excess funds of its own.

(6) INVESTORS' REMEDIES

1410. Interdicts. On the application of the Securities and Investments Board[1] ('SIB') (by delegation from the Secretary of State[2]) the Court of Session may grant interdict restraining certain contraventions or, as the case may be, make an order requiring the person concerned and any other person who appears to the court to have been concerned in the contravention to take such steps as the court may direct to remedy it[3]. The court must first be satisfied:

(1) that there is a reasonable likelihood that the person concerned will contravene any of certain provisions or conditions; or

(2) that he has contravened any such provision or condition and that there is a reasonable likelihood that the contravention will continue or be repeated; or

(3) that he has contravened any such provision or condition and that there are steps that could be taken for remedying the contravention[4].

The provisions and conditions concerned are:

(a) any provision of rules or regulations (including those made by SIB) relating to the conduct of investment business[5];

(b) any provision relating to misleading statements and practices, unsolicited calls, restrictions on advertisements or the employment of prohibited persons[6];

(c) any requirement imposed by an order excepting certain advertisements from the restrictions[7];

(d) the rules of a recognised self-regulating organisation, recognised professional body, investment exchange or clearing house to which the person concerned is subject and which regulates the carrying on by him of investment business[8];

(e) any condition[9] subject to which conduct of business rules and financial resources rules have been modified[10].

These provisions may provide more of a theoretical weapon than one greatly used in practice. They are unlikely to be weapons of first resort. Indeed, given the wide range of actions open to the SIB, the cost of pursuing an action under these provisions and the consequences for the credibility of SIB should such an action fail, it is likely that the provisions will be used only in cases of flagrant breach where investors have suffered substantial loss.

1 Nothing in the Financial Services Act 1986 (c 60), s 61, affects the right of any person other than the SIB to bring proceedings in respect of the matters to which s 61 applies: s 61(9).

2 Financial Services Act 1986 (Delegation) Order 1987, SI 1987/942. Certain of these powers are exercisable concurrently by the Secretary of State and the SIB.

3 Financial Services Act 1986, s 61(1), (8).

4 Ibid, s 61(1)(a)–(c).

5 Ie rules or regulations made under ibid, Pt I, Ch V (ss 47–63C). These include conduct of business rules, financial resources rules, notification regulations, indemnity rules, and regulations as to clients' money.

6 Ie any provisions of ibid, ss 47, 56, 57, 59: see paras 1331 ff above.

7 Ie an order under ibid, s 58(3): see para 1337, note 1, above.

8 No application may be made under this head unless it appears that the organisation, body, exchange or clearing house is unable or unwilling to take appropriate steps to restrain the contravention or to require the person concerned to take steps to remedy it: ibid, s 61(2).

9 Ie any condition imposed under ibid, s 50: see para 1340, note 3, above.

10 Ibid, s 61(1)(a)(i)–(iv).

1411. Restitution orders. If the Court of Session is satisfied on the application of the Securities and Investments Board ('SIB')[1] (by delegation from the Secretary of State[2]):

(1) that profits have accrued to any person as a result of his contravention of certain provisions or conditions[3], or

(2) that one or more investors have suffered loss or been otherwise adversely affected as a result of that contravention[4],

the court may order the person concerned to pay to the applicant such sum as appears to be just, having regard:

(a) in a case within head (1), to the profits appearing to have been accrued;

(b) in a case within head (2), to the extent of the loss or other adverse effect; or

(c) in a case within both heads, to the profits and to the extent of the loss or other adverse effect[5].

The court may require the person concerned to furnish it with accounts and other information, verified in such manner as it may direct[6]. Any amount recovered under the order must be paid out to such person or distributed among such persons as the court directs[7].

1 Nothing in the Financial Services Act 1986 (c 60), s 61, affects the right of any person other than the SIB to bring proceedings in respect of the matters to which s 61 applies: s 61(9).

2 Financial Services Act 1986 (Delegation) Order 1987, SI 1987/942; Financial Services Act 1986 (Delegation) Order 1991, SI 1991/200.

3 Financial Services Act 1986, s 61(1)(a), (8). The provisions and conditions concerned are those mentioned in s 61(1)(a): see para 1410 above.

4 Ibid, s 61(3)(b), (8).

5 Ibid, s 61(5), by reference to s 61(4)(a)–(c).

6 Ibid, s 61(7).

7 Ibid, s 61(6).

1412. Actions for damages. Without prejudice to the powers of the Court of Session to grant interdict or make restitution orders[1], certain contraventions are actionable at the suit of a person who suffers loss as a result, subject to the defences and other incidents applying to actions for breach of statutory duty[2]. However, no action in respect of such a contravention lies at the suit of a person other than a private investor, except in circumstances specified in regulations made by the Secretary of State[3]. 'Private investor' means an investor whose cause of action arises as a result of anything he has done or suffered:

(1) in the case of an individual, otherwise than in the course of carrying on investment business; and

(2) in the case of any other person, otherwise than in the course of carrying on business of any kind;

but does not include a government, local authority or public authority[4].

Head (2) effectively excludes any company acting as an investor. Therefore, although business investors are treated by the Securities and Investments Board for the purpose of the conduct of business rules and are arguably in many cases in no better position than private investors, they are only able to rely on their rights under the law relating to contract and delict.

It is submitted that it is highly likely that any breach of rules which causes sufficient loss to merit the bringing of an action under these provisions would involve not simply a technical breach of a detailed rule but would rather involve a failure to take the proper degree of care and diligence in performing investment services for clients — a failure which, under Scots law, would be independently actionable as a delict.

1 Ie subject to the Financial Services Act 1986 (c 60), s 61: see paras 1410, 1411, above.
2 Ibid, s 62(1). This applies to contraventions of (1) rules or regulations made under Pt I, Ch V (ss 47–63C) (these include conduct of business rules, financial resources rules, notification regulations, indemnity rules, and regulations as to clients' money); (2) conditions imposed under s 50 (modification of conduct of business and financial resources rules: see para 1340, note 3, above); (3) requirements imposed by an order under s 58(3) exempting advertisements from restrictions (see para 1337, note 1, above); (4) the duty under s 59(6) not to employ a person who is subject to a disqualification direction (see para 1338 above): s 62(1)(a)–(b). It also applies to certain contraventions of rules of a recognised self-regulating organisation or professional body: see s 62(2). For certain exclusions, see s 62(3).
3 Ibid, s 62A(1) (added by the Companies Act 1989, s 193(1)). For these circumstances, see the Financial Services Act 1986 (Restriction of Right of Action) Regulations 1991, SI 1991/489, reg 3.
4 Financial Services Act 1986, s 62A(2) (as so added); Financial Services Act 1986 (Restriction of Right of Action) Regulations 1991, reg 2. This definition does not *per se* exclude 'professional' individuals. Rather, it excludes only businesses (which are usually, but not always, professionals). The SIB no longer uses the term 'professional' for the purposes of its rules, but uses the term 'non-private' customer instead.

1413. Other direct and indirect remedies. Unlike the right to bring an action for damages[1], the other direct and indirect remedies available to investors under the Financial Services Act 1986 have not been modified in any way by the Companies Act 1989.

An agreement[2] made by or through a person who is not an authorised or exempted person[3] is unenforceable against the other person (the investor), who is entitled to recover any money or other property paid or transferred by him under the agreement, together with compensation for any loss sustained by him through the investment[4], although the court may allow the agreement to be enforced or money and property paid or transferred under it to be retained if satisfied that the contravention was innocent or that it is just and equitable to do so[5].

Proceedings for interdict and restitution orders may be taken in respect of the contravention of the prohibition on the carrying on of investment business by persons other than authorised or exempted persons[6].

The Secretary of State and the Securities and Investments Board ('SIB') have concurrent power to present a petition to wind up an authorised person or appointed representative who is a company, an unregistered or oversea company or a partnership if the person is unable to pay his debts or it is just and equitable that he should be wound up[7]. However, if the authorised person is a member of a recognised self-regulating organisation or is certified by a recognised professional body, that organisation or body must consent to the presentation of the petition[8].

In addition there are extensive powers of intervention and investigative and information powers[9].

1 Ie under the Financial Services Act 1986 (c 60), s 62: see para 1412 above.
2 Ie an agreement the making or performance of which by the person seeking to enforce it or from whom money or other property is recoverable under ibid, s 5, constitutes an activity falling within ibid Sch 1, Pt II (paras 12–16) (see para 1307 above), and is not excluded by Sch 1, Pt III (paras 17–25B) or Pt IV (paras 26, 27): s 5(7).
3 For the meaning of 'authorised person' and 'exempted person', see para 1306, notes 2, 3, above.
4 Financial Services Act 1986, s 5(1). The compensation is such as the parties may agree or the court may, on the application of either party, determine: s 5(2).
5 See ibid, s 5(3).
6 See ibid, s 6, and para 1324 above.
7 Ibid, s 72(1), (2); Financial Services Act 1986 (Delegation) Order 1987, SI 1987/942. A person who defaults in an obligation to pay any sum due and payable under any investment agreement

(defined in para 1332, note 2, above) is deemed to be unable to pay his debts: Financial Services Act 1986, s 72(3).

8 Ibid, s 72(5).

9 See paras 1414, 1415, below.

1414. Powers of intervention. The powers of intervention of the Securities and Investments Board ('SIB') (by delegation from the Secretary of State[1]) include:

(1) power to withdraw or suspend a person's authorisation[2];

(2) power to prohibit an authorised person from entering into specified kinds of transaction, soliciting business from specified kinds of persons or carrying on business in or otherwise than in a specified manner[3];

(3) power to prohibit an authorised person or appointed representative from dealing with his assets or specified assets in or otherwise than in a specified manner[4];

(4) power to require that assets or specified classes of assets belonging to an authorised person or appointed representative or belonging to investors and held by or to the order of an authorised person or appointed representative be transferred to and held by a trustee approved by the SIB[5]; and

(5) power to require an authorised person or appointed representative to maintain in the United Kingdom assets of such value as will enable him to meet his liabilities in respect of investment business carried on by him in the United Kingdom[6].

These powers are exercisable in relation to any authorised person or (except in the case of head (2)) any appointed representative of his if it appears to the SIB:

(a) that the exercise of the powers is desirable for the protection of investors;

(b) that the authorised person is not fit to carry on investment business of a particular kind or to the extent to which he is carrying it on or proposing to carry it on; or

(c) that he has contravened any provision of the Financial Services Act 1986 or rules or regulations under it, or has furnished false information or has contravened any prohibition or requirement imposed under the Act[7].

The powers may be exercised in relation to a person whose authorisation has been suspended[8], but may not generally be exercised in relation to a member of a recognised self-regulating organisation or person certified by a recognised professional body[9].

The SIB may of its own motion or on the application of a person on whom any prohibition or requirement has been imposed under these powers rescind or vary the prohibition or requirement if it appears that it is no longer necessary or that it should take effect or continue in force in a different form[10]. The power to impose, rescind or vary a prohibition or requirement is exercisable by written notice served on the person concerned[11]. The notice must normally give reasons[12], and must state the right to have the case referred to the Financial Services Tribunal[13].

1 Financial Services Act 1986 (Delegation) Order 1987, SI 1987/942.

2 See the Financial Services Act 1986, s 28, and para 1311 above.

3 Ibid, s 65.

4 Ibid, s 66. As to appointed representatives, see para 1361 above.

5 Ibid, s 67(1). Assets so held by a trustee may be released or dealt with only in accordance with directions given by the SIB or in circumstances which it specifies: s 67(3).

6 Ibid, s 68.

7 Ibid, s 64(1).

8 Ibid, s 64(3).

9 See ibid, s 64(4).

10 Ibid, s 69.

11 Ibid, s 70(1).

12 Ibid, s 70(3).
13 Ibid, s 70(5). As to the tribunal, see paras 1416 ff below.

1415. Investigations and information. There is an impressive array of investigative and information powers. The SIB (by delegation from the Secretary of State[1]) maintains a register of authorised persons, self-regulating organisations ('SROs'), recognised professional bodies ('RPBs'), recognised investment exchanges, recognised clearing houses, authorised unit trust schemes and recognised schemes, and persons prohibited[2] from being employed in investment business[3].

It may by notice in writing require authorised persons, SROs, RPBs, recognised investment exchanges and recognised clearing houses to furnish and verify such information as it reasonably requires[4].

The Secretary of State and the SIB have extensive concurrent powers to investigate the affairs of any person so far as relevant to any investment business which he appears to have been carrying on, including power to require that person or any connected person[5] to attend to answer questions and produce documents, subject only to the rules as to confidentiality as between client and professional legal adviser[6].

1 Financial Services Act 1986 (Delegation) Order 1987, SI 1987/942.
2 Ie under the Financial Services Act 1986, s 59: see para 1338 above.
3 Ibid, s 102. The information in the register (other than in relation to prohibited persons) is open to inspection, and a person is entitled to ascertain whether a particular person is a prohibited person: s 103.
4 Ibid, s 104.
5 'Connected person' includes a person's partner, employee, agent, appointed representative, banker, auditor, solicitor or principal, and a company's director, secretary or controller: see ibid, s 105(9).
6 Ibid, s 105(1), (3), (4), (6); Financial Services Act 1986 (Delegation) Order 1987. However, a lawyer may be required to furnish the name and address of his client: Financial Services Act 1986, s 105(6). Failure to comply with a requirement under s 105 is an offence: s 105(10). The SIB may authorise any of its officers or any other competent person to exercise its powers under s 105: see s 106 (amended by the Companies Act 1989 (c 40), s 73(5)). These provisions do not permit the investigation of transactions which took place before the provisions came into force: *R v Secretary of State for Trade and Industry, ex parte R* [1989] 1 All ER 647, [1989] 1 WLR 372, DC.

(7) THE FINANCIAL SERVICES TRIBUNAL

1416. Constitution of the Financial Services Tribunal. The Financial Services Tribunal has been constituted from a panel of not less than ten persons, including persons, at least one of whom is qualified in Scots law, appointed by the Lord Chancellor after consultation with the Lord Advocate, and persons appointed by the Secretary of State who are qualified by experience or otherwise to deal with cases which may be referred to the tribunal[1]. The Secretary of State nominates three panel members to serve as members of the tribunal to hear a particular case, and nominates one of them, being legally qualified, to act as chairman[2].

The tribunal may appoint counsel or a solicitor to assist it in proceedings before it[3]. The Secretary of State has made rules regulating the procedure of the tribunal[4].

1 Financial Services Act 1986 (c 60), s 96(1), (2). As to the terms of office of members, their expenses and the tribunal staff, see s 96(6), Sch 6, paras 1–3.
2 Ibid, s 96(3), (4).
3 Ibid, Sch 6, para 4(2).

4 Ibid, Sch 6, para 4(1); Financial Services Tribunal (Conduct of Investigations) Rules 1988, SI 1988/351.

1417. References to the tribunal. Any of the following persons may require the Securities and Investments Board ('SIB') (by delegation from the Secretary of State[1]) to refer to the Financial Services Tribunal the matter to which the appropriate notice relates:

(1) any person on whom there is served (a) a notice[2] of a proposal to refuse an application[3] for, or to withdraw or suspend, or to vary a suspension of, an authorisation by the SIB[3]; or (b) a notice[4] of a proposal to give a direction[5] to terminate or suspend the authorisation of a person authorised in another member state or to refuse an application[5] to vary such a direction[6]; (c) a notice[7] of a proposal to give a disqualification direction in respect of any person or to refuse an application for his consent to the employment of such a person in connection with investment business or for the variation of such consent; (d) a notice[8] of a proposal to publish a statement that an authorised person has contravened certain provisions[9]; (e) a notice[10] imposing, rescinding or varying a prohibition or requirement under the powers of intervention of the SIB[11];

(2) any person on whom a copy of a notice under head (1)(a), (b), (d) or (e) is served or on whom the SIB considers that such a copy would have been served had it been practicable to do so[12].

The requirement for a reference must be made within twenty-eight days of service of the notice, and on the making of the requirement the SIB must refer the matter accordingly[13], although it need not do so if it decides to meet the wishes of the person concerned and notifies him in writing accordingly[14].

Where the tribunal receives more than one reference concerned with the same or related matters, it may, if it thinks it expedient, and must if all the applicants so request, join the matters and order that they be dealt with as a single investigation[15].

On referring a case to the tribunal the SIB must send to the tribunal a copy of the relevant notice which it had served on the applicant, and of the applicant's request for the reference, and must notify the applicant that it has done so[16]. Within twenty-one days of referring the case the SIB must send to the tribunal and the applicant (or all the applicants in a joined matter) such further information and copies of such other documents as it considers would assist the tribunal[17], and within a further twenty-one days the applicant or each applicant must send to the tribunal, the SIB and other applicants a statement of his grounds for requiring the reference, specifying any disputed matters of fact, other matters he wishes to draw to the tribunal's attention and the names and addresses of any witnesses[18]. There is provision for the withdrawal of references[19].

1 Financial Services Act 1986 (Delegation) Order 1987, SI 1987/942.
2 Ie a notice under the Financial Services Act 1986 (c 60), s 29(1): see para 1311 above.
3 Ie under ibid, s 26: see para 1310 above.
4 Ie a notice under ibid, s 34(1): see para 1320 above.
5 Ie under ibid, s 33: see para 1320 above.
6 Ie under ibid, s 33(3).
7 Ie a notice under ibid, s 59(4): see para 1338 above.
8 Ie a notice under ibid, s 60(2): see para 1339 above.
9 Ie any provisions of rules or regulations under ibid, Pt I, Ch V (ss 47–63C: conduct of business: see paras 1356 ff above), or s 56 (unsolicited calls: see paras 1333–1335 above), or s 59 (employment of prohibited persons: see para 1338 above), or any condition imposed under s 50 (modification of conduct of business and financial resources rules: see para 1340, note 3, above).
10 Ie a notice under ibid, s 70, relating to the exercise of powers under Pt I, Ch VI (ss 64–71: powers of intervention): see para 1414 above.

11 Ibid, s 97(1)(a).
12 Ibid, s 97(1)(b).
13 Ibid, s 97(1).
14 See ibid, s 97(2), (3). For the power to refer where the SIB serves a substituted notice, see s 97(4), (5).
15 Financial Services Tribunal (Conduct of Investigations) Rules 1988, SI 1988/351, r 3.
16 Ibid, r 4(1).
17 Ibid, s 4(2).
18 Ibid, r 5.
19 See the Financial Services Act 1986, s 100.

1418. Investigation and hearing by the tribunal. The Financial Services Tribunal must investigate the matter referred to it by carrying out such inquiries as it thinks appropriate into and concerning the information, documents, records and matters placed before it[1]. For this purpose the tribunal may take evidence[2]. It must then notify the parties that they have fourteen days in which to make representations, either orally or in writing[3]. Any hearing will normally be in private unless the applicant or all the applicants request a public hearing[4]. Where the applicant or, in a joined matter, a majority of the applicants are either habitually resident, or have their principal places of business, in Scotland, the hearing will be in Scotland unless the applicant or all the applicants consent to the hearing taking place elsewhere[5].

1 Financial Services Act 1986 (c 60), s 98(1)(a); Financial Services Tribunal (Conduct of Investigations) Rules 1988, SI 1988/351, r 6. For the manner in which the tribunal makes its inquiry, see r 7.
2 As to the taking of evidence, see the Financial Services Act 1986, s 96(6), Sch 6, para 5, and the Financial Services Tribunal (Conduct of Investigations) Rules 1988, r 8. As to representation, see r 10.
3 Ibid, r 9. The parties' written representations must be exchanged: see r 11.
4 Ibid, r 12.
5 Ibid, r 18.

1419. The tribunal's report. The Financial Services Tribunal, having investigated a matter referred to it at the request of a person served with the relevant notice, must make a report to the Securities and Investments Board ('SIB'), stating what would in its opinion be the appropriate decision in the matter and the reasons for that opinion[1]. If the tribunal is minded to report that the appropriate decision would be different from that of the SIB, it must inform the parties and afford them fourteen days in which to make representations[2].

Where the reference is at the request of a person served with a copy of the notice or on whom a copy might have been served, the tribunal must report whether the reasons stated in the notice which relate to that person are substantiated[3].

In either case, the tribunal must send a copy of the report to the person who requested the reference[4]. The report must be made within prescribed time limits[5]. In preparing its report the tribunal must have regard to the need to exclude so far as practicable confidential information relating to a third person where publication might seriously and prejudicially affect his interests[6]. Provision is made for publication of the report[7]. Certified copies of a report are admissible as evidence of the tribunal's opinion[8].

1 Financial Services Act 1986 (c 60), s 98(1)(b). For the appropriate decisions which the tribunal may report, see s 98(2)–(4).
2 Financial Services Tribunal (Conduct of Investigations) Rules 1988, SI 1988/351, r 17.
3 Financial Services Act 1986, s 99.
4 Ibid, ss 98(5), 99.
5 Financial Services Tribunal (Conduct of Investigations) Rules 1988, r 16.

6 Financial Services Act 1986, s 101(1).

7 Ibid, s 101(2)–(4).

8 Ibid, s 101(5).

(8) COMPENSATION

1420. Introduction. The Financial Services Act 1986 (c 60) recognises that the conduct of business rules, the financial regulation requirements and client money regulations, however stringent, cannot guarantee that investors will be protected against all possibility of financial loss. Provision is accordingly made for compensating investors. The Secretary of State (who has delegated his powers in this regard to the Securities and Investment Boards ('SIB')[1]) is accordingly empowered to make rules for establishing a scheme for compensating investors where persons who are or have been authorised persons are unable or are likely to be unable to satisfy claims in respect of civil liability incurred by them in connection with their investment businesses[2].

The Secretary of State also has power to make rules concerning indemnity against any claim in respect of any description of civil liability incurred by an authorised person in connection with his investment business[3].

1 See the Financial Services Act 1986 (c 60), s 114, and the Financial Services Act 1986 (Delegation) Order 1987, SI 1987/942.

2 Financial Services Act 1986, s 54(1). For other provisions which the rules may contain, see s 54(2). For rules, see the Financial Services (Compensation for Investors) Rules 1990, made by the Securities and Investments Board under this power.

3 Financial Services Act 1986, s 53(1). Section 53 comes into force on a day to be appointed under s 211(1). However, some self-regulating organisations (for example the Financial Intermediaries, Managers and Brokers Regulatory Association ('FIMBRA')) have introduced a professional indemnity insurance requirement for their members. Many of the recognised professional bodies have, of course, had such a requirement for many years. Some professional bodies, such as the accountants' Institutes and the solicitors' Law Societies, do not permit their members to limit their liability to clients, and provide unlimited compensation.

1421. The compensation scheme. The compensation scheme set up under the Financial Services (Compensation for Investors) Rules 1990 is administered by a management company, Investors Compensation Scheme Ltd[1]. It is funded by annual levies paid by all directly authorised persons and members of self-regulating organisations[2].

The scheme may not be made so as to apply to members of recognised self-regulatory organisations except after consultation with the organisation, or to persons certified by recognised professional bodies except at the request of the body[3]. Further, the scheme may not apply to such members or persons unless the Secretary of State is satisfied that the rules establishing the scheme make sufficient provision:

(1) for the administration of the scheme by a body on which the interests of those members or persons are adequately represented; and

(2) for securing that the amounts that they are liable to contribute reflect, so far as practicable, the amount of the claims made or likely to be made in respect of them[4].

1 Financial Services (Compensation for Investors) Rules 1990, r 1.03(1).

2 Ibid, r 1.03(2), Annex 1, para 2, Annex 2. The Compensation Scheme and Fund was initially established under the Financial Services (Compensation of Investors) Rules 1988. At that time life assurance companies and building societies were not required to contribute, being covered by separate compensation arrangements. However, when the rules were redrafted in 1990 the contributors' base was expanded by bringing life offices and building societies within those liable

to meet the levy and the potential claimants' base was contracted to private investors (under the 1988 rules business investors could also claim in certain circumstances). The rules have since been amended by the Financial Services (Compensation of Investors) (Amendment) Rules 1991 to take account of the merger of the Association of Futures Brokers and Dealers ('AFBD') and the Secutities Association ('TSA'), to exempt certain oil market participants and to implement accounting and general levy changes.

3 Financial Services Act 1986 (c 60), s 54(3).

4 Ibid, s 54(3)(a), (b).

1422. Claims for compensation. Private investors[1] (who are the only category of investor given rights to compensation under the scheme[2]) have the right to claim compensation from the management company where a participant firm has been found to be 'in default'[3]. A firm is 'in default' where it is unable, or likely to be unable, to satisfy claims in respect of any description of civil liability incurred in connection with its investment business[4].

Previously, claims could be made in respect of investments made in connection with an authorised person after 27 August 1988, the date on which the scheme came into force. However, a recent High Court ruling[5] in England has extended the scope of the scheme to include investments made on or after 18 December 1986, the date on which the sections of the Financial Services Act 1986 defining 'investments' and 'investment business' came into force[6].

In principle, the amount payable by way of compensation is the amount of the investor's net claim against the firm in default[7], but the compensation fund is not unlimited (like those of some professional bodies). The management company will pay out only a maximum of £48,000 (comprising full compensation for claims up to £30,000 with 90 per cent compensation on the balance between £30,000 and £50,000)[8]. In addition, the management company is to pay interest on compensation sums in such circumstances and in such amounts as it considers appropriate[9]. There is also a limit of £100m on the total amount which may be paid by way of compensation in any financial year[10]. The payment of any compensation claim may be deferred or reduced if the management company considers that immediate payment in full would not be prudent, having regard inter alia to other pending claims[11]. Claims submitted towards the end of the scheme's financial year could therefore receive less favourable treatment than those submitted earlier. Claims submitted more than six months after the investor became or ought reasonably to have become aware of the participant firm's default, or where the investor has any responsibility for, or has directly or indirectly profited from, the firm's difficulties, may be rejected[12]. A substantial increase in defaults would therefore be required before the capping provisions on the total amount available for compensation purposes would come into effect.

1 The Financial Services (Compensation for Investors) Rules 1990 uses the phrase 'eligible investor', which it defines as (1) an investor who is not a business or professional investor, or (2) a trustee who is not a bare trustee or unit trust trustee and who is trustee of a trust which is shown to be principally for the benefit of individuals who are eligible investors not otherwise benefiting from the scheme or for charitable purposes: see the Glossary to the rules.

2 See para 1421, note 2 above.

3 Financial Services (Compensation for Investors) Rules 1990, r 2.02(2).

4 Ibid, r 2.01.

5 *Securities and Investments Board v Financial Intermediaries Managers and Brokers Regulatory Association Ltd* [1991] 4 All ER 398, [1991] 3 WLR 889.

6 Financial Services (Compensation for Investors) (Amendment) (No 2) Rules 1991.

7 Financial Services (Compensation for Investors) Rules 1990, r 2.06.

8 Ibid, reg 2.07(1).

9 Ibid, r 2.09.

10 Ibid, r 2.07(2).

11 Ibid, r 2.08. Payment may also be postponed if the management company considers that the investor should first exhaust his rights against the firm or a third party or pursue an application for compensation to some other person: r 2.02(5).

12 Ibid, r 2.02(3).

(9) CONCLUSION

1423–1500. Teething problems. At the time of writing the Financial Services Act 1986 has been in force for almost three years and has in that time suffered some serious teething problems. The legal structure and hierarchy of the regime, together with its, at times, very complex subject matter are perhaps responsible for what some have called the 'Byzantine Matrix'. It is hoped that the 'new framework' will in time permit further simplification. Meanwhile the spate of new rules, regulations, orders and amendments continues apace.

In view of section 57(2) of the Act[1] and Core Rule 5[2], the authors feel obliged to warn that no investment advice or advertisement is contained or implied in this part of the title, and none should be inferred.

1 See para 1337, note 2, above.
2 See para 1367 above.

2. INSIDER DEALING

(1) INTRODUCTION

1501. Background. Insider dealing, which for the purposes of introducing the subject may be regarded as the illegitimate use of confidential unpublished price sensitive information, has been the subject of discussion in Great Britain for a number of years. However, with the exception of limited and piecemeal controls upon dealings in options by directors or connected persons and upon disclosure of certain dealings by directors, connected persons or substantial shareholders[1], there was until 1980 no specific set of criminal sanctions for insider dealing.

A scheme of criminal sanctions was introduced in the Companies Act 1980[2], and that regime was made the subject of a separate statute following the consolidation of other companies legislation in 1985. The Company Securities (Insider Dealing) Act 1985 (c 8), as amended, contains a number of offences relating to insider dealing and these are expressed in the new terminology introduced in the 1980 Act. As the short title of the 1985 Act makes clear, the legislation is aimed at 'company securities'[3]. In relation to those securities, it creates a range of prohibitions. These can for convenience be labelled (although the legislation does not use this terminology) as prohibitions upon primary insiders, that is those who are in a position of access to unpublished price sensitive information, and secondary insiders (colloquially known as 'tippees') who obtain information from primary insiders. Directors and other connected individuals, along with public servants, can be regarded as primary insiders.

1 The relevant provisions (derived from earlier legislation) are now contained in the Companies Act 1985 (c 6), Pt VI (ss 198–220) (disclosure of interests in shares), and ss 323–330 (share dealings by directors and their families): see COMPANIES, vol 4, paras 346, 425.

2 See the Companies Act 1980 (c 22), Pt V (ss 68–73) (repealed).

3 Ie shares, debentures, options to subscribe and market options: see P L Davies 'The European Community's Directive on Insider Dealing: From Company Law to Securities Markets Regulation?' (1991) 11 Oxford Journal of Legal Studies 92.

1502. Basic concepts. Subject to certain defences[1], the Company Securities (Insider Dealing) Act 1985 prohibits primary and secondary insiders[2] from dealing, from counselling or procuring others to deal, and from communicating information[3]. The main offences which it establishes relate to 'an individual . . . connected with a company'[4] and 'a public servant'[5], and also to those who have 'knowingly obtained'[6] information from these primary insiders. For these individuals, dealing in securities[7] while in possession of 'unpublished price sensitive information'[8] is the basis of liability. The dealing must be on a 'recognised stock exchange'[9], although certain 'off-market deals'[10] and dealings outside Great Britain[11] are also subject to controls. Dealing by an individual who is contemplating a takeover offer or his 'tippee' is also caught[12], as is the counselling or procuring of others to deal and to communicate information to others one has cause to believe may deal[13].

Many of the offences require proof of knowledge of particular matters (for example knowledge of connection with a company, or that the information is unpublished price sensitive information, or, in the case of a tippee, knowing or having cause to believe that the information is confidential). A number of prosecutions have been brought under the Act. With few exceptions, these cases[14] have not involved the interpretation of any substantive points in the legislation.

1 See the Company Securities (Insider Dealing) Act 1985 (c 8), s 3, and paras 1526 ff below.
2 As to primary and secondary insiders, see para 1501 above.
3 See the Company Securities (Insider Dealing) Act 1985, s 1.
4 See ibid, s 1(1), (2), and paras 1503, 1511, below.
5 See ibid, s 2 (amended by the Financial Services Act 1986 (c 60), s 173(1)), and paras 1519–1522 below.
6 See the Company Securities (Insider Dealing) Act 1985, s 1(3), (4), and para 1512 below.
7 For the meaning of 'dealing in securities', see para 1510 below.
8 For the meaning of 'unpublished price sensitive information', see para 1504 below.
9 Company Securities (Insider Dealing) Act 1985, s 1(1), (2), (4)–(8), 2(3)(a). For the meaning of 'recognised stock exchange', see para 1503, note 4, below.
10 See ibid, s 4, and paras 1523, 1524, below.
11 See ibid, s 5, and para 1525 below.
12 See ibid, s 1(5), (6), and paras 1514–1516 below.
13 See ibid, s 1(8), and para 1518 below.
14 *HM Advocate v Bryce* (unreported; noted in (1981) 2 Co Law 178); *R v Dickensen* (unreported; noted in (1982) 3 Co Law 185); *R v Titheridge and Titheridge* (unreported; noted in (1983) 4 Co Law 117); *R v Kettle and Thorneywork* (unreported; see Financial Times 18, 20 September 1984); *R v Hancock and Brooks* (unreported; see Financial Times 9 November 1984 and 7 March 1985); *R v Naerger* (unreported; see The Guardian 30 April 1986); *R v Collier* (unreported; see Financial Times 2 July 1987); *R v Jenkins* (unreported; see Financial Times 18 July 1987); *Attorney-General's Reference (No 1 of 1988)* [1989] AC 971, [1989] 3 All ER 571, HL; *R v Cross* [1990] BCC 239, CA. Most of these cases are discussed in B Hannigan *Insider Dealing* (1988), from which the above newspaper references are drawn.

(2) DEALINGS IN SECURITIES OF A COMPANY BY INDIVIDUALS WHO ARE CONNECTED WITH THE COMPANY

1503. Prohibited dealings. The Company Securities (Insider Dealing) Act 1985 provides that an individual who is, or at any time during the past six months has been, knowingly connected[1] with a company[2] may not deal[3] on a recognised stock exchange[4] in securities of that company if he has information which:

(1) he holds by virtue of his connection with the company,
(2) it would be reasonable to expect a person so connected, and in the position by virtue of which he is so connected, not to disclose except for the proper performance of the functions attaching to that position, and
(3) he knows to be unpublished price sensitive information[5].

The use of the term 'individual' rather than 'person' makes it clear that a corporation such as a company cannot be guilty of this first offence, although it must be noted that those who counsel or procure[6] a company to deal or who communicate information to a company[7] may commit an offence.

1   As to who is connected, see para 1505 below.
2   For the meaning of 'company', see para 1506 below.
3   For the meaning of 'deal', see para 1510 below.
4   'Recognised stock exchange' means The Stock Exchange and any other investment exchange which is declared by order of the Secretary of State made by statutory instrument to be a recognised stock exchange for the purposes of the Company Securities (Insider Dealing) Act 1985 (c 8): s 16(1), (1A) (amended and added by the Financial Services Act 1986 (c 60), s 212(2), Sch 16, para 28(a), (b)). Such orders have been made: see the Insider Dealing (Recognised Stock Exchange) Order 1989, SI 1989/2165 (designating NASDAQ), and the Insider Dealing (Recognised Stock Exchange) (No 2) Order 1990, SI 1990/47 (designating OM London Ltd).
5   Company Securities (Insider Dealing) Act 1985, s 1(1)(a)–(c). For the meaning of 'unpublished price sensitive information', see para 1504 below. For defences, see s 3, and paras 1526 ff below.
6   See ibid, s 1(7), and para 1517 below.
7   See ibid, s 1(8), and para 1518 below.

1504. Unpublished price sensitive information. 'Unpublished price sensitive information' means information in relation to any securities of a company which:
(1) relates to specific matters relating or of concern (directly or indirectly) to that company, that is to say, which is not of a general nature relating or of concern to that company, and
(2) is not generally known to those persons who are accustomed or would be likely to deal in those securities but which would if it were generally known to them be likely materially to affect the price of those securities[1].

The Company Securities (Insider Dealing) Act 1985 makes no attempt to define 'specific matters', but much information relating to a company by its very nature relates to something specific. Examples of general information might include knowledge that a company is a likely takeover target without knowledge of any actual or contemplated particular bid, or knowledge that boardroom changes are expected without knowledge as to which particular individuals are affected. The Stock Exchange has published a *Model Code of Conduct for Securities Transactions by Directors of Listed Companies*[2], which lists examples of price sensitive information. The Act gives no such guidance, and it remains to be seen whether the courts will regard the examples listed as falling within the definition in the Act.

While the definition purports to be of 'unpublished' information, it actually refers to information not being generally known to 'those persons who are accustomed or would be likely to deal in those securities'. In practice there seems little point in construing this provision other than to mean generally known to investors and their advisers. The question of whether information is unpublished price sensitive information is in most cases likely to be easily answerable when viewed retrospectively, as it almost inevitably will be when there is a prosecution before the courts: if the price was affected then the information was price sensitive, and there is a strong inference that it was specific, and was not generally known to investors[3].

1   Company Securities (Insider Dealing) Act 1985 (c 8), s 10(a), (b).

2 See *Admission of Securities to Listing*, sect 5, ch 2, paras 10, 14–19.
3 See B Hannigan *Insider Dealing* (1988) p 57.

1505. Individuals who are connected. Individuals who are currently connected with a company are covered by the provision[1], as are those who were
connected at some time during the six months prior to the dealing. This
extension of the prohibition creates a somewhat arbitrary time limit which
means that certain recent ex-insiders cannot benefit from information obtained
while connected. Of course, ex-insiders outwith the time limit are at liberty to
deal, in so far as not caught by other provisions of the Company Securities
(Insider Dealing) Act 1985.
    For the purposes of the Act, an individual is regarded as connected with a
company if, but only if:
(1) he is a director of the company or a related company[2], or
(2) he occupies a position as an officer (other than a director) or employee of that
     company or a related company or a position involving a professional or
     business relationship between himself (or his employer or a company of
     which he is director) and the first company or a related company which in
     either case may reasonably be expected to give him access to information
     which, in relation to securities of either company, is unpublished price
     sensitive information, and which it would be reasonable to expect a person
     in his position not to disclose except for the proper performance of his
     functions[3].

1 Ie by the Company Securities (Insider Dealing) Act 1985 (c 8), s 1(1), for which see para 1503
  above.
2 For the meaning of 'director', 'company' and 'related company', see para 1506 below.
3 Company Securities (Insider Dealing) Act 1985, s 9(a), (b).

1506. Directors. 'Director' includes any person occupying the position of
director, by whatever name called[1]. While a body corporate can be a director, it
is not an individual and so is not caught by the prohibition[2]. Several provisions
of the Companies Act 1985 are expressly stated to apply to shadow directors[3] as
well as to directors[4], but the definition of 'connected person' for the purposes of
insider dealing does not include a shadow director. However, such a person may
well be caught by the prohibitions placed upon 'tippees'[5].
    The expressions 'company' and 'related company' are defined in the Com-
pany Securities (Insider Dealing) Act 1985. 'Company' means any company,
whether or not a company within the meaning of the Companies Act 1985[6].
That Act defines 'company' broadly to mean a company formed and registered
under the Companies Act 1985 or an existing company formed and registered
under the former Companies Acts[7]. 'Related company' in relation to a company
means any body corporate which is that company's subsidiary or holding
company, or a subsidiary of that company's holding company[8]. Accordingly,
in a large group of companies held by one holding company, directors of all
subsidiaries will be regarded as connected with the holding company[9] and with
other subsidiary companies (but not sub-subsidiaries) in the group.

1 Companies Act 1985 (c 6), s 741(1), applied by the Company Securities (Insider Dealing) Act
  1985 (c 8), s 16(2).
2 Ie the prohibition in ibid, s 1(1), for which see para 1503 above.
3 For the meaning of 'shadow director', see the Companies Act 1985, s 741(2), and COMPANIES,
  vol 4, para 407.
4 See eg ibid, ss 317(8), 318(6), 319(7), 320(3).
5 See the Company Securities (Insider Dealing) Act 1985, s 1(3), (4), and para 1512 below.
6 Company Securities (Insider Dealing) Act 1985, s 11(a).
7 See the Companies Act 1985, s 735(1).

8 Company Securities (Insider Dealing) Act 1985, s 11(b). For the meaning of 'subsidiary' and 'holding company', see the Companies Act 1985, s 736 (substituted by the Companies Act 1989 (c 40), s 144(1)), which is applied by the Company Securities (Insider Dealing) Act 1985, s 16(2).
9 See eg *R v Dickensen* (unreported; noted in (1982) 3 Co Law 185).

1507. Others. Officers[1] or employees of the company and of related companies are regarded as connected, subject to their being in a position of access to unpublished price sensitive information. As stated above, an individual who occupies a position involving a professional or business relationship between himself (or his employer or a company of which he is director) and the first company or related company satisfies the first part of the test of being connected[2]. The broad definition of 'related company'[3] makes these categories very wide indeed. For example, an employee of a merchant bank which is advising a holding company is caught.

However, the apparent width of these catgeories is reduced since the second requirement to be satisfied by an individual who is not a director is that the individual must occupy a position which may reasonably be expected to give him access to information which, in relation to the securities of either the company or a related company, is unpublished price sensitive information[4]. Moreover, the information must be such that it would be reasonable to expect a person in his position not to disclose except for the proper performance of his functions. It should be noted that a position of access to information in relation to either company is enough to give rise to a connection with the first company.

The question of a position of access is of central importance. An individual who obtains information but who was not in a position of access will not be caught by this provision, but may be liable as a 'tippee'. It is clear that not only senior employees are in a position of access, and so those occupying other than senior posts may nonetheless be caught. A very wide range of individuals have a 'professional or business relationship' with a company. The term 'professional' is of fairly limited application, but 'business' would seem capable of including a great variety of trading or commercial relationships. Shareholders, even major shareholders, are not routinely in a professional or business relationship with their company, although it is possible to envisage circumstances where such a relationship might arise. In view of the consultations which exist between companies and their institutional shareholders, it is perhaps surprising that the legislation does not include them as connected persons[5]. They may however be caught under the 'tippee' provisions.

1 'Officer' includes a director, manager or secretary: Companies Act 1985 (c 6), s 744, applied by the Company Securities (Insider Dealing) Act 1985 (c 8), s 16(2). Section 9(b) speaks of 'an officer (other than a director)': see para 1505 above.
2 See para 1505 above.
3 See para 1506 above.
4 Company Securities (Insider Dealing) Act 1985, s 9(b).
5 Clause 63 of the Companies Bill (1978), which did not reach the statute book, would have included shareholders holding 5 per cent or more of the issued share capital.

1508. Knowledge of connection. Connection of itself is insufficient: the individual must be 'knowingly connected'[1]. It will be relatively straightforward to find that directors and other employees were knowingly connected with their company, but difficulties of proof may arise as regards other individuals, particularly where the connection is with a related company[2] in a large group where the employee or other individual claims to have no knowledge of the connection. The term 'knowingly' relates to actual knowledge and may be capable of including wilful blindness[3].

1 See the Company Securities (Insider Dealing) Act 1985 (c 8), s 1(1), and para 1503 above.

2 For the meaning of 'related company', see para 1506 above.
3 G H Gordon *The Criminal Law of Scotland* (2nd edn, 1978), paras 8.22, 8.23.

1509. Additional requirements. The information must be information which the individual holds by virtue of being connected with the company[1]. It seems clear that an individual may be given information entirely independently of his relationship with the company, and hence not hold the information 'by virtue of' his connection. Again, and depending upon the source of the information, the individual may be exposed to liability as a secondary insider, or 'tippee'.

The information must also be such that it would be reasonable to expect a person so connected, and in the position by virtue of which he is so connected, not to disclose except for the proper performance of the functions attaching to that position[1]. This provision introduces an objective standard against which the confidentiality of the information may be measured, and it permits the disclosure of information in the normal course of work.

The individual must know the information to be unpublished price sensitive information[2] in relation to the securities of the company. While it may be relatively straightforward for the prosecution to establish that the individual knew the information to be price sensitive, it is likely to be more difficult to establish that he knew it to be unpublished, that is, not generally known to those persons who are accustomed or would be likely to deal in those securities[3].

1 Company Securities (Insider Dealing) Act 1985 (c 8), s 1(1): see para 1503 above.
2 For the meaning of 'unpublished price sensitive information', see para 1504 above.
3 See the Company Securities (Insider Dealing) Act 1985, s 10(b).

1510. Meanings of 'deal', 'securities' and related terms. The individual who satisfies the requirements discussed in the preceding paragraphs may not deal on a recognised stock exchange in securities of the company[1]. A person[2] deals in securities if (whether as principal or agent) he buys or sells or agrees to buy or sell any securities[3]. A person who deals in rights under a contract for differences etc[4] may be regarded as dealing in securities of the company[5].

Dealings through an investment exchange are included as dealings in a recognised stock exchange[6]. The effect of these provisions is to include not only dealings on the main market but also on the Unlisted Securities Market and the Third Market.

The term 'securities' is given a wide definition in the legislation. It means listed securities[7], and, in the case of certain companies[8], the following securities (whether listed or not), namely shares, debentures or any right to subscribe for, call for or make delivery of a share or debenture[9].

1 See the Company Securities (Insider Dealing) Act 1985 (c 8), s 1(1), and para 1503 above. For the meaning of 'recognised stock exchange', see para 1503, note 4, above.
2 Note the use of the word 'person' rather than 'individual'.
3 Company Securities (Insider Dealing) Act 1985, s 13(1).
4 See the Financial Services Act 1986 (c 60), Sch 1, para 9.
5 Company Securities (Insider Dealing) Act 1985, s 13(1A) (added by the Financial Services Act 1986, s 176).
6 Company Securities (Insider Dealing) Act 1985, s 13(1). 'Investment exchange' means an organisation maintaining a system whereby an offer to deal in securities made by a subscriber to the organisation is communicated, without his identity being revealed, to other subscribers, and whereby any acceptance of that offer by any of those other subscribers is recorded and confirmed: s 13(2). This part of s 13(1), and s 13(2), are prospectively repealed by the Financial Services Act 1986, ss 174(4)(a), 212(3), Sch 17, from a day to be appointed under s 211(1).
7 'Listed securities' means securities listed on a recognised stock exchange: Company Securities (Insider Dealing) Act 1985, s 12(b).

8 Ie any company within the meaning of the Companies Act 1985 (c6), a company registered under Pt XXII, ch II (ss 680–690) (companies not formed under the companies legislation, but authorised to register), or an unregistered company.
9 Company Securities (Insider Dealing) Act 1985, s 12(a). Despite the apparent width of this definition, some investments (eg unit trusts) are not included.

(3) DEALINGS IN SECURITIES OF ANOTHER COMPANY BY AN INDIVIDUAL WHO IS CONNECTED WITH A COMPANY

1511. Prohibited dealings. The Company Securities (Insider Dealing) Act 1985 provides that an individual who is, or at any time in the preceding six months has been, knowingly connected[1] with a company[2] may not deal[3] on a recognised stock exchange[4] in securities[5] of any other company if he has information which, in addition to satisfying the same threefold test as is stated in section 1(1)[6], relates to any transaction (actual or contemplated) involving both the company with which he is connected and the other company, or involving one of them and the securities of the other, or to the fact that any such transaction is no longer contemplated[7].

Accordingly, information regarding for example a business transaction or takeover offer between the two companies is covered. Transactions between the other company and a third party are not included. Proof that a transaction is or was contemplated, or no longer contemplated, may be difficult, and interesting questions will arise as to by whom the transaction was contemplated, including the matter of how a company can contemplate a transaction[8].

1 For the meaning of 'connected', see para 1505 above and for the meaning of 'knowingly', see para 1508 above.
2 For the meaning of 'company', see para 1506 above.
3 For the meaning of 'deal', see para 1510 above.
4 For the meaning of 'recognised stock exchange', see para 1503, note 4, above.
5 For the meaning of 'securities', see para 1510 above.
6 Company Securities (Insider Dealing) Act 1985, s 1(2)(a)–(c), corresponding with s 1(1)(a)–(c), for which see para 1503 above.
7 Ibid, s 1(2)(d). For defences, see s 3, and paras 1526 ff below.
8 Contemplation by 'responsible officers' of the company would probably suffice: see _Purcell Meats (Scotland) Ltd v McLeod_ 1986 SCCR 672, 1987 SLT 528, and _Tesco Supermarkets Ltd v Nattrass_ [1972] AC 152, [1971] 2 All ER 127, HL.

(4) DEALINGS BY 'TIPPEES'

1512. Prohibited dealings. The prohibitions in the Company Securities (Insider Dealing) Act 1985 are extended to those who have obtained information from connected individuals. An individual is within the scope of the provisions if he has information which he knowingly obtained[1] (directly or indirectly) from another individual who:

(1) is connected[2] with a company (or was connected in the six months prior to the obtaining of the information) and
(2) the former individual knows or has reasonable cause to believe:
   (a) the latter held the information by virtue of being so connected, and
   (b) because of the latter's connection or position, it would be reasonable to expect him not to disclose the information except for the proper performance of the functions attaching to that position[3].

The former individual is then subject to two prohibitions:

(i) he may not himself deal on a recognised stock exchange[4] in securities of that company if he knows that the information is unpublished price sensitive information[5] in relation to those securities; and

(ii) he may not himself deal in securities of any other company if he knows that the information is unpublished price sensitive information in relation to those securities and it relates to any transaction (actual or contemplated) involving the first company and the other company, or involving one of them and the securities of the other, or to the fact that any such transaction is no longer contemplated[6].

The use of the word 'himself' leaves room for argument about the scope of the prohibition. For example, the question arises as to whether it includes an individual who deals on behalf of a company. The definition of 'deal'[7] includes dealing as agent, and so it would appear that such an individual is caught by the provision. Unlike the prohibitions upon primary insiders, these prohibitions are not subject to the six-months time limit.

The Act uses the term 'knowingly' immediately prior to 'obtained'. However, it is difficult to see why the draftsman saw any need to exclude information which had been unknowingly obtained. It is arguable that the word 'knowingly' is intended to apply to knowledge on the part of the 'tippee' that the individual from whom the information was obtained is or was connected, and this would seem to be in the spirit of the approach taken in the Act generally. However, this construction appears to do some violence to the language of the provision, since it involves the use of 'knowingly' to qualify part only of it.

1 For the meaning of 'obtained', see para 1513 below.
2 For the meaning of 'connected', see para 1505 above.
3 See the Company Securities (Insider Dealing) Act 1985 (c 8), s 1(3).
4 For the meaning of 'recognised stock exchange', see para 1503, note 4, above, and for the meaning of 'deal', see para 1510 above.
5 For the meaning of 'unpublished price sensitive information', see para 1504 above.
6 Company Securities (Insider Dealing) Act 1985, s 1(4)(a), (b). For defences, see s 3, and paras 1526 ff below.
7 See para 1510 above.

1513. Meaning of 'obtained'. The question has arisen as to whether 'obtained'[1] means acquired by purpose and effort, or whether it includes simply having received the information. In the leading case[2], an individual was interested with others in acquiring a controlling shareholding in a company. He received information in a telephone call from the advisers to the company that the company had agreed to be taken over by others. The individual dealt in the shares of the company, and when charged under the 'tippee' provisions[3] it was argued that he had not 'obtained' the information. At trial the court accepted this contention, but the Court of Appeal and the House of Lords held that the information had been obtained, that term meaning no more than 'received'. This wide meaning of the term may well cover those who simply overhear a conversation or who catch sight of a document or the words displayed on a word processor screen. However, it must be recalled that to be liable the 'tippee' must knowingly obtain the information from a connected person, knowing or having cause to believe that the information was held by virtue of the connection and that it ought not to be disclosed except for the proper performance of the functions of the 'tippor'.

1 See the Company Securities (Insider Dealing) Act 1985, s 1(3), and para 1512 above.
2 *Attorney-General's Reference (No 1 of 1988)* [1989] AC 971, [1989] 3 All ER 571, HL.

3 Ie under the Company Securities (Insider Dealing) Act 1985, s 1(3), (4).

(5) DEALINGS BY INDIVIDUALS CONTEMPLATING TAKEOVER OFFERS

1514. Prohibited dealings. It was noted above[1] that under the Company Securities (Insider Dealing) Act 1985, an individual connected with a company is prohibited from dealing in securities of any other company inter alia where there is an actual or contemplated takeover offer by one company for the securities of another[2]. The Act provides further prohibitions, which to some extent appear to overlap with those just mentioned, upon individuals contemplating takeover offers.

Thus it provides that where an individual is contemplating, or has contemplated, making (whether with or without another person) a takeover offer for a company[3] in a particular capacity, that individual may not deal[4] on a recognised stock exchange[5] in securities[6] of that company in another capacity if he knows that information that the offer is contemplated, or is no longer contemplated, is unpublished price sensitive information[7] in relation to those securities[8].

1 See para 1511 above.
2 Company Securities (Insider Dealing) Act 1985 (c 8), s 1(2).
3 'Takeover offer for a company' means an offer made to all the holders (or all the holders other than the offeror and his nominees) of the shares (or a particular class of shares) in the company to acquire those shares or a specified proportion of them: ibid, s 14.
4 For the meaning of 'deal', see para 1510 above.
5 For the meaning of 'recognised stock exchange', see para 1503, note 4, above.
6 For the meaning of 'securities', see para 1510 above.
7 For the meaning of 'unpublished price sensitive information', see para 1504 above.
8 Company Securities (Insider Dealing) Act 1985, s 1(5). For defences, see s 3, and paras 1526 ff below.

1515. Scope of prohibition. There are a number of difficulties concerning the application of the provision set out in the preceding paragraph. First, there are likely to be difficulties in establishing the state of mind required to show that a person is contemplating or has contemplated, especially where no takeover offer is actually ever made. Secondly, it must be shown that a takeover offer is or was contemplated. Of course, contemplation of anything short of a takeover offer is outwith this provision. Thirdly, the question arises as to the meaning of the words '. . . making (whether with or without any other person) a takeover offer for a company in a particular capacity . . .'. Takeover offers are in most instances made by a company and not by an individual[1]. Where a board of directors (or perhaps a formal or informal committee of a board) is contemplating a bid, are the directors individuals who are contemplating a takeover offer in a particular capacity? This would appear to be the intended effect of the provision[1], so that the directors would be prohibited from dealing (either as principal or agent) in the securities in another capacity. But section 1(2) of the Company Securities (Insider Dealing) Act 1985[2] appears already to prohibit such dealings, and indeed does so in relation not only to directors but to other connected persons. If this is correct then section 1(5)[3] is of value only in relation to persons who are not connected[4] and hence are not caught by the earlier provision. However, it is unlikely that persons outwith the definition of 'connected persons' would be in a position to contemplate a takeover offer on behalf of a company.

It has been said that section 1(5) 'seems to be of value only to the extent that it covers the rare instances where individuals without any connection with a company personally launch a takeover bid'[5]. Where, for example, an individual is part of a consortium of individuals contemplating a takeover offer, he is prohibited from dealing in another capacity, for example personally.

Finally, the individual must know that the information that the offer is contemplated, or is no longer contemplated, is unpublished price sensitive information. It is uncertain as to when a particular contemplation will satisfy the definition of 'unpublished price sensitive information'.

1 See B Hannigan *Insider Dealing* (1988) p 68.
2 For the Company Securities (Insider Dealing) Act 1985 (c 8), s 1(2), see para 1511 above.
3 For ibid, s 1(5), see para 1514 above.
4 For the meaning of 'connected', see para 1505 above.
5 *Hannigan* p 68.

(6) DEALINGS BY 'TIPPEES' FROM INDIVIDUALS CONTEMPLATING TAKEOVER OFFERS

1516. Prohibited dealings. The Company Securities (Insider Dealing) Act 1985 provides that an individual who has knowingly obtained (directly or indirectly), from an individual covered by section 1(5)[1] information that the takeover offer is being contemplated or is no longer being contemplated must not himself deal[2] on a recognised stock exchange[3] in securities[4] of that company if he knows that the information is unpublished price sensitive information[5]. This provision merely echoes the earlier 'tippee' provisions.

1 For the Company Securities (Insider Dealing) Act 1985 (c 8), s 1(5), see para 1514 above.
2 For the meaning of 'deal', see para 1510 above.
3 For the meaning of 'recognised stock exchange', see para 1503, note 4, above.
4 For the meaning of 'securities', see para 1510 above.
5 Company Securities (Insider Dealing) Act 1985, s 1(6). For defences, see s 3, and paras 1526 ff below. For the meaning of 'unpublished price sensitive information', see para 1504 above.

(7) COUNSELLING OR PROCURING OTHERS TO DEAL

1517. Scope of the prohibition. The Company Securities (Insider Dealing) Act 1985 provides that an individual who is prohibited from dealing by any of the above provisions[1] is also prohibited from counselling or procuring any other person to deal in those securities, knowing or having reasonable cause to believe that that person would deal in them on a recognised stock exchange[2]. 'Counsel or procure' would involve positive action or advice rather than a mere communication of information[3]. Use of the term 'person' indicates that an individual who procures dealings by a company is covered.

1 Ie by any provision of the Company Securities (Insider Dealing) Act 1985 (c 8), s 1: see paras 1503 ff above.
2 Ibid, s 1(7). For defences, see s 3, and paras 1526 ff above. For the meaning of 'deal', see para 1510 above, and for the meaning of 'recognised stock exchange', see para 1503, note 4, above.
3 Communication of information is caught by ibid, s 1(8), for which see para 1518 below.

(8) COMMUNICATING INFORMATION

1518. Prohibited communication. The Company Securities (Insider Dealing) Act 1985 provides that an individual who is prohibited from dealing by any of the above provisions[1] by reason of his having any information is prohibited from communicating that information to any other person if he knows or has reasonable cause to believe that that person or some other person will make use of the information for the purpose of dealing[2], or of counselling or procuring[3] any other person to deal, on a recognised stock exchange[4] in those securities[5].

'Communicating' would appear to be capable of a wide meaning, so that, for example, drawing the attention of a person to a document, or word processor screen, ought to suffice. The mere leaving open of a means of access to information would appear not to be covered by this provision, but liability on the part of the person who obtains the information, as a 'tippee', may arise. Communication to a person whom the giver of the information had no cause to believe would deal, or pass on the information, or communication where the giver of the information had no cause to believe that the initial or later recipient of the information would counsel or procure another person to deal, is not struck at by the provision.

1 Ie by the provision of the Company Securities (Insider Dealing) Act 1985 (c 8), s 1: see paras 1503 ff above.
2 For the meaning of 'deal', see para 1510 above.
3 For the meaning of 'counsel or procure', see para 1517 above.
4 For the meaning of 'recognised stock exchange', see para 1503, note 4, above.
5 Company Securities (Insider Dealing) Act 1985, s 1(8). For defences, see s 3, and paras 1526 ff below. For the meaning of 'securities', see para 1510 above.

(9) ABUSE OF INFORMATION OBTAINED IN AN OFFICIAL CAPACITY

1519. Information to which the provision applies. The Company Securities (Insider Dealing) Act 1985 also contains provisions relating to information held by persons in an official capacity. The provision on abuse of such information[1] applies primarily to information which is held by a public servant[2] or former public servant by virtue of his position or former position[3], which it would be reasonable to expect him not to disclose except for the proper performance of the functions attaching to that position[4], and which is known by the individual holding it to be unpublished price sensitive information in relation to relevant securities[5].

1 Ie the Company Securities (Insider Dealing) Act 1985 (c 8), s 2.
2 For the meaning of 'public servant', see para 1520 below.
3 Company Securities (Insider Dealing) Act 1985, s 2(1)(a) (amended by the Financial Services Act 1986 (c 60), s 173(1)).
4 Company Securities (Insider Dealing) Act 1985, s 2(1)(b) (as so amended).
5 Ibid, s 2(1)(c). For the meaning of 'unpublished price sensitive information', see para 1504 above. 'Relevant securities' means securities (defined in para 1510 above) of a particular company: s 2(1)(c).

1520. Meaning of 'public servant'. The provisions relating to the abuse of information obtained in an official capacity apply primarily to a public servant or former public servant holding information to which the provisions apply[1]. 'Public servant'[2] means:
(1) a Crown servant;
(2) a member, officer or servant of a designated agency[3], competent authority[4] or transferee body[5];
(3) an officer or servant of a recognised self-regulating organisation[6], recognised investment exchange[7] or recognised clearing house[8];

(4) any person declared by an order for the time being in force under section 2(5) of the Company Securities (Insider Dealing) Act 1985 to be a public servant for the purposes of this provision[9].

'Crown servant' means any individual who holds office under, or is employed by, the Crown[10]. This would include those in the governmental regulatory bodies such as the Office of Fair Trading, and civil servants employed by government departments. The Securities and Investments Board is both the designated agency and the transferee body, and the Council of The Stock Exchange is the competent authority. While members, as well as officers or servants, of these bodies are included within the scope of the legislation, only officers and servants of the recognised self-regulating organisations, recognised investment exchanges or recognised clearing houses are caught.

It will be noticed that heads (2) and (3) deal with bodies which are within the aegis of the Financial Services Act 1986. The members and staff of the Panel on Takeovers and Mergers may have access to unpublished price sensitive information, but that body lies outwith the scheme of the 1985 Act. However, it may be argued that those individuals are in a professional or business relationship with a company and thus subject to the prohibitions in section 1(1) and (2) of the Company Securities (Insider Dealing) Act 1985 as connected individuals[11].

If it appears to the Secretary of State that the members, officers or employees of or persons otherwise connected with any body appearing to him to exercise public functions may have access to unpublished price sensitive information relating to any securities[12], he may by order made by statutory instrument declare that those persons are to be public servants for these purposes[13], falling within head (4) above. The following persons have been so declared to be public servants:

(a) the Governor, Deputy Governor, Directors, employees and individuals acting as employees of the Bank of England, and members of the Board of Banking Supervision;

(b) members of the Council, Committee, Appeal Tribunal or Disciplinary Committees or any Disciplinary Committee of Lloyd's, individuals by whom any such body acts, and officers and employees of Lloyd's;

(c) members of the Monopolies and Mergers Commission and individuals employed by, or engaged in work for or on behalf of, the Commission or employed by, or engaged in that work for or on behalf of, persons so engaged[14].

The Takeover Panel may be regarded as a body exercising public functions[15], but its members, officers and employees have not thus far been declared to be public servants.

1 Company Securities (Insider Dealing) Act 1985 (c 8), s 2(2) (amended by the Financial Services Act 1986, s 173(1)).

2 The Company Securities (Insider Dealing) Act 1985, s 2, formerly applied only to Crown servants.

3 'Designated agency' means a body to which functions of the Secretary of State are transferred under the Financial Services Act 1986 (c 60), s 114 (ie the Securities and Investments Board): s 114(3). This definition is applied by the Company Securities (Insider Dealing) Act 1985, s 2(4)(b) (added by the Financial Services Act 1986, s 173(2)).

4 'Competent authority' means the competent authority for the purposes of ibid, Pt IV (ss 142–157 (official listing of securities)) (ie the Council of The Stock Exchange): s 207(1). This definition is applied as stated in note 3 above.

5 'Transferee body' means the body to which functions of the Chief Registrar of Friendly Societies are transferred under ibid, Sch 11, para 28(1) (ie the Securities and Investments Board): Sch 11, para 28(4). This definition is applied as stated in note 3 above.

6 For the meaning of 'recognised self-regulating organisation', see para 1312, note 2, above. This definition is applied by the Company Securities (Insider Dealing) Act 1985, s 2(4)(c) (as added: see note 3 above).

7 For the meaning of 'recognised investment exchange', see para 1386, note 2, above. This definition is applied as stated in note 6 above.

8 'Recognised clearing house' means a body declared by order of the Secretary of State to be a recognised clearing house for the purposes of the Financial Services Act 1986: s 207(1). This definition is applied as stated in note 6 above.

9 Company Securities (Insider Dealing) Act 1985, s 2(4)(a)–(d) (as added: see note 3 above). For s 2(5), see the text to note 13 below.

10 Ibid, s 16(1).

11 For ibid, s 1(1), (2), see paras 1503, 1511, above.

12 For the meaning of 'unpublished price sensitive information', see para 1504 above and for the meaning of 'securities', see para 1510 above.

13 Company Securities (Insider Dealing) Act 1985, s 2(5), (6) (as added: see note 3 above).

14 Insider Dealing (Public Servants) Order 1989, SI 1989/2164. As to the Board of Banking Supervision, see the Banking Act 1987 (c 22), s 2.

15 *R v Panel on Take-overs and Mergers, ex parte Datafin plc* [1987] QB 815, [1987] 1 All ER 564, CA.

1521. Prohibitions applying to public servants. Public servants[1] are subject to very similar prohibitions as those applicable to primary insiders. They are prohibited:

(1) from dealing on a recognised stock exchange[2] in any relevant securities[3],

(2) from counselling or procuring[4] any other person so to deal in any such securities, knowing or having reasonable cause to believe that that other person would deal in them on a recognised stock exchange, and

(3) from communicating[5] the information held by them to any other person knowing or having reasonable cause to believe that or some other person will make use of it for the purpose of dealing, or counselling or procuring any other person to deal, on a recognised stock exchange in any such securities[6].

1 For the meaning of 'public servant', see para 1520 above.
2 For the meaning of 'recognised stock exchange', see para 1503, note 4, above.
3 For the meaning of 'relevant securities', see para 1519, note 5, above.
4 For the meaning of 'counsel or procure', see para 1517 above.
5 For the meaning of 'communicate', see para 1518 above.
6 Company Securities (Insider Dealing) Act 1985 (c 8), s 2(3)(a)–(c). For defences, see s 3, and paras 1526 ff below.

1522. 'Tippees' from public servants. The standard 'tippee' rules apply in relation to public servants. Thus, an individual who knowingly obtains information (directly or indirectly) from a public servant or former public servant who he knows or has reasonable cause to believe held the information by virtue of his position or former position as a public servant can be prohibited from dealing, counselling or procuring, or communicating the information[1]. To be prohibited, the 'tippee' must know that the information is unpublished price sensitive information in relation to the relevant securities[2]. Moreover, the information must be confidential, that is such that it would be reasonable to expect an individual in the position of the public servant or former public servant not to disclose except for the proper performance of his functions[3].

1 Company Securities (Insider Dealing) Act 1985 (c 8), s 2(1)(a), (3) (amended by the Financial Services Act 1986 (c 60), s 173(1)). For the meaning of 'public servant', see para 1520 above. For defences, see the Company Securities (Insider Dealing) Act 1985, s 3, and paras 1526 ff below.
2 Ibid, s 2(1)(c). For the meaning of 'unpublished price sensitive information', see para 1504 above, and for the meaning of 'relevant securities', see para 1519, note 5, above.
3 Ibid, s 2(1)(b) (as amended: see note 1 above).

(10) OFF-MARKET DEALS IN ADVERTISED SECURITIES

1523. Scope of the prohibitions. The Company Securities (Insider Dealing) Act 1985 extends the prohibitions on individuals set out earlier in relation to dealings on a recognised stock exchange[1] to include certain dealings otherwise than on a recognised stock exchange in the advertised securities of any company[2]. The term 'advertised securities' is given a wide meaning in the legislation: in relation to any particular occurrence, it means listed securities[3] or securities in respect of which, not more than six months before that occurrence, information indicating the prices at which persons have dealt or were willing to deal in those securities has been published for the purposes of facilitating deals in those securities[4]. Counselling or procuring a person to deal in advertised securities, or communicating information to be used for dealing or counselling or procuring, is also prohibited[5].

1 See the Company Securities (Insider Dealing) Act 1985 (c 8), ss 1, 2, and paras 1503 ff above, and s 3, and paras 1526 ff below. For the meaning of 'deal', see para 1510 above, and for the meaning of 'recognised stock exchange', see para 1503, note 4, above.
2 See ibid, s 4(1)(a) (amended by the Financial Services Act 1986 (c 60), s 174(3)), which is expressed to be subject to the Company Securities (Insider Dealing) Act 1985, s 6 (substituted by the Financial Services Act 1986, s 175) (price stabilisation): see para 1531 below.
3 For the meaning of 'listed securities', see para 1510, note 7, above.
4 Company Securities (Insider Dealing) Act 1985, s 12(c).
5 See ibid, s 4(1)(b), (c).

1524. Prohibited dealings. The prohibitions cover dealing through an off-market dealer and dealing as an off-market dealer. 'Off-market dealer' means a person who is an authorised person within the meaning of the Financial Services Act 1986[1]. In practice, this means persons who are authorised either by the Securities and Investments Board[2], by a self-regulating organisation[3] or by a recognised professional body[4].

An individual is taken to deal through an off-market dealer if the latter is a party to the transaction, is an agent for either party to the transaction or is acting as an intermediary in connection with the transaction[5]. To fall within the prohibition the dealing must be dealing otherwise than on a recognised stock exchange[6] in the advertised securities[7] of any company through an off-market dealer who is making a market in those securities, in the knowledge (of the individual dealing through him) that he is so doing[8]. In order to be regarded as 'making a market' in securities, the off-market dealer must in the course of his business as such hold himself out both to prospective buyers and to prospective sellers of those securities (other than particular buyers or sellers)[9] as willing to deal in them otherwise than on a recognised stock exchange[10].

Dealing as an off-market dealer is subject to the prohibitions if the dealing is dealing otherwise than on a recognised stock exchange in the advertised securities of any company and the dealer is making a market in those securities or is an officer, employee or agent of such a dealer acting in the course of the dealer's business[11]. An off-market dealer, or such a dealer's officer, employee or agent, deals in advertised securities if he deals in them or acts as an intermediary in connection with deals in such securities made by other persons[12].

1 Company Securities (Insider Dealing) Act 1985 (c 8), s 13(3) (substituted by the Financial Services Act 1986 (c 60), s 174(4)(b)). For the meaning of 'authorised person' in the 1986 Act, see para 1306, note 2, above.
2 See para 1310 above.
3 See para 1312 above.
4 See para 1313 above.
5 Company Securities (Insider Dealing) Act 1985, s 13(5).

6 For the meaning of 'recognised stock exchange', see para 1503, note 4, above.
7 For the meaning of 'advertised securities', see para 1523 above.
8 Company Securities (Insider Dealing) Act 1985, s 4(1)(a)(i) (amended by the Financial Services Act 1986, s 174(3)).
9 Ie the holding-out must be general.
10 Company Securities (Insider Dealing) Act 1985, s 13(4)(b).
11 Ibid, s 4(1)(a)(ii) (as amended: see note 8 above).
12 Ibid, s 13(4)(a).

1525. Prohibition on promoting off-market deals outside Great Britain.
It has been noticed that primary insiders (individuals connected with a company, and public servants) and their 'tippees' are prohibited by virtue of holding unpublished price sensitive information from counselling or procuring others to deal, or communicating information for others to deal or to counsel or procure[1]. These prohibitions apply both to dealing on a recognised stock exchange[2] and to dealing through or as an off-market dealer[3]. The Company Securities (Insider Dealing) Act 1985 provides that individuals so prohibited are also prohibited from counselling or procuring[4] any other person to deal, or communicating[5] information to others to enable them to deal or counsel or procure others to deal, on any stock exchange outside Great Britain other than a recognised stock exchange[6].

The intention of this provision is fairly clear: to extend the counselling, procuring and communicating offences to cover deals abroad other than on a recognised stock exchange. Counselling, procuring and communicating in relation to deals *on* a recognised stock exchange are of course covered by the earlier prohibitions. It will be recalled that the prohibitions on primary insiders and 'tippees' from dealing apply to actual dealing on a recognised stock exchange.

1 See paras 1517, 1518, 1521–1523, above.
2 See the Company Securities (Insider Dealing) Act 1985 (c 8), ss 1, 2. For the meaning of 'recognised stock exchange', see para 1503, note 4, above.
3 See ibid, s 4. For the meaning of 'off-market dealer', see para 1524 above.
4 For the meaning of 'counsel or procure', see para 1517 above.
5 For the meaning of 'communicate', see para 1518 above.
6 See the Company Securities (Insider Dealing) Act 1985, s 5(1)(a), (b). For defences, see s 5(2), (3), and para 1526, note 1, below.

(11) ACTIONS NOT PROHIBITED

1526. Permitted actions. Section 3 of the Company Securities (Insider Dealing) Act 1985 lists a number of actions which are not prohibited. In addition, sections 6 and 7 provide further, more limited, exceptions to the prohibitions. Under section 3, the prohibitions in the Act[1] do not prohibit an individual by reason of his having any information from:

(1) doing any particular thing otherwise than with a view to the making of a profit or the avoidance of a loss (whether for himself or another person) by the use of that information[2];

(2) entering into a transaction in the course of the exercise in good faith of his functions as liquidator, receiver or trustee in bankruptcy[3];

(3) doing any particular thing if the information:
(a) was obtained by him in the course of a business of a jobber[4] in which he was engaged or employed, and
(b) was of a description which it would be reasonable to expect him to obtain in the ordinary course of that business,

and he does that thing in good faith in the course of that business[5]; or
(4) doing any particular thing in relation to any particular securities if the information:
  (a) was obtained by him in the course of a business of a market maker[6] in those securities in which he was engaged or employed, and
  (b) was of a description which it would be reasonable to expect him to obtain in the ordinary course of that business,
and he does that thing in good faith in the course of that business[7].
Moreover, an individual is not, by reason only of his having information relating to any particular transaction, prohibited by specific provisions from doing specified things[8] if he does that thing in order to facilitate the completion or carrying out of the transaction[9].

1 The Company Securities (Insider Dealing) Act 1985 (c 8), s 3(1), states that 'Sections 1 and 2 do not prohibit . . .' and goes on to give a list of actions not prohibited. As has been seen, there are prohibitions other than under sections 1 and 2, namely in sections 4 and 5. However, section 4(1) applies the exceptions in s 3 to the prohibitions in s 4. Section 5(2) applies s 3(1)(a)–(c) to off-market dealings abroad, and section 5(3) is effectively a rewording of s 3(2) for off-market dealings abroad. Accordingly s 3 could be said to apply to all of the prohibitions.
2 Ibid, s 3(1)(a). See further para 1527 below.
3 Ibid, s 3(1)(b). See further para 1528 below.
4 'Jobber' means an individual, partnership or company dealing in securities (defined in para 1510 above) on a recognised stock exchange (defined in para 1503, note 4, above) and recognised by the Council of The Stock Exchange as carrying on the business of a jobber: ibid, s 3(1)(c).
5 Ibid, s 3(1)(c)(i), (ii). See further para 1529 below.
6 'Market maker' means an individual, partnership or company who (1) holds himself out at all normal times in compliance with the rules of a recognised stock exchange as willing to buy and sell securities at prices specified by him, and (2) is recognised as doing so by that exchange: ibid, s 3(1)(d) (added by the Financial Services Act 1986 (c 60), s 174(2)). For the application of this definition to the Company Securities (Insider Dealing) Act 1985, s 4, see s 4(2) (added by the Financial Services Act 1986, s 174(3)).
7 Company Securities (Insider Dealing) Act 1985, s 3(1)(d)(i), (ii) (added by the Financial Services Act 1986, s 174(1)). See further para 1529 below.
8 Ie prohibited (1) by the Company Securities (Insider Dealing) Act 1985, s 1(2), (4)(b), (5) or (6) (see paras 1511, 1512, 1514, 1516, above), from dealing on a recognised stock exchange in any securities; (2) by s 1(7) or (8) (see paras 1517, 1518, above) from doing any other thing in relation to securities which he is prohibited from dealing in by s 1(2), (4)(b), (5) or (6); or (3) by s 2 (see paras 1519–1521 above) from doing anything: s 3(2)(a)–(c).
9 Ibid, s 3(2). See further para 1530 below.

1527. Doing any particular thing other than to make a profit or avoid a loss. The 'defence' that a thing was done otherwise than with a view to making a profit or avoiding a loss[1] has been regarded by commentators on the Company Securities (Insider Dealing) Act 1985 as the main method by which a person who is otherwise prohibited can avoid liability. The wording of the provision leaves much room for speculation as to its intended scope, and it has been suggested that the provision enacts a substantial and wide exception to the net of liability[2]. It has been argued that any pressing need to obtain funds will permit the individual to argue that he dealt for that purpose, rather than simply to make a profit or avoid a loss[2]. Others have argued that the individual is protected only if the securities in which he dealt were his only source of funds for the pressing financial need[3].
It is suggested that these criticisms are based on a mistaken view as to the scope of the provision. The objectionable dealing will either be the purchase or the sale of, usually, shares. The defence permits buying or selling for a purpose other than to make a profit or avoid a loss. Trading while in possession of information, if the information is in fact price sensitive, will always result in the making of a profit or the avoidance of a loss. It is submitted then that the defence should be limited to circumstances in which another substantial and indeed

dominant motive, unrelated to the realisation of money for the shares, can be established. For example, it might be argued that a director who knows about a potential takeover bid for his company by another and who buys more shares for himself, or gets others to buy, acting in an attempt to frustrate the bid in good faith and in what he sees as the interests of the company, may be exonerated under the provision. Similarly, a director who is obliged to purchase qualification shares[3] would have the defence.

Conversely, a director may sell shares to others rather than the potential takeover offeror. Here his dealings would have still been caught by the Act were it not for the defence, for the disposal of shares while in possession of unfavourable information is of course a form of insider dealing although it is much less prevalent than the purchase form of dealing. Where securities are sold, the defence ought not to apply if the dealer sold them in order to realise more for his shares than would have been the case had he postponed dealing until the information was public. Moreover, it should be no defence that an unexpected financial burden has arisen — as has been pointed out, the dealer could have borrowed funds to meet this eventuality and could have given his shares as security[3].

It may also be observed that the defence relates to 'doing any particular thing' and so is capable of exempting not only dealing but also counselling, procuring and communicating.

1 See the Company Securities (Insider Dealing) Act 1985 (c 8), s 3(1)(a), and para 1526 above.
2 See D Sugarman and T M Ashe 'The Companies Act 1980, Part V' (1981) 2 Co Law 13 at 17.
3 See B Hannigan *Insider Dealing* (1988) pp 83, 84.

1528. Liquidators, receivers and trustees in bankruptcy. The exemption which permits action in good faith *qua* office-holder by liquidators, receivers and trustees in bankruptcy rather than in a personal capacity[1] is likely to be of limited application. Where, for example, a receiver has information that the company is in a much more severe financial plight than is generally thought, and he sells the shares to a new owner, the question may arise as to whether he is exercising in good faith his functions or whether his inside knowledge acts to show bad faith. It is suggested that in such circumstances the defence should not operate. Moreover, the exemption relates to entering into a transaction and so is unlikely to cover counselling, procuring or communicating information. It may also be observed that the exemption seems more readily applicable to the disposal of securities than to their purchase.

1 See the Company Securities (Insider Dealing) Act 1985 (c 8), s 3(1)(b), and para 1526 above.

1529. Jobbers and market-makers. Jobbers and market makers who obtain such relevant information in the course of business as it would be reasonable to expect them to obtain and who do anything in relation to securities in good faith and in the course of business are protected[1].

1 See the Company Securities (Insider Dealing) Act 1985, s 3(1)(c), and s 3(1)(d) (added by the Financial Services Act 1986 (c 60), s 174(1)), and para 1526 above.

1530. Facilitating the completion or carrying out of a transaction. An individual who is contemplating a takeover bid in one capacity is prohibited from dealing in any other capacity[1]. Clearly, the Company Securities (Insider Dealing) Act 1985 is intended not to prohibit those who are engaged in the activity of a takeover and who deal in securities for that purpose — their own knowledge that they intend to mount the bid is unpublished price sensitive information but they are permitted to deal for the purposes of completing or carrying out a transaction[2].

1 See the Company Securities (Insider Dealing) Act 1985 (c 8), s 1(5), and para 1514 above.
2 See ibid, s 3(2), and para 1526 above. This assumes that the bid can be regarded as a 'transaction'.

(12) PRICE STABILISATION

1531. Permitted price stabilisation. The Financial Services Act 1986 permits, in strictly controlled circumstances in accordance with the Financial Services (Conduct of Business) Rules 1990 of the Securities and Investments Board, the stabilisation by a 'stabilising manager' of the price of the securities[1]. This could for example take the form of permitting the stabilising manager to repurchase shares, which had been the subject of recent issue, in the market so as to keep the price at a particular level[2]. The Company Securities (Insider Dealing) Act 1985 provides that no provision of section 1, section 2, section 4 or section 5 prohibits an individual from doing anything for the purpose of stabilising the price of securities if it is done in conformity with such conduct of business rules and (1) in respect of securities which fall within any of paragraphs 1 to 5 of Schedule 1 to the 1986 Act and are specified by the rules; and (2) during such period before or after the issue of those securities as is specified by the rules[3].

1 Cf para 1388 above.
2 See B Hannigan *Insider Dealing* (1988) p 88.
3 Company Securities (Insider Dealing) Act 1985, s 6(1) (substituted by the Financial Services Act 1986 (c 60), s 175). Any order under s 48(8) of the 1986 Act (see para 1332, note 5, above) applies also in relation to the Company Securities (Insider Dealing) Act 1985, s 6(1): s 6(2) (as so substituted).

(13) TRUSTEES AND PERSONAL REPRESENTATIVES

1532. Permitted actions. Where a trustee or personal representative would otherwise be prohibited by sections 1 to 5 of the Company Securities (Insider Dealing) Act 1985 from dealing, or counselling or procuring others to deal, and he does any of these things he is presumed to have acted 'with propriety' if he acted on the advice of a person who:
(1) appeared to him to be an appropriate person from whom to seek such advice, and
(2) did not appear to him to be prohibited by section 1, section 2, section 4 or section 5 from dealing in those securities[1].
'With propriety' means otherwise than with a view to the making of a profit or the avoidance of a loss (whether for himself or for any other person) by the use of the information in question[2].

The effect of this provision is to permit a trustee or personal representative who is in possession of unpublished price sensitive information to deal, or counsel or procure dealing, if he acts on the advice of an independent person, such as a stockbroker, who did not appear to be in possession of the information.

1 Company Securities (Insider Dealing) Act 1985 (c 8), s 7(1)(a), (b). For s 1, see paras 1503 ff below; for s 2, see paras 1519 ff above; for s 4, see paras 1523, 1524, above, and for s 5, see para 1525 above. Where the trustee or personal representative is a body corporate, an individual acting on its behalf is given the same protection: s 7(1).

2 Ibid, s 7(2).

(14) INVESTIGATIONS AND LEGAL PROCEEDINGS

1533. Investigations into insider dealing. If it appears to the Secretary of State that there are circumstances suggesting that there may have been a contravention of the statutory provisions as to insider dealing[1], he may appoint one or more competent inspectors to investigate and report back to him[2]. Inspectors so appointed may require persons whom they think may be able to give relevant information to produce documents, attend before them and otherwise give all possible assistance, and may examine such persons on oath[3]. The inspectors may make an interim report[4], and the Secretary of State may curtail the investigation[5]. A person convicted on a prosecution instituted as a result of an investigation may in the same proceedings be ordered to pay the expenses of the investigation[6].

1 Ie contravention of the Company Securities (Insider Dealing) Act 1985 (c 8), s 1, s 2, s 4 or s 5.
2 Financial Services Act 1986 (c 60), s 177(1). The period and scope of the investigation may be limited and from time to time varied: s 177(2) and (2A) (added by the Companies Act 1989 (c 40), s 74(2)).
3 Financial Services Act 1986, s 177(3), (4). The failure of any person to comply may be referred to the court, which has extensive powers of enforcement: see s 178. However, a person cannot be compelled to disclose information or produce documents which he would be entitled to withhold on grounds of confidentiality as between client and professional legal adviser in the Court of Session: s 177(7). Bankers also have a degree of privilege: see s 177(8) (substituted by the Companies Act 1989, s 74(4)).
4 Financial Services Act 1986, s 177(5).
5 See ibid, s 177(5A) (added by the Companies Act 1989, s 74(3)).
6 See the Financial Services Act 1986, s 177(10), added by the Companies Act 1989, s 74(6)).

1534. Punishment of offences. An individual who contravenes section 1, section 2, section 4 or section 5 of the Company Securities (Insider Dealing) Act 1985[1] is liable (1) on conviction on indictment to imprisonment for a term not exceeding seven years or a fine, or both, and (2) on summary conviction to imprisonment for a term not exceeding six months or a fine not exceeding the statutory maximum, or both[2].

1 For the Company Securities (Insider Dealing) Act 1985 (c 8), s 1, see paras 1503 ff above; for s 2, see paras 1519 ff above; for s 4, see paras 1523, 1524, above, and for s 5, see para 1525 above.
2 Ibid, s 8(1)(a), (b). 'Statutory maximum' means the prescribed sum within the Criminal Procedure (Scotland) Act 1975 (c 21), s 289B(6) (added by the Criminal Law Act 1977 (c 45), s 63(1), Sch 11, para 5, and substituted by the Criminal Justice Act 1982 (c 48), s 55(2)) (ie £2,000: Increase of Criminal Penalties etc (Scotland) Order 1984, SI 1984/526, art 3): Company Securities (Insider Dealing) Act 1985, s 16(1).

1535. Potential civil remedies. Where a person transacts with another who has inside information there are difficulties in establishing any basis for a civil remedy. Normally the former person will have voluntarily instructed the sale or purchase of the securities. To afford a remedy to someone who by chance happened to deal with an insider, while leaving those who dealt with others without a remedy, seems anomalous. On the other hand, giving a remedy to all of those who dealt at a particular time irrespective of whether they dealt with an insider would be unacceptable.

The Company Securities (Insider Dealing) Act 1985 provides that no transaction is void or voidable by reason only that it was entered into in contravention of section 1, section 2, section 4 or section 5[1]. However, despite this provision it has been held that a gift of shares by a company director who had unpublished price-sensitive information about shares in the company was a sham, so that a later agreement for the sale of the shares on The Stock Exchange was unenforceable[2]. The possibility of any other basis for a civil remedy is remote. It is extremely unlikely that the courts would regard the Act as providing the basis for a remedy on the ground of breach of statutory duty. Certain insiders (for example company directors) will be in a fiduciary relationship with the company, with resulting obligations of trust and good faith. There is no doubt that a director who benefits from corporate property, information or opportunity is liable to account to the company to the extent of the benefit obtained[3]. It is unlikely that the company could ratify the retention of the profit by the director[4]. It may be possible for an individual shareholder to raise an action as an exception to the rule in *Foss v Harbottle*[5], but there is insufficient case law in Scotland from which to draw precise conclusions as to the availability of such action[6]. Action by a shareholder under the Companies Act 1985 on the ground of unfairly prejudicial conduct[7] is unlikely to succeed as the 'unfair prejudice' provisions relate to the carrying on of the affairs of the company or acts or omissions of the company, rather than acts of the directors as individuals.

No fiduciary duty is owed by a director to an individual shareholder[8] from whom shares are purchased, and despite some limited inroads into this principle[9] the courts in Scotland seem likely to adhere to it[10]. Where a person in possession of unpublished price sensitive information transacts without disclosing the information, there is no basis (in the absence of any misrepresentation or fiduciary duty requiring disclosure) for a contractual remedy by the other contracting party[11]. Other remedies based on constructive trust, or breach of confidence, may be argued[12], but appear to have little chance of success.

There is some basis for a statutory remedy under sections 61 and 62 of the Financial Services Act 1986. The former provision permits the court, following an application by the Securities and Investments Board, to order restitution where a person has profited in contravention of the rules or certain provisions of the Act or where an investor has suffered loss or been otherwise adversely affected by such contravention[13]. The latter provision permits an action of damages by a private investor who suffers loss as a result of a contravention of the rules and certain provisions of the Act[14]. These provisions are capable of being applied to insider dealing, but difficulties about the person to whom restitution should be made and about establishing any causal link between the dealing and loss are likely to limit the scope for so applying the provisions. Moreover, brokers, market makers and other professionals are subject to the provisions, but the actual person who dealt is usually not.

1 Company Securities (Insider Dealing) Act 1985 (c 8), s 8(3). For s 1, see paras 1503 ff below; for s 2, see paras 1519 ff above; for s 4, see paras 1523, 1524, above, and for s 5, see para 1525 above.
2 *Chase Manhattan Equities Ltd v Goodman* The Times 23 May 1991.
3 See eg *Regal (Hastings) Ltd v Gulliver* [1942] 1 All ER 378, HL; *Boardman v Phipps* [1967] 2 AC 46, [1966] 3 All ER 721, HL; *Industrial Development Consultants Ltd v Cooley* [1972] 2 All ER 162, [1972] 1 WLR 443; *Guinness plc v Saunders* [1990] 2 AC 663, [1990] 1 All ER 652, HL.
4 See *Cook v Deeks* [1916] 1 AC 554, PC.
5 *Foss v Harbottle* (1843) 2 Hare 461.
6 See A A Paterson 'The Aggrieved Minority and Scottish Law' (1981) 2 Co Law 155.
7 Ie action under the Companies Act 1985 (c 6), ss 459–461: see COMPANIES, vol 4, paras 482 ff.
8 *Percival v Wright* [1902] 2 Ch 421.
9 See *Coleman v Myers* [1977] 2 NZLR 225, N.Z. CA.
10 See eg *Kelly v Kelly* 1986 SLT 101, OH.
11 See *Spook Erection (Northern) Ltd v Kaye* 1990 SLT 676, OH.
12 See B Hannigan *Investor Protection* (1988) pp 119–136, dealing with the position in England.
13 See the Financial Services Act 1986 (c 60), s 61(3), (5), and para 1411 above.

14 See ibid, s 62(1), and para 1412 above. See also para 1387 above.

(15) PROPOSALS FOR REFORM

1536. EC directive on insider dealing. The Council of Ministers of the European Community has recently adopted a directive on insider dealing[1], which member states are required to implement by 1 June 1992. Unlike the Company Securities (Insider Dealing) Act 1985, which, as its short title makes clear, is confined to company securities, the directive applies to all 'transferable securities'[2]. Moreover, the requirement that information be confidential (that is, that it would be reasonable to expect the individual not to disclose the information except for the proper performance of the functions attaching to his position[3]) is not a part of the directive. Also, there will effectively no longer be any need to establish that an individual held information because of a connection with a company. Each of these changes will enlarge the scope of liability of individuals under the existing United Kingdom legislation, and one effect of this latter change will be to widen the group currently caught as primary insiders. The directive does not require 'tippees' from persons who were not connected with a company to be subject to liability, and it remains to be seen what view Parliament will take when the directive is implemented. The concept of 'unpublished price sensitive information' is replaced by that of 'inside information', which is in similar terms to that in the Company Securities (Insider Dealing) Act 1985, that is, the information must be of a precise nature which, if it were made public, would be likely to have a significant effect on the price of the transferable security or securities in question[4]. The directive focuses upon non-public information, while the United Kingdom legislation speaks of information not generally known to those persons who are accustomed or would be likely to deal in those securities[5], but this distinction will be of little import in practice.

1 EC Council Directive 89/592 (OJ L334, 18.1.89, p 30).
2 See P L Davies 'The European Community's Directive on Insider Dealing: From Company Law to Securities Markets Regulation?' (1991) 11 Oxford Journal of Legal Studies 92.
3 See the Company Securities (Insider Dealing) Act 1985, ss 1(1)–(3), 2(1)(b).
4 EC Council Directive 89/542, art 1(1).
5 See the Company Securities (Insider Dealing) Act 1985, s 10, and para 1504 above.

INDEX

HUMAN RIGHTS IN EUROPE

Abortion
European Convention on Human
    Rights, 25
Access
confidential personal records, to, 63
parental access to child in care, 64
Alien
political activity of, 6
Apartheid
international conventions on, 5
Armed forces
freedom of, 83
Arrest or detention
alcoholic, of, 29
arbitrary, freedom from, Universal Dec-
    laration of Human Rights, 4n
compensation for wrongful, 29
compulsory residence, 40
detention—
    deportation, prior to, 38
    end of detention period, what consti-
        tutes, 32
    extradition, prior to, 37
    freedom from, European Convention
        on Human Rights, 6, 85, 86
    indeterminate length, 35
    lawfulness to be decided speedily, 33
    minors, of, 39
    parole, life prisoners, 35
    setting off against custodial sentence,
        34
    unsound mind, persons of, 41
    vagrancy, 42
    voluntary surrender to, 42
    without trial, 32
drug addict, of, 29
European Convention on Human
    Rights—
    general rules, 29
    lawful, 29
files, access to, 36
infectious diseases, to prevent spread of,
    29
legitimate detention, what constitutes,
    29, 30
minor, of, 29
reasons for, obligation to give, 29
remand, prolonged detention on, 32
right to be brought before judicial person
    or body, 29, 30
    promptness, 30, 32

Arrest or detention—*contd*
trial within reasonable time, entitlement
    to, 32, 46, 47
unauthorised entrants, 29
unsound mind, persons of, 29
vagrant, of, 29
Artistic expression
freedom of, 73
Assembly, peaceful
right to, 6
Association, freedom of
right to, 6, 73, 75–77

Births, register of
transsexuality, 67
Broadcasting
freedom of expression, 73
licensing, 73
Business
provisional closure, fairness of, 60

Capital gains tax
discrimination, 86
Children and young persons
care—
    committal to, 64
    parental access and visitation rights, 64
    separation of siblings, 64
    termination of care order, promotion
        of parent-child relationship, 64
corporal punishment, 26, 90, 91
economic and social protection, 7
education, *see* EDUCATION
European Social Charter, 7
rights of, international conventions on, 5
Cinema
licensing, 73
Closed shop agreement
freedom of association, 77
**Committee of Experts for the
Improving of Procedures for the
Protection of Human Rights**, 13
Committee of Ministers
composition, 10n
European Commission of Human
    Rights, report by, 15
European Convention on Human
    Rights—
    application of, 10
    petitions alleging violation—
        Commission reports, 15

References are to paragraphs

Committee of Ministers—*contd*
European Convention on Human
    Rights—*contd*
    petitions alleging violation—*contd*
      decisions on, 15
      referral to Court of Human Rights,
        15
    supervision of application, 13
European Court of Human Rights,
    execution of judgment of, 20
Compulsory labour
see FORCED LABOUR
Compulsory residence
European Convention on Human
    Rights, 40
**Conference on Security and Co-
operation in Europe**
human rights and fundamental free-
    doms, respect for, 4
Conscience
freedom of, 73
    European Convention on Human
      Rights, 6, 72
    restrictions on, 78–84
    Universal Declaration of Human
      Rights, 4, 4n
Corporal punishment
European Convention on Human
    Rights, 26, 90, 91
Correspondence
prisoners, 69
private, 6, 62, 68
right of, 73
Council of Europe
Committee of Ministers, 10n
Consultative Assembly, 10n
establishment, 6n
European Convention on Human
    Rights, 6n
members, 6n
Court
right of access to, 44
Criminal law
retroactivity, protection against, 6, 61
Criminal offence
charge, nature and case of accusation to
    be given in language understood by
    accused, 43
defence—
    legal assistance, 43, 52
      payment for, 43
    preparation of, 43
    witnesses, examination of, 43, 55–59
hearing, *see* HEARING
innocence, presumption of, 43, 53

Cultural life
right to participation in, 4n
Custodial sentence
setting off time in custody against, 34

Deportation
detention prior to, 38
Detention
see ARREST OR DETENTION
Disabled person
training, rehabilitation and resettlement,
    7
Discrimination
European Convention on Human
    Rights, 6, 85, 86
international conventions on, 5

Education
corporal punishment, 26, 90, 91
international conventions on, 5
linguistic considerations, 89
parental convictions, 89, 90, 92
right to, 87, 89–92
    Universal Declaration of Human
      Rights, 4n
sex, 92
Elections
free, right to, 87, 93
    language groups, 93
    secret ballot, 93
Employment
children and young persons, 7
collective bargaining, 7
European Social Charter, 7
health and safety, 7
international conventions on, 5
maternity rights, 7
migrant workers, 7
organisations for protection of workers'
    interests, 7
remuneration, 7
territory of other contracting national,
    in, 7
vocational guidance and training, 7
women, 7
Equality before the law
Universal Declaration of Human Rights,
    4n
**European Commission of Human
Rights**
in camera, meetings in, 15
Chambers—
    establishment and composition, 14
    sittings in, 14
Commissioners—
    election to office, 11

References are to paragraphs

European Commission of Human Rights—*contd*
Commissioners—*contd*
  nationality, 11
  part-time nature of office, 11
  qualifications for office, 11
committees—
  establishment and composition, 14
  sittings in, 14
composition, 11
decisions taken by, 15
European Convention on Human Rights—
  application of, 10
  petitions alleging violation, 14
    application form, 15n
    friendly settlements, 15
    inadmissibility, 15, 15n
    individual, 14
    inter-state, 14
    lawyer, instruction of, 15
    legal aid, 15
    lodging, 15
    official languages, 15n
    report, 15
  supervision of application, 13
European Court of Human Rights, functions in relation to, 18
High Contracting Party, written representations on admissibility of application, 19n
legal aid, 15, 19
official languages, 11, 15n
plenary session, 14
proposed merger with European Court, 13, 13n
rules of procedure, 11, 15, 15n
seat, 11
workload, 16
European Community
European Convention on Human Rights, Community accession to, 9
European Convention for the Protection of Human Rights and Freedoms
aliens—
  political activities, restriction of, 6
  rights of, 6
application of, supervision, 13
applications, 15n
arrest or detention, rules pertaining to, 29–42
article 1 . . . 6
article 2 . . . 25, 31
article 6 . . . 43, 45, 60
article 15 . . . 31

European Convention for the Protection of Human Rights and Freedoms—*contd*
article 25, declaration under, 14, 14n
capital punishment, 26
child care, 64
civil and political rights, 6
collective enforcement, 6
Committee of Ministers, 10, 10n, 13
compulsory residence orders, 40
correspondence, private, 6, 62
court, right of access to, 44
deportation, detention prior to, 38
derogation in time of war or public emergency, 31
detention—
  deportation, prior to, 38
  extradition, prior to, 37
  files, access to, 36
  indeterminate length, 35
  lawfulness to be decided speedily, 33
  minors, of, 39
  remand, prolonged detention on, 32
  setting off against custodial sentence, 34
  unsound mind, persons of, 41
  vagrancy, 42
  voluntary surrender to, 42
discrimination, 85, 86
domestic law, incorporation into, 6
education, right to, 87, 89–92
elections, free, right to, 87, 93
enforcement, 10
European Commission of Human Rights, 10, 10n, 11, 13, 17
  in camera, meetings, 15
  decisions of, 15
  friendly settlements, 15
  legal aid, 19
  petitions, consideration of, 14, 15
  report of, 15
  Rules of Procedure, 15, 15n
  supervisory role, 13
  who may bring a case before, 17
  workload, 16
European Community, accession to, 9
European Community law, 9
European Court of Human Rights, 10, 10n, 12, 13
  ad hoc judge, 17
  advisory opinions, 23
  compensation, award of, 21
  costs and expenses, award of, 21
  High Contracting Parties, 17
  judgment of, 20
  judicial procedure, 17

References are to paragraphs

European Convention for the Protection of Human Rights and Freedoms—*contd*
European Court of Human Rights—*contd*
  jurisdiction, 17
  'just satisfaction', 21
  legal aid, 19
  members, 17
  'national' judge, 17
  parties to proceeding, 18
    legal representation, 18
  plenary jurisdiction, option for, 17
  statistics of, 22
European Court of Justice, 9
European Social Charter, 7
expression, freedom of, 6, 73, 74
extradition—
  detention prior to, 37
  procedure, 26
family life, respect for, 6, 62
family, right to found, 6
freedom, restrictions on, 78–84
  armed forces, 83
  information received in confidence, 82
  judiciary, authority and impartiality, 82
  legitimate aim, must have, 80
  necessary in a democratic society, must be, 81
  police, 83
  prescribed by law, 79
freedom of thought, conscience and religion, 6, 72
hearing—
  fair and public, entitlement to, 43–60
  independence and impartiality, 48
  legal assistance, entitlement to, 43, 52
  within reasonable time—
    commencement of period, 46
    right to, 32, 46
    what constitutes, 47
High Contracting Parties, 17
immigration, 65
impact of, 6, 94–96
innocence, presumption of, 43, 53
judicial person or body, right to be brought before, 30
judicial review, right to, 54
limitations, 6
marry, right to, 6, 71
meaning of 'human rights', 1
minors, detention of, 39
national laws, relationship to, 94–96
peaceful assembly and association, right of, 73, 75–77

European Convention for the Protection of Human Rights and Freedoms—*contd*
petitions, 15*n*
  admissibility, 14
  anonymous, 15
  contents, 15
  domestic remedies, 14, 14*n*, 15*n*
  inadmissible, 15, 15*n*
  individual, 14, 14*n*
  inter-state complaints, 14
  intimated in writing, 15
  lawyer, instruction of, 15
  legal aid, 15
  lodging, 15
  national courts, decisions made in, 15
  time limit, 14
power, 94
private life, respect for, 6, 62
property, right to, 87, 88
protection afforded by, 6
Protocols, 6, 6*n*
  First, 6, 87–93
  Second, 6*n*, 23
  Fourth, 6, 6*n*
  Sixth, 6, 6*n*
  Seventh, 6
public emergency, derogation in time of, 31
retrospective criminality, 6, 61
right, existence of dispute concerning, 45
signature, 6
trial *in absentia*, 50
United Kingdom domestic law, relation to, 6*n*, 8
violation, 6
war, derogation in time of, 31
European Court of Human Rights
Chamber—
  ad hoc judges, 17
  composition, 17
  'national' judges, 17
  oral proceedings, 17
  plenary jurisdiction, 17
  written procedure, 17
composition, 12
European Commission—
  functions in relation to Court, 18
  proposed merger with, 13, 13*n*
European Convention on Human Rights—
  advisory opinions on interpretation, 23
  interpretation and application, 10, 17
  petitions alleging violation, referral to Court, 15
  supervision of application, 13

References are to paragraphs

European Court of Human Rights—
　contd
judges—
　election to office, 12
　nationality, 12
　part-time nature of office, 12
　qualifications for office, 12
judgment, 20
　compensation, award of, 21
　costs and expenses, award of, 21
　execution, 20
　final nature of, 20
　just satisfaction afforded by, 20, 21
　reasons must be given for, 20
　revision, 20
　separate judicial opinions, 20
jurisdiction, 17
jurisprudence, 24
legal aid, 19
official languages, 18
parties to proceedings, 18
　individual applicants, 18
　legal aid, 19
　legal representation, 18
　official languages, 18
　presentation of own case, 18
Rules of Court, 12
Rules of Procedure, 18
seat, 12
statistics, 22, 24
who may bring case, 17
European Court of Justice
European Convention on Human
　Rights, 9
European Social Charter
declaration of aims, as, 7
social and economic rights, 7
Euthanasia
European Convention on Human
　Rights, 25
Evidence
unlawfully obtained, 60
witness, *see* WITNESS
Exile
arbitrary, freedom from, 4*n*
Expression
freedom of—
　European Convention on Human
　　Rights, 6, 73, 74
　'prescribed by law', meaning, 79
　restrictions on, 78–84
　Universal Declaration of Human
　　Rights, 4*n*
Extradition
capital punishment, 26
detention prior to, 37

Family
right to found—
　European Convention on Human
　　Rights, 6
　Universal Declaration of Human
　　Rights, 4*n*
right to marry, 6, 71
social, legal and economic protection, 7
Family life
respect for, right to, 6, 62
　access to confidential personal records,
　　63
　child care, 64
　'illegitimate' family, 62
　immigration, 65
restrictions on rights relating to, 78–84
Files
access to, 36
Financial means
discrimination, 86
Forced labour
European Convention on Human
　Rights, 6, 28
international conventions on, 5
meaning, 28
menace of penalty, 28
rehabilitation programmes, 28
**Fundamental rights, remedy against
　violation of**
right to—
　European Convention on Human
　　Rights, 6
　Universal Declaration of Human
　　Rights, 4*n*

Genocide
international conventions on, 5

Health insurance
appeals board, fairness, 60
Health standards
European Social Charter, 7
Hearing
defence—
　interpreter, assistance of, 43, 51
　legal assistance, 43, 52
　preparation of, 43
　witnesses, examination of, 43, 55–59
extra-judicial assurances, 60
fair, public trial as guarantee of, 49
fair and public, entitlement to—
　European Convention on Human
　　Rights, 43–60
　interpreter, right to services of, 51
　legal assistance, 52

References are to paragraphs

Hearing—*contd*
fair and public, entitlement to—*contd*
　Universal Declaration of Human
　　Rights, 4*n*
　witnesses, 55–59
in absentia, 50
independence and impartiality, 48
innocence, presumption of, 43, 53
interpreter, use of, 43, 51
judge, impartiality, 48
judicial review, right to, 54
legal assistance, 43, 52
　payment for, 43
　person not wishing to defend himself,
　　52
press, exclusion from judgment, 43
public, 49
　fair trial, as guarantee of, 49
　first hearing, 50
　questions of law, 50
public, exclusion from judgment, 43
within reasonable time, right to, 32, 46
　commencement of period, 46
　reasonableness, what constitutes, 47
witnesses, examination of, 43, 55–59
Home
meaning, 62
private, respect for, 6, 62, 68
violation of, 70
Homosexuality
private life, respect for, 66
Housing
housing and tenancy court, fairness of
　methods employed by, 60
Human rights
before 1945 . . . 2
after 1945 . . . 3
civil and political, 6
European Convention, *see* EUROPEAN
　CONVENTION FOR THE PROTECTION OF
　HUMAN RIGHTS AND FREEDOMS
international efforts to guarantee, 5
meaning, 1
social and economic, 7

Illegitimacy
discrimination, 86
Immigration
European Convention on Human
　Rights, 65
Impartiality
existence, test of, 48
judge, of, 48
meaning, 48
Information
right to impart and receive, 73

Innocence
presumption of—
　European Convention on Human
　　Rights, 43, 53
　Universal Declaration of Human
　　Rights, 4*n*
**International Covenant on Civil and
　Political Rights**, 4
**International Covenant on Econ-
　omic, Social and Cultural
　Rights**, 4
International law
customary—
　minority groups, 2
　Universal Declaration of Human
　　Rights, 4
extradition procedure, 26
monistic and dualistic approaches, 8, 8*n*
Interpreter
non-provision, 51
right to assistance of—
　hearing, at, 43, 51
　pre-trial proceedings, 51

Judge
impartiality, 48
Judicial review
right to, 54
Judiciary
authority and impartiality, maintenance
　of, 82
Justice
fair administration, 6

Language
discrimination, 85, 86
educational considerations, 89
League of Nations
minority treaties, 2
Legal aid
court, right of access to, 44
denial of, 52
European Commission of Human
　Rights, 15, 19
European Court of Human Rights, 19
'Legitimate aim'
law must have, 80
Liberty
right to—
　European Convention on Human
　　Rights, 6, 29–42
　arrest or detention, *see* ARREST OR
　　DETENTION
　general rules, 29
　judicial person or body, right to be
　　brought before, 30

References are to paragraphs

Liberty—*contd*
right to—*contd*
Universal Declaration of Human
Rights, 4*n*
state, deprivation by, 39
Life
right to—
European Convention on Human
Rights, 6, 25
Universal Declaration of Human
Rights, 4*n*

Marriage
right not to marry, 71
right to marry—
European Convention on Human
Rights, 6, 71
Universal Declaration of Human
Rights, 4*n*
Medical assistance
European Social Charter, 7
Minor
detention of, 39
Minority groups
customary international law before
1945 . . . 2
minority treaties, 2, 2*n*
national minorities, discrimination, 85
Movement
freedom of, 4*n*

Nationality
freedom of, 4*n*
'Necessary in a democratic society'
restrictions on freedom must be, 81

Opinion and expression
freedom of—
European Convention on Human
Rights, 6
Universal Declaration of Human
Rights, 4*n*

Parole
life prisoners, 35
Peaceful assembly and association
freedom of, restrictions on, 78–84
right of, 73, 75–77
trade union freedom, 76
closed shop agreements, 77
Police
freedom of, 83
Political opinion
discrimination, 85

'Prescribed by law'
law must be accessible and foreseeable,
79
meaning, 79
Press
freedom of, 73, 74
Prisoner
correspondence, 69
court, right of access to, 44
Private life
respect for—
access to confidential personal records,
63
correspondence, 6, 62, 68
prisoners', 69
European Convention on Human
Rights, 6, 62
home, 6, 62, 68, 70
homosexuality, 66
telephone conversations, 68
Professional bodies
reinstatement on roll, fairness of method, 60
Property
disposal, right of, 88
peaceful enjoyment of, 88
right to own, 87, 88
Universal Declaration of Human
Rights, 4*n*
use of, state control, 88
Public emergency
derogation from European Convention
on Human Rights in times of, 31
meaning, 31
Punishment
capital—
European Convention on Human
Rights, 26
extradition procedure affected by
threat of, 26
European Convention on Human
Rights, 6, 26
inhuman and degrading treatment, 26
European Convention for the Prevention of Torture and Inhuman or
Degrading Treatment or Punishment, 27
international conventions on, 5

Racial discrimination
European Convention on Human
Rights, 6, 85, 86
international conventions on, 5
Records
confidential personal, access to, 63

Religion or belief
discrimination, 6, 72
   European Convention on Human
      Rights, 85, 86
freedom of, 73
   European Convention on Human
      Rights, 6
   restrictions on, 78–84
   Universal Declaration of Human
      Rights, 4, 4n
Rent review board
methods employed by, fairness, 60
Residence
freedom of, 4n
Rent and leisure
right to, 4n
Retrospective criminality
European Convention on Human
   Rights, 6, 61

Security of person
right to—
   European Convention on Human
      Rights, 29–42
   Universal Declaration of Human
      Rights, 4n
Servitude
freedom from—
   European Convention on Human
      Rights, 6, 28
   Universal Declaration of Human
      Rights, 4n
Sex discrimination
European Convention on Human
   Rights, 6, 85, 86
international conventions on, 5
Sex education
European Convention on Human
   Rights, 92
Slavery
customary international law before
   1945 . . . 2
European Convention on Human
   Rights, 6, 28
Universal Declaration of Human Rights,
   4n
Social assistance
European Social Charter, 7
Social security
European Social Charter, 7
Universal Declaration of Human Rights,
   4n
Social welfare services
European Social Charter, 7
**Steering Committee for Human
Rights**, 13

Telephone
metering, 68
private conversations, 68
   unlawfully obtained used as evidence,
      60
tapping, 68
Television
freedom of expression, 73
licensing, 73
Tenancy
housing and tenancy court, fairness of
   methods employed by, 60
Thought
freedom of, 73
   European Convention on Human
      Rights, 6, 72
   restrictions on, 78–84
   Universal Declaration of Human
      Rights, 4, 4n
Torture
definition, 26
European Convention on Human
   Rights, 6, 26
European Convention for the Prevention
   of Torture and Inhuman or Degrading Treatment or Punishment, 27
inhuman and degrading treatment distinguished, 26
international conventions on, 5
Trade union
closed shop agreements, 77
freedom of association, 76
membership, discrimination, 86
Training
vocational—
   disabled persons, 7
   European Social Charter, 7
Transsexuality
private life, respect for, 67
Trial
fair—
   publicity as guarantee of, 49
   right to, *see* HEARING
in absentia, 50
interpreter, right to services of, 43, 51
   pre-trial proceedings, 51
judicial review, right to, 54
see also HEARING

United Nations
Charter, 3
trusteeship system, 3, 3n
Universal Declaration of Human Rights,
   4

References are to paragraphs

Universal Declaration of Human Rights, 4

International Covenant on Civil and Political Rights, 4

International Covenant on Economic, Social and Cultural Rights, 4

Unsound mind, person of

detention, 41

Vagrancy

detention—

European Convention on Human Rights, 42

voluntary surrender to, 42

War

derogation from European Convention on Human Rights, 31

lawful acts, deaths resulting from, 25, 31

Witness

anonymous, 43, 55, 59

Witness—*contd*

biased, 43, 55, 57

examination of, 43, 55–59

expert, 43, 55, 56

impartiality, 56

non-compellable, 43, 55, 58

Women

employment of—

European Social Charter, 7

maternity rights, 7

mothers, economic and social protection, 7

sex discrimination, *see* SEX DISCRIMINATION

Work

right to, 4*n*

World War I

minority treaties, establishment following, 2, 2*n*

World War II

international regulation following, 3

IMMIGRATION AND EXTRADITION

Abode

right of, 107

categories of entrant without—

Community law, 219–239

Community law, not under, 240–328

Channel Islands or Isle of Man, entry to UK via, 123

Commonwealth citizens, 118, 118*n*

entry clearance, 151, 153

European Community law, 117

exclusion order, 107

meaning, 117

patrials, 118*n*

polygamous wives and widows, 118*n*

children of, 118*n*

statutory nature, 118*n*

who has, 118

Administrative removal

appeal against, 201

challenging, 201

detention for, 199

European Community citizens, 195

illegal entry as ground for, 198

judicial review, 194, 201

liability for, 195

meaning, 194

member of Parliament, representation by, 376

Administrative removal—*contd*

procurement for, 200

refusal of leave to enter as, 197

ship and aircraft crews, 195, 196

what constitutes, 194

Admission

meaning, 146

temporary, 146

authority for, 168

breach of conditions, 187

refusal of leave to enter, following, 170

in temporary capacity, 146

Adoption

settlement, family reunion or creation by, 279

Air crew

administrative removal, 195, 196

immigration control, 129

Aircraft

administrative removal, procurement for, 200

airports, *see* AIRPORT

common travel area, journeys outwith, 133

conduct committed in, extradition procedure, 515

crew, *see* AIR CREW

deportee, removal by, 212

References are to paragraphs

Aircraft—*contd*
detention of passenger for examination,
  167
entry control requirements, 161
Hague Convention on Unlawful Seizure
  of Aircraft, 508
Montreal Convention for the Suppression of Unlawful Acts against
  the Safety of Civil Aviation, 508
operational ground staff, permit-free
  employment, 247
owners, liability of, 161
prevention of terrorism powers, 133
Tokyo Convention on Offences Committed on Board Aircraft in Flight,
  508
Airport
control areas, 161
designated, 133, 161
private security firms, role of, 138
Alien
entry of, *see* IMMIGRATION
Amnesty
illegal entrant, for, 112
Armed forces
immigration controls, 131
Arrest
constable or immigration officer, by, 168
Arrival
detention on—
  bail, 169
  examination, for, 167
examination on, 162
  conduct of, 164
  detention for, 167
  documents, declaration of, 162
  failure to comply with requirements,
    166
  medical, 165
  search warrant and arrest, 168
meaning, 146
Artist
change of employment, 256
entry clearance, 151, 254, 255
extension of leave, 257
Immigration Rules, 149
meaning, 154
police registration conditions, 175
work permit exemption, 154
Asylum
applicant for, removal of, 318
asylee—
  grant or refusal of leave to enter, 170
  meaning, 315
category changed by seeking, 171
claim for, 318

Asylum—*contd*
eligibility for, 318
grant of, 318
Immigration Rules, 149, 320
leave to enter, 170, 318
refugee status, and, 315
see also REFUGEE
Au pair
admission of, 310
change of category, 313
entry clearance, 151
extension of leave, 312
Immigration Rules, 149, 291, 310–313
meaning, 311
police registration conditions, 175
work permit exemption, 154
Auld alliance, 103
Aunt
settlement, family reunion or creation
  by, 289, 290
Authorisation
meaning, 146

Bail
breach of conditions, 187
detention for administrative removal,
  199
passenger detained on arrival, 169
Banishment
common law and statutory punishment,
  103, 105
Belgium
no-passport excursions to, 132
Border
controls, prevention of terrorism powers, 133
British citizen
abode, right of, 118
burden of proof, 118, 153
passport, 121
settlement, 121
**British Dependent Territories citi-
zen**
immigration control exemptions, 132
leave to enter, 120
meaning, 107
passport, 121
settlement, 121
British National (Overseas), 220*n*
immigration control exemptions, 132
leave to enter, 120
passport, 121
settlement, 121
British Overseas citizen
immigration control exemptions, 132
meaning, 107

References are to paragraphs

British Overseas citizen—*contd*
passport, 121
returning resident status, 120
settlement, 121
British protected person
immigration control exemptions, 132
leave to enter, 120
British subject
leave to enter, 120
meaning, 120*n*
passport, 121
settlement, 121
see also COMMONWEALTH CITIZEN
Broadcasting organisations
representatives of, 247
Brother
settlement, family reunion or creation
     by, 289, 290
Businessman
change of employment, 252
entry clearance required by, 250, 251
extension of leave, 253
police registration conditions, 175

Channel Islands
common travel area, 122
Community law rights, 220
deportation order made by, 123
entry to United Kingdom via, 123
Immigration Act, application to, 123
Child
adoption, family reunion by settlement,
     279
born in United Kingdom who are not
     British, 127
  entry clearance, 151
  Immigration Rules, 149
  settlement, family reunion or creation
     by, 284
dependant, as, 264
deportation of parent, 208
European Community law, 'primary
     right' holder, of, 223
illegitimate, family reunion by settle-
     ment, 279
meaning, 279
parent, meaning, 279
polygamous wives and widows, of, 118*n*
settled Commonwealth citizen, of, 125
settlement, family reunion or creation
     by, *see* SETTLEMENT
student, *see* STUDENT
Citizenship
acquisition—
  naturalisation, by, 121
  registration, by, 121

Colony
conduct committed in, extradition pro-
     cedure, 515
  designated colony, 520
Common law
generally, 108
nineteenth-century immigration law,
     105
Common travel area
exclusions from, Secretary of State's
     powers, 122
journeys outwith—
  leave to enter, 119
  prevention of terrorism powers, 133
  ships and aircraft, 133
local journeys, 122
meaning, 122
Commonwealth citizen
abode, right of, 118, 118*n*
deportation, with protection against,
     125, 126
East African dependencies, Asian popu-
     lation, 107
employment—
  conditions, 174
  vouchers, 107
entry clearance, 151, 261
immigration by, 101, 102
  appeals system, 329
  control exemptions, 132
  employment vouchers, 107
  Immigration Rules, 149
  statute law, 107
  statutory restrictions, 107
leave to enter—
  employment conditions, 174
  extension, 262
polygamous wives and widows, 118*n*
  children of, 118*n*
protected rights of entry, with, 125
settled—
  children, 127
  wives, 127
settlement, 121
United Kingdom ancestry, with—
  employment, taking or seeking, 261
  entry clearance, 261
young, on working holiday, 149, 151,
     154, 174, 241, 263
Commonwealth countries
extradition arrangements, 542
extradition from, 579, 580
extradition procedure, 'own nationals'
     exemption not applicable, 549
extradition to—
  ad hoc extradition, 524

Commonwealth countries—*contd*
extradition to—*contd*
  authentication of documents, 566
  designated Commonwealth countries,
    520
  extradition crime, definition, 522
  international law, 518
  liability for, 521
  municipal law, 519
  restrictions on, 523
  review, 571
Consul
family of, 130
immigration control, 130
Contumacy
extradition rules on, 536, 537
**Convention for the Prevention and
  Punishment of the Crime of
  Genocide**
extradition agreement, 508
**Convention and Protocol Relating to
  the Status of Refugees**, 116, 314
Criminal record
refusal of leave to enter due to, 171

Deception
refusal of leave to enter following, 171
Dentist
postgraduate training, in, 292
  change of category, 298
  entry requirements, 295
  extension of leave, 300
Depart, requirement to
variation, appeals, 329
Departure
control of, 147, 148
  administrative removal, *see* ADMINIS-
    TRATIVE REMOVAL
  curtailment of stay, 215
  embarkation card, requirements as to,
    192
  embarkation, place and manner of,
    requirements as to, 192
  extradition, *see* EXTRADITION
  hostage order, *see* HOSTAGE ORDER
  mental patient, removal of, 216
  passport, endorsement of, 193
  safety order, *see* SAFETY ORDER
  supervised departure, 215
  voluntary departure, 215
Dependants
entry clearance requirement, 264, 265
extension of leave, 266
meaning, 264
settlement, 266

Dependency
conduct committed in, extradition pro-
    cedure, 515
Deportation
alternatives to, 215
appeal against, 202, 211, 335
breach of conditions, following, 205
British citizen, deportee becoming, 214
Channel Islands, order made by, 123
Commonwealth citizen, 126
compassionate circumstances, 202, 210
control of departure decisions, limits on
    appeals relating to, 342
court recommendation, 202, 204, 206,
    209
  general principles, 206, 209
curtailment of stay as alternative to, 215
decision, 202
  appeal against, 202, 211, 335
  consistency in, 202, 210
  general considerations, 209
  grounds for, 204
  notification of, 211
    detention permitted by, 211, 213
    unsuccessful service, 211
European Community national, 203
family of deportee, 204, 208
  voluntary departure, 215
grounds for—
  breach of conditions, 186
  overstaying, 186
immigration control, exempt groups,
    132
Immigration Rules, 149
indefinite leave to enter or remain, 120,
    177
Isle of Man, order made by, 123
liability for, 203
marriages of convenience, 207
meaning, 147, 202
member of Parliament, representation
    by, 376
notice, 202
order, 212
  detention pending, 211, 213
  effect of, 212
  lapse, 214
  person subject to, refusal of leave to
    enter, 171
  revocation, 214
    appeal against refusal, 214
    no entitlement to enter conferred
      by, 214
overstaying as ground for, 204, 205
protected status, 126
public good, 204, 207

References are to paragraphs

Deportation—*contd*
public interest, 202, 210
refugees, 203, 321, 322
regulations, Secretary of State's powers
    as to, 138
Republic of Ireland, citizen of, 126
Secretary of State, order by, 202
'security' deportation cases, 335
supervised departure as alternative to,
    215
Detention
administrative removal, for, 199
arrival, on, 167, 169
deportation decision, following, 211,
    213
Diplomat
family of, 130
immigration control, 130
servants and staff, 247
Diplomatic asylee
see ASYLUM
Discrimination
nationality, on grounds of, European
    Community law, 221
Disembarkation
meaning, 146
Doctor
postgraduate training, in, 292
    change of category, 298
    entry requirements, 295
    extension of leave, 300
Drugs
Vienna Convention against Illicit Nar-
    cotic Drugs and Psychotropic, 508

East African dependencies
Asian population, 107
    special vouchers, 158
Embarkation
card, requirements as to, 192
meaning, 147
place and manner of, requirements as to,
    192
Emigration
number of emigrants, 101
Employment
breach of conditions, 188
businessmen, work permit exemption,
    154
change of, 248
    artists, 256
    businessmen, 252
    self-employed, 252
    writers, 256
entry clearance, liability for, 151
Immigration Rules, 149

Employment—*contd*
leave to enter, conditions imposed by,
    174
leave to remain, 140
migration for reasons of, 102
    'replacement labour', 102
permit-free—
    artists, 254–257
    businessmen, 250–253
    change of employment, 248
    entry clearance, 151, 246
    extension of leave, 249
    Immigration Rules, 149, 246–249
    independent means, persons of, 258–
        260
    meaning, 247
    police registration conditions, 175
    self-employed, 250–253
    writers, 254–257
post-entry control, 191
self-employed—
    entry clearance, 151
    Immigration Rules, 149
    work permit exemption, 154
students, 296
    dependants of, 302
visitors, 305
work permit, *see* WORK PERMIT
Enter, leave to
appeal, effect of, 332
appeals system, effect of, 329, 332
asylum, grant of, 318
authorisation by Secretary of State, 119
breach of conditions, 188
Channel Islands or Isle of Man, entry via,
    123
children, family reunion or creation by
    settlement, 280
conditions, 119
    variation of, *see* variation *below*
curtailment, general considerations for,
    181
deception, obtained by, 119
departure—
    nullifying, 120
    outwith common travel area, 119
    returning resident status, 120
deportation order, 119
duration, 119
    extension, 119
    removal of time limit, 119
    restriction, 119
employment—
    conditions, imposition of, 174
    restrictions, 119

Enter leave to—*contd*
fiancé or fiancée, 274–277
 variation after marriage, 277
grant of, 170
groups exempted from immigration
 control, 128
Immigration Rules, 170, 240
indefinite, 120, 173, 177
 absences and re-entry, 120
 deportation order, 120, 177
 prevention of terrorism, 177
 restrictions, 120
lapse, 176, 177
limited, 173
 police registration, 175
offences in relation to, refusal following,
 171
police registration, 119, 175, 183, 236
Prevention of Terrorism Act, subject to,
 119
refugee—
 appeal against refusal, 322
 seeking in different capacity, 317, 319
refusal of, 170
 administrative removal, 197
 entry clearance—
  person holding, 172
  person not holding, 170
 refugee, 322
 work permit holders, 242
Republic of Ireland, entry via, 124
returning residents, 176
settled, meaning, 120
settlement—
 family reunion or creation by, 270, 280
 variation for, 182
sponsorship, 160
spouse, family reunion or creation by
 settlement, 270
temporary absences, 119
temporary admission distinguished, 119
time limit, 173
 variation, 177
variation, 119, 149, 175, 177
 appeals, 329
 application for, 178
 decision to be given in writing, 178
 lapse, 179
 marriage, after, 277
 outside the rules, 177, 318
 refusal of, general considerations, 181
 settlement, for, 182
 sponsorship, 160
 without application, 180
visitors, 307
work permits, 154, 244

Entry
meaning, 146
Entry certificate
entry clearance, as, 150
Entry clearance
application for, 152
artists, 254, 255
burden of proof, 152, 153
businessmen, 250, 251
categories leading to settlement, 241
certificate of entitlement, 153
certificate of patriality, 153
change of circumstances since issue, 172
children, family reunion or creation by
 settlement, 280
Commonwealth citizens with UK ancestry, 261
dependants, 264, 265
false representation, 172
fiancés or fiancées, 274
form of, 150
Immigration Rules categories, 240
independent means, persons of, 151, 258,
 259
material fact, failure to disclose, 172
meaning, 150
passenger holding, refusal of leave to
 enter, 172
passenger not holding, refusal of leave to
 enter, 171
permit-free employment, 246
refugee travel document, 151*n*
refusal of entry, grounds for, 150
refusal of, 152
 representations by member of Parliament, 373
right of abode, 151, 153
 proof of, 153
self-employed, 250, 251
settlement, family reunion or creation
 by, 268, 270, 280
special vouchers holders, 159
spouse, family reunion or creation by
 settlement, 270
students, 292–294
validity, 150
visitors, 305
who needs, 151
work permit operating as, 244
writers, 254, 255
Entry clearance officer
powers, 141
Entry, right of
Commonwealth citizens, 125
European Community nationals, 255,
 236

References are to paragraphs

Entry, right of—*contd*
European Community nationals—*contd*
  families of, 236
  police registration, 236
  'primary right' holders, 236
  'secondary right' holders, 236
European Commission of Human Rights
East African Asians, 107
European Community citizen
abode, right of, 117
administrative removal, 195
Community law—
  direct effect of, 114
  relationship with United Kingdom law, 219, 235
  see also EUROPEAN COMMUNITY LAW
Community national, meaning, 222
depart, right to, 224
deportation, 203
employment, right to remain after, 239
enter, right to, 225
entry by, 101, 102
  refusal of, legal remedies, 234
establishment, right of, 226
European Convention on, 509
exclusion order, 171
expulsion, legal remedies, 234
family of, 134
  right of entry, 236
foreign state, to—
  political offences, 516, 531–535
  restrictions on, 516
  speciality, 516
free movement of persons and services, 114, 221
immigration by, 101
Immigration Rules, 114, 134, 149, 221
legal remedies of, 234
medical reasons, refusal of leave to enter due to, 171
nationality, 222
  Community law rights, and, 220, 220n
permanent incapacity for work, right to remain after, 239
police registration, 236
'primary right' holder, 222
  family of, 223
    residence permits, 230
    right to remain, 228
  residence permit, 230
  right to depart and return, 224
  right to enter, 225, 236
  right to reside, 226
    termination, 227, 238

European Community citizen—*contd*
Republic of Ireland, entry to United Kingdom via, 124
reside, right to, 226
  termination, 227, 238
residence permit, refusal of issue or renewal, legal remedies, 234
retirement, right to remain after, 239
return, right to, 224
right to remain after employment, 228
  termination, 229
rights of—
  alteration, 134
  public policy proviso, 232
    procedural limits, 234
    substantive limits, 233
'secondary right' holders, 223
  right to depart and return, 224
  right to enter, 225, 236
  right to reside, 226
    termination, 238
self-employed, 222
services, providers and recipients of, 222
  right to reside, 226
travel document—
  expiry, 233
  failure to hold, 233
workers—
  educational, training and residential facilities, 231
  equality of treatment, right to, 231
  frontier, 222
    right to remain, 228
  meaning, 222
  permanent incapacity for work, 228
  primary right holders, 222
  retirement of, 228
  right to remain after employment, 228
  seasonal, 222
  spouses and children, 231
  temporary, 222
  trade union membership, 231
European Community law
Channel Islands, 220
Community national, meaning, 222
depart and return, right to, 224
employment—
  equality of treatment, 231
  right to remain after, 228, 239
    termination, 229
  right to reside for purposes of, 226
enter, right to, 225
equality of treatment, 231
freedom of movement of persons and services, 221
Gibraltar, 220, 220n

References are to paragraphs

European Community law—*contd*
Immigration Rules, mediation by, 235–239
Isle of Man, 220
nationality, discrimination on grounds of, 221
precedence of, 219
'primary right' holders, 222, 230
   families of, 223
   right to depart and return, 224
public policy proviso, 232
   procedural limits, 234
   substantive limits, 233
refugees, 222
reside, right to, 226
   termination, 227, 238
rights relevant to immigration, 220
'secondary right' holders, 223
   right to depart and return, 224
stateless persons, 222
United Kingdom law, relationship with, 219, 235
see also EUROPEAN COMMUNITY CITIZEN

European Convention on Extradition
state party to, ad hoc extradition to, 517
United Kingdom not party to, 509

European Convention on Human Rights
free movement, principle of, 115
requirements of, 115

European Convention on the Suppression of Terrorism
extradition, 508, 532

Evidence
burden of proof, extradition from United Kingdom, 562
prima facie rule, extradition, 544–547

Examining officers
meaning, 145

Exclusion
meaning, 147

Exclusion order
breach of, 134
prevention of terrorism powers, 107, 117, 122, 134
refusal of leave to enter, 171
representations against, 134
revocation, 134

Extradition
ad hoc, 517, 524, 577
aircraft, conduct committed in, 515
alternatives to—
   deterritorialisation of criminal jurisdiction, 503
   terrorism, 503

Extradition—*contd*
alternatives—*contd*
   trial in *forum deprehensionis*, 505
   trial *in absentia*, 505
arrangements, 511
   general, 510, 511
   special, 510, 511
colony, conduct committed in, 515
Commonwealth country, to
   ad hoc extradition, 524
   authentication of documents, 566
   designated Commonwealth countries and colonies, 520, 566
   extradition crime, definition, 522
   international law, 518
   liability for, 521
   municipal law, 519
   restrictions on, 523
   review, 571
   Secretary of State's order to surrender or return, 575
contumacy, 536, 562
   conviction *in absentia*, 536, 562
      Republic of Ireland, in relation to, 537
   injustice in conviction, 536
      Republic of Ireland, in relation to, 537
Convention on the Physical Protection of Nuclear Material, 508
Convention for the Prevention and Punishment of the Crime of Genocide, 508
definition, 501
dependency, conduct committed in, 515
double-punishability, 515, 548
European Convention on, 509, 517
European Convention on the Suppression of Terrorism, 508, 532
extradition crime—
   definition by list method, 513
   double-punishability, 515, 548
foreign state—
   from, ad hoc, 577
   meaning, 512
   to—
      1870 procedure, 514, 517, 532
         restrictions on return to foreign state, 516, 532
      1989 procedure, 515, 516, 517, 532
      ad hoc, 517
      arrangement, 517
      England, conduct committed in, where conduct offence in Scotland but not in England, 515*n*
      extra-territorial offences, 515

References are to paragraphs

Extradition—*contd*
foreign state—*contd*
  to—*contd*
    international law, 506
    irrespective of where offence took
      place, 515
    opportunities to challenge surren-
      der, 516
    political offences, 531
    United Kingdom, priority of un-
      related crimes committed in,
      516
fugitive criminals, 513
genocide, 532
habeas corpus, application for writ of, 562,
  568, 575
Hague Convention on Unlawful Seizure
  of Aircraft, 508
historical background, 502–504
hovercraft, conduct committed in, 515
in absentia trials, 505, 536, 537, 562
injustice in conviction, 536, 537
inordinate delay or abuse of process, 562
International Convention against the
  Taking of Hostages, 508, 532
International Convention for the Suppression of the White Slave Traffic,
  508
international law, 503, 506. *See also*
  INTERNATIONAL LAW
judicial review, 568–573
legislative authority, 511
list method, definition by, 513
military law, offences under, 516, 534
Montreal Convention for the Suppression of Unlawful Acts against
  the Safety of Civil Aviation, 508
municipal law, 504, 510
nationality, trials which may be prejudiced by, 516, 532, 534
New York Convention on Crimes
  against Internationally Protected
  Persons, 508
'own nationals' exemption, 549, 562
  meaning of 'own nationals', 549
persecution, request made for purpose
  of, 516
political offences, 516
  1870 procedure, 532
  1989 procedure, 533
    variations under, 534
  general exemption, 531, 562
  Republic of Ireland, in relation to, 535
  terrorism, 532, 532*n*
political opinion, trials which may be
  prejudiced by, 516, 532, 534

Extradition—*contd*
previous acquittal or conviction, where,
  516, 538
Republic of Ireland, in relation to, 539
prima facie rule—
  1870 procedure, 545
  1989 procedure, 546
  Republic of Ireland, in relation to, 547
  traditional requirement, 544
purposes, 505
race, trials which may be prejudiced by,
  516, 532, 534
religion, trials which may be prejudiced
  by, 516, 532, 534
Republic of Ireland, 510
  authority to proceed, 555
  contumacy, 537
  double punishability, 548
  extradition crime, 528
  from United Kingdom—
    authentication of documents, 567
    executing warrant, 561
    hearing and committal, 564
    order by Secretary of State, not
      applicable, 576
    provisional warrants, 558
    review, 572, 573
  international law, 525
  liability for, 527
  municipal law, 526
  'own nationals' exemption not appli-
    cable, 549
  political offence exemption, 535
  previous acquittal or conviction, 539
  prima facie rule, 547
  restrictions, 529
  speciality, 543
  to United Kingdom, 581, 582
restrictions on, 516
  contumacy, 536, 537
  double criminality, principle of, 548
  political offences, 531–535
  previous acquittal or conviction,
    where, 538, 539
  prima facie rule, 544–547
  race, religion, nationality or political
    opinion, trials which may be
    prejudiced by, 516, 532, 534
  speciality, 540–543
speciality, 516
  1870 procedure, 541
  1989 procedure, 542
  arrangement with, 541, 541*n*, 542
  Commonwealth countries, 543
  general rule, 540, 562
  Republic of Ireland, in relation to, 543

References are to paragraphs

Extradition—*contd*
terrorism, deterritorialism of criminal
    jurisdiction, 503
tholed his assize, person claiming to
    have, 538, 562
Tokyo Convention on Offences Com-
    mitted on Board Aircraft in Flight,
    508
treaties—
    absence of, 517
    bilateral, 503, 531, 577
        expired or lapsed, 507
        states signatory to, 507
    expired or lapsed, 507
    multilateral, 503, 505, 508, 531, 577
United Kingdom, from, 504, 506–529
    authentication of documents—
        1870 procedure, 565
        1989 procedure, 566
        Republic of Ireland, in relation to,
            567
    authority to proceed—
        1870 procedure, 553
        1989 procedure, 554
        Republic of Ireland, in relation to,
            555
    burden of proof, 562–564
    committal, 562–564
    defences to, 562, 563
    evidence, production of, 562
    hearing and committal—
        1870 procedure, 562
        1989 procedure, 563
        Republic of Ireland, in relation to,
            564
    informal requisition or request, 556–
        558
    inordinate delay or abuse of process,
        562
    Order of the Secretary of State, 551
    'own nationals' exemption, 549
    provisional warrants—
        1870 procedure, 556
        1989 procedure, 557
        Republic of Ireland, in relation to,
            558
    requisition—
        1870 procedure, 550
        1989 procedure, 550
    review—
        1870 procedure, 568, 569
        1989 procedure, 570, 571
        Republic of Ireland, in relation to,
            572, 573
    Secretary of State's order to surrender
        or return—
        1870 procedure, 574

Extradition—*contd*
United Kingdom, from—*contd*
    Secretary of State's order to surrender
        or return—*contd*
        1989 procedure, 575
        Republic of Ireland, not applicable
            to, 576
    warrants—
        executing—
            1870 procedure, 559
            1989 procedure, 560
            Republic of Ireland, in relation to,
                561
        production of, 562
        provisional, 556–558
United Kingdom, priority of unrelated
    crimes committed in, 516
United Kingdom, to, 504, 530
    1870 procedure, 577
    1989 procedure, 577
    Commonwealth countries, from, 579,
        580
    foreign states, from, 577, 578
    Republic of Ireland, from, 581, 582
vessel, conduct committed in, 515
Vienna Convention against Illicit
    Narcotic Drugs and Psychotropic,
    508

Family
settlement—
    family relationship on grounds of, *see*
        SETTLEMENT
    family reunion or creation by, *see*
        SETTLEMENT
Fiancé/Fiancée
entry clearance, 151
settlement, family reunion or creation
    by, *see* SETTLEMENT
Foreign firm
representative of, 247
Foreign state
extradition to—
    bilateral treaties, 507
    fugitive criminals, 513
    international law, generally, 506
    multilateral agreements, 508
    see also EXTRADITION
meaning, 512, 517
Forgery
appeal limited by, 337
France
no-passport excursions to, 132
Free movement of persons and ser-
    vices
European Community law, 114, 221

References are to paragraphs

Free movement of persons and ser-
  vices—*contd*
European Convention on Human
  Rights, 114
Fugitive criminal
extradition to foreign state, 513
meaning, 513

Genocide
Convention for the Prevention and Pun-
  ishment of the Crime of Genocide,
  508
political offence, not regarded as, 532
Gibraltar
European Community law, 220, 220*n*
Gipsies
Gipsies Act 1609 . . . 103

Habeas corpus
writ of, extradition cases, 562, 568, 575
Hague Convention on Unlawful
  Seizure of Aircraft
extradition, 508
Home Office
immigration controls, 138
Homosexual relationship
close relative not created by, 269*n*
Hong Kong
British Nationality (Hong Kong) Act
  1990 . . . 107
British Nationals (Overseas), 220*n*
immigration by, 101
Hospital house officer
training, in, 292
Hostage
extradition in relation to crimes involving, 508, 532
International Convention against the
  Taking of, 508, 532
Hostage order
breach of, 187
generally, 216
prevention of terrorism, 117, 135
Hotel records
guests' duty to supply information, 184
hoteliers' duty to maintain, 184
Secretary of State's powers in relation to,
  184
Hovercraft
conduct committed in, extradition procedure, 515, 568

Identification
detention on arrival for, 167
Identity
examination on arrival to establish, 162

Illegal entrant
administrative removal, 195, 198
control of departure decisions, limits on
  appeals relating to, 341
deportation order, 202
illegal entrant, definition, 198
illegal entry, offence as, 185
Immigration
abode, right of, *see* ABODE
administrative removal, *see* ADMINIS-
  TRATIVE REMOVAL
appeals—
  adjudicators, 331
  after entry cases, representation by
    member of Parliament, 375
  aliens, application to, 329
  appealable decisions, 336–343
    notice of, 345
  Commonwealth citizens, application
    to, 329
  control after entry decisions, limits on,
    340
  control before entry decisions, limits
    on, 338
  control on entry decisions, limits on,
    339
  departure decisions, limits, on, 341–
    343
  deportation orders, limits on control
    of departure decisions, 342
  discretion of Secretary of State or offi-
    cer, against, 333
  first stage appeals, 345–356
    burden of proof, 354
    determination, 351, 356
    evidence, 353
    explanatory statement, respondent,
      by, 349
    grounds for, 333
    hearing, 352
      in absence of a party, 355
    nature of, 333
    notice of, 346
      appealable decision, 345
    parties to, 347
    preliminary issues, 350
    record of proceedings, 356
    summary determination, 351
    time limits, 348
  forgery as limit on, 337
  further appeals—
    determination, 363, 366
    disposal of application, 360
    evidence, 365
    hearing, 364
      determination without, 363

Immigration—*contd*
appeals—*contd*
  further appeals—*contd*
    Immigration Appeal Tribunal, to, 357
    leave for, 358
    nature of, 334
    notice of application, 361
    parties to, 362
    summary determination, 363
  illegal entrants, limits on control of departure decisions, 341
  Immigration Appeal Tribunal, *see* IMMIGRATION APPEAL TRIBUNAL
  members of Parliament, representations by, 329, 370–376
    administrative removal, in respect of, 376
    after entry cases, 375
    deportation, in respect of, 376
    entry clearance, where refusal of, 373
    entry, where refusal of, 374
    Home Office guidelines, 371
  non-appealable decisions, 344
  procedure—
    burden of proof, first stage appeals, 354
    determination—
      first stage appeals, 351, 356
      further stage appeals, 363, 366
    evidence—
      first stage appeals, 353
      further stage appeals, 365
    explanatory statement by respondent, first stage appeals, 349
    first stage appeals, 345–356
    further appeals, 357–366
    hearing—
      absence of a party, first stage appeals, 355
      determination without—
        first stage appeals, 351
        further appeals, 363
      first stage appeals, 352
      further stage appeals, 364
    notice—
      appealable decisions, 345
      first stage appeals, 345, 346
      time limits, 348, 359
    preliminary issues, first stage appeals, 350
    record of proceedings, first stage appeals, 356
    Secretary of State, on reference from, 367

Immigration—*contd*
appeals—*contd*
  procedure—*contd*
    'security' deportation cases—
      criticisms of, 369
      'Three Wise Men', representations to, 368
    summary determination—
      first stage appeals, 351
      further stage appeals, 363
    time limit—
      first stage appeals, 348
      further appeal, 359
  refusal of entry cases, representation by member of Parliament, 374
  refusal of entry clearance cases, representation by member of Parliament, 373
  removal destination, limits on control of departure decisions, 343
  requirement to depart, variation, 329
  'security' deportation cases, 335, 368, 369
  success rate, 329
  system—
    appellate authorities, 330
    criticism of, 329
    leave to enter or remain, effects of appeal, 329, 332
    personnel, 331
  Three Wise Men, *see* THREE WISE MEN
  wrong identity as limit on, 337
Commonwealth citizens, *see* COMMONWEALTH CITIZEN
control—
  adjudicators, appointment of, 139
  airports, 161
  bail, application for, 169
  breach of conditions and requirements, 186, 187
    deportation following, 205
  central, 138–140
  declaration of, 162
  definitions, 146, 147
  departure, of, *see* DEPARTURE
  deportation, *see* DEPORTATION
  detention on arrival, bail, 169
  documents, search for, 162
  entry clearance, *see* ENTRY CLEARANCE
  entry clearance officers, 141
  entry requirements, 161
  examination on arrival, 162
    identification, 167
    non-disclosure of material facts, 166
  examining officers, 145
  government departments, role of, 140

Immigration—*contd*
control—*contd*
  groups exempted from—
    air crew, 129
    armed forces, members of certain, 131
    consuls, 130
    deportation orders, 132
    diplomats, 130
    international acts, covered by, 130, 130n
    leave to enter, 128
    passports relevant to, 132
    seamen, 129
    settlement, relationship to, 128
    statutory instrument, by, 128
    unlawful entry, 132
  Home Office, powers of, 138
  hotel records, 184
  identification of passenger, 167
  identity, establishment of, 162
  illegal entry, 185
  Immigration Appeal Tribunal, *see* IMMIGRATION APPEAL TRIBUNAL
  immigration officers, 142
  Immigration Rules, issue of, 138. *See also* IMMIGRATION RULES
  institutions of, 138–145
  landing card, requirement to complete, 163
  local, 141–145
  Lord Chancellor, role of, 139
  medical inspectors, 143
  nationality, establishment of, 162
  overstaying, 186
    tracing overstayers, 188
  passport or travel document, 162
    endorsement, 120
  phases of, 148
  police, 144
    Home Office control, 138
  ports, 161
  post-entry controls, 185–191
    employment, 191
    generally, 189
    'passport raids', 190
    police checks, 190
    unofficial, 189
    welfare state facilities, 191
  private security firms, contracts with, 138
  Secretary of State, primary responsibility of, 138
  sponsorship, 160
  temporary admission, 169
  temporary release, 169

Immigration—*contd*
court decisions, 113
discretion of Secretary of State or officer, appeal against, 333
European Community citizens, *see* EUROPEAN COMMUNITY CITIZEN
European Community law, *see* EUROPEAN COMMUNITY LAW
examination on arrival—
  conduct of, 164
  detention for, 167
  documents—
    declaration of, 162
    search for, 162
  failure to comply with requirements, 166
  medical, 165
  search warrant and arrest, 168
family unification, 102
foreign workers, 101
Hong Kong citizens, 101
illegal entry, 185
  amnesty, grant of, 112
Immigration Appeal Reports, 113
Immigration Rules, *see* IMMIGRATION RULES
international law—
  Convention on the Status of Refugees, 116
  European Convention on Human Rights, 115
  International Convention on the Elimination of all Forms of Discrimination, 116
  International Covenant on Civil and Political Rights, 116
  international customary law, 116
  International Labour Organisation Resolutions, 116
  Universal Declaration of Human Rights, 116
Ireland, from, 101
Irish Potato Famine, 101
Jewish, 101
medical inspectors, *see* MEDICAL INSPECTOR
ministerial discretion, 110, 112
officers, *see* IMMIGRATION OFFICER
overstaying, 186, 188
patrials, 107, 118n
protected status, groups with, 125–127
public funds, 160, 160n
racial tension, and, 102
refugees, 101, 102
'replacement labour', 102
sponsorship, 160

Immigration—*contd*
tourists, immigration controls, 101, 102
tribunal decisions 113
United Kingdom, immigration to, historical background, 101–107
common law, 105
nineteenth century, 104, 105
statute law, 106, 107
twentieth-century, 102, 106, 107
until the Union, 103
work permit, *see* WORK PERMIT
Immigration Appeal Tribunal
appeal to, generally, 357
appointment of, 139
generally, 330
members, 331
president, 331
Immigration offence
refusal of leave to enter following, 171
Immigration officer
appointment, 138, 142
arrest by, 168
conduct of examination, 164, 170
controls on entry, duties as to, 161–170
enter, grant or refusal of leave to, 170
instructions to, 111
powers, 142
temporary admission, authority given for, 168
temporary release and bail, 169
Immigration Rules
adoption, child entering for, 279
appeals against, 333
asylees, 320
asylum, 149
au pairs, 149
categories, 149
   artists, 254–257
   au pairs, 291, 310–313
   businessmen, 250–253
   change of, 240
      au pairs, 313
   children, admission of, 279–285
   Commonwealth citizens—
      United Kingdom ancestry, with, 261, 262
      working holidaymakers, 241, 263
   Community law, entrants under, 219–239
   dependants, 264–266
   employment, persons in, 241–249
   fiancés and fiancées, 274–277
   grandparents, 285–290
   independent means, persons of, 258–260

Immigration Rules—*contd*
categories—*contd*
   marriage, 278
      family reunion and creation by settlement, 267–273
      fiancés and fiancées, 274–277
   parents, admission of, 285–290
   political asylees, 315–323
   refugees, 314, 316–323
   role of, 240
   self-employment, 250–253
   settlement—
      family reunion and creation by, 267–273
      leading to, 241
   students, 291, 292–300
      dependants of, 301–304
   United Kingdom passport holders, 324–328
   visitors, 291, 305–308
      dependants of, 309
   writers, 254–257
children born in UK but not UK citizens, 149
Community law as mediated by—
   entry, 236
   remain after employment, right to, 239
   residence, 237
      permits, 237
      termination of right to reside, 238
   United Kingdom and Community law, relationship between, 235
Convention on the Status of Refugees, 116
employment or business, passengers coming for, 149
enter, grant or refusal of leave to, 170
European Community nationals, 114, 134, 149, 221
   families of, 134
independent means, passengers of, 149
issue of, 138
marriage, passengers coming for, 149
outside the Rules, Secretary of State's power to decide, 110, 112, 149, 177, 318
reissue, 110
requirement for, 110
settlement, passengers coming for, 149
sexually discriminatory nature, 267
status, 110
students, 149
temporary purposes, passengers coming for, 149
transitional provisions, 110

References are to paragraphs

Immigration Rules—*contd*
visitors, 149
work permits, passengers on, 149
Imprisonment
offence punishable by, deportation rec-
    ommendation following convic-
    tion, 206
Independent means, person of
entry clearance, 151, 258, 259
extension of leave, 260
Immigration Rules, 149
police registration conditions, 175
work permit exemption, 154
International Bank
employees of, 130*n*
**International Convention against the
    Taking of Hostages**
extradition, 508
**International Convention on the
    Elimination of all Forms of Dis-
    crimination**, 116
**International Convention for the
    Suppression of the White Slave
    Traffic**
extradition agreement, 508
**International Covenant on Civil and
    Political Rights**, 116
**International Development Associ-
    ation**
employees of, 130*n*
International Finance Corporation
employees of, 130*n*
International Labour Organisation
resolutions of, 116
International law
extradition, 503, 506
    Commonwealth countries, to, 518
    Republic of Ireland, to, 525
    treaties, 503
immigration, 115, 116
International Monetary Fund
employees of, 130*n*
International organisations
employees of, 130*n*, 247
Ireland
immigration from, 101
Potato Famine, 101
Republic of, *see* REPUBLIC OF IRELAND
Isle of Man
common travel area, 122
Community law rights, 220
deportation order made by, 123
entry to United Kingdom via, 123
    restrictions on, 123
Immigration Act, application to, 123

Jews
immigration, 101

Landing
meaning, 146
Landing card
details required, 163
requirement to complete, 163
Language assistant
exchange schemes, 247
Leave to enter
see ENTER, LEAVE TO
Leave to remain
see REMAIN, LEAVE TO
Letter of consent
entry clearance, as, 150
Local journey
common travel area, 122
meaning, 122

Marriage
after being admitted for purpose other
    than, 278
convenience of—
    deportation order, 207
    meaning, 207*n*
Immigration Rules, 149
polygamous, 118*n*, 269
    potentially polygamous, 269
settlement, family reunion or creation
    by, *see* SETTLEMENT
spouse, *see* SPOUSE; WIFE
Medical examination
after entry, 165
breach of conditions, 187
immigration control, 165
referral for, 165
refusal of leave to enter following, 171
vaginal, no longer allowed, 165
who may make, 165
Medical inspector
appointment, 138, 143
instructions to, 111
powers, 143
Medical treatment
visitor seeking, 305
    conditions for entry, 306
    visitors' dependants, 309
Member of Parliament
immigration cases, representations con-
    cerning, 329, 370–376
    administrative removal, in respect of,
        376
    after entry cases, 375
    deportation decisions, in respect of,
        376

Member of Parliament—*contd*
immigration cases, representations concerning—*contd*
 entry clearance, where refusal of, 373
 entry, where refusal of, 374
 generally, 370, 372
 Home Office guidelines, 371
Mental patient
removal of, 216
Midwife
training in, 292, 293
Migration
reasons for, 102
Missionary
permit-free employment status, 247
Montreal Convention for the Suppression of Unlawful Acts against the Safety of Civil Aviation
extradition, 508
Municipal law
extradition—
 Commonwealth country, to, 519
 Republic of Ireland, to, 525

Nationality
Community law rights, 220, 220n
discrimination on grounds of, European Community law, 221
examination on arrival to establish, 162
trials which may be prejudiced by, extradition procedure, 516, 532, 534
Naturalisation
citizenship, acquisition by, 121
Secretary of State's discretion, at, 121
settlement as precondition, 121
Netherlands
no-passport excursions to, 132
New York Convention on Crimes against Internationally Protected Persons
extradition, 508
Newspapers and news agencies
representatives of, 247
Non-national document, 151
Northern Ireland
exclusion orders, 134
Nuclear Material
Convention on the Physical Protection of, 508
Nurse
training in, 292, 293

Offence
deportation recommendation following conviction, 206

Overseas government
employees of, 247
Overstaying
acquittal of offence, 205
deportation following, 204, 205
ignorance no defence, 205
offence, as, 186, 205
tracing overstayers, 188

Parent
meaning, 279
Passport
British citizens, 121
British Dependent Territories citizens, 121
British Nationals (Overseas), 121
British Overseas citizens, 121
British subjects, 121
collective, 132
endorsement—
 on departure, 193
 immigration control of British subjects, 120
examination on arrival, 162
failure to hold, 171
immigration control exemptions, 132
no-passport excursions, 132
'passport raids', 190
settlement, 121
United Kingdom passport holders, 324–328
 immigration control, subject to, 120
Patrial
abode, right of, 118n
meaning, 107, 118n
wives of, 107
Police
Home Office control, 138
illegal immigrants, guide to treatment of, 190, 190n
leave to enter, grant of, police registration conditions, 175, 183, 236
'passport raids', 190
post-entry control by, 190
private security firms, contracts with, 138
registration of aliens, 144
search warrant and arrest, 168
Political asylee
see ASYLUM
Political offence
extradition, restrictions on, 516
 1870 procedure, 532
 1989 procedure, 533
  variations, 534
 generally, 531
 Republic of Ireland, in relation to, 535

Political opinion
trials which may be prejudiced by, extradition procedure, 516, 532, 534
Polygamous wives and widows
abode, right of, 118*n*
children of, 118*n*
generally, 269
Port
control areas, 161
controls, prevention of terrorism powers, 133
designated, 133, 161
Postgraduate training
police registration conditions, 175
Prima facie rule
extradition, 544–547
Procurement
administrative removal, for, 200
Protected status
groups with, 125–127
Public good
exclusion conducive to, 171

Race
trials which may be prejudiced by, extradition procedure, 516, 532, 534
Racial tension
immigration control, 102
Refugee
appeals, 322
asylum—
    applicants for, removal of, 318
    claimed for, 318
    eligibility for, 318
    grant of, 318
    Immigration Rules, 320
control, application of—
    after entry, 320
    before entry, 317
    departure, of, 321
    on entry, 318, 319
Convention and Protocol Relating to the Status of Refugees, 116, 314
definition, 314
denial of asylum to, 315
deportation, 203, 321, 322
    judicial review of decision, 322
entry clearance, 151*n*
European Community law, 222
exceptional leave to remain, 318, 320, 322
immigration, 101, 102
    Immigration Acts, 316
    Immigration Rules, 116, 316–323
leave to enter, 171, 318
    appeal against refusal, 322
    outside the Rules, 318

Refugee—*contd*
leave to enter—*contd*
    sought in different capacity, 317, 319
leave to remain, appeal against refusal, 322
refugee status—
    loss of, 314
    refusal of, 322
        no appeal against, 344
removal, judicial review of decision, 322
restricted returnability, 323
rights to be given to, 314
tactics used to gain entry, 317
travel documents, 151*n*, 314, 323
United Kingdom law, 316–323
Release
temporary, 146
Religion
trials which may be prejudiced by, extradition procedure, 516, 532, 534
Religion, minister of
permit-free employment status, 247
Religious order, member of
permit-free employment status, 247
Remain, leave to
appeals system, 329, 332
    effect of appeal, 332
breach of conditions, 188
Department of Employment approval, 140
extension—
    artists, 257
    businessmen, 253
    Commonwealth citizens with UK ancestry, 262
    dependants, 266
    independent means, persons of, 260
    self-employed, 253
    writers, 257
generally, 199
Immigration Rules categories, 240
indefinite, 120
    absences and re-entry, 120
    deportation, 120
    restrictions, 120
    work permit holders, 244
lapse, 176
marriage after admission for purpose other than, 278
refugees—
    appeal against refusal, 322
    exceptional leave to remain, 320, 322
Secretary of State's powers, 138
settlement, family reunion or creation by—
    children, 280
    spouse, 270

References are to paragraphs

Remain, leave to—_contd_
work permit holders, 244
see also ENTER, LEAVE TO
Removal
meaning, 147
Removal destination
control of departure decisions, limits on
    appeals relating to, 343
'Replacement labour', 102
Republic of Ireland
citizens of, protection against deport-
    ation, 125
common travel area, 122
entry to United Kingdom via, 124
    appeal against refusal, 124
    European Community citizens, 124
    restrictions, 124
extradition, 510, 581, 582
    authority to proceed, 555
    contumancy, 537
    double punishability, 548
    extradition crime, 528
    from United Kingdom—
        authentication of documents, 567
        hearing and committal, 564
        order by Secretary of State, not
            applicable, 576
        review, 572, 573
        warrants, 558, 561
    international law, 525
    liability for, 527
    municipal law, 526
    'own nationals' exemption not appli-
        cable, 549
    political offence exemption, 535
    previous acquittal or conviction, 539
    prima facie rule, 547
    restrictions on, 529
    speciality, 543
immigration control exemptions, 132
leave to enter, where required, 124
Reside, right to
European Community nationals, 226
termination, 227
Residence permit
European Community nationals, 237
curtailment, 238
Residence requirement
breach of conditions, 187
Restricted returnability
meaning, 171
refusal of leave to enter due to, 171
visitors, 305
Returning resident
British Overseas citizen, 120
entry clearance, 151

Returning resident—_contd_
leave to enter, 120
readmission as, 176

Safety order
breach of, 187
generally, 216
prevention of terrorism, 117, 136
School pupil
training, in, 292
Search warrant
issue of, 168
Self-employed
change of employment, 252
entry clearance required by, 250, 251
extension of leave, 253
Servant
private, 247
Services
free movement of, 114, 221
Settlement
advantage over naturalisation, 121
dependants, 266
employment, 174
entry clearance, 151
excluded categories, 241
    change from, 241
family relationship, on grounds of, 268
family reunion or creation by, 267
    aunt, 289, 290
    brother, 289, 290
    child, 267, 268
        adoption, child entering for, 279
        adoptive parents, 279
        born in UK who is not British citi-
            zen, 284
        conditions of admission, 281, 282
        entry clearance, 280
        generally, 279
        leave to enter or remain, 280
        maintenance and accommodation
            requirements, 283
        meaning, 279
        parent, meaning, 279
        'serious and compelling family or
            other considerations', 281
        'sole responsibility' of parent, 281
        stepparents, 279
        welfare of primary consideration,
            279
    entry clearance, 268
    fiancé or fiancée, 267, 268, 274–277
        entry clearance, 274
        leave to enter, 274
            conditions of, 274, 276
            variation after marriage, 277

References are to paragraphs

Settlement—*contd*
family reunion or creation by—*contd*
  fiancé or finacée—*contd*
    maintenance and accommodation, consideration of, 276
    nature of marriage, 274
    'primary purpose' rule, 274
    variation of leave after marriage, 277
  grandparent, 285–288
    eligibility, 286
    maintenance, accommodation and dependency requirements, 287, 288
  homosexual relationships, 269*n*
  leave to enter and remain, 271
  marriage after admission for other purposes, 278
  nature of marriage—
    fiancé or fiancée, 275
    spouse, 271
  parent, 285–288
    eligibility, 286
    maintenance, accommodation and dependency requirements, 287, 288
  'primary purpose' condition
    fiancé or fiancée, 275
    spouse, 272
  proof of marriage, 273
  sexually discriminatory nature of rules, 267
  sister, 289, 290
  spouse, 267, 269–273
    entry clearance, 270
      conditions for, 271–273
    leave to enter and remain, 270
    maintenance and accommodation, consideration of, 272
    marriage after admission for other purpose, 278
    meaning, 269
    nature of marriage, 271
    'primary purpose' rule, 271
      burden of proof, 271
    proof of marriage, 273
  uncle, 289, 290
generally, 121
groups exempted from immigration control, 128
Immigration Rules categories leading to, 241
leave to enter—
  indefinite, 173
  variation, 182
nationality not affected by, 121
naturalisation following, 121

Settlement—*contd*
passengers coming for, Immigration Rules, 149
passports, 121
settled Commonwealth citizen, wife and children of, 125
special vouchers, 158
work permit holder, 244
Shipping
administrative removal, procurement for, 200
common travel area, journeys outwith, 133, 568
conduct committed on, extradition procedure, 515
crew—
  administrative removal, 195, 196
  immigration control, 129
  permit-free employment, 247
deportee, removal by, 212
detention of passenger for examination, 167
entry control requirements, 161
owners, liability of, 161
port, *see* PORT
prevention of terrorism powers, 133
Sister
settlement, family reunion or creation by, 289, 290
Slavery
International Convention for the Suppression of the White Slave Traffic, 508
Social benefits
migrants' access to, 102
Special voucher
allocation, 159
entry clearance, 159
generally, 158
number and distribution, 112
refusal, 159
  no appeal against, 344
who is covered, 159
Spouse
deportation of, 208
European Community law, 'primary right' holder, of, 223
marriage after admission for other purpose, 278
meaning, 269
settlement—
  family relationship, on grounds of, 268
  family reunion or creation by, 267, 269–273
    age limit, 269

Spouse—*contd*
settlement—*contd*
  family reunion or creation by—*contd*
    entry clearance, 270
      conditions for, 271–273
      proof of marriage, 273
    extra-judicial divorces, 269
    meaning, 269
    polygamous marriages, 269
    potentially polygamous, 269
see also MARRIAGE; WIFE
Stateless person
European Community law, 222
Statute law
generally, 109
twentieth-century immigration law, 106, 107
Student
au pair, change of category to, 297
change of category, 297
dependant of—
  conditions for entry, 302
  earnings, 299
  employment of, 303
  extension of leave, 304
  Immigration Rules, 301–304
  meaning of dependant, 301
employment of, 154, 296
entry clearance, 292–294
extension of leave for, 299
  doctor or dentist in postgraduate training, 300
Immigration Rules, 149, 291, 292–300
meaning, 292
migration by, 102
police registration conditions, 175
spouse, change of category to, 297
work permit, grant of, 157
young Commonwealth working holidaymaker, change of category to, 297

Teacher
exchange scheme, 247
Temporary admission
leave to enter distinguished, 119
Temporary release
breach of conditions, 187
Terrorism
deterritorialism of criminal jurisdiction, 503
European Convention on the Suppression of, 508, 532
hostage order, 135
International Convention against the Taking of Hostages, 508, 532

Terrorism—*contd*
political offence, not regarded as, 532, 532n
prevention of—
  exclusion order, 107, 117, 122, 134
  indefinite leave to enter, and, 177
  leave to enter, 119
  leave to remain, 119
  port and border controls, 133
  Prevention of Terrorism (Temporary Provisions) Act, operation of, 138
safety order, 136
Three Wise Men
appointment of, 331
generally, 330
'security' deportation cases, 368
Tokyo Convention on Offences Committed on Board Aircraft in Flight
extradition agreement, 508
Tourist
immigration controls, 101, 102
Trainee
work permit holder, 241
  extension of leave, 245
Travel document
European Community nationals, 233
failure to hold, 171
refugees, 314, 323

Uganda
Asians, expulsion of, 107
Uncle
settlement, family reunion or creation by, 289, 290
United Kingdom
abode, right of, 107
British citizens, 107
British Dependent Territories citizens, 107
British Overseas citizens, 107
exclusion order, 107
extradition to, 530
migration to—
  generally, 101
  nineteenth century, 104, 105
  twentieth century, 101, 102, 106, 107
  until the Union, 103
passport holders—
  change of category, 328
  dependants of, 326, 328
  entry, generally, 327
  extensions of leave, 328
  meaning, 324
  settlement, eligibility for entry for, 325
    dependants, 325

References are to paragraphs

United Kingdom—*contd*
patrials, 107
'replacement labour', 102
United Kingdom national
meaning, 220
Universal Declaration of Human Rights, 116
Unlawful entry
immigration control, exempt groups, 132

Vessel
see SHIPPING
Vienna Convention against Illicit Narcotic Drugs and Psychotropic
extradition, 508
Visa
entry clearance, as, 150
visa national, meaning, 151
who needs, 150*n*, 151
Visitor
business transactions by, 154, 242, 250, 305
Visitors
change of category, 308
conditions of entry, 306
dependants, 309
employment, prohibition on, 305
entry clearance, 151
  where advisable, 305
extension of leave, 307
Immigration Rules, 149, 291, 305–309
medical treatment, seeking, 305
  conditions of entry, 306
restricted returnability, 305
work permit granted to, 157

Warrant
extradition from United Kingdom—
  executing the warrant, 559–561
  provisional warrants, 566–558
Welfare state facilities
post-entry control, 191
Wife
dependant, as, 264
deportation of husband, 208
polygamous, 269
  abode, right of, 118*n*
  deportation of husband, 208
settled Commonwealth citizen, of, 125
settlement—
  family relationship, on grounds of, 268

Wife—*contd*
settlement—*contd*
  family reunion or creation by, *see* SETTLEMENT
see also SPOUSE
Work permit
allotment, 155, 156
  skilled workers, 155
  trainees, 155
Commonwealth citizens, 107
distribution, 112
employment vouchers, 107
  number and distribution, 112
entry clearance, 151
  operation as, 244
excluded work categories, 154
exemptions, 154
generally, 102
grant of, 154
holders, Immigration Rules—
  change of employment, 243
  concealment of material facts, 242
  extension of leave, 244
    trainees, 245
  false representations by, 242
  generally, 242
  leave to enter or remain, variation of, 244
  refusal of leave to enter, grounds for, 242
  settlement, 244
Immigration Rules, 149
issue of, 140
leave to remain, approval of, 140
no appeal against refusal, 344
number issued, 112
number, type and distribution, 154
permanent settlement following, 154
police registration conditions, 175
refusal of, no appeal against, 154
settlement, categories leading to, 241
trainees, 241
United Kingdom resident, by, 157
young Commonwealth citizen on working holiday, 241
Workers
seasonal, permit-free employment, 247
Writer
change of employment, 256
entry clearance, 151, 254, 255
extension of leave, 257
Immigration Rules, 149
police registration conditions, 175
work permit exemption, 154
Wrongful identity
appeal limited by, 337

References are to paragraphs

INDUSTRIAL AND PROVIDENT SOCIETIES, CREDIT UNIONS AND FRIENDLY SOCIETIES

Accounts
friendly society, 714
industrial and provident society—
  annual return, 634
  balance sheet, 632
  group accounts, 633
  publication, 635
  requirement to keep, 630
  revenue account, 631
Agricultural association, 614, 617
advances to members, 623
Agricultural co-operative
Agricultural and Horticultural Co-operation Scheme, 617
Agriculture
promotion of, 694n
Allotment society
community benefit society, as, 609
Ancient Order of Forresters, 679n
Art
society promoting, 694n
Assistant Registrar for Scotland
books, inspection of, powers as to, 644, 645
cancellation or suspension of registration by, 611
disputes, settlement by, 647
duties, 604
industrial and provident society rules, 612–616
  amendment, 616
inspectors, appointment of, 646
qualifications for appointment, 604
registration by, 610
special meeting called by, 646
Audit
friendly society, 714, 715
industrial and provident society, requirement for, 636
Auditor
appointment, 639, 715, 715n
disqualification from appointment as, 638
maximum fees chargeable by, 716
qualified, meaning, 637, 715n
removal, 639, 715
report by, 640
rights and duties, 716

Banking business
industrial and provident society, 622, 623
Benevolent society
friendly societies legislation, 601

Benevolent society—*contd*
friendly society, as, 679n, 681, 685
meaning, 694
valuations exemption, 717
Byelaws
industrial and provident societies, 612

Cattle insurance society, 693
animals covered by, 693
death only risk insured, 693
dissolution, voluntary, 700
friendly societies legislation, 601
friendly society, as, 679n, 685
investigation of affairs, 700
recovery of unpaid subscription or fine, 706
rules, 700
valuations exemption, 717
Charity
friendly society qualifying as, 681
Children
birth of, friendly society payments on, 686
insurance relating to death of child under ten, 692, 724
Club
community benefit society, as, 609
Co-operative Development Agency
status of, 607
Co-operative society
agricultural, forestry or fishing associations, 614
Agricultural and Horticultural Co-operation Scheme, 617
committee, managers and officers, 613
conduct of business, 607
democratic control, 607
distribution of economic results, 607
general principles, 607
housing, 617
inter-society co-operation, 607
meaning, 607
meetings, 613
membership, 607
  restriction on, 607
profits, 607
registration, cancellation, 607
restrictive trade practices, 614, 617
share capital, 607
wholesale, 614
See also INDUSTRIAL AND PROVIDENT SOCIETY

Collecting society
audit, 715
meaning, 682
meetings, 173
registration, 680*n*
rules, preparation of, 701
Community benefit society, 609
committee, 613
requirements of, 609
See also INDUSTRIAL AND PROVIDENT
SOCIETY
Company
credit union, conversion to, 673
friendly society conversion into, 726, 731
industrial and provident society—
conversion from, 650
conversion into, 651
transfer of friendly society engagements
to, 728
Cookery
society promoting, 694*n*
Corporation tax
friendly societies, exemption, 687, 689,
690
Credit union
accounts, display of, 671
amalgamations, 672
borrowings, 666
breach of borrowing limit, 666*n*
cancellation, 677
co-operative movement, affiliations
with, 656
committee members, 668
company, conversion to credit union,
673
current legislation, 603
deposits, 666
meaning, 666*n*
distributions, 670
dividends, 670
tax exemption, 659
employees, insurance against loss
attributable to, 668
general reserve fund, 670
guarantee arrangements, 668
heritable property, rules as to, 667
historical development, 602, 656
Industrial and Provident Societies Act
1965, application, 657
inspectors, appointment of, 675
insurance against loss, 668
interest earned by, tax exemption, 659
international credit union movement,
656
investments, 666
limited liability, 601, 662, 663
liquidation, 677

Credit union—*contd*
loans—
members, to—
interest earned on, 659, 661, 669
rebates on, 670
rules as to, 669
other credit union, to, 666
meaning, 601, 656, 661
meeting, registrar's power to call, 675
membership, 664
maximum, 664
minimum, 664
qualification for, 664
security of members, 656
name, rules as to, 663
offences, 678
defence to, 678
officers, 668
insurance against loss attributable to,
668
operation, 665–671
profits—
accumulation, 670
application of, 670
calculation, 670
distribution, 670
payments from, postponement, 670
social, cultural or charitable purposes,
use for, 670
protective insurance, 663
registrar—
cancellation of registration by, 677
information, power to require, 674
inspectors, power to appoint, 675
meeting called by, 675
operations, suspension by, 676
suspension of credit union by, 677
winding up, powers as to, 677
registration, 656, 662
before 1979 Act, 658
qualification for, 662
registration area, 605
rules, 663
scope of title, 660
shares, 665
transferable, when, 665
withdrawals, 665
statutory objects, 661
structure, 656
surplus funds, 666, 666*n*
suspension, 677
tax concessions, 659
transfer of engagements, 672
unregistered, 656
winding up, 677
See also INDUSTRIAL AND PROVIDENT
SOCIETY

References are to paragraphs

Death
friendly society payments on, 686, 723, 724
industrial and provident society member, of, 627, 628
nomination, *see* NOMINATION
Debts
industrial and provident society, recovery by, 625
Dividing society
friendly society, as, 682
meaning, 682

Education
society promoting, 694*n*

Fenwick Weavers Society, 608*n*
Fire assurance
friendly societies, 686
Fishing association, 614, 617
advances to members, 623
Floating charge
industrial and provident society, 641
Forestry association, 614, 617
advances to members, 623
Friendly society
accounting year, 714
accounts, 714
    rules as to, 699
agriculture, promotion of, 694*n*
amalgamation, 726, 727
    offences in relation to, 744
annual return, 718
art, society promoting, 694*n*
Assistant Registrar for Scotland, 604
    duties, 604
assistant registrars, 604
audit, 699, 714, 715
    display of, 714
    exempt societies, 715
auditor—
    appointment, 715
    rights and duties, 716
balance sheet, 714
    display of, 714
benefit conditions, rules as to, 699
benefits, maximum limits, 690
benevolent societies, 679*n*, 681, 685, 694, 717
birth, insurance payments on, 686
books, inspection of, 699
borrowing, 721
branch, conversion into, 729
branches, societies with—
    audit, 715
    meaning of branch, 697

Friendly society—*contd*
branches, societies with—*contd*
    registration procedure, 697
    rules—
        amendment of, 703*n*
        preparation of, 701
categories, 679, 679*n*
cattle insurance societies, 679*n*, 685, 693, 706, 717
    rules, 700
Central Area, business carried on in, 696
central body, rules as to, 699
charity, qualification as, 681
Chief Registrar, 604
child under ten years, insurance relating to death of, 692, 724
closed, 679
collecting societies, 680*n*, 682
committee of management, 709
    meetings, 713
    rules as to, 699
company—
    conversion into, 726, 731
    transfer of engagements to, 728
cookery, society promoting, 694*n*
costs, recovery from, 742
current legislation, 603, 683
    proposed reform, 684
death, insurance payments on, 686
death of member—
    certification, 724
    distribution, rules as to, 723
    nomination, 722–724
disputes—
    Court of Session, opinions on questions of law, 725
    internal affairs of society, 725
    meaning, 725*n*
    registrar, referral to, 725
    rules, mandatory provisions, 725
    sheriff court, settlement by, 725
disputes, settlement of, 699
dissolution—
    award, by, 739
    methods, 737
    offences in relation to, 744
    voluntary, 700, 737, 738
dividing societies, 682
    rules as to, 700
documents—
    inspection, 732, 733
        members' requisition, by, 732
    production, 734
    registrar, by, 733
education, society promoting, 694*n*

Friendly society—*contd*
employees, performance of duties, guarantee of, 686
endowment life assurance, 686
expenses, recovery from, 742
finance, 719–721
  borrowing by society, 721
  investments by society, 719
  lending by society, 720
Financial Services Act 1986 . . . 691
fire assurance, 686
funeral expenses, insurance payments for, 686
historical development, 602, 679
illness, insurance against, 686
industrial and provident society, incorporation as, 684
insurance benefits offered by, 686
  restrictions on, 687
interest, accumulation of, 702
investigation of affairs, 700
investment of funds in society with different object, 702
investments, 719
Jewish burial societies, 694n
juvenile, 729
land and buildings, powers as to, 702
legal proceedings by or against—
  costs or expenses, recovery of, 742
  enforcement, 741–745
  fines, recovery of, 741
  offences, 744
    prosecution of, 743
  penalties, 744
  property, recovery of, 745
  service, 741
lending, 720
liquidation, 740
literature, society promoting, 694n
loan fund for members, establishment of, 702
manager, 707, 712
marriage, endowments on, 686
meaning, 601, 679, 686
meetings—
  general, 713
  rules as to, 699, 713
  special, 713
  special resolutions, 713, 713n
member-owned premises, repair and decoration of, 694n
membership—
  corporations, 704
  eligibility, 704
  expulsion of members, 705
    irregular or unjustified, 705

Friendly society—*contd*
membership—*contd*
  honorary, 704
  liabilities of members, 706
  maximum, 704
  military service affecting, 705, 705n
  minimum, 704, 704n
  minors, 704
  non-payment of subscription or fine, 706
  questions of, disputes as to, 725n
  rules, conditions for set out in, 704, 705
  termination, 705
  terms of admission, rules as to, 699
  voluntary dissolution by, 737, 738
music, society promoting, 694n
name, rules as to, 699
nomination—
  certification, 724
  marriage, effect of, 722
  payment on death, 723
  power to nominate, 722
  revocation, 722
objects of, rules as to, 699
offences—
  penalties, 744
  prosecution of, 743
officers—
  appointment, 707
  committee of management, 709
  death of, prior claim of friendly society, 707
  election, 707
  fidelity bonding, 694n
  management by, 707
  manager, 707, 712
  money, in receipt or charge of, 707
  performance of duties, guarantee of, 686
  removal of, 707
  resignation, 707
  rules as to, 699
  secretary, 711
  security given by, 702
  treasurer, 710
old people's home societies, 679n, 685, 694, 717
penalties, rules as to, 699
pension business, taxation of, 689
property of—
  investment, 718
  trustees, vested in, 718
property, recovery of, 745
purposes of, 601, 686
reforms, proposed, 684

References are to paragraphs

Friendly society—*contd*
registered office, address, rules as to, 699
registrar, supervisory functions, 691
    transfer of, 691
registration, 683
    application for, 695
    area, 605
    branches, societies with, 697
    cancellation of, 736
    procedure, 695–697
    recording rules, 696
    refusal of, appeal against, 695
    registrable societies, 685
    restrictions on, 688
    rules confirmed by, 698
    suspension of, 736
Registry of, 604
reinsurance of society's risks, 702
rest centre, provision of, 694n
returns, annual, 699
rules—
    amendment of, 703
    applicable to all societies, 699
    cattle insurance societies, 700
    conduct of business, 691
        chief registrar, powers as to, 691
    confirmation, 698
    dividing societies, 700
    model, 698
    officers and trustees, 707
    powers under, 702
    preparation, 701
    society constitution formed by, 698
science, society promoting, 694n
secretary, 707, 711
self-regulating organisations—
    conduct of business rules, 691
    control over, 691
    recognition of, 691
shop clubs, 680n
specially authorised, 679n, 685, 702
    meaning, 694
    recovery of unpaid subscription or
        fine, 706
    valuations exemption, 717
sport, society promoting, 694n
supervisory functions, 604
suspension, 735
    registration, of, 736
tax exempt business, 687, 689
    annual limits, 690, 690n
tax exempt status, 679
thrift and savings societies, or clubs,
    680n, 694n
transfer of engagements, 726, 728
    offences in relation to, 744

Friendly society—*contd*
treasurer, 710
trustees, 707, 708
    appointment, 708
    corporation as, 708
    death, 708
    duties, 708
    removal, 708
    resignation, 708
unemployed members, assistance to,
    694n
unemployment, insurance against, 686
unincorporated nature, 679
unregistered, 680
valuation, 717
    appointment of actuary or valuer, 717
    exemptions from, 717
    periodic, 700
    required frequency, 717
working men's clubs, 679, 679n, 685,
    694, 717
Funeral expenses
friendly society payments, 686

Heritable property
credit union, ownership, lease or dis-
    posal by, 667, 678
friendly society, ownership of, 702
Horticultural co-operative
Agricultural and Horticultural Co-oper-
    ation Scheme, 617
Housing association
community benefit society, as, 609
dissolution, 652n
housing society, status as, 617
rules, amendment of, 616n
See also INDUSTRIAL AND PROVIDENT
SOCIETY

Illness
friendly society payments on, 686
Income tax
friendly societies, exemption, 687, 689,
    690
Independent Order of Odd Fellows,
    679, 679n
Industrial assurance
collecting societies, 682
Industrial and provident society
accounts—
    annual return, 634
    balance sheet, 632, 655
    group accounts, 633
    publication, 635
    requirement to keep, 630
    revenue account, 631
    year of account, 630

Industrial and provident society—
contd
agricultural supply or marketing society,
    agricultural charge, 641
amalgamations, 648
Assistant Registrar for Scotland, 604, 610
    duties, 604
audit, 613
    auditors—
        appointment, 639
        disqualification from appointment
            as, 638
        qualification, 637
        removal, 639
        reports of, 640
    exemption from, 636
    requirement for, 636
balance sheet, 632
    deliberate falsification, 655
banking business, 622
body corporate, as, 606
books, inspection of, 615
    members, by, 643
    order, by, 644
    production of documents, 645
    restrictions on, 642
borrowing powers, 613
byelaws, 612
co-operative society, 607
committee, 613
committee of management, 619
    duties, 620
    good faith, 620
    liability, 620
    obligations of, 620
community benefit society, 609
company—
    conversion from, 651
    conversion into, 650
constitution, 612
credit unions, *see* CREDIT UNION
current legislation, 603
    non-compliance with, 611
debt recovery, 625
deposits, 613
disputes, regulation of settlement, 615
disputes, settlement of, 647
dissolution, 652
    advertisement, 652
    disadvantages, 652
    offences in relation to, 655
finance—
    advances to members, 623
    banking business, carrying on, 622
    debt recovery, 625
    investments by societies, 624
    loans, 622

Industrial and provident society—
contd
finance—*contd*
    shareholdings, 606, 618, 621
        capital duty, avoidance of, 621
        interest on, 621
        maximum, 621
        minimum, 621
        nomination, 613, 620, 626–629
        redeemable, 606
        repayment of capital on termination
            of membership, 618
        share holding prerequisite of mem-
            bership, 606
        transferable, 606, 613
        withdrawable, 613
    floating charge, 641
        registration provisions, 641
    formed by two or more societies joining,
        606
    fraud, proceedings in case of, 620
    friendly society category, proposal for,
        684
    funds—
        investment, 613, 624
        in possession of officers, security for,
            615, 619, 620
    historical development, 602
    illegal purpose, existing for, 611
    inspection of affairs, 646
    inspector—
        appointment, 646
        powers, 646
    instrument needed to carry out objec-
        tives of society, 615
    investment by, 613, 624
    limited liability, 613
    liquidation, 653
        certificate of transfer of assets, 653
    loans, 613, 622
    managers, 613
    meetings, procedure at, 613
    member—
        death of—
            with a nomination, 627
            without a nomination, 628
        mental disorder of, 629
    members—
        advances to, 615, 623
        debt due from, 625
    membership—
        age restriction, 615
        formed by two or more societies join-
            ing, 606
        intestate member, 620
        mental incapacity of member, 618, 620

References are to paragraphs

Industrial and provident society—
contd
membership—*contd*
  minimum, 606
    number falling below, 611
  necessary requirements, 618
  register of, 618
  rights of members, 618
  shareholdings, 618
    maximum and minimum, 613, 621
    prerequisite to membership, as, 606
  termination, 613, 618
  terms of admission, 613
name—
  offences in relation to, 655
  rules as to, 613
nomination, 613, 620
  death, on, 627
  meaning, 626
  mental disorder of member, 629
objects of, 613
offences—
  dissolution of society, in relation to,
    655
  duration, 654
  false returns, making, 655
  falsification of documents, 655
  generally, 655
  inadequate information, provision of,
    655
  name, in relation to, 655
  officers, liability, 654
  penalties, 654, 655
  rules, fraudulent issue, 655
  society property, in relation to, 655
officers, 613, 619
  appointment, 619
  dismissal, 619
  funds, in possession of, 615, 619
  offences, liability for, 654
  powers, 619
  qualification, 619
ownership or tenancy of land, prohib-
    ition on, 615
profits of, application, 613
property held in trust for society, 610
property, offences in relation to, 655
purpose, 601
receivership unavailable to, 641
registered office, 613
registrar, abuse of discretion, 610
registration, 604, 606, 610
  acknowledgement, 610
  cancellation, 611
    appeal against, 611
  documents to be lodged, 610
  fraud, by, 611

Industrial and provident society—
contd
registration—*contd*
  mistake, by, 611
  property held in trust for society, 610
  recording requirements, 610
  refusal, appeal against, 610
  registrable society, 607
  requirements for, 610
  signatories, 610
  society no longer qualified for, 611
  suspension, 611
    appeal against, 611
registration area, 605
rules, 612–617, 613
  amendment, 616
  audit, 613
  books, inspection of, 615
  borrowing powers, 613
  committee, 613
  constitution and byelaws, 612
  copies to be given on request, 614
  disputes, regulation of settlement, 615
  fourteen points, 612, 613
  fraudulent issue of, 655
  funds in possession of officers, security
    for, 615, 620
  instrument needed to carry out objec-
    tives of society, 615
  investment of funds, 613
  managers, 613
  meetings, procedure, 613
  members—
    advances to, 615, 623
    age restriction, 615
    terms of admission, 613
    termination of membership, 613
  model, 612
  name, 613
  objects, 613
  officers, 613
  ownership or tenancy of land, 615
  preparation, 612
  profit, application of, 613
  registered office, 613
  registrar, negotiation with, 612
  seal, use of, 613
  shareholdings, 613
seal, use of, 613
secretary, 619
shareholdings, 606, 613, 618, 621
society no longer meeting its original
    description, 611
source and meaning of title, 606*n*
special meeting, call for, 646
sponsoring organisations, model rules
    supplied by, 612

Industrial and provident society—
contd
subsidiary companies or societies—
group accounts, 633
meaning, 633
supervision, 606
supervisory functions, 604
transfer of engagements to another
society, 649
Insurance
cattle insurance society, *see* CATTLE
INSURANCE SOCIETY
friendly society—
child under ten years, insurance relating to death of, 692, 724
insurance benefits offered by, 686
restrictions on, 687
Investment
industrial and provident society, by, 624

Jewish burial society, 694n
Juvenile friendly society, 729

Land
credit union, ownership, lease or disposal by, 667, 678
friendly society, ownership of, 702
Life assurance
friendly societies, 686
Literature
society promoting, 694n
Loan
credit union, by, 659, 661, 666, 669, 670
friendly society, lending powers, 720
industrial and provident society, to, 622
Loyal Order of Ancient Shepherds,
679n

Marriage
friendly society endowments on, 686
Mental disorder
industrial and provident society member, of, 629
Mental incapacity
industrial and provident society, member of, 618, 620
Minor
friendly society membership, 704
Music
society promoting, 694n

National insurance
introduction of, 679
Nomination
friendly society—
certification, 724

Nomination—*contd*
friendly society—*contd*
marriage, effect of, 722
payment on death, 723
power to nominate, 722
revocation, 722
industrial and provident society, 613,
620, 626–629
death, procedure on—
with a nomination, 627
without a nomination, 628
mental disorder of member, 629
meaning, 626

Old people's home society, 694
friendly societies legislation, 601
friendly society, as, 679n, 685
valuations exemption, 717

Party political association
community benefit society, as, 609
Pensions
friendly societies, 689

Receivership
industrial and provident societies, un-
available to, 641
Registrar, 604
Assistant Registrar for Scotland, *see*
ASSISTANT REGISTRAR FOR SCOTLAND
Chief Registrar of Friendly Societies, 604
conduct of business rules, powers as
to, 691
credit unions, powers in relation to, 674–
677
Rest centre
provision of, 694n
Restrictive trade practices
co-operative societies, 614, 617
**Rochdale Society of Equitable Pion-
eers**, 607, 607n
**Royal Commission on Friendly
Societies and Benefit Building
Societies**, 602

Savings society, 694n
Science
society promoting, 694n
Shop club
registration, 680n
Sport
society promoting, 694n

Taxation
credit unions, 659

Taxation—*contd*
friendly societies, exemptions, 687, 689, 690
Thrift society or club, 694*n*
registration, 680*n*

Unemployment
friendly society member, assistance to, 694*n*
friendly society payments on, 686

Winding up
credit union, 677
Women's institute
community benefit society, as, 609
Working men's club
friendly societies legislation, 601
friendly society, as, 679, 679*n*, 685
meaning, 694
valuations exemption, 717

INSURANCE

Accident
meaning, 844
Accountant
insurance intermediary, 811
Advertising
annuity policy, 810
linked long-term insurance, 810
Agreed value policy
meaning, 888
Annuity policy
advertisement of, 810
Financial Services Act, application of, 807
friendly society, 810
Assignation
assignatus utitur jure auctoris, 846
donatio mortis causa, 847
form and wording, 847
intimation to insurer, necessity for, 847
life policy, 854
policy, of, 845, 846
rights under policy, of, 845, 846
subrogation compared, 894
valid, prerequisites of, 847
written, must be, 847
Association of British Insurers (ABI)
Code of Practice for Intermediaries other than Registered Brokers, 815
Statement of General Insurance Practice, 816, 861
  proposal forms, 824, 867
    materiality, test of, 867, 872
    notification of loss, 881
    warranties, 873
  renewal notices, 825
Statement of Long-term Insurance Practice, 816, 861
  materiality, test of, 867, 872
  notification of loss, 881
  proposal forms, 824, 867
  warranties, 873

Average rule
insured's duty to account, 903

Banker
insurance intermediary, 811
Bankruptcy
Third Party (Rights Against Insurers) Act 1930, application of, 904–910
Building society
insurance intermediary, 811

Capital redemption contract
Financial Services Act, application of, 807
Carrier or custodier of goods
insurable interest in goods carried, 852
Cash
insurance premium payment by, 833
Causation
insurance claims, 879
proximate clause, 879
Cautionary obligation
insurance compared, 802
Cheque
insurance premium payment by, 833
Child
parents' insurable interest in life of, 853
Claim
agreed value policy, 888
average clause, 893
causation, and, 879
excess clause, 891
franchise clause, 892
general principles, 880
loss—
  betterment, allowance for, 886
  indemnity principle, 885, 886
    contractual variation, 887–893
  limit on, 886
    value of item lost higher than, 886

References are to paragraphs

Claim—*contd*
loss—*contd*
notification of—
by whom made, 883
place for notification to be given, 882
time limits, 881
partial, 886
particulars and proof of, 884
recoverable, generally, 885, 886
repairs, cost of, 886
marine insurance, causation, 879
reinstatement clause, 890
replacement value policy, 889
subrogation, *see* SUBROGATION
time limit, 881
Company
subrogation, 905
Consumer protection
insurance intermediaries other than registered brokers, 815
Insurance Ombudsman Bureau, 816
Personal Insurance Arbitration Service, 817
Policyholders Protection Board, 814
Contract
insurance as, 802
insurance contract, *see* INSURANCE
Contribution
double insurance—
generally, 913
liability, contract terms excluding or limiting, 916
notification of, contract terms requiring, 915
prerequisites for contribution, 914
effect, 912
indemnity insurance, 912
issue between two or more insurers, as, 912
prerequisites for, 914
same risk and interest, policies must cover, 914
valid and enforceable, policies must be, 914
Cooling-off period
insurance contract, 819–821
Cover note
broker with authority to supply, 825
cancellation, 825
indemnity insurance, 818, 825
insurance contracts, 825
oral, 825
policy terms—
requiring immediate notice, 825
unusual, 825

Cover note—*contd*
renewable indemnity insurance, 825
retrospective cover, 825
temporary cover, 825

Death
whole life policy, 804
Debtor
debtor's life insured by creditor, 854
Department of Trade and Industry
insurance company—
authorisation of, 807
intervention into business of, 808
Direct debit
insurance premium payment by, 833
Disclosure, duty of
See MISREPRESENTATION AND NON-DISCLOSURE
Double insurance
generally, 913
liability, contract terms excluding or limiting, 916
marine insurance, 913*n*
notification of, contract terms requiring, 915
prerequisites for contribution, 914

Employer's association
authorisation, 807
Endowment policy
See LIFE ASSURANCE
Excepted perils clause
effect, 837
subrogation, 909
Excess clause
meaning, 891

Fidelity bond
contract, insurance business, as, 802
Fidelity guarantee
uberrimae fidei contract, as, 802
Financial Intermediaries, Managers and Brokers Regulatory Association (FIMBRA)
promotion and marketing of insurance products, 809
regulation of insurance intermediaries, 812
Financial Services (Cancellation) Rules 1988 ... 819, 821
Fire insurance
indemnity insurance, as, 804
reinstatement clause, 890
First-party cover
meaning, 805

Franchise clause
meaning, 892
Friendly society
advertisement by, 810
authorisation, 807

Gift
insured, to, from party responsible for
    loss, 902
Guarantee
manufacturers', insurance compared,
    802

Heritable property insurance
heritable subjects, interest in passing to
    purchaser, 850, 850n
  subrogation, 900
reinstatement clause, 890
Hire
contract of, insurable interest of goods
    under, 852
Honour policy
marine insurance, 848
Household insurance
excess clause, 891
indemnity insurance, as, 804

Indemnity insurance
contribution, see CONTRIBUTION
cover note, 825
fire insurance, 804
household and property cover, 804
insurable interest, time of loss, 855
marine cover, 804
meaning, 804
motor insurance, 804
recoverable loss, 885, 886
renewable contract—
  cover notes, 825
  notice of renewal, 825
subrogation, see SUBROGATION
temporary cover, 818, 825
uncertainty, event insured against must
    contain element of, 804
Insurable interest
advantage or benefit, 849, 850
  expectation of, 850
carrier or custodier of goods, 852
child's life, in, 853
common law, 848
definition, 849
essential element of insurance contract,
    as, 848
factual expectation test, 850n
heritable subjects, interest in passing to
    purchaser, 850, 850n, 900

Insurable interest—contd
hirer of goods, 852
indemnity insurance, 855
leases of property, 852
life assurance, 853
marine insurance, 855
nature of, 849–857
prerequisite to insurance contract, as, 802
property, 849, 851
  possession of, 852
statutory provisions, 848
tenant under lease, 852
time and—
  insuring, time of, 856
  loss, time of, 855, 856
  prospective cover, 857
  retrospective cover, 857
  when policy effected, 854
Insurance
broker—
  code of conduct, 813
  complaints against, investigation of,
    813
  disciplinary committee, 813
  entitlement to term, 813
  financial criteria to be satisfied, 813
  independent intermediary or broker,
    806, 811, 812
    code of practice, 815
  Insurance Brokers Registration Coun-
    cil, 809
  list of those carrying on business as,
    813
  negligence, compensation fund for
    victims of, 813
  qualifications required, 813, 813n
  register of, 813
  regulation under Insurance Brokers
    (Registration) Act 1977 . . . 813
  temporary cover, authority to supply,
    825
  title of, entitlement to use, 811
causation, recovery dependent on, 879
classification, 803–805
company, see INSURANCE COMPANY
complaints, Insurance Ombudsman
    Bureau, 816
consumer protection, see CONSUMER PRO-
    TECTION
contract—
  agreed value policy, 888
  average clause, 893
  basis of contract clause, 823
  breach of warranty, 835
  consensus in idem, 818
  counter-offer, 818

References are to paragraphs

Insurance—*contd*
contract—*contd*
cover dependent upon payment of first
    premium, 818, 834
disclosure, duty of, *see* MISREPRESEN-
    TATION AND NON-DISCLOSURE
double insurance—
    terms excluding or limiting liability,
        916
    terms requiring notification of, 915
duration of cover, agreement as to, 818
enforcement of, 807
excess clause, 891
formation of—
    cover note, 825
    Financial Services (Cancellation)
        Rules 1988 . . . 819, 821
    Insurance Companies Regulations
        1981 . . . 819, 820
    law of contract, generally, 818
    proposal form, 822–824
    statutory notices and cooling-off
        periods, 819–821
franchise clause, 892
illegality, 835
indemnity principle, contractual vari-
    ation, 887–893
insurable interest, requirement of, 848
insurer unauthorised, where, 835
material facts—
    disclosure of, 823, 824
    non-disclosure of, 835
    See also MISREPRESENTATION AND
        NON-DISCLOSURE
material terms, agreement as to, 818
misrepresentation, *see* MISREPRESEN-
    TATION AND NON-DISCLOSURE
non-disclosure, *see* MISREPRESENTATION
    AND NON-DISCLOSURE
non-renewable, duration of duty of
    disclosure, 863
offer and acceptance, 818
    basis of contract clause, 823
oral, 828
premium, agreement as to, 818
prospective cover, 857
reinstatement clause, 890
renewable—
    duration of duty of disclosure, 863
    premiums, payment of, 834
replacement value policy, 889
risk—
    risk to be covered, agreement as to,
        818
    unjust enrichment, doctrine of, 835
sum insured, agreement as to, 818

Insurance—*contd*
contract—*contd*
suspensive condition, 818
term descriptive of risk, 878
uberrimae fidei, as contract of, 802, 858
unauthorised insurance business, 807
    enforcement of, 807
void—
    return of premium, 835
    void ab initio, 835
voidable, return of premium, 835
warranty, *see* WARRANTY
contract, as, 802
contribution, *see* CONTRIBUTION
cooling-off periods, 819–821
definition, 802
direct obligation imposed by, 802
double, 913–916
English law and practice, influence of,
    801
exchange, as type of, 801, 801*n*
first-party cover, 805
general business—
    classes of, 807
    company insolvency, 814
historical development in Scotland, 801
indemnity insurance, *see* INDEMNITY
    INSURANCE
insurable interest, *see* INSURABLE INTEREST
intermediary—
    accountant, as, 811
    banker, as, 811
    bonus or commission paid to, disclos-
        ure of, 812
    broker, *see* broker *above*
    building society, as, 811
    cold-calling, 812
    independent, 806, 811, 812
        code of practice, 815
        volume commission or bonus
            received by, 812
    Insurance Brokers (Registration) Act
        1977 in relation to, 813
    other than registered broker, code of
        practice, 815
    polarisation, 811, 812
    regulation—
        Financial Services Act 1986, under,
            812
        Insurance Brokers (Registration)
            Act 1977, under, 81
    regulation of, 806, 811–813
    solicitor, as, 811
    tied agent, 806, 811
        appointed representative of author-
            ised principal, 812

References are to paragraphs

Insurance—*contd*
intermediary—*contd*
  tied agent—*contd*
    breach of rules by, responsibility
      for, 812
    code of practice, 815
investment business, 807, 812
investment fraud, 810
life assurance, *see* LIFE ASSURANCE
long-term business, classes of, 807
marine, *see* MARINE INSURANCE
market manipulation, 810
marketing of insurance products, *see*
  PROMOTION AND MARKETING OF
  INSURANCE PRODUCTS
misleading statements, 810
misrepresentation, *see* MISREPRESEN-
  TATION AND NON-DISCLOSURE
money or money's worth, benefit
  received must be, 802
non-disclosure, *see* MISREPRESENTATION
  AND NON-DISCLOSURE
outwith insurer's control, event insured
  must be, 802
overinsurance—
  contribution, *see* CONTRIBUTION
  double insurance, 913
policy—
  agreed value, 888
  ambiguity in, 837, 842
  assignation, *see* ASSIGNATION
  average clause, 893
  cancellation before stipulated date of
    expiry, 836
  classification, 829
  constitution and proof, 828
  construction and interpretation—
    accident, meaning of, 844
    ambiguities, 837, 842
    construing policy as a whole, 843
    context of words, 837, 840
    excepted perils clause, 837
    generally, 837
    grammar, 837, 841
    ordinary meaning of word, 837, 838
    technical words, 837, 839
  contents, 827
  duration, 836
  embodiment of terms on which con-
    tract provided, as, 826
  excepted perils clause, 837
  excess clause, 891
  expiry, 836
  franchise clause, 892
  oral contract, 828
  premium, *see* PREMIUM

Insurance—*contd*
policy—*contd*
  reinstatement clause, 890
  replacement value, 889
  terms—
    immediate notice, requiring, 825
    unusual, contained in, 825
  unvalued, 829, 831
  valued, 829, 830
  warranty, 874. *See also* WARRANTY
  writing, whether in, 828
premium, *see* PREMIUM
promotion of insurance products, *see*
  PROMOTION AND MARKETING OF
  INSURANCE PRODUCTS
proposal form, *see* PROPOSAL FORM
provision of services—
  generally, 806
  independent intermediary or broker,
    806, 811, 812
  regulation, 806–808
  statutory controls, 806
  tied agent, 806, 811, 812, 815
  See also intermediary *above*
purpose of, 802
recognised professional bodies, *see* REC-
  OGNISED PROFESSIONAL BODIES
retrospective cover, 857
risk allocation, other forms distinguished, 802
schemes intended to confer benefit on
  others, 802
self-regulatory organisations, *see* SELF-
  REGULATORY ORGANISATIONS
statutory controls, 806
statutory notices, 819–821
subrogation, *see* SUBROGATION
third-party cover, 805
tied agent, 806, 811
  appointed representative of authorised
    principal, 812
  breach of rules by, responsibility for,
    812
  code of practice, 815
uncertainty, event insured must contain
  element of, 802
under-insurance, 893, 903
undervaluation, 903
Unfair Contract Terms Act, exclusion of
  insurance contracts from, 802
**Insurance Brokers Registration
  Council**
recognised professional body, as, 809
**Insurance Companies Regulations
  1981** ... 819, 820

References are to paragraphs

Insurance company
assets must be sufficient to meet liabilities, 807
authorisation, 807
  conditions for, 807
  failure to commence business after, 807
  necessity for, 802
  revocation, 807
collapse, consequences of, 806
controllers, 807
general business, long-term business finances to be kept separate, 807
head office outside EEC member states, 807
insolvency, Policyholders Protection Board powers, 814
Insurance Companies Act, failure to comply with, 807
intervention by Department of Trade and Industry, 808
investment business, 812
  authorisation to carry on, 807
liquidation, 807
long-term business—
  company liquidation, 807
  general business finances to be kept separate, 807
  investment business, 807
margin of solvency, requirement to maintain, 807
regulation, 807, 808
  statutory controls, 806
share capital, 807
unauthorised business, conduct of, 807
Insurance Ombudsman Bureau
awards made by, 816
decision binding on insurer, 816
fair and commonsense conclusion, 816
good insurance practice, obligation to take into account, 816
who may complain to, 816
Investment fraud
market manipulation, 810

Knock for knock agreement
subrogation, 897, 897*n*

Lease
property under, insurable interest, 852
Life assurance
annuity contract, 807
assignation, 846, 847, 854
capital redemption contract, 807
company insolvency, 814
contingency insurance, as, 804

Life assurance—*contd*
cover dependent on payment of first premium, 818
debtor's life insured by creditor, 854
disclosure, duration of duty of, 863
endowment policy, 804
  meaning, 804
Financial Services Act, application of, 804
insurable interest, 853, 854
  requirement of, 848
investment business, 807
investments linked to, 804
life assurance, 854
marketing, regulation of, 812
non-disclosure, 860
recoverable loss, 885
temporary cover, 825
uncertainty, event insured against must contain element of, 804
whole life policy, meaning, 804
Life Assurance and Unit Trust Regulatory Organisation (LAUTRO)
promotion and marketing of insurance products, 809
regulation of insurance intermediaries, 812
Liquidation
Third Party (Rights Against Insurers) Act 1930, application of, 904–910
Lloyds of London
authorisation, 807
Loss
claim for, *see* CLAIM
gift to insured from responsible party, 902
indemnification for—
  compensation for distinguished, 903
  subrogation as measure of, 900–903
subrogation, *see* SUBROGATION

Maintenance agreement
insurance compared, 802
Marine insurance
agreed value policy, 888
assignation of policy, 846, 846*n*, 847
average principle, 893
claims—
  causation, 879
  proximate clause, 879
double insurance, 913*n*
historical development, 801, 801*n*
'honour' policy, 848
indemnity insurance, as, 804
insurable interest—
  must exist at time of loss, 855

Marine insurance—*contd*
insurable intererst—*contd*
  not existing when contract made, 855
    requirement of, 848
interest or no interest policy, 848
loss, betterment, 886*n*
materiality, test of, 869
non-disclosure, 860
policies proof of interest (ppi), 835, 848
uberrimae fidei doctrine, 858, 858*n*
valued policies, 830
warranty, 874
writing, must be in, 828
Market rigging, 810
Material facts
disclosure of, 823, 824
Misrepresentation and non-disclosure
basis of contract clause, 823
disclosure, duty of—
  continuing, 863
  duration, 863
  material facts, 864
  new material fact, discovery of—
    after completion of proposal form, 863
    after policy issued, 863
    renewable contracts, 863
  positive duty of both parties, 858
generally, 858
immaterial facts, warranties, 873. *See also* WARRANTY
information which is not requested, 858
materiality—
  ABI statements of practice, 867
  doubtful, 865
  expert evidence as to, 864
  immaterial facts, 865
  material facts, 864
    waiver of disclosure, 866
  test of, 864
    ABI statements of practice, 872
    generally, 868
    marine insurance, 869
    motor vehicle insurance, 869
    reasonable insured, of, 871
    reasonable insurer, of, 870
    statutory, 869
misrepresentation—
  actionable, 859
  as basis of contract clause, 823
  contract induced by, 859
  insurer, by, 859
  material, 859
  meaning, 858*n*

Misrepresentation and non-disclosure—*contd*
non-disclosure—
  common law, 860
  disclosure to intermediary not passed on, 862
  extent of, 860
  life assurance, 860
  marine insurance, 860
  meaning, 858*n*
  motor vehicle insurance, 860
  statements of opinion, 861
remedy for, 858
Motor vehicle insurance
excess clause, 891
indemnity insurance, as, 804
knock for knock agreement, 897, 897*n*
materiality, test of, 869
non-disclosure, 860
reinstatement clause, 890
renewal notice, 825
subrogation, 911
temporary cover, 818
third party rights, 911

Non-disclosure
See MISREPRESENTATION AND NON-DISCLOSURE

Performance bond
contract, insurance business, as, 802
Personal accident insurance
recoverable loss, 885
Personal Insurance Arbitration Service
decisions of, 817
membership, 817
Policyholders Protection Board
establishment and purpose, 814
insolvent company's business, arrangements for, 814
powers, 814
Premium
agreement as to, 818
cash or cheque, payment by, 833
cover dependent upon payment of first, 818, 834
days of grace, 834
direct debit, payment by, 833
duration of policy, 836
form of, 833
instalments, payment by, 833
insurer's obligation to pay, 832
promissory note, payment by, 833
renewable cover, 834

References are to paragraphs

Premium—*contd*
repayment, 835
  breach of warranty, where, 835
  illegal contract, where, 835
  insurer unauthorised, where, 835
  void or voidable contract, 835
  where insurer ran no risk, 835
standing order, payment by, 833
time for payment, 834
Promissory note
insurance premium payment by, 833
Promotion and marketing of insurance products
advertising—
  annuity policy, 810
  linked long-term insurance, 810
bonus or commission paid to intermediary, 812
cold-calling, 812
contravention of rules, penalties for, 810
generally, 809
investment fraud, 810
market manipulation, 810
misleading statements, 810
regulation, 809
Securities and Investments Board, regulation by, 809
Property
indemnity insurance, 804
insurable interest in, 849, 851, 852
ownership, insurable interest, 851
Proposal form
Association of British Insurers statements of insurance practice, 824
basis of the contract clause, 823
form and content, 822
misrepresentation and non-disclosure, *see* MISREPRESENTATION AND NON-DISCLOSURE
warranty, *see* WARRANTY

Reasonable precautions clause
subrogation, 909
Recognised professional bodies (RPBs)
Insurance Brokers Registration Council, 809
promotion and marketing of insurance products, regulation of, 809
Reinstatement clause
meaning, 890
Renewal notice
temporary cover, 825
Replacement value policy
meaning, 889

Risk allocation
insurance distinguished from other forms, 802

Securities and Investments Board (SIB)
promotion and marketing of insurance products, regulation of, 809
Self-regulatory organisations (SROs)
promotion and marketing of insurance products, regulation of, 809
regulation of insurance intermediaries, 812
See also FINANCIAL INTERMEDIARIES, MANAGERS AND BROKERS REGULATORY ASSOCIATION; LIFE ASSURANCE AND UNIT TRUST REGULATORY ORGANISATION
Solicitor
insurance intermediary, 811
Standing order
insurance premium payment by, 833
Statutory notice
insurance contract, 819–821
Subrogation
ambiguous subrogation clause, 901
assignation compared, 894
company insured, where, 905, 906
contract silent as to, 901
control of litigation, 899
corollary of indemnity principle, as, 894
enforceability, 897
excepted perils clause, 909
individual insured, where, 905
insured must not prejudice right of, 898
knock for knock agreement, 897, 897*n*
life assurance, no application to, 894
measure of indemnity, as—
  basic principle, 900
  contractual variation of principle, 901
  gifts, 902
  insured's duty to account, 903
motor vehicle insurance, 911
'pay to be paid' clause, 907
purpose of, 895
reasonable precautions clause, 909
right arising automatically, 894
right dependent on settlement of claim, 896
statutory—
  contracting out, 907
  generally, 904
  insured, existence of, 906
  insurer, defences available to, 909

References are to paragraphs

Subrogation—*contd*
statutory—*contd*
  insurer, defences available to—*contd*
    restrictions on, 910
  insurer and insured, arrangements
    between, 908
  motor vehicle insurance, third party
    rights, 911
  Third Parties (Rights against Insurers)
    Act 1930, application of, 905–910
windfall profits, 900, 901, 901*n*
written notice of accident or claim,
  requirement to give, 909

Temporary cover
indemnity insurance, 825
life assurance, 825
Tenant
insurable interest of, 852
Third party
insured's right to sue, 898
motor vehicle insurance, 911
subrogation, *see* SUBROGATION
third-party cover, meaning, 805
Tied agent
provision of insurance services through,
  806
  appointed representative of authorised
    principal, 812
  breach of rules, responsibility for, 812
  code of practice, 815
Trade union
authorisation, 807

Uberrimae fidei
insurance contract as contract of, 802,
  858
Unjust enrichment
doctrine of, insurance premiums, 835
Unvalued insurance policy, 829, 831

Valued insurance policy, 829, 830
**Vehicle repair or recovery services,
  body providing**
authorisation not required, 807

Warranty
ABI statements of insurance practice, 877
breach of, 875
  return of premium, 835
categories, 876
creation of, 874
effect, 875
future facts, 876
immaterial facts, non-disclosure of covered by, 873
implication, arising by virtue of, 874
marine insurance, 874
opinion, of, 876
past or present facts, 876
policy, in, 874
proposal form, 874
purpose of, 873
terms descriptive of risk distinguished,
  878
use of term, 878
Whole life policy
See LIFE ASSURANCE

INTEREST

Arbitration award
interest on, 1035

Business charge
meaning, 1008, 1011

Cash advance
See LOAN
Child
legitim, claim for, interest on sum, 1031
  sum advanced during lifetime of
    deceased, 1031
Compound interest, 1038
contractual stipulation, 1002
Contract
breach of, interest as damages for, 1018–
  1020

Contract—*contd*
credit, implied terms as to, 1011
interest stipulated by, 1001
  agreed rate, where, 1037
  courts, enforcement by, 1002
  credit, implied terms as to, 1011
  express contract, 1002
  fluctuating interest rates, 1004
  general law, implication by, 1007
  implied contract terms, 1005
    credit, as to, 1011
    heritage, sales of, 1010
    sale, contract of, 1009
    types of, 1005
  interest rates, 1002
    legal rate or contract rate of interest,
      1003

References are to paragraphs

Contract—*contd*
interest stipulated by—*contd*
  loans, 1008
  mutuality, 1013
  particular facts, implication on basis
    of, 1006
  sale, contract of, 1007, 1009
    heritage, sales of, 1009, 1010
    implied contract terms, 1009
    moveable property, 1009
  wrongful withholding of sums due
    under, interest payable on, 1012
Credit
implied contract terms as to, 1011
Creditor
interest payable to, *see* INTEREST

Damages
breach of contract, for, interest as, 1018–
  1020
interest on
  date allowable from, 1032
  death or personal injury, awarded for,
    1034
  discretion of court, 1032
  generally, 1032
  interest on interest, 1032
  lump sum damages, 1033
  past or future loss, 1032
  taxation of, 1034
Death
damages, interest on, 1034
Debt
open account, 1011
Debtor
formal demand for payment, 1014–1017
interest—
  as compensation paid by, 1001
  See also INTEREST
intimation to, 1014, 1016
judicial demand for payment, 1014, 1015
wrongful withholding of sum, due to—
  intimation to debtor, 1014, 1016
  judicial demand for payment, 1014,
    1015
Decree
date from which due, 1032
discretion of court, 1032
interest on, 1032

Executry funds
interest on, 1031

Heritage
contract of sale, interest implied, 1009,
  1010

Income tax
damages, interest on, 1034
Interest
arbitration award, on, 1035
business charges, 1011
compound, 1038
  contractual stipulation, 1002
contract, breach of, interest as damages
  for, 1018–1020
contractual stipulation, 1001
  agreed rate, where, 1037
  contract rate or legal rate of interest,
    1003
  express contract, interest due by, 1002
  fluctuating rates of interest, 1004
  implied contract term—
    credit, as to, 1011
    heritage, sales of, 1010
    moveable property, sales of, 1009
  implied contract term, interest due by,
    1005
  general law, on basis of, 1007
  particular facts, on basis of, 1006
  types of implied term, 1005
  loans, 1008
  sale, contracts of, 1009
    heritage, sales of, 1009, 1010
    moveable property, 1009
  terms of, 1002
damages, on—
  date allowable from, 1032
  death or personal injury, awarded for,
    1034
  discretion of court, 1032
  generally, 1032
  interest on interest, 1032
  lump sum damages, 1033
  taxation of, 1034
date from which due, 1001
  contractual stipulation, 1002
  damages and decrees, 1032
  judicial demand, 1015
decrees, on, 1032
delayed payment, as result of, 1001
error, sum paid in, interest on, 1012,
  1012n
ex lege, 1001
ex mora, 1001
ex pacto, 1001
executry funds, 1031
fixed, contractual stipulation, 1002
formal demand for payment, 1014–1017
grounds for which awarded, 1001
interest on, 1032
intimation to debtor, 1014, 1016
judicial demand for payment, 1014, 1015

References are to paragraphs

Interest—*contd*
legal rights in succession, sums payable
     in satisfaction of, 1001
loans, interest on general implied, 1002
meaning, 1001
moveable property—
     contracts of sale, 1009
     deprivation of, interest payable for,
          1021
open account, 1011
principal sum—
     calculation of, contractual stipulation,
          1002
     decree for payment, 1003
     judicial demand, 1015
     parasitic upon claim for, 1001
rate, 1001
     appropriately calculated, 1037
     contract rate or legal rate, 1003
     contractual agreement, where, 1037
     court, fixed by, 1037
     express contract, interest due by, 1002
     fluctuating, 1004
          contractual stipulation, 1002
     intimation to debtor, 1016
     legal, 1037
     trust funds, 1023
     variation or substitution, 1003
rules as to, 1001
statute, by operation of, 1001, 1012
tribunal award, on, 1036
trust funds, 1001
     advances to beneficiaries, 1022, 1030
          ultra vires, 1030
     delay in payment, 1029
     failure of trust, 1029
     rate specified, 1023
     right to interest, implied, 1023
     trust deed, interest due by, 1022, 1023
     trustees' liability for interest, 1022,
          1024–1029
          terms of deed impossible to carry
               out, 1023
wrongful withholding of sum, due to,
     1001
     breach of contract, interest as damages
          for, 1018–1020
     contractual debts, 1012
     date payable from, 1012, 1014, 1016,
          1017
     equitable principle, as, example, 1017
     formal demand for payment, 1014–
          1017
     generally, 1012
     justifiable withholding, 1013

Interest—*contd*
wrongful withholding of sum, due to—
     contd
     'open accounts', 1014, 1016
     quantum meruit, sums due, 1012
     rent, 1012
     rules, 1012
     statute, debts due under, 1012
     sums paid in error, on, 1012, 1012*n*
     wrongful withholding, what consti-
          tutes, 1013, 1014

IOU
meaning, 1008
repayment, 1008

Loan
business charges, 1008
cash advance, as, 1008
interest on, 1008
     contractual stipulation, 1002
     general implication, 1002, 1007, 1008
IOU, treatment of, 1008
meaning, 1008

Moveable property
contract of sale, interest implied, 1009
deprivation of, interest payable for, 1021

Open account
meaning, 1011
wrongful withholding of interest on,
     1016, 1017

Personal injury
damages, interest on, 1034

Quantum meruit
wrongful withholding of sums due,
     interest payable on, 1012

Rent
wrongful withholding of sums due,
     interest payable on, 1012

Sale, contract of
See CONTRACT
Spouse
jus relicti vel relictae, claim for, interest on
     sum, 1031
Succession
interest on sum due as legal right in, 1031
intestate, 1031

Taxation
damages, interest on, 1034

References are to paragraphs

Tribunal award
interest on, 1036
Trust
failure of, 1029
fund—
    interest due on, 1001
        advances to beneficiaries, 1022, 1030
            ultra vires, 1030
        delay in payment, 1029
        rate specified, 1023
        trust deed, interest due by, 1022, 1023
        trustees' duty to invest, 1025
        trustees' liability for interest, 1022, 1024–1029

Trust—*contd*
fund—*contd*
    loss by *ultra vires* actions, trustees' liability, 1026
    no trust funds available for investment, where, 1025
    right to interest, implied, 1023
    trustees' liability for interest—
        co-trustees, liability for, 1028
        terms of deed impossible to carry out, 1023
    trustees using for own purposes, 1027

Wrongful withholding *See* INTEREST

INTERPRETATION OF STATUTES, DEEDS AND OTHER INSTRUMENTS

Absurdity
construction of Act to avoid—
    generally, 1124, 1125
    golden rule, 1109
    ut res magis valeat quam pereat principle, 1124
Acts of Parliament
See STATUTE
Adoption order
testamentary writing affected by, 1218
Affidavit
interpretation, 1262
Ambiguity
construction of deed, in, 1223
construction of statute to avoid, 1113, 1114, 1124, 1163
Annuity
alimentary, 1264

Blood relation
meaning, 1268
Bond
blanks in, 1228
Boundary
bounding charter, 1239
bounding title, 1239
description in conveyance, 1239
judicially construed, 1239
lateral, 1239
measurements, 1240
new, creation of, 1240
plans—
    colour, use of, 1240

Boundary—*contd*
plans—*contd*
    conflicting with boundary, 1240
    registration, 1240
Brussels International Convention Relating to the Arrest of Seagoing Ships
travaux préparatoires, 1154
Burden
presumption against enactment imposing, 1131

Canal
tow path included in, 1239
Casus omissus
not to be supplied by courts, 1107
Children
adopted, 1218, 1268
meaning, 1268
wills, interpretation of—
    conditio si institutus sine liberis decesserit, 1265
    conditio si testator sine liberis decesserit principle, 1265
    legal rights, 1264
Church seat
pertinent, as, 1242
Class
bequests to, 1268
Clerical error
deed, interpretation of, 1233
    rectification, 1234

Co-partnership, contracts of
interpretation, 1261
Common law
presumption against alteration by statute, 1126
Conditions, deeds of
construction and interpretation, 1260
Consolidation Acts
interpretation and construction of statutes, 1148, 1158
Construction
deed, of, *see* DEED
statute, of, *see* STATUTE
Contemporanea expositio
ancient statutes, 1112
modern statutes, 1113
Contract
naturalia as part of agreement, 1215
Convention
international, use as aid in construction
of statute, 1153
Conveyance
feu writ, 1237, 1244
implied terms, 1235
interpretation—
a coelo usque ad centrum principle, 1243
boundaries, description of, 1239
bounding charter, 1239
bounding title, 1239
measurements, 1240
new boundaries, creation of, 1240
plans, 1240
sea, 1239
See also BOUNDARY
disposition, 1237
description of subjects conveyed,
1238
dispone, meaning, 1237
feuduty—
imposition of, 1249
redemption, 1249
incorporeal rights, conditions involving, 1244
minerals, 1242, 1243
pertinents, 1242
plans, 1240
boundaries, conflict with, 1240
colours used in, 1240
measurements, 1240
registration, 1240
real burdens and conditions—
constitution, principles for, 1246
creation, 1245
enforcement, 1248
generally, 1245
interpretation, 1247

Conveyance—*contd*
interpretation—*contd*
real burdens and conditions—*contd*
real burden, meaning, 1245
real condition or restriction, meaning, 1245
reddendo, 1249
servitudes, of, 1242
statutory descriptions, 1241
subjects conveyed, description of,
1238
warrandice, 1250, 1255
pre-emption clause, 1244
redemption clause, 1244
where no term of entry specified, 1218
Conveyancing practice
as aid to interpretation of statute, 1161
Crime
offence distinguished, 1140
Crown
application of enactments to, 1212
Curator
deed by minor who has, 1229
De minimus non curat praetor
meaning, 1170
Declaratory Acts
retrospectivity, 1193
Deed
blank in material part, 1228
date of entry left blank, 1228
incapax, granted by, 1229
interpretation and construction—
adoption order, effect of, 1218
affidavit, 1262
alterations, 1227
pencil, in, 1230
ambiguity, 1215, 1223
blanks, 1228
capacity, 1229
clerical errors, 1233
co-partnership, contract of, 1261
conditions, deed of, 1260
construction as a whole, 1221
contra proferentem construction, 1232
conveyance, *see* CONVEYANCE
creditor's voluntary trust deed, 1262
ejusdem generis, 1224
entail, deed of, 1262
error—
clerical, 1233
rectification, 1234
extrinsic evidence, 1225
factory and commission or power of
attorney, 1262
family arrangement, deed of, 1262
floating charge, 1262

Deed—*contd*
interpretation and construction—*contd*
  foreign language, 1217
  generally, 1213, 1262
  ground annual, contract of, 1262
  holograph writings, 1218
  implied terms, 1235, 1236
    inappropriate implication, 1236
  ink, written in, 1230
  intention, ascertainment, 1216
  inter vivos settlements, 1214, 1262
  invalidating or defeating agreement,
    1215
  land certificate, 1259
  lease, *see* LEASE
  majority, reference to, 1218, 1231
  marriage, contract of, 1262
  meaning of terms which adverse party
    understood, 1215
  minority, reference to, 1218, 1231
  naturalia of particular contract, 1215
  overriding interests, 1218
  parole evidence, 1222, 1225, 1251
  pencil—
    alterations written in, 1230
    deed written in, 1230
  popular sense of words, 1215
  power of attorney, 1262
  prior communications, 1215, 1222
  purpose of, 1214
  renunciation, minute of, 1262
  rules, general, 1214–1234
  sense giving validity and effect to
    agreement, 1215
  servitude, of, 1262
  statute, effect of, 1218
  statutory declaration, 1262
  statutory meanings, 1231
  technical terms, 1215, 1217
  testing clause, use of, 1226, 1228
  trade usage, 1215
  typewritten, 1230
  usage, 1215, 1220
  waiver, minute of, 1262
  will, *see* WILL
  words, generally, 1215, 1219
land, conveying interest in—
  implied terms, 1235
  See also CONVEYANCE
later words, authentication, 1228
minor, granted by, 1229, 1231
nonage, capacity of person in, 1229, 1231
printed form, problems arising from use
  of, 1228
probative, blank left in, 1228
pupil, granted by, 1229

Deed—*contd*
Sunday, execution on, 1229
warrandice, implied terms, 1235
witnesses, incompetent, 1229
Dependants
term too vague to receive effect in will,
  1268
Dictionary
construction of statute, as aid to, 1152
Discretionary enactment
cases where found not to be mandatory,
  1180
generally, 1179
whether mandatory enactment may be,
  1175
Disposition
interpretation, 1237
Distance, measurement of
Interpretation Act 1978 rules as to, 1209
Document
prescribed form, 1178

***Ejusdem generis* rule**
statute, use in construction of—
  generally, 1166, 1167
  where inapplicable, 1168
Entail, deed of
interpretation, 1262
European Community
legislation, interpretation, 1205
Expressio unius exclusio alterius
meaning, 1165

Factory and commission
interpretation, 1262
Feu writ
clause prohibiting subinfeudation, 1244
  interpretation, 1237, 1249
Feuduty
clause of obligation of relief, implied
  terms, 1235
implied terms, 1249
imposition of, 1249
redemption, 1249
Financial year
meaning, 1171
Floating charge
interpretation, 1262
Foreshore
meaning, 1239
Forthwith
meaning, 1174

Gender
Interpretation Act 1978 rules as to, 1207

References are to paragraphs

Government department
explanatory memoranda issued by, as aid
    to interpretation of statute, 1149
Government report
as aid to interpretation of statute, 1149
Grammar
construction of enactments, in, 1104,
    1106
    golden rule, 1109
Ground annual, contract of
interpretation, 1262

Heading
Act of Parliament, in, use in interpret-
    ation, 1138
Heirs
meaning, 1268
Heritable security
interpretation and construction—
    bond of cash credit and disposition in
        security, 1254
    bond and disposition in security, 1254
    brevity and uniformity, aim of, 1255
    charge certificate, 1256
    discharge, 1257
    ex facie absolute disposition, 1254
    Halliday Report, 1254
    personal obligation, clauses relating
        to, 1255
    ranking, clauses relating to, 1255
    registration for execution, clauses
        relating to, 1255
    saving and enabling clauses, 1258
    standard conditions, 1255
    standard security, 1254, 1255
    title deeds, clauses relating to rights to,
        1255
    warrandice, clauses relating to, 1255
    printed form, issue to debtor, 1255
Heydon's Case
rule in, 1115
House
pertinent, as, 1242

Illegitimacy
status of, abolition, 1268
Incapax
deed granted by, 1229
Incorporeal rights
conveyancing, 1244
Injustice
courts' duty to avoid, when interpreting
    statutes, 1114
Intent
construction of statute according to—
    conflicting approaches, 1116, 1117

Intent—*contd*
construction of statute according to—
    contd
    generally, 1116
    section, object of, 1118
Inter vivos **settlement**
interpretation, 1214, 1262
Interpretation
conveyance, of, *see* CONVEYANCE
deed, of, *see* DEED
heritable security of, *see* HERITABLE
    SECURITY
lease, of, *see* LEASE
question of law, as, 1214
statute, of, *see* STATUTE
will, of, *see* WILL
Interpretation Act 1978
distance, measurement of, 1209
gender, rules as to, 1207
generally, 1206
number, rules as to, 1207
person, meaning of, 1211
post, service by, 1208
powers and duties, continuity of, 1210
Intestacy
presumption against, 1267
prior rights, 1264
Irritancy clause
lease, in, 1251
Issue
meaning, 1268

Land
real burdens and conditions transmitted
    with, 1245
Land certificate
map based by reference to Ordnance
    map, 1259
overriding interests, 1259
symbols used in title plan, explanation,
    1259
Lane
boundary on, 1239
Latter-will
interpretation, 1263
Lease
interpretation and construction—
    cardinal elements, 1252
    casualty, payment of, 1251
    consensus in idem, 1252
    construed as a whole, lease must be,
        1251
    contra proferentem, 1251
    definite period of let, 1252
    English form, lease drawn up in, 1251
    extraneous evidence, 1251

Lease—*contd*
interpretation and construction—*contd*
  general principles, 1251
  heritable subject, 1252
  irritancy clause, 1251
  long lease, 1251
  parole proof, 1251
  rent, 1252
  Rent (Scotland) Act 1984 . . . 1253
  termination, 1251
licence agreement, 1252
licence distiguished, 1252
new lease, implied renunciation resulting
   from, 1235
order for possession, 1253
Licence
lease distinguished, 1252
Licence agreement
lease of dwellinghouse, 1252
Liferent
alimentary, 1264
Lowest low-water mark
meaning, 1239

Majority
meaning, 1218, 1268
Mandatory enactment
effect, 1175
generally, 1176
permissive enactment mandatory in
  effect, 1175
statutory requirement held to be discretionary, 1178
statutory requirement held to be mandatory, 1177
where consequence of non-compliance
  not declared, 1175
March stones
boundary between, 1239
Marriage, contract of
interpretation, 1262
Mine
pertinent, as, 1242
Minerals
a coelo usque ad centram principle, 1243
pertinent, as, 1242
where not included in land sale, 1243
Minor
capacity to enter contract or grant deed,
  1229, 1231
Mischief
Heydon's Case, 1115
remedy of, by statute, rules as to, 1115
Month
meaning, 1171

Next of kin
meaning, 1268
Nonage
capacity to enter contract or grant deed,
  1229, 1231
Notice
prescribed form, 1178
Number
Interpretation Act 1978 rules as to, 1207

Offence
crime distinguished, 1140
Omission
Casus omissus not to be supplied by
  courts, 1107
inferring, 1108
statute, in, not to be inferred, 1107–1110
Orchard
pertinent, as, 1242

Parliament
intention of, in interpretation of statutes,
  1102
Parliamentary history as aid to construction of statutes, 1147, 1148
statutes, *see* STATUTE
Parole evidence
deeds, interpretation of, 1222, 1223,
  1225, 1251
Penal statute
interpretation, 1184
Pencil
deed written or altered in, 1230, 1263
Person
meaning under Interpretation Act
  1978 . . . 1211
Pertinent
meaning in conveyance, 1242
Plans
conveyancing, 1240
Post, service by
Interpretation Act 1978 rules as to, 1208
Power of attorney
interpretation, 1262
Practice
presumption against alteration by statute, 1127
Pre-Union Scots Acts
desuetude, 1201
interpretation, generally, 1200
Preamble
Act, to, construction, 1136
Presumptions
burdens, against imposition of, 1131
changes in existing law and practice,
  against—
  common law, 1126

Presumptions—*contd*
changes in existing law and practice, against—*contd*
 practice and procedure, rules of, 1127
common calamity, cases of, 1266
conditio si institutus sine liberis decesserit, 1265
conditio si testator sine liberis decesserit, 1265
correct usage of words, as to, 1133
division *per capita*, 1268
falsa demonstratio non nocet, 1268
intestacy, against, 1267
jurisdiction, in relation to—
 sheriff courts, 1129
 superior courts, 1128
  extension of supervisory powers of, 1130
legality, of, 1267
popular construction, in favour of, 1132
retrospection, against operation of, 1191
rights, against taking away, 1131
Private Act
meaning, 1202
strict interpretation, 1203, 1204
Procedure
alterations in, retrospectivity, 1192
presumption against alteration by statute, 1127
Proviso
Act of Parliament, in, construction, 1139
Punctuation
statute, in, construction, 1142
Pupil
capacity to enter contract or grant deed, 1229

Rank
words of, in construction of statute, 1169
Remedial statute
interpretation, 1186
Rent
as cardinal element of lease, 1252
clause of assignation, implied terms, 1235
Rent (Scotland) Act 1984 . . . 1253
Renunciation, minute of
interpretation, 1262
Repealing Act
decisions made under previous legislation, 1194
delegated legislation under repealed enactment, 1196
implied repeal, 1198
practice prevailing under repealed statute, 1199
re-enactment, 1196

Repealing Act—*contd*
repealing enactment repealed by, 1197
subordinate legislation under repealed enactment, 1196
substituted provisions, 1195
Repugnancy
will, interpretation and construction of, 1109, 1269
Retrospection
statute, of—
 declaratory Acts, 1193
 generally, 1189
 past transactions, legality of, 1190
 presumption against, rebuttal, 1191
 procedure, alterations in, 1192
 vested rights, 1190
Rights
presumption against enactment taking away, 1131
River
lateral boundary, 1239
 non-navigable, meaning, 1239
 tidal navigable, meaning, 1239
Road
boundary, on, 1239
Rubric
section of Act, of, construction, 1137

Salmon fishings
pertinents, as, 1242
Schedule
Act of Parliament, to, construction, 1141
Scotland
United Kingdom Act extending to, 1101, 1187
 older Acts, 1187
 uniform application, 1188
Sea
lateral boundary, 1239
meaning, 1239
Sea beach
meaning, 1239
Sea shore
meaning, 1239
Service
post, by, Interpretation Act 1978 rules as to, 1208
Servitude
interpretation, 1262
pertinent, as, 1242
Sheriff courts
jurisdiction of, statute ousting or adding to, 1129
Side note
section of Act, of, construction, 1137

References are to paragraphs

Spouse
common calamity, interpretation of will
    following death by, 1266
will or other testamentary writing, legal
    rights, 1264
Statute
deeds, effect of statute on interpretation
    of, 1218
desuetude, 1201
Great Britain Bill, Scotland included in,
    1101, 1187
in pari materia, 1156
interpretation and construction—
    absurdity, avoidance of, 1124, 1125
    Act not to be extended beyond object,
        1111–1113
    ambiguities, 1113, 1114, 1163
        construction to avoid absurdity,
            1124
    casus omissus not to be supplied by
        courts, 1107
    consolidating Acts, 1148, 1158
    construction—
        application of principle, 1120
        application of rules to scheme of
            Act, 1122
        external aids to, *see* external aids to
            construction *below*
        internal aids to, *see* internal aids to
            construction *below*
        limit to principle, 1121
        not to make Act invalid, 1123
    contemporanea expositio—
        ancient statutes, 1112
        modern statutes, 1113
    Crown, application of enactments to,
        1212
    de minimus non curat praetor, 1170
    declaratory acts, 1193
    desuetude, Acts falling into, 1201
    directory enactments, 1175, 1180
    discretionary enactments, 1175, 1179,
        1180
    distance, measurement of, 1209
    duties, continuity of, 1210
    ejusdem generis rule—
        generally, 1166
        inapplicability of rules, 1168
        rule of construction, as, 1167
    European Community legislation,
        1205
    expressio unius est exclusio alterius, 1165
    extending to more than one part of
        United Kingdom, 1188
    external aids to construction—
        administrative practice, 1162

Statute—*contd*
interpretation and construction—*contd*
    external aids to construction—*contd*
        consolidating Acts, 1148, 1158
        conventions, 1153, 1154
        conveyancing practice, 1161
        dictionaries, 1152
        earlier enactments, 1155–1159
        explanatory memoranda, 1149,
            1150
        generally, 1143
        historical setting, 1144–1146
        international conventions, 1153
        later enactments, 1155, 1160
        legislative history, 1147
        modern decisions, 1146
        modifications, 1159
        official reports, 1149
        older decisions, 1145
        Parliamentary history, 1147, 1148
        re-enactments, 1159
        statutes construed with other sta-
            tutes, 1157
        statutes, *in pari materia*, 1156
        statutory instruments, 1164
        textbooks, 1151
        travaux préparatoires, 1154
        uniform decisions, 1163
        usage, 1163
    faultiness of expression, correction
        1108
    gender, rules as to, 1207
    general principles, 1101
    golden rule, 1109
        limitations to, 1110
    grammar, rules of, 1103, 1106, 1109
    Heydon's Case, rule in, 1115
    inconsistency, golden rule, 1109
    injustice, duty of courts to avoid, 1114
    intent, according to—
        conflicting approaches, illustrations
            of, 1117
        generally, 1116
        object of section, 1118, 1120
    intention of Parliament, 1102
    internal aids to construction—
        generally, 1134
        headings, 1138
        interpretation sections, 1140
        preamble, 1136
        provisos, 1139
        punctuation, 1142
        rubric of section, 1137
        schedules, 1141
        short and long title, 1135
        side note of section, 1137

References are to paragraphs

Statute—*contd*
interpretation and construction—*contd*
  Interpretation Act 1978—
    distance, measurement of, 1209
    gender, rules as to, 1207
    generally, 1206
    number, rules as to, 1207
    person, meaning, 1211
    post, service by, 1208
    powers and duties, continuity of,
      1210
  literal reading, unintelligible result
    produced by, 1108
  literal rule, 1103–1106
  mandatory enactments, 1175–1178
  meaning clear, where, 1103–1113
  meaning not clear, where, 1114–1125
  mischief rule, 1115
  number, rules as to, 1207
  omission not to be inferred, 1107, 1108
  penal statutes, 1184
  permissive enactments, 1175, 1180
  person, meaning, 1211
  post, service by, 1208
  powers, continuity of, 1210
  pre-Union Scots Acts—
    desuetude, 1201
    generally, 1200
  presumptions—
    against change in law and practice,
      1126, 1127
    burdens, against imposing, 1131
    common law, against change of,
      1126
    correct use of words, 1133
    jurisdiction, in relation to—
      sheriff courts, 1129
      superior courts, 1128
      supervisory power of, 1130
    popular construction, in favour of,
      1132
    restrospectivity, 1191
    rights, against taking away, 1131
    rules of practice and procedure,
      against change of, 1127
  private Acts—
    generally, 1202
    meaning, 1202
    strict interpretation, 1203, 1204
  rank, words of, 1169
  remedial statutes, 1186
  repeals—
    delegated legislation, 1196
    desuetude, Acts falling into, 1201
    effect of, generally, 1194
    implied repeal, 1198

Statute—*contd*
interpretation and construction—*contd*
  repeals—*contd*
    prevailing practice as to, 1199
    re-enactment, 1196
    repealing enactment, repeal of, 1197
    revival of previously repealed act,
      1197
    special acts, 1198
    subordinate legislation, 1196
    substituted provisions, 1195
  repugnancy, golden rule, 1109
  retrospection—
    declaratory acts, 1193
    generally, 1189
    legality of past transactions, 1190
    presumption against, rebuttal, 1191
    procedure, alterations in form of,
      1192
    vested rights, 1190
  rules—
    golden rule, 1109
      limitations to, 1110
    literal rules, 1103–1106
    necessity for, 1101
    paramount, 1102
    special, enactments to which appli-
      cable, 1200–1205
  Scotland, drafting difficulties, 1101
  section—
    interpretation sections, 1140
    meaning of, determination by refer-
      ence to general scheme of Act,
      1122
    object of, 1118, 1120
    rubric of, 1137
    side note of, 1137
  service, interpretation of term, 1208
  statutes construed with other statutes,
    1157
  statutory duties—
    absolute, 1181, 1182
    qualified, 1181, 1183
  taxing statutes, 1185
  technical words, 1103
  territorial extent, 1187
  time, computation of, 1171–1174
  unambiguous words, 1105, 1112
  uniform application of Acts extending
    to Great Britain, 1188
  ut res magis valeat quam pereat, 1123,
    1124
  whole, statute to be read as, 1119–1122
invalid, construction not to make Act,
  1123

References are to paragraphs

Statute—*contd*
object of, interpretation not to extend,
   1111–1113
penal, interpretation, 1184
Pre-Union Scots Act, interpretation,
   generally, 1200, 1201
remedial, interpretation, 1186
statutory requirement—
   discretionary, held to be, 1178, 1180
   mandatory, held to be, 1177
taxing, interpretation, 1185
Statutory declaration
interpretation, 1262
Statutory duty
qualified, 1181, 1183
strict, 1181, 1182
Statutory instrument
use in construction of Act, 1164
Stop
accident, after, meaning, 1109
Superior courts
jurisdiction of, statute ousting or adding
   to, 1128, 1130

Taxing statute
interpretation, 1185
Tenancy
order for possession, 1253
Rent (Scotland) Act 1984 . . . 1253
termination by abandonment of possession, 1235
Testamentary writings
adoption orders, 1218
date born by, 1218
donation or disposition in contemplation
   of imminent death, 1263
falsa demonstratio non nocet, 1268
interpretation, object of, 1214
latter-will, 1263
legal rights, 1264
prior rights, 1264
restrictions affecting, 1264
subsequent to probative will, 1263
words with testamentary intention, 1263
See also WILL
Textbook
construction of statute, as aid to, 1151
Time
computation of, in construction of statute, 1171–1174
   financial year, 1171
   forthwith, meaning of, 1174
   month, 1171
   period of time after, or from, event,
      1173

Time—*contd*
computation of, in construction of statute—*contd*
   period of time before event, 1172
   week, 1171
Title
Act, of, long and short, 1135
Trade usage
interpretation of deeds affected by, 1215
Travaux préparatoires
aid to construction of statute, as, 1154
Trees
pertinents, as, 1242
Trout fishings
pertinents, as, 1242
Trust
alimentary liferent, 1264
annuity provision, 1264
Trust deed
voluntary, interpretation, 1262
Trustee
powers, generally, 1272
Tutor
deed granted by, 1229

United Kingdom
Act extending throughout, 1101, 1187
   uniform application, 1188
Parliament only sovereign legislature,
   1187
Usage
interpretation of deed, in, 1220
interpretation of statute, in, 1163

Waiver, minute of
interpretation, 1262
Wall
boundary, on, 1239
gable, 1239
mutual, boundary on, 1239
Warrandice
implied terms, 1235
**Warsaw Convention for the Unifi-
   cation of Certain Rules relating
   to International Carriage by Air**
travaux préparatoires, 1154
Week
meaning, 1171, 1172
Will
children—
   adopted, 1268
   conditio si testator sine liberis decesserit,
      1265
   illegitimacy, abolition of status of,
      1268
   rights of, generally, 1264

References are to paragraphs

Will—*contd*
disposition in contemplation of imminent death, 1263
donation, 1263
extrinsic evidence, interpretation, 1263
favourable interpretation, 1263
interpretation and construction—
  annuity provision in favour of beneficiary, 1264
  charity, gifts to, 1271
  descendants or nephews and nieces, *conditio si institutus sine liberis decesserit*, 1265
  general principles, 1263, 1264
  golden rules, 1109
  illegitimacy, abolition of status of, 1268
  ineffectual conditions or directions—
    charitable objects, 1271
    discretionary powers of trustees too wide, where, 1271
    public policy, conditions contrary to, 1270
    uncertainty, 1271
  intention, ascertainment of, 1263
  irreconcilable provisions, 1263
  jus relicti, 1264
  liferent in favour of beneficiary, 1264
  majority, meaning, 1218, 1268
  object of interpretation, 1214, 1263
  pencil, will written in, 1263
  presumptions, 1268
    adopted children, 1268
    bequest to number of persons, 1268
    between, meaning, 1268
    children, meaning, 1268
    class, bequest to, 1268
    common calamity, 1266
    conditio si institutus sine liberis decesserit, 1265
    conditio si testator sine liberis decesserit, 1265
    dependants, use of word, 1268
    falsa demonstratio non nocet, 1268
    intestacy, against, 1267
    issue, meaning, 1268
    knowledge of testator, as to, 1267
    legality, of, 1267
    majority, meaning, 1268
    next of kin, meaning, 1268
  prior rights, 1264
  repugnancy, 1269
  restrictions affecting testamentary writings, 1264

Will—*contd*
interpretation and construction—*contd*
  vesting, 1269
intestacy
  presumption against, 1267
  prior rights, 1264
latter-will, 1263
printed form, problems arising from use of, 1228
revocation, *conditio si testator sine liberis decesserit*, 1265
spouse—
  common calamity, 1266
  rights of, 1264
testamentary writing subsequent to, 1263
trustees—
  powers, 1272
  discretionary, where too wide, 1271
witnesses—
  beneficiaries, as, 1263
  printed form will signed without, 1263
Witness
deed, to, incompetent, 1229
will, to, 1263
Wood
pertinent, as, 1242
Words
construction of deed—
  foreign languages, 1217
  generally, 1219
  local or class usage, 1220
  popular sense to be followed, 1215
  technical terms, 1215, 1217
  verba sunt interpretanda contra proferentem, 1232
construction of statute—
  grammar, rules of, 1103, 1106
  literal construction not to prevail if opposed to legislature, 1106
  literal rule, 1103
  presumption as to correct usage, 1133
  technical words, 1103
  unambiguous words, 1105
  words of rank, 1169
Writ
blanks in, 1228
clause of assignation, implied terms, 1235
contra proferentem rule, 1232
feu, interpretation of, 1237
interpretation of, 1215

INVESTOR PROTECTION

Accountant of Court
exempted person, as, 1323
Accounting records
investment business, duty to keep, 1404, 1408
Advertising
authorised person, by, 1366
collective investment scheme, promotion of, 1326
DIE advertisements, 1367
direct offer, 1367, 1367*n*
exempt, 1367, 1367*n*
image, 1367
investment advertisement, meaning, 1337*n*
investment business, of—
  extra-territorial application, 1337
  restrictions on, 1337
    exceptions to, 1337
investors' remedies, 1410
issue and approval of, 1367
  overseas person, for, 1368
meaning of advertisement, 1337*n*
non-private customers, directed towards, 1367
off-the-page, 1363, 1367
overseas business, 1366, 1370
  private UK customers, for, 1369
private customers, directed towards, 1367, 1369
short form, 1367
SIB Core Conduct of Business Rules, 1366–1370
  application, 1400
  information about packaged products, 1363
  off-the-page, 1363
takeover, 1367, 1367*n*
third-tier rules, 1367
Advice
conduit, 1360
packaged products, SIB Core Conduct of Business Rules, 1365
Adviser
agent on behalf of client, 1353, 1362
principal dealing with clients, 1353, 1362
SIB statement of principle, 1353
Allocation
SIB Core Conduct of Business Rules—
  fair allocation, 1383
  timely allocation, 1382
Appointed representative
exempted person, as, 1323
meaning, 1361

Appointed representative—*contd*
prohibitions on, SIB powers of as to, 1414
SIB Core Conduct of Business Rules, 1361, 1378
Auditor
appointment of, SIB rules, 1405
Author
SIB Core Conduct of Business Rules, 1399
Authorised person
advertising by, 1366
automatic authorisation—
  collective investment scheme from EC member state, 1318
  EC national carrying on investment business in EC member state, 1320
  generally, 1315
  insurance company, 1316
  registered friendly society, 1317
collective investment scheme, promotion of, 1326
compliance orders, 1314
conduct, 1342
conduct of investment business, *see* INVESTMENT BUSINESS
Core Conduct of Business Rules, 1356, 1399
disqualification direction, 1338
exempted person, *see* EXEMPTED PERSON
fiduciary duties, 1354
Financial Services Act 1986, under, 1301
  necessity for authorisation, 1306
financial standing, 1342
misconduct by, public statement as to, 1339
necessity for authorisation, 1306
prohibitions on, SIB powers of as to, 1414
recognised professional body, authorisation by, 1309, 1313, 1314
register, 1415
routes to authorisation, 1309
Secretary of State, authorisation by, 1319
Securities and Investments Board, authorisation by, 1309, 1310
  refusal, withdrawal or suspension of, 1311
Securities and Investments Board statements of principle, 1342
self-regulating organisation, member of, 1309, 1312, 1314
withdrawal or suspension of authorisation, 1311, 1342*n*, 1414

Bank of England
exempted person under Financial Services Act 1986... 1321
Bankruptcy
trustee in, insider dealing rules, 1528
Bond
investment, as, 1308
Broadcast
sound, television or cable, investment advice, publication of, 1307
Broadcaster
SIB Core Conduct of Business Rules, 1399

Care
SIB statement of principle, 1344
Certificate of deposit
investment, as, 1308
Charges
fairness of, SIB Core Conduct of Business Rules, 1374
information to be given, 1363
Chartered Association of Certified Accountants
authorisation by, 1313
Chinese walls
SIB Core Conduct of Business Rules, 1358, 1395
Church of Scotland Trust
trustee of, exempted person, as, 1323
Churning
meaning, 1385
SIB Core Conduct of Business Rules, 1385
Clearing house
function of, 1322
recognised—
    application for recognition order, 1322
    exempted person, as, 1322
register, 1415
Cold-calling
agreement entered after, effect of, 1334
dealing restriction, 1335
investors' remedies, 1410
marketing restriction, 1335
misconduct, public statement as to, 1339
permitted, 1335
prohibition on, 1333
    extra-territorial application, 1333
    power to lift, 1335
regulations, 1335
Securities and Investments Board rules, 1340
Collective investment scheme
criminal acts by, 1330
establishment, 1307

Collective investment scheme—*contd*
European Community member state, from, authorisation, 1315, 1318, 1328
excluded investment categories, 1325
intervention by Securities and Investments Board, 1329
investigation, 1330
    confidentiality, 1330
    criminal acts, discovery of, 1330
meaning, 1325
open-ended investment company, 1325. *See also* OPEN-ENDED INVESTMENT COMPANY
operation, 1307
promotion, 1326
recognised, 1328
    promotion, 1326
    types of, 1328
Securities and Investments Board powers, 1328
    interventions, 1329
    investigations, 1330
single property scheme, promotion, 1326
Undertakings for Collective Investment in Transferable Securities (UCITS), 1328, 1399
unit in as investment, 1308
unit trust schemes, 1325. *See also* UNIT TRUST SCHEME
winding up, 1307
Commission
fairness of, 1374
information to be given, 1363
soft—
    Core Conduct of Business Rules, 1359, 1362
    meaning, 1359
Company
insider dealing, *see* INSIDER DEALING
Compensation
claims for, 1422
fund, establishment of, SIB rules, 1340
Securities and Investments Board scheme, 1408, 1420, 1421
Complaints
SIB Core Conduct of Business Rules, 1394
Conflict of interest
SIB statements of principle, 1348, 1355
Contingent liability transaction
customer agreements, 1375
meaning, 1375n
SIB Core Conduct of Business Rules, 1386

References are to paragraphs

Cooling-off period
provisions as to, 1336
Core Conduct of Business Rules
See SECURITIES AND INVESTMENTS BOARD
Court of Session
interdict granted by, 1410, 1413
  investment business carried on by
    unauthorised or unexempted per-
    son, where, 1324
  restitution order, grant of, 1411, 1413
  investment business carried on by
    unauthorised or unexempted per-
    son, where, 1324
  misleading statement or practice,
    where, 1324
Customer
assets, SIB statement of principle, 1349
classes of, SIB Core Conduct of Business
  Rules, 1398
clients' money regulations, 1409
dealing with, SIB Core Conduct of Business Rules—
  best execution, 1359, 1381
  churning, 1385
  dealing ahead of publication, 1384
  fair allocation, 1383
  order priority of customers, 1379
  switching, 1385
  timely allocation, 1382
  timely execution, 1380
information about, SIB statement of
  principle, 1346, 1347
investments, safeguarding, SIB Core
  Conduct of Business Rules, 1391
non-private—
  advertising directed towards, 1367
  private customer treated as, 1398
  SIB Core Conduct of Business Rules,
    1362
order priority, 1379
private, meaning, 1360*n*
relationship with, SIB Core Conduct of
  Business Rules—
  appointed representatives, 1361, 1378
  charges, fairness of, 1374
  confirmations and information to cus-
    tomers, 1377
  customer agreements, 1375
  customers' rights, 1376
  customers' understanding, 1372
  fair and clear communications, 1371
  remuneration, fairness of, 1374
  suitability of recommendation or
    transaction to customer's require-
    ments, 1373
remedies available to, *see* INVESTORS' REM-
  EDIES

Damages
action for, 1412
Dealing
insider, *see* INSIDER DEALING
meaning, 1510
publication, ahead of, 1384
Debenture
insider dealing, *see* INSIDER DEALING
investment, as, 1308
Debenture stock
investment, as, 1308
**Diligence, investment firms duty to
  act with due**
SIB statement of principle, 1344
Director
body corporate as, 1506
insider dealing, prohibition on, 1505,
  1506, 1507
primary insider, as, 1501
related company, of, 1505, 1506

Employee share scheme
excluded from collective investment
  scheme categorisation, 1325
Equities
soft commission, 1359
**European Bank for Reconstruction
  and Development**
exempted person, as, 1323
European Community
collective investment scheme, authorisation, 1315, 1318, 1328
insider dealing, directive on, 1536
member state—
  collective investment scheme from,
    1315, 1318, 1328
  national from, authorised to run
    investment business in that state,
    1315, 1320, 1320*n*
Undertakings for Collective Investment
  in Transferable Securities (UCITS),
  1328, 1399
Execution
SIB Core Conduct of Business Rules—
  best execution, 1359, 1381
  timely execution, 1380
Exempted person
Accountant of Court, 1323
appointed representatives, 1323
  SIB Core Conduct of Business Rules,
    1361
Church of Scotland Trust, trustee of,
  1323
European Bank for Reconstruction and
  Development, 1323
Financial Services Act 1986, under, 1301,
  1306, 1321

Exempted person—*contd*
General Synod of the Scottish Episcopal
    Church, 1323
meaning, 1321
money market institution, 1321
partnership, winding up, 1323
recognised clearing house, 1322
recognised investment exchange, 1322
Scottish Enterprise, 1323
Scottish Nuclear Ltd, 1323
Scottish Tourist Board, 1323
sheriff clerk, 1323
trustee in sequestration, 1323

**Financial Intermediaries Managers
    and Brokers Regulatory Associ-
    ation (FIMBRA)**
recognised self-regulating organisation,
    as, 1312
Financial Services Act 1986
authorised person, *see* AUTHORISED PER-
    SON
exempted person, *see* EXEMPTED PERSON
generally, 1301, 1423
investment business, 1307. *See also*
    INVESTMENT BUSINESS
legislation replaced by, 1302
regulatory structure, 1306–1324
scope, 1302, 1303
Financial Services Tribunal
constitution, 1416
counsel or solicitor, appointment of,
    1416
hearings, 1418
investigation by, 1418
reference to, 1417
refusal of authorisation, referral to in
    cases of, 1311
reports by, 1419
*Financial Services in the United King-
    dom . . . white paper*
recommendations of, 1305
Franchise arrangement
excluded from collective investment
    scheme categorisation, 1325
Friendly society
authorisation, automatic, 1315, 1317
SIB Core Conduct of Business Rules,
    1399
Futures
generally, 1303
investment, as, 1308
London International Financial Futures
    Exchange, 1322
Securities and Futures Association
    (SFA), 1312

Gower Report
proposals, 1304, 1305
publication, 1304, 1305

Indemnity rules
Securities and Investments Board power
    to make, 1340
Independence
SIB Core Conduct of Business Rules—
    appointed representatives, 1361
    generally, 1362
    inducements, 1357, 1362
    material interest, 1358, 1362
    polarisation, 1360
    soft commission, 1359, 1362
Inducements
SIB Core Conduct of Business Rules,
    1357, 1362
volume overriders, 1357
Information and advice
records and reporting, requirements as
    to, 1404, 1406
SIB Core Conduct of Business Rules,
    1365
    investment business, advice on, 1364
    packaged products, information on,
        1363
    periodic information, provision of,
        1377
Insider dealing
civil remedies, potential, 1535
communication of information to others
    who may deal, 1502, 1518
company, meaning, 1506
company securities, legislation aimed at,
    1501
confidentiality of information, 1509
contemplated transactions, 1511
counselling or procuring others to deal,
    1502, 1517
deal—
    meaning, 1510
    outside United Kingdom, 1502
debentures, 1510
defences to, 1527
director, 1501, 1505, 1506, 1507
    body corporate as, 1506
    shadow director, 1506
employee of company or related com-
    pany, 1507
European Community directive, 1536
facilitating the completion or carrying
    out of transaction, 1530
individual connected with a company—
    dealings by, 1502

References are to paragraphs

Insider dealing—*contd*
individual connected with a company—
  contd
  dealings by—*contd*
    in securities of another company,
      1511
    in securities of same company,
      1503–1510
  who is regarded as, 1505
information obtained in official capacity,
  abuse of, 1519–1522
insider information must be held as a
  result of connection with company,
  1509
investigations into, 1533
jobber, 1529
knowingly connected, individual must
  be, 1508
liquidator, action in good faith by, 1528
loss, thing done other than to avoid, 1527
manager, 1507, 1507n
market maker, 1529
meaning, 1501
off-market deals, 1502, 1523, 1524
  deals outside Great Britain, 1525
permitted actions, 1526
personal representative, permitted
  actions by, 1532
price stabilisation, 1531
primary insider, 1501
  off-market deals outside Great Britain,
    1525
  prohibitions on, 1502
profit, thing done other than to make,
  1527
prohibited dealings, generally, 1503
public servant, 1501, 1502, 1519–1522
  tippee rules, 1522
punishment of offences, 1534
receiver, action in good faith by, 1528
recognised stock exchange, dealing on,
  1502
reform, proposals for, 1536
related company, meaning, 1506, 1507
secondary insider (tippee), 1501, 1509
  off-market deals outside Great Britain,
    1525
  prohibitions on, 1502, 1512, 1513
  public servant, information obtained
    from, 1522
secretary, company 1507, 1507n
securities, meaning, 1510
shares, 1510
SIB Core Conduct of Business Rules,
  1387
statutory offences, 1501

Insider dealing—*contd*
takeover offers, and, 1502, 1514, 1515
  Panel on Takeovers and Mergers,
    members and staff of, 1520
  tippee from individuals contemplating
    takeover offers, 1516
tippee, *see* secondary insider *above*
trustee in bankruptcy, action in good
  faith by, 1528
trustee, permitted actions by, 1532
unpublished price sensitive information,
  1509
  meaning, 1504
wilful blindness, 1508
Institute of Actuaries
authorisation by, 1313
**Institute of Chartered Accountants in
  England and Wales**
authorisation by, 1313
**Institute of Chartered Accountants in
  Northern Ireland**
authorisation by, 1313
**Institute of Chartered Accountants
  of Scotland**
authorisation by, 1313
**Insurance Brokers Registration
  Council**
authorisation by, 1313
Insurance company
authorisation, automatic, 1315, 1316
Department of Trade and Industry
  supervision, 1316
self-regulating organisation, membership of, 1316
SIB Core Conduct of Business Rules,
  1399
Insurance contract
long-term, as investment, 1308, 1308n
protection policies, 1308
term assurance, 1308
Integrity
SIB statement of principle, 1343
Interdict
Court of Session grant of, 1410, 1413
Investigation
Secretary of State and SIB powers of,
  1415
Investment
advice—
  newspaper or magazine, given in, 1307
  sound, television or cable broadcast,
    1307
business, *see* INVESTMENT BUSINESS
dealing in, 1307
interest in, 1308
investment agreement, meaning, 1332n

Investment—_contd_
rights to, 1308
transactions—
  between companies in same group or
    enterprise, 1307
  designed to acquire more than 75 per
    cent of shares in body corporate,
    1307
  employees' share schemes, 1307
  excluded from investment business,
    1307
  industrial or commercial concern,
    arranged in connection with, 1307
international securities self-regulating
  organisation, 1307
trustee or personal representative by or
  for, 1307
Investment business
accounting records, 1408
advice offered by, 1307
adviser—
  agents on behalf of clients, 1353, 1362
  principals dealing with customers,
    1353, 1362
  SIB statements of principle, 1353
agent—
  on behalf of clients, 1353, 1362
  fiduciary duties of, 1354
appointed representative, _see_ APPOINTED
  REPRESENTATIVE
assets, management by, 1307
authorisation—
  automatic, 1309
    European Community member
      state—
        collective investment scheme
          from, 1318
        persons authorised in other, 1320
    generally, 1315
    insurance company, 1316
    registered friendly society, 1317
    Secretary of State, granted by, 1319
  fit and proper person, applicant must
    be, 1310, 1311, 1338
  necessity for, 1309
  recognised professional body, mem-
    ber of, 1309, 1313
    refusal and revocation of recog-
      nition, 1314
  refusal, 1311
  routes to, 1309
  Securities and Investments Board, by,
    1309, 1310
    withdrawal of, 1311
  self-regulating organisation, member
    of, 1309, 1312

Investment business—_contd_
authorisation—_contd_
  self-regulating organisation, member
    of—_contd_
      refusal and revocation of recog-
        nition, 1314
      suspension, 1311
      withdrawal, 1311
authorised person, _see_ AUTHORISED PER-
  SON
carried on by unauthorised or unexempted person—
    interdict, 1324
    restitution order, 1324
cessation of business, SIB Core Conduct
  of Business Rules, 1396
Chinese walls, 1358, 1395
clients' money, protection of, 1409
communications, fair and clear, must be,
  1371
complaints procedure, 1394
compliance with regulatory rules, 1393
conduct of—
  advertising, restrictions on, 1337
    exceptions to rules, 1337_n_
    extra-territorial application, 1337
    investment advertisement, mean-
      ing, 1337_n_
  authorised person, _see_ AUTHORISED
    PERSON
  cancellation—
    notice of, effect, 1336
    rules as to, 1340
    shortfall, 1336
  cancellation, provisions as to, 1336
  cold-calling—
    agreement entered after, effect of,
      1334
    permitted, 1335
    prohibition on, 1333
      extra-territorial application, 1333
      power to lift, 1335
    public statement as to misconduct,
      1339
    regulations, 1335
    rules as to, 1340
  concealment of facts, 1332
  Conduct of Business Rules, 1331
  conflicts of interest, 1348
  cooling-off periods, 1336
  customers—
    assets of, 1349
    information about, 1346
    information for, 1347
  disqualification direction, 1338
  financial resources, 1350

Investment business—*contd*
conduct of—*contd*
  integrity, 1343
  internal organisation, 1351
  market practice, 1345
  misconduct, public statement as to,
    1339
  misleading statements and practice,
    1332
    defences to, 1332*n*
    overseas person, by, 1332
    penalty for, 1332
    restitution order following, 1332
  notification of events, 1340
  prohibited person, employment of,
    1338
  public statement as to, 1339
  regulators, relations with, 1352
  rules—
    cancellation, 1340
    clients' money, as to, 1340
    compensation fund, establishment
      of, 1340
    conduct of business, 1340
    contravention, public statement as
      to misconduct, 1339
    financial resources, 1340, 1350
    indemnity, 1340
    notification regulations, 1340
    Secretary of State's power to make,
      1331
    Securities and Investments Board
      power to make, 1331
  SIB statements of principle, *see* SECURI-
    TIES AND INVESTMENTS BOARD
  skill, care and diligence, 1344
  unsolicited calls—
    agreement entered after, effect of,
      1334
    permitted, 1335
    prohibition on, 1333
      extra-territorial application, 1333
      power to lift, 1335
    public statement as to misconduct,
      1339
    regulations, 1335
    rules as to, 1340
customer, *see* CUSTOMER
customer agreements, 1375
dealing in investments, 1307
exclusions from, 1307
exempted person, *see* EXEMPTED PERSON
financial supervision, SIB rules—
  accounting records, 1404, 1408
  auditors, appointment of, 1405
  disapplication, where, 1402

Investment business—*contd*
financial supervision, SIB rules—*contd*
  financial resources of firm, 1403
  generally, 1402, 1408
  internal controls and systems, 1407
  reports, publication of, 1404, 1406
independence, SIB Core Conduct of
  Business Rules, 1357–1362
inducements, giving or receiving, 1357
information and advice, supply—
  firm, about, 1364
  packaged products, about, 1363, 1365
liability, SIB Core Conduct of Business
  Rules, 1376
material interest in transaction, with,
  1358
meaning under Financial Services Act
  1986... 1307, 1308
misconduct, public statement as to, 1339
packaged products, 1360
remedies against, *see* INVESTORS' REMEDIES
SIB Core Conduct of Business Rules,
  application, 1399. *See also* SECURITIES
  AND INVESTMENTS BOARD
soft commission, 1359
volume overriders, 1357
written description of, SIB Core Conduct of Business Rules, 1392
Investment club
excluded from collective investment
  scheme categorisation, 1325
Investment exchange
function of, 1322
recognised—
  application for recognition order, 1322
  exempted person, as, 1322
register, 1415
**Investment Management Regulatory
  Organisation (IMRO)**
recognised self-regulating organisation,
  as, 1312
Investors' remedies
agreements with unauthorised or unexempted person, 1413
compensation, 1420–1422
damages, action for, 1412
Financial Services Tribunal, *see* FINAN-
  CIAL SERVICES TRIBUNAL
interdict, 1410, 1413
intervention, SIB powers of, 1414
investigation and information, SIB
  powers as to, 1415
restitution order, 1411, 1413
winding up, SIB powers as to, 1413

Jobber
insider dealing rules, 1529

Joint venture
excluded from collective investment scheme categorisation, 1325
Journalist
SIB Core Conduct of Business Rules, 1399

Law Society
authorisation by, 1313
Law Society of Northern Ireland
authorisation by, 1313
Law Society of Scotland
authorisation by, 1313
Liability
SIB Core Conduct of Business Rules, 1376
Life assurance
company, appointed representative of, 1361
Life Assurance and Unit Trust Regulatory Organisation, 1312
Life Assurance and Unit Trust Regulatory Organisation (LAUTRO)
recognised self-regulating organisation, as, 1312
Liquidator
insider dealing rules, 1528
Lloyds
exempted person under Financial Services Act 1986... 1321
Loan stock
investment, as, 1308
London International Financial Futures Exchange
investment exchange, as, 1322
London Options Clearing House
investment exchange, as, 1322

Manager
insider dealing, prohibition on, 1507, 1507*n*
Market maker
insider dealing rules, 1529
off-exchange, SIB Core Conduct of Business Rules, 1389
soft commission, 1359
turn, 1359
Market practice
SIB statement of principle, 1345
Marketing of Investments Board (MIB)
establishment, 1305
Financial Services in the United Kingdom... white paper, 1305
merger with Securities and Investments Board, 1305
Organising Committee (MIBOC), 1305

Material interest
SIB Core Conduct of Business Rules, 1358, 1362
Misleading statements and practices
investors' remedies, 1410
Money market institutions
exempted under Financial Services Act 1986... 1321

Newspaper or magazine
investment advice, publication of, 1307

Occupational pension scheme
excluded from collective investment scheme categorisation, 1325
Off-market deals
insider dealing, 1502, 1523, 1524
deals outside Great Britain, 1525
off-market dealer, meaning, 1524
Oil market
SIB Core Conduct of Business Rules, 1399
Open-ended investment company
meaning, 1325
shares or securities in, 1308
See also COLLECTIVE INVESTMENT SCHEME
Options
generally, 1303
investment, as, 1308
London Options Clearing House, 1322
Over the Counter Market (OTC)
generally, 1303
Overseas business
advertising, SIB Core Conduct of Business Rules, 1369, 1370
Overseas person
advertising, SIB Core Conduct of Business Rules, 1368
Own account transactions
investment business, excluded from, 1307
SIB Core Conduct of Business Rules, 1390

Packaged product
information and advice on, SIB Core Conduct of Business Rules, 1363, 1365
meaning, 1360*n*
polarisation, 1360
Partnership
excluded from collective investment scheme categorisation, 1325
winding up, exempted person rules, 1323

References are to paragraphs

Personal equity plan (PEP)
excluded from collective investment scheme categorisation, 1325
Personal representative
insider dealing rules, 1532
investment transactions arranged by or for, 1307
Polarisation
SIB Core Conduct of Business Rules, 1360
Professional body
authorisation by, recognition of, 1313
meaning, 1313
recognition order, application for, 1313
Public servant
insider dealing, 1502, 1519–1522
  primary insider, as, 1501
  tippee rules, 1522
meaning, 1520
Publication
dealing ahead of, 1384
Publisher
SIB Core Conduct of Business Rules, 1399

Receiver
insider dealing rules, 1528
Recognised professional body (RPB)
investment business, relations with, 1352
register, 1415
Regulatory systems
compliance with, SIB Core Conduct of Business Rules, 1393
Remedies
investors', *see* INVESTORS' REMEDIES
Remuneration
fairness of, SIB Core Conduct of Business Rules, 1374
Reportable transactions
SIB Core Conduct of Business Rules, 1390
Restitution order
Court of Session powers, 1411, 1413
investment business carried on by unauthorised or unexempted person, where, 1324
misleading statement or practice, following, 1333

Scottish Enterprise
exempted person, as, 1323
Scottish Episcopal Church
General Synod, exempted person, as, 1323
Scottish Nuclear Ltd
exempted person, as, 1323

Scottish Tourist Board
exempted person, as, 1323
Secretary of State
authorisation to carry on investment business of individual or organisation, 1319
Securities
meaning, 1510
open-ended investment company, in, 1308
Securities Association, 1312
Securities and Futures Association, 1312
Securities Association (TSA)
recognised self-regulating organisation, as, 1312
Securities and Futures Association (SFA)
recognised self-regulating organisation, as, 1312
Securities and Investments Board Ltd
Court of Session, proceedings brought in, 1305
establishment, 1305
proceedings arising out of act or omission of, 1305
See also SECURITIES AND INVESTMENTS BOARD
Securities and Investments Board (SIB)
authorisation by, 1309, 1310
  application for, 1310
  compliance orders, 1314
  disqualification direction, 1339
  fit and proper person, applicant must be, 1310, 1311, 1338
  grant of, 1310
  refusal, withdrawal or suspension, 1310, 1311, 1314
  self-regulating organisation, of, 1312
    refusal or revocation, 1314
cancellation, rules covering, 1336
central compensation fund, 1408
clearing house, application for recognition as, 1322, 1322*n*
clients' money regulations, 1409
collective investment schemes, powers as to, 1328
  interventions, 1329
  investigations, 1330
compensation scheme, 1420, 1421
  claims under, 1422
cooling-off period, rules covering, 1336
Core Conduct of Business Rules, 1356
  administration, rules on, 1391–1401

Securities and Investments Board (SIB)—*contd*
Core Conduct of Business Rules—*contd*
  advertising, rules on, 1366–1370
    overseas businesses, 1369, 1370
  allocation—
    fair, 1383
    timely, 1382
  application of, 1399
  appointed representatives, 1361, 1378
  cessation of business, 1396
  charges, fairness of, 1374
  Chinese walls, 1395
  churning, 1385
  complaints procedure, 1394
  compliance, 1393
  confirmations, 1377
  contingent liability transactions, 1386
  customer—
    classes of, 1398
    customer agreements, 1375
    customer order priority, 1379
    customers' rights, 1376
    customers' understanding, 1372
    dealing with, 1378–1386
    information, disclosure to, 1377
    investments of, safeguarding, 1391
    non-private, 1362
    relationship with, 1371–1378
  derivative transactions, 1386
  execution—
    best, 1359, 1381
    timely, 1380
  fair and clear communications, 1371
  independence, rules on, 1357–1362
  inducements, 1357, 1362
  information and advice, rules on, 1363–1365
    disclosure to customers, 1377
  insider dealing, 1387
  investment firm, information about the, 1364
  market integrity, rules on, 1387–1390
  material interest, 1358, 1362
  off-exchange market makers, 1389
  packaged products—
    information about, 1363
    standards of advice on, 1365
  polarisation, 1360
  problems arising, 1362
  publication, dealing ahead of, 1384
  reliance on others, rules as to, 1397
  remuneration, fairness of, 1374
  reportable transactions, 1390
  scope of business, regarding, 1392
  soft commission, 1359, 1362

Securities and Investments Board (SIB)—*contd*
Core Conduct of Business Rules—*contd*
  stabilisation of securities, 1388
  suitability, 1373
  switching, 1385
  time, application as to, 1401
  establishment, 1305
Financial Services Tribunal—
  references to, 1417
  report of, 1419
Financial Services in the United Kingdom . . . white paper, 1305
financial supervision rules—
  ad hoc reporting requirements, 1406
  auditors, appointment of, 1405
  disapplied, where, 1402
  financial resources of investment firm, 1403
  generally, 1402, 1408
  internal controls and systems, 1407
  records and reporting, 1404
information and investigations, powers as to, 1415
intervention, powers of, 1414
investment business, relations with, 1352
investment exchange, application for recognition as, 1322, 1322*n*
investors' remedies, *see* INVESTORS' REMEDIES
merger with Marketing of Investments Board, 1305
misconduct by investment business, public statement as to, 1339
professional body, application for recognition order, 1313, 1313*n*
  refusal or revocation, 1314
register, 1415
rules—
  adequacy test, 1341
  cancellation rules, 1340
  compensation fund, establishment of, 1340
  contravention, public statements concerning, 1339
  core, 1341. *See also* Core Conduct of Business Rules *above*
  damages, restriction on right to sue for, 1341
  financial resources rules, 1340, 1350
  financial supervision rules, *see* financial supervision rules *above*
  holding clients' money, as to, 1340
  indemnity rules, 1340
  'new settlement' approach, 1341
  notification regulations, 1340

Securities and Investments Board (SIB)—*contd*

rules—*contd*

  rule-making powers, generally, 1340

  statements of principle, *see* statements of principle *below*

  statutory changes, 1341

statements of principle—

  advisers, classification of, 1353

  authorised person, conduct and financial standing of, 1342

  conflicts of interest, 1348, 1355

  customer assets, statement on, 1349

  failure to comply with, 1342

  fiduciary duties, and—

    classification of adviser, 1353

    conflicts of interest, 1348, 1355

    generally, 1356

    nature of fiduciary duties, 1354

  financial resources, statement on, 1350

  generally, 1342

  information about customers, statement on, 1346

  information for customers, statement on, 1347

  integrity, statement on, 1343

  internal organisation, statement on, 1351

  issue of, 1342

  market practice, statement on, 1345

  modification to adapt to particular circumstances, 1342

  purpose of, 1342

  relations with regulators, statement on, 1352

  skill, care and diligence, statement on, 1344

unit trust scheme, authorisation of, 1327

  revocation, 1327

unsolicited calls regulations, power to make, 1335

Self-regulating organisation (SRO)

Financial Intermediaries Managers and Brokers Regulatory Association, 1312

Financial Services in the United Kingdom . . . white paper, 1305

international securities, investment transactions by, 1307

investment business, relations with, 1352

Investment Management Regulatory Organisation, 1312

Life Assurance and Unit Trust Regulatory Organisation, 1312

meaning, 1312

Self-regulating organisation (SRO) —*contd*

member of, automatic authorisation, 1312

recognition—

  application for, 1312

  grant or refusal of, 1312

Securities Association, 1312

Securities and Futures Association, 1312

unsolicited calls regulations, 1335

Sequestration

exempted person rules, 1323

Share scheme

employees, investment transactions for, 1307

Shares

insider dealing, *see* INSIDER DEALING

investment, as, 1308

investment transactions designed to acquire more than 75 per cent in body corporate, 1307

open-ended investment company, in, 1308

Sheriff clerk

exempted person, as, 1323

Skill

SIB statement of principle, 1344

Stabilisation

insider dealing rules, 1531

SIB Core Conduct of Business Rules, 1388

Stock Exchange

investment exchange, as, 1322

Stocks

insider dealing, *see* INSIDER DEALING

investment, as, 1308

Suitability

of investment to client, 1373

Switching

SIB Core Conduct of Business Rules, 1385

Takeovers

insider dealing, 1502, 1514, 1515

  Panel on Takeovers and Mergers, members and staff of, 1520

Telephone

cold-calling, *see* COLD–CALLING

Time

SIB Code Conduct of Business Rules, application of, 1401

Tippee

insider dealing, 1509, 1512, 1513

  prohibitions, 1502

meaning, 1501

References are to paragraphs

Tippee—*contd*
off-market deals outside Great Britain, 1525
takeover offers, and, 1502, 1516
Transaction
contingent liability, 1386
insider dealing, *see* INSIDER DEALING
investment, *see* INVESTMENT
material interest in, SIB Core Conduct of Business Rules, 1358
own account, 1307, 1390
reportable, 1390
Trustee
insider dealing rules, 1532
investment transactions arranged by or for, 1307
Trustee in bankruptcy
insider dealing rules, 1528

Undertakings for Collective Investment in Transferable Securities (UCITS)
collective investment schemes, 1328
operators and trustees, SIB Core Conduct of Business Rules, 1399
Unit trust company
appointed representatives, 1361
Unit trust scheme
alterations to, notification, 1327
authorised—
   authorisation, 1327
   manager, 1327*n*
      replacement of, 1327
   meaning, 1325
   promotion, 1326
   revocation, 1327
   Securities and Investments Board powers, 1327

Unit trust scheme—*contd*
authorised—*contd*
   trustee, 1327*n*
      replacement of, 1327
establishment, 1307
Life Assurance and Unit Trust Regulatory Association, 1312
meaning, 1325
operation, 1307
Prevention of Fraud (Investments) Act 1958 . . . 1302
register, 1415
trustee, 1327
   investment business acting as, 1307
winding up, 1307
See also COLLECTIVE INVESTMENT SCHEME
Unlisted Securities Market (USM)
generally, 1303
Unsolicited calls
agreement entered after, effect of, 1334
dealing restriction, 1335
investors' remedies, 1410
marketing restriction, 1335
misconduct, public statement as to, 1339
permitted, 1335
prohibition on, 1333
   extra-territorial application, 1333
   power to lift, 1335
regulations, 1335
Securities and Investments Board rules, 1340

Volume overrider
meaning, 1357
SIB Core Conduct of Business Rules, 1357

Warrant
investment, as, 1308